T0340499

OUT

ALSO BY TIM SHIPMAN

All Out War

Fall Out

No Way Out

OUT

HOW BREXIT GOT DONE
AND THE TORIES
WERE UNDONE

TIM SHIPMAN

WILLIAM
COLLINS

William Collins
An imprint of HarperCollins*Publishers*
1 London Bridge Street
London SE1 9GF

WilliamCollinsBooks.com

HarperCollins*Publishers*
Macken House, 39/40 Mayor Street Upper
Dublin 1, D01 C9W8, Ireland

First published in Great Britain in 2024 by William Collins

2

A catalogue record for this book is
available from the British Library

HB ISBN 978-0-00-870996-9
TPB ISBN 978-0-00-871204-4

Set in Minion Pro
Printed and bound in the UK using 100%
renewable electricity at CPI Group (UK) Ltd

MIX
Paper | Supporting
responsible forestry
FSC™ C007454
FSC
www.fsc.org

This book contains FSC™ certified paper and other controlled
sources to ensure responsible forest management.

For more information visit: www.harpercollins.co.uk/green

For Ettie,
who was born between the Christmas Eve deal
and the Northern Ireland Protocol Bill,
and is already a better negotiator
than anyone in these pages

and for Charlotte,
from whom she inherited these skills

'Nearly all men can stand adversity,
but if you want to test a man's character,
give him power'

– Abraham Lincoln

'The Tory Party is an absolute monarchy
moderated by regicide'

– William Hague

'History has an open-door policy.
Any fool can walk right in'

– Mick Herron, Slough House

CONTENTS

PART THREE: OUT
Getting Brexit Done
December 2019 to December 2020

PART FOUR: DRUMMED OUT
The Downfall of Boris Johnson
January 2021 to September 2022

PART FIVE: OUT OF CONTROL
The Rise and Fall of Liz Truss
July to October 2022

PART SIX: OUT OF TIME
How Rishi Ran Out of Road
October 2022 to June 2024

PART SEVEN: OVER AND OUT
The 2024 General Election
June to July 2024

INTRODUCTION

This book is the fourth and final part of a sequence designed to tell the full story of the most explosive period of domestic British politics since the Second World War. *All Out War* (2016) was the first – and remains the only – all points narrative of the EU referendum campaign. *Fall Out* (2017) recounts how a new government, under Theresa May, set out to tackle Brexit, focusing on the 2017 election and how the loss of the Tory majority left May disastrously weakened as formal Brexit talks began. *No Way Out*, published earlier this year, but written at the same time as *Out*, is the story of May's three great negotiations: first, with her cabinet, then with the EU and finally with Parliament.

All four books provide evidence for a theory of power, that those who succeed in politics know where they want to go strategically; second, can devise tactics to get there; and third, have the necessary skills to execute their plans and take both MPs and the public with them. None of the prime ministers in these pages consistently managed all three. *Out* concludes the story with the 2024 general election where those failures of leadership were punished.

It begins with Boris Johnson's arrival in Downing Street in July 2019 in the midst of the most turbulent twelve months in Parliament for a century. Part One sees Johnson and Dominic Cummings pursue a strategy of unrelenting aggression to deliver Brexit 'by any means necessary'. This period saw the prorogation of Parliament, the government's defeat in the Supreme Court, the Benn/Surrender Act (delete according to taste) and Johnson's deal with the Irish and the EU, culminating in him forcing a general election.

Part Two tells the story of the 2019 Tory landslide from the perspective of the three main parties. In Part Three, Johnson finally gets Brexit done, but tensions immediately flare in his camp. The tale of his Christmas Eve Trade and Cooperation Agreement (TCA) with Brussels is intercut with details of how the Covid-19 pandemic led to the collapse of Johnson's relationship with Cummings. Part Four describes Johnson's downfall from the end of 2020 to mid-2022, including the breakdown of trust between him and chancellor Rishi Sunak and between the UK and EU over the Brexit settlement.

In Part Five, Liz Truss becomes Tory leader and pursues one vision of a post-Brexit economy, to the detriment of herself and that economy.

Part Six sees Sunak inherit Number 10 after a power struggle with Johnson and then strike a new deal with Brussels, the Windsor Framework. It covers Johnson's forced departure from Parliament and concludes with yet another leadership plot. Part Seven explains why Sunak called the 2024 general election and how Keir Starmer capitalised on years of political chaos.

In the conclusion, I try to draw some lessons about what this intense political drama meant; what it can teach us about the practice of politics and the effective exercise of power; and how it might have panned out differently.

This was a political, parliamentary, legal and diplomatic drama, but most of all it was a human drama which reinforced the unfashionable notion that, at crunch moments in political history, the actions of a few people are disproportionately influential. Over this period looms the character of Boris Johnson. Many who have strong views about him see only some of his contradictory multitudes. Here, you will find a more rounded picture than the hatred and hagiography peddled elsewhere, but whether you love or loathe you will leave with abundant evidence to support your view. You don't need to think Johnson a 'great man' to agree that he was the most consequential figure of the period.

This book focuses on the politicos around Johnson, Truss and Sunak, who made the decisions; the civil servants supposed to enact them; the EU officials they negotiated with; and the major factions in Parliament who sought to thwart them. My bias is towards those who were adept at the art of politics, whatever their goals. Confining observation to people called Dominic, visceral adversaries were successful in their own terms

– the punctilious Grieve prevented no-deal, the berserker Cummings ensured Brexit happened.

Brexit was not always a clean fight. Some people deceived the public, others just as surely deceived themselves. In the introduction to her trilogy on the English Civil War, still the best narrative of a conflict even deeper than Brexit, Veronica Wedgwood wrote, 'The day-to-day events of history arise at least in part from error and misjudgment. On this level falsehood itself is part of the truth.' This applies equally well to the period 2016 to 2024 as it does 1637 to 1649.

While at times Brexit seemed like a modern civil war, it was not. In the end, a democratic vote was upheld. However, in the twenty years that I have been reporting from Westminster, the period of *Out* was the most toxic. Witnessing – on both sides – fanaticism, incompetence, constipated communication, strategic ineptitude and bad faith was draining for MPs, ministers, their aides and, yes, journalists. Friendships were strained or even shattered; people's mental health suffered.

Yet I was conscious as each new madness unfolded that I would look back and conclude that these were the glory days of political journalism. I think of the words of Alistair Cooke, whose *Letter from America* was a lodestar for this budding hack. In the torrid summer of 1968, another time when political passions spilled over into something darker, he found himself in the kitchen of the Ambassador Hotel in Los Angeles seconds after Bobby Kennedy was assassinated. Cooke's description of RFK's deathly pallor ('like the stone face of a child, lying on a cathedral tomb') is vivid and shocking but what I remember most is how he felt about being present. 'It would be quite false to say, as I should truly like to say, that I'm sorry I was there,' he wrote. Nothing I've ever read better captures the grim voyeuristic fascination that journalists feel about their seat at history's ringside. It was the privilege of my working life to watch these events unfold and to be trusted by so many of the participants with their thoughts and feelings.

To misquote *Macbeth*, it would be quite wrong to say – as this book makes painfully clear – that Brexit was done well, let alone done quickly and, as events unfolded, a growing number of people doubted that it could or should be done at all, but this (as best as I can reconstruct it) is how it *was* done.

Tim Shipman, Blackheath, July 2024

ACKNOWLEDGEMENTS

Out is based on countless contemporaneous conversations and around 280 formal interviews with prime ministers, cabinet ministers, senior civil servants, Brexit negotiators, Downing Street political advisers, special advisers, Labour aides, frontbenchers and MPs, and senior figures in the Brussels institutions.

I have also drawn on a range of contemporary papers and other media. These include leaked cabinet minutes and government documents, letters from cabinet ministers to their prime minister, political strategy memos, emails, texts and WhatsApp messages – as well as several recordings of meetings made by the participants for their own use.

Special thanks to those who helped turn more than 300 hours of interviews into more than 3.3 million words of transcripts. Richard Assheton, Megan Baynes, Julian Bovill, Christy Cooney, Harry Duell, Daniel Gayne, Eleanor Langford, Anna Menin, Holly Pyne, Joseph Wardropper and Jan Westad were particularly industrious. I'm also grateful to Louis Ashworth, Frankie Crossley, Lizzie Deane, Tony Diver, Connie Evans, Todd Gillespie, George Greenwood, Sam Hall, Fergus Horsfall, Megan Kenyon, Ella Kipling, Lucy Knight, Michael Mander, Matt Mathers, Oliver Milne and Josh Stein.

I conducted most interviews on background, allowing me to reconstruct what happened without stating the origin of each scene or quote. Where I have described people's words, thoughts or feelings, they were imparted by that individual, someone in whom they confided or another witness. I am grateful again to the Brexit Witness Archive, a series of interviews conducted by UK in a Changing Europe.

I would like to express my gratitude to Guto Harri, who shared with me the transcripts of his 2023 podcast series on the final months of the Johnson premiership; Ailbhe Rea of Politico's *Westminster Insider* podcast, who shared a transcript of her programme on the Truss government; and Laura Kuenssberg who shared transcripts of several of her documentary series. Kevin Schofield came through with a helpful transcript as I was on deadline. Harry Yorke shared the text of his interview with Nadhim Zahawi. Steve Back was very generous in contributing the only recent image of Dougie Smith to posterity.

Unlike my first two books, which were written in parallel with rivals, other authors have trodden some of this turf first. I am grateful to Anthony Seldon and Raymond Newell, Harry Cole and James Heale, Sebastian Payne, Tom Baldwin and Andrew Gimson – all of whom shared copies of their books before publication.

At A. M. Heath, Victoria Hobbs was a rock as both agent and therapist when the going got tough. I am blessed, too, with the best (and most patient) editor, the incomparable Arabella Pike. At William Collins I would also like to thank Iain Hunt, a copy-editor of infinite ability, who trimmed the gargantuan manuscript with tact and good humour; Alex Gingell, who stepped into the breach; Graham Holmes, a typesetter nonpareil who handled numerous corrections with speed and skill; Sam Harding, who sourced the pictures; Matt Clacher for his brilliant graphics; and Katherine Patrick for her energy in promoting the book. Andy Taylor read the manuscript and contributed valuable observations.

My greatest thanks are reserved for my family who endured countless absences and ruined holidays as this project spiralled out of control and seemed, at several points, like it would never be completed. My wife Charlotte is (nearly) a saint and I will be forever in the debt of my in-laws – Kate and Michael Todman – for their help with childcare as my younger daughter learned the phrase 'daddy, fucking book'. I know how she feels. To adopt the words of Sir Steve Redgrave after *his* fourth ordeal, 'Anyone who sees me go anywhere near a [Brexit book] again, ever, you've got my permission to shoot me.'

T.J.S.

PART ONE

ALL OUT WAR REDUX

BORIS UNBOUND

July to October 2019

'If you find yourself stuck in politics,
the thing to do is start a fight'

– Attributed to Cicero in Imperium, *Robert Harris, 2006*
(Harris says it actually came from Lenin)

'If you do everything, you'll win'

– Robert A. Caro, Master of the Senate

'I think you used "all out war" a bit too soon'

– Steve Baker to the author, autumn 2019

1

'BY ANY MEANS NECESSARY ...'

The Madman Strategy

24 July to 24 August 2019

'His love of combat and delight in battles were a
great support to me in carrying out the policy
I regarded as necessary'

– Otto von Bismarck

After Boris Johnson returned from Buckingham Palace on Wednesday 24 July and gave his first speech to the nation as prime minister, the famous black door opened and he stepped into the foyer of 10 Downing Street. He was greeted by Mark Sedwill, the cabinet secretary, the chief whip Mark Spencer and a phalanx of civil servants and political aides applauding. As the camera pulled back, another figure was visible in the far corner near the window where Larry the Number 10 cat liked to warm himself on a heater. The man slouched inside dark casual trousers, black trainers and a grey T-shirt emblazoned with the slogan 'Open AI', the tech company set up by Elon Musk. He might have been mistaken for a maintenance man if it were not for the hawk-like eyes drilled into the bald skull, skin stretched tight like a cadaver. The man clapped slowly, perhaps less enthusiastically than some, an ironic smile wetting his thin lips. His positioning was arch, his separateness deliberate, his don't-give-a-fuck dress code performative. Thus did the world become aware of the return to frontline politics of Dominic Cummings.

A week earlier it had been briefed that Sir Edward Lister, Johnson's chief of staff in City Hall, the recently appointed head of his transition team, would become the Downing Street chief of staff. Lister at first rejected Johnson's request as he was now sixty-nine, but was persuaded to hold the fort until the new year. 'What he particularly wanted me to do, apart from general lobbying of MPs I knew, was put together the team at Number 10,' Lister recalled.

Yet while they were preparing for government in Admiralty House, Johnson took Sedwill and his whip-smart deputy Helen MacNamara into a side room and said, 'We've got Dominic Cummings coming here.' Neither civil servant had worked with him before, but they were aware of his reputation as the mastermind of the Brexiteer victory in 2016. Both thought it would be an interesting experience, more so when Johnson appeared crestfallen. 'You're not as horrified as you should be,' he said. And so began a relationship between Team Boris and the 'deep state' more complicated than it was often depicted.

Lister and the rest of Johnson's team entered Number 10 through 70 Whitehall as Theresa May's team left. Officials ran off with their phones to spread the news that the 'Dark Lord' was back: 'Dom then appeared in that ridiculous grey T-shirt.' Oliver Lewis, the former research director of Vote Leave who had fought to make this moment happen, beamed from ear to ear. The band was back together. In the minutes before Johnson returned from the palace, Cummings and Sedwill were deep in conversation, power seeking out power. 'They got on like a house on fire to start with,' an official recalled. Then they assumed their positions, Sedwill the master of ceremonies, Cummings looming, as a witness put it, 'in the corner clapping like a sinister Machiavelli'.

Not everyone was ecstatic. 'Eddie was not particularly happy,' a political aide observed. But those who believed delivering Brexit was the only thing that really mattered did not think Lister was the right man to run Number 10. He had sought to persuade Johnson that the civil service was not his enemy. Lister invited Sedwill to his club, Alfred's, off Berkeley Square, along with MacNamara. 'Boris had it fixed in his mind that the civil service was always going to sabotage him,' Lister said. 'Mark and Helen were totally pragmatic, and I was trying to reassure him that they were good guys and not bad guys. I failed because that's the reason he brought Dominic in. He thought I was too close to the civil service.' In one transition meeting, a member of Vote Leave raised concerns about 'the machine taking over'. Lister said, 'Don't worry, the officials know what to do.' To those who saw the civil service as the problem, this was far from reassuring.

Lister felt the threat to Johnson would come from elsewhere: 'I kept saying to him, "I don't think you should worry about the civil service. I think you need to worry about the party."' It was a point also made by Conor Burns, Johnson's parliamentary private secretary. Burns, who had written a university thesis about the downfall of Margaret Thatcher, told Johnson, 'There are two things, apart from blonde hair, that Mrs Thatcher and you have in common. You are beloved of the grassroots and tolerated by the parliamentary party so long as you're winning. The moment she didn't look like she was going to win, they took her out.' This would prove to be good advice.

The Vote Leavers were adept at studs-up political campaigning, the City Hall people from Johnson's time as mayor of London were hard-wired for governing. Neither had much experience of Whitehall. But for the Vote Leave fraternity, getting out of the EU, in defiance of Parliament, needed Cummings' willingness to go hard into the tackle. Instead, one recalled, 'Eddie started picking all the City Hall people for the transition team.' Nor was there a plan for governing. 'The first conversation I had with Eddie,' one aide said, 'was about whether you could claim air miles in government' (you can't). 'There was a lot of talk about what the proto-col was to go to see the Queen', rather than what happened afterwards. 'The whiteboard was blank,' a Vote Leaver said. 'There was no plan.'

The only new arrival who quickly won over the Vote Leave crew was Munira Mirza, who had been Johnson's deputy mayor for education and culture at City Hall and took charge of the Number 10 policy unit. A former revolutionary communist who had been on a political journey to the anti-woke right, Mirza was married to Douglas Smith, a veteran Tory Party fixer whose reputation for the dark arts surpassed even that of Cummings. Known simply as 'Dougie', Smith had graduated from running high-end sex parties to stitching up Conservative candidate selections, but had made himself useful to every Tory prime minister for two decades. Oliver Lewis pulled Mirza aside and said, 'This isn't going to work. I've done my bit. I'm leaving.' Smith told him to stay.

These concerns reached crisis point in a meeting between Johnson's transition team and senior civil servants in the week before the leader-ship result. It was held in Back Boris's basecamp, a house overlooking College Green which belonged to Andrew Griffith, a millionaire former Sky executive and MP for Arundel. Johnson was accompanied by Lister, his old spin doctor Will Walden, aides Lee Cain and Ben Gascoigne, and

Shelley Williams-Walker, his head of operations. Peter Hill, the prime minister's principal private secretary, and the Number 10 official spokesman James Slack were among the government contingent.

As Lister and Williams-Walker ran through a series of appointments and plans for Johnson's first three weeks in Downing Street, several of those present grew uneasy as simple questions received garbled answers, or no answers at all. Cain and Walden nervously caught each other's eye. Hill and Slack shifted uneasily in their seats. 'The meeting was a fucking car crash,' said one of those present. 'A clown car was driving towards the gates of Number 10.' This assessment was shared by both political aides and civil servants. Afterwards, Johnson told Cain, 'Fuck me, that was embarrassing. It's a shambles.' Cain replied, 'Unless you've got someone else who you think can be your chief of staff, you've got to get Dom.'

Johnson had already begun looking for alternatives to Lister. He twice asked Will Walden to become director of communications but Walden declined. He had a lucrative job at Edelman; he could only offer strategic counsel. Cain, Johnson's media spad, was threatening to leave unless he got the top comms job. Johnson also approached Paul Stephenson, from Vote Leave, who wanted to focus on his business, Hanbury Strategy. Cain got the job. A week later, Johnson pressed Walden to become chief of staff. He declined again but agreed that Lister shouldn't run Number 10. 'Who's going to do it then?' Johnson asked. Walden produced a list of eighteen names. They included Isabel Dedring, the City Hall hand who Johnson most respected, Mirza, Ben Wallace, Tim Montgomerie, Vote Leave founder Matthew Elliott, and several senior journalists. None had the drive of Cummings.

There were two problems: Cummings was on holiday in Greece and he was due to have an operation under general anaesthetic the following Wednesday, the day Johnson was due to take power. When he returned, Cummings spoke to Oliver Lewis. 'You have to do this,' Lewis said. 'Since 2016, the Tory Party has cut us out. But this is our one chance to get in and deliver Brexit. We have to grab it.' That morning, Johnson texted Cummings asking if he could come over.

The meeting which shaped Johnson government more than any other took place in Cummings' sitting room that Sunday, 21 July. Tellingly, the future prime minister travelled to Cummings' turf – a move which created ambiguity about who was the senior partner. In at least four public accounts of the meeting[1] and in conversations with friends,

Cummings said Johnson asked him to take charge of the government machine. In one telling, Johnson said, 'I am going to be prime minister shortly. Everyone thinks that we're snookered ... there's no way through to get Brexit and the government is going to collapse. You guys somehow found a way to win the referendum when everyone thought it was impossible; you should assemble your old team in Number 10. Let's find a way through this nightmare.'[2]

Johnson expressed the fear that he would be 'the shortest-lived PM ever' and that a second referendum would mean 'the end of the Tory Party'. He had to survive until 20 November to surpass George Canning's 119 days in office. He added, 'Everyone thinks I'm fucked and I'm going to be turfed out in no time. I can't see a way through.' This was what Cummings called 'Boris-SA', in 'self-aware' mode, realistic about his plight, open about his shortcomings and determined to defy his critics. 'I'm good at motivating people, I can tell the public a story and get them behind me, but I'm not good at organising.' Then there was flattery. 'You understand how Whitehall operates, you got all of these reforms done in the Department for Education,' he told Cummings, referring to his time as an adviser to Michael Gove. 'I don't understand Whitehall, I'm not a details person. A lot of people in Whitehall don't want us to solve this problem, they want a second referendum.' Defiance too: 'I don't care about the MPs screaming, I don't care about the media going crackers, I know they hate you, all I care about is winning.' Johnson had engaged his 'rat brain', the ruthless mindset he employed when his political survival was at stake.

When he heard about Cummings' impending operation, Johnson blurted, 'Jesus, you're not going to die are you?'

'I'm not going to die, but it means I can't move for a couple of weeks.' Johnson asked him to delay the operation until after 31 October.

Cummings had known what was coming and had prepared his terms. 'If I'm going to do it, it's only worthwhile if we have a clear agreement.' He wanted to know that Johnson was willing to do what was necessary on Brexit, but also that he would have a free hand to reshape the way government worked. 'First, you are deadly serious about getting Brexit done and avoiding a second referendum? Secondly, double the science budget; thirdly, create some ARPA-like entity; and, fourthly, support me in trying to change how Whitehall works and the Cabinet Office works, because it is a disaster zone.'[3] ARPA was the US military body which invested government money in long-shot technologies and helped create forerunners to both GPS and the internet.

For Cummings, changing how Whitehall worked was not just a desirable outcome of Brexit, he saw it as a precondition for exploiting the new freedoms leaving would bring. 'I think Dom always thought Brexit was a door you had to go through for greater reform of the country,' a colleague said. 'Whereas Boris saw it as the end reform, which would get him to where he wanted to be.'

Cummings presented Johnson with a diagnosis of May's mistakes on Brexit and a blueprint for remedying them. 'Brussels and the Remainers have played extreme and the government have been pussies,' he said. 'That has to change.' He pointed to eighteen months of paralysis, which saw May's efforts to pass a deal thwarted by both Brexiteers – who considered the deal she struck with Brussels in November 2018 to be BRINO: Brexit in name only – and Remainers in the parliamentary 'Bresistance', who devised ways of changing established precedent in the Commons, with the help of the speaker, John Bercow, to prevent a no-deal departure. To Cummings, it was the Bresisters who broke the rules first in a quest to reverse the 2016 referendum result. Vote Leave's margin of victory was famously close – 52 per cent to 48 per cent – but the 17.4 million votes cast to Leave were the most for any proposition or party in British history.[4] Cummings said, 'If they're going to tear everything up, we are going to tear it all up. When officials start babbling about Ireland, the Union, the rule of law, we keep bulldozing: prorogue, refuse royal assent. They're trying to overthrow the biggest democratic vote ever. We're entitled to use extreme measures to stop them. People will present legal advice, leak to screw you. You need to be prepared to purge, and you don't like firing people. Are you on board for that? If you're not, you're already fucked.' Johnson said he was ready.

There were other demands too. Cummings did not want to be chief of staff, but nor was he prepared to serve under anyone else with that title. 'You have to tell Eddie that he's not chief of staff.' Cummings insisted on the mundane title of 'assistant to the prime minister'. Lister would become Johnson's 'chief strategic adviser'. Cummings also insisted that every special adviser in government report to him. 'Vote Leave worked because I actually ran it,' he said. 'I know how to build teams. We can't do something like this if there isn't clear responsibility over spads.' A colleague remarked, wryly, 'Dom wanted to be chief of all the staff, but not the chief of staff.'

Johnson blithely agreed to all these points: 'Deal!' Cummings observed later, 'He wanted somehow to win and he was prepared to sign up to almost anything to try and get us in there to make it happen.'[5]

But Cummings did not trust Johnson. 'I know what you are like,' he said. 'I don't want you saying in two months' time, "This is all very complicated. I don't think we agreed that." So, I'm going to write it down.' Cummings emailed his terms, which he dubbed his 'terrorist demands'.[6]

Johnson wriggled: 'Just get in here and then we'll figure it out.'

'Unless you agree he won't come,' Cain advised. Johnson finally caved on the Monday evening.[7] 'Boris was really pissed off that he had to put something in writing,' an aide said. Cummings, the subordinate, had got what he wanted from the principal. In their sixteen months together, this power imbalance was never fully resolved.

After talking to Johnson, Cummings discussed it with his wife, the journalist Mary Wakefield. 'It's a national emergency,' she said. 'You're partly responsible for this situation and you've got a new prime minister who's saying he's going to do this properly. You have got to do it.'

That night Johnson told Walden he was going to hire Cummings and asked his opinion. Walden acknowledged that Cummings was a 'brilliant campaign strategist' but added, 'Government is a very different thing. You need to demonstrate who's in charge. Within the first week, I would dress him down publicly.'

'Why would I do that?'

'Because otherwise, within weeks, he'll be running the show. You cannot give him ultimate power.' It was obvious from Johnson's horrified expression that he had already done so.

Given his doubts about Johnson, why did Cummings return and agree to help him? It was an issue he addressed in a blog in 2021 after he left Downing Street. 'We knew his skills and his weaknesses,' Cummings wrote. 'We knew he was, in any objective sense, unfit to be PM.' He recalled that, when the referendum result was announced, Johnson admitted, 'Obviously it's ludicrous me being PM – but no more ludicrous than Dave or George, don't you think?' Yet Cummings and his associates concluded, 'The combination of a second referendum and Corbyn would probably be an even bigger disaster than Boris as PM.' By contrast, 'if we get Brexit done, all sorts of good things will happen and are possible.'[8]

If that was the public-facing explanation, there was also an arrogance about the Vote Leavers, who thought they were better at politics than the Tory establishment. Cummings claimed: 'We understand Whitehall much better than him and understand effective political action much better than him and the Conservative Party. Our team will handle rough seas much better than the others … From our perspective we'd been right about the big things in the referendum while the party establishment had totally fluffed it, then they'd ignored everything we'd said about how to do the negotiations, done the exact opposite, driven the country and themselves into a cul-de-sac, and now the new leader was begging us to save them.' If this was justified arrogance, Cummings was also personally dismissive of Johnson in a manner that ought to have raised alarm bells. Johnson's negative attributes ('his ignorance of Whitehall, his uninterest in policy and his desire to enjoy himself rather than work hard') were seen by Cummings as an opportunity to play puppet master: 'Precisely because he doesn't know what he's doing, we may be able to get him to agree things "the system" will think are "extreme" but we think are necessary.' In extremis, he wrote, if Johnson 'tries to move us out of Number 10, we can try to move him out of Number 10'.[9] Seldom has a partnership at the top of government been built on less stable foundations.

And yet, to start with, it seemed (and largely was) a masterstroke. Carrie Symonds was, in this first stage of Johnson's premiership, a resolute supporter of Cummings, indeed she was instrumental in his hiring. She called the Vote Leave director and said, 'Please do this. He doesn't have a plan. He doesn't have a clue how government works.' She told friends, 'I'm Dom's biggest fan.' A colleague agreed: 'She backed Dom at all the key moments. Until the election she was completely supportive.'

A year previously, Cummings had told a Vote Leave WhatsApp group that he would send a 'bat signal' when the team needed to save Brexit. The deal done, he sent an emoji to the group the night before he entered Downing Street. The Brexit Avengers would assemble again.

Cummings' return enraged the European Research Group (ERG) who feared he would achieve cosmetic changes to the Northern Ireland backstop arrangement for the Irish border and then ram through a modified version of Theresa May's deal in a fourth meaningful vote. Their view was coloured by the internecine warfare of the referendum campaign and a blog in which Cummings branded Eurosceptic MPs 'useful idiots' and a 'metastasizing tumour'. Most vocal was Steve Baker, who slipped into Downing Street that Wednesday evening. Cummings was in the prime minister's office, holding court at the seat of power. 'I know what you're like,' said Baker. 'I know if it's war, you're a psychopath and you'll win. Everyone's talking about how you're here to sell us out.' Cummings was placatory. 'Everyone needs to calm down. It's all bullshit. This is my mission: I'll get us out of the EU by 31st of October by any means necessary. That is what I'm going to do. If the prime minister and the cabinet are going to change that, I will leave.'

The following day Johnson offered Baker a job as minister of state in the Brexit department. He refused on the grounds that the department was not in charge of the negotiations and had ceded control of no-deal preparations to Michael Gove. 'It's a Potemkin job!' Baker yelled at Johnson, furious his efforts on the campaign had not been better rewarded. 'I delivered for you!'[10] A witness said, 'Steve came in and went completely fucking mad, slamming the desk.'

Baker had once pithily described Cummings as 'political special forces' – useful in a campaign firefight but liable to shoot the wrong people in peacetime. 'When I look at Dominic Cummings and see the smile on his face, I know he intends to put us through the most utter misery,' he told a Westminster friend that afternoon. 'He takes pleasure in the collateral damage. In great battles it matters how you conduct yourself. When we were facing the Soviet Union, cluster bombs were a brilliant device for taking out columns of armour with infantry around them. You can turn multiple football pitches into a sea of vile death. But it's not an appropriate weapon to use in Afghanistan where children might pick up the unexploded rounds, so we banned them. Giving fair warning and then acting with restraint is what I do. Acting without restraint and giving no thought to the injuries they inflict is what they do.' It might have sounded paranoid, but it was not a bad description of what then unfolded.

Remainers and pro-dealers also feared Cummings' reputation for taking nuclear weapons to a pillow fight – but for the opposite reason. They assumed his presence made a deal much less likely. The stage was set for three tumultuous clashes between Johnson and Brussels, Johnson and Parliament and Johnson and the Tory Party.

* * *

Cummings played no role in the first assertion of prime ministerial power, Johnson's reshuffle, which saw eighteen cabinet ministers removed. It was dubbed the 'Night of the Blond Knives'. Some recalled Johnson saying his favourite moment in film was the scene in *The Godfather* where Michael Corleone shoots all of his rivals. The purge was conducted by Eddie Lister with help from Will Walden and Lee Cain, the details drawn up on a whiteboard brought to Andrew Griffith's house and later moved to Admiralty House where Johnson spent the day and night before his arrival in Number 10. 'Dom was not in a single meeting on the reshuffle,' said one senior figure. 'Eddie was the hammer. It was a reshuffle to deliver Brexit.'

Johnson was clear from the off that only those prepared to countenance no-deal could serve, but he was ruthless too with his supporters, sending Liz Truss to the Department for International Trade and keeping Matt Hancock at Health, when both craved the Treasury. Johnson promoted non-white ministers, making Sajid Javid chancellor and Priti Patel home secretary, the first time minority ethnic politicians had held two of the four great offices of state. Cummings' only contribution was to tell the prime minister not to appoint Javid, who he did not rate. Carrie Symonds, Javid's former spad, lobbied for him and won – the seeds of confrontation sowed.

There were key jobs for the three young bucks who had joined forces to back Johnson. Oliver Dowden became Michael Gove's deputy at the Cabinet Office. Robert Jenrick was made housing and communities secretary. The big prize went to Rishi Sunak, who became chief secretary to the Treasury. Jenrick's elevation created another problem, since Johnson's ally Jake Berry had expected the communities post. Berry was offered minister of state attending cabinet. 'Jake was astounded – after everything they'd shared, being godfather to one of the kids – that Boris could step back from that,' a friend said. For three hours Berry dug in. 'Jake didn't handle it well, and neither did Boris. Jake was rude to him.' Berry was talked round, but when the new cabinet met for the first time there were so many ministers he had to sit on an extra table. 'Guess who got cut off in the official photograph? He wasn't best pleased.'

Mandarins told Johnson that Gavin Williamson couldn't have a job requiring security clearance after his dismissal for leaking from the NSC. 'Oh come on,' Johnson said. 'Bit unreasonable on old Gav.' MacNamara took him through the details of the leak inquiry. 'Education?' said the

PM. After Williamson's appointment, MacNamara teased him: 'Could we just have six months, Gavin, where I don't have to tell you off?' Williamson agreed.

The first minister of state to be fired was Stephen Hammond, organiser of the Rebel Alliance of ministerial Bresisters. Johnson was so averse to confrontation that Hammond had to sack himself. He recalled, '[Boris] suddenly started saying, "Stephen, you're a great health minister doing a great job."' For a minute he was lavished with praise. 'Then I suddenly looked at him and I said, "But actually, Prime Minister, what you're trying to tell me is that you don't want me in your government." And he said, "Yeah, that's right."'[11]

The purge was just as brutal among the aides as among the ministers. Going into the Cabinet Office that morning, one adviser recalled an official holding a folder. 'It had everyone's head shots in it of the former spads who'd left to go on the campaign. There were crosses through some people's faces. I was thinking: *Christ, am I about to have a cross through my face?*'

To the senior civil service it was an underpowered cabinet, in which loyalty was prized above ability. Johnson privately admitted as much to one senior civil servant: 'It's just a temporary thing until we get Brexit through,' he said. 'Once we've done that, we'll get on with being a proper government. It's going to be amazing.' He may even have believed this.

As a student of Otto von Bismarck,[12] Cummings saw the challenge facing Johnson in 2019 as analogous to the Prussian political crisis of 1862. Wilhelm I ascended to the throne and wanted military reform, but was opposed by a liberal-dominated parliament. The king appointed Bismarck to break the deadlock. He announced that great issues would not be decided by speeches but by 'blood and iron' and ruled by executive decree, bypassing the legislature. This fuelled political hysteria in Berlin, but he was supported by provincial voters. 'You've got a massive constitutional crisis, you've got a capital city that's having a nervous breakdown and the rest of the country feels completely differently and just wants it to go away,' Cummings told colleagues. 'Bismarck's view was that people had gone mad – run into that. Everyone is saying "let's negotiate, let's be calm" but there is no calming things down, there is only punching through.'

In a dinner with two veteran Tory strategists ten days before he went into Downing Street, Cummings explained his approach: 'We're going to go so hard for no-deal that, if Remainers want to try and stop us, they're going to have to do something so crazy they will become toxic and we will smash them in the next election.'

One of his dining companions said, 'Parliament will stop you.'

'We'll have to use every trick in the book to stop them,' Cummings agreed, 'but we can do that.' A witness recalled, 'Dom was very clear that you've got to prorogue Parliament. You've got to sack Tories. Every part of his plan played out, apart from the fact that Parliament did manage to block no-deal. But in the end that turned in their favour.'

On the evening of Thursday 25th, Cummings gave a pep talk to political advisers in Downing Street, making clear that delivering Brexit was the government's sole meaningful objective for the next ninety-five days. The following evening, he summoned spads to the pillared room on the first floor of Number 10 and told them to cancel any holiday. 'Officials have fucked things up, yes, but the heart of this problem is that ministers and special advisers have fucked up the last three years. It's our job to fix it. You've got a bunch of very, very clever people in Parliament working to ensure that no-deal cannot happen. Now you've got a bunch of very, very clever people in Downing Street who will try and make sure it can happen.'

The chief adviser said being pro-Remain 'was a perfectly reasonable attitude'. Remarkably, he claimed not to know whether Brexit was a good idea, it was a question he regarded as unanswerable. 'What is not reasonable to say is, "We've promised to have a referendum and we're going to respect the result and swear blind there won't be a second referendum and your vote for is for a generation. But, oh, we lost. Fuck that, we're going to undo it." You can't do that!'

Cummings laid out the plan: 'The public wants to see someone who is serious about solving this and that the prime minister actually cares about what the country cares about, so we are going to do two things. First, we are going to do Brexit by any means necessary.' He used the phrase – appropriated from Malcolm X – six times. Explaining what he meant, Cummings said, 'MPs have ripped up every constitutional convention under the sun. They're now taking control of the order book and they're trying to overturn the biggest democratic vote in British history. There are no fucking rules.'

'Second,' he went on, 'we are going to have the prime minister out and about on schools, hospitals and crime, setting out what we are going to do in a way that the country can understand. Voters are going to see someone really trying to solve the problem and when he's not doing that he's trying to deal with the NHS and the police. We will constantly link the two, saying, "We can't get this shit sorted out because the idiot MPs in Westminster have had a breakdown."'

Many saw these sentiments as unpalatable, Cummings' goal as undesirable, his manner of getting there reprehensible, but this was an object lesson in how to identify a goal, galvanise a team and pursue a political strategy. In his appeal to voters in northern Leave seats, with buzz issues like the NHS and crime, Cummings also showed he understood that Brexit had accelerated a realignment of the political map. In 2017, Theresa May, despite losing her majority, had made big gains in these areas. Johnson, his electoral modelling showed, could mobilise this new coalition of voters to make giant electoral strides.

To aides used to the secrecy and banality of the May regime, Cummings was a blast of cold air – refreshing and unsettling. One spad said, 'We haven't had a clear plan for three years.' A Downing Street politico said later, '2019 is my best experience working in government without question. Everyone knew what the plan was. There wasn't the normal infighting because everyone's priorities were the same.'

To understand why Johnson and Cummings pursued such an uncompromising approach, it is necessary to understand how the Vote Leave fraternity viewed Brexit and how those sentiments gave them a better grasp of public opinion than Remain-dominated political Westminster. Cummings compared Bresisters and Labour in 2019 to the Remain campaign in 2016: 'By being in London, by being surrounded by just themselves and talking to each other, they ended up losing connection with what the country thought. Therefore, we were able just to tell a simple story that this problem is going to be resolved, there's only one way of doing it, and it's the only way that the country can move on.'[13]

The Downing Street team regarded Brexit as worth achieving at any price. Their bedrock belief was that the biggest exercise in direct democracy the country had ever seen had to be respected. This carried extra moral weight, for them, since many who backed Leave usually did not vote at all. To ignore the views of people who had backed Brexit because they felt ignored, overlooked, disenfranchised and patronised by elites in the metropolis seemed, to Johnson's team, doubly dangerous, when it was the same elites who were intent on overturning the result.

Explaining the divisions in Britain in 2019 required a psychologist, not a political scientist, such were the depths of distrust on both sides. To Remainers, Brexit was a regrettable event secured by dishonest means, with consequences wholly deleterious to the public good at home and Britain's standing abroad. To them, Brexit had also created a new world they did not like, where practical economic problems became intertwined with alien values: dislike of institutions, expertise and immigrants.

To Cummings and the other Vote Leavers, Brexit was more than an argument over economics. To them, the campaign was a bonding moment of such volcanic power that it forged a loyalty to each other that transcended party. Their first allegiance was to Vote Leave, not the Conservatives or Johnson, and Brexit was not a process or a set of consequences, it was an almost tangible thing they had helped to create, which gave their careers meaning, something they had to protect from those who resented it or didn't understand it.

Remainers who find this sentiment bewilderingly absurd might consider how they feel about the nearest comparison, in the depth and intensity of feeling on the other side: the NHS, that great secular devotion of British progressives. Like the health service, Brexit was arguably economically wasteful and financially inefficient. Yet its supporters defended the institution against legitimate attacks on its failures. They felt their beloved thing above criticism, proud that it had been birthed by Britain. After 2016, the UK acquired a second national political religion. Just as many would do anything to 'save' the NHS, so the Brexiteers were prepared to do anything to 'save' Brexit.

Even the mandarins, at least initially, liked the clarity. To start with, Cummings got on well with Sedwill and came to regard his deputy, Helen MacNamara, as his most worthy adversary. They, in turn, admired his firm guidance about what was expected, direction which did not come from Johnson. When MacNamara asked the new prime minister what he wanted to do in office, there was no masterplan. Johnson replied, 'Win, Helen! Win for Britain.' But the officials liked the sense of purpose on Brexit and Johnson's desire to spread economic growth outside the South-East through his 'levelling up' agenda. After three years of paralysis under Theresa May, it was refreshing. 'It was a massive relief to have a government which was going to agree with itself on Brexit,' a senior civil servant said. 'Working for May was absolutely tortuous. They [Johnson's team] came in expecting a lot of resistance and I think were surprised on the upside that we were just desperate to have a government who actually wanted to do something. It was exciting. Whatever you think about Brexit, it's the biggest question we ever get to ask: what country do you want to be? What kind of economy do you want'

Sedwill was interested in outcomes, rather than punctilious observation of rules. While he feared no-deal, the cabinet secretary also felt his fellow civil servants were foot draggers. 'We were desperate to have Brexit done,' another official recalled. MacNamara had been on maternity leave during the referendum campaign and found the response of the Whitehall establishment – opposing Brexit and having an incomprehensible row in Parliament – completely alien. 'When has setting up a new government department been the answer to any question in life?' she joked. She regarded Vote Leave's end, delivering the referendum result, as wholly legitimate. Where she became Cummings' principal adversary was over the means he was to use.

There was an unspoken agreement between the mandarins and the Vote Leavers. 'The civil service position was: a Brexit deal that Vote Leave will accept is better than no-deal, a second referendum or Jeremy Corbyn as PM. The system can't cope with no-deal, but we've got a shared interest in stopping Comrade Corbyn getting control of the nuclear subs. If you can navigate through to some sort of deal, the deep state will support you, but it will all fall apart if it's no-deal.'

His team in place, Johnson gave a rambunctious debut at the despatch box that Thursday, 25 July, pledging to make Britain 'the greatest place on earth' and to leaving the EU on 31 October 'whatever the circumstances'. 'To do otherwise would cause a catastrophic loss of confidence in our political system,' he said. 'I would prefer us to leave the EU with a deal. I would much prefer it', but, he argued, a time limit on the backstop was not enough. 'It must be clearly understood that the way to the deal goes by way of the abolition of the backstop.' After three years of trying to see the upside of Theresa May's boring Boycottery, to see Johnson emulating Botham, Flintoff and Stokes, despatching the ball to all corners of the ground, led to an almost cathartic release on the Conservative benches. 'I've never seen Tory MPs so happy,' one said.

The Vote Leavers, who had seen Johnson at his best during the final stages of the referendum campaign, when he and Michael Gove had swung for the fences and taken the fight to David Cameron, detected the same posture in him now: 'His attitude is different.'

To write about Boris Johnson is to confront the contradictions of the human condition and the violently different conclusions others can draw about the same person. To his admirers Johnson was politically gifted, instinctive, irrepressibly optimistic, idealistic, often decisive, eloquent, loyal to his staff (even those who had failed him), keen to take people with him but also prepared to go it alone – a disruptor with a mongrel immigrant background who beat the English ruling class at their own game. He was all of this, of course – and much less. To his critics, he was lazy, inattentive, pampered, easily distracted, glib, offensive, narcissistic, desperate to be loved, pathologically ambitious, cynical, disloyal, indecisive and liable to agree with the last person he spoke to – someone who regarded it as more important to be clever and funny than right. He was all of this, of course – and much more.

All governments and all Downing Streets reflect the personality of their leader, but this was never more the case than under Johnson. In meetings he cracked jokes, creating a warmer atmosphere than Theresa May. 'It was a way of making people feel they were on the same side and headed the same way,' a cabinet source said. 'People had deep misgivings about a lot of what he wanted to do yet he kept most of us on board.' He was also someone who listened to the most junior person in a room. 'He doesn't stand on ceremony,' a cabinet minister said. 'He doesn't care who comes up with ideas.'

Johnson was also popular with the permanent staff in Downing Street: the custodians, police, the 'garden girls' administrative staff, the cleaners and canteen workers. 'He's decent and kind,' an aide said. 'He said "hello" to them; he was nice to them. You were never made to feel that you were below stairs.'

Johnson could be an effective chairman, summing up clearly and giving firmer direction than May, but other meetings were anarchy. The 8.30 a.m. senior Downing Street staff gathering with Johnson was moved, at one point, to 9 a.m. because he kept being late. 'You had people coming in from miles away to be there by 7.30 a.m. but he couldn't be bothered to walk down two flights of stairs,' one aide said. Another Downing Street political adviser said, 'He can be very unfocused, but he has an ability to cut through to the core of an issue even if it's uncomfortable for everybody.'

Where he was engaged, Johnson could take in a lot of knowledge and give clear direction. A long-standing aide said, 'If it's something that piques his attention, or something that's fronted by someone with a brain, who is challenging him, he likes that. If he's not interested, he switches off very quickly, he'll crack the gags. It's a lazy assumption to assume that he has no intellectual rigour for detail. But it's not untrue that he has a short attention span.' Where he was unengaged, the perennial complaint of officials was that Johnson did not read the papers in his red box. One senior political aide recalled 'nagging, nagging, nagging all the time for him to do his work'. Others disagreed. A Number 10 adviser said, 'It's crap about him not reading his papers, it's shit. Some of the comments which would come back were just brilliant, written in red.'

Johnson's critics and admirers made the same mistake. Those who saw him as a blunderer assumed he was a populist cipher for Cummings, a trope with long-standing heritage from Piers Gaveston and the Despensers in the reign of Edward II to the Duke of Buckingham under Charles I. Those who liked Johnson, but disliked what he did, assumed he would do the right thing if only his head was not turned by Cummings. The truth was more complicated. A cabinet minister said, 'People misunderstand the relationship. It's not one where Dominic says, "Jump" and the prime minister says, "How high?" It's one where Dominic still has to prove his case.'

That said, Cummings operated with rarely seen autonomy. 'Dom pursues a strategy, which is separate from the prime minister's strategy,' a Number 10 adviser recalled. 'It may be parallel, but it's not directly the same thing in a way that it obviously was for Ed Llewellyn', David Cameron's chief of staff. The problem was that Cummings was not a chief of staff, nor would he let anyone else be. 'There's nobody who turns up at 5 a.m. and reads all the key papers and puts the most important ones on top of the pile,' a Tory MP said.

Cummings was deeply sceptical about Johnson the politician but his assessment of Johnson the man successfully captured his contradictions in a way that both friends and foes could recognise:

The media generally portray Boris either as a) a clown and much simpler than normal senior politicians or b) a 'campaigning genius' ... The truth is he is neither. He is a much deeper and

more complex character … Behind each mask lies another mask –
but there's no masterplan … just the age old 'will to power'. He is
happy to hide behind the mask of a clown, mostly unbothered by
ridicule, while calculations remain largely hidden (including from
parts of his own mind). He rewrites reality in his mind afresh
according to the moment's demands. He lies – so blatantly, so
naturally, so regularly – that there is no real distinction possible
with him, as there is with normal people, between truth and lies.
He always tells people what they want to hear and he never means
it. He always says 'I can't remember' when they remind him and is
rarely 'lying'. He trusts nobody including his own family yet bears
almost no grudges. He will sacrifice anybody for his career yet
wants to make up with people who have screwed him over. He
will use anybody for anything but is more polite than most top
politicians towards junior staff. He is totally untrusted by anybody
in No10 yet has a superpower for making people feel sorry for him
… He's almost as comfortable with living in chaos as [boxer]
Floyd Mayweather but panics all day about the media. He
sometimes compares himself to historic titans (Octavian is a
favourite) and regularly admits it's ludicrous he's prime minister
… He is both much more useless than the media portray and
much more capable of self-awareness and ruthlessness than … his
enemies usually discern. He routinely says and does things so
foolish that people are open-mouthed, and is so hopeless at
getting rid of duffers, so determined to avoid difficult situations,
that people are usually shocked when he suddenly moves with
ruthless speed to remove them. He was desperate to be prime
minister but has almost no interest in the job. He complains
constantly about 'leaks and briefing' but he and his girlfriend can't
stop leaking and briefing.[14]

Others who watched Johnson up close saw a deeply troubled man. 'He's
so dark,' a senior civil servant said. 'There are three Borises. There's the
performer. The high he gets from being able to show off in front of
people is incredible. Then when he is not with people he needs to show
off to, if he's just sitting in a room with Dom or a few others, it's really
not fun. He can be dark and unpleasant and cross, sometimes petulant.
Then when he is on his own, he is unbelievably melancholy – really,

really bleak and self-loathing.' Even this witness regarded Johnson as the most interesting person they had ever met.

With a difficult upbringing, a father who beat up his mother, and a turbulent personal life, Johnson was a prime candidate for therapy, but gave no impression of ever having had any. His solitary nature was a factor in one of his biggest political problems: since he was not a clubbable character given to chit-chat in the tearoom, his relationship with MPs was a marriage of convenience where loyalty was transactional. They sensed that he did not regard them as his equals. 'They will do for him, by the way, not a shadow of a doubt,' a veteran Tory said in his first weeks. They did, in the end. The relationship with MPs would have been problematic even without the intense feelings unleashed by Brexit, but from the beginning, some backbenchers were implacable foes. 'I'd never realised, and he certainly didn't, how bitter some of them were,' recalled Eddie Lister. 'They were beyond reasonable. It was, "You are the force of darkness. You've destroyed the UK. I'm going to fight you every step of the way." They were ghastly. We didn't realise it was going to be that bad.' Cummings had a similar experience: 'The first time I walked into Parliament, I saw people weeping and shouting hysterically at each other in corridors. I had streams of MPs following along behind me, literally dancing with rage, just at my physical presence. A very large faction of Westminster had completely lost their minds.'[15] Johnson's political strategy sharpened these sentiments.

That first Thursday, Johnson held telephone conversations with German chancellor Angela Merkel and French president Emmanuel Macron in which he outlined his position that the backstop had to go. There had been suggestions that Johnson would make an early visit to Berlin or Paris to mend fences, but Cummings (vociferously) and attorney general Geoffrey Cox both advised against. 'They think we're going to go running to them,' an aide said. 'We're not.'

Johnson's first visits, at Lister's suggestion, would be to the four corners of the UK, prioritising Northern Ireland, Scotland and Wales over Brussels.

Cummings was leaving that first Thursday evening when Johnson asked him to come up to the flat. He had to be shown the way by an official. As they arrived the phone went; it was Macron. The official began scribbling notes 'on the back of a fag packet'. Macron said they needed to talk. Johnson replied, 'Well, I spoke to Jean-Claude [Juncker] earlier on and he said that there's nothing to talk about. So, we're just getting on with no-deal planning.' After a long pause, Macron made a couple of suggestions about how progress might be made. Johnson said, 'In the grand scheme of history, no-deal would be a small bump in the road.'

At the first cabinet on 30 July, Javid, the new chancellor, told ministers they would get the funds they needed to pay for no-deal preparations, a contrast to Philip Hammond's approach. After the meeting, a cabinet minister said: 'I can't work out whether this is going to be the greatest implosion in the history of British politics or the greatest triumph, but it's definitely one of the two.' Even afterwards, opinions would differ.

Johnson tore up the Brexit decision-making structure he inherited from May and replaced it with something like a plan Geoffrey Cox had drawn up for him during the leadership election campaign.[16] There would be an Exit Strategy committee, called XS in Whitehall and immediately dubbed the 'Brexit war cabinet' by the press. Chaired by Johnson, the membership was limited to six key ministers – Gove, Cox, Javid, Barclay and Dominic Raab. Gove, who became Chancellor of the Duchy of Lancaster (CDL), would chair a separate Exit Operations committee (XO), which met daily to plan for no-deal and drive through the referendum result. Cummings wanted XO run out of the Cobra emergency committee meeting rooms in the basement of the Cabinet Office, which had flatscreens for showing information, where a 'dashboard' of Brexit readiness could be displayed. He wanted decisions taken and immediately actioned by officials. Mark Sedwill felt 'relief' since, 'If you really want to drive a programme of that scale and ambition through Whitehall, you can't do it unless there's a really senior minister at the helm.'[17]

David Frost, special adviser to Johnson at the Foreign Office, was drafted in to take the lead role vacated by Oliver Robbins. Frost's Euroscepticism dated back to a four-year diplomatic posting to Brussels in the mid-1990s. Spells as Europe director of the Foreign Office and ambassador to Denmark followed. He then led on trade policy at the Department of Business between 2010 and 2013, before leaving government for stints with the Scotch Whisky Association and the British Chambers of Commerce (BCC). Remainers in Whitehall saw a mediocre and disgruntled ex-diplomat thrust into a post for which he was not qualified. But mandarins who worked with him, including Sir Simon McDonald, the Foreign Office permanent secretary, an emotional opponent of Brexit, said Frost was capable and could have landed himself one of the prized embassies if he had remained a diplomat. Working in Brussels 'had the reverse effect on me that it has on many other people,' Frost said. 'I felt Cameron just didn't try with the renegotiation. The dismissive way we got treated was the other thing that did it for me. It changed me from somebody who was an extreme sceptic to thinking: "There's no other choice but to leave."'

When he handed over, Robbins gave Frost a primer on how they had got to where they were, some pointers on how to handle the personalities in the EU and 'what works and what doesn't' in negotiations, but they did not discuss what to do next. Frost's big advantage over Robbins was his close relationship with Johnson. 'They do share a lot of the same views,' a civil servant said. The new chief negotiator spoke with both his master's voice and authority. As a political appointee he could say things a civil servant like Robbins could not.

In the first couple of weeks, Frost detected 'sullen hostility' from officials. He privately compared Johnson's arrival in Downing Street to the Norman invasion of 1066. 'William the Conqueror, by a mixture of good luck and skill, managed to seize power. But there were a lot of people who didn't want it and you had to rule through existing elites.' He saw this as institutional shock rather than hostility. 'They had been dealing with a different approach for so long that they couldn't process that we meant what we said, that we were going to do something different,' he said. 'At that point, everyone thought getting rid of the backstop was a totally unachievable fantasy and didn't take it seriously.' He was also surprised at how open officials were that they expected Britain to end up in the customs union. He decided shock tactics were needed. 'Frost said he didn't want anybody going to any EU meetings any more,' an official recalled. This was designed to 'shake the system' and 'shift the psychology in Whitehall [to show] that we were actually leaving'. It was watered down to exclude the most important meetings, but Frost made his point.

Johnson's team believed there were only three possible outcomes: a no-deal Brexit, a general election or a last-minute concession from Brussels. They were sceptical that a deal could be done and recognised it might be October before the Commission realised that Britain was serious about no-deal. They also knew they would have a constitutional battle to prevent Remainer MPs blocking it.

Frost and Johnson devised a three-stage plan for dealing with the EU. In the first phase, they would stake out their position and force Brussels to listen. Stage two was a holding operation, 'filling time and keeping them interested,' an aide put it. Frost planned a drip feed of positional policy papers. Phase three was the last three weeks, when they believed there would be a shared appetite for a deal. Phase one would conclude with Johnson writing to EU Council president Donald Tusk outlining Britain's proposals. First, they had to decide what to say.

That process began on 29 July, five days after Johnson became prime minister, when the Exit Strategy committee met for the first time. Frost presented a paper titled 'Approach to engagement with the EU on renegotiation', detailing plans to demand an end to the backstop and 'run down the clock' towards the October deadline. 'The fundamental premise is that the EU has not taken us seriously throughout this entire process,' a senior aide said. 'The only way to do it is to make them think that you're genuinely serious about no-deal.' Geoffrey Cox thought the Frost plan amounted to telling the EU to 'bugger off', but it was adopted.

If this was too much for some, it was not enough for the ERG, many of whom now wanted no-deal as the declared destination. The group had to be 'taken on a journey' in a series of Downing Street dinners at which the heavy lifting was done by Oliver Lewis. 'We'd love to rewrite the whole withdrawal agreement,' he said, 'but the EU is not budging. They might budge on the backstop.'

Tempers flared at the second XS meeting on 1 August when Cox confronted Johnson, telling him it was 'a complete fantasy' to think the EU would ditch the backstop. That was 'contrary to what they have published as their mandate'. The attorney general feared there was still a lack of understanding about the history of the negotiations and what was possible. 'These are legalistic things,' he said. 'They don't have the legal right to strip out the backstop.' Cox wanted the prime minister to have a clear view of what it would mean. 'I understand the need to be tough,' he added. 'If this is a bargaining tactic, fine, but it's not realistic as a destination. I will stand with you but you should know this is the path to no-deal.' Johnson did not say much. According to one of those present, 'He rolled his eyes, he shrugged his shoulders and he expressed a sort of saturnine resentment of being told things he didn't want to hear.'

Cox had campaigned for Brexit to recover Britain's legal and political sovereignty. He was prepared to pay a significant cost for that, but he wanted Johnson to be more honest than May about the trade-offs. The attorney general was also concerned by Johnson's desire to commission a second opinion about the £39 billion the UK had agreed to pay the EU on departure. Cox believed the Treasury had played a blinder in 2017 and got the European Council to agree a pared-back assessment of Britain's obligations. A second opinion was likely to raise the number. Johnson insisted on one anyway. 'They wanted a different opinion from some people they trusted,' a civil servant said. 'They basically cherry-picked a couple of Brexity lawyers and those people came back and said, "This is going to go up not down."' Nothing was ever published.

Throughout August and September, it was far clearer to ministers on XS what Johnson *did not* want. 'We didn't really know what the prime minister *did* want,' said one. Publicly, he called no-deal a 'million-to-one' shot, but privately he expressed a willingness to take that path. 'My view,' a member of XS said, 'was that he was entirely opportunistic. He was like a boxer, circling the ring, waiting to see if there was an opening, throwing a few jabs to see if there was a vulnerability in his opponent's defence.'

The criticism of Johnson was that he took a simplistic boosterish view of the world into highly technical negotiations. But ministers on XS say he did understand the issues. 'I was extremely impressed with the read-ing in that he had done and the manner in which he chaired meetings,' said one. However, for tactical and temperamental reasons, Johnson 'did not allow himself to be weighed down by' the potential problems, 'he had to brush them aside'. It is legitimate to criticise this as unrealistic, but it was also what had made Johnson a successful politician and allowed him to break through the conceptual straitjacket that had bound the May government. 'Sometimes a mindless bloody optimism is the only thing you've got,' the cabinet minister said. 'He came in spades with it – and he changed the game.'

A month after the first, fractious, exchanges in XS, it leaked to the *Telegraph* that Cummings had described negotiations with the EU as a 'sham', a story dismissed as a lie by Downing Street but which its author, Peter Foster, insisted came from multiple credible sources.[18] In conversa-tion with Mats Persson, the former director of Open Europe, who was now a special adviser at the Treasury, Cummings said he thought there was a '1 per cent chance' of a deal, but that he would not stand in the way of one. He told a confidant, 'My honest view is that it's either no-deal or an election. There's not going to be a fucking deal.' Asked about the dangers of no-deal, Cummings replied, 'I literally don't give a fuck.' A fellow Vote Leaver said, 'We knew the only way to get a deal was to look as if we didn't give a shit. It's the "madman theory", where Brussels really had to believe, "Shit, these guys really will just leave. They're not bothered."'

Summing up, a senior civil servant said, 'Dom didn't mind what the deal was. He didn't really mind if there was no-deal, what he wanted was to leave. But he certainly wasn't actively pushing no-deal. David [Frost] had the huge reputational issue that, if he didn't get a deal, it would look like a failure for him. The PM always felt that we'd get one but was not sure quite how.'

Either way, Cummings was confident that if Parliament blocked no-deal the resulting election would be fought on his terms. In July he told a Westminster confidant, 'If there's going to be an election it happens because Parliament has done something that is without precedent in four hundred years. It will be a very extreme event that stops us. If that happens, the election won't even be about Brexit, the election will be about: do MPs get to cancel votes? We have to leave and the current Parliament has to be destroyed.' Another Johnson aide said the goal was to 'lock Parliament in the boot of a car'.

The insouciance of the Vote Leave faction was not shared by much of the cabinet. Julian Smith, the Northern Ireland secretary, 'made it very clear early on that to strip out the backstop was disastrous for Northern Ireland,' a fellow cabinet minister said. Michael Gove, whose job was now to prepare for no-deal through the Exit Operations (XO) committee, also grew increasingly queasy. In meetings of XS, he even said several times that he had a 'nostalgic soft spot' for May's deal, since Cox had persuaded him of its merits. 'But I recognise that is gone,' he added. Johnson rated Gove's ministerial abilities highly but there was lingering awkwardness between the two men after the events of 2016, when Gove described Johnson as unfit to lead and stood against him for the party leadership. 'A couple of times I was in a room with them, there were periods of silence,' said a colleague. 'There was a bit of a crackling in the air, of tension.'

Gove's nervousness was shared by civil servants. To get them in a better place, the XS 'war cabinet' agreed a set of principles to circulate in Whitehall, so 'the system' understood what was expected of it. 'We had to actually write down, "The future is to be based on a free trade agreement" and "We will not agree to the backstop, will not agree to the customs union",' a senior aide said. Tom Shinner, in the Cabinet Office secretariat, refined the wording before leaving for the private sector. The XO committee then sent letters to every secretary of state, setting out that their number-one priority was to prepare for no-deal.

One other looming issue was what Johnson had told the DUP conference in November 2018. On the stage in Belfast, he got a standing ovation when he told the party faithful, 'We need to junk the backstop', and said he could never countenance a customs border in the Irish Sea. 'We would be damaging the fabric of the Union with regulatory checks and even customs controls between Great Britain and Northern Ireland,' he said. 'I have to tell you that no British Conservative government could or should sign up to any such arrangement.'

On the way home, Saturday 24 November, Johnson accepted a ride in the private jet of Christopher Moran, a property tycoon and Tory donor. Landing at a private airfield, Johnson jumped into Moran's Rolls-Royce, leaving Conor Burns and Lee Cain, who had accompanied him, with a £160 taxi ride into London. They were still en route at 10.30 p.m. when Johnson messaged Burns, 'Have you seen the *Sunday Times*?' The paper was splashing on a report that Moran owned Chelsea Cloisters, a luxury apartment block where 'more than one hundred prostitutes' plied their trade, known as the 'ten floors of whores'.[19]

Burns replied, 'Suboptimal', knowing he would have to declare the plane ride in his register of member's interests. Johnson paid the £1,308.32 cost of the flight to avoid declaring it – but was exposed anyway when Burns' entry dropped. Johnson's commitment to no customs border in the Irish Sea would be just as hard to dodge. In the meantime, the biggest threat was not a disgruntled DUP but a group of people whose number-one priority was to prevent no-deal.

The Bresistance movement consisted of a series of overlapping groups of MPs, using WhatsApp to coordinate their activities, all with slightly different priorities. In the early part of 2019, the curiously named Trains

and Buses group[20] had been a key coordinating body, but by the time
Johnson came to power, the thing that brought all of them together was
a conviction that no-deal had to be prevented. The key figures, known as
the No to No Deal group or the Benn group, met weekly in the offices of
Hilary Benn, the former Labour cabinet minister, who chaired the Brexit
select committee. The driving forces were Oliver Letwin and Dominic
Grieve who had devised a means of thwarting the government by taking
control of the Commons' timetable to pass a backbench bill – an enterprise made possible by John Bercow's willingness to interpret the
standing orders of the House in new ways. The group brought together
those backbenchers with the opposition front benches in the form of Keir
Starmer, the shadow Brexit secretary, and Jo Swinson, the leader of the
Liberal Democrats, plus Caroline Lucas of the Greens and others from
the SNP and Plaid Cymru. They were newly strengthened by the so-called
'Rebel Alliance' ministers who resigned in the dying hours of the May
government, of whom Philip Hammond, David Gauke and Greg Clark
were the most notable.

Having tied May's hands with the Cooper–Letwin bill (co-sponsored
by Labour's Yvette Cooper), which forced May to seek an extension to
the Brexit deadline, they quickly agreed there would need to be another
parliamentary effort to prevent no-deal under Johnson. Grieve, like
Letwin and his confidant Nick Boles, concluded the moment of maximum vulnerability was the period in mid to late October, after the party
conference recess. They knew Johnson had not ruled out proroguing
Parliament across the Brexit deadline on the 31st.

The problem was that the procedural innovations the alliance had
used to tie May's hands were no longer possible. In the spring, they had
only been able to seize control of the Commons timetable to pass their
own bill because the government had to bring forward a withdrawal bill
or a meaningful vote on a Brexit deal. If Johnson's House managers were
canny, and did not table legislation, that route was now closed off. 'We
were in a panic because we did not have the same mechanism,' one of
those involved recalled.

In early August, Letwin and Boles came up with a new idea, the 'SO24
route', exploiting another arcane Commons procedure. Under Standing
Order 24, an MP could ask the speaker for an emergency debate and had
three minutes to make their case. The speaker decided whether to allow
it. The motion to be debated, on the next sitting day, was usually 'That

the House has considered the matter of X'. The loophole for the rebels was contained in SO24B, which said, 'Where, in the opinion of the Speaker ... a motion ... is expressed in neutral terms, no amendments to it may be tabled.' That suggested that while the convention had always been that SO24 was a neutral motion, it need not be if the speaker said so. If a motion was not neutral, it could be amended and used as another pretext to seize control from the government.

The Bresisters were guided to this ploy by the House authorities, including Bercow himself. One said, 'We were encouraged to believe that the wording of the standing order would reward particularly close attention.' Asked about Bercow's role, the source said, 'My take, as a beneficiary of it, is that he bent as far as they would stretch but didn't quite break the proprieties. At no point did he say, "This is what you should do." On the other hand, he had thought through where possibilities lay. He'd explored them in great depths with the clerks.'

Having worked out how to seize the initiative in Parliament, the Rebel Alliance had to decide what they would do when they had it. This was a complicated process, since getting a Commons majority meant devising a plan backed by every faction: the Labour leadership; Keir Starmer; the SNP; Plaid Cymru; Letwin and Boles and their Labour allies Lucy Powell and Stephen Kinnock, who backed a soft Brexit; Grieve's group of Tory Bresisters, who now backed a referendum; Stephen Doughty, a key Labour MP who acted as a whip for the Bresistance and the People's Vote campaign, which was pressing for a referendum; Chris Leslie and Anna Soubry of Change UK; and the Rebel Alliance of ex-ministers who were less militant than the Grieve group. In Tory ranks, Guto Bebb was prepared to vote down the government in a no-confidence motion to prevent no-deal while other ex-ministers like David Gauke were not. Another MP ruefully remarked that even the Liberal Democrats had contrived to have 'three different positions on Brexit among eight MPs' at the 2017 election. Boles recalled, 'It was not so much herding cats as dragooning rabbits – with Dom Cummings flapping balefully overhead like a hungry vulture.'

In the meantime, a group of twenty-one Conservative MPs signed a letter to Johnson urging him to get a deal. It was arranged by Anne Milton and the Rebel Alliance's most high-profile new recruit, Philip Hammond. 'He found a backbone late in his career,' a fellow rebel observed. 'It was Boris who motivated him. Philip hates his guts.' The letter, published on 12 August, offered 'our complete and wholehearted support' in getting a deal but warned that Johnson's red lines 'set the bar so high that there is no realistic probability of a deal being done'. Seven former cabinet ministers signed the letter, which was leaked to the press by Number 10 to show the public what Johnson was battling against.

By mid-August, believing they had time to think over the summer, a number of the key players went on holiday. 'We agreed we would resume at the beginning of September,' one said. 'We assumed we had time.' They were wrong.

The Bresistance convinced themselves that Johnson was doing nothing to get a deal – because, on the surface, nothing seemed to be happening. 'The second phase was misunderstood domestically as us not wanting to actually do any negotiations and not being serious about it,' Frost recalled. 'We had this whole thing about people saying, "They haven't handed over any papers and there is no text."'

Concern about Johnson's approach was compounded by doubts about his team. Peter Hill, May's principal private secretary, was replaced by Martin Reynolds, who had been with Johnson at the Foreign Office but who did not know Number 10. Reynolds, sensing he did not command the same respect, tried to ingratiate himself with colleagues by encouraging social activities, earning himself the mocking moniker 'Party Marty' – which was to have embarrassing consequences.

Only in the second week of August did Frost begin discussing with Johnson what a new deal might look like. These conversations were kept very tight. The negotiator also began to talk regularly to Stéphanie Riso, now the key figure in the Commission president's office. He went to Brussels a couple of times and saw the French and the Germans but found them dismissive. He sensed 'Boris derangement syndrome'. Frost told a colleague, 'They just can't look through the persona and make rational judgements about what we are trying to do.'

The fear that Johnson and Cummings would take extreme action to force through no-deal gave rise to another idea to thwart them. On 5 August, the veteran *Guardian* columnist Polly Toynbee suggested the anti-no-deal alliance should consider something 'so outrageous it makes you gasp to contemplate it'. They 'would set up a temporary government of national unity to outvote Johnson' in a no-confidence motion. She explained, 'The only purpose of this "government" would be to ask the EU for a delay, to conduct a referendum and a general election.'[21]

The idea had first come up during a Trains and Buses dinner in February 2019, when Phillip Lee (who resigned as a Tory minister over Brexit) looked around the room at the former frontbench talent and said, 'This is a credible government. Wouldn't it be great if we could just swap places ... with the monkeys who are currently in cabinet?'[22] Toynbee's article was amplified by the summer 'silly season' in Westminster as Bresisters debated the prospects of a creature called 'gnu', the Government of National Unity (GNU). No question was more intensely pondered than who would be interim prime minister. Toynbee said it had to be an MP from Labour, a 'statesperson respected on all sides', rather than an 'active player', who might run for leader one day. She wrote, 'Rebel Tories suggest several names, but one stands out: Margaret Beckett, a previous interim Labour leader, who would be trusted to do only what the crisis demands.'[23] With their permission, Jo Swinson, the new leader of the Liberal Democrats, proposed the father and mother of the House, Ken Clarke and Harriet Harman. Hilary Benn's name was also floated.

The complication for the GNU crew was that, under the rules of the Fixed-term Parliaments Act, if Johnson lost a no-confidence vote he would not immediately have to resign. He could fight on for fourteen days before having to show that he could command a majority. Downing Street made clear that Johnson would not quit. This led to fervid talk that Bercow would allow an indicative vote to show that another leader, such as Ken Clarke, could command a majority, pressuring the Queen to ask him to form a government instead. Johnson's team got legal advice which concluded that the Queen's decisions, and the precedents they were based on, could not be challenged in court. 'You can't JR [judicially review] the Queen and you can't JR a convention,' a source said.

Despite the, at times, near-hysterical chatter, GNU never got off the ground. Dominic Grieve was among the sceptics. He could see a viable cabinet being created from Remainer grandees, but doubted it could sustain a parliamentary majority for long enough to achieve its goals. The real deal breaker, though, was Jeremy Corbyn. Egged on by their chief whip Nick Brown, Labour said they would only countenance a GNU if Corbyn led it. Brown had been at Gordon Brown's side when Nick Clegg demanded he stand down as Labour leader after the 2010 election. He was determined it would not happen again. 'Nick was very clear,' a close ally said, 'other parties don't get to pick who the leader of the Labour Party is.'

On 14 August, Corbyn wrote to fellow party leaders outlining his plan for a 'strictly time-limited' caretaker government. He said he would call a no-confidence vote and then try for a general election, which required the support of two-thirds of MPs. Labour would then campaign for a second referendum with the option to remain in the EU. Two days later, Corbyn said he was planning to convene a meeting, announcing that he was 'ready to serve'. He said, 'In Britain, when a government collapses, the leader of the opposition is called on to form a government.'

Jo Swinson, no fan of Corbyn, told an aide to call his office to find out when and where the meeting was due to take place. 'They didn't answer the phone all afternoon,' a Lib Dem official recalled. 'He'd been on TV saying he was going to convene a meeting. We couldn't get hold of them for twenty-four hours. That's the level of incompetence we were dealing with.' It confirmed to Swinson that Corbyn's operation was incapable of guiding the nation through a once in a century political crisis.

When the meetings did take place, 'Jeremy used to introduce things, then hand over to Seumas Milne,' a Lib Dem said. 'It was comical.' The Labour leader would ask, 'What do we think of this, Seumas?' Milne, who thought Labour should campaign on class issues, not Brexit, appeared totally uninterested.

This is where the events of spring 2018 came home to roost for Corbyn.[24] His disastrous handling of the aftermath of the Russian poisoning of MI6 double agent Sergei Skripal in Salisbury, the war in Syria and antisemitism running rampant in the Labour Party rendered him incapable of commanding a majority in the Commons. Had he behaved differently in 2018 he might have been regarded simply as a poor leader who could be trusted with one task. Instead, many MPs saw Corbyn as repugnantly unsuited to national leadership. A Liberal Democrat official was clear, 'Jo would refer to Jeremy as an antisemite in private.'

For their part, Corbyn's aides feared the GNU was a Trojan horse. 'I was always very concerned that this government of national unity thing was the vehicle through which a new party would be created,' one said. In the end, a Labour adviser admitted, 'You could see, as time went on, that this fantasy coalition just didn't work.' It was a view shared by Tory rebels. Greg Clark said, 'It was totally absurd from beginning to end. It amazes me that intelligent people could even begin to think that was a prospect. It was a waste of mental energy thinking about it.'

By mid-August, Johnson's team judged it the right time to take their argument to European leaders. On the 19th, the prime minister published his letter to Donald Tusk, outlining Britain's new negotiating position. The four-page letter set out Johnson's approach to what Frost and Oliver Lewis saw as the philosophical trap which Theresa May fell into. Their objections dated back to December 2017, when May signed a Joint Report with the EU,[25] which created the so-called 'backstop', a device to prevent a hard border between Northern Ireland and the Republic. In practice, the way Brussels saw it working was to keep Northern Ireland in close alignment with EU rules and regulations. In her deal of November 2019, May had secured what she considered a coup by persuading the EU to accept that the whole of the UK could enjoy the same access to the European market as the Ulstermen. To Johnson and the ERG this made the whole UK a 'rule-taker' from Brussels. To them it was an abrogation of Brexit. The letter marked a formal rejection of 'full alignment' with the EU in paragraph 49 of the Joint Report, which had impaled May on the horns of the backstop.

Johnson gave three reasons why the backstop was 'unviable'. 'First, it is anti-democratic and inconsistent with the sovereignty of the UK ... Second, it is inconsistent with the UK's desired final destination for a sustainable long-term relationship with the EU', in which Britain would diverge from EU rules. 'That is the point of our exit.' Third, he explained, 'the backstop risks weakening the delicate balance embodied in the Belfast (Good Friday) Agreement.' He concluded, 'The backstop cannot form part of an agreed Withdrawal Agreement. That is a fact we must both acknowledge.' He called for 'flexible and creative solutions' to replace it, including 'alternative arrangements', the phrase used by Brexiteers to connote technical means of tracking goods.

Tusk's formal response, the following day, said Johnson's letter contained no 'realistic alternatives' to the backstop. A Commission statement added, 'the letter does not provide a legal operational solution to prevent the return of a hard border on the island of Ireland'. Behind the scenes, however, one of chief EU negotiator Michel Barnier's aides detected an opening: 'Saying he would reject an "anti-democratic" backstop, some on our side saw a glimmer of hope that maybe a democratic backstop is acceptable.'

To several of the officials who had been in Downing Street since Brexit, this slapdown was both inevitable and necessary. 'They went on the same journey that May did, but just in two months,' an official in the private office said. 'They went through the same intellectual exercise, just massively compressed: the same set of difficulties, with the same set of choices, with the same parliamentary arithmetic.'

The letter was only the first move. Johnson now embarked on a charm offensive with European leaders, meeting Angela Merkel on 21 August, Emmanuel Macron on 22 August and then holding talks with Jean-Claude Juncker, the Commission president, at the G7 summit in Biarritz, between the 24th and 26th of August. 'The idea was that the PM would present what they would regard as a surprisingly acceptable and European face compared to all the stuff they had been hearing,' a senior aide said. 'That worked. In the bilaterals with the French and the Germans, they were beginning to engage on the backstop and understand we were saying something they couldn't just dismiss.'

Johnson's meeting with Merkel was, to the evident surprise of both, 'a lot of fun – extremely wry, friendly and humorous', one of those in the room recalled. The PM charmed the famously dour German chancellor. 'She found his way with words funny.' Merkel responded by 'pulling his leg'. Gesturing at the Bundestag, she said, 'I can control my parliament. Can you control yours?'[26] Nonetheless, Frost could see she was impressed with Johnson's command of the detail and his explicit desire to get a new deal. When Johnson hit his key talking point, that the backstop was 'anti-democratic', Frost felt it made the Germans uncomfortable. Before the meeting Merkel had publicly said the British had thirty days to devise a plan. 'She put a bit of pressure on him,' a German source said. At the end of the bilateral she explained that she had not meant it to come out that way – an olive branch.

When Merkel spoke to Juncker afterwards, the EU president said, 'I think he will deliver.' She was more cautious, aware of Johnson's unreliability. 'I'm not so sure. We know he changes quickly. He will do what is to his advantage.' Nonetheless, she was open to doing business. She also knew the talks would go to the wire, as Frost had predicted. 'It's always like that in the negotiation,' Merkel said. 'Everybody climbs up the trees, there is a lot of noise and it is one minute to twelve ...'

Downing Street was also clear-eyed about the likelihood of Merkel helping them. When Cummings addressed spad school on Friday 23 August, he pointed out: 'There is a 100 per cent record of failure when asking Merkel for help on EU issues in the last four years.'

Johnson's meeting with Macron was a more formal affair in which the French president turned up with a uniformed military adviser. The PM made the same points. 'They were quite surprised by him,' an aide said. 'They had built up a picture of him as Trump. And he just wasn't like that. He made a point of talking about Iran and Libya.' Johnson worked hard to defy the caricature he knew the other leaders had of him. A Europe adviser said, 'Bear in mind they had dealt with May, who read out her briefing notes and that was about it. She couldn't have a conversation with anybody. He was instinctively funny and wants to be liked and that's easier to be around than someone who is uptight.' Macron was reserved about Johnson's ideas for a new entente: 'A second fixed link across the Channel, a new hydrogen-fuelled Concorde aircraft, a new nuclear pact'.[27] The PM later concluded Macron 'would not hesitate to put his Cuban-heeled bootee into Brexit Britain'.[28]

Nevertheless, when Johnson described the meetings to cabinet, he said the talks 'helped to sharpen the understanding in Brussels of what the UK wants ... All those points have landed very clearly with our friends in Brussels. They get it.'

At Biarritz, Johnson repeated the trick with Jean-Claude Juncker. The two men looked each other in the eye and shook hands, feeling each other out. Juncker made suggestions and signalled a willingness to be flexible. 'If you get it through your Parliament it works for us,' he said. A senior EU official remarked, 'We knew [Johnson] was not a man of principles; we knew he wrote the [pre-referendum] op-ed for Remain and Leave. But we knew he had a strong self-interest to deliver.'

Nonetheless, on Brexit there was no breakthrough in Biarritz and Johnson's demands left EU officials depressed. 'Everybody came away with the idea that it was a train crash,' a different Commission official said. 'Either the British government changes position or it ends up with no-deal.' At the summit, Johnson also had a brief meeting with Donald Tusk. 'There was a good atmosphere but not much substance,' a Council official recalled. 'We went away from that meeting with the feeling that he was not really interested, that he was going through the motions.' That said, Tusk and his senior official, Jeppe Tranholm-Mikkelsen, had long been sceptical about Theresa May's approach. 'Some of us were not too unhappy with moving out of the logic of the old backstop,' a source close to Tusk said.

The real benefit of Biarritz for Johnson came when he showed he could play a constructive role in the Western alliance combating Vladimir Putin and climate change. Just as May had done at the G7 meeting in Canada in 2018, Johnson was more adept than the Europeans at dealing with Donald Trump. A witness said, 'In the leaders' meetings he was able to stand up to Trump and say, "Hang on a minute, there are some upsides to trade and the WTO has a role." On climate, he was able to use his prior relationship with this guy to move things along in a constructive way.' Eddie Lister, who observed the two leaders, recalled, 'He could manage Trump. He'd let Trump rant and then come in and say, "Donald, you know, I think if we could do this together, this would be the answer." And Trump would calm down. Trump's starting point was to beat you up.' Others who listened to Johnson's calls with the president remembered sniggering quietly as he referred to Macron as 'little Emmanuel'.

At Biarritz, Macron and the other leaders appeared to rethink their assumptions about Johnson. 'It always felt to me that the Merkels and Macrons thought for the first time that they wanted him to succeed,' a senior civil servant said. 'They realised they had a guy who could talk to the US, therefore they ought to give him a chance. He was able to land some points with Trump and get him to sign up to some stuff in a way they hadn't managed. That was quite a big turning point, because up until then all the mood music was "No, no, no, no, no".'

Johnson's team, happy with how things were going, were dining at an open-air restaurant on the seafront on the evening of Saturday 24 August, with members of the travelling British press corps, when news broke of a story in the *Observer*. The paper's political editor, Toby Helm, reported that Johnson had asked Geoffrey Cox for advice on the legality of proroguing Parliament for five weeks from 9 September, in an apparent attempt to silence MPs. Johnson critics had predicted the worst constitutional crisis since 1688. Now it was upon them.

2

WITHOUT BOUNDS

Prorogation and the Benn Act

August to September 2019

'If one characteristic of Lyndon Johnson was a
boundless ambition, another was a willingness,
on behalf of that ambition, to make efforts that
were also without bounds'

– *Robert A. Caro,* Means of Ascent

Boris Johnson made the most controversial decision of his premiership
wearing a pair of Bermuda shorts, black work shoes and formal socks, his
T-shirt damp with sweat. The prime minister had just played tennis in
this bizarre get-up on the court at Chevening when he sat down with his
senior staff to discuss a plan to prorogue Parliament. Knowledge of the
meeting, on Saturday 10 August, let alone the plan, had been confined to
a small circle of key advisers, now gathered around a large table upstairs,
in a room overlooking the lake. Sunlight streamed in from the garden
obscuring the screen set up at the end of the room. It was the prime
minister himself, in his incongruous outfit, who 'clambered up on a sofa
to try to close the shutters', one colleague remembered.

Isaac Levido, an Australian protégé of Lynton Crosby, who had been
hired to run the general election, spoke first, outlining the latest polling
on public attitudes. Looking back at him were Johnson, Eddie Lister,
Dominic Cummings, Lee Cain, Munira Mirza, aide Cleo Watson, Ben
Gascoigne, press secretary Rob Oxley and Dougie Smith from Downing
Street; the EU team David Frost and Oliver Lewis; Ben Elliot, the Tory
chairman; Levido's numbers man, Michael Brooks; and Nikki da Costa,

the head of legislative affairs who agreed to reprise her role under May a few days before Johnson came to power.

Carrie Symonds was also at Chevening that day, along with Ross Kempsell, a former journalist who had joined the policy unit and who Johnson liked to consult about his speeches. 'What the fuck is he doing here?' Cummings asked, furious the circle of trust had been extended by Johnson's girlfriend. In fact, Johnson had invited Kempsell. The adviser's growing role was a source of irritation to the Vote Leavers. Kempsell was dismissed in the papers as the prime minister's 'tennis partner', when they had only played twice. Far from being a patronage popinjay, Kempsell was a serious young man who had lost his father when he was only fourteen and worked his way up from lower middle-class poverty to Cambridge and then into politics through hard graft.

Levido explained that voters wanted a Brexit deal, but that leaving on 31 October was 'preferable to an extension'. He said, 'The voters are tired of the uncertainty, but they're also nervous about the uncertainty of no-deal. We'll need to work hard to explain the actions we're taking and the mitigations we'll put in place. Traditional Labour voters in the North are also worried about giving us their vote. They want to know what we would do for the rest of the five years post Brexit.' Then the crucial part: 'They remain against proactively calling for a general election. But if we're seen to be forced into it, their views change.' He told Johnson, 'You've got to show that you've done absolutely everything you possibly can to avoid that general election – and then they will permit it.' Cummings spoke about schools, police and the NHS; Frost and Lewis gave an update on the EU. After a tea break it was da Costa's turn.

Three weeks earlier, a couple of days after Johnson went into Number 10, Cummings had asked to see da Costa in a tiny room near the Cabinet Room. He said, 'I need you to know that we are doing Brexit by any means necessary. Do you understand that?' A Number 10 source explained, 'Dom wanted to see what Nikki was made of.'

Instead of being spooked, da Costa was relieved. She had endured the agonies of the May government and knew better than anyone the dogfight they were in with Parliament. She remembered a conversation she had with Clément Beaune, Emmanuel Macron's Europe adviser, at the start of the year. Beaune had stressed there were things the Europeans could do to move on Brexit, but they would only do so if the prime minister's hands were not tied by MPs ahead of the key summit. Da Costa explained to Cummings that she saw their job as getting Johnson to the European Council meeting on 16 October, fifteen days before Brexit day, 'with as many options as possible – then the EU will move'. Cummings told her to go and work on a plan. 'Don't talk to the others,' he said. 'We need to keep this tight.'

Da Costa explained all this at Chevening, admitting that most tactics had already been tried by May and had failed. 'We're down to a king and a pawn; that's all we've got left,' she said. 'You've got a budget, but it comes with some vote risks, and you've got a Queen's Speech, with a prorogation before it.' Da Costa impressed on Johnson that the Bresistance would try to bind his hands. 'When they come back, they're going to try and control you, PM, in the way they've controlled Theresa May and they're going to be more aggressive to you because they're going to fear you more. The strategy we pursue has got to be aggressive. We have to gamble.' A Queen's Speech, da Costa argued, 'is the best shot we've got'. Prevent another Bresistance power play and Johnson could go to Brussels and say, 'You need to move or we're going to leave.' She outlined plans to prorogue Parliament for five weeks. Cummings wrote the timetable on a whiteboard.

The audacity and controversy of the plan was clear to everyone in the room. Prorogation usually lasted less than a week, two at the most. But a long prorogation would allow Johnson to seize the initiative. 'Why don't we go in for the kill and prorogue for the whole period and never return,' a voice asked. Da Costa offered three reasons. First, 'You need to have Parliament back after the Council meeting to pass a deal.' Second, the government did actually need a Queen's Speech. It was already the longest parliamentary session on record. Da Costa had sent four separate submissions to May urging her to hold one. With Bercow, who had blocked the repeat of MV2, still in the speaker's chair, a new session of Parliament would give Johnson greater freedom of manoeuvre. 'If we need to revisit questions that had already been asked, a clean slate would be helpful.'

Da Costa explained the importance of the Northern Ireland Executive Formation Act (NIEFA), legislation rushed through in the dying hours of the May government. The bill had been amended by the Bresistance to set dates when the Commons had to be sitting, an attempt to make it impossible to prorogue Parliament to push through Brexit. That vote saw Philip Hammond finally rebel, abstaining on a three-line whip, the only occasion a chancellor has ever opposed their own government. Johnson's team had been in Admiralty House waiting to enter Number 10 when an official called da Costa to say, 'Peter Hill [the principal private secretary] personally called up to check that it got royal assent.' She explained, 'It's designed to give them a regular opportunity to take control of the order paper and command the prime minister to act.'

The first date in the Act was 9 September. That dictated the timing of prorogation. Da Costa proposed it began sometime between the 9th and the 12th and ended on 14 October. She had drawn up a memo outlining the case, which was formally sent to the prime minister five days later, on 15 August. It made the argument that Parliament would not have been sitting, in any case, for three weeks because of the recess planned for party conferences. Da Costa's plan envisaged extending that period by another five to seven days, for a total of up to thirty-four calendar days. She acknowledged that the longest prorogation since 1981 had been twenty-one days but made the point that MPs would have two weeks after the European Council meeting to pass judgement on any deal or hear from Johnson if there was a prospect of no-deal.

None of the ten people present that day who subsequently discussed it with the author was in any doubt that the primary purpose was to make it more difficult for Parliament to pass legislation preventing no-deal. Those present were sworn to secrecy and advised not to send emails or messages discussing the plan. 'There was an awareness that there could be legal consequences,' another Downing Street aide recalled. No one was in any doubt the plan would unleash a political firestorm.

Despite the risks, even the City Hall people were on board. One Sunday evening, shortly afterwards, Johnson was in his Number 10 study while his aides ate pizza. 'I can't have any, I'm on a diet,' the prime minister complained. 'Carrie has food upstairs.' Grinning, he pinched a slice and then another. 'No more!' A third slice disappeared. Cummings asked Eddie Lister for his views on prorogation: 'What do you think?'

Lister was reflective. 'I hate it,' he said, 'but I've studied it from every angle and really can't see an alternative.' Those present that night always remembered what Lister said – and that Johnson 'ate half a pizza' before going upstairs to Carrie.

What followed was seen by critics as the greatest act of constitutional vandalism since Charles I sent soldiers to arrest five members of the

Long Parliament. Allies believed it was the signature act of a leader who had to take bold decisions to defend and uphold, at all costs, the outcome of a democratic vote. Perhaps it was both.

Geoffrey Cox was not invited to the Chevening summit, but the attorney general had already given Johnson his view about the desirability and risks of using prorogation to get his way on Brexit. On 11 July, in the midst of the leadership election, Johnson had received a legal letter demanding that he undertake, if he was elected Tory leader, not to prorogue Parliament. The attorney general told him, 'The best thing to do, probably, is simply to ignore it.' However, Cox also gave his view of the dangers of prorogation becoming a matter for legal challenge. Politically, the AG felt that prorogation 'is very unwise indeed' but that equally, 'It would be unwise of a court to interfere.' If a court heard the case, it would be an intrusion into matters which had been regarded for centuries as the preserve of politicians and Parliament. However, Cox had appeared as a barrister in front of Brenda Hale, the president of the Supreme Court. He regarded her as an activist judge. The attorney general texted the prime minister that any decision by the highest court in the land to hear a case and rule on the government's decision to prorogue 'would represent the ultimate intrusion of the courts into matters political. However, with this Supreme Court, we cannot be confident that it would not interfere.'

On 13 August, Cox was invited to a fish supper in Johnson's Downing Street flat for another off-the-books discussion about prorogation. With the prime minister were Dominic Cummings, David Frost and da Costa. They were joined later by Carrie Symonds, but she was not present for the substantive discussion. 'Dom wanted to test where Cox was,' another invitee recalled. The AG's views would be significant since he had already shown his willingness to put law before politics and derail a prime minister's plans. His public ruling, on 12 March 2019, that Theresa May's Brexit deal left 'no internationally lawful means of exiting' the backstop had torpedoed her hopes of winning the backing of MPs.

Conversation at the dinner roamed over the negotiations and Cox repeated his view from XS: 'Our current trajectory is towards no-deal.' Then Johnson asked, 'What do you think of the prorogation proposal?' Cox had been sent the da Costa memo. 'Well, Prime Minister,' he replied. 'In my view, it is lawful. You have allowed them to be able to sit in the first week of September. They will also sit from the 14th of October onwards.' Others remember him saying the proposal would 'set the cat among the pigeons'. He continued, 'But I must warn you, Prime Minister, that with this Supreme Court, knowing what I know of it, having appeared in front of it on numerous occasions, I simply cannot rule out the real litigation risk that we would be incurring.'

To some of those present, including Cummings, Cox was 'hedging his bets'. One said, 'He did say the court's gone mad and they might hear it, but he also said he thought it was highly unlikely.' Another senior aide said, not without admiration, 'Cox was as slippery as an eel.'

What concerned the attorney general was a growing view among some judges that the courts were the supreme arbiters of the constitution, rather than Parliament. A new generation of 'liberal constitutionalists' believed the courts were 'equal interlocutors' in a constitutional dialogue with Parliament. Cox thought a majority of the Supreme Court tended towards this view. He said that if Johnson was determined to take the idea forward that, 'You should instruct me formally.' That meant sending a written brief asking for his views.

There was further discussion about whether Johnson would have to resign if he lost a vote of no confidence in the Commons. Cox said not, but warned it might get more difficult if a prospective interim prime minister formed a new majority. 'I wouldn't like to test it,' he said. His personal view was that, in those circumstances, 'The Queen would be put in an impossible position, and the prime minister probably would feel obliged to resign.'

The following day, 14 August, Cox was formally instructed, but not on whether a five-week prorogation was lawful or justiciable, only on a narrow point, whether the Northern Ireland Executive Formation Act (NIEFA) would prevent prorogation from 9 September to 14 October. Cox advised in writing that NIEFA did not prevent prorogation, despite the amendments attached to it by the Bresistance. But in his final paragraph, he repeated his warning at the fish supper: 'You must be aware that there are a broader range of issues affecting this question than simply whether NIEFA prevents it. The appetite of the Supreme Court to intervene will depend on the context.' It was this document which was leaked to the *Observer* ten days later. This was Johnson's third warning about the potential dangers of prorogation. He ignored it. Cox heard nothing more. The attorney general thought the supper highly irregular. He told friends later, 'You can't just ask a lawyer over dinner. It's like asking a doctor, "Have I got cancer?"'

Both Mark Sedwill and Helen MacNamara were blindsided; Johnson's team did not trust them not to try to sabotage the plan. Da Costa also felt she was protecting officials by not involving them. Later, one mandarin claimed the political team would have been better off consulting the civil service: 'The mistake Johnson made was not asking us, because we would have helped work out the answer.' Other civil servants were relieved to have been cut out. 'We were completely out of the loop,' said a Number 10 official. 'This worked out fantastically well, personally, because it meant I was nowhere near this bloody catastrophe.'

All that said, no one in the government legal service thought there was any legal grounds on which a court could rule on, let alone overturn, the decision. 'Everyone forgets this now because of what happened later, but no one said, "This is illegal and you can't do it",' a close aide to the prime minister said. Politically, however, it was toxic and a whistleblower decided the public had a right to know what was being done in their name. Cox's advice leaked.

Johnson and Cummings both knew prorogation would lead to a huge row. In part, that was what they wanted. They wanted voters to pick sides, Brexit over no Brexit, Johnson over Corbyn, the people over Parliament. As Cox observed, 'Dominic set out to show Boris as a Gulliver struggling to shake off the Lilliputian chains.'

The briefings about what Johnson might be prepared to do varied in credibility and combustibility but were designed to goad his enemies into missteps. Cain told journalists that if Johnson lost a vote of no confidence he would refuse to resign and dare the Queen to sack him, something unheard of since William IV dismissed Lord Melbourne in 1834. Aides said the PM would refuse to recommend a successor until after Brexit on 31 October. Cummings went further, telling colleagues and journalists, 'Unless the police turn up at the doors of Downing Street with a warrant for the prime minister's arrest, he won't be leaving.' If MPs passed their own law preventing no-deal, Johnson would ignore it. He would refuse to ask for an extension even if mandated to do so by Parliament. Cummings believed the only way MPs could stop Brexit would be to revoke Article 50 itself. If the Supreme Court ruled against him, they did not think there would be enough time to force Johnson's hand before 31 October.

This 'Brexican stand-off' strategy was designed so that, in a highly volatile environment, it could survive contact with events. Wins were wins which would enhance Johnson's standing with Leave voters, but defeats could also be spun as the heroic Brexiteer vainly battling the Remoaner establishment. The irony is that this total war approach meant challenging constitutional norms in a way the Vote Leavers had condemned when it was John Bercow doing the innovating.

The second issue was that these suggestions so shocked mainstream opinion that the pro-dealers believed they had no option but to act. Dominic Grieve saw Cummings as a man 'going on a sort of revolutionary frenzy', something he took as a 'declaration of war'. The former attorney general went to the house he owned in Brittany. But within twenty-four hours his wife was laughing at him: 'You're going to spend most of the holiday working.' The phone had barely stopped ringing with MPs horrified at what they were hearing. Then, in mid-August, Grieve and others were tipped off about da Costa's prorogation plan. 'We picked it up extremely quickly,' a rebel recalled. 'There were multiple leaks. At that stage, we had to move.'

Depending on where you stood on Brexit, an official revealing the secret tactics of a prime minister to his greatest enemies was either proof that Johnson and Cummings were engaged in an historic abuse of the constitution – or that disaffected civil servants put their personal views ahead of their duty to support a government seeking to uphold the stated will of the electorate. There was truth in both propositions.

Grieve, Letwin and other senior rebels returned to London. Stephen Doughty organised a meeting for 20 August, four days after Johnson's decision to prorogue and four days before the *Observer* story broke. Twenty rebels met at a location in central London. 'It was a big meeting,' one of those present said. 'We discussed what we were going to do to stop no-deal. It lasted a couple of hours.' Others phoned in from abroad, one MP from the slopes of Mount Vesuvius. When Dominic Grieve spoke there was no dissent: 'The options are quite clear, we've got to seize control of the order of the paper and do a bill.' The only way to get the Tories on board was to enforce a delay that was 'short enough not to allow a referendum'. Conservative Bresisters were impressed with Keir Starmer's flexibility. Despite pushing a referendum for months, the shadow Brexit secretary 'very quickly recognised' he had to drop the idea. 'You need the pressure of a hard deadline to force everybody to accept something less than what they want,' a Tory MP said. 'And every-body did it.' For the first time, the Bresistance was prepared to compromise, rather than let everyone's perfect solution be the enemy of a collective good.

It was agreed that Grieve and Oliver Letwin would write the legislation and the paving amendments to close off every possible tactic by Johnson to force no-deal. Letwin would then introduce a motion under SO24 to seize control of the Commons agenda to pass the bill. 'One of the prob-lems previously had been different people drafting different versions of bills or different amendments and them not cohering,' said another Bresister. 'So, a lot of us said, "All these people need to work together and draft the same thing and agree on its legal details, because this has to be watertight."' Grieve felt he had fronted too many things, so the legisla-tion would be introduced by Hilary Benn, the chairman of the Commons Brexit select committee. When he saw the product of Letwin and Grieve's efforts, he was delighted. 'The business motions which enabled the bills to be considered were a work of art,' Benn recalled. 'We had to repel all procedural boarders.'[1]

Until prorogation, the Rebel Alliance of former Tory cabinet minis-ters, including Hammond and Gauke, had argued that Johnson should be given the chance to get a deal before they sought to pass more legisla-tion. Now, they agreed to move against him. Greg Clark recalled, 'The prorogation was very significant. I thought Boris wanted a deal ... I felt he was entitled to achieve what he set out to, and that we shouldn't get in his way. Prorogation did two things. The very act of seeking to suspend Parliament for almost all of the time while the negotiations were taking place, seemed designed to facilitate no-deal. The second thing was that it removed the ability of Parliament to step in.' Anne Milton, channelling her disappointed mother-of-four vibe, remarked, 'It's not big and it's not clever.' Letwin called prorogation 'a civil war tactic, a 17th century tactic'.[2]

Philip Hammond's main contribution to the Benn Act was to write the wording of the letter which the bill required Johnson to send to Brussels. Some thought dictating the letter was overkill, but Hammond insisted Johnson would try to wriggle out of it if he could. 'We need a belt, two lots of braces and an elastic band around it,' he said. He also reached out to old contacts in Brussels, Paris, Berlin, Rome, Warsaw and The Hague to ensure the Europeans would accept the timetable for delaying Brexit until 31 January 2020. 'It would have been insane to write the Benn Act with an extension deadline that we hadn't tested on Europeans,' he said later. A Labour MP thought his intervention vital: 'Something shifted when it became clear that Hammond and Gauke were deadly serious. That was one of the biggest moments.' Doughty and Guto Bebb's whipping lists showed that prorogation flipped around ten Tory votes against Johnson. Hammond said, 'If I never do anything else in politics other than having prevented the government from crashing us out on 31 October, that will be a result as far as I am concerned,' he said. 'I genuinely feared and I still do believe that if we had not put the Benn Act in place, Boris would have gone to Brussels and made a final offer, take it or leave it, and then taken us over a cliff edge.'

Even before the 29 August summit, key Bresisters had sounded out the speaker. The first had been Yvette Cooper, who asked Bercow what the options were for those who wanted to resist a no-deal Brexit. The speaker was cautious: 'You should, in the first instance, consult the clerks about that.' Then Letwin turned up in early August. 'You know, Mr Speaker, I voted for Brexit three times,' he twittered in his busy, high-pitched voice. 'I support any deal that would safely get us out and would respect the wishes of people, however misguided you might think it is. But, having been minister for the national security planning, I am genuinely convinced that a no-deal Brexit will be an absolute disaster for this country. It will ruin us.' Letwin revealed he had been in discussion with Colin Lee, the procedural expert in the clerk's office about whether the method devised by the Bresistance – taking control of the order paper using Standing Order 24 – would be accepted. Lee had advised him that the decision would fall to Bercow. Letwin asked whether the speaker was open to the idea.

Bercow replied, 'The way I read it, Oliver, I think it is perfectly legitimate.' The speaker left himself some wriggle room: 'I don't want to absolutely guarantee that I would select such a proposition. I've got to see what you've got by way of numbers and who the people are.'

Letwin was ready for this argument. 'If there were, say, a number of prominent figures from the other side, the chair of a select committee ...' To Bercow, it was obvious he was talking about Hilary Benn. The speaker said, 'That would be highly relevant. That would be eminently respectable.' He said later, 'Oliver was very proper about it. Oliver didn't try to pressurise me at all.' Yet this was far more encouragement before the event than the speaker had given Grieve in January. It was effectively a green light for the Bresistance to take a stand.

Bercow was also visited by Philip Hammond and he took a call from Tony Blair. The former prime minister admitted he knew little of parliamentary procedure and asked if there was anything to be done. 'As somebody who wants to try to avert Brexit and give the country a chance to think again,' Blair said, 'I would like to think there is a legitimate way for this matter to be reconsidered.'

'Well, there are options, you know,' Bercow said. 'I talked him through it,' he recalled. It stuck in the speaker's mind when Blair said, 'The crucial thing is not to conflate Brexit and an election because if these two things are brought together and it's Corbyn versus Johnson, Johnson will win every time.' Blair had not lost his political antennae.

Bercow had not done anything demonstrably improper by having these conversations, but the reaction in Downing Street and the media would have been incendiary if it had been known that leading players on one team were sounding out the referee before the game. By contrast, when Johnson took over in Number 10, he invited Bercow, a keen tennis player, for a game at Chequers. Bercow had won their last game, at Chevening in January 2017, 6–0, 6–0, 6–0. He declined the invitation. 'I didn't think that was the right way to do it,' he recalled.

The Bresistance found out that the game was afoot before Geoffrey Cox. It was not until the day after their gathering in central London, 21 August, that the attorney general took a call from Nikki da Costa. 'The decision has been taken,' she said. 'He's decided to prorogue.'

'I'd rather hoped to be consulted about it,' a grumpy Cox said.

This was more than just high dudgeon, it also had serious legal implications. Cox knew that if there was a court case, the government would have to give the judges reasons for the decision which were credible and properly minuted. He said, 'It will be important that the documents recording his reasons are very carefully put together.'

Johnson's team was under the impression that they could not use a political justification for the five-week absence of Parliament. Cox believed it would have been perfectly possible to make a nakedly political argument that prorogation was necessary to give breathing space to enable Johnson to get a deal, to allow ministers to travel to Brussels, Berlin and Paris. If such a justification had been made, with supporting paperwork, it would have forced the court to rule on what was a good political reason for doing something and what was a bad political reason, a potential minefield for the judiciary.

Instead, the decision to prorogue was made with no input from the government's chief law officer and in a way that generated no convincing documentary evidence to back it up. That, more than the decision itself, is what would put Johnson in grave legal peril. When Cox explained this to da Costa, he was not sure she grasped the gravity of the problem. 'The first thing you do under judicial review is make sure your reasons are bombproof and can't be questioned,' he told one confidant.

On 23 August, Johnson was asked by the media whether he was considering proroguing and flat out denied it. Dominic Grieve was incensed, telling a colleague, 'That is an outright lie.' The whistleblower shared with the *Observer* emails between government officials discussing Cox's legal advice. The newspaper published the following evening.

When the story dropped, Rob Oxley, Johnson's press secretary, and James Slack, his civil service official spokesman, left the dinner with members of the parliamentary lobby in Biarritz for a hastily convened conference call with aides in London. They included an incandescent Cummings, who was railing against those he blamed for the leak. Sources on the call are clear that Johnson's senior adviser instructed Oxley to tell the press the story was 'total bollocks'. This he refused to do. Oxley was a Vote Leave alumnus but believed in constructive relations with the media. Cummings thought most journalists were 'wankers'.

Slack played diplomat. The official statement which Downing Street issued that night did not deny that Cox had been approached for legal advice, but it was a masterpiece of laser-cut misdirection. 'The claim that the government is considering proroguing Parliament in September in order to stop MPs debating Brexit is entirely false,' it read. This was literally true in two regards. The government was not 'considering' using prorogation – a firm decision had already been taken by the prime minister to do so. Second, the government's position would be that prorogation was for the purposes of staging a new Queen's Speech, not to stop MPs debating Brexit. As a whole the statement was misleading but it bought time by dissuading other papers and the BBC from picking up the story. The respite was short-lived. The 'denial' prompted disgruntled officials in Whitehall to tell several media organisations, including the BBC, on

Tuesday 27th that Johnson was due to make an announcement about prorogation the following day. On the same day, more than 150 MPs signed the 'Church House Declaration', vowing to 'do whatever is necessary' to prevent Parliament being prorogued. It was named after the headquarters of the Church of England which had become an alternative chamber for the House of Lords during the Blitz in 1940.

Downing Street's original plan had been for Jacob Rees-Mogg, in his capacity as Lord President of the Privy Council, to meet the Queen at Balmoral at noon on Wednesday 28 August. He was to be accompanied by Natalie Evans, the leader of the Lords, and Mark Spencer, the government chief whip. An hour later Johnson was to hold a conference call with the cabinet to seek retrospective support for the move. The leaks meant the conference call was hastily pulled forward. Again, the Bresistance knew what was going on before the cabinet.

At 11.30 p.m. the night before, Stephen Doughty, the Labour MP who acted as a Bresistance whip, was contacted by three people, two of whom were journalists who had been tipped off by officials. Doughty phoned his contacts and was told that the Queen's private secretary Edward Young had gone to Balmoral and that Rees-Mogg, Spencer and Evans were booked on a flight to Scotland in the morning. At half-past midnight, Doughty phoned the Buckingham Palace switchboard and said, 'I want to speak to the press officer or to the Queen's private secretary. I want to know if there is a meeting of the Privy Council tomorrow because it's not advertised on the website. I'm working with a number of privy councillors who want to know if it's happening.' The man on the switchboard paused. He seemed to be reading something. Then he let slip, 'Oh, yes, at Balmoral.'

Doughty called Ian Blackford, the SNP leader in Westminster, who was heading home to his croft on Skye. Blackford made inquiries with officials in Nicola Sturgeon's office. Then he alerted a few Scottish journalists, who sent photographers to the airport. By 5.30 a.m., Doughty was certain he had the facts. He called Laura Kuenssberg, but the BBC needed more corroboration to break such a big story.

Prorogation is a power under the royal prerogative and is ordered by the monarch on the advice of the Privy Council. It only takes effect when a royal proclamation is read to both houses of Parliament. Political and palace sources confirm that reassurances were given by Downing Street to the royal household, via the 'golden triangle' of aides – the cabinet secretary Mark Sedwill, Johnson's principal private secretary Peter Hill and the Queen's private secretary Edward Young – that the plan was regarded as lawful and constitutional. Sedwill was 'concerned' and had talked to Cox about how the constitution was 'a mix of law and convention' and about 'the role of the sovereign'. He consulted constitutional experts like Vernon Bogdanor and Peter Hennessy.[3] He was not alone in harbouring concerns. 'The palace was nervous about the length of the prorogation,' a Whitehall official said. 'Reassurance was sought and the message went back that everything was above board.'

But officials remained concerned about whether the Queen was aware of what she was getting into. 'We knew at that point that it was going to be legally challenged,' one mandarin said. MacNamara called Richard Tilbrook, the clerk of the Privy Council, whose job it was to brief the Queen, to impress on him that the monarch was being asked to do something controversial. Tilbrook flew to Scotland.

While many ministers might have travelled incognito – and Evans and Spencer were barely household names in their own homes – the statuesque Rees-Mogg stood out like a sore thumb. At Inverness airport, he had just been patched into a cabinet conference call when a man and his son approached him asking for a selfie. Word quickly spread.

Tilbrook, 'a woodland animal', shy and quiet, sat mute and horrified on the forty-five-minute minibus ride to Balmoral beside Rees-Mogg, Spencer and Evans, who officials later claimed were 'braying' about how prorogation was going to be a 'total triumph'. The highlight for the ministers was listening to funny stories told by the Queen's hairdresser, who joined them on the ride. Rees-Mogg said later: 'Holding the Privy Council in Balmoral is not routine but isn't particularly unusual, and it was going to be announced later that day, anyway.'

The monarch gave her approval to the plan. She had already spoken to Johnson by telephone that morning. But that was not the most notable of the prime minister's conversations that day. Ten minutes before the cabinet conference call, Geoffrey Cox was sitting in his study in Devon when his mobile phone rang. It was Johnson: 'Geoffrey.'

'Yes, Prime Minister.'

'Listen, I've already spoken to the Queen this morning and prorogation is going on. Please don't spook the cabinet by talking about the litigation risk.'

Johnson echoed the phrase Cox had used to warn him, on both the 11th and 13th of August, about the dangers of a legal challenge in the Supreme Court. It was clear he had understood and registered the danger. It was equally clear that he did not want the rest of the cabinet to know the full facts. Here was a sitting prime minister, on the verge of the most controversial constitutional move in a century, asking his attorney general to withhold relevant information from his cabinet, which accurately foreshadowed the humiliation of the executive by the judiciary. Had it become public, it might have led to cabinet resignations. Cox was uncomfortable with the request but considered the position Johnson had put him in. The Queen had already given her approval, he could not put the genie back in the bottle. He chose his words carefully: 'Well, Prime Minister, since prorogation is already in process, I will simply tell my colleagues that, in my view, it is lawful and leave it at that.'

'Yes, please.'

This was a deeply unedifying moment for Cox. Given what happened next, it was also one of the nadirs of Johnson's premiership. When senior civil servants found out what had happened, they were 'deeply uneasy' but, since the call was not a formal cabinet meeting, they concluded Johnson's actions were morally questionable rather than unconstitutional. Asked later about his request to the attorney general, Johnson said he could not remember it, but he did not deny it. He also understood Cox's concerns about the Hale court. Long afterwards, Johnson admitted privately that the AG and his team 'were a bit worried about Brenda [Hale]. They thought what we were doing was fine. But they thought Brenda was coming to the end [of her time at the Supreme Court] and may want to do some sort of weird flourish.'

Johnson began the conference call by announcing, 'I have spoken just now to Her Majesty the Queen to request that we end the current parliamentary session roughly between the 9th and the 12th of September and then have a new session of this Parliament with a Queen's Speech on Monday the 14th of October.' He continued, 'That will give ample time to all our colleagues in Parliament to debate the issue of Brexit both before the crucial summit on October the 17th, when I hope we will succeed in getting a deal, and after that as we run-up to Brexit day on October the 31st.' Johnson then expressed excitement at the 'dynamic legislative programme' he planned to introduce. He sounded like a suspect who worries he is being bugged, reading out the legal justification of his actions for the tape. What he did not know – one of his ministers was indeed taping the call.

Cox had not even done his turn when Julian Smith, the Northern Ireland secretary, jumped in. Smith found himself in a state of 'total fury', believing Johnson was putting Brexit before the Union. Prorogation, he privately thought, was a 'pollution of the well', which damaged the chances of getting a functioning government in Belfast. Cummings, he had heard, had said: 'I don't give a shit whether Northern Ireland falls into the sea.' Smith asked, 'Could we see the attorney general's legal advice prior to the Privy Council?' He needed to be satisfied that the prorogation plan allowed him to meet the legal requirement set out by Grieve's amendments to the NIEFA, to report to Parliament or before 9 October on efforts to re-establish the Northern Ireland executive.

Johnson said, 'We can definitely provide that, Julian, we are absolutely certain these are compatible with the EFA provisions.' The prime minister tried to move on to the more supportive Dominic Raab, but Smith was not finished. 'There's no prime minister in Northern Ireland,' he reminded Johnson. 'The number of sitting dates with this model will leave us very limited ability to pass the NI budget … We risk going into no-deal with no decision-making powers in Northern Ireland.'

Raab pronounced prorogation 'the right thing to do', arguing, 'it's only three or four extra days Parliament won't be sitting'. Johnson repeated his story: 'I don't think anybody looking at this could conceivably say that it's an attempt to pass Parliament.'

Nicky Morgan, the culture secretary, hailed the 'encouraging' news from Johnson's trip to Berlin, Paris and Biarritz. But she asked for MPs to be sent clarification of the need for prorogation. 'Some of the MP WhatsApp groups are going just bonkers about all of it,' she warned.

Johnson delivered another soliloquy for the jury. 'What this is not, this is emphatically not some attempt to prorogue Parliament to get Brexit through,' he said. 'On the contrary, that's absolutely not what we are doing.' Ministers listening wondered if the prime minister repeated it often enough, they might come to believe it.

Amber Rudd, the work and pensions secretary, began by taking aim at Cummings, expressing concern at 'the language coming out of Number 10', warning that it undermined Johnson's pledge on the steps of Downing Street to bring a divided country back together. She suggested that in an election campaign MPs would face 'pretty serious abuse' as they had in 2017, unless they 'tone that down'. Rudd's main concern, however, was that Johnson was not trying hard enough to get a deal. 'Could you be a little franker with your cabinet about what the strategy is to get a deal? What is the plan to get this deal through?'

The PM's reply was that 'getting a deal over the line' was precisely what was needed to bring about a 'moment of reconciliation'. Only then would the 'bickering and controversy end'. On the strategy, he said, 'We've landed two big messages with our [EU] friends. Number one is that we want a deal, and we're going to work really hard to get a deal out of them. But the second is that we are prepared as a country and as a government, as every single one of us said when we joined, that we are prepared to come out without a deal. It's that second point that really concentrated minds in the EU … At this stage they're really sucking their teeth and thinking can they actually now do what is necessary.' Dropping his voice, he sought to level with Rudd: 'I think, Amber, entirely frankly, there's a good chance we'll get a deal, there's a good chance that we won't. I've got to be absolutely realistic with you about that. We're working flat out, I can't be clearer than that at the moment.' Johnson repeated da Costa's argument at Chevening: 'Provided that they don't think that Parliament will come up with some means to frustrate Brexit, I think they are much more likely to offer us the deal we need.'

Only now did Cox join the conversation. He said, 'You asked me to advise on this question from the prospect of the law. In my judgement, there is nothing unlawful and certainly nothing unconstitutional about what is now proposed.' Answering Smith's question, he added, 'It has been designed in a fashion to comply with the Northern Ireland Executive Functions Act. And so, the cries that will be made that it is either unconstitutional or unlawful are political rhetoric.'

As someone who had tried and failed to get a breakthrough in Brussels, Cox praised the progress Johnson had made. 'I have no doubt that we have made more impact on the imagination and approach of the EU than we were able to do in the twelve months preceding that during which I sat in cabinet. There is now an opening window within the minds of the European Union. I wouldn't characterise it as more than ajar, but that is a long way more open than we ever succeeding in doing in February or in October. So, this strategy is the only strategy, in my view, that will lead to that door being prised open and to the golden prize of a deal.'

Of Cox's concerns that prorogation could be struck down by the Supreme Court there was no mention at all.

Robert Buckland, the lord chancellor, offered coded criticism in the form of a request. 'The prorogation period will be a long one,' he said. 'In modern history, prorogation usually lasts a week, perhaps sometimes longer, a fortnight. We need to be absolutely primed with all the right arguments to explain why this period, in modern terms, is somewhat longer than it has been previously.' Johnson said this was because the period of prorogation 'happens to span the party conference period. We'll make sure that colleagues are fully equipped with the right script.'

After the event, a senior civil servant explained that Johnson's request to Cox that he withhold important information from the cabinet was questionable but not unconstitutional: 'That was a call to brief the cabinet, not a meeting in which the cabinet was reaching a decision. That is the unbelievable sliver of veneer that makes it okay.' Yet even this was questionable since as Johnson drew the meeting to a close, he said, 'Cabinet approves the proposal for a Queen's Speech.' A chorus of yeses followed. As far as Johnson was concerned it was a decision-making cabinet and ministers had decided in his favour. The die was cast without any discussion of what might follow.

John Bercow was sitting by a swimming pool in the Turkish sunshine with his family when his wife, Sally, noticed a story online about prorogation. 'I'd had no wind of it,' he recalled. 'I issued a statement to the Press Association, saying I thought it was a "constitutional outrage". I stand by that view. I didn't expect them to try that.'

Bercow regarded the official justification as transparently dishonest. He said, 'It seemed to me, if it looked like a duck, walked like a duck and quacked like a duck, it was almost certainly a duck.' In his statement he said the plan was clearly designed to 'stop MPs debating Brexit'. In another interview he called it 'totally improper'.[4] Nicola Sturgeon, the SNP leader and first minister of Scotland, branded Johnson a 'tin pot dictator'. Mark Drakeford, the Labour first minister of Wales, accused him of wanting to 'close the doors' on democracy.

Both Amber Rudd and Julian Smith asked to see Geoffrey Cox's legal advice in full. It amounted to a single page, dealing with the narrow point about Northern Ireland. Rudd kept phoning the attorney general's office, but Downing Street ordered that the document not be handed out.

'Number 10 blocked her reading it but invited her to come and read it in a controlled condition because they were worried about leaks,' a legal department source said. Rudd was incensed and never did so.

The Brexit battles were now being fought on multiple fronts, of which cabinet tensions were the least important. Over the summer Joanna Cherry, a QC who was the SNP's justice spokesperson (and a member of Trains and Buses), joined forces with Jolyon Maugham QC, a vociferously anti-Brexit barrister, to make an application for judicial review to Scotland's highest court, the Court of Session in Edinburgh. They sought a ruling that prorogation to avoid parliamentary scrutiny would be unconstitutional and unlawful. The case had the backing of a total of 78 MPs and peers and was due to be heard on 6 September. On 28 August, as soon as the prorogation announcement was made, Cherry applied for an interim injunction to stop it. On the same day, Gina Miller, who had defeated the government over the use of the royal prerogative in 2018, made an application for judicial review on the use of prerogative powers to prorogue to the High Court in London. A third case was brought in the High Court in Belfast, by a victims' rights campaigner, Raymond McCord, claiming prorogation breached the Good Friday Agreement, though this, ultimately, was thrown out.

Cherry's request for an 'interdict' was rejected on 30 August, but the Scottish case was brought forward to 3 September. The same day, Sir John Major announced that he was joining Gina Miller's case in the High Court. The shadow attorney general Shami Chakrabarti had already been given permission to do so on behalf of the opposition.

A toxic battle erupted between Cummings and those in government he blamed for the leaks. Johnson's senior adviser was 'spooked' and 'fucking furious' about the *Observer* story and the evidence that Rees-Mogg's visit to Scotland had also been compromised.

Cummings summoned Jonathan Jones, the head of the government legal service, to see him in the Cabinet Room. It was the first time they had met. Jones had barely sat down when Cummings began reading out a list of names. 'Do you know these people?' he asked.

'Of course I know them, they are government lawyers.'

'They were all copied into an email about prorogation which then leaked,' Cummings said.

Jones stood his ground: 'There is no history of leaking from lawyers in government. It goes against everything we stand for.'

Jones had not been consulted about prorogation but he told colleagues he was 'troubled by the idea'. While he agreed it was not unlawful, the plan obviously created legal risk, particularly when the government clearly had an ulterior motive. He thought Johnson should have proper legal advice, spelling out the risks. The episode shattered trust between Jones and Number 10, who blamed him and his staff for undermining them. A colleague of Cummings said, 'There was a genuine fury that our own lawyers were briefing against us. It was very clear that Jonathan Jones and others were against the government; they made that very clear in meetings. Dom wanted to get new lawyers.'

Cummings was not done. At 8 p.m. on Thursday 29 August, he summoned Sonia Khan, a special adviser at the Treasury, one of those he suspected of leaking – though she had no knowledge of the prorogation. Khan was now working for Sajid Javid but had previously been Hammond's media adviser.

Appointing himself judge, jury and executioner, Cummings asked Khan if she had been in contact with Hammond or any of his associates. She replied that she had not had any direct contact with the former chancellor since July, when she began working for Javid. She did admit having a social meeting two weeks earlier with another former Treasury spad, Poppy Trowbridge. Cummings demanded to see both her work and private mobile phones. His allies claimed a flustered Khan tried to delete something from one of them. She denied this. He insisted that she hand them over. There were angry exchanges. He found a call to Trowbridge a week earlier and summarily fired Khan on the spot, telling her that her security pass was cancelled with immediate effect.

Cummings walked out of his office and summoned an armed policeman from the lobby in Number 10 and told him to escort Khan from the building. With other advisers watching in amazement, she was frogmarched out. One of those to witness her departure was Simon Walters, the *Daily Mail* journalist, who was in Downing Street for an audience with Cummings – an invitation which colleagues believed was the adviser's way of guaranteeing dramatic coverage for his brutal theatrics.[5] Khan's phone contained no incriminating messages, just proof of contact with people Cummings regarded as malign. But his action violated government HR procedures and resulted in Khan suing for unfair dismissal. The experience left her in shock and suffering anxiety. The government eventually settled her case out of court.

Javid demanded a meeting with Johnson early the next morning, furious that one of his aides had been dismissed without him being consulted. With Cummings sitting in, Javid complained that he had sought to humiliate Khan. 'It shows you are completely unfit to be in government,' he said.[6] Johnson squirmed, unable to placate his chancellor, unable to overrule his chief aide. Cummings' beef dated back to 18 August when the *Sunday Times* printed an entire Operation Yellowhammer document, detailing the perils of no-deal. The document was dated August 2019 under the May government. Number 10 claimed it was 'leaked by a former minister', by which they meant Hammond. Cummings' cronies suggested Khan was involved in the leak to justify her sacking, a claim that was totally untrue.

This vindictiveness from Cummings was increasingly on display in his Friday 'spad school' meetings with special advisers. To many, these became extended versions of the 'two minutes hate' depicted in Orwell's dystopian classic *Nineteen Eighty-Four*, in which citizens vent about enemies of Big Brother's regime. 'It was always an hour's monologue from Dom,' one said. 'Dom could only operate in two minutes hate mode. We all sat there getting revved up to hate the things that we were supposed to hate. But once we'd done Remainers and Corbyn, we ran out of stuff to hate. Then it became rants about all sorts of random stuff like BAE Systems. You'd learn quite a lot, but you're also thinking, "This is slightly deranged." It gradually morphed into picking on people – asking spads questions they were unprepared for, like how many arm's-length bodies their department has.'

Cummings ended one meeting by saying, 'I'll see *some* of you next week', sparking fears of mass sackings. 'I can remember being physically scared of him,' a political adviser said. 'He seemed to have absolute, arbitrary HR authority.' The following week, to the admiration and consternation of her colleagues, MoD spad Lynn Davidson, a nuggety Scot who was no stranger to high-stress work after a career in national newspapers, took Cummings to task. 'Something you said last week caused a lot of people a lot of anxiety.' A witness said, 'I'd never seen him challenged like this, by anyone. She got a bit more emotional; you could see that she was crying. It ended without a massive confrontation but then she didn't turn up the next week.' Davidson left government shortly afterwards.

Another front in the prorogation battle opened that weekend when tens of thousands of people took part in more than a hundred demonstrations around the country about the decision to suspend Parliament. Crowds chanted outside the gates of Downing Street brandishing banners saying 'stop the coup' and 'save our democracy'.

Johnson faced a dilemma. Dozens of Tory MPs were signalling that they would vote against him. In a war council at Chequers on Sunday 1 September, Cummings, backed up by Cain, pressed hard for the PM to strip any rebels of the Conservative whip. Expulsion from the parliamentary party was consistent with their plan to show the public that Johnson was trying everything possible to deliver the referendum result. Yet it would cause huge controversy; some of those likely to be affected had been senior cabinet ministers less than six weeks earlier. The PM questioned the decision, testing the idea, hearing the arguments. 'This is a really big thing, these are people who've served the Tory Party all their lives,' he said. 'Will ordinary people think this is reasonable?'

Cummings and Cain argued: 'These are people who are betraying the party. People want a prime minister who will finally stand up to it, not like Theresa May who got kicked around by it. It sends a signal about how serious you are. The public want you to deal with this.' Cummings' clinching argument was: 'These MPs are handing control to Jeremy Corbyn. That makes it a matter of confidence.'

Mark Spencer, the chief whip, agreed it was 'totally the right move', telling Johnson he needed to show the party who was boss: 'We need to make a statement.' Another aide recalled, 'The chief was a trooper. He was really solid. He went into battle.'

The Rebel Alliance's European Union (Withdrawal) (No. 2) Bill 2019 – better known as 'the Benn Act' – was published at 5.25 p.m. on 2 September. It was the result of very careful drafting by Grieve and Letwin, with the help of the clerks. They tried to anticipate what Johnson would do in response and close down every potential loophole. 'There was huge anxiety that we might get it wrong,' one of those involved said.

The bill allowed the prime minister to do a deal then seek Parliament's backing for it. It also allowed him to bring a motion before the House seeking the backing of MPs for no-deal if negotiations were unsuccessful. But if neither a deal nor no-deal passed the House by 19 October, the bill forced the PM to seek an extension until 31 January 2020. If the EU proposed a different date, the prime minister had to agree to that instead. The bill also demanded the government publish a report on 30 November about what it planned to do next. This too could be amended or rejected by MPs, giving Parliament a veto over Brexit strategy. Further reports had to follow on 10 January and every twenty-eight days until a deal was reached with the EU. To Johnson this was ordering him to do as both MPs and the EU instructed. The government would no longer govern.

At cabinet that afternoon, Johnson told ministers the rebel plans would take the pressure off Brussels. A briefing document shared with ministers stated, 'The EU will only get down to serious talks when they know they have to face the choice between a deal or no-deal, with the third option of extension/referendum/revocation definitively ruled out.' Johnson revealed that the EU was prepared to consider alternatives to the backstop and that Frost's team had been working on changes. 'We have preliminary worked-up legal texts plus assessments of the legal and process changes needed to replace checks otherwise required at Irish border,' the document said.

The same evening, 2 September, the PM launched a charm offensive with MPs, inviting them to enjoy the later summer sun in the Downing Street garden. One of the first to arrive was Theresa May. 'It was like seeing Banquo's ghost,' another MP said. 'I thought: Fuck! Has it all been a dream?' Asked by one MP whether the government would back down on its threats to deselect MPs, Cummings barked, 'What the fuck do you think I am here for?' There would be 'no surrender', he said. An MP who met Cummings for the first time that night said, 'He behaves like a cat whose tail has been trodden on.'

In the turbulent history of Brexit, 3 and 4 September 2019 were two of the most dramatic days of the lot. Tuesday 3rd began with Philip Hammond announcing that he would vote for the Benn Act. Taking aim at Cummings, he said, 'I am going to defend my party against incomers, entryists, who are trying to turn it from a broad church to narrow faction.' At this point the number of Tory rebels was in single figures.

At 10.15 a.m. Boris Johnson met fifteen potential Bresisters in Number 10. Hammond arrived with Anne Milton, David Gauke, Greg Clark,

Nicholas Soames and Tom Tugendhat. As the MPs waited outside the Cabinet Room, Cummings approached, even more provocatively vulpine than usual, and declared, 'I don't know who any of you are.'

The prime minister was accompanied by David Frost and Michael Gove. He positioned Amber Rudd next to him to help persuade her fellow pro-dealers not to join the Rebel Alliance. One of those present called it 'the most extraordinary meeting I have ever been in'. Opening proceedings, Johnson made the same case as he had to cabinet: progress was being made with Brussels and the threat of no-deal was 'focusing minds' in the EU. Passage of the Benn Act could mean a second referendum or even revocation of Article 50. It would also mean the loss of the whip for any rebels. His tone was ingratiating. 'Boris sat there saying, "Maties, maties, come on",' said one witness.

Milton acknowledged that no-deal might be a good negotiating tactic with the EU, but warned it would make life difficult in towns like hers where the Tories were fighting the Lib Dems. 'A seat like Guildford could be lost,' she said. Rather than reassuring her that she would have the support she needed from the party, Johnson was callously dismissive: 'If Guildford is lost, it's lost.' Milton felt like collateral damage for his desire to win Leave-voting seats in the North.

The rebels probed the prime minister for evidence that he was serious about getting a deal with Brussels. Gauke asked Johnson directly what the alternative arrangements to the backstop were. He got no answer. Such details would be released at a later date, they were told. 'Boris said he was confident he would get a deal but could not point to any evidence that supported his optimism,' said one MP. Hammond was visibly dismissive. 'You don't have a negotiating strategy,' he said. 'You don't really have a negotiating team. You're not really trying to get a deal. Even if you get a deal at the European Council on 17 October, there won't be time to pass the necessary legislation before the 31st.'

'No, there is time,' Johnson said. 'And there will also be time for you to pass legislation to stop no-deal after the 17th.' But when Greg Clark asked for a guarantee, none was forthcoming. 'Hammond kept talking over him, tutting and shaking his head,' a source told the *Mail*. 'Boris was doing the same. Their mutual loathing was very apparent.' When Hammond mentioned the 'EU legal advice' on extensions, the PM's aides filed that away for later, briefing after the meeting that he was taking dictation from Brussels. Hammond said he was simply citing the published view of the Commission. As the argument escalated, Johnson declared, 'You all just want to keep us in the EU.'

A furious Hammond hit back, 'We voted for the deal three times.' Twice more than Johnson.

'I will not tolerate a bill which hands over power to Corbyn,' the prime minister said.

'We are handing over power to Parliament.'

'You are handing power over to a junta that includes Jeremy Corbyn. Extension would be an extinction-level event for the Conservative Party.'[7] Cummings, who had been absent for most of the meeting, reappeared to 'troll' Hammond. Johnson banged the table and urged the rebels to 'trust' him. 'I assume everyone is with me,' he pronounced, optimistically.

The meeting, which lasted an hour and twenty-five minutes, was a disaster, hardening the resolve of those present to defy Johnson and leaving Rudd wondering whether she was sitting on the correct side of the table. After the meeting there was a call between Greg Clark and Cummings, on whether there would be time for emergency legislation after 17 October. The rebels claimed Cummings said, 'When are you fucking MPs going to realise we are leaving on October 31st? We are going to purge you.' Cummings later half-heartedly denied this.

By 2.30 p.m. when the Commons began sitting, the number of confirmed rebels had risen to fifteen.

The drama now switched to the chamber. When Johnson got to his feet to make a statement on the G7 meeting in Biarritz, shortly after 3.30 p.m., Phillip Lee stood up and crossed the floor of the House to sit with Jo Swinson. Lee was now a Liberal Democrat. The moment he sat down Johnson no longer had a Commons majority. Since the Lib Dems had failed to tip off journalists, the immediate impact of the defection was lost. 'It took a weirdly long time before anyone noticed he had gone,' a Lib Dem official admitted. 'That was slightly comical.'

Alistair Carmichael, the Lib Dem chief whip, first approached Lee in June. Lee concluded his brand of Conservatism had lost the battle for their party. He joined conference calls on the preparation of the Benn Act from his summer holiday. That weekend, as Johnson was deciding to strip the whip from the rebels, Lee decided he would change parties, 'because of the prorogation nonsense'. He said, 'I thought if they're lying to the Queen, this lot are capable of anything.'[8]

As Lee stood at the bar of the House, the smart watch on his wrist flashed red because his heart rate was so high. Then he began his walk to the Lib Dem benches. Seated next to Swinson, who had only found out the previous afternoon that he was defecting, Lee watched the expressions of his former Tory colleagues. There was stunned silence.

The defection was not even the most dramatic moment that day, but it put Johnson on the back foot as he read out his statement, most notable for the debut in the chamber of Cummings' preferred branding for the Benn Act. 'There is only one way to describe the bill: it is Jeremy Corbyn's surrender bill,' the prime minister said, adding that it 'means running up the white flag' and there were 'no circumstances' in which he would 'ever accept anything like it'. The response was so feverish Bercow had to tell MPs to stop 'ranting from a sedentary position'.

While this was going on, the Court of Session was hearing the case to block prorogation. The judges saw evidence that Johnson had approved talks with the palace about prorogation on 15 August, the note he had signed to da Costa and Cummings. But the government offered no witness statements about the reasons for prorogation. This was what Cox had been worried about. 'Everybody in Number 10, who might have sworn an affidavit as to the background of this decision, was unwilling to put their signature to it just being a reset,' a legal service insider said. A Number 10 source said, 'No one wanted to perjure themselves.' In fact, da Costa had never even been asked whether she would make a statement or give evidence in person and later concluded that it would have been better if she had done so.

It was 6.36 p.m. when Oliver Letwin got to his feet and spoke for his amendment allowing backbenchers, for the second time ever, to take control of the agenda of the House of Commons the following day. 'In the light of the government's decision to prorogue Parliament next week it has become an urgent matter for … this House to discuss whether it can accept a no-deal exit,' he said. 'I therefore ask you to grant an urgent debate under Standing Order 24.' Bercow did so.

When the debate got going, Jacob Rees-Mogg said he did not wish to question the speaker's impartiality but, in reference to a recent test match, added, 'as with the umpires at Edgbaston who saw eight of their decisions sent for review and overturned, accepting somebody's impartiality is not the same as accepting their infallibility'. He pointed out that only the year before Bercow himself had ruled that 'a debate held under Standing Order 24 could be held on a substantive and amendable motion only if the standing order is itself amended'.

Bercow responded that there had twice previously been Standing Order 24 debates with 'evaluative motions'. He was there to 'facilitate the legislature'. Appropriating Johnson's own language, he concluded, 'I will do it to the best of my ability without fear or favour – or, to coin a phrase, come what may, do or die.'

Rees-Mogg attacked Letwin's 'stunning arrogance' in seeking to supplant the executive, labelling the Bresistance 'the illuminati'. He said, 'Sovereignty in this House comes from the British people. The idea that we can overrule 17.4 million people is preposterous.' He was supported by the arch-Paleosceptic Bill Cash, who added, 'The European Union Referendum Bill, as enacted, was a sovereign Act of Parliament, which deliberately gave the right to the British people, and not to the British Parliament, to make the decision on the question of remain or leave ... Usurping the executive's right is unconstitutional; the abuse of emergency debates to do so is unconstitutional; and the bill itself is yet more unconstitutional.'

The mood in the chamber soured further when Rees-Mogg reclined horizontally on the front bench, apparently close to sleep – a pose even Brexiteers found disrespectful. Grieve compared the threat to withdraw the whip to the words of Sir Thomas More when told that opposition to the king would mean death, 'These are but devices to frighten children.' Rees-Mogg's behaviour emboldened some rebels. One said, 'Nicholas [Soames] is not somebody who likes being at odds with his whip; Richard Benyon ditto. You could see them during this debate going from wavering – and probably would have bottled it at the last minute – to being so fucking angry.'

For a serial rebel like Johnson, who had always escaped punishment for his own backbench behaviour, threatening to expel rebels was a big deal. Until the last moment he wavered. 'He absolutely hated it,' one aide recalled. 'Can't we spare Ken Clarke?' the prime minister asked, to a chorus of disapproval. 'He's always got away with stuff,' the aide said. 'He understood it was him or them. You could always rely on his sense of self-preservation, so he did it.' At 8.32 p.m., likely rebels received a text message which read: 'I would like to remind colleagues that the government considers this a matter of confidence. Therefore it is imperative that you are in the government lobby. Mark Spencer, Chief Whip.'

At 9.50 p.m., the House divided. For the second time in history, MPs voted to hand control of the Commons to the backbenches, by 328 votes to 301. Twenty-one Tories rebelled.

In Number 10 there was shock that the prorogation gambit had succeeded in provoking the one thing it had been supposed to prevent. Oliver Letwin recalled, 'The idea that they would prorogue after giving time for Parliament to ... achieve the effects we wanted, rather than the effects they wanted, struck me as bizarre. It arose from the fact that Mr Cummings didn't believe we knew what we were doing procedurally. Anyway, we did.'[9]

The twenty-one rebels were sacked by phone, some by message. As they gathered after the vote in David Gauke's office, phones began to ring, ping and vibrate, in alphabetical order. Spencer told Philip Hammond, 'I told you what was going to happen and it has.' The chief whip found Anne Milton: 'You know what I've got to say.' Milton had been deputy chief whip. 'Yes, you don't need to say it,' she said, before giving Spencer a hug. Stephen Hammond 'found it one of the most emotional and depressing moments in politics'. He had been a party member since university. 'It felt extraordinarily unfair. It felt extraordinarily wrong.'[10] The following day Milton took a call from her constituency association saying they had been told to start the selection process for her replacement. The same day, Gauke was informed by his chairman that he was no longer a member of the Conservative Party. It was six days before some of them got a formal letter confirming the loss of the whip. In the meantime, Graham Brady, chairman of the 1922 Committee, had written to the MPs asking if they would like to appeal the decision. One rebel said, 'But you can't appeal something when there's not a process. There's nothing to appeal. It was all so incompetent – absolutely dreadful.' Some waited even longer; Dominic Grieve was never told that he had been stripped of the whip. He was still receiving messages into November from his constituency agent about whether he could stand again.

Some rebels were suspicious. 'You would have thought the chief would have phoned me over the summer,' one said. 'They wanted to get rid of us. It suited them to wait and see who emerged from the woodwork. They wanted to find out who we were.'

*   *   *

Seemingly unable to win a Commons vote and with the main plank of his negotiating strategy removed, Johnson only had one play left – he would have to try to force a general election.

That evening, Cummings wandered the corridors of the Commons clutching a glass of red wine. He accosted Jeremy Corbyn in Portcullis House, tapping him on the shoulder and saying, 'Come on, Jeremy, let's do this election, don't be scared.' His tone, Labour sources attested, was 'boisterous' not 'threatening' but frontbencher Cat Smith described him as 'some loud bloke who stunk of booze, yelling at us'.

Johnson kept up the pressure on Labour in his debut at Prime Minister's Questions the following day, 4 September – a performance panned as evasive and blustering. The prime minister branded Corbyn a 'chlorinated chicken' for opposing a US trade deal and an election. When the Labour leader began to respond, Johnson shouted from his seat, 'Call an election, you great big girl's blouse.' Churchillian, it was not.

With the Bresistance in charge of the timetable, Hilary Benn introduced his eponymous bill. He said, 'The bill gives the prime minister the flexibility that he wants and needs to get a deal if he can. It does not render further negotiation pointless. I do not regard the threat of a no-deal Brexit as part of a credible negotiating strategy.'

In this, the crunch moment of all the parliamentary manoeuvrings in 2018 and 2019, that fundamental disagreement still split the two sides. The pro-dealers and Remainers regarded no-deal as the height of irresponsibility. But Johnson and his aides were equally adamant that his hardline approach had made the EU consider things they had previously refused to consider. They were not believed by the rebels. In the debate, Philip Hammond claimed there were no negotiations to disrupt: 'We have had confirmation from multiple sources across the European Union that nothing is happening, and confirmation from within government that nothing is happening. The government have declined to bring forward any proposals or serve any proposals on the European Union.'

This was not quite true, though it was the case that Frost and Johnson were happily running out the clock until the crunch talks they planned all along for late October. Hammond also denied Johnson's accusation that the rebels wanted to hand power to Corbyn: 'I would sooner boil my head than hand power to the leader of the opposition.' But Hammond did admit, 'The purpose of this bill is to instruct this government how to conduct the UK's future arrangements with the European Union.'

Opponents of the Benn Bill didn't just dislike the nature of those instruc-tions, sovereignty Brexiteers fundamentally didn't believe that was the role of backbenchers. Bill Cash thundered, 'This is a disgraceful reversal of our constitutional arrangements ... We have a system of parliamen-tary government, not government by Parliament.'

Summing up at the end of the debate, Brexit secretary Steve Barclay said, 'This is a bill that is intended to stop Brexit. I urge colleagues to oppose it.' He was ignored. The Benn Act passed second reading at 5 p.m. by 329 votes to 300. At 7.30 p.m. it passed third reading by 327 to 299. To steal Geoffrey Cox's analogy, the Lilliputians had chained Gulliver down.

The 1922 Committee meeting that Wednesday evening was a 'blood-bath', with MPs in uproar about the expulsion of the twenty-one and the multiple setbacks. Johnson, disingenuously, hid behind the robust human shield of 'Big Farmer' Spencer. 'I can't undermine the chief on whipping arrangements,' he said, as if he had had nothing to do with the decision. Anne Milton mouthed, 'Bollocks!' This, she told colleagues, was proof that Johnson was a 'dirty rotten liar'.

Former minister Tim Loughton told the prime minister, 'You and I are both classical scholars and we know that purges never work.'

Johnson fought back: 'Under Augustus Caesar there was a lot of bloodletting and then sixty years of peace.' This was both vainglorious and unwise. Comparing himself to the first emperor of Rome was hardly the best way for Johnson to convince MPs he wasn't drunk on power and prepared to undermine democracy to get what he wanted. There didn't seem like the prospect of even sixty days of peace.

At 7.51 p.m. Johnson was back in the chamber, arguing for a govern-ment motion to force a general election on 15 October, so he could go to the European Council meeting with a mandate. Under the Fixed-term Parliaments Act, he needed two thirds of all MPs to back the measure, not just those voting. He denounced the Benn Act as a bill that would 'force the prime minister, with a pre-drafted letter, to surrender in inter-national negotiations' and accused Corbyn of being 'frit'.

Corbyn replied that he would back an election once the Benn Act had received royal assent. Labour abstained. This position concealed a 'huge row' behind the scenes between Corbyn's closest aides on the one side and Keir Starmer, the shadow Brexit secretary, and Nick Brown, Labour's chief whip, on the other. Corbyn's team was relaxed about an election date before 31 October. His senior aide Seumas Milne believed Corbyn would get to negotiate Brexit himself, or that Johnson would pursue no-deal, which he thought would also help Labour. However, in a tense meeting of the shadow cabinet, Starmer and others insisted that any election be after Brexit day to prevent no-deal. After the Parliamentary Labour Party (PLP) meeting that Tuesday, one of Corbyn's aides said, 'We want to see more Tory blood and guts on the walls before we have an election.' This decision unnerved Tories. A minister said, 'I think Boris and Cummings have been completely wrong-footed.'

At 9.21 p.m. Parliament backed an election by 298 votes to 56, but Johnson fell well short of the necessary two-thirds majority. It was not just Labour that was divided. SNP leader Nicola Sturgeon clashed with her MPs at Westminster. She favoured an immediate election, which she thought would maximise votes for the nationalists, while most of the MPs wanted to see no-deal averted before giving their support.

The Benn Act had passed in the Commons, but it still had to get through the Lords. Battalions of ageing Tory peers took to the red benches with the fortitude of the redcoats at Rorke's Drift. Nikki da Costa knew, when she planned prorogation, that the Bresistance could push through a bill in a day in the Commons, but to do so in the Lords would mean tearing up the procedures of the upper house. Under Lords rules, every amendment had to be debated and every peer was entitled to speak. The only way to silence them was to pass a motion. Every motion to silence would use up twenty minutes. Marshalled by Nicholas True, the Conservative peers dug in to filibuster the bill until 9 September when it would die. 'It would require an almighty effort,' a Downing Street aide said. 'We might well have killed some peers, but the Lords were up for that.' Da Costa calculated that they would need to table around three hundred amendments to talk the bill out. Within a few hours, True and his team had already tabled nearly a hundred. It seemed like game on.

Later that night, however, True spoke to da Costa, who was in touch with Cummings and Johnson. 'The feeling was that the public wouldn't understand the procedural chicanery of a filibustering effort in the Lords,' one said. 'It would have looked like the same behaviour as the Remainers.' Da Costa didn't fight this but asked Johnson to meet the peers. They assembled in his parliamentary office. The prime minister recited Macaulay's poem 'Horatius at the Bridge', about a Roman who defended a vital redoubt. ('Now, who will stand on either hand and keep the bridge with me?'). 'It was his way of recognising that they were up for the fight with him,' a witness said, 'but he was going to ask them a very difficult thing, which was to stand down.'

At 1.30 a.m. the filibuster ended. It was announced that the bill would be sent back to the Commons by 5 p.m. the following day. The Bresistance had its Benn Act. The government had the political grievance they wanted.

The one piece of good news for Johnson on 4 September came from Scotland, where, in the Outer House of the Court of Session, Lord Doherty ruled that the question of whether the government was right to prorogue was non-justiciable, not a matter for the courts. The complainants appealed to the Inner House of the Court of Session.

Two days later, the High Court in London agreed. A panel of three judges – the lord chief justice, Lord Burnett of Maldon, the master of the rolls, Sir Terence Etherton, and the president of the Queen's Bench Division, Dame Victoria Sharp – rejected Gina Miller's case saying prorogation was a political matter that was 'not justiciable in Her Majesty's courts'. Further, they said there were 'no legal standards against which to judge' the 'legitimacy' of Johnson's actions and warned, 'This is territory into which the courts should be slow indeed to intrude.' So far, the judiciary was in agreement with Geoffrey Cox, who regarded prorogation as a matter for Parliament rather than the courts.

Between the two verdicts, Johnson suffered one of the most personally painful moments of his premiership. His brother Jo Johnson, the universities minister, the only one in government who did not pledge to support no-deal, contacted the PM that Wednesday evening to say he was planning to resign. Boris tried to talk him round, but failed. In his resignation letter, Jo cited an 'unresolvable tension' between family loyalty and the national interest.

The truth was that he chose a competing family loyalty, Jo's wife, the *Guardian* journalist Amelia Gentleman. 'There was an episode in the showers at the Hampstead lido where Jo and she had been swimming,' a family friend explained. 'She was in the shower and there were other women there. One said, "Did you see that Jo Johnson? I can't believe he's gone back to work for his brother. What a wanker. I was going to spit in his face." Milly burst into tears and that was the end.' The episode provided a wrenching example of the personal cost of politics, where blood and ideology, honesty to oneself and loved ones can clash.

Jo's resignation hit Boris hard. He appeared severely rattled on a visit that day to a police training academy in West Yorkshire. The event was supposed to mark the start of a Conservative general election campaign but Labour's refusal to back an election left him high and dry. Johnson arrived an hour late, then gave a rambling speech – criticised for politicising the police – notable only for the soundbite that he would rather 'die in a ditch' than request a Brexit extension. Even the *Telegraph* described him as 'genuinely dazed, lost, uncertain'. Comedy writer James Felton noted, 'He looks like a concerned relative has found him drinking heavily and shouting at pigeons in a bin.'

Asked about his brother's resignation, the prime minister said, 'Look, people disagree about the EU. The way to unite the country, I'm afraid, is to get this thing done. That is the reality.' It was left to Number 10 to issue a more heartfelt statement: 'The PM, as both a politician and brother, understands this will not have been an easy matter for Jo.' That evening Rachel Johnson attended a book launch for the BBC presenter Emma Barnett. She was visibly upset. 'They're both my boys,' she said, telling a friend she had spoken to Boris: 'He was so upset. It's like Cain and Abel.' Days later the two brothers met for two hours at their mother Charlotte's flat. She told Tom Bower, 'Boris felt let down by Jo quitting.'[11]

At the cabinet meeting on the Wednesday morning, several ministers, including Michael Gove, Amber Rudd and Matt Hancock, asked Johnson to grant a reprieve for the twenty-one, to be told that was impossible. 'He had all these howls from the wets and the One Nation lot,' a political aide said. Julian Smith raised the plight of the whipless rebels twice, which incensed Johnson. As they walked out of the Cabinet Room, he turned to the Northern Ireland secretary and indignantly declared, 'These people are cunts. They're utter cunts!'

Privately, the PM was having a wobble of his own and was 'not in a good place', telling friendly cabinet ministers that things had 'got out of control'. A close aide said, 'He got very jumpy because every newspaper was saying, "This is a massive mistake, a car crash, they're all maniacs."' Johnson was particularly agitated about taking the whip from Nicholas Soames, grandson of Winston Churchill. The day after the expulsions, he received a text from Amber Rudd. 'Maybe we could just bring her back,' Johnson suggested. Lee Cain shouted, 'Absolutely not! Do you know how weak you'll look?' Cummings asked: 'Are you zero tolerance on fuckers or not?' As a former Downing Street adviser observed, 'Sacking twenty-one Tory MPs is what gets Cummings out of bed in the morning. I don't think it's what gets Boris out of bed in the morning.'

Johnson was particularly unnerved because, unlike prorogation, Eddie Lister did not support the decision to strip the whip. 'I just felt that it was a bit of a pointless exercise,' he recalled. Eventually, Spencer, the chief whip, said there was a route back for the rebels, but only if they played ball. 'There's a long ladder and a short ladder,' he said. 'If they start voting with us, they get a short ladder back up.'

Johnson's critics dismissed him as a dilettante playing at populism, but those close to him could see the strain it was putting on him. 'The thing that no one has really spoken about is the amount of pressure that he was under in the months leading up to the election,' one adviser said. 'Removing the whip from the twenty-one was a hugely difficult decision for him. But out in the country, that was a demonstration of unity and purpose rather than division.'

Whatever his personal scruples, with his back to the wall Johnson was prepared to fight dirty. 'In the second half of 2019 he was completely desperate,' Cummings said later. 'He knew that he had only been put in there because no one could think of anything else to do. He did as we told him … As far as anything can be with him, it was reasonably stable – chaotic for the country, but he was focused.'[12] Another close ally said, 'Boris was both quiescent and upbeat. He's normally only quiescent when he's scared.' From the Corbynistas there was grudging admiration. Labour spinner James Schneider later told Cain, 'We should have done the same and purged our rebels.'

For a man at the heart of the political hurricane, Cummings seemed non-plussed. When special advisers gathered in Downing Street on Friday 6 September, he said, 'Other people are melting down. Well, let them. We need to be little Fonzis and stay cool. We are not going to panic.' In the space of a fortnight, the prime minister – egged on by his chief aide – had announced they were suspending Parliament for five weeks, suffered three Commons defeats, lost control of the parliamentary agenda, watched the Bresistance pass a bill banning no-deal, expelled twenty-one Tory MPs – many of them former cabinet ministers – and seen Jeremy Corbyn refuse to trigger the general election Johnson needed. Commentators who regarded Cummings as a political pyromaniac watched Number 10's tactical setbacks with glee, mocking the idea that he was the evil genius of the Cumberbatch film with the phrase #ClassicDom when things went wrong. But the more they gloated, the more Cummings was convinced he would have the last laugh. The chief adviser was 'cock-a-hoop', a colleague recalled, confident that these tactical setbacks only strengthened the power of his strategic narrative, that the political establishment was uniting to thwart Johnson and Brexit. 'What the critics didn't understand was that, Hulk-like, every defeat was making them stronger,' a Vote Leave ally said.

Keeping your eyes on a strategic goal in the middle of a political firestorm is a rare and often unheralded attribute in Westminster, but it was key to Cummings' success in 2019. Tory focus groups in a Midlands seat that week found that voters were 'very positive' about the decision to expel the twenty-one rebels. One poll found that 77 per cent of Tory voters backed the move. In Westminster, stripping the whip was seen as a disgrace but, as a senior Tory strategist noted, 'in the eyes of voters, it was a demonstration of his determination'.

When Cummings addressed special advisers that Friday he said, 'The Conservative Party promised a referendum and promised to respect that vote. That means some things are going to break.' The government would follow the Vote Leave tactic and 'double down', he said. 'People are saying that the last week has been mad. Trust me, it's not mad relative to where this is going.' The next month, he predicted, 'is going to be fucking weird'. About that, at least, he was right.

Cummings did not get everything right, however. He made four serious miscalculations, which might have unseated a less determined Downing Street team. The first was his belief that the government enjoyed the element of surprise around prorogation and that the Rebel Alliance would not have time to formulate a plan and pass a bill blocking no-deal. Instead, this was accomplished within thirty-six hours of Parliament returning. Dominic Grieve said, 'They were pretty sure we wouldn't have time to do anything. I think Cummings got it very badly wrong.'

Even internally, there had been some debate about timing. Oliver Lewis thought it unwise to offer Parliament any time between announcement and prorogation. He told Cummings they should get pre-approval from the Queen and then declare that Parliament was dissolved the second Bercow approved an SO24 debate. 'You have to do it up front in response to the threat,' he said. Bercow said later, 'The government was careless.'[13] Grieve, however, believed that, despite the evidence, Johnson's team did feel an element of shame about their plan. 'I think they were ultimately trying to maintain the view of constitutional propriety,' he said. 'To actually turn up on the Monday, and have somebody saying, "You're about to be sent away", was so outrageous that they weren't prepared to do it.'

Cummings' second mistake was to think that this legislation could not be binding on Johnson. He told colleagues that the only way Remainers could be sure to stop no-deal would be for them to seize control of Parliament again and pass a law revoking Article 50, but only after the prorogation period, between 21 and 31 October.

The reason for Cummings' second error lay in his third: a belief that it would not be possible to hear a case on such weighty matters in the Supreme Court and get a ruling which bound the prime minister's hands in less than about ten days. Without that, he believed, there was no way of enforcing any new law. In reality, it took just half that time.

The fourth error of judgement was to assume that Labour would be compelled to support a general election once the Benn Act was passed. Instead, Parliament decided to hold Johnson in political purgatory.

Even after the passage of the Benn Act, Johnson's team explored extreme measures to circumvent it. The prime minister asked Cox to task the government legal service with exploring whether the PM could ask the Queen not to give royal assent to the bill. The attorney general did not think this practical. Civil servants argued that, in reality, the Queen herself signed nothing and that the necessary formalities were conducted by officials. Cummings responded, 'Don't give me any of that shit. If you want to run around claiming that you've signed on behalf of the Queen, be my guest, because that's not going to work out well for you guys.' Johnson, however, was not willing to drag the monarch into such blatant controversy. The Act got royal assent and became law on 9 September. Cummings told colleagues Johnson had 'bottled it'.

Robert Buckland, the lord chancellor, considered resignation over Cummings' determination to ignore the law. On Monday 9 September,

Buckland issued an extraordinary tweet, making clear he had raised his concerns with Johnson. 'Speculation about my future is wide of the mark. I fully support the prime minister ... We have spoken over the past 24 hours regarding the importance of the Rule of Law, which I as Lord Chancellor have taken an oath to uphold.'

There was also talk in Whitehall that Johnson might try to force an election by resigning, or 'throwing' a no-confidence route. 'He can no-confidence himself, but that doesn't look good,' a senior Tory said. 'In an emergency, break glass and resign.' In reality, the polling Isaac Levido had outlined at Chequers suggested this would hurt the Tories.

Cummings told officials in Number 10, 'The more hysterical Remainers become with a campaign to arrest the PM unless he surrenders, the stronger our position with the country will get. Most MPs and journalists do not understand how much the country hates Parliament and wants someone to sort out this mess.' He remained impervious to the rage he engendered. 'I think the main difference between me and a lot of the people that I've ended up politically fighting against ... is that, for me, it's more important to win ... than it is to be friends with people.'[14]

The cabinet call on prorogation was the final straw for Amber Rudd. That Tuesday her special adviser, Jason Stein, contacted the *Sunday Times*. The political editor[15] said, 'Is this what I think it is?' Stein replied, 'Yes.' In the utmost secrecy they agreed he would go to Rudd's flat in west London that Thursday for an interview in which she would announce her resignation from the cabinet, the subterfuge to ensure that her side of the story was reported before Downing Street could brief against her. Rudd recorded a short version of her reasons on the photographer's iPhone before repairing upstairs for photographs. The reporter joked that it was the first time he had been in the bedroom of a cabinet minister but the only nerves he felt were whether the story would hold.

Only five people at the newspaper knew what was happening and a dummy paper was set up in the *ST*'s computer system so the story could be written, laid out and subbed away from prying eyes. That Saturday word began to spread that a cabinet minister was on the verge of quitting – the result of a lunch Rudd's brother Roland, a PR man, had with a leading broadcaster. Journalists and fellow ministers called and messaged Rudd. 'I know I'm not resigning,' Nicky Morgan wrote, 'so is it you?'

Rudd ignored them. Johnson repeatedly tried to contact her. She did not pick up. The plan had been to drop the story at 10 p.m., but Stein and the political editor decided to move the deadline forward an hour.

At 9 p.m. Rudd called Johnson to tell him she was going. Lee Cain was listening to the other end of the call and worked out what was happening. In an attempt to spike the *Sunday Times'* guns he contacted Harry Cole at the *Mail on Sunday*, who tweeted the news. Within seconds, the *Sunday Times* dropped the story online and released the iPhone video. Rudd said she was not only resigning from the cabinet but also quitting the Conservative Party in disgust at Johnson's 'purge' of the party and his 'failure' to pursue a deal with the EU. She claimed there was 'no evidence' the prime minister was actively seeking a deal because the cabinet had been 'not sufficiently informed' about his plans, calling it 'quite outrageous' she had not seen the legal advice. The 'short-sighted culling' of the twenty-one rebels she called an 'act of political vandalism', which amounted to an 'assault on decency and democracy'. She also denounced the PM's 'aggressive combative language' and warned that pitting Parliament against the people is 'really unwise' and would lead to 'dangerous outcomes'. She concluded, 'I no longer believe leaving with a deal is the government's main objective. My mother used to say, "Judge a man by what he does and not by what he says." I am concerned that he's not doing enough to make true what he says is his priority.'

As soon as the story broke, Johnson rang Robert Buckland while Mark Spencer called Morgan to check they weren't jumping ship as well. Both vowed to stay but asked for more information about the negotiations. That weekend, Morgan got a call from David Frost. She, Buckland and Matt Hancock all saw Johnson the following Monday. Frost revealed more about his conversations with Brussels, Johnson about his chats with Merkel and Macron. 'I really want there to be a deal,' he said, 'but we've got to be prepared for no-deal.' Johnson admonished Morgan for a recent article. 'You shouldn't really write for national newspapers,' said the author of two 4,000-word screeds on Brexit in the *Telegraph*, before having the decency to look sheepish. 'I know, I can't really talk.'

On 9 September, Dominic Grieve went after Cummings in the Commons, narrowly winning a vote on a motion that the government should release all written and electronic communications. This was an attempt to flush out the 'unofficial channels', believed to be WhatsApp messages, through which Johnson's aides had been plotting the prorogation. Unbeknown to Grieve, there was another secret channel used to circumvent scrutiny.

Cummings set up a series of threads in the messaging system Slack, which allowed colleagues to join group chats which were not subject to Freedom of Information (FOI) disclosure rules. Close aides used one, called 'cabinetmanagement', to discuss Johnson. 'There was a secret messaging system on Slack,' a political adviser revealed. 'Most of the senior people in Number 10 were on it. It was to have a place that couldn't be FOI'd or got at.' One channel was reserved for emergencies. 'Defcon', named after the Pentagon's numbered 'defence conditions' which signal the countdown to war, 'was for when shit was happening', the aide said.

Later that evening, Johnson tried and failed again to get backing for a general election. He taunted Corbyn: 'The surrender bill – the surrender Act – has now passed. It has gained royal assent. He has done his level best to wreck this country's chances of a successful negotiation. By his own logic, he must now back an election.'

Corbyn refused to do so, saying he would not let his party walk into 'traps laid by this prime minister'. This was the sixth parliamentary defeat of Boris Johnson's time as prime minister. He had suffered, in a week, more defeats than Thatcher, Major, Blair or Brown in their entire time in Downing Street.

Nonetheless, the Cabinet Office and Conservative campaign head-quarters (CCHQ) were now ramping up preparations for a general election. An email sent by Tory HQ raised more than £50,000 in less than an hour, 'the best response to a fundraising email I have ever seen,' one source said. Downing Street also began negotiations with executives from the BBC, ITV and Sky about live TV debates. Unlike the leadership contest, in which Johnson dodged scrutiny, his team wanted to get him into a head-to-head showdown with Corbyn – now possible under new broadcasting rules which allowed debates featuring only those party leaders most likely to become prime minister.

The final act of the prorogation drama was more Whitehall farce than Shakespeare, aided by Bercow's determination to seize centre stage. At 1.18 a.m. in the small hours of 10 September, Sarah Clarke, Lady Usher of the Black Rod, entered the Commons chamber to signal the start of the formal prorogation ceremony. The speaker, who had decided to partici-pate only with great reluctance, was at his most pompous, repeatedly snapping at Tory MPs. Addressing the House, the speaker said, 'This is not a normal prorogation. It is not typical. It is not standard. It is one of the longest for decades, and it represents, not just in the minds of many colleagues but for huge numbers of people outside an act of executive fiat.' When business minister Graham Stuart suggested he was out of order, Bercow snapped, 'You are a master of disorder, man … I could not give a flying flamingo what your view is.'

A group of opposition MPs, including Caroline Lucas and Clive Lewis, carrying 'SILENCED' signs tried to prevent Bercow from leaving his chair to go to the House of Lords to complete prorogation proceedings. Labour MP Paula Sheriff went as far as to sit on him. Conservative MPs left the chamber with the speaker to go to the Lords. Labour, SNP and Plaid Cymru MPs chanted, 'Shame on you!' and remained in the Commons singing 'The Red Flag', the Welsh hymn 'Calon Lân' and the Scottish patriotic song 'Wha Hae'.

It was usual for five Lords Commissioners to perform the prorogation ceremony, but it was boycotted by Baroness Smith of Basildon and Lord Newby, the Labour and Liberal Democrat leaders in the Lords. Just sixteen peers turned up.

When Bercow returned to the Commons he was cheered by the opposition MPs, who greatly outnumbered the Tories present. He then read the notice of prorogation: 'By virtue of Her Majesty's Commission which has now been read, we do, in Her Majesty's name, and in obedience to Her Majesty's Commands, prorogue this Parliament to Monday the fourteenth day of this October to be then here holden, and this Parliament is accordingly prorogued to Monday the fourteenth day of October.'

Johnson had succeeded, at least temporarily, in sidelining Parliament. He could not sideline the judges.

OUTLAWS

The Supreme Court

11–24 September 2019

The verdict was blunt and, for Boris Johnson, absolutely brutal. It was 11 September, a date resonant for seismic political events. A panel of three judges in Scotland's highest court of appeal unanimously declared that Johnson's advice to the Queen to suspend Parliament for five weeks was 'unlawful' and motivated by the 'improper purpose of stymying Parliament'. Lord Brodie, one of the judges, ruled, 'This was an egregious case of a clear failure to comply with generally accepted standards of behaviour.'

Joanna Cherry and Jolyon Maugham had used the Scottish courts precisely because Scottish law differed in key respects from England and Wales. Crucially, it did not share a deference to the exercise of the crown prerogative. The government had argued that this was a matter of politics, not the law. But one of the three judges, Lord Drummond Young, said, 'The courts have jurisdiction to decide whether any power, under the prerogative or otherwise, has been legally exercised.' His verdict went on, 'It was incumbent on the UK government to show a valid reason for the prorogation.' Lord Brodie concluded the 'principal reason for the prorogation' was 'to allow the executive to pursue a policy of a no-deal Brexit without further Parliamentary interference.'

The government had failed, again, to produce even one witness statement. The judges concluded, 'The prime minister's advice to HM the Queen and the prorogation which followed thereon was unlawful.' The words which shaped the public reaction to the verdict came not from the judgment, but from legal commentator David Allen Green.[1] He wrote that the judges made their decision 'on the basis that prime minister

Boris Johnson misled the Queen ... In effect ... the Scottish court has held that Mr Johnson lied to the Queen.' What might have been a matter of baffling constitutional obscurity became, instantly, a matter of morality in which a rogue prime minister had tricked a universally admired monarch – an issue comprehensible to the least engaged voter.

Dominic Grieve said that if the Supreme Court upheld this verdict, Johnson should resign 'and very swiftly'. Adam Price, the Plaid Cymru leader, said the prime minister should be impeached. There was a glimmer of solace for Johnson. A YouGov poll the same day found that 52 per cent of the public thought the prime minister should break the law to ensure that Brexit happened.

Downing Street's response was muted by their standards. 'We are disappointed by today's decision, and will appeal to the UK Supreme Court,' a spokesman said. 'The UK government needs to bring forward a strong domestic legislative agenda. Proroguing Parliament is the legal and necessary way of delivering this.' Kwasi Kwarteng, a business minister, voiced what many in Number 10 were really thinking: 'I'm not saying this, but many people ... are saying that the judges are biased.'

The ruling was not the end of the matter. The court did not declare the prorogation null and void but noted that the Scottish judiciary was now at odds with the English judiciary. Both this case and the Gina Miller case would now go to the Supreme Court in London. The future of the government hung, in part, on the verdict of the twelve 'Supremes' under the presidency of Brenda Hale.

The Supreme Court of the United Kingdom, on which sat English, Scottish and Northern Irish judges, was set up in 2009 by the Labour government, replacing the law lords as the ultimate court of appeal on civil matters for the whole country and on criminal matters outside Scotland. Lacking the right to overturn primary legislation, it was not remotely as powerful as the US Supreme Court, but the government's fate lay in its hands.

When the Scottish court announced its verdict, Baroness Hale of Richmond, who was two years into her term as president of the court, was at Yale Law School in the United States, attending a seminar on constitutionalism. 'As almost everyone there came from a country with a written constitution ... the general view was that the issue was justiciable, although not what the answer should be,' she recalled. Hale quickly concluded, 'We had to hear and decide the case.'[2] The maximum number of justices, eleven, would decide the prime minister's fate.

The court began a three-day hearing to consider the appeals for both R (Miller) v The Prime Minister and Cherry v The Advocate General for Scotland on 17 September. Opening proceedings, Hale said they would rule 'without fear or favour' but that the judgment 'will not determine when and how the UK leaves the EU'.

The first day of the hearing focused on the losers of each lower court case, with the Advocate General for Scotland, Lord Keen, doing battle for the government against Lord Pannick, representing Gina Miller. Keen argued that the Scottish Court of Session had exceeded its jurisdiction in ruling that prorogation was null and void. It had 'simply gone where the court could not go,' he said. He argued that previous prorogations in 1930 and 1948 had 'clearly been employed' when governments wanted to 'pursue a particular political objective' and that 'They are entitled to do so.' Keen said that if the Supreme Court ruled against the government, the prime minister would take 'all necessary steps' to comply with the judgment. But there was real tension when he was pressed by the judges on whether Johnson might then try to prorogue Parliament again.

When it was the turn of the owlish Pannick, the crossbench peer said, 'The exceptional length of the prorogation in this case is strong evidence that the prime minister's motive was to silence Parliament for that [five-week] period because he sees Parliament as an obstacle to the furtherance of his political aims.' Cranking up the rhetoric, Pannick added, 'No prime minister has abused his power in the manner in which we allege in at least the last fifty years.'

Pannick soon realised that this was not an argument which impressed Hale. 'Early on, we decided that the focus should be on the effect of the prorogation, rather than the motivation for it,' she recalled. 'If the matter was justiciable at all, and the effect was to frustrate the normal operation of Parliament at a crucial time in the nation's history, then it might be unlawful whatever the political motivation for it.' Pannick, she noticed, 'picked this up straightaway and adjusted his argument'.[3]

The second day of the hearing was a reversal of the first, with the two victors in each lower court case presenting their arguments. Geoffrey Cox had considered appearing for the government, but he was persuaded that he was too close to the case. It was a decision he was to regret.

Instead, the government was represented by Sir James Eadie QC, the Treasury solicitor, a role known in Whitehall as 'the Treasury devil'. Balding and bespectacled, Eadie was regarded as a first-class lawyer, but peering over half-moon glasses he presented a figure who was simpatico with the mood of the court, rather than an overt challenge to it.

Eadie used the morning session to state that a decision to prorogue was 'fundamentally political in nature' and power 'to be exercised by the executive'. If MPs wanted to challenge a government, they could use the 'nuclear option' of a no-confidence vote rather than the courts. 'My submission is that these are political judgments.' He warned that if the court took a different view they would be wading 'into the territory of political and parliamentary controversy'. It was not appropriate for the courts to 'design a set of rules' now about how long a prorogation should last. This was the standard legal view shared by both the attorney general and the lord chief justice. But it was a position immediately under fire in the Supreme Court. Government observers were concerned to witness an intervention from the bench by Lord Kerr, who asked, 'What if he decided to prorogue for one year? That is exercising me ... Scrutiny of the government's actions coming up to Brexit is reduced. Can it be [anything] other than the case that that represents a political advantage?'

Eadie said the prime minister was entitled to close Parliament whatever his reasons: 'Even if the prorogation ... was designed to advance the Government's political agenda regarding withdrawal from the European Union rather than preparations for the Queen's Speech, that is not territory in which a court can enter.' He cited the Attlee government, which prorogued Parliament in 1949 with the express intention of preventing the Lords from blocking its legislation. The government's case rested, in part, on A. V. Dicey's classic text *Introduction to the Study of the Law of the Constitution*, published in 1885. Dicey wrote that prorogation could not be challenged by a court and that if a dictatorial leader sought to prorogue for years, he would be prevented from doing so by other remedies, such as the need to regularly raise money.

Lord Wilson asked Eadie why no minister had given a witness statement. Eadie said he would present a written statement setting out what the government would do if it lost the case, but there was nothing he could do to disguise this glaring omission. As before, the only written statement was by Jonathan Jones, the head of the government legal service, putting into evidence Nikki da Costa's memo of 15 August and a scribbled note by Johnson the following day giving the go-ahead to discuss prorogation with the palace. 'The instruction came from Mark Sedwill that no official was to give evidence,' a civil servant recalled. 'He was just trying to protect us. Number 10 ran for cover.'

The tone of Johnson's note raised eyebrows. He wrote, 'The whole September session is a rigmarole introduced by girly swot Cameron to show the public that MPs were earning their crust', adding, 'So I don't see anything especially shocking about this prorogation. As Nikki notes, it is OVER THE CONFERENCE SEASON so that the sitting days lost are actually very few.' Where da Costa's memo suggested approaching the palace, Johnson had added a tick and scribbled 'Yes.' It was thin gruel. A minister said, 'Judges like evidence and we didn't give them any.'

In the afternoon, Aidan O'Neill QC for the Bresisters argued it was 'the province of the courts' to decide whether prorogation was constitutional. He said Johnson's decision was made 'in bad faith' and 'for an improper purpose', and suggested the government was engaged in 'low, dishonest, dirty tricks … given the attitude that has been taken by its advisers and the prime minister to the notion of the rule of law'. He added, 'The prime minister's action … has had the intent and effect of preventing Parliament … from holding the government politically to account at a time when the government is taking decisions that will have constitutional and irreversible impact on our country … We cannot have a situation in which there are no standards, in which prorogation can be used with impunity.'

Had Cox appeared he was prepared to launch a more robust challenge to the judges, warning that they risked upending constitutional norms if they meddled in politics. Cox knew several of the justices well. He had been tutored by Lord Lloyd Jones at Cambridge. Lord Sales and he had been opponents in court in some big cases. 'I would have been able to speak very frankly and bluntly,' Cox told friends later. 'I would have given the Supreme Court a very clear steer on politics and the law.' This might have made no difference to the outcome, but it would have raised the stakes and perhaps made the judges think twice about a course of action Cox came to believe had brought the court into disrepute.

On the third and final day, the court heard from the other parties to the case. Lord [Edward] Garnier, the former solicitor general, appeared on behalf of John Major. He argued that Johnson's prorogation was 'motivated by a desire to prevent Parliament interfering with the prime minister's policies'. Ronan Lavery QC, for Raymond McCord, whose case had not progressed in Northern Ireland, argued prorogation was designed to 'run down the clock' to force a no-deal Brexit, resulting in controls on the border with Ireland. In the closing arguments, Keen, for the government, said the courts were 'not properly equipped' to decide on matters of high politics. Pannick, for the petitioners, asked the court to declare prorogation unlawful so that Parliament could be recalled.

Dominic Grieve initially thought the government would win the case, but, as he watched, he changed his mind. It was not a surprise that the High Court and the Outer Court of Session had taken a conventional legal view of prerogative powers. But, in his mind, the stronger ruling was the second ruling in Scotland, in a court of appeal like the Supreme Court, whose job was to consider points of law rather than follow precedent. He thought the Supremes would react negatively to the government's failure to make the case for the length of the prorogation.

As Westminster waited for the verdict, the Labour Party conference began. With the government on the ropes, a successful conference for Corbyn could have helped his party begin to resemble a government in waiting. Instead, it was an exercise in incompetence and infighting to rival the Vaudeville show the Tories had staged for the nation.

Tom Watson spent most of Friday 20 September playing Super Smash Bros, a Nintendo video game, with his fourteen-year-old son. It was only when he went for dinner that Labour's deputy leader learned he was the victim of a political coup by some of Corbyn's closest allies. 'I got a text message in a Chinese restaurant in Manchester to say that they were abolishing me,' he said. That evening, as Labour prepared to finalise its Brexit stance and general election platform, Jon Lansman – a veteran of the Bennite plot to oust Denis Healey as Labour's deputy leader in 1981 – launched a similar attempt to defenestrate Watson. When the party's ruling National Executive Committee (NEC) meeting opened, Lansman, founder of the Momentum pressure group, asked for the usual standing orders to be suspended so that urgent matters could be discussed. Wendy Nichols of Unison, the NEC chair, was advised by Jennie Formby, the Corbynite general secretary, that the orders could be suspended. At this point, in a bid to 'keep his hands clean', Corbyn left the meeting. Lansman then tabled a motion calling for the deletion of the section in the Labour rulebook on the role of deputy leader and all references to the post. He accused Watson of disloyalty to Corbyn for advocating, the previous week, that Labour back a new EU referendum before a general election and support Remain if there was a second vote – both of which Corbyn had refused to commit to. 'It was a well-organised and meticulously planned hit job,' said one party source.

Not meticulous enough. Nichols ruled the motion out of order as no notice of it had been given to the NEC. But others sought to overrule her and have the motion considered. Lansman won the vote 17–10, but fell one short of the two-thirds majority required. Then Claudia Webbe, the hard left disputes committee chair, arrived. Lansman's allies attempted to rerun the vote, but this was blocked by Andi Fox, the NEC vice-chair. The hard left had a reputation for waging effective procedural warfare. But had Corbyn stayed and backed the coup, or had Webbe arrived on time, the attempt to oust Watson would have succeeded.

At the end of the meeting, Lansman was seen in conclave with Karie Murphy, Corbyn's flame-haired Glaswegian gatekeeper. The Watson gambit had been stitched up earlier by the pair of them, along with Murphy's lover Len McCluskey, the boss of Unite. Egged on by Murphy, Lansman announced that he would bring the motion again on the Saturday morning, when it needed just a simple majority to pass. 'Karie knows only two ways to deal with a situation,' said one half-admiring Labour insider. 'Take off his legs or take off his head.' This was personal. Murphy had once been Watson's secretary, McCluskey his onetime flatmate, but they were now mortal enemies.

The plotters forgot the old adage that those who seek to kill a king had better return with a body. The negative reaction was swift and overwhelming. Watson took to the *Today* programme to denounce the 'drive-by shooting'. He said, 'These things happen in Venezuela. They shouldn't happen in the UK.' Allies pointed out that, regardless of the outcome of Saturday's vote, he would remain as deputy leader until the end of conference on Tuesday and would make a speech which would 'read the last rites for the Labour Party'. Tony Blair branded the coup 'undemocratic, damaging and politically dangerous'. Gordon Brown contacted Corbyn to tell him that, if the vote went ahead, every living leader and deputy leader would publicly condemn him.

There was no Saturday vote. Corbyn faced a bombardment from John McDonnell and the leaders of Unison, the Transport Salaried

Staffs' Association and the GMB union to back off. Around 100 Labour MPs threatened to leave the party. 'Lansman is going to become the Lee Harvey Oswald of the Watson plot,' an insider said. 'Corbyn's office will set him up as the patsy, the lone nut who was behind it all.'

Brexit was also key to the other significant event in Camp Corbyn that week – the resignation, in secret, of Andrew Fisher, his policy chief, the author of his last election manifesto and the lone remaining aide from his first leadership election. The previous Saturday Fisher told a dozen colleagues that he was quitting in disgust and sent a long memo explaining his decision, which painted a picture of a leader's office that was laughably unready for power. Fisher denounced Seumas Milne and his allies for a 'lack of professionalism, competence and human decency which I am no longer willing to put up with daily'. He also complained that with one week to go before conference there was still no 'strapline' summing up the themes for voters. 'Tens of thousands of pounds have been spent on focus groups and polling for this and there is no end-product, just a blizzard of lies and excuses,' he wrote.

In his resignation note, Fisher also claimed that 'class war' had gripped the leader's office, a reference to the dominance of Milne and his sidekick James Schneider, both of whom were educated at Winchester and Oxford. Fisher said he would not be briefing the press and would tell others he was leaving 'for family reasons'. There it might have rested until one of the recipients summoned the author to an illicit meeting in a Westminster coffee shop and handed over the memo – an Exocet of a leak aimed squarely at Milne. Most of the shadow cabinet, including McDonnell, knew nothing of Fisher's resignation until the *Sunday Times* front page dropped that Saturday evening.

Fisher had concluded Labour had to back a second EU referendum. Milne, a dedicated Lexiteer, was accused of overruling the shadow cabinet to maintain Corbyn's ambiguity towards Brexit. 'Seumas is the problem,' a source in the leader of the opposition's office (LOTO) said. 'Andrew is unable to cope with it any more.' Another senior party official said, 'Brexit is the key faultline. Seumas and Karie have a view that we need to be more Leavey because that was the decision taken by the people. Andrew was pragmatic. He wasn't a cheerleader for a referendum but the reality is that's where our coalition of voters are.'

On the Tuesday before conference, Corbyn authored an article for the *Guardian* pledging that if he won the election he would negotiate a new Brexit deal and call a referendum. 'I will pledge to carry out whatever the people decide, as a Labour prime minister,' he wrote, signalling that he might not even play a prominent role in the campaign. Pro-referendum campaigners accused Milne of briefing the paper's editor Kath Viner, to whom he had once been very close, that Corbyn would be 'neutral' in a referendum campaign. The word was not in Corbyn's article but was prominent in the *Guardian's* headline.

At conference, the leadership proposed that a Labour government would secure a deal within three months of taking office, with a referendum held within six months. That deal would be a customs union, plus a close relationship with the single market, but not in it, meaning freedom of movement would end. Labour would then hold a one-day special conference after the general election to decide how to campaign in the referendum. This proposal enraged the pro-Remain grassroots. In shambolic scenes on the conference floor, Wendy Nichols, who was chairing the debate, first said the rebel amendment to impose an out-and-out Remain position had passed. When Jennie Formby, the Corbynite general secretary, leaned over to talk to her, she then announced that it had been defeated. Nichols rejected a formal card vote to spare Corbyn's blushes.

On the Wednesday evening, after the Supreme Court had heard from the four main parties, Brenda Hale decided to follow the same procedure her predecessor Lord Neuberger had adopted during Gina Miller's first case in 2017. 'I asked each member of the court to circulate a short paper, preferably on one side of A4, giving their answers to four questions,' she explained. 'Was the matter justiciable; if so, by what standards was the lawfulness of the advice to be judged; how did those standards apply to this advice; and if unlawful, what was the remedy? I asked that everyone circulate their memo at 9 a.m. on the Thursday morning, so that they were not reacting to one another.'[4]

When the memos appeared, it was clear that the justices agreed the matter was justiciable. During the day, they debated whether the prorogation was lawful. Hale admitted later that 'the precise criteria' for deciding this 'required fine tuning' but 'evolved gradually by discussion during the day'. The judges used the third day of the hearing to quiz lawyers for the government and Miller on the question of what the remedy should be if the government had acted unlawfully.

'Our deliberations that afternoon took much less time than they might have done,' Hale wrote in her memoir. 'It was clear that we were going to allow Mrs Miller's appeal and dismiss the government's appeal. Given the way the criteria were to be framed, the decision was likely to be unanimous.'[5] This was strikingly obtuse language, which did not answer the suspicion of government lawyers – that Hale, by plea or pressure, sought a unanimous verdict, which in a disputed area of law where the lord chief justice had ruled differently seemed unlikely. It remains unclear how many of the eleven judges thought the matter justiciable and the government's actions unlawful in their initial A4 answers.

On the Friday before the verdict, Dominic Cummings told the other special advisers there would be 'complete carnage' if the government lost the case. He also warned against plans to hold a new referendum, saying it would leave British politics 'in a smouldering ruin' and lead to 'smashing a load of eggs from which a load of nasty chicks would emerge'.

Over the weekend Hale and Lord Reed went away and jointly drafted a judgment. On Sunday morning they shared it with the other justices, who made comments via email. 'It was a truly collective endeavour,' Hale said.[6] On Monday, the final text was sent to the court and the president worked on her statement.

The scene in the Supreme Court on the morning of Tuesday 24 September was very British, low key and resolutely lacking the staged dramatics of big American court cases. Grey hair swept back, Hale sat in the middle of a horseshoe of judges and began to read the judgment – her tone that of a librarian explaining the need for quiet to a group of school children. She allowed herself one whisper of flamboyance: a silver spider brooch attached to the right shoulder of her black dress. Her husband had been buying her brooches for years 'to cheer me up and maybe others too'. The accessory which was to make her famous cost £12 from Cards Galore. Hale claimed to be 'completely unaware' that 'The Who had recorded a song about "Boris the Spider" who comes to a sticky end: If I had realised the speculation about hidden messages that it would provoke, I would probably have chosen something else.'[7]

Calling the case a 'one off', Hale took listeners through the chronology of prorogation and of the two resulting court cases. She was nearly five minutes in before anyone knew which way the verdict was going. 'The first question is whether the lawfulness of the prime minister's advice to Her Majesty is justiciable. This Court holds that it is.' The Supreme Court had sided with the Inner Court of Session and rejected the view of both the lord chief justice and the attorney general. Cox had a sinking feeling. Hale went on, 'As long ago as 1611, the court held that "the King hath no prerogative but that which the law of the land allows him".' Hale then said there was 'no doubt' that her court could rule on the existence and limits of that prerogative. 'A decision to prorogue (or advise the monarch to prorogue) will be unlawful if the prorogation has the effect of frustrating or preventing, without reasonable justification, the ability of Parliament to carry out its constitutional functions as a legislature and as the body responsible for the supervision of the executive.' Ministers watching now had a sense of gathering gloom as Hale echoed Bercow's view that 'this was not a normal prorogation'. She continued, 'It prevented Parliament from carrying out its constitutional role for five out of the possible eight weeks between the end of the summer recess and exit day on 31st October.' Hale made the point that proroguing, which stops all parliamentary business, 'is quite different from Parliament going into recess', where legislation continues, committees can meet and MPs can ask written questions. (This latter point was inaccurate.) She went on, 'The effect upon the fundamentals of our democracy was extreme. No justification for taking action with such an extreme effect has been put before the court.' The da Costa memo, the judges concluded, explained clearly why holding a Queen's Speech would be 'desirable' but 'it does not explain why it was necessary to bring Parliamentary business to a halt for five weeks', rather than the usual 'four to six days'.

The axe fell eleven minutes into Hale's statement. 'The Court is bound to conclude, therefore, that the decision to advise Her Majesty to prorogue Parliament was unlawful because it had the effect of frustrating or preventing the ability of Parliament to carry out its constitutional functions without reasonable justification.'

There was a final issue: what should happen next? The government had rejected the conclusion of the Inner House of the Court of Session that prorogation was 'null and void' on the grounds that it was a 'proceeding in Parliament' which, under the Bill of Rights of 1688, could not be questioned by a court. This seemed self-evidently the case to legal traditionalists like Cox. Even this was rejected by the Supreme Court, which said it was 'quite clear' that prorogation was not a proceeding in

Parliament. Hale explained, 'It takes place in the House of Lords chamber in the presence of members of both Houses, but it is not their decision
… It is not the core or essential business of Parliament which the Bill of
Rights protects. Quite the reverse: it brings that core or essential business
to an end.' Therefore, the court ruled that the order in council obtained
during Jacob Rees-Mogg's visit to Balmoral 'was also unlawful, void and
of no effect and should be quashed'. Hale concluded, 'Parliament has not
been prorogued. This is the unanimous judgment of all eleven justices.'

The ruling was a humiliation for Johnson and enraged Cox, eviscerat-
ing every legal and political judgment on which the government had
built prorogation. It sparked jubilation in the courtroom from the petitioners. Gina Miller hugged her lawyer Lord Pannick, while her
supporters outside in Parliament Square chanted, 'Johnson out.'

In Brighton, Jeremy Corbyn accused the prime minister of an 'abuse
of power' and having 'contempt for democracy'. He demanded an immediate election and said Johnson should resign. Jo Swinson said he was
'not fit to be prime minister', while Joanna Cherry, the MP who led the
case in Scotland, said his position was 'untenable'. Nigel Farage, the
Brexit Party leader, called prorogation 'the worst political decision ever'
and added, 'Dominic Cummings must go.'

In the City, the pound rose as the markets responded to a ruling which
could delay Brexit. In Brussels, there was gloating from Guy Verhofstadt,
the European Parliament's Brexit coordinator. He tweeted, 'At least one
big relief in the Brexit saga: the rule of law in the UK is alive & kicking.'
To complete the set, John Bercow popped up in the media village on
College Green. He praised the judgment and announced that 'the House
of Commons must convene without delay'.

In legal terms, the Hale court's was a 'revolutionary' ruling. That was
the verdict of Lord Sumption, who had retired as a Supreme Court justice
the previous December. In an article for *The Times*, he wrote, 'Ever since
the 18th century, ministers have made use of the power to prorogue or
(until 2010) dissolve Parliament for political advantage. There was a
consensus that they should not abuse the power, but what amounted to
abuse was itself a political question, not a legal one. What is revolutionary about the Supreme Court's decision is that it makes the courts the
ultimate arbiters of what political reasons are good enough.'

In this regard, the Hale court made new law. 'They invented a context
which is that parliamentary sovereignty requires that Parliament should

sit where issues of great controversy arise,' Cox said. In effect, the Supremes created a constitutional test which had not existed before. 'What this court has done was to apply what I consider to be its own view of constitutional morality.'

Other cabinet ministers saw the verdict as flawed, politically motivated and, in several regards, inaccurate. 'It was a dreadful judgment that made routine errors,' one said. 'They said a parliamentary recess was different to a prorogation because parliamentary questions could be answered in a recess. They can't. Hale in her statement got the name of the chief whip wrong, calling Mark Spencer, Mark Harper. It was amateur hour and showed that it was the judges wanting to do something, rather than doing their work properly.' David Davis, no friend of Johnson, pointed out that 'the most abusive prorogation' came under Clement Attlee: 'Attlee prorogued four times in almost as many months in his battle with the Lords. He was basically forcing them to buckle and to bend the knee ... and nobody argued you couldn't do it.'[8]

Yet Sumption's conclusion was that Johnson's behaviour justified the Supremes' decision. An unwritten constitution relies on convention, which works when politicians adhere to those norms, what the historian Peter Hennessy called the 'good chaps' theory of government. 'The present government has taken an axe to convention,' Sumption wrote. 'The natural result of constitutional vandalism on this scale is that conventions have hardened into law.'[9] A very senior civil servant put things more prosaically: 'The reason they lost is because they lied.'

Jonathan Jones concluded it was the lack of evidence to the contrary. 'This case might have gone differently if the decision had been taken in a different way,' he said later. 'In the end, it's the process and the justification for a decision that gives rise to the risk, rather than the substance of the decision itself ... The only person prepared to sign a witness statement was me ... That was the only evidence that the court had.'[10]

Dominic Grieve thought the central judgment 'faultless'. But even he regarded the ruling that prorogation was not a proceeding in Parliament as 'eccentric', when the Supremes could have simply issued a court order demanding that Parliament return immediately.

If there was one thing that surprised Cox and the government, it was the unanimous ruling. The petitioners and their supporters saw it as proof of Johnson's perfidy. In conversation with Julian Lewis, a devout Eurosceptic but old friend of the speaker, Bercow said, 'I think what it proves is that what the government has done is gross and unconscionable.'[11] Lewis drew the other conclusion, that the ruling was politically motivated and 'an absolute disgrace'. In the chamber, he asked Cox why not one of the Supremes had dissented. The attorney general said he could not 'fathom the inscrutable minds of their lordships in the Supreme Court'. But privately Cox said he was 'surprised by the unanimity' and speculated that the justices would have felt under pressure not to dissent. Robert Buckland, the lord chancellor, also heard talk in legal circles that the judge decided it would be better for there to be a unanimous verdict. Michael Howard, the former Conservative leader, was told that Hale had signalled at the start of deliberations that she wanted a unanimous verdict. Civil servants heard the same. 'There was obviously some pretty canny whipping going on in the Supreme Court by Brenda Hale,' a government legal source said. 'Word went round that she basically announced at the start that they were going to agree this unanimously or they weren't going to do it.'

When the verdict came, Johnson was in New York City where he was due to give a speech at the United Nations General Assembly the following morning. The prime minister, David Frost, Eddie Lister and other aides gathered in a hotel meeting room at 5 a.m. to watch the judgment on a laptop. 'We could tell it wasn't going to be good,' one said. 'But it was still a bit of a surprise. Quite crushing.' Johnson remained upbeat: 'Okay, we have to get back to London and deal with this.' A close aide said, 'He has this ability to absorb blow after blow.' This somewhat surprising sang-froid didn't last long.

Back in London, Mark Sedwill had set up a room near the cabinet secretary's office for a watch party. Gathered there at 11.30 a.m. on Tuesday were Cummings, Cain, Cox, Buckland, Jonathan Jones, Helen MacNamara and Michael Gove – along with sundry officials and advisers. That morning, Sedwill had told Cummings, 'I've heard some alarming rumours from the Supreme Court.' Cummings deduced that the cabinet secretary had been tipped off to brace for a crisis by another member of the 'deep state'. Sedwill seemed surprised. Like others, he had been told by Jones that, however unfortunate it might be, prorogation was lawful. Cummings was less surprised. When he consulted Richard 'Ricardo' Howell, the Vote Leave legal expert warned, 'Everyone is underestimating how insane the judges have become.'

The emphatic nature of the defeat was still 'a jaw dropper', one senior figure recalled. Gove corralled a smaller group into a side room for a transatlantic conference call with Johnson. The prime minister was now highly agitated. 'Boris went fucking mental,' a witness said, ranting at Cox, Jones and Cummings. 'You fucked me! You told me it would be fine. This is a disaster. I'm completely fucked! It's over! Now, what am I going to do?'

Cummings tried to calm him down: 'You're wrong, Boris. Remember what I said to you: "This is a win-win." Now the courts have joined the Remain campaign and now we all know where we are. What are you melting down about? This is great news. Lean in to it.' Another on the call said, 'When it's a survival thing, Boris was very, very prepared to take risks, but he gets in a total flap afterwards. He didn't know what the hell to do.'

If Cummings' pep talk stiffened the prime minister's spine, it was not what everyone in the room wanted to hear. Johnson had to be talked down from denouncing the court by Cox and Buckland, who stressed that he could publicly contest the verdict, but without impugning the motives of the judges. The message either did not reach the communications team in London, or it was ignored. 'We think the Supreme Court is wrong and has made a serious mistake in extending its reach to these political matters,' a Number 10 source told the lobby.

In New York, Johnson had to give his response for the broadcasters. A spad who watched him that morning vividly recalled, 'You could see Boris's terror on his face. The only other time I have ever seen that face was in one of the first budgets during Covid when he was shown the spending numbers. That morning in New York, he was absolutely terrified.' Johnson made clear he would not resign. He said the government disagreed with the ruling, but would abide by it. But he did not rule out a second prorogation. 'I strongly disagree with this judgment.' Without targeting the judges directly, he added, 'Let's be in no doubt, there are a lot of people who want to stop this country coming out of the EU.'

Not every minister and MP was so measured. In a cabinet conference call that evening, Jacob Rees-Mogg, one of the MPs with the best understanding of parliamentary procedure, denounced the ruling as 'a constitutional coup': 'It is the most extraordinary overthrowing of the constitution.'[12] Cox was less florid but argued the court had overturned decades of precedent. 'I don't believe any prorogation over the past one hundred years would have survived today's judgment,' he told cabinet. Johnson was less guarded in private, telling his ministers the judges had sided with Remain campaigners to 'frustrate Brexit'. Several ministers, with Buckland the most outspoken, warned the cabinet against questioning the independence of the judiciary. Even Johnson was 'seriously pissed off' at Rees-Mogg's intervention, suspecting it would leak, which it did.

The UN allowed the prime minister to bring forward his speech to allow him to fly home for Parliament, which was now due to reconvene at 11.30 a.m. on the 25th. There was just one reference to Brexit in his speech, when Johnson compared the toil of delivering the referendum result to the trials of Prometheus, the Titan god who gave the secret of fire to mankind but was punished by having his liver pecked out for eternity by an eagle. 'This went on forever … a bit like the experience of Brexit in the UK, if some of our parliamentarians had their way.' Afterwards he denied trying to thwart scrutiny by MPs. Breaking into cod-French he said, 'Donnez-moi un break is my message to those who say there will be no parliamentary scrutiny. It is absolute nonsense.'

The most awkward moment for Johnson came when he had to phone the Queen mid-Atlantic. After the verdict John Major, who helped bring the Supreme Court case and had been an adviser to Princes William and Harry, urged the prime minister to make an 'unreserved apology' to the monarch: 'No prime minister can ever treat the Queen this way.' Downing Street refused to say whether Johnson apologised, though multiple sources confirmed later that he did. Major's closeness to the palace, however, reflected undiluted fury among senior members of the royal family and courtiers in the royal household about Johnson's behaviour. 'John Major is very, very close to the Queen,' said a Tory source with close links to senior royals. 'He would not have started that court action without them knowing about it in the palace. John Major wouldn't have gone anywhere near it had the palace disapproved. The Queen has to do what she is told to do by the prime minister, but they did not want to prorogue Parliament in these circumstances. Nobody trusts Boris.' The source said Johnson would never receive the order of the garter, the traditional honour for retired prime ministers, while the Queen was alive.

The Queen's reaction was actually more sanguine than some. She thought Johnson a roguish and comic figure and took the disaster in her stride. One senior royal aide characterised her approach as, 'These things happen.' The Queen liked doing impersonations of her prime ministers, Gordon Brown being a particular favourite. A month after the Supreme Court ruling, she had an audience with a politician who was adept at impersonating Johnson. Enjoying herself, the monarch remarked afterwards of the PM, 'I think he was perhaps better suited to the stage.' The anger on the monarch's behalf, however, from the Prince of Wales in particular, was intense. 'Charles was absolutely furious,' a royal insider said. 'He was outraged that Boris should treat the Queen like that. She wouldn't ever say anything, but he was pretty robust in private.' The anger was shared by Prince William, whose private secretary was Simon Case, who had previously been in Number 10. 'I think that Simon Case wound William up,' a senior civil servant said. Another source who discussed the issue with courtiers said, 'They are not impressed by what is going on, at the very highest levels of the family.'

Johnson and the future King Charles III had already got off on the wrong foot. When Charles invited Johnson to visit him at Birkhall, his home on the Balmoral estate, at the end of the summer, the prime minister turned up in what courtiers described as a 'shambolic state' with Carrie Symonds. 'He was clearly not focused' on their meeting and Charles's aides felt Johnson was 'disrespectful'.[13] William was no less unimpressed by Johnson's behaviour. Constitutionally, the Queen had no choice but to accept Johnson's request to prorogue. But William's aides let it be known that in his reign as king there would be 'more private, robust challenging of advice' between the monarch and his prime ministers.[14]

Speaker Bercow opened the resumed sitting of Parliament, at 11.30 a.m. on 25 September, with a statement to MPs that the record of prorogation would be 'expunged' from the *Journal of the House of Commons*. He did so in what was 'the most peculiar atmosphere' he had known in the chamber in twenty-two years as an MP.[15] There was no Prime Minister's Questions, since questions are supposed to be tabled three days in advance, but Bercow invited urgent questions. Joanna Cherry urged Cox to publish the legal advice he gave Johnson. This he could not do, even if he had wished to, since the only written advice did not cover prorogation itself and Cox's verbal advice to the prime minister had been withheld even from the cabinet.

Cox defended his advice to Johnson as being 'in good faith' and distanced himself from Rees-Mogg's incendiary comments. His performance, from Bercow's seat, was carried off with 'shameless aplomb'. Cox said, 'This advice was sound advice at the time. The court of last resort ultimately disagreed with it, but in doing so it made new law, as it was entirely entitled to do.' He also made clear that if Johnson had attempted to prorogue all the way up to 31 October, 'I could not have stayed in the cabinet while it was done'. The attorney general explained, in future, 'the Court will be obliged to assess whether a particular political controversy is sufficiently serious, excites sufficiently heated controversy, as to warrant the House sitting'.

Cox the politician then took over from Cox the lawyer, launching what the speaker regarded as 'a wild and unstoppable rant'. His baritone boomed, 'This Parliament has declined three times to pass a withdrawal Act to which the opposition had absolutely no objection. We now have a wide number in this House setting their face against leaving at all. When this government draws the only logical inference from that position, which is that we must leave therefore without any deal at all, they still set their face, denying the electorate the chance of having their say.' Growing red in the face, Cox bellowed through a cacophony of dissent, 'This Parliament is a dead Parliament! It should no longer sit. It has no moral right to sit on these green benches.'

When Bercow intervened to quell the noise, Cox continued, 'They don't like the truth. Twice they have been asked to let the electorate decide whether they should continue to sit in their seats, while they block 17.4 million people's votes. This Parliament is a disgrace ... They could vote no confidence at any time, but they are too cowardly to give it a go ... This Parliament should have the courage to face the electorate, but it won't, because so many of them are really all about preventing us from leaving the European Union at all. But the time is coming, Mr Speaker, when even these turkeys won't be able to prevent Christmas.'

To Brexiteers this was a rambunctious and dazzling display of controlled rage, in which one of the Commons' most elegant speakers gave voice to their frustrations, delivering home truths to MPs and a judiciary which had rewritten the rules to thwart them. To Remainers, it was a disgraceful and uncouth attack on Parliament itself. Barry Sheerman, a Labour veteran, said Cox had 'no shame'. Hannah Bardell of the SNP called him 'flippant and ridiculous'. Bercow fumed.

When Cox looked at his mobile phone he saw a message from Cummings. It said, 'Well done.'

If Cox's ordeal was bad-tempered, it was nothing compared to the sulphurous atmosphere when Boris Johnson got to his feet at 6.30 p.m. The prime minister had worked himself into a fury watching the BBC coverage of his humiliation, complaining to aides, 'They are absolutely ecstatic that we have had a poke in the eye. They're totally out of tune with the country.' In the chamber Johnson was greeted with calls of 'resign' and responded by demanding an election to put an end to 'this paralysed Parliament'.

It was Johnson's flippant approach which attracted attention, but the prime minister also used his statement to make the clearest summary of the argument he and Cummings had been trying to put before the public for the previous two months. It was also notable for introducing the slogan on which Johnson intended to fight the general election: 'Get Brexit done.' He said, 'Three years ago, more people voted to leave the European Union than had ever voted for any party or proposition in our history. Politicians of all parties promised the public that they would honour the result. Sadly, many have since done all they can to abandon those promises and to overturn that democratic vote ... This government that I lead has been trying truly to get us out. Most people, including most supporters of the Labour Party, regardless of how they voted three years ago, think the referendum must be respected. They want Brexit done, I want Brexit done, and people want us out on 31 October, with a new deal if possible, but without one if necessary.'

Johnson said the Supreme Court was 'wrong to pronounce on a political question at a time of great national controversy' and posed the key challenge to MPs who wanted to frustrate his tactics: what did they think would happen if they succeeded? Johnson said, 'The truth is that opposition Members are living in a fantasy world. They really imagine that somehow they are going to cancel the first referendum and legislate for a second referendum, and Parliament will promise that this time it really, really will respect that vote. They think that the public will therefore vote to remain, and everybody will forget the last few years. That is an extraordinary delusion and a fantasy ... It will not happen.' Whatever else he said that day, this argument had force, even to many Remainers. To most Brexiteers and those who sought to be neutral, it was unarguably correct. The prime minister's speech was met with constant barracking and interruptions from Bercow seeking to quell the tumult. Johnson, a politician who, as London mayor, had turned a red city blue by appearing as a moderate figure, was now the most divisive politician since Margaret Thatcher.

The mood turned uglier still when Johnson took questions. Liz Saville Roberts of Plaid Cymru accused him of 'incontinent goading'. Joanna Cherry said he had delivered a 'populist rant one expects to hear from the leader of a tin-pot dictatorship'. Labour's Paula Sherriff condemned Johnson's 'inflammatory' language. Alluding to the murder, at the end of the referendum campaign, of Labour MP Jo Cox, she went on, 'We stand here under the shield of our departed friend. Many of us in this place are subject to death threats and abuse every single day. Let me tell the prime minister that they often quote his words – surrender Act, betrayal, traitor – and I, for one, am sick of it … He should be absolutely ashamed of himself.' This was greeted with applause.

In his fury at those who challenged him, Johnson became callously offhand. 'I have to say that I have never heard such humbug in all my life,' he responded to cries of 'Shame!' from MPs. 'He was tired,' one colleague explained. 'The speaker kept him there for three hours when he had rushed back on the red-eye.' A little later, Tracy Brabin, Jo Cox's successor as MP for Batley and Spen, said, 'May I ask him, in all honesty, as a human being … will he please, please moderate his language so that we will all feel secure when we are going about our jobs.' Johnson defended his view of the Benn Act and sparked further anger when he said, 'The best way to honour the memory of Jo Cox, and indeed to bring this country together, would be, I think, to get Brexit done.' His words unleashed fresh waves of fury. Jo Swinson called it 'a disgraceful state of affairs', telling MPs, 'Today, I have reported to the police a threat against my child.'

In the debate lasting three hours and eleven minutes, Johnson faced 111 backbench questions and referred to the 'surrender act' fifteen times. Bercow was forced to intervene on twenty-one occasions. Later that day, a government motion proposing that the Commons go into recess during the Tory conference was rejected by 289 votes to 306. It was the Johnson government's seventh successive Commons defeat. He still had not won a single vote since taking office.

Privately, Johnson acknowledged that he had made a 'mistake' in the debate, telling a meeting of the political cabinet the following afternoon, Thursday 26th, that his 'humbug' comment referred to the attacks on his use of 'surrender act' not the comment about Jo Cox. Nicky Morgan, Julian Smith, Ben Wallace, Matt Hancock and Buckland all urged a softer tone. When Liz Truss told Johnson, 'You've got to say what you like', he disagreed: 'No, it's right what people are saying.'

Cummings, vilified for persuading Johnson to pursue a divisive political strategy, was unrepentant, taking up residence in Portcullis House, where he was confronted by furious MPs and held court surrounded by a gaggle of reporters. When Labour's Karl Turner said that he had had 'death threats overnight', Cummings replied, 'Get Brexit done', then, 'I don't know who you are.' At a book launch that week, he goaded his critics further: 'We are enjoying this, we are going to leave and we are going to win.' Privately, Cummings compared the fuss over the use of 'surrender act' to 'bubble blindness' over the £350 million for the NHS on the side of the Vote Leave battle bus. 'Remain MPs keep babbling about the surrender act, reminds me of the good old days with £350m,' he texted one friend.

In his Friday meeting with spads, Cummings called Parliament 'a disgrace', saying Johnson would use 'surrender Act every day' and 'ram it down their throats'. As MPs considered impeaching Johnson, he also drew parallels with the US. 'We need to be like Bill Clinton when the Monica Lewinsky stuff was flaring up,' Cummings said. 'He ignored the Washington beltway bullshit and went around the country talking to people about their concerns. He ended up with higher approval ratings than when he first became president.' This was a bold comparison in a week when Johnson also faced scrutiny about an affair he had as mayor with Jennifer Arcuri, a blonde tech entrepreneur with a stripper's dancing pole in her flat.

As peak Cummings was reached, ministers thought he had broken the first rule of successful advisers: don't become the story. But a colleague said he was pursuing a 'Mourinho strategy', making himself a lightning rod to divert criticism from Johnson: 'When José Mourinho was manager of Chelsea, every press conference was a psychodrama where all the questions were about the manager. The players say that took the pressure off them and let them get on with their game.'

Arguably Cummings' most incendiary intervention after the Supreme Court ruling never leaked. It came in a one-on-one conversation with Helen MacNamara in G-39, a cupboard-like room on the ground floor of Number 10. Cummings was intent on finding a way around the Benn Act; the deputy cabinet secretary was equally determined to uphold the law. The ensuing battle of wills between Number 10's alpha male and alpha female was one of the most extraordinary of the entire Brexit era. MacNamara was concerned by Cummings' attitude to the Supreme Court ruling and his continuing exploration of inflammatory moves. She understood the politics, but she did not think the Vote Leave crew understood the consequences. The first loyalty of the civil service was the rule of law and the constitution not the government. 'The ship of state is cracking,' she warned. 'We are getting close to the point where a lot of officials are going to stop obeying orders. They are just not going to regard this government as a legitimate source of authority.' MacNamara made no threat to walk out herself. She presented this news as intelligence gleaned, an attempt to be useful. But this was, in effect, a warning from the second most powerful mandarin that, if Johnson continued on his current path, the civil service could mutiny.

A colleague of Cummings' with whom he discussed the conversation recalled, 'Helen thought it could end up with the prime minister having to resign. The civil service was very unhappy at the approach we were taking and at any suggestion of breaking the law, they were threatening to down tools. People don't know just how close it came to all just caving in and the civil service walking out.'

Cummings replied, 'I understand; I can feel the same vibes. I know a lot of people are very unhappy about the situation. But from my point of view, if a lot of people start resigning, that would be fine by me, because it makes it easier for me to replace them, which I want to do anyway. We're not going to change.' He was particularly withering about the government legal service, which he blamed for the prorogation leak and for questioning Vote Leave's tactics. 'Let them fucking quit,' he said. 'Let's just fucking fire them. Let's get some new lawyers in.'

Behind this bullish exterior, on one point, MacNamara detected vulnerability – when Cummings explained his fears about what would happen if the Bresistance and the People's Vote campaign got their way. 'If there is a second referendum, there will be rioting all over the place,' he said. In a previous conversation with Sedwill, Cummings had warned the cabinet secretary, 'You won't be able to send MPs outside the M25 without close protection units because they'll be getting shot. I know people who I worked with in the referendum campaign who are texting me saying, "Tell those cunts down there that if they stop Brexit, I'm going to come down and shoot them."'

MacNamara called him out on this. 'If there are riots, it will be because you will cause them, Dom. That's what you will do.'

Cummings acknowledged that he would have to fight an aggressive second Brexit campaign. To MacNamara he was someone who knew he would do anything to win and was worried about what this compulsion might mean. 'He was petrified about a second referendum,' she told one confidant. 'I think he is scared of himself. He didn't actually want to do the thing that he knew he would do.'

MacNamara had been sent to join Sedwill by Jeremy Heywood, in one of his last acts as cabinet secretary, precisely because she had far more experience of close combat in Whitehall than Sedwill did. Johnson found MacNamara 'utterly terrifying', an aide said, comparing her to the shark in *Jaws*, whose eyes roll into the back of its head when it attacks. This led him to nickname her 'Black Eyes'. Cummings told colleagues MacNamara was 'a serious person' and far more formidable than any MP. A fellow Vote Leaver said, 'I think Helen was one of the few people that Dom genuinely respected. She was fiercely intelligent and a really impressive political operator. She understands power, and she understands how to wield it. Not many people could out-strategise the team we had, but Helen was a very formidable and worthy opponent. She was thinking constitutionally, whereas Dom was thinking politically. We were in a knife fight and if you don't take a knife to a knife fight you're in trouble.'

The admiration was mutual, up to a point. MacNamara agreed with nearly all of Cummings' complaints about Whitehall, even with many of his solutions, but she thought him the wrong person to enact change. She summed him up to one friend: 'Ideas, nine out of ten. Execution, minus ten. Dom over-overestimates his own ability to manage other human beings, which is almost zero.' Those loyal to Cummings – and there were many in the political ranks – disputed that assessment, but his style was uniquely designed to trigger officials.

Talk that MPs blocking Brexit could lead to riots was seen as evidence that Johnson's team hoped to use civil contingencies legislation to suspend the Benn Act. Part two of the Civil Contingencies Act, which could be triggered with an executive order, would suspend all other acts of Parliament for a maximum of thirty days. Bresisters were aware of this danger. John Major went public to warn that the prime minister could use 'an order of council' to suspend the Benn Act, with a small number of privy councillors and without any input from the Queen. Cabinet ministers thought this bananas. 'That's used if there is an invasion or a flood or a hurricane,' one said. 'It's fantasy island.'

Prorogation and the Supreme Court ruling became symbols of Johnson's willingness to smash convention. Critics regarded it as wholly counter-productive. Tactically this was true; there was no hiding the humiliation and defeat. As a civil servant put it, 'All you've done is galvanise the opposition who, until that point, were a complete shambles. It was a miscalculation and they were lucky to get out of it as unscathed as they did. That period could easily have forced them into an election when they didn't have a deal and they've lied to the Queen. You're on the defensive, rather than the offensive.' Johnson himself concluded eventually that prorogation had been a 'brilliant stunt' but ultimately 'wasn't really necessary'. He told a friend four years later, 'All we needed to do was keep crowding Corbyn to either get Brexit done or give us an election. That in the end, was the thing that worked.'

Yet if prorogation was tactically damaging or pointless, it reinforced the Johnson-Cummings strategic framework. It was the centrepiece of government activity in the second half of 2019, which ensured the election was fought on their terms.

For all the sound and fury, the Supreme Court ruling did not change the game. As Oliver Letwin realised, 'Winning the prorogation case … though I think extremely important for constitutional reasons, never became a material factor … From a practical Brexit point of view, it didn't make two hoots of difference because … we had the Benn Act in place before Parliament was prorogued.'[16]

Johnson's options were dramatically narrowed by the Benn Act, but he still had one way out – to get a deal with Brussels. It was an article of faith among the Bresistance that Johnson did not want a deal and was doing nothing to get one. That belief had prompted the resignation of Amber Rudd. Letwin, Benn and Grieve all believed it was only the Benn Act that compelled Johnson to act. This was not the full story.

4

OUT OF THE BLUE

The Deal II

September to October 2019

'The main thing is to make history not to write it'

– Otto von Bismarck

As classical compliments go, it was double-edged, but it delighted Boris Johnson. Standing next to Leo Varadkar after a meeting in Dublin, the prime minister smiled as the Taoiseach compared him to Hercules, famous for his twelve labours, which bore more than a passing resemblance to getting Brexit done. Varadkar said, 'Negotiating FTAs [free trade agreements] with the EU and US and securing their ratification in less than three years is going to be a herculean task for you.' Then the kicker: 'We want to be your friend and ally, your Athena, in doing so.' In classical mythology, Athena helped Hercules with his labours but she also intervened after he had gone mad and killed his wife and children, knocking him out to prevent him doing more damage. It was an exchange with something for everyone across the Brexit divide.

Nonetheless a mutual love of the classics helped break the ice between two leaders. One of Johnson's daughters had studied in Dublin. 'They had a long one-on-one,' said one of those travelling with Johnson. 'Boris made a big effort with Varadkar. They hit it off.' It was 9 September, five days after the Benn Act passed, just hours before Parliament was due to prorogue, fifteen days before the Supreme Court verdict.

At this point David Frost's concept of where a deal might land was built on the idea of 'opt ins and opt outs', where Northern Ireland would partly align with EU rules in narrowly defined areas, while remaining in

Britain's customs union. It made sense to include agrifoods, since there was already an all-Ireland economy in these products. Frost and Johnson also wanted the backstop time limited by a democracy lock, giving the people of Northern Ireland a say over the arrangements. Finally, they wanted them to have a vote on whether to enter the new arrangements. 'Our strategy was that we were willing to see Northern Ireland be in bits of the single market for goods on the basis of consent,' a source recalled. The rest could be done through alternative arrangements.

Johnson showed more ankle to Varadkar. 'He hinted that we'd be willing to see the opt-in cover more than agrifoods,' a British official said. Both sides left the meeting with a belief that they could do business. 'We all thought we had taken a significant step forward,' one of those present said. 'When politicians meet politicians they look through the character and see the person. Boris is a bit of an introvert, although most people don't see that. They both recognised they weren't as dissimilar as they thought they were.' The meeting led Dublin to open substantive bilateral talks with the UK, without EU oversight, for the first time since 2017. On an RAF plane home Johnson paced the aisle, puffing out his chest and throwing his arms wide, declaring, 'We're going to get a deal.'[1]

In the aftermath of the Benn Act, Johnson came under pressure from his cabinet to push harder for a deal. On 7 September, the night Amber Rudd resigned, Julian Smith, the Northern Ireland secretary, used a speech at the British Irish Association dinner in Cambridge to freelance. Unauthorised by Number 10, he said the government should stick with the withdrawal agreement but attach a consent mechanism. 'That speech ended up going in Leo Varadkar's ministerial box,' an official said. 'I don't think he ever sent it to Number 10.' Smith thought the DUP's opposition to the backstop was out of touch with mainstream opinion in the province. Since his speech was on Chatham House terms, Smith got no publicity, but it landed well with the Irish. Johnson's team didn't even know where he was.

The following day Smith wrote a formal letter to Johnson urging him to do a deal. He warned the prime minister, 'For the Irish government, the EU, the DUP and many of our colleagues, there is a growing perception that the government is not sufficiently serious about reaching a deal. We need to counter this perception with decisive action and fresh thinking.' He told Johnson that if he looked more like he wanted a deal, the Irish 'would seriously consider showing more flexibility'. But he also said, 'We cannot ... rely solely on a complete Irish and EU reversal of position on the backstop – we will need to be willing to compromise too.' Smith called for a 'more creative approach to consent', but not one which gave the DUP a veto.[2] Smith understood that he was probably cutting short his ministerial career, but he thought Johnson's 'Rambo strategy' risked inflaming the security situation in Belfast, where the threat of bombs was real. He had lived and breathed Brexit for two years and hated the idea of no-deal. Johnson demanded to see him on Monday 9 September.

Smith did not know if he was going to be fired but the meeting went off without fireworks. Under the radar, Smith fed in ideas from officials who were expert on Northern Irish affairs, including Brendan Threlfall from Robbins' negotiating team, who had taken up exile in the Northern Ireland Office. With assistance from Mark Sedwill, the cabinet secretary, Smith ensured that realistic ideas were fed to David Frost, Robbins' successor. Johnson listened, then got on a plane to see Varadkar in Dublin, where he floated similar ideas.

On 16 September, Johnson flew to Luxembourg to meet Jean-Claude Juncker and the prime minister Xavier Bettel. The latter meeting became a high-profile disaster but that disguised progress over lunch with the Commission president. Juncker's judgement was that Johnson's ambition, for so long an obstruction to a deal, was now the best hope of one. He told aides, 'This guy will not stay prime minister if he does not get Brexit done.'

Juncker had a long meeting with Martin Selmayr, his chief of staff, to decide what could be offered to the British. Their conclusion was that it would have to be a version of the original Northern Ireland-only backstop, sweetened with political accountability. Both had noted Johnson's description of the 'anti-democratic backstop' as indicative of the direction of travel. 'We started thinking, does it mean we could have a "democratic" backstop,' another Commission official said. Juncker said, 'I will test this at this working lunch.' Juncker and Selmayr were also willing to review the backstop after five years. Half an hour into their conversation they concluded Johnson was not a Trumpian clone. 'I thought: this guy is not crazy, this is a serious guy,' Selmayr said.

To some in the Commission there was a general agreement on the way forward, but there was no agreement on detail and lingering doubts about Johnson's grasp of it. During a discussion about customs checks, Frost and Steve Barclay talked about checks in warehouses and at companies. 'We made a point that this was clearly a security risk in the Irish context,' a Commission source said. Johnson turned to Barclay and Frost and remarked, 'Is this really what we are proposing?' The Commission man said, 'He was a bit surprised that that was the British position.' EU officials claimed the prime minister seemed to 'slump' in his chair as Stéphanie Riso 'schooled' Johnson on why a common zone for food was not enough to create an invisible border.[3]

The mood, however, was positive. Johnson admitted he would be under time pressure after ruling out an extension beyond 31 October. Juncker said, 'Boris, you said already so many things you would never do in life! Advice from a politician of the continent, never say "never".' Johnson gave the Commission president the impression he would seek another extension if necessary – not something he would ever have admitted at home. After the meeting Juncker told colleagues, 'I can do business with this guy. We don't like what he wants, Brexit. But if you want to get it done there is no other way to get it done.' Juncker saw that the bulk of the deal would be the same as that negotiated with Theresa May. 'So I am even faithful to Theresa,' he joked.

Frost and his team put 'a few prosaic policy papers on the table' during the meeting, but did not share the sense that it was as significant as Juncker's team. 'We came back quite underwhelmed,' an official said.

Not for the first time, while relations with the Commission were better than the government let on, those with member states took a hit after the Benn Act. Johnson was booed when he emerged from lunch with Juncker. Then Xavier Bettel, the Luxembourg PM, insisted on holding a joint press conference outside, where protesters could be heard yelling 'bollocks to Brexit' and 'bog off Boris'. Johnson refused to take part. Bettel left an empty lectern and took the chance to condemn his absentee guest. He told the media he had suggested Johnson call a second referendum and said the UK was yet to table meaningful written proposals. 'I told him, "I hear a lot, but I don't read a lot." If they want to discuss anything we need to have it written [down] … People need to know what is going to happen to them in six weeks' time … You cannot hold their future hostage for party political gain.' Gesturing at the empty lectern, he added, 'So now it is on Mr Johnson.'

Away from the cameras, there were angry scenes. Frost had choice words for the Luxembourger sherpa. 'I don't think they realised how bad it was going to look,' a British official said. 'But they did feel that they could just mess us around. Boris was framed. It came out of the blue after a perfectly okay meeting.'

Johnson's negotiating team, the civil service and the EU were now all working on versions of a Northern Ireland-only backstop. In the third week of September, Brendan Threlfall joined Frost's team. A paper by Raoul Ruparel, the political aide with the best understanding of Brexit in May's Number 10, offered some ideas on how to achieve 'democratic consent' in the province. Ruparel wanted a 'hybrid' arrangement, where Northern Ireland was effectively part of both the EU and United Kingdom customs unions. Frost did not want Ruparel or his ideas. 'David decided he had too much baggage,' another of May's team recalled. 'I suspect, partly, because he was threatened by him, but I think they genuinely had a different view of the world.' Nonetheless, once the Benn Act became law, two private secretaries, Peter Hill and Jonno, began to push the idea of a hybrid relationship.

On 17 September, the first day of the Supreme Court hearing, Johnson spoke by phone to Angela Merkel. In a statement afterwards, Number 10 said, 'The prime minister reiterated that the UK and the EU have agreed to accelerate efforts to reach a deal without the backstop which the UK Parliament could support.' It did not shift the dial, but Frost thought the Germans were the first member state after the Irish to properly understand what he was trying to do.

Johnson was due to see Varadkar again the following week in New York at the UN General Assembly. In the intervening six days, Juncker and Selmayr worked on the Irish. After the Luxembourg meeting, Michel Barnier flew to Ireland, to begin working on a text for a reworked backstop. Juncker spoke three or four times a week to Merkel. 'I think we have a solution,' he told her. The German chancellor replied, 'You are the Commission. You have to tell us if this works.'

The New York meeting between Johnson and Varadkar, on 23 September, was not as successful as their tête-à-tête in Dublin. Frost told colleagues afterwards, 'It hasn't moved forward in any way.' The British team believed that events in Parliament had convinced the Irish they did

not need to compromise. 'The Benn Act did not affect our internal calculations that much,' a senior figure said. 'What it did do was visibly take
the pressure off the Europeans. You could see some of the willingness to
think hard disappearing.'

The Taoiseach left for New York telling the media he would 'try to get
a deal', but his deputy and foreign minister Simon Coveney complained
that 'credible proposals' were needed from the British. Coveney was
regarded as a Cassandra figure in London, willing to seek out the negative in every British action. Varadkar, however, had begun to moderate
his position, fearful of the impact of no-deal on the Irish economy. ('Irish
agriculture will be destroyed,' one cabinet minister cheerfully predicted.)
Not many in London understood the Irish political context. A cabinet
minister under May said, 'Coveney and Varadkar's party [Fine Gael] has
been criticised for 100 years and accused of selling out to the Brits and
allowing partition to happen. For them I think no backstop is worse than
no-deal. Simon Coveney and co are a little bit duplicitous when they say
this is about a return to the Troubles. What it is about is a return to the
divisive debates in the Republic of Ireland's history.'

Later, British officials accepted that the Irish had expected Johnson to
follow up the first meeting with more concrete proposals. 'I think they
were expecting the Dublin conversation to be built on more than it was,'
one said. 'They perceived us as pulling back slightly afterwards because
we weren't saying officially what Boris might have said privately.'

While no advances were made on the substance, the Johnson-
Varadkar bilateral was important in strengthening their personal bond.
Johnson was exhausted and preoccupied by the Supreme Court case. He
seemed vulnerable, a posture which Varadkar responded to, going off
script to offer ideas. The Taoiseach, who had his own political problems,
seemed to be reaching out as only one leader can to another. In the
matter of Brexit, they were in it together.

Johnson also met Donald Tusk in New York, after which Tusk
publicly lamented that there had been 'no breakthrough'. But Johnson
seemed far more engaged than he had been in Biarritz. 'It was clear that
the situation had changed,' a Council official recalled. 'We got the sense
he was actually interested in doing a deal. We attributed that to the Benn
Act. The domestic logic turned around. First he thought that he would
just run down the clock. Then he realised the only way to get to a general
election was to go for a deal.' In the meeting, Tusk gave Johnson a dead-

line: 'Time is running out. You need to come up with something credible, and you need to do so by the 3rd of October.' Both sides agreed not to leak the date. 'We didn't want to be caught issuing ultimatums,' the Council official said. 'But there was a very clear deadline set in the meeting. Johnson accepted the deadline.'

A conversation between the Irish and the European Council, a few hours earlier, gave Tusk's team hope. 'This was the first time that the Irish went into the idea of marrying the backstop with the idea of consent,' a Tusk ally recalled. 'That was the first time we thought it was ultimately going to work.' Tusk's view was that a solution needed joint Irish–UK ownership. He told his team, 'I will remain as Irish as the Irish, not more Irish than the Irish.'

Pro-dealers like Benn, Letwin, Boles and the others were utterly convinced that Johnson was only persuaded to try for a deal because the Benn Act had made no-deal impossible. They believed the EU did not regard Johnson's threats of no-deal as credible and consequently dismissed it as a negotiating device.

Downing Street figures like Cummings, Frost, Lewis and the prime minister himself were equally adamant that the negotiations were beginning to bear fruit around the time of prorogation and were set back by the Benn Act. A Downing Street source said, 'Movement starts to occur from them before the Benn Act appears. The Benn Act was a disaster, it was a catastrophe for us. That was the moment that the shutters came down in Brussels.' Another senior figure said, 'After the Surrender Act, negotiations basically just stop.'

The Supreme Court ruling on 24 September cut short Johnson's trip to New York and, in the eyes of Frost and his team, Britain's leverage with the Europeans. 'I think the Supreme Court judgment caused more problems than the Benn Act,' one said. 'I think it made even more of an impact on the Europeans. They thought they had the upper hand, politically, at that point.' Unnoticed in the melee over his ill-judged 'humbug' comments, Johnson's speech to Parliament on 25 September was a riposte to those who claimed he was getting nowhere: 'Some sixty-four days ago, I was told that Brussels would never reopen the withdrawal agreement; we are now discussing a reopened withdrawal agreement in the negotiations. I was told that Brussels would never consider alternatives to the backstop; we are now discussing those alternatives. I was told that Brussels would never consider arrangements that were not permanent; we are now discussing an arrangement that works on the principle of consent and is not permanent. I was told that there was no chance of a new deal, but we are discussing a new deal.'

The truth was: Johnson did want a deal, but his populist strategy meant he was not seen as an honest dealer in Brussels. EU diplomats referred to prorogation and the Supreme Court ruling as 'judicial hooliganism'.[4] Conversely, once the Benn Act passed, Commission officials knew they could play hardball in the talks since the consequences of failure would be an extension rather than no-deal. In the end, the events of September forced Johnson to intensify his focus on getting a deal. But by tying his hands, the Bresistance ensured he had less leverage. 'The detail of the Protocol's provisions was essentially imposed under duress,' Frost claimed later. 'By removing the "walk away" option, this massively weakened our negotiating hand – and we could see from the EU's behaviour that they knew it.'[5] In short, the Benn Act probably ensured that there was a deal but also that it would be less favourable to the UK.

The widespread assumption that Johnson had put himself beyond the pale led to renewed talks about a government of national unity (GNU). Unlike in August, the SNP was now prepared to support a Corbyn-led government. The Liberal Democrats, Tiggers (the Independent Group of MPs, formed in February of seven Labour and four Conservative defectors) and the Tory rebels still were not. The only Tory who entertained the idea of prime minister Corbyn was Guto Bebb.

In a meeting on 26 September, Nick Brown, the Labour chief whip, admitted, 'We know Jeremy can't command a majority in the House', undermining the entire premise of the discussions. A Lib Dem source said, 'Everyone said, "Yeah, we know that as well. That's why we're here. So can you support someone else?" "Oh, no, we can't do that."' What Corbyn was proposing was not what the Bresisters wanted. 'It wasn't a government of national unity,' said one rebel who attended. 'It was a Labour government propped up by us.' LOTO would not entertain the idea of anyone else. On 25 September, Margaret Beckett indicated that she was prepared to be a caretaker prime minister.

On 30 September, another rebel meeting was called. Swinson arrived early and was told to wait in a side room. When everyone else had gone in, Labour officials made her sit at the end of the table. 'It was clearly a punishment for pointing out the fucking obvious,' a Lib Dem source said. Swinson again pressed for Beckett or Yvette Cooper as GNU leader. The Labour whips' office responded by sending a party official to guard Beckett to ensure she took no calls from fellow MPs or journalists. 'Sat there all day and did fuck all,' a source said.

Constitutionally, it was correct that the leader of the opposition had the first opportunity to lead such a government. 'The rules are the rules,' John McDonnell said on 1 October. But practically it was impossible for Corbyn to get the numbers. Objections did not just relate to his views on security and antisemitism, there was also an issue of competence. A Lib Dem source said, 'Not only did Jo think he was unfit to be prime minister, she also concluded he would have been bad at even being a bad prime minister.' Even McDonnell fantasised about joining a GNU, angling for the job of chancellor. Lib Dem officials say he told former leader Vince Cable he could be home secretary.

John Bercow did think a GNU was viable and later suggested those who opposed Corbyn were 'overly squeamish'. He said, 'If, say, they had produced a cross-party government led by Jeremy, for the exclusive purpose of bringing about a referendum, and then Jeremy had tried to stay on ... they could have voted him out anyway ... Just like with the indicative votes, it fell because of people being opposed to something.'[6] With the silly season in full swing, there was even feverish speculation that Bercow himself could lead a caretaker administration.[7]

The Tory Party conference in Manchester began with new claims about Johnson's affair with Jennifer Arcuri. Johnson used his speech, on Wednesday 2 October, to announce that he was that day 'tabling what I believe are constructive and reasonable proposals', with the EU, 'which provide a compromise for both sides'. He declared, 'We will under no circumstances have checks at or near the border in Northern Ireland', an admission that some checks would be needed elsewhere. There would also be 'a process of renewable democratic consent by the executive and assembly of Northern Ireland'. He concluded, 'If we fail to get an agreement ... let us be in no doubt that the alternative is no-deal.'

Johnson accompanied the announcement with a blast of semi-comedic populist rhetoric. 'If Parliament were a laptop, then the screen would be showing the pizza wheel of doom,' he said. 'If Parliament were a school, Ofsted would be shutting it down. If Parliament were a reality TV show the whole lot of us would have been voted out of the jungle by now. But at least we could have watched the speaker being forced to eat a kangaroo testicle.' Road-testing his election message, Johnson said that rather than 'continuing to chew the supermasticated subject of Brexit … let's get Brexit done'. He also raised the spectre of Labour plus the SNP trying to 'bundle' Corbyn 'towards the throne' in a caretaker government 'like some Konstantin Chernenko figure, reluctantly propelled to office in a Kremlin coup'.

This knockabout disguised the fact that in the papers the government published the same day, 2 October, Johnson had given significant ground to the EU by agreeing that Northern Ireland would remain in alignment with the EU on goods as well as food – meaning in effect that it would stay inside the single market. This did not pass unnoticed in Brussels. 'That took a few people by surprise,' Stefaan De Rynck of the Commission recalled.[8] However, he was still insisting that Northern Ireland leave the customs union, proposing a regime of trusted traders who could register their consignments in advance. Those not in the scheme would face checks away from the border. To avoid a hard border between Northern Ireland and the Republic, Johnson was, in effect, proposing two soft borders: a regulatory border between Britain and Northern Ireland and a customs border between Northern Ireland and the Republic. The third element was to give the communities of Northern Ireland the right to decide every four years whether to stick with EU regulations or fall in line with the rest of the UK. Under Johnson's plan, both unionists and nationalists would have to support a decision to give it effect – in practice handing veto power to the Tories' DUP allies. Johnson held a series of meetings to square the DUP's Arlene Foster, and Steve Baker, chairman of the ERG, both of whom gave the ideas a cautious welcome. But in Brussels it was scathingly dismissed as 'two borders for four years'.

The following day, after an initially neutral reaction, a Commission spokesman said, 'Member states agreed the UK proposals do not provide a basis for concluding an agreement.' Since Britain had conceded regulatory checks in the Irish Sea, they wanted to agree the same on customs. Frost and Johnson were disappointed. 'We always thought they might say no,' a senior aide recalled, 'though, to be honest we thought it would land a bit better. They had to pretend they couldn't live with any of it.'

The Commission was not prepared to accept alternative arrangements for customs, fearing that goods sent from Great Britain to

Northern Ireland would leak into the Republic, undermining the integrity of the single market. In Dublin, the fear was that any inspection posts, however far they were from the border, would become targets for republican terrorism. 'I think they felt they could turn the screw one more time,' the aide said. 'That we were in a sufficiently weak position, we'd have to talk.'

There was also still a belief in some quarters that Brexit could be reversed. Varadkar had said publicly a week earlier that remaining in the EU was 'what the British people actually want'. Steve Barclay, the Brexit secretary, told colleagues that every meeting he had with his Irish or EU counterparts still began with 'a ritual statement of regret that Brexit is happening at all'. Frost said later, 'It was clear that the Commission doubted that we had the political backing to get a deal through ... In my opinion they were hoping that political developments would see Brexit reversed.'[9] Privately he, Barclay and Dominic Raab, the foreign secretary, all warned the Irish and the Commission this was a miscalculation. 'They are not in touch with the people of this country and if they listen to the people who lost the last referendum, there will be a disaster,' a minister said. 'They need to face political reality.'

Raab urged the Irish to 'get on the front foot' and accept up front the kind of customs arrangements that would have to be adopted in the event of no-deal, but a senior Irish civil servant said the Dublin government 'think it's better to have it forced on them after a no-deal, which they can blame on Britain'.

With the talks stalled, the madman strategy also faced a serious problem at home. Two days after Johnson's conference speech, the government had to issue a statement in the Scottish Court of Session, where Joanna Cherry and Jolyon Maugham had joined forces with businessman Dale Vince to bring a new case against the government. They wanted the court to rule that Johnson had to obey the Benn Act by sending a letter to the EU requesting an extension if MPs had not backed a new Brexit deal by 19 October.

Johnson had to decide how to plead in the Cherry case. MacNamara wrote a note, as tightly as she could so it was short enough to hold his attention, then walked it round to his office in hard copy. She busked her way in and told the PM, 'You have to read this.' When Cummings discovered what she had done he 'went crackers', accusing her of 'going behind my back'. MacNamara understood why he was cross but said, 'I had to. The prime minister needs to agree this.'

Johnson had a second problem, one generated by his habit of coping with crises by adopting two different positions at once. The prime minister had repeatedly said both that the government would obey the law and that he would not sign the letter mandated by the Benn Act. The statements were mutually contradictory. Johnson thought: *What the fuck am I going to do? I had to keep all the plates spinning.* James Slack, the PM's official spokesman, also pressed for an answer. 'There is a point at which I can no longer keep saying these two things,' he said.

The prime minister told cabinet that week he had 'four or five' ways around the Act. 'Some are cunning plans,' he said. Number 10 officials suggested to journalists that Johnson himself would not sign the letter – delegating the task to the lord chancellor, Robert Buckland, instead. As cunning plans went, it was more Baldrick than Blackadder.

Sedwill and MacNamara quietly reassured other senior civil servants that everything would be fine, while privately fearing a new constitutional crisis. Together they agreed to deploy Cox, the attorney general, and Richard Keen, the Scottish advocate general, to convince Johnson that he would have to tell the Scottish court he would send the letter. MacNamara held a meeting with Cox and Keen. They had both reached the conclusion that the law was 'clear, unambiguous and unassailable'. Keen had to instruct the Scottish counsel in the case, giving a personal undertaking that the letter would be sent. He needed to hear that directly from Johnson.

One evening the following week, Cox spelled out the legal reality to Johnson: 'You have to send the letter, you have to do it.' The prime minister was in one of his 'ranty, shouty' moods and was equally adamant that he would not. 'I'm not doing it,' he yelled. 'I'm going to ignore it.'

'Prime Minister, you just can't do that,' Cox said.

Johnson replied, 'Geoffrey, all my life people have been telling me "You can't do that." And I've always proven them wrong.'[10]

The civil servants broke things up, depositing Cox and Keen in Mark Sedwill's office with a bottle of wine. MacNamara bounced backwards and forwards with Johnson and Cummings for two hours. Then she brought the lawyers back to Johnson's study for round two. Watched by Sedwill, MacNamara and Martin Reynolds, Johnson's PPS, Cox and Keen clashed with Johnson and Cummings. The attorney general addressed Johnson with a 'booming' voice, his volume loosened by the claret, 'the rivets popping'. Cox told Cummings, 'I agree with you that the Benn Act is a total monstrosity which is fettering government, disabling its negotiating,' he said. 'It is wrong in every respect: the way it was passed, the way Bercow manipulated procedures – all of it was wrong. But it is a valid law. I've been thirty-seven years a lawyer. I simply can't break the law. It would go against everything I've believed in.' He went on, 'I'm very happy to go really far and hard on this letter saying, "This is Parliament's letter, not the prime minister's letter. We don't think you should grant the extension." But, Dominic, he's got to send a letter. If he doesn't send a letter, he will knowingly break the law.'

The less theatrical Keen made a greater impression than the Falstaffian Cox. 'It was Keen who persuaded Boris,' an official recalled. 'He was actually a much better lawyer. He had moral authority.' Keen explained that if no undertaking was given that the letter would be sent, the counsel representing the government would withdraw from the case. The advocate general, who was a party to the case, would then feel obliged to resign. Cox, notionally Keen's line manager, added his voice. 'In those circumstances I would have to go as well,' he growled. 'No law officer could preside over a situation in which a government, the legal affairs for which I am responsible, refused to obey the law.' This, Cox told friends later, was 'not a threat, just a statement of inevitable fact'. 'It has received assent,' Cox replied. 'It's a valid law. We have to obey it.'

Cummings was furious because Keen's focus was not what would be said to the court but to give assurances to his own legal team, who Cummings suspected of leaking. His fury boiled over. 'He was indignant, he was outraged,' a source said. 'He was shaking with rage.' The Vote Leave man erupted: 'This is just outrageous. This is your fucking client. You work for the British prime minister.' He thought Cox and Keen's behaviour appalling, effectively blackmailing Johnson. Cummings said later, 'I was appalled that Keen would come to a meeting with the PM half-cut and start demanding he give assurances to his own legal team that had huge political consequences and were not part of the official court proceedings. The episode was a classic example of how the civil service often talks about good process and the rule of law but itself adopts appalling, unprofessional processes. Drunken lawyers demanding personal assurances from the PM late at night was not the way to handle the biggest constitutional crisis in over a century.'

Cummings left the room. Some say he stormed out, others recall Johnson requesting a private word with him. 'Dom was visibly distressed,' a witness said. 'The prime minister chased after him and calmed him down.'

Cummings read the riot act to Johnson, demanding he fire both lawyers on the spot: 'They're trying to corral you into making statements which are going to fuck your whole political strategy. It's all fucking bullshit. They only care about their own reputation with the judges and the lawyers. That's not what we are here for. Are you going to destroy your own political position just so that Geoffrey Cox doesn't have a tricky dinner? It's all fucking mad. That Scottish cunt, you should just fire. We don't have to play nicey-nicey with the courts.'

The problem for Johnson was that it was not just Cox and Keen who were threatening to resign. Robert Buckland, the lord chancellor, had also made clear to Johnson that he would quit. 'Tories don't break the law,' he said. Julian Smith and Sajid Javid would likely have followed suit. Faced with the loss of his law officers, Johnson reluctantly agreed the Scottish court should be told he would send the letter. Cummings, the irresistible force, had finally met an immovable object. Privately he told colleagues, 'Boris was weak.'

Cummings did not back down, though. On the morning of Friday 4 October he called a meeting in Number 10 to discuss ways for Johnson to circumvent the Benn Act. Colleagues in a WhatsApp group called '6.30', after the time they met each evening to swap gossip, joked that 'someone could swim the Channel' with the letter to slow down its delivery or literally 'crawl to Brussels'. This was juvenile, but Cummings had a serious point. He believed the official advice was suspect. The inaccurate guidance before the Supreme Court case convinced him these were uncertain and untested matters of law and that the government should gamble. 'We were told prorogation was lawful and that was bulletproof and the legal advice turned out to be complete bollocks,' he argued. 'This situation is one hundred times more complex and unknowable than that. No one knows what the courts are going to say is lawful and unlawful.'

Getting wind of the pressure being applied to Johnson, officials insisted that James Eadie, the leading counsel to the government, also attend the meeting to spell out what would happen if the prime minister broke the law. Mark Sedwill was absent that day and Helen MacNamara was working from home in south-east London. She got a call from a private secretary just after 9 a.m. telling her to get to Whitehall as quickly as possible. One of her sons was ill and the other was going through a phase where he wore a Wonder Woman dress with a Little Red Riding Hood cape. She put the sick one, still in his pyjamas and dressing gown, into the car with a pillow – Wonder Woman riding shotgun.

Driving in, MacNamara phoned ahead to her private office, warning that they would have to look after her children. She gunned the car up the Old Kent Road, fearful she would be too late. MacNamara usually parked in Drum Court at the Treasury and then went through the Foreign Office to Number 10, but that was not going to be possible with two children in tow. She began to panic. She called the office of Simon McDonald, the permanent secretary at the Foreign Office. 'I really need you to help boost me through the gates, because I've got to be in this meeting.' She parked and then ran, holding the hands of one child who resembled Wee Willie Winkie and the other dressed as a female super-hero. As she was racing through the Foreign Office, a female civil servant tried to stop her to say 'how inspiring' she was as a woman who had reached the top. Clutching two children in fancy dress, she felt anything but the woman who has it all. Inside Number 10 she shoved her children towards a waiting Cabinet Office official and arrived just in time.

Cummings said he wanted to hear what would happen if Johnson didn't send the letter and broke the law. The prime minister interjected, 'What if I just wrote "Up yours!" on it?' Eadie and MacNamara exchanged a look. MacNamara explained that the Benn Act dictated the exact word-ing of the letter which must be sent. Cummings was adamant, 'Well we just won't send it.' Gesturing at Johnson, he added, 'They can put you in jail.'

MacNamara could see Cummings was bristling for a fight, but she was in no mood for equivocation either. She thought it ridiculous that she had had to come in on a day off to point out to the prime minister that he could not just break an Act of Parliament and get away with it. 'Well you can't do that,' she said.

'Where does it say you can't do that?' Cummings asked.

MacNamara warned that if the government set out to break the law, officials would down tools. 'The civil service can't work for you. If you want to do that, it's the law, none of us can work for you.' The mutiny threat was back.

Cummings had previously contemplated the ultimate photo opportunity to dramatise Johnson's desire to deliver Brexit. 'We'll just barricade the door and the police can fuck off. They'll have to break the fucking door down.' Another Vote Leaver said, 'There was serious conversation about what happens if the police come to arrest the PM. We couldn't think of a better visual of how determined Boris was to deliver Brexit.' Johnson chipped in, 'I'll barricade myself in.' He then recounted the story of an uncle who went mad and holed up in Newham Town Hall under police siege. 'They'll have to winkle me out with a flamethrower.' MacNamara thought they had both misunderstood how his scenario would play out. Far from protecting Johnson from a policeman with a warrant for his arrest, those guarding the building would be the ones arresting him. 'The police don't work for you in that situation, Dom, they work for me,' she said. 'They work for us. It's not your building. These aren't your people. The police work for the Queen. We all work for the Queen.' Johnson confirmed later: 'She did say that.'

Eddie Lister, who was also present, had another question: 'Can the Queen sack the prime minister?'

'Do you really want us to have to advise the monarch that she's going to have to ask you to stand down?' MacNamara snapped.

Johnson, losing his nerve, blurted, 'This might be getting a bit out of hand!' Another source said, 'He wasn't keen to serve at Her Majesty's pleasure.'

This was theatre, but Cummings' real concern was to find out what the lawyers thought the courts would do in such unprecedented scenarios. His strategy throughout had been to preserve ambiguity about Johnson's intentions to unsettle their opponents and keep the media guessing. A definitive statement of intent would scupper that. He knew Johnson would end up sending the letter, but he did not want the PM to admit that publicly. For weeks he had been working with lawyers on a second letter. 'It was several pages long and made several political points and threw chaos on whether the PM was undermining the application of the Surrender Act,' a source who saw it said.

When the Scottish court met on 4 October, the government refused to publish its submission but parts of it were read out by Aidan O'Neill, the QC for Vince, Cherry and Maugham, who then tweeted the document. It stated that the prime minister accepted 'he is subject to the public law principle that he cannot frustrate its purpose or the purpose of its provisions. Thus he cannot act so as to prevent the letter requesting the specified extension in the act from being sent.'

Three days later Lord Pentland, the judge hearing the case, ruled that he would take the government's undertaking at face value.

The civil service seemed less willing to do so. Mark Sedwill wrote a letter to colleagues, promptly leaked to Sky News, in which he acknowledged that Brexit was 'unsettling' officials. 'Rest assured,' he wrote, 'I am mindful of my own constitutional responsibilities, but I will continue to resist attempts to draw the civil service into the argument.'[11] This was a clear warning shot across Johnson's bows. A political aide said, 'This was the enemy moving. They would down tools rather than follow us in trying to deliver no-deal.'

On 1 October Eddie Lister travelled to Dublin with John Bew, a historian and defence expert, who was Johnson's foreign affairs adviser. His father Paul Bew had been given a peerage by Tony Blair for his role in the Good Friday Agreement. Together they were to deliver advance notice of the proposals Johnson was to outline in his party conference speech. Silver-haired and seventy, Lister was the sober face of the Johnson administration, the silk to Cummings' cyanide. Together with Bew, he had quietly developed a back channel with the Irish government, particularly Brian Murphy, Varadkar's chief of staff, impressing on them that Johnson wanted a deal and needed their help. 'John and I went to Dublin three or four times trying to improve relations,' Lister said, 'which we did.' Julian Smith also quietly worked the Irish. 'They certainly didn't trust Number 10 at all,' a civil service negotiator said.

The meeting on 1 October stretched this goodwill to breaking point. The government's proposals included a customs border between Northern Ireland and the Republic and a veto for the DUP over trading relations, both unacceptable to the Irish. The meeting was choppy, but Lister and Bew succeeded in winning an understanding that Dublin would not publicly trash Johnson's plans. That did not mean they were acceptable, though. David Frost travelled to Brussels on 2 and 3 October but did not make progress. He returned on the 7th, but it seemed like all EU leaders were reading from a script.

* * *

Cummings decided the only way to break through the impasse was to revive his berserker strategy, this time against the EU. He told Frost, 'Everyone in the EU thinks we're fucked because of the Benn Act. We need to get Paris, Berlin and Dublin thinking beyond this. We need to make them realise what's coming.' On the evening of the 7th, he sent Frost and Cain a copy of a message he was planning to send James Forsyth, the political editor of the *Spectator*, on the state of the negotiations. It was incendiary. 'It may set the cat among the pigeons,' Frost said, 'but let's give it a go.' Cummings told Johnson roughly what he was planning but not how explosive it would be.

At midnight, Forsyth posted a blog running the 800 words verbatim. No one waking on Tuesday 8th had a scintilla of doubt it was from Cummings. 'The negotiations will probably end this week,' he announced, blaming the Irish. 'Varadkar doesn't want to negotiate. Varadkar was keen on talking before the Benn Act when he thought that the choice would be "new deal or no-deal". Since the Benn Act passed, he has gone very cold.' Referencing the private conversations Johnson had with the Taoiseach, he added, 'Varadkar has also gone back on his commitments – he said if we moved on manufactured goods then he would also move but instead he just attacked us publicly. It's clear he wants to gamble on a second referendum.' Cummings acknowledged that 'Varadkar's behaviour' was 'arguably rational' if he assumed the worst that could happen was that Johnson won an election and then made the same offer to Brussels, but 'his assumptions are … false'. He added, 'Ireland and Brussels listen to all the people who lost the referendum, they don't listen to those who won the referendum and they don't understand the electoral dynamics here.'

Then came the threats. 'If this deal dies in the next few days, then it won't be revived,' Cummings explained. 'We'll either leave with no-deal on 31 October or there will be an election and then we will leave with no-deal.' He also claimed the UK would punish member states backing an extension: 'Countries which oppose delay will go to the front of the queue for future cooperation … Supporting delay will be seen by this government as hostile interference in domestic politics' which would put future cooperation 'in the toilet', Cummings wrote. 'We will focus on winning the election on a manifesto of immediately revoking the entire EU legal order without further talks, and then we will leave.' He concluded, 'Those who pushed the Benn Act intended to sabotage a deal and they've probably succeeded. So the main effect of it will probably be to help us win an election by uniting the Leave vote and then a no-deal Brexit. History is full of such ironies and tragedies.'

In Brussels, it seemed to be the start of a campaign to blame the EU for the breakdown of talks. Nonetheless, Cummings' hand grenade did shock into action some in Dublin and Brussels who wanted a deal. 'We felt we needed to do something to change the psychology,' a member of Frost's team recalled. A Number 10 adviser said, 'It was totally calculated. It was deliberately written in a way that everyone knew it was Dom. It was very much an effort to develop uncertainty in the minds of the EU. And it worked.'

When the cabinet met that Tuesday morning, Nicky Morgan, the culture secretary, pressed Johnson to disavow the suggestion that the Tories would 'fight the election on the basis of "no more delays, get Brexit done immediately"', a platform ministers took to mean explicitly advocating no-deal. Later Johnson received a delegation from the One Nation Group of Tory MPs – Damian Green, James Brokenshire, Gillian Keegan and Victoria Prentis – who pressed him to guarantee that no-deal would not be Tory policy in the next manifesto. Johnson told the MPs what he had told Morgan: 'Listen to me, not the briefings.'

The Cummings memo appeared on a day when Johnson had a pre-booked call with Angela Merkel. Johnson's team came to regard the call as the nadir of the negotiations. 'It was atrocious,' one of those listening said. 'Boris was terrible: weak, depressed and passive.'

To start with, Johnson urged Merkel to stage an intervention to revive the deal. 'We've made a big offer here,' he argued. 'We've put Northern Ireland into most of the single market in return for consent. You need to move ... Help us float this boat off the rocks.' The middle part of the call was, as one official put it, 'Germany saying "Nein!"' Merkel told Johnson he needed to work with Brussels and the Irish: 'You can't come to us to sort it out.'

Frustrated by hearing what could not be done, Johnson challenged Merkel. 'If this isn't going to work for you, how do you think we can solve this?' he asked. She responded with a blunt assessment of Britain's chances of getting what Johnson wanted, which concluded with a highly provocative claim. 'It would be easier for Germany to leave [the EU] than it would be for Britain because of Northern Ireland.' Merkel even suggested the province should remain in full alignment with EU rules 'for ever'. One of those listening to the call said, 'She definitely said it, although they tried to deny it straight after. That was what antagonised people at our end. It was outrageous.'

When the conversation finished, Johnson called his closest aides together and said, 'Right, it's no-deal.'

Fearing a hostile briefing from the German government or the EU, they resolved to get their retaliation in first. Cummings approved a provocative account of the call to pass to the media with the express intention of shocking the EU into action. Cain, hiding behind the title of 'Number 10 official', told journalists that Merkel 'made clear a deal is overwhelmingly unlikely and she thinks the EU has a veto on us leaving the customs union. It was a very useful clarifying moment … It means a deal is essentially impossible, not just now but ever.'

The briefing caused the pound to slide to its lowest level in more than a month. 'In fact, the conversation was much worse than it was briefed,' said one source. Donald Tusk, who had been flying to Berlin when the call took place, was briefed on it directly by the Germans. He publicly savaged Johnson: 'What's at stake is not winning some stupid blame game … You don't want a deal, you don't want an extension, you don't want to revoke, *quo vadis*?' A senior Council official said, 'That was a turning point in terms of Johnson understanding that he could not just charm himself through this, that the [European] Union was united and there was no way of getting around the Commission by reaching out to Berlin. You cannot do a separate peace with Germany and then throw it down the throat of the Irish.'

That evening, Johnson spoke to Varadkar. The Taoiseach seemed spooked by the no-deal rhetoric. A Number 10 aide said, 'That triggered a reaction from the Irish, this idea that we're really going for no-deal.' Another of Johnson's senior aides recalled, 'The Europeans were in a tizz by this point and wondering what the hell the Brits were doing. They were never quite sure that we hadn't found some way through the Benn Act. In retrospect it was a decisive day because there was reason for people to believe they had better try to patch things up.'

If the conversation with Merkel had been confrontational, 'The Varadkar call was really just a bit sad,' one of those listening said. 'It was awkward. It felt like they were not in the right place to do a deal.'

Johnson and Varadkar explained their bottom lines. 'I really want a deal,' Johnson said. 'But Northern Ireland must legally and under all circumstances remain in the UK's customs territory. I have to have Northern Ireland *de jure* inside our customs union.'

Varadkar replied, 'I understand. I get that red line but are you willing to have a genuine discussion about the practicalities? Can we land on the question of implementation.'

Johnson said, 'Yes.' This was the key which unlocked the talks. Varadkar summed up their separate needs. Johnson, he suggested, wanted Northern Ireland '*de jure*' with the UK. Varadkar needed '*de facto*' recognition of a lot of EU rules. A civil servant said, 'There were a whole bunch of people listening on the line who suddenly go, "Holy shit, that might be it".'

Johnson also pressed the need for democratic consent. 'I get it,' Varadkar said. 'It does create uncertainty, but I get why you're doing it.' The Taoiseach laid out his own bottom line. 'I can't have a situation with checks at the border. I can't defend that in any way, shape, or form.' Johnson understood. Sometimes progress comes simply from process. Varadkar had previously refused to engage with invitations to travel to the UK. But when Johnson suggested they meet, he agreed to cross the Irish Sea and even suggested a location.

Despite the positive ending, as the day drew to a close, Johnson seemed downbeat. 'He looked knackered, to be honest,' said someone who saw him that evening, 'like he was seeing everything fall apart.' To use a historical parallel he would appreciate, Johnson at this point was like Churchill in April 1940 – a political exhibitionist with an erratic and contrarian career building to his moment of destiny, but with little, so far, to show for it. 'Boris had been prime minister for just under three months,' a Tory member of the Bresistance said. 'Everything he had done had failed.' But his strategy was about to pay off in spades.

On Thursday 9th, Sajid Javid, the chancellor, opened his own 'back channel' to Dublin, calling his opposite number, Paschal Donohoe. In a thirty-minute exchange they discussed customs and concluded that a deal was still possible. Javid, who had responsibility for customs when he was financial secretary to the Treasury under David Cameron, was able to reassure Donohoe that London was wrestling with the regulatory issues. 'Saj played a useful role,' a Number 10 official said.

* * *

Johnson and Varadkar met on Friday 10 October on the Wirral. The moment Downing Street staff knew things were serious was when Cummings emerged that morning in a suit, the material hanging off him as if he was ill. 'He looked like someone on a stag-do who has to borrow a friend's clothes because of some terrible mishap,' a colleague recalled. Cummings had coupled the tent-like tailoring with trainers. Several officials, including Brendan Threlfall, had urged him to travel because of the mystique on the Irish side that he was the person most likely to kill a deal. 'He was actually the biggest pro-deal person at that time,' a civil servant recalled, 'because he realised it was better for the election campaign.' If Cummings' buy-in to the talks seemed a good omen, colleagues were concerned to see Lee Cain, who stayed in London, in a plum-coloured suit (which he insisted on calling 'Malbec'), one he had worn on the day of the Supreme Court ruling. 'I hated that suit,' a colleague said. 'Every time he appeared in it, something went wrong.'

The PM and his team took off from Biggin Hill, where rusty old fighter jets reminded some of previous conflicts in Europe. On the plane, Frost talked to Johnson: 'You're going to have to go further.' But even he did not know exactly what Johnson was planning to say.

The location for the divorce talks was a wedding venue, Thornton Manor, scene of Coleen Rooney's twenty-first birthday bash. 'It was a weird, weird place,' Eddie Lister recalled. A long table was prepared for a formal bilateral, complete with flags, but Johnson and Varadkar 'chatted warmly' about family links to Ireland then got down to business – alone.

While the leaders talked, anxious aides watched the buffet sandwiches begin to curl. Eventually they tucked in, demolishing a cheeseboard, the tension mounting. 'It seemed like a good thing that they were talking alone,' said one aide, 'but you don't know.' While they waited, Cummings explained the logic of his memo to Forsyth, to the Irish contingent, who included John Callinan, Varadkar's Europe adviser, and Martin Fraser, the Irish equivalent of the cabinet secretary. 'I think from both our points of view that it is better if we work this out,' Cummings said. 'It's easier for me to do the election if I've got a deal than without, but I can't sign up to your current position. So, if you are going to stick to that, I'll have the election on no-deal. You might think we are deluded but we won the referendum and we think we are the best people campaigning in Western Europe.' He could see that the logic of this position, stated calmly in person, rather than screamed in a blog, hit home.

The Irish delegation quizzed Cummings about how he would resolve the situation in Ireland. He replied, 'We come up with something that's so fucking complicated, no one knows what the fuck it means. You claim this. We can claim that. Both sides can claim victory, there is a deal.' In other words, a classic political fudge.

The plan had been for a twenty-minute tête-à-tête, but the clock ticked on for more than ninety minutes. Johnson broke the ice: 'My staff might kill me for saying this but if I said this what would you say back?' Varadkar played the game: 'If I move on this, might you move on that?'[12] Johnson laid out his case, Northern Ireland legally in the UK customs union, practically in the EU orbit but with a democratic brake. Varadkar confessed his concerns that failing to do a deal would leave his party vulnerable to a Sinn Féin surge in the Republic. 'It was two guys in a room,' he said later. 'Sometimes when you do these things without your officials present, it's easier. We found very quickly that we had shared objectives.'[13] After the meeting, Johnson told his team, 'We just got on quite well. I like him, he's a good guy. He's a free marketeer – on my wing of politics as far as they are in Ireland. He wanted to fix it. And he could see that we were sincere in wanting to come out with the UK whole and entire. You have got to understand from someone like Leo's point of view, the thing they don't want is bloody Sinn Féin.'

Three years earlier, Ivan Rogers had predicted that Britain's withdrawal agreement would come down to a 'walk in the woods' between the prime minister and their EU counterparts. Rigid and punctilious Theresa May, who adhered to the letter of her officials' advice, never had the personality or the imagination to break out of the straitjacket of convention. Johnson and Varadkar, by contrast, improvised a personal understanding, reaching together for a prize which had been elusively beyond the fingertips of their aides and officials. In so doing they demonstrated the galvanising power, at history's pivot points, of individual politicians who are prepared to take risks when they trust each other. From separate goals, policies, hopes and fears, they fashioned something which they owned and wanted to protect together.

Eventually, the leaders called in Frost, Sedwill, Callinan and Fraser to hear what had been agreed. 'It wasn't a done deal, but they had come to an understanding,' a British witness said. 'Both were looking slightly sheepish knowing they had conceded more than their teams planned.' This group talked for another hour, Frost and Callinan writing down what had been agreed. Cummings remained with the sandwich crusts. Varadkar accepted that the people of Northern Ireland could vote, in future, to leave the new arrangements, putting a theoretical time limit on the backstop. But the Irish government hated the idea that the DUP would have veto power and that, if they withheld consent, it would mean a hard border. He suggested that the consent plan involve a simple majority of voters in Northern Ireland, rather than the approval of both unionist and nationalist communities. Johnson also agreed to drop plans for an initial opt-in vote for Northern Ireland. Instead, they would vote on the new arrangements every four years.

On customs, Johnson conceded that technical solutions alone were not enough. He also offered to accept EU regulations on manufactured goods. Varadkar proposed and Johnson accepted a trade-off. He dropped plans for a light-touch customs border on the island of Ireland and conceded there would be no customs border between Northern Ireland and the Republic, in exchange for which the EU would agree to two customs territories on the island. Northern Ireland would leave the EU customs union with the rest of the UK and enjoy the benefits of any new British trade deals, but it would be treated for administrative purposes as if it had not left. A senior British source said, 'Both sides have moved – Ireland on customs and consent, us on regulatory alignment. They've ditched the backstop and accepted consent and a non-permanent deal, all of which the May lot said was impossible.'

Outside the hotel, the two leaders went for a walk in the grounds, like newlyweds beginning married life together. Inside, their aides worked up a battle plan for the two leaders to tweet, at the same time, that they both saw 'a pathway to a deal' and a gentleman's agreement to keep detailed briefing to a minimum.

When they got back to London, Cummings was both cheered and jeered by colleagues. He said, in his Durham deadpan, 'It's a lucky suit.'

Reports of a potential deal unnerved the ERG and the DUP. Owen Paterson, the former Northern Ireland secretary, wrote that holding the province in the EU customs union would be 'an obvious breach of the Principle of the Consent in the Belfast Agreement'. He was retweeted by Nigel Dodds, the DUP leader in Westminster. The following day Steve Baker, chairman of the ERG, issued messages on Brexiteer WhatsApp groups urging his flock to hold their fire until they had seen the final text of the deal. Publicly, Baker said, 'I am fully satisfied that the prime minister is determined to deliver a Brexit worth having.' Privately, he had another priority: 'If we do need to fire and block the deal, we need to shoot together to maximise the impact.'

One of the biggest questions about Johnson's time in office is whether his and Cummings' bombastic approach to negotiations – overtly threatening no-deal – helped or hindered the securing of a deal.

Commission officials are adamant that Johnson or Frost did not formally wave their biggest stick. 'It wasn't a very credible proposition to us and it wasn't a very rational proposition in our view,' said Stefaan De Rynck. 'I don't think there was ever any pressure on the unity of the twenty-seven following from the "tough strategy" in London. That has never impressed the EU.'[14] Instead, they saw threats of no-deal as a media strategy rather than a negotiating position. 'We didn't believe that he was nuts enough to do it,' one said. The striking thing, talking to Commission officials afterwards, was how tolerant they were of such theatrics. Juncker told his team, 'This guy is not nuts, he knows what he is doing, he is a communicator so he will make noise, which may sound awkward to some of us on the continent, but he will get it done.' They gave Johnson rather more credit, in this regard, than members of his own cabinet or the Rebel Alliance of Tory MPs.

However, in the Council, where officials were more attuned to domestic political pressures, there were people who took the threat of no-deal seriously. Donald Tusk, the most emotionally Brexitphobic of all the senior figures in Brussels, and his top officials, Jeppe Tranholm Mikkelsen and Piotr Serafin, regarded no-deal as the height of irresponsibility, but feared that Johnson might be driven to do it. 'We thought it was a real risk, not by design but by accident,' a senior Council official said. 'No one believed Theresa May would ever go for no-deal. With Johnson, we didn't think it was likely, but even if the threat is just 5 per cent, it changes things.'

Even senior civil servants like Sedwill, MacNamara and Jonno Evans, who were horrified by prorogation, felt the threat of no-deal was effective. 'The madman theory really worked,' one remarked. Another said, 'They bought it, I have no doubt about that.' In his memoir, Johnson admitted it was a 'bluff': 'I really, truly, deeply did not want a no-deal exit from the EU. But … I had a curious advantage … in that our partners thought that I might actually be mad enough to do it … In reality, I wasn't going to do any such thing. But I needed them to believe that I might.'[15]

The threat of no-deal had the biggest impact in Dublin. The Cummings memo, the call with Merkel and the success of the madman political strategy helped Tory poll numbers tick upwards despite the Supreme Court ruling (indeed, perhaps because of it). That changed things for Leo Varadkar. The Taoiseach had, for his own domestic political reasons, spent a year more worried about no backstop than no-deal. A cabinet minister, who left the government when Johnson became PM, said, 'The Irish suddenly thought they could end up with no-deal if Boris won an election. I think the prospect of Boris with a majority made Varadkar blink … Boris and Dom Cummings do deserve a lot of credit because that is the art of negotiation.' The Council official agreed: 'I think Varadkar began to become frightened of no-deal.'

Johnson's political art was delaying decisions as long as possible to see what turned up. Now that something had, he was able to grab the passing vine and jump. Those who spoke to him at the time said he was 'desperate' for a deal, having been given explosive warnings by Sedwill (who doubled as national security adviser) and Gove about the potential for terrorist atrocities if there was none. 'There are several hundred dissident Republican terrorists who would target any customs infrastructure,' a security source revealed. 'There would be a risk of civil unrest in places like Glasgow.' An aide said, 'If you had a border point at Crossmaglen, you would need five hundred people to protect you and within five minutes people would start trying to kill you.' In one conversation with a fellow Tory at that time, Johnson said, 'Any one of these risks we could cope with. Taken collectively, they would be a massive challenge to the UK state, and no one would choose to go down that route.'

The breakthrough with Varadkar did not mean Johnson had a deal. He still had to persuade the Commission. Cummings told colleagues, 'Now it's about whether Barnier is told to get a deal or fuck us over as they always have before.' After the meeting, Irish officials briefed the EU's Task Force 50, set up to conduct the negotiations with the UK. When he addressed EU ambassadors in Brussels that afternoon, Barnier gave only sketchy details but he soon came under pressure to move. The Irish contacted the French and Germans, saying they wanted to do a deal.

After the meeting, Frost drove to Manchester airport and flew straight to Brussels. He saw the Commission that evening. While the Brussels institutions were happy to be led by the Irish over the consent mechanism, Barnier regarded it as his job, not Varadkar's, to negotiate issues relating to the single market and the Taoiseach had crossed several of the Frenchman's red lines. There was immediately a problem. The Commission was not prepared to entrust GB to NI trade flows to technology. The jubilation of Thursday's breakthrough quickly turned to disillusionment. A Johnson aide recalled, 'That was a moment of frustration.' Another negotiator said, 'The purists in the Commission were unhappy with it.'

It was not just the Commission who were unpersuaded by Johnson's evolution to deal maker. That weekend, the *Mail on Sunday* revealed that Letwin and the Rebel Alliance (dubbed 'THE TORY BREXIT WRECKERS' by the paper) had another parliamentary trick up their sleeves. Grieve and Hammond were planning to pass a motion forcing Johnson to extend the Brexit deadline after 31 October, even if he secured a deal. This sparked fury in Number 10, given that the Benn Act was originally intended to force Johnson to get a deal.

The following day, Monday 14 October, three days before the crunch European Council meeting, the government presented its Queen's Speech. It included twenty-six bills, more than a third of which were related to Brexit and seven devoted to law and order, in line with the priorities Cummings spelled out in July. Fulfilling Johnson's pledges during the referendum campaign, a new immigration bill was planned to make EU citizens 'subject to the same controls as non-EU citizens', replacing freedom of movement with a points-based entry system.

After the Commission's initial rebuff, Frost summoned his best customs officials and regulatory experts from Defra, around forty people in total, to bolster the negotiating effort. It is telling that these people had not been there from the start of August. 'We told everybody don't tell London anything,' a senior member of the team recalled. 'We'll sort everything out here.' That prevented leaks and gave Frost control of the information flow to Johnson. From the top floor of the embassy in Brussels, he made a video call every evening to the basement of Number 10.

Frost alternated the role of chief negotiator with his deputy Beatrice Kilroy-Nolan and Tim Barrow. 'One of our strengths was that they never quite knew who they were going to get,' a British source said. 'It gave us some resilience that they didn't have.' The hard graft relating to Northern Ireland fell to Brendan Threlfall. 'The crunchy bits were done by Brendan,' a fellow civil servant said.

The other strength was that the British side was united, while they could see that 'they clearly didn't get on on the EU side'. Stéphanie Riso had moved on and been replaced by Paulina Dejmek-Hack, a Swedish-Czech former adviser to both Barnier and Juncker. A British negotiator said, 'She obviously didn't want to do it and felt, rightly, that she'd been dumped in the middle of this nest of vipers on their side, all of whom, I think, were probably a bit suspicious of her.' Frost and his team saw a woman who wanted to do a deal, while Barnier and his other aides gave the impression 'they wanted to make us suffer and not move on anything important to them'. The EU team dressed casually; Frost insisted his officials wear suits. A Council official, always sceptical about May's deal, said, 'It's not too strange that those who had been defending, day and night, the original construction were more attached to it than others.'

As before, the driving force for progress was not Barnier, but Juncker and his cabinet. Selmayr had resigned on 1 August, in part because Ursula von der Leyen had been nominated to replace Juncker and it was not deemed appropriate to have both the Commission's senior political and civil service jobs in the hands of German nationals. Selmayr went to Vienna to become the EU's senior official in Austria. The pivotal figure for the EU was now Richard Szostak, a protégé of Selmayr, who was half Polish and half British but fully European. Szostak was quietly spoken, his voice often dropping to a whisper, but with a formidable intellect and a fierce dislike of Brexit. 'He was very reluctant to move on anything,' a British source said. 'He'd clearly been told by Juncker to get it done, but to give away as little as possible. By being extremely difficult with us, he increased his credibility with his own team.' Witnesses say Szostak used long silences as weapons. 'You would say something and it would just sit there,' one said. 'You'd be desperate to fill the silence and try not to.' It was as if they were now negotiating with Theresa May.

From the 11th to the morning of the 14th, the Commission stuck to the pretence that they were in technical discussions. British customs experts, led by Jim Harra, who that month had become HMRC's first permanent secretary and chief executive, explained how the UK saw the customs arrangements working. 'They just dismissed one thing after another,' a source in the talks said

On Monday 14th, the day of the Queen's Speech, three days before the European Council meeting, the EU message changed: 'If you forget about your alternative arrangements, we'll see if we can work something out.' They tabled a plan that would keep Northern Ireland in the UK customs territory but with much of the EU customs code still applying. The negotiators would have to come up with a formula that identified goods from Great Britain that might go into the Republic of Ireland and treated them differently. The UK would be able to exempt from tariffs most goods passing from Great Britain into Northern Ireland, as long as they were subject to EU state aid rules, which restricted government intervention to prop up firms. That did not answer what would happen with customs processing or physical customs checks, but it did give Britain carte blanche to exempt tariffs on goods moving to Northern Ireland. 'We felt there was something to work with,' an official said.

In parallel with the customs negotiations, Frost led efforts to rewrite the political declaration on the parameters of the future trade deal. 'The task there was to strip out any language that sounded like customs union, to make clear we were aiming for a free trade deal,' a negotiator recalled. The EU's main goal was to preserve the level playing field provisions which Robbins had conceded – where the UK accepted EU rules on the economy, state aid, environmental issues and some taxes. The new draft was longer than the Robbins draft because it now included far more conditional clauses: 'could' and 'might', rather than 'will'.

On the 15th, Geoffrey Cox texted Johnson: 'It is essential I see the customs proposals before we go any further.' Given his role in March, the attorney general felt he needed to assess whether the new deal had succeeded where May's had failed in allowing Northern Ireland to escape the orbit of the EU. The prime minister replied, 'Yes, you must see it straight away.' Cox, like other ministers on the XS committee, was in the dark about the direction of the deal. When XS had met a week earlier, on 8 October, the attorney general had suggested to Cummings and Lewis a means of having a customs arrangement that would not come under ECJ jurisdiction. His idea was to deploy the technique Robbins had used to join the GB and EU customs unions in the original withdrawal agreement. 'It was stitched on not in EU law but in international law, which meant that all the GB customs union procedures were not subject to the EU's universal customs code,' Cox explained. If EU law was not involved, there was no role for the ECJ to interpret it.

When Cox saw the draft text negotiated by Frost's team, on the morning of the 16th, he was immediately concerned. Not only had his idea been ignored, Johnson was close to conceding, for most practical purposes, that Northern Ireland would be part of the EU's customs territory. There was a headline declaration that the province was in the UK's customs union – the *de jure* reassurance Johnson had won on the Wirral – but Cox smelled trouble. He texted Johnson: 'I'm afraid there are some potential legal problems.' The attorney general's team called Number 10 to say he needed to see the PM urgently. When they met at 11.30 a.m., Cox said, 'Prime Minister, I'm very anxious that you should understand the implications of this deal. It will mean a significant border down the Irish Sea in which customs procedures will have to be applied to goods coming from Great Britain to Northern Ireland.' Searching for a memorable analogy, the attorney general added: 'It might say raspberry jam on the label, but that doesn't mean it is raspberry jam, if you taste it and it's actually strawberry jam.'

How things worked in practice would be decided by the joint committee. In XS meetings Cox felt like the Roman statesman Cato, who ended every speech with '*Delenda est Carthago*' – Carthage must be destroyed. Cato's point was that Rome would never be safe while Carthage existed. Cox's point was that Britain's future would only be secure if the government won the key arguments in the joint committee. 'UK tariffs would apply to goods going in principle into Northern Ireland from GB,' Cox explained. 'But only if the joint committee said they weren't at risk of going into the single market.'

Cox explained the idea he had outlined the week before. Johnson called Frost in Brussels. 'The AG is concerned,' he said. With the phone on speaker, Cox said, 'It would submit us and Northern Ireland, to the ECJ's jurisdiction – the whole panoply of EU law in relation to customs.' Frost said, 'Prime Minister, it sounds as if it's a workable idea, but it's too late. I don't think I can go back and start negotiating on a different basis.' Cox, regretfully, pulled stumps. 'I've advised him. I can do no more. There will be a border in the Irish Sea and it will be more in appearance than reality that Northern Ireland is in the UK customs territory.' His views were minuted.

The next Cox heard, the deal had been agreed. Frost was not prepared to change his entire approach, but he did fight to get language inserted into the treaty that called for the Great Britain–Northern Ireland customs border to be 'de-dramatised', reducing checks to the bare minimum. The battles over the next fourteen months focused on arguments over what constituted an appropriate level of checks.

By the evening of Wednesday 16th, the night before the summit, there were just two issues to resolve – the final text on the level playing field in the political declaration and the issue of VAT in Northern Ireland. The Vote Leave campaign in 2016 had promised that Brexit would allow the UK to reduce VAT on goods such as sanitary products, without EU approval, an issue dubbed the 'tampon tax'. Cummings also wanted to scrap the tax on domestic fuel, which voters were told would save households £64 a year. The EU argument, pushed by Barnier, was that tax rates were inexorably tied up with other aspects of the agreement. Fuelled by sandwiches and pasta salad, negotiations went on until half past midnight. At one point a junior official was sent out to buy a bag full of white shirts for those who were running out of clean clothes. 'We'd reached the point where we were just talking past each other,' a British official said. Divisions were again evident in the EU team, Barnier resisting further concessions. 'They clearly had some sort of massive internal row in the delegation and essentially walked out and left us in the negotiating room wondering what was going on,' a British source said. 'We could hear them stomping down the corridor. They visibly did not want to be there and kept saying that to us. I think they were tired and fed up with the whole thing.'

Frost, Barrow and a handful of other officials sat powerless for an hour and a half, wondering if the EU side was trying to provoke them into walking out. At 2 a.m. the Commission team returned with a minor concession on VAT. Frost said, 'Okay, we accept for now and we'll go home and check-in in the morning.' He sent a note to Johnson saying, 'This really isn't brilliant on VAT. I think we really are almost there, but maybe we can squeeze one more thing out of them.' The EU's behaviour that evening soured relations, stung Frost and helped shape his approach to the trade talks the following year. 'My negotiating team was treated brutally as the supplicant representatives of a renegade province,' he complained. 'We put up with it because we wanted to get this done.'[16]

On the Monday evening, details of the customs compromise were shared with the DUP, whose votes Johnson would need to pass the deal in Parliament. 'We kept them very closely up to speed with what we were agreeing,' a government source said. The DUP had reluctantly agreed to a regulatory border in the Irish Sea. Now they were being asked to accept both customs declarations and checks on goods moving from Britain to Northern Ireland. On Tuesday night, Johnson endured a 'difficult' meeting with Arlene Foster, the DUP leader. On Wednesday 16th, a DUP delegation visited Number 10 between 11.30 a.m. and 1 p.m. They rejected the plan in the first meeting, but after a second group met John Bew between 4 p.m. and 7 p.m., it seemed as if they were on board. 'They basically bought it,' an official said. Frost received a thumbs-up message on WhatsApp.

Following consultations with their membership, Foster and Dodds changed their minds again, telling Number 10 they could not support the deal. 'This is the economic equivalent of the Anglo-Irish Agreement,' a DUP party adviser said, referring to the deal Margaret Thatcher struck which gave Dublin a role in the future of Northern Ireland. 'What Thatcher did politically in 1985, Johnson has done economically.'[17] Before his evening video conference with the PM, Frost got the message that it was falling apart. He later called the customs border in the Irish Sea 'the straw that broke the DUP's back'.[18]

He and Johnson had a difficult conversation about whether to press ahead. Political Westminster, and the DUP themselves, had come to believe in their own importance. In Downing Street, the calculation was different. Johnson did not want to get into a bidding war with people practised in saying 'No'. An aide recalled, 'They thought we would chase around after them like May's lot did. Boris is a better reader of people than Theresa. He said after the first meeting with the DUP that he did not think they were ever going to back the deal.'

Perhaps Johnson was just more ruthless than May, with her deep love of the Union. Johnson's aides dispute this. 'It was absolutely never part of the intention that we would have a breach with the DUP,' one said. 'We made huge efforts. Then it came apart. That's life.'

When Johnson addressed the cabinet on Wednesday morning he was in expansive form. 'It's a bit like *The Shawshank Redemption*. We're in the tunnel,' he said – imagining the fetid sewer through which Tim Robbins crawls to freedom in the 1994 prison movie.[19]

In March, Geoffrey Cox had pronounced May's deal politically sound but legally inadequate. This time he parked his political concerns and pronounced that Johnson had a legal way out of the backstop. 'Last time we were in the seventh circle of hell,' he said. 'This time I'm in an airy villa with a lovely view.' Cox had grave disquiet about the deal, but he viewed it as infinitely preferable to no-deal or no Brexit.

At 4.30 p.m., while Bew wrestled with the DUP, Johnson spoke to the 1922 Committee, comparing the talks to climbing Everest, saying: 'We are not quite at the summit, we are at the Hillary Step. The summit is not far but at the moment it is still shrouded in cloud.' He repeated the *Shawshank* line. One MP present was more prosaic: 'He's saying he's up to his eyeballs in shit but not to give up.'[20]

By the time of his video call with Frost that night, Johnson knew he did not have the DUP behind him, but he said, 'We've come this far. We've got to do it.' A senior aide recalled, 'One of the things Boris deserves more credit for is that he took that decision knowing the DUP weren't with him. Theresa May did the deal and it came apart afterwards.' Johnson gave the final green light at 6.30 a.m. on Thursday 17th, a few hours before the European Council began. Dialling in from Barrow's residence in Brussels, Frost told him that while talks on VAT were continuing, a deal was there to be done. Members of XS were patched into the call. The decision was taken not to inform the DUP. 'We weren't going to get anything better,' a source said. 'This was a good deal.'

At 6.45 a.m., the DUP issued a statement rejecting the deal. It said, 'We could not support what is being suggested on customs and consent issues and there is a lack of clarity on VAT.' Tory MPs claimed the DUP's ten MPs were split seven to three against the deal, but had agreed to jump together – a claim denied by the Ulstermen. Despite offering further talks, the DUP heard nothing more from Downing Street.

At 7.30 a.m. Frost called Paulina Dejmek-Hack, who was cycling to work, to tell her he needed one final concession. After consulting Commission lawyers together, they cooked up text which allowed the UK to zero-rate items, like tampons, which were not zero-rated by the EU. Frost was back in the Berlaymont, the Commission headquarters, by 9 a.m., wearing one of the fresh white shirts. Dejmek-Hack then rang Juncker to seek his approval. The Commission president agreed and a call was arranged between Juncker and Johnson. With the details settled, Johnson's communications team kept refreshing Twitter until Juncker announced the deal. 'We then pressed send on the prime minister's tweet,' one said. Which is how the rest of the world found out.

There was a final moment which symbolised the defiance of convention that carried Johnson and his team forwards. Cummings woke at 3.30 a.m. and was unable to get back to sleep. He was in Johnson's motorcade to the airport when Cain joked, 'You have all brought your passports, haven't you?' Cummings was seized by panic. In his tiredness, he had left his behind. At the airport he stuck like glue to Johnson and hoped for the best. 'Dom kept his head down and barrelled on through,' a colleague recalled. Cummings had improvised his own freedom of movement.

For Johnson, his first dinner with the other twenty-seven EU leaders was an anticlimax. 'He didn't even know what flavour the soup was until they briefed out that it was sauerkraut,' one source said. However, the major players were in the mood to be helpful. First Juncker, then Macron, hinted that they did not support any extension. The French president told a press conference he wanted to 'stick to' the 31 October deadline. 'I do not think we shall grant any further delay,' he said. Varadkar warned Johnson's domestic critics 'it would be a mistake' to assume an extension would get the unanimous approval it needed from the EU27.

The following evening Frost appeared at the weekly 'spad school' meeting where he got a 'huge cheer' from ministerial aides. Frost felt some satisfaction. Everyone had said the deal he had negotiated was impossible until two weeks earlier. In reality, he knew it was deeply flawed. 'We faced a choice: take this deal and try to get it through Parliament and sort out the detail in 2020 while we were negotiating the trade agreement,' he said later, 'or walk away, fail to deliver Brexit on 31 October, and almost certainly see the government collapse … We would have seen, at best, a second referendum, quite possibly Brexit taken off the agenda for good, and who knows what consequences in our domestic politics. We decided the lesser risk was to push the deal through … I do not believe Brexit would have happened if we had not taken it.'[21]

The celebrations didn't last long. Johnson quickly discovered, as May had before him, that doing deals with the EU was the easy bit. Negotiating with his own party was where it got complicated.

EXTENSION REBELLION

MV4 and 'Super Saturday'

18 to 27 October 2019

On Friday afternoon, 18 October, the Cabinet Room resounded to the sound of shouting. Boris Johnson was under fire from Mark Francois, the ERG vice-chairman. The vote on Johnson's deal was the following day and Francois wanted dramatic changes to the withdrawal agreement bill, now known to all as 'the WAB'. 'Francois's ask was to remove the entire transition period,' an aide said. 'He shouted at the PM. Whitehall advice was clear that this would have negated ratification entirely and caused a no-deal exit on 1 November.' Another witness said, 'He was at maximum Mark. He speaks at a volume that Mark does not regard as shouting but everyone else does.' Francois duly denied shouting. When Johnson complained about his obstinacy, Francois said, 'If we hadn't been obstinate last time, you wouldn't be prime minister.'

Francois's histrionics came after another delegation of Eurosceptics demanded the removal of something which they had 'lobbied the day before that we write in,' a government source said. 'Many of them don't know what they are talking about.' The demands were charted on a whiteboard in Number 10. Francois wrote them down in a notebook.

Meanwhile ministers, including Michael Gove and Dominic Raab, were quietly pointing out to Brexiteers that failure to secure a free-trade deal by December 2020 would mean the UK could still depart using World Trade Organisation rules, code for no-deal. Not quietly enough, as it turned out. ERG member John Baron told the BBC, 'We could leave on no-deal terms.' His remarks were seized on by supporters of a second referendum as proof that Johnson's deal contained a sting in the tail.

At a 4 p.m. cabinet meeting, business secretary Andrea Leadsom and Johnson agreed that an effort should be made to 'quash' Baron's remarks. Danny Kruger, Johnson's political secretary, chaired a meeting with the twenty-one Tories who had lost the whip. A former cabinet minister said, 'Most of them were positive and receptive to the deal, with one exception, Philip Hammond, who is genetically grumpy.' The former chancellor said he would only vote for the deal if Johnson ruled out what Baron had suggested: 'I won't be duped into voting for heavily camouflaged no-deal at the end of 2020.'

Late on Friday evening, Bill Cash was still refusing to sign up to the deal. His backing was needed to bring the rest of the ERG on board. 'If it was good enough for Bill, it was good enough for anybody,' Bernard Jenkin explained. Oliver Lewis was deployed to win Cash over, a 'horrific meeting' which went on in Number 10 until 1 a.m. Cash's demand was for a clause to be written into the WAB which would automatically disapply EU law during the transition period. Cox had to be woken up to give his view. 'This is ridiculous, it doesn't work,' the attorney general pronounced, adding that Cash's demand would immediately break the treaty Johnson had agreed.

In desperation, Downing Street summoned Steve Baker, who explained the interpersonal dynamic between Cox and Cash, who both thought themselves more knowledgeable about EU law. Baker shared Downing Street's belief that 'political disaster would follow' if Johnson's deal 'were not backed unanimously by Conservative Eurosceptic MPs'. He said, 'The stakes were so high as to induce occasional nausea. If half a dozen or more Conservative Eurosceptic MPs were standing with Farage and the Brexit Party, denouncing it as a betrayal, winning a Conservative majority would have been impossible.' Baker suggested they involve Barnabas 'Barney' Reynolds, a QC trusted by the Eurosceptics but also admired by Cox. Reynolds arrived at Number 10 around midnight. 'He sorted it out in ten minutes,' a source recalled.

Lewis came up with a solution to make Cash feel better. They would write into the WAB a 'sovereignty clause' declaring that Parliament was sovereign over Britain's laws, something Cash had first tried to insert into the Single European Act three decades earlier. 'Its time has come, Bill,' Lewis declared. 'This is how we protect Brexit, using your words from thirty years ago.' In a piece of circular symbolism, a sovereignty clause had also been what Johnson had demanded from David Cameron as the price of backing the Remain campaign, an idea Oliver Letwin tried in vain to deliver.[1] This time, it was enough.

The ERG steering group met on Saturday morning and agreed to back the deal after a plea from Priti Patel, the home secretary, dubbed 'Queen Spartan' by one witness. The 'stragglers' were Francois and John Redwood, who could only bring himself to abstain. Baker declared that Johnson had 'secured a tolerable path to a great future', a deliciously tepid endorsement. A Number 10 aide said, 'It felt like the first time in forty odd years that the Tory Party had united on Europe.'

There was one final tactical setback. While Cash was upstairs in Number 10, Oliver Letwin was downstairs. Johnson intended to seek approval for his plan in a fourth meaningful vote in the first Saturday sitting of Parliament since the Falklands War in 1982, an event dubbed 'Super Saturday' by the media. Letwin published an amendment calling for the Commons to withhold its approval until the entire withdrawal agreement bill was law. The effect of the motion was to render Saturday's big vote meaningless and trigger the provisions in the Benn Act forcing Johnson to write to the EU requesting an extension until 31 October.

The genesis of the amendment dated back to 15 September when Jolyon Maugham, the barrister who mounted the court challenge to prorogation, pointed out a loophole. There was a 'mismatch' between the wording of the Benn Act and the 2018 EU Withdrawal Act. If Johnson secured a deal and Parliament approved a withdrawal agreement before 19 October, he was no longer obligated to seek an extension from Brussels under the Benn Act. But the 2018 Act stated that to avoid no-deal there had to be further legislation passed enshrining the deal in law. Maugham warned that if MPs voted for the withdrawal agreement but then failed to pass the follow-up legislation 'the Benn Act will not apply' and 'we will leave with no-deal'. Nick Boles saw the tweets and phoned Letwin, who thought about it and agreed there was a 'real problem'. He consulted David Pannick and Lord Neuberger, a former president of the Supreme Court, who were providing pro bono advice to the Benn group. 'Everybody agreed there was a problem,' a source said. John Baron's claims that no-deal could still be achieved then prompted Letwin to act.

His plan to tie Johnson's hands was not universally popular. The Benn Act was designed to force Johnson to get a deal and now he had – but the Bresistance was again resorting to procedural trickery to force him into a humiliating delay. Tory MPs' WhatsApp groups shared a comment by Stephen Pollard, the editor of the *Jewish Chronicle*, who tweeted, 'There is a good case to be made that Oliver Letwin ... has had the most pernicious influence on British politics of any person in the past 4 decades.' Ben Bradley, the MP for Mansfield, added, 'I really hope that the man who brought us the ever popular Poll Tax and the hugely successful Fixed-term Parliaments Act hasn't just royally fucked this whole thing up too.' This took its toll on Letwin, not by nature a confrontational personality. 'I'm a peace seeker,' he said. 'Being surrounded by people who were very cross with me wasn't at all pleasant. In fact, it was very unpleasant.'[2]

In Number 10, 'Boris was pulling his hair out,' a Downing Street source said. Another complained, 'Nobody thought we would [get a deal] and we did it. And then they said it doesn't really matter.' The moral force with which the Bresisters had blocked no-deal was gone. Now their actions reinforced Cummings' claim that the establishment would do anything to stop Brexit. Letwin and Boles realised they were the only two members of the Benn group who wanted Brexit to happen. But they did not trust Johnson or Cummings. 'Our mission in life was to make no-deal Brexit impossible,' Boles said. 'There was the possibility it could still happen. We could not take that risk.'

To confuse matters further, Letwin argued that the vote could be used to indicate approval for the deal, even though the wording of his amendment said the opposite: that the House 'withholds approval unless and until implementing legislation is passed'. In negotiations which went on for hours, Johnson and chief whip Mark Spencer urged Letwin to pull or rewrite the amendment. 'They asked him to change the wording so it said what he claimed it said,' an aide recalled. 'Letwin was claiming black was white.' Playing the man as well as the ball, Johnson's team claimed that, in a series of conspiratorial calls, Letwin received 'instructions' from Pannick, who led the Supreme Court case against the government. A witness said, 'He [Letwin] walked through Number 10 giggling like an eight-year-old and had to keep calling Pannick on his mobile to find out what to do.' Pannick denied talking to Letwin that day but confirmed he had helped to write his amendment. Cummings told journalists, 'Pannick is the organ grinder. Letwin's just the useful idiot.'

Letwin's talks with Johnson dissuaded him from backing down. 'The whole point of [it] was simply to prevent the government having a vote that negated the effect of the Benn Act ... It became clear to me ... that

[Boris] genuinely believed that the way in which he was going to get Parliament to vote in favour [of his deal] was by threatening the abyss ... It was equally clear to me that he didn't mind terribly which way things went once the Benn Act had been disapplied.'[3]

As Super Saturday dawned, Johnson's split from the DUP meant his 'majority' was now minus 43. In a bid to win MV4, the whips launched a 'charm and harm offensive', offering rebels who had supported the Benn Act a way back if they rejected Letwin's amendment, supported the deal and voted for all stages of the withdrawal agreement bill and the budget, then due on 6 November. Those who refused were told their Conservative careers would be over. The twenty-one who lost the whip were 'love bombed' by Robert Buckland, Michael Gove and Nicky Morgan. Several, including Stephen Hammond, Nicholas Soames and Greg Clark, said they were willing to back a deal. Former leaders, including William Hague, lobbied MPs. Johnson spent twenty minutes trying to persuade Theresa May to make an intervention. Peter Kyle and Phil Wilson, who wrote an amendment attaching a confirmatory referendum to Theresa May's deal, told Conor Burns, a key Johnson ally, they could guarantee the numbers to win the vote if Johnson agreed to attach a referendum. Burns politely told them the idea would not fly. 'I didn't even need to put it to Boris,' he said.

Despite the whipping effort, it was clear early in the day that the government would struggle to defeat the Letwin amendment. At 9.12 a.m., Cummings messaged a small number of journalists to say, 'A vote for Letwin is a vote for delay and the whips will send everyone home. A vote for Letwin means MPs voting to render the entire day, that they demanded, meaningless. It would perfectly sum up this broken Parliament.' If the Letwin amendment passed there would be no MV4.

At 9.36 a.m. the prime minister got to his feet and made the case for his deal. He argued that Britain had been 'half-hearted' in its EU membership, a 'backmarker' on the euro and Schengen, sceptical of federalism and remote bureaucracy. But he went on, 'It follows logically that with half our hearts we feel something else: a sense of love and respect for European culture and civilisation ... a desire to co-operate with our friends and partners ... It is precisely because we are capable of feeling both things at once ... that the whole experience of the last three and a half years has been so difficult for this country and so divisive.'

The prime minister praised the EU for 'escaping the prison of existing positions and showing the vision to be flexible by reopening the withdrawal agreement'. Now he urged Parliament to embrace the same spirit of compromise. 'People simply will not understand how politicians can say with one breath that they want delay to avoid no-deal and with the next breath that they still want delay when a great deal is there to be done.' He concluded, 'Let us bring together the two halves of our hearts, to bring together the two halves of our nation. Let us speak now, both for the 52 and for the 48.' This was 'good Boris', the Johnson who had run London. But it was not enough.

Not even when Theresa May came to Johnson's aid, warning MPs that, if they failed to respect the referendum result, they would be 'guilty of the most egregious con trick on the British people'. Not when Johnson, in response to a question from Greg Clark, said he was prepared to legislate to ensure workplace rights in Britain were no worse than in the EU. Not even when Mark Francois tried to kill the idea that the ERG might back the deal but then torpedo the bill. He told MPs that in their meeting that morning, 'no member of the ERG spoke against it'. He added, 'We agreed that those who vote for the deal, vote for the bill through to the end … You have our word.' In the febrile atmosphere, trust was in short supply. Keir Starmer, responding to the pledge about workplace rights, said, 'I am not prepared, I am afraid – nor are the vast majority on the opposition benches – to take the prime minister's word. There is more than enough evidence that his word does not mean anything.'

At 12.49 p.m. Letwin made his case, warning that it was not 'responsible' of Johnson 'to put the nation at risk', by urging people to back the bill on pain of no-deal. The amendment would ensure 'we can be secure in the knowledge that the UK will have requested an extension tonight … to prevent a no-deal exit'. At 2.30 p.m., the Commons voted 322 to 306 in favour of Letwin's amendment. Just ten of the twenty-one expelled Tories backed it, with another eleven voting with the government. They included Alistair Burt, Nicholas Soames and Richard Benyon, who argued that, in getting a deal, Johnson had done what they had asked of him. The DUP's ten MPs voted against the government. 'The truth was without the deal having pissed off the DUP, we would never have got the Letwin amendment through,' a Rebel Alliance MP said. If the Democratic Unionists had backed Johnson he would have won 316 to 312.

Outside Parliament up to a million People's Vote marchers packed central London. They included former government economic adviser Uwe Kitzinger, now ninety-two, who on 4 January 1973 had been part of Britain's first ever delegation to Brussels as members of the EU. He had accompanied Christopher Soames, father of Nicholas. There was jubilation when the result came in. MPs, including Jo Swinson, John McDonnell, Sam Gyimah and Anna Soubry, went out to address the protesters.

There were also ugly scenes. Andrea Leadsom needed a police escort to get home and Jacob Rees-Mogg faced people screaming 'traitor' and 'shame on you' as he and his twelve-year-old son walked home surrounded by a dozen police in fluorescent jackets.

Johnson made a point of order, noting that the meaningful vote was 'voided of meaning'. He said, 'I will not negotiate a delay with the EU; neither does the law compel me to. I will tell our friends and colleagues in the EU exactly what I have told everyone in the eighty-eight days in which I have served as prime minister: further delay would be bad for this country, bad for our European Union, and bad for democracy.' He would table a new meaningful vote for the following Monday.

After the vote, James Slack and Lee Cain, Johnson's official and political spin doctors, held a fractious huddle with the parliamentary lobby, many of whom had come into Westminster on their day off to write for their websites. The daily newspaper journalists were even more furious when, under orders from Cummings, they refused to say what the government would do next. Slack repeatedly said the government would 'comply with the law' but not whether Johnson would send the letter mandated by the Benn Act. He had until 11 p.m. that night to comply. Instead, Cain invited two senior broadcasters and the political editors of three Sunday newspapers to Number 10 to give them the scoop.

For the politician who had said he would rather 'die in a ditch' than not deliver Brexit on 31 October, the day was a humiliation for Johnson, but it was one cloaked in the usual Vote Leave theatrics. Cummings produced his secret draft letter, in which Johnson told the EU they should ignore the letter sent under the Benn Act. 'It was laughably bad, a terrible schoolboy effort,' said one lawyer. Jonathan Jones was standing outside Waitrose in Ramsgate when the draft landed in his email. He thought it 'pretty shocking' and made clear: the letter had to be a genuine request; it couldn't just be undone in the following paragraph.

Cox told Cummings his draft letter was a step too far, though he believed there was more leeway for political games than Jones. 'I'm willing to stand up and fight in a court, that the government can't be circumscribed in the scope of its policy action,' the attorney general said. 'It only has to make the application for the extension. There's no harm in the prime minister making clear it's not his request and he would recommend against it', but the PM had to adhere to the law and he could not deviate from the wording of the letter which Philip Hammond had the foresight to write into the legislation. Cox wrote several drafts, which he and Cummings then batted back and forth.

The senior political aides gathered in Johnson's study, along with Sedwill and MacNamara. Johnson said, 'I don't want to send this.' Cummings, still enraged that they were being dictated to by Parliament, turned to Lewis and said, 'Sonic, what do you think?' Lewis said he 'would love' Johnson not to send the letter but that if he did not, the courts would have a judge or even Bercow send it. 'It's all rigged against us. It's a bit like the Borg in *Star Trek* – resistance is futile, because you can fight but the bad guys are still going to win.' Cummings gestured at Lewis and observed, 'Even the Nutter is saying we can't work if you don't send it, it's pointless.'

In the end, Johnson sent three letters to Donald Tusk. The first, deliberately derisory, was a photocopy of the text dictated by the Benn Act, unsigned; the second, a letter from Tim Barrow explaining that it was from Parliament, not the government; and a third personal letter, signed by Johnson, which warned the European Council president about the 'corrosive' impact of a delay. A little after 10 p.m. London time, Tusk tweeted, 'The extension request has just arrived. I will now start consulting EU leaders on how to react.' Johnson's sleight of hand was that of a stage magician – it distracted its intended audience, the media, just enough to ensure they focused on the theatrics rather than the substance – that Brexit was about to be delayed for another three months.

Despite the setback Johnson and Cummings remained confident they would eventually triumph. Adapting an old phrase of the IRA's, a senior Conservative said that night, 'Boris only has to win once. His enemies have to win every time and they won't.' Another said, 'A lot of china is going to get broken but we will win in the end.'

*   *   *

Even more china would have been smashed if Johnson had not secured a deal. In those circumstances, the Bresistance had plans to introduce a withdrawal agreement bill of their own, which would have contained a trigger for both a second referendum and a general election. It was to have been known as the Boles Bill, since it was Nick Boles' idea. Under the plan, the rebels would have moved an SO24 motion on Monday 21 October to seize control of the order paper, then passed the second reading of the bill the next day, before sending it to the Lords. Unlike the Benn Act, which was just an instruction to the government, a WAB would have spending implications but Boles discovered from the clerks that the need for a money resolution only kicked in at the committee stage of a bill. They could pass a second reading, secure a majority and then change the government.

The Boles Bill would have included the deal May thrashed out with Labour during the cross-party talks, a copy of which had 'fallen off the back of a lorry'. The bill was ingenious since it contained automatic trigger clauses which removed the requirement to hold together a fractious coalition through multiple votes over multiple weeks. A rebel MP said, 'As soon as the returning officer had declared the result [of the new referendum], Brexit would either automatically happen without Parliament sitting again or Article 50 would be revoked. Then the dissolution would have happened immediately the next day', triggering a general election.

'We had drafted an entire WAB which was ready to go,' a Labour Bresister said. Boles would have liked his name on a bill, but he was glad not to be the handmaiden of a second referendum. His own intention, had it come about, was to campaign for leave.

Estimates vary, but around 95 per cent of the text of the new withdrawal agreement was the same as that thrashed out by Oliver Robbins for Theresa May. This point is double-edged. There was a lot of diligent work to nail down important areas of agreement, for which the May government deserved credit. It is also the case that the changes to the backstop, that final 5 per cent, were not minor surgery but central to delivering something the Tory Party could support. 'We played ball with both,' a Barnier aide said. 'We found a solution for both.'

The extent to which Johnson had done anything new became a bone of contention between his team and May's allies. Officials pointed out that Brendan Threlfall's Northern Ireland unit had first presented the idea of Belfast in a hybrid relationship with both the UK and the EU to the Irish government on 16 May 2017. Philip Hammond told colleagues, 'Boris has gone back to what the Europeans offered Theresa in February 2018. He's played a political blinder, but I don't think, in negotiating terms, he's achieved anything at all.' May's chief of staff Gavin Barwell admitted that Johnson had broken new ground by securing the consent mechanism which 'would have allowed Geoffrey Cox to write a letter saying, "There is a way out of the backstop."' But he then asserted, 'There's no way the nationalist community are ever going to give consent to doing away with the Protocol.'[4]

The EU side shared the view of the Mayites that Johnson's negotiating achievement was unremarkable, but agreed with the Johnsonians that, politically, it was substantial. 'We could have done this deal in November 2017,' said one EU diplomat. 'But we had a prime minister who didn't know what she wanted and British negotiators who kept asking us what to do.'[5] A senior European Council official argued that May could not have secured the consent agreement, which unlocked the withdrawal agreement: 'I think that it was not possible. She was a spent force.' A Commission official concluded, 'I would say 98 per cent of the credit of the withdrawal agreement, of the orderly Brexit, goes to Theresa May and Olly Robbins, who were extremely good negotiators. I think the deal needed both Theresa May and her hard work and "the closer", Boris Johnson. But Boris Johnson and his team could never have negotiated the withdrawal agreement; they lacked the attention span; they lacked interest in the detail. Mrs May only lacked two things: a clear majority in the House of Commons, including the backing of her own party, and the capacity to sell bullshit for gold that her successor had.'

This was harsh on Frost, who showed he was capable of negotiating a trade deal the following year. He inherited a withdrawal agreement he disliked and limited time in which to change it. 'Given more time we would certainly have tried to do more, notably limiting the role of the [ECJ], but it wasn't possible in the time available.'[6]

But in referring to Johnson's salesmanship, the Commission official also captured (however backhandedly) the importance of Johnson's communication skills – with Varadkar, his MPs and the voters. May's fidelity to the letter of laws and conventions meant she was hidebound by her own process, rectitude and introversion. Johnson's Janus-faced wriggling from one half-truth to another as he deemed it convenient was widely seen as a negative in the negotiations and a black mark against his character. But his ability to speak out of both sides of his mouth at once, to co-exist like Schrödinger's politician in contradictory political spaces, to believe different interpretations of the same event, decision or clause, was not an impediment over which he had to triumph, it was the fundamental reason for his success. Northern Ireland needed a political fudge and it was Johnson's instinctive understanding of Varadkar's political needs which allowed him to seize the day on the Wirral.

Confronted by crisis, Johnson understood you could thrive in future only if you survived first. 'That is very much his philosophy,' a close aide said. 'Let's deal with today and deal with next week, next week.' It wasn't long, of course, before this habit and the contradictions he fostered presented him with new problems to solve.

When MPs returned to work, on Monday 21 October, John Bercow rejected the government's plan to stage a fourth meaningful vote. Saturday's motion, as amended by Letwin, had not been pressed to a vote and had effectively passed 'on the nod', meaning, for the speaker's purposes, that MPs had cast judgement on the deal. Bercow announced it would be 'repetitive and disorderly' to grant another vote.

The 22nd was bittersweet for Johnson. The government secured a major victory on the second reading of its 110-page WAB (so complex it required 124 pages of explanatory notes). The final result was more comfortable than Downing Street had expected: 329 to 299, a healthy majority of 30. It was the first time the House of Commons had voted positively for any form of Brexit. All but three of the Tories stripped of the whip backed the government. The exceptions were Dominic Grieve, Justine Greening and Guto Bebb. Nineteen Labour MPs voted with the government, fourteen more than ever voted for May's deal.[7] Andrew Fisher, Corbyn's policy chief, reflected later, 'That gave him the ability to go to the country and say, "I can get Brexit done", which helped wipe out the Labour Party. People like Caroline Flint, who voted for it, gleefully, lost her seat, as a result ... That was another one of the many tactical failures of people in this whole saga.'[8]

Johnson's pleasure lasted sixteen minutes. At 7.16 p.m. the government crashed to defeat in a vote on the programme motion. Ministers had allowed just three days for the passage of the entire bill in order to hit the 31 October deadline, which Bresisters regarded as a derisory period for scrutiny. Nick Brown, the Labour chief whip, went to see the prime minister, assuming there was a deal to be done. But when Johnson suggested he talk to Mark Spencer, Cummings signalled his disapproval. 'It definitely felt from our point of view that they didn't want their deal scrutinised,' a Labour official said.

A rebellion, led by Philip Hammond and Rory Stewart, killed the timetable by 322 votes to 308. This time nine of the whipless Tories voted against Johnson. They were joined by the DUP. One of them, Anne Milton, said later, 'I voted for his deal because I wanted a second referendum and his deal was a vehicle to get a second referendum. I voted against the programme motion because it was taking the piss.'

That morning Johnson had threatened to pull the bill and seek a general election if the programme motion failed. After his defeat, he merely announced he was 'pausing' it. But that was enough to prompt Donald Tusk to declare immediately that he would recommend a three-month extension and there was no need for a European Council to approve it. For speed, leaders could just sign a written agreement.

Number 10 did not want scrutiny because, as MPs dug into the detail of the deal, they raised concerns about the future extent of the customs checks between Great Britain and Northern Ireland. Steve Barclay, the Brexit secretary, admitted there would be some. Johnson, desperate to keep the ERG on side, denied it. The issue went to the heart of whether Johnson's deal-making could ever be a practical success as well as a political fudge. To Frost, these were issues which would be settled in the joint committee in 2020. 'It was a complete fudge where they have to say one thing and we have to say the other,' another member of the negotiating team said. 'There has to be some weight given to the fact that in legal text it says Northern Ireland is in the UK's customs territory. Equally, there has to be some weight applied to the fact that we have committed to apply the European Customs Code in Northern Ireland.'

To the Commission, however, the agreement was clear. 'The fudge lies in the presentation and in the text, not in the solution itself,' one of Barnier's aides said, arguing that Northern Ireland's legal membership of the UK customs area 'has no practical effect'. He went on, 'All the goods that come into Northern Ireland must abide by all the SPS [sanitary and phytosanitary] standards of the EU. They must be checked from GB to NI in terms of EU customs rules – all of them, without exception. Everything is subject to EU VAT rules and EU tariffs. There is a customs checkpoint between GB and NI. Where it exactly happens needs to be discussed in the joint committee, but the system is very clear.' All this left Johnson's critics with the choice of believing either that he did not understand what he had signed up to, or that he was misleading the public about it. One of his closest aides said, 'People tell him the reality of things, but he just thinks that most people don't care, which is probably true.' Oliver Letwin commented, 'The minutiae of what's in treaties was never of very great interest to Boris. The issue was, were we leaving or not?'[9]

MPs voted to support the Queen's Speech on Thursday 24th, by 310 votes to 294. This victory was greeted with apathy in Downing Street – retrospective confirmation that prorogation had very little to do with a new programme for government. By the time MPs voted, Johnson was focused not on the new session of Parliament but on dissolving it.

The prime minister opened cabinet that morning by announcing, 'I'm going to go for an election on December 12th. This Parliament has run its course, but I'm going to make them an offer.' MPs would have time to pass the bill first if they backed a dissolution. Those present said they had never seen Johnson so exasperated as he was that day, his dream of delivering Brexit by 31 October evaporating. He tore into obstructionist MPs: 'There they are sitting on their arses, luxuriating in their salaries. It's morally wrong and we will hammer them.'

Under the provisions of the Fixed-term Parliaments Act, Johnson needed to secure the support of 434 MPs, two thirds of the Commons, to force an election. That meant persuading at least 70 Labour MPs to back him. Cummings devised another radical plan to shame Corbyn and his party into action. 'We're going to push for an election every day,' he told Johnson. 'If they vote it down, we'll do it again the next day and the next day. We're going to make these motherfuckers vote every day to stop the public having a vote. The haven't got the balls for it. They'll crumble. If it takes two weeks or a month, we won't stop.'

Johnson was incredulous: 'You've lost your mind. We can't do that. Bercow won't allow it.'

'Fuck Bercow!' Cummings replied. 'You're the prime minister. We'll cause mayhem. Imagine the prime minister goes in and tries to introduce legislation to give the public a vote and the speaker prevents Parliament debating it. We'll have him arrested.'

'You've finally gone mad.' Johnson called Gavin Williamson, the shrewdest reader of Parliament in his cabinet and asked him to come over. When he arrived, the PM said, 'Dominic, tell Gavin your plan.' Cummings explained. 'It seems mad,' Johnson said. 'What do you think?'

Williamson smiled. 'It does sound totally insane, Prime Minister,' he said. 'I understand why you're concerned. But Dominic is completely correct; they will definitely crumble, and you should definitely do it. They won't last a week.' Cummings wanted to kiss him.

When Johnson outlined the plan to cabinet, Mark Spencer, the chief whip, said, 'They will look like dicks if they don't do it.' Not everyone was sanguine. Kwasi Kwarteng, a business minister, said, 'Call me superstitious but history is not kind in December elections.' Michael Gove hailed Stanley Baldwin's victory over Ramsay MacDonald in 1923. But as Kwarteng pointed out, Baldwin actually lost his majority. 'It was not kind to the governing party.' But there were no better options. Johnson told cabinet he had been 'trying very hard' with Emmanuel Macron, to get the French president to veto a delay, but he admitted, 'I just don't think it's going to happen.' He ended the meeting: 'If anyone else has any bright ideas, I'm all ears.' There was laughter. Ideas came there none.

In his weekly meeting with special advisers the following evening, Cummings announced, 'We will have a vote on an election on Monday and Tuesday and Wednesday and Thursday.' That weekend, Downing Street issued a lengthy statement by Johnson describing his deal as the 'light at the end of the tunnel'. By blocking his timetable, 'Parliament chose to ask for more tunnel,' he wrote. 'Parliament cannot hold the country hostage any longer.'

The most significant intervention that Saturday evening, however, was a story in the *Observer*, which revealed that the Liberal Democrats and the SNP were drawing up a bill to allow a snap election with just a simple majority of MPs in the Commons. The draft legislation proposed a 9 December election. Ian Blackford, the SNP leader in Westminster, said his party would support the plan as long as the EU granted an extension until 31 January 2020. In a letter to Tusk, Swinson and Blackford wrote, 'If that meaningful extension is secured, we will then work together to bring forward an election this year – but on Parliament's terms, not on the prime minister's.' This move blew apart the Bresistance alliance.

Throughout 2019 it seemed inevitable that the public would eventually pass judgement on Brexit at the ballot box, in either a general election or a second referendum. At the very moment an election looked inevitable, a long-standing power struggle within the People's Vote campaign erupted into an astonishing bout of mutual bloodletting to match anything seen during the Conservative Party civil war.

RUDD, SWEAT AND TEARS
The Implosion of the People's Vote Campaign
April 2018 to October 2019

Just before 9 p.m. on 27 October, the leaders of the People's Vote campaign – James McGrory and Tom Baldwin – received an email from Roland Rudd, the self-appointed chairman of the campaign, telling them they were fired. The start of a general election campaign to decide the fate of Brexit was just two days away, but Rudd informed the two political veterans that the board had approved their dismissal. 'You do not come back into Millbank', the location of campaign headquarters, 'or communicate with any staff without our prior approval,' he wrote. At 9.30 p.m. he emailed the group's sixty staff with the news.

On the eve of a campaign in which it might have had a considerable influence, the most successful grassroots organisation on Brexit had rendered itself irrelevant. 'Roland Rudd … basically dropped a hand grenade into the whole thing,' recalled Alastair Campbell, Tony Blair's former spin doctor.[1] Within days the rump of the campaign staff sat in the Grosvenor, a Thameside pub in Pimlico, trading legal threats with Rudd, the head of one of Britain's leading PR companies. As PR for a referendum went, it was disastrous. When Liam Fox bumped into Baldwin, the outgoing communications director, the cabinet minister joked, 'Pass on my personal thanks to Roland Rudd for destroying the People's Vote campaign at this very opportune time for Brexit.'[2]

Over the previous eighteen months, the People's Vote had turned the idea of a second referendum from a fringe pursuit of extremists into the political mainstream. They twice mobilised a million people to march through London and increased support in Parliament from around 30 MPs to more than 280. By the end, the campaign had amassed a treasure trove of data with the email addresses of more than 500,000 supporters, 600,000 Facebook and 150,000 Twitter followers – all of whom might have been mobilised in the election campaign.

The plan had been to run a tactical vote campaign in a hundred seats in support of Labour, Liberal Democrat and a handful of candidates kicked out of the Tory Party, including Dominic Grieve and David Gauke. 'We had a big platform, ready to go, and we were taken off the field,' said Campbell.[3] Baldwin said later, 'They decided to completely disable the campaign the day before a general election. It was, to put it mildly, a strategically suboptimal decision.'[4]

Nearly everyone who worked on the campaign gave the lion's share of the credit for its successes to McGrory and Baldwin, exasperating for Rudd, whose ego was visible from space. For months, personal animus and disagreements on strategy spiralled into a toxic cocktail of backbiting, leaks and smears extreme even for Westminster.

The People's Vote was an umbrella organisation bringing together ten different pro-Remain groups of which by far the biggest was Open Britain, which had emerged out of Britain Stronger in Europe, the official Remain campaign in 2016.

The tensions that were to tear the campaign apart were present even before the People's Vote launched at the Electric Ballroom in Camden on 15 April 2018. A few days before the event, staff received a 'bizarre series of calls' from Rudd, the chairman of Open Britain. 'He had only one demand, repeated ad nauseum, that Hugo Dixon be given a prominent speaking slot alongside the politicians and celebrities at the launch,' a campaign source recalled. A close friend of Rudd's dating back to their time together at Oxford University, Dixon ran a pro-European blog site. When it was pointed out that there was no value to giving such an obscure figure a speaking slot, Rudd insisted until he got his way.

Rudd's intervention was doubly strange since, in the two years since the referendum, insiders say the founder of Finsbury, the City PR firm, and the brother of Amber Rudd, the home secretary at the time, had called a total of just two Open Britain board meetings. He had held fundraisers but others, such as Tony Blair and Alastair Campbell, were concerned Rudd combined these events with his business interests. Campbell found himself sharing a table one evening at Rudd's £30 million mansion with the UK head of Huawei, the Chinese telecoms firm which the government regarded as a security threat.

Director of Open Britain and of the People's Vote was McGrory, who had been Nick Clegg's spin doctor during the coalition government and then chief spokesman for the Remain campaign. He and his deputy, Francis Grove-White, worked with MPs – Chuka Umunna, Alison McGovern, Jo Swinson and Anna Soubry – to form a 'contact group' to bring the different groups together. McGrory agreed to transfer all of Open Britain's assets to the People's Vote campaign, of which the most significant was the vast mailing list. The name 'People's Vote' came from Green Party MP Caroline Lucas. It polled better with the public than 'second referendum'.

Nine groups eventually joined forces in offices in Millbank Tower. The other significant organisation was the European Movement, chaired by Stephen Dorrell, the former Tory cabinet minister. Two youth campaigns – For our Future's Sake and Our Future, Our Choice (both named to create provocative acronyms: FFS and O-FOC) – brought energy from young activists like Femi Oluwole, Amanda Chetwynd-Cowieson, Will Dry, Richard Brooks and Lara Spirit. The other groups included several which were virtual one-man bands: Britain for Europe, Wales for Europe, Scientists for EU and NHS against Brexit. 'Mike Galsworthy had two such groups, Scientists for EU and NHS for Europe, and that was basically just him,' said Baldwin.[5] Then there was Hugo Dixon's InFacts website, which he had set up as a fact-checking organisation in the 2016 referendum and now produced a daily newsletter.

The only major organisation that refused to join was Best for Britain, run by Eloise Todd, which was explicitly pro-Remain as opposed to pro-referendum. A Best for Britain source said, 'Eloise and James McGrory hated each other, so we couldn't be friends. It was just stupid.' They eventually patched things up.

In June 2018, a tenth organisation came on board, the Joint Media Unit, set up by Alastair Campbell and the *Observer* columnist Henry Porter. With the help of Conservative peer Patience Wheatcroft and former MEP Edward McMillan-Scott, they raised £1 million to create a communications hub. Businessman Julian Dunkerton donated another £1 million for polling, giving the campaign huge resources to move the views of MPs. At Campbell's suggestion, Baldwin, the former *Times* journalist who went on to be Ed Miliband's spin doctor, joined as director of communications. Baldwin had watched the referendum result at home and bristled. 'I remember sending various drunken, possibly abusive, messages to people as dawn broke over Islington,' he said. Baldwin reported to McGrory, but the money went into an Open Britain bank account. 'It became clear to everyone that this was where the action was,' he said. 'It was like building an aeroplane as you are taking off; there are bits falling off and you are going very, very fast.'[6]

The first People's Vote march was held on 23 June 2018 – the second anniversary of the EU referendum – and the media began to take notice. The first was 'a bit of a shambles', but the campaign then hired Rachel Kinnock, daughter of Neil and Glenys and Ed Miliband's director of operations. She transformed them into professional, well-run events with a decent roster of speakers. Kinnock was one of several senior women brought into address complaints of gender imbalance in the top team. There was an inherent tension generated by the marches, however. Baldwin recalled that their strategy 'was to persuade people that a People's Vote was the democratic solution for this gigantic Brexit mess – whether you are a Remainer, a Leaver or not sure – a vehicle to solve the problem. But in order to get started we had to get noticed ... You have to mobilise this base of Remainers. But in doing so, you are then also becoming part of the polarising problem that you are trying to solve. We were simultaneously helping to create a crisis and then present ourselves as the solution to it. That is not an easy trick to pull off.'[7]

In Millbank, McGrory reorganised the disparate groups so they operated together in People's Vote teams running communications, field operations, policy, data and an attack unit. It was the first time pro-Europeans had properly joined forces in the thirty years since Maastricht had weaponised British Euroscepticism. The young staff had a strong sense of camaraderie and adopted the song 'Happy Birthday' as an anthem when major announcements were made, to the consternation of other occupants of Millbank. The irony was that the UK was developing the most vibrant movement in favour of the EU anywhere in the EU just as it was preparing to leave.

In 2018, they kept the focus on stirring up Remainers. 'I found out that we were putting filters on our Facebook ads so that they did not reach anyone who watched *Top Gear*, played Bingo, liked Piers Morgan or who had not gone to university,' Baldwin said.[8] On 20 October, they held a second mass protest, with 750,000 people, called 'March for the Future'.

Baldwin asked social media advertising to extend its reach beyond the confines set by these filters, but he was conscious that the marches could easily be caricatured as 'the longest Waitrose queue in history',[9] a grand day out for the cardigan-wearing middle classes horrified by Aldi-going Leave voters.

Managing the MPs proved more difficult than drumming up public support. Their high-profile backers were Chuka Umunna and Anna Soubry, 'divisive figures within their own parties'.[10] Umunna's role convinced the Labour leadership the People's Vote campaign was intended as a breakaway vehicle for Labour rebels. 'We were seen as some sort of New Labour plot or new party plot,' Baldwin said.[11]

To McGrory and Baldwin, winning over Labour was a necessary, but not sufficient, precondition for building a parliamentary majority for a second referendum. Baldwin used polling to shift opinion. The media focus since 2016 had been on the huge number of Labour-held constituencies which voted to Leave. However regular YouGov surveys, paid for with Dunkerton's £1 million, showed that while Labour seats went Leave, Labour voters did not back Brexit. By 2017, 70 per cent of Labour's vote was Remain. 'The polls that we were able to do showing a majority of Labour supporters for a referendum in people's individual constituencies was very influential,' Baldwin recalled.[12] They 'found only one constituency in the country where a majority of Labour voters were backing Leave, and that was Ed Miliband's seat in Doncaster North.'[13] He told MPs and journalists, 'Labour Leave voters are more Labour than they are Leave and Labour Remain voters are more Remain than they are Labour.'

While that moved Labour backbenchers towards the People's Vote during 2018, it was the campaign's decision not to support Commons votes on a referendum, designed to embarrass Corbyn, and their refusal to endorse the Independent Group of pro-referendum defectors in February 2019, which finally convinced LOTO they were not a front. John McDonnell, in particular, gave them a fresh hearing.

In parallel, Keir Starmer, who had originally thought a second referendum unobtainable, began to shift Labour towards backing a People's Vote. Alastair Campbell recalled, 'I had a meeting with Keir in my kitchen downstairs, and I remember Keir saying, "You are completely wasting your time. Politically, this is impossible." He was not going to get involved. Not that long later, I remember standing on the side of the stage, organising the speakers, and we had ... not just David Lammy, who was with us from early on, but John McDonnell, Diane Abbott, Keir Starmer, Emily Thornberry. They moved.'[14]

Tory referendum backers felt frustration that the focus was on Labour and the rallies. 'The big marches were impressive, but, fundamentally, the battle was in Parliament,' Phillip Lee said. 'The People's Vote ... didn't realise until late on it was about putting enough people through the lobbies at the right time ... it cast itself too much as the alternative Labour Party.'[15]

While the campaign gained public support, behind the scenes it became a bearpit of internecine warfare. In Millbank, tension was growing between the rapidly expanding PV staff – who by the end of 2018 numbered sixty – and a small faction around Dixon, who operated out of a large but usually empty office on the same floor, decorated with erotic pictures painted by his mother. 'There were definitely bare breasts in one of them,' remembered one female staffer. 'Women for a People's Vote would come in and have to sit under these boobs.'

Dixon, a yoga-loving Old Etonian, was close friends not only with Rudd but with Boris Johnson, a contemporary from both Eton and Balliol College, Oxford. He had even loaned Johnson his Greek island villa to write his biography of Winston Churchill, Dixon's great-grandfather. Dixon would also host 'Salmon en Croute' dinners at his Notting Hill mews home for broadsheet journalists at which he set out his personal theories on Brexit. Baldwin frequently had to spend the next twenty-four hours explaining why these musings were not campaign policy. Baldwin and Campbell also fielded calls from Sarah Sands, editor of the *Today* programme, asking them to stop Dixon phoning to volunteer himself as a voice for the campaign.

These divisions moved from tragicomic to calamitous when Rudd announced, without any process, that he was chairman of the People's Vote campaign as well as Open Britain. He named Dixon as his deputy chairman. 'There was no more legitimacy to the award of these titles than the Victoria Cross that Idi Amin pinned on his own chest,' Baldwin remarked. Campbell believed Rudd wanted 'status at west London dinner parties'.[16] On 22 January, the *Today* programme announced, to widespread hilarity in Westminster, an interview with Rudd, 'the chair of the People's Vote campaign, live from Davos', the winter resort which was home once a year to the global capitalist elite. At a time when opponents were seeking to portray the campaign as the obsession of an out of touch metropolitan elite, Rudd's performance caused dismay among politicians and staff. 'It was absolutely toe-curling,' Baldwin said.[17] One business executive sharing a ski lift with the leading PR man suggested, 'Roland, you need to get yourself a good PR man.'

In another example of Rudd's self-importance, his office phoned the campaign to announce he planned to attend a rally at Church House but said he would require a personal minder to meet him from his car and shepherd him to his reserved front-row seat.

Rudd had sought to strengthen his position in December 2018, when he forced through, on a vote of five to four, the appointment of three women to the Open Britain board, all of whom owed their position to him and one of whom was an employee of Dixon at InFacts. Control of Open Britain gave Rudd control of the database of People's Vote supporters and its finances, which were now self-supporting thanks to the £80,000 a week raised from small donations. Rudd's intrigues ended his relationship with Peter Mandelson, the godfather of one of his children. Mandelson had been attending weekly 'governance meetings' with Dixon, McGrory and Dorrell but Rudd sent him packing. From then on, they were attended by Baldwin and Campbell instead. Rudd began inviting Tom Brufatto and Mike Galsworthy, the directors of organisations that consisted of just two members of staff (themselves) to the meetings. Campbell found Dixon grating and stopped going, telling Rudd, 'You appear to have designed a system deliberately for dysfunction.' He was replaced by Patrick Heneghan, a former Labour campaign director, who was the People's Vote's head of field operations.

Rudd and Dixon attacked Baldwin and McGrory for meeting Tony Blair and demanded access to Baldwin's diary, insisting they not go to Blair's office in case they were photographed by the *Daily Mail*. Dixon also demanded to know every contact Blair, Campbell and Mandelson had with EU leaders – a request met with derision. Rudd, who seldom visited the campaign, began to demand a say over operational decisions, insisting that no one could speak at the next big demonstration unless approved by him and Dixon (who also wanted a slot).

Despite all this, the campaign gathered strength. On 23 March, less than a week before the UK was originally due to leave the EU, a third 'Put it to the People' march attracted a million protesters. When the indicative votes took place in April, a referendum secured 280 votes, the most of any option, though it fell 12 votes short of a majority.

When Article 50 was extended to 31 October, Campbell and Henry Porter pressed for the campaign to be put on a proper footing, so it could prepare to fight a referendum. A letter was sent to Rudd in late April setting out a process. It was ignored. An initial meeting was convened under the chairmanship of Stephen Dawson, a philanthropist and donor. Those present included the senior team at Millbank, the European Movement, the Joint Media Unit, and even Best for Britain and Galsworthy. Rudd refused to attend and Dixon said he was away for medical reasons. Rudd later complained bitterly about what became known as the 'Dawson process' interfering with 'my campaign'. Despite promises that he would meet Dawson, Rudd ignored calls and repeatedly cancelled meetings.

Between May and July 2019, the Rudd–Dixon camp and the McGrory–Baldwin camp had two major splits over strategy and tactics. The first concerned how to approach the local and European elections. In meetings at Finsbury's HQ, both sides agreed that the People's Vote would support any party that backed a new referendum. That meant an unambiguous endorsement for the Greens, the SNP, Change UK and Plaid Cymru. Labour's position had moved, but was not yet fully behind a referendum. Baldwin, McGrory and Heneghan believed that urging voters to oppose Labour would embarrass the two hundred Labour MPs backing the People's Vote. Without any consultation, however, Dixon wrote an article saying no Remain supporter should vote Labour. MPs such as Hilary Benn immediately threatened to withdraw their support.

Rudd had his own political history. In the 1980s he had been a member of the SDP and Dixon was involved in merger talks between the SDP and Liberal parties, which created the Alliance. The New Labour exiles began to view Rudd and Dixon's behaviour as evidence that their primary goal was not to secure a referendum, but to use the campaign to secure a realignment of British politics along the Remain/Leave axis. 'Roland was always very taken with the idea of a political realignment, perhaps because that is something he had wanted since his SDP days,' observed Alastair Campbell. 'It was not the purpose of the People's Vote campaign and the team there were right to resist any such mission creep. It felt like Rudd had given up on a referendum and was pushing hard for the Lib Dems to do as well as they could in a general election.'[18] Dixon's suggestion that Rudd was a 'British Macron', after the French president who had set up a new centrist movement, did nothing to allay these suspicions. If they wanted to build a new party, control of the database and mailing list was key.

The second falling out was over McGrory and Baldwin's summer strategy. With most Labour MPs on side, the key to winning a vote in Parliament was to encourage more Conservative MPs to get on board. That meant arguing that a referendum could be the solution to the political paralysis – rather than making the People's Vote look like a Remain ruse to overturn the result of the 2016 vote. To address perceptions that the campaign was dominated by a metropolitan elite, a summer of 'Let us be heard' rallies was planned in northern Leave-voting areas, culminating in a march in London in October. 'All these ideas were listened to by the Rudd-Dixon faction without – for once – any sign of disagreement,' a campaign source said.

However, on 8 June, Brufatto sent an email to members of Rudd's governance committee about plans for a pro-European March for Change on 20 July. A few weeks earlier, Brufatto had set up a new company explicitly for the purposes of data collection and fundraising for this march. 'They were coming to very small strategy meetings, hoovering up everything that was being discussed … meanwhile they were off setting up a rival campaign,' Alastair Campbell recalled. 'The little gang that Rudd was close to were constantly wanting to preach to the converted, so we could all tell each other how right we were. But it all played into the idea of a metropolitan elite telling Brexiteers they were thick – a caricature which helped our opponents. There was a Remainiac gravitational pull, which I felt we had to resist.'[19] Baldwin thought 'gathering the most Remainy people in Britain under an explicitly Remainy banner at a time when we were trying to show Conservative MPs and reluctant Labour MPs that a people's vote was a solution' to be 'strategic nonsense'.[20]

Despite viewing the breakaway march as malign in intent, McGrory and Baldwin ordered that no one in Millbank brief against it. Rudd agitated to change the name of the rally to 'No to Boris, Yes to Europe', an even more inflammatory stance as far as those wooing Tory MPs were concerned. That weekend, Rudd tweeted, 'We need to remain, reform and rejuvenate'. In case anyone missed the significance of what he was saying, he briefed Robert Peston, another friend from Oxford, who told his million Twitter followers, 'The chairman of the People's Vote campaign seems to confirm for the first time that the PV campaign is in favour of Remain, rather than simply a campaign to deliver a referendum … Quite a big and controversial shift.' While this seemed unremarkable to many, it was a direct contradiction of what the main campaign was telling MPs in order to win a vote in the Commons.

To McGrory, Baldwin and most of their staff this provided fresh evidence that Rudd was working to undermine the campaign for a referendum to position himself as a standard bearer for Remain supporters. It was an open secret in 2016 that he hoped to obtain a peerage or knighthood from his role in the Remain campaign. A realignment of politics might bring the old SDP man the recognition he craved. Someone who dealt with Rudd in this period said, 'He lives in the shadow of his sister. He's quite a vulnerable character. He has this charm and a desperation, wanting to impress.'

Rudd's allies countered that his position was driven by common sense. A source close to the PR man said, 'Roland's view was always that we should just say we're campaigning for Remain because the idea that in a second referendum we should campaign for Brexit is absurd.' This source said the People's Vote was 'a jolly for a load of former New Labour people … wrestling publicly with their own souls'. This he believed was alienating the Lib Dem wing of Remainia, a curious claim since McGrory was a long-standing Lib Dem. The Rudd ally said McGrory and Baldwin 'had no chance of winning the official designation of the Remain campaign' if there was a second referendum and accused them of fostering a 'toxic' culture where staff felt it was 'Okay to slag off Roland in the office'.[21]

McGrory again ordered that there be no response, but divisions were now bursting to the surface. Emails leaked to the media portrayed Rudd as a supporter of 'grassroots campaigners' who wanted to be more explicitly pro-Remain but were held back by the 'poisonous influence' of Baldwin and Campbell. Rudd, Dixon, Brufatto and Galsworthy all denied involvement in the leaks. When Richard Brooks, the young FFS campaigner, suggested Rudd should consider his position, Rudd told McGrory that any staff member echoing that sentiment should be sacked.

The March for Change took place the following day with a relatively paltry attendance of between 10,000 and 20,000 and was widely ignored by the media as a damp squib.

*   *   *

Behind the scenes, Stephen Dawson – with the full support of all parts of the coalition apart from Rudd and Dixon – had been quietly working on a plan to put the campaign on a war footing. Henry Stannard was recruited to write two reports: 'Project Marshall', the codename for the preparations for a new referendum campaign; and Project Root, a 'lessons learned' paper on what had gone wrong for Remain in 2016. Work began to identify target voters who held the key to victory in a referendum. There were questions to ask about the slogan, the message, who would run it and who would be the face of it.

Will Straw, who had run Britain Stronger in Europe, felt they lost that campaign because Remainers had not found a way of connecting emotionally with voters. He told a friend he worried about another referendum 'because I still don't think we have found that language'. A People's Vote strategist said, 'The successful slogans of the last few years, "Make America Great Again", "Take Back Control", even "Get Brexit Done" – all of them had personal agency and they also had change. Progressive slogans are often passive. We have to have a change story about ourselves and the country if we are going to win this. We are going to have to reach out to people who voted Leave last time and say, "We have listened to what you said, we have recognised you want the country to change. What we are offering is a faster, better, safer change. 2016 wasn't a waste because it's going to result in massive changes to this country anyway."'

They also recognised that a referendum campaign should not echo the debate in Parliament. Hilary Benn, a later referendum convert than many Labour MPs, said, 'You couldn't argue to the electorate, "I'm terribly sorry. You reached the wrong decision. Could you please go and cast your vote again?" That was not a credible position to adopt. But to say, "It's clear we are leaving. Unfortunately, the referendum itself offered no guide … to what kind of future relationship we are going to have with the European Union. What's on the table currently [is] quite some distance away from what was promised by the Leave campaign … can we check you are happy with it?"'[22] Boiling that down to a slogan would have been difficult.

On the other side Nigel Farage and Richard Tice were planning to run a new Leave campaign under the slogan 'Tell Them Again'. Dominic Cummings was convinced Vote Leave Redux would marmalise the Remainers. In Johnson and Farage, the Brexiteers would have two of the best stump politicians in the land.

Names floated to run a Remain campaign included the Labour MP Jess Phillips and Tory Rory Stewart. Others would have been brought in as well. 'It's really important in the networked age you don't have a single leader,' a campaign official said. 'When you start segmenting the electorate, you need people who have different reaches. You don't try and find somebody who can be all things to all people. Tony Blair is deeply unpopular but can actually reach people. Do you want him to be front and centre and the face of your campaign? No.'

Even with all this planning, the number of referendum supporters who thought they would win was limited. 'I was utterly convinced that people would ... think again,' said Phillip Lee, who was one of them. 'I always got the impression that the leading Brexiteers felt quite threatened by our little group. They knew that if we actually did succeed in getting it back to the people, that realistically Brexit would have not gone through.'[23] This was not a widely held view. Philip Hammond said, 'People like me and David Gauke ... didn't actually think we'd win it because, with the benefit of hindsight, it's blindingly obvious that you can't fight an emotional argument with a logical argument.'[24]

The Project Marshall team knew they would stand no chance at all unless they got properly organised. Dawson proposed a new campaign structure with a board consisting of representatives from all the different functional campaign groups, including Best for Britain, as well as a separate strategy committee led by Dominic Grieve and Margaret Beckett but also including experienced campaign professionals. 'The structure of the campaign and the governance system was not adequate in any way for fighting a referendum campaign,' Baldwin recalled. 'There was no way we would get the designation or deserve to get the designation.'[25] Ironically, Rudd would later use one of the internal reports which drew this conclusion to justify the sacking of McGrory and Baldwin – even though he resisted their plan to make the necessary changes. 'They refused point blank to even consider the kind of re-organisation needed to fight and win a campaign,' said Baldwin. 'But we did not have time to waste so we started doing it anyway. We invited Roland to the meetings, but he didn't turn up. We started doing the polling, the segmentation and the identification of key voters, all the things you need to do if you are going to win. But that was a trigger for a further explosion of anger and jealousy and rage.'[26]

On 19 August, barely an hour before an Open Britain board meeting was supposed to discuss Dawson's proposals, Rudd launched what his opponents saw as a 'hostile takeover' in the manner of the City deals he had spent decades facilitating. He sent the board a proposal to 'create a new company', which he called Baybridge 2019, 'to campaign to get a People's Vote and to be in the EU'. There would be a new board to set strategy, with four seats for Open Britain, plus an open competition for the appointment of a new chief executive. McGrory would have to apply for his own job. Despite fierce opposition from McGrory, Mandelson and three others, Rudd got the proposal approved and appointed three loyalists to the Baybridge board. A campaign which had mobilised millions had now become a rich man's plaything. 'Roland has the numbers and authority to make decisions as he sees fit,' his ally said.[27]

In Millbank, sixty staff signed a letter backing McGrory which accused the 'splinter group' behind the March for Change of having 'confused our supporters, diverted staff attentions and resources' and of 'seriously damaging morale'. Rudd responded by telling Open Britain board members that he had been meeting Dawson regularly and that the campaign was reliant on his fundraising. Staff wrote to Rudd, copying in the board, demanding he correct his false or misleading statements. The following week he turned up at Millbank to meet them, accompanied by board member June Sarpong, who had tweeted that she 'adored' Rudd. He was told repeatedly that staff would not work again with Dixon and his allies.

The infighting distracted the attention of the campaign at a time, in August and September, when it seemed that Boris Johnson was heading for no-deal – a propitious environment in which to recruit more MPs to back a People's Vote. 'We had promises from … dozens more Conservative MPs,' a campaign official recalled. Alastair Campbell said, 'Philip Hammond, who was clear he saw it as undemocratic to some extent, nonetheless said that if he had felt that the People's Vote was the only way to stop no-deal, he would've backed it. You had Tories who were moving in that direction.'[28] The chaos in the campaign made it easy to stay away. 'I was always against a second referendum,' Greg Clark recalled. 'The first one was divisive enough. If you call a referendum, and say you're going to abide by the results, you have to do it as a matter of honour.'

On Saturday 19 October, a million people joined the final People's Vote march through London. That evening the *Mail on Sunday* revealed leaked emails, which had been sent to Rudd in error in August,[29] showing that Mandelson and Campbell had wanted rid of him. In one, Campbell wrote, 'It should happen soon and be fast and brutal.' In another, Mandelson wrote to colleagues, 'We need to pin down Roland's slipperiness.'[30] The paper depicted this as the 'dark arts' of New Labour spin doctors, rather than an understandable response by political professionals to a dilettante PR man whose understanding of how to win was dwarfed by his self-confidence.

Yet Rudd did understand how to exercise corporate power. A week later, he struck. At 7.42 p.m. on the 27th, he emailed the Open Britain board to announce that he was sacking both McGrory and Baldwin to 'bring clarity to the campaign' and 'avoid any further pointless rows'. In their place he appointed Patrick Heneghan as acting chief executive. Mandelson replied, 'You have gone off your trolley, Roland, if you think this is a good moment to fire people without reason or due process.' Will Straw warned his action would demoralise and destabilise the campaign. Rudd ignored them both.[31] 'It was a catastrophic act of vanity,' Alastair Campbell said. 'They had both done an incredible job.'[32]

People's Vote staff vented their fury on Tuesday 29th, after Rudd summoned them to a Hilton hotel nearby where three beefy bouncers guarded the door. They could not protect Rudd from the open hostility of the staff, who voted 40 to 3 to declare no-confidence in both Rudd and Heneghan. One of the three votes came from Heneghan himself. Staff received letters from Rudd's lawyers threatening them with criminal charges if they sought to use the campaign's database or social media accounts. They responded by threatening a class action suit against Rudd.

On 12 November, Rudd fired Mandelson, Straw and Joe Carberry, another Remain campaign alumnus, from the Open Britain board. In a joint statement, they told Rudd, 'Your actions ... have done Boris Johnson's work for him. Whereas the People's Vote campaign has been a movement of millions, for you it has simply been a vehicle for your ego.'[33]

Later in November, Rudd resigned as chair of both Baybridge and the Open Britain board, but he continued to control both through his allies. On the 15th, the campaign fell apart completely, after both youth groups left the People's Vote. Baldwin said, 'It was disillusioning and devastating for the young people in the campaign who had worked so hard, to be denied the chance to play a proper part [in the general election]. I think we could have run a much better tactical voting operation than the one we saw. Roland Rudd's vanity and ego and appalling judgement took that away from them.'[34] Rudd's ally claimed the Baldwin faction was disgruntled that they had lost a power struggle. 'Frankly they were outmanoeuvred by Roland … He just wants to see Britain remain in the EU.'

The only way to keep Britain in the EU, of course, was to pass a bill to have a referendum in the House of Commons, or to help candidates who might back a referendum get elected in the general election. The burned-out shell of a campaign was no longer capable of doing either. Having seen his party obliterated in the 2015 general election and the heartache of the referendum loss in 2016, the destruction of the People's Vote campaign was the last straw for McGrory. Abandoning politics, he cut off contact with most of his friends and went to India for several months. Baldwin concluded, 'We achieved a lot together at breakneck speed, transforming what felt like a slightly soulless corporate Remain campaign in the referendum into a genuinely popular and energised movement. But this was an extraordinarily intense time in politics and it's fair to say everyone went a bit mad – some more than others.'

The last word, however, must go to one of the female MPs who had watched the alpha males on both sides lock horns like rutting stags. 'It was a lot of big swinging dicks,' she said. 'It was a lot of fucking ego. It was blokes, blokes, blokes, just being twats, twats, twats.'

PART TWO

KNOCK OUT

THE GENERAL ELECTION

October to December 2019

'People never lie so much as after a hunt,
during a war, or before an election'

– Otto von Bismarck

'The great man of the age is the one who can put into
words the will of his age, tell his age what his will is, and
accomplish it. What he does is the heart and essence of
his age; he actualises his age.'

– Hegel, Philosophy of the Right, *English translation 1942*

'Get Brexit done'

– Boris Johnson (via Dominic Cummings)

GOING FOR GOLD

The Liberal Democrats

Jo Swinson's decision to back a general election in 2019 – one of the half dozen most consequential choices of the entire post-Brexit period – came about because the Liberal Democrats had not listened closely enough to Lynton Crosby. One of the Australian strategist's favourite sayings was that 'polls are actors'. They don't just quantify the state of play, they change the way politicians and voters perceive things and how they subsequently behave. In May that year, the Lib Dems had paid for a superpoll – a new form of advanced statistical analysis, which combined national polling with thousands of demographic data points in each seat to make more reliable predictions about how individual constituencies would vote. The first results of this 'MRP' polling[1] came in May and they were stunning. The model projected the Lib Dems winning 73 seats. More telling, 'We were within 5 points of winning 200 plus,' a party source recalled. For a party which had gone from government in 2010 to near-obliteration in 2015 and had crawled its way back to just 12 seats at the 2017 election, this was heady stuff.

By the time of the party's annual conference in September, some Lib Dems were daring to dream that they might win 100 seats or become the official opposition. For Swinson, there was also a Brexit factor. Make big gains and the balance of power would shift in the Commons. A second referendum would become possible, even probable.

Some party veterans urged caution. In July, Paul Butters was having a drink with Timothy Wild of the Lib Dem press office in the Red Lion, the pub which guards the gates of the parliamentary estate on Whitehall. Butters was a barely reformed ex-spin doctor with the gift of the gab whose low cunning had singlehandedly kept the Lib Dems in the media through their bleakest years. Wild gave the party line: 'This is the biggest opportunity since David Steel for the Lib Dems to realign politics.'

'That's all true,' Butters said. 'But you're not going to pick up more than four seats.' He was by this point working for Best for Britain and had a near-bottomless budget for polling. He had seen how MRPs jumped around. On one occasion he warned Rhiannon Leaman, Swinson's chief of staff, the leader might lose her seat.

'I'll bet you a dinner at Roux you don't gain four seats,' he insisted. Brasserie Roux, just off Parliament Square, was, at the time, the best restaurant in Westminster, where the bill was large and the service slow.

By September, the Lib Dem MRP showed they were still competitive in 180 seats. At the start of October, the *Daily Mirror*'s Ben Glaze reported on a secret document sent to activists entitled 'Team 320'. Headed 'Building a liberal majority', the leaflet asked for donations of £100 a month so 'we can challenge to win a general election'.[2] Another MRP that month showed the Lib Dem tide receding. 'The October one had us winning low 30s,' an official recalled. 'But we were still competitive in around 80 seats.' The numbers pointed to the party trebling their seats, a return to the relevance they had enjoyed under Paddy Ashdown and Charles Kennedy. Beating the SNP to become the third largest party – with a prime minister's question every week – was a realistic goal.

The second reason for Lib Dem confidence was that, for the first time in their history, they had no money worries. In early September, Swinson won a commitment from David Sainsbury, the supermarket scion who had been a key funder of New Labour, that he would contribute £8 million. For the first time the Lib Dems could contemplate spending the maximum allowed by the Electoral Commission, set in 2019 at £19 million.[3] Party strategists wanted to contest 200 seats; now they could.

Swinson was not alone in thinking big. The other actor, alongside the MRP, was Chuka Umunna, the super-slick, super-confident, perhaps even super-talented, former Labour star, who had been the first Change UK MP to join the Lib Dems. Polling from his seat indicated he was going to win if they went now. Since Swinson had become leader, on 22 July, 'a flurry' of potential defectors 'wanted to speak to Jo,' an aide said. Chief whip Alistair Carmichael smuggled them in and out of Portcullis House unseen. 'We had to give them codenames,' one official recalled. 'It was a bit John le Carré. In meetings, you'd hear someone say, "When P comes over …", and all the other people in the meeting would be thinking, "Who the fuck's P?" It was ludicrous.'

In mid-August, Sarah Wollaston, the MP for Totnes, became the second Tigger to join the Lib Dems. Then, in early September, Phillip Lee crossed the floor, and Luciana Berger and Angela Smith both defected, though neither managed to garner the publicity they hoped for. Berger, the 'big get' for the Lib Dems, was trumped by the resignation, on the same day, 5 September, of Jo Johnson. She announced her defection to the London *Evening Standard*. 'It was embargoed until 11 a.m.,' said a senior Lib Dem. 'Jo Johnson announced he was resigning at a quarter to twelve. We got about forty minutes of coverage.' When Smith made her move two days later, she did so in the pages of the *Sunday Times*. Neither she nor most staff at the paper knew that Amber Rudd was quitting the cabinet on the front page that same evening.

The big reveal at the Lib Dem party conference in Bournemouth on 14 September was Sam Gyimah, the former science minister. Party officials booked a hotel room for Gyimah and his wife to wait in during the day, before he emerged at an evening rally. 'Our events team had booked the seediest, shittiest hotel in Bournemouth, miles from the conference centre,' a party official recalled. 'There was paint peeling off the walls. He must have thought he'd defected to a low budget porn production company.' Another party staffer recalled, 'The corridor to their room was like something out of *The Shining*.'

Gyimah's appearance was then delayed by the need to smuggle him into conference unseen. Sam Barratt, the communications director, set up a diversionary press conference with MEP Guy Verhofstadt to distract the hacks while Gyimah slipped in through a fire exit. Unfortunately, Verhofstadt's verbosity meant Gyimah's defection missed the first edition of some newspapers. Nonetheless, in four months, Swinson grew her party from twelve MPs to twenty.

It might have been twenty-one. In September, Michael Dugher, one of Tom Watson's closest friends in politics, suggested that he might join the Liberal Democrats. 'If you'd said to me two years ago, would Tom ever countenance doing anything with the Lib Dems, I would have said "no chance". Now I'd say "who knows?"' In *Left Out*, their account of Corbyn's leadership, Gabriel Pogrund and Patrick Maguire revealed that Jo Swinson, the Lib Dem leader, offered Watson the Lib Dem candidacy in Lewes. A friend of Watson's claimed he rejected the offer after thinking about it 'for five minutes'. The full story was a little different.

For more than two months, Watson had been in secret talks with the third party, leaving senior Lib Dems with the impression that he was seriously contemplating defecting. A senior figure revealed, 'Jo had a couple of long conversations with him face to face and other conversations on the phone.' One of the meetings took place in the House of Lords, a second in a Commons office. They swapped messages through the summer and autumn. Watson explained his transformation from the hyper-aggressive coordinator of the Hodge Hill by-election in 2004, where Swinson remembered the attacks he had ordered on the Lib Dem candidate, to a zen elder statesman. 'I'm a different person,' he declared. They talked about their shared support for a new Brexit referendum – and 'We did discuss him joining,' the senior figure said.

Swinson proceeded cautiously, at first just making clear that he would be welcome. Watson was a big beast, landing him would be 'an amazing political coup'. Watson had a codename too. His was 'Mr X'.

On one occasion all Lib Dem MPs were in a meeting room on the third floor of Portcullis House. Swinson left to see Watson next door in the office of Alistair Carmichael, the chief whip. The MPs' meeting was breaking up when Rhiannon Leaman rushed in and slipped a note to Carmichael. A party official recalled, 'It said, "Keep everyone here for ten minutes whatever you have to do." Every time anyone got up to leave, Alistair came up with some ludicrous reason that they had to stay, because we just couldn't risk them walking in to Mr X.'

A senior Lib Dem said, 'There was certainly a scenario that, early on in the general election campaign, the deputy leader of the Labour Party would announce he was joining the Lib Dems. I'm not saying that was more than 50 per cent likely at any point, but it was a lot more than 5 per cent likely. The moment passed.' Swinson later heard via an intermediary that he had decided not to defect. 'Maybe he was just stringing us along the whole time, but I don't think he was.'

The defectors had disproportionate influence because they were, mostly, more experienced politicians than the other Lib Dem MPs and, particularly in the case of Umunna and Berger, skilled media operators. A People's Vote official compared their arrival to 'a Premier League player dropping down a couple of divisions'. A Lib Dem official said, 'Watching some of our MPs in a meeting with Luciana and Chuka and

Sam and Phillip, was like watching a high school basketball team play the NBA. There was professionalism, strategic thinking, a sense of the big picture. They were plugged in to the business community. It was an eye-opening experience for quite a lot of people.'

Umunna's public profile was arguably higher than Swinson's, though she was relaxed about that. 'She'd just won a leadership election with a stonking great majority,' an ally insisted. 'She had been a golden child of the party for some time. She felt very safe and saw getting Chuka as quite crucial.' However, his presence inevitably had downsides. One Lib Dem said, 'Because he was charming, everyone treated Chuka like a doyen. And I sat there thinking, "Did we forget Change UK?" He just tried to launch a political movement and it was one of the most catastrophic things people have ever seen.' Umunna had been a Lib Dem MP for four months when he agitated for another catastrophic decision.

Swinson was keen on an election, but Umunna was 'the most vociferous' advocate of one. On the evening of Thursday 24 October Swinson summoned her 'strategic group' of MPs, peers and key aides, to decide whether to gamble. They included deputy leader Ed Davey, chief whip Alistair Carmichael and Jonny Oates, a former chief of staff to Nick Clegg, now a peer. Umunna and Phillip Lee were also present. Over the summer, Davey had wargamed the party's options. He concluded the best time for an election would be after Johnson had failed to deliver Brexit 'but where it could still be stopped'.

Swinson asked Umunna to spend Friday with the Commons clerks discussing the practicalities of an election bill. 'If there was going to be an election before 31 January, it needed to be called the next week,' a senior Lib Dem said. The weight of opinion was in favour.

Swinson's argument was also influenced by the EU's position on an extension. The Benn Act had forced Johnson to ask for one, but it could not compel Brussels to grant one. Swinson spoke to Clément Beaune, Emmanuel Macron's adviser on Europe, who said that France was not keen on another extension unless it was for a purpose. 'You wasted the last couple,' he said, but made clear an election would do the trick.

In Swinson's eyes, calling an election would be not only the safest way to guarantee an extension and avoid no-deal, but also – if the MRP was right – the route to a referendum. She envisaged Labour doing badly and Jeremy Corbyn being 'replaced by somebody it would be easier to work with'. By contrast, if Parliament kept Johnson in stasis, she believed the

Tories and Labour would agree a new programme motion for the WAB, the bill would pass and Brexit would happen. Swinson predicted Johnson would offer Labour MPs in Leave seats a 'fig leaf amendment on workers rights' to give them cover to back the bill. 'Anyone presented with those circumstances would conclude the gamble was worth it,' an aide argued.

The final factor proved to be Swinson's memories of 2010, when Nick Clegg's performance in the election debates had momentarily transformed Lib Dem fortunes. All she had to do now was to get on the same stage as Johnson and Corbyn. She boarded the Caledonian sleeper train from Glasgow to London with her five-year-old son, getting to her home in south-east London in time for an 8 a.m. conference call. There she fired the trigger on Election 2019. Politics is an unglamorous business. That day, Swinson's husband, the former MP Duncan Hames, went to hospital with abdominal pain, so the leader spent the day juggling child-care with a call on candidate selection and another with Ian Blackford of the SNP. The draft bill named polling day as 9 December, selected so Johnson would not have time to pass his withdrawal agreement bill. Blackford was planning to send a letter to the EU. They agreed to take joint ownership of both. Politics is also a brutal business. Swinson's spokesman Ben Rathe was due to go on his honeymoon on polling day. He broke the news to his wife, cancelled his honeymoon and then told the *Observer* there was going to be an election.

The SNP's decision to back the election had two motivations. The nationalists had won just 35 seats in 2017, partly thanks to the resurgence of the Scottish Tories under Ruth Davidson, 21 fewer than in 2015. The polls suggested the party would be able to regain much of that lost ground in 2019. The other reason was the looming trial of Alex Salmond, its former leader, who was facing fourteen criminal charges, including two counts of attempted rape. The case was expected to expose SNP infighting and put Nicola Sturgeon on the spot about what she knew.

The 'most vocal' Lib Dem opponents of an election were two former leaders: Vince Cable and Tim Farron. Nick Harvey, the party's chief executive, also argued against at the federal board meeting. Of the new recruits Angela Smith and Heidi Allen were both dissenting voices. Also vociferous in his opposition was ex-Tory Phillip Lee, whose view was, 'The government is snookered, so leave them snookered.' Lee had learned of the Lib Dem–SNP talks from the Trains and Buses WhatsApp group and feared straight away (and accurately) that he would lose his seat.

When the Lib Dem shadow cabinet debated the plan, Swinson's approach was: 'If we don't do this, Brexit is going to happen.'

Lee responded, 'If you do this, Brexit is going to happen.'[4] Having tried and failed to talk Swinson around, he ran into Guto Bebb and Keir Starmer, fellow members of Trains and Buses. 'I'm sorry,' he said. 'I've tried. But they're going to go for it. It's a bloody nightmare.'

On 28 October, Boris Johnson tried to force an election under the Fixed-term Parliaments Act. Once again, he failed to reach the threshold of two thirds of MPs after Labour abstained. Johnson won by 299 votes to 70, but was 144 short of the magic number. Afterwards, the PM signalled he was prepared to back the Lib Dem–SNP one-line bill. But he insisted that the election be on 12 December, after some students broke up for Christmas. The Lib Dems wanted the 9th when students, many of whom voted Lib Dem, would still be on campus.

The following day, 29 October, Jeremy Corbyn caved and the bill passed in a single day. The second reading, naming 12 December as polling day, was approved without a vote. At committee stage, Labour tabled an amendment for an election on 9 December. The Tories defeated this by 315 votes to 295. On third reading, unwilling to be seen to be blocking an election, Labour MPs voted with the government. The election was approved by 438 votes to 20. Farcically, the Lib Dems and the SNP abstained because they wanted the other date.

John Bercow chaired his final Prime Minister's Questions a day later, as the bill was fast-tracked through the Lords. It received royal assent on 31 October. The parliamentary battles over Brexit were over. The man who controversially shaped them had come to the end of the road as well. Bullying allegations against Bercow, later proven, prevented him getting a peerage. Tory wits contemplated handing him the British Empire Medal, the lowliest honour, instead.

The decision to hold an election came to be seen as a calamity for Swinson and the Lib Dems and for those who wanted to block Brexit. Phillip Lee branded it 'ludicrous, irresponsible, the worst political decision probably of a generation'.[5] Justine Greening called it 'a sliding doors moment' and a 'catastrophic error of judgement'.

No one should be spared criticism, but Swinson made her decision for the same reason as the SNP: both thought an immediate election would give them more MPs. That the SNP was proved right, and the Lib Dem leader was not, meant the 'blame', where it was apportioned, fell on her shoulders. It is also a matter of mathematical fact that the Lib Dems and Labour alone could not block Johnson's election bill. Conversely, the SNP alone had the votes, with the Tories, to force an election, though in practice they wanted political cover after being blamed for installing the Thatcher government in 1979.

While it was a bold gamble, the polling suggested a good result for Swinson's party, with considerable upside if she managed to sneak ahead of Labour in the early part of the campaign. Previously, Swinson had made selfless choices. 'Jo Swinson had an opportunity to do a deal with Corbyn, become deputy prime minister and lead the country towards a second referendum,' observed an unlikely admirer, Richard Tice of the Brexit Party. 'She took an incredibly principled stance ... instead of looking after her own personal interests ... and that was the Remain side doomed.'[6]

Were there alternatives? Some hoped to hold Johnson in stasis until he called a referendum himself. Others believed that if Brexit had been strung out until the Covid pandemic struck the UK, in March 2020, Britain might never have left the EU. Richard Corbett, the leader of Labour MEPs, claimed that Nick Brown, Labour's chief whip, told him, 'We are three votes away from getting a majority for an amendment for putting it to a referendum.' Corbett said, 'At that point the Liberal Democrats accepted an election ... It was a fatal mistake.'[7]

Yet, even Dominic Grieve did not believe the Bresistance could delay an election beyond Christmas. He thought Swinson's decision 'wholly mistaken' but, if no referendum was called and Johnson did not pass a withdrawal agreement bill in 2019, he thought an election 'inevitable' in January 2020.

As in the spring, efforts in autumn 2019 to create a 'Remain alliance' never quite took off. In September, David Gauke approached Swinson and Carmichael on behalf of fifteen of the twenty-one whipless Tories to offer a deal. 'If they would give former Tory MPs a clear run in ten to fifteen seats,' he said, 'we would endorse them in the other six hundred-plus seats and agree to cooperate closely with them if elected.'[8] They did not want to join the Lib Dems or back the revoke policy, but Gauke argued, 'It will demonstrate that the Tory Party has properly split and that moderate, Remain Tory voters should back someone else.'

By October, the Lib Dems had come to an agreement with Dominic Grieve not to stand against him in Beaconsfield. Grieve had first been approached by members of the local Lib Dem association. He then went to see Carmichael who agreed not to put up a candidate. The Lib Dems also stood aside to help Anna Soubry in Broxtowe.

Swinson took a different approach to Gauke, who was fighting as an independent in South West Hertfordshire, where the Lib Dems had no chance of winning. Two days before nominations closed, she told him he could be the Lib Dem candidate, but there was no question of them standing aside. 'They were focused on winning over the votes of Labour voters in their nearest target seat of St Albans,' where the wildly unpopular Tory Anne Main would lose, Gauke explained. 'They feared endorsing me would put such voters off.'[9] Gauke argued that the only way to stop Johnson was to attract disaffected Tory voters and said he would campaign for the Lib Dems in St Albans, but to no avail. Swinson's decision made no difference to his fate, but Gauke thought it a missed opportunity to appeal to pro-Remain Conservative voters who felt they had no political home.

Grieve spent £10,000 of his own money on a mailshot to half the constituency and, as donations flooded in, he was able to send a leaflet to the other households. Six hundred volunteers joined his campaign, dwarfing the official Tory effort. Grieve remained outwardly optimistic but he knew after a couple of days door knocking that he would lose. Many Tory voters said they wanted to support him but could not because they were frightened of a Corbyn government.

Heidi Allen finally joined the Lib Dems on 7 October. Just three weeks later she announced she would not fight the general election. Allen's behaviour was infuriating, but her decision to quit concealed a traumatic personal epiphany, which revealed much about the pressure on MPs. A week after she joined the Lib Dems, she received a 'really horrible' email from a constituent. It said, 'I definitely wouldn't have voted for you if I'd known that you'd murdered a baby.' Allen had bravely spoken in the Commons about having an abortion, during debates about services in Northern Ireland. 'The penny just dropped,' she said later. 'I'd been feeling like a machine for a very long time. I'd had two days' holiday all year.' In August a former Royal Marine was jailed for twenty-four weeks after threatening Allen, posting aerial images of her home on social media. 'It felt like my private and personal life had merged completely into one. I could feel myself shrinking as a person.' Of all the Tory defectors, Allen had the best chance of holding her seat as a Lib Dem,[10] but on 29 October, she told herself, 'This is just daft, Heidi, you've got to get out.'

Two days later, Antoinette Sandbach became the party's eighth, and last, defector of 2019. Two other Labour MPs, one in the south-east, one in the south-west were 'sensationally close' to changing parties.

Liberal Democrat strategy at the start of the campaign was still based on the giddy optimism of the summer. They had 220 target seats. 'Eighty seats were getting the full whack: literature, all the digital, all the direct mail,' an official explained. 'The 140 were basically moonshots. They weren't getting any paper [leaflets through the door], but many were getting direct mail and full digital support.' Swinson pushed for a big battleground against the advice of field director Dave McCobb.

As the campaign kicked off, the party was on around 23 per cent in the polls, three or four points behind Labour. Their approach was a 'pivot strategy'. If they could start strongly and get ahead of Corbyn, they were ready to expand the 80 top-tier battleground targets. That this never happened came down to several factors, which had their roots in the previous months: the party's Brexit policy, Swinson's unrealistic ambitions, and the campaign's failure to sell a national message.

Ask their political rivals where the Lib Dem campaign bombed and they were clear: when the party adopted revoking Brexit as policy. When Swinson won the leadership election, she was asked if she would vote for Brexit in Parliament if a second referendum produced another Leave win. She said, 'No, because I was elected on a firm manifesto pledge to fight for the UK's place in the EU.' It was a sincere statement of her views, but sounded, at best, politically naive, at worst, undemocratic.

Vince Cable had sharpened up the Lib Dem position, with his 'Bollocks to Brexit' slogan, but between 2016 and 2019 the party had not capitalised on its position as the most unequivocally anti-Brexit party. Six million people had signed a petition calling for Article 50 to be revoked. As the Lib Dem conference in Bournemouth approached, grass-roots members submitted motions to stop Brexit to the conference committee, which decided what would be debated. Swinson felt she should lead the process rather than have it imposed on her. There was also a fear that Labour would use its conference, a week later, to endorse a second referendum. The Lib Dems needed to go further to distinguish themselves. Tom Baldwin joked, 'I guess if Labour had gone for Revoke, the Lib Dems would have started a campaign to join the Euro.'[11]

When Swinson's three predecessors – Vince Cable, Tim Farron and Menzies Campbell – got wind of what was intended, they demanded to see her. A party source said, 'They all went in and said, "The Revoke policy is dire and this will really hurt the party. Please don't do it."' Farron said, 'I'm not putting my seat on the line for Revoke.'

Swinson was unmoved: 'I'm doing it, it's really important.'

The policy agreed said that if a majority Lib Dem government was elected, they would revoke Article 50. 'The debate was not "Should we back Revoke?", it was 'Should we have Revoke if we win a general election?" or, should it just be "Revoke right now".' Swinson thought the criticisms ridiculous. 'It's not like it was a secret that we want to stop Brexit,' she argued. Revoke was also the position of many donors, some giving for the first time. An aide noted, 'The donors we were getting were more likely to give if we were Remain on stilts.'

The bottom line was that Joanne Kate Swinson wanted to stop Brexit. In the 2016 referendum she had surprised herself at how she felt after the vote to leave. She had not thought she cared about the EU in the same way as she cared about saving the Union during the 2014 Scottish independence referendum. But the result in 2016 felt like a repudiation of her liberal values: working together with like-minded countries to tackle issues like climate change; a pulling up of the drawbridge on what she held dear. Europe became a defining element of her political identity. 'It just felt like one of these pivotal moments,' she said. Swinson lost her seat in 2015 but when Theresa May called an election in 2017, she thought 'for about a nanosecond' about standing. Swinson felt a visceral need to come back, to fight for her vision of the world.

The Revoke plan sailed through conference and by the end of September the Lib Dems, luxuriating in a 4-point bounce, were ahead in the polls for the first time among people who voted Remain. 'The policy was popular at that point,' an official said. The election framing they wanted was Johnson heading for no-deal, versus Revoke, but that was sunk when Johnson secured a deal. From then on, the policy was seen, by most voters, as extreme. 'I never met anyone on the doorstep congratulating me on that policy,' said Phillip Lee, 'but I met plenty of people who told me that it was anti-democratic.'[12] Paul Butters, canvassing in his native Wolverhampton, got spat at on one doorstep. The Revoke policy also made it more difficult to recruit defectors. Swinson had been wooing whipless Tory Margot James. 'I think Margot would have defected but that put her off,' a source said.

The signature moment of the campaign for Ben Rathe came on a train travelling back from a children's question time event in York. With a colleague, he found himself at a table for four next to a pleasant old couple from Middlesbrough. They had barely sat down when the wife, gesturing at her husband, said, 'You're going to regret sitting here. He's a talker.' Amid conversation about his kids and Christmas, the man turned to politics. 'You know,' he said, 'I don't get those Liberals, saying they're going to cancel it all. It's not very democratic, is it?' Rathe looked at his colleague, eyes imploring: *Don't tell him what we do*, but also, *We're fucked*. When the man asked about them, she said, 'We work at a charity.' It began to feel like the charity case was the Lib Dems.

After Revoke, the biggest problem for the Lib Dems was Swinson's repeated insistence that she could be prime minister. This had begun as the kind of brazen optimism which it often suits minor parties to adopt. In an interview with the *Mirror* before party conference, Ben Glaze asked her if she really could become prime minister and Swinson replied, 'Absolutely – and what's more, I think I would be a better prime minister than either Boris Johnson or Jeremy Corbyn.' On the conference stage, she offered herself to activists as 'your candidate for prime minister' and was rewarded with a standing ovation.

There were three reasons for this approach. Internal polling showed the public was interested in a fresh-faced woman, a contrast to the pale, male and stale leadership of the other main parties. The second reason was the influence on the Lib Dems of a Canadian political book called *Building the Orange Wave*, by Brad Lavigne, the campaign director for the New Democrats, the Canadian equivalent of Labour. It detailed how the leader, Jack Layton, had gone from a distant third place to become the leader of the opposition by making a bold pitch to be prime minister. In her acceptance speech as leader, Swinson had said, 'I stand before you today, not just as the leader of the Liberal Democrats, but as a candidate for prime minister. There is no limit to my ambition for our party and for our movement. I am ready to take our party into a general election and win it.' A Lib Dem source said, 'She virtually lifted the words from Jack Layton.'

Finally, insisting she could win gave Swinson a way of ducking the first question the Lib Dems were asked at the start of a general election campaign: would they join a coalition, or put one of the two main parties into government? Swinson found this particularly unpalatable, regarding both Johnson and Corbyn as unfit to lead. But saying she was not prepared to go into coalition with either of them would reduce the influence of the Lib Dems. In 2017, Tim Farron had ruled out a coalition and seen his relevance evaporate. 'Voters were able to remember two things about Tim Farron,' a party official recalled. 'One, he didn't like gay people. And two, he told everyone he wasn't going to win. That was it.' Olly Grender, a Lib Dem peer who came back for the campaign, recalled how Charles Kennedy also got into trouble for suggesting he would not win and urged Swinson to take a different approach.

When Swinson launched the Lib Dem campaign, on 5 November, she declared, 'As Liberal Democrat leader, what I am offering to the public is a Liberal Democrat government.' One of the Change UK defectors felt their heart sink. 'That was when she lost the room,' the MP said. After the launch, Sam Barratt watched the BBC's Vicki Young film her piece to camera, half of which was her discussing whether Swinson's PM claim was credible. Barratt's view was that what mattered was not what you said, but what voters heard. In a meeting that day he warned, 'This has not landed well.' The reply came, 'They're talking about our message.' Barratt responded: 'People saying you're mad isn't people talking about your message, that's people saying you're mad.'

Long after the election Swinson explained her approach: 'Obviously, I didn't think I was going to be prime minister. But by presenting the alternative, I hoped to get momentum for the party. Given where we were in the polls, with the possibility of getting into the debates, with the potential for the defections, with the massive amount of money that I'd fundraised, we did have an opportunity to say to people, "You could have something different", which would break the mould of British politics.'

This was a plausible argument at the start of the campaign, but not two weeks later as Swinson's continued insistence that she could end up in Number 10 became the subject of ridicule. It fell to Rathe to stage an intervention. 'You have to stop saying this because you sound ridiculous,' he told her.

'I think it gives people hope,' the leader replied.

'It makes you sound crazy. It gives everyone permission to switch off from everything else you say because you sound like you're not living on this planet.'

'So, what do I say instead?' she asked.

Rathe and another aide, Sara Mosavi, swapped ideas, their best argument being that Swinson had done a lot with a few MPs in the last Parliament. 'Give me more MPs and I can stop Brexit permanently.' Swinson admitted later, 'We probably should have done that a few days earlier.'

The other significant factor in Swinson's approach was a split at the heart of her campaign team between those who wanted to focus on the 'ground war' – local doorstep campaigning – and those who believed the 'air war' on the broadcast media was key to a breakthrough. The differences were exaggerated by the fact that Swinson was still putting her team together as the campaign began. Rathe had to work his notice and only joined at the end of September, Leaman a little earlier. Swinson had only just installed a new chief executive, Mike Dixon. 'The party itself was not in a fit state to run a general election,' Phillip Lee said.[13] The campaign director was Shaun Roberts, on his second spell with the party. His deputy, in charge of literature, was Denise Baron, an American who had been head of insight for the People's Vote. The front of the main leaflet said, 'Jo Swinson: Britain's next prime minister.' Sam Barratt listened dismayed as Baron argued in meetings, 'The air war doesn't matter.' He and Rathe both resisted. 'It really did matter,' one aide said, 'because that was the lens through which 99 per cent of people were going to view this election.'

The desire to focus on local leafleting also had a damaging effect on the communications team's ability to sell policy stories to the media. 'In the first week of the campaign, we launched every single one of our main six policies,' an official noted. 'The view was that we needed to get an early start. We wanted to stick it all on the leaflets. Everything was being dictated by the literature.' Barratt and Rathe argued they should hold back a meaty announcement for the manifesto launch and other policies for major interviews. Roberts and Baron disagreed.

The big policies did not even land well. The best of them – thirty-five hours a week of free childcare – which Barratt had intended for manifesto day, went exclusively to the *Guardian*, in the hope it would splash the paper. It ended up buried on page 10. 'That was the moment I realised we were getting royally screwed,' an official said.

There was another complication – Chuka Umunna. 'At the start of the election campaign there were two comms grids,' a source said. 'There was the party comms grid and then there was a Chuka comms grid. He had these random ideas and just went and did things.' With no policy, the communications team got broadcast and newspaper coverage for Swinson by focusing on a 'visual of the day'. These saw the leader start a fire at a kids' camp, don boxing gloves (a trick borrowed from Boris Johnson), drive a digger and go up in a crane. This was in the best traditions of Lib Dem comms. When Phil Reilly ran the party media operation under the coalition, he told his team: 'We need to be first, funny, or interesting.' Umunna, who sat on the campaign committee, disagreed. 'His view was that we should do serious, weighty press conferences,' an aide remembered. Rathe explained, 'We can't do that because no one will care because we are the Liberal Democrats.' Umunna had made the same mistake in Change UK. 'He could never get himself outside the mindset of, "They'll cover us because we're who we are",' a source said. 'He was used to getting covered in the Labour Party.'

More curious was Swinson's failure to harness the new talent. She could have presented the defectors as a group of 'sensibles' who had come together, in contrast to the hard leftists of Corbyn's Labour. A former Lib Dem strategist said, 'They should have turned it into Chuka, her and Luciana, whereas they made it all about her.'

In Conservative campaign headquarters, the Tory team watched as the Lib Dems 'carpet-bombed' their top targets with leaflets while alienating moderate voters who might have been minded to vote against Johnson. 'They made two big mistakes,' a Conservative strategist said. 'The Revoke position was just not credible. Even sincere Remainers knew that that was undemocratic. The other one was putting Jo Swinson front and centre of the campaign the way they did.'

It was the Lib Dems' misfortune that the Conservatives not only had a more popular central policy, they had also built their most harmonious election campaign team in living memory.

ISAAC NOT ISHMAEL

The Tories

Boris Johnson looked visibly worried. The prime minister was sitting with Dominic Cummings and Lee Cain discussing the election campaign. It was 6 November, a day late for the fitting symbolism of the Gunpowder Plot, yet it felt to Johnson like the campaign was blowing up in his face. To compound his frustration, the gaffes which had thrown it off course, were not even his own. Turning to Cummings, he sought reassurance: 'Dom, you're running the campaign, right?'

'No, Isaac's running the campaign,' Cummings replied.

'Yeah, yeah, I know, but you're really running the campaign, right?'

'No, no, Isaac's running the campaign.'

'What I mean is: it's Isaac's campaign, but you're overseeing it?'

Cummings snapped: 'No, this is Isaac's campaign, I've got all this shit to do, this is Isaac's campaign, he'll be great.'

Isaac was Isaac Levido, a protégé of Lynton Crosby, the 'Wizard of Oz', the political strategist who had masterminded Johnson's victories in London. It was not his first rodeo. In 2015, Levido had been in charge of enforcing Tory message discipline. On the surface Levido, thirty-six, an intense but drily humorous Australian, could not have been more different from Cummings: calm where Cummings was wired, softly spoken where Cummings shouted, hirsute where Cummings was bald, proud of his R. M. Williams boots, where Cummings' clothes were in fashion twice a decade in the same way a stopped clock accurately records the time. Levido had jet-black hair, a thick but sculpted beard and watchful eyes. What united them was a gift for reading opinion polls and devising an effective political message, the discipline and determination to stick to the script even in moments of adversity and the ability to inspire a team.

Levido needed all of these qualities after a disastrous twenty-four hours had seen one member of the cabinet forced to publicly apologise and another to resign. The apology came from Jacob Rees-Mogg, the leader of the Commons, who had made crass remarks about the 2017 Grenfell Tower fire[1] on Nick Ferrari's LBC radio show. The report into the tragedy, in which seventy-two people died – the worst loss of life to fire in domestic premises since the Second World War – found that fifty-five of those who perished had been told to stay in their homes by the London Fire Brigade. 'I think if either of us were in a fire, whatever the fire brigade said, we would leave the burning building,' Rees-Mogg opined. 'It just seems the common sense thing to do.' Much of what passes for news in general elections is confected outrage but there was nothing confected about the reaction from the Justice 4 Grenfell group.

On the morning of 6 November, James Cleverly was booked to do the morning round of broadcast interviews. But when viewers tuned in to Kay Burley's show on *Sky News*, they found the legendarily combative presenter announcing, 'There is an empty chair here. It was supposed to be filled by the chairman of the Conservative Party. Where is he?' Burley wanted to talk about Rees-Mogg and allegations that a cabinet minister lied about his knowledge of an aide's role in 'sabotaging' a rape trial.

The cabinet minister was Alun Cairns, the Welsh secretary. His aide, Ross England, a Tory candidate for the Welsh Assembly, made claims about a woman's sexual history in court, causing the trial to collapse. Cairns denied that he knew anything about it but BBC Wales found he had been sent an email about the case a year before. Rees-Mogg was banished to Somerset and told to stay off television. Cairns was forced to resign. 'We shot everyone in sight,' said a campaign official. 'Alun Cairns, gone, Jacob Rees-Mogg put in a freezer.'

For all his bravado, Johnson had been 'really wobbly' about forcing the election. 'He didn't think the country was quite ready for it,' an ally revealed. At the start of the campaign, the Tories had a lead of 11 points in the polls, but there were grounds for doubt that the campaign would be plain sailing. As the authors of *The British General Election of 2019* noted, 'It was unusual for a government to want to fight an election on the back of what was, ostensibly, a high-profile policy failure. Britain had not left the EU by 31 October.'[2] In calling the election, the Vote Leavers had the backing of Carrie Symonds. 'She actually supported us,' one said. But when things started badly, 'Carrie was in his ear,' an aide recalled. Levido had worked on Zac Goldsmith's campaign for London mayor in 2016, run by Mark Fullbrook, Crosby's business partner. Symonds, who was very close to Goldsmith, disapproved of the highly negative attacks on Sadiq Khan Fullbrook ordered. Levido, in turn, regarded Goldsmith as a poor candidate. That was not a problem he would have with Johnson. 'The guy can carry a day and a message like no one else,' Levido told friends. Whatever the PM's nervousness, Levido had been groomed for the role for months.

When it was announced that Cummings was going into Number 10, Levido had been watching test cricket with Paul Stephenson and Ameet Gill, the rival referendum campaign strategists who were now business partners. They persuaded him he should run the election for Johnson and pressed his case with others. Levido had already appeared on the radar of the Back Boris team, as a potential head of strategy. Even before Cummings decided to join the government, Crosby had called Eddie Lister and told him, 'Isaac's fucking great, you should bring him in.'

Levido grew up in a surfing village, his mother a nurse, his father a small-town lawyer who read voraciously about the Kennedys. After degrees in political science and accounting at university in Canberra, he worked for an Sydney insolvency firm then moved to the US in 2009, combining a master's at Georgetown University with working for the National Republican Senatorial Committee during the 2010 midterm elections. That led to a job with the Australian embassy covering Congress during the 2012 presidential election. He moved to the UK, called in a favour, met Crosby and then 'politely hassled' him until he got a job. After the 2015 general election, Levido opened an office for Crosby in Washington, D.C., but returned to help on the 2017 election. He left the PR firm CTF the same year to work for the Liberal Party in Australia, first for Malcolm Turnbull, then Scott Morrison.

Levido met Lister and then went for a pint with Lee Cain. Their first encounter was a little awkward, but Cain was soon calling the Australian, 'one of the best people I've ever worked with'. Cummings and Levido did not meet each other until the morning Johnson became prime minister. On Cummings' way to Number 10 for the first time, they had coffee in Patisserie Valerie in Marylebone to 'sniff each other out'. Cummings said, 'There's a reasonable chance there's going to be an election, it might be in a year, it might be in a few months. You need to grip CCHQ [Conservative campaign headquarters] and get the place into a position where we can fight an election. I don't want to run the campaign. I'm going to have to focus on the government.'

Levido enquired about Johnson's intentions: 'You guys are actually going to try and get a deal with the EU first, right?' His strong view was that to avoid the backlash which greeted May in 2017, Johnson needed to show the public he had tried everything to do Brexit.

Cummings said, yes, Johnson would try for a deal, 'but we obviously need to prepare for all eventualities'. He then explained how he wanted things to work. 'We'll have a very, very small group who decides the core strategic decisions. You run CCHQ, not me. I will coordinate between the campaign and Number 10. With Boris being what he is, I won't be able to babysit him and manage the building.'

Levido was game but he had to have control, not the appearance of it. 'A campaign can't be run by a committee. It needs one person in charge,' he said. 'I need to be able to make all the calls on staff, all the calls on supplies. I talk you through it but I'm in charge.'

To the surprise of his Vote Leave colleagues, Cummings agreed. To everyone's consternation, he then stuck to the agreement. From that moment Isaac, as in his biblical namesake, was the chosen one, Cummings a self-imposed Ishmael, exiled in Downing Street.

Levido stabilised his position that first difficult Wednesday with a long address to staff in CCHQ. He told them to hold their nerve; the campaign proper had not even begun. Levido had decided to use the power of incumbency to stage a theatrical launch the following week with a Johnson speech outside Number 10. The recent campaign in Australia had taught him in tight spots to 'ignore the commentators, don't panic'. His mantra was, 'Focus on things you can control.'

That evening Levido cemented the loyalty of his team, laying out some 'rules of campaigns' he had learned over the years. 'It's going to be a high-pressure environment,' he said. 'Don't be a cunt.' Cue: cathartic laughter. 'Be nice to each other. Everyone's going to be without a lot of sleep. Help your colleagues.' Levido offered lifestyle advice: 'Go for a walk round the block. Don't eat shit.' He told a story he had heard from Crosby's pollster, Mark Textor. 'Tex says someone on a campaign got scurvy because they had McDonald's for thirty nights.'

There was a serious message too. 'Everyone has their job, and a campaign is successful when everyone does the job they've been given. Don't worry about someone else's job. Just worry about doing your job.' This was Levido, the benevolent dictator. 'I know some of you have important jobs with ministers and you might feel like now you've got a job that's not. That's the job you're going to do. I won't suffer any bullshit with egos. I'm happy to throw you out the door. There are a lot of people that want to come into this building. You've been chosen for a reason.' He concluded with a call to arms: 'I'll ask a lot of you. I might be short at times. I hope I'm never unreasonable. But at the end of the day, we're standing in the most important building in Britain for the next five weeks. There's a huge amount at stake. It's not often you get a chance to make history. Relish it, try to enjoy.'

Cummings was not even present at the pre-election planning meeting in CCHQ on 24 October and neither was Eddie Lister. Instead, Levido and Cain led the ninety-minute session on the election 'grid' and messaging. They heard details of the manifesto from policy chief Munira Mirza and her co-author Rachel Wolf, a former aide to Michael Gove. Also present were Iain Carter, the head of the Conservative research department (CRD), Caroline Preston, the head of CCHQ communications, and Meg Powell-Chandler, who ran the grid in Number 10 and provided the perspective of the One Nation wing of the party.

Levido's plan was shaped by the failures of the 2017 election campaign and the success he had recently enjoyed as campaign director for the Australian Liberal Party. There would be a shorter manifesto 'far more politically stress-tested than the last one' after the 'dementia tax' fiasco that derailed May's campaign.[3] On that occasion, May's aides had been desperate to include difficult policies so she could claim a mandate after the election. This time, Ross Kempsell, from the policy unit, led an audit of pledges in previous manifestos, creating a six-hundred-line spreadsheet, to prevent claims that previous commitments had been dropped. Levido's view was that campaigns were a big communications exercise, with the leader and doorstep activists delivering the same message. 'Strategy' was understanding which issues and phrases could be used to change and reinforce opinions, to lock in the party's base supporters and reach others who were persuadable – and, just as importantly, not to waste time on those who were unreachable. That and relentless attention to detail, to spotting mistakes before they were made. 'A lot of people think campaigns are about thinking big thoughts, that if you take care of the big stuff the small stuff will take care of itself,' he explained. 'It's actually the other way around.'

His first priority was to convince voters that Johnson had a 'burning reason' for forcing the election. Addressing spads, he said, 'The reason we are doing this is to deliver a functioning government that will not only deliver on Brexit policy but on domestic priorities.' In a memo to Johnson, also sent on 24 October, Levido and Michael Brooks, his numbers man, noted, 'One of the reasons that the 2017 election was a political failure was the lack of a burning platform … Voters saw no reason for Theresa May to call an election – apart from naked self-interest stemming from her double-digit lead over Labour in the polls. There is a risk we fall into the same trap.'[4]

The second lesson of 2017, reinforced by Levido's experience helping Scott Morrison, was that the Tories needed to attack Corbyn's economic credibility, largely absent in 2017. Levido and Brooks – affectionately dubbed 'Rain Man' by Tory aides – had enjoyed success with similar assaults on Australian Labor Party leader Bill Shorten's energy and tax policies. Shorten crumbled under pressure.

The good news for Levido was that he had money to spend. Between 6 and 12 November, the Tories raised more than £5.6 million while Labour declared £218,500 for the same period. At a political cabinet meeting on 26 September, Ben Elliot, the party chairman, said Johnson had helped the party raise more that month than any previous September. 'A lot of money came off the bench,' a source said.

On 3 November, the Sunday evening before the election was called, Levido took Johnson and Cummings through his campaign grid, going over the plan day by day in the prime minister's office in Number 10. Brooks and Cain were also present, along with Darren Mott, a CCHQ lifer who was there to answer questions about the field operation; plus Lister and Ben Gascoigne. Levido went through a list of key decisions which needed signing off: the launch and rally; the grid and logistics; campaign days; target seats; communicating with MPs; the identity of key spokespeople; the TV debates and the prep for them; the slogan and bus design; and an update on research and messaging.[5]

'Think of the campaign as a court case, or trial,' Levido said. 'Opening arguments, closing arguments and a long evidentiary phase in the middle. Our opening argument and our closing argument have to be the framing message: "We did not want this election. We are having this election because Parliament is broken. Get Brexit done, move on, unleash Britain's potential."' Levido's draft grid set aside four days for the opening argument, 'Choice at this election', with individual days on 'delivery v dither and delay' on Brexit; a 'stronger economy v reckless spending', 'strong v weak' public services and 'controlled immigration v open border'. There were policy announcements planned on GP appointments, knife crime and immigration, followed by the launch of the campaign bus and a six-day 'benefits of Brexit' phase and then the manifesto.[6] The focus in 2017 had been on bold policy, this time policies were there to support a top-line political narrative. In meetings like this Johnson could be distracted or play to the crowd, but those present saw a politician who was 'incredibly focused'.

This was also the meeting at which 'Get Brexit Done: Unleashing Britain's Potential' was signed off as the campaign slogan. There was never any doubt about the first three words. 'As much as I would like to claim credit for writing that, it was actually the voters,' Levido said. 'That was a sentiment that we were hearing coming up time and time again. It was literally how people expressed themselves in focus groups.'[7]

At party conference, three weeks earlier, the strapline had been 'Get Brexit Done: Invest in our NHS, schools and police.' In the intervening period, Brooks tested several different versions. Levido wanted a slogan which would allow Johnson to talk about his great enthusiasms: big infrastructure projects and the sunlit uplands he perceived around Brexit. 'I need him on song,' he told colleagues. Among the other slogans tested was 'Get Brexit Done: Build a Brighter Future' but voters preferred the dynamism of 'unleashing' potential. 'The PM didn't actually like it at the beginning,' a source said.

At political cabinet on 5 November, Levido outlined his electoral strategy for ministers, twin pledges to 'get Brexit done' and then 'deliver the people's priorities'. He showed they could win a majority with a 50–50 strategy of defending 50 vulnerable seats and attacking 50 more, most held by Labour. The metric Levido followed most closely was the share of 2017 Tory voters the party had maintained. It had started the year at 90 per cent and stayed there until March and then 'fell off a cliff'. In a single weekend, MPs and activists reported a dramatic change in mood on the doorstep as voters realised Brexit was not going happen on 29 March. By the middle of June, 'We were bleeding more of our 2017 vote to the Brexit Party than we were retaining,' Levido told ministers. This changed during the leadership contest, as Leave voters heard all the candidates talking up the 31 October deadline. By the time of the political cabinet, retention was at 72 per cent, while Labour retained just 51 per cent of those who had supported Corbyn two years earlier.

The key voters were not actually Labour-to-Tory switchers in the northern Leave seats, which had become known as the 'Red Wall' because they were once a Labour firewall running the breadth of the country, but the 16 per cent of Tory supporters who were now backing the Brexit Party and the 12 per cent who had gone to the Lib Dems. In a memo for Johnson on 9 October, Levido and Brooks explained, 'There are very few voters still currently supporting Labour (around 4% of Labour's total support) that would prefer the Conservatives in government. Therefore, the opportunity for the Conservatives to increase their vote share is among Liberal Democrat and Brexit Party voters where a third (34%) and two-thirds (69%) of voters respectively would prefer the Conservatives to be in government.'[8]

Brexit Party voters were furious about the delays and wanted to leave, deal or no-deal. Lib Dem defectors were fearful of no-deal. Levido and Brooks polled which outcomes both blocks of voters would 'prefer', 'accept' or 'not accept'. Lib Dem defectors were plus 70 per cent, prefer or accept, on a new Brexit deal and minus 66 per cent on no-deal. The Brexit Party defectors were plus 75 per cent on no-deal but still plus 60 per cent on a new deal. In short, getting a deal was the glue which could unite both groups of lost voters and bring them home.[9]

While most media attention focused on whether Johnson could seize Leave-backing Labour seats in the north, Levido said the key to victory could be the Lib Dem surge, which could hurt Labour in Midlands marginals, allowing Johnson to seize seats that Theresa May lost and David Cameron never won.

Levido was also the beneficiary of work done by Mick Davis, the chief executive under May, who had recruited a hundred centrally paid campaign managers in the field after the 2017 debacle. They were sent to key seats. Unlike in 2017, when Tory ground campaigners were based in the wrong places as the battleground shifted mid-campaign, Levido decided to rely on remote campaigning in a lot of attack seats where the party had no historic base. 'They were just going to get mail and digital some phone calls,' a campaign official said.

The main lesson Levido had learned from 2017, when Crosby and Textor had clashed endlessly with May's chiefs of staff, Nick Timothy and Fiona Hill, was to build a harmonious team. 'What he hasn't done is come in and fire everyone,' a senior Johnson aide said at the start of the campaign. 'He's come in and steadied the ship.' When he made the presentation to political cabinet, Levido's final slide was a list of six 'key imperatives' for ministers to remember:

1. Unity and discipline are key and must be *demonstrated*
2. Competence is king and voters can *sense* it
3. Tone is *critical*
4. You must communicate *the why*, not just the what
5. It's about *the voters* NOT the commentators – do not get stuck in process
6. The election must be framed as a clear *choice* – consequence and outcome[10]

Michael Brooks, whose expertise lay in translating opinion poll findings into effective messaging, worked harder than anyone. The numbers man was there every night, with Levido often the last to leave, the boss class showing the troops they could put in a shift. Brooks rose again at 3 a.m. to look at the numbers on the tracker poll and draw up a summary for the first meeting of the day. That began at 5.40 a.m. with Brooks and Levido, one of Caroline Preston or Ben Mascall (a former Cameron and Remain press officer) to do a media summary on the evening broadcasts and the morning papers, someone from the digital team, plus the CCHQ veterans Alan Mabbutt, Darren Mott and Chris Scott, the head of voter comms and targeting. Brooks went over the numbers, Mott dealt with issues in the field. 'That first meeting was troubleshooting,' one attendee said. 'We'd try to have it wrapped up by 6 a.m. so we could listen to the top of *Today* and the other broadcasts.' That was Cain's cue to get on to the broadcasters, including Katy Searle at the BBC, if he did not like the prominence or slant of stories.

A smaller group met at 6 a.m.: Levido and Brooks, plus the press team, Meg Powell-Chandler, the grid supremo, and Iain Carter, the head of research. After a rundown of the first broadcasts, 'there was a bit of a talk about the day, but then also we'd start talking about tomorrow'. Stories being briefed to the papers would need to be sent out under embargo around lunchtime, so the policies needed to be copper-bottomed and the press releases written. At 7.15 a.m. Levido and Brooks spoke to the co-chairmen Ben Elliot and James Cleverly.

The crunch meeting came at 7.30 a.m. when Levido, Cain and Brooks had a conference call with Johnson, with Cummings dialling in. Cummings also got the overnight numbers. Preston or Mascall would do another media update and then Brooks talked numbers before a discussion of Johnson's day. The calls lasted anything from five minutes to half an hour. 'Isaac set the strategy and everybody was under no illusions that Isaac was the boss,' said a source in the meetings, 'but we would have proper discussion with him. We'd talk through the day. Even when we privately disagreed – which was very rare – we'd have a united front. It was the antithesis of 2017. It was very, very tight.'

Also unlike 2017, when May had sat mute through these sorts of briefings, Johnson had views. When the campaign was being buffeted, as it was in the early days, the prime minister had one obsession: 'How do we get it back to Brexit?' Strict interpretation by the courts of electoral funding laws meant Johnson was overnighting outside London more than leaders in past campaigns. The costs of a leader's travel (including expensive items like a helicopter or private jet) had to be assigned to the constituencies he visited. CCHQ was forced to plan an itinerary in which Johnson could visit twenty-five seats over three days, so costs could be divided twenty-five ways. Once a week, on a Sunday evening, Johnson and the quad – Levido, Cummings, Cain and Brooks – sat down for a face-to-face stocktake in Downing Street.

At 8.15 a.m. every day Levido spoke to the core group of ministers who were the senior spokespeople for the campaign: Sajid Javid, Brandon Lewis, James Cleverly, Rishi Sunak, Andrea Leadsom, Nicky Morgan and Matt Hancock: 'This is what's going on. This is what you'll say.' At noon there was a grid meeting, covering the next three days. Sometime between 4 p.m. and 6 p.m., the core group who met at 5.40 a.m. would speak again. Then at 8 p.m. the quad would talk again to Johnson. Levido and Brooks were regularly in the office after 11 p.m. The campaign director could have stayed in a hotel next to CCHQ but he sacrificed fifteen minutes of sleep to go home to his own bed in Battersea, a short cab ride away at 5 a.m.

Execution of the decisions made in all these meetings was coordinated from a central hub in the middle of the war room in CCHQ in Matthew Parker Street. Levido sat centre square, with Cain, Brooks, Caroline

Preston and Ben Mascall. Alongside them was Alan Mabbutt, the head of compliance, who was there to ensure plans complied with election law. As a veteran of multiple elections, he was also 'an incredible source of wisdom,' a colleague said. After Levido, the most important external hire was Paul Stephenson. The communications director of Vote Leave had taken unpaid leave from his firm Hanbury Strategy. He had no formal role but gradually took charge of the day-to-day press operation, freeing up Cain (a protégé at Vote Leave) to handle Johnson and talk to editors and senior broadcasters. Stephenson took personal charge of handling the Sunday newspaper political editors, who spent all week trying to cause trouble. In the three years since the referendum, Tory comms personnel had changed, got younger and many had not met Stephenson, though they knew his formidable reputation. 'No one said, "This is Paul, you have to work with him,"' a senior campaign official said. 'People would see Lee ask his advice and then others started going to him and everyone just realised he was fucking good.'

Levido's other key hires were two New Zealanders – Sean Topham, twenty-eight, and Ben Guerin, twenty-four – who were brought in to overhaul the Tory digital effort. Their predecessors Tom Edmonds and Craig Elder were hailed as a key reason David Cameron had been able to secure a majority in 2015, but the Tory operation had been overwhelmed in 2017 when Labour and outside groups backing Jeremy Corbyn swamped social media with freely shared ads while Theresa May and her team disdained Twitter and other digital platforms. Topham and Guerin had won praise for their contribution to the Australian election victory with memes that drew on pop culture references like *Game of Thrones*.

The pair showed their sophistication at the start of the campaign, releasing a 'Get Brexit Done' advert in an amateurish-looking Comic Sans font – an example of a technique known as 'shit posting'. The first goal was to attract attention. 'If you're scrolling through a news feed, you've got half a second to grab their attention,' Topham explained. 'People are not going to stop if they just see another blue, green graphic from the Conservative Party.' The second goal was to get a reaction. The response was a storm of derision from Remainer groups and Twitter warriors, which sent the advert viral. 'We didn't change the message, just the way it looks, and you have people freaking out about it and that amplified our message,' said a Tory source. The realisation that they were doing the Tories' work for them gradually dawned on Twitter users. 'Twitter that day went from "Oh my God, Tory graphic design is terrible",' another aide recalled, 'to "They've done this Comic Sans graphic. They are losing the plot", and then people were saying, "Oh, no! Don't share this!"'

Topham Guerin set up a creative digital agency inside CCHQ which combined eight of their staff with members of the existing Tory digital team. Topham led the creative team, Guerin the digital team. Sitting with Levido meant they could get instant answers on which ideas to proceed with and the campaign director could demand digital options when seeking to pounce on a development in the campaign. When they hit a good idea, the team yelled as one, 'Let's break the internet!' Adapting Marshall McLuhan, the medium was the message. 'Just because we're a conservative party, doesn't mean we need to communicate conservatively.'

The Tories also enjoyed another advantage: better polling. Just as Vote Leave's success in 2016 owed much to data analysis Cummings had carried out eighteen months earlier, the 2019 Conservative election was built on models he commissioned in 2018. Good polling was essential to drawing up a list of target seats and deciding where finite resources should be deployed. 'One of the biggest challenges is finding where the battleground is,' Levido told colleagues.

The second challenge was using data and analytics to map how things change during a campaign, to adjust target seats if necessary. In 2017 May's team had been far too aggressive and, since they were not monitoring seats they thought safe, they realised too late that some were slipping away. 'We understood what the true marginal seats were and who the real swing voters were,' Cummings said.[11]

Levido had three polls running simultaneously. Hanbury Strategy collected data which was fed into Cummings' MRP model, designed by Ben Warner, one of the data experts from Vote Leave. A second MRP poll by another supplier used Hanbury's raw data but run through a different model. Separately Michael Brooks had a tracker poll in the field every evening, with a 'three day roll' applied to flatten out volatility each day. Levido used the tracker to define his strategy and test messaging. The two MRPs produced a projected vote share in each seat. The Hanbury model was 'more bullish' on Tory prospects by around twenty seats (and would turn out to be the more accurate). A source said, 'We were using that to track the battleground and determine where the opportunities were popping up, where we should throw some resources.' This was all supplemented by constituency polls conducted by Lisi Christofferson of CTF Partners.

In thinking about their target voters, Levido and Brooks divided the electorate into nine different groups they wanted to reach. Five were 'persuasion' targets who needed to be won over and four were 'turnout audiences', who just needed to be encouraged to vote. They required different messages. Tory MPs found this segmentation much more accurate than in 2017 when they had knocked on doors and found voters supposedly sympathetic to the Tories unremittingly hostile.

Johnson defused one landmine laid by MPs. On 1 November, BuzzFeed reported, 'The UK's intelligence agencies have found no evidence that the Russian state interfered in the outcome of the Brexit referendum and the 2017 general election.'[12] The ISC had sent the report to Downing Street on 17 October, but Number 10 suppressed it, saying it needed to be scrutinised to prevent classified information being released.

Dominic Grieve, chairman of the ISC, urged Johnson to release the report before election day, arguing it was 'really unacceptable for the prime minister to sit on it'. While the headline finding was unexciting, the report contained embarrassing details about the influence of Russian money in British politics, much of it donated to the Conservative Party. There was no incentive for the government to risk publication. A judicious leak served their purposes admirably.

In the same week, Cain and Levido acted to deal with a second unexploded bomb: the danger of a breakout performance in the televised leaders' debates by Jo Swinson. They struck a deal with Labour and the broadcasters for Johnson and Corbyn to contest the main debate of the campaign without the leaders of the smaller parties. The Tory goal was to get Johnson face to face with Corbyn and prevent a repeat of 2010, when Nick Clegg's status had been hugely enhanced by sharing the stage with Gordon Brown and David Cameron – leading to the 'Cleggmania' surge, which momentarily catapulted the Lib Dems into contention.

Since 2010, leaders' debates had been a feature of every general election but, unlike in the US, there was no national debates commission to thrash out the details. The deal provoked fury inside the Lib Dems but also admiration. 'Stitching it up was smart,' a party official said. A Lib

Dem MP observed, 'It was really wrong of the BBC and ITV not to include her. I think it put us at a massive disadvantage.'

The main Tory split at the start of November was over whether the party should seek to 'unite the right' by doing a deal with the Brexit Party. Jacob Rees-Mogg was 'pushing hard' for a non-aggression pact with Nigel Farage in certain seats. Johnson, Cummings and most of the cabinet were opposed. While Johnson was not prepared to court Farage, others did. The outreach effort was led by Ben Elliot, the Tory co-chairman (and nephew of Camilla, the Duchess of Cornwall), Eddie Lister and Dougie Smith, the veteran Tory fixer whose reputation was that of Winston Wolfe, Harvey Keitel's character in *Pulp Fiction*. Another key link was Andrew Reid, a former Ukip treasurer who was a lawyer to Lynton Crosby. The campaign staff kept their hands clean. Levido said, 'I did not have a single conversation, discussion, exchange, text, anything with any representative of the Brexit Party at any point ever.'

Smith, who was in his mid-fifties, was arguably the most powerful man in Britain voters had never heard of. A former cabinet minister said, 'He is pathologically opposed to publicity.' Best known for running high-end Fever swingers' parties in the 1990s, Smith, largely unseen and almost wholly unchecked, influenced access to the Conservative candidates' list, appointments to public bodies and even the House of Lords. Armed with a salary from the Conservative Party and a Number 10 pass, he slid periodically in and out of Downing Street in casual trousers and a sweater. 'Sartorially, he is only two steps up from Cummings,' said one Number 10 aide. He was also one half of a power couple with Munira Mirza, Johnson's policy chief, and an old friend of Michael Gove. 'Dougie' had been on a political journey from his days in the Federation of Conservative Students, which even Norman Tebbit thought was too right-wing. There he had got to know Robbie Gibb, who went on to be Theresa May's communications director. Smith had also worked for Sir James Goldsmith, who set up the Referendum Party. 'Dougie loves power. That's it,' one senior Tory said. But Smith told people, 'I'm driven by values.'

It was while he was at the C-Change think tank that the *Sunday Times* ran a headline proclaiming 'Top Tory aide is king of the urban swingers', revealing his role in hosting opulent orgies in London mansions for couples and single women, in some cases personally selected by Smith. A

Tory spin doctor was an enthusiastic attendee and a cabinet minister also went along, before making his excuses and leaving. If anyone was suited to holding deniable conversations with political opponents, it was Smith, who didn't just know where the bodies were buried, he had usually chopped them up and dug the graves himself.

Farage made his opening offer in the *Sunday Times* on 8 September, offering Johnson a 'non-aggression pact', which he argued could garner a 100-strong majority for an alliance of the right. The Brexit Party leader announced he would not stand candidates against the twenty-eight Spartans who held out against Theresa May's Brexit deal. Farage also said he would leave alone Brexiteers such as Priti Patel who opposed a 'reheated' version of May's deal. He said that if Johnson made no-deal his goal, he would give the Tories a free run. Farage's offer came as a poll showed 73 per cent of Tory voters and 79 per cent of Brexit Party supporters wanted an election pact. 'An alliance between Boris and myself done intelligently, with a clear message, I think we'll be unstoppable,' Farage said. While he did not personally expect a ministerial job, he did suggest that 'one or two' of the 'extremely competent business people' standing for the Brexit Party could be ministers. Farage fancied becoming British ambassador to Washington ('There's some good parties there … an unlimited budget and a wine cellar!'), but he was self-aware enough to admit this was 'perhaps asking a little bit too much'.

Even as he made the offer, Johnson's team was working to scupper a deal. Cummings did not think they needed the Brexit Party. 'There was a meeting planned between me and a fairly senior member of their team that got cancelled very much at the last minute,' Farage said.

The Brexit Party leadership sent Rupert Lowe, the former chairman of Southampton football club, and Robert Rowland, a property tycoon, to talk to Elliot, Smith and Lister. 'They knew Dougie and Eddie,' a source recalled. Pollster Chris Bruni-Lowe armed Lowe and Rowland with a list of ten seats he thought the Brexit Party could win if the Tories stood aside. It included Hartlepool, where Richard Tice was standing. But when the pair returned, they were clutching scraps of paper on which they had scrawled rival numbers which made it look unrealistic. 'We've been shown counter-polling,' Rowland said. 'They've got quite a good point.' Some of his colleagues wondered which side he was on.

When Farage surfaced again, on 1 November, for the Brexit Party's election launch, he issued an ultimatum. Offering Johnson a 'Leave

Alliance', he said the Tories had two weeks, until nominations closed on 14 November to ditch Johnson's deal with the EU and campaign for no-deal. In those circumstances, Farage said his party would only run in around 150 Leave-voting Labour seats. If Johnson refused, he would stand candidates in every constituency in England, Scotland and Wales.

Farage made the pitch after dragooning Donald Trump as a character witness. In an interview with the US president for his LBC radio show the day before, Trump said Farage and Johnson would be an 'unstoppable force', adding, 'I wish you two guys could get together.'

Lowe and Rowland had several meetings with Smith, Elliot and Lister in an office block south of Westminster Bridge and in a flat on the South Bank. One, fittingly, seems to have taken place in the St Ermin's hotel, a former haunt of MI6 officers. These were 'congenial' until an 'unnecessarily confrontational' Tice turned up, playing the 'big cheese'.

The Tory contingent put pressure on the Brexit Party, a combination of carrots and sticks. The pressure was an appeal to history: 'You could destroy Brexit and let in Corbyn.' Brexit Party donors were leaned on to deliver the same message. The Tories could see this hit home with the Brexiteer 'ideologues', less so with 'the party builders' like Tice. There were two carrots. The first was an offer, not to stand down Conservative candidates in seats targeted by the Brexit Party, but to pull election resources, giving them a clear run. This was on the basis that Farage stood down in all but a handful of seats. Then there were the potential honours. The Tories are adamant these were requests by Brexit Party figures which they considered, not offers, which would have been illegal.

After one meeting, the Brexit Party team reported back, 'We have been offered these other things to stand down.' A party official said, 'Rupert Lowe was told he could be the head of the National Lottery. Robert Rowland said he had been offered a peerage. Nigel was to be given a knighthood.' Farage cleared the room and then erupted, 'I'm not taking anything from these cunts. I don't want anything from them. I just want to beat them.' He recalled later, 'I sent a very rude message to Boris. He did not respond.'[13] However, Lowe and Rowland gave colleagues the impression their heads had been turned. Rowland, who died in 2021, was keen on a peerage. 'Robert Rowland was the one that was asking for that,' a party source said.

The following day, 2 November, the *Daily Mail* went on the attack, splashing on 'BORIS: WE DON'T NEED YOU, NIGEL', accusing him of threatening 'to wreck Boris Johnson's election hopes'. A Brexit Party colleague recalled, 'That's the only time I've ever seen Nigel genuinely upset, because he texted Boris and said, "Unless you stop this shit, I'm going to go nuclear."' Farage went on the attack in another interview with the *Sunday Times* the next day. 'All sorts of baubles have been offered,' he said, detailing conversations about a peerage: 'That happened twice … The deal was that if I accepted that, we would only fight a few seats. That came from two very close sources – one from an adviser and one a minister … I said I was not interested.'

Tice, the chairman and an MEP, who had sought to run as the Tory candidate for London mayor the year before, was offered the Conservative candidacy in Rutland, a seat vacated by Alan Duncan. Tice said, 'Through a third party I was offered Rutland, if I left the Brexit Party and joined the Tories. Lots of MEPs and candidates, at the beginning of the election, were offered all sorts of inducements. There was all sorts of blackmail going on.'[14]

Farage certainly asked for seats. Tice said, 'Our view was that, if we did a deal with them, they should have stood down in about between 50 and 80 seats that they had never won in fifty to one hundred years and that we should stand in those and that we might win 15 to 20 seats.' He added, 'We were expecting some formal arrangement and, to be honest, some people in the Tory Party were talking about ministerial and cabinet positions.'[15] Even Brexit Party politicians regarded this as wildly ambitious. John Longworth, another of the Brexit Party's MEPs wooed by the Tories, suggested publicly that they should contest only twenty seats. Farage refused to speak to him for the rest of the campaign.

With time ticking down Steve Baker called Tice and complained, 'If you do this to us everywhere, we'll just lose to Corbyn and you'll lose Brexit.' Armed with more self-confidence than political experience, Tice was a harder nut to crack than Farage himself. 'Tice was deluded,' a senior Tory said. 'He thought he was going to win Hartlepool.'

Tory sources say Farage's real opening bid in private had been a free run in eighteen seats. This was still 'absurdly high' for those leading the discussions. By the time they sat down with Baker, Farage and Tice had lowered their expectations, but now wanted Tory-held seats rather than Labour targets. One said, 'During the meeting, the two of them were clear, they wanted us to stand aside in two safe Tory Leave seats so that they could have a clear run,' guaranteeing two Brexit Party MPs. Baker replied, 'That's a very big ask, I don't see that happening.' He was also surprised that Farage still envisaged his party getting ministerial posts. 'If you guys want to be ministers you will have to do a full coalition agreement,' he said. Their faces dropped. Baker told colleagues, 'They had no idea. They just thought: I'd like to be a minister.'

Smith, Elliot and Lister attended a meeting in Number 10 with Cummings, but not Johnson, to decide whether to give Farage a clear run in a couple of Labour-held seats. They agreed it was not necessary. There was relief – none of them knew if Johnson would have delivered on the deals they had discussed.

On 11 November, with three days to go before the deadline and the Tories refusing to step aside in any seats, Farage finally announced, 'The Brexit Party will not contest the 317 seats the Conservatives won at the last election. We will concentrate our total effort into all the seats that are held by the Labour Party, who have completely broken their manifesto pledge in 2017 to respect the result of the referendum.' Johnson welcomed Farage's concession, calling it 'a recognition that there's only one way to get Brexit done, and that's to vote for the Conservatives'.

Why did Farage give way? The Brexit Party leadership claimed to have negotiated a key concession from Johnson. '[Boris] made a short video where he said that they wanted a simple free trade deal, they didn't want regulatory alignment, and, critically, that there would be no extension of the transition period,' Tice explained. 'That was the promise we extracted from them ... We didn't get any seats out of them, but we did get that.'[16] Johnson had never suggested extending the transition period and had always wanted the ability to diverge from EU rules in a free trade deal – saying so cost him nothing. It was a 'fig leaf', a senior Tory said, but a valuable one since it gave Tice and the others a ladder to climb down.

The real reason owed more to Brexit Party internal strife. First, Farage was under fire from some of his own candidates – Longworth and Lowe among them – who warned he might become the man who destroyed Brexit. 'In our heart of hearts, we knew that we had a responsibility to the nation not to allow Corbyn in,' Tice said. 'I had emails from all my business colleagues begging me, for the sake of the country, to stand down. The abuse we got was ... very unpleasant ... I had two security guards, Nigel had more than that. We knew that if we didn't stand down, after the election we would have to leave the country.'[17]

Multiple Brexit Party sources, however, are clear that Farage did not have enough candidates to stand in every seat. Once Boris Johnson became leader, once keen candidates began to melt away. 'People start dropping off,' a party official said. 'You get the B-team, then the C-team, then the Z-team – just National Front people. When it gets to the deadline, they have nowhere near enough, around four hundred. They used this climbdown thing from Boris as cover. It was complete bollocks. They couldn't get enough candidates, that was the real reason behind it.'

Farage announced that he was not standing himself but would tour the country as a cheerleader for others. He made his declaration in Hartlepool, where Tice was running, a heavily Leave seat with a council run by a coalition of Tories and the Brexit Party. Some colleagues saw a bleak corner of deprivation hilariously unsuited to the expensively groomed City type and his girlfriend, the meticulously coiffured writer Isabel Oakeshott. 'Everyone was desperate for Richard to win,' a waspish party official said, 'so they both had to move there.'

Tory high command moved heaven and earth to stop him. 'The local Conservatives didn't want to put a candidate up,' Tice recalled. 'They wanted to give me a free run. Their first candidate resigned on the Monday before nominations were due in on the Thursday. They got another candidate. He was duly announced on the Tuesday. Thursday lunchtime, he had signed all his papers. Someone deliberately left them in their car and went on holiday … Regional Tory HQ scurried around, found someone to stand, raised £500 in cash, got ten people off the street to sign the form, and they got it in at 3.55 p.m. before the 4 p.m. deadline.'[18] By contrast, Rupert Lowe announced at 3.59 p.m. that he was not going to fight Dudley North, leaving no time for the Brexit Party to find a replacement candidate. Marco Longhi won the seat for the Tories for the first time. Tice eventually finished third behind Labour and the Conservatives with 21 per cent of the vote.

For Levido, the deal was hugely helpful, and not just in the seats where the Brexit Party stepped back. Brexit Party voters in Labour-held red wall seats also began to respond to Tory digital messaging that theirs was a 'wasted vote' and migrated to the Tories. Dehenna Davison, who was challenging Helen Goodman in Bishop Auckland, reported back to CCHQ that Brexit Party support had melted away in the days after Farage's announcement. Richard Holden, who was trying to overturn the 8,700 majority of Laura Pidcock, felt he was in with a chance in North

West Durham. As one strategist put it, 'We have shored up the western front and can now attack in the east.'

The deal also robbed the Lib Dems of the hope that the Brexit Party would split the Leave vote in Conservative–Lib Dem marginals, allowing them to swoop on Tory seats in the south. Swinson said later, 'I think the most important thing was the deal with Farage. That was a game changer.' Publicly, she kept her composure. Privately, she thought: *We're fucked.* She was right. 'In the first week', immediately after the deal, 'we lost five percentage points,' a Lib Dem official explained later. 'Then we lost one point in the middle two weeks and one in the final two.'

Farage did not stop causing trouble for Johnson. On 14 November, inflating his claims further, he said the Tories had offered no fewer than eight peerages to members of the Brexit Party to get them to stand down. Ann Widdecombe, a Brexit Party MEP who had been a Tory shadow home secretary, said she was offered a job on Johnson's EU negotiating team. Another Brexit MEP, Mike Greene, was offered a government education role by a member of Johnson's team. Three days later, the Metropolitan Police launched a criminal inquiry, which went nowhere. In July the following year Claire Fox would become the only Brexit Party figure to get a peerage. She just happened to be an old friend of Munira Mirza from her Revolutionary Communist Party days. As a onetime defender of the IRA, Fox was not a natural Johnson selection. Number 10 officials said Dougie Smith had been a vocal advocate of the move.

Smith also sought to fix candidate selections. At a meeting of the Conservative Party board at the end of October, Elliot handed him control of parachuting candidates into safe seats and key marginals, provoking a 'blazing row' and the resignation of Charles Walker, vice-chairman of the 1922 Committee. Smith's biggest scalp was Rupert Harrison, George Osborne's old right-hand man. Harrison had long been seen by many Tories, not least himself, as a future prime minister and had been eyeing the safe seat of Devizes, where he'd bought a home near his wife's family. Smith ordered the local party to delete three of the six names on the shortlist – triggering the resignation of the local chairman Brigadier Peter Sharpe – then made clear that Johnson expected the winner to be Danny Kruger, his political secretary.

The other key decision was what to do with the twenty-one rebel Tories who had backed the Benn Act. On 29 October, after voting again with the government, ten of the suspended MPs had the whip restored. Six of them announced they were standing down: Richard Benyon, Alistair Burt, Richard Harrington, Margot James, Nicholas Soames and Ed Vaizey. Another four fought the election as Conservatives: Steve Brine, Greg Clark, Stephen Hammond and Caroline Nokes. They would all hold their seats. Of the eleven who remained suspended, six did not stand: Guto Bebb, Ken Clarke, Justine Greening, Philip Hammond, Oliver Letwin and Rory Stewart. Sam Gyimah and Antoinette Sandbach both became Liberal Democrat candidates. David Gauke, Dominic Grieve and Anne Milton all stood as independents in their old seats. All five would lose.

Six members of the Gaukeward Squad later got peerages, including Benyon, Harrington, Soames and Vaizey from the group who were read-mitted. Ken Clarke and Philip Hammond, whose cabinet careers were the most significant, both went to the Lords as well despite not regaining the whip. The purge was brutally effective. Every rebel who resisted Johnson's imprint on their party was swept from the Commons.

At the end of October, Tom Watson requested a meeting with Corbyn. They met in the old shadow cabinet room in Norman Shaw South. 'I think it would be easier for me and easier for you if I was to stand down,' Watson said.

Corbyn would propose Watson for a peerage and, in return, he would not publicly criticise the campaign. They then discussed their vegetable patches and 'the challenges of growing horseradish, an invasive vegetable'.[19] Politics is a funny old game.

Johnson formally launched the Tory campaign on 6 November with a short speech on the steps of Downing Street, delivering his key message: he was 'chewing my own tie' with frustration that Brexit had not yet happened. Later, in a speech to activists in Birmingham, he promised to leave within weeks and then focus his government on the NHS and schools. Johnson said he would pass his 'oven ready deal' on Brexit through Parliament if he secured a majority. Johnson did not attack Farage by name, but he said those who 'cast aspersions' on his EU deal had a vested interest in Brexit not happening. 'They are like candle-makers at the dawn of the electric lightbulb', suffering from a 'terrible sense they are about to lose their market'.

The following day, 7 November, Ian Austin and John Woodcock jointly announced they would vote Conservative to keep the Labour leader out of Number 10. Austin declined the chance to stand for the Tories in his Dudley North seat but later accepted a peerage.

The Tories had their first party political broadcast (PPB) on 12 November. Well before the campaign, Levido's instructions to Topham Guerin were to produce TV slots that would 'go viral' online. 'I don't want to spend a lot of money on them, I don't want to get agencies in,' he said. 'I'm happy to give you a long leash.'

They came up with the idea of emulating *Vogue* magazine's 73 Questions slot, where a celebrity is quizzed about themselves, in a single continuous shot. Johnson would walk around the CCHQ war room and answer personal questions, some scripted, some deliberately sprung on him to get a spontaneous response. Topham said, 'It was an existing format that clearly worked well, that people were familiar with.' It took an expressive figure like Johnson to hold the attention of the viewer for four minutes and forty seconds. 'There are not many other politicians you can imagine doing that,' a campaign source said.

The digital team shot a test where Topham walked around the office, to work out the practicalities. They showed it to Johnson. 'That works, I'm up for it,' he said. The following evening, he went in to CCHQ for an hour and shot the film. It was at the end of the first take that they realised they might have something special. The plan was for Johnson to make a mug of tea. 'All right, we'll do another take,' Topham said. 'Oh, you've left the teabag in. You can just chuck it on the sink.'

Johnson replied, 'No, that's what I do. That's how I have my tea.'

They ended up shooting five takes, using the last one. 'When we played it back for a couple of the team who hadn't been part of it, they were transfixed,' Topham recalled. 'There was a sense of movement. He had that energy.' Not just that. As people watched Johnson leave his teabag in, the reaction was, 'That's so weird.' When the video went live, it sparked debate. Johnson was bewildered by the fuss. 'The boss has been defending himself all week,' said one adviser. 'I'm glad he's never made a brew for me.'

The PPB was a triumph, but it was a rare one that week. While the Tories were trying something new, Labour was replaying its 2017 campaign (on acid), announcing ever more eye-catching policies every day and running away with the lead on most broadcast news bulletins.

'REFIGHTING THE LAST WAR ...'

Labour

22 September to 26 November 2019

The signature moment of Labour's 2019 election campaign was never intended to be so pivotal. On the evening of 14 November, John McDonnell, the shadow chancellor, told the BBC's political editor Laura Kuenssberg that a Corbyn government would provide universal free broadband internet access by 2030. The following day, Corbyn unveiled the plan to nationalise the Openreach wing of BT and set up a new publicly owned company, British Broadband, which Corbyn hailed as 'our treasured public institution for the twenty-first century'. The £20 billion cost was to be funded by a tax on internet giants like Amazon, Facebook and Google. Free broadband was both an audacious 'retail' policy designed to appeal to consumers and a populist attack on the web corporations who avoided tax. It was not the first big budget announcement of the campaign. It would not be the last. But the way it was arrived at, the way it was revealed and the way it was received explain much about what was different between the 2017 and 2019 battles, the one a surprise breakthrough, the other a historic setback.

Corbyn said free broadband was central to Labour's manifesto, being launched the following week, which he portrayed as 'the most radical and exciting plan for real change the British public has ever seen'. He boasted, 'It's going to knock your socks off – you're going to love it.' The reaction elsewhere was predictable. BT, which saw its share price fall, suggested the scheme would cost closer to £100 billion. The reaction in the Labour Party was surprise, since most of the shadow cabinet had never seen the manifesto and had no idea what was in it. Jonathan Ashworth, the shadow health secretary, was booked on *Newsnight* that evening and took a call from a producer, who said, 'We need to ask you about Labour's new policy.'

'What is it?'

'Free WiFi.'

Ashworth said later, 'I knew nothing about it. This was a week when we were trying to focus on the NHS and we were suddenly going off in another direction.'[1] Labour's operations and communications teams were also blindsided. No effort was made to tie Corbyn's announcement to a photo opportunity to help to sell the policy to television viewers. Instead, Jack McKenna, one of his spokesmen, got a call the night before saying, 'Can you get to Lancaster? We're doing a speech on broadband tomorrow. It's the biggest announcement of the campaign.' It was the first he had heard of it. Only the following morning did the ops team check that the venue had a satellite signal or good broadband. A party official said, 'These policies didn't get the right coverage because we didn't know about them. We couldn't build anything around them. With the broadband policy, we didn't go to a rural area where old people need broadband. The day we announced the trains policy, Jeremy didn't get on a train' – a pledge to nationalise the railways within five years.

That week the policies came in a staccato burst, day after day, sometimes more than once a day. On the 12th there was an 'NHS rescue plan', with £26 billion for the health service over four years (£6 billion more than the Tories had pledged), funded by reversing cuts to corporation tax and raising personal taxes on the wealthy. Then came the formal launch of plans for a thirty-two-hour, four-day working week by 2030, an idea trailed by McDonnell at the party conference. Yet there was very little connecting the announcements, beyond a desire to spend money.

In 2017, the whole manifesto had leaked and it had given Labour a huge boost.[2] But when Seumas Milne, Corbyn's director of strategy and communications, penned an election strategy memo in 2019 he warned, 'We must avoid refighting the last war.'[3]

In the event, that is exactly what Labour did, except this time the public struggled to keep up with the bewildering blitz of pledges. After the election, Prof. John Curtice, the doyen of British psephologists, concluded that most of Labour's individual policies were 'popular' by margins of around two to one. However, if asked, more people 'thought they were unachievable than achievable'.[4] The commentator Stephen Bush said, 'It wasn't so much, "Wow, these policies are radical." It was,

"Wow, these policies aren't going to happen."[5] In Tory focus groups, participants asked, 'Who's going to pay for this?' Even rail nationalisation, a popular policy for twenty years, left people cold.

The other thing that was different from 2017 was the Tory response to Labour's announcements. Boris Johnson laid into the free broadband pledge, calling it a 'crazed communist scheme' as he launched his red, white and blue campaign battlebus at an event in Oldham. But beyond that, Tory campaign HQ did not seek a protracted row about the cost. When members of the press team produced quotes from city analysts opposing the policy, Stephenson told them not to send them out. Levido remembered 2017, when the Tories had been suckered into condemning every Labour spending pledge, even on niche policies like funding for local football clubs. 'They would draw us into attacking them over cost,' a campaign veteran said. 'Then, bang, they had a doorstep campaign about the wicked Tories refusing to fund something good.'

This time, the Conservative campaign accused Labour of a 'desperate attempt to distract from the fact they don't have a policy on the biggest issue facing the country.' In Labour HQ, James Schneider became concerned that the Tories were not locking horns as they had in 2017. 'We noticed that they weren't putting out any response comments to anything that we did,' he said. 'Broadband was the only one where they failed because Johnson couldn't help himself. But they basically shut up.'

The other story, where Stephenson's experience told, was the four-day-week announcement, coming at the same time as Labour's pledge for more NHS funding. The comms veteran went straight to the researchers and Jamie Njoku-Goodwin, the special adviser to health secretary Matt Hancock, and said, 'Figure out what the cost of the four-day week is going to be. I'll bet we can package it up as a funding cut for the NHS.' After waiting several hours for figures from the department, Stephenson did some quick calculations on a spreadsheet. The average NHS worker earned £32,257 for a 37.5 hour week. Cutting that to 32 hours a week would increase staff costs by 17.2 per cent across a workforce of 1.1 million. Labour's four-day-week would cost £6.1 billion – wiping out the extra £6 billion a year the party was pledging for the health service.

The Conservative research department (CRD) enjoyed a hit in the 'friendlies' – the newspapers backing the Tories – with a document claiming the 'cost of Corbyn' would top £1.2 trillion and lead to a '£2,400 tax bill for every household'. One Tory aide dubbed CRD their 'fake news unit'.[6] CRD had another hit in the papers that week, releasing a report on 14 November which built on a motion passed at Labour's conference that the party should 'maintain and extend free movement rights' beyond the EU. Oliver Lewis used official government methodology to calculate that Labour extending freedom of movement beyond the EU to the rest of the world would lead to annual net migration of 840,000 a year. This was a hit with the *Mail* and the *Telegraph*, but, like the Corbyn dossier, it barely troubled the broadcasters who devoted wall-to-wall coverage that day to new NHS A&E waiting times, which had reached their worst level on record. Then at 10 p.m. the Labour broadband plan dropped.

For the first part of the campaign Labour won the air war. It was their eye-catching announcements which were leading the main BBC evening broadcasts. In the first week, only Johnson's launch speech led the *News at Ten*. A Tory announcement about improving the high street was only the fourth story on the *Today* programme and *Good Morning Britain*. Farage's declaration that he was standing down half his candidates was the only time Brexit led the bulletins.[7]

Heavy flooding to large areas of Yorkshire and the Midlands, where dozens of marginal seats lay under water, also caused the Tories troubles. Johnson and his team procrastinated for days about a visit, with predictable results when he finally faced irate voters. 'Every day on the six and ten it was floods in Yorkshire, angry Yorkshiremen telling Boris Johnson that he's an arsehole, Labour wants to spend more money on this,' a Corbyn aide said. '"Get Brexit Done" wasn't on the news. It was as good as we could have hoped for.'

In CCHQ, Levido and his team held their nerve, surprised that neither Labour nor the Lib Dems had sought to set out an alternative framing for the election. 'They didn't have an opening argument,' he told colleagues. 'They've gone straight into the evidentiary phase.' The argument he worried Labour would make was this: 'Boris Johnson is only having this election to further his own political interest. He's abandoned getting Brexit done so he can get a big majority and fuck you over somehow.' A similar approach had worked against Theresa May in 2017. 'They focused all their resources on policies,' a senior Tory official said. 'They were not able to tell a story at any stage.'

*　*　*

Labour's biggest failure was not managing to tell a convincing story on Brexit. Corbyn made his launch speech on 31 October, the day Britain was supposed to leave the EU. Speaking at the Battersea Arts Centre in south London, he promised 'the most ambitious and radical campaign our country has ever seen' as he spelled out Labour's election strapline, 'It is now time for real change.' Brexit was an afterthought. 'Labour will get Brexit sorted by giving people the final say in six months,' he said. 'It really isn't that complicated.' It really wasn't that persuasive either. Andrew Fisher, still the head of policy, admitted, 'People agreed with the policies, but it didn't matter to them, because the only issue was Brexit.'[8] A close aide of Corbyn said, 'The strategy was: do Brexit at the start and then get off it.' In his August election strategy memo, Milne hoped to prevent 'a Brexit election: pitting Parliament and the establishment against the people' by presenting Labour as 'the real challenge to the establishment and the elites' where 'the crucial election choice becomes not in or out, but the many or the few'. They failed.

Margaret Hodge thought Corbyn guilty of a 'complete mishandling' of Brexit. 'That total fudge that we ended up with was just a disaster on the doorstep and showed actually what a useless leader he was.'[9] Ruth Smeeth, who lost her Stoke-on-Trent North seat, a key brick in the red wall, said, 'the crap position' on Brexit 'cost me in my constituency. It would have been much easier, I think, if the Labour Party had been fully fledged Remain or fully fledged Leave.'[10]

John Curtice concluded, 'One of the ironies about Jeremy Corbyn's leadership is that although this is somebody who was supposedly a radical politician … on the crucial central issue he was the last compromiser standing – on an issue where there was very little centre ground left. I think history will probably argue not … that Jeremy Corbyn failed his party because he was too extreme, but rather, because he was unwilling to take a clear position on a central issue facing the country.'[11] The endless parliamentary battles 'wore him down', an aide said of Corbyn, 'because he just wasn't that interested in it'. In spring 2019, as the Tories imploded, Corbyn's team assumed they would win the next election. But the Brexit extension after 29 March and the European elections changed that. 'From then on it was just torture.' Corbyn only backed a referendum as the cause collapsed. 'The People's Vote campaign was like a bee that stung its prey and then rolled over and died,' an aide said.

Labour's fudged position was both the consequence and cause of a civil war in Corbyn's inner circle which had been running for months between those who thought the priority was to protect seats that voted Leave – such as Karie Murphy, Ian Lavery and Andrew Gwynne – those who saw electoral upside in aligning with Remainers – including McDonnell, Watson, Fisher and Starmer – and those who wanted to avoid all talk of Brexit, the position adopted by Milne. McDonnell's realisation that the party should back a second referendum caused a deep split in his forty-year friendship with Corbyn. 'By being the reasonable guy, John made Jeremy look like the bad guy,' a Corbynite complained.

During August, McDonnell took election planning by the scruff of the neck and began chairing a daily morning call of campaign chiefs, including Lavery and Gwynne, with a further meeting at 9.30 a.m., also attended by frontbencher Jon Trickett, plus another call on Sunday evenings. This led to the party hammering an anti-no-deal message over the summer, while both Milne and Schneider were on holiday. When they returned, 'Seumas had an absolute hissy fit,' said a senior official.

Labour's Brexit procrastination reached crisis point at 9 a.m. on 22 September, the Sunday morning of the party conference. Corbyn's top team gathered in a meeting room in Brighton's Hilton Metropole Hotel to hear the results of a huge YouGov poll of twenty thousand voters commissioned by Niall Sookoo, Labour's director of elections, and Tim Waters, the party's head of data. The news was dire. Labour was on course to win just 138 seats, its worst result since 1917. Waters explained that the party was losing Remain voters to the Lib Dems, who had just announced their Revoke policy, while white working-class Leave voters would either stay at home or switch to the Tories.[12] Lavery, who learned he was on course to lose his Northumberland coalfield seat of Wansbeck, did not believe what he was hearing. 'People in the north just won't vote Tory,' he exclaimed. 'It just won't happen!' Waters explained that even if these voters were not switching to the Conservatives, the Lib Dem surge would split the Remain vote in Labour Leave areas, letting the Tories in by the back door. For every Leaver who abandoned Labour, three Remainers were doing so.[13] McDonnell took charge, pressing for a clear pro-Remain position.

McDonnell was also central to a plot to oust Karie Murphy from Corbyn's office after her botched coup against Tom Watson. Murphy was in Spain on 27 September when she was summoned home and told she had to move to Southside, party HQ, to take charge of election planning. She refused: 'The Brexit policy is going to fuck us and I ain't taking the rap.' However, on 7 October, Corbyn went to Southside to announce her appointment anyway. Witnesses said she had clearly been crying. Corbyn seemed furious as he revealed Murphy's new role to bewildered staff, before boasting that he had been 'eating more porridge every morning' to build his strength for the campaign.

The same divisions over Brexit were evident when Boris Johnson forced Corbyn's team to decide whether to back a general election. On three separate occasions they ducked the challenge. When Johnson first threw down the gauntlet, on 4 September, Corbyn demanded he take no-deal off the table first. In a meeting that day, in the whips' office, Milne, Murphy and Shami Chakrabarti all argued that Labour should back an election because the Lib Dems and the SNP would soon do so and it was better to move before Johnson delivered Brexit. Milne suggested they press for an election on 24 October. Opposition came from Nick Brown, McDonnell and Starmer. The chief whip warned that Labour risked disaster and that Corbyn faced a colossal rebellion from MPs frightened about holding their seats. He told the PLP that evening Johnson should 'stew in his own juices'. James Schneider, who was firmly in the pro-election camp recalled, 'All the people on the Remain side of the equation were opposed because they thought they could get a referendum. The rest of us said, "This is only going to get worse for us. He doesn't have a deal. Let's go for it." We would not have had to go through the abject embarrassment of having called for an election to then run away from it.'

Corbyn had demanded an election for months, but caught between two factions, he opted for inaction. On 22 October, the night MPs rejected the programme motion for the withdrawal bill, the shadow cabinet held further meetings. The 'young Turks' of the left – Laura Pidcock, Richard Burgon and Dan Carden – all badgered Corbyn to support an election, believing he could win it. Jonathan Ashworth said, 'Those colleagues who were very enthusiastic about Jeremy thought that once Jeremy gets out on the stump, he'll inject energy into the campaign and smash the Tories.'[14] A majority was against, Brown, Starmer and Emily Thornberry most defiantly so. Corbyn, again, refused to provide a lead.

Two days later, when Johnson demanded a vote under the Fixed-term Parliaments Act, things began to move towards the first December election since 1923. The crunch meeting took place at 7 p.m. in Corbyn's office. Brown, McDonnell and Diane Abbott all argued against an election, while Milne and Schneider declared that untenable. Andrew Fisher said, 'We've got to go for it. Yes, it's going to be tough and I'm not very optimistic about our prospects, but I'm less optimistic if we're seen to resist the election and then are forced into one.'[15] However, the consensus in the room remained opposed. Corbyn expressed no view.

Once the meeting dispersed, Milne had Corbyn practise various explanations for the TV cameras. Both could see that blocking an election would not hold. Milne gave Corbyn a new line, which completely ignored the previous discussion. 'Take no-deal off the table, and we absolutely support an election,' the leader told the BBC. All that was left was for the EU to grant Johnson the extension and it was game on. 'Within half an hour, they changed the position we'd agreed,' a Labour adviser said. The episode was Peak Corbyn: a political leader who refused to state a view, who held a meeting to determine his position and then, within minutes of it ending, allowed himself to be manoeuvred into doing the exact opposite. LOTO told the whips and the shadow cabinet that Corbyn had 'meant to say' he wanted an election.

Corbyn was confronted by Peter Kyle and Phil Wilson. Kyle said, 'You're not going to vote for a general election, are you?'

Corbyn, essaying his weary disinterest in the responsibilities of his position, replied, 'I don't know, it's not in my hands.'

'No, Jeremy, it is in your hands.'

'It's absolutely in your hands.'

When it became clear, that Saturday night, that both the Lib Dems and the SNP would back an election the following week, the die was cast. Both McDonnell and Starmer realised the game was up. Milne and Murphy encouraged Corbyn to move first, but it was not until Monday evening that LOTO told the whips Labour MPs should vote in favour. On Tuesday morning, 29 October, Corbyn presented the decision to the shadow cabinet. He had dithered and delayed so much that many were surprised. Only Thornberry put up a fight, but she was shot down by Ian Lavery, who declared, 'It's like having a boxer in the prime of his life and telling him he can't fight!' In truth, the Brexit wars had left Corbyn looking like an ageing boxer who has taken too many blows. When the vote came, he was not even in the chamber. 'A whip found him sat in the old shadow cabinet room with his feet up looking at the telly,' an adviser recalled. More than 100 Labour MPs, suspecting what was coming, abstained. Eleven voted against. Corbyn, who evinced little sign of ever wanting to be prime minister, was too exhausted to fight any more. An aide said, 'Ultimately, Jeremy selected suicide by electorate.'

Corbyn's abdication of leadership – refusing to grasp the nettle in three successive meetings – condemned his party. Many in his team came to believe that, instead of thwarting Johnson in September, they should have grasped the chance of an election. 'You have it at that point, when he didn't have a deal and it looked like we were heading for no-deal,' one aide said, 'or you have it a year afterwards.' But Corbyn's team was blindsided by their contempt for Johnson. Fisher admitted, 'What we didn't bank on, is that he would get a new deal.'[16]

Labour, guided by Starmer, used the time to push through the Benn Act and the Letwin amendment, moves which Remainers sincerely believed to be necessary, but which played into the Johnson–Cummings grievance strategy. 'We built our gallows and tied the noose around our own neck,' a LOTO aide said. These abstruse activities were off-brand for Corbyn, who had won support in 2017 as an outsider. Schneider worried, 'When people turned on their televisions, what most people saw of Jeremy would have been a few seconds of him in Parliament saying something quite arcane – he became part of the process.' Vote Leave 'stole our insurgent clothes', Fisher said. 'Jeremy was the anti-establishment candidate. Now, we were being lumped in with the Lib Dems and the others obstructing Brexit.'[17]

On the basis that you should always do what your opponent least wants you to do, Labour might also have sought to revive May's deal, with the extra concessions negotiated in the cross-party talks, then pass a meaningful vote or a withdrawal agreement bill with the backing of the Bresistance. 'If they had come out in support of May's deal before the campaign, we would've been fucked,' a senior Tory said.

The belief on the left of the Labour Party that Corbyn was fighting his last election distorted the list of target seats. Rather than try to shore up as many MPs as possible, the guardians of the Corbyn 'project' went for broke. For the hard left, this was a once in a generation opportunity to seize national power and, if they failed, they would be sidelined again, as they had been between 1985 and 2015. A senior official said at the time, 'We either win or we go down in flames.' The catastrophic YouGov megapoll did not change the view that they still had to 'go big'. As the campaign began, Niall Sookoo produced a list of 96 targets, 66 of which were attack seats, with just 30 to defend. What made sense for the Corbynites would end up being a disaster for Labour.

Corbyn's team never found an effective way of attacking Boris Johnson, who also wanted to scrap austerity and spend more money on public services, but had Brexit and a harder line on immigration with which to woo white working-class voters. Corbyn and his senior aides regarded it as a sine qua non of the new politics that Johnson was an incompetent liar and that the public would see him as such. In his August pre-election memo, Milne wrote, 'The Tories are ... led by a politician of proven incompetence, who is in hock to Donald Trump.'[18] Another adviser observed, 'Jeremy thought this guy was a charlatan, a chancer, that people would see through him. Jeremy had a very, very, very low opinion of Boris.' This attitude led Labour high command to underestimate both Johnson and his appeal to their traditional voters. When Johnson won the leadership in July, a LOTO aide said they waited for Milne to reveal the masterplan to take him on. There wasn't one. There were three possible lines of attack – that Johnson was a far-right demagogue; that he was a liar and untrustworthy; or that he was just another Tory who would put the moneyed classes first. Sookoo wanted polling on potential attack lines but was ignored. Schneider, who thought the 'just another Tory' line most likely to persuade red wall voters, said, 'We had endless meetings. We couldn't agree on anything.'

Corbyn's team was also riven by internecine warfare. Fisher kept the manifesto from Milne, Murphy refused to share the grid. Sookoo kept the list of target seats from Milne, Murphy and political director Amy Jackson.[19] Part of the problem was that they were exhausted after four years of perma-conflict with MPs, the media and each other. 'It was constant firefighting,' a LOTO aide said, 'whether it was antisemitism, whether it was Salisbury, whether it was Brexit, whether it was how we were going to whip, what we were going to do with rebels, who was going to resign – every single thing was constant firefighting. There was never any front-foot, strategic progress. It wears you down physically, mentally, psychologically. The whole idea of the Corbyn project was this hopeful, vibrant movement but we were living hand to mouth every week.'

The campaign's morning conference call began at 7 a.m., led by McDonnell, with Murphy, theoretically in charge of election planning, Milne, Fisher, Gwynne, Lavery and Sookoo also joining. But little strategy was discussed. Often, they did little more than talk about Corbyn's diary. By the time it started, Isaac Levido had already chaired two meetings and was on to his third.

Labour's ground war was compromised because the paid-for local campaigners put in place after the 2017 election had, thanks to the shifting battleground, spent two years deployed in the wrong places.

In 2017, Corbyn had benefited from arguably the most dynamic social media campaign ever seen in a general election. This time it misfired, badly. Corbyn had a talented social media man, Jack Bond, who had a huge roster of freelance content creators allowing Labour to successfully amplify their messaging through dozens of external groups, of which Momentum was the best known. But at the end of September 2019, a senior party official confided, 'The digital team is leaving because they can't cope with Seumas, Schneider and Carl Shoben.' A LOTO official said, 'One thing that has run through the project from the beginning is to use social media to bypass the mainstream media. But we made no effort to come up with a coherent social media strategy.'

Seen from CCHQ, Labour in 2019 still profited from content sharing by surrogate left-wing groups, but little of it was creative. 'There were a lot of people talking to a camera about this issue or that,' a senior Tory said. 'It gets quite boring quite quickly.' Labour had a more engaged activist base but Topham Guerin focused on quality and originality. Sean Topham said, 'If my campaign's objective was to get the most video views, then I would have lost. But I wanted to get lots of videos that created moments that had cut-through.'

The same chaos governed Labour's selection of a campaign strapline. The first effort, devised by Harry Barlow, an ad man who once worked for Ken Livingstone, was 'It's Time', a straight lift from Jacinda Ardern, who had won the New Zealand election in 2017. The idea was to peg each of Labour's main policies to it: 'It's Time … for Free Broadband'. But aides envisaged a Tory spoof ('It's Time … to Get Brexit Done') and dropped it. 'Real Change' polled adequately but, without any testing, it was then rammed together with the original idea to make 'It's Time for Real Change'. Arun Chaudhary, who had worked for Barack Obama, pronounced the episode a 'shitshow'.[20] James Schneider agreed: 'Our slogan … never really took off and we never filled it in with content or with other meaning.'[21]

Chaudhary and data consultant Paul Hilder, who had met on Bernie Sanders' insurgent presidential campaign in 2016, were hired to recapture the magic of 2017. They concluded it had gone; Corbyn was the least popular leader of the opposition in forty-five years. The messages which worked best were those delivered by ordinary people: the flood victim shouting at Boris Johnson. Hilder suggested they use them rather than the leader in their adverts. A project to revive Corbynism had concluded the best way was to cut out Corbyn.[22]

A December election meant bad weather and none of the mass outdoor rallies which generated excitement in 2017. Corbyn's crowds of five thousand were now crowds of five hundred. 'We did loads and loads of members' events,' a LOTO aide said. 'They were never big, they were never energetic and they were all inside.'

Yet the main problem was Corbyn himself. The rockstar politician of Glastonbury 2017 had become a pettifogging nuisance who spent his day complaining about his schedule and disputing his travel arrangements. In his first election campaign, Corbyn had not once joined the morning conference call. Now he did so every day, egged on by his wife Laura, whose influence was judged so malign by Milne that he nicknamed her 'Yoko'.[23] Corbyn did not make strategic observations about the type of target seats he was asked to visit but banal logistical points: 'That's a really long journey, that's not worth it.'

Corbyn's other obsession was his double-decker red battlebus. The leader had a 'tantrum' when he discovered that Jo Swinson had the use of an electric bus while his was powered by a diesel engine the Labour manifesto would pledge to outlaw.[24] He refused from that moment to set foot on it, forcing him onto trains where his phone constantly cut out during conference calls. To add to the farce, environmental protesters from the Extinction Rebellion protest group, dressed up as bees and superglued themselves to the Lib Dem bus, apparently unaware that it was the least polluting vehicle. 'They were quite combative,' a Lib Dem official said, 'then off camera they were quite apologetic.'

By the halfway point in the campaign, Corbyn seemed to be engaged in a work-to-rule protest against himself, turning up late and overstaying on purpose to minimise the number of events he had to do.[25] It was in this frame of mind that he readied himself for his first debate with Boris Johnson.

The first ever head-to-head encounter between the leaders of the two main parties came on Tuesday 19 November at Salford Quays. YouGov put the Tories on 45 per cent with Labour on 28 per cent. But the previous Friday, Levido had warned his team, 'We need to remember that we are in a worse position than we were at this stage of the campaign in 2017.' Both sides knew it was the first moment many voters would even register the campaign – doubly so because, for the previous three days, the nation had been consumed by the Duke of York's car crash interview with *Newsnight*'s Emily Maitlis on his involvement with the convicted paedophile Jeffrey Epstein. The format favoured Johnson since the debate was due to start with thirty minutes on Brexit, with the second half devoted to all other domestic issues. The Tories brought over American Brett O'Donnell, who had prepped Johnson for the debates during the 2016 referendum campaign, to run their debate camp.

Johnson won the first half and Corbyn edged the second, attacking on the NHS, but neither landed a knockout blow. A snap poll put them in a statistical dead heat (Johnson 51 per cent, Corbyn 49 per cent). At times it seemed like the main contest was between a Tiggerish Johnson blustering his way over his allotted time and moderator Julie Etchingham, who fought in vain to cut him off. Both candidates were ridiculed by the TV audience, who regarded Corbyn's stance on Brexit as literally laughable along with Johnson's claim to be trustworthy. Corbyn said he would offer 'a credible leave option' in a second referendum but refused on nine separate occasions to say how he would vote or whether he thought Britain should leave the EU or remain. Labour's four-day week and the antisemitism scandal were both jeered. Corbyn also attracted accusations of antisemitism when he pronounced Epstein 'Epshteen' in a cod Yiddish accent. He did better when he accused Johnson of holding 'a series of secret meetings with the United States' to 'sell our National Health Service'.

The biggest talking point of the evening was another piece of guerrilla social media provocation by Topham Guerin. The official Tory Twitter feed was rebranded 'factcheckUK', complete with a new fake logo, for the duration of the debate and pumped out a string of anti-Labour posts. While the Twitter handle @CCHQPress was unchanged, the Twitterati went into meltdown and Full Fact, a charity which monitored political statements for accuracy, complained to Twitter. Once again, the row had the effect of driving more people to Conservative messaging. 'It was only on for one hour and it led the BBC the next day,' a senior campaign official recalled. 'It was one of the moments where the BBC lost their fucking minds.' Levido added, 'We were in the middle of one of the momentous election campaigns in the last fifty years. It was the first ever head-to-head debate between two prime ministerial candidates. And what was running at the top of the broadcast news the next morning? That a Twitter account changed its name.' The Tory campaign director was happy with Johnson's performance, erratic as it had been, not least because he had repeatedly deployed 'Get Brexit Done'.

Jo Swinson prepared as if she was going to take part, recruiting serious players to help her prep the day before the debate. They included Sean Kemp, the brains of Nick Clegg's comms team who played Corbyn, declaring everything terrible and pledging to spend more money to fix it. James McGrory was an 'astonishingly good' Boris Johnson. They were working through attack lines when the ruling came through that the party's appeal against Swinson's exclusion from the debate had been rejected by the High Court. When they broke for a rest, Sam Barratt said, 'We're not in it.' Swinson's team had planned a 'cut through moment' to put her on the map. An aide recalled, 'She was going to say, "I'm only going to take thirty seconds. Because I'm going to give my other thirty seconds to Boris Johnson so he can look down the camera and apologise for his comments about Islamophobia. And to Jeremy Corbyn so he can apologise to the Jewish community for antisemitism. That's my thirty seconds. Off you go." The thing I most regret is not seeing that moment play out on TV.'

Swinson's campaign morphed from the disappointing to the ridiculous. On the day of the debate, she was asked by LBC's Iain Dale about her 'attitude to squirrels' in response to a spoof news article which claimed she used a slingshot to fire stones at these 'pleb bunnies'. The hoax article claimed to have unearthed 'harrowing' Facebook footage of her terrorising rodents and quoted an RSPA [sic] spokesman saying, 'I've never seen anyone so alive with twisted pleasure at the thought of harming another living creature. The glee is palpable.' It also featured a made-up quote from Swinson saying, 'I'm a crack shot. I don't go for the head because that's too clean a death.' In reality, Swinson put out seeds for squirrels on her windowsill when she was working from home. First Draft, a non-profit group fighting misinformation, later found it had originally been circulated among anonymous pro-Labour accounts on Twitter. It went viral ten days later when a Brexit Party account with nine thousand followers picked it up.[26]

The day after the first debate, the Lib Dems launched their manifesto at a nightclub in Camden. 'We had two glitter cannons, one of which didn't go off,' a party official recalled, 'which is an unfortunate metaphor of where we ended up.' Entitled 'Stop Brexit, Build a Brighter Future', it featured the party's pledge to add 1p to income tax to pay for a £7 billion cash injection for the NHS and the thirty-five hours of free childcare a week. A perplexed Laura Kuenssberg said to Ben Rathe afterwards, 'There was no new policy. You could have had free airtime on whatever policy you wanted because we have to cover it.' Rathe knew.

Labour launched their manifesto on 20 November, the day after the Lib Dems. Finalising the document was usually an agonising process, with every line thrashed out in a 'Clause V meeting' between the leadership, the unions, NEC members and shadow ministers. The panoply of expensive policies was nodded through during the six-hour meeting. Brexit was barely discussed. What Karie Murphy called Corbyn's 'difficult second album' took the themes of his first and, Spinal Tap-style, turned them up to eleven. There was billions for the NHS, universal social care, free broadband, a hundred thousand new homes, free bus travel for the under-twenty-fives, the abolition of university tuition fees and universal credit. Royal Mail, water, the railways and part of BT would be nationalised – paid for with £82.9 billion of tax rises on businesses and the top 5 per cent of earners, with the 45 pence rate of tax kicking in at £80,000 a year, rather than £150,000 and a new 50 pence rate starting at £125,000. McDonnell claimed the nationalisations would cost nothing because they would add assets to the government's books. Business groups said they would initially cost £196 billion.

At the launch in Birmingham, Corbyn called them 'popular policies that the political establishment has blocked for a generation'. There was a reason for that. Hilary Benn remarked, 'Our manifesto was so full of promises that we'd failed Nye Bevan's test when he said, "Socialism is the language of priorities." It looked like we had walked into the sweetshop, couldn't make up our minds and said, "We'll buy the lot."'[27]

Undeterred by fact check furore during the debate, the Tory digital operation had another surprise in store. Three days earlier, Topham Guerin had bought up the internet domain name 'Labourmanifesto. co.uk' for just £15. As Labour unveiled their plan for government, the Tory Twitter account posted a link to the page, coloured bright red and featuring an image of Corbyn looking confused. It read 'Labour's 2019 manifesto: No plan for Brexit. Higher taxes. Two more referendums.' CCHQ had also paid for a Google advert which meant internet browsers were directed to the website when they searched for 'Labour'. The Conservatives also ran adverts on the websites of the *Mirror* and LabourList saying, 'The Labour manifesto has no position on Brexit.' The Tories were amazed it was possible. 'Buying a whole bunch of domain names for bugger all is just campaign 101,' a Tory strategist said.

The following Sunday, McDonnell made a pledge that would break both the bank and his own, hard-won, credibility. The shadow chancellor declared that Labour would compensate every woman born between 1950 and 1955 who had been affected by changes to the state pension age – a group dubbed the WASPI women (Women Against State Pension Inequality). The price tag was a staggering £58 billion and the costings were nowhere to be found in Labour's manifesto, because the shadow Treasury team had not completed the work in time. 'That undercut the argument that our manifesto was fully costed, which worked so well in 2017,' a LOTO aide recalled.

By then, Corbyn had also made his worst misstep of the campaign, one made more inexplicable because it was planned. It occurred in the second debate, a four-way contest on 22 November which also featured Johnson, Swinson and Nicola Sturgeon facing thirty minutes each in front of a *Question Time* audience. Quizzed about Brexit, Corbyn said he would negotiate a 'credible' Leave deal – a claim interrupted by audience laughter – and added, 'I will adopt, as prime minister ... a neutral stance so that I can credibly carry out the result.' Host Fiona Bruce queried whether Corbyn would really not pick a side during another referendum. 'Yes,' he confirmed. 'First heard here on *Question Time*.' The Labour leader had made news on the one subject he had spent the campaign studiously avoiding. The idea was to emulate Harold Wilson, who had remained above the fray during the 1975 referendum on European membership, leaving members of his cabinet to front the rival campaigns. But after three years of heated public debate, voters couldn't understand why Corbyn had no view on EU membership.

'That was one of the key moments,' a senior Tory said. 'In our focus groups, voters were saying, "This is pathetic. That's the guy who's trying to be leader of the country." And that was a strategic move from them.'

The Tories responded with a series of ads pledging to 'get Britain out of neutral'.

Swinson had the most torrid time, however, in front of an audience supposed to be politically balanced but which had given Corbyn a standing ovation. For Swinson it was like fruitlessly attacking the goal at the away end. For half an hour she endured silence and derision. The first question, 'Do you regret starting off the campaign by saying you could be PM and do you now agree how ridiculous that sounded?' was greeted with applause. It went downhill from there. Swinson was pounded over backing 'harsh and uncaring benefit cuts' and imposing tuition fees during the coalition. Another questioner said, 'The reason people are poor is because of austerity, which you supported.' When she criticised Corbyn, a man in the audience intervened, 'Jeremy Corbyn has been fighting antisemitism and racism in all its forms since before you were born. You've got some brass neck,' another contribution which won wild applause and cheering.

Watching in the green room, Swinson's team felt paralysed as the onslaught continued. 'She was giving perfectly good answers,' one said, 'but she was just dealing with a crowd of Momentum activists.' Worse, every time Swinson had a bad moment, 'I could hear Nicola Sturgeon cheering in the next room,' the aide recalled. 'Every time she got heckled, every time she didn't get applauded. It was lacking class. It was more like a national puppy drowning than *Question Time*.' When Swinson came off stage, she was 'slightly stunned'. Sam Barratt sought out a BBC executive to complain about the biased audience. The corporation never admitted it had been infiltrated by left-wingers but for the next BBC debate checks on social media became part of the audience vetting.

There was a deeper problem though: Swinson herself. Her strident anti-Brexit stance and sometimes tetchy manner damaged her. Those prepping Swinson tried hard to make her sympathetic, but during the debate camp one texted a fellow Lib Dem, 'She sounds like a fucking robot.' Paul Butters was in an Asian-run 'desi pub' in Wolverhampton on the night of the debate. Two tables away was Labour's Pat McFadden. *Question Time* was on the television but with the sound down. There were no subtitles. But when Swinson came on screen, a man stood up and started shouting 'You fucking cunt' at the television. The two men exchanged a look and returned to their curry.

Allies saw a double standard in personal criticisms of Swinson. 'I do think she's good,' a fellow MP said. 'If you compare her to Jeremy

Corbyn, bloody hell. I think she was held to a much higher bar. Look at what Boris Johnson got away with. As prime minister he didn't even have to tell us how many children he's got.'

But Swinson's dealings with the media were awkward. When the Mirror interviewed her before the party conference, she arrived thirty minutes late and then evicted the paper's photographer – who had lost both his legs to a Taliban bomb while embedded with the Marines in Afghanistan – from a room so she could do her make-up. 'This man, who'd won a citation for bravery, had to get out,' a party source said.

While public dislike of Swinson grew during the campaign, MPs of all parties reported back from their canvassing that negative views of Corbyn were 'baked in' on the doorstep. One aide often on the road with the leader recalled, 'Whenever Jeremy was on stage, I'd speak to the regional organisers and staff and ask, "How's it going?" and they would say, "It's tough." Some people were not voting for us because of Brexit, but even if our Brexit position was different, they still wouldn't be voting for us because of the poppy, the anthem, the IRA.' Ruth Smeeth reflected later, 'If Jeremy hadn't been leader, I'd still be a member of Parliament.'[28]

No issue was more toxic than Corbyn's response to antisemitism. Luciana Berger, standing for the Lib Dems in Finchley and Golders Green, held by Tory Mike Freer since 2010, found a 'fear of Corbyn' on the doorstep. 'People who never voted Conservative in their life were voting Conservative because they wanted to guarantee that they weren't facilitating Jeremy Corbyn into Number 10. It came up here on most doorsteps.' Distaste for Corbyn's views was also common in seats with no Jewish populations, where it seemed to offend the British sense of fair play.

The most impactful intervention of the campaign came on the evening of 25 November. Ephraim Mirvis, the chief rabbi since 2013, had been picked precisely because he was a less flashy figure than his predecessor, the media savvy Jonathan Sacks, who in 2018 had compared Corbyn to Enoch Powell. But the depth of feeling about Corbyn, from what his aides called 'the Jews in the pews', convinced Mirvis he needed to act. He summoned a group of trusted allies, including academics on antisemitism and the Holocaust, to his home in Finchley on 24 November and asked how he could stage a public intervention against Corbyn becoming prime minister. Mirvis, as the leader of a charity, was restricted by law from telling the public how to vote. His lawyers said a public statement was 'out of the question'. Anthony Julius, best known as Diana, Princess of Wales' divorce lawyer, told Mirvis he could go ahead, as long as he didn't tell people how to vote. Only Michael Levy, who had raised millions for Tony Blair, counselled caution, warning that Corbyn could win the election and such an intervention would be disastrous for Britain's Jews.[29]

Mirvis wrote an article and his aides passed it to Henry Zeffman, a rising star on *The Times* political team. The newspaper's front page dropped with the force of a bomb going off: 'Corbyn not fit for high office, says chief rabbi'. Inside, Mirvis wrote that British Jews were 'gripped by anxiety' and that 'the question I am now most frequently asked is: What will become of Jews and Judaism in Britain if the Labour Party forms the next government?' Tackling the outbreak of antisemitism, he went on, 'A new poison – sanctioned from the top – has taken root in the Labour Party … It is not my place to tell any person how they should vote. I regret being in this situation at all. I simply pose the question: What will the result of this election say about the moral compass of our country? When December 12 arrives, I ask every person to vote with their conscience. Be in no doubt, the very soul of our nation is at stake.'

The timing was devastating. As the paper dropped on doormats on the morning of 26 November, Corbyn was preparing for the launch of his party's race and faith manifesto. Aides said he sat in bewildered silence, unable to deal with being accused of racism. Corbyn was very late for the launch and, on arrival, was heckled by protesters. He had previously been cajoled into several apologies for Labour's response to antisemitism. Yet, in a rambling speech, through bovine stubbornness and political ineptitude, Corbyn failed to say sorry.

Later the same day he faced the BBC's Andrew Neil, and appeared resentful and unprepared. 'That morning was the most chaotic of the whole campaign,' an aide recalled. 'It was complete carnage. Jeremy didn't want to be briefed and didn't want to focus. He wasn't in the right headspace.' What followed was inevitable and catastrophic.

Neil devoted most of the interview to antisemitism, trying four times to elicit an apology. Corbyn huffed and puffed and sighed like an irate teenager, a broken and defeated man who seemed determined to invest what remained of his personal pride in resistance, rather than resolving his political problem. 'You said that anyone who has committed any antisemitic act in the Labour Party, they've been suspended or expelled and you've investigated "every single case",' Neil said. 'The chief rabbi has called that "a mendacious fiction". And he's right, isn't he?'

'No, he's not right,' a sullen Corbyn retorted. On it went: his stock defence that he had spent his life 'opposing racism in any form', bristling and defensive when Neil tried to intervene. There was a hypnotic quality to it, viewers wondering if Corbyn would hold out, digging himself ever deeper. All he had to do was say, 'Andrew, I've repeatedly apologised, and I'm happy to do so again. More than that, I've acted.' But this was beyond him, either ideologically or professionally. The following morning, even the *i*, Corbyn's favourite national paper, splashed on his refusal to say sorry. The issue which had done most to cause the split and to disbar him as potential caretaker prime minister now ensured there would be no repeat of 2017. On the Labour campaign conference call, even his comrade in arms, Ian Lavery, snapped: 'Why can't you just say sorry? Just do it, man!'[30]

The coda came on 6 December, when the submission made by the Jewish Labour Movement (JLM) to the Equality and Human Rights Commission's inquiry leaked to the media, including seventy sworn testimonies by serving and former Labour officials. One witness reported twenty-two incidents of antisemitic abuse at party meetings where he was told 'Hitler was right'. The submission concluded that 'the Labour Party is no longer a safe space for Jewish people'. Two days later, Mike Katz, JLM's chairman, announced that his members had 'downed tools' during an election 'for the first time' because 'Jeremy Corbyn is not fit to be prime minister'. JLM had been a founding affiliate of the Labour Party and it no longer wanted Labour to win.

WOBBLES

From London Bridge to the Fridge

20 November to 11 December 2019

Even in 1987, as she secured her second three-figure landslide, Margaret Thatcher's campaign team had a serious wobble midway through the campaign. Ten years later, Tony Blair's inner circle wondered if they might still lose, even as they ran up the largest majority since 1935. And so it was with Boris Johnson's Conservatives. Labour's sustained broadcast dominance saw the polls narrow, particularly after the publication of Jeremy Corbyn's manifesto. For several days, double-digit leads evaporated in the Tories' daily tracking poll. On one day after the manifesto the Conservative lead narrowed to two points. 'It got close to touching,' a senior figure admitted. 'The PM was certainly concerned; any candidate is when it's getting tighter and tighter and tighter.'

Johnson's anguish continued for four or five days and led him to question whether there was enough in his own manifesto. Oliver 'Sonic' Lewis pulled Lee Cain aside and suggested Dominic Cummings take a more hands-on role: 'The messaging has gone off track. We're not talking about Brexit enough. We have to get Dom in here.' Cain was firm: 'He's not here. We need to make the best of it.'

Levido sensed the concern, felt it himself. A group of external political experts pitched to change the Tory slogan from 'Get Brexit Done' to 'Believe in Britain'. Similar noises were being made by MPs and candidates in Remain seats. Levido thought it the worst advice he received in the whole campaign. George Freeman, a transport minister from Mid Norfolk, bursting with more ideas than self-awareness, got in touch with Levido to say, 'Boris has told me to lead the strategy on the One Nation fight. Here is my memo. Tell me your thoughts. Where should I go?'

Levido replied, 'Really helpful. I think you should stay in the Norfolk area. That's where you can be really effective. Don't leave Norfolk. Don't go anywhere else. And don't talk to anyone.'

Johnson gave away one of the main headlines from the Conservative manifesto four days early. Pressed by an employee at a fabrication yard on Teesside whether he would help 'people like us', Johnson blurted out that he was going to cut National Insurance, raising the threshold at which workers paid the levy to £12,500. 'It was in his mind because the manifesto had been printed that morning,' a campaign official explained. 'We swapped Wednesday for Sunday in the grid. That's Boris!' The gaffe gave the Tories a strong second story on the broadcast news on the day of Labour's manifesto launch.

Johnson unveiled his manifesto on Sunday 24 November in Telford, a marginal seat the Tories had won by just 720 votes in 2017. The headline was a plan to spend £3.3 billion recruiting fifty thousand more nurses. The prime minister unveiled £23 billion of increased public spending and tax cuts, including what he billed as the 'biggest ever cash boost to the NHS'. He said Britain faced a choice between 'destructive socialism' and 'sensible One Nation Conservatism'. There was also £1 billion for child-care and a 'tax lock', pledging not to raise the rates of income tax, National Insurance or VAT, as well as to keep the pensions triple lock and free bus travel for pensioners.

Johnson mocked Corbyn's announcement that he would be neutral on Brexit, saying, 'He used to be indecisive, now he's not so sure.' He then embarked on a tortuous metaphor: 'Do you want to wake up on 31 December and find a nightmare on Downing Street? Let's go carbon neutral by 2050 and Corbyn neutral by Christmas.' The Brexit section of the manifesto, written by Oliver Lewis, hailed Johnson's deal of 17 October 'signed, sealed and ready'. Johnson said he would bring back the withdrawal agreement bill before Christmas so families could 'enjoy their festive season free from the seemingly unending Brexit box-set drama'. He concluded, 'Imagine the Friday 13th horror show if the Corbyn-Sturgeon coalition of chaos is triumphant ... We cannot let this nightmare before Christmas come to pass.'

The manifesto was not a game changer and the Conservative lead continued to shrink. 'The manifesto was carefully written,' Michael Gove recalled, 'to avoid some of the rows and distractions that had derailed

Theresa's campaign in 2017.'[1] Levido admitted later, 'The period immediately after the manifesto releases was the period when we were under
the most pressure ... It was the only time in the campaign that I felt there
was a narrative that Labour were offering change versus we were more of
the same.'[2]

The focus on health was one that, in years past, Lynton Crosby had
argued against, reasoning that the Tories should not raise the salience of
Labour's core issues. But a Tory strategist said, 'We wanted to persuade
a lot of traditional Labour voters whose number one hesitation for voting
for the Tories is that we're the Tories. Their hesitation was that we were
going to fuck the NHS, so we needed to neutralise that.'

This concern intensified three days later, when Corbyn landed
Labour's best attack story of the campaign. In an impromptu press
conference, he revealed that Labour had been leaked a document detailing trade negotiations between the UK and US. Corbyn claimed it as
proof that the NHS was 'on the table' in a post-Brexit trade deal between
the UK and Donald Trump. 'This is not only a plot against our NHS,' he
said. 'It is a plot against the whole country.' In fact, the documents
showed officials had discussed that option without ministerial backing.
More worrying, the security services determined that the documents had
been stolen from Liam Fox's private email by a hacker. Someone who
found them on an open source website alerted Labour.

The story knocked the chief rabbi's attack, the day before, off the top of
the news bulletins and achieved immediate 'cut through' in focus groups
conducted by both main parties. 'It was a concern,' a Tory official said. 'It
was coming up on the doorstep.' But even senior Labour figures did not
think it would swing the campaign. Jonathan Ashworth, the shadow health
secretary, who wanted a focus on patient issues instead, said, 'Politically,
voters didn't buy it. People understand what's happening when they can't
see a doctor or when they are waiting over an hour for an ambulance to
turn up, because it has affected them in their real lives. The problem with
the Trump-NHS campaign is that for a lot of voters it didn't feel real.'[3]

Cummings was sufficiently concerned about the narrowing of the
Tories' private polling, however, that on that same Wednesday, he posted
a blog warning Leave voters about the danger of a hung Parliament.
Cummings, who usually submitted to no authority but his own, wrote it
in collaboration with other campaign chiefs, including Levido. 'It was a
team effort,' said one.

Cummings seized on plans in Labour's manifesto, which he claimed would 'cheat' a second referendum. 'Their official policy is to give millions of EU citizens the vote in the second referendum. They don't plan to lose again and they've literally written into their manifesto that they will cheat the second referendum ... they will rig the question so the "choice" is effectively "Remain or Remain".' He urged Leave voters to 'make the time to speak to friends and family and explain why you will vote for Boris', pointing out that research had shown 'face to face' communication was the most persuasive. Addressing those who were thinking of voting for the Brexit Party, he explained that in Labour-held Leave seats backing Farage could split the Leave vote and hand victory to 'Corbyn, maybe by just a few hundred votes'. He concluded by warning, 'Trust me, as someone who has worked on lots of campaigns, things are MUCH tighter than they seem and there is a very real possibility of a hung parliament. Without a majority, the nightmare continues.'

That evening Tory nerves were eased by the publication of YouGov's first election model, using methodology which predicted a hung Parliament two years earlier. It showed a Conservative majority of 68, with Labour haemorrhaging 52 seats and the Lib Dems marooned on 13. However, in the week it took YouGov to complete the huge survey, the Tory majority had shrunk from 84 to 68. When Levido addressed his troops the following day he said, 'We knew the polls would tighten. We're sticking to our messages.'

Even as the polls remained a concern, the Tory machine rediscovered its mojo. On Thursday 28th, Channel 4 held a climate change debate. It looked like an ambush and Johnson declined to attend. CCHQ said Michael Gove would represent them, but the broadcaster refused on the grounds that it was a debate for party leaders only. Stanley Johnson, the prime minister's father and a longstanding environmentalist, never knowingly on message, said what a good idea the debate was. 'The Johnson clan do their own thing,' a weary Tory spin doctor observed.

Cain and Stephenson channelled Vote Leave vibes and told Gove to head to the Channel 4 studios and take Topham Guerin's cameraman with him. Gove, accompanied by Stanley Johnson and pursued by a boom mic, entered Channel 4's offices and asked to be included in the debate. He was turned down. After the stunt, he tweeted, 'Tonight I went to Channel 4 to talk about climate change but Jeremy Corbyn and

Nicola Sturgeon refused to debate a Conservative.' Channel 4 responded by placing melting ice sculptures representing Johnson and Nigel Farage at their podiums. If anyone said anything interesting that night, it was lost to history. Stephenson briefed the papers that the Tories would review Channel 4's broadcasting remit, while Cain issued a statement claiming Channel 4 had breached the broadcasting code with 'a provocative partisan stunt'. The Tory video of Gove's raid got more than 3.5 million views. Just 850,000 people watched the climate debate. 'That was a very Vote Leave day,' a 2016 veteran reflected, happily.

The tracking poll stabilised the following day, 29 November. Levido listened to Johnson's repeated demands to get the election back on Brexit by re-forming the treble act who had fronted Vote Leave. The prime minister was joined by Gove and Labour's Gisela Stuart to announce that, once the Brexit transition phase was over, he would ditch EU state aid rules, so 'we can intervene when great British businesses are struggling'. Sebastian Payne of the *FT* waspishly noted that the Tories were no longer pursuing a 'Singapore Brexit', with deregulation to the fore, but a 'North Korean Brexit'. One Tory staffer said, 'We literally rewrote forty years of economic policy there.'

The press conference was designed to resemble the final fortnight of the Leave campaign, when Johnson, Gove and Stuart had set themselves up as an alternative government to David Cameron's Conservatives. It had been set in the grid as a floating event for when Levido wanted a reset or to mount his closing argument. Addressing fellow Labour voters, Stuart said, 'In this election I will not vote for Jeremy Corbyn but I can vote for Brexit ... A vote for Boris Johnson this time around is a vote to get Brexit done. To do so does not make me and would not make you a Tory.' Six days later, Joan Ryan, who had quit Labour to join the Tiggers but was not standing again, became the eighth former Labour MP to tell voters not to back Corbyn. The Brexit press conference was the moment one Tory veteran concluded that Johnson was ready to win. 'There wasn't a single joke in it,' the source said. 'He knows it's all on the line.'

The prime minister needed all of his focus later that day when a terrorist went on the rampage, stabbing passers-by on London Bridge, scene of a terror attack at almost exactly the same stage of the campaign in 2017. Usman Khan, a twenty-eight-year-old released from prison on licence in December 2018, after spending eight years in jail for terrorism offences, was wearing an electronic tag and had been invited to attend a justice conference on prison rehabilitation at Fishmongers' Hall, on the north bank of the Thames. There he began his attack, before heading for the bridge. A man and a woman died after being stabbed. Two women and one man were hospitalised. Khan was restrained by a heroic group of civilians – one armed with a fire extinguisher and another wielding a five-foot-long narwhal horn seized from the wall of Fishmongers' Hall – before being shot dead by police. Khan had been jailed for his involvement in a 2010 plot to blow up the London stock exchange and for planning to establish a terrorist training facility in Kashmir.

For those who had worked on the 2017 campaign, the attack was an eerie reminder of when things had gone wrong for the Tories. On that occasion, the London Bridge attack had followed a suicide bombing at Manchester Arena, which took twenty-three lives. Corbyn, despite his dubious past on counterterrorism issues, had hammered the May government for its cuts to the police and nearly won the election. Tory campaign chiefs moved swiftly to ensure that did not happen this time.

Johnson was in his west London constituency when the attack occurred, just before 2 p.m., and had to rush back to Downing Street. After a brief conversation with Mark Sedwill, the cabinet secretary, Cummings went to Number 10 to take charge of the political response along with Cain. They joined Cobra committee meetings in the basement of the Cabinet Office, where Met commissioner Cressida Dick and intelligence chiefs briefed the prime minister.

In 2017, May's senior aides, Nick Timothy and Fiona Hill, had made a virtue of their government work, suspending the campaign for a week after the Manchester attack and again for a shorter period after London Bridge. Crosby found it difficult to get the information he needed in campaign headquarters. This time there was a swift conference call when the news broke and another within two hours where Johnson, Cummings and Cain were able to share details with Levido and Brooks in CCHQ. 'Our collective view was to suspend campaigning for the evening in London,' one participant said, 'but the public would expect us to go on.'

Johnson had a brief call with Corbyn, while Levido spoke to Karie Murphy in Southside. They agreed the campaign should continue and a seven-way debate on the BBC would go ahead. The Tories put up Rishi Sunak and Labour was represented by Rebecca Long-Bailey, the choice of most Corbynites as the next leader. Sunak came under attack from the six other candidates but acquitted himself well. Long-Bailey went straight into the 2017 greatest hits, attacking on police cuts, but her lacklustre performance was a sign of things to come for her as well.

Both Johnson and Cummings were 'fucking angry' about the failures which had let Khan out of jail to kill. Under legislation passed by Labour in 2008, terrorists had to be released halfway through their sentences without any assessment by the Parole Board of the threat they posed. The Tories scrapped automatic release in 2012 but Khan had been let out because he was sentenced under the old rules. Johnson was told Khan was granted permission by his parole officer to travel to London even though he was one of three thousand extremists on MI5's watch list. 'They came quite clearly to the view that automatic release for terrorists, to any normal person, sounds completely mental,' a senior Tory recalled. A cabinet minister said of Johnson, 'He does get really, really worked up about crime. You could see that his blood was up.'

The twenty-four hours following the attack was the moment when the experience of Cummings, Stephenson, Levido and Cain told most. By mid-afternoon, Cummings had called for policy options on sentencing and human rights law to be worked up. 'We have to respond with extreme toughness,' he said. The detailed work was done by Oliver Lewis and Rajiv Shah, a whip-smart special adviser at the Ministry of Justice. Stephenson sat beside them drawing up the media package to explain the new policies. 'We worked until gone midnight getting it together,' one said. Meanwhile, Cummings sought approval from the relevant secretaries of state and the security services.

There were further crisis meetings in Downing Street on the Saturday morning. By lunchtime Stephenson had briefed the Sunday papers about Johnson's planned crackdown: terrorists would serve their entire sentence, no longer be eligible for early release, and would spend at least fourteen years behind bars. Johnson would also vow to rewrite human rights laws to make it easier for intelligence officers to monitor terrorists. The prime minister said, 'These simple changes would have prevented this attack. I believe they will help stop further attacks.' By the afternoon, Johnson was back on the campaign trail.

While Vote Leave's populist attacking instincts were well suited to the occasion, Corbyn's history of questioning the security services left him floundering. The Labour leader first refused to support a shoot-to-kill policy by the police, which made it look as if he was questioning the

Met's handling of the incident. Under pressure from his aides, Corbyn then said he thought the police had 'no choice' but to shoot Khan dead. But when he appeared on *Sky News* that Sunday he was slow to recognise the political dangers in the Tory announcement, saying terrorists should 'not necessarily' serve their full sentence behind bars. 'Every interview he did was a gift,' a Tory official said. 'He was always one step behind.'

Labour's manifesto recommended stronger human rights protections for suspects, allowing Johnson to go on the attack again: 'It concerns me that Jeremy Corbyn is setting out plans to weaken our system and make it more difficult for our security services to stop people who want to do us harm.' A Tory official said, 'We were a lot better than them when we got into a fight.' Another said, 'That was not where the election was won, but it was the moment where it was not lost.'

From that point on the Tories stretched their lead. Before the terror attack the Conservatives had been taking around 7 or 8 per cent of Labour's 2017 vote. This would rise to 15 per cent.

Labour had already decided to change strategy. The previous Sunday, as Johnson was unveiling his manifesto, McDonnell chaired a meeting to push resources to a raft of new target seats which were in danger of falling. Fearing a revolt of candidates in the original 66 attack seats, they were left on the list, while the number of defensive constituencies was doubled from 30 to 67, most of them in the Midlands and North-East.

Adviser Andrew Murray came up with a new slogan, 'We're On Your Side', which sought to suggest both helping the less well off and reassuring working-class Leave voters about the party's motives. Nonetheless, it had no testing in focus groups.[4]

On the Monday, an ally of Milne briefed the BBC that Labour had adopted a new strategy to target Leave voters – against the wishes of John McDonnell, Andrew Fisher, Niall Sookoo and Tim Waters, the director of data and targeting.[5] Waters announced he was resigning.

Karie Murphy, Corbyn's gatekeeper, held a conference call on the Monday with regional campaign directors and Jennie Formby, Labour's general secretary. She said Labour would not win a majority but should 'concentrate resources where they will make a difference'. It was the first time someone in the inner circle had admitted to those outside that the strategy was in chaos. Over the next twenty-four hours, staff were told which target seats to abandon and which Labour-held seats to focus on.

The north-west region was the bloodbath: Bolton West, Morecambe and Lunesdale, and Southport were deprioritised, alongside Labour-held Warrington South. Hope was also quietly abandoned in Bolsover, where an eighty-seven-year-old Dennis Skinner was facing defeat. By Wednesday evening Milne had signed off a memo that Labour would be switching to promote more Brexit-friendly, northern and working-class voices – Rebecca Long-Bailey, Richard Burgon and Ian Lavery among them – to win back Leave voters in the Midlands and North. Lavery was sent on a tour of Leave-voting seats.

Trying to win seats on the original target list such as Telford, where the Tories were 17 per cent ahead, and Mansfield, where the lead was 24 points, had been 'ludicrously optimistic', a Labour staffer admitted. 'You've had people in West Bromwich and Ashfield saying they are getting no manpower, no leaflet budget, and it's all being ploughed into seats up the road which we've got no chance of winning.'

There were two other motives for the switch: ensuring the 'blame game' was lost by the Remain faction of McDonnell, Starmer and Thornberry; and pushing resources to key figures on the left so they would survive to fight over the entrails of their party. 'Laura Pidcock is getting disproportionate resources because she is the person who Karie has decided to support for the leadership,' one source said. Pidcock, at that time, had a 9 per cent lead in North West Durham. Videographers in Labour's community organising team threatened to go on strike after being told to divert resources away from target seats and instead make films of Long-Bailey, Corbyn's chosen successor.

That same weekend the Lib Dems slashed their target seats from 80 to 30. On a conference call with her senior campaign staff, Swinson asked, 'What are we talking, numbers wise?' They had individual constituency polls from Survation and an update to their MRP. The 30 surviving targets divided into thirds: the ten seats where they were safe, the ten where they would win if they 'did the right stuff' and ten more where 'we'll win if we have a good night'. Dave McCobb, from the field team, believed they were heading for a result in the teens. The constituency polling showed that some of the biggest names, including Luciana Berger and Chuka Umunna, were in trouble.

Swinson spent the first half of the campaign positioning herself equi-distant between the Tories and Labour. But in the vast majority of new target seats their opponents were the Conservatives, which dictated a change of tone. 'We had to get those soft Conservatives who hated Brexit, didn't really like Boris Johnson, but were probably going to vote Conservative because of Jeremy Corbyn, to vote for us,' a campaign chief said. On 1 December, Swinson did an interview with the *Sunday Times* in which she branded Johnson a 'liar' and added, 'Most people in politics have redeeming features, things I can agree with them on, things I can respect them for and Boris Johnson just seems to care about himself.'

Levido also used his two MRP models to reshape his battlefield. New targets were coming into play but he wanted to be sure his defensive seats were safe before devoting resources. He also knew a strong national swing would deliver some of these targets whether he spent money on them or not. He added 15 seats to his target list, bringing the total number which received central resources to 135. Levido also signed off a doubling of digital spending in target seats.

In parts of the red wall, and with blue-collar workers elsewhere, Johnson was getting a notably warm reaction. Danny Kruger said, 'I noticed it in Manchester. He passed a Kwik Fit garage, and all the mechanics saw it was Boris Johnson, and they came out cheering "Boris, Boris". This happened all over the place.'[6] One seat that now had an outside chance of victory was Blyth Valley, which had never voted Conservative before. 'An elderly guy' opened his door to Ian Levy, the Tory candidate, and said, 'I worked in the pit all my life. I never thought I'd see the day that I would vote Conservative, but d'you know what, Ian, I'm voting Conservative.' Levy gave him a leaflet. The man said, 'No, no, give us a bundle 'cos I'm taking them to the club tonight.'[7]

The most striking example of this phenomenon came when Johnson campaigned on Teesside on 30 November. During a visit to Wilton Engineering, he was greeted by a group of blue-collar workers in heavy boots, paint-spattered overalls and hard hats, brandishing a cardboard sign on which was painted, in bright red letters, 'We Love Boris.' It was at once a surprising, incongruous and clairvoyant image, the defection of the northern white working-class male made flesh.

By the first weekend in December there was just one cloud in the Tory sky – Donald Trump. The president had arrived in town for a Nato summit and Johnson's team was frantic about what he might say. Previous prime ministers had craved friendly intervention at election time from a president. But when it emerged that Trump was planning a television interview with Piers Morgan, who had appeared on the American version of *Celebrity Apprentice*, Johnson and his team tried everything to stop it. 'We used as many channels available to us,' a campaign official said, 'to express our opinion that it would not be a helpful thing if he did that interview.' The US embassy in London stressed to Trump that foreign intervention in the election might be counterproductive. During his time as foreign secretary, Johnson had got to know several of Trump's team. It was Jared Kushner, his son-in-law, who eventually persuaded the president to ditch the interview. 'Trump's people were saying to him, "You really could screw this up",' said a Republican strategist who was in London that week.

On 4 December, Jo Swinson survived her head-to-head encounter with Andrew Neil. But even this far into the campaign, he opened by showing the leaflet emblazoned with 'Jo Swinson: Britain's next Prime Minister', accusing her of 'fantasy politics? You know, I know, our viewers know, you're not going to be the next prime minister.' Swinson argued he should not second-guess the voters. Neil also took her to task for the Revoke stance and repeatedly got her to admit that she had voted for things during the coalition which her party was now opposing. The dreams of a breakthrough were gone, but Swinson got credit for keeping her cool, unlike Corbyn, and turning up at all, unlike Johnson.

The following day, tired of waiting for CCHQ to confirm Johnson, Neil used the final moments of his interview with Nicola Sturgeon to challenge Johnson directly. Looking straight at the camera, he said: 'We have been asking him for weeks now to give us a date, a time, a venue. As of now, none has been forthcoming. It is not too late. We have an interview prepared, oven-ready as Mr Johnson likes to say. The theme running through our questions is trust, and why at so many times in his career in politics and journalism, critics and sometimes even those close to him have deemed him to be untrustworthy.' Neil said that no broadcaster 'can compel a politician to be interviewed', but added, 'In every election they have. All of them. Until this one.' He concluded by saying, 'The prime minister of our nation will, at times, have to stand up to President Trump, President Putin, President Xi of China. So it was surely not expecting too much that he spend half an hour standing up to me.' The video got more than six million views.

The pundits erupted, convinced Johnson's behaviour was not only an affront to democracy but also a mistake. Levido wanted Johnson to do Andrew Marr's show that Sunday instead, but the BBC refused to give him air time unless he did Neil first. Carrie told him he should do it. Cummings claimed to colleagues that he heard her whispering in the background as Johnson told him, 'I've got to do Andrew Neil.' Cummings and Cain were both adamant there was nothing to gain. Alone, a while later, Johnson phoned back and said, 'Fuck that, you're right, torpedo it.' Afterwards, Cummings wrote, 'Why the fuck would we put a gaffe machine, clueless about policy and government up to be grilled for ages?' The 'upside' was 'zero'.[8]

The next day, 6 December, Johnson was back on the BBC, for his second head-to-head debate with Corbyn, moderated by Nick Robinson. Corbyn landed effective blows on Johnson's use of racist language in his newspaper columns, but faced a hard time on his past associations with terrorists. The best exchanges, however, were on Brexit. Johnson accused Corbyn of 'a failure of leadership' for not having a position on 'the greatest issue facing our country' and questioning who in Labour would negotiate their 'mystery deal' with Brussels when most of the shadow cabinet was pro-Remain.

Earlier that day, Corbyn and Keir Starmer held a press conference to release a leaked Treasury document which cast doubt on Johnson's claims that his Brexit deal would not leave a customs border in the Irish Sea. It suggested high street goods were 'likely to increase in price' in Northern Ireland and businesses would struggle to bear the costs of 'highly disruptive' border checks. The document, entitled 'Northern Ireland Protocol: Unfettered Access to the UK Internal Market', warned that 'the withdrawal agreement has the potential to separate Northern Ireland in practice from whole swathes of the UK's internal market'. It said, 'At minimum, exit summary declarations will be required when goods are exported from Northern Ireland to Great Britain.' And for trade from Great Britain to Northern Ireland there could be tariffs, it warned. Johnson had repeatedly claimed his deal would not require border checks, most recently on a BBC phone-in three weeks earlier, when he told one business in Northern Ireland that if they were asked to fill in a form, they should ring him, and 'I will direct them to throw that form in the bin.' At a campaign event in Kent, before the debate, Johnson insisted, 'There will be no checks on goods going between GB to NI, or NI to GB.'

In the debate, he found a better retort. When Corbyn raised this issue, Johnson hit back: 'I do find it slightly curious to be lectured about the Union by a man who has spent all his political life campaigning to break up the Union and who supported for four decades the IRA and their campaign violently to destroy it.' This won the first round of applause of the night. YouGov's snap poll again gave a narrow win to Johnson, by 52 to 48 per cent, a result which appeared to be an existential joke, suggesting the nation was still divided in the same ratios as in 2016.

Corbyn had, however, identified the Achilles heel of the 2019 deal which was to shape the Brexit debate for the next three years. When Johnson spoke to the *Sunday Times* that weekend, he admitted goods going from Great Britain into Northern Ireland which then went on into Ireland would face checks. Johnson refused to acknowledge that, without EU acceptance of alternative technical arrangements, Brussels would not distinguish between goods going from Britain to Northern Ireland and those which went on to the Republic. Either he did not know what he had signed or he was prepared to mislead. The evidence points to the latter.

Johnson got away with it because he was now into the closing argument phase of the campaign and was able to deliver his core message, with enough rhetorical flourishes to make news. He told the *Sunday Times*, 'What you have now is a One Nation Conservative government that can take this country forward and get the incubus of Brexit off our collective backs.' Comparing Britain to a slumbering giant, he said, 'You will hear one by one the pinging of the guy ropes as the Gulliver stands up again.' Asked what he wanted for Christmas, Johnson replied, 'I want Brexit! I want Brexmas!'[9]

The one curveball came when Johnson chose to sail close to the wind when answering a question, about the most romantic thing he had ever done, by suggesting Brexit would lead to a bonanza of bonking. 'I can tell you that whatever that [romantic act] may have been, it will be nothing compared to the way Cupid's darts will fly. Romance will bloom across the whole nation once we get Brexit done, I confidently predict.' Asked if he was predicting a baby boom, he replied, 'There was one after the Olympics, as I prophesied in a speech in 2012, it was quite amazing. There was a big baby boom.' This unsolicited soliloquy suggested strongly that Johnson was planning to start a family with Carrie. Put on the spot, he replied, 'I am not going to make any demographic projections.' Would there be the patter of tiny feet in Number 10? 'I don't comment about that sort of thing,' he said. Realising he had gone too far, Johnson joked that there might be the 'patter of tiny paws', since Dilyn, his new dog, had been seen by Number 10 staff humping Sajid Javid's dog Bailey in the Downing Street garden. 'There's some anxiety in both families that things may be moving too fast,' he explained. Johnson had indeed moved too fast. Carrie was already pregnant but the couple had not yet told Johnson's children from his marriage to Marina Wheeler. When they saw the paper, at least one registered dismay that they had to learn of it from the media. 'The kids were on his case and gave him a hard time,' a friend said.

That final weekend of the campaign, YouGov put the Tories on 43 per cent, ten points ahead of Labour. To drive home their advantage, Levido unleashed the full force of the Tory digital blitzkrieg which he had been planning since the start of the campaign, with a £500,000 online advertising offensive. The opening salvo was to buy a banner advert on YouTube's home page on 7 December, which featured an animation by Topham Guerin depicting bickering politicians shouting at each other in slow motion. The voice-over, said: 'This hung Parliament isn't working for you. They've been arguing amongst themselves for three long years. Now they're arguing about arguing. Arguing just for the sake of it. Their arguments have crept into your life, crept into your work, crept into your family. Their endless arguments have frozen our country, stopped us focusing on the things that really matter. You matter. Your vote matters. With your vote, you decide. Stop the arguing or let it carry on?' The music then changed to an upbeat choral track, Handel's 'Zadok the Priest'. 'End the argument. Stop the chaos. Vote Conservative. Get Brexit done. Get all of this done and move on. Vote Conservative on Thursday. Get Brexit done.'

It was a perfect encapsulation of the Tory campaign and with no mentions of Johnson was calibrated to appeal to Brexiteers and weary Remainers alike. By 9 p.m. that day, the advert, which cost around £120,000 to place, had been watched more than 1.5 million times. It would get to more than 3 million. The YouTube homepage that day received between 50 million and 60 million views. Sean Topham had told his team to find the best ideas online and adapt them for the campaign. To him, the Tory campaign was not competing with Labour for clicks but with Apple, Netflix and Disney to create memorable content. He said, 'We were also very mindful that going into the Christmas market you're actually competing against John Lewis and Waitrose, who are running ads in the same space and doing huge buys.'

The last week of the campaign had been planned in the first week, when the Tory team made ad buys for the final five days. The YouTube takeover was a tactic which had worked for Topham Guerin and Levido in Australia. Before the final push, the Conservatives had spent just 10 per cent of their £2 million digital budget, mirroring the approach taken by Vote Leave during the referendum campaign, when it spent £1.5 million in the final week on Facebook and digital content. The Tories also took over the home pages of the *Sun*, *Mail* and *Daily Express* on election day.

Labour, by contrast, ran a lot of videos and got lots of views and even put out a press release the night before the election saying they had won the social media campaign, but most of the content was forgettable.

The pièce de résistance of the Tory digital campaign was their final party political broadcast on 9 December. A spoof of the Christmas film *Love Actually*, it featured Boris Johnson in the role of Andrew Lincoln, wooing a female voter with a series of message boards. The idea had come up in the first creative brainstorm the digital team did at the end of October. Topham pitched Levido the *Love Actually* idea and the *Vogue* video on the same evening. They shot a tester video in a friend's doorway to see how it looked. Levido liked it. Johnson had never seen *Love Actually* so the prime minister was shown the clip from the film and also approved it. Two days later disaster struck. The Labour MP Rosena Allin-Khan had the same idea and issued her own version of the message board scene on Twitter. 'We'll have to go back to the drawing board,' Topham said. The digital team thought about other Christmas films they might ape. To get the film to the broadcasters, they had to make it by Friday 7 December. On the evening of Monday 2nd, Levido said, 'I'd like to think about doing it again because I don't think the Rosena Allin-Khan one had as much cut-through as people think. Only the bubble has noticed.' The following day he said, 'Let's do it.'

Filming took place on Wednesday 4th. Johnson had an exhausting day with the conclusion of the Nato summit and then a stop at the Red Bull Formula One team, where he changed a tyre for the cameras. That was followed by three hours of debate prep. Levido then despatched him to a mews in Kensington. 'He was not happy at having to go,' one campaign official recalled, 'it was fucking freezing outside.'

When Johnson's car arrived, he was presented with a steaming mug of tea – with the bag still in, of course. 'We were very mindful that we couldn't have him standing outside for too long or catching a cold for the final five days,' one of the team said. In the street, they had erected big black drapes either side of the doorway. 'Under no circumstances can anyone see this,' Topham said. No one wanted a repeat of 2015 when Ed Miliband had filmed a surprise endorsement from the comedian Russell Brand but a photograph snatched on a camera phone blew the secret.

The film opened with a couple watching the Tory YouTube film when the doorbell rings. The woman answers the door and finds Johnson on her doorstep. 'Oh, hi,' she said as he put a finger to his lips and displayed the first board: 'SAY IT'S CAROL SINGERS.' Having put 'Silent Night' on a portable stereo, Johnson continued through his cards:

WITH ANY LUCK, BY NEXT YEAR
WE'LL HAVE BREXIT *DONE*
(IF PARLIAMENT DOESN'T BLOCK IT AGAIN)
AND WE CAN MOVE ON
BUT FOR NOW LET ME SAY
YOUR VOTE HAS NEVER BEEN MORE IMPORTANT
THE OTHER GUY *COULD* WIN …
SO YOU HAVE A CHOICE TO MAKE
BETWEEN A WORKING MAJORITY
OR ANOTHER GRIDLOCKED HUNG PARLIAMENT
ARGUING ABOUT BREXIT
UNTIL I LOOK LIKE THIS

A frowning Johnson then unveiled a picture of a dog who shared a shock of blonde fur descending over his eyes. The woman laughed.

IT'S CLOSER THAN YOU THINK
WE ONLY NEED *9 MORE* SEATS TO GET A MAJORITY
AND ON 12TH DECEMBER
YOUR VOTE WILL MAKE ALL THE DIFFERENCE.

Johnson nodded vigorously.

MERRY CHRISTMAS.

This was accompanied by Johnson's trademark double thumbs-up gesture.

The PM took just two takes, then they filmed an over the shoulder shot in which the actress playing the female voter did reaction shots to each of the cards. Johnson went inside to get warm while the drapes were removed. Then he performed a final walk to the camera, in which he said, 'Enough, enough, let's get this done', before the final slogan appeared on screen: 'Vote Conservative, actually.' Johnson did not even mention Brexit; he didn't need to. The footage in the can, Topham's team edited through the night. He got to CCHQ at 4.30 a.m. When Levido came in at 5 a.m. they showed him the film.

Later that day four Brexit Party MEPs, including Annunziata Rees-Mogg, resigned from the party and urged their supporters to vote Conservative instead.

The *Love Actually* video was supposed to be released on 10 December but BBC Wales put it up the day before. It made little difference; the film went viral. Its prominence was boosted when Hugh Grant, a star of the original film, happened to be doing a media round on the Tuesday morning. Grant praised the 'very high production values' but added, 'Clearly the Conservative Party have an awful lot of money. Maybe that's where all the rubles went?' Grant pointed out Johnson had not used the card in the film which said, 'Because of Christmas, you tell the truth'. He said, 'I wonder if the spin doctors in the Tory Party thought that was a card that wouldn't look too great in Boris Johnson's hands.'

The video was the lead story on *MailOnline* for more than eight hours that day. It would get more than seven million views. For a production cost of just £50,000, Topham and Guerin had broken the internet again. By the end of the campaign, 'Facebook posts by the Labour Party and Jeremy Corbyn accounts were shared almost four times more than posts by the Conservatives and Boris Johnson (3.9 million vs 1.1 million),' the book of the campaign recorded. Corbyn's Facebook page had 98 million views, around 50 per cent higher than in 2017. 'Of the top 10 videos shared and viewed on Facebook, nine were posted on the Corbyn, Labour or Momentum channels.'[10] The one Tory entry was 'Brexit, Actually'. But Topham Guerin's output had more cut through into the mainstream national media than Labour's, taking it beyond preaching to the converted. More than a year later one Tory campaign veteran said, 'I can think of two PPBs since 2010 that I can actually remember. That's one of them.'

The final three days was no cakewalk for the Tories, however. On the morning of Monday 9th, the *Daily Mirror* ran a front-page story under the headline 'Desperate', with a photograph of a sick four-year-old boy forced to sleep on the floor of Leeds General Infirmary.

Johnson was up at 6 a.m. doing a tour of a fish market, after which he gave a series of regional media interviews. Things went wrong when he was quizzed by Joe Pike, an ambitious ITV *Calendar* reporter keen to make a name for himself. Pike asked if he had seen the picture. A brusque Johnson said, 'No, I've just been told about it', before talking about how much money the Tories were putting into the NHS. Pike offered his phone. 'Why not look at it now, Prime Minister?' At this point Johnson, seized by irritation, tiredness and the madness that can creep into campaigns, did one of the strangest things ever seen in an election interview. Pike, barely believing his luck, noted, 'You've refused to look at the photo, you've taken my phone and put it in your pocket, Prime Minister.' Johnson pulled out the phone, looked at the image and admitted, 'It's a terrible, terrible photo and I apologise to the family and all those who have terrible experiences in the NHS.'

'That is literally the only mistake he had in the campaign,' said one official. But it was ammunition for those who thought Johnson heartless and out of touch. The travelling pack was flying to Newcastle when the story blew up. Pike tweeted that Johnson had snatched his phone and refused to look at the picture, outrage fuelled by Robert Peston, the political editor of *ITV News*, with the BBC running hard to catch up. The *Guardian* claimed Johnson had refused to look at the image, while running a picture which showed him doing so.

Press secretary Rob Oxley and other aides who were with Johnson contemplated deploying a 'dead cat' – Lynton Crosby's idea that when things are bad 'you throw a dead cat on the table' to distract attention. They had not decided what to do when Johnson arrived at a tyre factory outside Sunderland. He was asked about the BBC licence fee and replied, 'At this stage, we are not planning to get rid of all TV licence fees, although I am certainly looking at it … I am under pressure not to extemporise policy on the hoof, but you have to ask yourself whether that kind of approach to funding a media organisation, still makes sense in the long term, given the way other organisations manage to fund themselves.' Johnson had supplied his own dead cat.

Campaign chiefs decided to despatch Matt Hancock, the health secretary, to the hospital in Leeds to try to meet the family of the boy. Which is where things went wrong again for the Tories. During the visit protesters tried to chase Hancock and his media adviser, Jamie Njoku-Goodwin, as they left. In the melee, someone screamed, 'You're not welcome here', more threatening since Njoku-Goodwin was black. As they tried to escape, Hancock was on the phone to Paul Stephenson in CCHQ, the screaming and shouting audible to those in London. Getting into the car, Njoku-Goodwin felt something hit him in the back of the head; he thought he had been punched. Oxley and others briefed the lobby. But when broadcasters checked the footage, it was clear no punches had been thrown. Njoku-Goodwin had been knocked by someone holding a placard. Journalists were furious they had been misled.

In London, Stephenson and his team leaned hard into the BBC licence fee story and succeeded in making it a major feature of most newspapers' coverage the following morning. The broadcasters, having the images of the boy and the Joe Pike footage, stuck with the NHS story. Cain was worried it might run for two or three days, costing the Tories a majority. 'We need to do something,' he said. He proposed pulling out a reserve dead cat and making a major announcement on immigration to try to knock Johnson's response to the four-year-old off the top of the bulletins.

Levido stopped him. He was a fan of the Vote Leave way, going for broke, but conscious this could alienate some voters. It was his job to see the entire chess position. 'We're not doing anything,' he said. They had plenty planned for the following day. Cain could have thrown his weight around. It was a reflection of the team spirit that he said to Levido, 'Respectfully, I disagree. I think you're wrong, but you're the boss.'

That evening the Tories held their final focus groups. They supported Levido's judgement. 'No one had heard about the Joe Pike incident,' one official said. 'We showed it to them. The almost universal reaction was: "Here we go again … I'm sick of these journalists on TV … He's just trying to answer the question."'

When he came on the evening conference call, Johnson was furious with himself and 'very apologetic' to his senior aides. 'He felt very bad about it,' one said. 'He was pulling his hair out about how badly he fucked up.' Levido tried to reassure him: 'You have been flawless in this campaign. Everyone gets tired and makes mistakes.' He showed Johnson polling to prove that very few people would be swayed. 'Hard undecided voters in the marginal seats are only 3 per cent now,' he said.

That night the *Love Actually* video began to transform their fortunes. The following day Johnson did a photo opportunity where he drove a huge digger emblazoned with a Union Jack through a fake wall reading 'Get Brexit done'. Both papers and broadcasters lapped up the footage. Cain sought out Levido and said, 'You were right.'

The Tories played two further cards in the final forty-eight hours. Levido's remaining concern was to hammer the idea that there were no 'consequence free votes' in this election. Michael Brooks wrote a memo warning that Corbyn might still gain power even if Labour won no more seats. It was handed to the *Telegraph*, who splashed the story on the morning of the 10th.[11] Brooks warned, 'The reality is that Jeremy Corbyn is much closer to becoming prime minister ... than many voters realise. Between them, [opposition] parties only need to win 12 more seats ... Labour do not need to gain a single seat, they can simply rely on the SNP to make gains in Scotland or the Liberal Democrats to make gains in southern Conservative seats.' That could be achieved with 'as little as a 1 to 2 per cent movement in the current vote in a handful of seats', Brooks wrote. Johnson followed up the morning after with a warning that a hung Parliament was a 'clear and present' danger.

The final shot in the Tory locker was fired on 10 December: footage of Jon Ashworth, the shadow health secretary, dismissing Labour's chances of winning the election in a call with a Tory friend, who had secretly recorded him: 'It's dire for Labour ... and it's the combination of Corbyn and Brexit ... Outside of the city seats ... it's abysmal out there ... they can't stand Corbyn and they think Labour's blocked Brexit.' An embarrassed Ashworth called Corbyn to apologise and issued a statement saying he had been joking. Both men knew it was all true. Ashworth recalled, 'This was a friend – not a friend any more, evidently – who was sending me increasingly desperate messages throughout the campaign telling me that he and his wife were going to emigrate to Canada in the event of Labour winning ... and I thought I'll just ring him and ... over-egg it all just to calm him down. It was a complete set-up.'[12]

*   *   *

If Rob Oxley thought Pike-gate was the nadir of his campaign, things got worse on the final day before the election, when he joined Johnson on an early morning milk round in Pudsey, West Yorkshire. The campaign had been in a stand-off with ITV's breakfast show *Good Morning Britain*, hosted by Piers Morgan and Susanna Reid, who had been demanding an interview with Johnson for months. *GMB* staged an ambush, sending a satellite truck. Reporter Jonathan Swain confronted Johnson as he put milk crates into a van: 'Morning, Prime Minister. Will you come on *Good Morning Britain*? Will you deliver on your promise to speak to Piers and Susanna?' Unaware that he was live, Oxley stepped in to block Swain and exclaimed, 'For fuck's sake!' Other journalists present could be heard giving a pantomime 'Oooh!' while back in the studio, Reid put her hands to her head and said, 'Wow, the look on his face, that minder.' Swain pursued the evasive Johnson, forcing the prime minister to escape into a large cold room. 'He's gone into the fridge!' a delighted Morgan squealed. After a stand-off lasting several minutes, Johnson emerged carrying a crate of orange juice and Swain extracted a pledge that he would indeed appear in future.

Oxley was distressed. A Vote Leave alumnus who had learned politics with the studs up, his occasionally brusque demeanour concealed a sensitive individual who thought deeply about how to do a good job and cared about his relations with the lobby. Everyone in Westminster (and his mother) had now heard him swearing on national television. The incident went viral and threatened to derail the Tory closing message. When Levido called him later, he was still down in the dumps. 'Are you calling to make me feel bad?' Oxley asked. Levido said, 'You've done a great job, just be calm. You haven't lost the election. Bring it home.'

In Matthew Parker Street, they put 'One More Day' from *Les Misérables* on the sound system. 'There was a bit of a singalong,' Levido recalled. 'Campaigns are very intense things, you have good days and bad days, it can be incredibly stressful. People were a bit delirious by this point.'[13] But they were ready to bring it home.

WIPEOUT

Election Night

12 December 2019

At 9.45 on election night, Boris Johnson sat at a round table in the first-floor study of Number 10 and announced that he had had a dream the night before in which the Conservatives won 345 seats and a majority of 40. His girlfriend, Carrie Symonds, and half a dozen aides wondered if the real result would be dream or nightmare. For fifteen more minutes their lives were in limbo, nerves wound tightly by word that financiers were selling the pound amid fears of a hung Parliament. This room had been Margaret Thatcher's office. It was the elm table at which world leaders had sat during the G8 summit at Lough Erne in 2013, a high point of David Cameron's premiership; the table where Cameron and his team sat as the EU referendum was lost and their political careers imploded. As the minutes passed to 10 p.m., when the polls closed, the team members gave their predictions. Dominic Cummings scrawled 359 on the sheet, characteristically the most bullish – a majority of 68. Lee Cain, Johnson's director of communications, went for a majority of 30.

It was a measure of Tory confidence that the digital team found time that morning to share a private joke. At Vauxhall Cross, home of MI6, Topham Guerin paid for an electronic billboard for one hour. 'We threw up a whole billboard in Comic Sans,' one said, a tribute to their opening stunt. 'The team went down and had a photo with it. That was just our having a bit of fun on the last day.'

* * *

One person not having fun was Luciana Berger. The clear challenger to Tory MP Mike Freer in Finchley and Golders Green, she had overtaken her old party, Labour. But on election day, Berger and her team became aware of an unusual number of Labour activists. The Red Roar, a Twitter account used by the Labour right to expose Corbynistas, published an email, nominally sent by Corbyn the night before, urging party members and Momentum activists to go there. Unable to forgive her opposition over antisemitism, the hard left was trying to deny her victory, even though it made more sense for Labour nationally if the Tories lost.

Frustrated and disgusted, she took to Twitter to accuse the Labour leader of 'trolling me'. She wrote, 'Given you were too busy (for 11 months) to talk to me about your support for an antisemitic mural, how about coming here yourself and we can chat about anti-Jewish hatred in @uklabour?' Berger said, 'My tweet reached over two million people. They had no chance of winning. If they had bothered to go next-door to Chipping Barnet they would have won Chipping Barnet. They didn't want me to win. It was more about vindictiveness.'

As reports of voter turnout were relayed to Westminster, all three main parties despatched everyone they could find to tight contests. CCHQ ordered special advisers to Richmond Park, where Zac Goldsmith was in trouble. South London Tories were diverted to Carshalton and Wallington, where Elliot Colburn was doing better than expected against Lib Dem Tom Brake, who had held the seat since 1997.

Tory optimism was stoked by reports coming in about the counting of postal ballots. It was illegal to say anything about votes before the polls closed at 10 p.m., but word spread that the early returns looked very good for the Conservatives. One Tory aide phoned a friend in the Lib Dems to gloat: 'You're fucked. You've lost Eastbourne. North Norfolk's gone. You're not going to win Cheltenham.' The only seat the Tories were writing off was St Albans.

At 5 p.m. the alarm went off in Lib Dem world that Brake was in danger. Messages went to advisers past and present to go to his aid. 'Everyone in the party got that email,' a former party official said. Pouring resources into seats like Esher, where they dreamed of ousting Dominic Raab, had left a party stalwart exposed.

By then Swinson was in trouble too. Despite every public MRP poll showing her holding her seat, her absence on the national campaign had left her vulnerable. By mid-afternoon, the Lib Dems' entire national phone banking effort was directed at voters in East Dunbartonshire in a bid to save Swinson. 'The leader gets all the phone banks, gets to ask anyone who's got any capacity in the country to help,' a former aide said. 'I know people that were told not to ring their own seats.'

The final Tory internal polling gave Levido heart. He was primarily looking at 'unaided' votes, those voters who don't know any of the candidates but are picking based on party affiliation alone. In the target seats the internals were showing a 4.5 per cent swing to the Tories among 'unaided definites'. The final Hanbury/Warner MRP model gave them 364 seats, a majority of 78. The second MRP had the number in the late 50s. Both Levido and Brooks thought the result would be at the 'high end' of the predictions, but they never told Johnson what the MRP was saying at any point.

At 2 p.m. Levido, Cain and Brooks went to Downing Street to see Johnson and Cummings. Johnson was a combination of 'confident because he was already talking about what would happen next' but also 'excited and nervous', one of those present said. Johnson kept saying, 'What are you hearing? What are you hearing?' The prime minister put Brooks on the spot about the numbers. Brooks said. 'We're talking about 350 to 360 seats but it depends on regional permutations.' Johnson suggested that he come to CCHQ for the exit poll at 10 p.m. Levido politely made clear that was 'not a good idea'. The team would be busy processing results and reacting; Johnson would be a diversion and his presence would be obvious to the media outside. He would stay in Number 10.

Some Labour officials prepared as if they were going to win. Helene Reardon-Bond, who replaced Karie Murphy as Corbyn's chief of staff, had been put in charge of devising a plan for government. It included four new ministries and a list of ministers, including Diane Abbott as foreign secretary. John McDonnell planned to make a speech the next morning at Bloomberg to calm the markets before brokering a confidence and supply deal with the SNP. In Southside, piles of Corbynista Victory Ale, brewed for the occasion, were stacked up.

Corbyn himself wanted a quiet night and had invited just two dozen family members and closest aides to join him at the north London headquarters of the charity Freedom from Torture, a poorly named choice as it turned out. One staff member arrived holding a Waitrose Victoria sponge with a Number 10 candle stuck in the top. Milne took one look at it and said, 'We won't be needing that.' He was one of the few who knew Labour's election model was predicting the party would secure just 180 seats. Milne had already written a press release blaming defeat on Brexit rather than Corbyn. The leader was ushered into a side room which had a window onto the main party. There he was joined by wife Laura, his three sons, Milne, Fisher, Reardon-Bond and Anjula Singh, Labour's head of press. An aide pulled the blinds closed.

The senior members of the Tory election team had dinner in a private room at the St Ermin's Hotel, a favoured haunt of the intelligence services, close to CCHQ. In addition to the war room warriors – Cain, Brooks, Stephenson, Oxley – James Cleverly and Ben Elliot were also present. Oliver Lewis spent the day at home playing Grand Theft Auto. He had been fighting for a Brexit government since 2012 and he just wanted to spend the day 'blowing shit up'. At 6 p.m., having achieved a 'sort of tranquillity' from virtual violence, he texted Stephenson asking how things were looking. 'Big Corbyn surge, think we're fucked', Stephenson replied. He spent much of the meal calming Lewis down.

As 10 p.m. approached, a Sky News journalist, Laura Jayes, over from Australia, tweeted that Johnson might lose his seat, quoting a senior Tory source. When one tabloid political editor relayed the story to his proprietor, all hell broke loose. Stephenson assured journalists the claim was 'bollocks'. Levido got Jayes' number off another Australian journalist and texted her, 'Hey Laura, Levido here. I'm not sure who your sources are re Boris's seat but they're a fucking load of shit.' Paul Butters, who had bet a fellow Lib Dem they would not gain four seats, texted, 'How's it looking?' The reply came, 'I think I'll owe a dinner at Roux.' When the restaurant closed a year later Butters was still waiting.

In the Thatcher study in Number 10, Johnson told aides that, having wooed Leave voters in the north, 'If we win, we've got to deliver.' He pointed at each member of the team – Cummings, Cain, Ben Gascoigne, Rosie Bate-Williams and Shelley Williams-Walker – 'You must deliver, we all must deliver for these people if they vote for us. We can't go back to the Tory Party of the old days.'

In the Tory war room, the nerves cranked upwards as 10 p.m. got nearer, TVs tuned to the BBC, ITV and Sky News. When Big Ben's bongs rang out there was a moment of total stillness, a beat lasting two seconds, the moment after a bomb has gone off and sucked the oxygen from the air. The number popped up on screen: 368 seats.

Instant mental arithmetic. A majority of 86.

Then: chaos, people jumping and hugging. Paul Stephenson, fists pumping the air like he'd won the FA Cup, embracing Ben Elliot. Oliver Lewis 'going apeshit', jumping up and down screaming, 'Five! More! Years!' so loudly he spent the rest of the evening drinking tea laced with honey. And in the middle of it all the figure of Isaac Levido, calm and poised, a slight slump to his shoulders, relief rather than joy coursing through him. At this moment others seemed to become aware of him, the fulcrum on which it had all turned. There began a throaty song: 'Oh, Is-aac-Lev-eeee-do', to the tune of 'Seven Nation Army', the 'Oh, Jeremy Corbyn' anthem of 2017. Still seated at the hub was Alan Mabbutt, unmoving and unmoved. He'd seen it all before.

In Number 10, Johnson leaped to his feet, 'pumping both fists like a footballer when they score a last-minute goal and that expression of joy seeps out before they compose themselves'. Carrie at his side was equally happy; behind them, laptop in hand, scarf round his neck, the eminence grise Cummings. The prime minister then cautioned, 'It's only the exit poll', but they all knew it was done.

The hard part over, Levido and Cain went to the Blue Boar bar with several aides and a journalist. Champagne in hand, Cain thought about the big calls Johnson had made to arrive at this moment of triumph. 'He was right to resign in July of 2018. That was a big call and if he hadn't done that, I don't think we'd be where we are now.' Cain had served his master for two years, done much in his name of which Johnson was unaware. Yet it was his role in persuading Johnson to quit after Chequers where Cain felt he had most made the difference, where he had known Johnson's interests even better than the man himself.

At 11.30 p.m., Ian Levy, the Tory candidate in Blyth Valley, faced his moment of truth. 'All the candidates were taken aside and shown the figures,' he recalled. 'I thought, "You've lost it, Ian, you haven't got it" – and then I look underneath and I saw 17,440 and I thought then, "Wow, I've done it, this is it."'[1] It was the first time the Conservatives had won there since the seat was created in 1950. In Number 10, Johnson was out of his seat again, arms aloft, victory now assured. The prime minister had pledged to keep off the booze until he had delivered on Brexit. He now allowed himself a glass of white wine. 'He now knows Brexit will be done,' a witness said. When Phil Wilson's Sedgefield seat fell to the Tories, CCHQ erupted in a rendition of Blair's election anthem 'Things Can Only Get Better'.

Hardest at work were the digital team who had to prepare a video for Johnson's victory party at dawn. Sean Topham and Ben Guerin had a 'man hug' when the exit poll dropped. Topham was pleased to see his young team taste victory. Most of them were not political, but video and advertising people in their early twenties. Good morale was good for creativity. They went into a side room to make a video call to their staff in New Zealand, to let them share the moment. Then, gone 2 a.m., they broke the news: 'We've got this rally. You need to cut these videos.' Two very tired video editors, several drinks to the good, got stuck in. They were finished by 4 a.m.

In Southside, staff were divided between the second floor, where the big screens, the pizza, crisps and Victory beer awaited, and the eighth, which was alcohol free, the working floor, where Jennie Formby, the general secretary, was hosting union leaders. Most of the staff were downstairs, just the press team and some policy people, twenty in total, ready to spin the results. James Schneider recalled, 'I'd spent the last half an hour rushing to get our lines agreed, what our approach would be if there were a hung Parliament ... to force Boris Johnson out of office.'[2] Another official said, 'There was so much nervous energy. Everyone thought there could be a hung Parliament.' Of what followed, he said, 'I've never really experienced anything like it.'

At 10 p.m., the same bongs, the same wait, but a different number: 191. Corbyn's Labour were on course to lose 71 seats, their worst general election performance since 1935. On the eighth floor of Southside, there was total silence, broken only by exclamations of 'Fuck, fuck' and the screams of a female press officer 'just hysterical', others crying in silence, consoling each other. 'When it hit, there was a shocked silence,' Schneider recalled. 'I felt very numb. We had standard lines for if we lost but not if we lost that big.'[3] No one spoke for 'what seemed like hours'.

At Freedom from Torture, the torture was just beginning. There was silence, then the sound of keening tears, Corbyn's wife Laura and his head of events, Frances Leah, both inconsolable, the atmosphere that of a funeral. Corbyn emerged from the side room, grey and shellshocked. He toured the party, now a wake. 'I'm sorry,' he said. 'This is on me.'

Milne fired off his talking points for shadow ministers who would now have to put a brave face on disaster on the rolling news. 'This defeat is overwhelmingly down to one issue – the divisions in the country over Brexit, and the Tory campaign, echoed by most of the media, to persuade people that only Boris Johnson can "get Brexit done" … Labour will have to learn lessons from this defeat, above all by listening to those lifelong Labour voters who we lost in working-class communities.' It was an accusatory finger pointed straight at the Remainer fraternity: McDonnell, Starmer, Fisher and Thornberry. It was also a backhanded compliment to Cummings, Levido and Johnson. No one had forced Labour to have an untenable position on Brexit or to run such a poor campaign.

At 2.20 a.m. Corbyn walked with his son Ben to the local leisure centre where the Islington North count was taking place. Jack McKenna, his press officer, went early to try to do a deal with the waiting press and photographers to let Corbyn have his dignity. By 3 a.m. he was on stage sharing small talk with Yosef David, the orthodox Jewish candidate of the Brexit Party, the human embodiment of the two issues which had destroyed his leadership. All three of Corbyn's sons, grown men, were tearful. Corbyn had won his seat with a majority of more than 26,000 but his purpose was to concede defeat. He did not announce his resignation as leader but made clear he would not fight another election. He had decided to stay to give the hard left time to organise for the succession.

Corbyn was driven to Southside as working-class bastions across the country were seized by the Tories, many for the first time in decades, some for the first time ever: Bishop Auckland, Wakefield and Workington – crumbling bricks in a red wall, blown apart by Brexit. In North West Durham, Richard Holden defeated Laura Pidcock, who had not even prepared a concession speech.

At 5 a.m., Corbyn found the inhabitants of the eighth floor still distraught, heads in hands, one young woman swigging a bottle of red by the neck. He sought out Karie Murphy in a side room. She was crying. He apologised for sacking her as chief of staff: 'I regret it, and I never should have done it.'

He made a speech to those that remained, reminding them who they had been fighting for, what they had achieved. 'There was the devastation on behalf of the people and the communities and the people we'd lost,' one of those present recalled. 'There was the second theme about remembering everything that we'd done: austerity is no longer up for grabs and the next leader of the Labour Party won't have to talk about austerity and foreign wars, we'll talk about poverty and equality and nationalisation and public ownership and state investment and the climate emergency.'

These sentiments were later boiled down into an op-ed for the *Guardian* in which Corbyn claimed to have 'won the argument', an article of faith for the hard left, ridiculous to others in Labour. 'That was misjudged,' a LOTO aide admitted. 'I think winning an argument doesn't put food on the table or close the food bank or end the zero hours contract or build the social home. I didn't want to talk about winning arguments whilst I was fucking bereft.'

Corbyn then went around every desk and spoke, one at a time, to all those who were left. 'You had people in floods of tears and he was just hugging them,' one staffer said. 'He was trying to be stoical for everyone else, asking people how they are.' Corbyn did not leave until 6 a.m.

It was the first election night Jo Swinson had ever managed to spend with her husband, Duncan Hames. In 2015 they had both lost their seats at opposite ends of the country. Now they were together in East Dunbartonshire. The chair of Swinson's local party had been concerned about her survival. His local Tory friends, who needed to vote for her rather than the SNP, were saying, 'We're not sure if we can, because we don't like Revoke.' It had prompted a door-knocking blitz and a wave of 'squeeze message' leaflets warning that voting SNP would let Corbyn in. Canvassing returns suggested it had worked. The Lib Dem MRP, the YouGov MRP and the Hanbury MRP all had Swinson winning. 'It's close but on the right side of close,' she was advised.

When the exit poll dropped, Ben Rathe and Sam Barratt were in London, working on a communications plan. When the numbers came in, the Lib Dems were projected to win 13 seats, just one more than in 2017, seven fewer than they already held after the defections. The really worrying figure, though, was the SNP projection: 55 (in fact the most inaccurate part of the exit poll). Rathe worked it out in slow motion. *There are only 59 seats in Scotland. Labour and the Tories will win something. Oh my God, is Jo going to lose?*

The mood darkened when the Lib Dems failed to regain Sheffield Hallam by just 712 votes. Nick Clegg's old seat, lost to Labour in 2017, was a key target. The Tories, in third place, got nearly 15,000 votes.

Swinson, waiting at home, grew nervous. It was never good news when there was no early news from the count. It reminded her of 2015, when she had lost, and 2010, when her majority had been cut in half. She did not want to write two speeches to cover herself, she found it hard to be authentic in either. She spoke to her chief of staff, Rhiannon Leaman, who was at the count and who did not want her to arrive early to brave the cameras. 'If you had to put money on it, if you had to say?' Swinson asked. Leaman replied, 'If I had to say, I'd say you've just not made it.' That was useful, the moment she was able to start processing her defeat. Another politician in this turbulent period, destroyed, in part, by her own decisions. The second guessing of her every move would come later. In the moment, all Swinson could think about was what she needed to do next: *What am I going to say? I need to conduct myself with dignity. I want to see my kids.* Also this: *I don't want to be hidden away.*

She went to the count. In the end, the margin was 149 votes. Nothing, a few canvassing sessions, a few text messages to friends asking them to knock on doors: the difference between survival and another political career ending in failure. Swinson did conduct herself with dignity. She had lost before. It was not something to be feared the second time, though it was far more public. When the news reached Nicola Sturgeon, who was live on camera, the SNP leader pumped her firsts and her face contorted into a rictus of gleeful schadenfreude – two leaders who had gambled on the election improving their position, only one of them successful. One clinging to her dignity, the other delighted by the success of a colleague or exposing her utter classlessness, depending on your perspective. Politics revealed again as the most brutal of sports.

When Swinson made it to London it was clear she had 'taken it hard'. A colleague said, 'She's incredibly resilient but she had just lost her job, her career and it's a very, very public way for that to happen.' Swinson felt responsibility. 'She was ringing round and texting people who had not been successful and lost their seats. She was clearly really hit hard, but she kept going.' Swinson's overwhelming feeling was of being 'knackered'. A great result meant the adrenaline dragged you through. Before she became a parent, catching up on sleep meant spending the weekend after an election in bed. With two small children, that was not an option.

As Friday became Saturday 14 December, the realisation hit that she had done nothing to prepare for Christmas.

Ben Rathe, who had given up his honeymoon for this, had a contract tied to Swinson, not the party. At 4 a.m. on election morning he lost his job. That weekend his email was turned off.

On Friday evening, Joe Perry, Labour's head of HR, emailed staff to warn that a reduction in short money funding could have an 'immediate impact' on their jobs. The party of the workers.

The winners write their own history and no one knew that better than Boris Johnson, biographer of Winston Churchill. It was gone 4 a.m. when Johnson got back to CCHQ from his own count in Uxbridge. 'A lot of people had had a lot of drinks,' an aide recalled. At 4.30, the prime minister gave an impromptu speech to the elated masses. 'No one can now refute,' he said, that he had a 'stonking mandate'. 'No one can possibly dispute that it is the will of the British people to get Brexit done!' Listing the seats that the Tories had taken from Labour, Johnson joked, 'We've turned Redcar Bluecar.'

There was reflection as well as triumphalism, an acknowledgement that he was guarantor of a precious political bond with a new set of Tory voters, forged from the legacy of the 2016 vote. 'We must understand now what an earthquake we have created,' he said. 'The way in which we have changed the political map in this country. We have to grapple with the consequences of that. We have to change our own party. We have to rise to the level of events. We have to rise to the challenge that the British people have given us.'[4] It was the tragedies of his premiership that Johnson allowed himself to be sidetracked from this mission by events and his own personal and political urges.

Johnson took Carrie back to Number 10 then returned to CCHQ, taking up residence in James Cleverly's office, hunched over Levido's laptop to write his speech for the steps of Downing Street. Cain and Levido were there, tossing ideas around, before they both fell asleep, stretched awkwardly on sofas not built for the purpose, Cain occasionally woken by Levido's thunderous snoring.

At 7 a.m. they printed off the speech and traipsed to the QEII Centre. Johnson was to address several hundred party workers under a huge banner emblazoned with 'The People's Government'. The phrase was

Cummings', of course, his framing for the next phase. In 2016 Vote Leave won a referendum and then slept for the weekend while Johnson played cricket and Theresa May stole a march. Cummings would not make the same mistake again. 'They were haunted by 2016,' a colleague said. The rally had made Levido nervous. When Stephenson came to him ten days out to propose something for the supporters, Levido replied, 'They're all going to be shitfaced. He can just do a speech in the street.' Levido controlled the budget. It was too soon to commit resources to a victory party. Eventually he signed off the plan, but with one change. Cummings wanted bright red banners, as if Vote Leave was a revolutionary government taking power. Levido decreed they had to be blue. Two days before the election, they viewed the venue. Levido kept muttering, 'Bad karma.'

As the sun rose over a Tory victory, Johnson told party workers, 'We pulled it off, we broke the deadlock, we ended the gridlock, we smashed the roadblock.' He said, 'A new dawn rises on a new day and a new government', a conscious echo of Tony Blair's words when he became prime minister, 'the people's government' slogan a homage to New Labour's proclamation (via Lenin) of being 'servants of the people'. Casting his eye over his young, drunk, troops, he hailed the biggest Conservative majority since 'literally before many of you were born'.

The key line was the next one, though: 'I have a message to all those who voted for us yesterday, especially for those who voted for us Conservatives for the first time. You may only have lent us your vote, you may not think of yourself as a natural Tory ... Your hand may have quivered over the ballot paper before you put your cross in the Conservative box, and you may intend to return to Labour next time round. If that is the case, I am humbled that you have put your trust in me and you have put your trust in us. I, and we, will never take your support for granted. I will make it my mission to work night and day, to work flat-out to prove you right in voting for me this time, and to earn your support in the future.' He finished with a typical Johnsonian flourish: 'Let's get Brexit done. But first, my friends, let's get breakfast done!'

At the far back right of the room, leaning against a wall, just as he had been that first day in Downing Street, was Cummings. Oliver Lewis, watching, thought to himself: *Geography repeats, just like history.*

That morning Johnson visited the palace. He did not need to, constitutionally, but there were good visuals to be had and his team wanted it to feel like a new government was taking office. At 11 a.m. Levido got a panicked call. 'Do you have the PM's work from this morning? He can't find the copy.' The campaign director replied, 'Yeah, it's on my computer.' Another moment of chaos. They got it to Johnson. He needed it to work on his statement in the street, which was timed for 4 p.m.

Addressing the nation, he repeated much of what he had said about the Tories' new voters in the North. This time he also addressed 'those who did not vote for us or for me and who wanted and perhaps still want to remain in the EU'. He said, 'I want you to know that we in this One Nation Conservative government will never ignore your good and positive feelings of warmth and sympathy towards the other nations of Europe, because now is the moment – precisely as we leave the EU – to let those natural feelings find renewed expression in building a new partnership ... I frankly urge everyone on either side of what – after three and a half years, after all – an increasingly arid argument, I urge everyone to find closure and to let the healing begin.' This was the best of Johnson, a rare sight of the man who had won the mayoralty. Rarely can it have been more important that the rhetoric about unity be delivered on.

In Downing Street on Friday, the prime minister summoned civil service chiefs, including Mark Sedwill and Helen MacNamara, to deliver the same message: things have to change. At a victory party at Browns restaurant that night, Johnson's old guru, Lynton Crosby, watched smiling as the candidate he had groomed for a decade spoke about the campaign run by his protégé, Levido. On Saturday Johnson began a tour of the new Tory seats in the red wall, including the Blair bastion of Sedgefield.

Standing as an independent, the former deputy chief whip Anne Milton finished fourth in Guildford, the seat she had held since 2005, with 7.4 per cent, 22,000 votes behind the Conservative candidate Angela Richardson. More than 500 locals urged Milton to stand and her campaign volunteers eventually numbered 120. Free of national party interference, her husband designed the leaflets and Milton went canvassing in 'a lovely pink rosette'. 'I knew that the chances of winning were almost infinitesimal,' she said, 'but it felt wonderful because I'd given people a choice and my integrity was intact.' One constituent sent her a picture of them holding their nose while they voted Conservative. Another wrote to say, 'Perhaps a loss while standing for what you believe is more straightforward than a win while standing for something you do not.' That summed things up perfectly for Milton.

Tom Brake lost Carshalton and Wallington by just 629 votes, a defeat keenly felt in Lib Dem HQ, where he had been known as an uncomplaining trouper for years. Paul Butters took to Twitter to describe Brake as 'an utter legend to every past and present Lib Dem press officer. He'd do every awful bid, agree every incendiary line (that you thought was brilliant) and do it all with a smile. His dedication to the cause was immense.' Having lost his job of twenty-two years, Brake went to Lib Dem headquarters, where he thanked every single member of staff, one by one, for everything they had done. Form is temporary, class is permanent.

A Labour aide was in Portcullis House the following Monday. 'I saw all these shiny new Tory MPs in exact carbon copy female suits and dresses and Russell & Bromley shoes and handbags getting their induction onto the IT system. There were hundreds of them. I thought: "Fuck this" and took the rest of the week off.'

That Thursday, the government presented another Queen's Speech. On Friday, the bill putting into law Johnson's Brexit withdrawal agreement with Brussels got its second reading, starting the process to deliver Brexit by 31 January. After three years of drama, MPs backed the bill by 358 to 234 votes, a majority of 124. As the result was announced, one Tory MP was caught on microphone exclaiming, 'Back of the net.' Every Conservative MP voted in favour.

Alluding to the 'oven-ready deal' he had promised during the election campaign, Johnson told MPs, 'The oven is on, so to speak, it is set at gas mark four, we can have it done by lunchtime, or late lunch.' In reality, the country would have to wait until their midnight snack.

Data expert Ben Warner's model was just one seat out. His MRP, run by Hanbury, had predicted 364 seats for the Tories and they ended up with 365, a net gain of 48. Labour did slightly better than the exit poll had predicted, winning 202, down 60. The SNP got 48 seats, seven fewer than the exit poll had predicted, but a net gain of 13 over 2017. The now leaderless Lib Dems won 11, one down on 2017 and two below the exit poll, but all the defectors had lost, reducing their numbers in the Commons by nine. It was still Labour's worst performance since 1935 and the Tories' biggest win since Margaret Thatcher's second landslide in 1987.

Warner's reward was a job in Number 10 working with Cummings where he would 'do data science' and help Downing Street use 'technology' to improve 'how best to make decisions'. Within three months Warner's appointment would prove to be critical.

Johnson's Conservatives won by securing the votes of 80 per cent of Leave voters, but also 20 per cent of Remain voters, the people who believed in delivering on a democratic vote or who wanted the issue put to bed. Levido's campaign held on to 70 per cent of the Remain voters who backed the Tories in 2017 while gaining a third of the Leave voters who supported Labour in 2017. Levido said, 'The overwhelming thing that drove the vote in our favour amongst soft voters was the perception that we'd get Brexit done and the overriding thing that drove the vote against Labour was Corbyn.' Most political parties trying to win a fourth successive election would have been hard-pressed to present themselves as the 'change' option, but that was also what Johnson, Cummings and Levido had achieved. 'The change we were offering was certainty and stability versus the mess that was going on,' Levido said.

Labour had never resolved whether they were appealing primarily to Remain or Leave voters. They tried first one and then the other. Reflecting later, Tom Baldwin said, 'Did Labour lose those red wall seats because it was too Remain? A lot more votes in those red wall seats were lost to no party at all because there is a great big segment of the electorate that is increasingly recoiling from the whole spectacle. I don't think it is as simple as saying that Labour lost red wall seats because it backed a People's Vote. I think Labour, possibly, backed a People's Vote too late and didn't make the case for a People's Vote strongly enough.'

Stephen Bush of the *New Statesman*, who travelled extensively during the campaign, attributed the Labour defeat to 'ABCD – antisemitism, Brexit, Corbyn and demographics'. Antisemitism and Brexit were linked. 'In February 2019, the Labour Party was ahead in most of the polls and its political strength was based on the fact that it was able to have a pro-Brexit position while holding on to the support of most Remainers,' Bush argued. 'What caused Remainers to move away from the Labour Party were seven people from the Labour Party standing up and saying, "We're leaving because of antisemitism and because of Brexit."'[5] Change UK did then, perhaps, change the UK.

Most Labour people thought their leader the biggest millstone. Corbyn was a highly discredited figure by 2019, as well as an exhausted one, but the Brexit framing of the election meant the circumstances were as bad as they could have been for him. 'I thought it was such a tragic way for Jeremy to go in this really grim winter election about Brexit,' an aide said, 'which is not what he or the project was about.'

*   *   *

The Lib Dem result looked like a disaster, though Swinson's Shakespearean fall in an election she had triggered disguised some advances. She doubled the number of seats where the party was first or second, secured 3.7 million votes, 1.3 million more than in 2017. She helped recruit 17,000 new members in the five months she was leader and boosted the Lib Dem share of the vote from 7.4 per cent to 11.6 per cent – a bigger increase than Paddy Ashdown, Charles Kennedy or Nick Clegg managed (though both Kennedy and Clegg scored over 22 per cent nationally). 'Were we right to be ambitious?' Swinson said later. 'Yes. We got the most members that we've ever had, we raised more money than we ever have before. We had our best set of results in a European election, we had polling, which has had us vying with Labour. In that scenario, I think if you're the Lib Dem leader and you target 20 seats that is extreme caution.'

Ben Rathe said, 'The single biggest reason we had a bad night was Jeremy Corbyn. We could not overcome the fact that soft Conservative voters were terrified to vote for us because they thought Labour might end up as the largest party. Jeremy Corbyn was not just responsible for Labour's crap election campaign, he was responsible for ours too.'

After her defeat, Swinson had plenty of time to consider her own mistakes. 'Should I have started off having a different answer to the question, "Who should be prime minister?" Probably. Should I have changed course earlier? Probably. Do I think that would have made such a difference? I don't really think so.' Her view was that the killer decision had been Farage's, standing down his candidates in Tory held seats.

It was the Brexit Party, too, who determined the scale of Johnson's win. When the official guide to the election was published, in 2021, work by John Curtice, Stephen Fisher and Patrick English showed that Farage's decision not to stand down in Labour areas cost the Tories a majority of around 130.[6]

The Conservative campaign was everything it had not been in 2017 – united, cohesive, with one clear strategy and minimal internal disagreements. It helped that the front man was one of the best campaigners of his political generation. It helped too that in Isaac Levido, Johnson had a campaign director with sound judgement and the wisdom and confidence to give the talents of Brooks, Cain, Stephenson, Topham and Guerin space and support to flourish.

Levido held his own in what could have become an undiluted Vote Leave operation, always remembering that Johnson had to coax votes from Remainers too. 'He, rightly, always had more of a concern for the Liberal Democrat-facing part of the vote coalition than the Vote Leave gang,' said a Vote Leaver. 'You've got to have balls of steel to walk in at thirty-six and own that room as he has owned it for the last few months. He was in charge, but I haven't heard him shout at anyone.'

Levido was good enough that no one ever briefed that he should be replaced by Cummings, who also had the good sense to let him get on with it. 'There were some pretty big fucking egos around,' a senior colleague said. 'Dom won the right to have an election in 2019, but Isaac won that campaign. It was Isaac and Brooksy's campaign. They were both brilliant and don't get as much credit as they probably should.'

The concern for some was that this A-Team was now breaking up. Levido and Brooks set up their own agency, Fleetwood Strategy. Stephenson returned to Hanbury. He had given his word to his wife and his business partner, besides he liked campaigns more than he liked governing; years as a special adviser to Philip Hammond and Andrew Lansley will do that to you. A senior campaign official said, 'When it goes back to peacetime, there are a bunch of people like Isaac and Paul who won't be there. I think they need more people like that.'

Cummings would return, with his often incendiary approach, to work hand in glove with Cain, whose instinct was also to 'have a scrap'. Predicting the future that week, a former cabinet minister said, 'If Boris's personal interests and the interests of the country are aligned, he could be a good prime minister.' There were times when that would be true, but even on election night, the cracks were beginning to show.

Securing a trade deal with the EU would take place against a background of internecine strife in Number 10 and the worst global pandemic in a century.

PART THREE

OUT

GETTING BREXIT DONE

December 2019 to December 2020

'All changed, changed utterly: a terrible beauty is born'

– W. B. Yeats, 'Easter 1916'

12

FALLING OUT

Ructions and the Reshuffle

December 2019 to January 2020

'A l'exemple de Saturne, la révolution dévore ses enfants'
(Like Saturn, the revolution devours its children)

– Jacques Mallet du Pan (1749–1800), French journalist

At the moment Britain left the European Union, Big Ben did not bong, the famous bell having been silenced for renovations – but Boris Johnson did. While thousands celebrated in Parliament Square, the scene in Number 10 provided a fitting capstone to more than three years of drama punctuated by farce. The television feed to the party went down, forcing the prime minister to lead his own countdown as the clocks struck 11 p.m. – midnight in Brussels, whose calendar always defined these deadlines. Johnson ushered in the age he had done more than anyone to bring about by seizing an ornamental gong, one more the size you associate with a battery-operated monkey than the opening titles to a J Arthur Rank film, but Johnson performed his task with gusto, and the hundreds of aides, officials and ministers assembled in the pillared state room on the first floor of Number 10 cheered their approval. Above his head, a portrait of Henry VIII peered down, the last national leader to take the country out of a major European institution.

Johnson praised 'the British people' for twice voting for Brexit and his chief aide Dominic Cummings for devising the slogans – 'Take Back Control' and 'Get Brexit Done' – which had brought him victory. 'I want you all to remember that you were here tonight after 11 o'clock in Downing Street when finally we got Brexit done,' he said. 'There are very few moments in our lives which really can be called an historic turning point – and this is it. This is a turning point in the life of our nation. This is a chance for genuine change and renewal.'

The prime minister used his speech to mangle Winston Churchill's words after the Battle of El Alamein, an earlier confrontation with a German-dominated force, 'This is not the end, as some people would say, this is not even the beginning of the end or even the second half of the middle, this is the beginning of the beginning.'

The gong was not even the most notable moment. Cummings, the most fearsome figure in government, took to the microphone to say a few words and found that he had none. What came, instead, were tears. He clutched a hand to his face, trying to compose himself, eventually croaking into the microphone, 'I can't say anything. Lots of people in this room know what happened. Thank you.' One briefly disloyal colleague remarked, 'It's like that scene at the end of *The Terminator* when Arnold Schwarzenegger says, "I know now why you cry ..."'

If the tears belonged to Cummings, the sadness was Johnson's as his chief adviser hogged the limelight. The PM studied the scene through narrow eyes. A Vote Leave alumnus recalled, 'He was massively upstaged and he was obviously fuming, absolutely furious.' Outwardly Johnson was jovial, calling Cummings 'Dom, matey' in front of his wife, Mary Wakefield. 'But when you get to know the guy, I saw he was thinking "You fucker." Very occasionally his mask slipped and you could just see his eyes calculating, "This is what the papers are going to say, fuck."'

The tensions were raw and basic – about power and who ultimately exercised it. Until the general election, there had been genuine ambiguity about whether Johnson was using Cummings or Cummings was using Johnson to get what they wanted. After it, Johnson felt, understandably, that he had won a large majority and had the right to rule, particularly since Cummings had mostly sat out the campaign. 'It played on Boris's mind through January,' a Number 10 aide said. 'The minute that general election was won he thought, "I'm safe." I do not like being a flesh puppet. The two speeches on Brexit night and the coverage afterwards perfectly encapsulated his rage about the whole thing: "Hang on, I'm prime minister, it's all meant to be about me."'

An aide who witnessed this scene said, 'It was a Gallagher brothers type relationship. Dom was Noel, writing the songs that Boris sang. But Liam was more popular than Noel.'

The clash of egos, views and ambitions was made the more acute since both Johnson and Cummings believed in the 'great man' view of history, Johnson from his reading of the classics, Cummings' from his studies at Oxford under Norman Stone. Johnson saw himself as the bastard child of Augustus Caesar, Winston Churchill and Pericles. Cummings' role model was Bismarck, manipulator of Kaiser Wilhelm, cloaking his own sophisticated statecraft behind his leader's powers in pursuit of his own political goals. Both saw themselves achieving great things. Until 12 December 2019, they had done so together. After that they would increasingly be at odds. Temperamentally, Cummings was motivated and energised by identifying, creating and sustaining enemies, a modus operandi that was exhausting to be around. Johnson evolved from being someone with the same enemies to someone who disapproved of Cummings' vendettas, until, finally, he became the subject of one.

One notable absentee from the pillared room that night, Carrie Symonds, by now six months pregnant and 'showing', hosted a separate party in the flat upstairs. With her close friends Henry Newman, Josh Grimstone and Alex Wickham, Symonds in a maternity gown held court as a dozen people listened to music and chatted. When Johnson arrived, they played the ABBA hit 'The Winner Takes it All' in his honour and Carrie's coterie began a pre-planned dance routine. Johnson tried to join in, but he was 'flailing', a witness said. 'He was super-analogue in this digital group. They were firing off pop culture references and he was a beat behind the whole way through. Carrie kept trying to bring him in. He looked like he would have killed for a curry and *Cash in the Attic*.'

Another found the scene discordant and poignant. Here was Johnson, marking the apogee of his political career, at a party with a group of his fiancée's friends, most of them more than twenty years his junior. He was not even the centre of attention in his own home, at a moment 'meant to be the crowning glory of his time in government, probably ever,' the friend said. 'He's the prime minister, got Brexit done ... and he's up in his flat, dancing to ABBA and his face looked like the French portrait during the revolution of the Count of Lyon, a mask-like face saying, "Fuck my life."' Symonds sensed she was 'losing the audience a little bit' and broke off the dance. 'Boris, Boris! I need to talk to you.' They disappeared together for ten minutes then Johnson left to go downstairs. 'He got totally shitfaced at that party,' an aide said.

* * *

The mood was bittersweet in Brussels too. Sweet for the Brexit Party MEPs who had got what they came for, bitter indeed for many others who had come to share the European dream of cross-border cooperation. None took it harder than Richard Corbett, leader of Labour's MEPs, a man so pro-European he had been banned from Labour's compositing room at conference. 'When we left the European Parliament,' a Brexit Party MEP said, 'he was the last person to leave. He was going around crying, literally in floods of tears, saying goodbye to all his mates. They were totally institutionalised.'

'It was very painful,' Corbett recalled. 'We weren't the only ones in tears. A lot of our colleagues, whom we had been working with for many years, were very unhappy.' The German Green MEP Terry Reintke came up with the idea that the European Parliament should rise and sing 'Auld Lang Syne'. 'Everybody standing together, linking arms, in a really heart-felt moment,' Corbett said. 'It drowned out the cheers of the Brexit Party mob.' Rory Palmer, Labour MEP for the East Midlands, suggested wearing scarves saying 'Forever United' with the Union Jack at one end and the European Union flag at the other. 'It was a very moving moment,' Corbett said.[1]

Cummings noticed an immediate change in Carrie Symonds. The pictures of shared jubilation in the Thatcher study, when the exit poll dropped, masked a near immediate froideur. 'She didn't speak to me after that all night,' he claimed. Cummings said later, 'Relations changed literally from 10 o'clock on the night of the election once the exit poll dropped … Within seconds, you could feel the room change … Within two weeks of the election, there were already discussions about how she was trying to force people out of the building.'[2]

Johnson and Symonds flew to Mustique, the private island in the Caribbean which had been a favourite of Princess Margaret, for New Year. It would later cause embarrassment when it emerged they had taken a freebie, courtesy of Tory donor David Ross, founder of Carphone Warehouse, and not declared it in the register of members' interests.

Johnson badly needed a relaxing time. He was trying to finalise his divorce from Marina Wheeler, the mother of four of his children, a divorce he had never wanted, while concealing that Carrie was pregnant. Friends say they were already engaged before they flew to Mustique.

Wheeler, who discovered Johnson's infidelity while undergoing treatment for cervical cancer, had decided to leave him in the spring of 2018 but did not finally do so until he resigned as foreign secretary that July. A family friend in whom she confided said, 'Marina wanted to go. She said, "It's not going to be retrieved. He absolutely thinks it will be. It will not." Boris had this vision that it would all be okay and, of course, it wasn't.' Her lawyers presented a settlement which committed Johnson to paying an eye-watering share of his future earnings to his ex and which left Marina with the ability to reopen parts of the deal in future. 'She heard about the baby,' a Tory woman said. 'He just had to sign on the dotted line.' When it was done, Wheeler's solicitor was overheard telling a colleague, 'I've never had a result like this before.'

When Johnson and Symonds returned to London, the PM seemed different, delighted with his election success and openly comparing himself to history's heroes. 'He went a bit mental,' a senior Number 10 figure recalled. 'He would rant that he was the king. "I'm Augustus. I have conquered everything."' To Cummings and Cain, Johnson's rat brain, his willingness to do anything to win, had been replaced by a leader enjoying the comfort of his laurels. The morning meeting began to resemble a *Spectator* magazine ideas conference with Johnson 'bouncing from one hot take to another' rather than focusing on a long-term plan. In January this led to a distracting obsession with the *Telegraph*'s campaign to get Big Ben to bong for Brexit. Johnson wanted to put public money into the scheme. 'It was clear very soon that we were losing him,' a senior aide said.

Johnson's divorce and his loss of a £250,000 a year contract with the *Telegraph* left him woefully short of money. At the same time, Symonds had commenced a renovation of their flat above Number 11, using the designer Lulu Lytle, whose boho chic did not come cheap. The Cabinet Office, which was responsible for maintaining the Downing Street estate, allowed £30,000 a year of public funds for the flat, but the bill quickly soared towards six figures. When he should have been planning for a decade in Number 10, or getting briefed on the first stirrings of a respiratory virus in China, Johnson was trying to get Tory donors to pay for his decorating.

'He was broke,' Cummings said later. 'He was having to find money to pay Marina, and at the same time, he had Carrie doing this insane renovation of the flat with Lulu running up these huge bills. He jumped into conversations with me in January where he would say, "You've got to help me get money to pay for this stuff. She's upstairs, she has spent £100,000. I'm fucked with my divorce. I can't pay for it.'"

'Go to Coutts,' Cummings advised. 'Get one of your rich friends to take out a loan.'

Many prime ministers borrow from a bank against their future earnings, but this wasn't possible for Johnson. 'They said no to him because of the divorce,' a friend said.

In Cummings' account, Johnson said, 'I want to get donations in to do it. But obviously it's bad PR so I have to keep it quiet.'

'That's illegal,' responded Cummings, who seems to have been genuinely horrified that Johnson could not see the ethical issues. 'What the fuck are you talking about? You idiots. The prime minister can't get secret donations. Are you out of your mind?'

Johnson would not, or could not afford to, see the problem. Eventually Helen MacNamara proposed setting up a trust to fund the renovations and other works to the Downing Street estate. When that failed, Tory peer Lord Brownlow coughed up £58,000 of his own money to cover Johnson's bills. For now, though, these arrangements were hidden from public scrutiny.

The Vote Leave crew claim Symonds was quickly gunning for them. 'She immediately was on at him about firing all of us which obviously is not a great way of starting a new government,' Cummings said.[3] He was warned by Dougie Smith, who had made it his business to befriend Symonds: power seeking out power. In Cummings' view, she 'wanted us there to win and solve the problem and make sure they weren't kicked out. But once the majority was won, she thought, "I want to control what actually happens downstairs with my friends in key jobs."' He claimed Symonds' influence led to a new species of prime minister, 'Boris-Carrie mode, which, like some demonic Russian virus, started overwriting previous Boris versions.'[4] Ever since the election campaign the chief aide and his allies had privately referred to Carrie as 'Princess Nut Nut', abbreviating this to an emoji of a princess followed by two peanuts in their message exchanges.[5]

Number 10 staff say they got texts from Johnson which read like they had been written by Symonds. 'You could tell when Carrie was messaging you from his phone, because the grammar and the spelling made sense,' one said. Others, including ministers, heard her voice in the background telling Johnson what to say during conversations. Symonds repeatedly denied these claims, but they were made by multiple credible witnesses. Civil servants confirm Carrie's attempts to influence issues she cared about, and to summon Johnson to the flat when he was in important meetings. 'She got involved in way too much,' a friend admitted.

Yet, in the preparation of this book, Johnson was adamant about one thing – that Carrie was unfairly targeted by his former aides who wanted to wound him by attacking her and that her influence did not affect government policy on major issues. 'It's not true,' he said. 'On Covid policy, she knew nothing and had zero influence. On Brexit policy, she knew nothing and had zero influence. It just is rubbish.'

To Carrie's camp, the tensions began not with her but with Cain, who they perceived as 'suspicious', 'hostile' and 'paranoid' about her because of her comms experience and her friendships with journalists like Harry Cole, her ex-boyfriend, Alex Wickham and Ross Kempsell. The latter two became godfathers to her two oldest children. When Johnson disagreed with Cain, Carrie's allies say he made her a scapegoat for Johnson's decisions. She concluded that Cain both believed she had intervened when she had not and liked to blame her to make it seem like she was a negative influence.

A special adviser who was close to Carrie said, 'Every spouse is going to have opinions; there's nothing improper at all about that. Because she has a background in politics, she might have had more opinions and stronger opinions than other spouses. If people think that she had too much influence, she's not culpable for that, Boris is culpable. He is the prime minister. If he's allowed Carrie to persuade him to make a decision, or change his mind overnight, that's on him, not on her.'

A senior official thought it unfortunate that a formal role was not found for her: 'I feel sorry for Carrie because politics and communications was her actual job. It wasn't as if she just got involved off the streets. She's also really good at it and she's got better judgement than Boris on a lot of things.' Where this mandarin felt Carrie 'crossed a line' was in trying to influence personnel decisions. 'She should never have had anything to do with people, appointments and interfering in reshuffles. I don't think she ever worked out how bad that was as the spouse.'

Some who briefed against Symonds believed Johnson was robbed of a wise, stable partner when he lost Marina, others saw both Boris and

Carrie as drama queens. 'Boris roams around and starts fires by accident and doesn't mind the chaos,' said a veteran Downing Street adviser. 'But for Carrie it is compulsive. She loves the intrigue of politics, the gossip and picking enemies. She saw Dom as her antagonist and had a Darwinian need to win. I don't think it gives her much pleasure, though, this thing that is inside her.' A family friend who knew both partners well said, 'He was traumatised and in pain at that time. He was going through a divorce he didn't want, his kids were not speaking to him, Carrie's pregnant and he's prime minister. It's what happens when you have a fractured family; he wants to keep the peace, but he can't. He doesn't want to hurt his children, but keeps doing things which are self-harming. You can't be on self-destruct mode as prime minister.' The same friend concluded more than a year after he left Number 10, 'Had he been married to Marina, I think he'd probably still be prime minister, let's put it that way.'

The divorce was made public on 18 February. Will Walden, who knew Marina well, handled the PR for both her and Boris, so Johnson could keep it separate from Cain's political communications. 'The real issue was that Boris didn't want to go,' another friend said. 'He loved her. There was a fuckload missing from his life.'

Yet many who saw Boris and Carrie privately witnessed a genuine bond between them. When she was deciding whether to stay with Johnson long term, she drew up a list of the pros and cons. The cons side was long. The pros contained just one phrase: 'I love him.' The mutual attraction was also obvious. 'It was not unusual, particularly in the September to Christmas 2019 period, for Boris to disappear to the flat for twenty minutes and come back visibly shagged out,' a senior Downing Street aide recalled. A custodian who was in Number 10 one night said the lift kept going up and down. He assumed it was malfunctioning, so he pressed the button and doors opened and they were just snogging like teenagers in the lift, going up and down.'

Cummings and Johnson had fundamentally different approaches to policy and governing. 'My attitude was: we've won the election, we've got a supermajority, there are a whole load of fundamental problems,' Cummings said later. '2020 is the year to do the hard things: like planning reform, which no one dares touch for decade after decade, because it's so politically difficult … Ignore the press, just head down, focus on this.' By contrast, Johnson's 'attitude was: I've done the hard thing, which was the election. Now it's time to enjoy myself. Very quickly, there is this clash of basic ideas.'

Someone who observed him closely said, 'Boris has always wanted to become prime minister and he has always wanted to have been prime minister – it's the bit in the middle which does not interest him.' This was not quite right, since Johnson revelled in 'being' prime minister, but Cummings wasn't alone in questioning whether he knew what he wanted to 'do' as PM. Beyond a speech on 3 February, primarily about Brexit, Johnson had little of substance to say in the first two months of the year. His stated priority on election night to deliver for red wall voters was encapsulated in his phrase 'levelling up', but it remained ill-defined even two years later. On the two major decisions he had to make that January – whether to give the go-ahead to the HS2 high speed rail line and allow Huawei, the Chinese telecoms company, to build part of Britain's future 5G network – Johnson accepted the conventional wisdom pushed by the civil service. In agreeing Huawei's access to 'non-core' parts of the network, announced on 28 January, he defied Donald Trump, who had warned it was a national security threat, as well as Priti Patel, the home secretary, and Ben Wallace, the defence secretary. On HS2, Johnson, who loved nothing more than 'building big stuff', gave the go-ahead, despite opposition from Cummings and Andrew Gilligan, his transport adviser. The project was already seven years late, with costs spiralling towards £100 billion.

'All he wants to do is not be a loser and not be put out in disgrace,' Cummings said later. 'Even in January 2020 he was saying to me, "God, you know, these people who say they want to do this job and go on and on? Well I want to write my Shakespeare book." By mid-January he was basically whingeing about what a difficult job it is.'[6] A few days earlier Johnson had confided that he hoped to leave Downing Street two or three years after the next election. Members of the policy unit asked to provide 'weekend reading' for the prime minister were told it should be 'an easy read: no more than four pages, or he's never going to read it – two pages is preferable'. A Number 10 source recalled Johnson saying, 'This job is too much like hard work. It's like pulling a giant 747 down the runway with a harness on your back. Every morning you get up and have to start pulling.'[7] Cummings read the riot act: 'You are prime minister and if you want to sit upstairs in the morning and do a bit of writing, that's up to you but I wouldn't run around the building telling everyone you are finding the job boring. Otherwise, you might find it hard to get people to do what you want.'

Cummings went through his to-do list: civil service reform, procurement, planning, science and technology, education, NHS changes. Johnson looked sceptical. The chief aide tried to spell out what the 2024 general election would look like. 'We've just won a "time for a change" campaign after the Tories have been in charge for ten years. That makes no sense. We did that because there was the biggest constitutional crisis for at least a century. Brexit, Corbyn. We can't pull anything like the same trick again. In 2024, everyone's going to say, "You said a bunch of shit in 2019, have you done it?" So 2020 is the year of annoying a lot of people, but laying the foundations for change. In 2024, your story will be, "We've done a huge amount as you can see, but we're halfway through. Let me finish the job."'

There was a pause after which Johnson said, 'You've just gone mad. Why do I want to annoy everyone now? I've just got an 80-seat majority.'

Johnson's governing style had also begun to grate on his aides. 'They wanted total control over attendance at meetings,' a close ally recalled, 'and Boris just doesn't work like that. He will invite who he wants. There were two headstrong personalities.' In the meetings, Johnson thrived on discursive conflict, when Cummings wanted clear decisions. 'The way Boris makes decisions is that he does like to cogitate all the different possible outcomes, mull them over, hear people thrash out their ideas. He sits over it like a chairman, goes away, thinks about it, and then comes back with a decision. It's not uncommon for him, at the start of a meeting, to talk for fifteen minutes. The thing you learn from working with him is that is what he really thinks and believes, so you have to pay attention. A big mistake that people make with Boris: they think he's just rambling.'

When Lee Cain took over Johnson's comms, Walden advised him how to handle the PM: 'Let 95 per cent of things go. You might not agree with them but most of it doesn't matter and he'll do it anyway, but the really important stuff that keeps the show on the road, throw the sink at it because that's the only way he listens. But if you do that with everything, he'll stop listening to you.' Increasingly, however, the Vote Leave contingent was not willing to let so much go. Someone with more respect for his prime minister than Cummings would have found a way of presenting his own agenda as integral to Johnson's own goals, or advanced the PM's wishes in exchange for backing his own.

Instead, Cummings, an overmighty subject in the medieval style, saw Johnson as a figurehead for the things he wanted to do in government. An ally of the aide said, 'Boris might be the face and voice, but he was certainly not the brains and that's the reality.' Johnson did have ideas, but two of them – 'levelling up' and 'global Britain' – were regarded by Cummings as meaningless vacuities. 'Boris wanted to make the Conservative Party the party of the hardworking classes, whether they had no money or lots of money,' a friendly cabinet minister observed. 'Mission number two was to create opportunity for all. He felt very strongly that opportunity was not spread equally across our country.'

Whatever their agendas, constitutionally the power was the prime minister's alone. Advisers advise, politicians decide. Johnson was to tire quickly of Cummings making decisions for him. Eddie Lister recalled, 'Dom felt he should be in charge of everything. He also had a fairly low opinion of Boris. I never understood why Boris was so keen on him. I don't think he needed him.'

Symonds, similarly, was growing tired of the Vote Leave total war approach. She wanted Johnson to be a more conciliatory figure, to reach out to the media and the corners of the party he had alienated in 2019. To her it seemed like Cummings craved permanent conflict, almost for its own sake. She was not alone. Even Paul Stephenson had quietly advised Lee Cain to pick fewer fights with the media. But to Cummings, reform had to be driven while Johnson had political capital in the bank.

At times he seemed out of control, treating Johnson and the special advisers as if it was Alcatraz not Whitehall. Cummings was also becoming the story, gaining more mentions in newspapers than any cabinet minister since Johnson took power. On 31 January he used his 'spad school' meeting to announce that, in future, they must pick up half the bill if they went for lunch, dinner or drinks with the media. 'The people's government doesn't take any favours,' he pronounced. Soon afterwards, the *Sunday Times* published a well-sourced but palpably ridiculous story suggesting Cummings had contacted Westminster restaurants asking staff to snitch on ministerial aides dining with journalists. 'He's got a network of spies who will report back if our people are in there with their media mates,' declared an ally.

*   *   *

A more serious disagreement erupted over real spies and Johnson's casual handling of sensitive intelligence documents. On a rare visit to the PM's flat in early 2020, Cummings found confidential papers lying around, including 'Strap' level material, the highest classification, readily identifiable because it was printed on pink paper. Papers classified top secret or higher, kept in red folders, were also found in the upstairs quarters at Chequers. Another Number 10 adviser recalled, 'The cleaners would find them stashed in cupboards.'

Cummings spoke to Martin Reynolds, Johnson's principal private secretary, and to Simon Case, who had returned from Buckingham Palace to the Cabinet Office. He demanded a new protocol whereby documents which might put lives at risk or identify intelligence assets would not be sent to Johnson's living quarters. 'Some of these things are about MI6 operations where, if it's reported, it could literally lead to our people getting strung up with piano wire,' a security source said.

Central to Cummings' concern was that Symonds was close friends with several journalists who visited the flat. It was agreed that sensitive Strap material was to be shown to the PM downstairs, then immediately returned. If time forbade that, 'someone should go with it and ask the prime minister to read it as a matter of urgency and then take it away'.

If it was not strange enough that the government had to take action to protect national security from the head of that government, serious security concerns were also raised about Johnson's decision to nominate Evgeny Lebedev for a peerage. The owner of the *Evening Standard* had backed Johnson when he was running for mayor of London. But Lebedev was also the son of Alexander Lebedev, a billionaire Russian oligarch once close to Vladimir Putin. Johnson had on six occasions been a guest at Palazzo Terranova, Evgeny's castle near Perugia in Italy, the scene of wild parties. In April 2018, at the height of the Skripal affair, the then foreign secretary ditched his security detail to spend a weekend with both Lebedevs. He had gone directly from a meeting of Nato and EU foreign ministers in Brussels, where they discussed expelling Russian spies from Western embassies in retaliation for the Novichok attack in Salisbury.[8] Johnson was seen returning home alone, dishevelled with no luggage, having apparently 'slept in his suit'. He admitted to another passenger he'd had 'a heavy night'.[9] Rachel Johnson told one journalist she did not know what happened at Evgeny Lebedev's parties because 'the women are sent home at midnight'.[10]

In 2022 the *Sunday Times* revealed that, in March 2020, the House of Lords Appointments Commission (Holac), which vets peerages, wrote to the prime minister advising him against granting Lebedev a seat in the Lords, objections based on intelligence provided by MI5 and MI6, relayed to the commission by Cabinet Office security officials. 'They considered that there could be a threat to national security,' a source told the paper.[11] Cummings has also revealed he strongly advised Johnson not to proceed with the nomination: 'I was there when the decision was made. I was in the room when other people said, "Prime Minister, you shouldn't do this." It was one of the many, many battles after the election I didn't win.'[12] Johnson is said to have responded to the advice by claiming, 'This is anti-Russianism.' Three months later, the security assessment was withdrawn and Lebedev's nomination went ahead.

Alexander Lebedev was frequently described in the media as a 'former lieutenant colonel in the KGB'. However, the security services believed Lebedev senior remained close to the Kremlin. Two cabinet ministers familiar with the intelligence and a third senior security official told the author that MI6, throughout this period, considered Alexander Lebedev 'an active member of the Russian intelligence services'. One said, 'You never leave. The view was that Evgeny was naive.' There is no suggestion that either Lebedev junior or Johnson was recruited by the Russians, but the arms of Putin's secret state were active in developing agents of influence and the prime minister's blasé attitude to the friendship concerned the security establishment. Johnson did not even admit he crossed paths with Alexander Lebedev until he appeared in front of the Commons Liaison Committee on his final day as prime minister in July 2022. He said, 'Look, I have certainly met him without officials.'[13]

This was not the only warning by the security services about figures close to Johnson. A senior figure in the government also revealed that, when Boris took over as prime minister, someone at the very top of the CIA, whose identity is known to the author, alerted his counterparts in SIS and security officials in Whitehall to concerns the Americans had about Stanley Johnson's interactions with the Chinese regime. Johnson's father was a regular at environmental conferences where Chinese government officials were present, and a vocal public advocate of closer relations with Beijing. A few months after this warning, in February 2020, it emerged that Stanley acted as a diplomatic back channel between the then Chinese ambassador, Liu Xiaoming, and Zac Goldsmith, the minister for environment and international development. After a ninety-minute audience, in which they discussed China hosting COP15, a biodiversity summit, Stanley emailed Goldsmith to say the Chinese were 'concerned' that there had been no 'direct contact' between 'the PM and Chinese head of state' about the coronavirus outbreak. Goldsmith thanked him.[14]

When Britain hosted the COP26 conference in November 2021, those working on the summit were asked by a member of the intelligence services to keep Stanley away from Chinese diplomats. One official on the COP team said, 'We spent the whole time saying to Stanley, "Please stop calling the Chinese ambassador." He was constantly going over for tea and taking books, and then he would come beetling over and try and have meetings with Alok [Sharma, the president of COP], which we stopped, because we obviously didn't want that shit happening.' This was at a time when the new ambassador, Zheng Zeguang, was banned from Parliament by the speakers of both Commons and Lords after China had imposed travel bans and asset freezes against five MPs. The COP official, debriefed afterwards by the intelligence services, was told, 'Thanks for keeping Stanley off the case.' He was not off it for long. Six days after the summit finished, on 18 November, Stanley posed again with Zheng at the Chinese embassy.[15]

Just five months later, Stanley announced on Instagram he was 'delighted to entertain' Zheng and his wife Hua Mei 'to lunch at home in London'.[16] That June, Stanley and his youngest son Max, thirty-six, dined at the diplomat's London residence.[17] Johnson Sr duly called for the ban against the ambassador to be lifted, telling the *South China Morning Post*, Zheng was a 'very agreeable, capable and intelligent man'.[18] In July 2023, Johnson was back, breathlessly telling his Instagram followers he had enjoyed a 'brilliant evening at the Chinese Embassy and Ambassador Zheng Zeguang to celebrate the 96th anniversary of the People's Liberation Army'.[19]

Stanley used his contacts to win the backing of the regime to film a documentary in the summer of 2023, *In the Footsteps of Marco Polo*, riding motorbikes across China with his son Max, a financier who lived for a decade in Hong Kong. The Johnsons rode through Xinjiang, the province where China brutally suppressed the minority Uighur people, a slaughter widely considered a genocide. No mention of this was made in the film, which was produced by One Tribe, a British company, in conjunction with China Central Television, owned and controlled by the Chinese Communist Party. In August, Stanley posted another picture of a dinner he and Max had with Zheng to 'celebrate the successful conclusion' of the project after 'seven weeks filming in China'.[20]

A trailer appeared online in the spring of 2024 but an industry source, who also filmed in China, said, 'It was commissioned while Boris was PM obviously. The Chinese spent a ton of cash buying access to Johnson, who was kicked out of office the minute the deal was signed. Even the Chinese crew were surprised by how happy they were to toe the party line.'

Asked about all this, Stanley said, 'I have never said things about China which I didn't believe in. We really need to think very carefully before we go down the route of saying we're going to be tough on China. You know, it just doesn't make sense.' Asked how he felt about the CIA voicing concerns about his Chinese links, he said, 'I'm sure they can read my MI6 file.'

Both Russian and Chinese efforts to get close to the Johnson family appear to have borne little fruit, though the behaviour of Boris and Stanley was naive. Johnson's initial support of Huawei being part of the UK's 5G network was in line with civil service and intelligence advice that the threat could be mitigated. It would be a more serious matter if he had contradicted the consensus Whitehall view. On Russia, after a brief spell as foreign secretary, when he sought better relations, Johnson was robust in word and deed about the Kremlin and took a leading global role opposing Putin's invasion of Ukraine. 'They didn't get much for their money,' a senior minister remarked. A TV industry insider added, 'It's a rather amusing story of the Johnson family adding the Chinese Communist Party to the list of those they have fleeced.'

Johnson conducted his first reshuffle on 13 February. It began with the removal of Julian Smith as Northern Ireland secretary and Geoffrey Cox as attorney general. Both had fallen out with Johnson and his aides over Brexit, though sacking Smith just days after he successfully negotiated the return of power sharing in Belfast was ruthless and unnerved both Dublin and Brussels. He was replaced by Brandon Lewis. George Eustice, a strawberry farmer, took over from Theresa Villiers at Defra. Anne-Marie Trevelyan joined the cabinet as international development secretary, replacing Alok Sharma, who moved to business. Oliver

Dowden became culture secretary, in place of Nicky Morgan who stood down for family reasons. Amanda Milling took over from James Cleverly as party chairman. Penny Mordaunt returned as paymaster general. Cox's replacement was Suella Braverman, a former chair of the ERG. It would prove to be the most significant appointment. With one exception.

The reshuffle would be forever remembered for the resignation of Sajid Javid, the chancellor of the exchequer. Cummings failed to get another scalp – Ben Wallace, the defence secretary, who he regarded as a 'security risk' because he was too quick to answer the phone to journalists. As an old friend of Johnson, whose leadership campaign he had run in 2016, Wallace was a nuisance to Cummings, because he had the PM's ear and views of his own about how to reform the MoD. Johnson could tell Cummings was cross when he refused to ditch Wallace. 'I can't stand you being sad like this, it makes me depressed. Tell me anything else you want.'

The chief aide seized his moment, urging Johnson to tell Javid all his special advisers were fired. 'They're all just useless and they are leaking everything … They don't want to work with Number 10. We don't need this shit after the six months we've just been through.' Cain and Cummings had devised a plan for a joint media unit, bringing together people from Number 10 and Number 11.

Johnson was incredulous. 'Who gives a fuck about spads?' he blurted, before noticing the looks his two senior aides were giving him. 'I didn't mean you, Caino, or you, Dom, obviously.' Once they had left Johnson's office, Cain remarked, 'Good to know where we rank in this operation.'

If the chancellor accepted the plan, he would be neutered; if he resigned Cummings and Liam Booth-Smith, who was slated to lead the joint unit, had identified Rishi Sunak, the chief secretary to the Treasury, as a capable successor. 'He was smarter, nicer and wanted to be part of a team to make the government work,' one of those in the loop said. Tensions between 10 and 11 Downing Street had been acute since Cummings summarily sacked Javid's spad Sonia Khan the previous August. Reports then reached Number 10 in the days before the general election that Javid had been telling colleagues, if the result was poor, that Cummings should be removed. Unfortunately, for the chancellor, 'Some of them rang people in Number 10 to say that Saj was trying to get a posse together,' one recalled. Javid had form for this, having led the cabinet charge (successfully) demanding the heads of Nick Timothy and Fiona

Hill after the 2017 election debacle.[21] When the story appeared, much later, Javid denied it then admitted to fellow MPs, 'I've made a terrible mistake. I'm fucked.' This also made its way back to Number 10.

Cummings, in turn, was irritated by Johnson's relationship with Javid, one of the few where he was unable to insert himself. The PM and Carrie, who had once been Javid's spad, had attended his fiftieth birthday in early December. Cummings and Javid clashed over the appointment of Andrew Bailey as governor of the Bank of England – a job Cummings wanted to go to the bank's chief economist Andy Haldane, who he thought more capable. 'I'll get my own back,' Cummings shouted at Javid's adviser Mats Persson.[22]

There were also policy differences. Javid had drawn up tight fiscal rules before the general election. With his majority in the bag, Johnson wanted to spend money and they were an inconvenience. On the Wednesday before the reshuffle, during a meeting in the Cabinet Room, the prime minister explicitly asked his chancellor to look at how he might tear up the rules. Bizarrely, Johnson had phoned Javid before the meeting to ask him to explain the fiscal rules. 'It was ahead of the PM having a meeting with his own team,' a Treasury source said. 'Saj walked him through the rules and briefed Boris on what to ask and what to say. Then he went into a meeting with his own team, which was a pre-meet before Saj came in for the proper meeting. So Saj pre-briefed the PM for his pre-brief' – *The Thick of It* as fly-on-the-wall documentary series. The rest of the day was compared by one aide to 'an Alan Ayckbourn farce'.

In the main meeting, Javid pushed back. His argument, summarised by one ally, was this: 'Fiscal rules are not your enemy, something to be hated. We came up with them because they are your friend. They force you to make choices. You can't say everything is your priority.' The only senior minister seemingly on Javid's side was the chief secretary, Rishi Sunak. In their brief time working together the two men would forge a close bond which later had important implications for Johnson.

Javid also resisted a plan, floated by Cummings, to impose a mansion tax on wealthy property owners. Number 10 asked Treasury officials to look at how it might work. The chancellor did not think taxing static wealth was Conservative. 'You don't level up by levelling everyone else down,' he said. But when the idea leaked, Number 10 accused Javid's team of briefing it to kill the plan. The Treasury, in turn, accused

Johnson's aides of trying to bounce him into the idea. One branded it 'proper DDR stuff' – equating Johnson's aides with the Stasi, the East German secret police. To Team Boris, this claim was evidence of 'paranoia' in Javid's camp. 'He psyched himself out of a job,' one said.

When Johnson spoke to Javid about the plan for a new joint communications unit, the PM made clear he wanted a close relationship with his chancellor. 'I want it to be like Dave and George.' But he said the briefings were causing friction and he wanted to build one unit so that they were getting the same advice. Johnson offered to resume weekly meetings and one-to-one dinners with his chancellor. But there had to be changes. Javid's reaction, according to someone in the room, veered between 'huffy' and 'pretty aggressive'. When he spoke up for his advisers, Johnson insensitively pronounced, 'They're just people.'

'They are our people,' Javid replied.[23] He felt cut off at the knees. 'You're all calling me CHINO,' he complained, referencing media reports branding him 'chancellor in name only'. Johnson worked on him. Eddie Lister recalled, 'I spent a happy hour and a half trying to persuade him not to throw his toys out of the pram.' Then Helen MacNamara had a go. But Javid dug in. If his spads were leaving, so was he. Johnson had a change of heart, prompting Lee Cain to threaten to resign. The prime minister invited Javid back into his office. 'You don't see what's happening, do you?' the chancellor said. 'Cummings is running rings around you. He's running your government.'[24] Javid eventually went out to the waiting cameras to say that he was resigning: 'No self-respecting minister would accept this,' he said.

Johnson was stunned. 'The PM thought Saj would accept the deal,' a Number 10 aide recalled. Another said, 'Saj played it extremely badly. He boxed himself in. He was seeing shadows everywhere. If Saj had just said: "I understand we should have one team between Number 10 and Number 11, but let's just me and you figure out how this is going to work and who should be in it, rather than me just walk out and start firing people", Dom would have been screwed. But Saj is just shit at politics.' Cummings told one confidant, 'Thank God for fools.'

Sunak was the natural fit for the role, already in the Treasury, more than clever enough and happy to be a subordinate player. Cummings had viewed him with affection since 2016, when he told Cameron and Osborne that he could not back the Remain campaign. He quickly showed his independence too. One of Johnson's only instructions was,

'You've got to fire Tom Scholar,' the permanent secretary at the Treasury. Sunak demurred: 'I'm not going to fire someone I've not had any experience of working with. It's just not right. If I find in a month's time, he is rubbish, I will do it then. But I'm not going to do it straight off the bat because someone said he was useless.' Confronted with the same choice, one of his successors behaved differently.

Javid's departure sent shockwaves through Whitehall. Special adviser Jamie Njoku-Goodwin told his cabinet minister, Matt Hancock, 'If they tell you that the only way to keep your job is to fire me, then obviously you do it.' MPs did not like the 'Torquemada tone' from Number 10. A former minister said, 'The people's government has a whiff of *The Death of Stalin*.'

Curiously, Johnson, who hated firing people, was grateful the vanquished made things easy for him. 'Do you know my favourite bit of the day?' he said to an official later. 'All those people I sacked from the cabinet, they all loved me. They never asked for anything. Half the people I appointed were cross with me and wanted something different.'

When it was over, Helen MacNamara went for a drink at the Harp off Trafalgar Square with a friend. It was 10.30 p.m. when her phone went; it was the prime minister. 'I need to get Whitto in,' Johnson said. 'We've got a Whitto-shaped hole.' It seemed clear what had happened. Johnson, thinking his work was done, had retired to the flat and had his ear bent by Carrie that there was no job for her old boss, John Whittingdale, the former culture secretary. The Johnson camp denies Carrie intervened and points out that not only was Whittingdale the best man for the job, the prime minister had promised to look after him because he was an early supporter in both leadership bids.

'We've literally appointed everybody,' MacNamara said. 'We've run out of jobs. We don't have any more salaries.' The number of paid ministerial positions was capped by law at ninety-five.

'We have to get rid of somebody,' Johnson said. 'You need to fix this.' MacNamara returned to Number 10 and found Ben Gascoigne, who had also had a call from Johnson. While all the jobs had been allocated in the culture department and the new ministers informed, some posts had not been publicly announced. Ranil Jayawardena, an early member of Johnson's leadership team, had made a nuisance of himself, demanding to be a minister of state. He would have to 'take one for the team'. When the press release came out the next morning there was a shock return as minister of state for Whittingdale. Jayawardena was thrown a consolation bone: deputy chairman of the Conservative Party.

The day after the reshuffle, Sunak invited Cummings to his office in the Treasury to go over the upcoming budget in detail. Officials watched nervously as they stood over a table strewn with papers, wondering how they would get on. They went through 'the real numbers', usually closely guarded by the Treasury. Sunak exuded a quiet authority for a man who had been a junior minister just seven months earlier. Cummings was unexpectedly deferential for one whose reputation was more hatchet man than numbers man. A Number 10 official said, 'That's the best meeting by a mile that we have had with the Treasury.'

The elevation of Sunak reduced immediate tensions, but it could not resolve policy differences between the advocates of fiscal responsibility and Johnson's urge to court popularity by spending money. Ultimately, it raised to prominence someone who many came to see as a viable alternative prime minister. 'If Sajid had stayed,' a close ally of Johnson reflected later, 'Boris would have had a broadly compliant chancellor. Instead it felt like Dom now controlled the Treasury. It was also another example of the HR tyranny. No one was safe because he had effectively taken out the chancellor of the exchequer.'

Claiming the scalp of a chancellor seemed only to embolden Cummings. Three days later, on 16 February, the *Sunday Times* splashed with the news that plans were afoot to scrap the BBC licence fee and replace it with a subscription model; force the BBC to sell off the vast majority of its sixty-one radio stations; reduce the number of the corporation's national television channels; scale back the BBC website; and ban BBC stars from cashing in with lucrative second jobs. One senior figure said, 'We are not bluffing on the licence fee. We will whack it.' When the story broke that Saturday night, the prime minister phoned the journalist and declared it 'a bit overcooked' before trying to smoke out the leaker. By Tuesday morning, *The Times* had declared it the work of Cummings. He and Cain both denied any involvement.

The following day, there was new acrimony. 'It was like the parents rowing in front of the children,' said one of those in Downing Street. The disagreement concerned the fate of Andrew Sabisky, who Cummings had hired as part of a drive to recruit 'weirdos and misfits with odd skills' to shake up Whitehall. On 2 January Cummings published, with his usual lack of brevity, a three-thousand-word blog calling for 'an unusual set of people with different skills and backgrounds to work in Downing Street: data scientists and software developers; economists; policy experts; project managers; communication experts; junior researchers one of whom will also be my personal assistant'. Those encouraged to apply were 'true wild cards, artists, people who never went to university and fought their way out of an appalling hell hole'. Those dissuaded were 'confident public school bluffers' and 'more Oxbridge English graduates'. Applicants for his personal assistant were warned, 'You will not have weekday date nights, you will sacrifice many weekends – frankly it will be hard having a boy/girlfriend at all. It will be exhausting but interesting and if you cut it you will be involved in things at the age of 21 that most people never see.'

There was much to commend this approach, as even some senior civil servants agreed, but it was not appreciated by those in the policy unit who had to wade through the thousands of applications which piled up. 'There were these enormous stacks of paper on the floor in the middle of the office,' one recalled. 'Every random nutter in the world had sent their CV to Number 10. It seemed to everyone like a totally pointless exercise.' It was also a cover for employing people who Cummings already knew. Sabisky, a 'super forecaster' adept at predicting future trends, was one.

Sabisky's arrival led to press scrutiny of his previous work. It emerged that he had claimed that IQ was somewhat racially dependent and given an interview stating that 'eugenics are about selecting "for" good things'. In a comment on Cummings' blog in 2014 Sabisky said compulsory contraception could prevent 'a permanent underclass'.

In a conference call with senior aides, 'Boris was absolutely furious,' said one source. 'He demanded that Sabisky be sacked.' Cummings refused, arguing that the government should not remove a talented individual because of a media storm. Some concluded Cummings was prepared to walk if he did not get his way. In a second conference call later that day, the prime minister put his foot down, insisting, 'He's got to go.' Sabisky was given the chance to resign. He did so.

The episode put another dent in the core relationship in government but that was soon overtaken because on the same day David Frost outlined Britain's opening position on a trade deal with the European Union.

A FROSTY RECEPTION

A Tale of Two Speeches

February to April 2020

'I have discovered the art of deceiving diplomats.
I tell them the truth and they never believe me'

– Camillo Cavour

The ceiling of the painted hall in the Old Royal Naval College in Greenwich is widely regarded as the finest mural in Britain. It was here, on 3 February, beneath the baroque kings, nymphs and naval triumphs, that Boris Johnson outlined what he wanted from a Brexit trade deal. As he gazed at the vast ceiling, the work of twenty years by Sir James Thornhill, perhaps he imagined himself up there alongside William and Mary or George I, toiling to complete what he had started four years earlier. Johnson certainly saw the Brexit project in the traditions of the painting, the centrepiece of which depicts the triumph of peace and liberty over tyranny.

As he rose to speak in front of a collection of EU ambassadors and other worthies, Johnson explained that the epic painting was begun in 1707, the year of the Act of Union, which brought four nations to live and work together until they were the dominant force in Europe. 'This is the settlement of a long and divisive political question,' he said, in this case about who sat on the English throne. 'The result is stability and certainty and optimism and an explosion of global trade propelled by new maritime technology … This is the newly forged United Kingdom on the slipway: this is the moment when it all took off. Today if we get it right, if we have the courage to follow the instincts and the instructions of the British people, this can be another such moment on the launching pad.

Once again, we have settled a long-running question of sovereign authority, we have ended a debate that has run for three and a half years – some
would say forty-seven years.'

If this did not persuade his audience of the parallels with Brexit,
Johnson's encomium to Thornhill, the British Michelangelo, may have
done. He 'spent twenty years flat on his back on top of the scaffolding, so
rigid that his arm became permanently wonky'. Brexit had been crippling
political toil for Theresa May. Johnson painted his own picture: of Brexit
Britain 'leaving its chrysalis', going 'out into the world', after 'decades of
hibernation', to become once more 'a campaigner for global free trade'.

The prime minister sought to allay fears that Britain wanted to 'slash
and burn' workers' rights or engage in a 'cut-throat race to the bottom'.
Britain was the first country to enshrine net zero in law and on issues like
paid maternity leave, paternity leave and flexible working, the UK was far
ahead of the rest of the EU – with a higher minimum wage than all but
three member states. Britain would not accept 'EU rules on competition
policy, subsidies, social protection, the environment … The UK will
maintain the highest standards in these areas – better, in many respects,
than those of the EU – without the compulsion of a treaty.'

Johnson's goal was to show his government had chosen a path which
Brussels had already offered. 'We have so often been told that we must
choose between full access to the EU market, along with accepting its
rules and courts, on the Norway model, or a free trade agreement, which
opens up markets and avoids the full panoply of EU regulation, like the
Canada deal. Well folks, I hope you've got the message by now. We have
made our choice: we want a comprehensive free trade agreement, similar
to Canada's.' The alternative was a relationship like Australia's, more
attractive branding for no-deal, with side agreements to prevent turmoil
in areas like aviation. 'I don't think it was ever rational to go for no-deal,'
Stefaan De Rynck noted. 'That doesn't mean that the government would
not have done it.'[1]

Johnson also hinted where Britain was prepared to give ground in the
negotiations. 'We are ready to consider an agreement on fisheries, but it
must reflect the fact that the UK will be an independent coastal state at
the end of this year 2020, controlling our own waters.' He delivered the
opening offer: 'Under such an agreement, there would be annual negotiations with the EU.' Brussels, egged on by the maritime nations France,
Spain and the Netherlands, wanted a twenty-five-year settlement.

Johnson's speech made him, for the time being, the good cop of the operation, putting the optimistic, outward-looking case for a free trade deal shorn of tariffs and barriers. His focus on Britain's high standards in employment and environmental legislation came because the EU showed no signs of dropping its demand that there be 'level playing field' rules, which would mean the UK adopting many of the same rules as the rest of the bloc even after Brexit, restricting the ability of the UK to diverge.

In meetings of the cabinet and the XS committee both Johnson and Frost made clear divergence was the goal, even if that meant the EU responded by imposing tariffs. 'Boris resigned because he thinks the whole point of Brexit is that we need to be able to do our own thing and maximise the benefits,' a confidant said. For Frost, 'the logic of Brexit' dictated that divergence was essential. 'It's a medium-term bet that being in control of your own affairs is better for you,' he said.

The Commission did not seem to be listening. Before Christmas, EU leaders agreed a joint negotiating position in which they wanted Britain to agree to regulatory alignment in exchange for a tariff-free, quota-free access to the European market. Johnson's team complained that the EU did not make such demands in other free trade agreements with the likes of South Korea. Another issue was 'governance'. The EU insisted that the European Court of Justice continue to govern Britain's trade relationship with the EU, when most trade deals are adjudicated by an independent arbitrator.

The two sides also disagreed about whether there was enough time to complete a deal before the end of the transition period on 31 December. When new Commission president Ursula von der Leyen met Johnson in Downing Street on Wednesday 8 January, she said it was 'basically impossible to negotiate' everything in that time. 'Without an extension of the transition period beyond 2020, you cannot expect to agree on every single aspect of our new partnership,' she said. A cabinet minister reflected, 'They think because we have a big majority that we can extend. The reason we have a big majority is that we promised not to extend.'

The Commission had still not understood the UK's political reality. In all their public pronouncements and their private preparations, Barnier's team gave the impression they still thought they were negotiating with Theresa May, a world view effectively expounded by Leo Varadkar, when Barnier visited Dublin on 27 January. 'The situation is that the EU is a union of twenty-seven member states,' he said, with the EU negotiator at his side. 'The UK is only one country. And we have a population and a market of 450 million people. The UK, it's about 60 million. So if these were two teams up against each other playing football, who do you think has the stronger team?' Frost recalled. 'There was an assumption that we were the weaker party and would have to accept certain things if we wanted an agreement. It took time for them to realise that that wasn't the case.'[2] Britain was the weaker party, but it was determined to play the cards it had with greater resolution.

In his speech in Number 10 on Brexit night, Johnson reflected on the cold shoulder presented to his chief negotiator, known to his colleagues as 'Frosty'. 'Every time our negotiation team goes to Brussels they throw a party like this,' Johnson joked. 'It's called a Frosty reception.'

In a bid to dramatise Britain's sovereign status, Dominic Raab, the foreign secretary, ordered British diplomats to break with their former EU allies and 'sit separately' at international summits. In a telegram sent to UK overseas missions in the last week of January, he told diplomats to ditch any ideas to 'seek residual influence' with EU countries and 'adopt a stance as a confident independent country' instead. Raab said, 'We need to signal to the world ... that 31 January represented an important change in our international position.'

Michael Gove, the minister in charge of Brexit preparations, was more explicit on 10 February when he summoned businesses to a Whitehall event, Preparing Our Border for the Future Relationship. He said they had to get ready for 'inevitable' border checks for 'almost everybody' from the start of 2021. There would be checks on food and goods of animal origin, and importers would have to fill in customs declarations plus safety and security certificates.

Even after Johnson's speech in Greenwich, Barnier did not seem to grasp that the government was no longer seeking frictionless trade, as May had been, and was in fact happy to accept friction at the border as the price of economic sovereignty. The great Cakeist was admitting that if you eat the cake, you couldn't have it too – and no one seemed to have noticed. Frost was frustrated that Johnson's opening position had been misunderstood and conscious that in the previous negotiations, May and Robbins had been outmanoeuvred because they let the EU frame the terms and process of the talks. Most of all he wanted Brussels to acknowledge that they were negotiating with a sovereign equal, rather than a separatist province of the EU imperium.

On 17 February, he travelled to Brussels to, literally, deliver a lecture to the EU on where he and Johnson were coming from, in a bid to try to explain the appeal of Brexit to uncomprehending Europeans. 'The EU had not absorbed that we genuinely wanted a Canada-style FTA rather than a high-alignment future agreement or that we were determined on leaving the transition period at the end of 2020,' Frost recalled. 'I don't think they really realised we were serious on either point until the deadline to extend the transition had passed in June. As a result, the first half of the year ... was largely shadow-boxing.'[3]

The speech was one of the most outspoken public interventions ever made by a civil servant. Frost called the EU 'a noble project', but argued that, in Britain, EU institutions seemed 'abstract' and 'technocratic' and 'hostile to national feeling'. In a country where institutions had evolved over centuries, it felt 'a bit unnatural' to 'be governed by an organisation whose institutions seemed created by design rather than by evolution'. He added, 'Much of this still does not seem to me to be understood here in Brussels and in large parts of the EU. I think one of the reasons why people here failed to see Brexit coming and often still see it as some kind of horrific, unforeseeable natural disaster is that – like the meteorite that wiped out the dinosaurs – is at root, they were unable to take British Euroscepticism seriously, but saw it as some kind of irrational false consciousness and fundamentally wrong way of looking at the world.'

Frost explained his own transition from being 'a typical pro-European' to Euroscepticism came about because 'I could see Britain was never going to be genuinely committed to the project.' By opting out of the euro and the Schengen agreement, 'Britain was like a guest who has had enough of a party and wants to find a way of slipping out. By 2016 we had already found our way to the hallway without anyone really noticing. It was only when we picked up our coat and waved goodbye that it felt like people said, "Oh, are you going?" as if they hadn't realised what had been happening ... Brexit is a re-establishment of underlying reality, in my view, not some freakish divergence from it.'

Frost then turned to the economics, disputing the views of those, Barnier included, who regarded Brexit as a 'lose-lose' or 'damage limitation' exercise. 'All these studies exaggerate – in my view – the impact of non-tariff barriers they exaggerate customs costs, in some cases by orders of magnitude ... Many Brexit studies seem very keen to ignore or minimise any of the upsides, whether these be connected to expanded trade with the rest of the world or regulatory change.'

Frost then laid out the negotiating position. 'We are clear that we want the Canada-Free Trade Agreement-type relationship which the EU has so often said is on offer – even if the EU itself now seems to be experiencing some doubts about that ... We understand the trade-offs involved – people sometimes say we don't, but we do.' Frost's 'deeper point' was this: 'We believe sovereignty is meaningful and what it enables us to do is to set our rules for our own benefit.' That might mean producing 'crops that reflect our own climate, rather than being forced to work with rules designed for growing conditions in central France'. He said, 'I struggle to see why this is so controversial.' Brexit, he explained, was an acceptance of 'short run cost' for 'huge gains' in future. 'We aren't frightened by suggestions there is going to be friction,' he said. 'We know that and have factored this in.'

Frost made the case that the EU should treat the UK 'as a relationship of equals'. He said, 'We bring to the negotiations not some clever tactical positioning but the fundamentals of what it means to be an independent country. It is central to our vision that we must have the ability to set laws that suit us – to claim the right that every other non-EU country in the world has ... That isn't a simple negotiating position which might move under pressure – it is the point of the whole project.'

The key passage pulled no punches: 'I do believe this needs to be internalised on the EU side. The EU needs to understand, I mean genuinely understand, not just say it, that countries geographically in Europe can, if they choose it, be independent countries,' he said. 'Independence does not mean a limited degree of freedom in return for accepting some of the norms of the central power. It means – independence – just that. I recognise that some in Brussels might be uncomfortable with that, but the EU must, if it is to achieve what it wants in the world, find a way of relating to its neighbours as genuinely sovereign equals.'

Frost thought there was a virtue in being frank. 'I didn't think it served us particularly well to conduct the negotiation in a secretive way,' he explained. Number 10 released details of other trade deals the EU had struck. The EU removed 99.5 per cent of tariff lines in its trade deal with Canada, 99 per cent in its deal with Japan and 98.7 per cent in its deal with South Korea. Not one of these countries was subject to any dynamic alignment on regulation. Canada's deal with the EU contained commitments not to use labour or environment rules to distort trade, but that was policed through a dispute mechanism, not by the ECJ.

Frost's defiance cut little ice in Brussels. 'Our job was to defend EU interests, not adjust positions because of UK speeches,' Commission official Stefaan De Rynck recalled.[4] To the EU, the issue was not British sovereignty, but the question of what a sovereign nation was prepared to give up to win preferential access to the European market. Barnier and his team saw Frost's focus on the former as an impediment to the latter. 'The difficulty with the Johnson government was its ideology on sovereignty which led to a very painful process to convince the UK that any international agreement implies international obligations, including with the EU,' De Rynck added.[5] Brussels also saw a double standard in Britain's refusal to give full diplomatic status to João Vale de Almeida, the EU ambassador in London, on the basis that he did not represent a country.[6] 'The discrepancy between saying, "We are sovereign equals, but then we're not going to recognise your ambassador here", it doesn't hold up,' De Rynck said. 'The UK needs to calm down in the way it interacts with the EU.'[7]

Where Johnson and Frost did have a point was that the EU seemed to have moved the goalposts. Brussels had spent three years urging Theresa May to pick one of the existing models for a relationship with the EU, once depicted in Barnier's staircase graphic. Now Britain had picked the Canada step, the EU wanted to impose tighter controls than those on Canada. A senior source said, 'They are trying to push for something with all the obligations of the Norway model with the market access restrictions of Canada – this is a total hypocrisy and a non-starter for the UK.'

When, the day after Frost's speech, Barnier published a graphic suggesting the UK had to remain in the EU's orbit, Lee Cain hit back, Tweeting the staircase image from the official Number 10 account with the words, 'In 2017 the EU showed on their own slide that a Canada-type FTA was the only available relationship for the UK. Now they say it's not on offer after all. Michel Barnier, what's changed?' An official recalled, 'We trolled him from government accounts. The commission went absolutely mental.' Barnier called the 'weaponising' of his staircase 'below the belt'. However, even mild-mannered civil servants, who despaired of the politicians in the first phase of the talks, privately thought Brussels was at fault. 'The EU has adopted a pretty unreasonable opening position,' said one Whitehall negotiator. 'If they stick to that, even the civil service will be recommending that we walk away.' Frost said later, 'Colleagues who began the process of negotiations … with a relatively positive view about the EU and how it works have been radicalised.'[8]

Some hoped that Barnier would have a harder time maintaining EU unity than in phase one. 'This time France, Spain, the Dutch and the Danes care about fish, others not so much,' an official said. 'Macron and Merkel care about the level playing field because they don't want a commercial rival on their doorstep. Others less so.' Yet Frost was very aware that divide and rule had not worked for Davis, Raab or Robbins. Strategically, he realised fishing rights were the best leverage he had and resolved not to resolve that issue in the early months.

Frost had advantages over Robbins: a prime minister who knew what he wanted and had conferred full authority on Frost to speak for him. Privately, Johnson told him to play 'ultra hardball' even if it put noses out of joint. It was a measure of Cummings' trust in Frost and Oliver Lewis, who he knew as a Vote Leave 'jihadi', that he left them to it. 'I don't want to be brought into Brexit conversations, I don't want to hear about Brexit, I trust you to get on with it,' he told Lewis.

On 27 February, the government published 'The UK Approach', a document setting out Britain's vision of the future deal and the future relationship.

It was not just the policy which was different under Frost. In dealings with the EU, where Robbins had been smooth, Frost cut up rough. But at home, where Robbins was secretive and uncollegiate, Frost created a sense of collective purpose which was better for morale. 'They have very different personalities,' a civil service EU adviser said. 'David was instinctively much more collaborative. Olly was a back channels guy, trying to fudge a package. Frost was very bright but he was pretty black and white and that is not how the Commission operates and they're not used to us operating like that either, so it was quite a shock for them. Olly was one of them, not because of his views on Brexit but, because of the way he operates … I'm not surprised the Commission preferred him.' A senior EU official said, 'David Frost seemed more interested in grandstanding than finding a solution.'

Frost told his Taskforce Europe team that Britain under May and Robbins had too often been a 'mouse' in the face of the EU negotiating 'tank'. He warned that their counterparts would behave like a 'moody teenager' if they did not get their way. He wanted Britain to frame the debate rather than let the EU 'hold the pen' as they had with Robbins. To prepare the team, Frost and his deputies set up a 'star chamber' where they could get each workstream negotiator 'match fit' and armed with the most effective ideas and arguments. The result was an 'esprit de corps' quite different from the mood in Robbins' team, where the secrecy of the chief negotiator had left many feeling marginalised.

Ahead of the start of talks in Brussels on 3 March, Frost gathered his team and the staff at the UK mission in the city to give them a pep talk. He told them to be polite and constructive but proud of what they were doing. 'You'll get all sorts of tactics,' he said. 'The staged walk-out, the pretend outrage at you and personal attacks. It's all part of the technique. Don't get fazed by it.' Frost had been horrified by what he had seen in the 2019 negotiations, with British representatives assuming that things couldn't be done and asked for, or backing off propositions Britain had put forward under fire from Commission officials. Describing what he wanted to see from his team: 'Don't be frightened, don't back off – just keep saying it until it sinks in. They're standing up for their interests, so you should too. Don't be embarrassed. It's okay to be tough, you're standing up for your country.' A civil servant said the pep talk made officials 'stand taller'. 'Frost convinced us that we are part of something with national and historical importance. Something to be proud of.' When the talks began a few hours later, the British team entered the Commission building sporting patriotic lanyards for their passes and wearing Union Jack lapel badges.[9]

The first negotiating session threw up a moment the British team would never forget. Frost outlined Johnson's key demand, that the UK be treated as an independent nation. Barnier responded with 'a hilarious meltdown', one British official said, the Frenchman launching into a 'massive rant' in which it is claimed he said, 'Why do you keep mentioning "sovereignty". All you do is mention this word.' To Barnier, sovereignty was something to be pooled and shared. The EU tended to use the word 'autonomy' instead for what Britain wanted. To Frost, sovereignty was something to be defended and respected. Yet the EU's chief negotiator was rattled by this unfamiliar British approach. In another meeting, an enraged Barnier literally shouted, 'I am calm!' after another heated exchange. These outbursts became known to the British team as 'Michel's calm and serene moments'.

There was also a moment in those first talks when the politicos in the room, Frost and Oliver Lewis, saw that the civil servants 'got it'. The official leading on the level playing field was a mild-mannered Treasury civil servant called Matthew Taylor. One of the EU officials talked about the need for a strong state aid regime to bind Britain's hands, making a comparison with China, which had no proper state aid controls. Taylor, emboldened by the star chamber sessions, responded robustly. 'Matthew, extremely politely, extremely controlled, went ape shit at the comparison with China,' a witness said. 'His argument was that the UK is a mature democracy which has operated in line with international norms through-out the post-war period, the idea that because we're leaving the EU it is legitimate to compare possible future actions to China is insulting.' Sitting at the back of the room, Lewis was cheering inside; even the officials seemed to be channelling Vote Leave.

The negotiating team was also bolstered by political advisers who had been largely absent before: Stephanie Lis, an experienced spinner, handled Frost's comms. Hugh Bennett and Chris Jenkins, the attorney general's special adviser, combined belief in Brexit with intellectual heft.

The negotiations were over almost before they started. On the day of the first round of talks fifty-one Britons were infected with the novel corona-virus named Covid-19, which had been slowly spreading globally since the turn of the year. The worldwide death toll was already 3,100. As March began, the spread became exponential.

Brexit was relegated from a government priority and from political debate. Meetings of the XS strategy committee and the XO operations committee were suspended. Some of the most talented officials, who had been seconded to Taskforce Europe, were sent to deal with Covid. Michael Gove, who had been focused on Brexit preparations, went to lead the virus response in the Cabinet Office. Oliver Lewis was sent to help run the shielding programme for the elderly and vulnerable.

One of the earliest victims of Covid in Whitehall was Frost, who was 'knocked out' for a month and it was five or six weeks before he was breathing normally and could walk upstairs without getting out of breath. Within six weeks, Boris Johnson had been warned hundreds of thousands of Britons would die and he was in intensive care, close to becoming one of his own government's statistics.

OUT OF BREATH

Covid-19

March to October 2020

Thursday 12 March 2020, in the view of Dominic Cummings, was 'one of the most, if not the most, insane day in Number 10 since 1945'.[1] It began with the prime minister's chief adviser trying to persuade the rest of Downing Street that much more radical action was needed to tackle the growing threat from Covid-19. At 7.48 a.m. he sent a text message to Boris Johnson, 'We've got big problems coming. The Cabinet Office is terrifyingly shit. No plans. Totally behind the pace. We must announce today, not next week, "If you feel ill with cold or flu, stay home." We must force the pace.' Then the killer blow. 'We are looking at 100,000 to 500,000 deaths between optimistic and pessimistic scenarios.'[2]

The night before, Cummings had texted a WhatsApp group, which included the prime minister and the chief scientific adviser, Sir Patrick Vallance, to argue for social distancing measures, warning that 'the risks of delay are much, much higher than the risks of going too soon'. There was 'pushback from within the system'.[3]

On the morning of the 12th, he urged Johnson to take charge and chair daily meetings to tackle the coronavirus in the Cabinet Room, rather than the Cobra rooms under the Cabinet Office. The government was about to face the worst global pandemic since the Spanish flu after the First World War, with a suite of emergency briefing rooms where it was impossible to look at real-time data. Johnson faced the toughest decision of his premiership: whether to order the effective curfew and quarantine of every household in the land.

Later that morning, however, Cummings recalled, the Covid conversations 'got completely derailed' because 'suddenly the national security people came in and said, "Trump wants us to join a bombing campaign in the Middle East tonight and we need to start having meetings about that."' Cummings went to Johnson and said, 'It's fucking crackers. We are going to have thousands of people dead here in the next few weeks. And various people want us to start bombing the fucking Middle East. They are out of their minds. We've got to sort out Covid.'[4]

The issue most exercising the prime minister that morning concerned an article in *The Times* the day before. Under the headline 'Downing St dog to be reshuffled', the paper suggested Dilyn, Boris and Carrie's Jack Russell cross, might be rehoused before Symonds gave birth to their first child. On 1 March, eleven days after Johnson's divorce was announced, Carrie had declared on Instagram both that she had a 'baby hatching early summer' and that the couple had 'got engaged at the end of last year'. The paper quoted a 'Whitehall source' asserting that Dilyn was a 'sickly' animal who had repeatedly fouled the couple's flat above 11 Downing Street. 'For a while there was dog shit everywhere.'[5] Regular visitors confirmed Dilyn's production of pungent poos, but Symonds went ballistic, tweeting, 'What a load of total crap! There has never been a happier, healthier and more loved dog than our Dilyn. 100% bs. The people behind this story should be ashamed of themselves.'[6]

Johnson responded to Cummings: 'I want an inquiry. I want to know who briefed it. Carrie thinks it's you.'

'What story? This is totally batshit,' Cummings said.

'There's a story in *The Times* that says the whole place is chaos. And me and Carrie are living like students with Dilyn shitting everywhere and the cleaners are all going mad.'[7] He stopped and looked at Cummings. Then he asked. 'Did you brief the Dilyn stuff?'

There was a brief pause. Cummings said, 'No.'

The hesitation was enough: *Fucking hell*, Johnson thought. 'I knew he was lying,' he told a friend later. The prime minister turned detective and discovered that Cummings and Cain had visited *The Times* to see executives a short time before the article was published. Dilyn's offence, multiple colleagues recall, 'was to keep humping Dom's leg'. To Johnson this was all proof they were responsible and that the story was designed to wound Carrie. 'People get very upset about dogs,' he told the friend. 'Dom's modus operandi is to hit the women to hurt the guy.' Johnson was thinking about the briefing campaign against Betsy Duncan Smith, which had contributed to the downfall of her husband as Tory leader in

2003. Cummings had worked for IDS but quit in disgust and publicly turned on his former boss.

The chief aide recalled, 'We had this completely insane situation in which part of the building was saying, "Are we going to bomb Iraq?"; part of the building was arguing about whether we are going to do quarantine or not do quarantine; the prime minister has his girlfriend going crackers about something completely trivial.'[8] Another Number 10 adviser said, 'It was like an episode of *The West Wing*, with so much mad shit happening at the same time.' Cummings added, 'Everything is going down the fucking toilet, but … he was looking at his phone getting texts from her about "Have you started the inquiry into the Dilyn leak?"'[9] Cleo Watson and Carrie's assistant Sarah Vaughan-Brown worked up a letter of complaint to the press watchdog but, when Johnson read it, he burst out laughing. 'I'm sorry, I can't write a letter that says Dylan is a treasured member of my family. He's a happy, healthy dog.' On your head be it, they thought. 'I'll take care of my Caroline. Don't you worry, leave it to me.'

The Covid meeting eventually went ahead and the decision was taken to press on with the lockdown plans. The attorney general, Suella Braverman, persuaded Johnson not to bomb Iraq. At 9 p.m. Cummings sat down with Ben and Marc Warner, the data experts who had helped with the referendum and the general election. Their message was stark: 'We are looking at all this data; we are looking at all these graphs. We are heading for total and utter catastrophe. We need to have plan B.'[10]

Ben Warner repeated the message the following day, Friday 13th, for Patrick Vallance. Even in the best-case scenario for the government's pandemic plan, the number of patients was going to 'completely smash through the capacity of the NHS, not by a little bit but multiple times'.[11]

The government's off-the-shelf pandemic action plan, designed to deal with flu, rather than a more virulent and deadly coronavirus, was a mitigation strategy, not a suppression strategy. The experts on the key committee – the Scientific Advisory Group for Emergencies, or SAGE – assisted by behavioural scientists on another called SPI-B, had made two other assumptions which proved false. First that the public would only tolerate extreme measures for a very short period – assumed to be a few days – which led to the view that lockdown or social distancing measures would have to be timed perfectly to 'squash the sombrero', the peak of infections on a graph which resembled the Mexican hat. 'That turned out to be complete nonsense,' Cummings said later.[12] Connected to this was the view that no Western society would tolerate wearing masks in public, something which was common in smog-hit cities in East Asia. 'A lot of behavioural science turned out to be complete charlatan bullshit,' Cummings said.[13] The second fallacy was that locking down hard at the start would simply lead to a much worse second wave of the virus in winter when the NHS was always stretched to breaking point in a normal year.

Underpinning Plan A was a belief that the spread of the virus meant a large proportion of the population would catch Covid and that by September, if 60 per cent of people had developed antibodies, there would be a natural 'herd immunity'. If this was not the policy's explicit goal, it was certainly seen as a by-product of it. That Wednesday, David Halpern of the Whitehall 'nudge unit', one of the behaviouralists on SPI-B, put the phrase in the public domain. It had also come up at cabinet, when Mark Sedwill told Johnson, 'Prime Minister, you should go on TV tomorrow and explain to people the herd immunity plan and that it is like the old chicken pox parties.'

Cummings intervened: 'Mark, you've got to stop using this chicken pox analogy. It's not right.'

'Why?'

Ben Warner said, 'Because chicken pox is not spreading exponentially and killing hundreds of thousands of people.'

Sedwill had not been out on a limb – he had simply repeated the message coming from the Department of Health, where it was assumed that no vaccine could possibly be developed for use in 2020. As late as that Friday, Vallance told Radio 4 that 'because the vast majority of people get a mild illness' the country could 'build up some kind of herd immunity so more people are immune to this disease and we reduce the transmission'.

The study which sparked the panic, by Prof Neil Ferguson at Imperial College, London (quickly dubbed 'Professor Lockdown' and, when caught breaking lockdown to conduct an affair, 'Professor Pantsdown'), predicted 250,000 dead with a worst-case scenario of 510,000 casualties. The Whitehall machine discussed a shortage of body bags and the need to find temporary storage facilities for the dead. 'The whole system was in this groupthink,' Cummings recalled, 'That we've just got to accept that there's going to be half a million people killed.'[14]

On Friday evening, Cummings and Ben Warner sat in the prime minister's study working out how to persuade Johnson that he would have to ditch the government's entire pandemic plan. On a whiteboard, Cummings sketched out the skeleton of what became 'Plan B'. Just after 8 p.m. Helen MacNamara, the deputy to the cabinet secretary, came in. She had been talking to Mark Sweeney, the Cabinet Office official responsible for liaising with the Department of Health. MacNamara was usually a vivacious character, who wrapped her razor-sharp brain in a cloak of humour and flirtation. She was seldom phased by anything. Sweeney, she revealed, had just told her, 'I have been told for years that there is a whole plan for this. There is no plan.' MacNamara added, 'I think we are absolutely fucked. I think this country is heading for a disaster. I think we are going to kill thousands of people.'[15] She could see immediately that Cummings was on the same page.

At 9.15 a.m. on Saturday 14 March, Johnson chaired a meeting in the Cabinet Room, at which Vallance explained that Britain had been four weeks behind Italy, where hospitals were overrun and images of patients in corridors beyond medical help were beamed around the world. Now it was more like two weeks. It was decided, in principle, that the government would have to announce a lockdown.

After the meeting, Cummings, both Warner brothers and Johnson's private secretary for health gathered in his study. The door was shut in Matt Hancock's face. Johnson was shown graphs revealing that the NHS was due to run out of capacity in April, but the virus was not due to peak, under Plan A, until June. Ben Warner said, 'The NHS is going to be smashed in weeks, and we have got days to act.' Cummings later told MPs, 'This is like a scene from *Independence Day*, with Jeff Goldblum saying, "The aliens are here, and your whole plan is broken, and you need a new plan", with Ben Warner in the Jeff Goldblum role.'[16]

There was just one problem. 'There is no lockdown plan,' Cummings said. 'It doesn't exist.' SAGE 'haven't modelled it. DH' – the Department of Health – 'don't have a plan. We are going to have to figure out and hack together a lockdown plan over the next week.'[17]

Johnson didn't like it. He had repeatedly told people his political hero was 'the mayor in *Jaws* who kept the beaches open', even as a great white shark was attacking people. Cummings was blunt: 'People will march on Downing Street and hang you from a lamp post if you try and be the mayor of *Jaws*.' The chief aide recalled, 'He was constantly trolleying backwards and forwards, so you never knew if you'd actually convinced him of anything. It wasn't really until about five days later that we really succeeded.'[18] Johnson did resist other demands. Priti Patel, the home secretary, wanted to ban flights from Covid hotspots and close the borders. Cummings agreed. Johnson refused.

That Sunday, Hancock told the BBC's Andrew Marr, 'Herd immunity is not our goal or policy.' Yet it was clear that herd immunity had been integral to the government's thinking before the Warners and Cummings realised it meant disaster. Herd immunity, Cummings said later, 'was seen as an inevitability … That was the whole logic of all of the discussions in January and February and early March.'[19]

The Department of Health continued to resist the change. On 18 March, Cummings invited two global data experts, Demis Hassabis from DeepMind, one of the world's leading artificial intelligence developers, and Tim Gowers, a professor of mathematics at Cambridge University, to join a SAGE meeting. Hassabis showed that herd immunity was a false god and that the government needed to act.

Cummings used the morning meetings in Number 10 to ram home how quickly the virus was spreading. 'I remember him standing up in the Cabinet Room with a whiteboard, hitting the numbers with a pen,' a colleague recalled. 'This is the logic of exponential growth. You have to understand this.'

Johnson, however, was wobbling as the scale of the economic dangers of locking down became clearer. On 19 March, Cummings messaged Cain to say, 'Rishi saying bond markets may not fund our debt.' The PM, he warned, was 'back to *Jaws* mode wank', dreaming again of keeping the beaches open. 'I've literally said same thing ten fucking times and he still won't absorb it. I'm exhausted just talking to him and stopping the trolley', the nickname given to Johnson when he veered from one decision to a contradictory stance. 'I've had to sit here for 2 hours just to stop him saying stupid shit.' Later that day, Cummings added, 'It's only a matter of time before his babbling exposes fact he doesn't know what to say.'[20] Cain replied, 'I'm exhausted with him.'[21]

Only on 23 March, nine days after the key Saturday meeting, did Johnson give his most famous televised address to the nation. His hero, Winston Churchill, had offered 'blood, toil, tears and sweat' as he vowed to 'fight them on the beaches'. Johnson added a third slogan to his name after 'take back control' and 'get Brexit done'. Looking directly down the barrel of the camera he said, 'You must stay at home.'

The clue that things were serious was in his hair – the blond haystack was neater than normal. 'It looked as if he had brushed it,' one aide said. 'You know when he's not messing it up that he's in the zone.'

Six days later Britain reached the grim milestone of a thousand deaths from Covid. The death toll had doubled in three days.

Cummings admitted later that 'it was a huge failure of mine' that the country was locked down too late, in part because he was 'incredibly frightened' that moving away from the original plan would cause a worse second wave in the winter. Others blamed Cummings for failing to get a grip on the developing situation in January and February. A senior government security official said, 'This stuff was buzzing around the NSC [National Security Council] in January. The first briefings came out at the beginning of January. Government was absent for nearly two months. Boris was knackered and Dom Cummings was keeping Boris away from sharp objects.' Another Number 10 political adviser said, 'We didn't understand the speed of the virus. It was like the Viet Cong during the Tet offensive – the virus was all around us before we knew it was there.'

Thus began the haphazard handling of the greatest crisis of Johnson's time in office. The hero of Brexit, whose political character was to be the bearer of stupefying optimism, faced a bleak and miserable task, requiring many of the skills he lacked – understanding of the Whitehall system, attention to detail, comprehension of the consequences of his actions and a willingness to learn from previous mistakes. Yet Johnson was somehow a big enough figure for this biggest of problems, a man who had always believed his destiny would place him at the fulcrum of great events. If he was not equal to the moment, he was not dwarfed by it either, as lesser egos might have been.

It is beyond the scope of this book to cover the Covid story. At the time of writing, the intricacies of the political, scientific and bureaucratic response were still being examined by the official inquiry. But the significance for this story is how the pandemic destroyed the partnership between Johnson and Cummings, which had delivered both Brexit and the general election victory, a breakdown that sealed the fate of the PM. The economic response to Covid also catapulted Rishi Sunak to a level of public prominence which made him a threat to Johnson. The backlash within the Conservative Party against the expansion of the state that Sunak oversaw then created the circumstances in which Liz Truss would emerge as leader.

*   *   *

On the morning of 17 March, as he prepared to unveil details of the biggest peacetime financial package ever offered by a British government, Sunak gathered his closest aides and civil servants together in his book-lined study in 11 Downing Street. 'The scale of what is required is beyond anyone's current imagination,' he said. 'We have to remove all limiting assumptions.' Throughout the weekend, Treasury officials had worked around the clock to prepare a package for business. 'They did three months' work in forty-eight hours,' a source said. It helped that Charles Roxburgh, the second permanent secretary, and Andrew Bailey, the new governor of the Bank of England, were both veterans of the response to the 2008 financial crash.

When he walked out with Johnson for a Downing Street press conference, aides were still finalising Sunak's comments as the statement came off the printer. The new chancellor had no time to rehearse or to prepare for questions but gave a remarkably assured performance as he outlined plans for £330 billion of government-backed loans for business, cash grants of up to £25,000 each, plus a business rates holiday and a mortgage holiday for the hard up. 'We will do whatever it takes,' Sunak repeatedly intoned. One of David Cameron's closest aides remarked, 'It was a better coming out as a politician even than Dave's.'

The furlough scheme to save jobs took longer. The plan for the government to pay a high percentage of wages was announced three days later, on 20 March, having been designed from scratch from orders issued by Sunak at 6 p.m. the day before. Officials again worked through the night to have the plans on his desk by 9 a.m. on Friday.

The dawn of Covid was a difficult moment for ministers and advisers already existentially exhausted after the previous four years. Mark Sedwill recalled, 'People underestimated the degree to which the civil service, in particular, had not had a break ... since the referendum. I do remember joking with the prime minister that he'd taken a year off, but I hadn't.'[22] One spad said, 'All of us went through two years of absolute hell during the Brexit wars and then the election, and there was a period of about a month where we all thought, "Great, the storm has passed, we've got through all the madness, now we can actually do the stuff that you want to do when you're in government." And then someone fucked a bat in Wuhan and it all went to pot.'[23]

Distracted by his divorce negotiations, his engagement and his fiancée's pregnancy, Johnson missed the first five Cobra meetings on Covid-19. Multiple witnesses attest that he referred to the Chinese virus as 'Kung Flu' and delighted in yelling, 'Aye! Corona!' On one occasion he suggested someone could 'inject me live on TV' to show the public there was nothing to fear from the virus. On 3 March Cummings messaged Cain, 'He doesn't think it's a big deal ... he thinks it'll be like swine flu.'[24] (Narrator: it wasn't.) Business leaders were surprised, during a conference call in which Johnson was trying to get them to build ventilators, to hear him dub this project 'Operation Last Gasp'.

Cleo Watson, who had been Cummings' personal assistant on the referendum campaign but was now deputy chief of staff, appointed herself 'Boris's nanny' and regularly took the prime minister's temperature to check for symptoms. 'This was generally done by me, towering over him ... one hand on a hip, teapot-style, and the other brandishing an oral digital thermometer,' she recalled. Each time, like a scene from *Carry On Covid*, Johnson 'dutifully feigned bending over'. She subjected him to 'questioning about whether or not he'd washed his hands', to which he replied, 'What do you mean by "recently"?'[25]

Johnson's casual approach was on display on 18 March, when it came time for his usual face-to-face weekly meeting with the Queen. In an interview with the BBC the following year, Cummings said he challenged Johnson: 'What are you doing?'

'I'm going to see the Queen.'

'What on earth are you talking about? Of course you can't go and see the Queen.'

'That's what I do every Wednesday. I'm going to go and see her.'

'There are people in this office who are isolating, you might have coronavirus. I might have coronavirus,' Cummings said. 'What if you go and see her and give the Queen coronavirus and she dies, what are you going to do? You can't risk that, that's completely insane.'

It was a lightbulb moment: 'Holy shit! I can't go.'[26] Johnson would not see the monarch in person again until June 2021.

Johnson's libertarianism, which made him reluctant to quarantine people, and his natural optimism, left him struggling to find the right tone. 'He's naturally cheerful,' said one colleague. 'He finds it difficult to deliver bad news.' A Tory aide said, 'Boris looks haunted. It's like when George W. Bush came in thinking he was going to be the education reform president and had to deal with the war on terror.' A former

Downing Street adviser spotted the key fact: 'Boris really doesn't want to shut stuff down. Fundamentally there is a Boris-Dom cleavage.'

With no television in the prime minister's study, Johnson would stand, 'hands on hips, feet well apart', watching the one in the private office just outside his door. A glitch meant it often switched to an animal channel. In quieter times Cleo Watson caught him 'straining his eyes to make out a basketful of kittens playing with a ball of twine'. Now she remembered the 'horrific out-of-body experience of standing outside the PM's office, watching live news footage of stretcher-filled car parks in Lombardy hospitals'.[27] Johnson knew Italy, he knew their health service was superior in many regards to the NHS. Politically, he could not afford Lombardy-style footage to be replicated in London and Liverpool.

Mark Sedwill sent an email to all special advisers and officials in Number 10 and the Cabinet Office. 'It basically said all the normal business of government has stopped,' a Downing Street aide recalled. 'That was the point when the government went into panic mode. We had been thinking about how to enact things with a fifteen-year time horizon. We had to switch to a twenty-four-hour time horizon. I felt out of my depth. I think a lot of people were actually very scared.'

These were dark times. The army raced to build 'Nightingale hospitals' for those who needed to be ventilated. But they were not all they seemed. 'People said they didn't have enough staff,' a senior aide observed. 'But they were never going to have too much staffing. You weren't going to come out of a Nightingale. They were holding zone morgues really. We also built mortuaries, but they never got any publicity. We built three in London. The biggest was in the Lea Valley. There were rows and rows of freezer containers.'

A woefully unprepared Whitehall had to 'come face to face with the fact that they had no effective data system to deal with Covid,' Cummings recalled. 'By the beginning of March, the data system for the prime minister was the head of the NHS reading out numbers that had been faxed to him on a bit of paper, and me scribbling them down on a whiteboard.' Marc Warner's company, Faculty AI, built a new one for the NHS. 'Very quickly, a bunch of senior officials saw the difference between the old world and the new world of cutting-edge data science and proper dashboards.'[28] He added, 'There wasn't a cloud system in Number 10, there wasn't even a document sharing system. In July 2019, when we walked through the door, the way that key Number 10 staff working for the prime minister worked was to email attachments of Word documents to each other ... Even a rubbish business could use Google Docs.'[29]

In the midst of unimaginable personal pressure, health calamity, economic catastrophe, bureaucratic inadequacy and technological deficiency, the prime minister became more decisive. 'He commands the room,' a cabinet minister said as lockdown was announced. But tempers frayed and senior political aides and officials exchanged caustic and profane comments about Johnson's handling of the crisis, with Matt Hancock another favourite target in WhatsApps that came to light during the Covid Inquiry, which launched in 2023.

The health secretary suggested in meetings that issues like the supply of PPE – personal protective equipment such as gowns and face masks – was under control but days or weeks later they would 'discover that was not in fact the case'. Helen MacNamara told Hancock she sympathised with him, saying it must be 'very hard' to be health secretary. He told her he was 'loving' the responsibility. To demonstrate his 'nuclear levels of confidence', Hancock adopted a 'batsman's stance outside the Cabinet Room,' she recalled. 'They bowl them at me, I knock them away,' he said.[30]

Eddie Lister remembered things differently: 'Matt Hancock would come to a meeting and say we have no problems with PPE. A month later we had no PPE. I remember I had to phone up the British embassy in Beijing and say, "You've got to send somebody and see if this factory really exists. Are we going to get these things?" The tourist officer for Wales went to negotiate.'

In May Cummings WhatsApped Johnson to say Hancock was 'unfit for the job ... The incompetence, the constant lies, the obsession with media bullshit over doing his job. Still no fucking serious testing in care homes, his uselessness is still killing God knows how many.'

Apart from terrible technology, the thing most people in Downing Street soon shared was Covid symptoms. 'Patient zero' in Westminster, Nadine Dorries, a health minister, tested positive on 10 March. Number 10 soon became known as 'the petri dish' and 'the plague pit' as key figures fell like flies. Reinforcements were recruited from the Vote Leave diaspora. Isaac Levido helped devise the government's 'Stay home – Protect the NHS – Save lives' slogan. Special advisers doubled up so they could cover for each other if they fell ill. Levido agreed to be drafted in full time if necessary. If Cain was sick, Paul Stephenson would help on comms. Tom Shinner, the civil servant who did the most to prepare Britain for a no-deal Brexit, was also rehired. Mark Sedwill said, 'People were capable of dealing with the pressure of Covid, because they dealt with the pressure of no-deal ... We had people who we had trained in crisis management, and contingency planning.'[31]

On 27 March, four days after the first lockdown began, both Matt Hancock and Chris Whitty, the chief medical officer, announced they were self-isolating. Within days, several ministers and most staff in Number 10 – a rabbit warren of offices perfectly designed to prevent social distancing – had caught it too, threatening to paralyse government. Sedwill kept his case secret even from close colleagues, a fact that only emerged months later. 'You'd go to a meeting expecting to see someone important and they were gone,' an adviser said.[32]

The night before, Boris Johnson had tested positive. He issued a video on the 27th saying he had 'developed mild symptoms', including 'a temperature and a persistent cough' and was now 'working from home'. But 'be in no doubt', he insisted, 'I can continue ... to lead the national fightback against coronavirus.' When he reminded Michael Gove that 'Pericles died of the plague', Johnson claimed his old frenemy's 'spectacles seemed to glitter at the thought, like the penguin in Wallace and Gromit'.[33] Within nine days it was touch and go whether he would live.

On the same day the PM went into self-isolation Cummings fled Number 10, the first steps in a 260-mile trip to Durham that became notorious when it emerged two months later. 'I suddenly got a call from my wife who was at home looking after our four-year-old child,' he said. 'She told me she suddenly felt badly ill. She'd vomited and felt like she might pass out. And there'll be nobody to look after our child. None of our usual childcare options were available. They were alone in the house. After very briefly telling some officials in Number 10 what had happened, I immediately left the building, ran to a car and drove home.'[34]

Johnson, isolating in his flat, went stir crazy and insisted on coming downstairs to his office, banging his chest, growling 'Strong as a bull!' at aides. Yet each day this bravado was accompanied by increasingly bad coughing fits. He chaired cabinet on a video link, 'coughing and spluttering'. Johnson finally faced the truth that 'something was definitely awry' when he, 'a functioning cheese-oholic', looked at a plate of cheese supplied by Carrie with 'complete apathy'.[35]

Concerned aides quietly reached out to St Thomas' Hospital over Westminster Bridge from Parliament in case he needed to be admitted. When the *Guardian* got wind of the preparations, Cain ordered the press office to issue a denial. But on Thursday 2 April Johnson struggled as he chaired the morning Covid 'war cabinet' and admitted he would not be able to end his seven-day isolation period the next day. After discussions with a doctor recruited by Chris Whitty, the PM was sent to bed with a reduced workload. The heavily pregnant Symonds was holed up at Chequers, isolating to protect her unborn baby, but a private secretary was sent to bring her back to Downing Street. 'She was really worried,' a friend said. 'He was coughing and she was taking his temperature a lot and he was obviously deteriorating. She was really fucking brave.'

Doctors at St Thomas' were told to expect the PM to be rushed to hospital on Thursday evening. They 'scrubbed up' and donned full protective clothing ready to admit him. Under a protocol drawn up after Tony Blair went to hospital with a heart scare in 2003, Johnson would have been smuggled in via a secret entrance, then moved along a 'sealed' route with corridors and lifts closed to prying eyes to a 'magic room' on the twelfth floor. The doctors only realised he was not coming when they saw him clapping for the NHS with Carrie at eight that evening. He looked hunched, his clapping laboured.[36]

The following day, Friday 3 April, Johnson recorded another video to explain to the nation that he still had a temperature, but it took several takes because he was coughing so much. MPs and journalists who watched it barely listened to the words. Johnson looked awful – grey with tiredness, his movements sluggish.

The prime minister was reluctant to go to hospital, fearing it would look like he was getting preferential treatment. Later, his aides concluded much more should have been done to help him. Unlike American presidents, British prime ministers do not have an official physician. A cabinet minister said, 'It was a fucking disgrace that he was left in the flat in Number 11 without official support.' A political adviser said, 'You can't fart in Downing Street for police and security crawling all over the building, trying to protect his life, but then he actually gets a serious illness and is basically left by himself.'

A medical check-up on the Saturday morning found Johnson's condition had deteriorated. Martin Reynolds cleared the PM's diary. By Sunday afternoon he was 'very, very unwell' and was finally taken to hospital, feeling 'completely decrepit'. Within minutes of arriving, he was fitted with an oxygen mask. Fearful of what might happen, Johnson told himself over and over: *Please don't say 'tracheotomy'*, where doctors cut into the throat to create an airway.[37] Number 10 issued a statement saying he had been admitted for 'precautionary tests' and that he would continue to receive a ministerial red box. It was worthy of the health updates dispensed by the Kremlin when Soviet leaders were incapacitated. Another Downing Street aide said, 'Caino was putting out North Korean-style press releases, about the PM working hard.'

Throughout Sunday, Johnson kept getting worse. He responded to some messages, wrestling with the hospital's poor mobile reception. With the PM banned from the public WiFi for security reasons, engineers were sent to boost the signal. That evening, Johnson phoned Reynolds and said he wanted Raab, the first secretary of state, to deputise for him. By Monday, the prime minister was too weak to even look at his phone. Cain had been isolating, but returned to work that day.[38]

At 5 p.m., Raab took the daily press conference and assured the nation Johnson was 'in good spirits'. In fact, the prime minister had now consumed 'litres and litres of oxygen' and was wondering, 'How am I going to get out of this?' He was told there was a '50–50 chance' he would need to be placed on a ventilator. 'It was a tough old moment,' he said later. He knew from the bustle around him that there were 'contingency plans in place' in case he died.[39] At 6 p.m., Carrie was called by the doctors to say he was not improving and that he might have to be ventilated. She wrote Boris a love letter, attaching a scan of their unborn child. At eight, Johnson was moved to intensive care on a different floor. 'I didn't want to sleep – partly in case I never woke up,' he admitted later.[40]

The events reinforced for many how he was not just the leader of a government but its heart and its talisman. That Monday night, aides and ministers exchanged bleak phone calls and messages with each other and with political journalists. Even opposition MPs were shaken by what was happening. There were many tears. One special adviser in the press team said, 'I'm going to pray.' She was not alone in doing so. Anyone who entered intensive care with Covid-19 had a survival rate of about 50 per cent. But if they had to be placed on a mechanical ventilator their chances fell to one in three. 'We all knew the odds,' said an aide. 'It was a coin flip at best. I thought we were going to lose him.' Another remembered, 'The general consensus was that he was about to die.'

For Carrie Symonds it was a moment of unimaginable horror and stress. 'She stayed in Downing Street all the way through,' a friend said. Cleo Watson referred later to 'the sheer bravery of Carrie heavily pregnant and reckoning with the possibility that she might be about to lose the father of her imminent firstborn child as a nation watched on'.[41] A Number 10 aide said, 'She was really on top of the doctors while he was in the hospital. I'd often wake up and she'd have sent me how he'd been in the night. It must have been very lonely.' Symonds provided twice daily medical updates to anxious staff in Downing Street and, via a hastily convened WhatsApp group, to Johnson's four children by Marina Wheeler, whom she had never met. Rachel Johnson called Marina to suggest that the children visit Boris in hospital for what might be the last time.[42] Downing Street officials said, when he knew he might be mortally ill, Johnson had asked to speak to Marina.

This was not just a personal crisis for Johnson and his family, it was also a constitutional crisis unprecedented since 1953 when Winston Churchill suffered a debilitating stroke. On that occasion the prime minister's incapacity was hushed up. When he heard that Johnson was out of action, Martin Reynolds shared the '50–50' prognosis with the other two members of the 'golden triangle' – Mark Sedwill and Sir Edward Young, the Queen's private secretary – whose role was to ensure continuity of government. Young informed the Queen. Sedwill summoned Raab to Downing Street for a briefing with the cabinet secretary and Helen MacNamara. A Number 10 aide said, 'He looked absolutely terrified.'

There is no such role in the British constitution as 'deputy prime minister' or 'acting prime minister', no agreed line of succession as there is in the US. Raab filmed an address to camera, visibly shaken. Sedwill arranged a conference call with a shellshocked cabinet. Only Michael Gove managed even a hurried homily to Johnson's health: 'I think I speak for everyone when I say our thoughts and prayers are with the prime minister.' Another cabinet minister said, 'Most of us were too shocked to say anything. I remember going for a walk and thinking, "Fucking hell, what if he dies?" It was a moment of panic and shock and grief.' For the nation too. 'I think the country actually came together around him in a way they'd never done before or since,' Eddie Lister recalled.

Sedwill was in charge of drawing up the succession plan if the prime minister died. 'If he was to be ventilated', the cabinet would have been told to select a stand-in prime minister for the duration of his absence. Lister said, 'There was a letter written, waiting to go to the palace to inform them that he'd gone into intensive care and was on a ventilator and that Dominic Raab would need to take over. The Queen was briefed and ready for that. She sent some nice messages back. Everybody knew it was desperate.'

If Johnson fell into a coma or died, the cabinet would have to formally vote for a successor. There could be no suggestion of the monarch taking soundings and inviting Raab to Buckingham Palace as prime minister. In their mind was the controversy in 1963 when a 'magic circle' of grandees told the palace to send for Lord Home, rather than Rab Butler, to replace Harold Macmillan. A Tory with contacts at the top of the royal household said, 'The palace was extremely edgy because they had their fingers burnt with the whole Alec Douglas-Home succession, which is like yesterday for them. They didn't want to get into the area where they were deemed to have exercised discretion. Sedwill and Edward Young would have told the cabinet to pick one of their number. A senior figure in Number 10 revealed, 'The plan was that the cabinet would have been locked in a room and not let out until they had picked someone.' The consensus is that, in these circumstances, the cabinet would have picked Raab to hold the fort. He had Johnson's blessing and the support of Cain, the most senior political aide left in the building. Another adviser said, 'If Boris had died, Raab would have been the caretaker and then I think Rishi would have won the subsequent leadership election.'

While all this was going on, a surreal public relations battle was playing out. Donald Trump announced to *Fox News* that he had asked American drug companies to 'contact his doctors at the hospital in London – they're talking right now'. In reality, St Thomas' had told the White House to talk to the Foreign Office; Johnson's doctors were busy enough. Chinese drug companies were also bombarding the hospital switchboard offering to help. All these offers were politely declined.[43]

Number 10 operated like a medieval court and it was now without both its Henry VIII and, with Cummings' departure, its Thomas Cromwell. For the next few days Raab, dubbed the 'designated survivor' by the papers, convened a quad of ministers – also including Sunak, Gove and Hancock – and won plaudits for his low-key, managerial approach, not imposing his own views, a chairman of meetings, rather than a chief executive for the government. 'We've all got our jobs to do,'

Raab told the quad. 'Let's get on and do them and make sure when the boss gets back that we've got on with the plan.' A fellow minister said, 'He deserves a lot of credit for the very tactful way in which he handled a very difficult situation. He didn't seek to maximise his power. He didn't order people about.' A political aide called Raab 'a really good caretaker manager'. Raab, not always known as self-effacing, appeared humble. At the end of one meeting, when civil servants had left, he turned to Lee Cain and Cleo Watson and asked, 'How am I doing? I don't want to overreach. Tell me if I fuck up.' Reflecting later, a cabinet minister said, 'Cabinet government worked.' However, Raab's elevation created a degree of envy. Fellow ministers pointedly referred to him in meetings as 'foreign secretary', rather than 'first secretary of state'.

Raab, the regent in the medieval metaphor, also made sure he had the king's senior functioning adviser on board for every major decision, insisting that the only papers placed in his ministerial box were those cleared by Cain, who could justifiably claim he knew Johnson's mind. 'Basically, the entire machine was reporting to Caino for a couple of weeks,' an ally said. 'Lee did end up running the country for a fortnight.' Had the circumstances been less critical for him, Johnson might have enjoyed the historical parallel. In 1953, Churchill's son-in-law Christopher Soames made many of the key decisions when he was incapacitated. When he returned, Johnson changed Cain's nickname from 'Commissar' to 'Chairman Lee', in the style of Chinese autocrats.

The prime minister had a better night than expected on Monday and on Tuesday morning, his temperature began to fall. Through three days and three nights on oxygen, he gradually improved though it was only on the morning of Wednesday 8 April, when a senior cabinet minister got a text message that Johnson was on the mend, that his colleagues felt confident he would live.

On Thursday afternoon he was able to leave intensive care. Johnson waved at doctors and nurses as he did so and then joined in with the clap for NHS workers at 8 p.m. from his regular hospital bed. He did have a ministerial red box, but it contained an iPad loaded with his favourite films (*Withnail & I* and the *Lord of the Rings* trilogy), Tintin books from his family and brownies from Carrie.

Johnson's resurrection, fittingly, came in Easter week. A member of the Johnson family texted Thérèse Coffey: 'He is risen.' The prime minister himself was clear that his revival had not been the result of divine intervention. 'The NHS has saved my life,' he told those who cared for him. 'The treatment has been exemplary.'

Guto Harri, his former and future director of communications, asked him later if he had ever thought he was going to die. 'I didn't,' Johnson replied. 'I never really thought that because of a childlike faith in doctors, but I could tell that the staff at the hospital were worried.'[44] However, in his memoir, Johnson said, 'I might have carked it.'[45]

By the time he left hospital, on 12 April, a total of 10,612 people in the UK had died of Covid-19, including around forty healthcare workers. Johnson gave one of his best ever televised statements, thanking the two migrant nurses – Jenny from New Zealand and Luis from Portugal – 'who stood by my bedside for forty-eight hours when things could go either way. The reason, in the end, my body did start to get enough oxygen was because, for every second of the night, they were watching and caring and making the interventions I needed.' The same day, Dominic Cummings drove to a town called Barnard Castle.

When Johnson recovered, friends say Symonds received a message from one of his children, cutting off contact again. The brief moment of shared terror had failed to heal the deep fissures in Johnson's life. From then on, a friend said, 'Boris always met his children separately', including Stephanie, his daughter with art adviser Helen Macintyre, who was now ten. 'Stephanie and her mum would always go to Chequers when Carrie was away, and she really used to hate that.'

Johnson undertook a period of convalescence at Chequers, feeling 'beaten up and absolutely exhausted'.[46] Cummings visited and told a confidant afterwards, 'He looks a fucking sight, like a guy who's been at death's door. He was in a very bad state.' Johnson confided in him: 'I thought I may well not make it', adding 'I'm now supposedly over it, but I feel terrible. I've got no energy. I'm tired all the time.'

Colleagues and ministers later judged the prime minister's return to Downing Street to have been at least a month too early. 'Being sick sent him into a spiral for a few weeks where he was all over the place. He couldn't make a decision,' a loyal political aide said. Johnson was still weak, exhausted and out of breath. 'It knocked him out for way longer than people ever realised,' a cabinet minister said. 'During his recovery, the nannying came on in leaps and bounds,' Cleo Watson recalled. 'I alternated between stern finger-wagging and soothing words in response to his regular "I hate Covid now. I want everything to go back to normal. Why does everything happen to meeeeeee?" temper tantrums.'[47]

One of the first issues Johnson had to deal with when he arrived at Chequers was Brexit. On 6 April, just as he was heading into intensive care, the *Sunday Times* had run an article by Nick de Bois, the former MP who had been Raab's spad when he was Brexit secretary, suggesting there should be an extension to the transition period. As a conviction Brexiteer he had credibility. 'First, it would be incomprehensible to many members of the public if his government devoted time and energy on these talks until the pandemic was under control,' de Bois wrote. 'Second, it will strike business, already on life support, as utterly illogical and inconsistent with the government's efforts to support business, to impose the prospect of greater disruption by not extending the transition period.' This view was winning support among senior civil servants and Gove, as the minister immersed in no-deal prep, also entertained it.

On 16 April, David Frost intervened to kill further debate. 'As we prepare for the next rounds of negotiations,' he tweeted, 'transition ends on 31 December this year. We will not ask to extend it. If the EU asks, we will say no.' He added, 'Extending would simply prolong negotiations, create even more uncertainty, leave us liable to pay more to the EU in future, and keep us bound by evolving EU laws at a time when we need to control our own affairs. In short, it is not in the UK's interest to extend.'[48]

The tweet coincided with Cummings' return to work. A Vote Leave ally said, 'Everyone thought Dom was behind that. Actually, it was Boris from his sickbed, texting, "This is what we're going to do." He was the person who was toughest on it all.' Having had to ditch the 31 October deadline the year before, Johnson would not delay again.

In Brussels, they watched with resigned despair. 'It was a ludicrous proposition not to ask for an extension,' said Stefaan De Rynck of the Commission, 'but also it's true that we never believed they would ask for an extension.'[49]

Frost believed that time was not the problem. Before Covid struck, the UK had already written a draft free-trade deal to illustrate its objectives, as had the EU. The problem was the decisions about where to compromise – and they would only ever be made at the last moment.

*   *   *

For the next six months, three parallel storylines played out. The first was the public-facing debate about when and how to lift lockdown: what to do about school exams, how to kickstart the economy and then – when infections began to pick up again – whether to stage a second or third lockdown. This, the A Plot of the Johnson government in 2020, with its regulations and tiers and 'eat out to help out', need not concern us much here. If this was a television drama series, the B Plot, which became the mainstay of the drama in 2021 and 2022, was initially submerged. That covered the 'parties' in and around Downing Street while the rest of the population was told it could not socialise. The third theme was the pursuit and exercise of power. This strand, in terms of the relationships at the heart of government, was the most explosive. The botched handling of the pandemic revived Cummings' case that a revolution was needed to sweep away the structures and failing personnel of the *ancien régime*. It was initially a project where he found common cause with Johnson, but eventually one that led to a parting of the ways.

Between mid-April and mid-May Johnson's government fixated on debates between ministers and aides split into 'hawks' and 'doves'. Cummings, Cain, Hancock and Gove were generally pro-lockdown and pro-caution. Sunak, Raab and ministers in other economic departments, like business and transport, were more concerned about the economy, a position also adopted by Eddie Lister. 'Rish at the start was not of the view that we shouldn't lock down,' a Sunak aide said. 'His point was that there needed to be an exit strategy.' Johnson's heart was with those who wanted things to reopen or stay open, his head sometimes turned towards caution by the reality on the ground. When an aide asked if he had lost his mojo during his brush with death, Johnson replied, 'I've always been comfortable with personal risk, I've just never been comfortable with risking the lives of others.'[50] Gove sometimes changed sides, his colleagues noting, with wry amusement, that the briefings to the papers tended to depict whichever side he was on as the 'hawks'.

While he was recovering, Johnson, like Treasury ministers, had been alarmed that so many people had listened to instructions to 'stay at home' and stopped working, threatening a 15 per cent fall in economic output. 'I've learnt that it's much easier to take people's freedoms away than give them back,' he said. Hawks argued that remaining locked down was storing up backlogs in the NHS which would cost more lives in the long run than Covid. Doves like Matt Hancock, the health secretary, argued that the immediate coronavirus death toll was the prime political problem. Robert Jenrick, the communities secretary, joined the hawks amid evidence that families confined to their homes had led to a huge upsurge in domestic violence. Gavin Williamson, the education secretary, pressed for schools to reopen quickly. Ministers had expected them to operate at 20 per cent capacity during lockdown. Instead, just 2 per cent of pupils turned up. Oddly, Mark Sedwill aligned himself firmly with the hawks. A cabinet secretary would usually position himself as an impartial arbiter, but a Tory adviser said, 'Sedwill was very, very anti-lockdown. It was quite unnerving to many cabinet ministers that the cabinet secretary was so aggressively lobbying for one side.'

Johnson's critics sought to paint him as indecisive, but the data and information available to him changed and, by the early summer, the pros and cons of lockdowns were clearer. A senior civil servant, who was privately critical of Johnson, nonetheless said, 'Anybody who suggests that Boris Johnson took decisions on Covid in a cavalier way wasn't there and didn't see quite how much he wrestled with balancing lockdown and other consequences. By that stage, it was becoming clear that people weren't turning up for other non-Covid health problems. It was starting to become clear what was happening in the economy, what was happening in society to kids not being at school. He could be difficult and could drive everyone mad, changing his mind. But at no point around Covid decisions did I see a man being flippant.'

By the end of the month, Johnson had decided to err on the side of caution. Ministers knew the prime minister was back to something like his usual self when he began spouting Latin in cabinet on 30 April, quoting the Roman orator Cicero: 'The health of the people should be the supreme law', a mantra he began to repeat as if it were holy writ. 'There was a lot of Latin and not a lot of translation,' one minister said.

Johnson announced the 'roadmap' for opening up in a televised address to the nation on 10 May, watched by 27.5 million people. The restriction on people exercising just once a day was lifted and a new system of five alert levels or tiers introduced. The government's slogan changed, replacing 'Stay at home' with 'Stay alert'. People were told to wear face coverings on public transport and in shops. New arrivals in Britain, except key workers and lorry drivers, would have to quarantine for fourteen days.

One thing had not changed in Johnson's absence from Number 10, with Hancock bearing the brunt of criticism for PPE shortages, problems with ventilators and his Panglossian claims about testing capacity. The prime minister was incredulous that many of the same issues remained. Faith in the health secretary's reassurances evaporated.

Hancock was one of life's positive characters, but his manner grated on many. Early in his first job in the education department, he met a civil servant he had last seen at Oxford University, when the future official had presented Hancock with his college's 'Captain Twat award'. Another Oxford contemporary told of the time Hancock arrived at a girlfriend's home for the weekend in a sports car. After enduring his brand of charm for two days, the girl's mother asked, 'Darling? Is it the car?'

Shortly after the prime minister's return to work he and Hancock had a 'tense' exchange about the Department of Health's 'grip' on the crisis. Hancock responded in a 'petulant' tone, 'That's not fair – give me a break.'[51] The health secretary was under pressure over the way Covid ripped through care homes and the slow development of a test, track and trace system and a new NHS app. A pledge he made to hit 100,000 tests a day by the end of April also caused tensions. Hancock, with a little bit of creative accounting, hit his target and said it was designed to drive the system to succeed, but others saw it as vainglorious.

Most of all, Johnson's inner circle felt Hancock far too optimistic about the ability of his department and the health service to cope. 'He has overpromised and been unable to deliver,' a colleague said. Hancock's team, in turn, was furious with both NHS England and Public Health England. 'On PPE, Public Health England not only didn't know what they had, they didn't know what they needed,' an adviser said.

Vallance and Cummings, with Sedwill, went to see the PM. On 24 March, Vallance had texted to say, 'I want to set up a vaccine taskforce, and do it outside the Department of Health and Social Care.' The chief scientific officer had already intervened to prevent the department signing off a 'duff' contract with AstraZeneca 'that would not have given us the rights to the vaccine, or would have left them questionable'. Cummings, who had read avidly about the Manhattan Project to build the first atomic bomb, wanted a similar dedicated project where the best brains would be free to work unencumbered by Whitehall bureaucracy. Hancock and the health establishment argued the UK should join the EU's vaccine procurement process. But when he explained to Johnson that the UK would not be compensated by Brussels for the costs of developing the vaccines and would have to share UK vaccines with them, Johnson took no persuading to go it alone.

Arguably the most momentous decision of 2020, setting up the vaccine taskforce, took 'about four minutes'. Eddie Lister recalled, 'Boris needs the credit for this. It was him who turned around and said to Vallance, "Who can do this?" They named half a dozen companies. Boris said, "I want it. I don't care about price. I want those vaccines." Rishi jumped in and said, "Don't worry about the money. A few million quid here or there doesn't matter because we are trashing the economy, we are losing millions every day." Boris said, "Get a commitment from them, we will have it before anybody else." Which is what they did.' Cummings credited Vallance: 'A lot of the things that were best in Covid, was the deep state thwarting Matt Hancock, the elected politician, for the benefit of the country.'[52]

In the immediate aftermath of his brush with mortality, Johnson was receptive to Cummings' argument that the civil service needed radical reform, with under-performing permanent secretaries weeded out. 'The system has been a complete car crash,' Johnson admitted. 'The motherfuckers nearly killed me. We were driving along and everyone was telling me I've got a Rolls-Royce. And then actually it was like that scene in the *Pink Panther* when Clouseau pulls the gear stick and the thing comes off in his hand and he throws it out the window.' Another aide remembers Johnson saying, 'Being near death reminds you that mother nature is tapping her foot, telling you to get on with it.'

This was music to his chief adviser's ears. A Number 10 official recalled, 'Boris agreed with what the problem was. He agreed with what the solution was. He agreed these people have to be removed. He agreed we had to bring new people in.' Cummings also found senior civil servants, particularly MacNamara, receptive to the need for a radical overhaul. 'We all knew the system had completely imploded,' said one official. 'We could agree on some terrible people who needed to be fired. We could agree on some principles of how the civil service needed to change. Let's do a deal.' Cummings got Tom Shinner to review the entire operation of Number 10 and the Cabinet Office.

Johnson and Cummings both concluded that the cabinet secretary had failed to step up to the plate in their absence. 'He was asleep at the wheel,' a senior member of Johnson's team complained. Sedwill's standing was not enhanced by working from home so much. 'He shoved off down to the West Country,' a Downing Street aide said. 'He spent quite a lot of time on Zoom calls with this fake background, and then the IT would glitch, and you would see he was actually sitting in his garden. He's got loads of teeth problems and kept saying, "What can we do about dentists? People have a right to access dentistry."' Another special adviser said, 'I don't think Sedwill covered himself in glory. Boris and Dom came back and things were going off the rails. They wanted someone to blame and it was Sedwill.'

This culminated in a showdown in May, after Johnson's broadcast to the nation, at which he asked Sedwill, 'Who is in charge of implementing this delivery plan?' He looked at the cabinet secretary: 'Is it you?'

Sedwill shot back, 'No, I think it's you, Prime Minister.'

Their relationship never recovered.

Johnson was so disgruntled with the civil service at the end of May that he turned on Martin Reynolds and said, 'I'm telling you if things don't change around here, I'm going to make Dom fucking cabinet secretary – and he can do whatever the fuck he wants.'

Cummings recommended Sedwill's removal, a step Johnson did not initially want to take, but in a bid to beef up the management of the Covid crisis, Simon Case, who had worked in Number 10 under David Cameron and Theresa May and was already on secondment to the Cabinet Office, was made permanent secretary in Downing Street.

Carrie Symonds announced the birth of the couple's new baby on 2 May, releasing a picture of her cradling the newborn on her Instagram account. Declaring 'my heart is full', Carrie wrote that he was named 'Wilfred after Boris's grandfather, Lawrie after my grandfather' and 'Nicholas after Dr Nick Price and Dr Nick Hart – the two doctors that saved Boris's life last month.' Ladbrokes said it had paid out nearly £10,000, apparently to friends who were in on the secret. Wilfred – at least Johnson's sixth child – was just the third born to the occupant of Downing Street in 150 years. Johnson was on course to be the first prime minister in history to score a hat-trick of a divorce, a wedding and a baby while living in Number 10. The last divorce and wedding had been the Duke of Grafton in 1770.

Johnson did almost nothing to exploit the personal events which had taken over his life. On the same day, David Wooding, the veteran political editor of the *Sun on Sunday*, published the first interview with the prime minister about his brush with death, but Johnson was sparing with the details.[53] A senior Tory strategist observed, 'I can think of numerous politicians who would have used the birth of a new child or a near death experience far more unscrupulously.'

Since his fans regarded him as superman and his critics thought him beneath contempt, few considered the effect of events on Johnson the man. Only those closest to him detected the emotional strain he was under, making immense life and death decisions while lethargic and run down from his own brush with the disease. Johnson was also under pressure to help with the baby. 'He was feeling quite shaky after Covid, and he now has a tiny baby, he's getting no sleep at all,' one Downing Street aide recalled. 'He'd often have these naps on the sofa in the office downstairs.' This and other witnesses say Johnson would be working when Carrie messaged him to say, 'Please come up NOW.' An aide said, 'I remember this car journey where she called him and he answered, and she went fucking ballistic. He was quite scared.' Neither the prime minister nor his spouse had the support they needed. Lynton Crosby told Johnson to put his job first. 'You're leader of one of the most important countries in the world, sixth largest economy in the world, you have a duty to get yourself organised,' he said. 'This is not co-parenting in the modern age. You're leading a fucking country and you have a duty.'

Johnson was far from alone in feeling these pressures. 'It feels just like a general election campaign, but one where you don't know the election date and you have to just keep going,' a special adviser said at the time. The prime minister concealed the strain. 'You have to be very close to Boris to see the pressure, but he was under a lot of pressure.'

May 2020 was, perhaps, the pivotal month of Johnson's premiership. The first episode, later dubbed the 'Domnishambles', began at around 4 p.m. on Friday 22 May, when a member of the Metropolitan Police contacted the government to let officials know that officers in the Durham constabulary were about to confirm to journalists that they had investigated whether Dominic Cummings had breached Covid rules by driving from north London to Durham at the height of lockdown.

The left-leaning *Guardian* and *Mirror* newspapers jointly broke the story that Cummings, his wife and their four-year-old son had taken the 260-mile trip at the end of March and had been seen by a neighbour on

5 April. Durham police said, 'On Tuesday, 31 March, our officers were made aware of reports that an individual had travelled from London to Durham and was present at an address in the city. Officers made contact with the owners of that address who confirmed that the individual in question was present and was self-isolating in part of the house … Officers explained to the family the guidelines around self-isolation and reiterated the appropriate advice around essential travel.'

At the time of Cummings' drive north, the government's lockdown rules were specific: 'You should not be visiting family members who do not live in your home … Leaving your home – the place you live – to stay at another home for a holiday or other purpose is not allowed.'

When Downing Street was contacted by the papers, Cummings' instinct was to ignore the story. 'He refused to comment and banned anyone else from commenting,' said one source. 'His attitude was that this was a non-story, it's left-wing papers and they can go fuck themselves. It was a five-day lesson in crisis mismanagement.' The following day, Number 10 issued a statement saying Cummings had gone north when his wife fell ill with coronavirus symptoms because he needed help to care for their son, contradicting the police: 'At no stage was he or his family spoken to by the police about this matter, as is being reported … Mr Cummings believes he behaved reasonably and legally.'

Mark Spencer, the chief whip, and Ben Gascoigne, Johnson's political aide, contacted cabinet ministers asking them to tweet their support. Michael Gove was first out of the blocks with Sunak, Raab and Hancock quick to follow. Enemies of Cummings were accused of drumming up calls for his resignation. Penny Mordaunt, a Cabinet Office minister, was dubbed 'Poison Pen' for telling her constituents there were 'inconsistencies' in Cummings' account. Eddie Lister, Lynton Crosby ('He's got to go, mate'[54]), Ben Elliot and Sajid Javid all told Johnson to throw him overboard. 'We kept saying, "You've got to ditch him,"' Lister recalled. 'He's quite loyal to people. He wouldn't hear of it.' Will Walden advised Johnson he could only keep Cummings if he apologised. 'I'll help you write the bloody statement, if you like,' he said.

Johnson did consider firing Cummings, but he thought: *I don't really want to. I like him and think we are going to do great things together. It has been great fun. He's my capital ship. I've got to protect him.* In the cabinet, Gove, Raab, Sunak and Hancock all backed Cummings staying, as did Dougie Smith, who saw the aide as a key ally. When Johnson asked

Gavin Williamson if he should sack Cummings, he replied, 'If you were going to, you should've done it on day one. It needed to be swift and brutal. It's far too late, Prime Minister.'[55]

Some thought Johnson had another motivation. 'What happened with Boris is that the hinterland of Marina and north London and other voices was dissipated by the negative establishment reaction to Boris post-referendum,' an ally observed. 'Then there was the divorce, which took his anchor points away. The reason he was so loyal to Dominic over Barnard Castle was not out of a personal love for him, I think it was fundamentally that there wasn't anybody else.'

When he emerged from his home in Islington, north London, Cummings berated the scrum of photographers: 'You're supposed to be two metres apart.' Johnson was angry with his most important aide but, like Cummings, never felt he should resign. An adviser said, 'His view was, "I am buggered if I am going to be forced into firing an aide", but he's extremely pissed off with him. Boris himself didn't choose to decamp to Chequers when he was sick, which he could have done.' Another factor was Johnson's personal distaste for the rules. 'He doesn't actually believe in locking everyone down,' an aide said. 'He understands why people might transgress and he can't bring himself to criticise it.' Johnson also shared with Cummings a key world view. 'Where they do meet is on the idea of apologies,' a Tory source said. 'Boris has always been clear that he doesn't ever say sorry.' Nevertheless, Johnson told Cain to tell Cummings to put out an apology. 'He's your chief of staff, you tell him,' Cain replied.[56]

On the Sunday morning Johnson called in Cummings and made him give a full account of his movements. They held a crisis meeting in the flat with Cain and Dougie Smith and agreed Johnson should try to draw a line under the affair. 'Boris would make clear that he was satisfied with Dom's account and try to shut it down,' said one insider. Smith argued that Cummings should not comment. 'Dougie was very much in the "tell them to fuck off" camp,' one said. Smith could not see how Johnson achieved any of the things he wanted without Cummings to drive them through.

But after being pounded with questions at a press conference on Sunday afternoon, Johnson failed to kill the story. 'Boris took one for the team,' an official added. 'After that press conference he came out and said that he had had his "arse whipped" live on national television and told Dom he would have to do the same.' To make matters worse, Patrick

Vallance, the chief scientific adviser, and Chris Whitty, the chief medical officer, had 'refused to do the presser,' a ministerial aide said. Ministers were also in revolt.

The decision that Cummings should make his own public appearance was confirmed at another meeting on Monday morning. Cummings did not want to do it, but Johnson insisted. 'It has cut through,' Cummings conceded. And how. Some MPs received more than 1,500 emails of complaint. While Cummings was driving to Durham, people were banned from seeing their dying relatives, isolated from their families, unable to attend funerals.

That day, 25 May, Cummings wrote a 2,500-word statement about what happened, while Johnson and Cain stood behind, leaning over his shoulder, making suggestions. Like Brexit night, when Cummings became the centre of attention, there was something discordant in the scene, a prime minister chipping in like the hired help as his adviser prepared to meet the press. The entire resources of Downing Street were concentrated on prepping Cummings, not Johnson. 'You could see it was annoying Boris,' an aide said. 'He could see the whole circus moving to this other guy.'

When it was ready, Cummings was put through his paces by the communications team, all firing questions at him. This was not a reassuring exercise as Cummings took delight in answering questions about the handling of the pandemic honestly. 'Someone asked, "What do you think of the Department of Health?",' one of those present said. 'He machine-gunned Hancock and said how useless the entire health establishment was. We had to say: "Don't say any of that."'

No one knew if Cummings would apologise when he faced the cameras, despite Johnson's encouragement to do so. The prime minister sent him a vitriolic text, which Cummings waved around in open defiance. 'His attitude was: "I don't answer to you",' said one of those present. 'Dom didn't bother returning Boris' calls.' Meanwhile, Cleo Watson had gone to Cummings' home to get some clothes which would make him look presentable. A white shirt was located from which an attempt was made to iron out 'decades of creases'. Later, as she was walking with Cummings down the back stairs to the Number 10 garden, Watson grew concerned and phoned his wife. 'Mary, we really need you to centre this guy a bit,' she said. Wakefield told her husband, 'Be nice, be nice. Don't lose your patience, be nice.'

Cummings' press conference was the most dramatic event in the Downing Street garden since David Cameron and Nick Clegg launched the coalition there in 2010. Jacketless, he sat at a table and read his statement, the main revelation being that he had driven north, in part, because he was worried about his family's security. 'I was subject to threats of violence,' he said. 'People came to my house shouting threats ... I thought the best thing to do in all the circumstances was to drive to an isolated cottage on my father's farm.' Some viewers found this self-serving, but for several days Cummings' colleagues had urged him to explain himself. From September 2019, at the height of the prorogation battle, it was not unusual for Cummings, Mary and their son to turn up in the middle of the night at Cleo Watson's flat nearby to announce that they had had a death threat through the letterbox. 'It was really frightening,' a friend said. The situation had been serious enough that Helen MacNamara suggested they move into a government flat in Admiralty Arch. The government's handling of the pandemic had led to more death threats in March.

Cummings confirmed he had not sought permission from Johnson before driving north. He said he then developed Covid symptoms 'including a bad headache and a serious fever' while his son had to be rushed by ambulance to hospital with a 'bad fever' on 2 April. By now, Cummings said, 'I could barely stand up.' On 12 April, recovered, he decided he needed to get back to work. 'My wife was very worried, particularly given my eyesight seemed to have been affected by the disease. She didn't want to risk a nearly 300-mile drive with our child, given how ill I had been. We agreed that we should go for a short drive to see if I could drive safely.' This was the infamous trip to Barnard Castle, thirty miles away, where the family were spotted again.

As the press dissected Cummings' explanations and sought to extract an apology, he began to get tetchy, eyes narrowing under the hot sun. Watson took to standing directly in his eyeline, 'bent over like a tennis linesman, gesticulating for him to sit up straight and, if not smile, be tolerant and polite when responding to the repetitive questions being fired at him.'[57] 'The expectation in Downing Street was that the word "sorry" would pass his lips,' a Number 10 official said, yet even Cummings' allies could not persuade him to apologise. He said, 'I don't regret what I did', a statement which undid whatever good his appearance had achieved.

In a foul mood, Johnson made clear his displeasure at having to do another press conference afterwards, the regular 5 p.m. Covid update. As he expressed regret for the 'confusion and the anger and the pain that people feel', a cabinet minister said, 'Why have we got the prime minister on television apologising for a special adviser. It's insane.'

Johnson had hoped Cummings' appearance would lance the boil, but as he watched the rumble in the rose garden he realised he had made a serious mistake. *I go out to bat for him. I do a press conference saying he's innocent. And then I have to listen to all this crap. I went out and spent a fucking shit ton of political capital. I should never have unleashed it in that way.* 'Boris made it very clear to Dom in words of four letters that he was unhappy about it,' a source said. That evening, Johnson's phone rang hot with MPs furious at the way Cummings had behaved and then performed. 'There was a lot of rage,' a source said. 'People hated defending that.' Johnson, in turn, was to discover that when Cummings said he was testing his eyes, it was actually his wife Mary's birthday. He thought: *The whole thing was a complete load of shit. They went on a birthday outing and he pretended he was the great Oculus of Barnard Castle. He did not need to get his eyes tested. It was rubbish.*

As the week went on, the Tories plummeted in the polls, Jeremy Hunt began phoning MPs, asking what they thought. In a WhatsApp message to her Blue Collar Conservatism group, the former cabinet minister Esther McVey wrote, 'I'm anxious to hear (in private) what people think about the Dominic Cummings situation and whether or not he needs to resign to protect the PM and the party', before adding: 'I would appreciate people not reply on here as it may leak.' In the time-honoured tradition, it then did so.

The Barnard Castle affair led to questions about whether the Vote Leave playbook was right for a public health crisis. 'It feels like they are running a general election campaign against the Covid-19 party,' a former Cameron aide remarked, wryly. A Tory adviser compared Cummings to the lead character in Monty Python's *Life of Brian*: 'He's proved he's not the Messiah, he's actually a very naughty boy.'

To the Vote Leave fraternity, Cummings was their leader, not Johnson, and he needed to be preserved at all costs. 'We took three years to get the gang in there,' one said that week. 'We can't throw that away now.' But the affair seriously damaged the pivotal relationship in government. Munira Mirza 'always said that the Dom-Boris relationship fell apart over Barnard Castle', a senior civil servant recalled. Another Downing Street adviser observed: 'It was clear to anyone working in that building that by April, May of 2020, prior to Barnard Castle, that their personal relationship went off a cliff. Dom was regularly swearing at Boris, having explosive emotional outbursts at him, calling him four-letter words, the very bad ones. It was a bullying relationship. Dom was very abusive to him. I'm sure it was the stress of the situation, but it was like when you have a very bad row with your partner. You can only say those bad things to people who you're very close to, in a strange way, and there were very emotional disagreements between them.'

The split occurred when Johnson was already worrying about his own future. 'Boris has become obsessed with the fate of Winston Churchill and Gordon Brown,' an ally remarked after Barnard Castle. 'You do this big important thing like Churchill winning the war or Brown saving the banks and then the electorate doesn't say, "Thank you very much, well done", they say, "That's great, now push off".'

If Cummings alone had broken Covid rules the Johnson government would probably have survived. Yet just two days before the Barnard Castle story broke an event was held in the Number 10 garden that had raised alarm bells even with the Vote Leave crew. On 20 May 2020 Martin Reynolds, Johnson's PPS, sent an email to more than a hundred Number 10 staff, inviting them to attend a party in the garden. 'After what has been an incredibly busy period it would be nice to make the most of the lovely weather and have some socially distanced drinks in the No10 garden this evening,' he wrote. 'Please join us from 6 p.m. and bring your own booze!' It was not until 1 June that groups of up to six people were allowed to meet outdoors. Cummings later said he had warned at the time the plan was likely to be against the rules and 'should not happen'.

The bring your own booze party came five days after another event where the prime minister and Carrie were pictured with Downing Street officials having wine and cheese in the garden. Then, on 19 June, Carrie messaged political aides in the building asking them to assemble for a birthday party for Johnson. Cleo Watson messaged Martin Reynolds at 9.09 a.m., 'Hi! PM birthday today – we've organised some sandwiches and cake for about 1 p.m. in the Cabinet Room if anyone from your team would like to pop in and wish him a happy birthday.' Reynolds sent a similar message to Simon Case and the private secretaries.[58] This was the event which was later judged to be illegal.

* * *

In mid-July, Johnson marked his first year in power. In twelve months, he had won the leadership, prorogued Parliament, been condemned by the Supreme Court, kicked out twenty-one Tory MPs, secured a Brexit deal, forced and won a general election, finalised a divorce, got engaged and become a father. 'This is not the premiership that Boris would ever have envisaged running,' a former Number 10 aide said. 'Boris is the sunny optimism guy and he's having to deal with all this shit. I don't think he enjoys the job as much as he thought he would.'

By July, Johnson's enthusiasm for Cummings' plans for Whitehall, as well as for the Vote Leave gang, had evaporated. 'You could tell he never really understood any of the civil service reform stuff,' a Cummings ally said. 'He is a sort of establishment man himself even if he rails against it. Over May and then into June, these huge headwinds came in.' The Tory right, egged on by its paper of choice, the *Telegraph*, began to argue that there should never have been lockdowns because the cost in economic, educational and health outcomes was too high, a debate which appeared divorced from the political realities of March. If Johnson had done nothing in the face of a credible threat of half a million deaths, there is every chance the government would have fallen.

At the time it was widely assumed that Johnson's brush with death had convinced him of the virtues of lockdown. If this was so, it was only the case briefly. The prime minister made a few remarks about the dangers of obesity ('Don't be a fatty in your fifties') but did not become more cautious. 'In fact, after the first lockdown, he was cross with me and others for what he regarded as basically pushing him into that first lockdown,' Cummings said. 'His argument after that happened was, literally, "I should have been the mayor of *Jaws* and kept the beaches open." That is what he said on many, many occasions.'[59] Hand in hand with his view of lockdowns went his view of the Vote Leave crew. Cummings and Cain had been strong advocates of household quarantine. 'I should never have listened to you,' Johnson said. 'It was all a disaster. Carrie's telling me we are making enemies.' A Vote Leave veteran said, 'By the end of July, we'd lost him and Carrie was back on manoeuvres.'

When the chief aide finally went in for the delayed operation on his back in July, he told Johnson, 'I think that I should go at Christmas.' The prime minister did not argue. Cummings said, 'I want to actually change things around here and you don't. You're more afraid of me having the power to change things than you are of chaos.'

Johnson laughed, 'You're right. Chaos is fine. Chaos means everyone has to look up to the king.' The gist of this conversation was well known in Number 10 at the time, not a post hoc Cummings confection.

Johnson spent much of August at Chequers receiving guests, who arrived to find that same chaos. 'Dilyn was charging around eating the furniture and shitting everywhere,' a witness said. 'They trashed the joint.' Another, Cleo Watson, recalled a midsummer meeting to decide strategy for the autumn. 'We made our way upstairs to be greeted by an appalling smell and what I took to be a small fig under the table. "Oh dear," the PM said, looking at me expectantly, "Dilyn's done a turd." I adopted the exasperated-teapot pose. "Well, you'd better pick it up then," I said. And he did.'[60]

On another occasion, the prime minister joked, 'Everyone hates the Vote Leave people. I can get rid of all of you, and everyone will just cheer.' Cummings publicly claimed Johnson also pronounced, 'Everyone had better remember, I'm the fucking Fuhrer around here.'[61] Downing Street denied the quote.

There were glimmers of self-aware Boris. Also in June, he noticed Cummings had stopped going to the 'gruesome morning meetings' which focused on whatever was obsessing the lobby. 'What a farce these meetings are,' Johnson admitted. 'I'm running the government like the old Speccie conferences, I love it, it's great fun, but my god it's no way to run a bloody country.'[62]

A feature of that summer was the 'pingdemic' when the NHS app informed people they should isolate because they had been in close proximity to someone who had tested positive. Johnson 'insisted on working from his downstairs office while isolating,' Watson said. 'Very soon, this required setting up chairs as barriers in the doorway, as he couldn't resist stepping over the threshold into our adjoining room to peer over shoulders at what people were working on (invariably in a pair of someone else's reading glasses he'd found lying around). So the prime ministerial "puppy gate" was created. He'd kneel on the seats, his elbows propped over the top, like a great unruly golden retriever, howling for attention.'[63] Cummings took to quoting Bismarck's remark about Kaiser Wilhelm: 'He is like a balloon: if you don't keep fast hold of the string, you never know where he will be off to.'

* * *

Parts of the planned Whitehall revolution took place. In early September, Cummings engineered the elevation of Simon Case from permanent secretary in Number 10 to replace Mark Sedwill as cabinet secretary. At forty-one, he was the youngest to hold the post since 1916, but Case had already served three prime ministers and been private secretary to a future king – though he had never run a major government department and was regarded as a queue jumper by fellow officials. Johnson promised Case the opportunity to 'transform Britain in eighteen months'. Yet it was already clear Case had serious concerns about the operation. In a WhatsApp exchange with Sedwill on 2 July, he complained, 'This place is just insane. Zero discipline ... These people are so mad ... They are madly self-defeating ... I've never seen a bunch of people less-equipped to run a country.' The criticism of Case from fellow mandarins was that, instead of challenging the chaos, he joined the team and did little to arrest the problems. Sedwill's fate was probably prominent in his mind. 'The fur will fly; watch yourself,' the outgoing cabinet secretary advised, revealing that he had complained to Eddie Lister about the briefings against him: 'It's hard to ask people to march to the sound of gunfire if they're shot in the back.'

On 21 August Cummings sent a series of WhatsApps about Helen MacNamara in which he said, 'I will personally handcuff her and escort her out of the building. I don't care how it is done but that woman must be out of our hair – we cannot keep dealing with this horrific meltdown of the British state while dodging stilettos from that cunt.'[64] The key word here was the one conspicuous by its absence: 'useless'. Cummings found MacNamara infuriating precisely because he rated her and she had been able to thwart him. She called the messages 'horrible to read'. When he gave evidence to the Covid Inquiry, Cummings apologised several times for his language, saying he was much ruder about men than he was 'about Helen'. His wife told friends, 'Dom is a misanthrope not a misogynist.'

Cummings threatened that a 'hard rain will fall' on the civil service, with whole departments decanted to northern cities and quangos like Public Health England scrapped. But his own pet project, a new 'mission control centre' in the Cabinet Office at 70 Whitehall, was stillborn. No one senior, including Cummings, went to work there and those who saw the dull, whitewashed office with plastic safety dividers between desks and a few flatscreens on the wall dubbed it the 'Starshit Enterprise'.

Johnson soon had second thoughts. Isolating again in his office, the 'fucking miserable' PM summoned a senior official, who had to hide behind the curtains to maintain social distancing, while he poured out his heart. 'I made a terrible mistake,' he confided. 'I should never have got rid of Mark Sedwill. I'm not sure Simon Case is up to it.' The official agreed Sedwill had been treated 'shabbily' but urged Johnson to give Case 'a break', 'See if you can work with him before fucking him'. Later, Johnson described the Cummings cull as a 'random act of mutilation' and complained that 'his great fucking war room did nothing'.

To Cummings, this was an example of how Johnson, the great disruptor, was really a creature of the establishment: 'His whole being wants to throw himself into the arms of polite young Balliol men and enjoy the trappings of power while they do the work and pull the strings. He believes in the system.'[65] Another senior Downing Street political adviser said, 'He's just not that interested in governing. You'd get these occasional spurts of exertion, particularly during the summer of 2020, where you'd get these long emails in the middle of the night from him with titles like "My Priorities", and there would be a list of fifty things, but not in priority order. He'd say things like: "schools ... make them better", no mention of how.'

For Johnson, there was a creeping realisation that unhelpful stories were still appearing in the papers with Cummings' fingerprints on them. On 25 August, *The Times* diary reported that Sir Humphry Wakefield, Cummings' father-in-law, had 'merrily informed' a visitor to his country seat, Chillingham Castle, that the PM was 'still struggling badly with having had Covid-19 and will stand down in six months'. Wakefield, a keen rider, remarked, 'If you put a horse back to work when it's injured it will never recover.'[66] Johnson concluded that it was Cummings who thought he was heading for the knacker's yard.

This was the backdrop as Johnson and Cummings embarked on their most explosive disagreement about Covid which was to last through September and October. During a 7.30 p.m. meeting in the prime minister's office on Wednesday 16 September, Chris Whitty and Patrick Vallance delivered a 'highly sobering assessment' of a 'sharp increase' in the Covid-19 infection rate. Hospital admissions had doubled since the start of September. In a 'reasonable worst-case scenario' Britain was on a path to between 200 and 500 deaths every day by early November, they warned. Draconian measures were discussed, including an immediate 'circuit-breaker' national lockdown and a ban on family-to-family contacts. Some aides suggested pubs and restaurants should be closed. Cummings rounded on Johnson, telling him, 'If you don't do it now, don't come back in a month and say, "We're going to do it", because that is just not a logical way of doing it.'

In another meeting two days later Rishi Sunak, the chancellor who had tried to kickstart the economy in August with subsidised restaurant meals, the Eat Out to Help Out scheme, moved to fight the closures. His opposition, temporarily, killed the idea.

On 20 September, Johnson approved a plan to introduce a 10 p.m. curfew for pubs and restaurants. It still made him uncomfortable, not least because fifty Tory MPs had joined a 'common sense' group, coordinated by the irrepressible Steve Baker, to oppose lockdowns. Into October, as the infection rate rose, Johnson resisted a full lockdown, so aggravating Cummings the aide printed out an A3 sheet of case rates and deaths, and carried it around with him, 'showing it to literally everyone,' a witness said. 'He opened up a meeting about civil service reform by getting it out and explaining why it showed we need to lock down.'[67]

In despair, Case messaged Cummings at lunchtime on 10 September, 'I am at the end of my tether. He changes strategic direction every day (Monday we were all about fear of virus returning as per Europe, March etc – today we're in "let it rip" mode cos [sic] the UK is pathetic, needs a cold shower etc.). He cannot lead and we cannot support him in leading with this approach. The team captain cannot change the call on the big plays every day. The team can't deliver anything under these circumstances. IT HAS TO STOP! Decide and set direction – deliver – explain. Gov't isn't actually that hard but this guy is really making it impossible.' Cummings replied, 'Totally agree, am getting lots of despairing messages from people in [meetings] with him.'[68] When Johnson suggested that Hancock work up plans for 'regional circuit breakers', Case said policy was being driven by 'whatever Carrie cares about, I guess', before adding, 'I was always told that Dom was the secret PM. How wrong they are. I look forward to telling the select committee "Oh, fuck, no, don't worry about Dom, the real person in charge is Carrie."'[69] Case warned the government 'doesn't have the credibility needed to be imposing stuff within only days of deciding not to … We look like a terrible, tragic joke.' Cain responded to that with a trolley emoji.[70]

On 1 October, scientists on SAGE demanded an immediate circuit-breaker lockdown. They were met with a dissection of their numbers and modelling by Sunak, who argued that pubs and bars were not a main cause of infections. 'He was quoting tables in the appendix at them,' a source said. 'That was the first time they had really been challenged on their data.' On 12 October, Downing Street announced that Covid regulations would be raised in 'tiers' according to local infection rates. The result was a chaotic system which spread resentment between those in different tiers. The rules even varied between councils in the same tier.

Cummings pressed Johnson to agree to a general lockdown. He said later, 'By this time ... all credible serious people in my opinion were saying essentially the same thing.' Johnson, he said, 'wasn't taking any advice; he was just making his own decision that he was going to ignore the advice ... The cabinet wasn't involved or asked ... If you took anybody at random from the top 1 per cent of competent people in this country and presented them with the situation, they would behave differently from how the prime minister behaved.' Johnson persisted with the view that it was more important to protect the economy. A senior adviser recalled, 'I watched Dom shouting at Boris down the phone, "How could you be so stupid." I remember being quite shocked. Boris and Dom are both brilliant and both impossible. In a relationship, you can have one person like that, you can't have two.'

On 15 October, a day after three tiers of restrictions were rolled out, Johnson told his closest aides he was 'rocked' by analysis that the average age of those dying was over eighty. 'That is above life expectancy. So get Covid and live longer.' He went on, 'I no longer buy all this NHS overwhelmed stuff.' When Cain questioned how this should affect policy, the prime minister said, 'It shows we don't go for nationwide lockdown.' A diary entry from Patrick Vallance on 25 October depicted a 'very frustrated' Johnson who started 'throwing papers down' because he did not like what he was hearing from the scientists. Johnson, Vallance wrote, wanted a 'let it rip strategy', and said, 'Most of those who die have reached their time' and 'had a good innings'. Johnson told the inquiry he was challenging his advisers and changed his position as the facts changed.

Events came to a head on the evening of Friday 30 October, when Johnson, Sunak, Gove, Hancock and Raab met to discuss plans for nationwide restrictions. The health secretary led the demand for more stringent measures but Sunak's opposition had also eased. The decisive intervention was Gove's. 'Michael said that if he didn't impose a second lockdown there would be a catastrophe,' a source close to Gove said later.

'Hospitals would be overrun, people would be turned away from A&E and people would be dying in hospital corridors and hospital car parks. He told the PM he would have to send soldiers into hospitals to keep people out. Was that the image of his post-Brexit Britain he wanted the world to see? It was devastating. The PM had no answer.'[71] They planned to announce the following Monday but within hours it was leaked to *The Times* and *Sky News* before Johnson had definitively made up his mind. 'Boris was apocalyptically incandescent,' said a Whitehall source.

Forced into a hasty announcement that Saturday, the prime minister demanded a leak inquiry. Cain, in conversation with Glen Owen, the political editor of the *Mail on Sunday*, said, 'Our rat, whoever it is, seems to be very chatty at the moment.' The 'Chatty Rat' was born.

Within days the security services were examining the phones of Gove, Hancock and other ministers and had seventy suspects on their list. The inquiry took months and never came to a firm conclusion. The Vote Leavers claimed it pointed to Henry Newman, a Gove spad who was close friends with Carrie Symonds. The Number 10 political team had also long suspected that a senior civil servant had been passing information to the Labour Party, who then gave it to journalists, a mole they dubbed 'Red Throat'. But the whips' office and Johnson suspected it was the work of Cummings or Cain themselves, who both denied any involvement. Yet even a close friend admitted, 'They had a "bounce to announce" strategy to leak things they wanted to happen.'

Whatever the truth of the leak, Johnson was furious at being 'bounced' into a second lockdown and emerged from the meeting on 31 October in a state of rage. Multiple witnesses claim he yelled from his study, loud enough that he could be heard outside: 'No more fucking lockdowns whatever the consequences. Let the bodies pile high in their thousands!'[72] Cummings said the following year, 'I heard that in the prime minister's study. That was immediately after he finally made the decision to do the lockdown on 31 October.'[73]

Johnson always denied making such incendiary remarks, but two weeks later, Cummings and Cain were gone. The Vote Leave contingent and the prime minister had come to see each other as madmen. Only when it came to Brexit, the project they had jointly authored, was this deliberate government policy.

THE MADMAN STRATEGY II

The UK Internal Market Bill

April to October 2020

The Brexit talks resumed on 24 April after both Johnson and Cummings returned from their Covid exiles. Like the rest of the world, at this point, meetings were conducted via video call. The negotiators suffered the same distractions familiar to those working from home during the lockdown. Both sides played 'through the Zoom keyhole', catching glimpses of the homes, bookshelves and lives of their counterparts. 'Everyone was texting each other saying, "Look at his books" or "What about that painting",' a negotiator said. 'No one was really listening to what was being said.'[1]

Those who *were* listening realised that both sides were dug-in to their opening demands. When they did debate the detail, the tone was 'tetchy'. The talks went nowhere. David Frost observed, 'I think you lose something in terms of informal contact … The ability to defuse things and move on, that is much harder over Zoom.'[2]

Officials in the Cabinet Office and other departments who had been sequestered to work on the pandemic, quietly returned to preparing for Brexit. XO, the cabinet's no-deal planning committee, met twice in the week beginning 4 May.

On 19 May, Frost decided to provide an adrenaline shot to the negotiations with another public intervention. He sent an open letter to Barnier, spelling out what he perceived to be the inconsistency and unfairness of the EU position, attacking the Commission's refusal to grant Britain the trading terms which had been offered to other countries. At the same time, he released draft legal texts prepared by the UK, to show member states what Britain was proposing. First, because Britain wanted a free trade agreement (FTA), 'our legal texts draw on precedent'. The draft

FTA was close to those the EU agreed with Japan and South Korea, the proposed fisheries agreement to the deal signed with Norway, the aviation and nuclear proposals close to that 'agreed with other third countries'. Frost wrote, 'Given this reality, we find it perplexing that the EU, instead of seeking to settle rapidly a high-quality set of agreements with a close economic partner, is instead insisting on additional, unbalanced, and unprecedented provisions in a range of areas, as a precondition for agreement between us.'

His second point was that Barnier was 'not willing even to replicate provisions in previous FTAs'. There were no 'mutual recognition' agreements, 'the EU agreed with or proposed to Canada, Australia, New Zealand and the US', or sector-specific provisions for key industries like cars, medicine and chemicals, 'agreed with or proposed to one or more of Canada, South Korea, Chile and the US, among others'. Nor was Britain being offered the kind of equivalence on sanitary and phytosanitary goods which were offered to Canada, Japan, New Zealand, Australia, Mexico and Mercosur. He added, 'Your team has told us that the EU's market access offer on services might be less than that tabled with Australia and New Zealand. Overall, we find it hard to see what makes the UK, uniquely among your trading partners, so unworthy of being offered the kind of well-precedented arrangements commonplace in modern FTAs.'

Frost's third complaint was to question why Barnier was continuing to insist on level playing field provisions when Britain's proposals were similar to those agreed in the EU–Canada trade deal, which granted the Canadians near-free trade without level playing field handcuffs. Winding up the rhetoric, Frost wrote, 'Your text contains novel and unbalanced proposals which would bind this country to EU law or standards ... To take a particularly egregious example, your text would require the UK simply to accept EU state aid rules; would enable the EU, and only the EU, to put tariffs on trade with the UK if we breached those rules; and would require us to accept an enforcement mechanism which gives a specific role to the European Court of Justice. You must see that this is simply not a provision any democratic country could sign.'

The EU's justifications for these moves, that Britain was being offered 'a future relationship of unprecedented depth', cut no ice with Frost. Once again, he said the Johnson government would rather have friction and tariffs than alignment. The second explanation, that Britain had to be treated differently because of its proximity, trade flows and integration with the EU market, was given short shrift. 'The US and Canada, for example, trade together ... without provisions of the kind the EU would like to see. This proximity argument amounts to saying that a country in Europe cannot expect to determine its own rules, simply on the grounds of geography, and that it must bend to EU norms. That is not an argument that can hope to be accepted in the twenty-first century.'

He concluded, 'Overall, at this moment in negotiations, what is on offer is not a fair free trade relationship between close economic partners, but a relatively low-quality trade agreement coming with unprecedented EU oversight of our laws and institutions. It does not have to be like this.'

There was much here that was reasonable, but commentators took Frost to task for his tone. Jill Rutter of UK in a Changing Europe compared Frost to 'a rather whiny child'.

Barnier's response was delivered with classic Gallic hauteur the following day, berating Frost for going public: 'I do not think an exchange of letters regarding the substance of the negotiations is necessarily the best way to discuss substantial points ... I would not like the tone that you have taken to impact the mutual trust and constructive attitude that is essential between us.' On the substance, Barnier insisted, 'The EU has always made clear that any future trade agreement between us will have to include strong level playing field guarantees.'

However, buried away in the letter, was an important signal, received and understood by Frost, but easily missed by the media. While Barnier was looking for the UK to uphold standards 'in the areas of state aid, competition, social and employment standards, environment, climate change, and relevant tax matters' that no longer meant actually adhering to EU law. If Britain was happy to maintain high standards, it did not matter if UK regulations were different.[3] Brussels had moved. David Davis, who had not been permitted by May to take such a confrontational stance as Frost, reflected, 'All you need to do to see what May could have done is look at what Frost did the moment he took over. He started cutting up rough and they started backing off slightly.'[4]

Barnier's colleagues insist he'd been trying, for some time, to signal areas of compromise. 'Even before the June meeting, Barnier had opened the door for saying, "We could reconsider how the role of the Court of Justice would be in a dispute settlement",' Stefaan De Rynck recalled. 'Various issues on our side had been put on the table as hints of landing zones if the UK would pick them up, and they didn't for three or four months.'[5]

No more progress was made until 15 June, when Johnson and Ursula von der Leyen had a 'high level' video conference. Charles Michel, the new Council president, and David Sassoli, the president of the European Parliament, also joined. Frost wrote Johnson a speaking note, with the key paragraphs bolded up where the chief negotiator most wanted a clear message delivering. Handing it to the PM he said, 'Those are the parts you've got to read out.' Johnson had come straight from another meeting and had not read the brief, so when it came to the call, he literally read out the script. 'It landed extremely well,' said one of those listening. 'He was extremely clear about everything. For the first time in a long time actually they heard the PM himself say some of the stuff and robustly.'

During the forty-five-minute call, the three points Johnson kept coming back to were: 'No European Court of Justice; no obeying EU law when we're not in the EU; and a good deal for our fishermen.' Von der Leyen seemed to take this in. 'I hear you,' she said. 'She was listening,' the British source said. 'Barnier was supposed to be a non-speaking part but then he spoke and disrupted the flow for her. I think they were trying to judge: are we really up for a deal or not? Boris convinced them of that.'

The Commission statement issued after the conversation said that Frost and Barnier would seek 'an early understanding on the principles underlying any agreement'. This was an attempt by the British team to force the EU to reopen its negotiating mandate and give Barnier more scope to compromise. In fact, the EU's position had already changed.

The real breakthrough was not publicised. As Barnier had hinted in May, the EU had decided to drop references to or the application of EU law and remove the ECJ as policeman of the trade deal. Frost had been arguing for five months that this should be a deal between two sovereign equals – and the Commission had now conceded the point. A British negotiator said, 'That was when we really felt they understood what this was about.' A colleague added, 'It was fairly clear that Barnier was told to move. At that stage we had won a political argument.' In return, Frost agreed that the UK would sign up to a treaty which brought together a 'suite' of agreements on trade, aviation, energy, security and fishing in one single text with a single arbitration mechanism, rather than multiple documents as he had been calling for – a classic demand made so it could be withdrawn later.

The politics was sorted, but hammering out the final economic details would be more complicated and even more contentious. Just how difficult quickly became clear. Johnson argued on the call that there should be a 'huge difference' in the number of fish in British waters which could be caught only by British fishermen. 'Absolutely,' came the reply. But within days it was clear the two sides had very different ideas about what 'huge' meant. 'The EU interpreted it as being 5 per cent and we interpreted it as being 80 per cent,' a British official said. 'One of our failings was that, because it was such an unreasonable position, we assumed that they had to move. In fact, they just never did.'

When Johnson vowed 'to put a tiger in the tank' to get a deal by autumn, Charles Michel fired a warning shot. 'We are ready to put a tiger in the tank, but not to buy a pig in a poke,' he tweeted, with commendable knowledge of English idiom.

On 25 June, ten days after the meeting, Frost felt he had to publicly face down a notion doing the rounds in the EU negotiating team. 'I want to be clear that the government will not agree to ideas like … giving the EU a new right to retaliate with tariffs if we choose to make laws suiting our interests. We could not leave ourselves open to such unforeseeable economic risk.' This was the first public mention of something which was to nearly derail the talks later. At this point, Barnier's deputies gave the impression they thought it a negotiating tactic. 'Don't worry about it' was the message from Paulina Dejmek-Hack and Clara Martínez Alberola, two of the key figures in Barnier's team.

Between mid-June and late July, when face-to-face talks finally resumed, in London, negotiations stalled over the EU's control of the process, the same issue which had caused issues for Theresa May in 2018. Member states told Barnier to operate a policy of 'parallelism'. Frost suggested draft legal text could be prepared immediately on the less contentious issues – aviation, energy, haulage, cooperation on crime and the trade in goods – while negotiations continued on the level playing field and fish. But parallelism banned EU officials from working on legal text until the UK had agreed to accept EU demands. 'They refused on the basis that we had to concede first,' a senior British source said. 'This began to seriously hamper progress.'[6]

There was also awkwardness between Frost and Barnier, partly a consequence of their different roles. 'Barnier had got used to dealing with

David Davis or Raab, with the number two doing the detail,' a British negotiator explained. 'All of a sudden, he was faced with [Frost] doing the detail. Even quite late, in July, he'd been attributing to us positions this government had never taken. He never really got to grips with the detail.' On one occasion, Barnier declared that Britain wanted passporting for financial services, a demand that had even been dropped by the May government. Frost, in turn, wound Barnier up by referring to the EU as 'your organisation', causing the Frenchman, a lifelong believer in the European project, to grind his teeth.

Frost found these initial interactions 'ritualistic'. Barnier refused to discuss legal text until Britain gave ground on the level playing field and fish, while Frost repeated that everything was linked and the trade-offs would have to happen together. 'He accused us of being arrogant or not listening to him,' a British official said. Barnier even threw the accusation of arrogance at Chris Barton, a self-effacing civil service expert in traded goods. His colleagues sniggered. Genuine discussions did establish understanding between the heads of working groups, and would eventually bear fruit, but at this stage EU officials didn't have the political backing to compromise.

Oliver Lewis was the main object of suspicion for the EU negotiating team, since he was assumed to be the voice of Cummings. In fact, as another senior figure recalled, Cummings was 'a pretty strong proponent of compromise. This idea he was always for crashing the HGV was not true at all. In September and October he thought we should compromise.' Believing Lewis to be the main blockage to progress, EU officials labelled him Johnson's 'political commissar' and Dejmek-Hack began to 'shadow' him, asking which sessions he was going to each morning. Once he realised what was happening, Lewis amused himself by appearing in meetings he had not mentioned to her. 'You'd see EU officials start texting and a few minutes later the door burst open and it was Paulina,' a British official recalled.

EU officials would have been even more concerned if they had noticed what Lewis was carrying when he appeared on the high-level conference call in mid-June. He had just returned from holiday and came to work with a doorstop-thick textbook on UK constitutional case law. He was very privately working on an idea which nearly blew up the talks and set negotiations onto a confrontational path for the next three years.

*　*　*

Lewis was a fan of one of Cummings' favourite Bismarck quotes: 'With a gentleman, I am always a gentleman-and-a-half, with a pirate, I try to be a pirate and-a-half.' As long ago as January it had been clear to the Vote Leave team that a piratical approach might be needed in Northern Ireland. The *Sunday Times* revealed on 23 February that Johnson's aides had been ordered to draw up plans to 'get around' the Northern Ireland Protocol with proposals to ensure that there did not need to be checks on goods passing from Britain to Northern Ireland. By the time of the reshuffle, on 13 February, Johnson and Frost believed the prime minister needed to remove Geoffrey Cox as attorney general because they wanted a law officer who could be relied upon to take a broader view of what was legal. In short, within three months of signing the withdrawal agreement treaty, Johnson was planning to violate it. 'There is deadly serious work going on about not obeying the Northern Ireland Protocol,' a Tory source said in February. 'That's why they had Suella put in there.'

Lewis had interviewed a handful of candidates to see where they stood on a range of legal issues. 'They wanted someone who was more realistic about the political context in which we were working,' a source said. 'Someone who was going to be a lawyer for the client, rather than for the lawyers.' Braverman was a legal traditionalist and held that Parliament was sovereign, and that international treaties only had effect in domestic law if Parliament said so. In effect, British statute overrode international law. This 'dualist' system tended to dominate in Commonwealth countries, but not in Europe, where international agreements usually applied automatically. 'It's a traditional view of how the law should work which has fallen out of vogue in the last twenty years,' a Number 10 official said, 'but in the last five hundred years that has been the absolute standard view of how the UK legal system works. We were keen on people who had that traditional reading.' Another senior figure said, 'None of us felt massively happy with the [2019] deal. We always thought that we might need a notwithstanding clause at some point. Obviously, the attorney was relevant to those sorts of decisions.'

'Notwithstanding clauses' are constitutional dynamite because they give ministers the power to ignore existing laws. 'We knew that we wanted to tear it up in a certain way, go really hard-core,' a Downing Street source said. Another said, 'The track record of Geoffrey was such that we didn't really see him as a safe pair of hands on that subject.'

Cummings had blogged about the potential impermanence of any deal long before he arrived in Number 10 and he and Lewis had discussed how Bismarck had blasted through international legal norms by being proactive and aggressive in international affairs. But the lesson of Bismarck was also that this was not possible unless you had a good argument to win public backing. 'We needed a reason to make things blow up,' a political aide recalled. In February, Frost and Lewis mapped out on a whiteboard how things might play out in Northern Ireland.

In July and August, the EU gave Lewis the opening he was looking for. The British negotiating team became irritated by what they saw as a deliberate attempt by the EU to use the situation in Northern Ireland to force UK concessions. The operation of the protocol was not part of the trade talks, that was supposed to be resolved in the joint committee, between Michael Gove and Commission vice president Maroš Šefčovič. However, Barnier's team hinted to the UK side that, if a deal was not done, the EU would be able to dictate which goods would have to be checked at ports on the Irish sea and which would have to pay tariffs.

Frost said, 'We saw the Northern Ireland Protocol start to be weaponised in the talks – not to shape the agreement, but to try to take away our no-deal option. We faced various threats that Northern Ireland would be "cut off" and we were even told that we would "not be able to move one kilo of butter from GB to Northern Ireland".'[7] He added, 'I think the credible walk away option was really important in 2020.'[8]

In response, Lewis proposed that Johnson follow a 'madman strategy', wielding a legal cudgel to prevent Northern Ireland being used as a stick with which to beat the government – in so doing he would be threatening the total breakdown of talks and the destruction of the protocol as a meaningful piece of law. It was reckless and bold, and Johnson and Cummings loved it. The chosen vessel for this fresh collision between Vote Leave's sensibilities and the usual way of doing things was the UK internal market bill, which was due in Parliament that autumn.

The genesis of this decision dated back to February, when Lewis joined a meeting in one of the Downing Street state rooms, in which officials from the Department for Business explained that, as a result of an arrangement Theresa May's government had struck with the SNP, the UK internal market would legally cease to exist at the end of the year when powers currently held in Brussels were passed back. Instead 'common frameworks' had been struck to ensure the Scottish government would not use their powers to undermine the Union. Lewis looked at John Bew, Johnson's foreign policy adviser who was from Northern Irish stock, and passed him a note: 'This is fucking mental.' A gentleman's agreement with a party whose main policy was to break up the Union was not going to work. Bew agreed, expletives deleted and passed one back: 'We're going to have to pass some legislation.'

The issue was ensuring that goods continued to flow between different parts of the UK – exactly the same issue between the Great British mainland and Northern Ireland. Lewis spoke to Frost, Cummings and other members of the Vote Leave team. 'I think I've got a plan here,' he said. 'We need a Cassis de Dijon case.' Cummings laughed and clapped at the audacity of it. He got it at once. Others looked blank.

Lewis's plan was to take inspiration from one of the foundational cases of European law to forge a path for Brexit Britain. The case, from 1979, came about because cassis, a French liqueur with alcohol content of 16 per cent, could not be sold as 'liqueur' in Germany, where the law stipulated that such drinks had a minimum strength of 25 per cent. The European Court ruled that products in one EU country were also legal in other EU countries. It then forced member states to agree on common standards, making it a key driver of the internal market. Lewis saw the possibilities of a law which drove integration between England, Scotland, Wales and, most importantly for the negotiations, Northern Ireland as well. Which was where his legal textbook – *Constitutional and Administrative Law* by O. Hood Phillips and Paul Jackson – came in.

Lewis and Braverman worked together, but in such a way that they did not alert officials. For public consumption, they helped Gove and his team write a bill which would strengthen mutual recognition – Cassis de Dijon-style – between England and Scotland. In secret, Lewis and Braverman drew up additional clauses enabling ministers to override the Northern Ireland Protocol. These they discussed in clandestine meetings at Braverman's house. After the leaks over prorogation, the last thing Johnson's team needed was the civil service getting wind of what they were planning. Braverman, initially, went to specialist lawyers in constitutional and international law outside government, bypassing the government legal service.

They both also consulted Frost since the goal would be to threaten to break international law to get the EU to move in a few, carefully defined areas. 'Our view was always that this was a tactic, rather than something we wanted to do,' said one of those involved. 'The optimal solution by far would be that the EU freaked out when we went full Bismarck and chose to move.' The three things which could trigger the notwithstanding clauses were: the possibility of tariffs on goods moving inside the UK, from Britain into Northern Ireland; the use of export forms on goods going the other way from GB to NI; and EU state aid rules applying in Great Britain. The plan was to argue that 'we deem these things, which are essential to the integrity of the country, to be above and beyond international law compliance'.

All three things 'utterly enraged' Johnson. Despite his setback in the Supreme Court the previous year, the prime minister was '100 per cent' behind the bill. Indeed, he grew steadily angrier throughout June as the full implications of what he had signed up to in 2019 became clearer. 'Fundamentally, Boris hated, hated, hated the whole Northern Ireland Protocol,' said one aide. 'He hated that he had to sign it, and it became increasingly clear to him what full implementation meant.' Johnson began approaching members of the negotiating team and saying, 'You're not going weak now, are you?' In one meeting on the implementation of the protocol, Gove and his special adviser Henry Newman explained that meat could not go from GB to NI, so they had decided to seek a transition period from the EU so Northern Ireland shops could source their meat from the Republic. 'Boris went absolutely mental, from zero to a hundred,' a witness said. 'He started shouting about how the UK has been built on the free circulation of pork pies.'

Lewis knew the gravity of breaking international law. 'This is a very serious thing that we're doing,' he told colleagues. 'We're doing it because the consequences [of the protocol] in Northern Ireland are a catastrophe.' The analogy he used about how to ramp up the pressure, however, was literally inflammatory. 'We're going to lock all the doors with us and the EU without them realising and then set the place on fire. We control the one window out and it's on our terms how everyone can get out.'

To move things forward, however, the Office of the Parliamentary Council (OPC) had to be tasked with writing the legislation and, under the influence of Jonathan Jones, the head of the government legal service, many of the young OPC lawyers objected to the plan. 'They were trying to use the civil service code,' an adviser recalled. 'Jonathan Jones was adopting this fringe legal view that it would somehow even be illegal for civil servants to work on preparing the bill.'

Jones recalled, 'I had been tipped off that there was a willingness in government to legislate, unilaterally, to disapply the bits of the protocol that it didn't like. Lawyers were very concerned about this, and I thought they were right to be concerned about it. The government was prepared … to do something that was deliberately and flatly and expressly contrary to the UK's international obligations.' No one disagreed that the bill would be 'contrary' to the treaty. 'Then the question became, "But is it okay to do that?" It's not really a legal question. It's your view as to whether there is a constitutional or moral or proprietary basis for breaking the law. The attorney general had persuaded herself that this was constitutionally proper. I had made it clear that I thought this was a problem, and I couldn't see how I could endorse that position.'[9]

Jones, along with Richard Keen, the advocate general in Scotland, demanded the external legal advice: 'Can you formally tell us as law officers, what's the legal basis on which you think this is okay?' This caused 'a bit of a flurry'. Number 10 had 'a hissy fit' and Frost demanded to know, 'On whose authority is that being done?'

'On my authority,' Jones replied.

He got a call from Braverman, who was 'furious', saying it was her job to be the law officer, reminding Jones of his 'obligations under the bar code, and the civil service codes and the Official Secrets Act'.

'I don't need any advice on those things, thank you very much,' he said.

After 'two fiery meetings' with Braverman, Jones was 'quite emotional', a witness recalled, while a second said, 'Jonathan was implacable and saying this is an "abomination" and "a disgrace to the United Kingdom".'

Lewis knew the key was to get a formal 'direction' from the prime minister. Braverman tried phoning Johnson but found him distracted, the sound of a crying baby and a yapping Dilyn in the background, then an irate Johnson: 'Get off, fucking dog!'

In late August, Frost drove Lewis and Chris Jenkins, Braverman's special adviser, to Chequers. They found Johnson still exhausted from his brush with Covid, the gallery room upstairs 'boiling hot' to help the PM recuperate. They needed his backing to thwart Jones, but they also needed Johnson to talk to Michael Gove to prevent him opposing the plan. Johnson took 'copious notes' then escorted them back downstairs, breathing heavily. When they reached the entrance hall, the prime minister 'collapsed on one of the hall chairs'. As he sat there, still 'slumped' and recovering his breath, his mobile phone rang. It was Gove. Johnson did not have his notes with him. 'We're sitting there thinking: this is going to be a train wreck,' one aide recalled. 'It was a tour de force – charming, accurate, perfect exposition. He performed as best as we could have hoped and got it over the line, all without notes, all while exhausted.'

On another occasion in August a Downing Street adviser tried to raise Braverman, but she had gone on holiday without her mobile phone, because she wanted to spend a week offline – an astonishing decision for a senior minister. Eventually, the adviser called her husband. 'I'm afraid I can't raise her,' he said. 'She's in a flotation tank.'

In the final week of August the plan went to GB(S), the Global Britain (Strategy) subcommittee of the cabinet, which had replaced XS now the UK had left the EU. This was the only Brexit strategy meeting which anyone remembers Cummings attending all year. Jess Glover, a director general in the transition taskforce, presented the plan, stressing how extraordinary the proposal was. She was blunt: this was a breach of international law, it would have serious ramifications for the UK's standing and questions about the rule of law. There might be a Supreme Court case. Braverman set out why she thought it was lawful and necessary. 'It's the only option we have,' she said. Some say Gove spoke disapprovingly, but he supported the plan on the basis it was a 'targeted' move, not a blanket disapplication of the protocol. Johnson, Braverman, Priti Patel, Liz Truss, Alok Sharma and George Eustice all backed the plan. The one dissenting voice was Rishi Sunak. 'It was basically all unanimous save for Rishi,' a source present said. The chancellor was the last to speak and concerned about the potential impact on the economy if it looked like the government's signature on a treaty was worthless. 'I have to say that breaking international law is a massive thing and it does have an impact on people's confidence,' he said. 'I have to raise my concerns about it.' But Sunak could read the room and he backed off.

Cummings brought the meeting to a close, unusually sounding a word of caution. 'We have to understand that this is a very different tactic to what we were doing last year. Last year we were deliberately ramping up issues like prorogation because we were seeking to raise the temperature. This is a very delicate decision we have made, an informed decision, but just play it very calmly. Do not seek to heighten the drama, leave it with Frosty. We just play it all extremely cool from this point onwards.'

That week, Mark Sedwill, who was in his final days as cabinet secretary, was overheard telling another official, 'They're looking for a green light to break the law.' In the key meeting he was silent. It was left to his successor Simon Case to write a 'comfort letter' to government lawyers telling them they could proceed with the drafting of the bill.

Within a week cool had turned to hot rage as the proposal leaked to the *FT*'s Peter Foster, who triggered Vote Leavers with both his scepticism about Brexit and his impeccable contacts. 'Sections of the internal market bill ... are expected to "eliminate the legal force of parts of the withdrawal agreement" in areas including state aid and Northern Ireland customs,' he reported. 'The move would "clearly and consciously" undermine the agreement on Northern Ireland that Boris Johnson signed last October.'[10] Those who had scoffed at the *Sunday Times* story six months earlier had to eat their words.

When the proposal became public, on the evening of 6 September, all hell broke loose. The leak, which Cummings again blamed on the government legal office, robbed Downing Street of the chance to roll the pitch and brief the story how they wanted it represented. 'I don't think we ever quite recovered the narrative,' a senior official said.

Frost and Lewis went into a crisis meeting with the Number 10 press team. Frost was clear: 'We need to own this now. You can't try to be mealy-mouthed.' A colleague said, 'We'd taken out the baseball bat and we had to say, "Yes, this is a baseball bat."'

On Monday 7th, Brandon Lewis, the Northern Ireland secretary, was summoned to the Commons to answer an urgent question. His name-sake Oliver Lewis (no relation) signed off a parliamentary briefing which confirmed that in a 'limited and specific way' the internal market bill did break international law. Even Braverman did not think he should say this 'in such blunt terms'. She suggested they stress the 'specific and limited' applications of the bill. Frost, however, was 'really clear' that he wanted to 'go nuclear'. He said, 'It's incredibly helpful for the dynamics of the negotiation if we put a gun on the table.' This was seen at the time as incendiary, a boastful two fingers to Brussels, but Number 10 concluded there was little point denying the obvious and did not want to be caught misleading Parliament. 'It is legal in domestic law, illegal in international law,' Frost said. 'That's how our constitution works.'

The EU negotiating team in London for the latest round of talks was outraged. Theirs was a union of laws whose principle was pooling resources to work together. This was anathema. It was even more surprising from a country which had been the chief advocate of the rule of law for centuries. When Frost and Lewis arrived at Lancaster House for pre-dinner drinks on Monday evening, they were met with a phalanx of European faces cast in stone, knuckles white as they clutched flutes of champagne like they were phials of hydrochloric acid. Frost made a joke about the weather not being very nice. The reply came from Clara Martínez Alberola, 'It's not the only thing that's not very nice this evening and that we have to talk about.' The dinner was 'just brutal'. Frost tried to dance around the issue, as if attempting 'normal diplomacy'. Barnier and his aides kept bringing it back to the main point. 'We need to talk about this Northern Ireland thing.' Frost eventually said, 'You have to understand that this reflects the prime minister's determined view to protect the integrity of the country. We must have a reasonable resolution on Northern Ireland which reflects the principles we agreed to last year.' Lewis then gave a fifteen-minute briefing, explaining, 'We don't want to use these powers, but we're prepared to.' Paulina Dejmek-Hack voiced the disbelieving anger of the Commission, when she said, 'This is not the way the UK negotiates.' As they were leaving, Lewis turned to Frost and said, 'We've finally convinced them that we're not Theresa May.'

Maroš Šefčovič called an emergency meeting with Gove for the following day, Tuesday 8 September. Gove took a 'kicking' from the commission vice president. 'I wish we could put it on Netflix,' said one EU official who was present. All twenty-seven EU governments dialled in to follow it. Gove was forced to listen as an Irish official, who appeared via video link, gave 'the speech of her life', pointing out that Dublin had not been contacted about the bill despite Britain's responsibility under the Good Friday Agreement to notify the Irish Republic of significant developments in Northern Ireland.[11]

Downing Street expected this reaction from the EU. What they did not anticipate was the buckets of ordure from Tory grandees. Former party leaders William Hague and Michael Howard and former chancellor Norman Lamont denounced the plan publicly and contacted Johnson to tell him he had gone too far. Accusing ministers of using arguments of 'lawbreakers everywhere', a 'dismayed' Howard said, 'How can we reproach other countries – Russia, China, Iran – if their behaviour becomes reprehensible when we ourselves have such scant regard for the treaties we sign up to, when we ourselves set such a lamentable example?'

Gavin Barwell said, 'It's rather ironic to me that a bunch of people who told me they couldn't vote for [May's] deal because the UK could never break international law, and the only way out [of the backstop] was to break international law, are now very happy and all advocating breaking international law.'

The backlash prompted a classic 'wobble' from Johnson. An aide recalled, 'It was the usual thing. Boris was absolutely gung-ho, more strongly for it than anybody. He had a wobble in the week after Brandon's statement. He didn't like people like Hague and Howard criticising him. But then he fired himself up. That's just how he is.'

It was too much for Jonathan Jones. The head of the legal service sat tight while the clauses were drafted but when the cabinet decided to introduce the bill they 'crossed the Rubicon'. He said, 'The government was putting itself deliberately on a course that would have contravened international law ... I felt I had to resign.'[12] On 8 September, Jones wrote a letter to Simon Case and Mark Sedwill saying he was off. Intent to break the law was his trigger. Braverman took the view that only when the notwithstanding clauses were used would a technical breach of the law have occurred. James Eadie, the Treasury solicitor, sided with the ministers. He saw no problem with the bill being written, or even passed into law, a judgement which reinforced Braverman's view that Jones had let his personal views distort his legal opinions.

The Vote Leave team was delighted when Jones left. His post-resignation tweets, which assailed the Johnsonites, confirmed for Braverman what she presumed his personal views to be. Jones told one confidant, 'I don't think she's any sort of lawyer. She was the worst possible choice as an attorney general.' A Braverman ally hit back: 'In his resignation letter he referred to a case that had been overturned on appeal. So, it shows he wasn't a particularly good lawyer.' Jones was not alone, though. On 16 September, Richard Keen resigned as advocate general for Scotland, telling Johnson he found it 'increasingly difficult to reconcile what I consider to be my obligations as a law officer with your policy intentions'. Two days later, barrister Amal Clooney, wife of film star George, quit as the UK's special envoy on media freedom, calling the government's actions 'lamentable'.

The impact of the UKIM bill was not as clear cut as partisans on either side would have it. Despite the turmoil and bad feeling, the publication of the bill did not damage the negotiations, which made more progress that week than they had for a couple of months. The EU briefed that the UK was a 'rogue state', but inside the windowless basement of the Department for Business, where the negotiators met when they were in London, a 'professional' atmosphere prevailed. Frost recalled, 'These UKIM provisions understandably caused fury on the EU side – though they were always very careful not to let outrage get in the way of the FTA talks.'[13] Frost's team believe the shock uncorked the talks. 'However much they hated it, I think that did change the psychology a bit.'

In Brussels they insisted that the loss of trust created by the UK's actions made the Commission drive a harder bargain on the level playing field than they would have otherwise. 'The UK internal market bill was a disastrous negotiating tactic by the UK,' Stefaan De Rynck from the Commission declared afterwards. 'It solidified the unity of the twenty-seven, at the crucial moment when we were going into the end game of the negotiations ... It's mindboggling, that kind of behaviour.'[14]

In the round, the bill may ultimately have been counterproductive, but on the issues it was designed to alleviate, it worked. On 17 September the British government published a formal statement on when the three killer clauses would be deployed, which Lewis (channelling Cummings) called 'our terrorist demands'. It said the notwithstanding clauses would be triggered if the EU was guilty of 'a material breach of its duties of good faith' in a way that undermined 'the fundamental purpose of the Northern Ireland Protocol'. It then listed five examples of such behaviour, including imposing tariffs or VAT on goods passing between Great Britain and Northern Ireland 'in ways that are not related to the real risk of goods entering the EU single market' and where 'insistence on paperwork requirements (export declarations) for NI goods going to GB' compromised 'unfettered access'. The EU eventually gave way on all five.

While the bill left some critics concerned the government did not know what it was doing, there were still worries in Number 10 that, with the crunch final stage talks approaching, Johnson remained functionally ignorant of key issues. Shortly after the UKIM bill was introduced in September, Frost and Lewis instituted a series of 'teach-in' sessions for the prime minister to go over the key issues ahead of the talks. The first was on 25 September on the customs union. After Frost outlined where the negotiations had reached and the likely end state for customs checks, others in the meeting were staggered when Johnson said, 'No, no, no Frosty, fuck this, what happens with a deal?'

Frost stopped studying his papers and looked up. Regarding Johnson carefully he said, 'PM, this is what happens with a deal, that's what leaving the customs union means ... That *is* if we get a deal, Prime Minister.' The no-deal scenario, which Johnson eulogised as the Australian option, was even worse. Cummings recalled, 'The PM's face was priceless. He sat back in his chair and looked around the room with appalled disbelief and shook his head. Horrified officials' phones pinged around the Cabinet table.' Simon Case messaged Cummings, 'I now realise how you managed to get Brexit done.'[15] Two other participants in the meeting confirmed Cummings' account.

MPs going to Number 10 to lobby for changes to the withdrawal agreement found Johnson similarly detached. 'They'll ask questions of Boris,' a Eurosceptic said. 'He'll look at his feet, he'll look at his hands and bluster. He'll say, "Frosty has got that." It is clear from the verbal ticks that he genuinely doesn't know.'

Twelve days before the next European Council meeting, due to start on 15 October, Johnson and von der Leyen had another phone call. The prime minister pressed for 'intensified' talks and sought to inject a fresh deadline. Amid concern in Number 10 that the EU might just run out the clock, he said the UK would leave without a deal unless it looked by 15 October like one was on the cards. 'We are ready to trade on Australian-style terms,' he told von der Leyen. The previous week progress had been made on state aid rules and governance, but there were 'significant gaps' on fish – code for deadlock.

As the crunch moment approached, member states became more proactive, led by Emmanuel Macron. France, with Spain, was the leading member of the 'Coastal Eight' group of countries who were piling pressure on Barnier's team not to give ground on fishing rights. The weekend before the Council meeting, Johnson called on Macron to compromise or watch Britain walk away from the talks. Annick Girardin, the French fishing minister, responded by saying, 'Fishermen would rather have no agreement than a bad agreement.' Girardin described fish stocks that would soon belong to Britain under international law as 'European resources'. The Coastal Eight were continuing to demand the same access to British waters as they had before Brexit.

Frost used a House of Lords committee hearing to shift his position, announcing that Britain was prepared to do a 'multi-year' deal on fish. In return, he wanted Barnier to use the Council meeting to get the approval of the member states to begin the final push for a deal. That meant an EU commitment to move to daily sessions of the talks and end 'parallelism', allowing detailed work on legal texts.

What followed was a rerun of the Strasbourg meeting in 2018, where member states rejected Theresa May's Chequers plan outright. Once more, the leaders were more truculent than the EU institutions. The draft Council conclusions called on Barnier to 'intensify negotiations with the aim of ensuring that an agreement can be applied from 1 January 2021'. Ursula von der Leyen had been taken ill and was unable to shape the outcome. Over dinner, the text was changed, following a pincer movement by Macron and the Dutch prime minister Mark Rutte. The plan to 'intensify' the talks was removed and replaced with 'continue'. There was an even more provocative addition. The Council 'calls on the UK to make the necessary moves to make an agreement possible'. The member states were signalling that they were done with compromises. If Britain wanted a deal, it would have to shift its position. Macron used his press conference to escalate tensions, boasting that the new wording was 'not meant to make the prime minister happy' and warning that unless Johnson met his 'terms and conditions' there would be no-deal. 'Under no condition can our fishermen be sacrificed during Brexit,' he said. 'If conditions aren't met, it's possible we don't have an agreement. We are ready for that.'[16]

When Frost and Lewis confronted members of Barnier's Task Force UK about the Council conclusions, the message was, 'Don't worry, these don't mean anything.' After years of being told that Council conclusions were holy writ, the British team threw these words back in their face. 'You can't spend five years lecturing us that these documents come from Mt Sinai then claim that these ones aren't real,' Lewis said.

Frost and Lewis went back to London to see Johnson. Again, Cummings made a rare appearance. 'As long as Michel Barnier is driving this, we're going nowhere,' Frost said. Only by walking away could the negotiating team 'create enough drama' to get EU leaders engaged. 'We've got to go for the blow up,' Lewis said. A senior source explained, 'All the serious eyes in Brussels were still on the pandemic. Nobody was watching the fact that Barnier, who is not very good, was just trotting out sound bites, standing in a ditch, arms folded.' Johnson told the pair, 'We have to be tough. Australia is a beautiful country.'

The following day, 16 October, Johnson recorded a televised statement in which he said there would be no more trade talks unless the EU adopted a 'fundamental change of approach'. He warned the country would have to prepare, yet again, for no-deal on 1 January. His official spokesman, James Slack, went further: 'The trade talks are over – the EU have effectively ended them yesterday when they said they did not want to change their negotiating position.'

Von der Leyen responded on Twitter that 'our negotiation team will go to London next week to intensify these negotiations'. But when Frost and Barnier had a video conference call that evening, Frost said there was 'no basis for negotiations' unless Brussels came up with a new plan over the weekend. Also on the call from the British side were Tim Barrow and Lindsay Appleby, another of the deputy negotiators, who would go on to be British ambassador to the EU. Lewis was sitting with Frost, but out of shot. For the EU Clara Martínez Alberola and Paulina Dejmek-Hack were in a separate room to Barnier. 'I'm not coming with any texts,' Barnier said. 'The European Council is clear.'

'Then don't bother coming,' said Frost. The moment was made more awkward by Barnier appearing not to grasp what Frost was saying. 'David had to say it two or three times until he really got it,' a witness said. When he finally understood, 'Barnier just lost his shit completely. He was screaming at us pulling out of the meeting.' The Frenchman yelled, 'You want to end the talks, don't you? Admit it, you just want to end the talks.'

Frost replied, 'No, Michel, we do not want to end the talks. But we can't have the talks proceed on the basis of the European Council conclusions. The European Council has basically said it doesn't want a negotiation, it wants concessions, and we can't engage in such a process.'

Barnier concluded that Johnson's team used the changes to the communiqué as 'a pretext' for abandoning the talks because they did not want to make concessions themselves. He regarded Frost's stance as 'almost childish'.[17] Incensed, he repeated his charge, once, twice, three times more: 'You want to end the talks, don't you? Admit you want to end the talks!' At this point Lewis began to laugh so much that he fell into shot. Frost had to kick him under the table.

Once he had calmed down, Barnier said the EU was ready to work on legal text, 'Our position is simply that, if we have to work on a legal text, then it should be done across all tables.'[18] Parallelism lived. Barnier told colleagues later the whole thing was 'theatre' but he was also annoyed with the member states for playing politics with his carefully crafted language. It was clear, even in Brussels, that Barnier was not gripping the negotiations in a way which promised a successful resolution.

The 'controlled explosion' of the walkout persuaded von der Leyen that she needed to intervene to steer things in the right direction. After a series of phone calls between the major players, her office got in touch with Barrow to say that Stéphanie Riso would be present at the next round of talks. Riso had been a key subordinate to Barnier during the May government's negotiations but had been promoted to be the key aide to the Commission president. Now she was returning to save the day.

When they met again with Riso present, Barnier announced, deferentially, 'We are very pleased to be joined by Ms Riso from the president's office.' He then handed over proceedings to her. Riso was a blast of fresh air. 'Let's cut the crap,' she said. 'What is the form of words that we need to say that means you can come back, your head held high to a negotiating table. What are those words and can we make sure they don't embarrass my president?' A British negotiator said, 'Suddenly there was serious engagement and dialogue back and forth. She sat there doing all the work, the EU team huddling round her, while Michel played on his phone.'

Barnier had one final key role to play, though. On 21 October, he made his final speech to the European Parliament as chief negotiator. It was his most important. Amid a Gaullist tour d'horizon, Barnier delivered the language thrashed out by Riso and Frost. The video showed him clutching a sheet of paper with the key paragraphs highlighted in fluorescent pen.

Adopting an emollient tone, Barnier said the EU wanted 'an agreement that is to the mutual benefit of each party, that respects the autonomy and sovereignty of each party and that reflects a balanced compromise'. Tearing up the Council conclusions that only Britain needed to move, he said compromises 'are needed from both sides to reach an agreement'. Barnier then slipped in the excised language and dumped parallelism. 'We are prepared to intensify discussions on all the issues and to do this on the basis of legal texts,' he said. Saying a deal was 'within reach', he explained that the EU's negotiating position was based on European interests which were 'compatible with respect for British sovereignty, which is a legitimate concern of Boris Johnson's government'. He added, 'Any future agreement will respect the decision-making autonomy of the European Union and the sovereignty of the United Kingdom … We have understood the red lines set out by Boris Johnson: on the role of the European Court of Justice; on the UK's legislative autonomy; on fisheries.'

Barnier continued to insist that 'fair play' level playing field rules must apply because of Britain's proximity to the EU and its forty-seven years of 'economic interconnection' – 'This situation is not comparable with any other.'

Barnier grumpily wrote in his diary that the whole episode was a 'psychodrama orchestrated by London'[19] and that he had been a defender of British sovereignty throughout the process, but it did not seem that way to the UK negotiating team. Nonetheless, after the Frenchman had finished, a friend of Lewis' who worked in the Commission texted him, 'Never has so much been said about British sovereignty on the floor of the European Parliament.'

It was game on again.

CUMMINGS AND GOINGS

(or the Cain Mutiny)

May to November 2020

On 12 November 2020 Boris Johnson had been prime minister for 478 days. He sat on a majority of 80 and was confidently pondering the prospects of ten years in power. He had survived a brush with death and, after a difficult start, weathered the world's worst pandemic. However, the events of that day would begin a string of events which brought his premiership to a crashing halt.

That evening he and Dominic Cummings had an argument which paved the way for the chief adviser's departure from Downing Street. Earlier that day Lee Cain had decided he was leaving after losing a power struggle with Carrie Symonds. Twenty-four hours later Cummings walked out of Number 10 for the last time.

Cummings believed that someone in Carrie's camp was briefing against one of his close allies. He told Johnson, 'You'd better get a grip on that, or things are going to blow up out of your control. When we leave, your girlfriend is going to say a bunch of shit and I'm going to hold you personally responsible for what she says.'

In the version of this conversation which Cummings relayed to his allies, Johnson, taken aback, said, 'I can't control her.'

'I don't give a fuck,' said Cummings. 'I'm holding you personally responsible, and you know what that means for you, don't you?'

'Are you threatening me?' Johnson asked.

'Yes, I'm fucking threatening you.'

The Johnson camp confirmed the conversation took place, though they stressed that the threats were to Carrie. If a more combustible exchange has occurred between a prime minister and chief adviser, it has never been recorded. The disintegration of the defining relationship in government, a partnership forged in the heat of the Brexit campaigns of both 2016 and 2019, was now complete. The prime minister was on notice: one wrong move and Cummings would try to bring him down. Twenty months later, through a combination of Cummings' desire to destroy and Johnson's tendency to self-destruct, he was gone.

The events which led to this explosive denouement began in May, when Lee Cain decided to permanently change the way government communicated with the public. He thought the Covid press conferences a success; they confirmed Vote Leave's view that it was better to talk directly to the public rather than through the filter of 'the mainstream media'. The director of communications drew up a plan to create a new media suite in 9 Downing Street, at a cost of £2 million, to hold press conferences, and decided to appoint a new Number 10 press secretary to front the televised briefings. Cain's blueprint for reform also involved firing a large number of civil service press officers across Whitehall, replacing them with a central media unit, to ensure government departments were communicating a single message more effectively.

Cain took the idea to Cummings, who sought Johnson's approval. He warned that the plan would be controversial. 'A whole lot of officials are going to go mental,' he said. 'We are going to start a process to hire someone to do this job. If you've got someone you want to be part of the process, say now. If you don't want to do the whole thing, tell Lee now.' Johnson said he supported the plan. 'Let Chairman Lee continue,' he said. Cain's preferred candidate was Sophy Ridge of Sky News. 'He did ask me,' she confirmed later. 'That's the easiest "No" I've ever given.'[1] Johnson suggested one name, Riz Lateef, a presenter for BBC London who he had known as mayor, who eventually applied. Cain was quickly inundated with applications from people wanting to be Britain's first ever version of the White House press secretary.

Everything changed at a dinner at Chequers in July where Johnson and Carrie hosted Rishi Sunak and his wife Akshata Murty. They were joined by Allegra Stratton, who had left broadcast journalism to be Sunak's spin doctor, and her husband James Forsyth, the political editor of the *Spectator*. Stratton had helped make Sunak the most popular politician in the country, with a slick social media operation and professional videos, courtesy of Cass Horowitz, son of Anthony Horowitz, the thriller writer. Stratton was a believer in 'good Boris', the One Nation conciliator who had won in London and who the pandemic had forced back into existence. Her views were in tune with those of Symonds, who believed Vote Leave's taste for permanent warfare to be damaging her partner, though this was the first she had heard of the plan for a press secretary. 'You used to be the most popular politician in Britain,' Stratton said, offering ideas to help him win back public approval. She declared the press secretary role her 'dream job'. Johnson said 'Great!' and urged her to do it, an awkward moment as Sunak, her current boss, sat watching. 'Rishi was quite pissed off about it,' a witness recalled. A ministerial aide said, 'Boris wants to be loved and he saw that Allegra had helped Rishi become popular. He wanted some of that.'

Cain was furious when he heard about the exchanges. He was no longer in control of a process he had set in train. He regarded Stratton as unsuited to the role, an intellectual where he wanted a street fighter. He believed Symonds was making a power play, challenging his authority. He encouraged others to apply. Ellie Price, a BBC regional political reporter, performed well and emerged as the challenger to Stratton. Carrie, in turn, believed that, since Johnson had offered Stratton the job at Chequers, Cain created the process in order to thwart her.

Cain arranged mock press conferences, which were filmed, with members of the Downing Street press team firing difficult questions at the candidates. Price took a 'folksy' and relaxed approach, Stratton was strident, combative. Those in the room, including James Slack, the highly experienced official spokesman, agreed Price was by far the better candidate. The final round was a 'chemistry test' interview with Johnson. Stratton, with whom he already had chemistry, emerged as the winner. On 8 October, the news was made public.

It made sense that Johnson had the final say over who spoke for his government, but for Cummings, the episode was precisely what he had sought to avoid. The Vote Leave version is that Johnson, at his most imperious, acknowledged he had changed his mind but added, 'What's the point of being king if you can't just do what you want?'

'I understand your point of view,' said Cummings. 'But from our point of view, what the fuck's the point of working with you if you're just going to cause all of this chaos? We've just wasted six months.'

It was not the first time Johnson had clashed with his aides over media-facing personnel. In September, Downing Street had grown tired of leaks about the government's travel corridors. Cain phoned Neil

Tweedie, a former *Telegraph* journalist who was special adviser to Grant Shapps, the transport secretary. 'If they carry on, we are going to have to start shooting people,' he said. Shortly afterwards Tweedie was blamed for a leak concerning quarantine for those returning from holiday in Spain. Cain called him and Tweedie, instead of taking his bollocking on the chin, hit back so hard that Cain fired him on the spot.

When Johnson heard he went ballistic. Tweedie was an old colleague from the *Telegraph*. He told Cain the spad had to be reinstated. Cain refused. Johnson, in a state of agitation, called Cummings late on Friday night from Chequers. Cummings was still at work in Number 10. 'You can't do this,' Johnson complained.

Cummings lost his temper, 'I haven't been involved. I'm dealing with different problems, some of which are caused by you. And now you're calling me up, arguing about a fucking spad who I've never even met and never talked to. Lee has fired him. He's fired. What the fuck are you doing calling me about it at eleven o'clock on a Friday night? Have you lost your fucking mind? If you don't think Lee's capable of making decisions, fire Lee, otherwise, what are we all doing here?'

Tweedie remained fired. In a piece for the *Mail*, published after Cummings and Cain had left, Tweedie condemned their 'schoolboy Mafioso language' and accused the pair of an 'abuse of power' which 'cast a malign pall over the heart of government'. He concluded, 'The Vote Leave mob, drunk on their success in the referendum and the election … revelled in their laddish, iconoclastic, adversarial approach … Ever alert to the inadequacies of those they regarded as inferiors, they were at the same time blind to their own glaring inadequacies as communicators and administrators.' The article might have been dictated by Symonds.[2]

Johnson was tired of being seen as Cummings' puppet. In October he snapped, 'Why do so many people around here care more what you think than what I think, I'm sick of it?'

Cummings responded, 'Because I've got a plan and I'll stick to it and I stick with people in tough times but they know you're listening to crazy nonsense from your girlfriend and you'll throw anybody under the bus.' He wrote later, 'Any normal politician would have been shocked and angry. Boris-SA [self-aware] just nodded.'[3]

By this time, 'Boris finally resolved that he had to get rid of Cummings,' a senior Tory said. One of Johnson's closest allies noted, 'From about the May time of that year, Dom had largely switched off. He wasn't driving anything. He was really interested in the ARPA stuff and nothing else. He didn't really appear at meetings. He checked out.' Henry Cook, one of Michael Gove's former spads who had impressed Johnson with his ability to capture his voice when writing speeches and op-eds during the general election, assumed more power. He was eventually made deputy chief of staff, alongside Cleo Watson and Katie Lam. But all that did was draw attention to what was really missing. 'We had three deputy chiefs of staff without a chief of staff,' a political aide recalled.

Over lunch at Chequers on 11 July, Johnson had discussed the chief of staff role with Sajid Javid, opening the way to a return. 'Not if Cummings is still there,' Javid replied.[4] More recently Johnson had phoned Lord Feldman, David Cameron's party chairman, and asked him to do the job. He was also unprepared to work with Cummings. Johnson was unhappy at the way Number 10 was functioning, detecting a lack of grip over the debacle concerning the downgrading of exam results in September and funding free school meals, a mess that twice put the government at odds with the footballer Marcus Rashford. 'He was very unhappy about that,' said a Number 10 official. The Vote Leavers blamed Johnson for that PR disaster. Cain had repeatedly told Johnson not to get into a stand-off with Rashford and had been ignored. Cummings recalled, 'He was told, "It's pointless fighting with Marcus Rashford because you'll never hold the line", does it anyway, collapses – then repeats the debacle weeks later.'[5]

Symonds encouraged Johnson to act. A Tory she had lunch with that autumn said, 'She told me her plan for the month was to get rid of Lee and Dom.' In the final week of September, Steve Baker told Times Radio that Johnson reminded him of Tolkien's King Theoden, who fell 'under the spell' of his advisers: 'Somebody needs to wake Theoden from his slumber.' In a meeting with MPs the following week, Johnson declared, 'I am not Theoden, I am Sauron', the malevolent necromancer who rules Mordor in *The Lord of the Rings*. There was only room for one 'dark lord' in Downing Street.

The final act of the drama began in the third week of October when Simon Case, the new cabinet secretary, approached Cain 'on behalf of the PM' about whether he would be interested in becoming chief of staff. Johnson had run the idea past Case and said it originated with Cummings and Cain, but it had also been suggested to Case by James Slack. Case said Cain seemed to be organised, disciplined and hard-working. Unlike

Cummings, he wanted to deliver for Johnson, not just for himself. He also thought it beneficial that Cain could be blunt with Johnson when necessary. 'What would everyone else think?' Johnson asked. Case asked around and received positive responses from Eddie Lister, Cleo Watson, Munira Mirza and Martin Reynolds. Some of these views were to change dramatically.

Seeing his opportunity, Cain wrote a note for Johnson on what was wrong with the Number 10 operation, sending it on 26 October. He helped Johnson to conclude that something had to change, setting in train events that would sweep both him and Cummings away. Cain's error, perhaps, was to be too frank in his criticisms of individuals. The team in Number 10 was 'underperforming' and 'fatally', he argued. 'We have too many people pursuing their agendas and not yours.' Cain also took aim at 'the lack of an agreed, understood and firmly communicated PM policy agenda' and said that Johnson, rather than let 'a thousand flowers bloom', needed to 'ruthlessly focus on three to five big ideas' to create 'a sense of direction that is currently lacking'. Meetings were 'flabby and unstructured' and staff were 'allowed to end-run', going directly to Johnson to get decisions made or changed, rather than through the private office.

Cain reserved his harshest words, however, for the policy unit under Munira Mirza, the private office, run by Martin Reynolds, and the whips' office. Complaining about the quality of special advisers, he wrote, 'The most egregious example of this is in the policy unit.' Cain said only 'one or two' of its sixteen staff were any good and most had jobs because of 'ideological purity (not even yours!), not competence'. He suggested Mirza was 'very talented' but 'not able to lead the team' and should take on a 'modified' role with the policy unit either shrunk under a 'new policy chief' or abolished altogether. Calling for 'Party Marty' Reynolds to be 'moved', Cain said the private office, which ought to be the 'engine room' of Number 10, 'lacks grip, drive and authority'. The part which looked, to others who heard about the memo, like a Vote Leave power grab came when Cain suggested the only people who ought to have direct access to the prime minister should be him, Cummings, the cabinet secretary, the principal private secretary and Eddie Lister.

Two days later, on 28 October, Cain had dinner at Chequers with the prime minister and Symonds. It was clear to him that she was hearing the chief of staff idea for the first time. 'They chatted about what was wrong with the operation, warts and all,' an insider said. Johnson said he agreed with Cain's assessments and would be keen for him to implement them. He did not offer him the job, but Cain left thinking he was in pole position. In his memo, Cain had made clear that his first proviso if he was to take the job was that he have 'the trust of you and Carrie'. The situation had acquired urgency because Cummings was leading the government's 'moonshot' programme for mass testing and had even less bandwidth than usual for running the Number 10 operation. Cain was already doing parts of the job and had won praise for his role, alongside Raab, in holding things together while Johnson had been in hospital. With Cummings focused on testing, Cain again assumed greater responsibilities. A Number 10 colleague said, 'People go to Lee when they want decisions taken. He knows what Boris thinks.'

Stratton's arrival felt like a challenge to Cain's authority. She took the job on the basis that she would report to the prime minister. Cain insisted she work to him. They clashed over whether Stratton would get a pay rise and an office (she didn't). Instead, she eschewed the press office and went to sit in another part of the building, a decision regarded as odd by her new colleagues. Cain insisted he appoint her deputy and said he wanted Ellie Price. Stratton saw that as an attempt to install the 'stop Allegra candidate'. She preferred Angus Walker, a former ITV colleague who was special adviser to Gavin Williamson, the education secretary. Stratton told Cain, 'I can't work with you.' She texted Johnson that she would quit and he should appoint Price instead.

In early November, Johnson asked Stratton back to Chequers for lunch with him and Symonds. There he said he was thinking about making Cain chief of staff. The two women told him it was a bad move. Both felt Cain's communications strategy was ineffective. Both also had concerns about the macho culture over which he and Cummings presided in Downing Street, which had made life uncomfortable for several young women advisers. 'Carrie just felt very clearly and firmly that he was wrong for Boris and for the government and for the agenda and for his relationships with people,' a friend said. 'She just felt he was at the heart of all the stuff that hadn't been working.'

Cain got wind of the conversation and wrote a letter of resignation. Johnson texted him to say he would not accept it. That Thursday, the PM waved Cain's letter at Stratton and made clear she would have to report to Cain. On her kitchen wall at home was a picture of Anthony

Scaramucci, who had survived as Donald Trump's communications director for eleven days. It did not look as if she would last much longer. On Sunday 8 November, Johnson cooked sausages while Cain mashed potato and swede into a lumpy accompaniment and the two ate together in the Downing Street garden. Over more than two hours they discussed the shortcomings of the operation. 'In the middle of this Covid crisis, it's your duty to the country to stay,' Johnson said.

The following day the mood in Number 10 was strange. One witness said Cain was 'walking around the building whistling', apparently confident. Stratton considered resigning. Johnson told her it was her duty to serve. 'It felt like a volcano was going to blow,' said one witness. 'You could see the smoke starting to swirl. The birds were flying away.'

At 7 p.m. on Monday, Johnson called in Cain and, according to the Vote Leave accounts, said he did want him to be chief of staff. He had sounded out Case and Lister. The cabinet secretary wanted more political grip. Lister, seventy-one, agreed to remain in Number 10 to help Cain bed into his new role. Allies of Cain say he asked for twenty-four hours to think about it and stressed again that he would need the backing of Symonds. Johnson's camp say he did not make a firm offer. 'It wasn't going to work,' said one of his closest allies. 'Lee was never offered it.'

Either way, the following evening, Tuesday 10th, the story leaked to *The Times*. Cain's enemies say he or Cummings briefed it to bounce Johnson into the appointment. Cain's allies accused Symonds of placing it to stop the plan in its tracks. Crucially, Johnson believed it was a Vote Leave operation. 'Boris was angry that it had been briefed without his authority,' a close ally recalled. 'Bounce to announce was the thing that fucked it for Dom and Lee's relationship with Boris.'

Ministers and MPs reacted with fury, contacting Johnson and his chief whip, Mark Spencer, to say Cummings had to go. Spencer said promoting Cain would 'lose the backbenchers'. At lunchtime on Wednesday, Laura Kuenssberg tweeted that Symonds was 'deeply unhappy about the plan', not something the political editor of the BBC would report unless she was certain. Carrie's friends claimed Vote Leave briefed her so Carrie would be blamed for their downfall.

Mirza was also furious. It seems likely that she and her husband Dougie Smith had seen Cain's memo with its criticisms of her. 'Munira was very against it,' a colleague recalled. 'Lee wanted to abolish the policy unit. I think the thing that killed it for Lee, was Munira saying, "No."'

The Cain mutiny exhumed long-standing ministerial hatred of Cummings and his culture of aggression. Allies of Symonds proactively told journalists they referred to the duo as 'the mad mullahs'. One senior cabinet minister branded Cummings David Koresh, after the cult leader who caused the slaughter at the Waco siege in Texas in 1993.

Symonds and Stratton both worked on Johnson. 'Carrie was depressed,' another friend said. 'She didn't think this was who Boris is.' Even allies of Cummings could see that things were slipping away. One said, 'Dom spent most of the last year telling people to fuck off. People who should have been his allies were not there for him.'

Symonds' cooperation and the change in attitude by Mirza and Smith answered Cain's query about whether Carrie would back him. In the Cain camp account, he confronted Johnson, who told him to deny the chief of staff story to the media. 'But you offered me the job,' he said. 'I've worked with you for four years, I am not fucking happy and I am going to quit. You have briefed against me.' Johnson asked him to stay, saying he could have any job he liked.[6]

The crunch moment came on Wednesday when Johnson had to break off these conversations to talk to the two most important women in his life – the Queen and his fiancée. At 6.30 p.m. the prime minister was in his study with Cain, when Reynolds told them the call was coming through from Buckingham Palace putting Johnson through for his weekly audience with the Queen, now a remote event because of coronavirus. Cain left the room. When Johnson reappeared, it was obvious he had been talking to Symonds. The PM was dishevelled and apologetic: 'I'm so sorry, Commissar. Carrie has been onto me. She says that you and Dom are totally against me. Oh my God, Lee, it's a disaster. What am I going to do?'[7] The 'trolley' had U-turned again.

Cain had reached the end of the road. 'Lee realised he would not have the support of Carrie to do the job,' a friend said. 'It was not a secret in the building that she had intervened.' Having pointed out that Johnson had reversed his position, apparently on the orders of his fiancée, he said, 'I've had enough', telling Johnson, 'The best thing you can do would be to accept my resignation.' He suggested James Slack replace him as director of communications. One minister acidly compared Carrie to Elizabeth I in *Blackadder II*: 'We've just seen who's queen.'

Oliver Lewis became deeply depressed. He could not believe that Johnson would turn on what he saw as the architects of their success.

When he heard that Cain was leaving, he went to the press office and found people in tears. Tired and angry, he announced to the room, 'Right, that's it, I'm done, I'm off', and went to clear his desk. Back in 9 Downing Street with Cara Phillips, his private secretary, he said, 'This is outrageous!' but realised he had missed a call from Johnson. Phillips' landline went. She said, 'Just FYI, the prime minister is currently walking over to talk to you.' Lewis was a key figure in the negotiating team but it is a measure of the sheer strangeness of Johnson's premiership that the prime minister was stalking around after his staff rather than summoning them to see him. Johnson asked Lewis to stay and assured him he was not going to weaken his negotiating position with Brussels, then asked, 'Where's Frosty?' Frost had already gone home. Eventually, he and Johnson spoke, with Frost saying he was not going to resign. But he was far from happy.

The accounts of the Johnson and Vote Leave camps, forever adversarial after this week, are irreconcilable. The chief of staff job was clearly a serious enough consideration that Johnson invited Cain to Chequers to talk about it and Cain penned a memo outlining how he would do the job. That Symonds was decisively opposed to the idea is also not in doubt. The most credible explanation for the rest of the confusion – one backed by partisans on both sides – is that Johnson had spent months playing off his aides and his partner and that the music finally stopped and he had to make a choice. A Number 10 adviser said, 'Boris loves to divide and rule. When he didn't want to do what Carrie wanted, he'd be up in the flat moaning about Dom and Lee. When he didn't want to do what they were telling him to do he'd be saying, he couldn't do it because Carrie was in his ear: "I can't control her." He's always thrived in chaos. But when it came to it, he had to side with Carrie.'

This approach of Johnson's was observed by many witnesses and, frankly, was less than either a talented and clear-sighted group of political aides or a loyal and politically experienced partner deserved. By making himself a firewall between them, there was no opportunity for the people who actually influenced his thinking to debate strategy, tactics or policy, for one side or the other to be seen to win and lose, which would have been a more honest way to proceed. Instead, neither side got a clear view of what the other was actually recommending or why, something which fed confusion, anger and paranoia on both sides. Having set himself up as the firewall, Johnson inevitably got burned.

Both Cain and Cummings were in the office on Thursday 12th, but the expectation was that they would both be gone by Christmas. Those in Number 10 reflected that Johnson and Cummings' relationship had never really recovered after Barnard Castle. The rows over lockdown and the 'chatty rat' had merely confirmed their different world views.

Critics pointed out that, however good Cummings' analysis, however good his suggested solutions to the sclerosis in government, he was the wrong person to deliver his own prescriptions. 'In Whitehall, to get stuff done you have to do it through the civil service but there has never been an acceptance of that from Team Dom,' one critic said. 'He kicked out a load of civil servants to set up his own ridiculous control room in the Cabinet Office – but he didn't even sit there himself. He always wanted to set up parallel structures that reported to him. For someone who was so keen on management books, he was remarkably ineffective.' Regarding officials as ignorant of political reality, he underpriced that some were more effective at Whitehall bureaucratic warfare than him.

Cummings told friends the people he got on best with were officials from 'the deep state'. But those who did not work closely with him obstructed him while ministers hated and feared him. 'They never saw themselves as serving the prime minister,' one said. 'The prime minister was an instrument to them. They were not interested in his agenda; they only cared about their own.' It is hard to dispute this.

From the Vote Leave side, the explanation about what went wrong was simpler. The thing that had changed was the attitude of Carrie. When Cummings and Johnson talked on Thursday evening, the adviser felt like she was present too. In the Vote Leave telling, the conversation began in conciliatory fashion, with Johnson bemoaning his lot. 'This whole thing with Caino is a shitshow,' the prime minister admitted.

Cummings asked, 'Are you going to make Allegra director of communications? I know you are doing what you've promised Carrie, but what part of your brain is telling you it's a good idea to lose Caino, who saved your arse on many occasions?'

Johnson, as he sometimes did in private, at least pretended to sympathise with Symonds' critics. 'She's doing my head in,' he said. The prime minister discussed the prospect of getting Simon Case to use his influence with the royal household to get Carrie a job with the Duchess of Cambridge working on her net zero campaign. Case later admitted he discussed work 'opportunities' for Carrie with the Royal Foundation which administered the Duke and Duchess of Cambridge's Earthshot prize for environmental innovation.[8]

Then Johnson asked, 'When is the last time you spoke to …' He named a *Telegraph* journalist.

'I've never heard of them,' said Cummings. 'I've never spoken to them.' Then, in Cummings' account, he noticed Johnson looking at his phone. 'You're reading out questions from Carrie to ask me about the media,' he said. 'What has she done to your fucking mind? Listen to you. You're asking me to get the cabinet secretary to get her a job. Then you are literally reading out questions, that she's texted you.'

Outside the office staff could hear raised voices. Johnson did not deny it. 'I know, she's driven me crazy.' A pause. 'But are you with me?'

'Are you out of your mind?'

What came next, Cummings' explicit threat to Johnson ('Yes, I'm fucking threatening you'), is not disputed in its essence, only in its emphasis and the manner of its delivery. Another very senior figure in Number 10, who spoke immediately afterwards with the prime minister, confirmed that there was a confrontation: 'It was the day before Cummings left.' Johnson recalled it as a telephone conversation but there were several conversations the following day as well.

There was also a coded threat to Carrie. Her messages with Cummings had mostly been friendly, but allies say the last one he sent her was very different in tone. While suggesting he did not personally think she was responsible for Johnson hiring Stratton, other people in Number 10 did and that would end up being a 'big problem' for her and Johnson. She took this to mean that Cummings would ensure it would become a problem for her. 'He threatened to attack Carrie in the media,' Johnson told one confidant. 'That's what he did.'

The following day, fittingly, given the horror show now unfolding, was Friday the 13th. The briefing war began in earnest, with both sides giving as good as they got. Johnson and Cummings had two or three further conversations, made more surreal by the fact that Cummings had had a wisdom tooth extracted and spent the day clutching cold cans of Diet Coke to his face. Johnson thought he was faking it, comparing it to John Major's wisdom tooth operation during the fall of Margaret Thatcher. An ally of Symonds said Johnson 'was very uncomfortable with' Cain and Cummings remaining 'in the building'. Another branded them 'squatters' who had to go. The Vote Leavers were adamant it was Carrie, not Boris, who wanted them gone.

It was also open season on Symonds by allies of Cain and Cummings. One claimed she called Johnson's private office 'more than twenty times a day demanding that he leave meetings to call her back', a gross exaggeration, dismissed as untrue by civil servants. Friends of Symonds were furious about the way she was depicted. One said, 'They wanted her to look like Lady Macbeth.'

Cain's allies were incensed by what they saw as a cabal of 'posh southern women' who had ousted a hard-working man from Ormskirk in Lancashire. 'This bloke is a working-class outsider who went from dressing as a chicken to becoming the prime minister's director of communications,' said a Tory strategist who worked with Cain during the general election. 'He got the job on merit without going to a fancy school or Oxford or being on the BBC. There's something distasteful about the glee with which they greeted his demise.'

Johnson called in Cain and Cummings. Both told friends the forty-five minute meeting was 'warm with lots of laughter' as the trio recounted their Brexit battles together. Another political aide who was present for part of the meeting said, 'Boris and Dom were joking about him enjoying "leave" and chilling out.' Johnson had become angry over the media briefings against Symonds and raised the issue. A senior Number 10 source said, 'The prime minister was clear with them on Friday that the briefings had to stop and it was clear that they had not stopped.' Yet the upshot of the meeting was that the three parted on relatively cordial terms. Johnson suggested that if Stratton was not a success, he would be 'calling you guys back'. Cummings would remain on the government payroll until 18 December, working his notice at home. But there was talk of him returning part-time in January, perhaps running the British version of ARPA. Johnson expressed a desire to 'get the old gang back together' for the next general election. This was not Vote Leave spin, since the prime minister used the same phrase that day when discussing the meeting with civil servants.

Cummings went to see Rishi Sunak and his chief adviser Liam Booth-Smith to explain that he was leaving, but he also told them he had agreed with Johnson that he would help out with the Covid roadmap over the next few weeks. 'It was all, "Dom, will you stay home for a week while everything calms down", but then Carrie got wind of amicable discussions and went nuclear,' a Vote Leave source said.

After the meeting, Johnson visited Cain in his office and signed a pair of boxing gloves emblazoned with 'Get Brexit done', before making a speech wishing him well. 'He's the only one of my staff who always answers phone calls, no matter what time of day or night,' Johnson said, adding, 'I sometimes wait for days for Dom to return them.' It was another gathering which risked breaching the social distancing guidelines. Three Downing Street insiders later told *Panorama*, 'There were about thirty people, if not more, in a room. Everyone was stood shoulder to shoulder, some people on each other's laps.'[9]

It was claimed that Carrie convened a gathering in Johnson's flat above 11 Downing Street, playing loud music, including ABBA's 'The Winner Takes It All' to celebrate Cummings' departure. Those who were upstairs say there was 'no party' but a crisis meeting to discuss how to handle the departure of two such senior figures.

The mood in the building was bitterly divided. The Vote Leave loyalists were crying and drinking heavily, bereft at their project coming to an end. An official who visited the building said, 'You have one lot of people walking around with massive grins and another looking like their whole family had just died.' A Number 10 staffer who was delighted remarked, 'The thaw has come to Narnia.' A cabinet minister said, 'Boris has finally decided that he wants to be the prime minister rather than a kidnap victim.'[10]

But a Westminster figure who was a fan of American football, where the team's quarterback is protected by hulking brutes weighing up to 300 lbs, had a different perspective: 'Dom and Lee were Boris's offensive line, quite literally at times. Without them he was always going to be sacked.' An official asked Johnson, 'What are you going to do now Dom and Lee have gone? You've lost your human shields.'

He replied, 'It's okay, now I've got Allegra.'

Cummings, still fearful of what the Carrie camp might brief, decided to stage a theatrical departure to blast everything else off the front pages. He walked out of the black door, to an incendiary burst of camera flashes, carrying a cardboard box. Later, it was claimed that he had made off with key government papers which he planned to use against Johnson. He told friends the box was full of 'random shit people have given me'. Even the unsentimental Cummings wanted something to remember his time there. He never spoke to Johnson again. That weekend the toxic briefings continued. Cummings, assuming the Symonds–Stratton axis was to blame, vowed to make the Johnsons pay. A witness to Johnson's friendly exchanges earlier with the departing duo said, 'She tried to burn the bodies and she fucked it up. It was one of those moments of sheer stupidity and triumphalism. If they [Carrie and Boris] didn't do what they did that weekend, and shut up, I think the guy would still be prime minister.' Carrie denied that she did any such thing.

Afterwards Cummings concluded that Johnson no longer wanted to fight with Carrie: 'He turned out to be more frightened of his girlfriend than he was us.'[11] If that was Johnson's calculation, it would prove mistaken. What one colleague remembered most clearly from those final days was this: 'Dom's favourite gesture at the moment is to pull the pin from an imaginary hand grenade and then throw the grenade over his shoulder as he leaves the room. Everyone is braced.'

Two weeks after Cummings' departure, Johnson took Cleo Watson aside in the Cabinet Room for what she described as 'an exchange that I am sure may have been familiar to many of his girlfriends'.

Johnson said, 'I'm not sure this is working any more.'

'Okay, you seem to be trying to break up with me. I'll get my things.' Johnson wriggled: 'Aargh … I don't know … yes, no, maybe … wait, come back!' Eventually: 'I can't look at you any more because it reminds me of Dom. It's like a marriage has ended, we've divided up our things and I've kept an ugly old lamp. But every time I look at that lamp, it reminds me of the person I was with. You're that lamp.'[12]

Watson reflected grimly that she had evolved from 'the Gazelle' in some newspapers to an 'ugly old lamp' in Johnson's separation anxieties. She said goodbye to the press team. Johnson 'gave a painful, off-the-cuff speech to a bewildered clutch of advisers' and then she left.

Covid was the proximate cause of the cleavage in the team that won the referendum, but it was simply the catalyst for a personality clash which was always coming. 'It is absolutely clear to me that if Covid hadn't happened Boris and Dom would still have fallen out,' a veteran Downing Street operator said. 'Even without Covid or Carrie, Boris hated being on the bridle, under control.' In 2019, however, it was a position he had been happy to adopt. When a minister visited the PM at Chequers that Christmas he found Johnson still bitter, referring to Cummings as 'that fucker'. The minister said, 'You used each other. It was an abusive relationship you both went into with your eyes wide open.'

THE NIGHTMARE BEFORE CHRISTMAS

The Deal III

22 October to 24 December 2020

The British team knew Stéphanie Riso meant business when she turned up in the negotiating room with a projector. This beamed the legal text they were debating onto the wall. Riso grabbed a pointer stick, like a 1950s schoolteacher, and tapped the wall. 'Can we live with this word? What does this word mean? English is not my first language, what exactly does this word mean?'

'We had finally got proper engagement back and forth,' a British official recalled. 'She engaged in the detail. Up until that point the meetings had been us making a case and Barnier going, "No, no, absolutely not", then having it explained to him that we were agreeing with him. She was several levels above. She would be on her laptop writing with all the officials on the EU side congregated around her desk – and then you've got Barnier by himself playing with his phone.'

Barnier continued to make the opening statement in each session, 'but he would then tune out slightly,' another British negotiator said. 'She was trying to be courteous to him, but it was more and more obvious that she was giving the instructions. It got quite awkward. He was usually listening through interpretation which didn't help; he was the only person in the room who was, so he was always visibly behind what was going on. And you never quite get the detail in the same way.' The need to placate Barnier hamstrung the talks because 'he likes early nights, so negotiations could not go on beyond nine o'clock in the evening'.

In his memoir, Barnier hinted at his irritation at Riso's arrival, without admitting the extent of her influence. In his entry for 30 October, he reported that the British team 'asked to meet Stéphanie Riso', who was 'continuing to follow the negotiations closely'. Barnier complained, just as he did about the crucial contacts between Selmayr and Robbins, 'the British think that they have opened a second line of negotiation'. Over lunch that day on the thirteenth floor of the Berlaymont, Frost said, in what Barnier thought 'a rather arrogant tone', that 'all the important subjects of negotiation will be dealt with at the level of' von der Leyen and Johnson. That afternoon, Barnier went to see Riso to 'apprise' her of the situation, complaining, 'I will not accept these methods.' Riso, to placate him, promised she would 'make it clear to the British that there has been a misunderstanding ... and that from now on she will involve Clara or Paulina in all her meetings with the British.'[1] There had been a misunderstanding, but it was Barnier who had made it.

While Frost and Riso began to make progress, it was clear to the Brits that there were huge tensions within the Commission taskforce. Riso and Clara Martínez Alberola did not get on. 'Those two started to have bitchy arguments in front of us on minor things,' a witness said. 'It was obvious they didn't like each other.' Riso cut a lonely figure, cycling alone in a high-vis jacket to the Bourget, the Commission building where the talks were held, down the road from the Berlaymont. In casual conversations before and after meetings, it was clear she was feeling the heat from member states who thought she was 'conceding too much' or 'being too lenient to the Brits'. The British team read reports in the European press that she was interfering, which they assumed were briefed by Barnier.

By mid-November, the most intractable problem was fishing quotas. While Frost was demanding that more than half the fish in British waters be reserved for UK-based fishing vessels, the EU offered only the repatriation of up to 18 per cent of stocks. 'It's ridiculous,' a Downing Street official told journalists that week. Johnson repeatedly told aides he could not settle for such a deal, citing the example of the former Tory prime minister Edward Heath, whose name was a byword for betrayal in fishing communities. 'I'm not prepared to be another Ted Heath.'

To read Michel Barnier's account of these exchanges is to step inside a parallel universe where an independent Britain's territorial waters and fish were still the property of the EU, which had generously consented to give some back. The Frenchman recounted telling Frost the EU was 'prepared' to reduce its fishing by 18 per cent as if this were a historic act of generosity, then accused Britain of 'hiding behind its newfound sovereignty to refuse any serious commitment'.[2]

On 14 November, Barnier met von der Leyen for a stock take, reporting 'deadlock' on the level playing field, fisheries and governance but that he could see 'landing zones' on other issues. He said he had deliberately held back concessions on market access, including 'cabotage' for lorries and a 'fifth freedom' for aviation access and rules of origin. Von der Leyen said, 'Stéphanie thinks we should put it all on the table now.' Barnier was concerned 'the British will pocket our concessions without offering anything in return', but the president had spoken. After seeing Frost on 20 November, he concluded he should return to 'the old-fashioned method of resistance' instead.[3]

Nonetheless as the next round of talks began again on 28 November, this time in London, the British press was reporting that the outlines of a deal might be agreed within a week. Senior government sources said von der Leyen was being 'quite helpful' and was 'keen to unblock things'.

The mood soured quickly on 2 December after Emmanuel Macron started ringing fellow EU leaders, accusing Barnier of 'going soft' and urging that member states take a stand. That night, officials working for Frost and Barnier talked until 1.30 a.m. 'It ended up with people screaming at each other in the corridor,' a source said.

Then the bombshell dropped. On the afternoon of Thursday 3rd, in what was supposed to be a routine update on progress, Barnier produced legal text on the level playing field that, to Frost, took the talks back months. The UK was prepared to agree clauses saying Britain would not lower its standards on environmental laws and workers' rights. But the EU was demanding an 'equivalence clause', where the EU would be able to impose tariffs if Britain diverged from EU rules and gained a major economic advantage. Frost had tweeted opposition to such a move in June and no one had mentioned it since. He thought the whole thing had been dropped. Now it was back with a vengeance. 'It said that if they move their standards either up or down we have to go with them, and if we don't, they have the right to punish us,' a senior British source said. It meant that if the EU said twenty pigs could live in a sty and Britain wanted only six, Britain would have to change its rules or the EU could impose 'lightning tariffs', without having to go to the independent arbitration panel.

After the ambush, members of the EU team disappeared to their own room. The four senior negotiators on each side had a meeting. Riso, who was 'looking like total death', said, 'We cannot budge on this clause. It's non-negotiable. We must have it.'

Frost replied, 'We just can't have it at all. This is a total no-go. It's a baseball bat to bash us into alignment with EU law for ever.'

A crestfallen Riso looked at the floor as Barnier 'started ranting and raving', yelling, 'We have to have it. You must understand, Brexit has consequences!' The British negotiators sat silently while Barnier lectured them with 'crap soundbites'.

Frost was in regular contact with Johnson via text, but now walked to Number 10 for a face-to-face meeting with the prime minister, who read the text and said, 'There's no way we are going to do that.' Frost returned to the conference rooms in the basement of BEIS. Windowless and airless, this 'terrible, terrible place' was dubbed 'the bunker' by the Brits and 'the cave' by the team from Brussels.

Frost, along with Tim Barrow and Oliver Lewis, holed up in the UK team's space, discussed what to do. After a while there was a knock at the door. Cara Phillips, Lewis' private secretary, said, 'Steph's here.' Riso sneaked in. She said, 'We're going to have to put cards on the table here. I have a massive issue with this. What's the way around it?' The British were stunned Riso had risked her career to go behind Barnier's back. They were momentarily speechless. 'I'm not joking around here,' she said. 'It's been made extremely clear from von der Leyen's office that this must be secured. What are we going to do?'

Lewis and Frost had been tossing around ideas for the final treaty, including the possibility of an amending clause which might, in some circumstances, permit the reopening of the treaty. This would eventually become something Lewis dubbed the 'rebalancing clause' or 'freedom clause'. The idea was in its infancy, but they shared some of the thinking with Riso, and also raised the UKIM bill, which had not been talked about in the negotiations since the explosion nearly three months earlier. In the intervening period, Maroš Šefčovič and Michael Gove had been meeting in the joint committee to decide how the Northern Ireland Protocol would be implemented in practice. Frost suggested that if Riso could ensure concessions from Šefčovič, there might be room to negotiate. There was a joint committee pencilled in for early December and that would be the legal moment where the protocol could be reopened and certain things changed. 'We're not doing UKIM because we want to break international law, we are willing to withdraw the notwithstanding clauses if you make these moves,' they said. 'That will give us political room to move on certain things on the retaliation clause.'

Frost and Lewis demanded: 'The protocol text being changed to make genuinely clear there will be no customs processes imposed from goods going from GB to NI; second, no export forms from NI to GB; and third, clarity over when EU state aid rules will apply to GB firms with NI subsidiaries.' Riso considered it and said, 'I can work with this. Let me go and do my thing.'

At this point a civil servant arrived to warn them that Barnier was roaming the conference rooms looking for Riso. 'We smuggled her out of the UK room so that he didn't realise that she'd been doing the grand bargaining with us,' a source present said.

That evening, more legal text arrived, outlining EU plans for its fishing vessels to keep their quotas of British fish for ten years. Britain was prepared to stomach a three-year transition to lower quotas.

At the same time a group of newspaper executives in Downing Street to see Johnson were surprised when the prime minister gave an impromptu rendition of 'Waltzing Matilda'. The message was clear: Johnson was preparing to do business with the European Union on the same terms as Australia – no-deal by another name.

After further fruitless discussions on Friday morning, Frost briefed Johnson at 3 p.m. 'That's not acceptable,' the prime minister declared. 'It's all about control.' A source familiar with the exchanges said, 'It's what people voted for twice – in the referendum and again in the general election. It is written in the manifesto. That's what we need to deliver. They've never understood it. They've never got it.' In a metaphor for the deterioration of relations, the two sides had shared takeaway pizza and meals from Leon early in the week. By Friday the Europeans were being offered 'manky sandwiches in plastic'.

The talks were suspended and Johnson called von der Leyen on 5 December from Chequers. A conversation originally intended to put a rubber stamp on an embryonic deal became instead a last-ditch attempt to save it. They spoke again on Monday 7th. 'From a negotiation point of view this process is dead,' he told her. 'We need to apply the political defibrillator. We need to revive this process like that scene in *Pulp*

Fiction, where they stick the adrenaline straight into Uma Thurman's heart,' he added, deploying one of his rich panoply of cultural references. Von der Leyen replied, 'I haven't seen that film.' She and her team had to huddle around an iPhone while one of her aides googled the YouTube footage so she knew what he was talking about.

Johnson wanted to directly involve Angela Merkel and Emmanuel Macron to try to break the deadlock. Von der Leyen was initially sympathetic but the French and German leaders made clear they had no intention of getting involved. Twice that week Johnson was informed he would have to negotiate with the Commission alone. Merkel and Micheál Martin, the new Taoiseach, were both keen on a deal, but diplomats said Macron was telling fellow leaders, 'Keep pushing and the British will fold.' The Lutheran Merkel was disinclined to help. Despite their good first meeting, Johnson's willingness to tear up the deal he had signed the previous year meant she saw him as a political libertine. A cabinet minister observed, 'Boris is from Mars and Merkel is from Venus.'

Eddie Lister, who watched these relationships deteriorate, recalled, 'They were fine at the beginning and then went steadily downhill, partly because they couldn't stand David Frost, because he was doing his job. They couldn't stand Boris. The personal animosity was awful between him and Macron. It got sour as we got closer to the deal. It became obvious that Macron would never allow us to walk away from Europe without a lot of pain. The relationship with von der Leyen was not good. They didn't like each other very much.' A civil servant in the negotiating team felt the Europeans harboured resentments at Johnson dating back decades. 'There was so much baggage,' the official said. 'Animus going back to the *Telegraph* columns in the 1990s, which are still talked about. Then they hated that he did a deal and then immediately said, "We didn't really mean it." They didn't want to give Boris a win on anything.' Johnson was also at fault. 'He couldn't really resist taking pot shots.'

Johnson could not back down, since he was already feeling the heat from the ERG. On that Friday, Steve Baker used his 'Clean Global Brexit' WhatsApp group to urge the prime minister to 'deliver an exit worth having'. Andrew Bridgen, the first MP who put in letters calling for a leadership challenge to Cameron and May, warned the PM might be toppled. Despite this sabre-rattling, David Jones and Sir Bill Cash, two veteran Brexiteers, were in close contact with Lewis and professed themselves content with the government's approach.

Johnson also enjoyed the backing of his ministers. At cabinet that week he compared what the EU was demanding to twins. 'The UK is one twin, the EU is another, and if the EU decides to have a haircut then the UK is going to have a haircut or else face punishment.' Robert Buckland, the most Remain-minded minister, backed him: 'As the father of twins myself, I can say that they don't want to wear the same clothes or have the same haircuts.' Twelve other ministers spoke in support.

On 9 December, Johnson took a delegation to Brussels for dinner with von der Leyen, an event that became infamous as 'the fish supper'. On the menu were scallops and turbot – fitting for a negotiation stalled over fishing quotas – but it was Johnson who was filleted.

EU officials told MEPs afterwards that in a fifty-minute pre-dinner meeting, attended only by the two principals plus Frost and Riso, the prime minister went in 'all guns blazing, urging her to sideline Michel Barnier', calling him 'unimaginative' and an 'obstacle' to a deal. In this version of events, Johnson also made a joke about how the British and Germans both know 'how difficult the French can be'. Von der Leyen made clear that Barnier had all twenty-seven member states behind him.

Over dinner, Johnson, flanked by Frost, Barrow and Lewis, proposed 'several' ways of resolving the impasse over the level playing field, including a 'pay for freedom' proposal, where the UK followed the broad direction of EU regulation but with an escape route. If the UK wanted to diverge, the two sides would agree a quick 'review mechanism' to set tariffs that each would impose on the other. Crucially, the UK said retaliation should be confined to the area in dispute and tariffs imposed only where the EU could show that Britain diverging had done them real harm. 'I'm prepared to be generous on fish,' Johnson said as he offered to lower Britain's demand that EU fishing quotas be cut by 45 per cent. Realising he might have gone too far, he said, 'I hope I haven't thrown too much overboard.'

Frost chipped in, 'It's a bit too late for that, boss.'

Johnson was met with blank expressions from VDL, Barnier, Riso and Martínez Alberola. 'They just sat with their arms folded,' a British official said. 'It was "talk to the hand" the whole time.' Barnier, who 'thought it was hilarious' they had served fish, seemed to be calling the shots again. In his account of this meeting, he crowed that Gove and Šefčovič had come to agreement in the joint committee on the implementation of the withdrawal agreement in Northern Ireland, 'A lot of wasted time and controversy only to end up simply honouring their own signature'[4] – no mention that Gove had won all the concessions he asked for following the deal with Riso. Of what followed, Barnier had nothing to say, which is hardly surprising.

To the British, there was just one glimmer of hope. Von der Leyen looked 'sort of embarrassed' by the display of truculence. Things had gone so badly that Frost cornered Riso and asked for a 'wash-up' at the end, a rerun of the quad meeting beforehand. Johnson managed to get some one-on-one time with von der Leyen as they walked, very slowly, downstairs.

As the two leaders and their sherpas talked in von der Leyen's office, Barnier – who was being man-marked by Lewis, who had been forced to listen to one of the Frenchman's anecdotes about running the Abbeville Winter Olympics for the fourth time – became aware that a conversation was happening without him. He scribbled a note, which he gave to a waiter to deliver to von der Leyen. There was a knock at the door and a piece of paper was thrust inside. The Commission president read it and showed Riso. 'This is a problem, but what can you do?' It was a threat from Barnier. Frost told colleagues, 'He was outside demanding to be let in. She got a note ... which said, "If you don't let me in, I am going to resign."' The meeting broke up rather than accommodate Barnier's ego. Johnson took a lift downstairs with von der Leyen but their conversation went fruitlessly over the same ground.

When the prime minister returned to Tim Barrow's residence, a 'frustrated' Johnson drank red wine while Frost, a former CEO of the Scotch Whisky Association, clutched a glass of his old product. Johnson said, 'I kept throwing pennies in the well and no sounds came back.'

With Downing Street briefing that there was no better than a 20 per cent chance of a deal, on 11 December Johnson and Gove conducted a crisis meeting in the Cabinet Room on the UK's preparations for a no-deal Brexit, summoning civil service director-generals from across Whitehall to 'stress test' contingency plans which had been thrashed out in table-top exercises. The results were stark. It was decided that Britain would have to throw open its borders for the first 'four or five' months of 2021, waving through most freight traffic to minimise chaos. Emma Churchill, the official in charge of the borders delivery unit, outlined plans for seven new inland sites to handle border checks away from ports and keep the lorries moving. These were dubbed 'Farage's garages' by locals. Gove was warned that several weeks of disruption would be inevitable in Kent because small firms were still not familiar with the new customs paperwork. 'It's all very real now,' an official said.

Another war game, dubbed Capstone, outlined the worst-case scenarios. The previous month Gove had led an exercise to plan for the Royal Navy to intercept and board French fishing vessels in the Channel. As a former journalist, Gove's no-deal planning was shaped by horror headlines, which he drew up detailing the most politically damaging stories that could unfold. 'One of his biggest worries is a new Battle of Trafalgar with clashes between French and English fishing fleets and the navy and French fishermen,' said one friend.

Ministers held talks with leading food suppliers, including the big supermarkets, and told them to prepare for no-deal. Food producers warned there would be shortages of vegetables for three months and emergency planners predicted panic buying on a bigger scale than the pandemic. Health ministers told suppliers of medicines, medical devices and vaccines to stockpile six weeks' of supplies at secure locations in the UK. Gove had by then chaired two hundred XO meetings, spent £4 billion and devised a 'decision matrix' where the Cabinet Office secured pre-approval from other ministers for every course of action that might be needed, to save time when problems arose. He was under huge personal stress, with allies saying he had trouble sleeping as he considered the possibilities.

On several occasions Frost and Lewis discussed whether they should do the deal they were negotiating, or whether it might be better to go for no-deal. Both preferred the option of a deal. Johnson sought to convince them he would play hardball: 'You have to believe me. I'm prepared for no-deal,' he said. Both believed Johnson but thought he would be reluctant to do so without cabinet backing. This, they thought, would probably have been forthcoming, but not straightforward. 'I think they would have gone along with it,' one said, 'and then badmouthed him in the usual way.'

This period was miserable. 'Everyone was worn out, because there were no breaks,' a British negotiator said. 'We'd been going without weekends since the beginning of November and everyone was fed up.' The Bourget was a 'horrible' place which looked like a 'car park'. One participant said,

'If 1970s bureaucracy had form, the Bourget would be it.' At least it had windows, more than could be said for the dungeon under BEIS in London, where time seemed to stand still. 'It is hard to explain how bleak it is,' a British source said. 'You don't know what time of day or night it is. A colleague went outside for a walk when it was raining – and he said, "It's just glorious out there."'[5]

Stress levels rose further when the 'Kent variant' of coronavirus, 60 per cent more transmissible than the original strain, began to spread. 'That sent everyone into black despair,' a British source said. Frost, unlike Robbins, sought to maintain morale by being very open with his whole team about what was said in each negotiating session, keeping everyone in the loop. But the responsibility was weighing on him. He let people go home to see their families but brought them together as often as he could, not an easy task since some were jumpy about Covid. 'If you weren't staying in the Residence, which was only about ten of us, the hotels just gave you a paper bag of food in the evening,' an official said. 'Once you were back in your hotel, you couldn't get out of your room because of the curfew, which was pretty horrible for weeks on end.' As Christmas approached, people were increasingly worried about whether they were going to get out in time. Someone put up a picture of an RAF jet with a countdown showing the number of 'hours to freedom' on Christmas Eve, when it was assumed they would be collected and flown home.

Despite the poor morale, Frost and Riso began a secret diplomatic dance to try to formulate a compromise on the level playing field. On two or three occasions Frost and Barrow went to see Riso in her office in the Berlaymont. Von der Leyen sent her *chef de cabinet*'s car to collect them and smuggle them in via a basement car park and a lift, allowing them to bypass Barnier's office. 'For two weeks we deliberately tried to do meetings without him,' a British official said. Riso was privately dismissive of Barnier. In one of these meetings she confirmed what had been in his note on the night of the fish supper. Von der Leyen twice dropped in and also expressed irritation with Barnier. A British account of her words, circulated at the time, summarised her view as: 'You see what I've got to deal with. Don't take him seriously. He's not representing our position; we have to manage it.'

When Riso wanted to visit the UK delegation space, Frost's team deployed junior officials like Cara Phillips in the corridors outside to act as a mobile blocking force, watching round corners to ensure the coast was clear. On at least one occasion they had to intercept Barnier. 'It was a whole bunch of junior officials holding up Barnier, giving him small talk while we smuggled Steph out through a back door,' a source recalled. While one civil servant did the talking another was texting, 'Hurry up!'

On another occasion Riso visited Frost at Barrow's residence. By then the TV cameras were routinely following Frost around Brussels and one was parked outside when it came time for her to leave. Riso could not be filmed or the subterfuge would be destroyed. Frost staged his own exit to distract the TV crew. 'She left on her bike once the cameras had cleared off,' a source said.

Lewis was able, with Riso, to develop the ideas he had sketched out on a white board with Frost for a 'freedom clause', giving both sides the ability to reopen the treaty. In its early stages, Lewis wiped the board clean whenever anyone else came into the room. The clause stated that if either side felt the other was abusing divergence, or the punishment of divergence, they could request a review that would reopen the treaty in a specific area without blowing the whole thing up. Riso enjoyed the intellectual stimulation of the discussions. At one point she leaned back and said, 'Nothing like this has ever been written in an international treaty before. It is deeply problematic from all sorts of perspectives. But it is logically completely coherent with the style of relationship we are trying to build.' She added, 'Let's be honest, there are so many potential self-destruct clauses and termination clauses in this thing that it would be a miracle if lasts six months. What's another tripwire?'

In the meetings where Barnier was present, one witness recalled, 'He didn't have a scooby what was going on.' On one occasion he began to lecture Lewis that there had to be a role for a tribunal in the event of a dispute. 'Mr Barnier,' he replied. 'I completely agree that there should be a formalised process. I'm saying that there should be a formalised process with the option to reopen if that formalised process doesn't command the confidence of the two parties.' Riso cut across this. 'Thank you very much, Michel. I think we can make this work.'

The other person confused by the plan was Johnson. The British team had divided the key issues into Block A, Block B, Block C and so on. Block E became a synonym for the freedom clause. Johnson would phone Lewis during the meetings and say, 'Sonic! Explain this Block E again, why do we need it?' Lewis would have to talk the prime minister through

THE NIGHTMARE BEFORE CHRISTMAS

it without the EU representatives hearing his full account of why it would allow Britain to diverge further in future.

While Riso was generally helpful, she was also 'highly strung' and 'there were a couple of moments where she lost it,' a British negotiator said. 'There was a 2 a.m. moment where she stormed out in a huff over the level playing field. We were all fed up and fractious with each other, but she was the first to actually walk out. She threw her arms up and said, "That's the end!" It was genuine – it wasn't staged confrontation. We deliberately took a decision not to do any of those histrionics.'

Lewis was absent when the clause was finally agreed. He received a text from Frost saying, 'They have agreed to Block E.' On the same day there was a Zoom call with Johnson, in which the PM seemed to finally grasp what his team had achieved. Celebrations were short-lived. That evening, Frost texted again to say, 'We've got a problem with fish.'

Under pressure from Macron, the Commission dropped another last-minute demand. On the afternoon of 21 December, the EU had produced its final card, a clause von der Leyen called 'the hammer', granting Brussels the right to retaliate across the board if Britain sought future reductions in access to its waters for EU fishermen.

Johnson saw this as undermining the very basis of his vote to Leave. 'It's not about fish – it's about freedom,' as one aide put it.

There ensued a series of crisis calls between Downing Street and the team in Brussels, Johnson patched-in to the delegation room on a spider phone. Simon Case, the cabinet secretary, asked if Lewis had any other ideas: 'Sonic, have you got something like Block E you could deploy on fish?'

At 8 p.m. Johnson told von der Leyen, 'I cannot sign this treaty, Ursula. I can't do something that is not in my country's interests.' One of those listening said, 'It was the most direct that he was with her. He said that unless they changed track, we would trade on Australian terms', the code for no-deal. 'That was the closest it came to all falling over.' Adopting an antipodean twang and saying, 'Australia is a beautiful country' seemed to be getting Johnson nowhere. He then spoke 'terrible German' to von der Leyen, *Viel hummer, kein hammer* (lots of lobster, no hammer). One of those listening said Johnson also sought to explain the problem with reference to the surreal cartoons in one of Britain's best-known comedy shows. 'We can't have this Monty Python situation, where we are trapped in the car with a giant hammer outside the gates to clobber us every time we drive out,' he said.

This was met with silence and then, 'OK, thank you, Boris.'

Johnson's lobster/hammer intervention became legendary in Number 10, where his new chief of staff, Dan Rosenfield, bought matching hammers 'with the EU and Union Jack flags on either side', a colleague recalled.

Frost and Lewis contemplated failure. 'There were some pretty dark times in the final two days,' one member of the team admitted. In the end, the lobster call convinced the EU to move on fisheries. The following day, it ditched demands that EU vessels should continue to enjoy their current quotas for seven or eight years. Frost's priority by this stage was to reduce the number of years it would take to bring down the EU quotas, rather than the percentages. Lewis and he had one of their very few arguments over the issue, the Vote Leave man insisting they move as quickly as possible to a situation where the UK could legally deny access to its waters to European fishing vessels, to take back control.

Senior civil servants say Johnson did, finally, knuckle down and study the detail. 'In those last couple of weeks in December, Boris read the draft legal text cover to cover,' a senior mandarin said. 'He really knew he had to understand it. He was reading and asking, "Why is it this word, not that word?" It was the one time you really saw him with wedges of paper, setting aside large amounts of time to read through and really understand it and ask questions.'

However, the more he understood, the more nervous Johnson seemed. Getting him on side for the compromise that was going to be necessary was not easy. The prime minister could smell the cries of betrayal from Nigel Farage and co., who had made fishing a touchstone issue. The prime minister was seized by indecision. 'There were times, not very often, but on a few days, where we did get a bit frustrated with the leadership from London,' one of those camped in Brussels said. 'It was about a willingness to make choices about things.' Frost had tough conversations with Johnson in which he said, 'If you're not going to agree to this, then it's over. If you're not going to tell us to agree, then we'll have to come home.' A senior civil servant detected Frost also losing his nerve. 'Frosty was really windy about doing the deal, saying, "I'm not sure we should be doing this deal,"' the official recalled. 'I think Boris did want to do the deal but was really spooked because Frosty sounded very negative. He was really nervous about fish. Sonic in Brussels was the one who pulled Frosty around. Sonic started talking to Boris directly without Frosty knowing.'

Johnson seemed to the negotiating team to be desperate for a deal, to the point where he even shunned more theatrics. 'There was a point when Frosty said him and Oliver should come home for consultations,' a source familiar with the conversations revealed. 'David was halfway out of the building when the PM said it would be best if they stayed.'

On 22 December, James Slack stayed up into the small hours of the morning, preparing two press statements – one for a deal and one for the collapse of the talks. It still felt like either could happen.

On Wednesday 23rd, Johnson and von der Leyen had four phone calls. That morning she said the EU would accept a transition of six years to lower fishing quotas. Johnson said: 'Five!'

A seemingly endless silence ensued, broken by the Number 10 switchboard operator apologising that the connection had gone down. A disembodied German voice then piped up, 'No, I'm still here – five and a half years?' Johnson agreed.

After lunch, in their fourth call of the day, the EU agreed that the hammer would be heavily restricted so a fish dispute would only mean sanctions relating to fish. 'Steph [Riso] persuaded VDL to take the risk on that and to limit retaliation to fisheries,' a British official said. 'The Norwegians face tariffs on fish, so it wasn't inherently unreasonable.'

In return the Brits conceded more than they ever intended. There would be just a 25 percentage point reduction in EU fishing quotas – a far cry from the original 80 per cent sought by Johnson. Frost and Lewis were not happy with the numbers, but Riso was a shrewd reader of Johnson, who had been texting Barnier and von der Leyen behind Frost's back, to hurry things along. They had two choices: accept the offer or go for no-deal. 'I know you are not bluffing. I know you are both prepared to go for no-deal,' she said. 'But we all know your prime minister is weak, he is bluffing, he will collapse, you should take this deal.' The duo left the room to talk it over and concluded that she was right. It was time to close. 'They were worried Boris was going to crater,' said another Vote Leave veteran. Cummings, by now a highly critical observer, wrote, 'Frost/Lewis suddenly had to make concessions (including fish) because the PM collapsed at the final moment after all his tough talk. The tough, formidable Steph Riso was one hundred times more able than Barnier. She realised his weaknesses ... He had already made various disastrous phone calls that had alerted people to his panic, an international version of the familiar domestic WhatsApp trolleying.'[6]

By then Frost had also thrashed out a last ditch deal on electric cars covering how many non-UK and EU parts there could be on a car before 'rules of origin' regulations meant tariffs could be slapped on those vehicles. The EU wanted no transition. Frost fought for and won a deal that gave car plants time to adapt. Up to 60 per cent of the parts would be allowed from outside the UK and EU to start with, reducing eventually to 45 per cent. 'If we hadn't got that, the implications for Nissan and Toyota really don't bear thinking about,' a Number 10 source said. 'It would make what they are doing close to unviable.' Riso had promised she would be able to give the deal to Frost, 'but we won't be able to tell you until the final day'. She was as good as her word.

On Wednesday evening, Johnson, who had been sustained by takeaway burgers from Five Guys, updated the cabinet. No minister was more relieved at developments than Gove, who was anxiously waiting to see if his no-deal preparations would be tested. Contacted by a member of Frost's team, he said simply, 'Rejoice!'

Frost remained in Brussels, going line by line through what the revised quota plan would mean for each species of fish. There was one final moment of farce. The EU's legal text was based on an earlier offer of 22 per cent of fish stocks being returned, rather than 25 per cent. That meant the precise quotas for 105 different species of fish and shellfish would have to be recalculated. The problem was, that would involve a fresh set of approvals from member states, each of which had an interest in different native species. Journalists, who had been told to expect a 7.30 p.m. press conference waited as the deadline moved to 9 p.m., then 1 a.m. At midnight they were told to go to bed.

Johnson got a good night's sleep and got up on Christmas Eve for a run with his dog Dilyn. But he began to lose patience. Frost had been up all night with two hundred officials, while in Downing Street staff had slept in the office, expecting a 7 a.m. press conference. Still things dragged on. At lunchtime Tim Barrow sent sandwiches to both negotiating teams.

In London, a senior figure at the BBC spoke to Number 10, urging it not to announce the deal during the broadcast of the corporation's big Christmas Eve film, *Kung Fu Panda*. About 12.30 p.m. Johnson spoke again to von der Leyen and said, 'We really need to get this over the line now. We've got to get Frosty and his team home for Christmas.'

An hour later Frost WhatsApped the prime minister to say, 'I think we've got there.' It was around 3 p.m. local time when Frost rang Johnson and said, 'I think you should accept this, because if you don't it's all over.'

The prime minister said, 'Okay. Do it.'

Twenty minutes later in a video call with von der Leyen. Johnson asked, 'So do we have a deal, Ursula?'

She replied, 'Yes, we do.' Downing Street staff at the back of the room burst into spontaneous applause.

Johnson then had some fun at Frost's expense. After congratulating him on signing a deal that also encompassed crime, social security, some services, as well as trade, in rapid time, he added, 'I'm afraid there's a problem with the RAF flight and I don't think we're going to be able to get you home.' An 'awful silence' ensued until James Slack piped up, 'I think he's suffered enough, PM.' For weeks thereafter Frost felt like a Vietnam veteran, waking every morning with flashbacks to fisheries negotiations.

Throughout the process, Lewis had been in touch with arch-Eurosceptics such as Sir Bill Cash to reassure them that the rebalancing clause would allow any future candidate for prime minister to run on a pledge to change Britain's relationship with the EU. 'A politician can get elected on a specific mandate and say, "I can get the treaty changed",' he said. Cummings, watching from exile, messaged Lewis to ask, 'Is it a good deal?' He received the reply, 'Yes.' Cummings asked some questions and concluded, 'It sounds like you've done it.'

Lewis spent Christmas Day on the phone to Mark Francois and other members of the ERG, organising to have the text of the deal printed and sent to their homes in taxis so their star chamber could opine. The lawyers eventually pronounced themselves satisfied. Another government Brexiteer said, 'From my perspective, it does the job. Vote Leave's argument was that it is possible to trade freely with Europe without having to follow the EU's law. The deal does this. It's a triumph of the philosophy Boris championed in 2016.'

In short, Johnson had achieved the goal he set himself. There would quickly be questions about whether his focus on sovereignty was the right one economically. But in his own terms the deal was a success. Frost had seen off two eleventh-hour efforts to skewer the UK and Britain would be able to trade with zero tariffs.

Missing was EU recognition of UK regulators. The EU side was also surprised that Britain did not ask for more on services. Stefaan De Rynck,

Barnier's adviser, recalled the member states saying, 'We would really like to have more generous mobility arrangements for students or for specific categories', or, 'We would like a non-discrimination clause for longer-term visas'. The Commission told them, 'A mobility arrangement is very hard because the UK government is not interested.' This British decision meant future European tours by bands and musicians were derailed by borders bureaucracy. 'I had expected the UK to be a bit more ambitious on services,' De Rynck said. 'It doesn't affect only musicians, it affects service providers across the board from the UK.'[7]

The most glaring failure was on fish, where the quotas were far smaller, and the transition period far longer, than Johnson or Frost wanted. 'It's the one thing we called wrong in the negotiations,' a senior figure said later. 'We all thought that their position on fisheries was so ridiculous and indefensible that in the end they'd have to come off it and get a lot closer to where we wanted. They never did and they timed us out on it. By that point nobody wanted to lose the whole thing over fish.'

Even in a moment of political achievement for Johnson, after a period of overwhelming stress, fate delivered a cruel personal blow. He and Carrie spent Christmas at Chequers with their friend Nimco Ali, who had cleared her presence with the Cabinet Office to ensure it was compliant with the Covid rules on childcare support bubbles. There, on New Year's Eve, Carrie suffered the quiet trauma of a miscarriage, a loss seldom understood by those who have not experienced one. It was a fact she kept private until the following July when she announced she was expecting their second child.

By then, Johnson's deal had proved to be less than perfect and he was again doing battle with the EU, while, at home, he crested the high political wave from which he then precipitously plunged.

PART FOUR

DRUMMED OUT

THE DOWNFALL OF BORIS JOHNSON

January 2021 to September 2022

'Character is destiny'

– Heraclitus

'The key element in tragedy is that heroes and heroines are destroyed by that which appears to be their greatest strength'

– Robert Shea

'A man who lies to himself and listens to his own lie comes to a point where he does not discern any truth'

– Fyodor Dostoevsky, The Brothers Karamazov

FATAL DISTRACTIONS

From Wallpaper to Paterson

February to November 2021

'The PM ... suffered the inevitable conclusion
of his bin-fire of the vanities'

– *Mick Herron,* The Secret Hours

Boris Johnson's temper was out of control. After two months of leaks designed to undermine him, the prime minister snapped. Dominic Cummings had threatened him the previous November. Since then, stories had appeared in the newspapers revealing his private text messages to world leaders, his plan to pay for the refurbishment of the Downing Street flat, even Dilyn the dog pissing in a handbag. Johnson believed there was a conspiracy to bring him down. The prime minister had people paid to fight back for him, not least his new Number 10 director of communications Jack Doyle. But instead of leaving the job to them, Johnson picked up the phone to a senior executive at News UK and did so himself. Then he called another editor – and a third. 'It was a knee-jerk thing,' said a government source. 'The prime minister was very angry and let rip.'[1]

Cummings was on holiday in Northumberland, his phone out of range, when the morning papers dropped on 23 April 2021. The front page of the *Sun* screamed: 'BORIS: DOM'S A TEXT MANIAC'. Inside, under the headline 'Dom Corleone', the paper had mocked up Cummings as a mafia chief, though he looked more like Nosferatu than Brando or Pacino. *The Times* splashed with 'Cummings is accused of leaking PM's texts', quoting 'a No 10 source' saying, 'Dominic is engaged in systematic leaking … We are concerned about messages from private WhatsApp groups which had very limited circulation. The prime minister is saddened about what Dom is doing. It's undermining the government and the party. It might be that Dominic feels bitter about what's happened since he left but it's a great shame.'

The story which triggered Johnson's rage was a report, from the BBC's Laura Kuenssberg, on 21 April, that he had offered to 'fix' a tax issue for James Dyson, the vacuum cleaner tycoon. His workforce had worked on the government's ventilator challenge but most were in Singapore and he wanted assurances they would not face higher taxes for travelling to the UK. When he didn't get the guarantees he wanted, Dyson texted the PM. 'I will fix it tomo!' the prime minister replied, adding later, 'Rishi says it is fixed!!' When Dyson sought a further assurance, Johnson replied, 'James I am First Lord of the Treasury and you can take it that we are backing you to do what you need.'

While this was hardly a scandal, Johnson was disturbed to see his private communications leaked. A week earlier messages from Mohammed bin Salman, the crown prince of Saudi Arabia, revealed that he had lobbied the PM to intervene to support a Saudi attempt to buy Newcastle United football club. The PM had been advised by Simon Case, the cabinet secretary, to change his mobile phone number to stem the flood of MPs, lobbyists and business people messaging him. On one occasion he had even been contacted directly by a Universal Credit claimant asking for help with their benefit claim, which DWP duly provided.[2] Johnson rejected Case's advice.

The problem for the prime minister was that around thirty officials in the Treasury and Number 10 saw the exchange between Johnson and Dyson, so Cummings could plausibly deny it. When he got back in range to sixteen missed calls and messages galore from journalists, Cummings rang a couple of contacts in Number 10. 'We've been meeting with the PM and he's convinced there is a massive conspiracy and you and Caino are trying to destroy him,' one said. 'He's told us all you've given Laura these texts from James Dyson. We've told him you're not even on the original distribution list, but he just says, "You don't understand, these people are out in the jungle with a knife between their teeth, like Colonel Kurtz in *Apocalypse Now*."'

The prime minister was half right. Cummings had begun what he told friends was a campaign to 'fuck up' Johnson, by exposing some of the prime minister's most questionable behaviour in Downing Street. He wrote a blog post accusing the prime minister of 'unethical' behaviour and falling 'below the standards of competence and integrity the country deserves'. He said he had never received the Dyson messages and claimed Johnson tried to stop the leak inquiry into the 'Chatty Rat' briefing about the second lockdown. According to Cummings, Johnson held a meeting with him, Case and Cain in which the cabinet secretary said 'all the evidence' led to Henry Newman, then an aide to Michael Gove, but who Carrie Symonds had since helped bring into a senior role in Number 10. 'The PM was very upset about this,' wrote Cummings. 'He said to me afterwards, "If Newman is confirmed as the leaker then I will have to fire him, and this will cause me very serious problems with Carrie ... perhaps we could get the cabinet secretary to stop the leak inquiry?"' Cummings said he told the prime minister this was 'mad and totally unethical'.[3]

Downing Street denied Johnson had interfered in the leak inquiry and called the allegations against Newman 'false'. Indeed, the Cabinet Office official who interviewed Newman said the evidence against him didn't even rank as flimsy. More than one Number 10 person had pointed the finger at him, but when Newman asked if this was Cummings and Cain, his questioner fell silent and looked embarrassed.

However, Cummings didn't deny responsibility for a third area where Johnson was under siege, the funding of the Downing Street decorations, for the simple reason that he was one of several sources who had been providing information to the *Daily Mail* on 'wallpapergate'. 'The PM stopped speaking to me about this matter in 2020,' Cummings wrote, 'as I told him I thought his plans to have donors secretly pay for the renovation were unethical, foolish, possibly illegal and almost certainly broke the rules on proper disclosure of political donations if conducted in the way he intended. I refused to help him organise these payments.'[4]

For his campaign to undermine Johnson, Cummings chose the *Mail*, edited by Geordie Greig, who disliked the prime minister and had campaigned for Remain when he was editor of the *Mail on Sunday*. 'If we'd had a different editor things would have been very different,' a Johnson aide observed later. 'It was an organised campaign by the deposed spads in exile.' The point of the spear was Simon Walters, a story-getter known to engender fear in the political class, who found him unbiddable and relentless. He had already proved an enthusiastic purveyor of negative stories on Symonds.

The first story to bear Cummings' fingerprints was an amuse bouche, on 19 February, recounting what Walters called Dilyn the dog's 'watergate'. The Jack Russell had cocked his leg over the open handbag of Katie Lam, at her Number 10 leaving party in the rose garden. When Lam pushed the dog away there was a confrontation with Symonds.[5] If the leak about the canine leak was designed to irritate, Walters' exclusive on 2 March was far more serious for Johnson, revealing that the couple had dramatically overspent the annual taxpayer-funded allowance permitted for refurbishing their flat above 11 Downing Street. The paper reported that Johnson had complained Symonds' spending was 'totally out of control' and that there was 'no way' he could afford to pay the bill from the designer Lulu Lytle, of 'over a hundred grand'.[6] Johnson raged, 'She's buying gold wallpaper!'[7] It was a killer detail which sent the story from one of interest to the Westminster village to one that cut through with voters. It was also untrue. The wall in question had been painted red in celebration of Johnson's 'red wall' wins in the 2019 election.

The story revealed that Johnson was trying to set up a trust to cover the costs of the makeover, based on a similar scheme for the White House. He had asked Lord Brownlow, a peer with close links to the royals, to run the trust, which would also fund maintenance of the rest of the building, including the state rooms.[8] The idea had apparently been the brainchild of Helen MacNamara. While Number 10 was a historic building which might have benefited from such a scheme, it was also clearly a means for Johnson, broke from his divorce, to get Tory benefactors to pay for his fiancée's extravagance. It later emerged that Alistair Darling, the former chancellor, had declined an offer to run the trust, an appointment which might have contributed a veneer of cross-party respectability to the arrangement.

Walters followed up with further stories on the 5th, 6th and 13th of March and the 11th and 21st of April. He revealed that Johnson and Symonds had also enjoyed £12,500 of daily food deliveries from Daylesford, the luxury organic farmshop in the Cotswolds owned by Lord Bamford's wife, Carole. A Number 10 spokesman said, 'The costs of food for personal consumption are met by Boris Johnson.' But questions were growing about how he could afford such largesse.[9] Walters detailed how Conservative Party funds were used to pay the redecoration bills, with Brownlow paying the money into party coffers to cover the costs – effectively donating to Johnson in secret.[10] CCHQ paid the money to the

Cabinet Office, which then settled Lytle's bill.[11] An email from Brownlow to Tory co-chairman Ben Elliot, Tory chief executive Darren Mott and Mike Chattey, the party's head of fundraising in October 2020, proved that he had handed over the money 'to cover payments the party has already made on behalf of the soon to be formed "Downing St Trust".'[12] This was enough to prompt the Electoral Commission to demand answers from Elliot, who had privately dubbed the affair 'wallpapergate'. Brownlow's donation, at that point, had been declared neither by the party to the Electoral Commission, the deadline for which had been 30 January, nor by Johnson in his entry in the register of members' interests.[13]

That revelation, on 21 April, came the day before Johnson snapped and began denouncing Cummings to the papers. By then his ex-chief adviser had opened a second front in the offensive. At a Covid press conference on 15 March, Matt Hancock had denied herd immunity had ever been part of the government's Plan A to deal with the pandemic. Asked about the health secretary's comments, Downing Street agreed. An incensed Cummings contacted close associates to say, 'These people have got to be removed. They're flat out lying about the biggest disaster since Hitler. We should try and get rid of these motherfuckers by any means.' In this version of events, Cummings had until then only been trying to damage Johnson, now he was actively determined to remove him. Not everything that followed was his doing, but one of those who knew the background to some of the revelations which were used to undermine Johnson in the months ahead said, 'Most of it *was* him.'

Removing a leader with a huge majority, when the rollout of the AstraZeneca vaccine was erasing Johnson's mistakes in the spring of 2020, would not be easy. Cummings' rationale, to those he could trust, was that a drip feed of negative stories would grind down Johnson's inner circle. He deliberately gave Walters fresh lines for Saturday's paper, meaning Johnson's aides had to work late on Fridays dealing with them. 'Carrie has reprogrammed his rat brain and he has surrounded himself with idiots,' he told co-conspirators. 'If we put him under pressure, he'll fuck up because he's got her in one ear and idiots in the other ear.'

In his blog on 23 April, Cummings piled psychological pressure on Johnson's team, threatening to release records of all his communications in Downing Street to MPs.[14] Allies claimed he had text and WhatsApp messages, emails and even audio recordings that would embarrass Johnson. Three days later the *Mail* splashed with Johnson's comments from the previous October about letting 'the bodies pile high'. The prime minister tersely denied he had said the incendiary phrase but both BBC and ITV found corroborating witnesses.

Cummings was hell-bent on destroying Johnson, but that inevitably led to the question of who or what he wanted to install instead. On 2 May, the *Sunday Times* revealed conversations between Cummings and his Vote Leave allies, in which he made plain that Rishi Sunak was his preferred replacement. The ex-adviser told them Vote Leave needed a 'new host' for their ambitions, a turn of phrase which reinforced the idea of a colonising force in the Conservative Party. Cummings denied using this term, but Vote Leave insiders confirmed the story sent him 'apeshit' because his true intentions had been revealed.

Sunak's allies were quick to say he would not entertain the idea of a return to government for Cummings, yet the effect was to sow divisions between the two senior figures in government, and stoke the paranoia of Johnson's advisers. Cummings also kept in touch with civil servants in the PM's private office and political aides. 'We knew, because we had a lot of spies inside the building, how damaging' the leaks were, a Vote Leave source said. 'The political world thought this stuff hadn't affected him, but inside the system was crumbling around him.'

Cummings gave evidence to a joint hearing of the health and science select committees on Wednesday 26 May. In seven hours of testimony, Cummings said 'tens of thousands' of people had died needlessly thanks to Johnson's indecision over lockdowns. He said he had heard the prime minister say 'let the bodies pile high', he claimed to have lobbied for Matt Hancock's sacking 'every day' and he dismissed Johnson's position on herd immunity. 'I am completely baffled as to why Number 10 is now trying to deny that that was the plan,' he said. 'The whole point is: that was the original plan, but we realised what the consequences of it were going to be, and we decided that it was intolerable and we had to try something else.'

Nonetheless, at this point, even Cummings' allies did not think he would succeed in bringing Johnson down. The stories were embarrassing and irritating but nowhere near fatal. The PM had made the correct calls on vaccines and to leave the third lockdown quicker than the rest of Europe. The Tories were ten points ahead in the polls. 'He thought the vaccine was going to save him,' a Downing Street insider said. Yet Cummings had two advantages. First, he was not motivated by a desire for preferment or the perks of high office and could not be bought off. Second, while Johnson wanted people to love him, Cummings didn't care what anyone thought of him.

The team in Number 10 which had to deal with all these developments was new but not harmonious. In January Johnson had recruited as chief of staff Dan Rosenfield, a former civil servant who had been principal private secretary to both Alistair Darling and George Osborne at the Treasury. He was recommended by Paul Deighton, the chief executive of the 2012 Olympics' organising committee who helped sort out the PPE mess during the pandemic. Rosenfield had lost a power struggle in Deighton's firm Hakluyt and it suited the peer to find him an exit route.

The appointment came as a surprise to many, including Rishi Sunak, since it had been announced that Eddie Lister would take the helm for three months while a search was conducted for a permanent chief. 'Eddie gets appointed and everyone is happy,' a Treasury source said. 'Seven days later Dan Rosenfield is now chief of staff. The appointment was the beginning of the end of Boris Johnson's premiership. Not because Dan is a bad man, but it didn't work.'

Rosenfield was clever but totally clueless about the Conservative Party and his Whitehall experience came entirely from the civil service side. 'He asked how the Tory Party chooses its candidates, whether it was the members,' a senior colleague recalled. 'It was obvious when he came to conference that he had never been to one before.' An MP said, 'Dan didn't know any MPs. He had no grasp whatsoever of the parliamentary party.'

Political aides quickly complained of Rosenfield's instinct to cut them out of decisions and work through his old network of mandarins instead. 'When something happens, he rings up officials in the department and says he wants to speak to the director responsible,' said one ministerial aide. 'He doesn't go to ministers or special advisers.' Another said, 'If you're a civil servant, the Whitehall process is a game, but when the game is done, the slate is wiped clean because nobody is going to lose their job for losing the game. If you're a political person, you do lose your job if you lose the game. Your word is your bond because that's the only thing that binds these advisers together.' A Treasury aide added, 'Rosenfield would renege on promises made to Liam [Booth-Smith] and Rishi all the time ... He was like a mini-Boris, running around saying "Yes" to everything when he was supposed to be the one getting a grip.'

Rosenfield took the desk nearest to the prime minister's study in the outer office. He insisted on installing a Bloomberg terminal, used by City slickers to keep up with financial news and message each other. 'It was the single most emblematic thing of his complete cluelessness,' a political colleague said. 'Nobody in politics is on Bloomberg instant messenger. It just symbolised that his prime locus was not Westminster and Whitehall, but the City. He liked the idea that as the PM's chief of staff he could whack off messages to CEOs. But it just underscored his utter irrelevance.' Another colleague said, 'He insisted on having a wardrobe put in his office, so he had somewhere to hang his suits, because he cycles in. When a wardrobe was found, he didn't like it, so he insisted something was custom-built overnight. Facilities moved heaven and earth to sort it out; the next morning he was angry because his office smelt of wood stain.'

A die-hard Manchester United fan, Rosenfield blotted his copybook early by pressing Johnson to support plans for a new European super league, which his club was backing. When the mutinous reaction of fans forced the teams to ditch the project, Johnson, who knew so little about football he did not even pretend to support a team, was needlessly embroiled and had to publicly denounce the plans. Rosenfield overcompensated for his early missteps with gauche pronouncements to his new colleagues, calling male advisers 'matey'. On a Zoom call with spads, he declared they would be 'getting twatted' together. One recalled, 'It was painful.'

Rosenfield also enjoyed the baubles which came with the job. Others in Number 10 looked askance in September 2021 when he attended the premiere, at the Royal Albert Hall, of the new James Bond Film, *No Time to Die*. 'People were told they could arrive five hours early and walk up the red carpet or come through a back entrance,' a senior figure recalled. 'He actually went five hours early to walk up the red carpet and get noticed.'

In his defence, Rosenfield had an unenviable job, trying to follow the power vortex that was Cummings. In terms he would have understood, it was a bit like David Moyes replacing Alex Ferguson at Old Trafford. 'Whoever comes next is going to be temporary unless they're a José Mourinho-level genius,' a member of the policy unit observed. Nonetheless, for a moment it felt like 'the grown-ups are in charge'. Rosenfield was shocked when he learned the details of wall-papergate. 'He couldn't believe anyone had allowed such a crazy arrangement to go ahead in the first place,' an ally said, 'or that so much time had been spent on trying and failing to sort out the mess.'

Rosenfield formed a close alliance with Jack Doyle, appointed director of communications in April 2021 when James Slack left to become deputy editor of the *Sun*. Doyle, the son of a policeman who had cut his teeth as a crime and then political reporter for the *Daily Mail*, had been both Cain and Slack's deputy. Doyle and Rosenfield were quick to do away with the idea of televised press conferences for the lobby, which meant Allegra Stratton was surplus to requirements. Stratton was sent to work on the COP26 climate summit.

Outside of these two appointments, however, the influence of Carrie Symonds was plain to see. Her friends Henry Newman and Simone Finn, a glamorous Tory peer who once dated Michael Gove, both took senior jobs. Henry Cook, who like Newman had once worked for Gove, was also a key player in the new regime. The most glaring issue in Nadine Dorries' book *The Plot* was to surmise that their arrival in Number 10 provided evidence of Gove's Machiavellian activities, when their patron was actually the prime minister's wife. However, Johnson was now surrounded by aides from a different generation with very different reference points to his own. Ben Gascoigne, who had been with him since City Hall, had to be persuaded not to resign. He eventually left in April 2021.

Cummings wasn't the only one lobbing hand grenades. After months of hints, Jennifer Arcuri finally gave an interview to the *Sunday Mirror* on 28 March, confirming she'd had a four-year relationship with Johnson while he was mayor. She claimed he asked to borrow £3.10 on their first date and said that one raunchy picture she sent him was 'enough to make a bishop kick a hole in a stained-glass window'.[15] By now this sort of thing bounced off Johnson and the public was understandably more focused on the end of the third Covid lockdown the following day.

Neither Arcuri nor Cummings did much to dent Johnson's prospects in the local elections on 6 May, when the Tories gained thirteen councils and 235 councillors. In the first big test of Keir Starmer's leadership, Labour went backwards, losing eight councils and 327 councillors. Overall, the Tories got 36 per cent of the vote, seven points ahead of Labour. On the same day, the Tories won the Hartlepool by-election with a 23 per cent swing, called when incumbent Mike Hill stood down after being kicked out of the Labour Party amid sexual misconduct allegations.

It was the first time the Conservatives had won the seat. Starmer spent much of the following day on the verge of resigning. 'I had a moment where I thought we are not going to be able to do this,' he admitted later.[16] Instead, it became the inspiration he needed to overhaul the party, tack to the centre and do what it would take to win the general election.

From January 2021 to the summer, Johnson was on a high. He could regularly be heard lustily singing 'Strong Britain, Great Nation', a surprise YouTube hit by a school choir, which opened: 'We are Britain, And we have one dream, To unite all people, In one great team.'

On 28 May, Lord Geidt, the former private secretary to the Queen who had become the prime minister's ethics adviser, issued his ruling on wallpapergate. Johnson, 'unwisely, in my view allowed the refurbishment of the apartment at No 11 Downing Street to proceed without more rigorous regard for how this would be funded', his report concluded. But it also stated (inaccurately as it transpired) that the PM had no idea that Lord Brownlow had paid £58,000 towards the makeover. He cleared the PM of breaching the ministerial code.

The following day, Saturday 29 May, Johnson and Carrie got married in a private ceremony in Westminster Cathedral. The prime minister ordered his team to withhold the information from the press, but the *Sun on Sunday* was tipped off by a passer-by who saw the couple emerge. A reporter got confirmation from a member of the clergy.

June allowed Johnson to play the statesman at the G7 summit in Cornwall, though it was not all plain sailing. On the 17th the Tories lost a by-election in Chesham and Amersham, caused by the death of MP Cheryl Gillan. The Lib Dems overturned a majority of more than 16,000 with a swing of 25.2 per cent, the first time a non-Tory had won there since the seat was formed in 1974. Two weeks later, on 1 July, Labour just held Batley and Spen, caused by the departure of Tracey Brabin to become mayor of West Yorkshire. Despite Tory optimism, Kim Leadbeater, sister of the slain Jo Cox, scraped over the line by 323 votes.

Between the two by-elections Matt Hancock was forced to resign as health secretary after CCTV footage was passed to the *Sun* of him kissing and fondling Gina Coladangelo, a friend since university who was also married with three children, when social distancing was in force. Johnson first told Hancock he would stand by him, then ordered him to quit. 'The thing I've worked out about Boris is that he doesn't want the media to force people to resign,' a political adviser said. 'It's about control. He wants to be the person who fires them.'

All remaining Covid restrictions were lifted in July, a moment dubbed 'Freedom Day' in Number 10. Looking back, Johnson was to argue that his successes in 2021 proved he did not need Cummings. In his mind he was politically unassailable for a year after the Vote Leavers left before things started to go wrong. 'Cummings went absolutely spastic with fury when we defeated Labour in Hartlepool and when we continued to be ahead in the polls even though he was trying to kill us,' a Johnson familiar said. 'To ascribe the sole success of the government to the period he was there, is absolute rubbish.' But with Cummings and Cain had departed any political direction. For months Number 10 talked up a speech on 'levelling up'. But when it came, on 15 July, it was a damp squib, lacking major announcements or intellectual heft. Cummings kept up his campaign. On 20 July he briefed Laura Kuenssberg about the incident in March 2020 when Johnson had to be talked out of going to see the Queen as Covid-19 ripped through Downing Street. When Kuenssberg called Number 10, they denied the incident. Johnson's reflex to deny anything negative, regardless of the number of witnesses, was exactly what Cummings had predicted. One day it would catch him out.

August brought storm clouds, but far from Downing Street, in Afghanistan, where a precipitous American military withdrawal, opposed by Britain, led to disaster. US forces held the airport outside Kabul to evacuate their forces – to hit a 31 August deadline, imposed by President Joe Biden, of total withdrawal in time for the twentieth anniversary of the September 11 terror attacks. But as they pulled out, the Taliban swept across the country in just a few days. The capital fell on 15 August. Thousands of Afghans who had assisted Western forces as translators or members of the security services fled for their lives.

On Saturday 14th, as the British ambassador, Sir Laurie Bristow, prepared to board a plane to leave Afghanistan, a military officer said, 'I don't think so, do you?' Chief of staff Dan Rosenfield said Bristow had to stay. Dominic Raab, the foreign secretary, refused to accept his instruction and stated that he was only prepared to be overruled by the prime minister himself. Johnson told Raab, 'Consider yourself overruled, there is no way the ambassador is leaving.'[17]

The following Monday, with the airport surrounded by escapees and Taliban, Biden used a press conference to reject any suggestion the withdrawal could have been handled better. In London, a minister said the president 'looked gaga', while an aide described Biden as 'doolally'. Frustrations grew more acute when Johnson requested a call with Biden on Monday morning and the president did not ring back until 10 p.m. on Tuesday. At his family property on Exmoor, Johnson was wrestling with a television which was on the blink as he tried to watch Biden, complaining, 'Why won't he speak to me?' Johnson openly referred to the president as 'Sleepy Joe', the nickname he had been given by Donald Trump. While most people in Number 10 had wanted Biden to win the election, Johnson told one confidant his 'lizard brain', where his darkest thoughts resided, had been cheering on Trump.

As the 'Afghani-shambles' unfolded Tom Tugendhat, who had fought with the SBS in Afghanistan and Iraq, made the speech of the year, talking of his 'anger and grief and rage' at the 'abandonment of not just a country but the sacrifice that my friends made'. Tugendhat, like other veteran MPs, was frantically engaged behind the scenes in trying to facilitate the escape of his comrades in arms from the Afghan army, paying local drivers to get them to land borders with neighbouring countries, dubbed 'Uber escapes'.

The most heated recriminations concerned the response of Raab and the Foreign Office. When the crisis began, the foreign secretary had been holidaying in a five-star resort in Crete. On 13 August, Raab dialled in to Cobra from his beachside hotel. After that meeting he was told by Dan Rosenfield to come home. But Raab spoke to Johnson and got permission to stay with his family for two more days, a dreadful judgement by the prime minister. It was a shame that Rob Oxley, Raab's savvy media spad, who thought his boss should fly home immediately, was absent on honeymoon. A fellow holidaymaker at the five-star Grecotel Amirandes Boutique hotel said he had seen Raab 'lounging around on the beach on the very day Kabul was falling into Taliban hands', sunbathing, playing paddle ball, swimming, 'running on the beach and washing the sand off his legs'. Raab said this could not be true because 'the sea was closed' that day, one of the least persuasive excuses ever proffered by a cabinet minister.

While he was away, officials worked from home and thousands of emails to the Foreign Office crisis centre from people seeking safe passage out of Afghanistan went unread. The foreign secretary eventually landed back in Britain at 1.40 a.m. on Monday, after Kabul had fallen. Stephen Lovegrove, the national security adviser, swanned home a day after Raab. The permanent secretary at the Foreign Office, Sir Philip Barton, was also on holiday. Raab told him not to fly back, apparently so he would not make the foreign secretary look bad. Barton didn't return until the evacuation was over.

The last British soldiers came home on Saturday 28 August. Operation Pitting – the largest British evacuation since the Second World War – had saved 15,000 people, including 5,000 Britons and their families, plus more than 8,000 Afghan former UK staff and their families. But Foreign Office negligence in preparing exit routes was blamed for 9,000 eligible for rescue by the UK being left behind.

Tragedy was the handmaiden of farce. Whitehall became transfixed by the fate of former Marine Paul 'Pen' Farthing, who was trying to evacuate two hundred cats and dogs rescued by his Nowzad animal charity. As he tried to get visas for his staff, Farthing was recorded threatening to 'destroy' Peter Quentin, a special adviser to Ben Wallace, if he did not approve the flight. Wallace regarded Farthing's plan to charter a plane for his animals as an abomination. Johnson denied overruling the defence secretary to approve the animal airlift. But Dominic Dyer, a friend of Farthing's, lobbied Carrie Johnson, another friend, to get the plane in the air. 'Boris and Carrie DID help rescue my friend Pen, his staff and dogs from Afghanistan,' Dyer tweeted. 'They should speak up – and be proud of it!'[18] The following year, Raphael Marshall, a Foreign Office employee, gave written evidence to MPs that the FCO had 'received an instruction' from the PM to evacuate the animals. An email to the Foreign Office evacuation team said, 'The PM has just authorised their staff and animals to be evacuated.'

The Afghan debacle was followed by a cabinet reshuffle in which Raab was demoted to justice secretary, though Johnson had planned to do that in July, even before the capitulation in Kabul. Liz Truss became foreign secretary, Michael Gove took charge of a new ministry for levelling up. Johnson loyalist Nadine Dorries was promoted to culture secretary and Jacob Rees-Mogg made Brexit opportunities minister.

While Afghanistan suggested a nation in retreat with its tail between its legs, the government's integrated defence and security review, presided over by John Bew, helped shape a new strategy for post-Brexit

Britain's place in the world – a country forming nimble new alliances to tackle specific problems. Foreign policy flexibility was to prove one of the clearer benefits of Brexit. In September, Johnson agreed the Aukus defence pact with the United States and Australia, a tacit attempt to respond to growing Chinese global activism. Under the deal, the US and the UK would assist Australia in acquiring nuclear-powered submarines. That led Australia to scrap an existing contract with the French. Emmanuel Macron reacted with Gallic fury, withdrawing his ambassador from Washington and Canberra. French officials said they had not bothered to leave London because the UK was insignificant. Johnson delivered an equally characteristic riposte, telling the French 'to *prenez un grip* and *donnez-moi un break*'.[19]

Tory conference that October was arguably Johnson's political peak. Under the slogan 'Build Back Better', he mapped out a post-Brexit world in which wages kept rising as business stopped 'mainlining' on cheap immigrant labour. In his speech, Johnson invoked Winston Churchill, Margaret Thatcher and tennis star Emma Raducanu, and found time to tease Michael Gove, who had been filmed dancing alone in a suit in an Aberdeen nightclub, dubbing him 'Jon Bon Govey'. A cabinet minister wryly noted, 'I had had twelve conferences as an MP. That was by far the most stable – partly because Boris was the PM and he wasn't destabilising everyone. I remember thinking: this guy is going to be here forever.' The author sought to capture Johnson's pre-eminence and ideological breadth, tweeting, 'Boris Johnson now squats like a giant toad across British politics. He has expanded the Overton window in both directions. Praising bankers and drug companies, while tight on immigration and woke history. Cheered for lauding the NHS and pro LGBT. Where does Labour find a gap?' Nine months later Johnson would be gone, crushed like the toad beneath the harrow.[20]

The prime minister made a success of hosting the COP26 summit that November. Britain seemed the natural home of climate talks: forty thousand people sitting around for a fortnight talking about the weather. Allegra Stratton helped Johnson boil the goals down to 'coal, cars, cash and trees' and progress was delivered in all four 'baskets'. Leaders from more than 120 countries, covering 88 per cent of the world's forests, agreed to end and reverse deforestation. More than 100 countries agreed to cut methane emissions. Most strikingly, more than 40 committed for the first time to phase out coal power – though the summit ended with

Alok Sharma in tears as India, with the support of China, watered down the conclusions to see coal production 'phased down' rather than 'phased out'.

Johnson's enthusiasm for green issues was credited to (and blamed on) Carrie, though this was wrong. Even at Oxford, Michael Gove recalled Johnson introducing himself as a 'green Tory'. 'Boris is very into net zero, though he doesn't broadcast that,' a friend of the couple said. 'Carrie is much more concerned with animals.'

Interlude: In the midst of this apotheosis of the team who brought Britain Brexit, there was also personal loss. On 2 July, Michael Gove and his wife Sarah Vine issued a joint statement announcing that they were to divorce after 'drifting apart'. No marital breakdown has but one cause, yet Vine was clear Brexit itself had been a significant factor. 'My whole life fell away,' she wrote. 'I didn't speak to many close friends ... Marriage can take strain, but it cannot take that much.' Vine told *Tatler* six months later, 'Politics creates a toxic environment and puts immense pressure on families and marriages ... I can't look after my family and myself and be a wife of politics ... My ulterior motive throughout my entire life was to stop my husband being prime minister because I can't think of anything worse.' She added, 'Despite all the rumours, his only mistress was politics. That's what he is in love with.'[21]

Those seeking further clues read Vine's column after Matt Hancock left his wife just a month earlier: 'The problem with the wife who has known you since way before you were king of the world is that she sees through your façade.' While political wives remain 'the same person', for the husbands, 'Climbing that far up Westminster's greasy pole changes a person. And when someone changes, they require something new from a partner. Namely, someone who is as much a courtesan as a companion, one who understands their brilliance and, crucially, is personally invested in it. Not someone who thinks it's all a monumental nuisance and wishes they would get a proper job that doesn't involve people poking cameras in your face and commenting on your poor choice of footwear.'[22]

Boris Johnson lost his mother on 13 September, the artist Charlotte Johnson Wahl, to whom he had been close. In the words of her friend Mary Killen, her son 'absolutely worshipped her'.[23] As a young boy with hearing difficulties, he had bonded with his mother over a shared love of painting. Many saw Johnson's creation of the character 'Boris', at once bombastic and vulnerable, as a way of coping with his mother's nervous breakdown in the 1970s. She had been suffering from Parkinson's disease when she died. Another friend, Miriam Gross, saw Charlotte as Boris's 'role model'. She said, 'I think she felt particularly protective and anxious about Boris and regarded him as very vulnerable. She must have been a huge support for him, because she completely understood him, including his weaknesses.'[24] Now that huge support was gone.

Johnson's family, in all its complexity, was present at Charlotte's funeral in Notting Hill. Boris, Rachel, Leo and Jo Johnson carried their mother's coffin. Boris, Carrie and Wilfred sat in the front right pew, Carrie in an ostentatious black hat, periodically thrusting her son into the prime minister's lap for a bottle feed. Rachel, Leo and Jo sat front left. A couple of rows back was Marina Wheeler in what mourners described as 'a buffer zone' of grandchildren, with his first wife Allegra Mostyn Owen and his first girlfriend Alexa de Ferranti also present. At the back, his father Stanley accompanied Stephanie, his daughter by Helen Macintyre.[25]

Some who saw him in the months ahead say Johnson was, understandably, 'teary' when talking about Charlotte. One said, 'I think there was a lack of compassion for this man who had been dealing with a lot of trauma. When you lose your mum, it shows you your own mortality.'

A week after his mother's death, Johnson gave a speech to the UN General Assembly, comparing mankind's attempts to deal with climate change to those of a teenager emerging from a period of immaturity – which was loaded with autobiographical themes. Mankind, he said, was at the 'fateful age' where it was able to 'engage in all sorts of activity that is not only potentially embarrassing but also terminal. In what seemed like self-analysis, Johnson added, 'We still cling with part of our minds to the infantile belief that the world was made for our gratification and pleasure and we combine this narcissism with an assumption of our own immortality. We believe that someone else will clear up the mess we make, because that is what someone else has always done … We have got away with it so far, and therefore we will get away with it again.'[26]

Some think the loss of his mother affected Johnson's judgement in the months ahead. Certainly, he took no time off work. The prime minister was about to embark on a period in which the Johnsonian belief that he would always 'get away with it' turned 'embarrassing' issues into a situation that was politically 'terminal'.

*   *   *

On 2 November, the prime minister flew back from COP26 to attend a dinner at the Garrick Club in Covent Garden with a host of former *Daily Telegraph* leader writers. They dined on roast pheasant and Grand Marnier soufflé amply lubricated by claret. Johnson gave a speech noting that he had only written two *Telegraph* leaders, the second (and last) of which had supported the Ayatollah Khomeini after declaring a fatwa against the novelist Salman Rushdie. After ruminating about his achievements in government, Johnson was heckled: 'You haven't been very conservative.'[27] He laughed raucously. He must also have been joking when, as one participant told the *New European*, he admitted 'buyer's remorse' about his marriage to Carrie.[28] Others at the dinner rallied to say the story was untrue. Jack Doyle went into overdrive, calling the paper's editor-in-chief, Matt Kelly, at 10.30 p.m. to say Johnson was prepared to sue for defamation – a hollow threat it transpired.

Charles Moore claimed he did not, at the dinner at least, raise the case of his old friend Owen Paterson, who had been the subject of his column three days earlier. The former environment secretary was facing suspension from the Commons, having been found guilty of 'paid advocacy', secretly lobbying on behalf of two firms who paid him handsomely. Paterson got £49,000 from Randox, a health care company based in Northern Ireland. During the pandemic the company was awarded a £133 million contract for Covid testing kits and a £347 million contract for testing work – after Paterson pressed their case with James Bethell, the health minister responsible for private sector deals. In 2016 Paterson took a second job with Lynn's Country Foods and lobbied the Food Standards Agency about their 'naked bacon' produce.

During the investigation by Kathryn Stone, the parliamentary commissioner for standards, Paterson's wife Rose took her own life, he believed, because of the stress and shame of the probe. When Stone's report was published on 26 October it found Paterson had egregiously breached the rules on lobbying and recommended he be suspended from the Commons for thirty days. A ten-day ban was enough to trigger a recall petition in his Shropshire North seat, which in turn could force a by-election likely to end his career. The sanction had to be voted on by the whole house. Moore and a group of Tory right-wingers thought the system unfair and that it was wrong Paterson had no means of appeal.

The morning after the Garrick Club dinner Johnson, who had previously resisted intervening to help Paterson, changed his mind. Mark

Spencer, the chief whip, Jacob Rees-Mogg and Declan Lyons, Johnson's new political secretary, presented a plan which would see the government table a motion to delay the vote on Paterson while a committee of nine MPs decided whether there should be an appeal mechanism. The idea had been gestating since the weekend, but Johnson's absence at COP26 meant this was the first time it had been discussed with everyone present. The move which began the disintegration of his government should have been more carefully considered. Andrea Leadsom agreed to table the motion and John Whittingdale said he would chair the committee. In essence, they wanted to change the rules to save Paterson. The trio rejected the idea of simply voting down Paterson's punishment or reducing it to less than ten days as fraught with peril. 'We all agreed we could not be seen to be defending Owen Paterson's conduct personally,' one of those involved said. 'But we all felt a profound sympathy for the fact that his wife had committed suicide. He's paid the ultimate price. Second, a lot of his colleagues felt very strongly that the process had been flawed and therefore there needed to be an appeal system.'

As a fan of classical literature, Johnson ought to have been more attuned to the speed with which hubris could become nemesis. 'He was high on his own supply,' a minister observed. To make Paterson a cause célèbre was foolish since those who read the report concluded he was 'bang to rights'. Paterson had been an anachronism even when he was in David Cameron's cabinet, best known outside Eurosceptic circles for declaring during a badger cull, 'The badgers have moved the goalposts.'

There was a second reason, Johnson's aides believed, why he was sympathetic to Paterson. The parliamentary commissioner had investigated the prime minister over his holiday in Mustique, paid for by a Tory donor, and Stone was champing at the bit to investigate whether Johnson had made the correct declarations about the funding of the flat makeover. Stone represented everything Johnson disliked about the rules and of which the disorganised PM was always liable to fall foul.

Dan Rosenfield and Jack Doyle told Johnson to read the report, since he had not done so. Two witnesses said he pronounced it 'quite bad' and 'quite damning'. The chief of staff raised the key objection: 'Why would Labour play ball with this? And what happens when Labour say, "Fuck off I'm not putting anyone on the committee."'[29] But having garnered a reputation for cluelessness about politics, Rosenfield was ignored. 'Dan argued against the Paterson course of action, to be fair to him,' a cabinet minister said. 'But he was ignored on the basis of, "You don't really understand the Tory Party."' Spencer, whose job it was to understand Parliament, declared that MPs on all sides were fully on board. Johnson was persuaded. 'His view was fuck this, let's rip the plaster off.'[30]

At 11.12 a.m. lobby journalists were sent a message announcing the plan and arguing, 'This isn't about one case but providing Members of Parliament from all political parties with the right to a fair hearing.' Rees-Mogg and Spencer had badly misread the mood of Conservative MPs.

Johnson began to realise he had made a mistake as he sat down on the front bench between PMQs and his statement on the G20. Next to him was Alister Jack, who had taken Scottish questions earlier. 'See you next week,' Jack said.

'Where are you going?' Johnson asked.

'I'm going up to COP, I'm speaking there later.'

'What about the vote?'

Jack laughed. 'Good luck with that!'

'Really?' said a startled prime minister. 'Is it a bad one?'

'It's ridiculous, honestly,' said Jack.

The amendment passed that afternoon, but 13 Tories voted against the government and another 98 abstained. Christian Wakeford, who won the red wall seat of Bury South in 2019, marched up to Paterson in the division lobby and called him 'a fucking selfish cunt'.

Angela Rayner, Labour's deputy leader, promptly announced that Labour would play no part in the 'sham process' or the 'corrupt committee', a stance quickly echoed by the SNP and the Lib Dems.

Back in Number 10, Spencer and Rees-Mogg admitted they had no plan and Rosenfield wanted the whole scheme to be scrapped. Dougie Smith was among those arguing the opposite. 'Never U-turn!' he growled at one of the architects of the mess. While Johnson considered his options, Paterson took to Sky News and, with the clanging tin ear which was the hallmark of his media appearances, announced, 'I would do it all again.'

The following morning, Thursday 4 November, Rees-Mogg signalled a retreat, telling MPs, disingenuously, 'I fear last night's debate conflated the individual case with general concern, this link needs to be broken.' Paterson announced his intention to stand down, complaining about the 'cruel world of politics'. Kwasi Kwarteng got into hot water for calling on Stone to 'consider her position', the kind of rash media intervention for which the business secretary was renowned, which would have even more serious consequences in a future job. Friday's *Daily Mail* splashed with the question: 'IS ANYBODY IN CHARGE AT No 10?' On the Saturday, John Major described the handling of the affair as 'shameful' and Johnson's government as 'politically corrupt'. Ministers told *The Times* the chief whip should be sacked.[31]

When Johnson saw Jack the following week he said, 'You might have been more forceful!'

'What's the point?' said the Scottish secretary, whose fierce loyalty gave him licence to speak his mind. 'You don't listen to anyone.'

The Lib Dems won the by-election in Paterson's seat and MPs endorsed a new code of conduct banning MPs from acting as paid lobbyists. The Paterson debacle severed good relations between Johnson and his MPs, raised questions about the competence of his team and caused deep divisions between older and younger Tory MPs. The old guard, who had known Paterson well, resented their lucrative second jobs being removed. The newer intakes could not forgive the cliquey naivety of the pro-Patersonians. A cabinet minister remarked, 'The first rule of politics is that if you listen to Charles Moore and do the complete opposite of what he says, you won't go far wrong.'

Since Cummings' departure from Downing Street, there did not seem to be anyone in Number 10 capable of saying no to Johnson and curbing his wilder flights of fancy. Rosenfield had made the right call but been ignored. Increasingly the building was divided between his allies and the friends of Carrie Johnson. To one cabinet ally, the key to the Paterson disaster was the absence from Downing Street of Eddie Lister: 'When Ed left, it began to unravel. He was the person giving Boris the best advice and the only one he listened to.' There was also deep resentment that MPs had been made to vote for something and then defend it in public, before having the rug pulled from under them by a Number 10 U-turn. This was to be a toxic theme of the next eight months.

At cabinet on 11 November, the prime minister was unusually contrite. A keen tennis player, he admitted the mess was 'an unforced error'. Later that week a Savanta ComRes poll gave Labour a six-point lead, their biggest to that point under Starmer.

Johnson had made mistakes before, but this one had come from a clear blue sky. A Tory strategist said, 'Boris opened this can of worms himself.' Cummings had, so far, failed to bring down the prime minister. The Paterson affair was the moment Johnson began to accomplish that task for himself. After he had left Number 10, he would privately admit Paterson was the moment the rot set in.

Later that month, Johnson shot himself in the foot again when he gave a speech to the CBI and lost his way. His refusal to use an autocue meant he was beholden to a paper script. 'It was an honest mistake from the duty clerk who didn't print the page numbers at the bottom,' an aide recalled. 'So it got jumbled up.' Johnson paused for an agonising twenty seconds, shuffling papers as he tried to find his place, muttering 'forgive me', before launching into an eccentric disquisition on children's television: 'Yesterday I went, as we all must, to Peppa Pig World. I don't know if you've been to Peppa Pig World … Hands up who has been to Peppa Pig World … Not enough. I was a bit hazy what I would find at Peppa Pig World but I loved it. Peppa Pig World is very much my kind of place.' To sniggering from the audience, Johnson continued, 'It has very safe streets, discipline in schools and a heavy emphasis on mass transit systems, I noticed. Even if they're a bit stereotypical about Daddy Pig. In the past such a stream of consciousness might have been regarded as charming, but it convinced some MPs the prime minister was losing it.

The sense of a government veering off the rails was reinforced by three other developments. Tensions between Johnson and his chancellor Rishi Sunak led to open wounds at the top of government. Within three weeks of the Paterson disaster, stories began to break about another sleaze scandal which became known as 'partygate'. In parallel, throughout 2021, it became clear that, thanks to the way events were unfolding in Northern Ireland, Brexit was not really 'done' after all.

FROSTY THE NO MAN

The Brexit Dreadnought

January 2021 to July 2022

Just before 4 p.m. on Friday 29 January 2021, the EU made arguably their worst tactical misstep of the entire Brexit process. The evening was drawing in, officials preparing to call it a week, when Brendan Threlfall spotted a tweet from the Belfast-based BBC correspondent John Campbell saying the EU had decided to trigger Article 16 of the Northern Ireland Protocol, allowing one side or the other to suspend aspects of the deal in an emergency. Threlfall WhatsApped the tweet to one of his counterparts in the Taoiseach's office. It was the first the Irish government had heard of this bombshell as well. In one fell swoop, the Commission had erected a vaccine border on the island of Ireland and managed to unite Britain, Ireland and many other capitals against them.

In an intervention simultaneously inept and toxic, the Commission announced they were pulling the emergency brake to prevent the export of Covid vaccines from the EU, where there were shortages, an action they justified 'to avert serious societal difficulties due to a lack of supply' in member states.

There were two issues: the first was the AstraZeneca vaccine, developed with Oxford University, which was being sold at cost, unlike the other vaccines, and seen as Britain's gift to the world during the pandemic. The British government had not only backed the vaccine but also signed a contract stipulating that one hundred million doses had to be supplied to the UK before AZ began fulfilling deals with others. The EU had a four-hundred-million-dose deal, but a problem with one of AZ's European factories meant supply would be 60 per cent lower than expected. To complicate matters, Britain had paid to fit out a Halix factory in the Netherlands to manufacture the drug. As such, it was technically part of the British supply chain, not the EU's, but the Commission felt entitled to the output of a factory inside its borders. 'The EU couldn't understand why it was rolling off the production line for us while they were getting nothing,' a Number 10 official said. 'Our contract was superior. They agreed their contract nine months later. They were way behind schedule. They were furious.'

The EU, driven by Emmanuel Macron, had backed other suppliers, including two French companies whose vaccines had not worked out. AstraZeneca found itself the target of a disreputable briefing war led by Macron, who publicly claimed it was 'almost ineffective' in the over-sixty-fives, an assertion which was both irresponsible and inaccurate. The European Medicines Agency had approved it for use in all age groups, but against the advice of the EMA, France, Germany, Italy and Spain all temporarily suspended use of the Oxford vaccine.

Even before the row, things were 'very niggly' on the ground in Northern Ireland, with businesses surprised at the burden of paperwork required to move goods between Great Britain and Northern Ireland. But in January 2021 even Arlene Foster, the leader of the DUP, went on the record to say the protocol could be made to work. David Frost observed, 'Although there were some short-run shortages in Northern Ireland supermarkets, they mainly disappeared quickly and were arguably no worse than those in the rest of the UK.'[1] A minister added, 'It settled down. What blew it up was the vaccine export ban.'

Frost explained, 'We had been told repeatedly – incorrectly, but repeatedly – over the last five years that it was impossible to bring into play any new processes at the land border. We had been told there could be no new restrictions on North/South movements. This was why we had the protocol. Then the EU turned round and said – in pandemic conditions that were already extremely fraught, and just hours after President Macron had denounced the AZ vaccine as "quasi-ineffective" – that it proposed to ban exports of vaccines across the land border.'[2]

This created a second serious problem, since it blocked the next consignment of the Pfizer vaccine, manufactured in Belgium. 'We had bought and paid for them,' a Downing Street aide said. 'They were contractually owed to us under EU law.' It was not yet known that vaccines from different firms could be mixed and matched. Ten million of the most vulnerable people in the UK had been given the Pfizer jab.

Blocking the consignment would prevent them having the booster injection which gave them greater protection against the disease. 'We could send a van over to get it,' one aide suggested to Johnson in a later meeting. 'You could drive it.' The prime minister, predictably, liked this gung-ho approach.

Quite how the EU decision was made remains shrouded in mystery, since it was quickly dismissed by the Commission as 'an error'. In Whitehall, the understanding was that it was signed off by the 'cabinet' – or private office – of Ursula von der Leyen, the Commission president, but doubt remained how high up the food chain the decision went. The media focus on Britain's problems with Brexit and the border in Ireland meant the EU's issues were underappreciated. 'They wanted to stop vaccines leaving the EU and they couldn't stop anything from going into Northern Ireland,' a British official said. 'Once they got into Northern Ireland, you can do Northern Ireland to Great Britain. They realised the only technical way they could stop their vaccines going into the UK was to suspend the protocol. And it's true, that's the only way they could do it. But they just didn't realise the effect of doing that would just explode.' To many who had witnessed the serial ineptitude of much of British politics over the previous five years, and the patronising commentary often accompanying it from Brussels, the revelation that the EU was capable of similar miscalculation was perversely reassuring.

A spirited discussion ensued in London about how Boris Johnson should respond. In a video conference, with the prime minister in the Cabinet Room, Frost argued the EU triggering Article 16 was actually good news. 'We've been handed an opportunity to use this,' he said. It meant the UK could 'reserve the right' to use it too in future. To Frost, that was the sensible strategic move, one which would give Britain more leverage in the debates ahead about implementation. 'We should not let our outrage overwhelm our interests,' he urged, remarking later that the EU had 'set a very low bar for the use of Article 16', showing that it was in fact possible to control goods going across the land border, something the UK could have agreed to. 'We'd have had the moral high ground.'[3] Johnson took a different stance, revealing Brexit to be no longer his political priority. A slightly bad-tempered prime minister overruled Frost, making clear the far bigger prize was a successful vaccine rollout. 'We've got to use this to stop the EU blocking vaccines against us,' the PM said. 'Our vaccine stuff is a big success story. That's the big political issue.

That's the big domestic issue. We should use this to make sure that our vaccine programme carries on.' Johnson smelled redemption for the mistakes he had made in handling Covid. Nothing could get in the way of being the Western country with the fastest jabs rollout. 'Boris was straight onto the bigger prize,' a civil servant recalled.

On Northern Ireland, Johnson thought the EU's approach should be condemned for endangering the Good Friday Agreement, which Frost opposed. 'Frosty realised it created a problem,' an official said. 'Article 16 was now toxic. It's obviously a nuclear button but it backfired within hours and that made it harder to use.'

The rest of the year would be taken up with internal debates about when and how Britain could use Article 16 – or how to develop an even larger nuclear weapon.

Despite his refusal to go to war in the way Frost wanted, the prime minister was at his rambunctious best that day. Both Johnson and Micheál Martin, the Irish PM, spoke personally to von der Leyen to express 'deep unhappiness'. Johnson sought to extract a direct pledge from the Commission president that she would not block the consignment of Pfizer jabs. 'Just to be clear, are you saying you are stopping the export of the Pfizer doses?' he asked.

Silence.

'There are ten million vulnerable, elderly Brits. Not just Brits, actually, EU citizens living in the UK who have had their first dose. If you do this, you will be denying them the life-saving medicine that they're expecting. Can you guarantee that this export ban will not be applied to the Pfizer doses?'

Von der Leyen gave no such reassurances. Johnson tried again and again, channelling Jeremy Paxman v Michael Howard – a third, a fourth, a fifth time. Still she would not give the guarantee. 'Then this conversation is over,' said Johnson and put the phone down on her. An aide watching said, 'That was the best I ever saw him.'

After he had hung up, Johnson spoke to Martin. There were expressions of outrage from both Sinn Féin and the DUP, with Arlene Foster calling it 'despicable'. Even the Archbishop of Canterbury condemned the EU's move. Brussels swiftly backed down. 'They got in touch a few hours later and said, "Don't worry, the Pfizer doses will come,"' the Downing Street adviser recalled. Von der Leyen was forced to tweet that she had agreed an 'export authorisation mechanism' which would protect the protocol. Her office then issued a statement saying, 'The Commission is not triggering the safeguard clause.' The media too readily flags changes of course as a 'humiliating U-turn', but even the Europhile *Guardian* said as much in its intro to the story that night.[4]

Unusually for him, Johnson banned his team from making the full details of the row public. 'None of this to be briefed,' he ordered. 'Literally, none of this. We need to get it sorted. I don't want to provoke them into something.' Once again, Brexit leverage took a back seat to the vaccine programme. 'I never heard him give that instruction before,' a Number 10 aide said. The same order went out when it became clear the EU had pilfered some of the Dutch-manufactured AstraZeneca doses supposed to be bound for Britain. 'We ended up losing a few million from the Dutch Halix plant,' the aide revealed. 'We didn't give them permission; they took them. We ended up forgoing those. Again, we didn't make a fuss about it because we wanted the Pfizer jabs.'

Privately, Johnson seethed and even claimed in his memoir to have 'commissioned some work on whether it might be technically feasible to launch an aquatic raid' by the special forces to seize the 'kidnapped' jabs. One present said this was an outburst of jocular exasperation in one meeting and, 'There never was any planning.' It was an idea which died two weeks later when the military top brass visited Number 10. Lieutenant General Doug Chalmers, the deputy chief of the defence staff, said, 'Well, PM, it's certainly feasible', but concluded, 'If we are detected we will have to explain why we are effectively invading a long-standing Nato ally.' Johnson admitted, 'The whole thing was nuts.'[5]

There was a long-term Brexit dimension to the vaccine production, of course. David Davis saw his decision to resign in 2018 as leading to a Brexit where Britain had freedom to innovate: 'Why do vaccines matter? Obviously, they matter because thousands of lives are saved. But it's [also] become an exemplar of how, in new industries, the UK can lead innovation … You can do it with gene technology. You can do it with artificial intelligence. You can do it with self-driving cars … The resignation worked.'

But for the future of the protocol and medium-term UK–EU relations, the episode was a disaster. 'Unfortunately the damage had been done,' Frost recalled. 'The whole moral basis for the protocol had been destroyed in unionism's eyes. It had shown that the EU's interests came first, whatever the protocol said.'[6]

* * *

Frost remained disgruntled by Johnson's decision not to leverage the use of Article 16 for Brexit purposes – just at the time when the protocol was throwing up problems on the ground. 'This was a huge opportunity and we failed to take it,' he reflected later. 'As a consequence, we found ourselves in the only possible alternative position: that was to say that the protocol was not workable, but without being able to effectively point the finger at the EU for making it so.'[7] Worse, the status quo had been both returned and discredited and Britain then 'had the responsibility of managing' it.[8]

A plan to make Frost national security adviser had also been pulled, after Theresa May and others complained he had no security background. In mid-February, Frost went to see the prime minister, intending to resign. 'I think it's time to go,' he said. 'I came in to do the negotiation. The job's done, it's now time for others to take it over.' Privately he told friends, 'I've had enough.'

Frost was also at loggerheads with Michael Gove, who had been the point man in the joint committee with Maroš Šefčovič throughout 2020. Frost believed Gove had not been aggressive enough in using the threat of the UK internal market (UKIM) bill to extract concessions from Brussels when they were fleshing out the aspects of the protocol which had been left vague. He was already suspicious since Gove had backed May's deal and, as a Johnson loyalist, mistrusted him because of the events of 2016. 'Michael was forceful, formally,' a source familiar with Frost's thinking said. 'But not really. He kept sending tough letters to the EU and backing off them. The mistake was that we accepted too much when we didn't have to, the EU's presumption that applying their customs code to all goods crossing the Irish sea, that they had to be treated the same way. David thought we could have pushed harder and got some differentiation between UK and Ireland, between north and south goods.'

In 2020, Frost had been the tip of the negotiating spear with Brussels but after the Christmas Eve deal, the focus had switched to the joint committee. Protocol dictated that Šefčovič's interlocutor had to be a minister, not an official like Frost. This had created huge awkwardness when Gove hosted Šefčovič for a dinner in the Cabinet Office. The EU vice president wanted to talk one-on-one so Frost and other officials were forced to retreat to an anteroom. The meal took two hours while Frost sat impotent with rage waiting to see what had been agreed.

Johnson resisted Frost's attempt to walk away, telling him, 'No, you need to stay. If we have to make you a minister, we will.'

It was a time of great ferment in Downing Street. Henry Newman was taking over the role of protecting the Union, as Oliver Lewis was leaving. 'Sonic' had engaged in the new role with energy, drawing up a strategy to be more aggressive with the Scottish Nationalists. But, like Cleo Watson, he quickly felt isolated by the departure of other Vote Leave colleagues. Others regarded him with suspicion, amid briefings that he was a leaker – untrue in the author's experience – and he decided to walk. 'There's a new gang in charge,' he told friends, 'and I'm not part of the gang. They think I'm a jihadi.'

While the Goveites reasserted their control of the Union, with a more cautious policy stressing the benefits of membership for Scotland, Frost's power play ensured Gove lost control of Brexit negotiations and opened the door to a fresh hardball offensive there. Frost was given responsibility for the negotiations and made a Cabinet Office minister so he could talk to Šefčovič. He would also attend cabinet. 'Frosty got that cabinet job because he threatened to resign,' an ally of Gove complained. Gove himself put it more pithily: 'David wanted to take back control!'

Having negotiated the 2019 and 2020 deals, Frost knew the protocol as signed had serious problems, but he expected that it would survive until the first consent vote in 2024. He had tried to ensure its design and that of the Trade and Cooperation Agreement would create a structure in which Northern Ireland was incentivised to mirror Great Britain on regulation rather than the EU. 'I expected that we would do so much domestic reform and change within Great Britain between 2020 and 2024 that it would be self-evidently attractive to Northern Ireland to end the protocol and put some other arrangements in place,' he said.[9] He hoped his job would be to focus on post-Brexit reforms and otherwise settle things down. 'The plan was never to have a massive row immediately after signing it,' he told a friend later. 'I didn't expect it to come apart in the way it did quite so quickly.'

Some of the issues he confronted ought to have been predictable, others resulted from the EU choosing to implement the letter of the protocol in a manner which seemed overzealous to the British. Others arose because of events. Since Britain was no longer in the customs union, EU rules around goods crossing its borders were applied to the movement of goods between Great Britain and Northern Ireland. Traders were hit with burdensome customs paperwork, checks and duties. For agrifoods there were complex certification requirements. A single supermarket truck of goods might have to provide five hundred certificates – even when the cargo was supposed to stay solely in Northern Ireland. All this soon deterred some retailers from sending goods to the province at all. 'What surprised us is how strong the disincentive was,' Frost said later.[10] Goods moving east from Northern Ireland to Great Britain were much less restricted than those moving west, but they still required an export declaration. Chilled meats like sausages were banned altogether, impacting on some religious communities, who had trouble buying kosher or halal meat from the mainland. There were other nuisances. Parcels from people or businesses in Great Britain sent to friends, family and consumers in Northern Ireland were all subject to customs declarations.

Some 80 per cent of medicines in Northern Ireland came from Great Britain, but drugs approved for use by the UK's medicines regulator were not automatically available in Northern Ireland. By June thirty drugs were no longer available and cancer patients in Belfast found themselves denied a life-changing new drug available everywhere else in the UK. When the protocol was enacted in full, the situation was due to get worse with expensive and burdensome checks on all medicines; companies having to manufacture drugs with two completely different labels and supply chains; and pharmacies needing to check every package with scanners.

Those who saw Johnson's public protestations that his deal meant no customs checks as evidence of ignorance or turpitude, had a point. But it is also the case that while customs 'controls' were always part of the deal, the number of actual 'checks' – and with them the level of disruption – was a decision for the EU. 'We never succeeded in getting across the difference between controls and checks,' a minister said. 'Everyone still has a mental picture of the customs guy in a box stamping a form. That was the root of the confusion in the election. Modern customs processes are virtual in most cases; it's just somebody sending you an electronic notification to declare the contents of a consignment. You can't identify a point at which they're made at all other than to the computers ... We accepted there were going to be controls but we thought the actual number of checks was going to be extremely low – and in the end we'd be in charge of that, because we don't do as many checks as the EU would like us to do.'

What Frost and Johnson had not realised was that the EU would demand far more checks than expected and that the complexity of the processes, even where there were no checks, would put off businesses who did not have the patience for the new bureaucracy. Frost concluded, fairly or unfairly, that the EU was prepared to put strain on the Belfast Good Friday Agreement because they saw their interest 'as maintaining leverage over the UK, causing us political difficulties and creating incentives to keep us closely aligned with the EU'.

Frost said later, 'The protocol is not a clear, black and white document in every area … In Article 5 it says the provisions of the Union Customs Code should apply, and then in Article 6 it says we should all do our best to minimise checks and controls in the ports of Northern Ireland. You have to read those two things together; you can't just look at the first … There is a margin of appreciation here. If you are undermining the logic of it, then you are not working within the spirit of the protocol … Something can be legal but not consistent with what we are trying to do.'[11]

On 3 March, almost Frost's first day in charge, the British government unilaterally announced it was taking 'temporary technical steps' to extend some 'grace periods', agreed with the EU to ease in the new rules, until 1 October. These included areas like pet passports and non-commercial parcels. Gove had taken the decision before he left. In Brussels, though, it looked like Frost was pursuing a tougher line and trying to tear up the treaty he had negotiated. Twelve days later, the EU launched legal proceedings against the UK for failing to apply the treaty, proceedings which would ultimately be overseen by the European Court of Justice (ECJ). 'They went nuclear immediately,' a British negotiator said. 'We thought: if they do that every single time there is a problem we can't make this work.'

Levels of trust, already low, fell off a cliff. 'Boris immediately tilted towards the unionist view of the world and endorsed it,' an aide recalled. 'They didn't think Boris wanted to enforce the treaty.' Frost thought the EU going to court was a 'totally disproportionate reaction'. He said later, 'There is a tendency to be mesmerised by the minutiae of actions on Northern Ireland, but I just reject the proposition that extending a grace

Election night 2019: Boris Johnson celebrates his landslide victory in the Thatcher study of Number 10 with Carrie Symonds and Dominic Cummings

Brexit night, 31 January 2020: Johnson bangs a gong at 11 p.m. as Britain leaves the European Union, but it was Cummings who stole the headlines

Johnson recorded a video when he was isolating with Covid. Two days later he was in intensive care

First of all in my own case, although I'm feeling better,

Under Johnson and Sunak Stéphanie Riso became the key figure on the EU side and was prepared to bypass Michel Barnier to do a deal

David Frost and Oliver 'Sonic' Lewis negotiated both of Johnson's Brexit deals, and Lewis returned for the Windsor Framework as well

Cummings and Lee Cain met on Vote Leave and forged a formidable partnership in Number 10, but the breakdown of their relationship with Johnson spelled the end of his premiership

Kwasi Kwarteng, Truss's chancellor, brandishing the text of his 'mini-budget', which was anything but

Liz Truss gives her disastrous press conference after ditching her economic programme

After just forty-nine days Truss leaves Downing Street with husband Hugh and her two daughters, the shortest-serving prime minister in British history

Rishi Sunak and Ursula von der Leyen, the Commission president, bonded over their time at Stanford University

The only recent picture of Tory fixer Dougie Smith

Liam Booth-Smith, Sunak's chief of staff, in what one colleague called his 'shit John Travolta' outfit

David Cameron joins Emmanuel Macron, Olaf Scholz and Joe Biden for a photo which exposed Sunak's early departure from the D-Day commemorations

Sunak was better prepared and went on the attack during the TV debates with Keir Starmer

Nigel Farage's entry into the race leeched votes from the Tories and stirred heated emotions

Le Deluge: Sunak calls the 2024 election in a downpour, the first of several campaign gaffes

Morgan McSweeney, Keir Starmer's election director and chief strategist, helped him win his landslide

Sue Gray, who wrote the report into partygate and then prepared Starmer for government

Brexit looming in the background: Starmer with Nick Thomas-Symonds, who was tasked with leading his EU negotiations

period for the paperwork that goes with parcels makes you an international problem state.'[12]

For the British team, the EU's use of Article 16 and Macron rubbishing the AstraZeneca vaccine had a similar effect. In March and April, Frost sought to explain to Šefčovič, 'You've got to understand how damaging this behaviour has been.' He found the vice president calm rather than confrontational, someone who wanted to find a way through, but also a bureaucrat who believed that if only the bosses got together one-on-one they would both be able to compromise. A source said, 'We were gradually coming to the view, in April, May and June time that the protocol as it stood was unworkable and that we were going to have to use Article 16 to diffuse bits of it.'

Johnson was bullish. Liz Truss was also in favour of using Article 16, Gove and Rishi Sunak against. Frost agreed, in principle. By June he believed the UK would have to use it, but argued, 'We should keep the moral high ground and make an effort to renegotiate consensually first.' Frost went to see Johnson, who was now tougher than him. The prime minister had absorbed that notwithstanding clauses, as used in the UKIM bill, were the biggest weapon in his armoury. He wanted to try the same approach again.

Frost regarded that idea as a 'nuclear weapon' best left off the table. He had no legal or moral difficulty with it, but his view was that it was the 'shock effect' of the previous bill which had helped achieve their goals. He was still in touch with Oliver Lewis, who also believed that UKIM was a 'one off' and a rehash would not work. One of the last things he had said to Johnson before leaving Downing Street in February was, 'Don't do UKIM again. The EU didn't see it coming last time. Next time, they would.' Lewis was concerned that what had been a very high stakes gamble, with very clearly defined objectives (which were achieved), had now morphed in Johnson's mind into a simple solution to all his problems with the EU. 'I don't think it's necessary,' Frost said. 'We should try everything else first.' Reluctantly, Johnson agreed to a less confrontational approach. Britain would produce a 'command paper' instead, outlining how things might change to make the protocol workable.

Before that, Boris Johnson had to navigate the G7 summit in Carbis Bay, Cornwall, where he was playing host for the first time to the leaders of the world's most developed countries. Downing Street was concerned the agenda not be hijacked by the problems in Northern Ireland and fearful that US president Joe Biden – who prided himself on his Irish heritage – would make public comments critical of the UK's position. In the end, the summit was a triumph, with Carrie Johnson wheeled out as prime ministerial consort, with one-year-old Wilfred in tow, hogging the attention of the photographers. Biden privately told Johnson he would not tell him how to manage his country's internal affairs.

Johnson's encounters with von der Leyen, Charles Michel, the Council president, Angela Merkel and Macron were bruising, with the threat of tariffs flashed around, the EU fraternity apparently 'reading from a script'. Frost attended these meetings pointedly wearing Union Jack socks. Yet the French president gave Number 10 an unexpected opportunity to score points when they met on the morning of Saturday 12 June. Johnson complained that the EU's interpretation of the Northern Ireland Protocol would prevent processed meat, such as sausages, from being sent to the province from Britain. 'How would you like it if the French courts stopped you moving Toulouse sausages to Paris?' he asked.

Macron claimed that it was 'not a good comparison because Paris and Toulouse are part of the same country', according to a UK source who was present.

Johnson replied, 'Northern Ireland and Britain are part of the same country as well.'

When the story broke, a French diplomat said Macron was well aware that Northern Ireland was part of the UK but appeared to confirm the view that France saw it differently: 'It is not possible to compare the four nations that make up the UK with a unitary state such as France and its individual regions.' French officials said Macron used their meeting to offer Britain a 'reset' in relations – but only if Johnson 'kept his word' and enforced the protocol deal. A British official responded, 'We are enforcing the deal. That is the problem.'

Dominic Raab, the deputy prime minister, was unleashed on the airwaves to accuse Macron of 'offensive' behaviour. 'Could you imagine if we talked about Catalonia, the Flemish part of Belgium, one of the länder in Germany, northern Italy, Corsica in France as different countries. We need a bit of respect here.' Johnson said he would 'not hesitate' to use Article 16 to keep goods flowing.

*   *   *

The Monday after the summit, 14 June, Johnson and Frost had dinner in Downing Street with Scott Morrison, the Australian premier, to thrash out details of a trade deal. On the menu was Australian wine and Welsh lamb, two of the key moving parts in the deal. Morrison was accompanied by George Brandis, the Australian High Commissioner.

The crunch issue concerned the import of Australian beef and whether the quotas allowed to enter the UK would be measured by the 'product weight' of the cuts of meat, or the 'carcass weight equivalence' of the whole animal, bones and all. This was important because 10 tons of prime steak had a carcass weight of 13 tons, meaning the quotas were filled more quickly. The plan was to open the doors to Australian beef over a ten-year period based on carcass weight equivalence.

Johnson's desire to do a deal went too far. Three hours into the dinner, when Morrison pressed on beef quotas, Johnson conceded a deal based on product weight. Brandis wrote down what had been agreed and then left the room, ostensibly to use the toilet. He handed the paper to an aide, who immediately photographed it and sent it to the High Commission, where another colleague turned it into a formal trade document. This was printed in Number 10 and put in a folder for Brandis, who took it back into the dining room. Morrison asked Johnson to sign an agreement in principle and Johnson agreed.[13]

The next morning, Australia's chief negotiator Dan Tehan taunted Liz Truss, the trade secretary who had not been allowed into the dinner, over breakfast: 'Your boss has already conceded the whole kingdom.'

The command paper, designed to seize the initiative with the EU, was published on 21 July. 'The official machinery didn't want to renegotiate in any way,' a minister recalled, 'on the grounds that we had signed the treaty.' The essence of the paper, which would be Britain's stated policy for another fourteen months, was that the customs border was the land border, but for practical convenience, the UK would police goods going into Ireland in the Irish Sea. Second, goods of both types could circulate within Northern Ireland. If Britain was staking out a new position, they might as well make big demands. 'We wanted the ECJ taken out of the system altogether, with Northern Ireland becoming part of a TCA-like arrangement on the arbitration of disputes.' Frost argued that the EU's legal proceedings meant this was not just an ideological aspiration but a legitimate concern.

The package was signed off by a cabinet committee and Frost gave the EU a day's warning before it was made public. On 6 September the grace periods were extended. This time, no unilateral action was needed. 'Both sides agreed to freeze all current actions and see what could be done,' a British negotiator said. It would be another five weeks before the EU sent an official response.

In the intervening period, Michel Barnier announced he was running for the French presidency, triggering one of the most blackly comedic footnotes of the Brexit period. At a hustings for the centre-right Les Républicains party in Nîmes on 9 September, the human embodiment of EU orthodoxy suddenly began channelling the Brexiteers. Barnier demanded 'a referendum on the question of immigration' and a moratorium on all new arrivals from outside the EU. He insisted France must regain its 'legal sovereignty in order to no longer be subject to the judgments' of the ECJ and the European Union.

On hearing the news, Frost joked, 'He seemed to have been paying closer attention to our arguments than he let on at the time.' Nigel Farage branded Barnier 'the biggest hypocrite ever born'. Jean Quatremer, the veteran Brussels correspondent of the left-wing *Libération* newspaper, declared, 'Having dreamed of being a new Jacques Delors, he has ended up as Boris Johnson.'

Barnier's analysis, of course, was more sophisticated than the headlines allowed, but his embrace of Euroscepticism clearly horrified the *Observer*, the centre-left Sunday paper which secured an interview with Barnier on publication of his book, *My Secret Brexit Diary*. Outlining his 'lessons of Brexit', Barnier compared the red wall Leave voters to the *gilets jaunes* in France, the yellow-jacketed protesters whose anger about a fuel tax rise had morphed into a nationwide rebellion against the political establishment. 'Many regions in the UK, in France and Belgium and elsewhere have a sense of being abandoned by power; deprived of public services, of industry, of a future,' he told the paper. 'This is what I call a "popular" sentiment, which is not the same thing as populism. Populist politicians are using it for their own purposes.' Quite what Barnier thought he was doing it for was left unexplained. He even took aim at the EU: 'People in the bubble of Brussels think they are always right. They don't want to listen. They don't want to change anything. This is precisely the way to provoke more Brexits elsewhere in Europe.'[14]

When the French edition of his book had been published in May, Barnier also criticised the EU's vaccine programme, telling Politico, it was mired in 'administrative problems, bureaucracy ... and an almost-ideological mistrust of private-public partnerships ... We don't know how to take risks. The British took risks by financing the private sector. The Americans took risks.'[15] In the book, he noted that Leave voters thought 'they were voting against globalisation, against a Europe that did not protect them enough, against a Europe that had deregulated and de-industrialised. The same reasons that so many French voters in Marseille and Picardy vote for [French hard left leader] Jean-Luc Mélenchon and Marine Le Pen [of the Front National]. We must pay attention to this.'[16]

Despite copying this exact playbook when it came to his own (unsuccessful) campaign, Barnier consoled himself that he was still a good European since he did not want to prevent freedom of movement: 'I'm talking about immigration from outside the EU.'[17] It is curious that Barnier, thoughtful as he was about voter discontent, did not have greater understanding of British leaders operating in the same political environment, or admiration for the way the UK had avoided the rise of an openly racist party like the Front National in France. But Barnier thought he was popular, not populist. French voters disagreed.

On 13 October, the Commission published its response to the command paper. The EU ideas focused on reducing the paperwork for goods entering Northern Ireland, offering simplified certification for food, plant and animal products moving between Great Britain and Northern Ireland. The EU claimed this would cut the number of checks in this area by 80 per cent. 'Flexible customs formalities', it was claimed, would reduce paperwork by 50 per cent on goods going GB–NI. In return, the UK would have to offer the EU 'access to IT systems' monitoring the flow of goods, bring in labels on products saying they were only destined for the UK market and construct 'permanent border control posts'. The EU also promised 'enhanced engagement' with the authorities and businesses in Northern Ireland and, most significantly, agreed to change its own rules to allow the uninterrupted flow of medicines from Great Britain into Northern Ireland.[18]

To Frost it was a 'rather feeble set of ideas'. He told Johnson, 'It doesn't get anywhere close to what we need.' As far as Frost was concerned, the EU still did not understand where they were coming from. The problem in Brussels was that Britain was not carrying out checks at the border and was failing to implement a treaty it had willingly signed. The problem for Johnson was the difference in law between Northern Ireland and the rest of the UK.

The government was already quietly working on plans to deploy a bigger weapon in the talks. The next phase of the Brexit wars began in September when Suella Braverman, who had been on maternity leave since March, returned to work as attorney general telling colleagues she was politically 'very keen' to use Article 16. During her absence she had even expressed concern to Michael Ellis, her maternity cover, that she might 'miss all the fun'.

Braverman decided the advice from the government legal service was inadequate and sought outside legal counsel from a 'crack team' of experts in constitutional and international law. They concluded that the way Article 16 was drafted set the threshold for its use too high. The UK could only act unilaterally if measures imposed as a result of the protocol were deemed to be causing 'serious economic, societal or environmental difficulties'. Britain would also have to show there was no other way to deal with the issue. As a solution it was only temporary, and the EU would have a legal basis for retaliation. 'If we wanted to cease the operation of some EU SPS [sanitary and phytosanitary] rules, we might have been able to use Article 16,' a source said. 'But on something like the EU customs code it would not be enough.'

By October, Frost had concluded he was going to have to use Article 16 but resisted a 'big bang' bill to blow things up altogether. He advanced a different theory, stolen from British tactics at the end of the First World War, known as 'bite and hold'. 'The British Army worked out the best tactic in the end was not to throw everybody over the top of the trench but to try and take a mile or two of land, then stop and consolidate. And then do it again,' a source said. 'That was Frosty's military metaphor for what we might try to do.' Use the protocol to achieve a small defined goal and wait to show the Commission that it worked on the ground, then try something else. The hope was that initial outrage would dissolve into tacit consent.

As the work was being done, Johnson 'started blowing himself up', an aide recalled. November brought the Paterson affair and the Peppa Pig speech. Partygate was just around the corner. The prime minister began to see a row with the EU as a potential distraction. Sensing his weakness, the Eurosceptics intensified the pressure to back up Article 16 with legislation. At the beginning of December, at a cabinet committee meeting,

Frost presented the options, saying they were now in position to invoke Article 16. 'Boris was quite keen",' a minister present recalled. 'We all looked at each other around the table slightly.' Another said, 'People were raising eyebrows.' Braverman was eager to trigger Article 16 and to write a bill, feeling the endless debate was becoming '*Groundhog Day*'. Gove accepted the justification for using Article 16, on the grounds that there had been some diversion of trade, with Northern Ireland businesses increasingly selling to the South – but not the wisdom of deploying it. Coronavirus cases were flaring up and it felt like another lockdown was looming, one which would pitch the leadership against an increasingly activist base of libertarian MPs. The effect on supply chains from lockdown and a spat with the EU was uncertain. Frost said, 'I think it might be better to wait until the new year.' The prime minister agreed to wait. A colleague recalled, 'Frosty thought Boris would bluster and then bottle it at the first sign of gunfire.'

Not wanting to give the impression that Britain had backed off, Frost conceived the idea of a 'mini-interim deal' to build confidence and write down in black and white the issues that needed dealing with in 2022. After his final round of talks, on 17 December, an unusually detailed press statement was issued setting out the British demands. Frost thought anything that moved the needle in the right direction was worthwhile, as long as it was not declared to be permanent.

In response to the talks, the Commission put forward proposals to ensure the long-term supply of medicines from Great Britain to Northern Ireland, rejecting Frost's call for them to be excluded from the rules under the protocol. Instead, Brussels said it would change its own laws to accommodate the changes. In his statement, Frost said this was 'a constructive way forward', but beyond medicines, little had been achieved in 2021. The 'burdensome customs and … arrangements for goods moving between Great Britain and Northern Ireland' had caused 'a chilling effect on trade'. The 'simplest solution', he argued, 'is to put in place substantively different processes for goods which all sides agree will stay in the UK and those which do not'. The media referred to this as 'red and green lanes'. He also wanted to change the 2019 rules on state aid, which stipulated that 'the government cannot deliver aid to Northern Ireland, for example for Covid recovery support, without asking for the EU's permission'. Discussion on VAT and excise policy had been 'relatively constructive' but had not led to a solution. Most fundamentally, Frost went on, 'Neither Northern Ireland nor the UK more broadly gets any say on the way EU legislation is imposed on Northern Ireland. This remains a fundamental issue of democratic accountability. Nor is it reasonable or fair for disputes between the UK and the EU relating to the protocol to be settled in the EU Court of Justice, the court of one of the parties. The withdrawal agreement already provides for the use of an independent arbitration mechanism instead, and the simplest and most durable way forward would be to agree that this should be the sole route for settling disputes in future.'[19]

Outlining his proposal, Frost said, 'Our preference would be to reach a comprehensive solution dealing with all the issues. However, given the gravity and urgency of the difficulties, we have been prepared to consider an interim agreement as a first step to deal with the most acute problems … A solution needs to be found urgently early next year. For as long as there is no agreed solution, we remain ready to use the Article 16 safeguard mechanism.' However, others suggest that what Frost was prepared to sign would have been 'a crap deal'. A senior civil servant said, 'Looking back on it, it would have been a pretty weak, poor deal, which fudged a few of the grace periods and a few of the side issues, but at the time the EU just said no way.'

Nobody noticed the significance of this since it was Frost's final act as a minister. On 9 December, the same day Johnson returned to the office after the birth of his and Carrie's second child, Frost had been 'hanging around', a colleague recalled, saying '"I want to go." This is on the afternoon that [Johnson's] daughter's just been born. They agree, "Let's get through to the new year and see how we get on."'

The day after Frost's statement, 18 December, Glen Owen of the *Mail on Sunday* broke the news that Frost had resigned, blaming 'the Gove people' for 'stitching me up'. Frost had evolved from Brexit negotiator into a full-spectrum libertarian conservative with ambitions beyond his Brexit brief. In a hastily penned resignation letter, he said, 'I hope we will move as fast as possible to … a lightly regulated, low-tax, entrepreneurial economy.' An outspoken opponent of the July 2021 rise in National Insurance, he also voiced concerns that not enough was being done to take advantage of the benefits of Brexit. Aides in Number 10 thought that was supposed to be Frost's job.

The final straw for Frost had come on 8 December, when the virulence of the Omicron variant of Covid forced Johnson to announce a move to the so-called 'Plan B'. People were told to work from home again and the government also proposed requiring proof of vaccination to enter night-clubs and settings where large crowds gathered. Frost had warned Johnson a month before that he could not support vaccine passports.

As a minister attending cabinet, his resignation had a far greater impact than it would have done when he was an official. The timing could not have been much worse for Johnson who became mired that same week in allegations of misconduct over parties in Number 10 during the first lockdown. It also fuelled a backbench rebellion over vaccine passports. 'Frosty's resignation was a hammer blow,' a Johnson ally said. 'Boris was very angry around the office.' Baby Romy was not sleeping, the stress was mounting. Frost and Johnson did not speak properly for three months.

Braverman sought to change Frost's mind, telling him, 'We're on the brink of getting what you've been working for all year. This is going to damage the project on the protocol because you are the only person who can front it.' Frost had not enjoyed being a minister but told people he was frustrated to leave when he did. He felt like the protocol he had helped negotiate 'hung round my neck' and he had wanted to leave things in a better place. Outsiders saw him as a zealot on Brexit, when he was less hardline in private than Johnson or Braverman.

Nonetheless Downing Street staff and fellow ministers thought Frost also reluctant to make the compromises needed to resolve the issues with the protocol. Some thought him ungrateful to Johnson. 'He'd been given everything you can be given by a prime minister,' said a senior political aide. 'It is quite major to go from sherpa to the Rt Hon Lord Frost, member of the cabinet. Some people who worked for him certainly thought he could not see a clear path through [on Brexit] and thought it was better to get out.' A cabinet minister agreed: 'The thing about Frosty is that he wants to be in control but is also scared of the consequences of being held respon-sible. I'm convinced one of the reasons he resigned is that dealing with the grim consequences of border control posts at Dover, and whether or not you have … checks on goats coming into Grimsby, was just not him.'

Frost's vision of a Singapore-on-Thames-style Brexit was shared by Liz Truss, his successor as Brexit supremo, and, with Johnson increasingly mired in scandal as 2022 dawned, it was an agenda which would have to wait until she was prime minister. In taking the job, the foreign secretary was already thinking ahead. 'Liz enthusiastically accepted,' an aide recalled. 'She saw it as a way to get the ERG on side.'

Truss brought her experience of the trade department to the role. Like many Brexit ministers from David Davis onwards, she believed smart bilateral diplomacy might create a way forward. Truss planned to win over friendly countries like Lithuania and then try to come to an arrangement with Spain over Gibraltar. 'Once we resolve those issues, show they work, that's an operating model for Northern Ireland,' she told aides. 'There's a landing zone if the EU are willing to flex.'

Truss invited Šefčovič to join her at Chevening for a two-day summit on 13 and 14 January 2022. They held three sessions of talks, one over a dinner of Scottish smoked salmon, Welsh lamb and apple pie from Kent. They also went for a private walk around the estate. Truss outlined her view that there were pragmatic solutions the two sides could agree and her belief that the EU had a duty under the Good Friday Agreement to help find them. Privately, she made the case that the inability to send post or receive medicines was 'morally not right'.

The principals 'got on famously at Chevening,' a Truss aide said. So famously that drink was taken to excess, an issue which troubled officials about Truss. Jamie Hope, her policy director, found himself sharing a Jack and Jill bathroom with a 'slightly drunk' Šefčovič. Hope spent the night listening to the rattling and banging of the old house wondering if the noises meant a half-cut Commission vice president was trying to force his way into his bedroom.

While Truss and Šefčovič dined together, their aides ate in a separate room, arguing over what a joint statement might say. Runners went in to find out what the principals had agreed, then Adam Jones, Truss's spin doctor, negotiated with Renáta Goldírová, Šefčovič's communications adviser, over every word of the text. 'She was quite formidable and did not understand Adam's English humour at all,' a colleague recalled. The British wanted a line saying the 'operation' of the protocol was not working for Northern Ireland, an implied criticism of Brussels. The EU team wanted to stress the need for 'full implementation' of the protocol, where they felt the UK was falling short.

After dinner, Truss took Šefčovič into a side room to try to resolve the differences, then to play snooker. When he finally said, 'I'm going to bed', she turned on a winning smile and flirtatiously announced, 'It was a lovely dinner, we're going to solve that statement in the morning.'

Šefčovič looked horrified. 'His face dropped,' a witness said. 'He realised that one way or the other, there was going to be a statement.' It could not have been blander: 'The meeting took place in a cordial atmosphere … We share a desire for a positive relationship between the EU and the UK underpinned by our shared belief in freedom and democracy.'

A second meeting, in Brussels, on the 24th, also ended positively, with Šefčovič saying the political goodwill could 'lead to a timely agreement on durable solutions'. That paved the way for the joint committee to meet for the first time in six months. But even after a third meeting at Carlton Gardens on 11 February, little practical progress was made.

In one exchange, Truss said, 'Nothing we are suggesting will cost the EU any more at all. What's not to like?'

Šefčovič replied, 'Well, you signed the protocol.'

A former British negotiator, watching from afar, remarked, 'You can have as many positive meetings as you want, as long as you don't mind not achieving anything.' A senior figure in Downing Street agreed: 'They were nonsense negotiations.' Truss explained, 'Šefčovič didn't have the political authority within the Commission to do a deal. He also had officials who were actively negative. [Richard] Szostak was the absolute key – a proper character.'

Truss's line began to harden after she visited Belfast on 27 January, where she met Michelle O'Neill, the Sinn Féin first minister, and Paul Givan, the DUP deputy first minister, who set a deadline of 21 February for Truss to resolve the problems with the protocol. 'She was blown away by how complicated, how difficult and how arduous the whole thing was,' an aide recalled. There was a whiff of Dominic Raab discovering Dover was an important port about this observation.

A week later, on 3 February, Givan announced he was resigning as deputy first minister in protest at the operation of the protocol, saying it had upturned 'the delicate balance created by the Belfast and St Andrew's Agreements'. That brought down the whole power-sharing executive. The stakes had got higher.

Truss liked Šefčovič but found him intransigent and unable to negotiate in the way that was needed. 'Šefčovič never had the ability to change his mandate and therefore just couldn't talk about stuff,' a Truss aide said. 'She thought the galvanising thing would be to get VDL involved.'

Truss also found her EU counterparts highly reluctant to engage with the issues. On a trip to Prague in May 2022, she sought to enlist the support of the Czech foreign minister Jan Lipavský, whose country was about to take over the presidency of the European Council. She had a good rapport with Lipavský but when the protocol was raised, he said, 'I don't think we need to talk about that.'

Truss interjected, 'You've experienced the break-up of a country, you understand all the emotional things that go alongside it. I think that's something that gets lost in the bureaucracy.'

Lipavský was sympathetic but immovable: 'I agree there are two sides to this coin. I'm happy to talk about it, but not now. Don't let it ruin our bilateral relationship.'

To break the deadlock, Truss backed a project Suella Braverman had been working on since September – domestic legislation which would become known as the Northern Ireland Protocol Bill. If the Commission would not rewrite the text of the protocol treaty, the only other solution was to pass domestic legislation to countermand parts of it. Just as with the UKIM bill in 2020, this meant adopting Braverman's interpretation that laws passed by Parliament trumped international law. As the new year began, the attorney general had identified the legal basis for the new bill. 'It was half to two thirds done by January,' a source said.

'There were two legal arguments,' a senior Number 10 adviser explained. The first was that both the UK and the EU had obligations to protect the Good Friday Agreement, a treaty lodged at the United Nations and supposed to protect the sovereign government and the economic rights of the people of Northern Ireland. These, the government could argue, had been undermined and the protocol bill would protect the peace deal. Some of these ideas had been developed at the time of the Belfast Agreement by Paul Bew, the peer who was father of John Bew, Johnson's foreign affairs adviser. This provided a moral and politically useful argument in the court of public opinion, but the lawyers argued it wasn't sufficient grounds for overriding the protocol if the issue went to court.

The second legal justification, pushed hard by Braverman, was the 'doctrine of necessity', an orthodox principle of international law that allowed nations to suspend international treaties in an emergency. 'It gave us a lot more breadth and a lower threshold than Article 16,' a minister said. There had already been violence and disorder in Northern Ireland. The figures on the diversion of trade were stark, with data showing that 'businesses in Northern Ireland had pretty much ceased trading with GB and were diverting their trade to the Republic, both import and export.' As the situation became more acute, so the legal justification for unilateral action increased. Braverman told aides that, unlike Geoffrey Cox, who had put loyalty to the law above helping Theresa May, 'We need to build a legal case for our client, the prime minister.' By April, there was a working document, by May a draft bill.

From this moment, the bill disapplying EU law became the preferred solution of the ERG and the Tory right. Braverman expressed the view that it would be 'an end in itself' which would deal with 'all the problems'. But as she and her aides had to acknowledge in private, 'You couldn't do it indefinitely. It would always be subject to the doctrine of necessity argument' and would have to be 'periodically reviewed'. Braverman saw the bill, however, as a way of forcing the EU to either accept a change in facts on the ground and come to a new agreement, or put things into a 'permanent frozen conflict'.

Truss quickly realised that supporting it was a shortcut to win right-wing support. She told her spads, 'International law does matter and we need to be careful, but if what you are doing is fundamentally right, you start making the EU look less reasonable and their position becomes untenable.' She said later, 'The bill was designed to solve the problem and be a cudgel because my view of the EU is that, until they feel the pressure, they don't do anything. If Parliament is sovereign then you can override international law.'

Johnson's enthusiasm for the bill was partly a function of his fury at the EU for the way they operated the protocol. 'You've got to understand how infuriated Boris gets,' a source familiar with Johnson's thinking said. The prime minister told himself: *They are deliberately pissing me about. They didn't need to do all this shit: all this stopping the shortbread and the sausages, it's just ridiculous. They know it's winding me up and they know they can point to it as a failure of Brexit, a failure of my negotiations: 'Johnson got it wrong.' It's very painful for me because I felt I'd got a good deal and I could make it work. I thought that once we were out and we're running our own country, it would be fine. What I didn't realise was the way the civil service would continuously follow the letter of the law in favour of the EU. We religiously enforce whatever the French want. I like the bill, more and more. It's the only thing that fixes this problem.*

Some interpreted Johnson's support as a bid to placate his MPs, who were now circling him for the kill. 'He was a wounded lion, trying to escape the trap he was in,' a Number 10 adviser said. A cabinet minister agreed: 'The decisive thing was Boris's political position weakened over-all, so reliance on the original ERG base became greater.' Johnson and the ERG had always been awkward bedfellows since he had been front man for Vote Leave. 'The ERG vision of a Brexit end state was a much more Trussian, neoliberal, small state, Thatcher redux version. Boris liked some of that but not all of that. He had a better understanding of how the victory was won and upon whom it depended. He never wanted to be tied down by anyone – but partygate and everything else meant that he became more reliant on them.'

More intriguing, is the view, strongly held by an aide who had been with him through both the 2019 and 2020 deals, who believed Johnson's backing for the bill resulted from his sense of ownership of his Brexit deals. 'Boris didn't do it for the Conservative Party politics or for votes, he did it out of a sense of repentance,' this adviser said. 'He did care about the Union actually. I think he had that sense of responsibility for what he'd done in 2019. That wore quite heavily on him.' It was another example of where the caricature peddled by his enemies matched only one facet of Johnson's character.

Another of his personality traits remained a factor, however: the prime minister's position kept changing. 'He might be gung-ho in an afternoon and then various people would get at him,' a political aide said. In one meeting he told Truss, 'Liz, you've pushed this too far.'

There were also dissenting voices in Number 10. John Bew worried that the bill, which he called 'a high attrition negotiating strategy', was unlikely to produce a settlement both sides would be happy with, since the EU was not going to agree a 'full-tonto ECJ' agreement expunging European court oversight. He believed Article 16 was not a big enough weapon but told colleagues they should try to find a solution that, unlike the bill, was actually 'landable' with Brussels.

However, Bew and other moderates went along with the plan, in part, because they were furious at the way the EU and the Irish government were using Johnson's vulnerability to turn the screws. 'There was bad faith and bullshit from the EU,' a Number 10 official recalled. 'The Irish government was trying to fuck around with our relationship with the US, trying to piss on our chips. It was a fantasy that we were being scolded all the time by the Americans about Northern Ireland. We had senior Americans telling us the Irish were trying to screw us with them. All this fucking around drove the bill.'

Some of these frustrations were voiced by David Frost in a speech to the Policy Exchange think tank on 27 April. 'The reality is that, at most of the crucial moments of the last five years, Ireland chose to throw its weight behind EU interests and to prioritise protecting the single market, instead of working collaboratively with us to find solutions that can actually work in Northern Ireland,' he said. He argued Ireland had not 'got good value from the EU for acting like this' and said Dublin 'talking up the supposed "all Ireland economy"' had succeeded in 'disrupting the balance in Northern Ireland'.[20]

In the local elections on 5 May, Sinn Féin emerged as the largest party in the Northern Ireland Assembly for the first time. Michelle O'Neill's party held their 27 seats but the DUP saw their vote share fall by 7 percentage points and they dropped three seats, falling from 28 to 25, while the cross-community Alliance Party made big gains, up 9 to 17. The result reinforced the sense in the DUP that unionism was embattled. Overall, unionists won two more seats and a slightly higher vote share than nationalists, but the trend was clear – they would soon be in a minority in the North. Jeffrey Donaldson, the DUP leader, refused to re-enter power sharing until the problems with the protocol were ironed out.

A week later it was clear the current talks were not going anywhere. Truss and Šefčovič spoke by phone at 8 a.m. on 12 May, a 'tetchy' exchange. 'Parts of the protocol aren't working. We need to change it, that's the reality,' Truss said to aides. On the call, the foreign secretary described the protocol as 'the greatest obstacle to forming a Northern Ireland Executive', insisting the commission 'bore a responsibility to show more pragmatism'. Having advanced the British case for a red and green lane system, Truss listened as Šefčovič said there was no room to expand the EU negotiating mandate or introduce new proposals to reduce trade friction. She concluded the call with a threat to take unilateral action: 'If the EU will not show the requisite flexibility to help solve those issues, then as a responsible government we will have no choice but to act.'

Šefčovič hit back, describing unilateral action to disapply an international agreement as 'simply not acceptable'. He warned it would 'undermine' trust between the two sides, the Good Friday Agreement and Northern Ireland's access to the single market. 'The EU and the UK are partners facing the same global challenges, where upholding the rule of law and living up to international obligations is a necessity,' he said.

Truss's support for the bill convinced EU officials she was more interested in promoting her leadership prospects than in getting a deal.

In parallel Johnson and his home secretary Priti Patel were plotting an equally controversial course on tackling illegal migration, which led to tens of thousands of people every year paying people smugglers to transport them across the Channel in barely navigable boats. When an armada of small boats ferried the British Army home from Dunkirk in 1940, it was regarded as a 'miracle'. Now 'small boats' were a symbol that Brexit had not delivered the 'control' of borders which Brexiteers had promised.

On 14 April 2022, Johnson gave a speech announcing that the government was establishing a scheme to send those deemed to have arrived illegally to Rwanda, where they could apply for asylum. Seven out of ten arrivals in small boats in 2021 were not refugees, he argued, but economic migrants, 'men under forty, paying people smugglers to queue jump'. The numbers coming, under 10,000 in 2020, had risen to approaching 30,000 in 2021 and were on course to hit more than 45,000 in 2022. Johnson boasted of the 185,000 genuine refugees Britain had taken in since 2015.[21] But he added, 'The quid pro quo for this generosity is that we cannot sustain a parallel illegal system … We can't ask the British taxpayer to write a blank cheque to cover the costs of anyone who might want to come and live here.'

Even in Johnson's inner circle, there was concern about the optics. Guto Harri recalled, 'When I first chaired a meeting on how we were going to communicate this policy I remember looking around the room and everyone was anxious because the first thing that came to mind for most people when you said, "We are sending people to Rwanda", was the horrible, haunting image of machete-wielding genocidal tribes that went for each other decades ago and caused an absolute shocking carnage. I hadn't appreciated how much Rwanda had moved on.'[22]

Some saw the idea as an eye-catching way to distract attention from Johnson's multiplying scandals, but illegal immigration had exploded as a political problem, in part because of the prime minister's own policy on *legal* migration. Johnson had been promising an Australian-style points-based system since the time of the referendum, but it is one of the supreme ironies of the Brexit years that the system he put in place was among the most liberal in the world – it just no longer discriminated in favour of EU citizens. The scheme, introduced at the end of 2020, allowed skilled workers who spoke English, from anywhere in the world, to enter the UK if they had a job paying an annual salary of £25,600 rather than £30,000 under the old scheme. While low-skilled entry was limited to the social care sector and seasonal agriculture, the main skill requirement was reduced from a degree to the equivalent of A-levels. From July 2021, a 'graduate route' was also opened, allowing those studying in the UK to stay on after their degree with their dependents. Consequently, the 331,000 work visas issued in the twelve-month period ending in June 2022 was nearly double the 168,000 on average pre-pandemic between 2014 and 2019. In total, nearly 1.2 million visas allowing residence in the UK were issued in the year to June 2022, the highest number on record.[23] Johnson, who had backed an amnesty for illegals when he was mayor of London, quickly found that Theresa May, who had argued that 'control' had to mean control of numbers as well as the levers at the border, was more in touch with Leave voters than he was.

The Rwanda scheme was quickly assailed in Parliament and the courts. On 15 June, the first flight due to leave was cancelled minutes before take-off after a ruling by the European Court of Human Rights that British judges, who had given the plan the green light, had not properly looked at conditions in Rwanda. It would be two more prime ministers and two more years before a plane was airborne. Opponents lined up to condemn the government as callous and the scheme as unworkable. Vocal public opponents included the Archbishop of Canterbury, Theresa May ('I do not support the removal to Rwanda policy on the grounds of legality, practicality and efficacy.') and, just days before the first flight was supposed to leave, the Prince of Wales, who was a few short months from becoming king.

On 10 June, *The Times* splashed on the revelation that Prince Charles had, on several occasions in private, referred to the plan as 'appalling' and feared it would mar the Commonwealth Heads of Government meeting, where he was to represent the Queen, later that month.[24] Number 10 and their counterparts in the royal household went into overdrive 'trying to work out the choreography, how the two could share a stage and not embarrass each other,' recalled Downing Street's director of communications. On the flight out, as is traditional, the prime minister took questions from a 'huddle' of journalists flying with him to Kigali. 'Boris gave an off the record briefing where he had a dig at people with condescending attitudes towards countries like Rwanda that had moved on in leaps and bounds. He never mentioned Prince Charles by name, but he didn't need to. A situation that was always going to be awkward was potentially horrendous now.'[25]

At the summit there was a public display of mutual respect, Charles and Boris shaking hands, smiling at each other. In private, Johnson took the heir to the throne to task for 'shitbagging' his flagship plan. 'Did you actually criticise government policy?' he asked.

Johnson told an aide that Charles replied, 'Well maybe, inadvertently, without intention I may have said something.'[26]

Both men were due to give speeches, Johnson focusing on the shared values and booming economies of the Commonwealth. Charles revealed that he wanted to respond to the widespread fury about colonialism unleashed by the Black Lives Matter campaign, by acknowledging the evils of slavery. Johnson, despairing that even the monarchy had been captured by 'woke' ideology, was blunt: 'I wouldn't talk about slavery if I were you, or you'll end up having to sell the Duchy of Cornwall to pay reparations to the people who built the Duchy of Cornwall.' When Johnson emerged from this encounter he told Harri, 'I went in quite hard.' Charles ignored the prime minister, telling the summit, 'I cannot describe the depth of my personal sorrow at the suffering of so many as I continue to deepen my own understanding of slavery's enduring impact.' A relationship fundamentally soured by prorogation was now in freefall. 'I don't think relations ever fully recovered,' Harri said.[27]

Back at home, the driving forces of the Northern Ireland Protocol Bill were Braverman and her special adviser Chris Jenkins, who consulted widely with the ERG and its legal allies from the star chamber. But there were concerns the plan was too blunt an instrument. 'Liz let the ERG virtually write it,' a government source said. Ministers did not let Sir James Eadie, the first Treasury counsel, rule on whether the policy was legal. 'This is unprecedented,' a former minister said. Truss's response was that the bill was not the ERG's: 'They didn't want any EU regulation.' She fought to get 'the purists, like Bill Cash' to agree references to the ECJ. 'If you're in Northern Ireland and you're producing goods to go to the Republic and you voluntarily subscribe to EU law, then there is a referral mechanism to ECJ,' Truss explained. 'From a sovereignty point of view, you can wear that because you're not forcing somebody in Northern Ireland to follow EU law, you're saying, "If you want to have access to those markets, then you have to." To me that was reasonable.'

David Frost supported the plan in public. Privately, however, he viewed it as a 'nuclear weapon' which would make progress more difficult. To Frost, it was better to use Article 16 in a targeted way to deal with specific problems, not least because it was part of the protocol and 'unarguably legal in all respects'.[28]

Frost's public pronouncements were resented in Number 10. 'Frosty is slightly ludicrous,' one Johnson ally said. 'He was in government and had a chance to do this stuff and he walked away. It's like a footballer who hasn't scored a goal for a decade watching in the crowd and complaining that the striker has missed the target.'

Frost's view was partly informed by Oliver Lewis, who was clear that the UKIM bill had only worked because it had included five specific and limited objectives, all of which were achieved. 'If you're going to play hardcore with the EU you've got to have a strategy,' he warned Johnson. Lewis saw no sign of a targeted strategy now, just a demand for a general disapplication of EU law. Braverman's focus was on building a very large weapon, rather than thinking about where it was targeted. 'UKIM was a targeted prescriptive punch on the nose,' Lewis told one friend. 'NIP was more dashing around waving machetes.' Watching from afar, Dominic Cummings thought the bill a classic product of the MPs he so despised. 'Our bill did exactly what we wanted,' he told allies. 'It did unlock things. Theirs is a nonsense bill, which is hardcore enough that it fucks everyone off but not hardcore enough to make a difference. The ERG nutters never had a fucking clue what they were on about.'

The bill caused splits in Johnson's Downing Street team. David Canzini, a resolute Brexiteer and close confidant of many ERG MPs who was now deputy chief of staff, egged on Truss. Guto Harri, the new director of communications, who had fallen out with Johnson over his passionate support for Remain in the referendum, urged caution. The PM vacillated. 'The object of the exercise with some people seems to be to have a fight,' a senior ally told the *Sunday Times*. 'The object of the exercise for the prime minister is to restore democratic processes to Northern Ireland. The PM does not want to use nuclear weapons, whatever the knuckleheads tell him.' Harri was blamed for the quote. Canzini began introducing himself as 'Mr Knucklehead'.

*   *   *

The key decision-making body on Brexit was now 'GBS', the Global Britain Strategy cabinet committee, chaired by the prime minister, and the post-Brexit reincarnation of XS. It met on 9 June in a windowless conference room on the lower ministerial corridor in Parliament.

The day before, Bill Cash and other members of the ERG went to Downing Street to see Johnson. Cash argued the bill needed to include notwithstanding clauses and pressed for two other measures to be written into the legislation. First, he said it must repatriate VAT policy so changes made in London would apply in Northern Ireland as well as England and Wales. He also called for a dual regulatory model, where businesses in Belfast could decide whether to follow UK or EU rules. Truss and Brandon Lewis, the Northern Ireland secretary, were also present. Cash left depressed. He rang Braverman, who supported all three measures, and said, 'Suella, I'm crestfallen. We are only going to get any change in Northern Ireland if we include these three things. I made the case to them and they basically said "no". Liz didn't say anything. Brandon didn't say anything. I feel like no one supported me. I feel like Boris wasn't really present in the meeting.' Johnson was undoubtedly distracted. He had faced a no-confidence vote by Tory MPs two days earlier.

Cash told one of Braverman's aides, minutes later, that she said, 'If we can't get that, I'll have to resign.' The attorney general phoned Truss, who said, 'Suella, why don't you have a go with Boris. He's not really in the mood.' They both believed Johnson had been 'got at' by John Bew and others who thought the bill too provocative.

Braverman called Johnson from her ministerial car at eight the following morning, the day of the meeting. 'Boris, I think if you don't include these measures, there's no point in doing this. It's going to be a futile exercise and ultimately it will get overridden in the courts. We're not going to have the effect that we want to have, which is to restore an open border between Northern Ireland and Great Britain.'

By the end of the conversation, Braverman's advocacy had convinced Johnson to say yes. She immediately feared she had made a strategic error. As the first cabinet minister to speak to him that day, she had left seven hours for others to get to Johnson and change his mind. She rang Cash to give him the good news. In the intervening hours the attorney general's office and Number 10 exchanged draft clauses.

Everyone trapped in the windowless conference room for the GBS meeting that afternoon recalled a stultifying atmosphere, a lack of natural light and a bad-tempered discussion. 'It was a horrible room,' said one cabinet minister. When Braverman walked into the 'dungeon' she was armed with a version of the bill and bristling for a fight. Officials warned her Johnson had changed his mind again.

Truss opened, presenting the bill, since the foreign secretary was technically the lead minister. Braverman followed, arguing that on the three contentious issues, 'This is absolutely essential. We have got to do it and if we don't do it, this is going to fail.' The attorney general said the notwithstanding clauses would protect the government as and when the EU took the UK to court for violating the treaty. 'The unquestionable legal merit of those clauses is that it is unambiguous to a judge and a court, however interventionist or hostile they want to be,' Braverman explained. 'You could be up in front of the worst Brenda Hale of all time – even she can't argue with a notwithstanding clause. It leaves no room for judicial interpretation.'

Michael Gove arrived late and missed part of Truss's presentation. The hardliners felt later that he had not read the room. The levelling up secretary, a devout unionist, gave an impassioned speech, parrying Braverman's legal arguments with practical arguments. 'This is like putting a gun to our heads,' he said. 'Why the hell would we do this? We should do this through negotiation. We should keep going with the joint committee. This is an absolute disaster. We're going to start a trade war.' Gove argued that a trade dispute with the EU would drive up food prices at a time when the rising cost of living was already the biggest domestic political issue. 'Everyone is going to suffer. It's absolute madness.' Gove thought the ERG's claim that the EU only ever responded to strength, misguided: 'The EU will break any rule and tell any lie in order to advance European integration. What they will not do is to break rules on our behalf to facilitate the erosion of the single market.'

Braverman went on the offensive: 'Michael, you don't know what you're talking about. This is absolutely the necessary proper and politically essential course of action.' The prospect of a trade war was 'speculative', she argued. 'It's a classic EU threat. They would lose out more than us.' This was, to put it politely, highly debatable, but Braverman believed Gove had gone soft.

Back and forth they went, interrupting each other, the tone heated. The outcome of the meeting hung in the balance. Dominic Raab said he agreed with Braverman and Truss. Kwasi Kwarteng, the business secretary, rowed in behind them too. Michael Ellis, the paymaster general, 'murmured in agreement'.

When Johnson spoke he seemed sceptical, as Truss and Braverman had feared. Like Frost before him, the prime minister had dusted down a First World War analogy, comparing the notwithstanding clauses to the class of pre-war battleships which sparked an arms race with the Kaiser's Germany. 'They're the Dreadnought in your armoury,' he said. 'They are a show of strength.' Johnson wondered whether they would be unnecessarily antagonistic to the EU. 'Boris was very worried that we would have friction and more trade barriers between Ireland and Northern Ireland,' a witness said. Priti Patel, the home secretary, was also 'hostile' to the bill, apparently taking her lead from Johnson's equivocation.

It was left to Braverman to make the obvious point about party management. 'Politically, the Eurosceptics in the party have been advocating for this,' she said.

Johnson snapped, 'Fuck the Eurosceptics.' The Eurosceptics joined the ever-growing fraternity who Johnson had dismissed in this fashion. They would not be the last.

Again, Patel backed him up. 'You shouldn't be dictated to by fringe groups in Parliament.' From a member of the Spartans, this was striking.

In addition to Gove, those against included Anne-Marie Trevelyan, the trade secretary and a former ERG whip, and Rishi Sunak. The chancellor often kept his counsel in such meetings, preferring to share his views with Johnson one-on-one, but the Treasury was concerned the bill would not give legal certainty on taxes.

Despite the prime minister's nervousness, ministers backed the radical approach with the bill. Johnson approved the notwithstanding clauses. The dual regulatory device and VAT demands would also be included. It was the prime minister's fourth different position and third U-turn of the day. He told himself (and others) later he had emphatically backed Braverman. A government source said at the time, 'We are not scrapping the protocol, we are acting domestically to fix it.'

The Northern Ireland Protocol Bill was published on 13 June. Truss endured calls where Šefčovič 'was shirty in a slightly pantomimey fashion'. Two days later, the EU launched fresh proceedings against the UK 'for breaking international law'. In a bid to show that it was trying to make progress through negotiation, the Commission also published position papers on customs and sanitary and phytosanitary issues (SPS).

Senior figures in the EU spent the next four months warning that if the bill was passed and enacted they would have no choice but to impose tariffs on the whole of the UK – effectively using the Northern Ireland dispute to torpedo the entire Trade and Cooperation Agreement signed on Christmas Eve 2020. The bill had sparked an arms race. The Kaisers in the commission had built their own Dreadnought.

To those working on the substance of the Brexit negotiations this escalation was depressing. 'If you use unilateral action you need to have a plan – and we didn't,' one senior official said. 'Then the EU obviously responded with, "Okay, we'll blow up the TCA then", but it was obviously just madness on both sides. It was so over the top.'

Johnson, Braverman and Truss did not believe the EU would retaliate. Johnson hoped Britain's strong links to Eastern Europe after the Russian invasion of Ukraine, four months earlier, would help. A cabinet minister said, 'Boris thought Europe would not want to trigger a trade war because of all the economic difficulties, and the good odour in which he now stood with the Poles, the Baltics and the Nordics.' This assumption led to complacency in Whitehall, where senior civil servants originally shared the optimism of Number 10. 'The government was not preparing for full-on tariffs and general breakdown in our relationship with the European Union,' the cabinet minister said. 'That's the direction we were headed but there seemed to be no strategic planning whatsoever.'

This changed at the committee stage of the bill in the Commons, in July 2022. Fearing the EU was serious about robust retaliation, departments started to make assessments of what would happen in a trade war. Not wanting to spook the public when it leaked, most of this work was done under the veneer of an exercise to prepare for problems with supply chains and energy costs caused by the war in Ukraine. A government forged out of Brexit now had to pretend it was not a factor.

A Brexiteer with experience of dealing with the EU painted a picture of what might follow: 'The EU has quite a good way of putting pressure on external partners. When it wants to screw with the Americans it has a bunch of PhDs who do a mapping exercise on the congressmen who are the most troublesome for the White House – what are the industries which are most important for jobs in those areas? What's the tariff line that corresponds to that industry? As soon as there's a spat with the

Americans, the EU will come out with a list of tariff rises. Sure enough, a few days later, the White House has these congressmen going absolutely mental. It's not hard to replicate that strategy over here.'

The bill was supposed to persuade the DUP to return to power sharing. As ever, hope triumphed over experience. Truss had tried to get them to agree to go back into the executive if the bill was published, but this soon evolved to if the bill was introduced; then if the bill was passed by the Commons; and then if the bill became law. Jeffrey Donaldson said in the debate on second reading in June 2022 that if the bill passed he would make moves to return. 'It was important to Tory MPs that the DUP were fulfilling their side of the bargain,' Truss said later. 'They basically agreed over the summer to do it and hadn't. My view was that we should put pressure on them to restart the Assembly before the bill came back to the Commons.'

A spat in July between DUP grandees and John Bew led to mutual recriminations. In Number 10, senior advisers felt the DUP leadership was overplaying its hand and had miscalculated both their influence over the prime minister and his ability, as his political strength ebbed away, to deliver what they wanted. 'They made a fundamental mistake,' a Downing Street source said. 'There was a lot of overreading of their own leverage.' Bew tried to explain this to the DUP but instead they put their fate in the hands of Johnson. 'They decided to take a punt on a weak prime minister,' a Number 10 source recalled, 'on a cabinet that was divided, on the government winning trench warfare in the Lords or a future government using the Parliament act to force it through. They made a fundamental strategic error, not for the first time.'

By then, however, Johnson and his team had made the fundamental strategic errors that would bring him down – over how to respond to the scandal which became known as 'partygate'.

PARTIED OUT

Partygate

November 2021 to April 2022

The phone call that did most to unseat Boris Johnson was made to Dominic Cummings in October 2021. A Vote Leave ally got in touch to say, 'A lovely golden nugget is falling into our laps.' The friend had been contacted by someone from ITV, which had obtained footage from a mock press conference on 22 December the year before, at the height of the second lockdown. In the video Allegra Stratton, the prime minister's press secretary, was asked by a fellow member of the press team about 'a Downing Street Christmas party on Friday night'. Clearly embarrassed to be put on the spot, Stratton laughed nervously and said, 'I went home.' With Stratton lost for words, the questioner tried again, 'Would the prime minister condone having a Christmas party?' Stratton asked her colleagues, 'What's the answer?' They then chipped in from the back of the room 'it wasn't a party' and 'it was cheese and wine'. Her head in her hands, Stratton tried, 'It was a business meeting.'

The footage was dynamite. There was just one problem for ITV: the source of the leak made it difficult to broadcast. Amber de Botton, the channel's head of politics, tried in vain to persuade her bosses that they had a public interest defence and the footage should run but the lawyers were cautious.

Cummings and his confidant discussed what to do. Here was a golden opportunity to open a new front in the battle against Boris. The labyrinthine plot that sparked partygate began when Cummings' friend suggested they talk to the *Daily Mirror* and use the video to prove that there were Number 10 parties. Once the details were in the public domain, ITV would have legal grounds to broadcast the footage. This approach provided one other benefit. Cummings said, 'This could work out better. We could trap the fucker into lying about it? He'll just tell Jack and everyone to just deny it all.'

The beneficiary of the plot was Pippa Crerar, the political editor of the redtop, an affable Scot with a reputation for both straight shooting and diligence. She knew Johnson as well as any lobby correspondent after a spell as City Hall correspondent for the London *Evening Standard* while he was mayor, understanding both his mercurial political talents and his legion of character flaws. Having broken the story of Cummings' escape to Durham the year before, she was the obvious outlet for a Vote Leave black op, giving them more deniability. It was also more likely that Johnson and his team would deny the story out of hand if it came from a hostile paper like the *Mirror*.

Crerar was a good choice. Months earlier, in January or February, she had been tipped off about the parties and begun working on the story, but her source did not give the information first hand and she had not been able to stand it up to her satisfaction. But she was primed when Cummings' ally invited her to a clandestine meeting and played her the video. She was not allowed to take a copy, but it was enough to give her the impetus to revisit her other sources and the *Mirror* the confidence to run the story. 'The video was a metaphorical brown paper envelope,' she recalled, 'not enough evidence on its own to publish a story, but enough to encourage me to investigate further.' She spoke to half a dozen Downing Street people, most of them still working in the building, to piece together what had happened.

When Crerar contacted Downing Street on the afternoon of 30 November to say she was going to reveal details of lockdown-busting parties, a crisis meeting assembled in Dan Rosenfield's office between the chief of staff and Jack Doyle's communications team. Rosenfield had not been in Number 10 at the time and asked Doyle, his deputy Rosie Bate-Williams and Max Blain, the prime minister's official civil service spokesman, what had happened. The three spin doctors admitted things may have got out of hand but none argued that Covid rules or guidance had been broken. Doyle and Rosenfield agreed that would be the line. They went to see Johnson and had the same conversation. Doyle assured both of his bosses the rules were followed by the press office.

Every comms expert will tell you that in a crisis those involved need to establish the facts and then come clean, or risk accusations of a cover-up.

Yet neither the prime minister nor the chief of staff made any effort at this stage to ascertain how widespread the social gatherings were or to issue a holding line until the danger was assessed. 'We were lucky that Doyle and Rosenfield were morons,' a Vote Leave source said.

The *Mirror* splash, dated 1 December, dropped after 10 p.m. on the 30th. It featured a picture of Johnson drinking gin at an event that day and the headline: 'BORIS PARTY BROKE COVID RULES'. The front page story read, 'Boris Johnson and his staff have been accused of breaking Covid rules by enjoying crowded parties last year.' It detailed how Johnson gave a speech at a leaving do during the second lockdown, the existence of a 'festive bash' during Tier 3 restrictions, which included a 'festive quiz' and 'secret santa' – and how people got 'totally plastered' the night Cummings left Downing Street. The headline on the page 4–5 spread was 'DOWNING 'EM STREET'. Crerar quoted a source saying there were 'many social gatherings' in Number 10 which Johnson either attended or turned a blind eye to and there were 'always parties' in the Johnson family flat. Another source claimed, 'Carrie's addicted to them.'

As Cummings predicted, the instinct of Johnson and his team was to bat the story away. Doyle issued a simple statement saying, 'There was no Christmas party. Covid rules have been followed at all times.' Sarah Vaughan-Brown, Carrie's spokeswoman, said it was 'total nonsense' that she held parties in the flat. The following day, the story was the focus of PMQs. Johnson repeated the same line, telling MPs, 'All guidance was followed completely.' The denials were in. The race to prove them untrue was on.

Cummings' friend called him, 'Pippa's put it to Downing Street and Jack has denied the whole thing. We've got them.'

Cummings replied, 'This whole thing is now going to run for months. All these journalists have watched *All the President's Men*. They all know the script now that there's an on the record denial. When the truth drips out, it's going to be a train wreck and he's going to have to keep lying internally. It's going to break him. Character is destiny, he will lie.'

With the denials in, ITV broadcast the mock press conference footage, since it clearly contradicted the official line from Downing Street. In truth, the video revealed Stratton's hideous embarrassment about the indefensibility of the parties, rather than a gung-ho attitude, but seeing Downing Street staff apparently joking about rule-breaking took the story into the stratosphere.

The footage referred to a gathering on 18 December 2020. The Number 10 press team met after work every Friday evening, but on this occasion emails and WhatsApps were sent out by junior civil servants in the press team urging people to attend. About forty people gathered in a foyer outside the press office. 'Everyone was packed shoulder to shoulder,' said one who attended. 'If it looks like a party, sounds like a party, stinks of booze and goes on until 2 a.m., it is a fucking party.' Johnson did not visit the Christmas gathering but, as Cummings pointed out, 'To get upstairs [to his flat] he has to walk past that area.'

Doyle offered to resign but Johnson refused to accept. Once again the decision about how to respond was taken in a tight circle of Johnson, Rosenfield and Doyle. Declan Lyons, the political secretary, and other political aides like Finn, Henry Newman, Henry Cook and Meg Powell-Chandler were cut out. 'They stuck to the same line that all guidance was followed at all times,' one colleague recalled.

Taking matters into her own hands, a tearful Stratton emerged from her home in north London to a waiting pack of photographers and announced her resignation on camera. 'The British people have made immense sacrifices in the ongoing battle against Covid-19,' she said. 'I now fear that my comments in the leaked video … have become a distraction in that fight. I will regret those remarks for the rest of my days and offer my profound apologies to all of you at home for them.' Johnson's 'human shield' was gone. Stratton, who had not even attended the party, was for months the only person in Johnson's orbit who seemed to have acted with any integrity or dignity.

At Prime Minister's Questions that Wednesday, Johnson said he was 'furious' to discover the video but stuck to the line: 'I am sure that what-ever happened, the guidance was followed and the rules were followed at all times.' He flatly denied that there had been a party on the night Cummings left Downing Street.

That same day in Portcullis House MPs were seen brandishing letters they were planning to send to Sir Graham Brady, chairman of the 1922 Committee, demanding a vote of no confidence in the prime minister. Fifty-four were needed to trigger a vote yet only Brady and his long-standing secretary, Sybil, knew how many had been submitted. But a prime minister who had seemed imperious and impregnable at the start of October was in deep trouble just two months later.

The lockdown party stories were particularly toxic since the nation was once more thinking about the restrictions of lockdown. Three days before the *Mirror* splash, Johnson had been at the very same podium where Stratton was filmed, warning the country that a 'third wave' of the virus was coming, the highly virulent Omicron variant, capable of infecting even those who were double vaccinated.

On 8 December, the day after the Stratton story broke, Johnson gave a press conference to re-impose self-isolation for those who tested positive and made face masks mandatory again in shops and on public transport. On the same day, the PM launched an investigation of his own, with Simon Case at the helm, a cabinet secretary 'very cross' at being asked to pass judgement. 'You need an independent investigation,' he told Johnson in front of several witnesses. 'No civil servant working for you will be seen as independent. I will not be seen as a credible figure.'

In reality Johnson needed a private, internal inquiry to find out what had happened. From Australia, Lynton Crosby told him, 'Get your chief of staff immediately to get every diary, every meeting, every event, every CCTV and collate exactly what happened. Only when you're totally clear will you be able to fix it.'[1]

In the morning meeting in Number 10, Henry Newman said, 'Someone needs to sit down and do an audit of everything we know before we start making statements.' One of those present observed, 'It was a tumbleweed moment.' Four different witnesses recall Newman's comments, but they led only to an embarrassed silence.

The second time Keir Starmer raised the issue at PMQs Johnson wound down afterwards in an office behind the speaker's chair. He quizzed Rosenfield in front of a cabinet minister. 'Dan, I've asked you, but were people having parties in Number 10?'

The minister recalled, 'Dan said, "I've asked around, Prime Minister. No, they weren't." And he clearly hadn't fucking asked around. He hadn't asked the right people. He certainly hadn't gripped the civil service, who eventually accounted for about 150 of the fixed penalty notices. Dan took no responsibility ... he should have said to the PM, "I've asked around, they were pissing it up on a Friday night. I've got to the bottom of it. We're going to have to put our hands up here and we need to get out on the front foot and apologise."'

Blaming Rosenfield for failing to investigate and Doyle for a lack of candour about what went on is not to absolve Johnson. Quick and full disclosure formed no part of the playbook he had pursued in public life.

'One of the things that had both served him extremely well and ultimately was his undoing was his determination never to answer a question
if he could possibly avoid it,' said an MP close to Johnson. 'His view
always was that once you've answered one, you open up another three or
four.' This meant the prime minister avoided adopting a proactive
communications strategy which might have saved him. Conor Burns, his
former PPS, had begun turning up to PMQs prep every Wednesday. The
line of attack he suggested was this: 'If I had thought these gatherings
were against the rules, why did I have the official photographer recording
them?' Burns said, 'Get it out there, apologise and then move beyond it.'
Johnson's riposte was timeless: 'Once you concede, they've got you.'

The Metropolitan Police had, so far, refused to investigate, saying the
Stratton video did 'not provide evidence of a breach' of Covid rules. But
the stories kept coming, a form of Chinese water torture. On 9 December
the BBC revealed Jack Doyle had doled out awards at a Christmas party
the previous December. Three days later Number 10 was forced to admit
that Johnson had attended a semi-virtual quiz when indoor gatherings
were banned. On 15 December, a photograph emerged of Shaun Bailey,
the Conservative mayoral candidate for London, at a party in CCHQ,
complete with bargain basement snacks.

A day later it was revealed that Johnson attended a do in the Downing
Street garden on 15 May 2020, which Number 10 called a work event. On
19 December a photograph was published showing Johnson and Carrie
with Wilfred at a table on the terrace next to the Cabinet Room, with
Cummings and Martin Reynolds, and fifteen others visible in the background. Both cheese and wine were being consumed.

This fuelled the paranoia of Johnson's team since it was clear the
picture had been taken from a first-floor state room being used by Rishi
Sunak's political team. One of the chancellor's aides provided a different
explanation: 'I am convinced that photo came from one of the cleaners
or security people. You could tell from their faces how disapproving they
were.' The door to the state room was next to the entrance to Johnson's
flat, a vantage point that also enabled Sunak's advisers to see how often
the prime minister's red box remained unopened outside his door. 'I
cannot tell you the number of times we would be there all in at 7.45 a.m.
and the box would be sitting there with the newspapers on top, not
touched from the night before,' one said. 'You would hear Boris coming
up the stairs at 5 p.m. To be fair, some of this was him recovering from

being ill but it was a consistent thing. There was one occasion where something big happened. I vividly remember seeing him coming out of the flat with no shoes on at quarter to six, shirt untucked, hair all over the place, being walked back down the stairs by Martin Reynolds.'

On 16 December, the Lib Dems won the North Shropshire by-election with a gargantuan 34 per cent swing. The same day Sir Roger Gale, a long-term Johnson critic, became the first MP to publicly confirm that he had submitted a letter of no confidence.

To cap it all, Case was forced to recuse himself from the inquiry because it emerged that a Christmas party had been held in his own office on 17 December 2020, involving an online quiz with the six people who were already in the office joining in from their desks and another half dozen working from home attending virtually. Case did not take part, but walked through the room.[2] The cabinet secretary went to see the prime minister and said, 'In light of this, there is no way I can carry on and do a report that would carry anybody's confidence.'

In his place, Simone Finn and Henry Newman recommended the appointment of Sue Gray, the former head of propriety and ethics, who had delivered the verdict which ended the cabinet careers of Damian Green over 'pestminster' and Andrew Mitchell over 'plebgate'. Rosenfield made the appointment. Johnson was later furious with Finn for involving Gray, but she regarded the civil servant as preferable to the alternative – Cabinet Office permanent secretary Alex Chisholm, a very by-the-book official.

Gray had a reputation as a civil servant of independence and rare bravery – having left her Whitehall career in the 1980s to run a pub in Newry, Northern Ireland, during the Troubles. But, as her surname suggested, 'Sue' (like 'Boris', one name was enough) was adept at operating in the dark corners of Whitehall, a fixer who was as good at hiding bodies as she was at digging them up. When the call came, from Darren Tierney, now the head of PET, she was second permanent secretary at the Cabinet Office. Gray said, 'No thanks', repeatedly. But the decision had been taken. This was instruction, not request.

Case recused himself from the discussions. When he heard about Gray's appointment he told colleagues it was 'a terrible idea' since Gray would be put in an invidious position. He thought the requirements of the Civil Service Code, which demands honesty, integrity and impartiality of officials in serving the government of the day, would run up against the need to do the right thing for the prime minister. Others thought he was all too happy to see the hospital pass land in Gray's lap.

Johnson and his team, who had spent the first lockdown in a bizarre bubble, both physically and mentally divorced from the experience of most of their countrymen, seemed oblivious of the depth of feeling the scandal was generating. 'The whole thing is nonsense,' an uncomprehending prime minister ventured. For years, Johnson's superpower seemed to be brazening out crises, both personal and political, unscathed. Ben Gascoigne sought to boost morale by recounting the scene at City Hall when one of Johnson's periodic personal dramas was plastered across the front pages. Johnson emerged from his office and said, 'Don't worry. The show – and it is a show – will go on.' The anecdote perfectly captured the insouciance with which Johnson always confronted adversity. But his consequent belief that he would always bounce back now served him badly.

Others who spent the pandemic toiling in Number 10 admitted later that they had a blind spot when it came to the 'parties'. Lister said in mitigation: 'You've got all these youngsters working there. They go back to their one-bedroom flat, or bed-sit. Of course, they're going to stay in the office and have a drink with their mates. Now, is that a party?'

A senior political adviser said, 'Number 10 had a very different experience of the pandemic because we were together, which was very unusual for office workers. When the first story came out, those of us who were there didn't say, "Fuck, they're on to us!" We didn't feel like there had been mass rule-breaking. We collectively convinced ourselves nothing really had happened. Then, you started to look back and think, "You know what? Maybe that wasn't quite right. Maybe someone should have thought about how that would look." The vast majority of these occasions would start with something that was appropriate and within the rules. On Friday night, you'd have a glass of wine at your desk. People worked late. At 10 p.m., 11 p.m., you'd be three or four glasses in and someone would be sitting against your desk rather than behind the Perspex screen. In hindsight, that was socialising. It didn't feel like socialising or partying. I'm sure that hampered the initial reaction, because we felt, "We weren't partying. It's so unfair."'

As pictures emerged of Johnson raising a glass at events it reinforced a view some voters had of him as an extrovert bon viveur. It was assumed that he had been the party king, but the public view was broadly wrong. 'He was not someone who would dodge work to go and have a drink,' an aide said. A cabinet minister explained: 'He's not averse to a glass of wine but he doesn't like parties with people he doesn't know, so the idea that Boris's idea of fun is to join lots of spads and civil servants for a five-hour drinkathon, that was grotesque and unfair.'

In a bid to get on the front foot, Isaac Levido and Ross Kempsell pressed for Johnson to establish a 'war room' with lawyers to look at the evidence and prepare for new revelations. But it never got off the ground. There was no attempt to argue that people working under unbearable stress in a national health crisis had let their hair down a little too much.

Senior cabinet members bluntly told Johnson he needed to change his Number 10 team if he was to save his premiership. Members of the whips' office put the boot in too. A former cabinet minister observed, 'He needs to know he needs to change, he needs to want to be able to change and he needs to actually be capable of changing. I'm not very confident about any of those three.' Condemning Number 10 as a medieval court, he added, 'We need an end to the Tudor twattery.' Iain Duncan Smith, the former Tory leader, said, 'People in Downing Street should be prepared to take a bullet for the PM but at the moment it appears to be him taking a bullet for them.'

As 2021 became 2022 the mood in the Tory Party was grim. Cummings predicted that the 'silent artillery of time' would do for Johnson, saying, 'He's done, gone by this time next year, probably summer.' At the time, the consensus view was that Johnson would find a way to wriggle free, but Cummings wasn't leaving the bombardment to chance, by now openly telling journalists his allies had 'a grid' of potential stories designed to wound.

'They ran a very effective briefing campaign,' said an aide who remained loyal to Johnson until the end. 'It was deliberate, it was totally coordinated, but it was also very, very undemocratic and outside the rules of normal politics, because this guy was elected, he was leader of the Conservative Party, he was prime minister.' Summing up the Johnsonworld view of Cummings' operation, the aide said, 'It was mainly Dom, with a bit of Lee [Cain] on the side, bit of Cleo [Watson]. To be fair to Lee, he went on to start his business and probably eased off the gas a bit.' Cain and Watson kept their heads down, but she was friendly with

Amber de Botton, the key figure at ITV, and Nissy Chesterfield, Rishi Sunak's press secretary.

On Friday 7 January, Cummings wrote a blog opening a new front. The focus, he argued, should be on an event on 20 May 2020 when Downing Street staff had been invited to 'socially distanced drinks' in the garden. 'I and at least one other spad … said that this seemed to be against the rules and should not happen. We were ignored. I was ill and went home to bed early that afternoon but am told this event definitely happened.' The other spad was Lee Cain. The post was the first time Cummings had explicitly said he was trying to oust the prime minister: 'The only way to avert this existential threat to many seats, including much of the "Red Wall", is to replace the trolley with a team that can actually deliver.'

The following day, the *Telegraph* revealed that the invite to this apparent party had been sent by Martin Reynolds. The *Sunday Times* then ran a front-page story saying Reynolds had encouraged staff to 'bring your own booze' and that both Johnson and Carrie had been present – the first time the prime minister had been placed at any of the questionable events. On 10 January, ITV got the full email which read: 'Hi all, After what has been an incredibly busy period we thought it would be nice to make the most of the lovely weather and have some socially distanced drinks in the No10 garden this evening. Please join us from 6 p.m. and bring your own booze! Martin.' Around forty staff attended where drinks and picnic food were served. Just hours before this gathering, Oliver Dowden had told the public at the daily Covid press conference, 'You can meet one person outside of your household in an outdoor, public place provided that you stay two metres apart.'

This flurry of revelations wrongfooted Downing Street. Rosenfield's half-hearted investigation had not turned up any details of the gathering and only when Johnson's diary was checked was it confirmed the prime minister had attended. Reynolds had not bothered to warn his colleagues the email existed. 'How the fuck has this happened?' a furious Johnson shouted at aides. 'How hasn't this been sorted out.' They studied the floor. Around this time, a senior cabinet minister walked in as Johnson was reproaching Jack Doyle: 'You told me there weren't any fucking parties!' This, more than any other revelation, caused splits between Johnson's political aides and the senior civil servants – divisions Cummings was able to exploit. 'People wanted to kill Reynolds,' one insider recalled.

Civil servants in the press team, involved in organising the party, feared they would be thrown to the wolves. Their political colleagues, in turn, were still suspicious about a senior figure in the private office being 'Red Throat', leaking to Labour. A close ally of Johnson later told the author Sebastian Payne: 'A lot of the partygate stuff was leaked by junior civil servants, particularly in the press office. There's about thirty of them, all quite young and junior. One person leaking had quit on bad terms the previous summer. Another was selling pictures to the *Mirror*.'[3] Cummings also had a network of officials in Number 10 and the Cabinet Office leaking to him via WhatsApp. A Vote Leave source said, 'Most of it was us, but not all of it. There was also a bunch of deep state people. One of the terrible things that Boris did, is that he fucked over a whole bunch of junior Downing Street staff and they wreaked revenge on him. His theory was that if it looked like everyone was [going to parties], it's not his fault. But it poisoned the entire building against him.'

Facing an existential political crisis, Johnson deployed his new human shield: Michael Ellis, the paymaster general, who was regarded by his colleagues as a comic figure from a Vaudeville production of Parliament. Ellis, known as 'Sir Michael' because of his quivering desperation for a knighthood, had begun his professional life as a defender of Northampton burglars. But as someone prepared to endure any humiliation in the interests of self-advancement he was perfect for Johnson when he needed someone to answer an urgent question on partygate. Armed with little more than misplaced self-confidence, Ellis brazened it out. When he repaired to the tearoom afterwards, Andrew Bridgen – the backbench dean of dissent – said, 'Congratulations. I think Prince Andrew wants you to help him now.' Two days later, Bridgen announced he had submitted a letter of no confidence, the fourth successive prime minister he had sought to remove, as if his life's goal was to complete a line of regicidal bingo.

Bridgen was hardly alone, though. Years of grievances led MPs to withdraw their support. Johnson told aides of a visit by Andrew Mitchell, the former development secretary: 'He was furious because of what I had done to DfID [merging it with the Foreign Office], he was furious because I hadn't put him in the cabinet, furious because he hadn't got a knighthood – a seething vat of sulphuric acid.' As he walked out, Mitchell turned and said, 'They're going to get you, you know.' It wasn't long before Mitchell was calling for Johnson's head.

Labour now led by 14 points in one poll. Party officials, preparing Keir Starmer for Prime Minister's Questions that week, seized on another finding. 'At the start of the week, more people believed the moon landings were faked than believed Boris Johnson's explanations about these parties,' one said. 'By Wednesday the figure was 6 per cent, which is about the same number who believe in the Loch Ness monster.'

In PMQs, in what was perhaps the most humiliating moment of his premiership, a chastened Johnson stood up in the Commons to read a statement admitting he had attended the 20 May bash for twenty-five minutes after being asked to thank staff for their hard work. He said he 'believed implicitly' it was 'a work event' but admitted, 'With hindsight I should have sent everyone back inside. I should have recognised that even if it could be said technically to fall within the guidance, there would be millions and millions of people who would not see it that way.' Starmer called on Johnson to 'do the decent thing and resign'.

Afterwards the PM headed to the tearoom. Some MPs present said he claimed privately that he had done nothing wrong. But he was confronted by at least one MP who had watched loved ones die of Covid, unable to visit them. 'Boris was white-faced and close to tears,' this MP said. 'He was absolutely contrite.'

If Johnson hoped his apology would buy him time, he was mistaken. Later that day, Douglas Ross, the leader of the Scottish Conservatives, along with two of his predecessors Ruth Davidson and Jackson Carlaw, called for the PM to resign. The following day, 27 out of 31 Tories in the Scottish Parliament joined them, along with William Wragg, chairman of the public administration and constitutional affairs select committee, and former ministers Caroline Nokes, Tobias Ellwood and Tim Loughton.

Two major revelations were still to come. The first emerged on Thursday 13th. Two parties – leaving bashes for James Slack, the former director of communications, and a photographer – had taken place on 16 April 2021, on the eve of the Duke of Edinburgh's funeral. The disclosure forced Number 10 to send an apology to Buckingham Palace. While the Queen sat poignantly, alone in her grief as she adhered to Covid rules at funerals, Number 10 staff had gone to the Co-op on the Strand to fill a suitcase with wine. Fortunately for Johnson, he was absent at Chequers. 'Everyone was lathered,' said one who did attend. Shelley Williams-Walker, Johnson's head of operations, played DJ then sat on and broke a swing belonging to Wilfred, the prime minister's toddler.

At the end of that week came reports that Johnson regularly stopped to talk to staff enjoying 'wine time Fridays' in Number 12 Downing Street, right by the stairs he had to climb to get to his flat. 'The idea that he didn't know there was a drinking culture is utter bollocks,' one said. Wine time Fridays dated back to the Cameron era but Johnson's aides went one better, spending £142 on a wine fridge with a capacity of thirty-four bottles – dubbed 'a fridge too far', as the revelations continued.

The boozing had immediate cut-through with the public. By 14 January 2022, YouGov found that 72 per cent of voters had an unfavourable view of Johnson, surpassing Theresa May's worst-ever figure. On the 17th, Cummings said the 'bring your own booze' event alone meant 'the PM lied to Parliament about parties'.

Johnson's fightback took three forms. The first, 'Operation Red Meat', was designed to drum up policies to appeal to backbenchers who were fast losing faith. 'Stop talking about dead cats and start throwing some red meat on the green benches,' culture secretary Nadine Dorries beseeched. There was talk of a reshuffle, action on immigration, the cost of living and a levelling up bill. The BBC licence fee was frozen.

Johnson also drafted in two new sets of advisers. They included the former whips Chris Pincher and Chris Heaton-Harris, plus Conor Burns. Grant Shapps, the transport secretary, dusted off the spreadsheet he used to count supporters and opponents. Together they set up a shadow operation to lobby MPs – a tacit admission that Johnson had lost faith in his chief whip, Mark Spencer. They even took Spencer's constituency office in the Commons as their headquarters, meeting there every morning and at least once a week with the PM.

They were assisted by Johnson's fixer Ross Kempsell and Charlotte Owen, a junior special adviser, who made up for her lack of experience with charm and political intelligence. Blonde and nearly six feet tall, Owen was popular with MPs – both the men of a certain age and women who were repelled by the 'macho' approach of Spencer's whipping operation. She and Pincher ran things in Parliament with Nigel Adams installed in Number 10. Armed with better information about MPs and their grievances, Johnson hit the phones.

The group's existence and a nickname – Operation Big Dog – was revealed by Anna Isaac of the *Independent* on 14 January. 'Big Dog', it was claimed, was not a reference to Johnson, but his nickname for the diminutive Adams. Yet even a year later, Adams had never once heard anyone call him Big Dog.

The importance Johnson attached to the operation was evidenced by the fact that he would hand peerages to Kempsell and Owen, both only in their twenties, in his resignation honours. 'Without Charlotte and Ross, Boris would have gone months before, without question,' one of the MPs said. The PM had also been consulting Eddie Lister (now Lord Udny-Lister) about how to shake up his team. Lister agreed to be an arm's-length sounding board, but refused to return while Rosenfield was in the building.

The second group of new advisers, dubbed the 'Brains Trust', consisted of Tory strategist Isaac Levido, his mentor Lynton Crosby and Will Lewis, Johnson's former editor at the *Telegraph*, who began providing advice on communications separate from the discredited media team in Number 10. Kempsell joined their discussions too.

Despite these moves, Johnson was in emotional torment. His mood veered between complacent confidence and a fatalistic fear that his political magic was broken. 'It reminds me of when he came back after he had Covid,' one Downing Street official said. 'A lot of his trains of thought didn't make a lot of sense. He's quite up and down.'

The Big Dog sniffer operation caught its first whiff of sedition on Monday 18 January when a dozen members of the 2019 intake disillusioned with Johnson met in the office of Chris Loder, the MP for West Dorset, a gathering described as 'group therapy more than strategy'. But they were already under surveillance. A staffer from the office of Rebecca Harris, a whip, was lingering in the corridor as they went in. 'We probably should have pulled it,' one MP said. 'But we're new to this.'

Unbeknown to the plotters, one of their number had 'grassed on their mates,' a Big Dog operative revealed. The double agent was debriefed in a 'safe house', the flat shared by Adams and Chris Heaton-Harris five minutes from the Commons. 'We got all the names, when the meeting was going to take place, so we had people in the corridor. We got verbatim notes from their meeting.'

The following day, around twenty MPs gathered in the office of Alicia Kearns to decide what to do. There was talk of a joint letter or statement calling for Johnson to quit. Gary Sambrook, the MP for Birmingham Northfield, was to the fore. Some were unwilling to show their hand, so they held a secret ballot to determine how many had already submitted a letter to Graham Brady. Ten had already gone in and ten more were soon to follow. The involvement of Kearns, the MP for Rutland and Melton, was a gift to Team Boris. Chris Pincher gleefully announced, 'It's a Pork Pie Plot!', the most famous product of Kearns' constituency.

The whips and the shadow whips responded with a combination of carrots and sticks. Kearns was told by an intermediary that there was a road to a government job if she ceased her activities.

The Pork Pie Plot highlighted the lack of party discipline or sangfroid under fire in the 2019 intake, who had been forced by Covid to stay away from the Commons for much of their first year. 'They hadn't been whipped properly, didn't really know what the game was,' a Johnson loyalist said.

The same day as the Pork Pie Plot was uncovered, Rosenfield summoned parliamentary private secretaries (PPSs) – the backbench MPs who work as assistants to ministers – to a meeting. One after another, they denounced the prime minister's chaotic operation and at least three called for senior resignations. Paul Holmes, an aide to Priti Patel, the home secretary, said the operation was 'a failure' and that 'heads must roll'. Mark Fletcher, PPS to Kwasi Kwarteng, agreed. Then Jane Hunt spoke up. A mild-mannered aide to Steve Barclay, the Cabinet Office minister, she told Rosenfield, 'I wouldn't piss on you if you were on fire.'

Rosenfield admitted to Downing Street colleagues that they may need to 'fall on their swords', although one remarked, 'He didn't give the impression he would be leaping onto the first sword.' It was also increasingly clear to the shadow whipping operation that Johnson would face a vote of no confidence in the weeks ahead. 'Bring it on!' the prime minister told aides. In an interview with Beth Rigby of Sky News, a hangdog PM repeatedly apologised for the party on the eve of the royal funeral. Quizzed about the bring your own booze event, he insisted, 'I'm saying categorically that nobody told me, nobody said this was something that was against the rules.'

It was watching this squirming performance that persuaded David Davis he needed to speak out. Having asked Lindsay Hoyle, the speaker, for 'a free hit' at the end of Prime Minister's Questions two days later, Davis got to his feet and intoned the words with which Oliver Cromwell dismissed the Long Parliament and Leo Amery helped destroy Neville

Chamberlain in 1940: 'You have sat here too long for all the good that you have done. In the name of God, go.' Johnson's allies were withering, comparing Davis's quest for the limelight to Michael Heseltine: 'Margaret Thatcher used to say, "The trouble with Michael is he wants to be the bride at every wedding and the corpse at every funeral." That's DD.'

In fact, Davis's intervention helped to unify the Conservatives, coming after Christian Wakeford, the Tory MP for Bury South, defected to Labour just before PMQs. The anger that act provoked in his colleagues caused a closing of the ranks. Wakeford, who had been dubbed 'Wokeford' by colleagues for his earnestness on social issues, had been in talks with Labour for months but only agreed to jump in a meeting with Starmer two days earlier. Johnson was in his car driving to the Commons when Declan Lyons broke the news to him. Seven Tory MPs withdrew their letters of no confidence against the PM.

On 24 January ITV reported that Johnson had attended a 'party' on his birthday on 19 June 2020, at a time when indoor gatherings were banned. Among the thirty people present were Carrie, who had organised the gathering, Rishi Sunak, who had turned up for a meeting in the same room, and Lulu Lytle, who had been in the flat finishing the redecorations. It was probably the most wretched birthday gathering of Johnson's fifty-six years, with curling M&S sandwiches laid out on a table and jugs of fruit juice and cans of beer – but it became the most significant. Reports claimed a Union Jack cake was served while attendees sang 'Happy Birthday'. In fact, the cake, which ministers say was supplied by Chloe Westley, a special adviser in the comms team, remained in a tupperware box. The prime minister attended for less than ten minutes.

Efforts to defend Johnson proved farcical. Conor Burns told *Channel 4 News* the prime minister 'was in a sense, ambushed with a cake', a phrase which symbolised a government stranded in the no man's land between tragedy and circus. Nigella Lawson, the television chef, announced that her next cookbook would be called 'Ambushed by Cake'. Johnson went 'apeshit' when he saw a clip of the Burns interview. At PMQs, Starmer again urged him to resign. It took four days for anyone to notice *The Times* had reported the birthday gathering in the week it happened, after being proactively briefed by his team, a fact Johnson would claim as proof no one saw the gathering as a breach of the rules.

It was also claimed there was a gathering in the Johnsons' flat that evening. A Downing Street aide received text messages from Carrie Johnson saying she was in the flat with two friends, with Boris joining them later. 'I'm with the gays,' the message read.[4]

The image of the prime minister's wife as a distributor of cake caused an upsurge in media usage of the nickname she had acquired during wallpapergate, 'Carrie Antoinette'. A former minister, previously a Johnson supporter, joked, 'I think the prime minister should resign – and she should take her husband with her.'

The coverage convinced friends that Carrie would not be sorry to see the back of Downing Street. One who knew the couple well said, 'She was telling friends the pressure on her was too much and she'd be happier if he left.' A friend of Carrie added, 'She just wants to focus on her children.' That said, she was not urging her husband to resign, quite the contrary. 'Carrie did not think Boris had done anything wrong,' a friend revealed. This was significant since she was one of the few people who could have persuaded Johnson to face up to the political peril he was in.

Cummings' attack grid repeatedly tried to focus media attention on the gathering in the flat on the evening of 13 November 2020, the night he left Number 10. Vote Leavers claimed the music from the flat was so loud that ABBA's 'The Winner Takes It All' could be heard downstairs in the press office and from the road behind Number 10. Both Carrie and Johnson vociferously denied there had been any party, a position reinforced by three others present that night. Johnson erupted with indignant rage when interviewed for this book: 'There was no fucking party!' He and Carrie believed his enemies had 'deliberately conflated' that night with the celebrations on Brexit night, when ABBA was played and Vote Leave's Cleo Watson was present. 'I think it was all made up by Lee and Dom,' a source familiar with Johnson's thinking said, 'because Cleo had the memory of that party. We kept thinking that people would realise this was bullshit and that it would all disappear. The police were getting a huge amount of testimony from people like Lee and Cleo.' There were rumours that Cummings had acquired video of the party in the flat. 'The video was of them all dancing upstairs on Brexit night,' a political aide insisted.

Downing Street claimed the event on 13 November was actually a job interview, with Johnson quizzing Henry Newman, then working for

Michael Gove, about a position in Number 10. It can now be revealed that those present were all government special advisers: Newman, Allegra Stratton, Josh Grimstone, Declan Lyons and his partner Sophia True. They describe a crisis meeting where Johnson sought advice from trusted advisers away from the ears of the Vote Leavers loyal to Cummings. Alcohol was drunk but it was a formal enough affair that Lyons even sketched out a brief agenda. 'There was nowhere else to go,' one said. 'Cleo [Watson] was still in the outer office. Lee [Cain] was still in the press office. We were talking about building a future team and stabilising the parliamentary party. Boris wanted everyone to come into Number 10, which, with the exception of Josh, did happen.'

This is one of those occasions where there is no reconciling different stories. At least three people gave evidence to the police that they heard ABBA music that night emanating from the Johnsons' flat. Those present are equally adamant that this claim was invented.

Days before Sue Gray was due to produce her report, Met Police commissioner Cressida Dick announced that Scotland Yard was opening a criminal investigation into partygate because of the apparent 'serious and flagrant breaches' that had occurred. Johnson got just a few hours' notice.

Martin Reynolds gathered the civil servants in Number 10 to reassure them. Many were getting abuse as the scandal spread. 'People were getting shouted at in the street, their neighbours weren't talking to them, and their friends weren't talking to them,' a senior political aide recalled. 'Martin had very carefully calibrated it, and what he said was written out very clearly.' Rosenfield gathered the thirty-odd political special advisers in the Cabinet Room, having been advised to use the same script. 'He didn't stick to the script at all. He said, "It's a fixed penalty, like a car park fine." It leaked, before we'd even left the room. You must be so disliked for that to happen.'

The photographs and witness statements Gray had collected had been passed to the Met by the Cabinet Office, an arrangement set up by Tierney and Case before she was appointed. During the Met investigation the only contact the police had with government was with Tierney.

The Met investigation – Operation Hillman – soon led to investigating officers taking evidence about twelve events, seven of which Johnson had attended. A prime minister who, Guto Harri recalled, was at first more concerned about Sue Gray – whom he branded 'the psycho' preparing 'an orgy of pain, abuse and humiliation' – then realised that the police findings might well make it impossible to continue in his role'.[5]

In early February, the police said they were sending a questionnaire to ninety people present at the events, including both Johnsons, Sunak, Case and Reynolds. By March the figure was over a hundred. Downing Street confirmed on 11 February that the prime minister had received the questions, which had to be 'answered truthfully' and had the same legal status as information given under caution – the first time a sitting prime minister had even been interviewed under caution. Like other high-profile Met probes, it proceeded with a minimum of openness to an unsatisfactory conclusion. The future of the government now rested in the hands of a less accountable and arguably an even less competent body.

The police inquiry initially bought Johnson time not least because it coincided with Operation Fightback gearing up. At PMQs the following day, the shadow whipping operation ensured there was vocal support for Johnson as he fended off Starmer for the third week in a row about partygate. When the prime minister returned to his Commons office afterwards, he pumped his fist in a mock victory celebration, saying, 'Come on! Good noise from the colleagues.' He was increasingly spending time in the Commons, rather than Number 10. He told MPs partygate was a 'witch-hunt' got up by Labour and the media, that he did nothing wrong and would bounce back.

The Big Dog team was now meeting three times a day, starting at 9 a.m. in Mark Spencer's office, boosted by occasional visits from Nadine Dorries and Jacob Rees-Mogg. A second (virtual) meeting of the inner core followed mid-morning, with another in person at about 4.30 p.m. On Shapps' spreadsheet, up to 160 MPs were initially identified as at risk of opposing Johnson in a no-confidence motion, just 20 short of the number needed to oust him and much higher than the 117 who opposed Theresa May in December 2018. The group believed they now commanded more than 115 supportive MPs.

When the Met probe began Gray and the police came to an agreement that she could publish an interim report after the police had seen it. She did so on 31 January.

Gray bumped into Conor Burns, with whom she had worked in Northern Ireland, before publication. 'Sue told Conor that we should all read her conclusions carefully,' a source said. 'Yes, there would be blame apportioned to Boris, but anyone who reads it with an open mind will see that it is not a "get Boris" report.' Senior civil servants would share the blame.

The report, a dozen pages, was carefully worded but quietly devastating. The document provided a list of sixteen gatherings, including some that had not been previously reported in the media. Gray condemned 'failures of leadership and judgment' in both Number 10 and the Cabinet Office and, by implication, Johnson, Case and Reynolds. She wrote, 'A number of these gatherings should not have been allowed to take place or to develop in the way that they did', and that some of the behaviour surrounding them was 'difficult to justify'. Gray said there was a 'serious failure' to observe the standards expected of government employees or ordinary citizens during lockdown.

Turning to the culture of drinking at the top of government, Gray said, 'The excessive consumption of alcohol is not appropriate in a professional workplace at any time.' She condemned the fact that 'some staff wanted to raise concerns about behaviours they witnessed at work but at times felt unable to do so'. The 'structures and support' in Downing Street were not fit for purpose. While this was embarrassing for Johnson, it was aimed at the mandarins.

Johnson was delighted that he was not singled out for attack in the report, but it was also an eye-opener for the prime minister. 'It was the first time he had the full picture about what had been going on,' one aide said. In the Commons debate which followed, Johnson apologised for the third time, telling MPs he was 'sorry for the things we simply didn't get right and also sorry for the way that this matter has been handled'. Ian Blackford, the SNP leader in Westminster, was thrown out of the chamber by the speaker, Lindsay Hoyle, after he repeatedly stated that Johnson had misled the House. Andrew Mitchell joined his old friend David Davis in saying he had lost confidence in Johnson's leadership.

Theresa May also chose the moment to slide a stiletto between Johnson's ribs. Adopting the glaring disapproval of a maiden aunt confronting a nephew who has removed his trousers in church, she said people 'had a right to expect their prime minister to have read the rules, to understand the meaning of the rules' and to 'set an example'. She finished with a sting in the tail: 'Either my right honourable friend had not read the rules or didn't understand what they meant … or they didn't think the rules applied to Number 10,' she said. 'Which was it?' He told her to 'wait [for] the conclusion of the inquiry'.

Starmer dismissed Johnson as a 'man without shame' and, in an observation that even the prime minister's weary associates sometimes made, added, 'Just as he's done throughout his life he's damaged everything and everyone around him.' In retaliation, Johnson played the man rather than the ball, claiming the Labour leader had 'spent most of his time [as director of public prosecutions] prosecuting journalists and failing to prosecute Jimmy Savile', the former DJ and television presenter who was exposed as a paedophile. According to MPs sitting behind him, Johnson repeated the barb after Jacob Rees-Mogg, who was sitting next to him, first yelled it across the despatch box. Starmer had been head of the Crown Prosecution Service when the decision was made not to prosecute Savile, but he was not the reviewing lawyer for the case and played no role in the decision. The attack, when Johnson was supposed to be the one apologising, provoked widespread fury, including in Conservative ranks.

Three days later, Johnson was in his official car when he took a call from Munira Mirza, the head of the Number 10 policy unit, a close ally since he was mayor. She implored him to make a public apology for the Savile comments. Her husband, Dougie Smith, told a Number 10 political aide Mirza had 'a hissy fit' and he had 'never seen her so worked up about something'. Johnson refused, saying it would make him look weak and stupid to recant. 'If you don't, I'll resign,' Mirza threatened.

Johnson softened: 'Don't be ridiculous. I'll apologise.' They agreed a form of words. Mirza was relieved he could be reasoned with. But Johnson failed to stick to the agreed formula. There was no apology. Instead he claimed, lamely, that he was 'not talking about the leader of the opposition's personal record when he was DPP. I was making a point about his responsibility for the organisation as a whole.' By mid-afternoon Mirza had decided to walk, writing an excoriating letter: 'This was not the normal cut-and-thrust of politics; it was an inappropriate and partisan reference to a horrendous case of child sex abuse. You tried to clarify your position today but, despite my urging, you did not apologise for the misleading impression you gave.' She concluded, 'It is not too late for you but, I'm sorry to say, it is too late for me.'

For many this was the moment which truly shook the foundations of his premiership loose. Johnson had once named Mirza one of the five most important women in his life. Colleagues compared her departure with the last raven leaving the Tower of London. Many did not believe she had really gone over the Savile comments. In reality she had been growing disillusioned and it was the 'final straw'. 'Dan Rosenfield had wanted Munira out because he thought the policy unit was weak,' a senior Johnson adviser said. 'She was also angry about Rosenfield trying to get shot of her and constantly cutting her out of meetings.'

Johnson and his closest aides quickly saw it as something more sinister. The prime minister felt Mirza's demands on the phone sounded like a hostage negotiator. Panicking, he called Lynton Crosby and said she was 'reading from a script', adding, 'I don't believe a word of it.'

Johnson's team was already wary of Dougie Smith, amid suspicion he had 'crossed over' to support Rishi Sunak's leadership ambitions. Smith was said to have told friends months earlier that they should 'get ready for Rishi'. There is more than a whiff of sexism in the suggestion that Mirza was a puppet in her husband's power games. Fairer was the view of a cabinet minister, who said, 'Put it this way, if Dougie told her to stay, she'd have stayed.'

What happened next is one of the most contested moments of Johnson's premiership. It is claimed Smith called Johnson to threaten him. In fact, it was Johnson who called Smith. The prime minister was discombobulated. 'Dougie, I'm so upset about Munira,' he said. 'I'm completely devastated. What do you think I should do?'

Smith saw little point in gilding the lily. 'I've always given you good advice.' Pause. 'I think you should resign.'

Johnson, incredulous, blurted, 'You must be joking!'

Smith was not. 'I think you're finished,' he said. 'You can tough it out to the bitter end if you want to and terminally damage your brand. Or you can gather yourself together, say Covid means you haven't been on top form and that's why you've made some mistakes and stand down. Once that happens your reputation will recover and, at some point, there's a decent chance you can come back.'

'I can't do that,' said Johnson.

'Boris, in his usual pleading way, wanted someone to say, "Don't worry",' a cabinet minister said. 'Instead, Dougie said, "You're fucked, you need to face up to reality."'

Smith told Johnson that if he clung on he would become 'toxic' like Richard Nixon resigning the US presidency after Watergate. Then the punchline: fail to resign and 'They will get you,' he predicted. The minister said, 'Dougie told me he didn't tell Boris he would bring him down. He just explained the facts of life and told Boris that he was finished.'

This was not what Johnson heard. Another cabinet minister who saw Johnson fifteen minutes later said, 'Boris was quite shaken. He said to me, "I just had Dougie Smith on the phone. He told me I had to go and go now." Boris said, "Dougie told me I'm toxic and if I don't go, he's going to get me."'

The call was deeply dispiriting for Johnson, who still thought he was being unjustly punished: *Dougie's my adviser. Why is he saying this when I've done nothing wrong and it's all bullshit? Munira has known me for a very long time. The justification that she picked for resigning is pretty bloody peculiar. To resign because I've said something in the heat of the moment in the chamber, is bizarre. Christ, the things I've said, which she hasn't batted an eyelid at.*

This exchange with Smith became Exhibit A in Team Boris's hypothesis that he was the victim of a labyrinthine conspiracy to install Sunak in his stead. Smith had been instrumental in helping the chancellor secure his Richmond, North Yorkshire, seat after the retirement of William Hague. Nadine Dorries, who wrote that a cabal of middle-aged men had formed a 'Movement' to make and break Conservative leaders, pointed out that Smith and Cummings had known each other for two decades, having first become friends on the campaign against the euro in 1999. Johnson also recalled that on one occasion, before he became leader, when he visited Cummings to try to persuade him to join the team, 'Dougie was there'.

A veteran Downing Street operator said, 'Boris was in a state of heightened agitation. He immediately put the most lurid and paranoid spin on it. Boris can't help it; he will always try to spin whatever has happened in a way that exculpates himself. That's just what he does.'

There was undoubtedly a convergence of interests between Cummings, Smith and the Sunak camp, but discerning where a few calls becomes a 'plot' is not possible. A cabinet minister said, 'They clearly both wanted him [Johnson] out of there. They're both alpha males but Dougie is impressed with Dom's brain and was definitely happy that Dom was taking the heat. Cummings ridiculed the idea of a grand conspiracy, keen to depict himself as the driving force behind the campaign to oust Johnson.

Later on the day of Mirza's resignation, 3 February, Jack Doyle quit as communications director, seizing the opportunity to bury his own bad news beneath Mirza's bombshell departure. Doyle had endured a torrid time, suffering a major family bereavement while he tried to keep the show on the road, all the while knowing that he would probably have to quit for the mistakes he had made at the start of the partygate saga. It was a reminder of the terrible toll which politics can take on individuals of talent who make a mistake in the path of a political hurricane.

The same day Rosenfield shared a car with Johnson. The chief of staff had told friends a week earlier he was trying to overhaul the operation, but it was clear he would have to join the exodus. He agreed to go quietly in return for a peerage. Rosenfield had been meeting old friends from the City for months – one encounter in 5 Hertford Street took place in full view of a journalist. When the government held an investment conference with blue-chip companies, Rosenfield joked with colleagues it was 'my milk round'. The following day, 4 February, it was announced that both Rosenfield and Reynolds would leave. A new 'Office of the Prime Minister' would be created, in response to Gray's suggestion that the centre needed beefing up. After he left, Reynolds took one look at the Bloomberg terminal on Rosenfield's desk and said, 'At least can we get rid of that screen, it's costing us £1,000 a month.'

To add to the pressure on Johnson, a biography of Carrie by Lord Ashcroft reheated claims that she had fiddled her expenses when she worked at CCHQ, by taking cabs and putting them under other people's names, accusations she always denied. The most lurid claim, however, serialised in the *Mail on Sunday* on 5 February 2022, was that one of Johnson's aides had walked in on him and Carrie in flagrante in 2018. Conor Burns was later named as the witness. The rumour was without foundation since no one had seen either of them unclothed.

Burns was in Northern Ireland that Friday when he took a call from Ashcroft who said the story was to go live the following evening. Burns told him what had really happened. It was an evening when Johnson, then foreign secretary, was hosting drinks receptions in his ministerial office. Having cleared up, Burns had supper with Mark Worthington,

Margaret Thatcher's former private secretary, and was about to go home when he saw Johnson's ministerial car in New Palace Yard. Burns and Worthington went back to Johnson's suite of offices. The door was closed between the two rooms. Burns knocked on the door. 'Hello, who is it?' Johnson's voice.

'Conor.'

'Hang on!' There was a delay of ten to fifteen seconds before Johnson opened the door. Carrie was with him, one bottle of wine empty, another nearly finished.

The next day Burns took Ben Gascoigne aside and said, 'If anything is going on, that really is not the smartest place for anything to be going on.'

'Did they have their clothes on?' Gascoigne asked. They did.

The next Burns heard of it was when Ashcroft phoned on 3 February. He denied seeing the couple in a compromising position and explained that Worthington would back him up, something which gave Ashcroft pause. Burns' phone went again. It was Johnson: 'The fucking *Mail* are going to run this story about me and Carrie and you.' Burns fled to his car, where his close protection team listened in, silently laughing. 'You've got to phone Ted Verity,' the editor of the *Mail on Sunday*, Johnson instructed. 'Tell these fuckers you did not see her noshing me off.' Burns made the call: 'There was no blow job.' Ashcroft watered down the story.

While Burns was having a much-needed drink, Johnson was trying to appoint his third (and final) leadership team to resurrect his premiership. He went into conclave with the Brains Trust at 7 a.m., when they met for bacon sandwiches. They were still going as they wolfed 'godawful takeaway' late in the evening.[6]

Tory MPs wanted the prime minister to appoint Lynton Crosby as his chief of staff, to kick the machine and impose discipline on Johnson himself, but the Wizard of Oz was not interested in a permanent role. Instead, he dialled in from Australia while the others gathered in Rosenfield's office to pick the new team. Others present included Nigel Adams, Ben Gascoigne, Ross Kempsell, Will Lewis and Isaac Levido, who had chaired the first meeting to prepare for the next election, due in 2024, the day before in the boardroom at CCHQ.

He might have been at the end of a phone line, but the most influential voice was Crosby's, who appeared underwhelmed by the group Johnson had assembled. 'Who else is there?' he asked. When Adams called out his name, Crosby replied, 'Nigel who?'

'Nigel Adams. I'm the minister who protects the prime minister.'

The Australian endorsed the appointment of David Canzini – the softly spoken former CTF Partners man who wore a goatee beard on his face and robust conservative opinions on his sleeve – to boost the political operation and liaise with MPs. Though Johnson did not know him, Canzini was popular with Brexiteers, having helped run the 'chuck Chequers' campaign in 2018. Canzini began quietly reaching out to rebels. 'What would it take to get you to rescind your letter?' he asked. One MP suggested that a knighthood might do the trick. Another asked for an awkward court ruling to go away.

The most visible (and arguably most critical) job was the hardest to fill, the replacement for Doyle as communications director. The first choice, proposed by Adams, was George Pascoe-Watson, the former political editor of the *Sun*, now a partner at Portland Communications. He quickly declined. Johnson, who was surrounded by Carrie's young friends in the political operation, fancied a grey beard of his own generation and sounded out Neil Darbyshire, who he had known at the *Telegraph* and was now an executive at the *Mail*. Darbyshire's wife kiboshed the plan. Andrew Porter, the former political editor of the *Telegraph*, and Sarah Sands, the former editor of the *Today* programme, were also approached. Johnson asked Will Lewis to take on the role, but he preferred to remain an informal adviser. Ben Gascoigne even phoned Will Walden, Johnson's mouthpiece at City Hall, but Walden, who had been blamed by Carrie for pro-Marina quotes in a *Times* article, had severed links with the psychodrama. 'Anybody who put their hat into the firing line was going to be attacked by Dom,' a witness said. 'That was a big factor in people not wanting to go for it. It had a chilling effect on the recruiting process.'

That left Guto Harri, the former BBC political reporter who had been Johnson's original mayoral spin doctor. Harri, a professional Welshman and resolute Remainer, had fallen out with his old boss over Brexit. But he was the kind of upbeat and amusing character who Johnson liked to have around and both sides were prevailed upon to give the relationship another go. The deal was sealed in a one-on-one meeting, where Harri arrived and clicked his heels, subaltern style, and said, 'Prime Minister, Guto Harri reporting for duty, sir!' Johnson arose as if to take the salute and then stopped himself. 'What am I doing? I should take the knee,' he said – a reference to the gesture which caused GB News to sever their links with Harri. 'All I want to know now, Boris, is: will you survive?' The prime minister responded by launching into an impromptu rendition of Gloria Gaynor's 'I Will Survive'.[7]

Harri was rusty, however. His feet were barely under a desk in Number 10 before he had given an interview to a Welsh language website in which he described his new boss as a 'very likeable character' and 'not a complete clown'. In a world of instant online translation and social media (neither of which had been a factor when Harri had last been in the front line), the comments went viral. Johnson went ballistic.

The third iteration of Team Boris was no more harmonious or effective than the second. Steve Barclay was made chief of staff after Johnson decided he wanted a minister to do the job. But he quickly put noses out of joint. 'He took it upon himself to exclude everyone from meetings,' a colleague said. Among those who were kicked out was Adams, who had recommended his appointment. A senior cabinet minister said, 'The whole structure was dysfunctional. Point one: it is impossible to be both an MP and chief of staff. Not even a George Osborne at the top of his game or a Peter Mandelson at the top of his game could have done it.' Barclay was not remotely in their class as a political operator. 'Steve very quickly realised he'd made a mistake,' a ministerial aide agreed. 'He had to be enemies to everyone. You have to be a fighter for the PM and no one can like you but he very quickly realised how damaging that was for him because he was still a cabinet minister and an MP.'

Barclay took a shine to Canzini, who became deputy chief of staff in all but name, further alienating Johnson's established allies. 'Canzini's quite charming,' one said, 'and he gives the impression that he knows everybody and everything; he doesn't, he knows the ERG lot and that is it. There was a Radio 4 profile about how close he was to Boris, who had only met him twice.' Canzini's arrival ruffled the feathers of Adams, Ben Gascoigne and Declan Lyons. He also got off on the wrong foot with Harri, but they later bonded.

Harri was considered too garrulous with journalists. 'Guto is legitimately fond of Boris,' a cabinet minister said. 'He's a quick thinker but he's not at all strategic. He's not a Tory. You got the sense that a professional PR man had been brought in. Rather than thinking, "At last, an opportunity to serve a great cause", he thought, "This will be fun!" He was a rhinestone cowboy, not a committed gunslinger.'

Sam Cohen, a former assistant private secretary to the Queen and now Johnson's 'gatekeeper', enjoyed the support of Crosby, the title of 'director of government relations' and glowing write-ups in the papers which focused on her nickname in the royal household, 'Samantha the Panther'. But she lacked relevant experience. 'I think she probably thought she was coming in to be in charge,' a political colleague said. 'But it was quite clear that it was her first time in government and first time in politics.' Another veteran observed, 'I think she was told that she could get rid of us, and then realised that we were going nowhere.'

The Number 10 veterans had an even lower opinion of the other Samantha, Sam Jones, previously adviser to the PM on the NHS and now Number 10's COO, who had been recommended by Rosenfield. Colleagues recall an incident where it was suggested that time was put in the prime minister's diary for him to prep for the Commons Liaison Committee, the panel made up of all the select committee chairs. Jones asked, 'What is the Liaison Committee?'

Others wondered how Crosby, who had no formal post and was still a businessman with commercial clients potentially affected by decisions taken in Number 10, was able to turn up for the key meeting of the day at will. 'He was coming in for meetings he would not have been allowed to attend in David Cameron's day,' one said. The answer, of course, was that that was how Johnson, no stickler for either process or propriety, wanted things.

The prime minister was determined to cling on, but virtually every member of the cabinet, beyond Dorries and Rees-Mogg, was privately clear the police held the key to his future. 'You can't have the prime minister convicted of breaking his own laws,' one said.

Just as Theresa May was liberated from the miseries of Brexit by security issues in the spring of 2018, the first major war in Europe for decades granted Johnson a political fire break. The invasion of Ukraine by Vladimir Putin's Russia on 24 February 2022 was not just an opportunity to cos-play Winston Churchill, though Johnson's instincts were informed by his hero's resolution and rhetoric in 1940. It was also a moment which showed that Britain could play a positive role in continental politics, and remained a cornerstone of European security, even after Brexit. Johnson stepped up and became the leader his admirers had wished him to be all along. It was both his apotheosis and an episode that threw the unfo-cused self-indulgence which characterised much of his time in office into darker and starker relief.

It was 4.10 a.m. on 24 February when Johnson was awakened by his military adviser, Jamie Norman, to be told Russian troops had crossed the border and missiles were raining down on the Ukrainian capital, Kyiv. The news was a shock but not a surprise. British intelligence had been warning for months that Putin, who had assembled 169,000 troops – the biggest build-up of lethal force in Europe since the Second World War – was not bluffing. Unlike Afghanistan, this was a crisis for which Number 10 was prepared.

Shortly after Johnson woke, Volodymyr Zelensky, the president of Ukraine, phoned him to say, 'They're attacking everywhere.' Harri, listening in, recalled, 'Zelensky was breathless, he was anxious, but very calm. It was harrowing. It was haunting. Boris could not have been clearer that we were there to help Ukraine in whichever way we possibly could. I think he was imagining himself in that bunker in his own capital city with foreign troops advancing and his life at risk.' The two leaders already had a close bond, but it quickly grew deeper. In that first call Johnson asked, 'Are you safe? Is there anything we can do?' Zelensky replied, 'I'm okay, I've got good people but you never know when Russian special forces are crawling all over the city. I hope this is not the last time you and I speak.' Then the line went dead.[8]

When ministers met later that morning, it was sobering. 'I will never forget the cabinet meeting,' Nadhim Zahawi recalled. 'We were being told Zelensky, at best he's got two weeks, at worse he's got three days. And Boris said, "We must help, it doesn't matter."'[9]

At 7 a.m. on Friday 25th they spoke again, Zelensky recounting how Russian soldiers had wiped out a group of thirteen Ukrainians occupying the tiny outpost of Snake Island in the Black Sea. Urged to surrender, they replied, 'Go fuck yourselves', before being slaughtered. 'Heroes,' said Johnson when he came off the phone, adding, 'Jesus, that guy is brave.' The prime minister offered to help move Zelensky to safety. 'He doesn't take me up on that offer,' Johnson said later. 'He heroically stayed where he was.'[10] When the Americans made the same offer, Zelensky replied, 'I need ammunition, not a ride!'

Zelensky, once a television comedian famous at home for a comedy sketch in which he played the piano with his penis, had emerged as the defiant voice of his country, a deft communicator using social media to defy Putin's disinformation machine. Harri turned to Johnson and joked, 'Who would have thought that a former chat-show host would turn into a statesman of great principle and stature. It wouldn't happen here!' Johnson, who had made his name with the public as a guest host on the comedy show *Have I Got News for You*, flashed a sharp look. But it was hardly fatuous to suggest that in Zelensky he saw not just a Churchillian figure, but a Johnsonian one. In their second call, the prime minister said, 'We are praying for you.' A close ally noted, 'Boris tends to leave God out of things. He was very moved.'

When the prime minister climbed the stairs from his office to the white room on the first floor of 10 Downing Street at 11 a.m. that Thursday to record an address to the nation, it was as a leader who seemed to have a clear purpose for the first time since the general election. An official photographer was poised to record him glancing at the pictures of previous wartime leaders, David Lloyd George and Winston Churchill, which lined the yellow staircase, but Johnson kept walking. At the top, he paused for thirty seconds. Instead of messing up his hair as he often did before a public appearance, Johnson let an aide 'run a brush through it'. In his televised address, the prime minister announced, 'A vast invasion is underway by land, by sea and by air.' Pure Churchill. Consciously echoing Chamberlain's dismissal of Hitler's invasion of Czechoslovakia, he said, 'This is not, in the infamous phrase, "some faraway country of which we know little" … This hideous and barbaric venture of Vladimir Putin must end in failure.'

By that evening, Russia was spreading propaganda that Zelensky had fled Kyiv. The president and his closest aides took to the streets and filmed a shaky video: 'The PM is here, the party leader is here, the president is here … We are all here, our soldiers are here, our citizens are here. We are all here protecting our independence, our country, and we are going to continue to do so. Glory to Ukraine!' Put on social media at 9.25 p.m., the broadcast transformed Zelensky into a war leader and galvanised international support. It may have been the most important tweet of the twenty-first century to that point.

In a cabinet meeting that evening, and in calls with foreign leaders, Johnson's mantra was, 'Putin must fail.' Realising this sounded like 'Take back control' and 'Get Brexit done', he told cabinet, 'We are quite good at three-word slogans.'

In pursuing a strong pro-Ukraine line, Johnson's reshuffles had helped him. At the Foreign Office he had Liz Truss, rather than the more cautious Raab. On the first day, the foreign secretary summoned the Russian ambassador, Andrey Kelin, for a dressing down. When Kelin claimed Nato was a threat to Russian security, Truss said he was speaking 'total rubbish' and told him to leave: 'You should be ashamed of yourself. Get out now! I've heard enough.'

At the Ministry of Defence, Ben Wallace was also a round peg in a round hole. A former Scots Guardsman, he fought for nine months to send lethal aid to Ukraine, doing battle with cautious securocrats and diplomats with only Johnson at his side. They were egged on by John Bew, Johnson's foreign affairs adviser. In a building of Vote Leave political arsonists and modern-day Regency chancers, Bew, an academic historian and biographer of Castlereagh and Attlee, seemed like a fish on a bicycle. But he was a tough Ulsterman with a righteous realpolitik belief that autocratic adventurers had to be met with strength and resolution, which accorded with the prime minister's world view.

At the heart of Whitehall opposition to lethal aid was a fundamental misreading of Putin. Senior officials like Stephen Lovegrove, the national security adviser, and Simon Gass, the chairman of the Joint Intelligence Committee (JIC), believed that to do so would be 'provocative' and hand the Russian leader an excuse to invade. Wallace's analysis, based on Putin's public statements, was that the Russian leader was determined to invade regardless of Western actions. 'Read Putin's essays,' he told security officials. 'He's going to do this at some stage. We need to help the Ukrainians defend themselves.'

Johnson was in lockstep with Wallace, believing, from bitter experience as foreign secretary, that the only language the Kremlin understood was strength. Perhaps it was also true that Johnson, who had a well-developed sense of his own historical destiny, also understood Putin's need for greatness, his belief in restoring the unity of the ancient Rus uniting Russia and Ukraine. A Number 10 aide said, 'Boris thinks this is about Putin being respected and being the centre of attention.'

Between March and December 2021, Wallace and Johnson were thwarted by officials on the National Security Council, a body the PM found infuriating. 'The Foreign Office and national security people were just throwing up unnecessary bureaucratic hoops to jump through,' said Wallace. Things changed in December when the JIC and the NSC saw satellite imagery of troops massing on the Ukraine border with the support units needed to sustain an invasion. With the exception of Brexit, Johnson had shown little understanding of how to bend the civil service to his will during his time in power. But on Ukraine, with help from Wallace, as a friendly cabinet minister observed, 'He took on the blob and won, it was a shame he could not do it on other matters too.'[11]

Early in 2022 Wallace pushed hard for two thousand 'next generation light anti-tank weapons', known as NLAWs, to Ukraine. British personnel were sent to Ukraine to train their soldiers in how to use the shoulder-launched weapons. The first were delivered to Ukraine on 19 January and by the start of April they had received four thousand. On 1 February, Johnson flew to Kyiv to see Zelensky.

In a call with Putin the following day, Johnson endured long explanations of the Kremlin's historic grievances. But when Putin blamed the West for missteps that alienated Russia after the fall of the Berlin Wall, Johnson hit back, pointing out Russia's history of provocations. 'These were very long and substantive discussions about the history,' said one of those listening in. Johnson told Putin, 'If you do this, it will be an utter catastrophe. It will mean a massive package of Western sanctions. It will mean we continue to intensify our support to Ukraine. And it will mean more Nato, not less Nato, on your borders.' Their jousting took a comically sinister tone. Johnson later revealed, '[Putin] threatened me at one point, and said, "Boris, I don't want to hurt you but, with a missile, it would only take a minute" or something like that. Jolly.'[12]

In the final fortnight, both Wallace and Truss went to Moscow. Both the head of the Russia desk and the head of the security in the Foreign Office told Truss not to travel, but the headstrong foreign secretary refused to listen. On 10 February, she endured four hours with the vulpine Sergei Lavrov, Putin's foreign minister. In their press conference, Truss was publicly humiliated when she mistook two ancient provinces of Russia for parts of Ukraine. But over a lunch of borscht, halibut and apple, Lavrov said, 'You would have made a very good minister in the old USSR because you deliver clear messages over and over again and you're very stubborn.' The foreign secretary was photographed in Red Square in a fake fur hat, a tableau stolen from Margaret Thatcher, who had visited Moscow thirty-five years earlier.

The weekend before the war began, Johnson, Truss and Wallace attended the annual security conference in Munich, where Johnson demanded 'an overwhelming display of solidarity' from the West. He said later, 'The German view was at one stage that if it were going to happen, which would be a disaster, then it would be better for the whole thing to be over quickly, and for Ukraine to fold … I thought that was a disastrous way of looking at it.'[13] In the city where Chamberlain had capitulated to Hitler in 1938, Zelensky won a standing ovation as he asked for greater military support.

There was quiet satisfaction in Downing Street that the conflict reaffirmed Britain's importance to the White House. 'Every Democrat administration comes in saying Germany is the heart of Europe and they want to deepen ties,' a senior Johnson adviser said. 'That lasts until the first security crisis hits.' At the end of a forty-minute call on Valentine's Day, Johnson told Biden the UK would do everything it could to help. The president responded, 'We're not going anywhere without you, pal.'

The UK had greater flexibility to push for a tough line on Moscow now the country was outside the EU. 'We weren't forced to worry about the slowest-moving EU countries,' an official said.

On the final weekend, intelligence chiefs predicted a 'lightning war' to take Kyiv, oust Zelensky and install a puppet government. They predicted, accurately, that Russian armoured forces would be in the capital within three days. What they failed to predict was that the Ukrainians would hold their ground and slowly turn the tide. The G7 leaders held a conference call just hours after the invasion. Johnson was first to push for Russia to be kicked out of the SWIFT international payments system, which processes cross-border financial transactions. Germany, which had to pay for Russian gas using the system, was initially opposed, along with Italy, which was lobbying for exclusions from sanctions for luxury goods so that brands such as Gucci and Prada could continue selling to Russia's super-rich. Belgium demanded the same exemptions for diamonds.

Before the G7 meeting, Johnson spoke to Olaf Scholz, the new German chancellor, and 'pushed very hard to get him to put SWIFT on the table', a Number 10 official said. Scholz was dismissive: 'Boris, we don't need any last-minute changes.' Johnson also pressed for Germany to ditch the Nord Stream 2 gas pipeline from Russia, urging 'We've got to get Nord Stream out of the bloodstream.' On the G7 call, Johnson said, 'We should all ban Aeroflot.' One of those watching said, 'There were literally no takers.' Mario Draghi, the Italian prime minister, complained that he was under attack from the UK media. Johnson replied, 'Join the club.'

Privately, Johnson described Emmanuel Macron's visits to see Putin as 'nauseating'. After the French president criticised Britain's response to the Ukraine refugee crisis, Johnson let rip in a morning meeting in Downing Street: 'He's a cunt, he's a weirdo, he's Putin's lickspittle. We need to go studs up. We need an orgy of frog bashing. I'm going to have to punch his lights out.'[14]

Britain's closest partners were members of the JEF – the joint expeditionary force – Denmark, Estonia, Finland, Iceland, Latvia, Lithuania, the Netherlands, Norway and Sweden. Each country would send what they could. Iceland had few military resources but, Johnson noted, 'They can send renewable energy and supermodels.'

The first UK sanctions, announced on Thursday, involved asset freezes against eight oligarchs, five major Russian companies, a ban on Aeroflot and limits on high-tech exports to Russia. More than a hundred individuals would later be sanctioned.

On Saturday 26th, the PM had a third call with Zelensky, congratulating him on 'an incredible act of heroism'. He said, 'The whole world is praying for you and applauding you. You are becoming a global hero.' Zelensky asked for weapons and for a SWIFT ban. 'You know your Shakespeare, Boris,' he said. 'To SWIFT or not to SWIFT, that is the question.' Later that night Britain, the US and the EU announced that they had agreed to expel Russian banks from SWIFT.

Ukrainian forces repelled Russia's initial offensive against Kyiv, in no small part thanks to the Northern Irish-built NLAWs, which were credited with knocking out many of the 164 Russian tanks destroyed, damaged or captured in the initial assault. While British commanders call the NLAWs 'en-laws', the Ukrainians pronounced the word 'en-love'. In mid-March the Ukrainian leader serenaded Johnson with the song 'When You're Young and N-Love' and then a bastardised Beatles rendition of 'All You Need Is N-Love'. In the final week of March, Zelensky told Johnson, in one of their daily phone conversations, that Ukrainian soldiers shouted 'God Save the Queen' when they fired the weapon.

The bonds between the Johnson government and Zelensky deepened on 8 March, when the Ukrainian president addressed the House of Commons by video link. Predictably he channelled Churchill: 'Just in the same way you didn't want to lose your country when Nazis started to fight your country, you had to fight ... We'll fight in the forests, on the shores, in the streets.' The two men spoke every day, sharing 'a deep bond' and a 'dark, gallows humour'.[15]

A month later, on 9 April, Johnson defied the advice of the security services to visit Kyiv, not long after Russian troops had pulled back. He had tried to go in the first days of the conflict but Simon Case implored him not to, warning that there was a non-zero chance he would be killed. When it was finally agreed that he could go, Case made the prime minister sign a statement saying he was going of his own free will and was willing to take the risks. Johnson signed with alacrity, perhaps thinking of the many times Churchill had driven Alanbrooke and others mad by visiting the front. The trip was so secret the prime minister and his security detail were armed only with a burner phone for emergencies as they flew to Poland and took a train into Ukraine. In the greatest walkabout of his career, Johnson was hugged and cheered like a hero by the people of Kyiv. With election night, it was probably the high point of Johnson's time as prime minister.

Within a few days of the invasion, Scholz had announced the mothballing of the Nord Stream 2 pipeline from Russia to Germany and a historic military pivot away from the self-flagellation and Second World War guilt, which had constituted Berlin's foreign policy for eight decades. Scholz, a figure of overweening caution and zero charisma, announced a *Zeitenwende* – historic turning point – agreeing to send weapons into a war zone for the first time in decades. The German chancellor also declared that Germany would ramp up defence spending to meet the Nato goal of 2 per cent of GDP.

For two months Johnson, a leader who often did not know what he wanted to do with his power, pursued a focused and successful mission to galvanise world opinion to back Ukraine and impose the toughest sanctions on Russia. A man quickly bored and distracted applied himself to a problem with an energy and gusto of which few leaders were capable. Johnson cajoled Scholz, stiffened Biden's resolve and helped bind the countries of Eastern Europe and the Baltics into the Western alliance. If Johnson had not achieved everything of which he believed 'Global Britain' was capable, he had, briefly, shown that the UK post Brexit did not have to stumble as the country had done after the Second World War, when, in the words of former US secretary of state Dean Acheson, 'Britain lost an empire and failed to find a role.'

The war transformed Johnson's reputation. By early March his personal ratings had risen by 11 points. On 17 March, Roger Gale, the first MP to say publicly that he had submitted a letter of no confidence, announced, 'Is now the time to change our leader? No, it isn't.' Douglas Ross, the Scottish Tory leader, said he was withdrawing his letter. At least six other MPs did the same. Cummings and his co-conspirators were momentarily concerned his slow-moving coup had stalled. 'Ukraine was such a big deal that he actually could still have saved himself if he'd had a total reboot,' a Vote Leave source said. But for Johnson, Ukraine was not the pivot point he hoped.

While Johnson played statesman, the police inquiry continued unabated. On 29 March Scotland Yard revealed it was sending out the first twenty £50 fines for government officials who attended lockdown parties, a batch that covered those who had attended James Slack's leaving do the night before Prince Philip's funeral. One of those caught was Helen MacNamara, who apologised for bringing a karaoke machine for the leaving do in June 2020 of Hannah Young, a private secretary. As MPs left for their Easter break, two days later, a minister remarked, 'It feels like the calm before the storm, Boris's Phoney War.'

The Blitzkrieg arrived on 12 April, when Johnson received an email in his personal inbox informing him that he had received a fixed penalty notice and a fine for attending his own birthday party. Carrie Johnson got a similar message. To the consternation of his aides, Rishi Sunak was also fined. The two senior figures in government and the prime minister's wife had all been found to have broken the government's own lockdown laws. The decision pitched Downing Street into turmoil and began a spiral of events which would lead to Johnson's downfall. Events that day also highlighted the now bitter divisions and lack of trust between Johnson and his chancellor, which had been in freefall for eighteen months.

OUT OF STEP

Boris and Rishi

October 2020 to May 2022

For seven hours after he was hit with a fixed penalty notice Rishi Sunak agonised over whether to resign from the cabinet. The chancellor believed that both he and the prime minister should resign, but he also recognised that the chances of the prime minister doing so were zero.

Boris Johnson was at Chequers when he received notification of the fine via email. Sam Cohen alerted the rest of the inner circle on WhatsApp. Nigel Adams went into Number 10 and found no one there. He called Ben Gascoigne and said, 'Get your arse in here.' Ross Kempsell arrived. Guto Harri was on an Egyptian felucca sailing on the Nile when he heard. He rang Johnson and they agreed he would do a brief clip for the broadcasters. When Adams spoke to the PM, Johnson said, 'There are helicopters circling above Chequers. I'll come in.' Adams thought this a disastrous idea: 'We don't want an O.J. [Simpson] situation of driving down the M4 with helicopters following. We'll come to you.' They grabbed Rosie Bate-Williams from the press office to handle the broadcast clip. Then they alerted Steve Barclay, the chief of staff, and Chris Heaton-Harris, the new chief whip, who both made their way independently to Chequers.

There was consternation and anger among the prime minister's team that he had been fined. Senior officials in Downing Street had confidently told journalists for weeks they did not think he would be, that the Metropolitan Police would be reluctant to involve themselves so directly in politics, that Johnson's legal defence was watertight. In truth, the police had told them nothing. The PM argued on his form that he had attended each event for a short period, before they became proper parties, in a work capacity, thanking staff for their hard work. His closest advisers assumed the most problematic one was the 'bring your own booze' party in the garden, but Johnson insisted he had not seen Martin Reynolds' provocative email. There was disbelief that the prime minister had, instead, been fined for the birthday party, which only intensified when it became clear that Johnson, Carrie and Sunak had all been issued with a penalty while Simon Case, who was pictured opposite Johnson laughing when he raised a beer, was not.

Johnson was to claim that Sue Gray agreed. The prime minister said to aides she had told him the birthday party did not 'reach the threshold of criminality' and that she had advised the police not even to bother looking into it further. He said, 'She told me twice there was nothing.' Both a senior mandarin and a cabinet minister confirmed that this was something Johnson had said. The senior civil servant said, 'The person who was most surprised by Boris Johnson being fined for that event was Sue Gray.' When it was announced later that Gray was going to work for the Labour Party, Johnson claimed, 'She trapped me.' Gray, however, was absolutely categorical that she 'never, ever' said any such thing and, more importantly, did not believe Johnson was in the clear. 'The only gathering that Sue thought probably did not breach the rules was the work meeting which took place in the garden', where Johnson and Cummings were pictured with glasses of wine on the terrace next to the Cabinet Room. 'This is absolute rubbish. She had no idea what the police were going to think.'

Sunak was disbelieving that he had been fined for entering the Cabinet Room to attend a Covid meeting and then encountered the birthday gathering. 'The only three people fined were Boris, Carrie and Rishi,' a senior official recalled. 'None of the officials who turned up for the meeting were.' Scotland Yard never provided an explanation of its reasoning. In Downing Street, they concluded that the Met had taken a simplistic and literal approach. 'The police looked at the word "party" in "birthday party". There were all these leaving drinks for people. But they don't say "party". On the face of it, it's completely bonkers.'

Sunak was both teetotal and punctilious; he deeply resented that he had been sucked into what he saw as the prime minister's vortex of misrule. A Sunak ally told *The Times* that day, 'He feels very badly let down.' Even Johnson thought it absurd. 'What had he done? I thought it was absolutely ridiculous,' Johnson told a friend even after he had fallen out with Sunak.

When Sunak called close aides at 10 a.m. to reveal the news, they were 'incredulous'. One said, 'Not a part of us remotely thought he would get a fine. There was no gaming out of that.' 'I almost cried,' said another. 'I couldn't believe it.' When his special advisers gathered, it was clear the chancellor was teetering. 'He fundamentally doesn't believe it right that someone in a position such as his, who has just been fined by the police for breaking the law, can stay in their job,' one said. 'What is he going to say in his next interview? What is he going to say to all the backbench MPs who think he is moral and upstanding?'

While Sunak pondered the morality of the situation, Dougie Smith considered the politics and urged the chancellor to resign. 'You should quit now, get clear of this shitshow,' Smith advised. 'Boris is going down. Take responsibility.' Smith was not the only veteran in Sunak's ear, however. '[William] Hague told him not to go,' an adviser revealed.

Now installed at Chequers, Heaton-Harris spoke to Sunak. 'Rishi told Chris he was absolutely devastated and he was going to resign,' a member of Johnson's team recalled. 'He had his letter ready. We were thinking we were going to have to make Steve Barclay chancellor.' Johnson took to the book-lined study which overlooks the front lawn at Chequers – biographies of Labour prime ministers (fittingly) to the left of the fireplace, those of Conservative premiers to the right. He called Liam Booth-Smith to tell him Sunak could not resign. Booth-Smith tried to give Johnson 'some comfort', but the situation was still in flux.

At tea time Sunak was still dithering. *The Times* and other papers were planning to splash on the chancellor on the verge of resignation. 'If you're not going to resign, we need to tell them that,' an aide said. Sunak said he would like to 'sleep on it', a breathtakingly naive comment in an age of twenty-four-hour news, and a clue that his methodical approach would be found wanting in pressurised situations. If the papers got it wrong, it would not just be them who looked stupid, but Sunak himself.

Late afternoon the prime minister called his chancellor. Heaton-Harris sat in on the conversation, a witness to corroborate Johnson's account if it went wrong and things descended into a briefing war. 'Boris talked him down,' another said.

In the end, Sunak decided that to quit would make it look like he had deliberately set himself against Johnson, putting 'the PM in an impossible position,' an aide said. 'It would have looked like a move against the PM.

He felt that in all scenarios the party would hate him for causing chaos.' Sunak was not ready to sign Johnson's political death warrant. Part of him, too, recognised that he was not yet ready to inherit the crown either.

Harri tried to keep Sunak's team on the same side and liaised with Nerissa Chesterfield to agree the statements the two men would issue. 'I have to say in all frankness, at the time, it did not occur to me that this might have been a breach of the rules,' the prime minister said to the pool camera crew, before making clear that he was not going to resign. 'I feel an even greater sense of obligation to deliver on the priorities of the British people.' Carrie Johnson issued a statement offering her 'unreserved' apologies. Privately, she believed the fine absurd. 'She thought it was a conspiracy against her and Boris by Cressida Dick,' a friend said. 'She was livid.'

Sunak, often seen as the one lacking political antennae, did rather more to show he understood the boiling public anger. 'I understand that for figures in public office the rules must be applied stringently in order to maintain public confidence,' he said. 'I respect the decision that has been made and I have paid the fine. I know people sacrificed a great deal during Covid, and they will find this situation upsetting.'

The following week, Johnson faced another grilling in the Commons from Keir Starmer. When he repeated the claim that it 'did not occur to me then, or subsequently' that he was breaking the rules, the Labour leader accused him of dishonesty. Speaker Lindsay Hoyle forced Starmer to withdraw the comment. But the mood on the Tory benches was turning again. Mark Harper, a former chief whip and lockdown rebel leader, called on Johnson to resign. The prime minister had a torrid time when he addressed the 1922 Committee.

The oddity of the birthday event, Sunak's decision not to resign and Johnson's determination to plough on as if a sitting prime minister had not just been fined for breaking laws he had imposed on the rest of the country, meant no ministers were yet ready to speak out. Cabinet ministers who had confidently declared that if Johnson got a fixed penalty notice he would have to go, now rowed back and said everyone had better wait until the end of the police inquiry or Gray's full report before passing judgement. The caravan moved on, but it did so with a faultline between Johnson and Sunak which was never healed. Indeed, it was one which had been yawning open, at that stage, for eighteen months.

* * *

The first tensions between prime minister and chancellor had become evident to their aides in the autumn of 2020, when the attention of cabinet briefly turned from Covid-19 to the government's spending review. The vast sums being spent on furlough and other support schemes led Sunak to replace his intended three-year settlement with a one-year envelope. He did not consult cabinet. 'He's already acting as if he's prime minister,' a cabinet colleague complained. With the passage of the pandemic uncertain, Sunak argued, any plans might have been rendered meaningless in months.

With money tight, a battle royal began for what little there was. Dominic Cummings wanted more for defence and the intelligence services, with Ben Wallace's energetic support. Johnson, who had pledged in the manifesto that defence spending would rise by 0.5 per cent above inflation each year, demanded special treatment and a three-year settlement. The prime minister, with the COP26 climate conference coming at the end of 2021, also wanted more for renewable energy. Finally, Johnson dreamed of building a bridge to Northern Ireland, a pipe dream inside a white elephant thrown into a bottomless money pit, as far as virtually everyone else in government was concerned. 'Rishi's position on everything,' an aide explained, 'was "what do you need to prioritise?" He was not afraid of making difficult choices, whereas Boris just wanted to do everything that sounded good and positive and generous.' Sunak disagreed with prioritising defence or renewables. The Treasury regarded the MoD as a sink hole of financial mismanagement, where billions were wasted annually on ill-thought-out procurement projects which invariably ran over time and over budget, but Johnson and Wallace eventually won an extra £16.5 billion between 2020/21 and 2024/25, a sum described as 'the largest sustained increase in the core defence budget for thirty years'. Away from who was winning and losing the arguments, senior aides detected a move from ministers and others with an agenda towards Sunak. 'People were beginning to bet their house on Rishi,' a senior Number 10 adviser recalled.

Initially, both men respected the other for the traits they did not possess themselves. A Johnson aide said, 'Having seen them up close, the truth of their relationship is that Sunak knows he is politically inexperienced, and he knows that Boris has a much more confident grip of the Westminster ins and outs. Boris can smell all of that. Part of Sunak knows that he needs someone to help him with that, almost like a tutor

… Boris knows that he needs a highly numerate, technical, liberal, credible figure to square off the Davos class he doesn't appeal to.' Cabinet colleagues agreed the government needed both Johnson's wild political boosterism and Sunak's careful, diligent management. With Gove they were probably the cleverest three ministers in the cabinet. Colleagues hoped Sunak's parsimonious approach would satisfy the markets and southern voters who wanted fiscal discipline, while Johnson enthused voters who wanted high spending on public services. A Downing Street aide agreed: 'My view was that Boris and Rishi would be electoral dynamite in 2024. The important thing was to keep them together.' Another Johnson aide said, 'They really are cup and saucer. They have complementary skills.'

However, their success was partly a function of the fact that neither man enjoyed confrontation. Under the surface there was turbulence but, for a while, tensions between 10 and 11 Downing Street were ironed out by Declan Lyons and Liam Booth-Smith, who regularly smoked together round the back of Number 10. A fellow cabinet minister said, 'Rishi's starting point was wanting to believe in Boris, being rather in awe of some of Boris' talents and then progressive disaffection.'

Things began to go wrong in the first six months of 2021 as a chasm opened between Sunak and Johnson over how to handle the country's emergence from a year of lockdowns. In his budget in the first week of March, Sunak attempted to rein in the vast spending of 2020 and set out his own road map to plug the emerging black hole in the nation's finances. Corporation tax would increase gradually from 19p in the pound to 25p. Income tax thresholds were frozen, a breach of the spirit but not the letter of the manifesto pledge not to raise the headline rates of income tax, VAT and National Insurance. Sunak was concerned that the fast rollout of the vaccination programme meant pent-up spending would be released into the economy, driving up inflation. Every percentage point rise in interest rates added £25 billion to the annual cost of government borrowing. Treasury spin doctors made a virtue of Sunak 'being honest with the British people' about the sacrifices that would be necessary. The problem was that Johnson did not share this approach and nor did a large number of Tory MPs, who were horrified by the planned rise in business taxes. Number 10 stopped the Treasury going further. A cabinet source said, 'Rishi wanted corporation tax up from 19 to 25 per cent in one go. The PM and his team blocked that.'

The differences were systemic and personal. Prime ministers always want to spend money, chancellors want to rein them in. The fundamental problem was that Johnson and Sunak did not agree on how to go about running a government. In June 2021, tensions surfaced in the *Sunday Times*, which revealed that two of Johnson's recent announcements – plans for a twenty-first-century version of the postwar Marshall Plan to fund green growth in the developing world and a pledge to build a new national flagship to replace the Royal Yacht Britannia – emerged out of the blue with no sign-off from the Treasury. To Johnson the new 'national flagship', an obsession of his old paper the *Telegraph*, was evidence that post-Brexit Britain was playing a global leadership role again. A picture was painted of a floating symbol of Britain's soft power, drumming up trade. To Sunak it was a ludicrous white elephant. He refused to find the £200 million cost, telling the MoD that they could pay for it. Wallace was equally dismissive. 'No one in the Treasury had a clue about the new Marshall Plan until it appeared in the media,' said a senior Whitehall official. One of Sunak's aides complained, 'It got to a point where policy was getting cooked up because Boris wanted to do a speech.' One of Johnson's senior aides did admit, 'We keep announcing things without telling them.'

The Treasury was also under pressure to find more for Covid education catch-up and to pay for the huge backlog of NHS operations, cancer treatments and court cases delayed by the pandemic. Johnson's schools recovery tsar, Sir Kevan Collins, said £15 billion was needed, but Sunak found only £1.5 billion, and Collins resigned.

There were also divisions over pensions. Sunak wanted the elderly to share in the sacrifices their children and grandchildren made during the pandemic, but he was overruled by Johnson when he tried to scrap the pensions triple lock, which dictated the state pension would rise in line with inflation, wages or 2.5 per cent, whichever was the highest.

In an interview with Andrew Neil on the new GB News television channel, Sunak argued he was protecting taxpayers. 'It's not my money, it's other people's money, and I take my responsibility to that very seriously,' he said. Johnson's allies saw the decision to speak to Neil, who the PM had dodged in the election campaign, as a coded act of disloyalty. Johnson favoured untrammelled spending on 'levelling up' in the red wall seats in the north of England, funded by borrowing, since he backed neither tax rises nor spending cuts. Sunak feared this would fuel inflation, a seemingly distant threat, since it had only just risen above 2 per cent, but he told Neil, 'That's one of the many risks that it's my job to worry about.' Allies of Johnson began to pop up in the papers saying Sunak was 'not a team player'.

These philosophical differences were embodied in and exacerbated by the personal characteristics of the two men. Johnson was a figure given to grand pronouncements and a seat of the pants politics, driven by instinct and a near-feral understanding of the desires of his target voters. Sunak was a details man, happier buried in the appendix of a document than crafting its foreword, driven by a desire to solve problems that was forged in a pre-political career with Goldman Sachs and two hedge fund firms. 'He was a trader before politics,' a Tory who ran a business group said. 'He is happiest analysing trends and details in the numbers.'

Johnson, a creature of the heart, while not tall was a grand figure in every sense, his stomach often well upholstered, his hair skew-whiff, his clothes sometimes ill-fitting. Sunak, a creature of the head, looked like he had parted his hair with a scalpel and wore expensive suits which hugged his tiny physique like a glove (his bizarrely short trouser legs contributed to the image of an immaculately dressed schoolboy). Johnson was a captive of his urges, frequently placed on a vegan diet or a course of yoga by Carrie but given to lapses in which he devoured slabs of cheese, washed down with good Italian red. Politically he was happiest gorging on a vast infrastructure project. Sunak was punctilious, happily married, apparently loyal to his wife, fasted twice a week and did not drink alcohol. His most exotic indulgence was a penchant for cinnamon buns and Mexican Coke, even sweeter than Coca-Cola, a taste acquired in California. 'The guy doesn't really eat much,' said a friend. 'He'll have some chicken broth in the evening. He'll sustain himself throughout the day with a Granny Smith apple and some cashew nuts.' This parsimonious regime was nothing to do with Sunak's Hinduism; rather, it flowed from the chancellor's belief that flushing things out of the system was good for his health.

The personality and policy clashes soon morphed into a rivalry rather than a partnership. When a Number 10 aide once said to Johnson that it was good he had talented 'young lions' in his cabinet, Johnson's eyes narrowed and he said, 'I prefer tired old lions.' Perhaps, too, Johnson, who had signed away most of his money to his ex-wife, looked at the independently wealthy Sunak, with his near-billionaire spouse, with a green-tinged eye. Sunak, in turn, became weary of Johnson's tendency to delay decisions, his refusal to make hard choices and his contentment residing at the epicentre of a whirlwind of chaos.

At the G7 summit that June Sunak had led the way in securing an international agreement for multinational tech giants such as Amazon to pay tax in the countries where they did their business rather than where they banked their profits. The chancellor had single-handedly persuaded the Americans to get on board, without which any deal would have been meaningless, a result he achieved through polite but persistent diplomacy and attention to detail. It convinced him that he could do a bigger job.

The tensions came to a head in July 2021 when Johnson decided to use the political capital he had earned from the vaccine rollout to tackle an issue he had pledged to solve in his speech in Downing Street after the election – the funding of social care. He saw an issue where he might boost his political legacy. Those hit by dementia or infirmity ended up selling their homes to pay for care and the manifesto had vowed to end that injustice. It also appealed to Johnson that Theresa May had failed utterly to deal with the issue after her solution nearly cost the Tories the 2017 election.[1]

At the same time, Johnson had encouraged other ministers to come forward with ambitious plans, which then materialised with no input from the Treasury. 'The PM knew what he was doing,' a Sunak ally recalled. 'He'd be creating enemies for the chancellor. Boris would say he wants their thing, but Rishi doesn't. It became a good way of managing his cabinet.' This created the vibe between the prime minister and his chancellor of a naughty schoolboy being told off by the prefect. On social care, however, Sunak had less wriggle room since it was a manifesto commitment. 'Rishi was deferential,' the ally said. 'He would always take the view that this guy won us an election. It wasn't a question of whether we do it, it's how we do it. We were haggling over price.'

From the beginning, Johnson was 'pretty set' on a plan devised by the economist Sir Andrew Dilnot to cap care costs at £50,000 a person, so families did not have to sell their home to pay for care. Sunak and Booth-Smith pointed out that would disproportionately benefit voters in the south, where property is worth more, and that the final bill would run to billions. 'Boris didn't get it at all,' another Treasury aide said. 'He just wanted to stop talking about Covid.' Booth-Smith had polling which showed that the public did not view social care as a pressing issue. Johnson got increasingly annoyed by 'Liam and his numbers'.

At a meeting in mid-April 2021, billed as the big decision-making moment, Number 10 tried to bounce the chancellor. Unfortunately for Johnson, Sunak and Booth-Smith were forewarned and armed, having seen a note that the policy unit had prepared for the prime minister with annotations attached, after it was mistakenly sent to the Treasury two days before. It was immediately apparent that they had 'gerrymandered' the Treasury research. A nineteen-page document had been reduced to just two pages. When Rosenfield and Mirza made the case, Sunak hit back: 'We have got your note and your annotations so we know that you've made stuff up and you're hiding seventeen pages of it from the prime minister. Those pages say you categorically should not do this, politically.' The meeting broke up after less than ten minutes.

Johnson's team did not give up. Rosenfield told Booth-Smith, 'We need to do something. I need to get Boris to start winning. I need a win.'

After a strong performance in the local elections and the Hartlepool by-election that May, Johnson was 'in full on Fuhrer mode' and insisted he wanted to move on social care before the summer recess. Sunak did not believe it should be a priority, but his attitude was: 'If that's what you want to do, that's fine, but where is the money coming from? You can't leave a £12 to £15 billion commitment unfunded.'

As Johnson approached the second anniversary of his arrival in Number 10, the prime minister and Sajid Javid, the health secretary, were both enthusiastic about creating a separate health tax to pay for the plans. At the same time there were also predictions that NHS waiting lists would rise from five million to thirteen million. Reforming the care sector was seen as a way of helping to get 'bed blockers' out of hospital and into the community. Sunak suggested health and social care should be dealt with together, so the lion's share of the money could initially pay for the backlog of operations caused by Covid and then cover the costs of the care package as they increased in later years. He advocated a rise in National Insurance to pay for the plan, which polling showed worked because it was a tax associated with the health service.

In June, Booth-Smith wrote a memo for Sunak, warning his boss that even this plan would be a total disaster and that Johnson would end up blaming the chancellor. 'The idea that he will own this is for the birds,' he said. 'They will eventually turn on it and turn on you.' A few days before the formal announcement, he tried again, sitting Sunak down: 'This is going to be a car crash. The NHS can't deliver it. DHSC [the health department] won't own it. Every political instinct I have tells me this won't work.' Instead, he suggested 'moving the numbers around' to find a short-term fix for the NHS.

That Friday, Sunak's inner circle – Booth-Smith, Chesterfield, Rupert Yorke and Cass Horowitz – had dinner in the chancellor's Downing Street flat, with him and his wife, Akshata Murty. 'We all said he should resign,' one of those present recalled. 'We could see that inflation and interest rates were going to rise. We knew the cost of living was going to become an issue. We said, "You can't add a tax on top of that. You will get killed for that. It will become your tax."' Murty agreed: 'If you don't think it's the right thing to do, you can't support it.' Booth-Smith was already thinking ahead to how Sunak would present himself as and when he ran for leader. He argued, 'This is a moment of definition. It will show people that cutting taxes and keeping them low isn't a wave-of-a-wand thing, it is something that requires effort and discipline and sacrifice. It's bad politics in support of a bad policy.' They discussed the pros and cons for several hours. By the time the aides left, Sunak had still not made up his mind. He talked to his wife. On Saturday morning he told them he was staying: 'For better or worse I'm a loyal person. I don't think anyone will thank me for leaving now. I can't jump ship because I don't like one policy thing the PM is doing. I work to him.'

The day before the planned announcement, Sunak called Johnson and tried one last time, 'We should pull it and just announce NHS money.' An ally observed, 'Rishi gets loads of shit for being disloyal but he told Boris, "You've done the sensible thing by accepting expensive stuff has to be paid for, and I will support you. I will back you in cabinet and I'll do all the media rounds you need. My view is that this is a bad idea and we shouldn't do it. But, I'm 100 per cent with you if you want to do it."'

The prime minister, frustrated by this last-minute sabotage, considered his options and phoned the chancellor back: 'We're doing it. I need you to back me.' Sunak agreed. Then Sajid Javid caught Covid and the event to launch the policy had to be abandoned and with it, the reshuffle Johnson had planned for the same week. In it, Liz Truss had been due to become education secretary. 'If that had happened, she would probably never have been prime minister,' a political aide reasoned later.

* * *

As one Johnson–Sunak flashpoint died away, another blew up over the economic recovery from Covid. By late July 2021, the chancellor was infuriated at the sclerotic pace at which the government was easing travel restrictions, leaving families' summer holidays hanging in the balance. Sunak thought Britain was saddled with more draconian rules on testing and isolation than many EU countries when the UK could have obtained a competitive advantage as a result of the faster vaccine rollout at home. In a provocative move, just days before the cabinet was due to decide the rules for August, he wrote a formal letter to Johnson warning that Britain's border rules were damaging the economy and tourism and hospitality in particular. In the letter, Sunak said that UK border policy was 'out of step with our international competitors'.

The letter leaked to the *Sunday Times*, which duly splashed on the new division between Number 10 and Number 11. The leaker claimed, 'Rishi has called time on the travel restrictions.' The problem was that the first Johnson knew of the letter was when details of it appeared in the paper. Officials had failed to flag it for his attention, or to put it in his ministerial red box – evidence of further Downing Street dysfunction. The PM was doubly furious because he and Sunak were both keen to lift the restrictions. By writing to him, the chancellor had made it look as if he alone was heroically fighting for freedom.

At the morning meeting in Number 10 the following day, the prime minister erupted with rage, those present describing him variously as 'apoplectic', 'raging' and 'fucking tonto'. In a fit of frustrated impotence, Johnson suggested, in front of a dozen or more witnesses, that he might sack Sunak. 'Where's Rishi? I need to speak to Rishi,' Johnson demanded when the chancellor failed to appear, before launching into a soliloquy on the stupidity of his chancellor's actions. 'It was a failure of political judgement, it was bound to be leaked.'[2]

The prime minister suggested he might demote Sunak to the least appetising post in cabinet. 'I've been thinking about it. Maybe it's time we looked at Rishi as the next secretary of state for health. He could potentially do a very good job there.' Johnson was known for making off-the-cuff comments 'half in jest' with just enough devilment that his spin doctors could say he was joking. But several of those present were struck by his vehemence and his reckless openness at a time when growing scrutiny was falling on tensions with the Treasury. The rant duly leaked to the *Sunday Times,* which ran a front-page story on the divisions for the second weekend in a row.

It was understandable that Johnson was looking over his shoulder at Sunak. That week the monthly survey of grassroots opinion on ConservativeHome showed his popularity had plummeted by 36 points to a net positive rating of just 3 per cent. Sunak, by contrast, was still riding high on plus 74, just behind Liz Truss. Asked who should be the next leader, 31 per cent answered Sunak, with Truss (12 per cent) and Penny Mordaunt (11 per cent) the only others in double figures.

Johnson and Sunak finally thrashed out a compromise on social care on 2 September over an Indian takeaway in the prime minister's Downing Street flat. They decided to slap a 'social care levy' on top of National Insurance, settling on 1.25 per cent, which raised £12 billion. Johnson announced the plan to the Commons on Tuesday 7th.

Neither Johnson nor Sunak ended up happy. The prime minister was content to borrow to fund the care package and resented that the chancellor had made him put up taxes again. Sunak was infuriated that, so soon after the budget, Johnson had returned with a begging bowl. Both blamed the other for the tax rise.

When Sunak joined Johnson on the Commons terrace to address the 1922 Committee of Tory backbenchers, he was dutiful, stressing the importance of 'support and loyalty' to the prime minister, 'the leader of our party and the country'. From the cabinet there was barely a peep of dissent. Just three ministers spoke out against the plan: Jacob Rees-Mogg, David Frost and Liz Truss, who suggested the government should borrow rather than put up taxes. She was shot down by Sunak: 'I am genuinely shocked if anyone thinks the answer to the question is more borrowing.' A foretaste of debates to come. After cabinet, Simon Case, the cabinet secretary, told Liam Booth-Smith that watching Sunak fight for a policy he did not believe in 'was the most immense show of loyalty from a chancellor to a prime minister I have ever seen'.

For Sunak's team, things were never the same again between Johnson and his chancellor. 'They rubbed along as the yin and the yang of the government well enough until then,' one of the chancellor's closest aides said. 'But social care changed things.'

Relations did not improve when Johnson reshuffled his cabinet on 15 September, moving Dominic Raab to the Ministry of Justice (with the consolation prize of the title of deputy prime minister) and made Truss foreign secretary. Johnson was deliberately building up Truss, who openly craved the chance to be Britain's first female chancellor, as a rival to Sunak – and Sunak knew it. 'He was rattled,' a special adviser said. Johnson did not rate Truss as highly as Sunak but he liked her boosterish positivity, a contrast to the chancellor's Cassandra-like warnings about the economy. 'Rishi has become Dr No,' a former minister observed, 'while Liz is Mrs Yes, Yes, Yes!' To twist the knife, mischievous Johnson allies suggested he had appointed the six-foot five-inch tall Simon Clarke as chief secretary to the Treasury because it amused the prime minister to surround his five-foot six-inch chancellor with ministers who towered over him in public.

In their discussions around the care package, Sunak extracted an agreement from Johnson that they would cut income tax before the general election, as long as there was spending restraint in the short term to build up a war chest for 2024. However, it was not long before Johnson demanded more money from the Treasury. With the COP26 summit just a month away, the prime minister needed to ensure that Britain was a leader in tackling climate change before hosting world leaders and urging them to do more. Ahead of the summit, the government published a hydrogen strategy, designed to shift consumption away from fossil fuels; a boiler strategy, to get households to swap their gas boiler for a heat pump; and a major net-zero strategy. Sunak, who had already committed £12 billion in his budget for green infrastructure and new technologies, made clear the money had to be found from existing budgets. To Sunak, the endless demands for more money were those of a child in a sweet shop. To Johnson, the parsimony of Sunak and the Treasury was the behaviour of a 'dog in the manger chancellor', a phrase he began to use with close allies.

Once COP26 was out of the way, in November, attention turned to the levelling up white paper, where Michael Gove was trying to put policy flesh on the bones of Johnson's flagship idea for wooing the red wallers. Sunak refused to let Gove have a penny more than the £4.9 billion he had already assigned to the issue. Without new investment Johnson's central slogan remained a frustratingly elusive concept. A senior cabinet minister said, 'Rishi thought we were raising expectations too high, that levelling up was important, but the scale of spending in Boris's mind to make a reality of it was not available.'

Johnson's habit of breaking his word and changing his mind drove the ordered Sunak mad. 'In Rishi's mind,' a cabinet colleague explained, 'they'd have these conversations, and he would say to Boris, "Okay your top priority is social care?" "Yeah, absolutely my top priority." "Absolutely sure? You realise it will cost all this money?" "Uh, yeah, yeah." "Okay. You are the prime minister. This is your priority. I will deliver it." Then two days later Boris would be saying, "The Gover needs all this cash for levelling up." That happened in Rishi's telling over and over and over again.' A Sunak aide said, 'There's only so many times you can make an agreement with someone, and they can break it and lie to your face and you can trust them. It kept happening. Boris didn't want to be confronted a lot of the time with reality.'

Sunak was not alone in bemoaning Johnson's approach to decision-making. 'You would listen to what Boris wanted,' the cabinet minister said, 'but you wouldn't commission the furniture and order the wallpaper until you were absolutely sure.' One of Johnson's closest aides also tried to help, telling Liam Booth-Smith, 'You can never believe his first answer. You have to leave him and go back a couple of hours later when he's on his own and ask him again. Invariably you'll get, if not the opposite, a modified version of what was said previously. That is the answer you need to use.' But even then, Johnson kept coming back for more money. 'One thing was done, and then in two months he'd come back and say, "I need £15 billion for some fucking space rocket or something",' a Treasury source complained.

Things came to a head in a meeting ahead of the spending review, between Johnson and Sunak, at which their respective chiefs of staff Dan Rosenfield and Liam Booth-Smith were present, along with policy chief Munira Mirza. This was supposed to be a 'rubber-stamping' exercise of what had been agreed. However, after a 'perfunctory two minutes of faffing', Johnson pulled out a sheet which had been prepared for him and read out a list of additional spending commitments he needed 'to make this thing work'. There were around a dozen items totalling around £25 billion. Sunak, reeling in his seat, said, 'Everyone get out.'

Outside the room, Rosenfield delivered his 'matey, matey' routine to a furious Booth-Smith, who declared, 'You have completely overplayed your hand. That was not smart.'

Inside the room, the irresistible force of the prime minister clattered hard into the immovable object of his chancellor. After forty-five minutes the aides were called back in. 'The chancellor and I have discussed what is necessary,' Johnson said. 'I'm going to go through what we've agreed, so you're all clear and then that is the end of it.' He read out the revised list. It totalled just an additional £500 million, 2 per cent of the extra money Johnson had been demanding. It was a brutal outcome for Rosenfield, who had egged on his prime minister only to see him capitulate.

By mid-October, Westminster was gripped by a BBC documentary series in which Tony Blair and Gordon Brown bared their souls – a psychodrama playing out between a slickly political prime minister, fixated with the media, and a detail-obsessed chancellor who plotted both a different economic direction and his own succession to the top job. A senior Tory remarked with concern, 'I'm worried we are falling into the same thing with Boris and Rishi … only this time it is the prime minister with the "great clunking fist".'

When the levelling up white paper finally appeared at the start of February 2022 it was a smorgasbord of policy ideas which Gove had been forced to steal from other departments since he could also appropriate the funding that had been assigned to them. A plan to exempt high street businesses from paying business rates was vetoed by Sunak. Again, it felt like he was thwarting the central tenets of Johnson's mission, though the prime minister's own failure to crystallise what he wanted and drive it through was as much to blame. 'There's no underpinning philosophy,' someone who worked closely with Johnson explained. 'The only policy in Number 10 is spending money.' A Tory who worked for several months in Downing Street said, 'They've elected David Owen not Margaret Thatcher.' Sunak worried, reasonably, that Johnson's attachment to rising wages would fuel an arms race between wages and prices. 'Some people don't seem to understand the dangers of inflation,' he said, pointedly and presciently.

By the end of 2021 Sunak had acquired an independent power base. The joint unit set up by Cummings the year before was allied fully with the chancellor. A senior Tory observed, 'Cabinet ministers are either barons, with their own power base, or they are knights, who are dependent for patronage on the boss.' Sunak began as a knight, but as chancellor he evolved into the most powerful baron. He concluded the prime minister would not learn from his mistakes or change his laissez-faire approach to spending or his chaotic management style. The chancellor felt confident enough to cause fresh divisions on lockdowns, partygate, Ukraine and the cost of living. 'Rishi's view was that Downing Street was a shitshow, unable to make decisions, unable to stick to them,' a friend revealed. 'He found the whole thing immensely frustrating. Most Treasury people think the country would be better run if it was run by them.'

As collaboration turned to recrimination, Sunak seemed more offended than others by Johnson's habits. 'Rishi isn't a saint,' the cabinet colleague explained. 'He can be difficult. He's occasionally petulant when crossed. If you go in hard, he can be a bit snappy and wounded. He's fonder of his own ideas than other people's. But he values candour, and he believes in a certain code of honour. He was offended by what he saw as the casualness of Boris towards office and the truth. In Rishi's mind there's a little bit of José Mourinho – he is "the special one" – but on the other hand, there's a bit of, "I'm blessed, my parents invested everything in me. I've got to demonstrate to them and the world that the talents that I've been given are put at the use of the country and public service", and in his mind that requires certain things.'

To Johnson and his aides Sunak's moral code made him a prig. Sunak's evident distaste for Johnson's approach to partygate cut no ice with the PM who told aides, 'Rishi lives in the building the same as I do. If I knew about all these parties [which Johnson denied], so did he.'

In early December 2021, Liam Booth-Smith said to his fellow special advisers in Number 11, 'They're going to try and lockdown again. I can feel it.' The Omicron variant of Covid, which originated in South Africa, led the scientists to push for restrictions. Sunak spoke to a doctor friend in the US, who put him in touch with one in South Africa. He had written a thread of evidence suggesting Omicron was not very contagious or dangerous. Sunak took the data to Rosenfield: 'You don't need to freak out. Get the data and give us everything they've got.' When ministers met the scientists on Friday 10th, Sunak tore into them, contesting the data. 'I think we've won that,' he told aides.

But Tuesday 14th, his aides were anxious that the battle was not won and a second Christmas lockdown was looming. Sunak was due to fly that afternoon to San Francisco for a long-planned official trip to meet health technology firms and business investors in Britain. 'You can't leave,' Booth-Smith said, 'because they will do this and you will have no sway.' Sunak was adamant: 'I am not cancelling this trip.' His plane had already taken off when Declan Lyons and Ben Gascoigne arrived from Number 10, expressing concern that things had moved and there would be an announcement by Friday. When Sunak landed, Wednesday morning UK time, Booth-Smith told him, 'They're going to do this, you have to come back.' Sunak was 'absolutely furious'.

The chancellor stayed up until the small hours of the morning to call the prime minister and seek to dissuade him. Then he flew home, landing on Friday morning and going straight into a meeting with the scientists, led by Chris Whitty, who was pushing for a circuit breaker lockdown. 'He tore them to pieces,' a witness said.

When he got Johnson alone, Sunak made the argument that neither Tory backbenchers nor the cabinet would accept a lockdown. 'A week ago, you agreed this was a terrible idea. It is absolutely unnecessary. You don't want to do it. I don't want to do it. The cabinet don't want to do it.' He suggested Johnson hold a full cabinet meeting. 'Take it to them and make them be the ones to make the decision.' The prime minister, whose personal instincts were anti-lockdown, agreed.

Cabinet on Monday 20 December 2021 was probably the only occasion in the passage of the pandemic when cabinet government lived up to its name. Javid and Gove argued for new restrictions. Johnson had phoned Jacob Rees-Mogg and David Frost the night before to urge them to lead the charge against them. Sunak said little, pointing out that the PM knew his views, and also not trusting his colleagues not to leak his comments. Some ministers saw a tricksy customer who wouldn't nail his colours to the mast. Rees-Mogg, Grant Shapps, Alister Jack and Mark Spencer 'put in a shift' to ensure the plan was blocked. 'Ultimately, it was Boris's decision,' a cabinet minister said. 'He faced down the usual threats about deaths being on his watch', telling the meeting, 'I've heard these arguments before. This time I'm prepared to take the risk. I believe we've got to look after children's education, the economy.'

There was no thanks for Sunak, however. 'I don't think Boris ever liked it when Rishi was tough,' a Treasury aide said. 'He resented Rishi being right, even when it benefited him.'

Three days later, Sunak's team purchased a web domain from GoDaddy called 'readyforrishi.com'. They had long assumed he might one day have a crack at the leadership. This was the first concrete measure that proved they were beginning to do more than think about it. But they pleaded innocence about the timing. 'People buy up shit because they think they can make some money, so you have to buy it off them,' an aide said. 'There was no scheming or plotting and put a knife in the back tomorrow, or in a month's time. This person came to Cass [Horowitz] and said, "I've got ready for Rishi" and Cass decided to buy it, just in case.'

By that stage partygate had been running for seven weeks and Sunak was growing increasingly frustrated with Number 10's failure to close down the story, and seemed genuinely dismayed at the culture of impunity in Downing Street. He began to speak more freely in private about Johnson's foibles, joking with a friend that, with his back to the wall, the prime minister was working harder: 'Boris is so worried that he has started to read his papers.'

Sunak wasn't the only one growing bolder. The BBC's political editor Laura Kuenssberg triggered a social media storm when she quoted an anonymous 'senior Downing Street source' saying, 'There is a lot of concern inside the building about the PM … it's just not working.' The BBC website originally flagged the comments as from Number 10, not something Kuenssberg had said, and this was changed, sparking speculation that the quote had actually emerged from Number 11. Johnson's allies blamed Booth-Smith – unfairly, the Treasury insisted.

Johnson's Big Dog group, who were doing their own whipping, detected that Sunak's parliamentary outriders were also becoming more active, with his PPS Craig Williams, James Cartlidge and Julian Smith, the former chief whip, all quietly suggesting the party might be in better hands under Sunak. Gavin Williamson and Mel Stride were also identified as key cheerleaders for Sunak as well.

In the final week of November 2021, the Conservative clan gathered for the *Spectator* magazine's annual Parliamentarian of the Year awards. Handing out the 'disruptor of the year' to the politician 'who has done most to cause chaos for the government' (Angela Rayner), the magazine's editor Fraser Nelson felt compelled to joke, 'We had to exclude the prime minister from consideration.' Unfair competition, after weeks of self-inflicted damage. Sunak won politician of the year (joking grimly that the award 'only cost £400 billion'), and Liz Truss the politician to watch.

It was an open secret in Westminster that Truss was also positioning herself for a future leadership contest, holding one-on-one meetings with ministers, 'fizz with Liz' drinks with MPs and 'biz for Liz' chats with donors at 5 Hertford Street. Truss's ambition was such that when a former minister lamented the partygate chaos at one gathering, the foreign secretary responded cheekily, 'It will be better when I'm in charge.' Ben Wallace thought them both too blatant, telling friends, 'The first rule of combat is that the enemy should not see and hear you coming. Someone should tell that to Liz and Rishi.' Nadhim Zahawi, the education secretary, was also contemplating his options, while Jeremy Hunt, the former foreign secretary, was vying with Tom Tugendhat, the chairman of the foreign affairs select committee, for the backing of the One Nation Conservatives group. On the right, Priti Patel, the home secretary, was also taking soundings.

Sunak and Truss were clearly the frontrunners, however. At the Tory winter ball fundraising dinner that same week, Sunak and Truss were 'working the room all night'. One donor stumped up £35,000 to play cricket with Sunak; another £22,000 for karaoke with Truss. By contrast, at a recent auction by Surrey Conservatives, two books by Dominic Raab, the deputy prime minister, fetched a princely £8.

When Munira Mirza resigned, claiming disgust over Johnson's comments about Jimmy Savile, there was no longer any disguising the split at the heart of government. Asked at a Covid press conference about the prime minister's remark, Sunak said. 'Being honest I wouldn't have said it.' Johnson loyalists saw this as a coordinated assault from Sunak's allies. Suspicions of a conspiracy were heightened when Sajid Javid endorsed Sunak's position, saying Starmer had done a 'good job' as director of public prosecutions and deserved 'absolute respect'.

The chancellor's team then failed to give Number 10 prior sight of an article he had written for the *Sun* in which he reinforced the criticism and indicated he would do things differently if he were leader. That weekend there were reports that Sunak supporters, among them Booth-Smith, had met in an Italian restaurant to discuss a Sunak leadership campaign and how they might lend MPs' votes to Truss's rivals to keep her out of the final two. However, Dominic Cummings, who was in regular but not frequent contact with Booth-Smith, did not think the Treasury was doing nearly enough to hasten Johnson's departure. 'My impression, talking to some Treasury people, is that they weren't pushing out a bunch of stuff,' Cummings told one confidant. If Vote Leave were in the Treasury, I think there would've been a different grid.' In the Boris bunker, however, Sunak seemed complicit. A Johnson ally thought it impossible that Sunak didn't have 'tacit knowledge, if not direction, of this campaign happening on his behalf ... I find it very difficult to believe that he wasn't speaking to Dom, for example. There was a blindness on Team Boris about the fact that somebody so close to him was so advanced in their plotting.'

Sunak's activities irritated his colleagues and cabinet rivals, who privately expressed the view that Johnson should move him in the next reshuffle. A Johnson adviser said, 'Rishi's just not ready to be prime minister. He risks being the Ole Gunnar Solskjaer of Westminster', a reference to the recently dismissed Manchester United football manager, who got the big job too soon.

Johnson tried to hold Sunak close, inviting him to a pre-meet before the morning meeting in Number 10, alongside Barclay, the new chief of staff, and Guto Harri. Even here, his ambitions were never far from the surface. Someone had supplied bacon rolls. Johnson 'tucked in enthusiastically', joined by Barclay and Harri. Sunak declined, sparking memories of Ed Miliband, whose leadership of Labour never recovered from pictures of him wrestling with a bacon butty. 'Being able to eat a bacon sarnie is critical for your advancement prospects in the political arena,' Harri teased. Sunak laughed. The following day he scoffed a bacon sandwich. His team also briefed how he had assimilated into his North Yorkshire seat. 'Sunak drinks exclusively Yorkshire tea, is a devotee of the pork and apple pie from Kitson & Sons butchers in Northallerton and has picked up several verbal tics from his adopted home. Around No 11 he is often heard to say "now then" and "job's a good 'un",' the *Sunday Times* reported.

Privately, however, Sunak saw little point in these morning meetings, telling his aides, 'Boris just talks about the papers and then we all leave and do our real jobs.' The only time it seemed like Johnson was interested in his views on partygate, a Treasury aide observed, 'was when Boris was calling him up asking him: "Don't throw me under the bus in this interview today."'

Johnson's major beef with his chancellor was his failure, even his refusal, to set out a growth strategy for the government. In January 2022, he invited Sunak to Chequers and made his pitch. 'Why don't you set out your vision for tax cuts?' Johnson appealed to Sunak's vanity and his admiration for Margaret Thatcher's greatest chancellor: 'I want you to be the Nigel Lawson of your era. Tell the country how we're going to get growth, how we're going to get things moving and why Brexit Britain has made the right decision.' To the prime minister's surprise, Sunak seemed hesitant, temporising. 'Rishi kept putting it off and off and off,' a senior Downing Street adviser recalled.

From Johnson's perspective, Sunak had either been captured by the Treasury or the chancellor did not want to help his prime minister out of the partygate hole, or Sunak was saving up all his good ideas for when he was prime minister. 'I think basically he had people in his ear saying, "Don't give Boris anything. He's fucked. Just bide your time,"' a source familiar with Johnson's thinking said.

Lynton Crosby was roped in to do some messaging testing, coming up with 'a plan for a stronger economy'. But the failure to agree what was in the plan meant the joint speech was up in the air when both men left Downing Street.

One bugbear of Johnson and his aides was Treasury reluctance to do away with Solvency II, a set of EU regulations which came into effect in 2016, forcing insurance companies to hold more capital. 'Boris couldn't get Rishi to do it for love nor money,' the adviser said. 'He kept saying, "We're working on it."' It was not until September 2023, eleven months into his own premiership, that Sunak published plans to move away from Solvency II in the UK.

The Russian invasion of Ukraine, in February 2022, created three new fissures between Johnson and Sunak, the first immediate, the other two strategic. The prime minister's strong push for Russia to be kicked out of the SWIFT payments system was opposed by the Treasury. Officials warned in National Security Council meetings that such an action would have security implications since it would encourage Russia to set up its own payment system, possibly with China and India, meaning Western regulators and intelligence officers would find it more difficult to track the movement of shady money.

Johnson was such a robust advocate for Ukraine that anyone would have looked less enthusiastic about arming Zelensky's forces than the prime minister – but the PM quickly became suspicious that Sunak did not want to take sides. In an early cabinet discussion about sanctions, the chancellor was a voice of caution, telling ministers, 'Of course we can do sanctions but we should be careful because this will have

economic consequences.' Sunak saw it as his job to make sure the consequences had been considered. He, rightly, believed that Johnson was
poor at seeing the future implications of decisions he made today. In
private he was even less enthusiastic about the war in its early stages,
believing Russia would win. A friend of the chancellor said, 'He thinks
Putin will still be there and that there will have to be a deal with him and
if that's the case is it really worth the pain to the economy?'

The final issue was the huge economic shock delivered by the conflict
to a world economy already on its knees after the pandemic. The war sent
the price of oil and gas, and with it domestic energy bills and inflation,
soaring. It also exposed decades of failure by both main parties to build
national security into energy provision. The chancellor also pushed hard
to get Johnson to level with the public that their energy prices could rise
to £4,000 or £5,000 a year. 'You've got to prepare the country for it,' he
warned.[3] In his opening televised address to the nation, Johnson, who
loathed delivering bad news (either to colleagues or the public), did not
talk about the pain the public would likely have to endure.

The two men then disagreed about what to do to mitigate the cost of
living and where to invest for future energy security. Johnson wanted
billions in new nuclear power stations to wean the UK off Russian oil and
gas. A Sunak aide said, 'He's expected to just rustle up a few nuclear
power stations from thin air.'

It was not just Johnson who was uneasy about Sunak. With inflation
rising to 8.7 per cent by the end of January (the highest for four decades),
other cabinet ministers wanted to see Treasury action to curb the soaring
cost of living, which the Office of Budget Responsibility (OBR) was
warning was about to suffer the biggest rise in sixty-six years. When
Kwasi Kwarteng, the business secretary, gave an interview suggesting his
officials were in discussions with the Treasury about a bailout package
for firms hit hard by soaring gas prices, Sunak's team accused Kwarteng
of 'making up' the claim. When Johnson backed the business secretary, a
fellow Old Etonian, a Sunak spinner had to apologise to Kwarteng.

Cabinet critics saw Sunak's orthodox approach, at a time when firms
had been hit by a fivefold increase in the cost of fuel, as politically naive.
'We can't allow a temporary increase in global gas prices to send otherwise viable businesses to the wall,' a Tory adviser said. And that was
before the National Insurance rise kicked in, adding £600 to the average
household's taxes, with the energy price cap also expected to add another

£500 to costs from April 2022. Ministers and the Tory right pressed for a VAT cut on fuel. Sunak resisted since he wanted a war chest for a pre-election income tax cut. He insisted help be targeted at the poorest. MPs wanted something universal since even middle-class households were feeling the pinch.

Johnson wanted to abandon the National Insurance rise. He met Sunak on the morning of Friday 28th in the Cabinet Room. The chancellor got Johnson to agree they would stick with the NICs rise and vetoed a VAT rise. Instead, he was planning to expand the warm homes discount and provide a council tax rebate for the most needy. With pump prices heading towards £2 per litre and predictions that the energy price cap could hit £3,000, Kwarteng argued that every household should get £500 of energy bill relief. Sunak planned for a loan of just £200, clawed back from consumers in future years. He failed to see that he was spending political capital on an announcement which was set to fail.

The spring statement on 23 March was a disaster for the government generally and the chancellor personally. Sunak's handout gave properties in bands A to D a council tax rebate of £150 when the energy cap rose from around £1,300 to nearly £2,000 in April. Having refused to ditch the National Insurance rate rise, he sought to woo the Tory tax cutters by increasing the threshold above which National Insurance contributions started to be paid, from £9,880 to £12,570 from July 2022. Sunak's own advisers had warned him this would not allay the public's fears. One said, 'A few of us said. "Nobody understands the threshold stuff." Even if you say 70 per cent of people are going to be better off, everyone is going to say, "I thought my national insurance is going up, so how does that work?" The comms of it was impossible.'

With two weeks to go before he made the statement, Sunak realised his offer was 'not going to cut the mustard'. The chancellor did not think he had the sums to cut income tax, but he decided to pre-announce a 1p cut in income tax, which would not kick in until April 2024, just before the expected date of the general election. Johnson's team had no idea about this gimmick until the morning of the statement and regarded it as 'bonkers', since the chancellor was simultaneously killing the impact of a pre-election tax cut while getting no benefit from putting money back into people's pay packets when they needed it.

Sunak was bullied into the final measure – slashing 5p off fuel duty – by his advisers. Nissy Chesterfield, whose job it was to spin the plan, could see what the headline would be: the OBR warning that the tax burden was going to be the highest for seventy years. A fuel duty cut would give them some good news to sell to a beleaguered public. She persuaded Booth-Smith and they both went to see Sunak. The chancellor was unsure. 'It will make no difference to people,' he argued.

'It's not about how much better off people are feeling,' she argued, 'it's a signal that you understand what people are going through.' Over the next twenty-four hours, Sunak came around and told his team they would cut fuel duty by 3p in the pound. 'Let's take the win,' Booth-Smith said. 'It's got to be 5p at an absolute minimum,' Chesterfield argued. 'People are going nuts.'

Cabinet on the day of the statement was a fractious affair. Sunak had barely finished outlining the difficult economic position when first Kit Malthouse, the policing minister, then Jacob Rees-Mogg, the Brexit minister, demanded he reopen the spending review to slash spending. Michael Gove attempted to ride to Sunak's aid, urging ministers to focus on their own departments rather than berating the chancellor for global economic conditions beyond his control. Seeking divine intervention he quoted the Serenity Prayer: 'God grant me the serenity to accept the things I cannot change, courage to change the things I can, and the wisdom to know the difference.'

Johnson was privately supportive of Sunak, telling cabinet, 'If Rishi hadn't done what he did during Covid, we wouldn't even have an economy left.' Publicly, he suggested more would need to be done to help with the cost of living, undermining the chancellor on the day of the statement.

Having won plaudits in 2020 for throwing the full force of the state into protecting the country from the pandemic, Sunak's spring statement was seen as too little too late to help families in growing distress over the cost of living. It fuelled a narrative that the chancellor's personal wealth left him out of touch with the public. The media backlash the following morning, from usually supportive papers such as the *Mail* and the *Telegraph*, stunned Sunak's team. The Institute for Fiscal Studies and the Resolution Foundation both argued that lower than expected debt interest payments had given him headroom to do more for the poor. The failure to come out with a big bazooka on energy costs overshadowed the £9 billion he spent on a fuel duty cut and the shift in National Insurance thresholds. 'He didn't grasp the politics,' one frustrated supporter said. 'You have to be seen to be doing something. That was the biggest waste of £9 billion I've ever seen because he got no political credit.' Later, one of Sunak's inner circle admitted, 'We shouldn't have done both thresholds and income tax. It was all too complicated.'

These errors were compounded by a publicity stunt in which Sunak was filmed filling up a Kia Rio at a petrol station and then, when paying, tried to put his can of coke against the card reader, suggesting he was a stranger to contactless checkouts. It then emerged that he had borrowed the car from a member of the public.

Johnson was, by now, egging on all those who might make trouble for Sunak. In late March, Jacob Rees-Mogg visited the prime minister to outline his plans to tear up EU regulations as part of a bill porting EU law into British law. Rees-Mogg said he had concluded that the civil service was trying to keep the UK in 'the lunar orbit' of the EU and that Rishi Sunak had 'gone native'. Johnson encouraged him to give everything 'a massive kick'. Rees-Mogg warned, 'I might have to step on some rather big toes.' He paused. 'Actually, some rather little toes of people in big departments.' Johnson laughed and told him to 'go ahead'.[4]

Two weeks after the spring statement, on 7 April, Sunak suffered another major setback which raised fresh questions about his political judgement. The *Independent*'s Anna Isaac revealed that his wife Akshata Murty was non-domiciled for tax purposes and that, while living in the UK, she stated her home residence was India, a revelation that left MPs open-mouthed with incredulity. A chancellor of the exchequer raising people's taxes while his wife, who was worth upwards of £700 million, paid an annual fee of £30,000 (more than the national average income) to avoid £20 million in taxes on her foreign investments, might have been a new dictionary definition of 'cut through' or hypocrisy. Sunak saw nothing wrong and since he did not perceive the political danger, he had not told his closest aides, leaving them blindsided when the news broke. The first even Booth-Smith knew about it was when Isaac emailed Nissy Chesterfield to ask for a comment. When they went to Sunak, he was horrified: 'How do they know this?'

When Sunak became a minister in 2018, he sat down with Helen MacNamara, the head of propriety and ethics, and talked her through his own finances and those of his wife. He moved his own investments into a blind trust and revealed both that his wife was a non-dom and that they held green cards, handed to those with permanent residence in America and an obligation to file a US tax return. 'They over-declared,' one of his aides said. 'That meant people in government knew the tax status of Akshata, something they didn't need to know because of the rules. He also told them about the green card ... And now they have been screwed.' Sunak also informed his permanent secretary in both departments where he had worked, the Treasury and local government.

One of Sunak's ministerial allies, speaking without the authority of him or his aides, accused Johnson's aides of leaking Murty's tax status: 'I know someone is briefing full time against Rishi in Number 10. There are people in there who want to get rid of him because if the PM gets into trouble they want there to be no alternative leader.' Two weeks earlier, after the prime minister told British firms to stop doing business in Russia, there had also been reports that Infosys, the firm owned by Sunak's father-in-law, N. R. Narayana Murty (and in which his wife had shares), was still trading in Moscow.[5]

At first, Sunak's inner circle absolved Johnson's aides of the blame for the non-dom story. A close aide said, 'I think it was a leak from within government to Labour and then to the media.' A cabinet minister said, 'That information was only available to a very small number of people and the PET team in the Cabinet Office. It was either someone who didn't like him, who was in the Treasury, a very tight group of people in his office, or it came out of the Cabinet Office. The Cabinet Office leaks like a sieve.' Only later did they discover that Anna Issac had once worked for one of the members of Johnson's Brains Trust, a connection which bred suspicion. 'The prime minister can ask to see an update on all of his ministers' financial updates,' a Sunak aide pointed out. Team Boris, in the form of Nadine Dorries, placed the blame at the feet of Dougie Smith, who she suggested had leaked the story to keep his candidate on a short leash, a manoeuvre which seemed counterproductively Machiavellian even for Dark Arts Dougie.

Wherever the leak originated, the effect was the same. MPs and friends who had invested time and effort in a potential leadership campaign were horrified that Sunak could be so naive. One long-standing friend said, 'His wife is his biggest blind spot. You can't be a chancellor and you can't be prime minister where your wife is a non-dom, particularly at a time when you are increasing everyone's taxes ... The idea that he thought he would get through an entire leadership contest without this coming out is bananas.' Advisers who had clashed with Sunak's team could not contain their glee when the story broke. Hostile spads called the chancellor and his wife 'Rishi Notax and Akshata Murky'.

The following day, to make matters worse, it emerged that Sunak had held a US green card, which implied a long-standing allegiance to America, even while he was chancellor. He had met his wife while studying at Stanford University in California and they kept a home in Santa Monica. Holding on to the green card suggested Sunak was keeping his options open about a life across the pond, and it gave ammunition to his enemies, who portrayed this conviction Brexiteer as a rootless cosmopolitan, too wealthy to understand the economic suffering of voters.

When the non-dom story broke on the Wednesday night, a senior figure in Conservative campaign headquarters advised Sunak's team their defence would not hold and that Murty would have to materially change her tax arrangements to kill the story. They were ignored. 'I want to protect my wife and I think her privacy matters,' Sunak told his team. Asking her to alter her personal tax affairs was 'not an option', he said. Instead, Sunak again considered whether to resign. He was fast turning into a modern-day Hamlet, repeatedly contemplating whether to be or not to be a minister.

Dougie Smith had another solution: stand and fight. 'Dougie's playbook is to dismiss all criticism as a "smear",' a Tory strategist said. Sunak gave an interview to the *Sun* in which he parroted Smith's lines: 'To smear my wife to get at me is awful.' He explained, 'She loves her country. Like I love mine, I would never dream of giving up my British citizenship. And I imagine most people wouldn't,' he said. He also sought to excuse her tax arrangements as 'complicated' and claimed they did not involve her paying less tax – when in fact not paying tax on her foreign earnings would have saved her at least £4.4 million the previous year. The interview landed, as one senior Tory put it, 'like a cow pat'. Another said, 'The idea that there's no advantage in being a non-dom is nonsense. And telling people it was overcomplicated is nuts. It's very simple. Man raises taxes, wife doesn't pay taxes.'

By Friday morning, Murty had got her own PR adviser and issued a statement saying she would now pay that tax in the UK. However, she insisted, as an Indian citizen, that she would keep her non-dom status – protecting her from hundreds of millions of pounds in inheritance tax. The Sunak spin operation said the decision was made in a desire to protect her own reputation, rather than that of her husband. 'She has a life here. She goes to the shops, she takes the kids to school, she goes to the gym. She doesn't want to be seen as someone who has broken the rules. It was nothing to do with him.'

The decision was a relief to his inner circle who had wanted Sunak to sort things out more quickly. 'We didn't deal with it fast enough but when the personal meets the political it is much more difficult,' a close aide admitted. A cabinet minister also observed, 'He married into a super-rich family and he clearly isn't the primary decision-maker.'

Johnson was 'super supportive', Sunak's team admitted, twice calling the chancellor and telling his own aides to offer 'full-throated' backing. But the prime minister, who gave up his American citizenship so he didn't have to pay US taxes, was also 'a bit baffled' by Sunak's retention of his green card. When aides tried to explain to Johnson that Sunak had willingly paid tax in both countries until the year before, an uncomprehending prime minister said, 'Tell me about this green card thing again. I don't understand …'

The prime minister made clear that he would stand by his chancellor and Sunak appears to have reciprocated in kind. A cabinet minister recounted, 'Boris said to me that Rishi said, "I'll always stand by you." Boris said, "Rishi told me that he had my back, because I had his back." When people said Rishi was on manoeuvres to be leader, Boris didn't believe them.' This would have repercussions later. 'One of the things that upset Boris so much was how much he stood by Rishi during that time as chancellor, when he was coming under attack.'

Johnson also believed the affair highlighted Sunak's inexperience. 'I liked Rishi, I considered him my friend and partner,' Johnson wrote in his memoir. 'But I had not seen the evidence that he knew how to cope with the scale of the [top] job … I thought Rishi's best bet would be to hang on, help get us through 2024, and then take over in due course. We had discussed his career several times, and he assured me of his complete support "for as long as you want" … I assumed he understood that he was not yet ready, that we were a good fit.'[6]

That then was the state of play when Johnson and Sunak were fined – the leading politicians in the country maintaining a veneer of cordiality while their teams butted heads, both men damaged by political missteps.

On 19 April, in his first Commons statement since his fixed penalty notice, Johnson apologised repeatedly during the debate, by one count on forty-two occasions. However, he then spoke to the 1922 Committee and was much more forthright in defending himself. 'He didn't think he had done anything wrong,' an MP present said.

On the same day the speaker Lindsay Hoyle approved an application from Starmer and other leading opposition MPs to table a motion for debate followed by a vote on 21 April, on whether Johnson should be referred to the Parliamentary Privileges Committee to investigate whether he knowingly misled Parliament. Downing Street initially sought to kill this off, but it soon became clear they faced a backbench revolt by MPs who were sick of defending their wayward prime minister in public. Chris Heaton-Harris tabled an amendment to delay the decision until after Sue Gray's report was published and imposed a three-line whip on Tory MPs. Even this attempt to buy time was rejected by Conservative rebels and Heaton-Harris was forced to lift the three-line whip. The party managers told Johnson's aides the party would not swallow an attempt to vote down the entire enterprise. The prime minister reluctantly agreed. Guto Harri was incredulous. 'That was the moment for me when I thought: this party is going to self-destruct, this is mass suicide by Conservative MPs. This is the moment when they are showing their propensity to self-harm and a willingness to see one of the most successful leaders they have ever had, at winning elections at least, destroyed.'[7] Two days later, Johnson acknowledged it might have been better to fight it.

Once again, the inner circle had forced MPs to hold the line when they did not want to and then retreated, just as they had over Paterson. Johnson was on a trade trip to India as events unfolded, absent again just as he had been at COP26 while the Paterson gambit was devised. In the end, the Commons approved the motion without a vote. A landmine was placed under Johnson's futures. Harri recalled, 'Agreeing to go along with that committee was the moment when it was all lost. Tory MPs could have voted it down.'[8]

The Ukraine moratorium on public criticism of Johnson was also over. Tory backbencher Nigel Mills said his position was 'untenable'. Lord Wolfson, a justice minister, resigned. On the 19th, two of the best backbench organisers broke cover. Mark Harper said Johnson was 'no longer worthy' of his position, while Steve Baker declared, 'the gig is up' and said Johnson should be 'long gone by now'.

Four days later, it was announced that further fines had been issued for the 'bring your own booze' event in the Downing Street garden. Johnson did not receive one. Junior civil servants – who had admitted being at the parties and whose names had been passed to Scotland Yard by Sue Gray – were being fined for attending events they had been asked to go to by their line managers, while politicians appeared to be escaping because the police had not bothered to establish who else was at the events.

Parliament and the Met went into purdah for the local elections, but still the bad news came for Johnson. Neil Parish, the MP for the rural seat of Tiverton and Honiton, was exposed for twice watching pornography on his phone in the Commons chamber. He claimed, with total sincerity, that the first time he had been googling a tractor called 'the dominator', but then admitted he liked what he had seen and had revisited the site.

Two days before the elections, Johnson was sick with food poisoning. It was also the day he was finally scheduled to do an interview with ITV's *Good Morning Britain* – fulfilling the pledge made eighteen months earlier outside the walk-in fridge. 'He was throwing up and had to change his suit because he got sick on his lapel,' an aide explained. In a metaphor for his political plight, Number 10 negotiated a 'distress signal' with the interviewer Susanna Reid. 'If he raised a glass of water, they would cut the cameras so he could run out to be sick again.' Many Tories watching felt nauseous themselves as an under-par Johnson endured a grilling over partygate. Afterwards, the PM went straight to the morning meeting and declared, 'I just got beaten up by Susanna Reid.'

In the morning meeting on election day, Johnson recognised he was about to be beaten up by another uncompromising group: the British electorate. 'We are going to get our arses kicked,' he told aides. 'But let's be clear, we would have got our arses kicked tonight if no one had ever heard of partygate.' That was not the prevailing view among MPs, particularly in the 'blue wall' seats of the Tories' southern heartlands, where public fury over partygate was pronounced.

The Tories ended up losing 481 seats and eleven councils, a triumph of expectation management by the party's director of communications, Alex Wild, who had convinced journalists they might haemorrhage a thousand seats. A senior Tory official said, 'If the red wall had started to crumble that would have been serious. But no matter how much beer and chicken curry he offers them, they're not buying Keir Starmer.'

That was a reference to another CCHQ triumph. The day the election results came in Durham police announced they were investigating a beer and curry session during lockdown attended by Starmer. Kempsell and Wild's attack unit, with the help of local MP Richard Holden, had dug up a Facebook post revealing a pub quiz had also been held, to undermine Labour's claims, when it was first reported, that it was simply a pause for food in the working day. Holden wrote to the police suggesting they should reopen their inquiry. Wild managed to get the *Mail* to run the story on the front page ten days in a row in April. When the news dropped, CCHQ quickly found footage of the Labour leader calling for Johnson and Sunak to resign simply for being investigated by the police.

Starmer and Angela Rayner, who had also been present, insisted they had not broken the rules, but announced they would resign if given a fixed penalty, to demonstrate that they were not the same as Johnson.[9] The announcement gave Johnson a spring in his step. 'It's time to get off the ropes,' he told aides. In Prime Minister's Questions he dubbed Starmer 'Sir Beer Korma', a nickname so bad it was almost good. But 'beergate' was only ever a distraction from Johnson's troubles.

Boris Johnson had just come off the phone with Volodymyr Zelensky, the Ukrainian leader, when he was informed that he would not be facing any further fines from the Metropolitan police over the parties scandal. It was 19 May. While some aides were jubilant that his job was safe, the man himself seemed nonplussed. 'Mentally, he had already moved on,' said one aide. 'There was no fist in the air or a high five from him. He was surprisingly subdued.' Johnson told aides, 'Now we've got to get on with everything else.'

Westminster and the public were less keen to move on. Operation Hillman had involved twelve detectives, 345 documents, 510 photographs or CCTV images, and 204 questionnaires. It had cost taxpayers £460,000 – all to see whether the prime minister and his staff had broken their own rules. In the end 126 fixed penalty notices were issued for offences on eight different dates, 53 to men and 73 to women. Some 28 people had received between two and five fines. This made Downing Street the address with the most Covid-19 penalties in the entire country.

Even then, the police's conclusions seemed inconsistent. In total, 83 people were issued with a fixed penalty notice but more than 300 were estimated to have attended the various gatherings. It emerged later that

Johnson did not even receive a questionnaire over his presence at three leaving parties and the prime minister had attended several, including the 'bring your own booze' bash.

The other problem for Johnson was that getting on with everything else meant agreeing a plan with Sunak to do more on the cost of living. The chancellor backed a windfall tax on the energy companies, whose profits soared thanks to the rising price of oil and gas, an idea backed by more than 80 per cent of the public according to the Tories' polling. However, Johnson's new advisers – Barclay, Canzini, Harri and Andrew Griffith – all opposed the measure as 'unconservative'. Sunak insisted on discussing the issue in bilateral meetings. 'Then he would turn up with an army of Treasury officials,' a Johnson aide said. 'Boris was always battered in those meetings.' Another recalled a meeting where 'Boris asked how much the windfall tax was going to raise, and Rishi refused to say. Not, couldn't tell him, refused to tell him.'

An alternative plan was drawn up by Gerry Grimstone, a Tory peer who was the former chairman of Barclays and Standard Life, for the energy companies to voluntarily contribute to a cost of living fund, to fund petrol vouchers for pensioners. The boss of BP, Bernard Looney, agreed to contribute £1 billion. 'Rishi blocked it because he is only keen on ideas he thinks of himself,' a Johnson loyalist claimed. The PM eventually agreed to sanction a windfall tax, but only if the Treasury agreed to spend some of the money on massive new investment in nuclear power stations and offshore wind farms.

The Politico Playbook email on the morning of 19 May quoted at length from some analysis by Sam Coates of Sky News, in which he pointed out that MPs and ministers were bitterly divided about whether to cut income tax or VAT, or levy the windfall tax. Coates wrote, 'This is a Conservative Party that isn't sure what it is doing', describing MPs running around Parliament 'like headless chickens'. He concluded, 'Boris Johnson needs to impose a narrative, a story, to work out who his government is for and how he is going to help them.'

Johnson read this out loud in the morning meeting and then 'lost it', launching into an intemperate rant, blaming Sunak for thwarting his vision. 'Fuck this shit!' he said. 'We need to clear out the Treasury.' Johnson said he wanted to get rid of Tom Scholar, the permanent secretary, and his deputy Charles Roxburgh and put John Redwood on the monetary policy committee of the Bank of England. 'The Treasury has just become a bank manager,' he added, mimicking the Little Britain sketch of petty but unbending authority: 'Computer says No. We need to go for Singapore-on-Thames', the free marketeer dream of a deregulated economy off the coast of a social democrat Europe. 'We need to get out of people's way. We're costing business too much. Rishi has signed too many cheques but got very little value for money.' Two days earlier, Johnson had embarked on a similar venting exercise. 'This is meant to be a radical government. If Rishi is a Thatcherite, let's have it!'[10]

Sunak would hit back in meetings, pointing out that it had been Johnson's decision to spend vast sums of taxpayers' money on new hospitals, more police, doctors and nurses. 'We had a song for a long time,' the chancellor said. 'Do we not want to sing it any more?'[11]

Johnson and Sunak remained personally cordial, but their relationship was now in a bad place. The prime minister frequently complained that Sunak 'just blocks everything to thwart me'. Sunak, despairing of the PM's lack of seriousness, cut Johnson off. 'By the end, Rishi never used to take Boris's phone calls,' said a friend of the Johnsons. 'He would call and Rishi would just ignore him. Carrie was telling him, "You're the prime minister, you can sack him." But Boris didn't have the balls to do it. Carrie used to call Rishi "the princess next door".'

Johnson was not a good butcher, however. Several aides and his wife urged him to replace Priti Patel, the home secretary, as well as Sunak. Johnson openly bemoaned the 'lack of energy in energy', where Kwasi Kwarteng was in charge. 'Special KK,' as the PM called him, 'sits there like a Buddha, but fuck all is happening,' he complained.

While Johnson kept his comments behind closed doors, other ministers laid into Sunak. Truss denounced the National Insurance rise and told allies she would run for the leadership on a 'reverse Rishi's tax rises' ticket. In a meeting on the Northern Ireland Protocol, tensions over Brexit played second fiddle to cabinet splits over tax. Sunak was talking about the need to encourage business investment as a way of stimulating economic growth when Brandon Lewis, the Northern Ireland secretary, exclaimed, 'Then cut corporation tax.' He was joined by Kwarteng, who immediately blurted, 'Yes!' Guto Harri concluded later, 'Had the whole government not imploded, I doubt the chancellor would have lasted the summer.'[12]

Johnson sought his own advice on the windfall tax, from a panel of four economists. Gerard Lyons, a former adviser to Johnson, was joined by Lord King of Lothbury, the former governor of the Bank of England, Rupert Harrison, George Osborne's right-hand man when he was chancellor, and Baroness Shafik of the London School of Economics. King was withering about the Bank's performance in approving quantitative easing the previous autumn – a decision approved by Sunak – but said a handout package need not be inflationary now the money supply was shrinking. Harrison suggested any boost needed to put a sum equivalent to at least 1 per cent of GDP into the economy. Lyons called for 'timely, targeted and temporary' help but contested the Treasury view that both tight monetary and tight fiscal policy were needed. The economists backed significant fiscal loosening.

Three days later, on 26 May, Sunak announced a further £15 billion package, part funded by a £5 billion windfall tax on energy firms. Every household would get £400 off their energy bill – a handout, which replaced the £200 loan he had offered in the spring statement – while eight million of the lowest income families would get an extra £650, pensioner households an additional £300 and those on disability benefits £150. The stimulus effect was around 1.5 per cent of GDP.

Sunak's second cost of living intervention was much more popular than his first, but by then the world had been digesting Sue Gray's final report for twenty-four hours. Within six weeks he and Johnson would both be gone.

OUT OF EXCUSES

(or Bye Bye Boris, Part II)

25 May to 6 July 2022

'When a regime has been in power too long, when it has
fatally exhausted the patience of the people, and when
oblivion finally beckons – I am afraid that across the
world you can rely on the leaders of that regime to act
solely in the interests of self-preservation, and not in
the interests of the electorate'

– Boris Johnson

The paper was still warm from the photocopier when Boris Johnson was handed Sue Gray's final report on partygate. It was Wednesday morning, 25 May, and the prime minister was in his office with Steve Barclay, his chief of staff, and Guto Harri, his director of communications. Samantha Jones, the permanent secretary at Number 10, rushed the report in, pages still loose. They had expected it at 8 a.m. It was now 10 a.m. and they had only an hour to prepare Johnson's statement to the Commons and pass it to Lindsay Hoyle, the speaker, and Keir Starmer, who by convention got prior sight of it. Johnson and Barclay began to read while Harri flicked to the conclusion, the former journalist looking for the top line.

The silence was shattered as Johnson's dog, Dilyn, began to bark in the Downing Street garden, 'going absolutely apeshit', as one witness put it. Johnson could not concentrate. 'Can someone deal with that fucking dog?' he snapped. Ben Gascoigne, now deputy chief of staff, was sent to calm the recalcitrant canine. No sooner had he returned than Dilyn started yapping again. Johnson repeated his outburst. The third time it happened, an irate PM yelled, 'Will someone put that fucking dog down!' Harri suggested his military adviser, Jamie Norman, a former special forces commando, could dispatch Dilyn 'with his bare hands'.

The episode was emblematic of much of Johnson's premiership: moments of great seriousness and high tension shot through with comedy and low farce. It also revealed the tension he was feeling. The night before, Johnson had been 'literally hysterical' as he tried to craft the speech to MPs on which his political career likely depended. 'In the old days we would have recommended a slap or a bucket of water thrown over someone,' Harri recalled. Johnson only calmed down when his spin doctor announced, 'We're going to order a drone strike. We'll take Sue Gray out.'

The sixty-page report contained no killer blow but it laid bare the culture of chaos which thrived in Johnson's ecosystem. 'The senior leadership at the centre, both political and official, must bear responsibility for this culture,' Gray wrote. She condemned the way parties were renamed 'events' in emails and messages, proof she said that officials knew they were in the wrong.

When Johnson presented the report to Parliament that afternoon, he delivered a performance of forelock-tugging contrition about how he was 'humbled' and took 'full responsibility for everything that took place on my watch', repeating his apology for the birthday party for which he had received a fixed penalty notice. The prime minister said he had been unaware that events he attended briefly for work reasons descended into rule-breaking 'after I had left, and at other gatherings when I was not even in the building'.

Johnson did not tell MPs that Downing Street had requested a meeting with Gray earlier that month at which Steve Barclay suggested there was no longer any point in releasing her findings because the details were now 'all out there' as a result of the police investigation, an entreaty she rejected. With people she was planning to name, Gray conducted a so-called 'Maxwellisation process', giving them a chance to respond to the sections on them. This led to some changes. Gray was lobbied on Tuesday evening to make changes by Sam Jones and Alex Chisholm, the permanent secretary in the Cabinet Office, in their role as line managers of some of those who were to be named as attending the parties. Tom Scholar and Sarah Healey, the permanent secretaries at the Treasury and Culture, charged with providing pastoral care to officials, also weighed in.

Around thirty people were warned they would be named. In the end only fifteen were identified, suggesting half the names were removed as a result of lobbying by the mandarins.

Despite the excisions, Gray's report, detailing 4 a.m. drinking, a brawl between two civil servants (over a woman), vomiting and red wine up the walls, was damning. It might have been even more embarrassing. Downing Street officials said two couples were caught having sex in the building on the night Cummings and Cain left in November 2020. Gray did not investigate this but witnesses say a male and female employee disappeared into a room together and barricaded the door with a table upon which the sounds of enthusiastic coitus could be heard.

Even Johnson was shocked to read that Number 10 custodians and cleaners who tried to stop the parties were abused. 'That was the only time he was really angry,' an aide said. 'He knew the press office were always drinking on a Friday, at the end of a tough week. But he didn't realise they were drinking until two o'clock in the morning, and shagging, and he was mortified at the idea of them being rude to staff.' When Johnson returned to Number 10 from the Commons, aides took him to apologise to the custodians, who sit in a room off the foyer behind the famous black door. One, who had to clean up the mess, said he had been asked, 'How can you work there?' by relatives who assumed he was a participant in the revels. The prime minister repeated his apologies in the post room and to the cleaners the following morning. He even went to say sorry to his protection squad officers. One of them, polishing his gun, smiled and said, 'Don't worry, sir, no one is ever rude to us.'

Insiders say the laissez-faire approach came directly from Johnson. 'He absolutely thinks none of the rules apply to him,' said a source who knew him well. 'He's been telling everyone for months, "I've done nothing wrong." The reason the apologies sound so fake is that he doesn't think he needs to apologise.'

Others came forward. Two Conservative sources said a female employee at Chequers left after 'personality clashes' with the Johnsons. 'Staff at Chequers had a lot of problems,' one said. 'The dog was chewing everything and pissing all over the place.' A second said, 'One of the housekeeping left because she found it a nightmare.' Another aide said, 'It was general carnage, with chasing around after Dilyn trying to stop him eating some seventeenth-century book off a shelf.' It was not just Dilyn. 'Wilfred being potty trained was another problem.' Another, who visited not long after the Johnsons left, confided, 'They trashed the joint. You can still see some of the damage.' A Johnson aide conceded, 'Dilyn is a spritely dog', but contested the claims that the house was trashed: 'It wasn't like the Who had just come off stage in the middle of Chequers.'

Johnson and many of his senior team believed he had escaped from the Gray report, if not unscathed, then not 'fatally winged', as one put it. 'I just thought: is that it?' said one of his closest MP allies. 'There's nothing here that endangers him.' Johnson expressed dismay at the backbenchers who were losing confidence in him: 'Why is everyone wetting the bed. What on earth are they playing at?' Those who had worked with Johnson for years had seen him escape seemingly impossible situations and emerge to win over the public. 'Boris's fundamental belief was that it would blow over and that he would survive,' another ally recalled. 'He thought Keir Starmer was useless and that he would marmalise him in the general election.' Johnson later told friends, 'I thought the media hysteria would deflate once people saw what crap it all was.' This would prove to be a fatal misjudgement.

People like Nigel Adams had been warning Johnson for months: 'Forget about the public, the only people who can actually kick you out are the MPs.' The parliamentary party, who Johnson had never properly wooed in the first place, had never liked him but had now lost trust in his Houdini qualities as well. There were six weeks until the summer recess. 'If we had made it to recess, he would have been safe,' a senior supporter said later.

It was not to be. Gray's report brought all the doubts about Johnson, partially allayed by Ukraine, back to the top of MPs' inboxes and the forefront of their minds. A trickle of MPs – Julian Sturdy, John Baron, David Simmonds, Stephen Hammond, Elliot Colburn, Bob Neill, Alicia Kearns, John Stevenson and Steve Brine – announced they were submitting letters of no confidence. Paul Holmes, a parliamentary aide to the home secretary, resigned over the 'toxic culture' in government. Jeremy Wright, the former attorney general, called on Johnson to resign and, not to be outdone, Andrew Bridgen revealed he had resubmitted his letter. By 30 May, twenty-seven Tories had done so publicly. By the time of the Queen's Platinum Jubilee in June, the number was forty-one, just thirteen short of the threshold to trigger a vote. A former cabinet minister involved in the plotting said, 'The dangerous thing for Boris is that it's not coordinated. It's just people who have had enough.'

Johnson's problem was that he was not just facing the ire of one faction of backbenchers, but several. A loyalist minister said, 'You had the One Nationers and the Remoaners who would never forgive Boris; the discontented, badly managed 2019-ers; plenty of mad fuckers who just put in letters constantly. Too many mistakes pushed people who didn't normally take action. They were being told, "If we carry on down this path we're going to be wiped out – it's your duty to take action."'

Johnson thought that Tory MPs had become 'psychologically vulnerable' to the pressures of social media condemnation and allowed themselves to be spooked by 'crap on Twitter and Facebook' into coming after him. 'They were radicalised and told "kill Johnson",' said a source familiar with Johnson's thinking. 'It was very, very difficult for them to resist. A lot got to the stage where they felt the only way that they could purify themselves spiritually in the face of the rage on Facebook was to do this insane thing.' Had Sunak not, apparently, imploded after the spring statement, non-dom and green card revelations, the numbers might have risen more rapidly.

It was not just MPs turning against the prime minister. A snap YouGov poll on the day Gray's report was published found that 59 per cent of voters (though only 27 per cent of Tory supporters) thought Johnson should resign – two points higher than on the day he was fined. YouGov modelling published that Friday implied that in an election the Conservatives would hold just three of 88 battleground seats, with Johnson's Uxbridge and South Ruislip constituency falling to Labour.

At an away day for those in target seats that week, MPs were asked to think about what changes were needed for the Tories to win the next election. 'Many of them concluded that a start would be to find a new leader – although unsurprisingly no one piped up in the public session,' a source said.

Sunday 5 June 2022 was the high point of the jubilee celebrations and one of the lowest moments of Boris Johnson's premiership. When the Queen appeared on the balcony of Buckingham Palace to greet the crowds filling the Mall, Johnson was in the VIP seats between Carrie and Keir Starmer and behind the Duchess of Cambridge. The prime minister had not told a soul in Downing Street that he had received a call shortly before departing for the palace from Brady, informing him that the threshold of fifty-four letters had now been reached. His job, Brady informed Johnson, was to hold a vote 'as soon as practicably possible'. Brady received a mini lecture about why this was an 'act of folly' by MPs.

Nigel Adams, Chris Heaton-Harris, Lynton Crosby, Ross Kempsell and Guto Harri assembled that night in Johnson's flat to drink tea and plan the salvage operation. Johnson asked how bad the situation was. Adams, citing the latest evidence from the spreadsheet, compiled by Grant Shapps and Charlotte Owen, warned him there would be around 150 votes against him. Shapps' model assigned a likelihood percentage to waverers based on information from the team, a system which compensated for the lies people told the whips and the lies they told themselves.

No other Tory prime minister who faced a confidence vote had gone on to win a general election, let alone with a revolt of that scale. They figured Johnson could survive as long as he secured 200 votes, which meant up to 168 against. 'I tell you, a majority of one will be enough for me,' Johnson said.[1] The 'win by one' message was briefed to select journalists.

Johnson's team saw no virtue in giving the rebels longer to mobilise or making it look like they were running scared. 'Let's crack on with it tomorrow,' he texted Brady.[2] The vote would be announced first thing Monday and the ballot would take place between 6 p.m. and 8 p.m. A Second World War scholar, Johnson knew 6 June was the seventy-eighth anniversary of D-Day. He now found himself in the role not of Churchill, but Rommel, the commander of the defenders, wondering if he could drive the attackers back into the sea.

Further questions about Johnson's conduct were raised on 31 May when Lord Geidt, the government's independent adviser on ministers' interests, published his annual report, suggesting the prime minister being issued with a fixed penalty notice 'might have constituted a breach of the overarching duty within the ministerial code of complying with the law'. Geidt was angered that Johnson had not even sought to address whether he had breached the code and added, 'I believe a Prime Minister should respond accordingly, setting out his case in public.' The adviser made clear he was going public with this demand having been completely ignored by Number 10. As a former private secretary to the Queen, Geidt was a stickler for rules. He did not say so, but privately he threatened to resign unless Johnson publicly explained himself.

Johnson published a letter, later that day, clearing himself and Sunak of breaching the code, claiming a fixed penalty notice was not a criminal conviction and blaming 'a failure of communication' for ignoring Geidt. The adviser realised too late that he was not independent, since he reported to Johnson, who remained cavalier towards the rules. An old friend said, 'Christopher had never dealt with anyone like Boris. Someone that slippery was quite outside his frame of reference.' When it came to partygate, 'He had no idea how to hold Boris to account and he worried that it was constitutionally questionable for an unelected adviser to bring down an elected prime minister.' Geidt thought Johnson had breached the code but he pulled his punches.

Geidt finally contrived a reason for resigning two weeks later, on 15 June, when asked about whether deliberately breaching World Trade Organisation rules in a steel dispute with China was a breach of the code. Geidt, who was also concerned about the dispute over the Northern Ireland Protocol, grasped this opportunity to denounce law-breaking, saying he had been put in 'an impossible and odious position', and announced he was off. In truth, he was delighted to have found a reason to leave which did not involve Johnson's personal conduct.

While media attention focused on the Queen during Jubilee week, beneath the surface the tectonic plates of politics were shifting. Harri attended a performance of *Julius Caesar* at the Hay literary festival, the staged assassination of a once beloved leader by a group of disillusioned allies, and joked with colleagues the open-air performance proved that 'toppling a strong leader who has won great victories ended badly'. In this production, Brutus was played by a woman. That week Andrea Leadsom had accused Johnson of 'unacceptable failings of leadership'. The whips believed she was acting as an outrider for Penny Mordaunt, who had helicoptered into Hay to promote her own book.

The nerves of Conservative MPs were not helped by footage on Friday 3 June as Johnson and Carrie arrived at St Paul's Cathedral for the thanksgiving service to mark the Queen's Platinum Jubilee. A few cheers from the crowd were swiftly drowned out by a wave of booing, footage viewed eleven million times on YouTube. In what appeared to be a deliberate joke at the prime minister's expense, Johnson also had to read a lesson from Philippians, selected by the palace, extolling the virtue of 'whatever is true, whatever is honourable ...'

Afterwards Harri, a Welsh rugby fan, reassured Johnson the initial cries of 'Boris! Boris!' were 'like the English rugby crowd singing Swing

Low Sweet Chariot' while the boos were equivalent to a Welsh crowd responding with 'You Can Shove Your Fucking Chariot Up Your Arse'. But a jubilee crowd of royalists ought to have been a Johnson crowd as well. It was the moment several former supporters faced up to how unpopular their populist leader had become. Several sent letters to Brady, but with the proviso that he made no announcement about a vote of no confidence during the jubilee pageantry. Number 10 also sent a friendly MP to tell Brady not to interrupt the celebrations. Irritated, he replied, 'I'm well aware of how to do my job.'

Jeremy Hunt, perceived at that point as the biggest leadership threat, told friends it was his 'public duty' to take over if Johnson fell. But Cameroons like George Osborne, who saw Hunt as their best hope for a centrist restoration, were unimpressed by his lack of killer instinct. 'George's view is that power is never given, it has to be taken,' a former minister said. 'But Jeremy has rejected that advice.'

Johnson was confident of survival. The *Sunday Times* that weekend quoted a former cabinet minister, who opined that if the PM refused to go, 'It is the job of the chief whip to present him with a brandy and a revolver', before adding: 'The problem is that Boris would probably drink the brandy and shoot the chief.' When an aide read this quote to Johnson, he loved it. 'Exactly, I'd shoot the fucker,' he said.

The assault on Johnson's position began at first light, even before Brady had made the announcement, when Jesse Norman, an Old Etonian and longtime ally of the prime minister, channelled years of irritation at not making cabinet, anger at his recent dismissal as a minister and months of disappointment at Johnson's behaviour into one of the most excoriating no-confidence letters ever penned by a British politician. He accused Johnson of 'presiding over a culture of casual law-breaking' in Downing Street and condemned as 'grotesque' the prime minister's claim to have been 'vindicated'. Norman, a biographer of the great constitutionalist Edmund Burke, also railed against Johnson's populist belief that he was a direct tribune of the people. 'You are not a president, and you have no mandate other than as an MP, and from the confidence of your colleagues,' he wrote. 'For you to prolong this charade by remaining in office not only insults the electorate, and the tens of thousands of people who support, volunteer, represent, and campaign for our party; it makes a decisive change of government at the next election much more likely. This is potentially catastrophic for the country.' Many in Number 10 laughed at Norman's pompous clarification at the end of his letter that 'this is not a leadership bid' (no one but Norman thought such a thing viable), but more than a few recognised the accuracy of many of his criticisms.

After Brady issued his press release at 8.15 a.m., John Penrose resigned as the prime minister's anti-corruption tsar, saying Johnson had broken the ministerial code – 'a clear resigning matter' – and declaring it 'the beginning of the end' for the PM. 'I think it's over. It feels like it's when not if.' Only now did Jeremy Hunt try to publicly encourage things along, tweeting at 10.50 a.m., 'Conservative MPs know in our hearts we are not giving the British people the leadership they deserve.' It was time, he said to 'change or lose'. A furious Nadine Dorries publicly accused Hunt of 'duplicity' and of 'being wrong about almost everything'. She regretted including the 'almost'.

In Downing Street, Johnson's team printed off a letter for each of the 358 Conservative MPs, each of them topped and tailed by hand (not by Johnson), and stuffed them into envelopes. They were taken to the Commons where Chris Pincher oversaw operations, shoving them in MPs' pigeonholes along with a briefing note, written by Ross Kempsell, which laid out Johnson's track record as a vote winner. Pincher controlled a huge network of whips and other Johnson loyalists, who were dispatched to speak to MPs with whom they had close links, these networks all recorded on Shapps' spreadsheet. Johnson made follow-up calls to the waverers. There was no coordinated plot to oust him, something which might have finished him that day. Equally clear, however, MPs who felt little affinity for the PM and only installed him because he was a winner were pulling their support in droves.

At 5 p.m., an hour before voting began, Johnson addressed the 1922 Committee, fighting for his job. Adopting his usual posture of optimism, he said, 'I have won before and I can win again', and warned that removing him would lead to 'some hellish *Groundhog Day* debate' about returning to the single market.[3] He concluded, 'The prize tonight is enormous. We can get on with taking this country forward. We are only halfway. The best is yet to come.'

His pitch seemed to have had the desired effect when Charles Walker spoke. No fan of Johnson, Walker told him, 'There are times when you have driven me wild.' This being the Tory Party, where you can take the boy out of the public school but not the puerile sense of humour out of the man, this was greeted with a suggestive 'Ooooh', as if they were in a scene from *Carry On Up the Commons*. Then Walker got serious: 'Defenestrating a sitting prime minister is a bloody shocking, horrible, terrible thing and we have to ask ourselves tonight: "Can we live with it?"' Johnson's team began to think things would be okay. Veteran right-winger John Hayes, who backed Gove for leader in 2019, warned that MPs should not overturn the general election result. 'I certainly wasn't in the vanguard who supported you,' he told Johnson, 'but the party made its choice and so did the public. If 180 MPs trump the electorate, I would regard that as indefensible.' However, when quizzed about partygate, Johnson needlessly gave ammunition to his critics. Arguing that he was right to attend drinks events to praise staff for their efforts, he said, 'I'd do it again.'

Three hours later the prime minister received a text message from Sir Graham Brady, chairman of the 1922 Committee: 211 MPs had stuck with him, 148 were opposed. As a percentage of the parliamentary party, Johnson had done worse than Thatcher, May or Major, none of whom survived for long. Before the vote, Shapps had sealed his prediction in an envelope: 149, one vote out. 'It is done,' Johnson said, upon learning his fate. No sooner were the words out of his mouth than the only conversation in SW1 was whether, in fact, he was 'done'. Yet Johnson remained confident, knowing he could not be challenged again for twelve months. His trickiest internal rival, Sunak, appeared to have been neutralised. In a speech to the Onward think tank, the day after the vote, the chancellor joked that he could now speak more freely. 'Until recently, anything I did or said was framed by others as some tilt at the leadership ... not so much a problem any more!'

Eschewing the idea of a reshuffle to make peace with the parliamentary party, the prime minister sought to convince MPs he would be pursuing a more conservative agenda. Number 10 inflated divisive issues such as Rwanda, Brexit and looming national rail strikes to force politicians and voters to take sides.

Johnson also survived a two-week grilling at PMQs from Starmer. Two days after the confidence vote, the Labour leader was accused by a shadow cabinet member of 'boring voters to death' by missing the open goal. A week later, Starmer overcompensated with a scattergun assault in which he compared Johnson, variously, to *Star Wars* villain Jabba the Hutt, a contestant on *Love Island* and an ostrich.

At a meeting of Conservative special advisers on Friday 24 June, Isaac Levido presented polling showing that Starmer was failing to hit home with voters. Labour had led nationally since the previous December, but a poll for the *Observer* even after the confidence vote showed Johnson leading Starmer on the issue of who would be the best prime minister. Despite this, there was a fragility about Johnson's position. His political aide David Canzini sat in the London Grind coffee shop overlooking London Bridge that week and said, 'There can't be any more fuck-ups.'

Johnson weathered the squall caused by Christopher Geidt's resignation on 15 June, but then found himself at the centre of fresh controversy when, on the 17th, *The Times* wrote a story about a plan Johnson had to appoint Carrie as his chief of staff while he was foreign secretary and in a secret relationship with her, an idea his aides had to block. The story had clearly been briefed by the Vote Leave crew. Carrie reacted with fury and Johnson told aides, 'This makes me look like a twat and it makes me look corrupt.' Guto Harri, once the director of communications for News UK, was prevailed upon to lobby his old company to take the story down. In a classic example of the Streisand effect,[4] removal from *The Times'* website brought far more attention to the claims than they would otherwise have had. 'He was obsessed with this because Carrie was,' an aide said. 'He should have been thinking about Pincher.' Harri concluded later that he would have been better off using up his banks of goodwill when Johnson was really in trouble.

Johnson was still in Rwanda, attending the Commonwealth heads of government meeting, when the Tories suffered a double by-election loss on 23 June. Labour won back the red wall seat of Wakefield, a vote forced by the imprisonment for child sex abuse of the MP Imran Ahmad Khan, while Liberal Democrats overturned a Tory majority of 24,000 in Tiverton and Honiton, the seat vacated by the tractor porn peruser Neil Parish. That result was the biggest by-election reversal in British political history.

The same day Johnson had just finished a pre-dawn swim at his hotel in Kigali, when party chairman Oliver Dowden called to say he was quitting. 'Don't be ridiculous,' the PM said, his rat brain already calculating whether this was a plot to unseat him.

'I'm serious,' said Dowden. 'I've got to do the right thing.'

'If you were doing the right thing, you would stay on in your job and defend me,' Johnson said, first thoughts for his own survival.[5] Dowden told friends later that the PM 'got more and more aggressive'.

When Dowden said, 'It was entirely my own decision', Johnson laughed. With Dowden off the line, Johnson said, 'You could hear the gun being held to his head by Dougie.' He then contacted Chris Heaton-Harris, the chief whip, and with Harri began a series of calls to check whether Dowden's resignation was the first of a full-blown cabinet coup. Johnson rang Sunak, who said it was the first he had heard of the resignation. Johnson seemed to have woken the chancellor and was not sure whether to believe him.

Dowden texted to reinforce the point: 'If I had wanted to bring you down, I would have resigned over the confidence vote.' Then: 'There is no plot, Prime Minister: Rishi doesn't know that I am resigning.'[6] Johnson's aides assumed he was protesting too much. In an uncharacteristically blunt resignation letter, Dowden said, 'We cannot carry on with business as usual. Somebody must take responsibility and I have concluded that, in these circumstances, it would not be right for me to remain in office.' Pointedly, he said he remained loyal to the Conservative Party, rather than to Johnson himself. Friends believed Dowden had not voted for the prime minister in the no-confidence vote two and a half weeks earlier, a proposition he never denied. 'Even loyalists have their limits,' one said.

After being reassured that Sunak was not quitting as well, the prime minister hit the phones to Dominic Raab, Priti Patel and Steve Barclay, all of whom were loyal. Sajid Javid was hosting a health round table and had his phone on silent, so missed an increasingly frantic set of calls from the chief whip. When he eventually rang back, Johnson asked, 'Can I cross you off the suicide watch list?'

While the Wakefield loss looked like a classic mid-term defeat for an unpopular government, the defeat in Tiverton and Honiton showed that Johnson's central appeal from 2019 had gone. 'This is one of the great Brexity parts of the country and Brexit has now evaporated as an electoral argument and as the defining theme of the party,' a senior Tory said. Thanks to partygate, the Conservative candidate, Helen Hurford, felt compelled to avoid media appearances, only turning up for one hustings, at Tiverton High School, after the organisers threatened to 'empty-chair' her with a scarecrow.

Johnson tried to keep perspective, comparing his difficulties with those of his friend Volodymyr Zelensky. 'What are Zelensky's problems at the moment and what are mine?' he asked one aide. He also visited

Rwanda's genocide museum and heard from one African leader at the summit that he was wrestling with the prospect of 4.5 million people facing starvation. 'To say a man called Oliver Dowden doesn't want to be party chairman any more doesn't really touch the sides,' the aide said.

Then and later, Dowden, Sunak and their aides were adamant they were not in cahoots. On the day, Dowden told only his wife that he was going to resign, but Johnson's team smelled a rat. Dowden's primary motivation was 'just to get out' he told friends, but he was undoubtedly keen to see Johnson toppled, and stung by the decision to make him chairman, a job he 'hated'. When the vote of no confidence was held, the party chairman was only told, by the chief whip Chris Heaton-Harris, ten minutes before the news broke, nearly twenty-four hours after Johnson's inner circle found out. He thought: *What's the bloody point? If I'm not trusted, I'm not going to go out there and say, 'Everything's fine and dandy' and get a load more shit chucked over me. I don't want to be the Comical Ali at the end of the regime.* His resignation was also premeditated. On election day Dowden asked both of his special advisers to be present because he knew they would be at the heart of a media storm when he quit. He told them over a pub lunch, 'If this goes wrong, I'm planning to resign.'

The party chairman was one of Sunak's closest friends in politics. Two years earlier Dowden had taken Sunak aside and declared, 'You should be prime minister one day and, when the time comes, I'm going to help you.'

One of Johnson's shrewdest aides reflected, 'I think Rishi became a receptacle for a lot of other people's ill will [towards Johnson].' To the twin bogeymen of Dominic Cummings and Dougie Smith could now be added Dowden, who had been a close collaborator with Smith since his days working in Cameron's Number 10 and then on public appointments in the arts when he was culture secretary. 'Dougie and Oliver Dowden were credited with getting Sunak elected in Richmond,' the Johnson ally said. 'If you become a Tory MP, you remember who you think pulled the strings to get you selected.

At the end of the summit in Kigali, Johnson gave an interview to the *Today* programme in which he said he would win the next election and claimed, with an ebullience which seemed wholly divorced from reality, that he was 'thinking actively about the third term' in power. For his MPs, though, the most telling moment was also Johnson's most honest.

Defending his record, he said, 'If you're saying you want me to undergo some sort of psychological transformation, I think that our listeners would know that is not going to happen.'

Back at home, Harri and Steve Barclay questioned why Johnson had allowed Dougie Smith to keep his Number 10 pass after Munira Mirza's resignation. 'Neither of us have ever met this guy,' Harri said. 'Why does he have a pass?' Johnson initially urged them to 'just let it be'. Harri quietly got Sam Jones to find out how often Smith had been in the building. Security records showed Dougie had used his pass twice in the previous month. Ben Gascoigne and Alister Jack also urged him to cut Smith loose. Johnson eventually agreed. 'Just revoke his pass,' Harri told Jones.

Two hours later, the prime minister changed his mind: 'Let's not antagonise him.' Some assume Smith issued further threats. In fact, he didn't need to. 'Dougie, early on in the Boris premiership, made Carrie his friend,' a cabinet minister explained. 'He exchanged a lot of messages with Carrie. Carrie probably said too many indiscreet things about other people, because she didn't realise who she was dealing with. But Dougie then had a lot of Carrie text messages that she was worried he might use if Boris sacked him. I know she was very nervous about her comms trail with Dougie.' It was a decision Johnson's team would come to regret. 'It was an error,' a close aide said, 'because Dougie was clearly always working as an agent of Rishi.'

That week the whips got wind of a lunch held at Ma La Sichuan, a Chinese restaurant near the Home Office, by three prominent allies of Theresa May, at least one of whom was now quietly whipping for Sunak. They were overheard by a Labour MP discussing Johnson's future. When a minister left, he said loudly, 'Viva la revolución!'

Within three weeks of the confidence vote, rebels said upwards of thirty letters of no-confidence had been re-submitted to Brady. The chairman of the '22 was facing calls to change the rules so Johnson could be challenged within twelve months, just as he had been in the dog days of Theresa May's premiership. Elections to the 1922 executive were seen as an opportunity to back a slate of MPs who would seek to oust Johnson.

The PM convinced himself that his critics were divorced from the everyday concerns of voters. 'If you look at the by-elections, people were absolutely fed up hearing about things that I'd stuffed up,' he said. 'What they wanted to hear was: What is this guy doing?' To answer that question and bind Sunak to Johnson, Harri and others began to brief that the prime minister and chancellor would soon be giving a joint speech on the economy, outlining a new plan for growth. But even ministers were tiring of the endless relaunches. 'The bond of trust is broken between the PM and the party and the PM and the voters,' one said. 'He got Brexit done, he handled Covid fine and got the vaccine programme and he's done well on Ukraine but people think he's a liar and a shady bugger and that's binary, it's black and white.'

That was the state of affairs in the final week of June – a party which had lost two seats and a party chairman, MPs and donors who had lost faith in their prime minister, and a leader who would not and could not change – when Chris Pincher, the deputy chief whip went drinking in the Carlton Club, the cathedral of conservatism on St James's Street.

The club was busy that night. In an area under the stairs known as 'cad's corner', Pincher, fifty-two, was drinking champagne with several other men. Neatly bearded and well-dressed, he was a dapper figure with a plausible manner and a relentless work ethic which made him a natural and able whip. He was also a man with demons. He lived alone and drank too much. 'The problem was he didn't have a lot else going on in his life – he'd not got a partner,' a fellow member of the Big Dog group said. 'He had an understanding of the history of the party. He was across everything. But he also had a drink problem.' Increasingly inebriated, Pincher allegedly groped two men, grabbing one of them by the left buttock and groin. Later, in the Macmillan bar, witnesses described him propositioning others, including younger advisers and researchers. One of them reported Pincher to Sarah Dines, a fellow whip, who then, crassly, asked the man if he too was gay. 'What's that got to do with it?' he replied. 'But, yes I am.'

Dines said, 'Well, that doesn't make it straightforward.' She later said she had been trying to ascertain whether there had been a prior relationship between Pincher and the man. Dines reported the incident to Chris Heaton-Harris. At 1 a.m. Mark Fletcher, the MP for Bolsover, told Pincher to leave the club and helped forcibly remove him.

Within minutes Heaton-Harris was alerted and the next morning he spoke to at least two MPs who witnessed Pincher's behaviour. Pincher was summoned to explain himself. He admitted he had crossed a line, but no formal complaint had been received. No action was taken against him until the *Sun* got in touch that afternoon. Noa Hoffman, an enterprising young Australian journalist, had been a member of the paper's lobby team for just three days when she got the scoop which would help to unseat a prime minister. Pincher quit that evening, admitting in his resignation letter: 'Last night I drank far too much. I've embarrassed myself and other people.' He apologised to 'those concerned'.

Several of Johnson's aides told the prime minister he would have to suspend the whip from Pincher, pending a proper investigation, despite concerns about another by-election (Pincher's majority in Tamworth was lower than in Tiverton and Honiton). Declan Lyons, having learned from his mistakes during the Paterson affair, told the chief whip, 'We must remove the whip now.' He recalled William Gladstone's dictum that 'the first essential for a prime minister is to be a good butcher'. Heaton-Harris, however, along with his flatmate Nigel Adams, was friends with Pincher. 'A lot of people were compromised,' a political colleague said. Heaton-Harris failed to take action.

Downing Street said Johnson 'regards the matter as closed' after Pincher's resignation. 'Boris is actually quite sentimental and kind,' a senior cabinet minister observed. 'He doesn't delight in cruelty ... he knew that Pinch was absolutely uber loyalist for him.' Harri felt sorry for Pincher and briefed the papers he had 'done the right thing'. On Friday morning, concerned about Pincher's state of mind, the communications director compared him to Dr David Kelly, the chemical weapons expert who killed himself in 2003 after finding himself in the eye of a media storm over weapons of mass destruction, warning the press team that if they briefed against Pincher they might end up with blood on their hands. Somehow a government, already under the cosh for its response to a string of ethics crises, had now positioned itself on the side of a potential sex pest. One man's demons were fast becoming the whole government's crisis.

That morning Simon Hart, the Welsh secretary and an instinctive loyalist, hinted on his broadcast round that he wanted to see Pincher stripped of the whip. A few hours later, at the briefing for lobby journalists in the media suite in Number 9, the prime minister's official spokesman, Max Blain, said Johnson was not aware of any previous allegations against Pincher, a bald untruth. Realising his error, he retreated to any 'specific' allegation. But even this line, given to him by Harri, had not been checked with Johnson. Asked about Pincher's appointment in February, Blain said, 'In the absence of any formal complaint it was not appropriate to stop the appointment on the basis of unsubstantiated claims.'

Lynton Crosby, Steve Barclay, Ben Gascoigne and Declan Lyons all told Johnson he would have to act. Female MPs and ex-ministers were lining up to condemn Downing Street. Later that afternoon, one of Pincher's alleged 'victims' complained through Parliament's Independent Complaints and Grievance Scheme. Only then did Johnson agree to remove the whip. Not only had he waited twenty-four hours too long, ministers had again been asked to go out to defend the indefensible only for the inevitable U-turn to follow.

Pincher's attempts to find male company had already caused one break in his career, in 2017, seven years after he entered Parliament, when Alex Story – a former Olympic rower cum Tory candidate – described him as a 'pound shop Harvey Weinstein' after Pincher made unwanted advances while wearing a bathrobe. Pincher resigned and was eventually cleared by a Conservative Party investigation, returning to the front bench in 2018 when Theresa May made him deputy chief whip. It was a post he returned to in February 2022 under Johnson.

On that occasion both Heaton-Harris and Nigel Adams pressed Pincher's case. However, his appointment was delayed after Steve Barclay, the new chief of staff, raised concerns about rumours surrounding Pincher's conduct which had been brought to his attention. An MP who claimed to have been subjected to an unwanted advance also contacted Heaton-Harris to warn him. Pincher's case was referred to the propriety and ethics team, but after several hours they said there were no grounds for withholding the appointment. Just as at the start of the partygate saga, a red flag had been raised and no one in Downing Street, least of all the prime minister, made any real effort to ascertain the full facts before making a decision. In truth, Johnson's team felt he needed an operator like Pincher and were prepared to turn a blind eye to allegations which had not been substantiated.

After Pincher was stripped of the whip, it was open season in the Sunday papers. The *Sunday Times* quoted the man assaulted by Pincher at the Carlton Club: 'I had my drink in my hand and then he then went down and grabbed my arse and then slowly … moved his hand down the front of my groin. I froze … it ended after about two or three seconds.'

More importantly, the paper revealed several other incidents where claims of sexual misconduct had been made against Pincher. In 2017, a few weeks after Alex Story went public, Pincher sat next to a junior back-bench MP, before placing his hand firmly on the man's inner leg. The MP – who was married with children – considered it an unwanted physical pass. He removed Pincher's hand. The following day the MP asked to see his whip in Westminster Hall. He did not make a formal complaint but raised concerns about Pincher's mental health and urged the whips' office to keep an eye on his behaviour when drinking. The whip confirmed that the conversation took place. Pincher, through his lawyers, denied acting inappropriately.

The revelation was significant for two reasons. This was the incident Barclay had been told about during the February reshuffle. Second, the newspaper had been trying to print the story for several months but had been prevented for legal reasons. Only when Pincher was publicly exposed did the paper's lawyers relent. However, *Sunday Times* journalists had been in frequent contact with Downing Street about the allegations. Claims that Number 10 knew nothing of previous Pincher problems were nonsense.

The paper also detailed another incident in 2018 in which Pincher was alleged to have behaved inappropriately towards a second young Conservative MP, messaging the MP asking him to come up to his parliamentary office. Subjected to an unwanted physical advance, the MP believed Pincher had been drinking heavily, told him to 'sod off' and left the room. He too chose not to make a formal complaint. However, it was this MP who, upon hearing that Pincher might be made chief whip, had messaged both Heaton-Harris and a Number 10 official to warn against appointing him during the February reshuffle. The government confirmed these exchanges but pointed out that no formal complaint had been made. Pincher denied the allegation and said he did not know who the MP was. Afterwards, Johnson allies revealed that Heaton-Harris spoke to Pincher on the day of the reshuffle but that the MP was only keen to stop him becoming chief whip (something which was 'never' on the cards), rather than preventing him taking a job as deputy.

Despite both Number 10 and Heaton-Harris being alerted, Downing Street maintained that weekend that Johnson was not informed of the MP's allegation until after the reshuffle, and had only ever heard unsubstantiated rumours about Pincher. This caused Dominic Cummings to break his recent silence. That Saturday he wrote on Twitter, 'If [Johnson] didn't know about Pincher as he's claiming, why did he repeatedly refer to him laughingly in No10 as "Pincher by name Pincher by nature" long before appointing him …?' This line of attack was reinforced by a story in the *Mail on Sunday*, which reported that Johnson said of Pincher in 2020, 'He's handsy, that's a problem.'

Thérèse Coffey, the work and pensions secretary, was given the hospital pass of representing the government on the political shows that Sunday. Quizzed about what Johnson had known and when he had known it, she claimed ignorance – wholly honestly since no one in Number 10 seemed able to answer the question themselves. 'I have not spoken to the prime minister,' she told the BBC, saying her information came from 'someone in the Number 10 press office'. Johnson had been abroad at the G7 and Nato summits, away again as his premiership shook.

With the stench of death hanging over him, Johnson had two salutary conversations. The first was with Benjamin Netanyahu, the Israeli prime minister, who had suffered his own share of political near-death experiences. 'I'm in the departure lounge,' Johnson confided.

'Oh no, Boris,' Netanyahu insisted. 'This is just the start of one big glorious comeback. You've got to knock out that spectacular book and then you'll be back, my friend, before Hanukkah.' One aide who heard the call thought: *I didn't think Jews believed in the Resurrection.*

The second was with Simon Case. A reflective Johnson finally admitted what Eddie Lister had encouraged him to see when he took over in Number 10. 'I got it all wrong with the civil service,' he said, his voice almost a whisper. 'I didn't understand that, in the end, the only people I could trust were my civil servants.' Case, a historian of Whitehall, knew that both Harold Wilson and Edward Heath had drawn similar conclusions in their final hours.

Sajid Javid's faith in Johnson had crumbled slowly like coastal erosion. The morning of the no-confidence vote, the health secretary had been due on the broadcast round. Before going on air, he consulted his wife and special advisers about whether he could honestly say he still had confidence in the prime minister. He decided to give Johnson one more chance.[7] After 148 MPs voted against him, Javid saw the PM after cabinet and told him, 'If things don't change now, it's over.'

'It was a convincing win, Saj.'

'That's not true. It was a really shit result,' Javid said. He delivered an ultimatum: 'PM, this is your last chance. You've got to put all this chaos behind you and show people things can change.'

Johnson, still irritated, said, 'Saj, I get it.'[8]

Instead, that June weekend, Javid opened his *Sunday Times* to see a briefing from Downing Street about a presentation he had given to cabinet on the NHS, in which he 'struggled to answer questions from his colleagues'. In the meeting, Johnson urged Javid to outline his plans for NHS reform: 'I know we've given you the biggest hospital pass of all time, Saj. You're in charge of a third of government spending, equivalent to the GDP of Greece. But we can't fix this by water-cannoning money at it. What do you want to do? What's the reform? You hum it, we'll sing it. Haul it up the flagpole, we'll salute it. Hand us the nettle, we'll grasp it!'

Javid resorted to pre-scripted lines ('We're running a Blockbuster NHS in an age of Netflix') which prompted Kwasi Kwarteng to intervene: 'None of us know, Saj, what the reform plan is.' The newspaper quoted a senior Number 10 aide saying Javid's performance was 'an audition for sacking'. The furious health secretary confronted Guto Harri, who he blamed for the drive-by shooting.

Johnson and Javid had already clashed ahead of a decision to end free universal Covid testing on 1 April, which was costing an astronomical £2 billion a month. Javid had argued for thirty million people to keep free tests. 'You're asking me to disarm when the enemy is still lurking out there,' he complained. Johnson snapped back, 'I'm epileptically bored with Covid. What people are getting now is not killing them. It's a matter of stupendous irrelevance as long as we have a good set of eyes in the crow's nest, so we don't miss another iceberg.'[9]

As the disastrous Number 10 response to Pinchergate unfolded, Javid asked himself again whether the time had come to withdraw his support. On Sunday evening he invited two of his special advisers to his home in west London and consulted party grandees. Each thought 'the time is coming' when he should walk, but that he should sit tight for now and see if the prime minister made it to the safe harbour of the summer recess.[10] Yet again a senior colleague of Johnson's succumbed to the intoxicating delirium of hope over cold, hard experience.

* * *

The events which would finally shake Javid from his indecision began that same Sunday. Simon McDonald, the former permanent secretary at the Foreign Office, watched Thérèse Coffey's interview and wondered about what to do. When Boris Johnson had been foreign secretary and Pincher was Europe minister, there had been another complaint about his inappropriate behaviour. 'Details of the key meeting are seared in my memory,' he recalled. 'A group of colleagues came to see me to complain about his behaviour. Immediately afterwards, I consulted the Cabinet Office and opened a formal investigation. The complaint of inappropriate behaviour was confirmed. I went to see Mr Pincher to explain the consequences. He agreed to apologise to those affected and undertook not to repeat the behaviour. He claimed to be mortified that anyone could misinterpret his actions so horribly, and that nothing like this had ever happened before. It was the most awkward meeting I had as permanent under-secretary.' What is more, McDonald knew Johnson had been told about it. That Sunday, 'I contacted people to try to get Number 10 comms to correct its line-to-take,' he said.[11] The person he contacted was Philip Barton, the permanent secretary at the Foreign Office. He in turn 'got his office or his press office to talk to Max Blain [Johnson's official spokesman] and team on the Monday morning to say, "Be very careful."'

The message seems to have reached senior levels because, that evening, the propriety and ethics team went back through their files. They found a formal note about the investigation, but not that Johnson had been informed of it. 'There was no record anywhere in Number 10 of Boris being warned, no paperwork,' an aide recalled. Had someone gripped the issue, it is possible that Johnson might yet have survived. But no one did. Most importantly, no one seemed to have told the briefing team, a group of junior officials whose job was to prepare government spokesmen before media interviews. Will Quince, the children's minister, had been entrusted with the morning broadcast round on Monday 4 July. He was sent out armed only with the lines prepared on Friday which had also been given to Coffey – with suboptimal results – dismissing what was now hard fact as 'speculation' and 'rumour'. Quince told the BBC he had been given a 'categorical assurance' by Number 10 'that the prime minister was not aware of any specific allegation or complaint made against the former deputy chief whip Chris Pincher'. This was not only untrue – thanks to McDonald, Number 10 had been warned that it was untrue. When he found out that he had been asked to peddle rubbish, Quince went ballistic. 'It was another totally unforced error,' a senior civil servant said.

Mid-morning on Monday, Simon Case spoke to Barton and asked what McDonald had told him. The cabinet secretary informed the PM's office that the media line would have to change. At 11.30 a.m., in the morning lobby briefing, Max Blain sought to redress the damage, telling journalists, 'The prime minister was aware of media reports that others had seen over the years and some allegations that were either resolved or did not progress to a formal complaint, but at the time of the appointment of the deputy chief whip he was not aware of any specific allegations.' Responding to the claims in the *Sunday Times* that red flags had been raised during the February reshuffle, the official spokesman added, 'He did take advice on some of the allegations that had been made, but there was no formal complaint at that time and it was deemed not appropriate to stop an appointment simply because of unsubstantiated allegations.' Johnson was hiding behind the fact that those accusing Pincher had not registered a formal complaint. As McDonald knew, even that was not the full truth.

That Monday, McDonald was contacted by a BBC journalist. He returned her call at 6 p.m., saying he would not volunteer information but would confirm details she was able to put to him. 'On the train afterwards, I read with disbelief Number 10's latest version of what the PM had known and when,' he said.[12] McDonald spoke to his wife about writing a newspaper article laying out what he knew. He agonised about whether to go public. McDonald knew how his intervention would be depicted. He knew Johnson despised him, saw him as the embodiment of a Remoaner establishment who had never come to terms with Brexit, who disapproved of the prime minister's personal conduct.

Johnson thought this because, in part, it was true. McDonald was so horrified by the effect of Brexit on his staff in the Foreign Office that he announced to them that he had voted Remain, in the hope that this would make them see they were not alone. He had only been permanent secretary for a year when Johnson became foreign secretary. To say they had not got on is to stretch the limits of the word 'understatement'. When Johnson became PM, he merged the Foreign Office with the Department for International Development and informed McDonald that he would be taking early retirement. Things were bound to get ugly. If he handed the information to one paper, it would be easier for the others to brand him a bitter partisan. He decided it would be better just to release it on Twitter, Westminster's noticeboard of choice. Olivia McDonald thought her husband was playing with fire. 'Be careful what you wish for,' she warned. Johnson was teetering, her husband might help bring him down. McDonald texted the BBC journalist to say she should keep her eye on his Twitter account.

At 7.30 a.m. on Tuesday, McDonald tweeted a letter he had written to Kathryn Stone, the parliamentary standards commissioner, stating that Number 10 was 'still not telling the truth' about Pincher. He gave details of the investigation and then delivered the killer blow, revealing that Johnson 'was briefed in person about the investigation and outcome of the investigation'. McDonald claimed this constituted a formal complaint. 'The original Number 10 line is not true and the modification is still not accurate,' he wrote. The iceberg had pierced the hull of RMS Johnson.

McDonald's phone exploded with calls and texts. He agreed to speak on the *Today* programme at 8.20 a.m. Before he went on air, he listened to Dominic Raab being grilled. The deputy prime minister was confronted by McDonald's tweet. 'That's news to me,' he said. When McDonald spoke to *Today*'s Justin Webb, he was pressed on Johnson's knowledge of the affair. 'I know that the senior official briefed the prime minister in person because that official told me so at the time,' he said.

Johnson had spent the morning at a prayer breakfast in Westminster. When he got back to Number 10, the inner circle went into a crisis meeting. It was quickly established that the official who had spoken to the PM about Pincher in 2019 was Helen MacNamara. Blain and Guto Harri asked Johnson whether he remembered being told by MacNamara about the Pincher incident at the Foreign Office. Johnson said, 'I don't remember.' Those present said his confusion seemed genuine, not an attempt to dodge accountability. The prime minister's aides were furious the meeting was not properly minuted.

Michael Ellis was again sent to the Commons to answer an urgent question, the political equivalent of defending a Northampton burglar caught red-handed with the family silver in his swag bag. The prime minister 'did not immediately recall' MacNamara's briefing, he said. Max Blain had barely opened his mouth at the 11.30 a.m. lobby briefing when Jason Groves, political editor of the *Daily Mail*, spoke for the hacks: 'Are you planning on telling us the truth today?' Confirming the 'brief conversation', Blain said, 'The prime minister was informed but not asked to take any action. The minister carried on serving in that department for a number of months.' Number 10 persisted with the claim that it was not a formal investigation, but they had surrendered the right to be heard.

Downing Street was now a bunker, with political aides and officials waiting for the next blow, some of them quietly briefing the press about which of their colleagues was to blame for the disaster. 'It was every man for himself,' one said. 'A hideous atmosphere.'

Sajid Javid had also been at the prayer breakfast in Westminster Hall, where he watched Boris Johnson intently as Rev Les Isaac delivered a sermon about the need for politicians to rise above self-interest 'for the common good'. Javid said, 'I started to think, "I have to go now."' The McDonald revelations and cabinet that morning confirmed his decision.

For reasons that defy understanding, cameras were allowed to film the start of cabinet that day. Ministers stared blankly into the middle distance like a row of Easter Island statues, others contemplating the grain in the table, which now seemed aptly coffin-shaped. When the cameras had gone, Johnson announced plans for a series of economic press conferences to set out the government's approach to the public finances and explain what they were doing to help with the cost of living.

For several weeks Downing Street had been briefing that Johnson and Sunak would do a speech together to outline the government's growth plan under the strapline 'Rebuilding a strong economy'. The problem was, as one aide put it, 'The idea to have a speech pre-dated any idea about what to put into it.' The cabinet meeting was the final straw in proving it was not possible to get the two men on the same page. Johnson launched into a 'boosterish' speech about 'how everything's going to be brilliant'. Sunak and Gove both said the government would need to be honest with the public that soaring inflation would mean the next year or two would be painful. 'Boris's response was to say something like, "Yeah, yeah, we'll do all that as well",' a cabinet source said. 'But it was perfectly obvious he was not prepared to make difficult choices.'

Unknown to the rest of the cabinet, Johnson and Sunak had shared dinner the previous Sunday evening, remaining at loggerheads over when the government could afford to cut tax. Number 10 wanted a speech or joint press conference to announce a new growth strategy;

Number 11 did not see how they could agree what to announce. From Sunak's point of view, Johnson would not face up to the fact that the government could not just borrow to fund unlimited spending. To Johnson, a man he had come to believe was plotting against him was truculently blocking everything he suggested.

Over dinner they briefly discussed the Pincher affair. 'This is not tenable,' Sunak said, criticising the response from Number 10. 'You need to deal with it fast.' He made clear he would not go out and defend Downing Street disinformation. Johnson's aides said the chancellor made no constructive suggestions about how to handle the crisis.

After the dinner, Sunak began to conclude he could not remain in Johnson's cabinet, so incompatible were their views. That night he called Oliver Dowden and said, 'I'm thinking of resigning', but decided to sleep on it.[13] A close aide recalled, 'The thing that was genuinely the straw that broke the camel's back was the economy speech Boris wanted to give.' The aide said, 'We said, "No, this is a disaster. If you do it, it will blow everything up." Boris wanted to cancel the corporation tax rise. It was unserious.'

It was not just the economy, though. Sunak had developed a highly moralistic distaste for Johnson's personal behaviour and sophistry. 'Rishi couldn't stand him by the end and went around telling everyone that he was the worst human being he had ever met,' a fellow minister said. Some think this was a function of the fact that Sunak was a devout and practising Hindu, a faith which encouraged hard work and devotion to duty, neither of which Sunak detected in Johnson.

The chancellor also found the Johnson psychodrama distracting from the serious business of government. Another close aide said, 'From Rishi's perspective, he'd spent many interviews, when he should've been talking about positive stuff that we were doing as a government, talking about bloody partygate.' On Monday evening, Sunak sat down with Liam Booth-Smith, his closest aide, and concluded he would probably have to go. He called Dowden to tell him. The claim from the Johnson camp that this was a premeditated plot does not stack up. Cass Horowitz was away at a wedding and Nissy Chesterfield had flown to Corfu, unimaginable if this was the culmination of a secret plan drawn up in advance. She was already by the pool at 8.30 a.m. the next day when Sunak called to say, 'I think I need to resign.' It was clear from his voice he meant it. Either way, the comms director said they would have to cancel a series of events the following day to highlight the rise in National Insurance thresholds, which had been planned for six weeks. 'There will be nothing apart from questions about Pincher,' she said.

Sunak asked to see Gove in his office after cabinet that Tuesday. He said he was very concerned by McDonald's letter and revealed something of his economic disagreements with Johnson. 'What do you think?' he asked.

'It's very, very difficult,' said Gove. He had thought Number 10's response to Pincher terrible, but it was only when McDonald surfaced that he thought it terminal too.

That afternoon, Sunak again consulted his aides and decided he had had enough. They would make the announcement around 6 p.m. to minimise the amount of time the papers would have to do more than just report events. Then Chesterfield heard from a journalist that Johnson was expected to do a clip for the six o'clock news apologising for his handling of the Pincher affair. It would look far more aggressive to trump that with a resignation announcement. Sunak would have to delay.

Meanwhile, around 3 p.m., Javid called Gove. 'Let's cut to the chase, Michael,' the health secretary said. 'I'm thinking of resigning. Why don't we both go?'

Gove felt conflicted. He did not want to bring down a second prime minister. He did not want to end Johnson's ascendancy for a second time. 'Given everything that's happened in the past, I don't think I can, Saj,' he replied. 'But if I change my mind, I will let you know.' Gove did not get the impression Sunak and Javid had talked. He then went to the Royal Opera House and turned his phone off. Perhaps appropriately, he was there to watch a double bill of *Cavalleria Rusticana* (about a Sicilian blood feud) and *Pagliacci* (which dramatises the downfall of a clown).

Both the Sunak and Javid camps were and remained adamant there was no coordination between them. Javid had texted Sunak after the prayer breakfast but the two did not get around to speaking. A Sunak confidant said, 'We genuinely did not know about Saj. There was no contact between us and them.' Johnson's team did not believe a word of it. 'Bollocks!' a cabinet loyalist said. 'Rishi was Saj's chief secretary when he was chancellor. They went to the premiere of the *Star Wars* film together. Rishi did not want to be wielding the dagger. It was perfect for him.'

* * *

Chris Mason, who had replaced Laura Kuenssberg as the BBC's political editor, was summoned to Johnson's Commons office to do the interview for the six o'clock news. While the cameras were setting up in the grand office on the upper ministerial corridor, the prime minister sat in Sunak's room next door practising his lines. As he was doing so, Javid was signing his resignation letter and the chancellor was writing his. Johnson had to do the clip knowing there was no way it would lead the news for long. The health secretary had just got in touch, saying he wanted an urgent private meeting with the prime minister. Johnson and Javid met soon afterwards and spoke for an hour but the PM was unable to change his mind.

As Big Ben struck the hour, the news began with Johnson's admission that he should never have made Pincher deputy chief whip and that it was a 'bad mistake' not to have acted on the warnings. Two minutes into the bulletin, Javid tweeted his resignation letter. Johnson's pre-recorded interview was still running when the BBC's onscreen headline switched to 'BREAKING ... Sajid Javid resigns'. In his letter, Javid said voters 'expect integrity from their government' and that it would be 'competent in acting in the national interest', but added, 'the public are concluding that we are now neither'. Javid said that, since the no-confidence vote, Johnson had failed to provide 'humility, grip and new direction' and that it was 'clear to me that this situation will not change under your leadership – and you have therefore lost my confidence too'. He praised Johnson's contribution in 'seeing off' Jeremy Corbyn and 'breaking the deadlock on Brexit'. But he concluded, 'the party is bigger than any one individual' and that he had to 'serve the country first'.

Johnson was sad about Javid's departure but grateful for the prior warning. He wrote a generous response. It was the lead item on the news for precisely nine minutes.

In 11 Downing Street the sight of Javid resigning led to rapid recalculations. Sunak could wait or pounce. 'We decided we needed to get it out there,' one said. Sunak's team claimed the chancellor tried to make a WhatsApp call to Johnson to alert him. Johnson's aides insisted the second resignation was dropped on them cold. Sunak's aides hastily printed off his resignation letter and delivered it next door. At 6.11 p.m. he tweeted it to the world.

In the letter, Sunak wrote, 'The public rightly expect government to be conducted properly, competently and seriously. I recognise this may be my last ministerial job, but I believe these standards are worth fighting for and that is why I am resigning.' Sunak said he 'respected' Johnson's 'powerful mandate' from the 2019 election and had 'always tried to compromise in order to deliver the things you want to achieve. On those occasions where I disagreed with you privately, I have supported you publicly.' But he made clear that if the government was going to deliver a low-tax, high-growth economy 'this can only be responsibly delivered if we are prepared to work hard, make sacrifices and take difficult decisions'. The implication was clear: the prime minister was not prepared to do so. 'I firmly believe the public are ready to hear that truth,' Sunak wrote. 'In preparation for our proposed joint speech on the economy next week, it has become clear to me that our approaches are fundamentally too different … I have reluctantly come to the conclusion that we cannot continue like this.'

Sunak decided he would not do any interviews or give a resignation speech in the Commons. He did not want to be seen to be turning the knife. 'He made a calculation that if it was only him, the ministerial ranks would hold fast,' an ally said. In the event, things moved more quickly.

When the news broke Johnson 'went absolutely bananas' about Sunak's betrayal. Reading Sunak's letter he muttered to himself the final words of Julius Caesar as Brutus slipped in the knife: 'Kai su, teknon.' ('You too, child.')[14] For public consumption he declared the summary of their exchanges 'fucking lies' and its author much worse. Behind the profanity there was deep and lasting hurt that the chancellor had turned on him after their mutual declaration of 'I've got your back' after the non-dom revelations. 'Boris was genuinely shocked at the end, really bitter and really hurt by Rishi,' a close aide said.

A few days later, Johnson found a brief video on social media. He sent it to Guto Harri with the message, 'Thinking of sending to Rishi …' The communications director clicked the link. After a couple of seconds of jangly music, a voice said, 'You're a cunt!'[15] The video was never sent.

Johnson had gathered a group of his supporters together for thank-you drinks in a large room next to his office. They watched the news with shock and anger. In one of his more bravura performances, the PM addressed them, seeking a silver lining in the cloud. 'We fight on!' he shouted to cheering. 'Those of you who champion free markets and tax cuts might find in light of the very recent news that we might be able to deliver some of those now!'[16] Clinging desperately to the bright side of life, he could still turn a room.

Heaton-Harris began another cabinet ring round to gauge the scale of the mutiny. Gove was initially unavailable but then publicly said he was staying. When Liz Truss saw Javid and Sunak resign, she called her special advisers Sophie Jarvis, Adam Jones and Jamie Hope and asked, 'What do I do?' They told her that loyalty to Johnson was her trump card in a future leadership contest. 'Do you feel like you need to go?' one asked. Truss was 'pretty silent', one spad recalled. Then Jarvis said, 'What do you always say?'

'Stay on the bus,' Truss replied. So she did.

Johnson now had an emergency reshuffle to perform. He told aides that as long as he could form a government he would stay. The first summons went out from Nigel Adams to the education secretary Nadhim Zahawi, a text message which read, 'Get your arse over here.' Salivating at the prospect of promotion to the Treasury, Zahawi bombarded Adams with questions: 'What am I getting Nige?' Adams told him to wait. Appointments were for the prime minister.[17] Thus began one of the more farcical sagas in a week of them.

Even before he got back to Number 10, Johnson decided Barclay should replace Javid at health. He had previously been a junior health minister and had nearly got the role when Matt Hancock resigned.

For the job of chancellor, Johnson said, 'Let's go for Kit Malthouse or Liz Truss.'

'Why?' an aide asked.

'It would fuck off Rishi so much,' Johnson replied.[18]

Truss might have considered herself the frontrunner, but Johnson judged he should not move her because of the situation in Ukraine. The job went to Zahawi, who Johnson had called 'my Beaverbrook' when he took over as vaccines minister. This time he had another urgent mission: 'I want us, in a couple of weeks' time, to present an economic plan, post-pandemic.'

'I'll get on it now,' Zahawi said, before heading to the Treasury, where he demanded to see everything officials had been working on. 'We've got fourteen days,' he announced.[19]

Zahawi, fifty-five, was a long-standing fixture in Tory politics but had only made it to the cabinet relatively late in life. Born in Iraq, he was fond of telling people how he had come to Britain without a word of English, aged eleven, and built the hugely successful YouGov polling company. His was not a rags to riches story since his father had run a bank, but Zahawi seemed to many Tories to embody the virtues of meritocratic capitalist individualism. '[My cousin] had to go on the frontline, had to fight in the Iran–Iraq war, and was taken prisoner of war for eleven years,' he recalled. 'That could have been me … I still get goosebumps talking about it.'[20] Suggestions that his business interests were too exotic for a cabinet minister perhaps delayed the fulfilment of his political promise. However, he had done a widely admired turn as the vaccines minister during the pandemic and Johnson put him in the cabinet in September 2021. PET gave Zahawi a clean bill of health. It would emerge later that he had not declared, as he should have, that he was under investigation by the National Crime Agency and HM Revenue and Customs over his taxes.

In their face-to-face chat Johnson was reassured that Zahawi, unlike Sunak, shared his desire to cut taxes and use supply side reform to drive growth, and they agreed to press ahead with the set-piece speech. When the new chancellor left, Johnson said, 'Rishi was ankle-chaining me.' Andrew Griffith said, 'This is an unlock.'[21]

Harri briefed the lobby that Barclay was a 'massive upgrade' on Javid, who was 'out of his depth' and 'felt the health job beneath him'. Javid, it was claimed, repeatedly lobbied Johnson to make him foreign secretary instead. Sunak 'had no real plan for growth and was just obsessed with balancing the books'.

To replace Zahawi at education, Johnson appointed Michelle Donelan, who had impressed as universities minister and was already slated for a cabinet post on Lyons' reshuffle plan. She was about to become the shortest-serving cabinet minister in history.

Even as they were plugging holes in the dyke, more were opening up. Alex Chalk, the solicitor general; trade envoy Andrew Murrison; party vice chairmen Bim Afolami; and five parliamentary private secretaries: Saqib Bhatti, Theo Clarke, Virginia Crosbie, Jonathan Gullis and Nicola Richards – all resigned that night. Johnson's team pointed out that some of these individuals were barely household names in their own homes.

Zahawi had just two hours' sleep as he read into his new brief and prepared for the morning media round. It was arguably the most expensive in history. The new chancellor signalled that he wanted to scrap the rise in corporation tax (at a cost of £16 billion), cut income tax (£5 billion), give teachers a 5 per cent pay rise (£12–£15 billion if replicated for all public sector workers).

Even as he was speaking, Will Quince resigned, still furious that he had been sent out to peddle falsehoods. Zahawi was still on *Today* when Laura Trott, a rising star and PPS to Grant Shapps, also quit. There were no longer enough fingers for the dyke. Robin Walker resigned as schools minister at 9.43 a.m., John Glen as city minister at 11.06. At 11.43 a.m. it was the turn of Victoria Atkins, the prisons minister. These were all people more simpatico with Sunak than Johnson, yet it was no longer about ideology but competence and integrity. Rob Halfon, the blue-collar Tory who chaired the education select committee, and ex-miner and hardcore Brexiteer Lee Anderson both called for Johnson to go.

Michael Gove chose his moment with ruthless aplomb, having taken soundings from MPs and ministers across the party. The levelling up secretary believed Johnson was finished and may not even realise it. He phoned Simone Finn, the deputy chief of staff in Number 10, who had been his girlfriend twenty years earlier, and asked for some time with Johnson before or after the PMQ prep meeting where Gove was a regular. 'Not if you're going to resign,' she said, only half-jokingly. Gove said he was not quitting but didn't say what he was planning. Other accounts have suggested Finn became Gove's willing accomplice, bulldozing others to let him into the room. In fact, she had gone to a meeting elsewhere when Gove arrived. Sam Cohen let him in.

For the second time in six years Gove appointed himself executioner for Johnson's career. Politely, deferentially even, but firmly, he said, 'I'm terribly sorry about this, Prime Minister, but I think you have to go. I think you should announce you're standing down today.' He proceeded to outline the intelligence he had gleaned. 'There are going to be a slew of junior ministerial resignations, many more than you may have been told. I anticipate they will include some of the best people in the party, people who are huge fans of yours. But you will not be able to get an administration together, it will be insupportable. If you survive that, the '22 will change the rules and you will lose a vote of confidence. I don't want to see you go that way.'[22]

Johnson, who had never quite forgiven Gove for his betrayal in 2016 and had never quite forgiven himself for standing down rather than fighting on that occasion, replied, 'You've delivered the bullet in a polite way', before signalling that he was not going anywhere. The story he told was one familiar to Johnson's aides. He had been using it since the turn of the year to illustrate how he would deal with a coup. One of Johnson's uncles, a planning officer in East Ham, was in dispute with his superiors and 'failed to take his meds one day' and barricaded himself in the town hall with a shotgun. Sometimes, in the retelling, the weapon became a flamethrower. The uncle was eventually seized by the police. 'That is going to be me,' the prime minister said. 'I'm going to fight, they're going to have to prise me out of here.'

Gove, taken aback, nodded his acquiescence and listened while Johnson rehearsed his argument about why it would be a terrible idea to get rid of him. The levelling up secretary made clear he was not going to resign and said he would discuss his intervention with no one. Once Gove had left Johnson's office he exploded with rage again, as he had at Sunak, livid that his old frenemy had chosen to destabilise him before what was arguably his most important showdown with Starmer. One of the Praetorian Guard, listening in a nearby room, heard Johnson yelling profanities. Another styled these eruptions 'the vagina monologues', because of the prevalence of the C-word.

In a moment of bizarre surrealism which even Dalí would have balked at, Gove then attended the PMQ prep meeting in the Cabinet Room as well. A source in the meeting said it was 'completely mad' and that the team was openly 'game-planning' what to do if cabinet ministers resigned in the chamber or MPs defected to Labour while Johnson was on his feet. Gove even contributed several suggestions. The prime minister was defiant. 'We fight on whatever,' he said. 'I have a mandate from fourteen million people. If people quit, we can replace them.'

Gove returned to his ministry and told aides Johnson had 'gone mad'. It was not long before the news of Gove's gambit leaked. David Canzini was overheard telling MPs about it in Portcullis House.

Prime Minister's Questions was a bloodbath. It was only one minute old when Jo Churchill, an environment minister, resigned with a broadside at Johnson: 'Integrity, competence and judgement are all essential to the role of prime minister, while a jocular self-serving approach is bound to have its limitations.' In the chamber, Starmer deployed some of his best one-liners, as the Tory benches sat mute and horrified. After subjecting Johnson to a torrid time on the Pincher affair, the Labour leader dismissed Sunak and Javid as 'the first case of sinking ships leaving the rat' and labelled wavering ministers 'the charge of the lightweight brigade', a line which even Johnson enjoyed. When Starmer dismissed the prime minister's team as 'a Z-list cast of nodding dogs', the look on some Tory MPs' faces suggested they agreed. Johnson tried to fight back, attacking Starmer for propping up Jeremy Corbyn and voting forty times against Brexit, but the lines, once hits with his backbenchers, died on his lips.

The most blistering moment, however, came from the Conservative benches. Gary Sambrook, a member of the 1922 Committee executive, quoted Johnson's claim to him and others in the tearoom on the Monday night that one of the MPs present should have intervened to stop Pincher. Sambrook called this 'insulting ... to the people who did try and intervene that night'. To a silent house hanging on his every word, he went on: 'He always tries to blame other people for mistakes. There is nothing left for him to do other than to take responsibility and resign.' As Sambrook sat down the opposition benches erupted in applause and had to be silenced by the speaker. David Davis reiterated his call for Johnson to 'do the honourable thing and put the interests of the nation before his own interests'.

Straight after PMQs it was Javid's turn to sink the knife, making a personal statement which resigning ministers are granted. Comparisons with Geoffrey Howe, who had eviscerated Margaret Thatcher in 1990, were inevitable. Javid was not a great orator but he borrowed themes from Howe who had compared the Iron Lady to a cricket captain breaking the bats of her own players. 'I am instinctively a team player,' Javid intoned while Johnson was forced to sit and listen, his face carved into a pose of blank granite stillness. 'But treading the tightrope between loyalty and integrity has become impossible in recent months ... I also believe that a team is as good as its team captain, and that a captain is as good as his or her team, so loyalty must go both ways. The events of recent months have made it increasingly difficult to be in that team.' Criticising the litany of lies which had emerged from Number 10, Javid said, 'It is not fair on ministerial colleagues to have to go out every morning defending lines that do not stand up. This week, again, we have reason to question the truth and integrity of what we have all been told ... Enough is enough ... The problem starts at the top, and I believe that that is not going to change. That means it is for those of us in a position of responsibility to make that change.' If Javid had intended it as a leadership pitch, he was to be disappointed, but as an additional nail in Johnson's coffin it did its job.

As Johnson went off to prepare for an afternoon appearance in front of the Liaison Committee of select committee chairmen, usually an ordeal but which now looked like a welcome distraction, the resignations and demands that he quit continued: Stuart Andrew, Liam Fox, Mims Davies. The most wounding blow came at 2.24 p.m. when five high-fliers from the 2017 intake – Kemi Badenoch, Lee Rowley, Neil O'Brien, Julia Lopez and Alex Burghart – resigned together, calling on Johnson to 'step aside' for the 'good of the party and the country'. Just as the endorsement of Sunak, Dowden and Robert Jenrick in 2019 had shown that Johnson had won the backing of the future stars of the party, now he had lost them. Johnson was profoundly hurt by Burghart's betrayal since he had once been the prime minister's personal parliamentary aide. 'It went down like a shit in a phone box,' one loyalist remarked. 'Boris went fucking bananas, called him a cunt. PPSs are uber, uber, uber loyal. James Duddridge would have run through a brick wall if Boris asked him to. The only one who shafted him was Alex.'

That afternoon, Johnson endured a surreal two-hour session answering the Liaison Committee's questions on everything from Pincher to petrol, while a delegation of half a dozen ministers had gathered in Number 10 to call for him to go. As the trickle of resignations became a flood, the newly installed chancellor, Nadhim Zahawi, texted Dominic Raab, the deputy prime minister, and Chris Heaton-Harris, the chief whip, who was already in Downing Street: 'This is becoming a stampede'.[23]

Soon, kettled in the wood-panelled small dining room upstairs, were Zahawi, Priti Patel, the home secretary, Simon Hart, the Welsh secretary, Kit Malthouse, the policing minister, Anne-Marie Trevelyan, Grant Shapps and another who had been promoted the night before – Michelle Donelan. When he returned to Downing Street at 5.30 p.m., Johnson huddled in his office with uber loyalists Nadine Dorries, Ben Elliot and Alister Jack. Dorries told him, 'You send them packing.'

The prime minister's closest aides and members of the Big Dog team and the Brains Trust set up camp in the Thatcher study on the first floor, where Johnson had watched the exit poll on election night. Shelley Williams-Walker, the head of operations, drew up a list of those permitted to enter what became known as 'the bunker' and barred entry to other interlopers. The team still believed there were enough MPs who could take ministerial jobs and maintain a functioning government.

At 6 p.m. Graham Brady went into Downing Street via the link door from 70 Whitehall. That afternoon the executive of the 1922 Committee had met. Upon hearing that he was in the building, Johnson said, 'He can fuck off if he thinks I'm leaving.'

When Brady sat down in the Cabinet Room, Johnson sought to pre-empt the discussion: 'So you've changed the rules?' he said.[24]

Brady explained that the '22 had decided against an immediate change but that there would be new elections to the executive the following Monday. The new executive would be likely to change the rules and it was 'almost inevitable' that a vote of confidence would follow on the Tuesday. 'It is fairly obvious you would lose it,' he said. Johnson dug in, insisting he still had 'great things' to do and made clear that if MPs wanted to defy the will of the electorate by removing him, 'They're welcome to try.'[25] The prime minister was now, metaphorically, holed up with his uncle's shotgun.

Brady said, 'It would be better for the country, the party and for you personally if you didn't push it to that point.'[26] He left before 6.30 p.m., the time of the prime minister's weekly (virtual) audience with the Queen. The fact of this conversation had led to growing speculation through the day that Johnson's last card would be to try to force a general election. That idea had been wargamed in the bunker. Andrew Griffith, the abrasive head of policy, had suggested it.

Several senior ministers contacted Simon Case, the cabinet secretary, asking how Johnson could be removed. 'They thought he had gone mad,' said one ministerial aide. Among their concerns were rumours that Johnson might ask the Queen to dissolve Parliament. Case was in touch with Edward Young at Buckingham Palace, where there was concern the Queen might be dragged into a constitutional controversy and also with Brady. Case took it upon himself to tour Number 10, pointing out to Johnson's political aides that under the so-called Lascelles principles, which dictate when the monarch can refuse a dissolution, there could not be an election. According to the convention, devised by Alan 'Tommy' Lascelles, private secretary to George VI, a dissolution should not be granted if Parliament is still viable, an election would be detrimental to the economy and if an alternative prime minister could command a

Commons majority. Case pointed out that all three criteria were met. The palace did not stage an intervention to force Johnson's hand, but courtiers were relieved when Case did. Since the Queen would have had to grant a dissolution if asked to do so by her prime minister, if Johnson had looked like trying it, the game would have been to prevent him asking the question. In those circumstances it was likely that Brady would have engineered an immediate vote of no confidence while it was politely made clear that the Queen would not be answering the telephone.

Throughout Wednesday, Carrie Johnson had been supportive, urging Johnson to consider his position carefully. 'She was his rock,' one minister said. 'She was a supportive spouse and was prepared to do whatever he wanted.' Another source said, 'She certainly wasn't urging him to stay, but she wasn't telling him to go either.' At one point Alister Jack told Johnson, 'Get up to the flat to see your wife. This number of resignations is highly distressing for your family.'

Those in the building that day say it also had a far greater impact on Johnson than he wanted to admit. 'He needed support on a human level, because this was a very traumatic event for him,' a cabinet minister said. 'He masks his feelings very well. He was absolutely devastated and in a state of shock. I could tell when he looked away, the pressure he was under.' Johnson's principal stated emotion, to those he confided in, was one of disbelief. 'He was just slightly stunned that these people were walking away from him when he stood by them, or he'd done things for them. He couldn't understand why they were knifing him.' This was most acute in his feelings about Sunak.

By 7 p.m., when Johnson agreed to see the kettled ministers – dubbed 'the self-appointed death squad' by one of the bunker aides – thirty-nine ministers had already resigned.[27] Minding the seditious six, on a rotating basis, were Heaton-Harris, Charlotte Owen and Simone Finn. They were fed endless pots of tea. David Canzini also looked in on several occasions. Witnesses say he was overheard whispering that he too thought Johnson should go and that the focus should be on a timetable for the handover of power.

Zahawi had been pacing the dining room muttering, 'He's got to go, he's got to go', as if trying to steady his nerves about what needed to be done. Zahawi also had a quiet conversation with Heaton-Harris, who admitted, 'Boris isn't listening.' They were both concerned the PM was not facing reality and allowing the ultras – Adams, Griffith, Gascoigne and Lyons – to convince him he could survive. 'We have to work together to help him transition out of this,' Zahawi said. Patel, Trevelyan and Donelan agreed. Griffith came into the dining room and argued that Johnson could still form a government. 'You may have enough numbers now,' replied Zahawi, 'but in one hour the numbers will have fallen, and in five hours, they'll have fallen even more. It's the herd beginning to move.'[28]

Griffith insisted each minister would have to go in alone to see Johnson. There would be no mob ousting.

First in was Zahawi. 'Look, I'm working on the plan, as we agreed,' the chancellor said. 'I think I'll have a great plan in two weeks' time, but unfortunately, Prime Minister, I don't think I've got two weeks. As a friend of yours, someone who loves you and respects you, and is eternally grateful for the opportunity you gave me, I just need to tell you that I think the herd is stampeding. I can't bear to see you being treated this way. They are going to drag your carcass out of this place.'[29]

Johnson convinced his new chancellor that there was still a slim path to survival, or at least that he had the right to try. 'No, Nadhim,' Johnson said. 'We can make this.' The two found common cause when Zahawi told Johnson that, in his first hours in the Treasury, he had learned that Sunak had been blocking viable policies for helping combat the cost of living crisis. By the end of the meeting they were discussing the big speech again and hugging. Zahawi emerged from Johnson's study and ran into another cabinet minister, telling them he was 'tremendously excited' about the economic plan he and the PM were going to announce.

Next to see Johnson was Shapps, who did not tell the prime minister to resign but laid out his fears that he no longer had the support to survive. 'Grant told him he could only guarantee him 28 votes if there was a new vote of no confidence,' a minister said. 'The ceiling was 60 votes.' Michelle Donelan, appointed education secretary to replace Zahawi, went in to resign but was persuaded to stay. Kit Malthouse, the policing minister, was 'hostile' but also 'waffled'. He wanted Johnson to go but seemed unable to say so unequivocally.

Priti Patel, the home secretary, and Anne-Marie Trevelyan, the trade secretary, both told him the game was up, but made clear, 'If you want to fight, we will stand with you.' Johnson seemed strangely upbeat. 'The PM was quite perky,' a minister said. 'He knew the situation was untenable by then but he hadn't completely decided what to do.'

After waiting for five hours Simon Hart, the Welsh secretary, finally saw Johnson. He had arrived with a resignation letter in his pocket and said he would make it public the next morning if Johnson didn't quit. The prime minister asked for a reprieve until Tuesday. 'I can turn this around.' Hart disagreed, telling him, 'I think the game is up.'

By now, Zahawi was having fresh doubts as well. 'By the evening, someone at Number 10 had briefed out that he and I would be making a speech the next day,' he recalled. 'It was impossible, it would have destroyed his reputation and mine to try and make an economic speech within forty-eight hours of being appointed the chancellor of the exchequer.'[30]

Inside Downing Street most were now convinced Johnson was coming to terms with his fate, but from outside it looked as if he was planning to squat in Number 10. 'He wants to be a martyr and go out like Mussolini or Ceaușescu,' said a minister who saw him that day. In the Number 10 bunker, Harri, Lyons, Heaton-Harris and Kempsell made clear they would stand with Johnson if he wanted to fight, but few privately thought it a good idea. However those who had been around in 2016 and who had seen Johnson drift into regret and recrimination about his decision to stand down after Gove had withdrawn his support, knew it was a decision he had to reach himself. 'He regrets pulling out in 2016 when Gove chopped his legs off,' a close ally said. 'He will wonder for the rest of his life what would have happened if he had had a go.' Another said, 'We could all see where it was going to end but he had to get there himself.'

The biographer of Shakespeare provided a third act twist before the final curtain fell. Johnson's anger at Gove 'festered all day', the four-letter expletives continuing to fly. They found voice in one last theatrical flourish. As the day went on Johnson began to voice the view that Gove and Sunak had been engaged in a plot lasting months to destabilise him, in cahoots with Dougie Smith and Dominic Cummings. 'He observed that there was a lot to come out about that,' a witness said. 'Someone filled his head with it.' When word reached the bunker that Gove might resign, the idea was floated that he should sack the levelling up secretary before he got the chance to jump. 'If you're going to survive, you need to look strong,' one aide said. Another added, 'You must know that everyone in this room is in favour.' Johnson went around the room and let everyone pronounce. The bunker was a court of hanging judges with Nigel Adams,

Chris Heaton-Harris and Guto Harri the most gung-ho. A few, including Ben Gascoigne and Gove's former spad Declan Lyons, questioned the decision. 'What problem does it solve?' Gascoigne ventured. But those who were there say the mood was one of blood lust. 'I could feel the atmosphere had changed,' a witness said. 'It was a packed room, quite raucous. Everyone got a bit carried away on the Michael thing.'

The prime minister went downstairs to his office with Adams and Harri and called Gove on his mobile. It was 8.59 p.m., a moment of collective catharsis. Gove asked, 'Are you resigning?'

Johnson replied, 'No, Mikey, I'm afraid you are. I'm going to have to ask you to take a step back.'

Gove, undeterred, sent the ball back, 'Prime Minister, if anyone should be stepping back, it is you.'

A Number 10 official said it was 'revenge, pure and simple'. Harri briefed the press that Gove was 'a snake'. Others regarded this as 'pretty childish'. While some of his closest allies felt Gove's sacking was a just pay-off for his perfidy in 2016 – and again that very morning – Johnson felt 'sad' about the whole thing, telling one friend, 'It's a tragedy, but it had to be done.'

Shortly after Gove's defenestration, his stunned allies in the Department for Levelling Up sought to mobilise opposition to Johnson. Kemi Badenoch, who had quit eight hours earlier, messaged a DLU ministers WhatsApp group to say, 'Resign before midnight. DO IT. DO IT. DO IT.' This was accompanied by a laughing emoji.[31]

By now the reshuffle whiteboard had been set up in the Thatcher study to try to put together a new government. Brandon Lewis, the Northern Ireland secretary, arrived in Downing Street with the intention of joining the group telling Johnson to go. He was late because he had to fly back from Belfast but he had been in touch with Zahawi, so he knew the lie of the land. He also found Johnson in a 'very positive' frame of mind. The PM offered him the levelling up department. It was the first Lewis had heard that Gove had been sacked. Lewis had seen the whiteboard and knew Johnson was struggling to fill a cabinet. He either demanded, or was offered, the Cabinet Office, a promotion which came with the chancellorship of the Duchy of Lancaster. He agreed not to resign but to think about it.

One bunker dweller asked Simon Case what the minimum number of ministers would be to count as a functioning government. 'There is no quorum anywhere in our legislation,' Case explained. 'In the end, the prime minister can take on all secretary of state jobs if he wants to.'

Greg Hands turned down the offer of party chairman. A number of proposed names had the initials 'PET' next to them because they were likely to come under scrutiny by the propriety and ethics team. 'The situation was so grave that even known sex pests were being considered for roles despite the Pincher scandal,' said a cabinet minister who saw the board. By 10 p.m. there had been forty-three frontbench resignations.

Even in this desperate environment some overplayed their hands. Ranil Jayawardena, victim of a last-minute reversal in the 2020 reshuffle, was considered for minister of state at the Home Office and the Ministry of Justice had he not demanded more. 'He would have had a promotion,' one witness said, 'but it wasn't good enough for him. He wanted to be a privy councillor. He wanted to be deputy president of the board of trade. We were all trying not to laugh.' Jayawardena remained a junior minister in the trade department.

There was time for one last screw-up. Someone in the bunker called David T. C. Davies, the junior minister at the Wales office, to offer him the job of secretary of state. Davies phoned Hart, a friend, 'I didn't think you'd resigned,' he said. 'I haven't,' Hart replied. Furious, he phoned Heaton-Harris, who apologised, but the damage was done. Hart sat on a park bench and tweeted his resignation letter. He was the first cabinet resignation of the day.

When did Johnson give up? Those who were there say it was around 10.30 p.m. It was increasingly obvious that he could not create a credible government. Simon Clarke, a committed Boris fan, turned down the job of levelling up secretary. He threw in the towel when it became clear that Alberto Costa was the best candidate available to become solicitor general. Costa was a journeyman MP with an amendment about EU citizens' rights to his name, some constituency activism and little time in any government role. Johnson thought this was scraping the barrel: *Can I go to the Queen and say that I've got the best possible government I could have from the ranks of the Conservative Party in Parliament?* He said, 'I can't do this, it's all too ghastly, it's not me.'[32]

To one of the PM's aides, the last burst of Johnsonian bravado on Wednesday night put him in mind of the opera *La Bohème*, in which the heroine, dying of TB, rouses herself to sing one of the greatest arias before expiring. 'You think, "If she can sing like that, she can't possibly die" – and then she keels over and dies. The end.'

At around 11 p.m. the bunker team broke up. Adams and Heaton-Harris returned to the flat they shared and turned on the television, where they watched Suella Braverman, the attorney general, announce to Robert Peston that she was not resigning, but she was running for the party leadership. 'What the fuck?' said Adams. Heaton-Harris phoned Braverman and gave her the hairdryer treatment. There wasn't a corpse, let alone a cold one, yet she was already campaigning for the job.

Johnson went upstairs to the flat, his decision apparently made – but he still needed to talk to Carrie and Lynton Crosby, the man who more than any other had helped him rise to the top and the wife who had joined him at the summit.

'Mate, I've been thinking about this and I don't want to destroy the Conservative Party,' Johnson said. 'I think I should stand down. What do you think?'

'Do you have the numbers?' Crosby, straight to the point. Politics is knowing how to count.

'No, the guys have looked at the numbers and say I can't win.'

To Crosby, it was clear Johnson had already made up his mind. For the second time in six years he recommended he throw in the towel. 'From everything I know, Boris, it sounds like going is the right decision.' He added, 'If you're going to go make sure you do what you can to protect your legacy: Brexit, vaccines, leading the world on Ukraine.' When Johnson hung up, Crosby turned to his wife, Dawn, and said, 'I think he's going to pull stumps.'

Carrie did not try to talk her husband out of it: 'It's your decision.' A friend said, 'She was very upset for Boris. She was in bits for him. She thought it had been unfair. She just wanted him to be happy.' They agreed Johnson should sleep on it.

The fifty-fifth prime minister of the United Kingdom of Great Britain and Northern Ireland woke early the next morning, Thursday 7 July, not long after 5 a.m. At 5.30 a.m. Guto Harri texted him to say, 'It's not looking good.'

'I know, I'm writing my speech,' came the reply. By 7 a.m. his aides began assembling in the Thatcher study. By half past, Johnson had presented the first draft of his resignation address to the nation. Over the next two hours Declan Lyons helped Johnson polish the text. On the way to work that morning he had spoken to his mother in Warrington, who had not been following events closely and was baffled that the prime minister was going. For these voters, Lyons urged Johnson to make clear that he was leaving against his will: 'It's important to put on record that you don't think you should be resigning.' The final version combined scorn for the MPs who had made the 'eccentric' decision to get rid of him, with Zahawi's observation that he had been trampled underfoot by a 'herd' of panicking colleagues.

Johnson might have appropriated Zahawi's language but he did not tell the chancellor that he was planning to resign. Seeing the state of play, Zahawi felt he needed to break cover again. At 6 a.m. he called Barclay. 'What do we do?' the chief of staff asked. 'It's a disaster. It's over.'[33]

The chancellor agreed. At 8.43 a.m., Zahawi tweeted a letter, on Treasury headed paper, saying he was 'heartbroken' that Johnson had not heeded his advice to go. 'Prime Minister: this is not sustainable and it will only get worse: for you, for the Conservative Party and most importantly of all the country,' he wrote. 'You must do the right thing and go now.' It was an intervention which was already superfluous and would open Zahawi to ridicule and seriously damage his chances of succeeding Johnson. He was not the only one spinning on a sixpence, however. Both Brandon Lewis and Michelle Donelan announced they were resigning, along with care minister Helen Whately, security minister Damian Hinds and science minister George Freeman. 'Their resignations were slightly pointless,' a ministerial colleague said. 'They were positioning themselves for what was to come next. They were trying to jump on the bus and the bus had already left the station.'

Number 10 was a bear pit of internecine warfare. Canzini was accused by others in the inner circle of working with his former business associate Mark Fullbrook, who was quietly advising Zahawi on a leadership run. 'When Canzini walked into the study on Thursday morning, he got told unceremoniously to leave,' a source said. 'Chris [Heaton-Harris] kicked him out.' Guto Harri was attacked for presiding over the inaccurate briefings which had caused such chaos. One colleague summed up his contribution over the last six months with the nickname 'Harri-kari'.

At 8.30 a.m. Johnson spoke to Graham Brady. 'I reflected on our conversation last night,' the prime minister said. 'I've changed my mind. I will be going.' Johnson still seemed unrepentant, however, presenting himself,

Brady said later, as 'a great leader', dismissing the criticisms of MPs as 'complete nonsense and trivia'.[34] Johnson's next call was to the Queen.

Wanting to stop the cascade of resignations, Harri rang Chris Mason, the political editor of the BBC, who was broadcasting on an extended edition of the *Today* programme when the call came in. At 9.10 a.m. he told the world, 'The prime minister has agreed to stand down.' Later, Johnson wrote, 'If Caesar had twenty-three stab wounds from his assassins, I ended up with sixty-two', the number of ministers who had resigned.[35]

Johnson's draft speech was 'much punchier' than the one delivered. One section which was cut highlighted his belief that he only had to make it to the summer recess to survive. 'There is still part of me that thinks that if we could have turned off Twitter and sent the MPs off to the beach, we could have sorted this out and gone on to thrash Labour at the next election,' he would have said.

Another excised passage tackled the demand of Tory MPs that he should 'go with dignity'. This, wrote Johnson, 'as though I was off to a Swiss euthanasia clinic. I think dignity is a grossly overrated commodity, and I prefer to fight to the end.' A third deleted section revealed his lingering irritation with MPs: 'I can't ask good friends and colleagues to superglue Humpty together again, when they are frankly hesitant, or not supportive.'[36] A source who was very close to Johnson said that week, 'He hates the Tory Party. He absolutely hates them. He sees them as thwarting him. He's convinced the British public is still behind him.'

When Alister Jack arrived in Downing Street he had found some loyalists 'blubbing'. He sought to change the mood: 'Don't worry, Prime Minister, you were born in New York. You can still go and be president.' It was Jack's fifty-ninth birthday. Johnson insisted they crack open a bottle of champagne. Around 11 a.m., Johnson phoned Zahawi and, to the chancellor's surprise, asked him to remain. 'Why did you write me that letter?' the prime minister asked.

'I just thought that your team were panicking and delusional about the problem.' Zahawi apologised.

Johnson said, 'No, Nadhim, it was me. I just needed to reflect and I think I've made the right decision.'[37]

At 12.30 p.m. a surprisingly jaunty Johnson went to the podium in Downing Street and addressed the cameras while his closest aides and a couple of dozen MP supporters watched from the wings. 'It is now clearly the will of the parliamentary Conservative party that there should be a new leader of that party and therefore a new prime minister,' Johnson announced, placing the blame squarely at the door of the MPs, before explaining that he had fought to stay because it was his 'duty' and 'obligation' to deliver on the 'incredible mandate' he had been given in 2019. Johnson embarked on a recitation of his greatest achievements: 'getting Brexit done', 'the fastest vaccine rollout in Europe', 'the fastest exit from lockdown' and 'leading the West in standing up to Putin's aggression in Ukraine'. He then made the case for levelling up.

Johnson could not disguise his irritation that he had been forced out. 'In the last few days I have tried to persuade my colleagues that it would be eccentric to change governments when we are delivering so much and when we have such a vast mandate and when we are actually only a handful of points behind in the polls even in mid-term after quite a few months of pretty unrelenting sledging ... but as we've seen at Westminster, the herd is powerful and when the herd moves, it moves.' There was a hint of admiration when he referenced the 'brilliant and Darwinian system' which had finished him – and which would now 'produce another leader'. Johnson vowed to give his successor 'as much support as I can', which you did not have to be excessively cynical to assume would amount to 'not much'. He finished by addressing the people, from whom he wrongly believed his constitutional authority had derived: 'I know that there will be many who are relieved but perhaps quite a few who will be disappointed and I want you to know how sad I am to give up the best job in the world' – he paused for a beat to deliver the most Boris line of the lot – 'but them's the breaks.'

Of his personal mistakes over Pincher and partygate there was no mention whatsoever. However, it was also true that in quieter moments, Johnson had privately admitted fault. 'He's not deluded. He dates it from Paterson,' a friend said. 'He has great regrets about Paterson and the handling of partygate.' It might have done his reputation good to acknowledge this publicly, but that had never been Johnson's approach to politics. As the man himself had said, there was to be no deathbed psychological conversion. Watching the speech, a prominent Westminster figure observed, 'He was right. The Tory Party has finally developed herd immunity to Boris Johnson.'

Johnson chaired a cabinet meeting around 3.30 p.m. and showed he still had his sense of humour. Alister Jack praised Johnson's loyalty and

Trevelyan his optimism. 'There are three things about you, Boris,' Jack said. 'You are kind, perhaps too kind. You are loyal, perhaps too loyal. You are fearless. Each of these brought you down.' To Paterson and Pincher Johnson had indeed been too kind, to failing aides and advisers he had indeed been too loyal. Jacob Rees-Mogg found time to denounce the departed Sunak: 'Good riddance to the socialist chancellor.' Johnson sheepishly confessed his desire to stay in Number 10 was perhaps evidence that he had been too optimistic the night before. He compared his determination to cling to office to that of the Japanese soldier Hiroo Onoda, who hid in the jungle for years and refused to accept Japan's surrender after the Second World War. Johnson then quoted the surrender declaration of Japan's Emperor Hirohito at the end of the war: 'The situation has developed not necessarily to our advantage.'

That evening, Johnson and Carrie both attended a birthday party for Alister Jack in Dover House, home of the Scotland Office, where guests watched him beating the retreat. 'They put in a proper shift,' said one minister present. 'Boris is a real trouper. He didn't just go and lick his wounds, he went out, faced up to everyone.' It was, another attendee recalled, 'a beautiful sunny evening – it was a good way to end'.

Johnson also spoke to Volodymyr Zelensky, perhaps the only politician who now shared the prime minister's assessment of himself. Johnson sought to reassure the Ukrainian president his successor would continue Britain's strong support for his cause. 'You're a hero, Volodymyr,' the PM said. 'Everyone in this country loves you.' Zelensky said he was 'personally disappointed' that Johnson was going: 'You're a hero, Boris. Everyone in this country loves you.'[38] Johnson's tragedy was that he always hoped for the same sentiment to prevail at home. By his actions he ensured that, if it ever had, it no longer did so.

The greatest political survivor of his generation had not survived. Why? The story Johnson told himself was that he was the victim of a plot, a hydra-headed conspiracy between Sunak, Cummings and Dougie Smith.

The question is simple, the answer multi-faceted. First there were Johnson's own characteristics, which set the tone in Downing Street and led to a culture where people felt able to push beyond both the letter and the spirit of the rules. Perhaps he did not know the full scope of partygate. Certainly, he failed to understand the impact it had on a public whose experience of the pandemic was very different from his. While Johnson had his own brush with mortality, government at that time was a souped-up version of the usual experience of national leadership, bigger and more frightening but an extreme version of their existing reality. For much of the public, it was a period of existential shock which had a profound and damaging effect on people's lives, their relationships, education, development, mental health and friendships. It felt to many voters like the Number 10 'parties' were a collective thumbing of the nose at their sacrifices. Inside the Downing Street bubble, Johnson did not, perhaps could not, comprehend this.

One of Sunak's closest aides, who had watched Johnson up close, had a simpler explanation: 'I think he would have done literally anything to save himself. But the reason he didn't is that he didn't have a clue what he was doing.' To Dominic Cummings, who had done as much as anyone to undermine Johnson, it was all a 'Greek tragedy' where Johnson 'surrounded himself by Yes men' and told 'lies all the time – it became pathological – he couldn't stop'.

To some degree, though, all these factors had been present throughout his career and Johnson had survived every previous crisis which engulfed him personally and professionally. There are friends of Johnson who say his second wife Marina would have forced him to take a more placatory stance. 'I think if he was still married to her, he would still be prime minister,' one long-serving ally declared in 2023. There are some friends of Carrie Johnson who say she had checked out of political life when it mattered. 'The drip, drip, drip of the Simon Walters stories was all so horrific that she switched off,' another woman in Number 10 said. A cabinet minister added, 'She was bruised by the constant briefing from Dom.' Other friends say she reinforced Johnson's view that he had done nothing wrong. 'She basically was like, "We're not apologising for anything",' one said. 'They just thought they were going to spin their way out of it.'

Others say the belief that Carrie had authorised briefing against Cummings and Cain was what unleashed the Vote Leave counterattack. This does not wholly hold water, since Carrie was a clear supporter of Cummings early on and negative briefings about her had been appearing for eighteen months before the Vote Leave fraternity left Number 10 in November 2020. Yet her lavish spending on the Downing Street flat was a distraction and lent an air of rule-breaking to Johnson's government.

In several conversations with the author, Johnson went out of his way to defend Carrie against her critics. Marriages are complicated and opaque to external observers, sometimes even to those within them.

The tritest answer to why Boris Johnson didn't survive is that he did not do everything that was necessary to save himself, which most senior Tories believed was possible even as late as March 2022. First, he was late to recognise how serious was the threat to him. A cabinet minister said, 'I think in his mind he couldn't quite believe that parties that he didn't attend and bum-pinching, when he wasn't the one pinching bums, could result in someone with an 80-seat majority, who was leading the West's struggle against Putin, being kicked out.'

This meant he never delivered the simple apology which might have saved the day and the announcement that he was firing those responsible. As Guto Harri concluded later, 'The cover-up is invariably worse than the crime. Coughing up to some people having had far too many drinks as key workers under extreme pressure during a global pandemic would have been extremely painful, but it would have been done and dusted by that Christmas. But telling Parliament and the public that there were "no parties" was a fatal mistake.'[39]

The primary reason for this was that Johnson thought he would get away with it, as he had every other transgression, because he did not regard Keir Starmer as any sort of political threat. He believed the Labour leader was out of step with the voters – and that that should be obvious to all Tories. 'He genuinely does not like Keir,' an aide said. 'There's nothing contrived. He sees this man as part of a privileged metropolitan narrow-minded elite that is uncomfortable with the raw instincts of the vast majority of British people.' In his memoir, Johnson compared Starmer to 'a bullock having a thermometer shoved unexpectedly up his rectum'.[40] Johnson was six points behind in the polls the day he resigned. A cabinet minister said, 'He just didn't rate Starmer. He thought to be within six points of him, with everything that had happened, as far as Boris was concerned, that was a dream. He'd come from 17 points behind to beat Ken Livingstone.' Another minister said, 'Boris believed 100 per cent that he was going to wipe the floor with Keir, and I think he was right about that. His mistake was to assume that Tory MPs would see it and accept it.'

Instead, the never warm and wholly transactional relationship between Johnson and the parliamentary Conservative Party broke down. After he was ousted, Johnson conceded to a friend: 'I was complacent. Too many of the MPs hated me, 150 had never been on my side because of what I'd done to Dave and because of what I had done to Theresa.'

This was a process exacerbated by Covid, which prevented Johnson inviting his backbenchers to Chequers, kept the 2019 intake in a state of semi-detached resentment towards their older colleagues and led to votes on lockdown restrictions in the autumn of 2020 which antagonised some of the most organised plotters on the right of the party. Eddie Lister said, 'Lockdown was the biggest single mistake, because all those new MPs were thrown loose for a good six, seven months. They went feral.' Another Downing Street politico said, 'The ultimate exam question is: how you go from the triumph of December 2019 to defeat in July 2022? Covid started a set of events within the parliamentary party that meant it was always going to be very hard to bring that whole thing back together. There were far too many votes on difficult things that frankly he shouldn't have been putting to Parliament, like vaccine passports. We could have picked our battles a bit more intelligently.'

Most MPs could see Johnson was a great campaigner and a serial winner, but they also thought his overweening self-confidence meant he would keep making the same mistakes – chaotic governance and lack of candour when caught out – again and again. 'It is true that Boris might have won the election if he had survived as leader,' one MP said. 'But it is also true that he would have given the party half a dozen more reasons to get rid of him before we got to an election.' Just as he was surprised when Marina Wheeler pulled the plug on his marriage, so Johnson was amazed and resentful when Tory MPs did the same to his premiership.

Another explanation, proffered by Johnson after his departure from Number 10, was that he never got a team as good as he had at City Hall. After Cummings' departure, a senior cabinet minister observed, Johnson decided 'he did not want to be beholden to anyone like that again' and that meant 'There was no one who could say to Boris, "Look boss, that is a truly fucking mad idea." Cameron relied on George [Osborne], Letwin and Hague. Blair had brilliant consiglieris in [Jonathan] Powell and [Alastair] Campbell, and had [Alan] Milburn, [John] Reid, [Tessa] Jowell and [Charlie] Falconer. To succeed as a prime minister, you need two or three other senior politicians who you can bounce things off.'

After he was ousted, Johnson acknowledged that he had needed the Vote Leave crew at the beginning but wished he had moved on after the general election. A key aide recalled him saying, 'I needed them to get

Brexit done but I held on to them too long.' A cabinet minister said, 'He acknowledges that the Pincher appointment was a mistake … He regrets backing Rishi earlier in the year. He was complacent about the Sue Gray report.' None of which absolves Johnson himself. One long-standing ally admitted, 'He didn't know how to grip things. He doesn't know how to run things. He collected all of these people who were entertaining but couldn't implement his will.'

The two men who could have been that consiglieri were unavailable. Simon Milton died young. Eddie Lister was pushing seventy when Johnson became prime minister and was not a constant presence. 'If only I'd had Eddie throughout …' he told one confidant, his voice trailing off, his gaze in the middle distance.

To Lister the explanation was simpler – in the end, Johnson had too many enemies to survive when he got into difficulties. 'You've got all the Theresa May supporters, who think he stuffed them,' Lister explained. 'You've got the Remainers who think he's stuffed them on Brexit. You've got all the people he sacked from the cabinet and all the ones he hadn't promoted to the cabinet, who thought they should be. And then the general malcontents.'

A minister asked: 'If you're so convinced everyone is trying to shoot you, why leave so many boxes of ammunition lying around?' A former Downing Street aide put it best: 'Boris Johnson is the third prime minister to be brought down by Boris Johnson.'

Interviewed for this book in 2023, Johnson veered between declarations that he had done nothing wrong, to introspection about his mistakes and swiftly back again. In his memoir, published in October 2024, he finally conceded that 'the plot' only succeeded because of 'my many goofs': 'I made too many duff appointments, a couple of whom turned out to be homicidal maniacs [Cummings and Cain, presumably]. I badly mishandled our response to some of the crises … I did nothing like enough to explain myself to the parliamentary party and keep them onside.' He wished he had warned his staff 'about the vital importance of not only obeying the rules but being seen to obey them', a failure he came to 'greatly regret'. He concluded, 'I was complacent and thought I could charm people into sticking with me' and was 'sometimes arrogant' and 'should have realised that, as prime minister, you serve not just at the pleasure of the people but of your colleagues'.[41]

* * *

Who, in the end, was he? Andrew Gimson, the biographer who understood Johnson-the-man best, saw traces of Benjamin Disraeli, a wayward adventurer and political 'impresario' who charmed voters and colleagues, a 'risk-taker' who helped split the Conservative Party over the corn laws, just as Johnson did over Brexit. In both cases, almost all the 'intelligent, high-minded, reputable people' took the opposite side of the argument, while Disraeli and Johnson found themselves in a foxhole with the 'backwoodsmen' of their party. Both enraged the establishment with the way they passed their signature policies: 'The measure – the Brexit Bill, the [1867] Reform Bill – needed to go through, and there was no altogether reputable way to do it,' Gimson wrote. 'Disraeli and Johnson saw the way the world was moving and contrived to move with it. This is not one of the most elevated political arts, but if revolution is to be avoided it is one of the most necessary.'[42] Those who deplored Johnson and Cummings' behaviour in 2019 must explain how they would have stopped Brexit without doing even more damage to faith in democracy.

Gimson correctly identified that Johnson's political platform and the coalition of voters he assembled to support it – dismissed by his critics as crude 'populism' or 'English nationalism' – was a direct descendant of Tory democracy, advocated by Disraeli, Randolph Churchill and his son, Winston. 'Tory democracy is an alliance between a section of the ruling class and the working class to enrage and outwit the middle-class prigs,' Gimson wrote, a fair summary of the Brexit years and the 2019 election. 'The programme of this alliance is patriotism plus practical measures to improve the lives of the workers', wrapped in love of the monarchy and the armed forces and a belief in 'saying what the hell you like, especially if it shocks the liberals'.[43]

Gimson also quoted Karl Marx on Lord Palmerston, the nineteenth-century foreign secretary, who became prime minister late in life and had an affair at the age of seventy-nine. Palmerston was 'an exceedingly happy joker' who was 'endowed with a restless and indefatigable spirit' and whose goal was 'not the substance, but the mere appearance of success'. Palmerston embarked on 'show battles' with a view to 'disentangle himself from them in a showy manner … the whole ending in violent parliamentary debates'. Marx might have been writing about 2019. There are echoes of Johnson's 2020 battle for an EU deal here as well: 'He manages international conflicts like an artist, driving matters to a certain point, retreating when they threaten to become serious, but having got … the dramatic excitement he wants. The movement of history is nothing but a pastime, expressly invented for the private satisfaction of Palmerston/Johnson.[44]

Anthony Seldon, who has made the office of prime minister his life's study, called Johnson 'Britain's most iconoclastic and outlandish prime minister since David Lloyd George', another leader who dealt with war, a pandemic which nearly killed him (both men were fifty-five) and turbulence over Ireland and its borders. Lloyd George was also an orator, won a December landslide election, abused patronage, messed with the constitution and made an art form of adultery. 'Both saw themselves akin to the US president, with a direct mandate from the people, and had little love for their party or Parliament,' Seldon concluded. 'Both fell because they lost trust and credibility with the public, amid accusations that they had tarnished the office and public life.'[45]

Those who saw Johnson as the unique villain of his times would regard comparisons with these figures of historical note as repellent, but they do show how the costume of attractive rogue is a well-worn one at the top of British politics. If politics, propriety and the British polity all suffered, so too did Johnson himself. 'His mum died, he nearly died,' an MP ally said. 'It was brutal. I'm struggling with what I went through, Boris faced multiple betrayals by friends. His work, his life's dreams, gone.'

Johnson's friends said he 'got the big calls right' on the three signature crises of his premiership: Brexit, Covid and the war in Ukraine. There is a strong case that on Brexit, however unpalatable his methods, he did what was necessary to 'get it done' but was disingenuous when it came to the details, particularly where it concerned the Irish Sea border. There is equally a case that a deal on Northern Ireland always needed a fudge and Johnson's ability to coexist in multiple different realities helped that process as much as he hindered it. In this analysis he succeeded, not in spite of his reputation for sophistry, but because of it. On Covid he was slow to lock down in March and October 2020 but deserved plaudits for the vaccine programme and for resisting restrictions before Christmas 2021. Ukraine, where he was genuinely at the leading edge of opinion, was arguably his finest hour. Yet, in the final analysis, Johnson made so many bad 'small calls' that they undermined the faith of both MPs and voters in his competence – a battalion of duck-sized horses overwhelming three horse-sized ducks, in the popular parlance.

Nonetheless, Johnson was the most compelling political figure of his age in the UK. He was not as good a platform speaker as David Cameron, let alone Tony Blair or Barack Obama, though he was a highly gifted phrasemaker. As a manager he was borderline hopeless, a lesser figure than Gordon Brown, Theresa May or Rishi Sunak, let alone those multi-term prime ministers and presidents. Yet he was matched only by Bill Clinton in his ability to connect with ordinary voters and Ronald Reagan in stealing blue-collar workers for the centre-right.

In the end, however, he could not defy the consequences of his own personality. For years Johnson had prospered with a blustering style of near-demented optimism and, when the going got tough, a steadfast refusal to answer uncomfortable questions about his behaviour. Barrelling through and doubling down was combined with speaking simultaneously out of both sides of his mouth. It was what 'got Brexit done' and what enabled him both to win the 'red wall' and to swathe southern England in blue. Yet Johnson's belief in his immunity from the normal rules of political propriety and gravity also bred the complacency and hubris which was his undoing. Johnson's fall, from the heights of the October 2021 party conference to his defenestration just nine months later, was the most precipitous in modern British political history. If William Shakespeare, the subject of Johnson's second biography, had been writing plays today, it seems likely that the court of King Boris would have given him decent subject matter. The public, of course, would have been divided on whether it was one of the Bard's tragedies or comedies.

Johnson's departure marked the end of a modern odyssey that began in February 2016, when he decided to back the Leave campaign, a period in which he evolved from a popular, but politically slight figure, best known for getting stuck on an Olympic zip wire, into a divisive leader whose actions and views have – for good or ill – changed the course of a nation's history. Critics ridicule Johnson's self-reverential Churchillian cos-play, but even they can scarcely contest that he was the most conse-quential politician of his generation.

When Michael Gove had dinner with him just before they joined Vote Leave, what he saw that night led him to conclude, 'Churchill wanted to put himself at the centre of events. I think it's the same with Boris.' Johnson created a political moment and then, very briefly, rose to it, before crashing back to earth. Four years on, an aide to the prime minster said, 'This is Boris's world now. The rest of us are just living in it.'

That was not the legacy he wanted. But it would have to do.

PART FIVE

OUT OF CONTROL

THE RISE AND FALL
OF LIZ TRUSS

July to October 2022

'Risk comes from not knowing what you are doing'

– Warren Buffett

'Some of us would take our time, if we knew that
we are rushing to our deaths'

– Mokokoma Mokhonoana

'There is only one basic human right, the right to do as
you damn well please. And with it comes the only basic
human duty, the duty to take the consequences'

– P. J. O'Rourke

KNIFE FIGHT IN A PHONE BOX

The Leadership Election

7 July to 6 September 2022

'This isn't a knife fight in a phone box'

– Tom Tugendhat, 13 July 2022

The frontrunners to replace Boris Johnson had been preparing for some time, but when the vacancy arose it happened so fast that none of them was ready. Not for the want of trying. Rishi Sunak's aides had first registered a website – 'readyforrishi.com' – on 23 December 2021 just three weeks after the partygate scandal broke. On 6 July 2022, two days after Sunak resigned, they added another – 'ready4rishi.com'. A month earlier, on 8 June, Liz Truss, who was to make much of her loyalty to Johnson in the contest that followed, registered 'lizforleader.co.uk' just two days after he was weakened by the no-confidence vote.

By the time Johnson resigned, on 7 July, Sunak's aides had already booked a suite at the Conrad Hotel, next to St James's Park tube station, to get their campaign off the ground. It was to be run by Liam Booth-Smith, Sunak's chief of staff, and Oliver Dowden, who took on the role of campaign chairman. Mel Stride, the chairman of the Treasury select committee and keeper of the 'numbers', and special adviser Rupert Yorke hit the phones to MPs. For the crucial MPs' stage of the contest, which would winnow the number of candidates to two, Sunak could soon call on the services of no fewer than four former chief whips: Gavin Williamson, who had been instrumental in installing both May and Johnson, Julian Smith, Mark Harper and Mark Spencer.

But Sunak's inner circle knew that was only half the battle. At their first campaign meeting Dowden and Booth-Smith were clear that they expected to be trailing with the membership whichever right-wing rival they faced at the start of the grassroots phase of the campaign.

Cass Horowitz, Sunak's social media manager, began work on a launch video, which featured old family photos exhumed by his wife, Akshata. When it appeared, rivals assumed Sunak had the video prepared months before, but Horowitz, as the guardian of 'brand Rishi', was used to turning such projects around quickly. 'Liam was rewriting the script half an hour before he did it,' a colleague recalled. 'Rish filmed it in the bedroom of the hotel on the evening of the *Spectator* party. Cass made him do it again afterwards because it wasn't good enough.'

Having put up taxes to the highest level in seventy years and played a leading role in unseating the party's folk hero, Sunak had an uphill battle to win, but as he pressed the flesh at the magazine's annual summer bash that evening, the former chancellor was regarded as the clear frontrunner to top the ballot of MPs. Afterwards, an aide said, 'He was determined final numbers needed to be way over a hundred', but an early briefing (perhaps by a rival to undermine him) that he hoped to win over 200 colleagues may have been nearer the mark as a target if he was to go into the grassroots stage with the necessary momentum.

The *Spectator*'s garden was packed that night with potential leadership candidates: Nadhim Zahawi, Tom Tugendhat and Kemi Badenoch. Suella Braverman had already announced her intention to run. Their thunder was stolen, however, when Josh Grimstone, Michael Gove's special adviser, marched up to Guto Harri and pronounced him 'a fucking disgrace' for his role in the sacking of Gove and the briefing that his boss was 'a snake' – having alerted a couple of journalists to his intentions so the confrontation could be recorded for posterity. Harri stood his ground and made clear Gove had been removed as a blunt act of revenge for his betrayal in 2016.

The video went live the following afternoon. It began with Sunak explaining the values he learned from his mother who had emigrated to Britain as a young woman. But it quickly framed the contest as a battle between two economic visions, between reality and fantasy. 'Do we confront this moment with honesty, seriousness and determination?' he asked. 'Or do we tell ourselves comforting fairy tales that might make us feel better in the moment but will leave our children worse off tomorrow?' The party, it would transpire, was rather attracted to the Brothers Grimm.

While Boris Johnson was holed up in his Downing Street bunker, Liz Truss was incommunicado on a plane to Indonesia, where she was attending the G20 foreign ministers' summit in Bali. When the plane refuelled in Dubai, Truss spoke to her spads. Johnson was teetering but still in charge. Adam Jones and Jamie Hope, her media spad and her policy adviser, agreed that she had to keep going, to be seen to 'get on with the job'. As soon as she landed after the second leg, they realised it was a mistake. 'You've got to come back,' Jones said. 'This is going to move very, very quickly. You need to start making calls.'

Truss's instinct was to go to the first session of the summit, so she was not open to attack by other cabinet ministers. When she returned to her hotel, she turned on the TV to see Johnson resigning. Another foreign minister messaged her, 'Get back home woman and start hustling!' Unfortunately, the crew of her government plane had not had their mandatory rest time, so she had to wait until the next morning. As she walked along the beach to gather her thoughts, Truss revealed 'I started crying', sad that her period as a foreign minister was coming to an end.[1] The summit was compared by rivals to John Major's wisdom teeth, which had kept him out of Westminster during Margaret Thatcher's removal. It worked for him too. She jumped on the plane to return home, making calls to MPs during the second layover in Dubai and wrestling with intermittent WiFi.

Asking her colleagues for their support did not come easily to Truss. 'I'm not sure I can do this,' she confided in one aide. Jones said, 'She wasn't naturally clubbable. I remember a minister saying, "There is no such thing in government as a Trussite." She was slightly socially awkward. She had strongly held views and beliefs but was often someone who personally struggled to bring people with her. She relied on spads and supportive MPs to do a lot of the corralling.'[2] Truss held 'Fizz with Liz' drinks dos (though a friend pointed out, 'She much prefers a cold sauvignon blanc') but had done little to think about how a campaign would work and needed help building support in the parliamentary party. She told one confidant, 'I think I would be a very good prime minister, there are just two problems: I am weird and I don't have any friends. Can you help me fix that?'[3]

On a trip to Australia in January 2022 she went for a 6 a.m. run with Jones around Sydney Harbour. Partygate was in full swing. 'It's looking dicey for Boris, isn't it?' Truss said, raising the subject for the first time. 'We did have a conversation about whether she should run and what we needed to do about it,' Jones recalled.[4] 'Have you thought about what you will do if the balloon goes up?' he asked.

'I've got no idea,' she replied.

'Who would our campaign manager be?'

'Probably Thérèse Coffey, but I've got no idea.'

Coffey, Truss's closest friend in politics, was her first call. She would oversee the campaign. Nadine Dorries would cheerlead on Twitter and peddle the 'Rishi betrayed Boris' narrative, with Dehenna Davison as Truss's advocate in the 2019 intake. But Truss did not land until Friday evening. She was more than a day behind. It felt like more. At this stage she was 'very worried' about her chances of making the final run-off. 'I think in herself she thought she probably wouldn't,' a close aide recalled.

Liz Truss was not one to be deterred by adversity, however. She had already seen the end of her career flash before her eyes on several occasions. Her most memorable moment at Defra had been a party conference speech (branding it 'a disgrace' that the UK imported so much cheese) so bad it had garnered a cult following on YouTube. As justice secretary she had been slow to defend the judiciary when they were named 'enemies of the people' by the *Daily Mail*. As chief secretary to the Treasury she was frozen out of the budget preparations by the chancellor, Philip Hammond. Since June 2018, when she had made a speech at the LSE outlining her world view, Truss had turned her fortunes around with a well-judged but brazen PR campaign, positioning herself as a born-again Brexiteer and crusader for new trade deals, a pitch designed to appeal to the right in Parliament and the Tory grassroots. She told the *Mail* in November that year she wanted to be the first female chancellor, but 'I don't want to be there just because I've got a pair of boobs.'[5]

This was a far cry from Truss's time as a teenage Liberal Democrat, backing the abolition of the monarchy. But after a peripatetic childhood in Glasgow, where she acquired a broad Scottish accent, and then Leeds, she was used to being told she was not good enough.

Her impudent determination, to those who accompanied her, was never better displayed than on a visit to the United Nations in 2019 with Boris Johnson, when the Supreme Court ruling on prorogation came in.

Roundly ignored by Johnson's team, Truss was desperate to make it into the room for the prime minister's meeting with Donald Trump. She argued that because US trade representative Robert Lighthizer was due to be there, so should she. Representations through spads and the private office came to nothing. At a breakfast with business leaders, Truss was ushered out but followed Johnson, pushed her way through a crowd and tapped him on the shoulder. 'Boris, I need to be in this bilat,' she said. 'These people are telling me I can't be – why not?' Johnson caved. When the time arrived, Truss's advisers squeezed into a tiny room. 'You could just tell every single person around Boris was thinking, "What the fuck are they doing here?"' one of her team recalled. 'It was so awkward.' Truss, whose EQ was as low as her chutzpah was high, just kept smiling. She was a woman in a hurry. 'Liz had one speed and that was ramming speed,' recalled a former special adviser. 'And, if you didn't keep feeding that desire to keep going, she would go off and create bloody mayhem.' Even before she became a leadership contender, there were concerns that she had no internal brake. 'She was very good at getting stuff done,' one of her inner circle explained. 'But the way she did that was by setting the dial at 150 per cent, in the knowledge that advisers, the media, Number 10 and the deep state would dial it back to 80 or 90 per cent. She'd end up getting most of what she wanted.'

From June and through the summer a proto-leadership team began to meet once a fortnight in the Boot and Flogger pub near London Bridge, consisting of Jason Stein, Ruth Porter, Guy Robinson and James Bethell, a Tory peer who was to become a minister during the Covid crisis. Porter spent part of her formative years at the Institute of Economic Affairs, Truss's favourite think tank. Stein had been Truss's civil service spokesman at the Treasury before spells as Amber Rudd's special adviser and on Jeremy Hunt's 2019 leadership team. 'She was always clear she was going to do it because her daughter always wanted her to do it,' a close friend said. Truss said she 'felt compelled' to run but even her husband had his doubts about the wisdom of it. 'Hugh said it would be impossible to lead the party, given the level of infighting and nihilism demonstrated by the removal of Boris.'[6]

Now playing catch-up, Truss gathered her team at her home in Greenwich on the Saturday morning after Johnson's fall. Her special advisers – Adam Jones and Jamie Hope – were joined by Porter, her former spad and ideological buttress, Stein, her former comms expert and spirit animal. Sophie Jarvis, Truss's other spad and the primary 'Truss whisperer', hit the phones from a Swedish campervan holiday.[7] 'It was totally chaotic,' one adviser recalled. 'She always wanted the top office but the idea that she was actively planning for it is nonsense.' The politicians present from the start included Thérèse Coffey, Ranil Jayawardena, Vicky Ford, Wendy Morton and Truss's PPS Rob Butler. Kwasi Kwarteng and James Cleverly, both of whom lived nearby, also helped. Jon Moynihan, a financier and party donor, would raise the cash. At this stage they didn't even have a bank account.

Truss and her aides had discussed how they would position her if there was a contest, specifically how they would match up with Sunak: 'It was basically three things: one, loyal to Boris; two, traditional Tory economics; three, someone who is tougher and has the courage of their convictions.' Now they had to quickly set up a whipping operation, get the website live, devise a campaign slogan and record a launch video.

She told the team assembled in Greenwich, 'It's going to be me versus Rishi. Rishi is not cutting taxes. I don't need to go nuts, but I need to cut a bit to set the parameters. We're going to scrap the NI rise, scrap the corporation tax rise, and we're going to scrap the green levies.'[8]

Truss had huge ambitions to transform the political economy of the country. Hers was a version of Brexit beloved by much of the European Research Group (ERG), the trade-dealing, deregulating version which had been dubbed Singapore-on-Thames. This was distinct from the Vote Leave version, which had championed extra money for public services (both on the side of the bus and in government). Boris Johnson had straddled this divide, using both visions when it suited him, but Truss was a fully signed-up Singaporeesta. However, she was not yet prepared to tell her party how far she wanted to go.

That evening Truss went to Kwarteng's house, two streets away, and sat in his garden. Over a magnum of sauvignon blanc, the business secretary pledged his fealty. The two had talked for months about what they would do if they got power. It was obvious he would be her chancellor. They discussed how to avoid the 'heebie-jeebies' which had afflicted Johnson and Sunak, Blair and Brown. 'I was hired because I was going to do her bidding,' Kwarteng admitted. 'I was very explicit about that. I was an enabler.' He would kick himself later for not pushing back more.

The two had been elected at the same time in 2010 and had been ideological bedfellows ever since. Some presumed their relationship ran to more than that, something they both always denied. They had both been leading lights in the Free Enterprise Group of young Tories (alumni also included Dominic Raab, Priti Patel and Chris Skidmore) and co-authors of *Britannia Unchained*, a manifesto for deregulation to kickstart growth as long ago as 2012. Kwarteng's parents had emigrated from Ghana as students, but he was a blue blood politically, rising from Eton via Trinity College Cambridge (where he got a double first and won *University Challenge* almost single-handed), Harvard and JPMorgan Chase, then the world of hedge funds. Truss was quicker into the ministerial ranks and the cabinet, proof that the galvanising fury of other people's disregard can outrun even the best educations. Neither suffered fools or self-doubt.

Classically intelligent, Kwarteng's advance was slowed because of a reputation for laziness punctuated by impulsiveness. Officials in the Department for Business, Energy and Industrial Strategy (BEIS) commented negatively on his 'refusal to take a red box' of official papers home with him. A political adviser said, 'We heard absolute horror stories from his private office that he would just have an oral box at the end of the day. He would just get the private secretaries to come in at six o'clock and do a thirty-second oral summary, and make a snap decision, which is not a good way to run a government.' Kwarteng denied this 'oral box' claim but admitted he preferred an 'electronic box' rather than hard copies of papers. The same spad said Kwarteng could be easily influenced: 'The trick with Kwasi is, you make a comparison to something in Conservative Party history and go, "This is exactly like when Peel did this" and he'll say, "Oh great, well then let's do that." Other than that, he was utterly work-shy.' A cabinet colleague who thought the job should have gone to Simon Clarke said, 'Candidly, I don't think he was the right choice to be chancellor. That was partly because he is brilliant but lazy; partly because he just wasn't going to tell her difficult things.'

The next day, Truss filmed her launch video in her back garden – but only after Jones and Stein had turned manual labourers to remove weeds and builders' waste from view. 'It all felt remarkably slapdash,' Jones recalled.[9] In it she pledged her mantra would be to 'deliver, deliver, deliver' growth in the economy, as well as low taxes. She repeated the message in an op-ed for the *Telegraph*, while Kwarteng took aim at Sunak in the *Sun*: 'We can't simply be accountants trying to balance the books the whole time.' Her team were soon installed in 11 Lord North Street, a Westminster townhouse owned by Tory peer Greville Howard – from where the leadership campaigns of Boris Johnson, Andrea Leadsom and Iain Duncan Smith had been run. It was most famous for being the house where Michael Portillo was caught installing forty phone lines in 1995 as he prepared an abortive challenge to John Major.

Sunak and Truss were the presumed favourites when the contest began. For those trying to get traction to challenge them, there was first-mover advantage. Suella Braverman stole a march on Priti Patel for the backing of the ERG. Braverman had not expected Johnson to fall, but when he did, she received several invitations to run from MPs on the Eurosceptic right. Her tough stance on the Northern Ireland Protocol Bill distinguished her from Patel, of whom one Brexiteer minister remarked, 'On the protocol, she wasn't really supportive.' When the ERG tabled an amendment to the borders bill, which would have given the government the power to ignore so-called Article 39 rulings of the European Court of Human Rights, Patel, as home secretary, led government opposition to the measure. 'She flatly refused,' another cabinet minister said. 'She did not want it. Boris and Priti had a chance to stop the boats and because they didn't take those steps, the bill was pretty useless.' Braverman became the most outspoken advocate of the plan – which was effectively an extension of the notwithstanding clauses in the NIP Bill to the area of asylum and immigration.

On the other wing of the party, first out of the blocks was Tom Tugendhat, chairman of the foreign affairs select committee. In an op-ed for the *Telegraph* on Friday morning, the former soldier, who had fought in Afghanistan and Iraq, talked up both his military experience and the need for renewal. 'I have served before, now I hope to answer the call as prime minister.' In an interview with the *Sunday Times* that weekend, Tugendhat had lined up a series of SBS commandos to testify how he had dodged death during the first major firefight behind enemy lines in the Iraq War.[10] Counter-intuitively the outspoken Remainer's campaign chairman was Anne-Marie Trevelyan, who had whipped for the ERG during the Brexit battles in Parliament. Tugendhat's team was a broad church. It featured Cameroon campaign director Daniel Korski, Nick Faith, the former boss of Policy Exchange as communications director, and several Brexiteers, including Vote Leaver Eline Storeide, his parliamentary Girl Friday. Tugendhat's whips were former Rebel Alliance numbers man Stephen Hammond and Aaron Bell, but he soon attracted the support of Johnson ally Jake Berry, head of the Northern Research Group of red wall MPs.

Tugendhat's ability to carry the military mantle was enhanced that Saturday when Ben Wallace, the defence secretary, who was top of the cabinet approval ratings with the Tory grassroots on the ConservativeHome website, ruled himself out. Wallace's marriage had broken up a year earlier. When his teenage children asked him not to run, he put family first. Graham Stuart, who had been drumming up support with MPs, became Truss's campaign whip instead.

Tugendhat was not the only fresh-faced challenger. Indeed he was about to be eclipsed by a fresher face still – just as Matt Hancock, the One Nation challenger in 2019, had been by Rory Stewart. Kemi Badenoch, a local government minister, set out her stall in *The Times* that Saturday, stressing the need for fiscal discipline and honesty. 'The truth will set us free,' she wrote. It was organisation and the backing of Michael Gove which was to give her credibility, however. He thought her the most talented junior minister he had ever had. Gove felt he owed Badenoch since, heavily pregnant, she had introduced him at his own campaign launch in 2019, just forty-eight hours after the revelation that he had once taken cocaine. Earlier in 2022, over dinner, Gove told her, 'You could be prime minister one day.' He wrote supportive articles and played Tugendhat in their debate prep sessions.

Badenoch's campaign team consisted of the young ministers who had resigned en masse earlier that week – Lee Rowley, her numbers man, plus Neil O'Brien, Julia Lopez and Alex Burghart. Before that, Badenoch had watched the result of the no-confidence vote against Johnson at Gove's official residence in Carlton Gardens, along with Simon Clarke, Burghart, Claire Coutinho and Laura Trott. The vote had failed to put an end to the bleeding one way or the other and the feeling that night was that the new generation should offer their own candidate when the time came. They were not terribly subtle about it, however, meeting in Lopez or Burghart's offices on the lower ministerial corridor, close to that of Johnson loyalist Nigel Adams. 'If you're running a leadership campaign, you do it off site,' a loyalist remarked. 'It was blatant.'

As a young Conservative intellectual, Badenoch took some votes from Sunak, as a Brexiteer she capped Braverman's upside, but it was Truss, who most closely matched her culture warrior credentials, who was most hurt by her entry into the race. Truss's team saw it as a plot by Gove and

Sunak to keep her out of the final two. But Badenoch's game was the two-stage leadership bid – establish credibility and secure a big job to position for a frontrunner bid at a later date.

Badenoch's energy and organisation soon meant she eclipsed more established runners like Jeremy Hunt, Sajid Javid and Grant Shapps plus the newcomer to the top table, Nadhim Zahawi. The (acting) chancellor had been briefly considered the most likely candidate to surge through the middle in a party divided between fans of Sunak and Truss, but his political pirouettes in Johnson's final days undermined his credibility with colleagues. 'Being prime minister is 95 per cent judgement,' a Johnson aide said. 'He showed a catastrophic failure of it.'[11]

The candidate exhibiting the least judgement was Rehman Chishti, the MP for Gillingham and Rainham in Kent, who appeared to have taken a look in the mirror one morning and mistaken himself for Barack Obama. In a shaky video, filmed selfie-style in his garden, Chishti said he was running to fight for 'aspirational conservatism'. Chishti's candidacy was the ultimate expression of aspiration. He would fail to secure the support of a single fellow MP.

Truss was slower to build momentum than Sunak. She was far from the only right-winger or the only woman in the race. 'We thought we would have more early supporters,' an aide said, 'but it was clear that more than expected were in the Suella and Kemi camps.' Truss needed a new pitch to see them off and unite the right under her own banner: 'experience, thick skin, track record'.

The 1922 Committee in conclave with the Conservative Party board decreed that candidates had to secure the backing of 20 MPs to even make it onto the ballot paper, up from eight in 2019. On Monday 11 July it was announced that from the second MPs' ballot, survivors would need 30 votes. Despite Graham Brady's desire to get the election done and dusted by mid-August, the grassroots membership wanted to drag out the contest until October to allow for hustings around the country. They compromised on a result on 5 September, with the new prime minister installed a day later. Every campaign team had until 4 p.m. on Tuesday 12th to get the necessary support.

When nominations closed, eight names had made the cut. Both Shapps and Chishti fell short, but the biggest casualty was Javid, who had never found a way of harnessing his inspiring back story and experience in half a dozen cabinet jobs into a compelling narrative about why he should lead. 'This time he got to 19 signatures with ten minutes to go and someone who had said they had signed his form, didn't sign it,' one of his team revealed. Shapps failed despite displaying the chutzpah to ask Tugendhat to back him. 'At that point we had 21 publicly declared supporters and Shapps had seven,' a member of Team Tom recalled.

Sunak launched his campaign at a slick event in Westminster on the morning of the first ballot, Wednesday 13 July. He was introduced by Dominic Raab, the deputy prime minister. Shapps was also present, having abandoned his own campaign. A Truss aide threatened the end of their careers, if she won: 'If you're on the stage, you're in a grave.'[12]

The first PR coup of the day, however, went to Truss, when Jacob Rees-Mogg and Nadine Dorries emerged from Number 10 after the first cabinet meeting with Boris Johnson as a lame duck leader, to tell the waiting cameras they were backing Truss. 'She's probably a stronger Brexiteer than both of us,' Dorries declared. Rees-Mogg added, 'When we discussed taxation, Liz was always opposed to Rishi's higher taxes.' Dorries, the self-appointed bad cop, took to Twitter and accused Sunak of using 'dirty tricks' and the 'dark arts' to oust Johnson.

In Sunak's headquarters, his team watched as the two Johnson loyalists 'used the set of Downing Street to do a party political broadcast on behalf of Liz Truss', a performance they firmly believed had been sanctioned by the prime minister. In the days ahead the Ready for Rishi team became convinced Johnson had also given the green light to 'an organised conspiracy from inside Number 10 to deliberately leak documents' which might harm Sunak. Before long, the leaks began about how he had secretly tried to block the plan to fly migrants to Rwanda, and other pet projects, when he was chancellor.

When Graham Brady read out the results, Sunak came top but there were surprises behind him:

88 Rishi Sunak
67 Penny Mordaunt
50 Liz Truss
40 Kemi Badenoch
37 Tom Tugendhat
32 Suella Braverman

25 Nadhim Zahawi
18 Jeremy Hunt

Hunt and Zahawi were eliminated, the runner-up in 2019 not even getting the votes of all twenty MPs who nominated him. Hunt texted Truss to say she had been a 'brilliant foreign secretary', but he had made the 'tough call' to back Sunak. Furious, she pronounced it, 'Another nail in Rishi's coffin.'[13]

Tugendhat's was a creditable result, but he trailed Badenoch for the best newcomer award. The big story, though, was the very strong showing of Penny Mordaunt, who had also launched that morning, with a patriotic performance which played up her role as a Royal Navy reservist and promised real Tory values. Comparing the party to Paul McCartney's performance at the Glastonbury festival, she said, 'We liked hearing those new tunes, but we really wanted to hear the old favourites.' Mordaunt was careful not to name her favourite songs but to let her audience imagine she shared theirs. As a blank canvas she became the candidate on whom it was easiest for MPs to project their hopes. Thus was born 'Mordmentum' – the media delighting in a plot twist they had not seen coming. ConservativeHome conducted a series of head-to-head polls in which Mordaunt beat every other candidate.

Mordaunt's campaign began scarcely less chaotically than Truss's. Despite having flirted with the idea of running since 2018, she had not built a strong team. Her right-hand woman, Laura Round, had departed government and was at a music festival for Freud Communications when news of Johnson's resignation came through. She called Mordaunt, who told her to 'come on over'. Round quickly recruited Simon Finkelstein, a nephew of the *Times* columnist Danny, as head of policy. He began churning out op-eds from his holiday sunbed. John Millman, who worked at InHouse Comms with Theresa May's former spinner Katie Perrior, was her next call. The following Monday the three met in the Portcullis House office of Craig Tracey, Mordaunt's whip, along with Andrea Leadsom, the candidate's closest senior ally. None of them knew each other. 'Nice to meet you all,' said Round. 'I've decided we are all going to have to just trust each other.' She looked around the room and saw expressions which combined terror and excitement.

Round, Leadsom and Tracey set up a WhatsApp group called 'Three Generals' to run the campaign. Nicola Richards, who won West

Bromwich East in 2019, deputised for Tracey. They were soon joined by MPs John Lamont, John Penrose, Kieran Mullan, Damian Collins and George Freeman. David Davis and Damian Green gave the supporter base ex-cabinet heft. But there were still teething troubles. Mordaunt's launch video, which sought to play up her links to the Navy and her belief in 'teamwork' ('a little less about the leader and a lot more about the ship'), had to be re-edited after it used unauthorised footage from the armed forces. However, attracting Brexiteers, One Nation Tories, social liberals and fellow women, Mordaunt had the broadest range of support in the field. Her emergence was a mortal threat to Truss. Round took a call from the BBC's Chris Mason, telling her, 'Truss's team are properly rattled.'

Truss needed Braverman to drop out so she could peel off Brexiteers and right-wingers. Under pressure from ERG grandees to keep going, Braverman refused to quit. The next morning, she released a video promising that, as prime minister, she would pull the UK out of the European Convention on Human Rights (EHRC).

Confronted by the threat of not reaching the final two, where Truss was confident she could beat Sunak with the membership, her team decided they needed to knock some of the gloss off Mordaunt. On 14 July, David Frost – who also lived around the corner from Truss in Greenwich – went on TalkTV to issue a blistering account of Mordaunt's performance when he was Brexit minister and she was his deputy in the Cabinet Office. Revealing 'grave reservations' about her candidacy, Frost said, 'I'm sorry to say this, she did not master the necessary detail in the negotiations last year. She wouldn't always deliver tough messages to the European Union when that was necessary and I'm afraid she wasn't fully accountable or always visible. Sometimes I didn't even know where she was. I'm afraid this became such a problem that after six months I had to ask the PM to move her on and find somebody else to support me.'

Truss finally staged her formal campaign launch the same day. Seeking to contrast herself with Sunak, she said, 'I'm loyal to Boris Johnson.' Seeking to contrast her cabinet experience with Mordaunt's, she said, 'I am ready to be prime minister from day one.' And seeking the ERG's second preference votes, she vowed to take a tough line with Brussels on the Northern Ireland Protocol. Truss could not shake the awkwardness of her public performances. When she left the stage, she turned the wrong way and appeared lost as she searched for the exit.

In the second ballot, that evening, both Braverman and Tugendhat went backwards and the attorney general was eliminated. Tugendhat had achieved his goal of remaining in the race so he could participate in the first debate, his chance to cut through with the public. Sunak cleared the 100 MPs mark. Truss advanced but Mordaunt widened the gap between them, while Badenoch's continuing buoyancy also hurt her:

101 Rishi Sunak (+13)
83 Penny Mordaunt (+16)
64 Liz Truss (+14)
49 Kemi Badenoch (+9)
32 Tom Tugendhat (-5)
27 Suella Braverman (-5)

Truss and Braverman had spoken that morning, before the ballot. They had been allies on the Northern Ireland Protocol Bill. Truss saw a kindred spirit: 'She's got balls.' Braverman believed Truss was the only other candidate who would genuinely tackle the things she cared about most: Brexit and immigration. Truss supported the notwithstanding clauses on the NIP Bill and Braverman pressed the case for the same approach to be taken to the small boats. A Truss aide recalled, 'Liz said, "If you come out and endorse me, what do you want?" Suella said, "Home secretary." and that was done. Liz never regretted it for one second.'

As soon as the result was in Truss and Braverman spoke again. Some of Truss's team thought she should pull the offer since Braverman had not endorsed her before the vote, something which might have put Truss ahead of Mordaunt. 'Liz may have said, "Look, it was home sec this morning, it's justice now."' But Braverman was quick to endorse and 'earned her corn' getting actively involved in the campaign.

Later that evening, ERG chairman Mark Francois told their WhatsApp group, 'I do hope that all of our Group will now feel able to unite firmly behind Liz, to help deliver the vital Northern Ireland Protocol Bill, expand on the opportunities offered by Brexit and secure the future of the Conservative Party.' Braverman chipped in that Badenoch could be prime minister one day but that 'Liz is undeniably the better placed candidate to get to the voluntary party round, and fight there for the things that all three of us believe.'[14]

* * *

Just as Truss seemed to have revived her prospects, they were nearly killed off. Her performance in the first debate, broadcast by Channel 4 on Friday 15 July, was almost career-ending. She wore a pussycat bow top, which could have been stolen from Margaret Thatcher, but her delivery was a disaster: stilted sentences punctuated with robotic gestures.

Tom Tugendhat seized his opportunity and distinguished himself from the other candidates by refusing to say Boris Johnson was an honest man. He won the snap public poll at the end of the debate with 36 per cent, well ahead of Sunak on 24 per cent, with Truss last of the five candidates on 7 per cent. The irony is that Tugendhat had prepared for his big moment in a debate camp run by Brett O'Donnell, the American who had helped Johnson before the referendum debate in 2016 and for the leadership contest of 2019. Will Walden, Johnson's former spin doctor, also helped put Tugendhat through his paces. When Tugendhat shook his head and said 'No' to Johnson's trustworthiness, the green room 'erupted' with cheering from his supporters. 'We knew that was the debate, there,' one said. Another of his team was overheard calling Truss a 'mannequin'.

Truss's comms team – Adam Jones and Jason Stein – had spent the week trying to persuade Sunak's spinner Nissy Chesterfield to join them in boycotting the debate. She kept them waiting until Thursday evening before texting Stein to say, 'We're going for it.' By then it was too late to prepare Truss properly. Her debate camp, at the house in Lord North Street, was run by MPs and not well structured.

Truss's team admitted to journalists, 'She's not a good public performer', but insisted the party and public wanted a 'serious person'. They told Truss she had done well. She knew from looking at their faces that she had 'bombed'.[15] When the foreign secretary glanced at social media, she screamed at Jones and Stein, 'Why the fuck did you say I did okay? Twitter is in meltdown.'

In another example of her awkwardness, the following day, Truss phoned Tugendhat to congratulate him, a stilted conversation which his staff listened to on speaker. 'There was this bizarre pause to which Tom said, "So is there anything I can help you with, Liz?" She said, "I just wanted to touch base and see how things are going."' The call ended without Truss asking for his support.

Truss deleted Twitter from her phone and that Saturday she called what one aide called 'the biggest crisis meeting of the campaign at her house' with her closest allies. 'We need to do two things,' they told her.

'We need to go for Penny and we need to drastically improve your debate performance.' Another confessed, 'We even put "kill Penny" in the grid.'

Mordaunt had given them an opening during the debate, when she claimed she had 'never been in favour' of gender self-ID, the focus of an increasingly toxic public debate about trans rights. Under that policy, people could change their gender without medical intervention, something opposed by women's rights groups who saw it threatening women-only spaces like rape crisis centres and single sex prisons.

Mordaunt's position was curious since she had long been identified with the issue, partly influenced by her brother who was a trans rights activist. In one Commons debate she had declared, 'Trans women are women', a position not supported by her rivals. Mordaunt's misfortune was that both Truss and Badenoch had, like her, been equalities ministers and knew the issue inside out – and Braverman had found herself in the middle of the debate when she became the first cabinet minister to take maternity leave. That necessitated a change in the law, but the bill as originally drafted referred to Braverman not as a mother but as a 'pregnant person', to her enduring fury. Mordaunt's allies claimed the offending term was written by a Downing Street aide, not her.

Mordaunt, nonetheless, knew she had a problem, since she had written a Twitter thread the previous week, arguing that people who were legally a woman were not always biologically a woman. This sparked a backlash from ministers and Number 10 advisers who claimed that her approach in government made her 'too woke' to be prime minister. At Mordaunt's campaign launch she tried again to park the issue: 'It was Margaret Thatcher who said that "every prime minister needs a Willie". A woman like me doesn't have one.'

After the debate Adam Jones, Truss's spin doctor, was overheard telling a journalist that Team Truss knew Mordaunt was lying about her views and 'we have the docs to prove it'. Jones was not the one who led the dark arts operation to leak the papers. Another aide contacted journalists from the *Sunday Times* and the *Mail on Sunday* and arranged for them to collect a stuffed brown envelope from an address in north London that Saturday morning. Both papers carried front-page stories which quoted leaked documents from July 2019 showing Mordaunt had argued for the self-ID rules to be loosened, removing some of the medical checks before a gender change – leaving only a test of whether someone was of 'sound mind'. Seven months later, self-ID was scrapped.

On television that morning Badenoch observed witheringly, 'I'm not going to call her a liar; I think it's very possible she genuinely did not understand what she was signing off, because it's a very complex area.' Claws bared.

Fellow ministers Victoria Atkins and Baroness Williams rallied to Mordaunt's cause, but only Williams went on the record. The damage was done. 'It was a hit job,' a close ally remarked. 'It was definitely a turning point. It got more difficult to get people on board. It did affect people who didn't have a chance to meet Penny and don't know her.' Mordaunt told her supporters she would not fire back. She did not say so out loud but her private inspiration was Michelle Obama's catchphrase, 'When they go low, we go high.'

While Truss's team spent Saturday doing their best to stall Mordaunt's progress, the candidate rested. Sunday would be spent trying to improve her performance in the second debate that evening on ITV. Truss threw herself into a punishing eight-hour prep session led by Rob Butler, her PPS, who had been a newsreader for Channel 5 and the BBC before becoming a media coach. Jason Stein was also a skilled tutor, having prepared Formula One drivers and Premier League footballers for their encounters with the media. Stein faced down Kwasi Kwarteng, James Cleverly and Simon Clarke, who all wanted to get involved.

Butler played the moderator while he worked on Truss's delivery, voice, tone and body language, telling her where to rest her hands when she was speaking, urging her to talk about her background rather than just policy. Stein led on attack lines, jokes and played the role of Sunak. Adam Jones played Mordaunt and gave Truss lines that worked. No one else was allowed in. 'It was a horrible, swelteringly hot day,' one of those involved said. 'She was grumpy. She doesn't like being told what to do. She doesn't like being rehearsed.' But as the day went on, they could see dramatic improvement. 'We practised, practised, practised,' another said. 'We went through every conceivable scenario.'

In the car to the studios, Stein now acted, as a colleague put it, 'like her "upper" drug', deliberately engaging Truss in mindless small talk about falafels to keep his candidate calm. One said, 'Adam went with her to the first debate and he stresses her out because he's always on the phone. Jason handles her very well.' Stein's attention to detail extended to briefing the driver that Truss's favourite song, 'Dancing in the Dark', should come on just as they were arriving at ITV. She also took Kwarteng's advice to 'have half a glass of wine before going on air'.[16]

What followed was probably Truss's best public performance as candidate or prime minister. It was a slug fest. Sunak attacked her for 'fantasy economics'. She hit back, 'Rishi, you have raised taxes to the highest level in seventy years, that is not going to drive growth.'

The format dictated that each candidate had to ask the other a question. Sunak asked Truss what she 'regretted the most' – being a Lib Dem or a Remainer? Butler, Stein and Jones watched full of confidence; they knew it was the third time she had answered the question that day: 'I was not someone who was born into the Conservative Party. I went to a comprehensive school, but my fundamental belief and the reason I am a Conservative is I saw kids at my school being let down, and not get the opportunities, not get the proper educational standards you may have got at your school, Rishi.'

Stein and Jones had argued with the production team before the programme about their question, querying Sunak's more conciliatory stance on China, an unpopular position with many Tory MPs. 'You can't ask that, it's too harsh,' a producer said. ITV tried several times to get them to shift. Team Truss asked for examples of what might be acceptable. The producer refused to say. 'If you're not going to give us a better steer, China is the question,' Stein said. It was a good decision. Sunak was uncomfortable.

Sunak won the snap poll, with 24 per cent, ahead of Tugendhat, but Truss did much better with 15 per cent. Tugendhat had come close to winning the backing of Priti Patel that weekend, which might have helped him gain broader support, but it was not to be. The real winners of the debate were arguably Labour, who had seen the two most likely prime ministers kick lumps out of each other. After the show Sunak turned to Truss and said, 'Why are we doing this?'[17] It was a question Tory MPs, troubled by the blue-on-blue civil war, were now asking. Many wanted no more TV debates at all. The back channel between the two camps was reopened. Stein and Chesterfield agreed their candidates would not take part in the third, upcoming, Sky News debate the following Tuesday.

Truss was becoming more disciplined. A minister said, 'She realised she needed to be better at not saying something. When you're brimming with ideas you want to tell everyone about them, but she learned quickly that you need to say a few things repeatedly and that's how the big job is different.' It helped that she did not have to do her own dirty work.

On the morning of the third ballot, 18 July, Mordaunt came under fire again. The *Mail* attacked her for meeting members of the Muslim Council of Britain. The *Telegraph* reported that she was seen as a 'Walter Mitty character' at the Department for International Trade, 'who often went missing', making 'no overseas visits' between January and March. Her boss, the secretary of state Anne-Marie Trevelyan, who was backing Tugendhat but had told Truss she would switch to her once he was knocked out, then told LBC, 'There have been a number of times when she hasn't been available and other ministers have picked up the pieces.' While three of Sunak's former Treasury ministers and three of Truss's former Foreign Office ministers were backing them, none of Mordaunt's DIT colleagues supported her.

As the battle to replace Boris Johnson intensified, he embarked on a farewell tour, self-congratulatory and self-pitying in equal measure. The previous weekend he had played host at Chequers to 130 guests – still loyal ministers, MPs and aides – who supped sparkling wine and ate barbecued burgers while Johnson flamed Sunak: 'This year if all goes well we will launch the first UK satellite in history to enter space from UK soil ... and I leave it to you to imagine who I would like at this stage to send into orbit.'[18]

This gag was judged so successful by Johnson that he wheeled it out again in a speech at the Farnborough air show on the morning of the 18th. There, the demob happy prime minister recounted the valedictory joyride he had taken the week before in a F-35 Typhoon jet. His account of performing 'a loop the loop and a barrel roll and an aileron roll' was a metaphor for what he had put his party and country through. That evening the government called a confidence motion in itself, to demonstrate that the Tories retained the right to govern even as they changed leader. It was an opportunity for Johnson to essay his greatest hits – getting Brexit done, the election landslide, getting 'the big calls right' during Covid, arming Ukraine – and take a dig at those on his own benches who still wanted him gone. 'This Conservative government is undefeated at the polls and never let that be forgotten,' he said, pointedly, before admitting sadly that 'I am more popular on the streets of Kyiv right now than I am in Kensington.' This time it was Keir Starmer he wanted to send into orbit.

Johnson sat huffily crossing his arms and shaking his head as Starmer worked his way through the case for the prosecution: 'He's been forced out in disgrace. Judged by his colleagues and peers to be unworthy of his position and unfit for office … A vengeful squatter mired in scandal.' When Tory MPs protested, Starmer told them to 're-read their resignation letters'. He compared the Tories to 'a once-secure Premier League side burning through managers as it slides inevitably towards relegation'. Labour's Kevin Brennan put it best, suggesting the debate was Johnson's 'opportunity to speak at his own funeral'.

At 8 p.m. the effect of the 'kill Penny' onslaught was clear. Mordmentum stalled, Mordaunt's total falling by one in the four days since the second ballot. It was a truism of Tory leadership contests that you could never go backwards. Truss was catching her but Badenoch was catching her.

115 Rishi Sunak (+14)
82 Penny Mordaunt (-1)
71 Liz Truss (+7)
58 Kemi Badenoch (+9)
31 Tom Tugendhat (-1)

Tugendhat was eliminated after a spirited campaign. He had been warned by his whips that he might lose half of his supporters, but in the event just one peeled away. Anticipating his elimination, he had met Truss that morning. She said that if he backed her and brought thirty supporters with him, she would make him foreign secretary. Tugendhat agreed since he was more closely aligned with Truss than Sunak on foreign affairs, particularly China. But he said he wanted to vote for Badenoch, a close friend, in the fourth ballot. Truss was bemused but agreed. It was a misstep by Tugendhat.[19]

Badenoch gained just one vote in the fourth ballot the following day, (presumably Tugendhat's) and Truss picked up fifteen, just half of Tugendhat's supporters. Mordaunt advanced again but her margin over Truss was now just six votes, with another fifty-nine in play in the final round of MP voting.

118 Rishi Sunak (+3)
92 Penny Mordaunt (+10)
86 Liz Truss (+15)
59 Kemi Badenoch (+1)

Sunak was clearly in the final round, but as it was now a three-way fight, and one so close between the other contenders, suspicions arose that his team would try to fix the result of the final ballot. Gavin Williamson's presence prompted the same accusations as in 2019 that he used proxy votes to manipulate the numbers. Sunak's supporters always insisted that they did not mind who they faced. In both Truss and Mordaunt's teams this was regarded as nonsense. Both assumed their candidate was the one Sunak did not want to face. 'The numbers were really odd,' a Trussite said. 'Rishi only went up by three. It did not smell right. They were trying to get Penny in the last two.'

In Mordaunt's camp, however, there was a strong belief that Sunak's team believed they could take out Truss during the run-off using a 'dirty dossier' on the foreign secretary. This was not Sunak's style, indeed he banned his team from personal attacks on Truss. But some of those who wanted him to win were undoubtedly capable of such a move. 'They had a file on Liz's private life,' a Mordaunt aide said.

Personal claims about Truss and her sexual proclivities had circulated in Westminster ever since she had admitted an affair with Mark Field more than a decade earlier. In more recent times, it was baselessly claimed the foreign secretary liked to receive her ministerial red boxes in the bath. Internet chatter focused on a lascivious conspiracy theory about the meaning of an oval necklace Truss was fond of wearing. Truss was also accused by Sunak backers of 'predatory' behaviour towards a younger male staff member and even 'that a sex tape existed of her'.[20]

One claim doing the rounds about Truss caused colleagues to sit down Jamie Hope, her policy adviser. 'We just wanted to let you know that there's this rumour floating around that you've been having an affair with Liz,' a fellow aide said. Hope went bright red and burst out laughing. 'Then everyone else burst out laughing,' a witness said. Hope told his girlfriend the news. She also burst out laughing. Harry Cole of the *Sun* later told Hope, 'You know what saved you? Every time I called Adam Jones to ask about it, he said, "Have you ever met Jamie Hope?" And then just laughed his arse off.' None of which stopped Dominic Cummings tweeting about a 'spad shagger' among the leadership candidates – though Truss was not the only one he was referring to.

Truss was not alone in being the target of the misogynist rumour mill. Tory sources circulated a salacious and highly sexist story about another female contender, suggesting that, while smoking with colleagues in her younger days, she once declared, 'I'm actually worried I like anal too much, I'm worried my arse is going to fall out.' Men were not immune either. Westminster women discussed with grim fascination the well-endowed cabinet minister whose girth was compared by one former lover to a Coke can. Conscious of his lengthy appendage, he politely enquired, mid-coitus, 'There's more, if you want it.'

Sunak celebrated wildly when the result of the final ballot was declared at 4 p.m. on 20 July. His campaign Twitter account released a video of him sitting tensely in his Portcullis House office and then punching the air and shouting 'Yes!' when it was announced that Truss had beaten Mordaunt. He hugged Liam Booth-Smith and then addressed a room full of supporters, telling them they had 'smashed it'. An aide said, 'I've never seen him so fired up.'

137 Rishi Sunak (+19)
113 Liz Truss (+27)
105 Penny Mordaunt (+13)

For others, it was a crushing outcome. Twenty minutes before the result, Laura Round, Mordaunt's campaign manager, called her whip Craig Tracey as she walked around St James's Park. 'Where are we, do you think?' Tracey replied, 'I think we've got it.' Mordaunt watched the declaration with her supporters. 'She had a poker face,' a witness said, when it was announced that she had not made it. 'The room was in shock. Some of the MPs were in tears. People must have lied. We thought we had the numbers.' Round felt like she had been run over by a truck. 'It was like a war,' she told a friend.

Truss had drinks with her MP supporters on the Commons terrace, then took her aides for an Honest Burger in Covent Garden. They laughed about a gaffe in which an aide tweeted for Truss, 'Thank you for putting your trust in me. I'm ready to hit the ground from day one.' Little did they know it would turn out to be a rare example of a campaign pledge delivered in full.

Minutes after the result was in, both Truss and Sunak received a text message from Simon Case, the cabinet secretary. 'Congratulations on reaching the final two,' he wrote. 'As in 2016 and 2019, the PM has authorised access talks for the final two candidates, so that you can access civil service briefing via me on issues such as government formation, government organisation and policy issues.'

Just as in 2019, the MPs who supported Mordaunt were not asked to indicate where their second preference votes would have gone. Sunak's camp was confident that a clear majority of them would have backed him. His position with the membership would have been much stronger if he had been shown to have the support of more than 200 MPs.

By the time the result was declared, Sunak already knew topping the MP ballot might be the summit of his success. His campaign had commissioned private polling. It was disastrous. Booth-Smith and Dowden took Sunak into a private room at a central London hotel to show him the numbers. He was losing to Truss among party members by 49 per cent to 22 per cent – 69 per cent to 31 per cent of likely voters. Booth-Smith explained, 'We have to win every "don't know", and probably shave five off her. I can't see how we do it.'

As Sunak absorbed this, his chief of staff now said he had a 'choice to make' about the kind of campaign he wanted to run. Booth-Smith, an advocate of 'where there is life, there is hope', suggested they run hard in the belief that Truss might win and then implode. 'Her plans are crazy,' he said. 'They are going to trash the economy. We know this. If you are consistent in hammering home this message and pay a price, by December, she's probably in a lot of trouble. Maybe at that point, if it doesn't work, there might be an interesting space.'

Sunak was naturally more pessimistic. 'It's not going to happen. Of course she's going to cause a lot of damage, but people won't want to do anything. It won't be as bad as we think. Everyone else gets the luck.' Nonetheless, he wanted to run a campaign where he made a virtue of telling the truth as he saw it. Booth-Smith had one other goal, to 'break the myth' that the right-winger always won Tory leadership elections by a margin of two to one. That meant dragging Sunak's numbers into the low 40 per cent range.

As the campaign went on, MPs and journalists could not understand why Sunak was not cutting his cloth more closely to the views of the membership. The answer is that his team believed that would position him better for the future. They were not alone in predicting disaster for Truss. Those around Boris Johnson believed he was only backing her because he suspected she would implode – though they identified the most propitious time for a Johnson comeback as June the following year, after poor results at the local elections. 'Boris was supporting Liz, not out of great enthusiasm for her, just because she wasn't Rishi,' a close ally recalled. 'But more importantly because he knew she was going to flop. She was just meant to take her time fucking up. By the summer, people would be saying, "Please bring back Boris".' In the end, both Sunak and Johnson were too conservative in their predictions.

That same day, Boris Johnson faced his final Prime Minister's Questions. It was testament to his divisive impact on British politics: edgy and bad-tempered as he sought to project a legacy and others took the opportunity to boo their villain off stage. Johnson argued his was 'mission largely accomplished' but when Keir Starmer quoted the less than complimentary views of various leadership candidates, Johnson called the Labour leader a 'great pointless human bollard'. Shakespeare, it was not.

Johnson offered some statesmanlike advice to his successor: 'Number one, stay close to the Americans, stick up for the Ukrainians, stick up for freedom and democracy everywhere. Cut taxes and deregulation wherever you can and make this the greatest place to live and invest.' But he also could not resist references to the plotters who had come for him: 'Focus on the road ahead, but always remember to check the rear-view mirror. And remember above all it's not Twitter that counts, it's the people who sent us here.' His final words as prime minister were appropriated from Arnold Schwarzenegger in *Terminator 2*: 'Hasta la vista, baby.' Left unspoken was that character's most famous line: 'I'll be back.'

Asked later why he had been so blatant, Johnson told a friend, 'One of the reasons for that was just to wind everybody up.' Pause. 'And also, because there might one day be truth in it.'

Johnson's most eloquent opponent in the press gallery, Rob Hutton, the sketchwriter of *The Critic*, noted, 'the Cyberdyne Systems Model 101, and its successor the T-1000, are better known for causing huge amounts of random damage than for achieving their goals.'[21] When Tony Blair called it a day, the Labour benches exploded into applause and David Cameron urged Conservatives to their feet to join in. At the end of Johnson's valediction, Tory MPs clapped, though some – Theresa May included – sat with arms folded. Andrea Jenkyns wept.

For the run-off stage, Sunak's headquarters moved from Smith Square to donated office space in Holborn, a location Nissy Chesterfield insisted be kept secret because its glass and steel corporate vibe was not the message they wanted to send to the media.

Sunak's MP supporters and those who were primarily dealing with them – Mel Stride and Gavin Williamson – pushed for some 'sunlit uplands' in the form of tax cuts to compete with Truss. They did not think just saying 'it's all very difficult' was enough. One option examined by Sunak's aides was to extend his pledge to cut the basic rate of income tax by 1p in 2024. 'We thought: why don't we look at whether we can keep that going down each year,' one said. 'There would be another penny coming off income tax for the next five years.'

Sunak was reluctant. 'I haven't been in the Treasury for weeks,' he said. 'I don't know the latest numbers. I don't want to be making these promises that I don't know I can deliver. I can't give you the sunny uplands if I don't know.' This was a bad way of winning a campaign, but consistent with his character and the image he wanted to project.

What Sunak was good at, his team reasoned, was convincing members to support him when they heard him. He was polished and presentable and clearly believed what he was saying and was more self-deprecating than many expected, opening his stump speech with the man who told him, 'Wow, you're even shorter in real life.' Sunak talked about his parents' values, joking with members that he had mentioned his mother's work as a pharmacist so often that she had told him, 'I wish I still had my pharmacy, I'd have queues out the door.' He was good at winning over those who had wrongly imagined him as the horned enemy of Brexit and Boris. 'They saw someone they didn't actually think they were going to see,' an aide who accompanied him to members' events said. They resolved to fight to the end, trying to get him in front of as many members as possible.

That it was likely to be a futile enterprise was clear to the world on 21 July when YouGov published the first poll of the membership. Truss was leading by 62 per cent to 38 per cent – not quite as bad as Ready for Rishi's internal survey, but the first time most of Sunak's campaign staff had any idea of the depth of the hole he was in. 'We were all in the office [when it dropped], it was quite bleak,' a senior aide recalled. Sunak's response was matter-of-fact: 'It is what it is, let's crack on.' But, as the aide observed, 'From that point on, MPs and the lobby saw the polls and thought, "You're done, there's no way you can come back from that."'

With nothing to lose Sunak went on the attack in the BBC head-to-head debate with Truss on 25 July in Stoke-on-Trent. As Truss and her entourage left her house in Greenwich, past a huge pack of photographers, one of her team recalled, 'I remember thinking this is how it must feel to walk out the tunnel at an away team, you are going off to war. That was our psychology: it was just all out war against Rishi.' Jonathan Gullis, the local MP, arranged for Team Truss to take over the boardroom of Port Vale football club. There Rob Butler and Jason Stein put her through her paces, this time accompanied by Jamie Hope.

Truss knew that if she held her own, she was on course to be prime minister, make a mess of it and new questions would be asked about her performance. 'I have never seen any human being as nervous for anything as she was,' an aide recalled. 'She was antsy, asking the same questions over and over again. She knew that she wasn't a good debater, and she knew how many people would be watching. Stein was so effective a fake Sunak, dismissing her plans as fantasy economics, that Truss and he 'got nose to nose', the candidate jabbing her finger in his face and saying, 'Don't you dare mansplain to me!' Over two days, they did four complete debates – and rehearsed plans to ask the audience, 'Put your hand up if you want to pay more tax', a gambit she did not find a chance to use.

Sunak turned up with a minibus full of supporters and aides, Truss walked in with Stein alone. Just before she went on stage, he put on 'Dancing in the Dark' and Mark Ronson's 'Uptown Funk' and they danced to loosen her up.

When the candidates were let loose at each other, Sunak criticised Truss's plans for a 'short-term sugar rush' of unfunded tax cuts and asked his opponent why she was content to 'cause misery to ordinary people' by risking higher inflation by borrowing billions. She hit back, accusing him of 'scaremongering' by peddling a new 'Project Fear'. Sunak seized on this as a chance to score points over Brexit: 'I remember the referendum campaign and there was only one of us on the side of Remain and Project Fear and that was you.'

It was not the substance of Sunak's attacks which drew attention, however. The former chancellor was hyper-aggressive, talking over his opponent, his tone disbelieving and dismissive. In the first twelve minutes he interrupted Truss more than twenty times. It looked like the head boy incredulous that he was losing an election to the girl who flunked the maths test. In the green room it triggered those who saw Sunak as entitled and those alert to sexism. Before the debate ended, Stein sent a quote from a campaign spokesman to Steven Swinford of *The Times*: 'Rishi Sunak has tonight proven he is not fit for office. His aggressive mansplaining and shouty private school behaviour is desperate, unbecoming and is a gift to Labour.'

Sunak's team was taken aback at the vehemence of the quote, which soured relations for the rest of the campaign. 'Rishi was getting frustrated that they weren't challenging her,' a close ally said. 'He had had to do difficult stuff in the last two and a half years and therefore had more of a sense of the reality.' They were also amused that Stein had gone off the handle just before Truss said she would have Sunak in her cabinet (an offer he had already decided to decline).

Truss and her allies were elated by the debate. When she came off stage she was whisked straight into her car and the protection squad raced her home at 120 mph. 'We felt like we had gone in as the away team and beaten them three-nil,' an aide said. 'That was an amazing moment, that was a high point of the campaign.'

With six weeks still to go, the BBC showdown was the last proper contest of the campaign. A debate on TalkTV was abandoned halfway through when the host, Kate McCann, suddenly fainted live on air. A dozen hustings up and down the country, organised by CCHQ, would follow but there were no head-to-head debates.

The focus was no longer on the air war, but on the ground game, somewhere Truss's team were lacking. After the BBC debate, she received a text from Mark Fullbrook, Lynton Crosby's former business partner, who had stepped in at the same stage for Boris Johnson in 2019. He had helped Zahawi and then Mordaunt but was still casting around for a candidate who might win. By 26 July he was part of the team.

Not everyone in Truss's inner circle was convinced Fullbrook was a good hire. Jamie Hope remembered him asking for the Foreign Office's help on behalf of a client with connections in Libya. Stein regarded

Fullbrook as a bullshitter. They fell out after Truss's team decided they should pull out of a final debate on Sky News a week later. Fullbrook stepped in and said, 'Let me handle that one. I'm going to get the chairman of the party to write to both candidates and say enough is enough now and we'll use that as cover.'

When it became clear this had not happened, Stein was incandescent. He was forced to contact Sky to say Truss would not be at the debate and offer a twenty-minute interview with audience questions instead – a bad night for Truss which could have been avoided. He WhatsApped both Adam Jones and Ruth Porter to complain about Fullbrook's 'total dereliction of duty', writing, 'I cannot be clearer how unprofessional Mark has been about this … He has screwed over Liz. It is a sackable offence. We now have to offer Liz up for a high-risk interview that never needed to happen – Mark is responsible.' Stein phoned Truss to tell her, 'The man is not to be trusted and he is reckless.' The seeds of divisions which would help to derail the Truss premiership were sown.

Stein and Fullbrook also clashed over whether Truss should attend the final of the women's European football championships at Wembley on 1 August. The nation had taken the England team, the Lionesses, to their hearts. Stein, who in addition to his political duties had been given control of government sports policy, thought Truss should go, Fullbrook disagreed. On 28 July Rob Oxley, special adviser to Nadine Dorries, the culture secretary, called Stein and expressed surprise that Truss had declined an invitation to sit in the royal box for the final. Stein tried again, messaging the 'CORE WorkingGroup (noLiz)' WhatsApp group to say, 'DCMS view is 20 million people are watching and it will look prime ministerial. They want to check we have really thought this through. My view has always been that she should be there.' Hugh Bennett, a former adviser to Jacob Rees-Mogg, chipped in that the German premier and foreign minister would be there. Fullbrook insisted it was a waste of time. 'She doesn't need to be there,' he replied. 'She just needs to be watching it on TV in a pub and we get pictures out. This is a final decision by Ruth and I.' Stein went to Truss who agreed with him: 'You're right, I should go.' She did, dancing in celebration with Dorries and Thérèse Coffey when the Lionesses won the trophy.

*   *   *

Truss now had all the momentum. At the first hustings on 28 July in Leeds, where Truss grew up, she had the audience eating out of her hand when she told members she wanted to 'channel the spirit of Don Revie', Leeds United's legendary manager.

Fullbrook helped to organise 'Operation Rolling Thunder', an allusion to the Vietnam War, where the campaign carpet-bombed the media with a series of big name endorsements. Ben Wallace, the defence secretary, was first to break cover on Friday 29th, followed by Tom Tugendhat a day later, then Brandon Lewis. Nadhim Zahawi and Sajid Javid, both chancellors, followed on Monday and Wednesday. Wallace slammed Sunak over defence spending, Lewis criticised his position on the Northern Ireland Protocol Bill. The *Telegraph*, which had been more balanced than Sunak's team expected, now endorsed Truss as well.

The biggest fish, though, was Penny Mordaunt, whose endorsement was dubbed 'Project Exeter' and was kept secret until she appeared on stage that Monday evening to introduce Truss. Sunak had been trying to woo Mordaunt too and had long conversations with her. As late as that morning she had been requesting policy documents from him. When she backed Truss, his team saw this behaviour as duplicitous. Those who had tried to 'kill Penny' now applauded as she called Truss a 'great friend'.

Mordaunt's endorsement helped to stem the bleeding from the Truss campaign's worst own goal. That morning, a press release was sent to journalists launching a policy to 'introduce regional pay boards so pay accurately reflects where civil servants work', suggesting this would save £8.8 billion by paying public sector workers around £1,500 a year less outside the south-east, a death knell for the levelling-up agenda. Truss was apoplectic. 'There were raised voices and a lot of swearing,' a witness said. 'I've never seen her so angry.' Adam Jones berated himself for failing to spot the problems and the policy team for feeding him 'weapons grade shit'. Truss had studied and rejected the plan years earlier when George Osborne had binned it. 'I saw what a shitshow it was,' she said. Worse, the embattled Sunak campaign was able to show its political smarts, spotting the black hole in the costings. Instead of just attacking Whitehall officials, the £8.8 billion savings meant the policy would have had to include doctors, nurses, teachers, soldiers and firefighters as well. Team Sunak put together a briefing document and the media tore the plan to pieces.

Stein told Truss to scrap the idea with another of his sporting metaphors: 'Take the bogey, don't make a triple bogey trying to save par.' The plan was ditched on Tuesday lunchtime, prompting a Sunak backer to taunt, 'The lady *is* for turning.'

There were other Truss gaffes. Asked at another hustings whether Emmanuel Macron was 'friend or foe', she said, 'The jury is out', and vowed to 'judge him on deeds not words'. The diplomatic difficulties were not worth the price of the cheap applause line.

However, Sunak's team was not crowing for long. A video soon leaked to the left-of-centre *New Statesman* in which Sunak boasted that while chancellor he had tried to reverse formulas 'that shoved all the funding into deprived urban areas'. A Truss ally responded with a quote which would have done Labour proud: 'He's like a reverse Robin Hood, he wants to rob the poor to pay for the rich.'

Sunak had also been forced into a flip-flop of his own on 27 July, announcing that he would scrap VAT on energy bills, a proposal he had blocked when chancellor. Kwasi Kwarteng delighted in describing this as a 'screeching U-turn'. Despite the campaign's decision to draw attention to the problems with Truss's tax cuts, Booth-Smith had concluded that he had to offer something to members if Sunak was to clear the 40 per cent threshold. 'The research was clear, the party wanted a message on tax and all they were hearing from us was we didn't want to do anything,' a senior source said. 'We should have done that earlier. That was a mistake on our part.'

Hostilities continued. On 8 August Dominic Raab put his name to an op-ed in *The Times*, the only paper to endorse Sunak, warning that Truss's plans were an 'electoral suicide note' that would 'see our great party cast into the impotent oblivion of opposition'. Truss's team responded with a briefing to the Sunday papers that Raab had been in line for a big cabinet job until he revealed his 'utter hatred' and 'barbarism'. Stein, for it was him again, said, 'To see him sent out as a suicide bomber is a sad end to his career.' Raab rejected this as 'a Jedi mind trick'. Truss was assumed to have the hide of a rhino, but she admitted later, 'To hear colleagues I had worked with for years describe me variously as "immoral" or "an electoral suicide note" was upsetting. I shut myself off from the media because I just couldn't take it.'[22]

It was Raab's plans for a British Bill of Rights, coupled with Sunak's failure to recast the race, which led, four days later, to the defection of Robert Buckland from Sunak's camp to Team Truss. Buckland, a popular and usually loyal character, who had been brought back into the cabinet as Welsh secretary, wanted a return to the Ministry of Justice and had been persuaded by his wife to put his own interests first for once. Colleagues were left open-mouthed at his cynicism. No prominent supporter had ever changed sides in a leadership election before (though plenty had pledged themselves to more than one candidate).[23] MPs doubted he would get what he wanted. They shared a quote from *A Man for All Seasons*, the play and film about another former lord chancellor, Sir Thomas More: 'It profits a man nothing to give his soul for the whole world. But for Wales?' They appreciated the joke even more when Truss kept Buckland at the Wales office.

A week later, 19 August, Sunak got his final endorsement, when Michael Gove finally came out for him, branding Truss's plans a 'holiday from reality', but it was far too late to have any positive effect.

That weekend Boris and Carrie Johnson finally celebrated their marriage, at the Cotswold home of Anthony Bamford, the Tory peer and boss of JCB. A video leaked to social media of Johnson dancing with his wife and son, Wilfred, to the sound of 'Sweet Caroline' by Neil Diamond. The couple were probably fortunate that another video did not leak. As part of her wedding preparations, Carrie had got her bridesmaids to perform their dance to ABBA's 'The Winner Takes it All' – only this time the lyrics were rewritten. The song directed daggers at Sunak, who both Johnsons blamed for his removal from Downing Street. It began:

We're not here to talk/About leader contests
That's no job for us/Traitors bugger off/(Cough) Rishi!

The rest of the song poked fun at Johnson's age and Carrie apparently losing her engagement ring in a bin. For the chorus they sang: 'The winner's clear to see/Boris and Carrie.' The groom's speech also referred to his defenestration, describing it as 'the biggest stitch-up since the Bayeux Tapestry'.

Johnson, who spent the month after his removal 'between anger and denial', was pleased that Truss was on course for victory. 'He was prepared to endorse her publicly if it looked like she was in danger of losing to Rishi,' a Truss confidant revealed. 'But it never looked like it was going to come to that.' One ally said Johnson even 'felt sorry' for Sunak, recounting how Johnson told him, 'He's been manipulated by these characters, Dougie, Dom and Lee to do me in, which he has, but there's nothing in it for him. It was never their agenda to get Rishi in as PM, it was about taking me out.'

At the end of July, Johnson even suggested to Truss that they do a job swap, so that he could continue his role in helping Ukraine: 'I should be foreign secretary!' This was billed as a joke by aides, but it was considered semi-seriously, both concluding it would not work.

As August went on some MPs were getting 'seller's remorse' about Johnson's departure. A former minister said, 'People have seen the alternatives now and they aren't convinced. It's like the married man moving in with his mistress and then discovering that she farts in bed at night.' Johnson did little to burnish his legacy, however, taking off on holidays to Slovenia and Greece. When he joined Nadhim Zahawi on a trip to Wales to see executives from Airbus, an encounter at which a prime minister would not usually be seen dead, a ministerial aide said Johnson was 'giving off David Brent vibes', after Ricky Gervais's sitcom character who returned to *The Office* having lost his job.

Truss was also in close contact with George Osborne. 'They spoke quite a lot during the leadership contest,' an aide recalled. 'She always had an idea in the back of her mind that she would bring him back.' The scenario Truss discussed with her team would have seen Osborne return as foreign secretary, with a seat in the Lords, if she was in political difficulties after six or seven months. None of them realised she would be in dire straits after just seven weeks. It would be left to her successor to play a similar card.

In his final campaign interview, on 30 August, Sunak told the *FT* he had 'won the argument' but he knew he had lost the leadership. He sent Robert Jenrick to relay a message to Truss, via Simon Clarke, that he was conceding defeat and calling off the dogs. 'We all need this government to succeed and the next few weeks are going to be crucial,' he said.[24]

A close aide of Sunak said, 'I think he'd reconciled himself that he wasn't going to win it quite early on.' All those involved took pride in fighting even when it looked forlorn. 'What was really heartening was on the bank holiday, a week before the results, the office was full.' In the penultimate week of the campaign Sunak took part in twenty-nine events with members. That week the same aide said, 'At the end of this we know we can walk into either Downing Street or the sunset with our heads held high because we did what he believes in. There is no free money. And in pretty short order he is going to be proved right – and she and all her people know that too.' Another Sunak supporter predicted, with some prescience, that Truss would end up 'like Jim Callaghan', who went cap in hand to the IMF in the 1970s.

Just before the candidates took to the stage for their final hustings, at Wembley Arena on 31 August, an aide turned to Truss and said, 'How surreal is this? You're about to be PM.'

'My whole life has felt surreal,' she replied.[25]

Truss and Sunak were given the result a little before 12.30 p.m. on Monday 5 September in a side room at the QEII conference centre. Unlike three years earlier with Johnson and Hunt, there was no meaningful chat between the candidates, not even a handshake. With poker faces they went to sit in the main auditorium as Graham Brady announced that Truss had secured 57 per cent of the vote, with Sunak on 43 per cent. She swept past her challenger without a look to take to the stage for her victory speech. Truss stated, 'During this leadership campaign, I campaigned as a Conservative and I will govern as a Conservative. I will deliver a bold plan to cut taxes and grow our economy.'

Truss and her jubilant team drank champagne on the roof of Deliveroo's headquarters while the Ready for Rishi officials licked their wounds. There was some satisfaction among Sunak's aides. He had cleared the 40 per cent threshold and gained around 12 points since the start of the campaign. The weeks of pressing the flesh had worked, to a degree. One senior figure said, 'Rishi wasn't really fighting Liz Truss, he was fighting the Conservative Party's love affair with Johnsonism. Truss was just a cipher. They had to see those ideas being implemented for us to win that argument.' Until the Conservative Party had seen Trussonomics fail, they would believe in it. That faith was about to be tested.

Boris Johnson addressed the nation one final time outside the door to Number 10 the following morning, bruised clouds over his head portending a storm, both actual and metaphorical. Watching from the sidelines his most faithful retainers, a small number of MPs and wife Carrie. One close friend said she was 'quite relieved to be leaving'. Her husband was not. Allies said he was still 'fulminating' about his eviction.

His valedictory was a combination of light-hearted word play and churlish irritation. 'Well, this is it, folks,' he said. 'The baton will be handed over in what has unexpectedly turned out to be a relay race. They changed the rules halfway through.' After another run-down of his greatest hits, Johnson concluded, 'I am now like one of those booster rockets that has fulfilled its function and I will now be gently re-entering the atmosphere and splashing down invisibly in some remote and obscure corner of the Pacific. And like Cincinnatus I am returning to my plough.' This was 'hasta la vista, baby' for the classicists, since the Roman statesman did not spend long with his plough before returning, by popular demand, for a second spell in charge (this time as dictator).

Johnson then flew to Balmoral for his final audience with the Queen, a jolly affair in which, palace officials said, he mistook the monarch's enjoyment of his company for her approval of his premiership. The Queen praised his apparent sangfroid, telling Johnson, 'There's no point in bitterness.' He later fondly recalled confessing his neurosis about seeing magpies, bringers of bad luck. The Queen advised, 'If you see a single magpie, you just say, "Good morning, Mr Magpie, today is Monday the 12th of March", or whatever the date is. That sorts it out.'[26]

Truss, the teenage republican, flew on a separate aircraft for security reasons while her aides nervously watched the skies. 'Fog over Aberdeen airport delayed Liz's landing to see the Queen,' an aide said. There was biblical rain in the car on the way to Balmoral. The last time they met the Queen had 'remarked that being a woman in politics was tough', Truss recalled. This time she warned that the job could be ageing and offered two words of advice: 'Pace yourself.' Truss reflected, 'Maybe I should have listened.'[27]

Back in Westminster, 'We didn't know until ten minutes before Liz read out her Downing Street statement whether or not it would be out on the street or inside because of rain showers,' the aide recalled. All this as the new prime minister, the fifteenth of Queen Elizabeth II's rein, planned to tell voters, 'I am confident that together we can ride out the storm.'

What she did, instead, was to open all the windows and dare the hurricane to approach. And rather than pacing herself, she charged headlong towards the storm.

24

GOING BIG

(or Shock and Awe-ful)

13 August to 24 September 2022

'It's got to be shock and awe ...'

– Liz Truss, August 2022

It began with a dog-eared piece of paper, which some came to see as a metaphor, but at the time was a sign of confidence. The leadership election was not even half done when Liz Truss formed her government and began serious preparations for Downing Street. It was 6.30 p.m. on 9 August, five weeks before the result was due to be announced, when she scribbled down a list of the cabinet. 'There's not even a whiteboard,' an aide said. 'There are a lot of crumpled bits of paper.'

The big jobs were settled. 'KK', Kwasi Kwarteng, was listed as chancellor; 'JC', James Cleverly, as foreign secretary; 'SB', Suella Braverman, as home secretary. Their deal held. Tom Tugendhat agreed to be security minister rather than foreign secretary if it came with a cabinet seat. There were a few changes later. Sajid Javid was listed as Northern Ireland secretary, Iain Duncan Smith as leader of the Commons and David Frost running the Cabinet Office. None would end up serving. 'IDS wanted a department,' a campaign source said. 'And Frosty wanted to be foreign secretary.' Truss ended up boasting that she was the only Tory prime minister 'not to have appointed Michael Gove, Gavin Williamson or Iain Duncan Smith'. That went for Dougie Smith, too.

If filling the great offices of state had been easy, the other pivotal role, chief whip, was more problematic. One of the men in the running had attracted claims from women MPs and journalists that he was a sex pest.

'Liz wanted a woman,' an aide recalled. Most of all she wanted her closest friend in politics, Thérèse Coffey, to do the job. Coffey wanted a department and to be deputy prime minister. She dug in and got her way. Andrea Leadsom and Anne-Marie Trevelyan were considered and rejected. By the time the list was drawn up, the job was Wendy Morton's. She had been one of the first MPs present at Truss's home when she got back from the G20 foreign ministers' summit in Bali and 'Wendy had done a good job whipping during the campaign,' the aide said. Morton didn't even want the job; she wanted to go back to the Foreign Office, where she had been happy as a minister of state. The appointment was to prove one of Truss's most catastrophic decisions.

None of it seemed that way when Truss, confident she was going to become prime minister, gathered her team at Chevening on 13 August. The Palladian house in Kent, the grace and favour home of the foreign secretary, is far grander than Chequers, a 115-room mansion which is the focal point of a thirty-acre estate with gardens sweeping down to a lake, which had virtually dried out in the hot summer of 2022.

Harry Cole, the political editor of the *Sun* who was writing a biography of Truss with James Heale of the *Spectator*, visited Chevening to interview her. Cole found a rarefied atmosphere reminiscent of a scene from Trollope or Henry James. 'You had this alternative seat of power being established,' he recalled. 'It was a bit like wandering through a Regency novel. There were lots of people wandering around in couples and foursomes, talking about all the things they were going to do, drinking tea.'[1] The grinding practicalities of Whitehall seemed a world away. The sun was out and everything seemed possible for Truss.

Yet, beneath the veneer of elegant calm, hairline cracks were developing in Team Truss which would become lethal fissures during her premiership. The other key role in Number 10 was chief of staff, but Truss could not find someone qualified who wanted the job. 'For a woman who plotted meticulously her path to power,' a close aide said, 'she had no one in mind, literally didn't have a clue.' There had been talk of David Frost taking the job, but he ruled himself out. It was offered, on the sly, to lobbyists Scott Colvin and Michael Hayman, both of whom rejected it. Truss did not think Ruth Porter a big enough personality or a hard enough hitter. Kwasi Kwarteng texted Truss to say, 'Ruth isn't up to it.' David Canzini was vetoed when the Tory whips' office, who were still loyal to Boris Johnson and saw him as disloyal in the final hours of his premiership, said they would back Truss only if she did not employ Canzini.

Mark Fullbrook was present and willing. To the dismay of some of his new colleagues, Truss concluded, 'He's good with the MPs; it's a political job.' He was the kind of Tory greybeard who was good company for men of his own age – a wealth of experience, good-humoured and with a roster of amusing stories. Yet Fullbrook had no experience of Whitehall or the civil service. He had also tried to get first Zahawi and then Mordaunt onto the ballot ahead of her. This was still causing irritation to some a couple of weeks later, at a celebratory dinner the Sunday before the result was announced. Truss said, 'I want to thank Mark Fullbrook because I couldn't have done it without him, without the incredible infrastructure you put in around the country, and all that operational expertise that was all ready to go ... for Penny.' When Fullbrook said, 'I know how good this team is because they beat me –', the heckle came, 'We beat you twice.'[2] Another special adviser said, 'Mark is very easy to get on with, but I don't think there was a single meeting where he said anything other than the most basic opacities about anything, bigging himself up but offering actually nothing.'

Truss had a different conception of the chief of staff job. 'I don't need a chief of staff in the old mould because I've got Nick Catsaras and I've got myself. I don't want officials talking to anyone but me.' Catsaras had been her private secretary at the Foreign Office and was to become principal private secretary in Downing Street. She trusted him totally. Truss saw Catsaras, in effect, as a civil service chief of staff.

Most of the team found out about Fullbrook from the newspapers. Jason Stein, a trusted political adviser for years, neither wanted nor expected the job, but he thought Fullbrook unsuitable. In the car with Truss on the way to Biggin Hill on 19 August, he erupted: 'It's a massive mistake. Throughout the campaign I saw him taking credit for things that were nothing to do with him. He's going to lead you to inevitable defeat.' Truss gave as good as she got. It was a 'massive shouting match'. When they got out of the car, one of the protection squad officers said, 'I haven't heard a domestic like that since David and Sam Cameron.' It was not for nothing that Stein was dubbed, by one of his fellow advisers, 'the pin in the Liz Truss hand grenade'.

Truss usually listened to Stein, who was young but had (mostly) good judgement, but she had Kwarteng, Nadhim Zahawi and Brandon Lewis all telling her to hire Fullbrook. He got the job and Stein found himself frozen out for the next few weeks. He was not alone. At Chevening, the team of special advisers who had helped Truss turn her career around and put her in position to win the leadership were sidelined by new, more ideological, hires and by the arrival, in force, of the civil service.

For two years Truss had been guided by Sophie Jarvis, her vivacious 'mini-me', her face and voice in Parliament; Adam Jones, her spin doctor; and Jamie Hope, her policy adviser. Jarvis, who shared Truss's libertarian philosophy but who fate had handed her boss's quota of emotional intelligence, was given the title of political secretary, but she then discovered she would be reporting to Iain Carter, a former CCHQ policy chief, who neither woman knew well but Truss appointed director of political strategy. Colleagues said Carter was brought in by Hope, who disliked Porter and wanted to create a rival but then Carter became close to Fullbrook, who Hope disliked. In the end, Carter failed to get the access he needed to Truss and Jarvis felt aggrieved as well. 'Liz ran a very divide and conquer operation, pitting staff against each other, without even meaning to,' one political aide complained.

Jones was told he would become director of political communications. But the comms job was to be split in two. Simon McGee, who had been a journalist and then a civil service press officer in the Foreign Office under Boris Johnson, was brought in from the private sector as a civil service communications director. Perhaps this was because Jones had carried the can for an ill-judged briefing during the Australian trade talks that Truss's opposite number would be made to sit in an 'uncomfortable chair' to speed up the talks – an image from Monty Python and the Spanish Inquisition. When Jones heard about McGee, he asked Truss, 'What does that mean?' She replied, 'You two work it out.'

Jones, like Stein, was kept out of key meetings at Chevening to prevent leaks to the media. Stein, arguably the best comms man in the whole set-up, was told he could not speak to the media at all. The irony was not lost on anyone who worked for Truss, who had been regarded by both the May and Johnson operations as the most prolific leaker in cabinet. 'She was investigated at least three times,' said a former Number 10 aide, 'and found guilty at least once. I remember her sheepishly going in for a dressing down by Boris.'

Jamie Hope fell victim to the most blatant case of sidelining. Ruth Porter helped bring in Matthew Sinclair, an economist for Deloitte, as

Truss's chief economic adviser. Hope was told to focus on other domestic and foreign policy. 'Does that mean I sense-check politically Matt's work and Matt economically checks my work?' he asked. 'No,' Truss replied. 'He does his thing, you do your thing', as if domestic policy had nothing to do with the economy. Hope's policy unit was hollowed out. Truss did not know Sinclair at all, but he was an ideological soulmate. 'I love him,' she said after their first conversation on the patio at Chevening. 'He's so sound.' It was not a love which endured. Hope had not even been told Sinclair was joining the team. The view of the old guard on Sinclair was quick to calcify: 'A very, very nice man, but not political and an ideologue to the hilt', as one put it.

A senior figure said, 'She basically neutered everyone. She couldn't manage anyone and didn't recognise that and employ anyone to do it for her.' To one degree or another, all Truss's closest allies felt vulnerable and she showed little human understanding of how to motivate a team. One aide told her, 'You don't handle people very well and you are afraid to give them bad news, so you just fudge everything.'

'You're telling me what I already know,' Truss admitted.

Yet instead of using the valuable preparation time at Chevening to build a coherent team spirit between her existing advisers and the new hires, which any new government needs, Truss functioned with extreme secrecy, creating and fostering division. Aides who had been used to dropping into her office for a chat were told they had to book audiences with her. 'Each day, the night before, you'd be told whether you were required and what time to arrive for,' said one spad. 'They would say, "Please show up for your 10 a.m. meeting, but please don't show up too early." You'd see Kwasi leaving as you arrived. You'd do your thing then you'd be offered lunch.' This consisted of 'whatever her husband Hugh had been out to get that morning – heavy on the crisps'. After that, 'You'd be told you can head off and you just knew there was a fleet of other meetings happening later on.'

Truss rejected this characterisation, bemoaning the lack of heavy hitters around her, saying she felt 'like a one-man band', something she found 'a frustrating and isolating experience'.[3] She said, 'I personally ended up doing a lot of the work. This idea I shut people out ... honestly, I felt like I was doing a lot of it myself. If Jamie or whoever had wanted to suggest an alternative chief of staff, they could have done. The idea that they weren't in the room – there was no room.' However, she did admit,

'In an ideal world people wouldn't go straight into Number 10 in the middle of a crisis – not having worked there before or not having worked with each other before.'

There is always an element of tension when a leadership start-up grows so it can govern, but this chaos was not just about bruised egos, it had a material effect on Truss's behaviour. In their time together in the Foreign Office, Jarvis, Jones and Hope were useful sounding boards for Truss, but were also able to rein in her wilder flights of fancy.

When the war in Ukraine broke out, Truss was gung-ho to sanction every major Russian in the UK with links to the Kremlin. Hope convinced her this required a very high legal bar and it was better to proceed more methodically – targeting Roman Abramovich, the oligarch who owned Chelsea football club, could backfire unless the case was legally water-tight. 'Then you go from the foreign secretary who sanctioned more Russians than anyone in history to the foreign secretary whose sanction regime blew up in their face,' he warned. Truss listened. Another spad said, 'We had the sort of group that, if she was barking up the wrong tree, could say, "Hang on, Liz, we don't think that's right." She'd say, "No, rubbish, rubbish", then she'd call another meeting three hours later and say, "I thought about it and we should actually do this", and of course, it was her idea.' That handbrake was gone.

There was another factor, too. To put it bluntly, many in Westminster regarded Truss as 'weird'. Her personal manner could be unnerving for those who did not know her well. An odd combination of coldness and warmth, Truss was prone to eye contact that lingered too long, as if she was struggling to read the other person or was staring them down. Her views were delivered with a bluntness of manner and an element of teas-ing which made it difficult to know sometimes if she was serious about one of her provocative statements. Her preferred mode of engagement, particularly with men, was a kind of coquettish semi-sarcastic flirtation.

Truss's personal manner failed to inspire those who did not know her well. One private secretary broke down in tears after bringing the prime minister the wrong sort of coffee (Truss insisted on double espressos from Pret a Manger). The police, doorkeepers and custodians at Number 10, who had liked the polite May and the affable Johnson, found Truss haughty and rude. 'The guys on the door had a competition to see if they could get her to say "hello" or "thank you" and there was no winner,' a source said. Staff at Chequers told a similar story. When a senior Tory asked who their least popular PM was, the reply was instant: 'Who do you think? And she only came a couple of times.'

These were all mannerisms her triumvirate of spads were used to navigating and Jarvis, in particular, became Truss's 'representative on earth', buttering up MPs who struggled to connect with Truss herself, keeping both the ERG and the One Nation wing of the party on board during the preparation of the Northern Ireland Protocol Bill. 'Liz operates at one hundred miles per hour and sometimes bits fall off the car,' a colleague said. 'Sophie was the one who would grab the wing mirror and tape it back on.' Jarvis was Truss's 'ideological true north', Jones and Hope expert at turning their ideas into something politically practical for the media. Truss called Jones a 'centrist dad' and Hope an 'unsound mercenary pragmatist' because of their more moderate political views. Hope was also 'evil Tintin' because of his cowlick haircut.

Truss had previously always had prime ministers reining her in, balancing the views of other departments. Now she was in charge, that disappeared. 'Through her career there had always been a check on her,' one close aide said. 'The prime minister, civil servants, Theresa May, David Cameron, Nick Clegg, whoever it was, someone was always there to block things. During the campaign, up to Friday 12th August, there were people to say no to her because she didn't think that she would win. But once she knew she was going to win, she thought, "This is now my moment. I am the decider." There was no one strong enough around her to stop anything.'

Another development contributed to Truss's isolation – she changed her mobile phone number. Aides recall becoming overwhelmed by the number of messages she was receiving: MPs, donors, journalists and old friends bombarding her with congratulations and suggestions. 'There was a day when she handed it over to us and said, "I literally can't deal with this. I got a thousand text messages today. Somewhere in there are things I really need to reply to." But there was no way to set up a system where someone else was trawling through all the messages.'

The Cabinet Office sent officials from MI5 and GCHQ to brief both Truss and Sunak at the start of the campaign. 'We said, we should definitely expect that bad people are trying to find out what's going on,' a security official said, spelling out how Russian and Chinese spies would seek to access their messages and voicemails. 'We recommend you change your telephone numbers.' They also told Jamie Hope to examine what would be compromised if Truss's messages were accessed. A senior civil servant said all this work was precautionary and denied reports that Truss's private thoughts were accessed by Russian intelligence.[4] The result, however, was that most ministers and MPs no longer had any means of communicating with Truss. An important umbilical link to opinion in her party was lost.

It was in this bubble that Truss embarked on the most important conversations she would have at Chevening – working out what to do about the soaring cost of energy and what to put in the 'mini-budget' she and Kwarteng were planning to follow the energy announcement. On 26 August, Ofgem, the energy regulator, announced that the average annual household bill would rise by 80 per cent to £3,500 a year in October and could hit £5,300 by March. It was clear the government would have to act, but how? Truss spent the leadership campaign resisting universal 'handouts'.[5] Her initial plan was to increase the £400 Rishi Sunak had proposed to give every household to £1,000. In the Treasury, the caretaker chancellor, Nadhim Zahawi, was working on plans to beef up Sunak's windfall tax on the oil and gas companies. This was anathema to Truss and Kwarteng, who told him to stop.

Two weeks earlier, Labour had announced an energy price freeze, a policy, at that point, costed at £29 billion. It was becoming clear to Truss and her chancellor-to-be that they would have to do something similar if they wanted to park the cost of living as an issue. The prime minister in waiting was also driven by the need to boost Britain's energy security in the long term, a view reinforced by her discovery that Whitehall officials had been running a series of war-game exercises codenamed 'Yarrow'. The second of these, 'Noble Birch', had just tested whether Whitehall could operate if there was an electricity blackout.

Before the transition talks began, Truss planned to install James Bowler, a civil servant she had got to know in the trade department, as cabinet secretary. However, Simon Case swept into Chevening and immediately impressed her. In their first meeting, Truss tested him on what she should say in her first speech as prime minister. Case did not miss a beat. 'I think the overriding thing for people this winter is the uncertainty around energy bills,' he said. 'I think it will mean businesses going to the wall. It will mean people out of work. If you don't solve it now, it's going to affect everything and undermine your premiership.'

Case talked about other prime ministers and how their time in Number 10 had been shaped by wars or the pandemic. 'You don't want this to be the thing people point to and say, "The government failed to solve energy bills."' The cabinet secretary presented policy options and suggested the best people in the Treasury and the business department to drive them through. 'She could see he was her address book of government and he became invaluable,' one of those present recalled.

In addition to a major intervention on the cost of living, Truss wanted to start cutting tax. During the campaign she had only pledged three cuts: scrapping Sunak's National Insurance rise, blocking the planned rise in corporation tax, and scrapping green levies – with a collective price tag of around £30 billion.

Details of what would become the mini-budget were thrashed out in meetings at Chevening between Truss and a 'quad' of economic ministers, which included Kwarteng, Chris Philp, who was to be chief secretary to the Treasury, and Simon Clarke, the current chief secretary, who represented a red wall seat. He had originally been pencilled in for the business department. But Clarke suffered from agoraphobia and did not like the open plan BEIS offices on Victoria Street. He asked for a different role and was considered a better fit as levelling up secretary than the blue blood Jacob Rees-Mogg, who got the business brief. Truss set up her economic 'war room' in the tapestry room on the first floor at Chevening, overlooking the lake, tables arranged in a giant square. For the first meeting, John Redwood, the most Thatcherite MP on the Tory benches, was also present since he had been lined up for a minister of state job at the Treasury. It was not the cabinet role he wanted and he did not come again.

Truss was encouraged in her radical 'Trussonomics' by a trio of visitors – Institute of Economic Affairs economists Julian Jessop and Andrew Lilico plus Boris Johnson's former adviser Gerard Lyons – who had long craved someone in power sympathetic to their views. These 'Trussketeers' descended on Chevening as if it were the stable in Bethlehem, bearing gifts of tax cuts, supply side reform and a shared distaste for the stifling 'orthodoxy' of the Treasury and its watchdog, the Office of Budget Responsibility (OBR). This was an agenda to which Truss was well disposed. As one of her (resolutely Brexiteer) Foreign Office spads put it, 'I spent more time in government fighting the Treasury than I did fighting the EU.' Truss was similarly disparaging of the way the governor of the Bank of England was 'virtually unsackable' and how criticising the flurry of cheap money he had presided over was 'akin to questioning papal authority'. The Treasury, the Bank and the OBR, she charged, 'have the same mindset – pro-EU, pro-China, pro-immigration', 'fatalistic about Britain's decline', anti-manufacturing and 'more interested in balancing the books than growing the economy'.[6]

Lyons and Jessop presented a paper on ways of boosting growth, but it also warned, 'The markets are nervous about the UK and about policy options. If immediate economic policy announcements are handled badly then a market crash is possible.' Truss heard what she wanted to hear and ignored the caveats. 'The meeting was confident, perhaps even overconfident,' Jessop said later. 'They were very gung-ho about what they would be able to do. I suspect that may have led them to do too much too quickly.'[7]

The plan was fleshed out with senior aides over coffee and biscotti in Truss's living room in the third week of August. Truss and Kwarteng also met in the Guildford Arms or the Richard I pub, on nearby Royal Hill, a fitting location to plan a 'crusade' to transform Britain.

One conviction the Trussketeers did reinforce – particularly Gerard Lyons – was Truss's decision not to ask the OBR to do a formal forecast of the public finances ahead of the mini-budget. This stemmed from three beliefs, one practical, one political and one ideological. Truss's core mantra was that the independent watchdog was as much the guardian of the economic status quo as the Treasury and that the OBR would not engage in dynamic modelling. This meant that people like her who believed that cutting taxes could generate higher revenues and supply side reforms could boost growth were not rewarded for these actions in the OBR's model. 'They give very little, or no, credit for dynamic effects,' another cabinet minister said. 'For example if you cut corporation tax you would expect some stimulation in the wider economy, but they don't account for that.' Supporters pointed to the coalition government cutting corporation tax from 28 per cent to 19 per cent and increasing receipts from £25 billion to £58 billion.

Truss called the OBR's approach 'abacus economics', focused on dividing up the pie, rather than growing the pie. More fundamentally, she thought it was one of many 'unelected organisations and individuals claiming independent expertise' whose 'pronouncements' were 'treated as irrefutable statements of fact' by the public and the media, when she saw them as 'pursuing a self-interested agenda'.[8]

Politically, Truss's team argued that the OBR's forecasts were 'always wrong'. Practically, they pointed out that while there had been a formal forecast alongside the spring statement, Sunak had not had an OBR forecast for his second cost of living intervention. Why, then, should she? The OBR had been created by George Osborne as a way of showing the public that the government was not marking its own homework. To cast it aside at a major fiscal moment was to invite the criticism that Truss was dodging scrutiny.

Case was not the only senior civil servant who attended the Chevening meetings. Cat Little, the acting permanent secretary at the Treasury, was also present, along with Beth Russell, the director general of tax and welfare; and Philip Duffy, the director general of growth and productivity. 'Senior Treasury officials made clear there was a risk', in not using the OBR, a Tory said. 'The cabinet secretary made it clear that there was a risk.' A senior civil servant said, 'At Chevening, we definitely told them about the OBR. We did it in the way that we always do these things, which is to say there is no legal requirement to have an OBR forecast. There is a legal requirement to do two OBR forecasts a year, but budgets have been done without the OBR. Now, here are all the reasons why you want to do an OBR forecast: people don't believe your numbers, this is the thing that gives markets confidence that your sums are right. Much as you hate it, it was set up for a good reason.'

One of Team Truss's public arguments – that she wanted to act very fast on the energy package and it would not be possible for the OBR to turn around a formal assessment quickly enough – was torpedoed on 26 August. The Treasury select committee published a statement from the OBR confirming that 'it began work on a forecast on 29 July and would be in a position to publish such a forecast alongside a potential emergency fiscal event in September'. The fact that this statement had been elicited by Mel Stride, the committee chairman, one of Rishi Sunak's whips, deepened Truss's suspicion that there was a conspiracy against her. Turning the screws, Stride said, 'These forecasts provide transparency on the health of the nation's finances to Parliament, the public and critically, to international markets, upon which the UK substantially relies for its borrowing.' It would be vital to publish 'as full a forecast as possible'.

In fact, the argument that the OBR could not do a proper analysis was probably right – but that should have led to Truss slowing things down and combining the mini-budget with her planned 'medium-term fiscal plan' which spelled out the supply side reforms and spending cuts, rather than abandoning OBR oversight. As one of her key aides explained, 'In order to have a legitimate OBR answer, you have to have spending assumptions. And they are what you have to agree for the medium-term fiscal plan later in the year. If you try to do that in two weeks, you're going to fuck it up. If we'd tried to hurry it, it would have been worse, not better. The bigger question, in my mind, is: should we have waited to do all of the policy stuff until we could get an OBR assessment and have the full picture?' The correct answer was surely yes.

Instead, Truss felt there was no time to waste and raced headlong to put all her chips on half a strategy. 'The plan was to get on with the stuff we needed to do immediately,' she said. 'The legislation had already been passed to raise corporation tax, so we needed to change the law to get it back down. The three biggest measures – the energy guarantee, corporation tax, National Insurance – we needed to do sooner rather than later to send a signal that Britain was open for business.' In her memoir she remained unrepentant: 'I don't regret not commissioning a forecast that I knew would be wrong and that would have inevitably undermined our plans from the outset.'[9]

Some of Truss's allies were concerned by her approach. Simon Clarke said, 'She was well within her rights to point out that the guardians of Treasury orthodoxy are bad at conducting dynamic modelling of the positive impact of both lower taxes and supply side reforms. But this was not the time to try to test that weakness.'[10] Another confidant said, 'I don't think the OBR should exist, I don't think it's ever got anything right, ever. I think it's wrong that they leave you in a binary choice that you either put up taxes or cut spending. But you've got to deal with the world as you find it not as you wish it.' Celia McSwaine, Kwarteng's spad, recalled, 'It set this narrative that we weren't fiscally responsible, and we didn't care about the markets … We were on the back foot in terms of demonstrating fiscal competence from that point on.'[11]

The original plan, in July, had been for a three-year spending review to identify cuts in Whitehall budgets to balance out the tax cuts Truss wanted. Kwarteng, Clarke and Philp all saw them as a package. 'Tax cuts yes,' a cabinet minister said, 'but spending reductions, a fiscal framework and supply side reforms' to stimulate growth. Shortly after Johnson resigned, Clarke spoke to Truss. 'I highlighted the need for credible savings options to accompany her tax cuts, warning that without these we would be monstered,' he said. 'She agreed. We settled on a new spending review. We discussed the relative merits of requiring 5 and 10 per cent reductions in expenditure. Her only caveat, quite reasonably, was that it would be better to identify specific saving plans in the run-up to a budget once safely in office, as opposed to in the heat of a brutal campaign.'[12] Neither was to happen.

The kind of cuts being discussed would have been controversial but substantial savings could have been made, particularly to the £250 billion-a-year benefits bill. Benefits were due to be uprated in line with the Consumer Price Index that September. Philp made a 'fiscal and moral' political argument that, while the state pension and disability benefits should rise by the expected 10 per cent, working-age and able-bodied benefits should only rise in line with wages, which were up 5 per cent. That would have raised between £4 billion and £5 billion and resulted in a permanent reduction in public expenditure. 'Why should someone that is not working get a 10 per cent rise, when someone who gets up at six in the morning to go and sweep the streets gets a five per cent rise? – how is that fair?' he argued. 'Plus, we're trying to get people off welfare and into work. If you jack up welfare by 10 per cent while wages rise at 5 per cent, you are weakening work incentives.'

Clarke wanted to tie future NHS spending to improvements in delivery. A freeze on income tax thresholds would have dragged millions into the higher 40p rate of tax but raised billions. Clarke was also a sceptic about the HS2 high speed rail line, the cost of which had spiralled. Adopting such savings would have created a highly charged political debate about priorities with the Labour Party rather than one about the fundamental economic viability of the government.

The need for spending cuts was Kwarteng's one clear disagreement with Truss before the mini-budget. Celia McSwaine recalled, 'He was really conscious of the need to emphasise fiscal discipline, particularly with the scale of the tax cuts that we were planning to set out. That was even more important in the context of not having an OBR forecast ... He raised that point repeatedly, but unfortunately just lost the battle.'[13] One of Truss's aides agreed spending cuts were 'the only thing he warned about in advance' but recalled that Kwarteng's resistance was weak: 'Kwasi did try and get some spending cuts in with the growth plan but he was told "no" and he didn't put up a fight.' A cabinet minister observed, 'She wasn't interested in spending reductions at all. She literally wouldn't talk about it, in a way that was quite weird. I think she thought it would be unpopular.' Truss said later, 'My view is that we weren't ready' to outline cuts.

Some ministers claim senior civil servants were 'totally silent' and wanted to 'give Liz a bit of rope to hang herself', but others are clear the mandarins were warning of the need for cuts to balance the ledger. Clare Lombardelli, the Treasury's chief economist, was 'unbelievably nervous' about the issue, a political aide recalled, 'sweating spinal fluids'. In one meeting Simon Case, the cabinet secretary, said, 'Shouldn't we have a conversation about spending cuts? Otherwise, people will see through it instantly.' Jamie Hope agreed. A witness said, 'Simon told her that, for the project to have any credibility, you have to be able to prove we're not just making unfunded tax cuts.' Truss appeared to concede the point, suggesting a list of potential cuts was drawn up, but nothing came of it. Another aide said, 'Simon Case was really pissed off.' The cabinet secretary told a colleague, 'This is economically illiterate', and described Truss as 'completely mad'.

Much of the detail of the plan for the mini-budget was kept from political aides 'because of her ridiculous paranoia about anything leaking'. What did filter out, unnerved those who were excluded. Hope, Adam Jones and Iain Carter were all aghast when they discovered that ending the cap on bankers' bonuses was part of the budget. In a cost of living crisis, 'It's mental,' Jones said. 'The mini-budget never got the political or comms interrogation that it needed,' another adviser said.

Before they came to Chevening, Hope had talked to Truss about tax cuts and changes to the way the economy ran over the next two years, five years and ten years. It gradually became clear, she wanted to do much of it over her first two weeks. In a meeting on the Friday before she became prime minister, Truss said, 'We have to hit the ground running.'

After her departure from Downing Street, a narrative developed that Truss got carried away when she became prime minister. However, ministers and aides were clear that the key decisions were taken in the bubble at Chevening. Simon Clarke later recalled walking the grounds on the August bank holiday, Truss 'stalking ahead impatiently through the yellowing grass' as she spelled out her vision. He predicted on this walk that the next few months would be 'bracing'. Truss went further, suggesting 'it would be a calamitous six months of turbulence and we would have to batten down the hatches'.[14] Clarke said later, 'It was those weeks at Chevening ... that truly mattered to the fate of her premiership ... Her distaste for "abacus economics", always present, won out over caution. The whole package was an exercise in Reaganomics without, fatally, the support of a reserve currency. Indeed, it was launched at the very moment when the strength of the dollar left sterling desperately exposed.'[15]

A cabinet minister said Truss became 'massively emboldened', getting a 'head rush' combining 'dangerous levels of self-confidence and a nagging insecurity that she didn't have much time'. A senior aide added, 'She decided she wanted to do a fiscal event because she had to undo the NICs rise. Then she got in her head, "If I'm going to do that, I may as well do one or two other things. Why waste the opportunity?" Bankers' bonuses was decided at Chevening. Stamp duty was decided at Chevening. Once it evolved into a full-blown "everything is on the table" fiscal event, the Treasury warned very loudly and they were ignored. Kwasi went along with whatever she wanted.'

One of Truss's team went even further, suggesting that what came over her was effectively the manic state of a mental breakdown: 'She wasn't depressed, but she had a breakdown. She was giddy with expectations. She developed a serious detachment from reality, she was more demanding and intolerant of people. She didn't want to be challenged. Two things change people – power and money. Those are the two torches of life which tell you what a person is about. At the start of the leadership campaign, she listened to a lot of people because she was unsure of herself. When it dawned on her she was going to win, she jettisoned this approach and it made her psychologically unfit to be prime minister.'

It is a truism of politics that to become a leader you have to impress the base, but once installed you pivot towards the voters. This was no part of Truss's plan. Adam Jones said, 'One of the many strategic mistakes we made and Liz made was not pivoting hard enough from a campaign aimed at the Tory membership and Tory MPs to the wider electorate and the public and governing. I think Liz herself found that switch very difficult. She became slightly punch drunk on love from Tory members.'[16] The other aide said, 'She had a good campaign plan; what she didn't have was a governing plan. When she sat down to create a governing plan, she went fucking mad.'

Once installed in Number 10, Truss was just as radical and just as cack-handed in the way she organised the centre of government. After visiting the Queen at Balmoral, on Tuesday 6 September, Britain's fifty-sixth prime minister returned to a building in turmoil. Dozens of civil servants in Number 10 had received a peremptory email at 9.30 a.m. that day telling them to leave the building. Two dozen of Boris Johnson's political aides, including most of the policy unit, were also culled. They were told to be gone by 11 a.m. and handed boxes to clear their desks. 'We ended up with a policy unit that had four people in it,' said one of the survivors. 'It was absolutely insane. I was responsible for five departments – a job previously done by ten people. She got rid of all the civil servants who knew what they were doing and replaced them with lowest common denominator process advice from the Cabinet Office.' Dominic Cummings tweeted that the reorganisation was a 'fiasco', adding, 'New PM shooting her team in both feet.' The data unit, which had helped save the day during the pandemic, was moved out of Number 10.

In her memoir, published in the spring of 2024, Truss complained that, on arrival in 10 Downing Street, she was struck by 'just how small the operation was', contrasting the thousands who worked for her in government departments with 'just over one hundred staff working directly for the prime minister's office'. Like those who saw Boris Johnson failed by the system when he caught Covid, Truss concluded, 'The prime minister is treated like a president but has nothing like the kind of insti-tutional support that we would expect in a presidential system.'[17] She complained, 'Despite now being one of the most photographed people in the country, I had to spend time organising my own hair and make-up appointments … There was also no medical support … When I had a cough, my diary secretary had to go out in the middle of the night to buy me some medicine.'[18] These were legitimate gripes, but Truss's claim to the author that the building resembled 'the *Marie Celeste*' was, in large measure, a situation she had personally exacerbated by evicting dozens of officials on day one. A cabinet minister said, 'It was like she'd stripped off all the wallpaper, then the paint and floorboards too. There was basi-cally zero institutional memory left.'[19] A senior aide noted, 'On one hand, she knew exactly what she wanted to do – and yet as someone who had been a minister for ten years, who had served three prime ministers, she had no idea how to run Number 10.'

Team Truss pointed out the huge powers handed to Nick Catsaras. 'He is practically her kindred spirit,' a senior aide said. But to Number 10 staff banished to the Cabinet Office, it did not feel empowering. The mood in the civil service was 'sulphurous'. There was anger at Case for not warning people what was coming. Some dubbed him Varys, the smarmy eunuch in *Game of Thrones* whose loyalties seamlessly shifted to accommodate each new regime.

In another unorthodox move, Truss decided to use the Cabinet Room as her office, with senior aides billeted next door in the study where Boris Johnson, Theresa May and David Cameron had all worked. The press office was banished from the suite of rooms it had occupied under the previous four governments in 12 Downing Street to a small room which the visits team had once occupied. Adam Jones, instead of sitting with Simon McGee and the rest of the spin doctors, took a desk in the study room next to Truss, alongside Catsaras, Mark Fullbrook, Ruth Porter and a diary secretary. Sophie Jarvis, Jamie Hope, Matthew Sinclair, John Bew, Iain Carter and sundry private secretaries sat in the 'outer' private office.

The old press office was taken over by Thérèse Coffey in her capacity as deputy prime minister. Those venturing past in the weeks to come found rooms which had been packed with dozens of staff populated by just a handful. Coffey (who also had an office in the Department of Health, where one of her first edicts had been to ban the 'Oxford comma' from paperwork) would put up flags to greet visiting dignitaries. On one occasion a baffled Truss was confronted by an Irish tricolour. One of her daughters had to explain: 'Thérèse is seeing Varadkar.' An official said, 'She seemed to think it was the office of the vice president.'

Officials were removed because of past behaviour of which Truss disapproved. Stephen Lovegrove, Johnson's national security adviser, was exiled to a defence procurement post, apparently because he had opposed arming Ukraine in 2021. In another meeting, she cleared the room and berated Catsaras because 'a civil servant who used to work for Gove' was in the meeting.[20] Despite efforts by Sophie Jarvis and Adam Jones, Olivia Oates, an adviser to Simon Clarke, was jettisoned because she was engaged to Liam Booth-Smith, Sunak's chief of staff. Truss saw enemies everywhere, a mindset which became self-fulfilling.

* * *

By far the most significant firing was that of Tom Scholar, the permanent secretary at the Treasury who had helped to see Britain through the 2008 global financial crash. Truss and Kwarteng regarded him as the embodiment of the 'Treasury orthodoxy' they wanted to overthrow. Allies said Truss also blamed Scholar for the way she had been treated as chief secretary, when she was frozen out of budget decisions. 'That was Philip Hammond's decision,' a senior civil servant and Scholar ally said later. 'Hammond didn't want her in the room because he thought she would just leak everything – he was probably right.' But, as a cabinet colleague observed, 'Liz treated it as a great affront and wanted Tom out. I don't think he treated her very nicely when she was there.' Truss claimed this was a misreading of her views: 'I wasn't dead set on getting rid of Scholar. Kwasi was particularly keen. I spent much of the campaign talking about the Treasury orthodoxy – and he was it – but I don't have any massive personal feelings about him at all.'

Another factor was Truss and Kwarteng's irritation at the way government rules had been bent to allow Scholar to work remotely for weeks at a time in Argentina, where his wife and family moved. The arrangement had begun under David Cameron and ended in 2018 but, when Covid struck, ministers joked he was the 'pioneer of working from home'.

Kwarteng called in Scholar on his first day in the Treasury. It was an awkward conversation. 'Liz won against the orthodoxy,' the new chancellor said, 'so she will govern against the orthodoxy. There will have to be some changes.'

Scholar said, 'What do you mean?'

'We need a change at the top,' Kwarteng explained. 'You are the embodiment of the Treasury orthodoxy.'

Scholar was taken aback, shocked but perhaps not surprised. 'You're getting rid of me?'

'I thought you knew that,' the chancellor said. Kwarteng thought the cabinet secretary had rolled the pitch with Scholar, squared him off.

'He hasn't said anything,' Scholar explained. Case had made no such warning. There was a way for these things to be done: a few months of transition and then a quiet statement of regret that it was not working. Scholar could see how this was going but he felt duty bound to offer a warning. Truss and Kwarteng had already decided to ignore the OBR, getting rid of him would not calm the situation. He said, 'You're about to do a substantial budget, a more substantial budget even than you think. It's going to unsettle the markets. I am your link man to the City institutions and the markets. I can try to land it for you with them.'

If Kwarteng thought much about this argument, he did not let on. The decision was made. Scholar was dismissed. Another mistake had been made. Scholar's removal was greeted with dismay in the civil service and particularly in the Treasury, where officials calculated that if he was not safe, no one was. It seemed like an attack on experience and expertise. The fallout meant that Treasury officials who had concerns about the government's budget plans were far less likely to voice them.

Kwarteng later resiled from many decisions he took as chancellor, but not the dismissal of Scholar. 'From my point of view, he'd done his thirty years and it was a good time for him to bow out,' Kwarteng said. 'At the time there was a bit of rumbling, but nobody said that this means the budget will unravel and it'll be a disaster. Since then, it has been written up as this great act of hubris – and that is wrong.'

When Truss's first cabinet met on Wednesday 7 September, MPs were surprised to see that not one of her spin doctors or political aides, from chief of staff Mark Fullbrook down, was present. Only Nick Catsaras was there. Aides said Truss's administration would be about substance not spin. Fullbrook had made 'GSD' or 'Get Shit Done' the motto of the political team. 'Liz doesn't want a presidential-style Number 10,' Jones told sceptical journalists, who correctly predicted that when cabinet leaked there would be no spin doctors present who had a clue what had been said. 'She wants it to be relentlessly focused on delivery – policy-making and legislating. You'll see fewer prime ministerial visits, fewer events in Number 10.' Truss, he revealed, also wanted to 'rethink' the government's news grid – 'Do fewer announcements but do them better and empower cabinet ministers to have more ownership of departmental announcements.' Out was 'the long-standing obsession that a succession of Number 10s have had with day-to-day news management'. In was 'communicating a clear long-term vision and then setting grid announcements in the context of that vision – not on over-management of the news cycle'. The lobby had heard it all before.

Truss scrapped the morning meeting in Number 10, where every prime minister had begun their day for decades, preferring a Monday meeting to 'task' senior civil servants and her directors of strategy, policy, economics and communications. The meeting had undoubtedly become too obsessed with the news cycle under Johnson but scrapping it removed her government's ability to respond quickly to new developments and left it frequently flat-footed. Truss's other meetings were cut to a very small cast list, meaning she was seldom exposed to dissenting views from more junior officials.

Truss refused to read the papers (a claim most prime ministers make – but she stuck to it). It wasn't long before she spotted a stack of papers on a side table in the private office and instructed Adam Jones to 'get those away'. After several weeks in the job, she told her director of communications to 'stop trying to manage the news'. Once an enthusiastic briefer of 'colour' for the long reads in the Sunday papers, Truss (with Fullbrook and Porter's backing) now banned her staff from doing the same, a diktat which held for less than a week. 'I did not want us to be briefing the journalists of the Westminster lobby system with their preferred diet of triviality,' she wrote in her memoir. When her aides disagreed, she accused them of 'appeasement'.[21]

This approach has always been superficially attractive to new governments, which resent their co-dependent relationship with the media. However, all governments need to tell stories about themselves and the better ones realise that helping journalists to tell them is more productive than leaving a group of temperamentally mischievous people to their own devices. The supreme irony was that Truss had put herself in pole position for the leadership almost entirely through a canny manipulation of the media – offering her views in a series of provocative interviews and engaging with enthusiasm in the horse trading of information with political editors. When she publicly opined that there was 'too much focus on the optics' in modern politics, St Thomas' Hospital braced for the admission to A&E of lobby journalists laughing their heads off as they recalled her near-obsessive use of Instagram.

One of her closest aides reflected, 'This wasn't a slight shift in the way Liz Truss operates, this was a whole pendulum swing. Physically and in practice, she was distancing herself from the news. I think there was an element of her which thought, "I've spent the past couple of years getting to where I want to be by caring about communications, being intensely political. Now I don't need that stuff any more."' Another put it like this: 'She knew how the game worked and during the campaign she played ball. She just got drunk on power very quickly.'

The group gathered around the cabinet table had several fresh faces – Kemi Badenoch at trade, Tom Tugendhat, Kit Malthouse at education and Michelle Donelan at culture. But with Gove, Sunak and Johnson all gone, this was the least experienced and most intellectually under-powered Conservative cabinet since the days of Heath. Truss was by far the longest-serving cabinet minister at her own top table.

The coda was this: within two hours the cabinet's decision to pause legislation for a new 'Bill of Rights' had leaked. This time there were no spads or spinners to blame. Not for the last time under Truss, the press operation knew less than the lobby. The new system didn't work but it would be several weeks before Truss was persuaded to change.

Most of this was hidden from view, however, as Truss's administration began with a bang. Tory MPs were underwhelmed by her speech on the steps of Number 10, but she surprised on the upside in her first performance at PMQs. Keir Starmer had spent months trying to get Johnson to admit to demonstrable facts and appeared startled when Truss readily owned her more radical views. Labour had pushed Sunak towards a windfall tax; Truss said she hated them. She returned Starmer's peroration that she was 'nothing new' with interest: 'There is nothing new about a Labour leader who is calling for more tax rises.' It was one of the high points of her time as prime minister.

No one in Downing Street thought much of it when a routine briefing for the new prime minister was cancelled that afternoon. Truss was busy with her plans for an energy price freeze and the rest of her reshuffle. She could get her 2.30 p.m. scheduled 'bridges briefing' another time. It was the Whitehall codename for the death of the Queen. 'Little did we know,' a Number 10 official said.

Truss had promised action on the soaring cost of energy bills. At the last minute she decided it needed to be universal. She had looked at Sunak's two interventions on the cost of living – in the spring statement and again in June – and concluded that the media and the public were not satisfied with targeted, time-limited measures. Kwasi Kwarteng argued, 'If we go down the targeted support route, we'll be dragged to the Commons every two months for more and more and the government will grind to a halt. It will be complete gridlock every time Ofgem put the price up.' Celia McSwaine, the chancellor's spad, said, 'She didn't want to be dogged by this issue in the same way that she'd seen Boris and Rishi, when he was chancellor, dogged by it.'[22] Two days before the announcement, the prime minister said, 'I don't want to talk about energy for two years. It's got to be big. It's got to be shock and awe.' There were practical reasons too. 'BEIS cannot administer targeted schemes, so that was a problem. It's very difficult because people's energy bills aren't the same as their income.'

Truss was furious at the way the Treasury and the OBR wanted to score the intervention. 'What we were providing was essentially an insurance against prices going high.' But the OBR scored it as if she was handing everyone thousands of pounds up front.

'They don't take into account the fact that those prices come down,' she said. 'I fundamentally object to the Treasury approach.'

Two days before they moved into Downing Street, Truss's team had been installed in Dover House, the official Whitehall waiting room for incoming prime ministers. There they decided the level at which to freeze energy bills. Present were Truss and her Treasury ministers, Kwarteng and Philp, her advisers Ruth Porter, Matthew Sinclair and Jamie Hope, plus officials – Sarah Munby, the permanent secretary at BEIS and Maddy McTernan, who ran the energy supply taskforce.

Kwarteng and Philp wanted to at least 'claw back' some of the costs. As business secretary, Kwarteng had heard from power industry bosses who suggested the handouts be treated as a loan, with customers asked to pay back some of the money over decades. 'You pay off £1,000 over twenty years, so that's fifty quid a year on your bill for twenty years,' a minister said. One of those present recalled, 'Kwasi expressly said that this would help the bond markets see that there is some income that will partly offset the massive liabilities that we are creating.'

Truss rejected this approach, with very little debate. 'I am not going to do that,' she said. 'That sounds like a new tax. Why would you even do that?' She argued that Sunak had been able to spend £400 billion on Covid assistance without spooking the markets. 'She kept on saying that we had a lower debt-to-GDP ratio than other G7 countries, so we should let the balance sheet do the work,' a cabinet minister said.[23]

Kwarteng said, 'This is £120 billion, can we talk about this?' A witness said, 'When you're making a decision with that much money, you would think that a ten-minute conversation, initiated by her designated chancellor, would be something that you would entertain. But she just shut it down. That was typical of how decision-making was done.'

The last thing to be agreed was the number above which energy consumers would not have to pay more for the next two years. 'There was a debate about whether it should be a £3,000 cap or £2,500,' said one of those present. The difference between these two decisions was 'a £10 billion decision', with the lower cap more expensive.

Truss peremptorily declared, 'Make it £2,500.'

Philp, the new chief secretary to the Treasury, interjected, 'Are you sure you don't want to talk about it?'

'No,' said Truss. 'Do £2,500.' Throughout these conversations, she told aides, 'These are extraordinary times and it requires an extraordinary intervention from government.'

Truss wanted to separate the energy announcement from her main economic plans, so she could reassure the public about soaring energy bills before 'doing the fun stuff', the tax cuts she wanted to introduce later. The free marketeer prime minister, arguably the most hostile to 'tax and spend' and 'handouts' since the Second World War, agreed to spend in excess of £120 billion – nearly double the cost of the furlough scheme – on a universal handout.

At the time, there was frustration among Truss's team that what happened next robbed the energy intervention of the publicity they needed to inform the public how they were to be bailed out. It is also the case that it drowned out the hard questions which would inevitably have followed about how the plan was going to be paid for.

Less than twenty-four hours later Truss was at the despatch box, giving MPs the outline of her plans to freeze bills, when she was passed a note by Nadhim Zahawi. It said Buckingham Palace was due to issue a statement about the Queen's health. Zahawi signalled Labour's Angela Rayner to join him behind the speaker's chair where Simon Case was waiting. Starmer was now on his feet and a message was passed to the Labour leader that the Queen was 'unwell'. He did not need to be a codebreaker to work out that he needed to wrap up. Case took them into a small anteroom and explained the situation. Then he called Nicola Sturgeon, since the Queen was in Scotland. The palace statement read, 'Following further evaluation this morning, The Queen's doctors are concerned for Her Majesty's health and have recommended she remain under medical supervision. The Queen remains comfortable and at Balmoral.'

Truss and her team had known the Queen's death was a possibility the evening before when plans for her to host a virtual Privy Council to swear in the new cabinet were delayed and then scrapped. Case had to pull Truss out of the room. He told the ministers, 'Her Majesty is not available', but they saw the grave look on his face and drew their own conclusions. Number 10 staff were quietly advised to have a black tie to hand. While Truss prepared to go into the chamber on Thursday, Case took her aside and warned that death was 'a matter of hours'. Aides were sent to her Greenwich home to fetch black dresses.[24]

The Queen died at 3.10 p.m. on 8 September and the final call from the palace, bearing the news a country was coming to dread, was made to Number 10 at 4.30 p.m. Truss was in the Downing Street flat surrounded by close aides. 'On only my second full day as prime minister, it seemed utterly unreal,' she admitted later. 'Amid profound sadness, I found myself thinking: *Why me? Why now?*'[25] It thrust her into a world of ceremony which was 'a long way from my natural comfort zone'.[26]

The prime minister wrote her speech about the Queen herself, having rejected a civil service version prepared under David Cameron. Two hours later, the news was made public. At 6.50 p.m. Truss told the nation, 'Queen Elizabeth II was the rock on which modern Britain was built' before becoming the first PM in seventy-one years to say, 'God save the King'. The consensus, though, was that her hastily written oratory lacked emotional bite. One opponent said, 'It was like Year 8 had been asked to give a presentation on the Queen using Wikipedia.'

In the mourning period which followed, Truss was overshadowed by Boris Johnson, who issued an eloquent statement and then gave one of his best speeches in the Commons. Johnson had told aides that spring that he was already working on his speech for the Queen's demise. He wanted to popularise the name 'Elizabeth the Great', but that week he claimed to have suffered 'writer's block', before dashing off his words from scratch at 5 a.m. on Friday morning. Missing the chance to make the speech from the despatch box by three days was exquisite torture for the former prime minister. 'He totally adored her,' said one former Number 10 adviser. However, a Tory close to the royal household suggested mischievously that, 'Her Majesty wanted to hang on long enough to see Boris off the premises.'

Charles III flew down from Balmoral on Friday 9th and Truss had her second audience with a monarch in four days. Beyond a curious squatting curtsy, which one observer likened to 'tea bagging', Truss survived the ordeal of ceremonial activities in the days ahead. Nonetheless, as a poor public speaker, it was hardly her best platform to introduce herself to voters. The preparations for the funeral – Operation London Bridge – had been years in the making and the civil service took over, leaving Truss's political team at a loose end during the official mourning period which would last until 19 September, the day of the state funeral.

On Saturday 10th, senior privy councillors – including all living former prime ministers – gathered at St James's Palace for the accession council ceremony, where Charles read a formal notice of the Queen's death and Penny Mordaunt, just appointed Lord President of the Council, read a list of the new King's duties. As archbishops, judges and peers rubbed shoulders and the ousted Tory prime ministers made awkward small talk, a cabinet minister offered his condolences to one of the Queen's closest aides. 'It must have been very difficult,' he said. The courtier explained that the Queen's final days had been happy ones. She had enjoyed a gathering of her family and treasured staff two evenings before her death. The courtier confided that when Boris Johnson was mentioned, the Queen, mischief in her eye, had said, 'Well at least I won't have that idiot organising my funeral now.' This, it seems, was said to amuse but it was a widely shared sentiment in the royal household.

On Monday 19th, Truss joined Tony Blair and John Major, both knights of the garter, at the second, more intimate, funeral service ceremony in St George's Chapel, Windsor. She had a warm relationship with Blair, but Major was 'sulking about Brexit' and ignored her. She then flew to New York for the UN General Assembly, a dramatic comedown after the pomp of home. On the way to the UN, 'I got stuck behind a bin lorry.'[27]

The period after the Queen's death led to tensions with the palace. Ministers wanted a public information campaign about the energy package, a move blocked by civil servants because it was a period of political purdah. News then leaked that Truss was planning to lift the ban on fracking, a means of extracting gas from shale. Case was questioned privately by courtiers and blamed overzealous spads. A source close to the royal household said, 'Downing Street is not supposed to be doing anything. Everyone who works with Charles knows he has temper tantrums about things like this.'

* * *

The biggest political problem about the period of mourning, however, was the time it gave Truss and her most ideological advisers to 'hang more baubles on the tree' of the mini-budget. Aides say she became 'imperial' in her manner. 'She was high on the adrenaline,' a close aide said. 'The Queen's death meant she became closed off. It elevated her – not that she would ever use this phrase – to deputy monarch during that period.'

While the civil service focused on the funeral, political aides allowed themselves to dream big thoughts about the budget. Celia McSwaine said, 'Number 10 started to get much more ambitious. It got to the point where every day there would be a new request from Number 10 for a new policy to be included – things like investment zones ... and maybe we could add something on childcare. Maybe we should do some planning reforms to help accelerate infrastructure. It became very difficult to keep track of what was in the package day to day because so much was being added and taken out.' McSwaine asked a member of the private office, 'Is it always like this before we do a budget?'

The official replied, 'You're trying to do in three weeks what we normally do in four or five months.'[28]

There was no meaningful cabinet discussion of any of this. 'The cabinet basically only discussed ceremonial matters,' a minister recalled. Even those in the loop only managed to snatch meetings at short notice. 'It was literally when a gap opened up in her schedule. We didn't have a big economic planning session.' Reflecting later, Kwarteng said, 'It was very exciting, you felt you were part of a project. People got carried away, myself included. There was no tactical subtlety whatsoever.'[29] He added, 'We should have been much more cautious and much more deliberate.'

Efforts to get Truss to rein things in were greeted with, 'I've only got two years!' Asa Bennett, her speechwriter, recalled, 'She felt then the stakes were so high that there was no time to dither or delay.' But Hugh Bennett said, 'That wasn't enough time to really explain to people why we were doing what we were doing, why they were the right decisions for the country.'[30]

The Queen's funeral was on Monday 19 September. Truss insisted the autumn statement take place on the Friday, rather than wait until after the party conferences. Major announcements are almost never made in Westminster on a Friday, since they disappear into the weekend news vacuum. 'The Queen's funeral fucked with people's heads,' a Treasury source said. 'The logical thing would have been to think of a date in November.' Truss was having none of it: 'We'll do it on Friday.' A cabinet minister said, 'She hated dissent.'

Alongside the headline income tax measures, ministers were asked to come up with schemes to boost growth. Truss pressed for 'shovel ready' infrastructure projects to be named in the mini-budget. These included wind farms and one hundred road improvement schemes, which it was assumed would be popular with MPs. Plans for investment zones, where planning rules would be suspended, in exchange for tax cuts in those areas, were also dramatically expanded in the period after the Queen's death.

The prime minister demanded the list of roads within twenty-four hours, sending the Department for Transport into a spiral. Truss became enraged with Anne-Marie Trevelyan, the transport secretary, when officials were unable to produce a list. 'There was much eyerolling at the DfT's uselessness,' a fellow minister recalled. Matthew Sinclair tore his hair out trying to get the list together, telling one colleague that he spent more time on something which almost nobody noticed than everything else in the budget combined – a perverse use of time for a macroeconomic adviser. 'Ministers were losing their minds because their departments wouldn't give them lists of projects,' a spad said. 'How the fuck is this so hard? I suspect they were worried that anything they put on the list was something they would have to deal with later.' This all reinforced Truss's view that Whitehall lacked the can-do spirit when it came to boosting growth.

Truss also got 'very testy with Simon Clarke about investment zones,' a fellow cabinet minister observed. 'She felt that he wasn't going fast enough. I remember thinking: I bet this is how Thatcher treated Howe – quite rude to him.' The investment zones faced resistance from Treasury officials, who disliked a scheme which would see 'different tax outcomes' inside and outside the zones. The lack of dynamic modelling meant the Treasury only saw upfront costs, not the potential benefits later. Another cabinet minister said, 'Liz wanted hundreds of them and the liability was hundreds of billions, potentially.' The Treasury insisted on a cap on the numbers to ensure quality. Truss wanted no cap at all. When Clarke questioned this, she 'sashayed around' the cabinet table, smiled at him flirtatiously and said, 'You've got to live a little.'

*   *   *

In the headlong rush to pile policies into the budget, most of Truss's pragmatic political aides were kept in the dark about what she was planning. Adam Jones got wind that a 1p cut in income tax was on the table before he flew to New York with Truss. The PM was 'aghast' that anyone in the comms team knew. The first most of them knew about Truss and Kwarteng's intention to scrap the cap on bankers' bonuses was when it leaked to the *Financial Times* on 14 September, another story which irritated the King's advisers. It also staggered those not in the loop. 'Why the fuck are we doing this?' one asked. There was no backtracking, though. 'Liz and Kwasi both think the bonus cap is a shit policy that should never have been introduced,' a senior aide said.

The secrecy hampered policy-making. Jamie Hope was told to work up plans for the rollout of superfast broadband and better childcare. He needed £20 million for the broadband plan, a rounding error in the general scheme of things. Truss wrote on the note left in her ministerial box, 'No additional spending.' The answer was the same on childcare. Hope asked Matthew Sinclair why he could not have the funds. 'Oh, I can't tell you that,' the prime minister's economic adviser replied.

One political adviser found out about plans to double the threshold at which stamp duty was paid to properties worth £250,000, after pocketing a stray piece of paper left lying around at Chevening. On 20 September, the day after the Queen's funeral and three days before the budget, the aide concluded that the plans were 'fucking mental' and decided to try to stop Truss in her tracks. Using a burner phone to avoid detection, he called Steven Swinford, political editor of *The Times*, to leak the story, hoping that pre-publicity would lead to it being scrapped. The leak failed because other news organisations struggled to follow it up. When journalists phoned the comms team asking for a confirmatory steer, Jones and McGee had no idea whether the story was true or not.

The days leading up to the budget were a blur, with the business energy relief package unveiled on the Wednesday, Thérèse Coffey's 'ABCD' plan for the NHS on Thursday (ambulances, backlog, care, doctors and dentists) and the budget on the Friday morning. 'We've got to cram two weeks' news into four days,' Jones told journalists.

Throughout this period, there was no polling or testing of the decisions in focus groups – and none of the usual pitch rolling between Treasury ministers and Conservative MPs, where reactions are gauged and ideas sought. An aide added, 'They thought the reason why the Boris

Johnson government failed was because he was obsessed with popularity. They felt they were on a mission to reverse twenty-five years of social democracy.' True believers do not need the validation of polls. 'None of it was compromised by collision with anyone who disagreed,' a cabinet minister recalled. 'Liz's interjection in every meeting was, "This isn't bold enough. This isn't radical enough."'

No effort was made to tell the political team who needed to communicate the budget to the public what was in it. It was only on the morning of Thursday 22 September, the day before, that Adam Jones, Ruth Porter and Jason Stein learned about the most explosive item in Kwarteng's speech – a decision to scrap the 45p top rate of tax, which kicked in on those earning £150,000 a year. Truss said later, 'I was amazed we were criticised for not trailing the budget when the whole point is you're not meant to.' The decision to give the richest 1 per cent a tax cut in the middle of a cost of living crisis was bold to say the least, but the additional rate was regarded by Truss as 'a virtue-signalling tax', which raised little (around £2 billion a year) but sent a message to the world that Britain did not welcome the successful and wealthy.

The origins of scrapping the 45p rate dated back to late August when ministers began brainstorming policy ideas. One contribution was a paper, on which Chris Philp held the pen, but to which others contributed, outlining the options for tax cuts. Another was to take 1p off the basic rate of income tax to reduce it to 19 per cent. When the blame game began later, some used this document to point the finger for the 45p plan at Philp. 'They were tossing lithium and hydrochloric acid' on a combustible situation, a cabinet minister said. However, Philp's paper also called for a 'fiscal plan' to generate headroom in the public finances and it expressly warned about the dangers of spooking the City. The third paragraph read, 'Unless we balance and show elements of restraint, we will lose the confidence of the bond market.' Truss, a minister said, 'wasn't interested in any of that'.

After a brief discussion at Chevening, Philp thought the idea had been dropped. It was only in a meeting shortly before the mini-budget, when he saw a copy of the budget 'scorecard' containing the item 'additional rate: £2bn' that he realised it had been revived by Truss and Kwarteng.

Scrapping the 45p rate was finally agreed between the prime minister and her chancellor alone. Even Nick Catsaras was not present. Truss recalled, 'We were both keen on it. It was always there on the list of options. We were looking for everything we could do to get Britain's economy going and send a signal that Britain was open for business. This is a tax that raises very little money and it sends a signal to people that we don't like aspiration, we don't like people trying to earn more, and that's the whole culture we were trying to battle.' When he was asked later what had happened, Catsaras told a colleague, 'Kwasi and Liz got in a room and decided this thing and that was that. They cooked this up themselves.' A former Number 10 official observed, 'Usually advisers are the crazy ones and the politicians take the pragmatic view, but in the Treasury they are calling Liz and Kwasi "the terrorists".'

It was only on 15 September, eight days before the mini-budget, that Kwarteng messaged his media special adviser, Cameron Brown, 'Liz wants to announce 19p and abolish 45p next week – thoughts?'

Brown replied, 'That's a big fat rabbit – you're not fucking about, are you?' The Treasury wanted a cut in the basic rate to create a 'retail' offer for voters. Brown, highly experienced at the sharp end of Whitehall comms even at twenty-eight, told Kwarteng he needed to do both or neither of the income tax moves. If he was putting money in the pockets of the richest, he had to deliver at the lower end too.

The great irony is that the measure was selected precisely because it was economically insignificant and politically potent. Truss and Kwarteng had tasked Matthew Sinclair with finding measures which had 'little fiscal cost but were meaningful'. An adviser said, 'If you've got this dire growth picture, if you've got a lever that doesn't cost you very much to pull fiscally, you pull it.'

Kwarteng's determination to be Truss's 'enabler' meant he went along with the idea. Previous governments had suffered as a result of differences between prime ministers and their chancellors. Margaret Thatcher fell out with both Geoffrey Howe and Nigel Lawson; John Major and Norman Lamont were daggers drawn over Black Wednesday; Tony Blair and Gordon Brown were the ultimate political frenemies; Philip Hammond and Rishi Sunak regarded Theresa May's and Boris Johnson's grasp of economics with disdain. The ideal in modern times had been David Cameron who let George Osborne run the economy and political strategy in exchange for total public loyalty even when they disagreed privately. The result was austerity, a strategy which worked well politically while seeding economic problems later. But even under Cameron there had been tensions. Under Truss and Kwarteng, that creative tension was lost. They did not even disagree in private.

The chancellor did get warnings. Gerard Lyons, the Trussketeer economist, contacted Downing Street on the Monday before the budget after taking soundings from hedge fund managers. He warned that the markets had not priced in tax cuts that went beyond the changes to National Insurance and corporation tax outlined in the leadership campaign. Lyons said later, 'I warned them clearly about the febrile state of the markets – to not spook the markets, to keep them onside, to outline clear fiscal principles and to address their concerns about institutions.'

However, civil servants, including Treasury officials like Cat Little and Beth Russell, were reluctant to criticise the plans or warn that they would tank the markets. 'They'd just seen their boss [Scholar] beheaded in front of their eyes,' a special adviser realised. Both Case and Catsaras 'tried to keep her [Truss] on the straight and narrow'. But the approach of most officials was to try to steer rather than confront. A political aide concluded, 'They were giving Liz and Kwasi enough rope to hang themselves. It was malicious compliance.'

The only official prepared to fight was Clare Lombardelli, the chief economist at the Treasury. 'She was basically the only person who shoved her head above the parapet,' another political adviser said. 'The others tried their best to shape things as Liz wanted, while gently saying, "We could do it like this, as opposed to like this." But Clare Lombardelli would sit there silently, and Liz would go, "What do you think, Clare?" And she would tell her exactly what she thought. As a result, Liz didn't like Clare Lombardelli.'

Others believe that even a full-frontal warning from the entire Treasury team would have been dismissed by Truss, who was predisposed to disbelieve what she thought of as a discredited orthodoxy. 'I'm not sure anyone could have stopped her,' one of her longest-serving advisers concluded. Truss fed off the prospect of negative fallout, using it as evidence that the establishment would always fight real economic radicalism. 'She was told, "Don't do this, no one will like it." And her attitude was basically, "I don't care."'

Prime ministers are usually grounded by their spouses, but unlike Samantha Cameron and Philip May, Truss's husband Hugh O'Leary was an ideological soulmate, someone who reinforced her views rather than challenged them. 'Hugh often gave her good advice,' a Truss ally said, 'but ideologically they're total bed fellows.'

Imposing better process and ensuring the communications team was properly integrated into the operation for the most important public announcement the government was ever likely to make, could have been a job for the chief of staff, but Mark Fullbrook was absent for a lot of the period. During that time his mother was seriously ill and his father died. He was at his father's deathbed holding his hand when he received a call asking about how he had been questioned by the FBI as a witness as part of an investigation into an alleged criminal plot to bribe an American politician. A week later, a plan to pay him through his company was revealed and then quietly dropped. 'Mark was having a horrible time because his dad died,' a colleague said. 'On a human level you really feel for him. But I think communications and political people didn't get to interrogate the budget in the way that it should have been.' Even before his bereavement, Fullbrook was far from integral to the budget preparations. 'It wasn't Mark's fault because he wasn't in the room, but it was Mark's fault *that* he wasn't in the room,' a colleague said.

Adam Jones stumbled across the key news. The communications director forced his way into a budget meeting in the final week, insisting that he needed to know what was in the statement, but heard only details of the items which were likely to be popular, including plans to freeze alcohol duty. As he walked out, he asked Matthew Sinclair, 'I'm hearing some rumours about big tax cuts.'

'Oh, do you mean the 45p rate?'

'What do you mean, the 45p rate?'

At this point they were intercepted by Truss, who snapped, 'We're not having any leaks. So, can you not talk about that. Adam can see everything when it's all agreed. It's still not agreed.' It was only with twenty-four hours to go that he was allowed to know the truth.

Even then, there was an effort to rewrite Kwarteng's budget speech to make it more nuanced. The chancellor sent the text to Philp, who inserted four or five paragraphs saying that the tax cuts would need to be offset with spending reductions. These balancing paragraphs were removed. Truss's defence later was that the statement might have been even more incendiary. 'We left a lot out – scrapping inheritance tax, moving to a flat tax,' she explained.

Kwarteng put final touches to his growth plan over a takeaway curry from Pimlico Tandoori in the Number 11 dining room, with close aides and Treasury officials. One of them quietly wondered to himself: *Why are we calling it a growth plan when we are heading for a recession. People will say it has failed.* The chancellor was on a mission, though. 'We can finally say, and do, what we think is right,' he said. 'We're about to undo twenty-five years of social democratic tinkering.' He then practised the speech with books piled high to simulate the Commons despatch box. Even Kwarteng's team was on edge. One of them contacted Nissy Chesterfield for advice about how to handle the rollout and admitted, 'This is going to be much bigger than you think. It's completely insane.'

From Truss, however, there was no evidence of doubt. On Thursday, she told her quad, 'I'm prepared to take the difficult decisions. We have to be unapologetic about doing what we know is right.' That evening she told a senior civil servant, 'My one worry is that I'm not going far enough.' To political aides, she kept repeating the phrase, 'Go big, or go home.'

In the end, she would do both.

When Kwarteng got to his feet in the chamber at 9.34 a.m. on Friday 23 September, Matthew Sinclair had assembled members of his economic unit and some invited guests for a viewing party in one of the state rooms upstairs in Downing Street. Jamie Hope and Iain Carter were watching from the private office downstairs. Celia McSwaine was in the box reserved for officials in the Commons chamber, up behind the speaker's chair. That morning Kwarteng had been 'over the moon' as he addressed cabinet, telling colleagues, 'Some of the rabbits have survived.' An aide recalled, 'He told them everything apart from the 45p thing.'

Kwarteng began with confidence, looking like a man who had been delivering budgets for a decade, but soon he and McSwaine, the two in the chamber, got an uneasy feeling as they absorbed the reaction of Tory MPs. 'If the chamber is quiet, that's a really, really bad sign,' she said. 'And from the get-go, our backbenchers were deathly silent.'[31]

Kwarteng outlined a plan of staggering audacity. In the leadership election, Truss had proposed to cut £30 billion of taxes. The supposedly 'mini' budget contained tax cuts of £45 billion and increased borrowing of £72 billion to fund the energy price freeze. When the chancellor revealed that the 45p rate was to be abolished altogether, one Tory MP exclaimed, 'Jesus Christ!' On the front bench, a cabinet colleague struggled not to choke. 'I thought the rabbits were going to be a new road here and there. I thought: Are you fucking mad?'

He was not alone. Neither Hope, the head of policy, nor Carter, the director of political strategy, had any idea about the 45p plan until the words left Kwarteng's mouth. The two advisers had spent more than two years together in CCHQ tearing apart Labour's unfunded policies and now their own government was engaged in the same pursuit. 'Did you hear that?' they asked each other. 'Why are we giving a tax cut to millionaires in a cost of living crisis?' Hope's view was that it was 'totally nuts'. In retrospect, McSwaine concluded that the surprise made it seem even more radical: 'When you're trying to announce new radical things, you want to actually do it in a very boring way so that people are reassured about the change. By making it a rabbit, we ... almost emphasised the degree to which it was controversial.'[32]

Chris Philp was embarrassed by events. Before Kwarteng reached the controversial parts of his speech, the pound had begun to slowly rise against the dollar. The chief secretary tweeted from the front bench, 'Great to see sterling strengthening on the back of the new UK Growth plan'. Within minutes, the currency began to slide as City analysts and journalists waded through the OBR documents and the scale of the unfunded commitments became clear. By 10.44 a.m. the pound had hit its lowest level against the dollar since 1985, ending the day below $1.09.

In her response, Rachel Reeves, the shadow chancellor, called the plan 'casino economics: gambling the mortgages and finances of every family in the country to keep the Tory Party happy'. By holding the budget on a Friday, Truss's plan had been to overshadow the start of the Labour Party conference the following day. Instead, she and Kwarteng handed the opposition a large stick with which to beat the government. Reeves' deputy, Pat McFadden, raced to central lobby, to speak to the waiting broadcasters. He recalled, 'Liz Truss and Kwasi Kwarteng were like two excited students who suddenly got hold of the keys to a Ferrari, namely the British economy, and they took it for a joyride and crashed it into a ditch.'

Concerned Conservative MPs quickly dubbed it the 'Kami-Kwasi budget'. A former minister told the *Sunday Times*, 'Everyone who isn't mad hates it.' Those with long memories compared the bonanza to the 'Barber boom', named after Ted Heath's chancellor Anthony Barber, which had sent inflation spiralling and put Labour into power again in

1974. A former Downing Street aide who advised City businesses and Sunak declared, 'The gulf between the free-marketeers and what the free market actually thinks of the free-marketeers is hilarious. The City boys don't have any confidence they know what they are doing in Downing Street.' Even the RSPB got in on the act, calling the enterprise zones an 'attack on nature' because habitat regulations protecting endangered species would be suspended there to encourage house building. They were backed up by the Woodland Trust and the Wildlife Trust.

That afternoon, however, Kwarteng and Truss were both upbeat as they visited a housebuilding firm in Kent together. Truss said, 'I was ecstatic to have finally done the things we had talked about and planned for so long. That afternoon was probably my happiest moment as prime minister.'[33] The chancellor followed budget day tradition and was filmed, alongside Matthew Sinclair, buying drinks for his officials in the Two Chairmen pub, a stone's throw from the Commons. Kwarteng then went to a champagne reception for Tory donors, arranged by CCHQ, at the Chelsea home of financier Andrew Law, who had given the party £3.6 million. Others in attendance included a who's who of the finance sector. Kwarteng gave a five-minute speech in which he declared it 'a great day for freedom'. Those present said hedge fund managers, delighted at the budget, egged him on to go further. In response, Kwarteng confirmed that more tax cuts were planned, but also made clear that there would be spending cuts in the medium-term financial plan. Guests told Kwarteng to 'double down' – an approach from which some stood to make enormous profits by shorting the pound. 'He was high on adrenaline,' one of those present said. 'His big thing was: "Look, we're not going to do stuff incrementally. We really believe in this stuff."' After the reception, at least two prominent hedge fund bosses told City associates that Kwarteng was 'a useful idiot'. A source who was present at a dinner a week earlier attended by hedge fund managers revealed, 'They were all supporters of Truss and every one of them was shorting the pound.'

On Friday evening, the advice from Treasury officials and EDS – the economic and domestic affairs secretariat in the Cabinet Office – was, an aide recalled, 'The market reaction is at the negative end of what we expected but within the scope of expectations – I don't think anyone realised how bad it was at that time.'

Truss and her allies argued afterwards that it was the Bank of England, rather than the mini-budget, which left the pound weak. On Thursday, the day before the budget, the pound fell to its lowest rate in thirty-seven years after the Bank of England raised interest rates by just 0.5 per cent. They had been expected to do so by 0.75 per cent as the US Federal Reserve had earlier that week. 'The bank missed market expectations,' Truss was to write.[34] The Bank also announced a £40 billion sale of government gilts at the same time, the first quantitative tightening after years of easing. This, in turn, pushed up the cost of government borrowing. There were warnings that interest rates would rise as high as 5 per cent, sending mortgage costs soaring. Another straw in the wind emerged on Saturday in the form of Julian Jessop, one of the three Trussketeer economists, who felt the need to distance himself from the budget he had helped to inspire. 'My advice would have been to delay the announcement of the cuts in income tax (which is what seems to have most spooked the markets) until a full budget later in the year,' he wrote, warning of a 'doom loop' of rising interest rates and more borrowing.

Truss seemed impervious to these chill winds. She was in very high spirits that Friday, buoyed by the reaction of the Tory press. The *Mail* splashed on 'AT LAST! A *TRUE* TORY BUDGET',[35] hailing the '£45 billion dash for growth', while Allister Heath, editor of the *Sunday Telegraph*, pronounced it 'the best budget I have ever heard a British chancellor deliver, by a massive margin'. A Truss adviser said, 'She was over the moon, bouncing round the office absolutely delighted', gleefully telling those around her, 'This is only the beginning.'

That weekend, the prime minister saw her biographers. Harry Cole found her 'pretty calm, pretty zen' and dismissive of the fuss about the unfunded budget. 'This is all ridiculous,' she said. 'We've got one of the lowest debt to GDP ratios in the G7.'[36]

At that point, Liz Truss had been prime minister for seventeen days. Just twenty-seven days later, she resigned.

25

GOING HOME

(or 'Hitting the Ground')

25 September to 20 October 2022

'Go big, or go home ...'

– Liz Truss, September 2022

In a hotly contested field it was, one of Liz Truss's closest aides concluded later, 'the biggest head in hands moment'. Kwasi Kwarteng was in Laura Kuenssberg's hot seat on the BBC's flagship Sunday programme. The markets had delivered him a raspberry, his job was to calm them down. Before the interview Adam Jones, the Number 10 director of communications, and Cameron Brown, the chancellor's media adviser, agreed Kwarteng should project an image of fiscal responsibility and try to talk about the supply side reforms the government was planning to boost economic growth. Instead, he blurted out that there was 'more to come' on tax cuts and declared, 'This is only the beginning' – an intervention which sent the markets into freefall when they reopened on Monday morning. Kwarteng said he would neither bring forward his planned November budget nor ask the Office of Budget Responsibility to publish its forecasts of his plans.

'Only the beginning' was a phrase Truss herself had been using in private, but even she realised 'more to come' should not be the government's public message. 'She was furious about it,' one insider said. One of his aides explained: 'It was Kwasi just saying shit. People ask why he said it. He was telling the truth. That's part of Kwasi's problem, that he tells the truth.' Kwarteng admitted later, 'I made some silly remarks which I am totally culpable for.'

The Asian markets opened first. It seemed like everyone was selling sterling. The pound plunged to $1.035, its lowest ever level against the dollar. The interest rate paid on government debt soared, pushing the cost of a new mortgage above 6 per cent.

'We got into the Treasury really early in the morning,' Celia McSwaine recalled. Kwarteng had called a meeting of all the Treasury's director generals. Clare Lombardelli, the chief economist, 'gave this very grim presentation about the market reaction that happened that morning'. McSwaine said, 'A hush descended over the room as everyone took in the full scale' of the disaster. 'She said it very calmly, but we were left in no doubt that this was a very, very serious situation.'[1]

Kwarteng had a serious attack of the jitters. 'Kwasi became very, very nervous and skittish from the Monday onwards,' one of Truss's closest aides recalled. 'He realised that he'd fucked up on Kuenssberg and was in back-pedalling mode. Until then you couldn't have put a bit of cigarette paper between him and Liz. But Kwasi was generally shitting himself. He realised the enormity of it slightly earlier than Liz.'

By Monday lunchtime, 26 September, Kwarteng felt he needed to issue a statement to clarify that he would publish an update of the government's growth plans on 23 November, along with an assessment by the OBR. Even that statement was initially resisted by Truss, whose instinct was to stand firm and say nothing.

This all happened at precisely the moment when Labour finally seemed to have got their act together as a potential party of government. Keir Starmer told the party faithful assembled at the party conference in Liverpool that they would re-introduce the 45p additional rate of income tax. A Labour official said, 'Truss told us she would hit the ground. What she didn't say was that she would take the pound with her.'

After a decade of fractious conferences between moderates and Corbynistas, the hard left stayed away and peace broke out. When delegates sang the national anthem, with none of the predicted booing, Pat McFadden – the most devout centrist during the dark years – walked out of the auditorium and declared, 'My work here is done.'

Tuesday brought an extraordinary intervention from the International Monetary Fund (IMF), which issued a statement treating Britain as if it were the basket case economy that had gone running for aid, as the

Labour government had been forced to do in 1976. 'We do not recommend large and untargeted fiscal packages at this juncture,' the fund said, announcing that it was 'closely monitoring' developments and calling on the chancellor to 're-evaluate the tax measures'. If that was an unusual but reasonable economic observation within its remit, the criticism that 'the UK measures will likely increase inequality' was a political judgement about decisions that were rightly those of national governments. 'It was blatantly political,' Truss said. 'They were making a comment, not about the financial stability of our policies, but about the equity of them, which is not their role.' The IMF intervention was a perfect Rorschach test; those already convinced of Truss's irresponsibility saw a humiliating international dressing down. Those, like the prime minister, who perceived a global establishment dictating a stifling orthodoxy, had their view reinforced too. The prime minister was clear who she blamed, telling aides, 'I can see the hand of Tom Scholar in this.'

The real impact of Scholar's departure was that the City had not been ready for much of what Kwarteng announced. 'Tom's big focus wasn't actually policy, it was liaising with the Bank and external markets and making sure the subterranean pipework of the system was working,' a Treasury official said. 'That is precisely what has gone wrong this week.'

The same day, the chancellor staged an intervention with Truss, trying to get her to change tack. 'Even after the mini-budget we were going at breakneck speed,' Kwarteng recalled. He told the prime minister, 'You know, we should slow down.'

Truss was still fired by an intoxicating cocktail of paranoia and extreme urgency. 'I've only got two years!' she protested.

'You will have two months if you carry on like this,' the chancellor warned.[2] Inside he thought: *She's going to blow up*. Privately, he confided in an aide, 'I want her to win, I want her to succeed, but there won't be a government if we keep going at 100 mph and fight on every issue. With all the vested interests, the rent seekers, the Left, the establishment, the institutions, we're fighting everyone. We need to pick our battles.' The aide found the conversation sobering: 'Kwasi is quite a bombastic, overt, confident individual, but he was the sensible, rational one in the room. I love him to bits but he's not normally that.'

The issue which had split them was an attempt by Truss to secure a long-term supply of energy. Since August, she had been meeting executives from the Norwegian gas giant Equinor in a bid to secure a gas futures deal. She wanted deals with Norway that would lower energy costs and the amount of subsidy the government needed to pay to households. The chancellor and his deputy, Chris Philp, saw a new disaster, believing the deal was terrible value for money.

Truss wanted to borrow billions more to buy gas for twenty years at a 'strike price' of £180 per therm. At that time the going rate was around £380 per therm and at one point it had risen as high as £600. However, prior to the Ukraine war the average price in America had been between £70 and £80 per therm. Treasury officials estimated that Truss's proposed deal would have cost £130 billion over the lifetime of the deal. A minister said, 'We knew prices would be high over the winter and then would come down in the future. It was estimated that over a lifetime, that contract would lose £32 billion.' Locking in at £180 and funding it with borrowing would be a recipe for further market turbulence in the short term and an economic disaster in the long term.

Kwarteng told Truss, 'This is madness. It's going to cost us £30 billion.'

'It secures the price,' she responded. 'Gas prices might stay high.'

'But they might not.'

On a day when the chancellor went to the Treasury campus in Darlington, Truss arranged a meeting with Jacob Rees-Mogg, whose business beat covered energy. The prime minister wanted to get him on side and sign the deal that weekend. Chris Philp got wind of the meeting, briefed the business secretary and turned up. 'What are you doing here?' Truss snapped. 'You weren't invited.'

'I hope I will always be welcome,' Philp muttered. He thought Rees-Mogg considered the Equinor deal a bad idea, but in the meeting the business secretary, who put loyalty first, agreed with Truss. Philp objected strongly and Truss signalled 'frostily' for him to stop talking. Afterwards, Philp phoned Kwarteng, who was finally able to persuade the PM to back off. In the end, gas prices fell quicker than the Treasury had anticipated. Had Truss signed the deal, the government would have lost up to £60 billion.

Kwarteng suggested to Truss that she form a quad of senior ministers to stabilise things: the two of them, plus Thérèse Coffey, the deputy prime minister, and Nadhim Zahawi, the Cabinet Office minister who had an eagle's eye view of Whitehall. Kwarteng had previously dated Amber Rudd and recalled the words of her father, a veteran of the Second

World War, about survival when the bullets are flying: 'However bad the problem, you have got to have a plan. That's the start. You can't run around like a headless chicken.' The chancellor thought they could escape the mess with some calm planning, but 'Liz didn't want to know,' a source said. 'Everything was in her head. She had absolute power.'

The Trussonomics crisis reached its most acute moment on the morning of Wednesday 28 September, five days after the mini-budget. A combination of that and a lower than expected interest rate rise, coupled with the announcement from the Bank of England the week before that it would sell government bonds, led the City to sell these 'gilts', driving down the price. This, in turn, threw pension funds into turmoil. The problem was an investment vehicle called 'liability-driven investments' (LDIs). The use of LDIs dated back to the early 2000s, when pension funds were underfunded. The pension funds would give government gilts to companies, freeing up cash to invest in riskier assets. The idea was that if interest rates fell, making it harder to fund pensions, the value of the bonds would rise to balance things out. However, when there was a sharp fall in the value of gilts – which were supposed to be a safe asset – providers were expected to pay the shortfall (known as a 'margin call'), threatening to tip some of the pension companies into bankruptcy. 'People were dumping the bonds,' a minister said. 'They had to do a fire sale to get some money back, which made things worse, so the Bank effectively said, "We'll buy this shit off you" to keep up the price.'

This house of cards combined with market jitters over the mini-budget to create a perfect storm. The astonishing thing is that no one in authority appears to have seen it coming. Simon Case, the cabinet secretary, first received a call from Andrew Bailey, the governor of the Bank of England, the previous Sunday evening. He had been warned by junior officials at the Bank that there was a problem and warned Treasury officials. On Monday, Case called Clare Lombardelli, the chief economist, and said, 'We need a teach-in on LDIs.'

She replied, 'I'm just finishing mine.'

By that afternoon, panic was spreading. 'We were learning fast,' a senior civil servant said. 'But nobody really understood what the liability was. Nobody, including the governor, or anybody at senior level, had ever heard of these things.' Truss, a former chief secretary, said, 'I literally didn't know anything about it – literally nothing.' Simon Clarke, who had spent a year at the Treasury, said, 'I never even heard the phrase. The extent to which, institutionally they were blind and that politically we were blindsided is total.' A political aide concluded, 'I think Treasury suffered from assuming this was someone else's job now. They saw this as something that the Bank does.'

Staggeringly, as Truss was to discover, it turned out that the value of total assets in LDI strategies was 'equivalent to around 60 per cent of the UK's GDP'. The Bank of England told the prime minister they wanted to make a public statement on the Monday. 'At no point during any of the preparations for the mini-Budget had any concerns about liability-driven investments (LDIs) and the risk they posed to bond markets been mentioned at all to me, the chancellor or any of our teams by officials at the Treasury,' Truss said later.

The Bank of England statement was written with the help of Matthew Sinclair but Truss and Kwarteng argued about whether to issue it. She said, 'I was concerned on the Monday that a statement by the Bank of England would be an overreaction and would actually cause more trouble. Kwasi was convinced he had to do it. I wasn't telling him not to. I was convinced over the day that we had to do it.'[3]

To make matters worse, Bailey said he would 'not hesitate' to increase interest rates, having failed to do so by enough the week before. The governor also announced that the Bank would provide an 'assessment' of the government's policies at the next meeting of the monetary policy committee. Truss thought neither the Treasury nor the Bank had 'provided reassurance to the market' or 'taken sufficient action to avert' disaster. 'That, in my view, was a failure to do their job.'[4]

At 9.15 a.m. that Wednesday, Bailey called Kwarteng and delivered the blunt message that without massive intervention from the Bank of England, the entire pensions industry was on the brink of insolvency. 'We had some of Britain's biggest insurers saying they were hours away from collapsing,' a Treasury adviser said. The chancellor agreed the government would indemnify an intervention to buy up government bonds. The Bank announced that it would buy 'on whatever scale is necessary' to stabilise the market. It amounted to £65 billion. 'Were dysfunction in this market to continue or worsen, there would be a material risk to UK financial stability,' the Bank declared. While the government got the blame, it should have been shared since the Bank was now buying bonds having announced the previous week that it would sell them. Unhelpfully, the governor said he would only prop things up for two weeks. Truss, in effect, had been given fourteen days to sort out her economic policy or see her government collapse. She thought Bailey 'ruthless' in 'pushing back' at the government because he was 'clearly annoyed during the leadership election that I had questioned the bank's mandate'.[5]

Even then, insiders say, Truss refused to countenance holding a crisis meeting. 'She doesn't see it as a crisis,' a Whitehall source said at the time. 'Her view was: the markets will do what they do.' While the prime minister and chancellor met late morning, there was no emergency Cobra meeting. Instead, there were discussions about Truss flying to Ukraine to see Volodymyr Zelensky before the Tory conference to distract media attention.

Labour could hardly believe their luck. Pat McFadden, the shadow chief secretary to the Treasury, said, 'What I saw happening in real time was the Tories setting fire to their own economic credibility. You got all this rhetoric through the years: "We are the party of sound money. We might not have the biggest hearts in the world, but we know how to run things and we can be trusted with the public finances." And they just took a sledgehammer to the whole thing.'[6]

In Kwarteng's view this, rather than the collapse of the currency, was the decisive moment. 'People go on about the pound,' he said later. 'What screwed us was the gilt market wobble. That is what did for the government.'

The pension industry crisis gave institutional opponents of Truss's plans a way to force a change of direction. A cabinet colleague agreed: 'The OBR more or less stuck the knife in, the Bank of England even more. These groups thought it was heresy. You could have pitch rolled with an atom bomb and they wouldn't have bloody heeded it.'

On Friday 30 September, Truss and Kwarteng met the OBR to talk about their medium-term fiscal plan. In Truss's account, the OBR said tax rises were a 'more certain source of income' than cuts to public spending and offered a 'very Keynesian' analysis that government spending had more effect on growth than money in the private sector. To the prime minister's fury 'they were not prepared to "score" supply-side measures' with the exception of higher immigration.[7]

The Bank bailout reinforced the growing public view that the prime minister and her chancellor had no idea what they were doing. For Kwasi

Kwarteng, public criticism came very close to home. Graffiti was chalked on the pavement outside his house, saying, '1 + 1 = 4'. An ally said, 'It was the most Greenwich graffiti ever.'

By now, Truss was losing the backing of even supportive backbenchers, who believed she had the right approach. MPs shared videos of comedian Eric Morecambe massacring a piano solo ('I am playing all the right notes, but not necessarily in the right order'), as a metaphor for her performance. Around twenty MPs were thought to have submitted letters of no confidence in the prime minister.

Allies of Sunak began to mobilise to say, 'I told you so', but then with a view to topple Truss. One supporter, Simon Hoare, tweeted that the disaster had been 'authored' in the Treasury. 'This inept madness cannot go on.' One of Sunak's most senior aides announced that the former chancellor would not be going to conference to 'give Truss all the space she needs to own the moment', a deftly worded knifing. A cabinet minister noted, 'The Sunak counter operation was quite advanced by this stage. [Mel] Stride and [Gavin] Williamson were actively coordinating to sabotage the plan.' Julian Smith was named as another 'henchman'. Others observed with justified suspicion Michael Gove's intention to speak at nine different party conference fringe meetings to 'let off a few grenades'. Rumours circulated that some of Sunak's allies might vote against Kwarteng's finance bill. Team Truss hit back, calling the former chancellor a 'petulant child' and pointing out that budget votes are always confidence motions and rebels would lose the whip. 'There is a group of them who believe only the headboy should be in charge,' a cabinet minister complained. An aide of Truss admitted that she 'was going around saying Rishi's mates in the City were taking their revenge on her'. In her memoir she referred to 'a sustained whispering campaign by the economic establishment, encouraged and fuelled by my political opponents in the Conservative Party who refused to accept my mandate to lead'.[8]

However, even Truss loyalists accepted that she had provoked the wrath of her internal enemies by excluding able people from cabinet in the interests of ideological purity. 'Firing people like [Grant] Shapps and [Steve] Barclay was gratuitous and actively exposed her flank in a way she just didn't need to,' a cabinet minister said. Even Kwarteng had argued that she should hang on to Shapps and Greg Hands.

Trying to keep this fractious mob in line was Wendy Morton, a chief whip described as 'reading out talking points' when she met MPs. She was soon known in Truss's circle as 'Wendy Moron'. The cabinet minister said, 'The whips' operation in the chamber was pitiful. It felt like amateur hour. I really like Wendy, but she was in no way up to the task.' This minister wanted Alister Jack, 'who was as hard as bloody nails and a very good operator', as chief whip. Jack might well have improved things for both Boris Johnson and Truss in that regard.

With party conference approaching, Jason Stein realised with horror that Truss had no idea she was slated to do fourteen interviews on the Thursday morning with BBC local radio outlets. The commitment was a long-standing diary item for Tory leaders before conference, but Truss hated interviews and she had not appeared in public for nearly a week. 'She's going to go fucking mental,' he warned colleagues.

'It's in the diary,' an official said.

'She doesn't see her diary!'

When Truss found out she said, 'I'm not doing all this.' On this occasion, it was explained that she had to.

The first interview set the tone, with the presenter asking Truss, 'Where've you been?' Another went in with, 'Are you ashamed of what you have done?' There followed a cringeworthy collation of awkward silences, robotic soundbites and stuttering explanations. She insisted the 45p tax cut was 'the right thing to do'. It was as if Truss had decided to provide every media trainer in the land with a 'how not to do an interview' video for their clients. Dan Snow, the television historian, proclaimed it, 'the worst provincial campaign of any of our leaders since autumn 1216 when King John, marching about dealing with a rebellion and two invasions, caught dysentery in Norfolk, lost the crown jewels in The Wash and died in Nottinghamshire'.

This should not have been Truss's first major media appearance since the budget. The communications team had wanted to wheel her out to say, 'I'm working very hard to keep the markets stable.' The trouble was, they did not believe Truss would deliver that message. 'I'm not sure if in her own mind she accepted she was in a lot of trouble until the Wednesday,' a senior aide said. 'Which is why we took the decision not to do some broadcast stuff early in the week. At that point, the danger was of her doing a Callaghan and saying, "Crisis, what crisis?"'

MPs were losing their nerve at what had now been dubbed the 'Trussterfuck', a process accelerated when YouGov dropped a poll that night giving Labour a 33-point lead over the Tories, who were marooned on just 21 per cent. As Tory conference began that weekend, Truss's personal approval rating had sunk to -59, a depth never plumbed by Boris Johnson or even Jeremy Corbyn at their most unpopular.

Kwarteng and Chris Philp also began circulating letters to cabinet ministers demanding 'efficiency savings' ahead of a meeting with the OBR, also on Thursday, in which they discussed £40 billion of cuts.

Truss remained incredulous. As she headed to a British Gas site in Kent on Friday to highlight the government's energy price cap intervention, she expressed irritation that the City had ignored that the energy package was the biggest item in the budget. 'Markets surely get that?' she said. Leaving that evening for Birmingham, she said to an aide, 'People forget the counterfactual here. Doing nothing was not and is not an option. Change is difficult, I get that, but we need it.' Before the weekend was out, it was Truss who was forced to change.

Her first task at conference was to survive twenty minutes with Laura Kuenssberg on the Sunday morning. Truss tried to dismiss concerns about soaring mortgage rates as 'a global phenomenon' and said, 'I do stand by the package we announced.' Where she did give ground was to say, 'I do accept we should have laid the ground better, I do accept that.' The prime minister was blaming her communications team for the problems with a policy they had only been told about twenty-four hours before the public. It left Adam Jones 'pissed off'. Truss refused to say whether she would cut public spending, telling people to wait until Kwarteng's medium-term fiscal plan at the end of November.

Asked if she was absolutely committed to axing the 45p rate of tax, she said, 'Yes', arguing that it would make Britain 'competitive internationally'. It was a pledge that would hold for just twelve hours. Kuenssberg questioned whether Truss had discussed the decision with the cabinet. 'No, we didn't. It was a decision that the chancellor made.' Aides claimed the PM was simply explaining that tax announcements were formally Kwarteng's responsibility. But the chancellor felt a twinge of fear that he was being hung out to dry.

When Kuenssberg finished her grilling, the prime minister had to sit and listen while Michael Gove savaged her budget from just a few feet away, saying it was 'not Conservative' to fund tax cuts from borrowing and was a betrayal of the 2019 election manifesto. Calling himself 'profoundly concerned', Gove said, 'There are two major things that are problematic with the fiscal event. The first is the sheer risk of using borrowed money to fund tax cuts. That is not conservative. The second thing is the decision to cut the 45p rate, and indeed at the same time to change the law on how bankers are paid in the City of London. At a time when people are suffering ... cutting tax for the wealthiest, that is a display of the wrong values.' He called on Truss to 'correct course'. At a lunchtime fringe event, he was more explicit, saying the government should drop the plan.

Gove's was a brutal and effective intervention which added needle to an already difficult relationship. 'Liz hates Michael,' a cabinet ally said. 'It goes way beyond simple dislike. She loathes him.' As a junior minister when Gove was education secretary, Truss did not think he backed her when her planned reforms to childcare ratios were blocked by the Liberal Democrats. Gove saw a minister who went flying in with both feet and thought ideological zeal would be enough to drive through a reform which needed subtlety and careful preparation.

Downing Street aides briefed that Truss had sought to make peace with Gove after firing him from the cabinet. The previous Monday they met for a drink in Number 10. Gove told Truss 'how much he admired her' and praised the energy price support package, though he made clear that he did not support the abolition of the top rate of tax. Truss, in turn, asked if he was interested in a new role. Nothing was explicitly offered but the PM alluded to a senior diplomatic post working with a major ally. The ambassadorships to Israel and the United Arab Emirates were both due to become vacant. She had not heard from him until he popped up on the BBC. What Team Truss did not reveal was that when she fired him she made pointed comments about Gove's private life, implying, without any evidence, that he was gay. 'Michael, you can enjoy yourself now,' she said. 'Go to Heaven every night if you want to.' Heaven is one of London's best known gay clubs. Gove's marriage had broken down and he had been filmed dancing in an Aberdeen disco, but it was not a gay club. For a woman who complained about scuttlebutt regarding her own private life, it was an odd way to win someone over.

Gove's allies said he had told both Truss and his whip that he would oppose the 45p tax cut publicly. One MP, who spoke to Gove, said he was also trying to find a coalition of the willing to replace Truss: 'Michael thinks Boris and Rishi should come together and get the show back on the road.' Sunak returned to London that Thursday having spent conference with former aides at his constituency home in Yorkshire. Few yet predicted a second act in his political career.

The following weekend Truss authorised briefings against Gove. In the *Mail on Sunday*[9] and the *Sunday Telegraph*[10] he was a 'sadist' who had 'stabbed the PM in the back' and whose plotting would lead to a Labour government. The *Sunday Times* carried an astonishing character assassination: 'Michael is troubled and has never found his place in the sun. There is something deeply troubling about the darkness inside him. It grips him and corrupts his soul. The more he plots, the more baggage he collects and the more conflicted he then becomes about who and what he is. His answer to everything is more tax, more salami slicing, more failed economics. The Tory Party has rejected him.' Reading this, even one loyalist minister concluded, 'Michael was left with no choice but to fire back.'

Gove was not alone in stirring up trouble for Truss. Mel Stride and Julian Smith continued fomenting rebellion. Damian Green, leader of the One Nation group, saw Truss and asked for a change of tack. Penny Mordaunt told allies she was ready to fire up her campaign again. Also prominent at conference was Grant Shapps. When she sacked him, Truss told Shapps he was 'one of the best media performers', but because he had not supported her, 'there is no room at the inn'. Shapps treated himself to a new mobile phone, the Samsung Galaxy Fold (RRP: £1,649), which flipped open so he could better see the spreadsheet where he was now recording the views of colleagues about Truss. By Tuesday evening, Shapps had recorded 237 recent conversations with MPs. His to-do list included 57 coffees with colleagues. Shapps's spreadsheet already contained more than 6,000 historic 'data points'. Recent additions included Truss losing the support of the G-Group of twenty right-wing conservatives. One of the most prominent, Peter Bone, had been made deputy leader of the Commons by Johnson, voted for Truss, joined her transition team and was then sacked. 'She has taken somebody who was loyal to her and crossed the road to make an enemy,' a senior MP said.

What Shapps found was sufficiently bad for the prime minister that by Wednesday he had broken cover to publicly warn that Truss 'has ten days' to turn things around or MPs 'might as well roll the dice and elect a new leader'. Shapps saw himself as a possible caretaker prime minister, though the memories of the time he had used an alter ego – Michael Green – to sell get rich quick schemes on the internet meant this was not a view shared by his colleagues. One rebel noted, wryly, 'I'm not sure his get rich schemes were any more dubious than the chancellor's.'

It was also at conference that MPs discovered that Truss and her party chairman, Jake Berry, had dismissed Isaac Levido, as director of the next election campaign. Levido had kept quiet, but the bullet had been delivered a couple of weeks earlier, with appalling timing, the day before his wedding. For MPs growing concerned about holding their seats, this was finally proof that the regime had gone mad.

Multiple Number 10 officials said Truss had struck a deal with Mark Fullbrook, her chief of staff, that after a few months he would move from Downing Street to CCHQ to take charge of the election campaign. The contract was said to be worth around £5 million. Fullbrook's business partner was Alice Robinson, the wife of Berry. It looked like too cosy an arrangement. One Truss aide called it 'straight up corruption'. When details surfaced in the media, a furious Berry first threatened to sue for defamation and then announced that he was going to hold an open tender for the post, letting it be known that he had invited Levido's company, Fleetwood Strategy, to apply. Another U-turn loomed.

Throughout her career, Truss had survived and prospered because she was tactically pragmatic and dropped plans which were not working. At lunchtime on the Sunday of conference, 3 October, Jones and Stein briefed the *Mail* and the *Telegraph* that 'the lady's not for turning', an echo of Margaret Thatcher during her controversial economic reforms of the early 1980s. Berry was sent out to warn MPs that if they voted against the budget they would be stripped of the whip and deselected. At 4 p.m. that day Truss met her speechwriter Asa Bennett to discuss her platform speech later in the week. At that point it still included a section which read, 'We will abolish the 45p rate of income tax, which was bringing very little money into the exchequer. I'm not prepared to keep a tax just for the sake of virtue-signalling.'

Truss loathed her first and only party conference as leader, much of it spent cooped up in her hotel suite. 'She was up and down a lot, there were a lot of violent mood swings,' an aide recalled. On one occasion she predicted, 'They're going to drag me out in six weeks.' She was not a natural conference creature and 'absolutely hated' the round of meetings with newspaper editors and conference parties which pepper a prime minister's diary. 'I didn't like being holed up in the conference venue,' she admitted. 'I hate being boxed in.' She felt surrounded and under fire by 'all of the people who were upset losing the leadership election'. Truss seemed to have 'no idea' about what was expected, complaining after meetings, 'I want to slit my wrists.' She would call Fullbrook or Adam Jones in 'to shout at them'. Rounding again on the communications, she called Jones' handling of the budget 'a mess'.

Jamie Hope warned her that if she U-turned there was no way back. The same message was delivered by Simon Clarke, who told Hope, 'She mustn't backtrack because if she does, you know we're finished.'

But as Sunday went on it became clear to her that the media focus on the 45p tax cut was drowning out any coverage of the more popular measures. At a cost of £2 billion, it accounted for only 4.4 per cent of the £45 billion of tax cuts, but was responsible for 90 per cent of the negative publicity. The whips and Kwarteng's Treasury team were hearing the same things from MPs. 'The party was in a very, very mutinous place,' Celia McSwaine recalled. 'Abolishing the 45p rate of income tax was proving so toxic on the doorstep. None of the other tax cuts had cut through.' In Kwarteng's suite his aides, 'running on caffeine and adrenaline' and surrounded by 'stale sandwiches', worked on the speech the chancellor was due to make on the Monday. MPs were periodically invited up 'to give this terminal diagnosis to the 45p rate'.[11]

The tipping point came at 7 p.m. when Truss received Graham Brady in her suite. The chairman of the 1922 Committee did not gild the lily, the prime minister had 'a big problem'. Despite a working Commons majority of 71, Truss was facing a major rebellion on 45p. 'You might get it through, just,' Brady said, 'but it's probably the last vote you'll win.'

She called Stein to her room and asked, 'What do you think?' He said, 'It's got to go.' There was also talk of sacking the chief whip.

Kwarteng was having dinner with the lobby team from the *Sun*, when his special adviser, Cameron Brown, messaged him that Truss wanted to see them. He then began signalling across the table. Brown held up four fingers and then five. He was trying to communicate that they had been summoned to see Truss in her suite at 8.45 p.m. This digital semaphore was spotted by Harry Cole, the political editor, who concluded that the four and five referred to the 45p rate. When Kwarteng left without receiving his main course, his journalistic antennae were abuzz.

Back at the Hyatt, in her suite on the twenty-fourth floor, Truss and her aides considered her options. She said, 'We can't go to Parliament next week with this still a running sore. I can't do my conference speech then say something different later.' The natural conclusion was that she should bite the bullet and ditch the 45p tax plan immediately. 'Get Kwasi here,' she said.

Kwarteng arrived at Truss's suite to find her mob-handed with Fullbrook, Porter, Stein, Jones, Jarvis, Hope and Carter also present. 'What's up?' he asked, gazing at the ranks of enigmatic aides. 'This looks like an interview ... I love that', his bonhomie forced. 'What's going on?'

Truss wasted no time. '45p rate,' she said, her voice grave. 'We need to rip the plaster off.'

Kwarteng replied, wanly, 'I totally agree with you.' But when he tried to continue, Truss cut across him: 'I think we need to do it, like, now.'

'So what do I say?' Kwarteng asked, assuming he would be making the announcement in his conference speech.

Truss said, 'Basically, what I think we need to do is say, "This has become a distraction from what is a really great package. Although I, Kwasi Kwarteng, and I, Liz Truss, massively support getting rid of this ridiculous rate, which is higher than Ireland's, it's clear that it's becoming a distraction from a massively positive package."' Then the key part for Kwarteng. 'I think, basically, you should just say that tomorrow ...'

'In the speech –'

'... on the media.'

'On the media round?' Kwarteng sounded alarmed.

'Yes, for the following reason. I've just done a media round this afternoon. All they're asking about is the 45p rate. You're going to look like an idiot if you go on the media in the morning and then you say the opposite in the speech. I think we make a virtue of necessity. We tell the cabinet tonight. We tell MPs at the time we are telling the media, we say we've listened. The problem is, because of all the market shit it's just created this pressure cooker. We need to do something to relieve the pressure. That's my view.'

Throughout this monologue, Kwarteng contributed a series of affirmative grunts, part sigh, part agreement. Sitting mute next to him was Cameron Brown, knowing that his boss had been given a hospital pass, unable to say anything to contradict the decision which had clearly already been made. Kwarteng would be made to own the U-turn. The chancellor reached for Shakespeare: 'My view is that if you're going to do it, it were done and twere best it was done quickly.'

'That's exactly what I was thinking,' said Truss. 'Lady Macbeth!' Kwarteng laughed nervously.

Fullbrook sought to check that the chancellor actually was in agreement. 'Do you agree?'

Kwarteng said, 'I want to do it! I think we have to junk it.'

Fullbrook added, 'There is no point defending it for a week if we think it's going to go.'

There then ensued a conversation about how Kwarteng should sell the U-turn, one of the most humiliating in recent political history. He said, 'We U-turned on dementia tax in the middle of a bloody election and this is two years out. This is just one measure out of about one hundred.' There was no acknowledgement that the chances of them fighting that election were vanishing fast. Even Truss seemed to believe the chancellor would even have 'an opportunity' to talk about 'all the great stuff we are doing' – a stance that redefines 'optimistic'.

Jones tried to argue that the announcement should be saved until Monday lunchtime so as not to embarrass the *Mail* and the *Telegraph* (and by proxy, himself) whose first editions were reporting Truss's resolution to stand firm. The prime minister overruled him. Kwarteng's speech, including a commitment to 'stay the course', had also been briefed to the papers. It was agreed that Truss would tell the cabinet at 7 a.m., while Kwarteng tweeted the news at 7.25 a.m. just before he began his morning media round.

In the event, even that plan proved naive. In the intervening three hours, Cole had been roaming like a predator through various drinks dos, including one hosted by Berry elsewhere on the twenty-fourth floor. By midnight he was confident enough to write that the policy was going to be ditched. The first most ministers and aides knew of the decision was from reading Twitter at 12.20 a.m.

Around the same time, Penny Mordaunt told a fringe party, 'What have we learned from conference so far? Our policy is great, but our comms is shit.' When Kwarteng took to the stage on Monday afternoon, he let out a cathartic groan: 'What a day.' More were to come. That evening, he told another prominent Tory, Truss's chances of survival were 'only 40–60'. The prime minister's take on the night's events? 'Drama just seems to follow me wherever I go.'[12]

* * *

Cameron Brown woke at 5 a.m. to six missed calls from Harry Cole and a torrent of texts from colleagues saying, 'It's been leaked!' Fullbrook summoned the team to his suite. Brown arrived to find Ruth Porter, Iain Carter, Sophie Jarvis, Jones, Stein and Wendy Morton, the chief whip, already present. Together they drafted a statement. The chief of staff had ordered fifty mini croissants from room service. 'Nobody touched them,' an aide said. 'We weren't in the mood.' Fullbrook asked Morton, 'What do you think MPs will make of this statement?'

There was a pause while the spads waited to see what pearl of wisdom would drop from Morton's lips. 'Some will like it,' she said. 'Some won't.' A witness, dripping with sarcasm, said, 'That's just the sort of insight you want from your chief whip in that moment.'

The rest of Tuesday 4 October wasn't much better. That evening, party donors attended a 'funereal' drinks do. Malik Karim, the party treasurer, made a speech about how difficult things were and introduced the prime minister. 'There was complete silence,' one of those present reported. 'No applause at all. The mood of the donors was like Bernie Madoff's investors', a reference to the US Ponzi scheme boss who stole millions and ended up dead in jail.

The sour atmosphere also brought the splits in her team to the fore. Chief whipping boy was Mark Fullbrook who found himself on the receiving end of briefings to the papers that he was dubbed 'Chief Wiggum' after the corpulent police chief in *The Simpsons* who is too lazy to fight crime. Another aide leaked WhatsApp messages from the Hyatt complaining about abuse of a hotline set up for Truss. 'I am getting many room service orders. Please can you reiterate that my number is for the PM requests only.' Fullbrook, the croissants going stale on his sideboard, replied, 'That was me, apologies.' The aide said, 'Rome was burning and he was fiddling room service pretending to be the PM.' Truss's final room service bill was £11,000.

Truss's speech on Wednesday 6 October was on the same stage where she had triggered hilarity eight years earlier with her thoughts about cheese imports and pork products. This was a more coherent oratory. She defended her plans to cut taxes and deregulate and announced, 'I have three priorities for our economy: growth, growth and growth.' On 45p she said, 'I get it – and I have listened.'

But the main theme was an attack on 'the enemies of enterprise' and the 'anti-growth coalition' she detected among 'Labour, the Lib Dems and the SNP, the militant unions, the vested interests dressed up as think tanks, the talking heads, the Brexit deniers and Extinction Rebellion'. She framed this new division in cultural terms which were familiar from the Brexit wars: one between patriotic reformers seeking to build a better Britain against a cabal of liberal elitist naysayers. 'They taxi from north London townhouses to the BBC studio to dismiss anyone challenging the status quo,' she said. 'From broadcast to podcast, they peddle the same old answers. It's always more taxes, more regulation and more meddling. Wrong, wrong, wrong.'

Truss also explained her personal journey and her libertarian credo. She said she knew 'how it feels to have your potential diminished by those who think they know better', adding that she was used to being treated differently 'for being female, or for not fitting in'. As a leader, she said, 'I'm not going to tell you what to do, or what to think or how to live your life.' The speech was one of Truss's best, admittedly a low bar, and MPs liked the branding of the 'anti-growth coalition'. But while she pledged that plans were coming down the tracks on childcare and other supply side reforms, there was no new policy at all for the media to get their teeth into. 'All she has done is bake in a historic error on 45p in the public mind, like Gordon Brown dithering over the election or Theresa May saying "Nothing has changed". It was the least professional conference I have ever been to,' one Tory said. A minister heading for the lifts in the Hyatt spotted the author, turned and walked back to deliver this verdict: 'They're fuckwits. They think they've turned it around. But they don't understand politics.' Ultimately, it was the most disruptive Tory conference since 2003, when MPs had plotted to oust Iain Duncan Smith as leader (he was gone two weeks later).

For those who believed in her crusade, the 45p U-turn, not the decision to include it in the mini-budget, was the defining disaster of her leadership. 'I still believe, frankly, that we should have not given way on the 45p,' Simon Clarke said later. 'That was the moment when we let the air out of the balloon. That was a very defensible policy.' Privately, a cabinet minister went further: 'She bottled it. The die was cast, because it shattered her authority. Once there was blood in the water, the sharks were moving. Her speech was actually quite good, but it didn't matter because it was only words. No one believed in her ability, at that point, to deliver it.' Another cabinet minister complained, 'She was really tough before the shit hit the fan, and then she was the first person to retreat. She was bold as brass going into the melee then, when it got sticky, she was the first one out. It left everyone totally dumbfounded. You expect the leader who's led you over the top to stick it out.'

When they got back from conference, Truss hoped MPs had calmed down but she faced a difficult time at a meeting of the 1922 Committee of backbenchers. 'There was a deliberately staged series of questions,' she recalled. 'It was clearly just an ambush and there were people orchestrating it who were also in the room who weren't saying anything.' Truss blamed Sunak's outriders, convinced her rival had prepared the ground during the leadership election for a counterattack later. 'The other side of the debate pursued a scorched-earth policy of talking endlessly through the leadership campaign about "This is immoral" and "There'll be difficulties with the markets", so essentially [they were] priming something bad to happen. I didn't launch any kind of personal attacks on Rishi during the campaign. But I was called "immoral" and "nutty".' Trussites who believed in her plans and saw this all as a plot might have asked themselves how Sunak was so certain she would be a failure.

Truss developed a healthy contempt for cowardice of her colleagues: *If they're going to blanch at any sign of trouble, then they're just not up for this. We have a massive problem around stagnation and a lack of economic growth. To win the election in eighteen months' time we need to act now. I went hell for leather but there are people in the parliamentary party who are keener on what positions they hold, than they are on following that strategy. Why on earth have we got to the stage where cutting taxes is controversial in the Tory Party!?*

Truss was also unhappy with her team. There was a 'blazing row'[13] between Truss and Adam Jones in the Downing Street flat around the budget comms. Truss now re-admitted Jason Stein to her inner circle. Until 19 September, he did not even have her new mobile phone number. Initially exiled to the second floor of Number 10, he moved to the inner private office next to the Cabinet Room. She began to tell cabinet ministers, 'Deal with Jason.' When Jones left to get married, she told Stein he would have to do the comms job, along with his other work. Simon Case invited Stein to his office for tea. The cabinet secretary said, 'It's become clear to me there are only two people in this building that she listens to and that's you and Nick Catsaras.' From then on, they had daily meetings. In one of them, Case said, 'She genuinely could be a good prime minister if she allows herself the time to become a good prime minister. Everything's in a rush.'

Truss decided to part company with Jones when he returned, something he only learned after she had left Downing Street. She also became irritated with Wendy Morton and Matt Sinclair, her chief economic adviser, who she saw as a 'chatterbox'. 'If he answers another question Kwasi asks me again, I will stab him in the leg,' Truss threatened on one occasion. Another aide explained, 'If she didn't like people she would say, "I don't want them in the room."' Before one meeting on economics, Truss barred Sinclair. When it was pointed out that he was her chief economic adviser, she snapped, 'Well, I don't want him there.' A meeting on party management elicited the instruction, 'I don't want Wendy there, I don't like her.' Interviewed for this book, Truss denied this and said some criticism of Morton was 'unfair'. She said Sinclair was 'quite chatty – but I like him'.

Before conference, Truss and Kwarteng decided to appoint Antonia Romeo, the feisty permanent secretary at the Ministry of Justice, as Tom Scholar's replacement at the Treasury. Truss recalled, 'A message was relayed to me from the governor of the Bank of England that the markets might react badly if we installed Romeo since she had not previously worked at the Treasury.'[14] The job went, instead, to James Bowler, who had missed out on the cabinet secretary post.

On Friday 7 October, two days after Truss's conference speech, she and Kwarteng discovered the depth of the hole they were in. The Office for Budget Responsibility delivered its verdict on the mini-budget: there was a £72 billion black hole in the nation's finances. The prime minister saw this as 'revenge for being sidelined' and the (almost immediate) leaking of the figure as 'deliberate abuse of market-sensitive information in order to undermine confidence in the government'.[15] Her critics thought she was doing that just fine without any help.

The final fortnight of Truss's premiership was consumed by arguments about how to fill the black hole. At the same time, Treasury officials calculated that reversing the rise in National Insurance and halting the rise in corporation tax would only boost growth by between 0.4 and 0.9 percentage points after five years. The chancellor's target was a 2.5 per cent uptick in growth.

Trussite confidence in the OBR's methodology was undermined further by the way they arrived at the £72 billion figure. Treasury official Cat Little, acting permanent secretary after Scholar's removal, had told ministers the number was likely to come in 'at the lower end' of a range between £30 billion and £50 billion. Instead, it was £22 billion higher than the upper estimate, meaning the government had been working on false assumptions – a shambles which reinforced Truss's suspicions about the economic institutions. A furious political aide said, 'The reason you have a butt-covering range is so that it can't possibly be outside the butt-covering range – and it was, by a huge amount.' That was not all. 'The OBR also made a very low assumption of immigration,' a minister complained. 'Immigration is a key driver of growth in their model. Every year, for the last twenty years, net migration averaged 250,000 per year and they modelled it at 120,000. You can knock out £15 billion just by changing the immigration assumption from 120,000 to 250,000. As it happened, the actual immigration figure in 2022 was 500,000. If they had put it up to 500,000 that would have knocked £30 billion off it.' It seemed to Truss later that this was a conspiracy to undermine her.

The strategy to plug the hole had two elements – a plan for announcements on supply side reforms designed to boost growth, covering childcare, immigration, business regulation, housing, mobile broadband, energy, financial services and agriculture; and spending cuts. Truss had to somehow try to deliver on two hugely controversial fronts when her MPs were least likely to vote for anything unpopular.

Unlike before the budget, the cast list for economic meetings on the medium-term fiscal plan had expanded to include Jamie Hope, the head of policy, Sophie Jarvis and Iain Carter, all of whom had been kept in the dark about the budget. Case, Catsaras and Nick Joicey, another of Truss's favourite civil servants, the director general of the domestic and economic affairs secretariat (also the husband of Labour's Rachel Reeves), insisted on the change.

Ruth Porter led on getting the eight supply side reforms ready, but others realised they would never get a Commons majority. 'It became clear none of them was possible,' an aide said. Truss wanted to make it easy for broadband providers to lay new cables without permits. 'Turns out that the broadband engineers are the worst offenders for fucking things up in streets, leaving potholes,' an aide said. 'MPs hate their streets being dug up.' A plan for 'broadband vouchers' was axed due to lack of money. Housing and planning reform was ditched as politically impossible. One idea Jacob Rees-Mogg had for business deregulation would have allowed motorists get their first MOT after four years rather than three. But the knock-on effect would be to 'make a load of small, self-employed businesses running garages unemployed'. Another aide recalled, 'MPs just didn't want to do anything. "The broadband's good enough" was one thing I heard.' Hope and his deputy James Harries sent Truss details of what it was realistic to do. She replied that these plans were 'not ambitious enough'.

Efforts to find the £72 billion were not helped by the prime minister when, at PMQs on 12 October, she insisted she was 'not planning public spending reductions'. Truss's point was that spending would rise even if inflation meant there were real terms cuts, but her words suggested to the markets that she didn't take the crisis seriously. That evening, Jacob Rees-Mogg went on *Newsnight* and criticised the OBR for failing to do dynamic modelling. The impression was that the government had learned nothing. Matthew Sinclair watched Rees-Mogg and thought: *We're fucked. That's what you say if the strategy is: "Fuck you, we're going to keep going" – but we're not.*

That week, Kwarteng flew to the US for IMF meetings in Washington. Truss was 'quite resistant' to him going, 'because I thought the situation in Britain was very difficult. We had an issue to deal with – who cares about the IMF?' The chancellor believed staying home would fuel the crisis. 'If I hadn't gone, it would have been a massive deal,' he said. 'You were damned if you did and you were damned if you didn't. It would have been the first time since God knows when that a British chancellor hadn't gone to the annual meeting at the IMF and that would have been the story.'[16] In D.C. he was treated to lectures by experts who saw Britain as a case study in how not to handle the crisis.

Andrew Bailey, also in Washington, caused another run on the pound when he announced that the Bank of England would not continue its intervention on LDIs beyond the following Monday, when it would have been more logical to continue until the government's fiscal plan was unveiled at the end of the month. Worse was to come, though, when Joe Biden, the US president, said 'it was a mistake' to axe the top rate of tax. 'I think the idea of cutting taxes on the super-wealthy … I disagreed with the policy.' Truss saw this as 'utter hypocrisy' since the top rate of US federal income tax was only 37 per cent and kicked in at more than three times the level of the 45p rate. 'I was shocked and astounded that Biden would breach protocol by commenting on UK domestic policy,' she complained later, not without justification.[17]

Kwarteng woke up on Wednesday morning, read his emails and called Philp, who was in London. 'Chris, why the fuck have I just been sent a copy of the scorecard showing corporation tax going up?' he asked. Philp made some enquiries. Treasury officials said they had been asked to model a corporation tax increase by Number 10. But they had only done so because mandarins had leaned on Truss and her aides.

The same day, Cameron Brown, Kwarteng's media spad, who was visiting his father in California, picked up talk that Truss was 'sniffing around' for alternative chancellors. Sajid Javid's name had come up. He told Kwarteng.

'She can't do that, because if she does get rid of me, she's gone,' the chancellor declared.

On Thursday a headline in *The Times* announced that Number 10 was considering a U-turn on business tax. Truss had not taken any decision to put up corporation tax. It was clear to her political team that the story had been briefed by civil servants in the Treasury who were trying to bounce her into a decision. 'The market then priced it in,' said one political adviser. 'That was when the penny dropped with her.'

Truss asked Philp to come and see her to discuss possible spending cuts. On his way, he was called by Cat Little, who said, 'I have got to speak to you now.' Gravely, she said, 'I should let you know, Chief Secretary, that Number 10 are very concerned about financial markets and what is going to happen next Monday when the Bank of England's intervention into the bond market ceases.' Philp thought Little was trying to stop him sending examples of spending cuts to Number 10. Treasury officials later claimed a list of potential cuts could not be shared with Downing Street until they had been signed off by the chancellor, who was still abroad.

By the time he saw Truss, it was clear that Treasury officials had taken advantage of Kwarteng's absence to agitate for an increase in corporation tax instead. James Bowler, the new permanent secretary, visited Truss to warn that the markets would crash. For several days business leaders, donors, city financiers and Tories with City contacts had been telling Number 10 that the only way the markets would be satisfied would be if

Truss announced a U-turn on corporation tax and delivered the chancellor's head on a plate. She was resistant, knowing that such a move would unpick the entire basis of her government.

Truss kicked officials out of the Cabinet Room and asked Philp whether she could see options for spending cuts. Brandon Lewis, the justice secretary, arrived. They discussed cancelling the entire prison building programme to generate capital savings. 'It was clear at this point that Liz was beginning to freak out,' a minister said.

All this prompted a discussion about whether the chancellor should fly home. Celia McSwaine, who was with Kwarteng, argued that he should stay in Washington or it would look like panic and would raise questions about his future. Kwarteng thought: *Is there no drama they won't turn into a crisis? It will look out of control, weird and crazy.* They did not win the argument. When the chancellor cancelled drinks and dinner with journalists, it was obvious what was going on. Just as it was when Priti Patel had flown home to be fired by Theresa May, political Westminster was soon glued to the flight tracker of his red-eye flight. As he took off, Kwarteng didn't know his fate was already sealed. 'I should have stayed,' he later concluded.[18]

That evening, Truss was greeted by the new King at Buckingham Palace for her first weekly audience with the monarch, with the immortal line, 'Back again? Dear, oh dear.'

The *coup de grâce* was delivered by Simon Case. The cabinet secretary had been in regular contact with Andrew Bailey, the governor of the Bank of England. When the two spoke that morning, they agreed what the prime minister needed to do. Case went to the Cabinet Room and read Truss the riot act. Stating that he had consulted the governor before seeing her, he announced that unless she acted, the pound would plummet to such a level on Monday morning that 'we will struggle to fund government debt'. He warned, 'Global markets are moving against you.' Case impressed on Truss that time was running out. 'The buyers were going to put in their bids on Friday night for the Monday morning for when the market opens,' a close aide said. 'They said, "Our assessment is that it's going to be really bad on Monday."'

The prime minister was deflated. She felt the establishment 'had me at gunpoint'.[19] She told Case, 'I've realised I just can't beat the institutional investors. I can't beat the markets. They control us.' She later presented his intervention as an establishment ambush, tantamount to constitutional bullying, but it came about because she, not trusting the Treasury, had requested Case liaise with Bailey. 'She had asked Simon to keep in touch with him,' a senior civil servant explained. As the crisis peaked, the cabinet secretary and the governor spoke once, often twice, a day.

Truss repeatedly tried to contact Kwarteng, who proved elusive. When they did speak, the chancellor urged her to hold her nerve. Truss erupted: 'Kwasi, I'm being threatened with a market meltdown. This is fucking serious!'[20]

Adam Memon, Kwarteng's policy spad, who was in London, got hold of the chancellor in Washington and relayed the official warnings. Jamie Hope talked to Mark Fullbrook, urging him to impress upon Truss that she needed to move. But not everyone supported a corporation tax rise. In a crisis meeting in the Thatcher study, Matthew Sinclair argued passionately that it was the last tax that should be put up. Instead, he pressed Truss to raise VAT. Other political aides thought this 'fucking mad' and 'quite insane', proof that Sinclair was an ideologue who did not grasp politics. 'We were going through all these doomsday options,' one of those present recalled, 'and Matt was the only one who thought we shouldn't do corporation tax.' Stein slapped Sinclair down: 'We're in a cost of living crisis, we can't just put everyone's prices up.'

Truss did not believe the warnings she was getting. The prime minister asked ministers to take soundings, like a cancer patient with a terminal diagnosis seeking a second opinion. 'She sent Chris Philp, Brandon Lewis, Andrew Griffith and all these other ministers out to talk to their mates in the City to try to find out if the Bank of England and the Treasury were telling the truth about the markets,' an aide recalled. 'She was so sceptical of this Treasury orthodoxy.' Philp talked to Michael Hintze, a financier and Tory donor, and to Andrew Griffith, the City minister, both of whom urged calm. But even Griffith acknowledged that the Bank wanted to stabilise the pension market and would 'continue looking at actual end of week decisions'. In other words, a signal needed to be sent. These were not the only voices, however. One aide characterised City feeling as: 'If you don't U-turn on corporation tax, the economy will be rubble.' Truss, suspicious but resigned, said, 'I ignored them before and crashed the market so I can't risk it again.'

She knew what this might mean for herself. 'If the Conservative Party bin me after six weeks and I'm the Brian Clough of prime ministers, then so be it,' she told her private secretary Nick Catsaras.[21] Clough, a managerial legend, had lasted just forty-four days as Don Revie's replacement at Leeds in 1974, an episode dramatised in the book and film *The Damned United*.

Even putting up corporation tax would not save Truss. That measure only reduced the size of the black hole by £18 billion. What was more, it was becoming clear that she did not have the votes to pass her finance bill. The whips, Graham Brady and Thérèse Coffey had all been in touch saying that Kwarteng had to go.

In a meeting at around 3.30 p.m. that Thursday, in the 'den' off the Cabinet Room, the prime minister discussed her options with Fullbrook and Stein. In a bid to get a grip on the parliamentary party, it was proposed that Coffey move to become chief whip, with Grant Shapps made health secretary, an acknowledgement that he should never have been fired and that he was too dangerous left on the backbenches. Wise as this might have been, it looked like a plaster applied to a gunshot wound. Truss suddenly said, 'I think the problem is Kwasi.'

The prime minister realised her chancellor would have no credibility if she ditched most of his policies. 'The market won't take him seriously again,' she said. In the air, unspoken, was the possibility that her own credibility would be shot as well, but ditching Kwarteng seemed the only way to save her own skin. When she realised what she was going to have to do, Truss became highly emotional. She said, 'This is very, very painful', and then got up and left the room. Kwarteng had been her closest political ally for more than a decade. 'It was really tough for her,' a source said. 'It wasn't something she relished at all. The only time I ever saw her cry was when she knew she had to sack Kwasi.'

When Truss had composed herself, they discussed who could replace Kwarteng. Nadhim Zahawi was the initial frontrunner. He had done the job for two months and knew his way around the department. Then Truss alighted on Jeremy Hunt, an idea which won immediate support from Stein, who had worked on Hunt's 2019 leadership bid. Hunt shared few of Truss's views, but she judged him someone who would not just be credible with the markets. 'Jeremy is somebody that I felt I could trust,' she said. 'He's not somebody who briefs or leaks.'

* * *

It is difficult to imagine the stress Truss felt that night. 'I could hardly sleep,' she confessed. 'There was the clock on nearby Horse Guards, which chimed every quarter of an hour … You could time exactly how long your insomnia lasted. And I did.'[22] As she lay awake, her political predicament reminded her of a game she played in her teens: 'It was like a game of Tetris when you start losing control and the pieces are getting closer and closer to the top.'[23] Since her arrival in Number 10 Truss had hated the 'gilded cage' of Downing Street and the flat above, a place she found 'isolating'. The prime minister considered herself a 'prisoner' in a 'soulless' building she hated. 'I'm not sure it would be rated well on Airbnb,' she noted. 'The place was infested with fleas … I spent several weeks itching.' This she blamed on a previous occupant – Dilyn, the Johnsons' dog. Outside, she could hear 'the constant backdrop of chanting and shouting' from protesters.

When Kwarteng landed at Heathrow, he was whisked away in a ministerial car, but it was immediately obvious to the chancellor and to McSwaine that they were being tracked by the Sky News helicopter, which could be heard above them. They were driving towards Downing Street when Steven Swinford of *The Times* tweeted that the chancellor was about to be fired. McSwaine saw the tweet and passed her phone to Kwarteng. He 'took a minute to take it in,' she recalled, then he said, 'Well, that's that then.'[24]

In a highly emotional twenty-minute meeting in the Cabinet Room, a 'teary-eyed' Truss told Kwarteng, 'You're going to have to go.'

'I know,' Kwarteng replied, his voice as cold as a knife. 'I've seen it on Twitter.' The chancellor argued his case. He wanted to stay to repair the damage. 'I'm your firebreak. This will make you weaker, not stronger.'

Truss explained the view of the mandarins and the markets. They had lost the City and the party. 'I'm doing this to save myself,' she admitted.

'If you fire me, you know they'll come for you next,' he said.

'They're already coming for me, Kwasi.' Spoken with sad finality.[25]

'But at least you'll have some sort of shelf life,' he argued. 'If you can get to Christmas, you have a break, people come back and there's something of a reset. It might get worse, it might get better – but you have a chance that it might stabilise. But this is insane. I'm the fall guy, I get that, but whatever shelf life you thought you had, it is going to be shortened by this act, not lengthened. If you get rid of me, they're going to ask you why you're still here.' Seeing Truss unyielding, Kwarteng asked who would replace him. He assumed it would be Zahawi or Sajid Javid. When she said 'Jeremy Hunt', Kwarteng exclaimed, 'Are you mad?'

At conference, Kwarteng had told journalists, 'If she sacks me, she's finished.' As he left the room, after just thirty-eight days in the job, he thought Truss might survive a few weeks: *I'm the only person who has ever been fired for doing exactly what they were told. It's like seeing someone take a gun out of nowhere and blow their brains out. It's blind panic.*

This was a Shakespearean moment, up there with Gove knifing Johnson in 2016 or Johnson sacking Gove in 2022. It was also one many of her closest aides regarded as a mistake. Jamie Hope had arrived at work early on the Friday and was ushered into the Cabinet Room by Ruth Porter to be told that Kwarteng was going. He thought it strange there was no debate about a decision so shattering to Truss's own project. One aide said, 'If you're losing a chancellor within forty days that implies it's less the chancellor's fault and more yours.' Another reflected, 'If you put two shots into the back of your friend's head, you lose all credibility with the MPs who are already quite upset.'

Truss had offered the job to Hunt three hours before she even saw Kwarteng. Even this was a farce. When the prime minister called Hunt, he did not answer and did not have Truss programmed into his phone, evidence of their personal distance. He was on holiday with his wife in Belgium. 'She texted him and I think he thought it was a prank,' a political aide said. Stein contacted Christina Robinson, Hunt's former spad and occasional spokeswoman, with whom he had worked in 2019. 'You're fucking joking me,' she said on being told the news. When Truss finally got through, Hunt asked for a moment to consider the offer. Stein called Robinson again and said, 'We are worried he's going to say no.' Robinson reassured him: 'It's yes, don't worry, but he's got to square it with his wife.' Stein went into the Cabinet Room and announced, 'He's going to say yes.' Truss, Catsaras and Porter exclaimed, 'Yes!' Hunt called back soon afterwards to accept.

Truss and Hunt's conversation was very brief. He put down a marker. 'We're going to need to do some very difficult things,' he said, 'and you're going to have to support me.' Truss said she would.

The appointment was seen by cabinet Trussites as a hoisting of the white flag. 'Jeremy is one of the nicest men I know, but he was antithetical to the whole project,' said a cabinet colleague. 'You might as well have called in the receivers.' Truss realised she was abandoning her beliefs but her focus now was 'dealing with the instability issue'. She said, 'I'd come to the conclusion at this stage that, regrettably, I wasn't going to be able to do my agenda.'

The new chancellor caught the Eurostar home, arriving in London at 1 p.m. At 4 p.m. he met Truss in Downing Street. In their first meeting, he said she should also change the chief secretary. Hunt wanted Rupert Harrison, George Osborne's former Treasury adviser, now a banker, to get the job and a seat in the Lords. Truss rejected the idea on the grounds that handing Harrison an immediate cabinet job would 'piss too many people off'. Hunt was told Harrison could have a peerage plus another ministerial position. Harrison still wanted to be an MP and became chairman of a new panel of economic advisers instead. Hunt suggested Mel Stride as his deputy. That received a 'hard veto'. Stride was seen as one of the key plotters against the prime minister. Hunt was offered a list of three people – Ed Argar, Will Quince and Jeremy Quinn – and told to pick whoever he liked. All three were ministers of state, all three had backed Hunt in 2019. 'Let's go with Ed,' said Hunt. Argar was the paymaster general, so he and Chris Philp, to Philp's distress, did a job swap. Once again Downing Street could not get hold of the chosen man. Stein eventually got through and passed his phone to Truss. Argar, thinking he was talking to Stein, said, 'Hi matey, what the fuck do you want?'

Truss said, 'Hi Ed, it's Liz, you're becoming chief secretary.'

Argar blurted, 'Fucking hell, thanks for that.'

Truss had her new team. She now needed a new policy but it would be one devised by Hunt. If some in Downing Street saw the new chancellor as a human shield, Hunt's allies realised – just three months after finishing last in the leadership contest – he was now the most powerful man in Britain.

Truss finished the day by appearing, for a paltry eight minutes, at a press conference in Downing Street. It may have been the most abject media performance ever given by a prime minister. She admitted she'd gone 'further and faster than markets were expecting' and announced that corporation tax would rise to 25 per cent in line with Sunak's original plan. There was no contrition. She took just four questions and then walked out after refusing to apologise to her party. She later compared the 'ghastly experience' to 'officiating at my own funeral'.[26] A more adept prime minister could have launched into a 'masochism strategy', taking every question head on until the journalists were begging to be released, but a close aide explained, 'We had to keep it short because she was no good at press conferences.' They would have been better off not holding one at all.

Hunt went straight to the Treasury on Friday afternoon. He found the civil servants shellshocked having lost both a permanent secretary and a chancellor in the space of five weeks. James Bowler, who had only been in charge for a few days, gathered a dozen of his top officials – Cat Little, Beth Russell and Clare Lombardelli among them – and they began to go through the options. As the meeting began, Hunt told them, 'One thing I want you to be absolutely clear about is that we are going to do the right thing for the country – even if that means we are going to have to do things that are absolutely impossible electorally. We have a shared responsibility to do the right thing.' His goal was to align their incentives with his own. In one sentence the political-civil service stand-off was at an end. To reinforce the point, he added, 'If I end up being a chancellor, like Ken Clarke was, who does the right thing but ends up going to electoral oblivion, so be it, because the situation is so serious.' This turned out to be one of the more accurate Treasury forecasts of the era.

Hunt went in again on the Saturday morning. Since the Treasury revolved around fiscal events, he found the officials most wanted to work out what would be in the autumn statement. The chancellor also braved 'the media round from hell', where he signalled that he would not fix the government's finances with Greek-style savage spending cuts. Hunt said there would be 'difficult decisions ahead' but 'they will be done fairly' and 'we will do everything we can to protect public services'.

Hunt called up former chancellors to seek their advice. In the Treasury there was an assumption that reversing the corporation tax cut and changing the chancellor would be enough to calm the situation. But Sajid Javid asked, 'Have you thought about the markets on Monday?' Robert Jenrick also messaged Hunt to warn, 'Look out for the markets on Monday.' In a conference call that evening, the new chancellor agreed it would be necessary to announce some measures on Monday to reassure the City. The one predecessor he decided not to contact that weekend was Rishi Sunak, who he felt would be conflicted.

The day he was sacked, Kwarteng was eating a curry with a friend when his phone rang. It was Sunak. 'I'm really pleased you picked up, I didn't think you would,' he said. They talked for twenty minutes about Treasury budget 'scoring', Sunak saying he had heard Kwarteng was well liked by his officials. Kwarteng thought this a nice gesture, but also a smart one. Between the commiserations and compliments, he felt Sunak was sounding him out about how long Truss would last.

That Saturday, Adam Jones got married in a church near Scarborough, a service attended by many of his colleagues. The experience was surreal. He had seen Swinford's tweet about Kwarteng's dismissal just before he went into the rehearsal the day before. Jones felt guilty about not being there to help. But his growing conviction that this was probably the end of Truss made it easier to accept his absence from the centre of the drama. He felt 'zen' as he and his new wife departed for their honeymoon in Mauritius.

Was there an alternative? Kwarteng thought so: 'I think we should have actually worked together. You've got to have a very calm approach ... I thought summoning me back a day before ... just shone a huge light on the fact that there was this turmoil.'[27] Kwarteng, who was speaking to Andrew Bailey every day, thought the danger of a market cliff edge the following Monday was more 'in their heads' in Number 10 than real. The problem, as one cabinet minister pointed out, was that Truss and Rees-Mogg had publicly demonstrated their mistrust of the Bank: 'Whatever you think about the governor of the Bank of England, it does not help for a minister to say, "He's shit." Investors look at that and think, these guys are crazy.' Another cabinet minister agreed: 'She could have got the governor in and got assurance the Bank of England would extend [support for the bond market]. She could have done partial U-turns, she could have flagged the spending cuts. That would have preserved the bulk of her political and economic intent. As it was, she completely jettisoned all of it, thinking it was safer.'

Throughout this whole period, when the economy teetered on the rim of the volcano, the prime minister never met or spoke to the governor of the central bank. Not once. 'I actually had a meeting set up and wanted to meet him, but I was advised that would be a bad idea,' she said later. 'That advice came from the cabinet secretary ... In retrospect, I probably should have spoken directly to the Governor.'[28]

That weekend, those who saw Truss believed she was close to mental collapse. 'In her final ten days, she was tormented,' an aide said. 'She

would say constantly, "I keep thinking about all the mistakes I made.'"
This was not the stonehearted politician Truss presented herself as.

The holding and exercising of power is a very lonely business, particularly so when a leader has made all the decisions themselves and has no one else to blame. Ultimately, it was not something for which her colleagues felt Truss was psychologically prepared. 'She just was not suited to that level of pressure,' a senior cabinet minister observed. 'She just could not cope with it.' Another cabinet minister said, 'She went from recklessness to panic in quite a quick spin. I was struck by how quickly Liz went to pot in that forty-eight-hour period. She totally capitulated. She had been given all this very negative news and just thought there was no alternative, but there were alternatives.'

It is a truism of politics that only others who have been in the same position can ever understand what a leader goes through. Two of Truss's predecessors got in touch on Saturday 15 October to try to help. Theresa May called her to say, 'You need to sound more sorry and wear more serious clothes.'

Boris Johnson was also 'constantly in touch with her,' an ally said. Still fixating on the plot he believed had unseated him, Johnson urged Truss to fight back. He texted her: 'You should go out there and say: "The people who plotted against one pm [*sic*] are now trying to get rid of another. They know who they are. The world knows who they are. They don't care about anything except their own jobs and their own careers. We cannot afford to waste time on this nonsense. We owe it to the British people to focus entirely on them and their needs. And that is what we are doing. We will get on with helping them with the cost of energy. We will tame inflation and create conditions for growth. I say to the plotters, 'You have had your time you have had your chance. Grow up and think of the people who sent you to Westminster.'"'

On Sunday 16 October, the PM received Hunt, his family and his Treasury team at Chequers to thrash out what they needed to do to stabilise the economy before the markets opened on Monday morning. Hunt brought several officials apart from Clare Lombardelli, since she had clashed with Truss as chief secretary and again before the mini-budget.

Hunt did not think, at this stage, that Truss regarded herself as 'toast', but she knew her libertarian tax-cutting project was dead. As he laid out how much of her mini-budget he would have to junk – nearly all of it –

she accepted his judgement. He could see it was an excruciating experience for Truss but his respect for her grew. Despite her personal views, he was convinced she wanted to act in the national interest. She told her new chancellor, 'You have got to do what you need to do. Don't worry about me.'

Hunt explained the situation to the political team. 'The atmospherics were of shock,' one said. 'It was clear that Hunt held the whip hand. He was very matter-of-fact, but he understood how powerful he was.' Together they agreed the choreography. They would slip the news to the BBC at 6 a.m. that the chancellor would make a statement to camera later that morning to reassure the markets, which opened at 8 a.m., another to Parliament in the afternoon. Hunt phoned the speaker, Lindsay Hoyle, to explain that this was one announcement which could not wait for Parliament to sit at 2.30 p.m. 'The markets might have been in freefall again,' a source said.

An Opinium poll that weekend predicted a Labour Commons major-ity of 411. Andrew Bridgen popped up to say Truss should go, a view echoed by MPs Crispin Blunt and Jamie Wallis.

Those present at Chequers did not know that Truss and her husband Hugh also had a conversation that day while their daughters played in the swimming pool. Having predicted that the party would be ungovern-able before she even entered Downing Street, Truss regarded Hugh as 'a bit of a soothsayer'. As they walked on the lawn, he asked, 'How can you continue with this when you are not going to be able to do what you believe in?' The prime minister knew he was right.

At 11.15 a.m. on Monday 17 October Jeremy Hunt addressed the nation. He was wearing a smart suit with two flags behind him – the Union Jack and a red standard emblazoned with the logo of the Treasury. There was more than a little of the vibe of a military commander who has seized power in a *coup d'état* telling his citizens that no one had been harmed in the seizure of the television tower.

'We will reverse almost all the tax measures announced in the growth plan three weeks ago that have not started parliamentary legislation,' he announced, gravely. That meant the National Insurance rise would remain scrapped and the stamp duty cuts would go ahead, but he was ditching a raft of other measures, including cuts to dividend tax rates, VAT free shopping for tourists and the freeze on alcohol duties. The basic rate of income tax would no longer be cut by 1p. 'It is a deeply held Conservative value – a value that I share – that people should keep more of the money that they earn,' he explained. 'But at a time when markets are rightly demanding commitments to sustainable public finances, it is not right to borrow to fund this tax cut.'

Much of this had been expected, but Hunt had another unpleasant surprise up his sleeve. The energy price support for families, which had been guaranteed for two years, was cut to just six months. Truss's last remaining achievement was gone. In seven short minutes, Hunt had read the last rites on Trussonomics. Later that week, his ally Steve Brine referred to him as a 'fantastic prime minister'. It was barely a Freudian slip. Hunt had gone from a high-flier under Cameron to an exiled select committee chairman after being vanquished by Johnson in 2019, to humiliation in the 2022 leadership contest. Now, he was arguably the most powerful chancellor since Stanley Baldwin ran the Treasury while also prime minister in 1923.

The pound strengthened and the price of UK government bonds rallied but there seemed little hope of reviving Truss's fortunes. That morning, a poll by Redfield & Wilton gave Labour a 36-point lead, the largest for any party with any polling company since October 1997.

Hunt was due to address the Commons at 3.30 p.m., but before that Labour was granted an urgent question, an attempt to drag Truss to the despatch box to face the music. She sent Penny Mordaunt instead, who claimed the prime minister was detained on 'urgent business'. Keir Starmer said, 'I guess that under this Tory government everybody gets to be prime minister for fifteen minutes.' Giving a masterclass in how to appear supportive while undermining Truss, Mordaunt revealed the prime minister was not, in fact, 'hiding under a desk'. MPs began to think there was a security crisis. In fact she was meeting Graham Brady.

Truss sat next to Hunt on the front bench while he was 'shredding' her policy platform. It felt like 'an out-of-body experience,' she said. 'It was uniquely painful.'[29] Her only public comments came in an interview with the BBC's Chris Mason, in which she said, 'I do want to accept responsibility and say sorry, for the mistakes that have been made.' She insisted, 'I will lead the Conservatives into the next general election.' The *Mail*'s splash headline that night screamed, 'IN OFFICE, BUT NOT IN POWER', Tony Blair's line about John Major.

* * *

Jake Berry, the party chairman, set up a 'war room', where key allies would fight to shore up support among MPs. Truss had lost faith in Wendy Morton's whipping operation. 'The whips were giving everyone "Rag ratings",' a source said, assigning 'red, amber or green' status to MPs depending on their levels of hostility. 'They were flagging people as amber if they were just a bit grumpy. Being annoyed about a piece of legislation is not the same as wanting to oust a sitting prime minister.' At this point 'more than half the parliamentary party was red or amber'. A Number 10 source said, 'It was a shitshow. Some of the prime minister's closest supporters were on amber. They had Oliver Dowden [Sunak's best friend in SW1] as green!'

On Monday afternoon, Truss addressed the One Nation group of Tory MPs for forty-five minutes. Having appointed Hunt, one of their number, she was well received. There was even some levity. When Matt Hancock said, 'There are a lot of talented people on the backbenches', he was greeted with hoots of laughter and a shout of, 'Who did you have in mind, Matt?' But there were two lumps of grit in the oyster. Richard Graham raised concerns about Truss's support for fracking. Guy Opperman questioned why one of her aides had briefed against Sajid Javid, who had been labelled 'a shit minister' in the *Sunday Times*. The banging of desks from colleagues suggested anger was widespread.

A meeting, the next day, with the hardline Brexiteers of the ERG also went well. Truss explained that she had fought for the vision of Brexit Britain as a high growth country, one shared by many of those present.

However, Tuesday also showed how difficult it would be to stabilise the economy. A document was pulled together featuring eighty-six potential spending cuts, the scale of which was staggering. The black hole was big enough that the entire prison building programme was at risk. Treasury officials were also targeting the Ministry of Defence, which they regarded as the worst squanderers of cash in Whitehall. Getting wind of this both Ben Wallace, the defence secretary, and James Heappey, the armed forces minister, threatened to resign. Across government, ministers mouthed support for the need to save money and then launched into 'fiscal nimbyism' to save their own budgets.

Truss's operation was now failing to perform basic tasks. Members of the war room team met officials for a 'grid meeting' to discuss future Number 10 activity. As it concluded, one revealed, 'We've never met before', a ridiculous state of affairs six weeks into a new government.

By now, the Trussketeer economists were in full flight, giving interviews to defend their own reputations. A Sunak aide, watching from afar,
was encouraged: 'The moment Gerry Lyons decided to shit on them, you
knew it was over.'

At 3.30 p.m. on Tuesday, David Canzini walked into the pillared war
room, upstairs in Number 10, and there was a spontaneous round of
applause. The veteran Tory campaigner had been recruited by Berry and
Mark Fullbrook. Help was also on hand from loyalists like Brandon
Lewis, the justice secretary, and a phalanx of advisers, including Giles
Dilnot and Hudson Roe, special advisers to the foreign secretary James
Cleverly. Dilnot was new to government but, as a former BBC reporter
and communications chief to the children's commissioner, one of the
most experienced spin doctors in Whitehall.

That evening Truss launched her own 'weird' charm offensive, wheel-
ing out her teenage daughters at a drinks do, in a bid to win over MPs.
The sum of these events was that by Wednesday morning the war room
and the whips had moved a decent number of MPs 'from amber to
green'. One of those involved said, 'Every day we were able to tell the
prime minister that it had moved more in her direction. She was always
very positive. What brought her down was Wednesday's shambles.'
Others saw it as displacement activity for people who wanted to help but
could do little to change the trajectory of events.

Wednesday 19 October 2022 has claims to rival 12 March 2020[30] as the
day which most resembled *The Thick of It* in the entire post-Brexit
period. It provided the capstone not just to six weeks of Trussite turmoil
but to six years of Brexit bedlam.

Truss faced a make-or-break Prime Minister's Questions against Keir
Starmer. In a bid to make it a success, Jake Berry went into battle with
Hunt and the Treasury, who had wanted to save an announcement that
the government was standing by the 'triple lock' to uprate state pensions
until the chancellor's fiscal announcement on 31 October. Declaring that
pensions were safe would give Truss something to trump whatever the
Labour leader said at the despatch box.

In the PMQ prep meeting Truss was warned that Sajid Javid was planning to use the first question of the session to name Jason Stein as the
source of the briefing against him the previous Sunday. Simon Case
sought to resolve the issue, telling Stein to see Darren Tierney, the head

of propriety and ethics. 'Tell him what you've done, he's going to give you a slap on the wrist and a written warning.' Case then handed Truss the wording she could use in PMQs: 'There is a long-standing convention we don't comment on staffing matters, but action has been taken and I am very happy to brief the right honourable gentleman on what action has been taken.' Case added, 'Then you sit down.' By 9.30 a.m. Javid was prepared to withdraw the question.

By 10.30 a.m. he had changed his mind. Stein believed Ruth Porter had 'wound up' Javid. Porter was adamant she was trying to resolve the situation in his favour. Either way, Javid now wanted Stein to be suspended before he would back down. Stein was apoplectic, believing Porter wanted to ruin his reputation because he had become influential again with Truss. A colleague said, 'Jason and Ruth were both storming around like upset children.' The prime minister reluctantly agreed to suspend Stein, telling him to return to work two days later. Porter called Javid with minutes to spare and he withdrew his question.

When PMQs began, Truss took a hammering from Starmer but was combative, quoting Peter Mandelson's claim, 'I am a fighter, not a quitter'. The pressure from MPs appeared, momentarily, to subside. However, news of Stein's suspension leaked while Truss was on her feet. This was merely the *amuse bouche* to the feast of chaos which then ensued.

The next flare up had begun the night before when Truss had an angry meeting with Suella Braverman, the home secretary. In a bid to fill the black hole, Truss wanted to announce a liberalisation of immigration laws, admitting more high-skilled migrants – one of the most effective ways of boosting the growth figures in the OBR's model. A new visa to admit immigrants in elite sport, IT and science would raise £14 billion, roughly equal to the size of the entire police budget. Having complained about the nature of the game, Truss was now playing it.

Braverman wanted no part of a policy which would open the border further, indeed she wanted new measures to limit numbers. 'The OBR wanted a statement from the home office on migration policy,' a senior figure said. 'Suella wanted to start pulling some of our levers on salary thresholds and students and Liz didn't want to do it.' The home secretary fought to include statements from the manifesto about reducing overall numbers. 'They thought that would spook the OBR,' the source said. Braverman also threw Truss's arguments of a week earlier back at her:

'The OBR is totally wrong in its assessment of the impact of migration on the economy. It only looks at GDP, not GDP per capita, which falls the more people come in.'

Truss basically agreed, writing in her memoir that the OBR's positive view of immigration took no 'account of the strain on public services'. She thought their calculations 'fiction' and complained, 'If the numbers were reduced as Suella had outlined, the OBR claimed this would add £10 billion to the deficit.'[31] Truss, through necessity, however, was now aligned with the Treasury orthodoxy. They parted on bad terms.

At 7.25 a.m. the next day, the home secretary emailed the proposed ministerial statement from her work email to her Gmail account, an action precluded under the ministerial code of conduct. She then sent it to Sir John Hayes, the veteran right-winger who she regarded as a good 'barometer' of thinking on the Tory right, copying in Hayes's wife. Or so she thought. Unfortunately for Braverman, the email went instead to a Commons staffer working for Andrew Percy, the MP for Brigg and Goole. Since the statement was technically a cabinet document and was not yet agreed policy it was confidential, not least because details of a change in immigration were market sensitive. By sending it to Hayes, who was not a member of the government, she had breached the ministerial code a second time. Braverman had regularly taken advice from Hayes. His frequent trips to the Home Office had attracted the attention of the permanent secretary, Matthew Rycroft. A fellow minister recalled, 'You'd walk into her office and find Hayes there, swanning around like it was *his* office.' A Number 10 official said, 'She was basically asking his advice as to whether she would still be the darling of the right wing if she agreed to this thing?'

Percy spoke to the chief whip, Wendy Morton, who referred the issue to Simon Case. The cabinet secretary went to see Truss. It was reported at the time that he presented it as a clear-cut breach of the code and encouraged the prime minister to dismiss her home secretary. In fact, Case told Truss, 'On the facts as we have them right now, as I understand it, this might be a breach of the ministerial code.' Case said he could go away and collect more facts, talk to Braverman and report back. In offering to launch an investigation he was, in effect, offering to kick the issue into the long grass. A source familiar with the exchange said, 'Simon didn't quite say that he could make it go away but that was certainly what he communicated. At the very least he could have bought some time.'

Truss, however, was happy to see the back of Braverman. 'I think I know which way I want this to go, thank you,' she told Case.

This decision was partly shaped by another leak, several months earlier, in which Chris Hope at the *Telegraph*, the main outlet for MPs on the pro-Brexit right of the party but who was not renowned for his security contacts, had got wind of the highly classified details of a sensitive terrorist case. They were known to only nine members of the government, one of whom was Braverman, then the attorney general. A leak inquiry had not fingered her but no one in Downing Street doubted it was her. 'Concerns had been raised that she might have been sharing restricted documents with people she shouldn't have,' a senior government source said.

Truss saw Braverman in her Commons office. 'This is a breach of the code and you're going to have to go,' the prime minister said.

Braverman urged her to 'slow down', calling the decision 'a complete overreaction'. She said, 'Your government's falling apart right now. You lost your chancellor on Friday. You can't lose your home secretary on Wednesday.'

Truss displayed the same fatalism as she had with Kwarteng. 'Suella, they're going to come for you. It's going to be torture if you stay on. Go nicely and I'll bring you back in January.' Truss recalled later, 'She disagreed quite a lot. There was shouting.'

Braverman said, 'You're not going to be here in January, Liz, if you make this decision.' She was the shortest-serving home secretary since 1834. Downing Street, not wanting any trouble, penned an effusively warm reply to her resignation letter, which had not yet been received, and sent it to Braverman. It told her she should be 'really proud of what you have achieved' and left the door open to a return with the words, 'I expect to see you back in high office soon'. Truss's aides waited and waited, irritation turning to anguish.

At 4.32 p.m. Braverman tweeted her letter, an inflammatory rocket aimed straight at Truss, which effectively called on her to resign as well. 'Pretending we haven't made mistakes, carrying on as if everyone can't see that we have made them, and hoping that things will magically come right is not serious politics,' it said. 'I have made a mistake; I accept responsibility; I resign.' Truss's response was shorn of any warmth and published soon afterwards.

To replace Braverman, Truss called on Grant Shapps, the former transport secretary who had spent the intervening six weeks leading the resistance against her. 'There was some talk about whether we should do deals with terrorists,' said one aide, 'but in the end it was decided it would be better to pick off a senior rebel.' Shapps packed up his spreadsheet and got to work.

If the chaos had ended there, Truss might have lived to fight another day. But her government was undone by a clever tactic from the Labour chief whip Alan Campbell. Tory MPs were split over fracking, which was seen by the free marketeers as a key weapon in the fight for energy independence and by environmentalists as a political and ecological disaster. During her leadership campaign, Truss had pledged to overturn a moratorium, which the 2019 Conservative manifesto had vowed to preserve. Campbell tabled a motion opposing fracking but also added a clause that would have allowed the opposition to repeat the Brexit Rebel Alliance trick of seizing control of the parliamentary timetable to pass their own legislation.

This put Number 10 in a difficult position. Opposition day motions were usually ignored, a moment for mass abstentions, but the second clause was an open challenge to the authority of the government. At a meeting in Downing Street that morning, it was agreed it was 'essentially a confidence vote'. But when this view was communicated to the whips' office, the nuance was lost. Craig Whittaker, the deputy chief whip, emailed Conservative MPs to inform them they were on a strict three-line whip. 'This is not a motion on fracking,' it read. 'This is a confidence motion in the government.'[32] Anyone voting against the government would lose the whip and be deselected. Whittaker thought the Labour whips had 'pulled an absolute blinder'.[33]

An issue on which the party was bitterly divided had been elevated to a test of strength and a bellwether vote on the survival of the prime minister. As the debate went on, it became clear that there was still likely to be a serious rebellion. One of the first to publicly defy Truss was Chris Skidmore, one of her co-authors of *Britannia Unchained*.

Panic ensued. 'It felt like either the Russians had decided to launch nukes or something was about to explode somewhere,' a senior official said. A crisis meeting was held, with Thérèse Coffey, David Canzini, Sophie Jarvis, Iain Carter and others trying to get a clear idea from Wendy Morton on the scale of the rebellion. 'She had no clue about the numbers,' said one source in the building. 'Not a fucking clue.'

Half an hour before the vote, Morton told Whittaker, her deputy, 'Number 10's been on the phone and they want us to drop it from being a vote of confidence in the government. What do you think?'

'Absolutely not,' said Whittaker, who was sure there were only six certain Tory votes against them, with another two possibles. 'Which government in their right mind hands control of the order paper to the opposition on any day? Trust me, it's a vote of confidence.'[34] They phoned Coffey and Whittaker told her to forget about it. He had previously complained to a cabinet 'Thérèse thinks she's chief whip.' Now he was overheard on the phone to Jarvis urging high command to hold its nerve. 'Let me do my fucking job,' he said. 'We are going to win. The majority will be approaching 100. Stop interfering.'

But there was little faith in Morton's operation. The decision was taken to change the whip. Charlotte Owen, who had been part of Johnson's Big Dog operation, sent a message to the PPS on the government bench, who passed a note to the climate minister Graham Stuart at the despatch box. Stuart used his winding up speech to say, 'Quite clearly this is not a confidence vote.' All hell broke loose, with MPs in a frenzy about whether they could rebel or not.

Jacob Rees-Mogg, the principal driver of the fracking policy, asked Whittaker, 'What on earth is going on?' When he explained, the business secretary said he would get Stuart to make a point of order to reverse his announcement.[35] In the division lobby, there was tumult, with Rees-Mogg and Coffey trying to steer colleagues to back the government, actions which led to accusations that ministers had tried to physically pull potential rebels into the correct lobby. 'No one was manhandled,' Whittaker insisted later. But Rees-Mogg was overheard threatening rebels with a 'snap general election' if they failed to back the government.

The chaos was capped with Morton, who felt undermined by the change being issued over her head, 'in floods of tears' rushing through the voting lobby, yelling, 'I am no longer chief whip.'

When he discovered Stuart had made no point of order, Whittaker, livid that political defeat had been snatched from the jaws of victory, stormed towards Truss's office shouting, 'I am fucking furious and I don't give a fuck any more.'

With just a few minutes to go, Penny Mordaunt, as leader of the House, stepped in and demanded to know where the chief whip had gone. 'I think she's just resigned,' someone said. 'She's in with the PM.'

Mordaunt found Truss and Morton deep in conversation but, bizarrely under the circumstances, quaffing glasses of fizz. 'You have got to take some responsibility,' she snapped at Morton. 'People have no idea what to do. You have to tell them how to vote.' A witness described her as 'frogmarching the chief-not chief' to the lobbies with less than a minute to spare before the doors closed.

The government won the vote with a majority of 96. While 40 Tory MPs had failed to back Truss, only six voted against the government, exactly as Whittaker had predicted. He said later, 'It was a textbook whipping day. Somebody at Number 10 got the wobbles.'[36] For nearly two hours no one knew if Morton and Whittaker had resigned. It even seemed that the prime minister had failed to vote, until it transpired that Truss had failed to swipe her pass in the voting lobby.

Veteran MP Sir Charles Walker had seen enough. He walked into central lobby, parked himself in front of a camera and let rip at the people who had installed Truss. 'I think it's a shambles and a disgrace,' he raged, on the verge of tears. 'I think it is utterly appalling. I'm livid and, you know, I really shouldn't say this, but I hope all those people that put Liz Truss in Number 10 – I hope it was worth it. I hope it was worth it for the ministerial red box. I hope it was worth it to sit around the cabinet table, because the damage they have done to our party is extraordinary. I've had enough. I've had enough of talentless people putting their tick in the right box, not because it's in the national interest, but because it's in their own personal interest to achieve a ministerial position.' It was probably the most startling vox pop given in Parliament during the Brexit years.

At 10 p.m. Truss phoned Morton five times in a bid to sort out what sanctions would be brought against the rebel MPs. 'Wendy wasn't answering,' a witness said. When the PM eventually got through Morton said, 'Sorry, Prime Minister, I'm in the smoking room.' Her main concern was 'there is stuff on [gossip site] Guido [Fawkes] about me which we need to get changed'. Morton had been to the whips' office after the vote and announced she was quitting. All the other whips agreed that if the chief had to go over a whipping issue they would have to resign too. Truss 'spent a long time talking them all down,' an aide said.

Alex Wild, the acting press secretary, tried to get Morton to sign off a statement clarifying that she had not resigned. He sent it to her at 10.30 p.m. Half an hour later, having heard nothing, he sent a question mark. 'I'm just looking at it,' the chief whip replied. At 11.53 p.m. he asked if she was content with the wording. At 12.17 a.m. she said edits were needed. Another seven minutes went by before she pointed out that there was a double 'a' in the final paragraph. Some 114 minutes had been wasted to make a grammatical change while the government was held up to public ridicule.

While that was going on, Nick Catsaras asked several political aides to stay in Number 10 because there was likely to be an emergency strategy meeting with the prime minister. Matthew Sinclair's big idea was to turn the medium-term fiscal plan into a 'back-me-or-sack-me' challenge to Tory MPs. Most others thought Truss would not even make it to that point and, even if she did, that she would lose a confidence vote. Nearing midnight, they were told to go home and come back at 6 a.m. Many others had been in the pub for hours. Hugh Bennett recalled, 'I think we all needed a pint.'[37]

Truss also needed a drink. She cancelled a planned meeting with Jeremy Hunt and sat down with her husband. Over a bottle of sauvignon blanc and a pork pie, she came to terms with the fact that she was finished.[38] 'There was an atmosphere in the House of Commons, not in a good way,' she recalled. 'I could just tell.'

Hunt had also concluded that Truss had to go. Jake Berry was summoned by two civil servants from the Cabinet Office to a meeting at which the chancellor made clear that the markets and the pound were on the verge of another plunge. Berry had already received reports that, the night before, Hunt had attended a dinner at the Carlton Club at which he had held up a picture of a graph on his phone to the assembled grandees. 'It showed the pound would tank if Truss stayed,' a witness revealed, 'and would zoom if Rishi took over.'

The night that Richard Nixon fired H. R. 'Bob' Haldeman, his White House chief of staff, the outgoing president called Haldeman as usual that evening for their normal chat, as if nothing had happened. At 11 p.m., Truss rang Stein. 'Liz, you do know you suspended me?' he said. 'I'm not in the building any more.'

'Don't worry about all that, we'll get it sorted,' she said.

'But it isn't sorted, is it?' Evidence, perhaps, that the bonds of political kinship are often both weaker and sometimes strangely deeper than those of normal friendships. Evidence, perhaps too, of a prime minister clinging to familiar flotsam while her ship sank around her.

* * *

After a restless night, in which she barely slept again, Truss was up at 5 a.m. on Thursday messaging aides. They were soon in the office. The prime minister saw some of her confidants in the flat. She also received another text message from Boris Johnson, urging her to fight on.

The final decision came in a conversation in the Cabinet Room with Mark Fullbrook and Nick Catsaras. Truss then went upstairs again to talk to husband Hugh, who said, 'You would have regretted never running for leader and trying to do the things in which you believed, but you won't regret leaving now that it has proved impossible.'[39]

Eventually Simon Case went up to the flat. Truss then came downstairs, bright and breezy, the burden of decision lifted. She swept past her policy chief with a jaunty 'Good morning, Jamie Hope! How are you?' as if she hadn't a care in the world.

'I'm okay. How are you?'

'All fine, thank you. I have a meeting now.'

She took others aside and asked their view: 'It's difficult, isn't it?' Everyone knew what was coming. One political aide present said, 'I was broken. It was not one of those defeats where it was easy to spin a story to yourself.' But not for the prime minister. 'She was gutted but, at that point, she had done her normal rebounding act.'

The 9 a.m. meeting that day in the pillared state room was a scene from *The Thick of It* as imagined by Salvador Dalí. At least one of those present regarded it as the strangest meeting they ever attended in government. Truss was concerned she had lost every national newspaper bar the *Daily Express*, whose readers liked the confirmation of the pensions triple lock. 'That one front page cost us £5 billion,' said a senior Tory. 'It would have been cheaper to just buy the newspaper.'

Jamie Hope and Sarah Ludlow were asked to outline plans for policy over the next few months. They looked at each other incredulously. Ludlow said, 'I think it's a bit ambitious to be thinking weeks and months ahead. We need to be thinking about what the prime minister does in the next couple of days.' In the end it was nearer two hours.

Despite the chaos of the night before, those present were incredulous that the 'whip's report' was just the fourth item on the agenda. 'I was sitting there thinking, "There isn't just an elephant but a fucking T-rex in the room and no one is acknowledging it,"' said one aide. 'It was completely mad.' When it was her turn, Morton began her remarks by saying, 'Can I just say my whips' office is devastated by what happened.' The witness said, 'It was as if none of it was anything to do with her.' The chief whip was then quizzed by Coffey, who pointed out she had moved some of the business on the parliamentary timetable. Asked what it was, Morton replied, 'I haven't got that on me, Deputy Prime Minister', an answer that reinforced the view of many in the room that she was clueless about her role. Morton then got up and announced that she had to be somewhere else. As she reached the door, she turned and said, in a 'medium-pace Yorkshire accent', 'Just remember. I. Am. The. Chief. Whip.' She left, leaving officials open-mouthed.

The moment some staff knew it was over came late morning when they noticed Truss had changed her clothes. 'She started the day in a red-ochre outfit and then I spotted she had changed into a dark blue suit,' one said – suitable attire for a political funeral. That was how she received Sir Graham Brady, chairman of the 1922 Committee, who was photographed slipping in by the rear entrance to Downing Street at 11.43 a.m. Truss had summoned Brady but he told friends he was 'reaching for his phone' to request a meeting even as he was summoned. A cascade of MPs had contacted him overnight – some with formal letters of no confidence, others with WhatsApps and emails – saying Truss had to go. The prime minister asked, 'Do you think the situation is retrievable?'

Brady replied, 'No, I don't think so, Prime Minister.'

Truss concurred: 'I don't either.'

At 1 p.m. Truss summoned her closest allies to the Cabinet Room and told political aides and officials that she was going to resign. 'She was very together,' an ally said. Truss thanked her team for their hard work but explained, 'It's clear that I can't govern the parliamentary party. It's clear that I don't have the support of the MPs and I think that makes my position untenable. Instead of dragging it out, I am going to go while I still have some grace about it and not be forced out. I cannot deliver what I said I would deliver, and that's that. I wish we had more time, working together here, but it is what it is.' Concluding, she said, 'Politics is a blood sport', a quote made famous by Labour's Aneurin Bevan. Those standing close to the prime minister heard her add, *sotto voce*, 'And I'm the fox.'

When, at lunchtime, her daughter Liberty called from the school playing field, urging her mother not to resign, Truss had to tell her it was too late.[40] Both daughters had seen their lives upended. Frances was beginning her A-level studies when she moved to Number 10. 'We never had time to talk about the massive life change,' Truss confessed. 'I'm pleased they managed to fit in a sleepover with their friends. And they did get to visit the nuclear bunker.' But Truss's overwhelming feeling was one of guilt. 'My biggest worry was that I had let them down,' she said. 'Most children find out about the fallibilities of their parents over a number of years. Mine saw all mine publicly exposed in very short order.'[41]

Truss called the King to say she was resigning and then asked Hugh to leave work and come to Number 10. He was the only one in the street supporting her when she addressed the nation at 1.35 p.m. Still visible on the road beneath her feet were marks indicating the position of the lectern put down for her arrival as prime minister six weeks earlier.[42]

She spoke for less than a minute and a half, telling voters, 'We set out a vision for a low-tax, high-growth economy that would take advantage of the freedoms of Brexit. I recognise though, given the situation, I cannot deliver the mandate on which I was elected … I have therefore spoken to His Majesty The King to notify him that I am resigning as leader of the Conservative Party … I will remain as prime minister until a successor has been chosen. Thank you.' To Truss, this bookend to a 'surreal' premiership, 'seemed like just another dramatic moment in a very strange film in which I had somehow been cast'.[43]

Truss had been prime minister for forty-four days, the exact length of time Brian Clough lasted as manager of Leeds United. When she left Downing Street she had served for forty-nine. She was, by a distance, the shortest-serving premier, smashing the dubious honour previously held by George Canning, who died after 119 days at the helm. Lord Bath technically assumed office for only two days (10–12 February 1746), but was unable to find more than one person willing to serve in his cabinet. A satirist wrote, 'The minister to the astonishment of all wise men never transacted one rash thing; and, what is more marvellous, left as much money in the Treasury as he found in it.' Truss could not say the same.

Adam Jones was on a bike ride around Mauritius with his new wife when he got a call to say, 'She's resigning in an hour.'

At the end of the day, Truss and a dozen aides had drinks in the Downing Street flat with her husband and two daughters. One close aide said, 'The sadness the staff feel is akin to a loved one dying.' The woman herself was more sanguine. 'Don't worry,' she told them. 'I'm relieved it's over … at least I've been prime minister.'[44]

To the rest of her parliamentary party, stunned at the speed of the implosion, there was a numbed relief that it was over, a sense that it all had to have been a fever dream. One MP told the *Guardian*'s Peter Walker that Truss and her acolytes had 'fled the burning Waco compound as the FBI shot it up, leaving dozens of others still trapped inside'.[45] The same analogy had been thrown around by MPs at the fall of Boris Johnson, by Johnson's team about Dominic Cummings, but to many it better fitted the ideological Kool-Aid of the Trussites.

Fullbrook messaged the 'New game plan group', a WhatsApp gathering in search of a purpose with startling news, 'For the record I have proposed everyone in this group for an honour.' This was greeted with incredulity by some. Sarah Ludlow replied, 'Thanks but no thanks.' Jamie Hope, more self-aware than many about the mistakes that had been made, added, 'Don't think I've earned one so please don't put me on the list.' Fullbrook replied, 'No worries.' He then invited aides to decompress at his villa on the Caribbean island of St Lucia.

On her final weekend as prime minister, Truss invited her depleted phalanx of aides and MPs to Chequers with her family, 'an afternoon of bruised clouds and close heat foreshadowing the storm which broke as we dispersed,' recalled Simon Clarke. Truss, he said, displayed 'quiet dignity and [an] absence of self-pity'.[46] Her attitude then, as it was afterwards, was unrepentant about what she chose to do, her regrets confined to how she went about it. Those too would dissipate with time. 'We were doing the right things,' she told her guests. 'The problems that we face are not going to go away and we need to make difficult decisions to get our economy and country into the best place to take on our competitors and adversaries.' She admitted, 'The party wasn't ready for this.'[47]

In politics, it is not possible to divorce ends from means in this way. Particularly when it comes to the economy, the extent to which you do things and the speed at which you do them is not an abstract, it is the essence of what you are doing. For Truss, the most experienced cabinet minister in her own government, not to comprehend this had fatal consequences. Like Boris Johnson, she emerged as leader because she was optimistic and bold and was prepared to ignore the rules. Like him, these were also the root causes of her undoing.

If there is a lesson in this book, it is not that some ideologies are right and that others are wrong, but that success belongs to leaders who build effective teams to pursue clearly defined goals that they can not only explain to the public but also persuade them to support. Leaders need a strategic target, a tactical plan to get there, the ability to execute it and the communication skills to take people with them. Unlike Theresa May, Truss knew her own mind and had clear goals, but she mistook victory in the leadership election, where she won over the grassroots membership, for a mandate that encompassed her MPs and the public. With them she made little effort to persuade.

In this context, Simon Clarke concluded later, 'It was a mistake to have excluded from government so many of those who had backed Rishi Sunak. Her administration had too few allies when its momentum faltered … There was a sizeable group of MPs who were unpersuadable from the beginning. From those who shivered at the thought of making the case for lowering the top rate of income tax … to those who did little to hide their desire for revenge for the summer's reversal.'[48] One of her closest aides said, 'There definitely wasn't enough done to get MPs on board before the mini-budget. She went too hard and too fast.' Another added, 'It doesn't matter how well you're doing with the membership, it's the parliamentary party that matters. You have to govern.'

More perversely, some of her aides talked as if she had inherited Johnson's public mandate from the 2019 election. 'We have a majority of more than 70 and we've never done anything with it,' one said in August. It was not Truss's majority. Indeed, civil servants who worked on the transition correctly calculated – as a result of the posture of some pro-Sunak MPs – that Truss really only enjoyed a practical majority of around ten, not a cushion which would survive contact with excessive radicalism. She stepped into this minefield needing highly effective party managers. Instead, her appointment of Wendy Morton as chief whip, arguably her worst personnel decision, hastened her demise.

Unlike Johnson in the first six months of his premiership, Truss did not build an effective team or think much about how to achieve her goals. Her predecessor hired Dominic Cummings, in part, because he was aware of his own shortcomings and wanted to compensate for them, deciding to work with someone who could impose a disciplined strategy upon him. By contrast, Truss cast aside the aides who had helped get her where she was, freezing out Sophie Jarvis, Adam Jones, Jamie Hope and Jason Stein from meetings on the central policy by which her premiership would be defined. In so doing, she removed the brake on her own behaviour with consequences which were inevitable. 'The Number 10 system is designed to really jump for the PM,' a political adviser said. 'As a minister you push for 100 and get 20, she pushed for 100 and got 50, then pushed again and got 70, and it was too much, too fast.' Truss, with Kwarteng in tow – too politically and personally aligned to do anything more than mouth the odd warning – careened out of control. 'She just got drunk on power and wouldn't listen,' a close aide concluded.

The team she did build was the seventh Conservative regime since 2010 – following the coalition, David Cameron's majority rule, two distinct May operations and three groups of Johnson aides. Arguably, it was the most internally divided. 'She weakened everyone, created all these power struggles,' an aide said. Celia McSwaine said, 'As an administration it was very chaotic to work within ... We really could have done with more experience in the Number 10 and Number 11 teams. We were learning on the job.'

Truss also abandoned the pattern which had revived her career and turned a second-tier minister into the leader of her party. She had done so with deft manipulation of the media and by listening to comms experts who could land her messages and understood the 'optics' she railed against as PM. It was as if she thought that phase of her life was only necessary to get into a position to enact her ideological vision.

She then pursued that vision in a context-free fashion like someone who had spent half a lifetime mouthing to herself, 'When I become prime minister, I'm going to ...' and was determined to stick to the blueprint regardless of the prevailing economic circumstances. Like many Tories, who habitually recalled only the aspects of Margaret Thatcher's government which suited their world view, Truss donned like a cloak the Iron Lady's determination in 1981 to get a basket case economy back on track, but did not digest that major tax cuts had to wait until both inflation and debt were under control. The top rate of tax was only reduced from 60 per cent in 1986, seven years into Thatcher's premiership. Truss wasn't prepared even to wait seven weeks.

Instead, she embarked on the most radical redrawing of Britain's political economy in decades without squaring the City. This was doubly important because Truss had not used the leadership contest to outline her plans in full. She seems to have been fooled by the cross-party consensus that the energy package needed to be huge into believing she could borrow tens of billions of pounds without consequences.

Truss was initially 'very low' after her departure from Downing Street but soon bounced back to a state of Tiggerish defiance which veered towards denial. When the author asked how she was in January 2023, she replied, 'I'm fine. What would be the point of being anything else?' She told allies, 'I lost a battle, but I haven't lost the war',[49] as she busied herself with paid speeches and plans for a new think tank.

She re-emerged four months later with a four-thousand-word essay in the *Sunday Telegraph*, edited by her ideological ally Allister Heath. In it she wrote, 'Knowing what I know now, undoubtedly I would have handled things differently. I underestimated the extent to which the market was on edge and, like many others, was not aware of how fragile our system had become.'[50] But she barely managed to admit fault and certainly did not apologise for the mess she had left behind. Her memoir, which followed in 2024, contained one paragraph acknowledging that she made mistakes, but she confined her *mea culpa* to the admission that she was 'not always good at translating' her 'internal dialogue' about tax cuts boosting growth 'into something for wider public communication'. She admitted, 'I assumed people understood what I was trying to do more than they did.'[51] By that point, her resentment at the Treasury, the City, the OBR and the Bank of England had calcified into a universal theory of her demise which blamed the 'deep state' for thwarting her.

Truss was not blessed with perfect fortune. The Bank of England's failure to raise interest rates by the expected amount before the mini-budget put pressure on the pound even before Kwarteng got to his feet. The ignorance in the Bank, and particularly the Treasury, about the latent risks to the pension system smacks of incompetence. The first big event of her premiership did not play to Truss's strengths and distracted public attention at a crucial time. 'Not to be glib or crass, but the timing of the Queen's death was incredibly unlucky,' one aide recalled. 'It meant Liz didn't get the political credit for the energy intervention.

But, ultimately, Truss was the one to blame. A sympathetic cabinet ally said, 'For good or for ill, the decisions were hers and hers alone. Her agency from beginning to end was total. The issue was the lack of checks and balances. If anything, she would have wanted what happened to have been more radical, not less.' Truss had a huge advantage over many prime ministers in that she knew exactly what she wanted to do. 'In her diagnosis of the situation at home and abroad and what should be done about it, Liz Truss was fundamentally and importantly right,'[52] Simon

Clarke said. But she was quite incapable of plotting a path from A to B. 'The strategic goal was right,' Kwasi Kwarteng said later. 'Her insight and diagnosis of the problem was right. Where we fell woefully short was to have a tactical plan. My biggest regret is we weren't tactically astute and we were too impatient. There was a brief moment and the people in charge, myself included, blew it.'[53]

Both cabinet colleagues and her closest aides concluded in the end that Truss was temperamentally unsuited to the premiership. A senior cabinet minister said, 'I don't think she had the right personality for it. And in a way it is a credit to how effective the system was that she got moved on. It was a Shakespearean drama, in that the strengths which got her to the top … were the ones that saw her demise. The strengths turn into weaknesses. What I find extraordinary is that every single thing that went wrong she was advised against. People said Jacob was a liability at BEIS and it was his insistence on fracking that was the proximate cause [of her downfall]. The chief whip, she was warned against. She couldn't pivot into being a leader of a government.' Mario Cuomo, the former governor of New York, said, 'You campaign in poetry, you govern in prose.' The cabinet minister concluded, 'The problem was, she wanted to govern in poetry.'

There is a question as to why colleagues who had known her for years didn't see all this coming, since the clues had been there, as Cole and Heale's biography makes painfully clear. One minister, explaining the process of revelation, said, 'You and I know Antarctica is very cold, but neither of us have ever been there. If we were dropped there from a helicopter in our boxer shorts our experience of that would be completely different. There is knowledge and understanding and there is knowledge that comes from experience. Yes, I understood that she was a sort of crazy individual – but it was only when we were actually in the moment that I thought, "Actually, she is fucking crazy." You can never know how human beings are going to react in a particular situation, particularly when they've got considerable power.'

Most of all, she was impatient. After her demise one of her cabinet ministers consulted a child psychologist, who told him extreme impatience was 'a function of autism'. The doctor illustrated this with a test. 'You give a child who is not autistic and a child who is autistic £20 to last a week. The autistic one will spend the money in five minutes – the non-autistic child will eke it out,' the minister explained. 'She demanded that everything was done immediately.'

Disaster was not inevitable; it was Truss's haste which made it so. A senior civil servant observed, 'It's not that her destination was wrong, it's that her journey was too far and too fast. If you are publicly criticising the Treasury and the Bank of England and the OBR, the people that own our debt out there look to you to tell us, "This is all okay." They all want a smaller state with low taxes; that's exactly how they flourish. It's just they thought she was doing it in a reckless way.' One of the PM's political advisers said, 'Stuff probably does move too slowly [in government], but sometimes, on really big policies, it's good to do that. Rushing [the mini-budget] out on the Friday between the state funeral and the conference recess was just a mad decision.' Another said: 'The path along the clifftop was really narrow, and we tried to sprint down it.'

So, what might she have done? Most cabinet ministers involved in the discussions at Chevening and in the period after the Queen's death believe the fatal error was to decouple the tax cuts from spending reductions and a fiscal plan, which would have reassured the City. 'If she had done all of those things, my personal view is: that works,' said one. Celia McSwaine, Kwasi Kwarteng's adviser, agreed: 'We should have published our forecasts alongside the mini-budget, even if that had meant delaying it. And I do think we should have delayed it ... I think we should have outlined some spending cuts alongside to make it clear how we were planning to pay for the tax cuts. We should have been honest with MPs and the public that you can't have tax cuts for free.'[54]

Truss's conviction that she was there to deliver sweeping change created two fundamental errors. Her view that the advocates of 'orthodoxy' had been holding the country back for years meant that when some voices were timidly raised against her plans, she was pre-programmed to dismiss them; it merely reinforced her view that she was correct. The second mistake was analogous to the Brexiteers who railed against the EU's political project but then seemed surprised when Brussels put politics ahead of economics when it came to negotiating a Brexit deal. Having railed for years against the powerful stranglehold of the Treasury, the Bank of England, the IMF and the OBR, it was perverse for Truss to believe that they would be pushovers when she challenged their thinking. Since she believed she was fighting implacable foes, she ought to have prepared twice as carefully for the battle.

Truss was right to say later, 'The centre of political gravity moved to the left in Britain, so a lot of the things that I was espousing, apart from

Conservative Party members, there wasn't a massive constituency for them in the media or the Conservative parliamentary party.' But rather than acknowledge that it was her job to make these arguments, she used her *Sunday Telegraph* article to direct the blame at her own spin doctors. 'I fully admit that our communication could have been better,' she wrote. This was too much for Adam Jones, Simon McGee and Jason Stein, all of whom Truss had explicitly excluded from knowledge of the budget until it was too late. In April 2024, Jones gave a critical interview to Politico's Aggie Chambre calling Truss's behaviour as an ex-prime minister 'slightly unedifying'. When Truss launched her book, *Ten Years to Save the West*, a few days later, only McGee turned up.

Truss's own aides regarded her view that the 'deep state' had thwarted her as risible. One said, 'She just doesn't realise how much she torched the reputation of the party in the country. She's completely detached from reality.' Asa Bennett, her speechwriter, concluded, 'There will be some people who will blame so-called proponents of orthodoxy ... [but] when you're prime minister, you have to take responsibility for the actions of the government you're presiding over. You have the final say on what's happening in the budgets that you've worked very closely with your chancellor on. And I think she knows this.'[55] A cabinet minister who bumped into her at Christmas 2022 said, 'Her take was that the system didn't let her implement her plan. Actually, the system let her implement her plan in an unadulterated form. The problem wasn't that they stopped her, but that they let her.' A peer who worked in various 'deep state' jobs agreed: 'The "deep state", if it exists, failed to stop the then government delivering the hardest possible Brexit. The "deep state" then failed to stop the Truss budget that crashed the British economy. If the Deep State exists, it's totally useless!'

While Truss raged against the machine, her ideological allies bemoaned that the ideas they cherished were discredited by the way she herself had executed them. Chris Philp said, 'What is disappointing is that there was a way to make the growth agenda work. Lower taxes to stimulate growth could have been accepted by the financial markets if accompanied by specific and reasonable commitments to restrain spending growth, to at least partially offset the tax cuts. The case for stimulating growth through tax reductions has been seriously damaged.' Adam Jones added, 'The tragedy of Liz's premiership, I think, is the extent to which it has set back and damaged the cause of people who believe broadly in free markets and a smaller state and deregulation.'[56] Privately, feelings were raw. One cabinet minister said, 'Whenever someone in the next ten years says, "We are going to go for growth and we are going to have tax cuts and deregulation to drive that", everybody is going to say, "Liz Truss tried that and it didn't work." It is quite hard to say, "She didn't do it properly." I am angry that I have been associated with what people will see as a car crash. She wasn't willing even to discuss some of the ideas that would have made it work, even with Kwasi, her closest political friend and the person she had chosen to be her chancellor.'

These wails were greeted with amusement by those on the left. Rafael Behr of the *Guardian* wrote, '[The] Truss government failing was, for libertarian Brexit ultras, like dawn breaking for a doomsday cult the morning after the night when the Rapture/alien rescue was supposed to happen … Some cult hangers-on slink off to nurse disappointment, but the hardcore confect a whole new mythology to explain why, despite all evidence to contrary, they were right all along. The absence of Rapture proves that work of the cult is needed more than ever.' The irony is that it was Truss herself who continued to lead this faction, spending her post-premiership demanding the same action she had in her pre-premiership – almost as if her premiership had never happened.

While the focus of her time in office was the mini-budget, Liz Truss became prime minister because of Brexit. A Remain voter in 2016, who (after a period of soul searching) enthusiastically campaigned to stay, became a born-again Brexiteer afterwards, one of the most outspoken advocates of no-deal under May. Her blunt personae and Johnsonian-style boosterism as trade secretary made her culturally a Brexiteer too, leaving her the candidate best placed to unite the right of the party in the summer of 2022. Truss was also, by then, the boldest advocate of one form of Brexit. Her vision of a buccaneering nation, cutting taxes and slashing regulation at home while championing free markets abroad was what a certain strain of Brexiteer had always wanted, the shining city on a river known as 'Singapore-on-Thames'.

There is an argument too, that Brexit helped to finish Truss. She only secured victory by co-opting Suella Braverman and her supporters, whose Brexit passion was stronger border controls and reduced immigration. When that clashed with Truss's desire to raise immigration to stimulate growth it led to a schism which undermined her at a key moment and led to her demanding her home secretary's resignation the following day. Had she survived in office more than one more day, the incompatibility between these two Brexiteer Jerusalems would have become even more stark.

Brexit, with its binary war between Leave and Remain, had also papered over other ideological splits in the Tory Party – between the free marketeers and the fiscal hawks and the One Nation paternalists who wanted higher spending, between the globalists and the anti-immigration nationalists – which erupted again under Truss, rendering the parliamentary party nearly ungovernable.

If Liz Truss's premiership was shaped by Brexit, it in turn shaped Brexit. As an experiment in one theoretical expression of Brexit it was a failure, discrediting the Singapore model. To some Remainers, she had exposed as fallacious claims that leaving the EU would lead naturally to a new economy. To some Brexiteers, her failed execution of the idea left them with the view (often voiced by socialist purists) that their big idea had 'never been done properly'.

Unseen in the economic meltdown, however, Truss had also quietly reopened negotiations with the European Commission on the Northern Ireland Protocol. The decision over what to do next would lie with her successor. As she left Number 10 for the last time it was clear that would either be her predecessor or the man she had beaten to the job in the first place.

PART SIX

OUT OF TIME

HOW RISHI RAN OUT OF ROAD

October 2022 to June 2024

'Victory is no longer a truth. It is only a word to
describe who is left alive in the ruins'

– Lyndon B. Johnson

PRINCES IN THE (MILLBANK) TOWER

17–22 October 2022

'We're sitting here, you and I, like a coupla regular fellas.
You do what you do. I do what I gotta do'

– Vincent Hanna (Al Pacino) to Neil McCauley (Robert De Niro),
Heat, 1995, Michael Mann

The BAFTA building on London's Piccadilly, the spiritual centre of British drama, was a fitting location for the next act – the most dramatic game of political chicken since Tony Blair and Gordon Brown made their deal at the Granita restaurant in 1994. At a party to celebrate the two hundredth anniversary of the *Sunday Times*, on Monday 17 October, a member of Boris Johnson's Brains Trust revealed that several of his team were now urging the former prime minister to endorse Rishi Sunak, whose resignation had helped bring him down. 'Several of us think that is the serious and sensible course of action,' he said. 'If he thinks he can't win, the statesmanlike thing to do would be to back Rishi and say the feud is over.' A member of Johnson's family agreed: 'Boris has to back Rishi! That's the way to solve this.'

At that point none of those involved knew that, in less than three days, Liz Truss would announce her resignation. Johnson certainly did not, or he might not have been sunning himself in the Dominican Republic.

Sunak was at his constituency home in North Yorkshire. He had invited his closest aides to stay with him for three days. Liam Booth-Smith, Nissy Chesterfield, Rupert Yorke, Cass Horowitz, Eleanor Shawcross, Douglas McNeil, James Nation and Will Dry had all made the journey, arriving on the Sunday of conference, a day which had ended with the prime minister's U-turn on the 45p rate of tax. 'We'd obviously seen the budget and the reaction to it,' one said, 'but we were always going to submarine, and not cause any trouble.' Truss's plummeting poll numbers did, however, elicit a whiff of schadenfreude.

They spent Monday lazing by the pool, or playing table tennis. That evening, however, the conversation turned to what Team Truss should and would do next. 'There was a view amongst the policy people, including Rishi himself, that they just didn't see how it was sustainable. In Asian markets, the pound was still on the floor. Where was the confidence going to come from? At that point we were all thinking they were going to have to go further; it couldn't just stop at 45p.' None, however, believed Truss was mortally wounded. Someone said, 'She'll still be there at Christmas, the question is what happens after Christmas.' They agreed that Sunak should say nothing.

The 'bat signal' did not go up until the day of Truss's resignation, ten days later. When it did, Nissy Chesterfield was in Wales with friends. Having worked for Truss at the Department for Trade, she watched PMQs, where her old boss announced she was a 'fighter not a quitter' and concluded she was 'going full Liz'. As the day went on, Chesterfield and other Sunak aides took calls from friends in Number 10 saying, 'It is utter chaos, this whole thing is going to fall apart.' On Thursday morning, journalists began to call, asking, 'Is Rishi ready?'

When Truss quit, Sunak was in Teesside having lunch with his two daughters. Liam Booth-Smith, his chief of staff, called him to talk about what they should do. Sunak was not sure. 'My head has not been in it,' he said. 'I don't know if I want to do this.' The leadership election had been physically gruelling and emotionally draining. He had started taking his cricket seriously, hoping to break into the local village team.

As the day went on Sunak spoke again to Booth-Smith, Oliver Dowden, his best friend, James Forsyth, *The Times*'s political columnist, and his wife, Akshata. It was gone 6 p.m., five hours after Truss quit, when they all gathered in a small hotel room near St James's Park tube in Westminster. 'When he walked in, he looked knackered,' a witness said. 'I think it was psychological tiredness from working out whether to go or not.' Sunak said, 'If we're going to do this thing we need to get on the phone now. We need to sew up the MPs as quickly as possible. We need to get way bigger numbers than we did before, where's the plan, let's go.'

Mel Stride began coordinating the ring round. By Saturday morning they had well over 100 MPs in the bag.

The 1922 Committee agreed new rules that Thursday to limit the number of candidates to those with the backing of 100 MPs by Monday, when the MPs would vote. Some saw this as an attempt to thwart Boris Johnson. 'They moved the goal posts,' an ally said.

Johnson made dozens of calls to MPs and cabinet ministers from his Caribbean villa but was handicapped by the time difference and his inability to meet people in person. A minister said, 'He has been seeking to assure people that he would build a good team around him and, unlike the last time, would start off his tenure by bringing some grown-ups with him into Downing Street.' The man who said he could never change was vowing to do so. The scent of power is a drug.

MPs were also queasy about the Privileges Committee investigation into whether Johnson had lied to the Commons over the partygate scandal, which meant he could be suspended from the House, triggering a bid to oust him as an MP – a bruise which Sunak's outriders were quick to punch. 'Rishi's people were telling MPs that they couldn't vote for Boris because the privileges inquiry would finish him,' a Johnson ally complained. They, in turn, were forced to clarify that Johnson would not try to scrap the investigation if he returned to Downing Street. A former minister said, 'Boris is telling people he will get them to vote to scrap the standards inquiry,' prompting the MP to call the manoeuvre 'Paterson 2'. 'Boris has learned literally nothing,' the minister said.

While the candidates scrambled for votes, senior Tories were trying to put in place a plan for the economy which would survive contact with events. Treasury sources said the Halloween budget would go ahead to ensure there was a 'proper financial statement' before the next meeting of the Bank of England's monetary policy committee on 3 November, when interest rates were predicted to rise. Jeremy Hunt was determined he should be the one presenting the fourth major economic statement of the year. On Friday, he spoke to both Sunak and Mordaunt and then Johnson over the weekend, briefing them on the gravity of the situation. Johnson and Mordaunt told him he would stay as chancellor if they won. Having gone through the numbers with Sunak, Hunt said, 'It would be useful to know if you plan to keep me as chancellor.'

'Look, I don't need to keep you as chancellor because I've got enough credibility of my own with the markets,' Sunak said, glib and self-confident, 'but I will keep you as chancellor, yes. There are some things I want to talk to you about how this job has to be done.' Sunak wanted to ensure the problems between him and Johnson were not repeated if he became prime minister. An early power play.

Johnson flew home overnight and landed on Saturday 22nd. 'He was being egged on by other people,' a family friend recalled, detecting ambiguity in Johnson's approach. 'It was the people around him who wanted it for him. They were more into it than he was.'

Johnson's case was not made easier by a column in the *Telegraph* that morning in which Charles Moore, a close friend, wrote, 'I can see Boris storming back in different circumstances, with a Labour government in disarray and a lacklustre Tory opposition seeking renewal. I don't see it working right now.' The same message was imparted by several big Tory donors, who foresaw more turbulence which would let Labour in.

Johnson and Mordaunt spoke soon after he was installed in his new office space in Millbank Tower. Both sought to persuade the other to stand aside to pool resources against Sunak. 'We thought we were going to get to the final two, where we should have been before,' a Mordaunt aide said. 'Boris came into the fray and that obviously fucked us.'

Johnson told Mordaunt 'I really respect you' and promised that she would be 'a key part of the team'. MPs were calling for her to be deputy prime minister or foreign secretary. This was Johnson at his most winning, promising a new mistress his fidelity and devotion. He brought his A-game. Mordant was immune to his advances.

'Boris, you're an incredible politician. You've done incredible things for the party, for Brexit, and you know that I really respect you. But I cannot back you,' she said. 'What you have to understand is that *my* supporters will not back you. Your supporters *will* back me. That is a key difference in this situation. You are a massive asset to the party and if you want to have a frontline role, I would be delighted.'

Mordaunt campaign officials said, at this stage, they had 55 to 60 votes, with Johnson not much further ahead, yet that was more than double the number of publicly declared votes for her. 'The problem we had was, a lot of them wouldn't tweet about it, which was frustrating,' an aide said. 'We didn't push them to do it. That was probably a mistake.'

On Saturday a close ally of Mordaunt admitted she was unlikely to get the numbers to get on the ballot paper. Laura Round, her right-hand woman, suggested doing a deal with Sunak, but Mordaunt chose not to pursue the idea. 'I can't,' she told her team. 'I can't be seen to have folded.' An adviser said, 'A lot of MPs who decided to back Penny said, "I'll back you, but you have to promise me you're not going to fold for some plush job." And she promised them. And she kept her word.'

Throughout the week intermediaries had been working on Johnson and Sunak to try to 'get the old gang back together'. Isaac Levido encouraged a rapprochement. Ross Kempsell and Nigel Adams told Johnson he needed to 'speak to Sunak'. Ben Wallace, the defence secretary who declined to run again, called for unity, demanding that all three candidates work together. On Saturday he phoned Johnson and urged him to talk to both Sunak and Mordaunt. 'I want to see a triumvirate,' he said publicly. 'All three of them have to come together and put aside their egos and recognise that without unity we will have a constitutional crisis and that the new leader will not be able to command a majority.' A former Number 10 aide, who knew Johnson well, said, 'I can see why it would suit Boris. But why would Rishi do that? Boris is a bastard and would come back and do all the things Boris does. He'd be causing chaos within a week, subtly undermining everything Rishi does.'

Nonetheless, in the two days after Truss resigned, various 'random odds and sods' from the Johnson camp got in touch with people they thought were close to Sunak to propose the two principals talk. One back channel saw Nigel Adams contact Julian Smith. It was not clear to Sunak or Booth-Smith if any were authorised by Johnson. 'That went on, in a ridiculous way, for thirty-six hours,' a Sunak aide said. Booth-Smith replied to these entreaties, 'If they want to reach out and have a conversation, they should do so properly and we can have a conversation. Until that point, we're going to keep prosecuting our case.'

Around 3 p.m. on Saturday a formal approach was finally made from Johnson's head of operations, Shelley Williams-Walker, who talked to her opposite number Lisa Lovering. The two had worked together in government. Sunak and his senior team had a quick meeting and agreed they should respond positively. They sent the message back that it would be better to meet soon and suggested Johnson come to Parliament. 'It's the weekend and no one's here, it's fine,' they said.

Johnson's team refused. They were a few hundred metres down the road in Millbank. 'Just come here,' they said. This did not appeal to

Sunak's aides who knew there would be a battalion of television and press cameras ready to greet their arrival. There were also protests outside Parliament which would have made it difficult for Sunak to exit via the main gate, while Johnson's team could easily enter Parliament via Black Rod's entrance, nearest Millbank, before anyone knew what was happening. It was also a power play. Johnson's team wanted it to look as if the prince was visiting the court of the king.

At ten minutes before three, Kempsell alerted the lobby that Johnson had secured the 100 supporters he needed and 'therefore could be on the ballot'. The use of 'could' suggested it was not a done deal. As an announcement designed to project strength it was curiously equivocal. The same effect had been conveyed by pictures released that morning of Johnson on the telephone to MPs, a tribal chief calling in his favours. But Sunak's accumulation of named supporters projected greater strength.

Johnson hoped Sunak would agree to subordinate himself again. His allies hoped that, even if that was not the case, the younger man would 'bend the knee', give Johnson the respect he craved, perhaps even apologise for helping to bring him down. This was not how Sunak saw things. As the afternoon went on, he became sure he did not need to do business with Johnson. MPs were flocking to his side. At 4 p.m. he called a national newspaper editor and said, 'I've got the numbers. I don't need Boris.' His team persuaded Sunak it made sense to be seen to talk to Johnson, but as one explained, 'There were no circumstances at all where there was a deal to be made. The only deal we wanted was him [Johnson] stepping aside.' Sunak sought an endorsement, not a running mate. 'If there was any offer, it was simply to say, "We want to respect your legacy. We want to honour your time in office. We want to continue some of the amazing work you've done", but the party needed to move forward.' Sunak had seen the chaos that surrounded Johnson. 'Why hitch your wagon to that again?' an aide asked.

A plan to meet at 3.30 p.m. was put on ice. Another, around 5.30 p.m., came and went. Even months later, both sides would claim the other as the cause of the delay. One of Sunak's aides insisted Johnson's operation needed more time to drum up support. Others admit they were in no rush to hold a meeting which Johnson needed more than they did. 'Rishi was not really bothered about seeing Boris and it was more of a courtesy in the end,' one close ally said. Booth-Smith sent Sunak home to have a shower and make more calls to MPs. They reconvened at six and decided, as the crowds and the photographers had thinned out, that it would be fine to go to Millbank. 'You will go into that meeting in a much stronger position than he will,' Booth-Smith reminded his man.

The meeting finally went ahead around 9 p.m., after some spy-movie tradecraft by Sunak's team who used two cars, one a decoy with police outriders, while he and Booth-Smith sat beyond the blacked-out windows of the second, thirty seconds behind. The first arrived at Millbank from one direction attracting the remaining media, while the second quietly drew up at a rear entrance once they had been distracted.

They were greeted in Johnson's nondescript offices by Johnson, Nigel Adams, Ross Kempsell and Williams-Walker. It looked a bit like 'a call centre'. Johnson was 'very smiley and friendly', a witness said, Sunak cooler, keen to get down to business. 'Okay, great, shall we do our thing and talk?' he said. The two men went into a conference room on their own, a long table with flags behind. Kempsell, Adams and Booth-Smith went and had a cup of tea, 'talking about anything other than politics'. Johnson's seconds tried at one point to speculate about what the two men were discussing but Booth-Smith said, 'Just let them talk. There's nothing we can talk about here that is going to have a material impact in there, so let's just let them figure it out.'

The encounter, lasting around an hour, saw power politics and personality collide to determine the future direction of a party and a country. It was a meeting packed with resolution, passive aggression, flashes of anger, moments of humour and an acute feeling that, at that moment, they were the only two people who mattered. It was the apprentice not his old master who held the trump cards, the former prime minister surviving on his wits and his chutzpah to try to unsettle a rival with the prize in his grasp. Both men knew Sunak was significantly ahead. Johnson was claiming to be in three figures but only around 70 MPs were declared. Sunak already had more than 120 supporters publicly confirmed.

According to accounts relayed to their aides, it was 'a circular conversation', with both men making the same arguments time and again, refusing to back down, 'talking at and over each other'. Johnson outlined what he saw as his moral and constitutional right to rule. 'I have a mandate. I won the election. I should be able to discharge that mandate.' He admitted the last few months had been 'a bit bonkers'. He said, 'We've just been through a terrible time. The party needs to come together. I'm the obvious frontman.' He urged Sunak to support him, in return for his job back as chancellor and a greater say over policy. 'You come back and produce the growth agenda we talked about. Let's get our act together. Come on! I can't do this without you. You have to back me.' Then, the kicker, 'You know I will win with the membership.'

Sunak responded with words to the effect, 'No, your time is over. You'll tear the party to pieces as you did before. You are wrong for the country and wrong for the party and it's over. I admired the stuff we did together. I want you to have a really important role in public life at home and abroad. But the country needs something different. You can either support me or we can take it to the members.'

Between the demands for support were flashes of Johnson's anger at his defenestration, unable to hide the resentment he felt towards Sunak. 'Why did you do it?' Echoes of his incomprehension at Gove's betrayal in 2016 – unable to countenance a role for his own behaviour in his demise. Sunak, bluntly, countered, 'You should ask that question to the sixty other people who resigned as well. You know it wasn't just me, despite your best efforts to paint it as being me.'

Alongside the hurt were coded threats. Johnson could play the betrayal card and damage Sunak's standing with MPs. 'Matey, I know you were doing this and doing that and if you hadn't I would still be there,' was how one source characterised Johnson's approach. 'I'll have to tell people about all the things you blocked.'

Sunak was unfazed: 'I've got no problem with the truth being out there. I'm happy to do a debate where we tell everyone exactly what happened. It's not me that should be worried, it's you. If you hadn't lied, you wouldn't have got in such a mess. Maybe you should take accountability for your own behaviour.'

Neither participant felt that tempers flared, but to those sitting outside it was intense. 'I certainly heard raised voices,' one said. 'You can't hear the actual words, but you can hear the volume and the tone. I heard Sunak shouting at Boris, and I heard him shouting back. It was pretty passionate.' A Borisworld source said, 'It was a bit like the scene in *Heat*, with Pacino and De Niro, when he and Rishi got together. "I've enjoyed this, but if I see you out there I'm gonna have to take you in", and "If I see you out there I'm gonna have to take you down". We know how the film ends. Boris said to Rishi, "You know if we go out there, I'm going to wipe the floor with you with the party in the country", and Rishi says, "If you do, I'll just stop you forming a government, as I did in the summer, so what are we going to do about it?" And Boris blinked.'

The Sunak side denied these threats were explicit by either of them. Neither was a fan of overt confrontation. However, Sunak and Booth-Smith did share the supposition that Johnson would win with the members if it got that far. 'The idea that we didn't know that is ridiculous,' a senior Sunak aide said. 'But we would have beaten Penny 60–40.'

Sunak landed a blow by arguing he was better qualified than Johnson to deal with the situation they faced. 'His argument was that he knew an awful lot about economics,' Johnson told his team. 'And that there was an economic mess and that he needed to sort it out.' Johnson accepted the validity of this point but stressed that was why he wanted Sunak back at the Treasury. Sunak tried to explain why he could not work with Johnson. 'I've already fought a campaign on a message that was categorically proven to be one hundred per cent correct.' He suggested Truss's approach of limitless borrowing was, in effect, what Johnson had wanted to do as prime minister, the policy Sunak had blocked as chancellor. If Johnson was to fight him now, he might find himself defending an approach which had brought soaring inflation and mortgage rates. 'This is why I took the view I took in your government,' Sunak said. 'If I'd let you spend what you wanted to spend you would have done this to the economy, not her.'

Johnson, for his part, felt he scored a hit when he warned Sunak that Cummings and Dougie Smith turning on him could happen to Sunak as well. Recounting the meeting, the former PM said, 'The only moment when I think he really focused on what I had to say was when I said that I thought that they were using him and you are already hearing Dougie say that Kemi Badenoch is the new thing. That was the only moment he really paid attention.' Sunak had no recollection of this point being made at Millbank and one close aide to Johnson said it came up in a separate phone conversation. 'They've had conversations where Sunak has admitted, in private, that he shares the same vulnerability,' one said.

When they emerged, the former PM announced to their aides, 'We've done the deal. Rishi has agreed to become chancellor, foreign secretary and CDL and anything else he wants. Deal done!'

Liam Booth-Smith looked momentarily alarmed until he saw his boss's face. Sunak smiled, wanly, impervious to Johnson and his blandishments. 'Interesting, that,' he said.

'Oh come on, Rishi,' Johnson pleaded.

Nigel Adams joined in: 'Come on, why can't we just toss a coin for it?'

Which is when Johnson offered one of the signature moments of his time in politics. 'No, no, no,' he exclaimed. 'Let's have an arm wrestle, come on, Rishi, let's arm wrestle.' He raised his arm, wise-cracking to the last, the big man offering to literally fight for the keys to 10 Downing Street and the leadership of the sixth largest economy on earth.

Sunak finally cracked and laughed, aware he couldn't compete with Johnson's humour, his confident ebullience, even perhaps his sense of entitlement. There was a pause, a moment those present would remember. How would he respond? Sunak walked over to Johnson, slapped him confidently on the back and said, 'See you at the debate on Wednesday, Boris.' With that he turned on his heel and walked out, Booth-Smith racing to catch up. Sunak's chief of staff would tell colleagues it was 'Rish's Hollywood moment'. Sunak was not 'a cool guy' but he had somehow conjured a moment which left Johnson a little startled. He had the self-possession to turn the tables and remind Johnson that, if he wanted to fight, there would be a battle ahead, one Sunak would relish.

'We came away from that meeting thinking they seemed wobbly,' a Sunak aide said. 'They didn't seem confident, or sure whether he was going to run or not.'

There were two endorsements that Sunak regarded as not just desirable but essential. That evening Kemi Badenoch came out for him in the *Telegraph*, announcing, 'I'm a big fan of Boris and he got the party through a very difficult situation in 2019. We are now in a different political climate that requires a different approach.'[1]

At lunchtime on Sunday the *Telegraph* posted an article by Suella Braverman, announcing that she too was on board. 'I have backed Boris from the start … His resignation in July was a loss for our country. But we are in dire straits now. We need unity, stability and efficiency. Rishi is the only candidate that fits the bill and I am proud to support him.' The piece was not just an endorsement, however, it was a promissory note redeemed.

Sunak, like Truss before him, had done a deal. A senior aide said, 'Boris was offering these people everything, whatever cabinet job they wanted. But it smacked of desperation. We made a very categorical commitment to both Suella and Kemi.' Badenoch was told she would either get trade or culture. 'Kemi hates Boris,' a source said. 'He destroyed the party. She's a very moral type of individual. She didn't resign because Boris was behind in the polls but because he kept lying. Suella is more "what's best for me".'

Braverman wanted to be home secretary again and Sunak was prepared to give her the job back – but her real goal was to get him to agree a hardline policy on immigration. 'The agreement they came to wasn't on jobs, but on policy,' a Sunak aide said. These were Braverman's demands:

- A commitment to reduce net migration by closing down the graduate route, restricting the number of dependents and increasing the salary threshold from £25,000 to £40,000.
- A commitment to prioritise the small boats crisis by introducing legislation with notwithstanding clauses so asylum courts could ignore modern slavery laws.
- A 'robust approach' if the European Court of Human Rights sought to prevent expulsions to Rwanda and the government to 'start the conversation' about leaving the European Convention.
- Retain the Northern Ireland Protocol Bill and the Retained EU Law Bill and pass them unchanged to the existing timetable.
- The Department for Education to issue 'unequivocal and enforceable' guidance on trans ideology which would stress the binary nature of biological sex and protect single sex spaces.
- Break up the Home Office, separating homeland security policy from migration.
- Braverman to have full control of spad appointments and to be consulted on her junior ministers and parliamentary aides.

She found Sunak tougher than expected. His parents had moved legally to Britain from India. He regarded it as a matter of fairness that those who came illegally did not gain an advantage over those who played by the rules. When Braverman pushed him to consider leaving the European Convention on Human Rights, Sunak said he wanted to try tougher domestic legislation first, believing the country would need to be taken on a journey, to see that everything else had been tried – just as Johnson had over Brexit in 2019. But on this issue even Sunak's advisers – Booth-

Smith and the deputy chief of staff Will Tanner – thought leaving the ECHR might be where they ended up. To them it was an 'issue of timing', not of principle. This difference of emphasis was to prove a running sore.

The deal was hidden in plain sight in Braverman's *Telegraph* article, which read like a series of terrorist demands but was a summary of what they had agreed. 'We will only stop the boats crossing the Channel if we can actually pass vital legislation to limit the impact of Modern Slavery laws, the Human Rights Act and the European Convention on Human Rights,' she wrote. 'We can only deliver the Rwanda Scheme if we stop the Strasbourg Court thwarting our policy-making powers.' She also publicly called for 'a firm line on trans ideology in our schools'.[2] Again, Sunak was closer to her views than most of his party grasped. He was seen by many MPs as a cultural remainer, a wishy-washy man of establishment compromise, yet on the economy, on immigration and on social issues he was far more conventionally right-wing than Johnson, who advocated higher state spending, had once backed an amnesty for illegal immigrants and believed a tough line on trans ideology risked turning the Tories into the nasty party again. Sunak told Braverman he was prepared 'to do whatever it takes' to stop the boats. In government, they were to disagree fiercely about what that meant.

Only on Brexit did Braverman tread on tiptoes. 'On the Northern Ireland Protocol, Rishi has reassured me that he will maintain the current Bill in Parliament with a view to fixing the border,'[3] she wrote. Sunak vowed not to scrap Truss's NIP Bill, but to him it was leverage, not an end state. Fixing things might require a different approach. Braverman gave him just enough space to do so.

The Badenoch and Braverman endorsements were a double sucker punch to Johnson's hopes. 'Boris understood that the only way he could beat Rishi was to unite the emotional right and the intellectual right,' a Sunak ally observed. The leading light in each of those groups had now backed Sunak. To make matters worse, he had also secured the support of David Frost. 'Boris Johnson will always be a hero for delivering Brexit' but 'we must move on', he tweeted. 'It is simply not right to risk repeating the chaos and confusion of the last year. Let's get behind Rishi.'[4]

Having flown home with just two days to drum up support, Johnson had not had the time to put together a new team, which might have demonstrated that he was serious about doing things differently. His cheerleaders were Jacob Rees-Mogg, Nadine Dorries and James Duddridge, his former PPS, loyal and determined allies, but they had seen little wrong with Johnson 1.0 and were poorly placed to argue that Johnson 2.0 would be different. One ally, told their help was not needed, said, 'People just thought he hadn't learned anything.'

Nigel Adams and Chris Heaton-Harris initially led the whipping operation from the flat they shared in Vauxhall, before moving things to Millbank, where they were joined by Ross Kempsell and Charlotte Owen, with Amanda Milling, Daisy Peck and Emma Dean all helping out. At one point they took a call from Mark Francois, demanding Johnson attend an ERG plenary session the following day where the group could decide who to support. Johnson took the phone and said, 'That's very kind of you but most of the ERG have already signed up to nominate me and I'm not sure it's the best use of my time.'

The final tally for Johnson was 104 MPs, enough to fight on, but his closest confidants were not sure it was enough to ensure the parliamentary party fell in behind him. That morning there was another effort to get Mordaunt to stand aside, but she still insisted he back her. 'We knew she was talking bollocks,' a Johnson ally said.

That Sunday, Adams and Heaton-Harris sat down with Johnson and Kempsell. 'There's good news and bad news,' they said. 'The good news is you're going to be over the line, we've got you there. You're going to be on the ballot. You'll be prime minister by Thursday or Friday,' the trio of aides explained.

Adams delivered the kicker: 'But we think you shouldn't do it.' Heaton-Harris and Kempsell indicated this was the view of them all. Adams continued, 'There's one thing winning and that would be a Lazarus story. And we're with you if you want to do it. But we don't think you should.'

Johnson gave little away, said even less, taking notes of their argument, a felled king writing down the terms of his abdication. 'He would have just been going back into a shitstorm of more colleagues hating him than liked him,' one explained later. 'If we had well over half of the MPs prepared to nominate him, I think we would have gone ahead. It had to be half to stand a chance.' It was Sunak who was getting close to securing half the MPs.

This was Boris Johnson's third serious tilt at the premiership. For the second time in seven years his closest advisers were telling him to give up his dream. Johnson believed passionately in his mandate from the public in 2019, but he also thought: *We aren't there by enough. We are a parliamentary democracy (not a presidency). I don't want it all to happen again. The MPs plainly need to get something out of their system.* Bluntly, he doubted he could command a majority in the Commons. The decision made, Adams said, 'You should probably say it by tonight. You owe it to these people who have worked to get you on the ballot to tell them.'

Johnson began to write his statement, explaining why he was pulling out but, characteristically, even this was chaotic. He joined a Zoom call organised for those who'd pledged to support him, some of them having taken their careers in their hands by doing so, and as Johnson started to talk, Kempsell went into a spiral. The press release was about to drop announcing his withdrawal. 'Ross was worried that Boris wouldn't have told them before the press release dropped. It was very touch and go.' The call did not go well. 'People were crying, a couple of people were angry,' a witness said.

Ben Wallace was furious, as was James Cleverly, who had been foreign secretary for just seven weeks. Fearing exactly this outcome, his aides had urged him not to publicly declare for either candidate until Johnson was on the ballot. With most cause for grievance, Nadhim Zahawi was forced into another of his political pirouettes. At 9 p.m. the *Telegraph* published an article by Zahawi urging the party and the country to 'get ready for Boris 2.0, the man who will make the Tories and Britain great again'. Two minutes later the press release went out declaring that Johnson was abandoning his renewed bid for power.

Johnson had another reason for withdrawing. That afternoon he spoke to one of the most influential figures in the British media about whether their organisation would get behind him or back Sunak. The answer was not what Johnson wanted to hear: 'I don't think now is your time,' came the answer. Just before 8.30 p.m., Nissy Chesterfield took a call from a senior figure at a national newspaper who said, 'Keep an eye out for our copy.'

'What do you mean?' she asked.

'Boris is pulling out.'

Half an hour later Johnson did so, announcing that he had concluded continuing to fight would make it impossible to unite the Tory tribe. 'I think Boris would have won, but at what cost?' one friend said. Kempsell briefed the lobby, 'Boris came to the clear conclusion that the best way of protecting party unity was to support Sunak from outside of government. The national interest was not served by ripping each other's throats out. It's incredibly hard for him to step back from the impulse to win.'

Events had moved with such dizzying speed that Sunak's team were scattered in several locations when Johnson withdrew. Having not had time to make preparations for becoming prime minister this quickly, Booth-Smith began to write a speech for Sunak to give in Downing Street, a process assisted by Danny Finkelstein, the Tory peer and *Times* columnist. They finished it late on Monday night.

Johnson's withdrawal briefly gave life and hope to Mordaunt, whose team tried to line up the newly liberated MPs. But many, seeing the direction of travel, chose to back Sunak instead. The herd was moving again. At 8 a.m. on Monday, Mordaunt had raised her supporter count to 85. By 11 a.m. it was 95, but then the numbers began to fall away as backers such as George Freeman flipped to Sunak and urged others to do the same. Some die-hard Johnson fans were too bruised to consider voting for Mordaunt. 'Rishi really squeezed,' a Mordaunt aide recalled. 'His people were saying, "We can't have another leadership election" but Penny felt very strongly that the membership should have a say.' She also came under pressure from Jake Berry, the party chairman, to stay in the race. He had sold the rights to a leadership debate to raise funds for party coffers. Mordaunt fought on until just before 2 p.m., the deadline to secure the backing of 100 MPs, when she texted Sunak to say she too was pulling out. Her list of backers had, by then, fallen to 90.

Afterwards some were sceptical that Johnson really had the 102 backers needed to get onto the ballot paper. 'There were probably a significant number of them that were not certainties,' a Sunak aide said later. 'If you worked out who the people were who hadn't publicly declared for anyone, it still didn't add up to a hundred. There obviously will have been some people who were bullshitting.' On the Sunday night, after he dropped out, Johnson's team gave their list of MPs to Mordaunt to try to help her over the top. One of her team claimed it included one MP who was listed under her maiden name and her married name. Nigel Adams showed Bob Blackman of the 1922 Committee emails from MPs saying they were nominating Johnson, to confirm that he had the necessary support. 'They had to send an email from a parliamentary email address and they were printed out,' a source said.

Putting down a clear marker that Johnson still had 'unfinished business' in Number 10, a close ally told the *Sunday Times*, 'This has taught him that he can get on the ballot paper if he wants to, that he's got the backing of the membership if he wants it. His email inbox was unmanageable with party members urging him to do it.' Sunak was on notice: trip up and Johnson would try to mount a comeback.

Failure was a long hard fall for Johnson, but it was no less so for Liz Truss, when she left Downing Street to offer her resignation to the King on Tuesday 25 October. By then, Number 10 was a 'ghost ship', just Sophie Jarvis and the newly unsuspended Jason Stein left of her political aides to help the family pack up its belongings. In the final moments before she left for the palace, they were in the Cabinet Room, as Truss lamented the direction of her party: 'The parliamentary party has gone so far to the left, that if we have a spare pound, we spend it on public services, not on tax cuts.' She felt herself 'the only Conservative in the room' a lot of the time. Truss departed to address the nation before driving with her family to Buckingham Palace, leaving behind just three thank you notes for the one hundred Downing Street staff: one for her official spokesman Max Blain, one for her diary secretary and a third for a canteen lady. Few others in the building mourned her passing. 'She had no emotional intelligence whatsoever,' a Number 10 staffer recalled.

Truss drove in a car with her protection team, while her two teenage daughters were in a second government car. 'The moment she ceased to be prime minister, the second car was supposed to be withdrawn because only she was entitled to police protection.' Truss's daughters could have been 'left standing outside the palace,' an ally said. 'It was a fiasco.' Frantic calls were made to the government car service. Eventually sanity prevailed but as an illustration of what failure looks like it was telling.

Rishi Sunak's speech in the street on his return from the palace was more public information film than party political broadcast. Explaining why he was standing in front of the old black door, just seven weeks after losing a leadership election, he cut to the chase: 'I want to pay tribute to my predecessor Liz Truss, she was not wrong to want to improve growth in this country, it is a noble aim. And I admired her restlessness to create change. But some mistakes were made. Not borne of ill will or bad intentions. Quite the opposite, in fact. But mistakes, nonetheless. And I have been elected as leader of my party, and your prime minister, in part, to fix them.' Having dealt with Truss's toxic economic legacy, Sunak addressed the other bull elephant in the room. 'This government will have integrity, professionalism and accountability at every level,' he said. 'Trust is earned. And I will earn yours. I will always be grateful to Boris Johnson for his incredible achievements as prime minister ... I understand too that I have work to do to restore trust after all that has happened.' Sunak pledged to deliver on the 2019 manifesto, answering the claims of Johnson loyalists by saying it was 'not the property of one person'.

Thus began the *Krypton Factor* premiership, in which one of life's geeks set about solving seemingly impossible problems under time pressure. The best part of it was that Sunak was Britain's first non-white prime minister – and almost no one regarded it as remarkable at all.

From the off, though, Sunak's high principles ran headlong into political reality. Within hours his claims to integrity seemed hollow as he reappointed Braverman as home secretary. He had tried to offer her the Ministry of Justice but she stood firm. Ministers, civil servants and political advisers angered by the decision were quick to brief against her, reviving questions about the MI5 leak inquiry. 'She's got a department full of lawyers who don't think she can be trusted with the advice that is given to her,' a senior official said. Political aides dubbed Braverman 'Leaky Sue' but civil servants preferred 'Suella De Vil', after the puppy kidnapper in *101 Dalmatians*. One traumatised official said, 'She's managed to achieve the impossible: making us feel nostalgic about Priti Patel.'

Sunak's cabinet was more balanced across the different factions of the parliamentary party than Johnson's or Truss's. Booth-Smith pushed to install Gillian Keegan at education, the first Tory from a comprehensive to hold the post. Dominic Raab's loyalty was rewarded with justice and the deputy prime minister title. Sunak henchmen Mel Stride, Gavin Williamson and Mr Spreadsheet himself, Grant Shapps, would all attend cabinet. Michael Gove was back at levelling up. But Truss ally Thérèse Coffey also kept a cabinet job along with James Cleverly, who remained at the Foreign Office, and Nadhim Zahawi, despite backing Johnson's abortive comeback. In a break from tradition, Sunak decided to make every reshuffle call himself rather than leaving the hiring and firing of junior ministers to the whips. The cabinet was light on women, but Sunak made Elizabeth Perelman as his principal private secretary, the first woman to hold the post since it was created in 1868. Eleanor Shawcross, who raced back from a holiday to be present for Sunak's arrival in Number 10, would lead the policy unit.

Sunak's team had seen a lot of polling evidence that voters were sick of politics. They planned to get their heads down and stay out of the news, surprising on the upside when they had something to announce. On Sunak's second day in charge, Gove told a roomful of journalists he was 'grateful' that 'after twelve months of turbulence, after a rolling news buffet, an all-you-can eat story extravaganza, that boring is back'.

Sunak and Booth-Smith, now the Downing Street chief of staff, also sought to change the culture in Number 10. In an address to staff, the new prime minister said, 'I'm sorry you've had so much disruption. I know how much that will have affected you all. I want to make people proud to walk through the door.' Booth-Smith set about reversing the upheaval caused by Truss. 'People had PTSD,' he told colleagues. In the first week he found those exiled to the Cabinet Office and told them, 'Return to your old desks.' The press office reoccupied its traditional real estate in Number 12. Having seen his wife excluded from government by the Trussites, the chief of staff made a point of telling Jamie Hope and other special advisers they would be welcome to stay.

At the 1922 Committee and in his first cabinet, Sunak delivered a simple message: 'Unite or die.'

The prime minister set an example, starting work a little after 7 a.m. and going through until 9.30 p.m. or 10 p.m. It helped that nearly everyone in his team had worked in Number 10 before. 'Previous Downing Streets wasted six months peacocking around and fighting each other,' an aide said. 'Everyone knows how it works.' Sunak and his chief of staff also had to fend off ministers who wanted to explain why they had mistakenly backed Truss. Booth-Smith amused himself by saying, 'Don't worry about it. It's totally fine. You were just doing it for your career.'

Sunak delayed the planned Halloween budget until 17 November to give him time, with Jeremy Hunt, to devise an announcement which would set the tone for his premiership. 'That first few weeks was all economy,' an aide recalled.

At 9.30 a.m. on his first Friday in charge, together in the Cabinet Room, their teams went 'line by line' through 104 proposals for saving money or raising tax. Sunak's arrival had gone some way to satisfying the markets. A fall in the cost of borrowing meant the black hole had shrunk to £50 billion, but it still called for the most painful tightening of the public finances since George Osborne became chancellor in 2010. Sunak told Hunt the budget had to be 'fair' and 'honest' with taxpayers about the problems ahead. The chancellor used a Mark Twain aphorism when he addressed cabinet on budget day: 'When in doubt tell the truth. It will confound your enemies and astound your friends.'

Hunt outlined a £55 billion blizzard of tax rises and spending cuts which raised the tax burden to its highest since the Second World War and prompted the Office for Budget Responsibility to warn that living standards would fall by 7 per cent over the next two years, 'wiping out eight years of growth', returning family incomes to 2013 levels. This time, the good news didn't leak: extra money for schools and the NHS. Hunt, cleverly, pushed most of the Whitehall spending cuts to 2025, after the next general election. While taxes would rise by more than £7 billion over the next two years, so would public spending, by £9.4 billion. Economically, the OBR said that would add 1 percentage point to GDP. Politically, it meant that if Labour wanted to boost spending they would have to outline tax rises to pay for it. The newspaper front pages the next morning were brutal, but Sunak's team took comfort that they all sported different grievances. No single issue blew up to derail the whole package.

By then Sunak had also lost Gavin Williamson, who quit as Cabinet Office minister amid claims he sent abusive messages to Wendy Morton, the former chief whip, and told an aide to slit his own throat when he was defence secretary.

The prime minister believed in hard work. But he also tried to make his own luck. On his desk was a bronze statue of Ganesh, the elephant-headed Hindu god who symbolises new beginnings and is seen as a bringer of good fortune. 'Whenever you start something new in life you do a prayer to Ganesh,' Sunak told friends. He would need both hard work and good luck if he was going to solve the next problem in his inbox – finally getting Brexit done.

THE THIRD PROTOCOL
The Windsor Framework
October 2022 to March 2023

'Success is often achieved by those who don't
know that failure is inevitable'

– Coco Chanel

The first decision was whether to try at all. Rishi Sunak had bought a little time with the autumn statement. He and Suella Braverman, the home secretary, were wrestling to devise legislation to deter trafficking gangs from sending more migrants across the Channel. The prime minister did not need to go looking for further problems to solve. However, as November began, it seemed obvious to him and his chief of staff, Liam Booth-Smith, that some problems would 'find him'.

Tensions with Brussels over the Northern Ireland Protocol left the Paleosceptics and the ERG spoiling for a fight. 'It became clear to all of us that this was going to be an issue,' a senior aide recalled. 'They were going to cause trouble. Boris was going to make it a thing. We could dodge and weave and hope you can hold some sort of phony peace until the election.' But Sunak and his team quickly came to the view that the Tory right would keep up a grinding guerrilla war. 'If we're going to have this fight,' Booth-Smith told him, 'the most important thing is we decide when and we decide on what terms.'

The chief of staff set out two requirements for success. Public opinion had to be on the government's side. That meant getting a good deal, but not necessarily everything the ERG wanted. He also demanded 'over-whelming information asymmetry'. They had to keep the talks secret and surprise Eurosceptic MPs on the upside. 'The ERG had a preconceived view of Rishi,' one adviser said. 'They kept saying "There won't be treaty change" or "They won't get anything on sovereignty". They talked themselves in circles.' The time was also right. Both the UK and the EU would go to the polls in 2024. The last chance to make progress would come in 2023. And what no one knew – negotiations had already begun.

The decision to recommence talks with Brussels had been taken under Liz Truss, who reached out to Ursula von der Leyen, the Commission president, during the UN General Assembly in New York, where she also had her first bilateral with Joe Biden. During her brief time in charge, Truss also hosted the Taoiseach Micheál Martin at Chevening. Contact had been initiated by Tim Barrow, now the national security adviser, who got on well with von der Leyen. 'That unlocked the negotiations,' a source said.

Truss was still of the view that she needed to pass the NIP Bill. 'We'd rather you didn't do that,' von der Leyen said. Nevertheless, the meeting was 'very positive', Truss told her team. The decision to engage was held very tightly. Beyond Barrow, the only others in the circle of trust were John Bew, the Ulsterman who ran foreign affairs in Downing Street; Mark Davies, a longstanding civil service negotiator on EU matters; and Simon Millet, the private secretary who covered Brexit. Barrow's main contact was with Stéphanie Riso, von der Leyen's right-hand woman and the key to the 2020 deal.

Those who accompanied Truss to New York denied that Biden leaned on her to resolve the situation before the twenty-fifth anniversary of the Good Friday Agreement in April 2023. But behind the scenes, it was a running sore between the UK and White House staff working for a president who regarded himself as a professional Irishman. At least one senior American diplomat said Brussels should give ground on the implementation of the protocol and the UK should give up the ERG's theological objections to the role of the European Court of Justice in adjudicating problems. He added, 'The problem is her [Truss's] brand is conflict, and what we need is a solution.'

Truss's time as foreign secretary, pushing through the Northern Ireland Protocol Bill, had also left a residue of mistrust in European capitals. An Irish government official described her attachment to the bill as that of 'a mad woman running into the street with a gun'. However, cautious contacts quietly resumed in September 2022. Truss soon became 'very disillusioned by the lack of pragmatism from the EU,' one of her former aides said. 'The negotiations were always about political will, not technical substance – and the political will to compromise from the Commission was never there when Liz [was] leading things.'[1]

When Sunak took over, the problems were the same. Northern Ireland was legally a member of the UK customs union, but practically a member of the EU customs union. The customs border in the Irish Sea, and the sheafs of paperwork which went with it, deterred companies from sending their products to the province. The result was irate unionists.

On 7 November, Sunak met von der Leyen in Sharm el-Sheikh, at COP27. The meeting established trust with the Commission. The strange alchemy of political relationships is under-analysed. Johnson–Varadkar worked where May–Varadkar had not. Johnson–VDL had been a difficult and mutually uncomprehending partnership. In place of Johnson's pugilism and puns, von der Leyen found a man she could do business with. 'She lives in a rural part of Germany and obviously he's in Yorkshire; they bonded over that,' a Downing Street official said. 'Her kids used to ride ponies and Rishi's kids like riding. Von der Leyen's son is studying over here.' Most of all, both leaders had studied at Stanford in California, a formative part of Sunak's identity, an experience about which they both enthused.

Sunak's message, outlined by a close ally, was simple: 'I'm not Boris. I'm not Liz. I think we can get something done here, but you have to recognise the real-world implications of what's happening in Northern Ireland. I can't do it without your help.' In return, he made clear his government would abide by any treaty he signed. Unlike Johnson, Sunak spoke no German, but his aides called it a 'very productive' meeting and saw 'a lot of goodwill' to 'work with us'.

Sunak also had productive talks in Egypt with Emmanuel Macron and Giorgia Meloni, the new prime minister of Italy, who was facing a similar influx of seaborne migrants. She bonded with Sunak over her admiration for Sir Roger Scruton, the late conservative philosopher, who he had pronounced a 'great influence' when working on local government and housing issues. On his flight home, aides urged the now exhausted PM to sleep, but he declared sadly, 'I've not been given the gift of being able to nap.' Instead, he asked for extra papers to read. Sunak continued the charm offensive on 11 November, when he attended the opening of the British–Irish council and met Micheál Martin.

Central to Sunak's plan to fix the protocol were three of the key figures in Truss's circle of trust. Tim Barrow was the front man, the figure with the contacts in Brussels: diplomatic, charismatic and calm. John Bew was the foreign policy expert and proud unionist whose father had been a key player in the Good Friday Agreement. He knew the DUP well, though there was a degree of mutual suspicion between them. Mark Davies would lead the negotiating team. At his side, throughout, was Brendan Threlfall, the leading official on Northern Ireland matters. He and Bew were Cambridge contemporaries where they had both been talented footballers. Colleagues thought Bew was on a redemption mission after his role in the 2019 deal which created the protocol. 'He had guilt from what happened in 2019,' one said. 'He felt he was part of "get Brexit done", at the expense of Northern Ireland unionism, even though he's a North Ireland unionist and voted Remain.'

Sunak also wanted his homework marked by a 'true believer', one who had already shown he had the brains and imagination to be an asset in the negotiating room. Liam Booth-Smith called Oliver Lewis during the first leadership contest in July asking him to meet Sunak's policy team. A little later, Lewis met Sunak and gave him a fifteen-page potted history of the Northern Ireland elements of the Brexit deals plus some thoughts on strategy. The Northern Ireland Protocol Bill was the wrong approach, he said, and Sunak would need to 'engage with the ERG' but that did not mean giving them everything they wanted. 'You can explain a good deal in their terms,' he added, 'as long as you're framing it as Bill Cash would.'

He also delivered a warning: 'If you decide to negotiate with the EU, you are dependent on the EU's goodwill.' Sunak would have to pick one of two approaches, a 'wide but shallow' deal, or focus solely on winning concessions on sovereignty around the role of the European Court of Justice in arbitrating on EU rules being implemented in Northern Ireland – the ERG's biggest bugbear. 'If you do that, you're not going to get anything else,' he said. 'The EU will only go for one or the other.'

Lewis also talked to David Frost, encouraging him to see Sunak. Frost agreed privately that the bill was a problem, but took the view that now it was going through Parliament, the government should not pull it. 'The worst thing you can do is back down,' he said.

Two weeks after Sunak became prime minister, Lewis got another call from Booth-Smith asking him to come in. It was 8 November, the day after the PM's meeting with von der Leyen. The talks were on. Sunak wanted him for 'the Frosty role' but Lewis had a problem. He had created a tech start-up and had promised his investors he would stick with it. To avoid any conflicts of interest, they decided he would not be paid for his work on Brexit, and his appointment would be cleared with both propriety and ethics and ACOBA, the watchdog on appointments. Lewis squared all this with Simon Case, the cabinet secretary, then joined a series of high-level discussions in the Cabinet Office with Barrow, Davies, Threlfall and Lindsay Appleby, Britain's ambassador to the EU. They mapped out options on a whiteboard.

While these preparations went on in secret, a splash in the *Sunday Times* made things worse for the prime minister, quoting a 'senior government source' musing about putting Britain on course for a 'Swiss-style relationship' with the EU. Switzerland had access to the single market through a series of bilateral agreements, which was not remotely Sunak's plan, but the paper highlighted quotes from Jeremy Hunt saying 'unfettered trade' with the EU would be better for growth. Booth-Smith urged Hunt to be more careful: 'You're the chancellor of the exchequer, nothing is off the record. Go and see the prime minister, tell him you said it. Talk to the ERG. Calm them down.' Hunt did so. What might have been a disaster for the nascent negotiations brought prime minister and chancellor closer together. Nonetheless, Sunak had a steeper hill to climb to convince his party he was not planning to sell them down the river. 'That did more than anything to set the ERG on edge,' a source said.

Inside the Commission, Sunak's arrival led to a change in attitude. Von der Leyen and Maroš Šefčovič, the vice president and point man for the UK, were no longer hiding behind their 'mandate'. A Number 10 official said, 'The Commission had degrees of imperial autonomy. They had got themselves legally comfortable with making unilateral decisions. We were dealing with twenty people who we could have relationships with. They had both the scope and the willingness to do something.' An EU negotiator agreed: 'The mandate was whatever we wanted it to be, really.' The failure of Truss's plans for extreme deregulation had also eased fears of mass divergence by Britain. 'They were worried we were going to be

Singapore-on-Thames, and that's clearly not happening,' a former cabinet minister said.

General Lord Ismay, the first head of Nato, had famously joked the alliance's purpose was to 'keep the Russians out, the Americans in and the Germans down'. One official said the new talks were designed to keep 'the Irish out, the Brits and the Commission in, and the French and Germans down'. This time there would be little interference from member states. The absence of Simon Coveney, a fixture in previous Irish governments, was also helpful. 'He always wants to insert himself in everything, in a way that is toxic,' a British source said. David Frost's departure also removed Europe's 'bogeyman'.

In her talks with Sunak, von der Leyen 'had a clear message from the outset that she had no specific attachment to the protocol,' a British negotiator recalled. 'That was a Juncker thing. She had come to the view that their approach hadn't worked, and they were going to have to be flexible in terms of the practicalities on the ground.' The Commission president's priority was to defend the single market, but she could see the protocol was an impediment to that. 'If it's not working, because we were not implementing most of it and they thought we were going to blow the whole thing up', she believed it was better to try a different approach.

The war in Ukraine had also shown that Britain still had a key role to play in Europe. Ukraine 'totally changed everything for her personally,' the negotiator said. 'They actively wanted to get an agreement,' a senior figure in Number 10 agreed. 'They were just waiting for someone they could do business with.' After the first exchanges did not leak, trust began to build. Sunak had shown he was not going to 'tub-thump to try and impress twenty backbenchers'.

Von der Leyen devolved almost total dictatorial power to Riso to do the deal. 'VDL told her to get it done,' a British official recalled. 'VDL said she didn't want anything more to do with it.' Having been absent from Brexit discussions since the Christmas Eve deal nearly two years earlier, Riso made little secret of the fact that she regarded this as a penal deployment before her next big job. However, when the British team sat down in the negotiating room, 'It was the Riso show. She was the Queen,' a British negotiator said. 'She was on her own and exposed throughout the whole thing. You talk human to her and she claps her hands and all the EU drones reprogramme and start moving in directions they previously said were impossible.'

Lewis had said to Sunak he would put his life on hold, 'but you've got to be serious. I'm not going to do it just for bluster so you can then walk out.' Riso's participation gave him the confidence to commit. He told Sunak, 'The fact that Steph is involved means you have a realistic chance of getting them to move. You can't dawdle, she's only there a few months and once she's gone the bureaucrats will just come back in.'

The British team was much less hierarchical. Barrow was the roper, the charmer, talking high-end strategy with Riso. Lindsay Appleby went deeper into the detail. Mark Davies and Brendan Threlfall negotiated word by word, line by line. 'They were exceptional,' a colleague said. Lewis was the wild card, providing political input to the 'core group' and floating from big concept talks with Riso to micro-solution brainstorming with the civil servants. This division of labour occasionally led to tensions but there were no serious arguments and it allowed people to sub in and out on different issues, swapping the roles of good and bad cop. From November to February, the British team were in Brussels two or three days a week, the details held so tight that it was January before anyone really grasped that serious progress had been made.

Before engaging with the EU, Sunak's advisers sat down with the prime minister to ascertain what he wanted. Focusing on the practical problems on the ground, rather than the theoretical issue of EU legal oversight, gave the government a way of responding to the seven tests the DUP had set out the previous year – with the potential prize of a return to power sharing in Belfast. Sunak said, 'I want to go wide. I want to solve the practical, real-world problems that exist in Northern Ireland for businesses.' A senior figure in Downing Street explained, 'We prioritised the DUP over the harder Brexiteer stuff as a conscious choice. The ECJ did not appear on the DUP seven tests and businesses [in Northern Ireland] didn't give a shit.'

Even Lewis, the self-styled 'Brexit nutter', agreed it was not the right time for a row about the ECJ. But he was clear with Sunak: 'We can't come back later and say we want to take back the ECJ.' This was almost certainly the correct approach to achieve practical gains but it would have been political suicide for Sunak if the decision had leaked. Lewis warned Booth-Smith, 'There are going to be a lot of people who scream as a result of what we decided. I'm not going to promise you what I delivered in 2020, which was near uniform Tory approval.' But he added, 'I do think that the chance of kids being blown up by pipe bombs will go down dramatically.' The chief of staff agreed. When the going got tough they reminded each other: 'Remember, we're stopping kids being killed, that's why we're doing it.'

Every negotiation develops its own internal logic. The two sides soon saw themselves engaged in a collective endeavour and did not want to see it derailed. Both sought to get the Americans to butt out. British officials saw a pro-Dublin administration which cared little for the sensibilities of the unionist community – a view reinforced by the almost comically biased appointment, on 19 December, of Joe Kennedy III, Robert F. Kennedy's grandson, as Biden's envoy to Northern Ireland. Officials in London rolled their eyes when Kennedy privately boasted he was 'close to the IRA'. One noted, 'The Americans like to think of themselves as honest brokers, but they are not.'

The Commission told the Americans to ensure that Kennedy confined his role to boosting the economy of Northern Ireland and stayed well out of matters to do with the peace process and the protocol. John Bew conveyed a similar message to a friend in the state department. 'It is not helpful for anyone to make it look like there has been a deal because the Americans told us to do it,' said one negotiator.

The story of every other deal between Britain and the EU was one of dancing around the edges before a brutal trade-off over the key issues at the death. This time the crucial agreement, at least in principle, came first – and it was so secret they kept a lid on it for three months.

The origin of what became known as the 'Stormont Brake' dates from 14 November, exactly a week after Sunak's meeting with von der Leyen in Egypt. While thrashing out ideas on how to improve governance of the treaty, Threlfall suggested, 'Let's attack the pipeline of EU law', which would impose new regulations in the years to come. He proposed Stormont be given the right to disapply new EU regulations, perhaps with a vote in a committee of the Northern Ireland Assembly. Davies did not think the EU would go for it, but Threlfall had only been back on the Brexit beat for a week after twenty months at the Department for Levelling Up. With fresh eyes, he was no longer ground down by years of Brussels rejecting ideas which had merit.

Threlfall and Bew had helped devise the consent mechanism in the October 2019 deal, Johnson and Frost's signature achievement, which gave Stormont the right to vote every four years on whether to continue with the protocol. Since then, the way the protocol was being implemented on the ground had created a new crisis of consent in the unionist community. This, Sunak could argue, was undermining the Good Friday Agreement, the same play which worked for Johnson.

Bew saw the brake idea as a way of killing two birds with one stone. Not only did it deal directly with the issue of consent, it also answered the ERG charge that the protocol was a ratchet for keeping the province perpetually in close regulatory alignment with the EU. 'The brake emerged as an answer to both the fear of divergence and the democratic deficit,' a senior official said. The civil servants believed it was better than anything they could wangle on the ECJ itself. There was another advantage to Threlfall's idea. 'It was easier for the EU to concede something on that, rather than conceding ... an ERG thing on the ECJ.'

Following a discussion with the prime minister, the core group agreed to make the brake their 'big ask'. Tim Barrow went to see Riso to make the pitch. She responded, 'I think we might be able to work with this.' Even more significantly, she revealed, 'We're prepared to do it under section 164', a clause which said the two sides could agree to amend the agreement 'to correct errors, to address omissions or other deficiencies, or to address situations unforeseen when the Agreement was signed'. Until that point the Commission's position was that the protocol itself could not be changed, only the way it was implemented. Now Sunak knew he could get changes to the text, something the ERG believed he would fail to accomplish.

'The sign off on [the brake] came right at the end, but the principle was agreed in November,' a senior figure in Downing Street said. 'It was the first thing we agreed – and no one knew about it.' The agreement was deemed so precious it was not even referred to directly in the talks that followed, except in the loosest terms. 'We didn't talk about it ever again,' a source said. Inside the British government, the Stormont Brake became known as 'Operation Rabbit' since they hoped it would prove to be the rabbit from the hat when Sunak finally showed his hand. There was a WhatsApp group for those in the know called 'Run Rabbit Run' and in-jokes about the 'rampant rabbit'. An official said, 'It is very rare in government that you keep a secret, but that was really significant.'

*   *   *

Oliver Lewis went to Brussels on 11 December for one-on-one talks with Stéphanie Riso, his primary goal to reassure her. 'We do actually want to do a deal,' he said. 'We're not stringing you along. The prime minister is serious, he is not a continuation of what you have seen up until now. But we are going to need you to move.'

Riso, in turn, made clear that Britain needed to drop the Northern Ireland Protocol (NIP) Bill. As Lewis had predicted, Brussels saw the new bill as a wrecking device, not an attempt at leverage. 'Obviously there is nothing we can work with here,' she said. 'You're going to have to just withdraw this. This is just a slap in the face.'

There were practical difficulties with the NIP Bill, quite apart from the widespread view that it was a breach of international law. It was stuck in the House of Lords, where ninety-two amendments had been tabled by opponents. Overturning them and ramming it through would take a huge amount of political capital. The day Lewis met Riso, the *Sunday Times* splashed on news the bill was 'on ice until the new year'.

Sunak's near-pathological desire for secrecy had echoes of Theresa May's approach to Brexit. The talks were designated 'a national security issue,' a source revealed, 'which helps culturally' in Whitehall to preserve secrets. But unlike May, Sunak kept his key ministers in the loop. Chris Heaton-Harris, a former ERG chairman and Northern Ireland secretary, was brought into the circle of trust, along with the foreign secretary, James Cleverly, another Brexiteer. While Heaton-Harris worked on getting power sharing back in Belfast, Cleverly dealt with Maroš Šefčovič on day-to-day Northern Ireland matters and quickly showed he was not interested in public grandstanding. 'The relationship with Maroš improved massively when we agreed not to carry out a running commentary,' a British official said.[2]

Heaton-Harris's deputy was Steve Baker, the man who had done more than any other to lead the ERG into battle. By 2022 he was a changed man. The Brexit wars had been a bruising experience for Baker, a deeply moral person, who had found it hard to reconcile the brutalist political tactics he used to pursue his deeply held views on Brexit with his Christian beliefs. When he took his second ministerial position, he made a public apology to the Irish for the way his political activities contributed to the bitter divisions over Brexit. 'I caused a great deal of inconvenience and pain and difficulty,' he said. 'Some of our actions were not very respectful of Ireland's legitimate interests. I want to put that right.' Micheál Martin called it 'honest and very, very helpful'.

Baker wanted to make a positive contribution. But he also warned both Downing Street and EU diplomats in London that the ERG would require movement on the ECJ to back any deal. 'Just because Mark Francois is not shouting about the ECJ does not mean this has gone away,' he told the German ambassador in London. Sunak and his team did not tell Baker everything, but Booth-Smith talked him through aspects of the plan and asked for ideas. On more than one occasion, the prime minister briefed Baker in the secure bunker in the basement of Downing Street. Sunak also brought back Jonathan Caine, the Tory point man with Ulster since John Major's day as a minister of state.

Just before Christmas, domestic politics and the talks collided over the issue of border control posts (BCPs). In talks with Barrow at the British residence in Brussels, Riso pointed out the UK had failed to build a single BCP, a requirement of the protocol. Even the NIP Bill included plans for red and green customs lanes, which required control posts for the red lane. Riso's irritation flared: 'You claim you're being honest with us yet there are no BCPs. We are getting roasted by our guys who ask, "Why are you falling for these tricks once again. They claim they've changed, but they're not even building things from two years ago."'

The following day Davies and Threlfall warned Lewis, 'We've got a real issue here.' Lewis told Riso he would resolve the problem, but for several days it stalled when Baker tried to veto BCPs, leading Bew to intervene. The government quietly laid a statutory instrument to create what were euphemistically referred to as 'SPS huts', where checks could be made on animal and plant material entering Northern Ireland. An EU official remarked, 'I don't care what they are called as long as bricks are put on top of other bricks.' When senior ERG figures found out border posts were to be built, some went apoplectic, demanding the passage of the NIP Bill to stop this outrage – until Lewis pointed out that their beloved bill also required them.

Sunak's team had also established a covert back channel to the DUP, which it suited neither side to advertise. 'There'd been long-standing engagement, which no one knew about,' a senior Number 10 official said. Bew, Threlfall and Davies were the point men. Bew's grandmother's house was near DUP headquarters, allowing a degree of covert contact.

The DUP leadership 'were sending us documents that were extraordinarily generous interpretations of the seven tests,' a negotiator said. 'You could do anything for them to be complied with. We had the seven tests printed out, everyone had the seven tests in their bundles.'

By the end of the first week in January 2023, Rishi Sunak had been prime minister for ten weeks. He had succeeded in calming the markets and stopped the precipitous collapse in Tory support, but his low-key style had yet to deliver anything notable and he was already looking over his shoulder. That week, Boris Johnson was honoured with a dinner at the Carlton Club, where he unveiled a new portrait, a rite of passage for all ex-prime ministers. In the same week Lord Greenhalgh, an old City Hall hand, said Johnson would 'return' to Number 10 by the end of the year.

That same week, there was helpful mood music from Dublin. Leo Varadkar – who had now returned as Irish prime minister – told reporters he would be 'flexible and reasonable' and admitted, 'When we designed the protocol, when it was originally negotiated, perhaps it was a little bit too strict.'

The talks remained under the radar, held in the EU's nearby language school instead of the Berlaymont. 'They cleared out the first floor,' a British negotiator said. 'That's where we did the talks, in classrooms.' The rooms were off an atrium. 'Nearly every fucking night they had massive parties,' said a member of the British team. 'From 8 p.m., people were trolleyed, loud and dancing to Queen and ABBA. On one occasion there were a whole bunch of people in Leprechaun costumes, smoking outside, as we marched out in our suits.' The British negotiators took over several meeting rooms in the basement of their embassy, where officials were told to keep quiet about their presence.

The British team argued their demands were real world issues on the ground, while the Commission's were simply theoretical risks to the single market. The EU negotiators insisted their concerns were also practical, pointing to UK imports of oranges from South America, where citrus black spot disease was found. EU officials argued that if an infected orange was taken to Seville, it could destroy the entire Spanish crop. Commission officials complained that apples carrying EU food labels were being sent into Northern Ireland in parcels, bypassing customs checks. Lewis and Sunak agreed Britain could tolerate greater controls when the EU could demonstrate a credible threat of 'disease or pestilence', as long as the legislation was drafted in such a way that the UK always had ultimate sovereignty.

One day Riso and Lewis found themselves in a corridor together drinking coffee and began exchanging war stories. 'It didn't dawn on me until three or four weeks after the vote that Northern Ireland was going to be a huge issue,' she admitted. Lewis let slip a fascinating historical footnote – what might have been if Boris Johnson and Vote Leave had taken charge in 2016. He and Richard 'Ricardo' Howell, the legal wizard who advised Vote Leave on treaty law, had devised a plan. 'We came up with a whole bunch of ideas on how you could solve Northern Ireland by taking the old treaty clauses the EU used to solve trade between West and East Germany back in the 1950s and 1960s. For matters of trade, it was continued internal trade. We would have taken that and copied it over for North and South in Ireland.'

Riso said, 'Oh, you guys actually did have a plan then.'

The first public acknowledgement that serious progress was being made came on 9 January, when Cleverly and Šefčovič announced, at Lancaster House in London, that a deal had been done on data sharing. Britain had developed a computer system to monitor the flow of goods into Northern Ireland from Great Britain. It showed that EU concerns about these consignments bleeding into the Republic and threatening the integrity of the single market were unfounded. EU technical experts examined the computer system – a rare triumph of government IT – and requested twenty-two changes to improve the scope and speed of the data. They needed 'real-time' access, also a better search facility. British officials insisted the EU could have agreed this by mid-2022 but had been dragging their feet. In a statement, the two sides agreed that access to the UK's data system was 'a critical prerequisite to building trust'.

Cleverly had much better relations with Šefčovič than Truss, a personal warmth aided by a mutual love of *Yes Minister*. Brexit deals tended to be founded on the kind of linguistic circumlocutions and fudge that made Sir Humphrey Appleby Britain's favourite fictional mandarin.

Both sides had worked on the same red lane/green lane idea – trusted traders, who regularly sent goods into Northern Ireland, could use a green lane where they were monitored but there were no checks. Others

would have to go through a red lane. The two sides used different termi-
nology, however. The Commission's negotiating team on customs, led by
Richard Szostak, referred to 'express lanes'. An EU official admitted they
scrapped the name 'green lanes' on the grounds that using the colour of
the Irish Republic and Sinn Féin might alienate the orange half of the
population. This was bizarrely revealing of the Commission's ignorance
about what actually irked unionists.

Progress was encouraging but both sides downplayed the imminence
of a final deal, resisting media clamour to confirm they were in the fabled
'tunnel'. The Downing Street comms team insisted it was just 'a scoping
exercise'. In Number 10, they were worried the talks might yet collapse.
Asked later if there were moments when it looked like this was happening, one negotiator said, 'All the fucking time.'

The politics on both sides of the Irish Sea was still toxic. When
Cleverly visited Belfast on 11 January, he became embroiled in a row with
Sinn Féin over whether the party leader Mary Lou McDonald had been
banned from the meeting. The Foreign Office pointed out that Michelle
O'Neill, Sinn Féin's leader in Northern Ireland, was invited, but claimed
McDonald 'invited herself'. To complicate things, the foreign secretary
had not yet met Micheál Martin, now the Irish foreign minister, who had
done a job swap with Varadkar at Christmas. It would have been a breach
of protocol to meet a member of the official opposition before him. Thus
protocol thwarted progress on the protocol.

The situation was exacerbated by a trip to Belfast the following day by
Keir Starmer, who made a point of meeting McDonald. The Labour
leader offered his support to Sunak to pass a deal in the Commons, but
he could not resist a dig, branding the prime minister weak in the face of
the ERG, 'a Brexit purity cult which can never be satisfied'. This irritated
even civil servants, who believed it would make it far more difficult for
Sunak to secure a deal and sell it to MPs.

Under the radar, the British negotiating team had made two further
advances. The first was to get the EU to accept that the deal was underpinned by the Vienna Convention, which had put in black and white
how international treaties should be interpreted. In the EU, when
member states said a treaty was incompatible with the convention, the
ECJ ruled that EU law, not international law, should prevail. It was a
hobbyhorse of Bill Cash and other Paleosceptics. In trade deals with third
countries, the Vienna Convention was supposed to hold sway, but the

EU was reluctant to concede this to the first country ever to leave. In one session, a British negotiator said, it was 'three hours of [Riso] just effing and blinding at us: "I'll never agree to this, I know exactly what you people are doing, you're just going for the ECJ. The reason we're here is because you fucking promised me nothing on the ECJ. I told you again and again the ECJ is the alfa and omega to us. I'm not touching it, fucking bastards."' Eventually it was agreed.

The second advance was that the negotiating team succeeded in minimising the role of the ECJ by reducing the number of areas over which the court might be asked to make a judgment, a side of the deal which, even when announced, Number 10 did little to trumpet. 'We were exempting huge swathes of EU law from Northern Ireland so the ECJ's remit doesn't apply,' a negotiator said. The protocol operated on the basis that businesses sending goods into Northern Ireland had to comply with EU rules on products that might enter the Republic, with no checks on North–South movements. The new deal changed that. Goods complying with UK standards could now enter Northern Ireland and some North–South checks were put in place, including market surveillance on goods labels. While this was not exactly border posts, it showed that the idea of an open border on the island of Ireland could be more flexible than the EU had insisted throughout the May and Johnson years. This was kept even more hush-hush. 'They told us, we could not specifically advertise this point,' a British source said.

When Britain's negotiating team returned to London on Thursday 19 January they were upbeat that the basis of a deal was in place. Mark Davies, the lead negotiator, told a colleague, 'I've been working on this since 2017 and it finally feels like we have cracked it.' One official sat down in the bar of the Corinthia Hotel in Westminster that day and said, 'We have a deal.' At the same time, European Commission sources briefed EU member state officials – including the Irish – that a 'framework deal' had been thrashed out. The customs arrangements were basically finalised, but some of the legal text was being refined. There was no complete text but, as a negotiator put it, 'We had drafts, there were papers going around. The contours were very much there.'

Downing Street put up a wall of silence, flatly denying to journalists that there was anything close to a deal, as Sunak examined the papers. The paralysis was made worse by the absence of Booth-Smith on his honeymoon. At this point, the prime minister became spooked by noises emanating from the ERG about the need for movement on the ECJ. Sunak wanted more. A negotiator said, 'He'd become worried about the fact there was so little of substance on the ECJ. They did flap a bit.' This was not just, in the eyes of those in talks, unrealistic, it was also going back on what the PM had asked them to do. 'January 25th was when it went South,' the official said.

MPs suggested that companies found to have breached the terms of the red and green lanes could have their infraction proceedings heard first in a Northern Irish court, rather than face legal action from the EU. Lewis had to explain that the treaty stated the ECJ was the 'sole and final arbiter' of questions on EU law. Others called for the protocol to be scrapped altogether and disputes to be settled by the independent arbitrator set up as part of the Trade and Commerce Agreement (TCA). The problem was, the protocol was not about free trade, it was designed to keep the border open. The legal advice was that a trade arbitration panel was not the appropriate body. Lewis warned Sunak that by delaying he risked the good bits of the deal being unpicked. 'You're not going to get anything on the ECJ,' he said. 'Entropy is our enemy here because you're negotiating with a small number of people in the Commission. The longer you leave it, the more chance the rats elsewhere in the Commission or the Council will get to it. We will lose stuff as a result.'

Riso took a firm line, arguing that the plan had been to deal with practical, not theoretical, difficulties and the role of the court was not something raised by businesses in Northern Ireland. Szostak was even more implacable. Brussels, he argued, could not be seen to water down the role of the ECJ at a time when the EU had grave concerns about democratic governance in Poland and Hungary.

Sunak's other push was to broaden the range of goods going into Northern Ireland that were exempt from EU regulations. The EU had already agreed this could apply to food. 'If you can exempt foods why can't other goods come into British standards with labelling?' the negotiating team pushed. 'The EU were just flat out rejecting it,' one said.

Riso played the practical card again. 'The whole reason we're talking about food is that obviously food is an issue,' she said. 'It's pork pies and sausages. The queues, the lorries, we can't deny it's a problem. But you can't name a single good where you have deviated from EU standards that you can't get into Northern Ireland. It's a theoretical problem.' She added, 'Also, you can't name a single good where your plan is to drop standards. Name me one example where you need this exemption from our regime. It's done to placate the ERG. This isn't a real-world issue and we're here to solve real-world issues.' Without specific examples, Downing Street was effectively asking for blanket exemptions from EU law, desirable, but at this point not negotiable.

For more than a week, the talks were deadlocked as Sunak pondered. A details man to the point of obsession, he buried himself in the small print. Ever since November he had been demanding detailed briefings on every conceivable aspect of the talks, to a degree which drained the team in Brussels. 'He'd say, "Make it a three-pager", but some were twenty pages because he wanted all the detail,' one said. At one point Lewis went to the PM and urged him to set 'five key objectives' for this phase and then 'trust your team to deliver'. Sunak gave them twenty goals. 'I'll take that as a win,' Lewis joked. Sunak told his team he wanted to run the negotiation like a budget. Unlike a budget, however, this was not simply a case of manipulating data and figures – the enemy had a vote. Sunak's rationalisations could be rejected by the EU. It was as if the budget red book had come alive and started arguing back.

A week later Riso arrived in London. 'The PM wanted to meet her,' an aide said. Their conversation barely touched on the deal. 'He got into a theoretical debate with Riso about the future of subsidies and the state aid regime. We all left saying, "What was the point of that?" But it convinced them that we meant to engage. She was worried he'd got cold feet because he was spooked by the ERG.'

Confident he was still serious, von der Leyen agreed to speak directly to Sunak, who had effectively appointed himself chief negotiator. A senior figure recalled, 'Rishi went after every single piece he could on customs.' He managed to increase the threshold at which companies would automatically be allowed to use the green lanes, insisting on a figure of £2 million of annual turnover, a benchmark the Commission accepted. 'He pushed stuff on fucking pet passports,' another incredulous adviser said. Sunak's advocacy ensured that pet owners in Great Britain with microchipped animals could sign up for a lifetime travel document, available online in minutes, or tick a box when booking a flight or ferry.

Such micro-managing frustrated cabinet ministers and senior officials. As one civil servant put it, 'Rishi is yet to understand that he can't be secretary of state for every department.' But it was refreshing for most

of those involved in the talks to see a prime minister who fully understood the deal he was negotiating and who was taking personal ownership
of its success. 'He was very different to Boris,' said one who had worked
for both, 'he knew the details inside out and backwards, not only the
high-level concepts but line by line the individual percentage tariffs.'

However, Sunak's attitude did concern some officials, who believed
he was missing an opportunity to announce the deal and seal a win,
before the DUP and ERG could mobilise. To chivvy the prime minister
along, some began to speak to journalists, heightening the fears in
Number 10 that Riso and von der Leyen would get cold feet. 'The leaks
began hampering our ability to keep the integrity of it all together,' a
senior figure said. 'We were trying to get the last two or three things that
really mattered, that only Rish could unlock, and stuff was potentially
falling off the other side of the table.' The stress was beginning to tell on
Sunak. 'That was a dark cloud hanging over him,' a long-standing
adviser recalled. 'He was getting quite stressed about the politics and
landing it.'

On 9 February, at Ditchley Park, a country house used by the Foreign
Office, a cross-party group which included Michael Gove and shadow
foreign secretary David Lammy gathered for a two-day summit to discuss
'How can we make Brexit work better with our neighbours in Europe?',
in the company of diplomats, defence experts and bankers. Details were
leaked to the *Observer* that weekend.[3] Other Brexiteers present included
Michael Howard, Norman Lamont and Gisela Stuart. Peter Mandelson
and David Lidington attended from the Remain camp. Oliver Robbins
and Tom Scholar represented civil service alumni and a host of other
academic and think tank 'experts' were also invited.

Central to the discussion was how a Tory or Labour government could
use a review of the TCA in 2025 to reduce barriers to trade and how to
resolve the protocol impasse. A discussion document said Brexit was
'acting as a drag on our growth and inhibiting the UK's potential'. Gove
was very 'honest' about the problems, according to attendees, but argued
leaving would still prove the right decision in the long run.

While opponents of Brexit seized on the participation of senior
Brexiteers as evidence that even they admitted Brexit was damaging, the
exercise was seen in Number 10 as a useful distraction. Concerned that
details of the Stormont Brake would leak, a Downing Street official said,

'We put all the Brexit cottage industry up at Ditchley to stop people feeding them. We cut them out. That was an active choice.'

Bew, Davies and Threlfall continued to talk to the DUP. Sunak had also had private meetings with Jeffrey Donaldson, the party leader. With crunch point approaching, the PM needed to know whether the DUP would back the deal. At 4 p.m. on 16 February, the team in Belfast reported back on their progress. It was scleroticly slow. 'You've got an eight-part agenda,' an exasperated Sunak said. 'You're on part two and you've been there for six hours.' Then: 'I'm coming.'

The prime minister was due in Belfast the following day to meet the leaders of all the main parties in Northern Ireland. Those on the ground tried to dissuade him from arriving early. Sunak was having none of it. 'Get the plane!' He turned to Booth-Smith: 'Get your overnight bag. I need you to come with me. We need to sort these people out.'

Accompanied by Heaton-Harris and key aides, Sunak flew to Belfast and by 8 p.m. they had set up a secure office in the five star Culloden Hotel. Booth-Smith called Bew and Threlfall, who were still with the DUP. 'The prime minister is here,' he said. The reply came, 'We know. It's all over the news.'

'Come to us,' Booth-Smith said, a message relayed to the DUP contingent, who were reluctant. 'It's too much pressure, too much heat,' was the reply. 'Fine, we'll come to you,' the chief of staff said. That, Donaldson believed, was even worse. 'We should meet tomorrow,' he told Bew. Booth-Smith called Timothy Johnston, the DUP's chief executive, who was with Donaldson. He was polite but firm. 'The prime minister is here. He's come to Northern Ireland. He's requested to speak with your party leader and your party leader is refusing to meet. Is that true?'

'No, no, no. That's not true. You need to understand this is a highly tense situation.'

'Well, he's your prime minister and he's here asking to speak to your political leaders, to try and solve a problem to do with a part of our country together, and you don't want to meet because you're worried about some press cameras and your party.' Turning the thumbscrews, Booth-Smith went on, 'You either want to solve the problem or not', then he hung up. Johnston was a tough figure, blooded in years of hardscrabble Ulster politics. He felt a little bad about playing hardball. The chief of staff waited five minutes before calling back and saying Sunak wanted to speak to Donaldson. 'Jeffrey, I'm here, I want to talk to you and your party. You told me that this is really important. We're trying to solve an issue for Northern Ireland. Then you refuse to meet me. Why?'

Donaldson expressed concern about the television and press cameras. 'I've just got to this hotel and I'm a prime minister and there's not a single camera outside,' Sunak said. 'I'm looking out the window. I can get you here.' It was 9.30 p.m. Sunak sent his police security detail to collect Donaldson and his team. The protection squad bundled the DUP into a van and drove them to a rear door of the hotel, away from the media. 'They found a discreet entrance and smuggled them in under the cover of darkness,' a British source recalled.

There followed five hours of talks that encapsulated the experience of four prime ministers in dealing with the Democratic Unionists, a highly charged encounter blending cold-eyed logic and high emotion, in which political styles, pragmatism and ideology, clashed. In addition to Booth-Smith, Heaton-Harris, Bew and Threlfall, Sunak was accompanied by political secretary James Forsyth and press secretary Nissy Chesterfield. Donaldson brought Johnston, MP Gavin Robinson and Emma Little-Pengelly, a member of the Northern Ireland Assembly.

The first round of talks did not begin until 10.30 p.m. and lasted until fifteen minutes past midnight. Sunak took the DUP through what had been agreed in 'granular' detail. Some in the room thought Donaldson and his colleagues 'seemed pleasantly surprised' by what they heard but talks which began 'friendly and respectful' turned 'quite frank' as Sunak sought to put the DUP on the spot. The prime minister was a practical, goal-driven politician. The people sitting opposite him were more experienced at saying what they could not support, rather than what they would. The clash of styles led to friction and frayed tempers on both sides. A source who was briefed by the DUP delegation said, 'The PM patronised and talked down to them. He read out his deal and seemed very proud of himself for what he had done. He was very much telling them what was happening rather than opening up a discussion.'

Gavin Robinson was incensed by a briefing in the media, which he assumed came from Number 10, that Sunak had satisfied all seven of the DUP's tests. In fact, these briefings had emerged from civil servants in Whitehall, who could not understand why Downing Street was not putting public pressure on the DUP. 'He should have got out there weeks earlier,' one official said. 'The handling was appalling.' Robinson pulled out his phone and waved it at Sunak. 'You can't just come to Belfast and treat us this way,' he complained. Sunak's aides understood. 'They lived through thirty years of domestic terrorism,' one said. 'Many of them have friends and family members who died or have been mutilated. For them it's much more visceral.'

Sunak was frustrated too, however. 'It was very testy, but always respectful,' a Downing Street official recalled. 'They didn't like that we just turned up and made them have a meeting that they didn't want to have and forced their hand. But no progress would have been made otherwise.'

'What do you need to go back into power sharing?' the prime minister said to Donaldson. 'I could have just pushed this off, avoided all the pain, zero risk to me. I'm doing this because I want to help Northern Ireland. So what do you need? What are your problems? Just be very clear, speak very plainly, very directly.'

Donaldson danced around the issues, refusing to be pinned down. 'They couldn't speak clearly or plainly,' a Number 10 witness said. 'They didn't really know what they wanted.' Another added, 'He went fast for them. It was unsettling for them.'

Sunak continued to press for answers. A list began to emerge of DUP asks, Booth-Smith and Forsyth acting as stenographers. The British team had hinted at the Stormont Brake, suggesting some sort of democratic brake might be possible, but claimed it would be difficult. One of the DUP team admitted, 'If you get a veto on EU law, that's got the wow factor. We need a wow factor.' Knowing he was getting closer, Sunak said, 'Find me a printer. Get me a printer now!' It was 2 a.m. Booth-Smith went downstairs and liberated a printer from the hotel lobby, took it back upstairs, then typed up the list of asks, printing one for Sunak, one for Donaldson. 'Right, let's read it now,' the prime minister said. Addressing Donaldson, the PM asked, 'If we get these things, you are going to get back in. Is that correct?'

The DUP leader squirmed again. 'For five minutes Jeffrey found every way humanly possible to try and not say "yes", but the PM wouldn't stop asking the same question,' a Sunak aide said. 'And then Jeffrey said, "Yes, okay, we'll go back in." At that point we thought they were in play.' The same witness later admitted, 'Everyone has massive optimism bias.'

The prime minister did not get to bed until 2.45 a.m. Most of his team got three hours' sleep. They were up again at dawn. Sunak had another long day, meeting the leaders of the Northern Ireland parties. He was having a fasting day. 'He drank a lot of tea,' an aide said. They fed the others shortbread and Battenberg cake. Doug Beattie of the Ulster Unionists emerged saying he did not expect a deal for weeks. Sinn Féin's Mary Lou McDonald talked of 'significant progress'. Donaldson made the kind of warm noises Sunak had hoped for, telling reporters, 'Progress has been made across a range of issues' and he was 'hopeful' agreement could be reached.

The following Tuesday, 21 February, Donaldson addressed the ERG, praising Sunak for making progress, particularly on the green lanes, but added, 'The protocol is like an anchor attached to the good ship UK, trying to drag us back.' He said Sunak had told him he believed the final deal would fulfil all seven of the DUP's tests. But asked by Jacob Rees-Mogg to mark Sunak's homework, Donaldson said the PM had satisfied him on just 'three or four' of the tests. He said he was 'pleasantly surprised' at the areas where the EU had moved but Donaldson stressed he had not seen any legal text. He was upset that EU law was not disapplied on goods made in Northern Ireland even if they were sold into the UK market. Donaldson also confirmed the worst fears of the sovereignty purists in the ERG, that 'any dispute still has the ECJ' involved. It was the first detail most of the MPs had heard.

The next day, Sam Coates of Sky News revealed the UK had banked another win. In future, Westminster, not Brussels, would set VAT rates, taxation and state aid policy in Northern Ireland. It was an area where Sunak, as a former chancellor, personally fought for more.

The other key gain from Sunak's second offensive was one of the last things agreed – access to Northern Ireland for medicines approved only by British drug watchdogs, rather than the European Medicines Agency, which maintained control under the protocol. The heroine of the hour was Cara Phillips, Oliver Lewis's former aide who had smuggled Riso to the British delegation room in 2020. In a meeting with Riso, Phillips piped up, 'You do realise medicines degrade with time.' The threat to the single market of drugs from Great Britain entering the Republic was diminished if they had a limited shelf life, a point Riso grasped immediately: 'It's like food, it is perishable.' What had seemed an intractable issue was resolved in a few days. Riso understood how it would look to block Sunak's demand. 'Steph freaked when she realised vital medicines were not getting into Northern Ireland,' a British source said. 'It was a disastrous look for them.'

For all the gains and the goodwill, by 23 February it was clear that Sunak was likely to find himself at odds with Boris Johnson. He declared the NIP Bill 'the best way forwards'. Johnson said, 'It fixes all the problems. It solves the problems that we have in the Irish Sea, solves the problems of paperwork, VAT and so on. So I'd go with that.' In Whitehall there was irritation. 'Boris is being a bloody nuisance, winding up the DUP,' an official said. Two days earlier, Robert Buckland, Johnson's former lord chancellor, cornered him in the Commons chamber to point out that the bill did not remove the oversight role of the ECJ, it simply gave ministers the right to disapply it. He also suggested that doing a deal was a good way to cement relations with the Biden White House. Johnson replied, 'Fuck the Americans!' The land of his birth joined business, Northern Ireland and special advisers as recipients of this epithet. His spokesman called it 'a jocular conversation'.

Sunak and his team began to prepare the ground with opinion formers on the right. Bew and Booth-Smith worked on David Frost, and the chief of staff also talked to Bill Cash. Some in the ERG took a harder line even than the DUP. While Donaldson's red line was that EU regulations should not be imposed on Northern Ireland without democratic consent, ERG chairman Mark Francois said he wanted 'EU law expunged from Northern Ireland'. Simon Clarke said the same.

Booth-Smith also had conversations with Bernard Jenkin, in which the Paleosceptic grandee made the point that if Britain imposed its own rules in Northern Ireland, the EU would retaliate with tariffs. 'That would also happen with the protocol bill,' Booth-Smith said. 'That's just how global trade works.' Jenkin said the ECJ would decide whether Britain had broken the rules. 'That is categorically not true,' Booth-Smith said. The ECJ's role was to adjudicate on points of EU law, not decide on whether a treaty had been violated, which was a role for the TCA arbitration panel. He told colleagues, 'There's no point trying to convince people who don't want to be convinced.'

On Friday 24 February, rumour was rife in Westminster that the deal could be signed imminently. Ursula von der Leyen would shake hands with Sunak at Windsor and then meet Charles III. The Commission president, a fan of the King, was on a private visit to the UK to see her son, a student at Oxford. When the news broke, the Eurosceptic right pronounced it a disgrace which would embroil the monarchy in politics. Jacob Rees-Mogg complained about 'constitutional impropriety'. Those who were outraged had been comfortable with Elizabeth II being dragged into prorogation (Rees-Mogg was one of the embroilers) while those who saw no issue had been horrified by Johnson's activities in 2019 – Brexit making monkeys of everyone, again.

By Saturday morning, Sunak was ready to publicly make the case for what he was doing, summoning the author and Caroline Wheeler, the political editor of the *Sunday Times*, to a dawn interview in Number 10. Sunak hinted at the Stormont Brake: 'I want to correct the democratic deficit because sovereignty is really important, and that's why the idea that the EU can impose laws on Northern Ireland without them having a say isn't acceptable.' Facing down his critics, he added, 'I'm a Conservative, I'm a Brexiteer and I'm a unionist – and anything that we do will tick all of those boxes, otherwise it wouldn't make sense to me, let alone anyone else. I voted for Brexit, I believe in Brexit but this is about this unfinished business on Brexit.'

In a parallel operation, details of the legal advice presented to Boris Johnson about the NIP Bill were also leaked, making the case that disapplying aspects of the protocol under the 'auspices of necessity' could only provide 'temporary justification' and was not the end-state solution the hardliners desired. 'There would be a high likelihood the EU would challenge this argument in international arbitration' and that 'the UK would have to pay reparations to the EU, even in arbitration' should Brussels take out infraction proceedings. The killer line was a direct quote from the full legal advice. In those circumstances, 'the UK would have an international law obligation under the [Withdrawal Agreement] to comply with any ruling' of the ECJ. A Whitehall official explained, 'Even with the bill passed into law, it could still be subject to the ECJ.' This ran a coach and horses through the ERG's position. Sunak added, 'The bill definitely helped create the environment for these talks to happen. But the [Johnson] government also consistently said, when it introduced the bill, that a negotiated settlement would be preferable.'

Officials were withering about the ERG demand for the bill to be pushed through anyway. 'If we do this, the EU has made it very clear it will stop talking to us about this or anything else. We can wave goodbye to cooperation over small boats and it will stop talking about anything apart from national security.'

That Saturday, Sunak also met Steve Baker and took him through the deal. The following day Booth-Smith parked Baker in his office in Number 10 with a pot of coffee and the full text. 'My office is yours all day,' the chief of staff said. 'Read it. Take your time. Any questions, let us know.' Baker went away satisfied, a foretaste of how a lot of MPs reacted. 'He wanted it to be over,' said a Number 10 official. 'That was the overriding feeling outside a group of fifteen true believers who wanted the war to never end and another twenty or thirty more who wanted to find any reason to vote against because they didn't like the PM. The overwhelming feeling, was: "If it's anywhere near half good, make the madness stop, make it go away."'

The Irish government was also informed of the plans that weekend, a full week after the DUP. A Downing Street source said, 'We thought the Irish would massively oppose it so we didn't tell them until five minutes to midnight.' To the joy of Bew and others, Tony Connelly, the reporter whose scoops from Irish officials had disrupted previous Brexit deals, was absent covering the war in Ukraine.

Those who did not get special handling raged at the prime minister's refusal to take them into his confidence. None was more irritated than Boris Johnson, whose allies wound him up about the disrespect Sunak had shown him. 'If they drop a text on us, this is going to go very badly for them,' one Johnsonite fumed. Sunak told the *Sunday Times*, 'People will always want to know every single detail, but ultimately you can't conduct a very complicated negotiation in public.'

On the morning the deal was announced, Monday 26 February, Sunak called Johnson in person and talked him through it. 'This is what I'm going to do …' He did not ask for Johnson's support, since it was clear it would not be forthcoming. Some ERG members wanted Johnson to swallow his pride and back what was clearly better than the deals he had signed. 'Rishi seems to have done quite well in improving Boris's deal,' said one red wall MP. 'I hope Boris helps complete what he started. It's better for his legacy if he does.' He would be disappointed.

The prime minister also tried, in vain, to call Liz Truss. The Downing Street switchboard is renowned for being able to contact almost anyone in the world. 'Even Switch couldn't get hold of her,' a Number 10 source revealed. Truss, it seemed, did not want to be reached.

At cabinet that morning, held virtually, Sunak thanked Heaton-Harris and Cleverly for their hard work. 'We've secured what many said was impossible: making legally binding changes to the Protocol Treaty itself,' he said, hailing the Stormont Brake as a 'powerful new mechanism'. Ministers lined up to praise him. Heaton-Harris said it made Northern Ireland a 'hugely attractive place to run a business'.

Politically, the two most important contributions, ones which were, unusually, both flagged up in the cabinet readout emailed to the lobby, came from Suella Braverman and her successor as attorney general, Victoria Prentis. 'The home secretary congratulated the prime minister and highlighted the new Stormont Brake as an important measure to help safeguard sovereignty,' the statement recorded. Sunak had briefed Braverman in person that morning and – despite making performative noises about resignation in the days beforehand – she felt obliged to support him. The readout went on, 'The attorney general welcomed the agreement, saying it was a permanent solution which was binding and subject to international law. She said the Northern Ireland Protocol Bill was not a permanent solution and would still leave the jurisdiction of the European Court of Justice unaffected in international law. She added that the legal basis for the Bill, the doctrine of necessity, had now fallen away thanks to the successful negotiation of the agreement.' In a few sentences, Braverman, the trickiest cabinet minister, was handcuffed to the deal and the leaked legal advice was confirmed.

At 3.30 p.m., Sunak and von der Leyen appeared for a press conference at a hotel in Windsor. 'We have made a decisive breakthrough,' Sunak said. 'Together we have changed the original protocol and are today announcing the new Windsor framework.' It was important for Sunak to portray it as a new legal text. After the backstop deal and the Northern Ireland Protocol, this was in effect the Third Protocol, one negotiated with the same secrecy as Frederick Forsyth's fourth.

The effect of Sunak's personal diplomacy was clear when a reporter asked von der Leyen why he had succeeded where his 'three predecessors had failed'. Matthew Parris, the *Times* columnist, wrote that she 'glanced shyly at the British prime minister and murmured that "we have so much in common" … Eyes modestly cast down and looking quite a catch, Rishi Sunak replied that this was "not about me" – and glanced back at the demure blonde at the other lectern. Electricity flowed.'[4]

Just before 5 p.m. the government published a twenty-seven-page document on the Windsor Framework, a five-page political declaration agreed by both sides and the seventy-four-page legal text. It was now clear how the Stormont Brake would work. If and when the Northern Ireland executive and assembly were restored, the brake could be triggered on the same basis as the so-called 'petition of concern' which was already embedded in the Good Friday Agreement. That stipulated that a concern could be raised by 30 members of the 90-strong assembly from at least two parties. At that time the DUP held 25 seats. The paperwork showed the brake 'will not be available for trivial reasons: there must be something "significantly" different about a new rule, whether in its content or scope, and [Members of the Legislative Assembly] will need to show that the rule has a "significant impact specific to everyday life" that is liable to persist'. It could be used for a whole new law or a limited part of one. Unlike the petition of concern, which required a cross-party confirmatory vote, the Stormont Brake would be triggered automatically and the new rule suspended immediately. It could then only be applied in Northern Ireland if the UK and EU both agreed in the joint committee, giving the UK a permanent veto. 'This new safeguard in the treaty is not subject to ECJ oversight, and any dispute on this issue would be resolved through subsequent independent arbitration according to international, not EU, law.'

At 6.30 p.m., Sunak got to his feet in the Commons to explain the deal. He praised von der Leyen and 'my predecessors for laying the groundwork for today's agreement', a contribution which sparked gales of laughter. Explaining the details, the prime minister said the only checks in the green lane would be 'those required to stop smugglers and criminals'. Goods from Northern Ireland to Great Britain would no longer require export declarations and would now be 'completely unfettered trade'. All this 'permanently removes the border in the Irish sea', he claimed, which was over-egging things.

Sunak spent some time on the most toxic area, the movement of food. 'Instead of hundreds of certificates, lorries will make one simple, digital declaration to confirm that goods will remain in Northern Ireland. Visual inspections will be cut from 100 per cent now to just 5 per cent. Physical checks and tests will be scrapped, unless we suspect fraud, smuggling or disease.' To reassure the EU that food imports would not go into the Republic, high-risk products would be labelled 'not for EU', while 'the ban on British products like sausages entering Northern Ireland has now been scrapped. If it is available on supermarket shelves in Great Britain, then it will be available on supermarket shelves in Northern Ireland.'

On parcels, Sunak said, 'If the protocol was fully implemented, every single parcel travelling between Great Britain and Northern Ireland would be subject to full international customs. You would have needed a long, complex form to send ... even a birthday present ... and you could only have shopped online from retailers willing to deal with all that bureaucracy ... Today's agreement fixes all of this.'

Sunak then hailed the changes to medicines, pet passports, VAT and state aid, pointing out that just 2 per cent of UK subsidies would need EU approval and they could only complain if subsidies had 'a real, genuine and material impact on Northern Ireland's trade with the EU', a much higher threshold than under the protocol. Agriculture and fish would no longer fall under the common agricultural and common fisheries policies. A plant passport scheme would prevent a repeat of the ban on oak trees, which upset unionists during the Platinum Jubilee.

Turning to the key issue of sovereignty, on which his most implacable opponents would judge him, Sunak claimed that 1,700 pages of EU law had been scrapped altogether and that just 3 per cent of EU law would apply in Northern Ireland. 'Some members of this House, whose voices I deeply respect, say that EU laws should have no role whatsoever in Northern Ireland,' he said. 'I understand that view and I am sympathetic to it, but for as long as the people of Northern Ireland continue to support their businesses having privileged access to the EU market, and if we want to avoid a hard border between Northern Ireland and Ireland, as we all do, there will be some role for EU law.' That, then, was the pragmatist's argument against the absolutist sovereignty-first position. Sunak also praised Bill Cash for 'his support' in negotiating the underpinning of the Vienna Convention. Addressing the DUP, he urged them to take their time to study the deal but stressed, 'I have kept the concerns raised by the elected representatives of Unionism at the forefront of my mind.'

The prime minister concluded by trying to slay the NIP Bill once and for all. 'As I and my predecessors always said, the Bill was only ever meant to be a last resort ... Now that we have persuaded the EU to rewrite fundamentally the treaty text of the protocol, we have a new and better option. The Windsor Framework delivers a decisively better outcome than the Bill, achieving what ... the Bill does not offer. It permanently removes any sense of a border in the Irish Sea. It gives us control over dynamic alignment, through the Stormont Brake, beyond what the Bill promised. The Bill did not change a thing in international law, keeping the jurisdiction of the European Court of Justice and leaving us open to months, maybe years, of uncertainty, disruption and legal challenge.'

Sunak won clear backing from Keir Starmer. The Labour leader told MPs, 'I have been clear for some time that if the prime minister were to get agreement with the EU and if that agreement is in the interests of this country and Northern Ireland then Labour would support it. And we will stick to our word ... When the prime minister puts this deal forward for a vote, Labour will vote for it.' His only harsh words were reserved for Boris Johnson. 'We must be honest, this comes with trade-offs. The Member for Uxbridge and South Ruislip told the people of Northern Ireland that his protocol meant "no forms, no checks, no barriers of any kind" on goods crossing the Irish Sea after Brexit. That was nonsense.'

Most MPs took a positive view of the deal. Michael Gove, who had been kept in the dark, declared himself 'pleasantly surprised' by the ground the EU had given. Number 10 was even more pleased when David Davis, the former Brexit secretary, said, 'It has got pretty much everything Boris was trying to get with the so-called protocol bill but without effectively going into civil war with the European Union.'

That evening, Steve Baker, Davis's old DExEU colleague, gave an emotional interview to *Newsnight* in which he said the Windsor Framework 'bookends a seven-year chapter of my life which I'll be glad to close'. He revealed, 'Seven years of this cost me my mental health. In November 2021, I had a major mental health crisis, anxiety and depression, I couldn't go on ... Holding these tigers by the tail – Brexit, Covid recovery group, net zero scrutiny group – all took its toll ... The way I've led rebellions, no one should have to do.' Baker had been the pivotal figure of backbench dissent for half a decade. 'This is an important moment for me personally,' he explained. 'Because I can authentically say, "He's done it."' Baker called Windsor 'an amazing achievement' and 'an incredible opportunity' to 'move beyond this awful populism we've suffered'. To his former ERG brethren, he pleaded, 'Just be sensible and grown up, do the right thing ... You bet I'm emotional.'[5]

Freed from the firm grip of their handler, the tigers of the ERG showed little sign of wanting to abandon the fight which had defined their careers – but they also showed little of the organisation which had come from

Baker. It would take the ERG's star chamber of legal experts three weeks to deliver a verdict, in which time Sunak and his team succeeded in winning over the vast majority of Conservative MPs.

Some hardliners were quick out of the box to condemn the deal. By 6 p.m. Ian Paisley Jr had announced that it provided no basis for the DUP to go back into government and declared the Stormont Brake was 'in the boot of the car under the spare wheel and impossible to reach'. Jim Allister, leader of Traditional Unionist Voice, which had been leeching votes from the DUP with an even more hardline approach, announced, 'Effectively the protocol stays and all that has gone is the government's protocol bill.' Others seized on the Commission's statement that the Stormont Brake would only apply as 'a last resort' and in 'the most exceptional circumstances', taking EU spin as holy writ in a manner they had long condemned in others.

Jeffrey Donaldson, however, reserved his party's position. 'We continue to have some concerns,' the DUP leader told the BBC. 'We will examine the legal text, we will look at all of this in the round and come to a decision … We are reasonable people but we want to ensure that what the prime minister has said is matched by what is actually in the agreement.'

David Frost embodied the disappointed fatalism of much of the Brexiteer right. In a piece for the *Telegraph*, published on the evening of the 28th, he argued the deal 'should go ahead', acknowledging that there was much that was 'worth having' and that it would make the protocol 'easier to operate', but concluding it was 'a bitter pill to swallow' because the government was 'still only partly sovereign over all its territory'. Frost paid a backhanded compliment to Downing Street by calling the deal 'oversold', not something of which the May government could ever have been accused when promoting its own deals.

Of the 1,700 pages of EU law that had been 'disapplied' in Northern Ireland, Frost wrote, 'In fact, what has happened is that the EU says it will pass a law itself (it hasn't yet) setting the conditions under which UK-standard food and drink may move from Great Britain to Northern Ireland. In this Kafkaesque world, "disapplication" of EU law is actually a new EU law.'[6] A Number 10 official noted, 'There was a little bit in him just a bit upset because people were a bit shitty about *his* deal.' Frost's article did not get much pick-up in England, but was front-page news in Belfast, making it harder to convince the DUP.

Reflecting later, Frost's objection was that Sunak portrayed Windsor as a definitive settlement, rather than a step along the road. 'I think they were quite mendacious,' he said. He saw commitments to consult the EU about changes to regulations in Great Britain to avoid unnecessary divergence as a device to 'hold GB in alignment in certain areas'.

Two days later, Thursday 2 March, the prime minister and more than two hundred Conservative MPs were back in Windsor, for a Tory away day in the hotel where the deal was signed. Sunak urged MPs to help bring an end to the Tory 'psychodrama'. Theresa May was present, Liz Truss and Boris Johnson were not. The star turn, however, was Andrew Strauss, the former England cricket captain who took a divided team and made them into world beaters. He told MPs a good team environment 'provides you with a lifeboat' to pull together. 'If the team environment is not good, then all you have is eleven heads bobbing up and down in an ocean of fear and self interest.' If the allegory for their own fate was not clear enough to the MPs, Strauss went on, 'Teams, whether they be sports teams or corporate teams or, dare I say it, political teams, are inherently dysfunctional. People have their own individual goals and ambitions and fears and insecurities. It is therefore up to the leaders of these teams to shake people out of their natural self-protection mode and get them motivated by something that isn't in their own limited self-interest.' Isaac Levido delivered a similar sermon, explaining that voters were sick of seeing a divided Tory Party.

At 'the exact same moment', Johnson got to his feet in Westminster to give a paid-for speech denouncing the Windsor Framework, declaring that Sunak's Brexit deal would act as a 'drag anchor' on post-Brexit freedoms, tying the UK to EU regulations, crushing efforts to innovate and diverge, and that he would find it 'very difficult' to vote for it. He called for the government to 'have the guts' to 'deploy' the NIP Bill again.

On 20 March, two days before the Windsor Framework was to be put to a vote in the Commons, the DUP finally said they would be voting 'no', despite the belief of Sunak and the negotiating team that they had met all seven of the DUP's tests. 'We assumed that if you solve the problems in the seven tests, the DUP would be on board,' said one government source. Senior DUP figures expressed irritation that this view was widely communicated to journalists long before they, the true arbiters, had seen any legal text. Sunak's team also misread the significance the DUP put on the tests, which had been drawn up eighteen months earlier in a different political environment. Many were vague. 'If we'd known they were going to assume this level of importance we would have rewritten them and sharpened them,' said one senior DUP figure.

Peter Kyle, Labour's spokesman on Northern Ireland, thought the government had only themselves to blame. 'The DUP were raising concerns about the protocol quite soon after the deal was delivered in 2020 and they were ignored,' he said. 'By the summer [of 2021], they were quite stridently saying that they had problems. They were ignored. Then they pulled out of the executive in February [2022]. In the months between February and the May elections for Stormont, they didn't have a single meeting with the prime minister and not a single statement to the House of Commons. Imagine if the Scottish Parliament or the Welsh Senedd had collapsed and there'd been no statement to the House of Commons. Then, they refused to appoint a speaker, and everything grinds to a halt, and Boris Johnson visits. If you act functionally within Stormont, you're ignored. Act dysfunctionally, and the prime minister gets on a jet and flies over to meet you. It's a complete perversion of how politics should work.'

There was always a strong possibility they would say 'no', the word most associated with the DUP since the days of Ian Paisley Sr. 'The PM knew these guys didn't even back the Good Friday Agreement,' a close aide pointed out. 'All he really wanted was that they did not reject it out of hand.' Donaldson did not rush to judgement. But as the aide observed, 'We gave them every opportunity to take "yes" for an answer and they still decided not to.'

For a methodical English politician like Sunak, the DUP's stance seemed not just unreasonable but counter-productive to their own political ends. In only ever rejecting what others put before them, they denied themselves the chance to shape their own world. The Stormont Brake only had power if the DUP went back into government. By dogmatically demanding an end to all EU law in the province, by clinging to a pure past which had never existed, they were giving up the ability to block new EU rules and regulations. 'They don't have a strategy,' a Number 10 adviser said. 'It's like they're fighting over who gets to be emperor during the last days of Rome. History will continue. They should be a part of that.'

The day after the DUP said no, 21 March, the ERG's star chamber of lawyers issued their ruling. At 133 pages, it was nearly twice as long as the legal text of the deal. On the one hand it was devastating for Sunak, rubbishing his negotiation as near worthless in some regards and worse than the protocol in others. On the other hand, it was such a hatchet job, which made no attempt to welcome even the bits the DUP liked, that it failed to capture the mood of either the country or the Commons.

ERG chairman Mark Francois emerged from a conclave in Portcullis House and read out a statement in which he quoted himself by name in the third person, intoning, 'The star chamber's principal findings are: that EU law will still be supreme in Northern Ireland; the rights of its people under the 1800 Act of Union are not restored; the green lane is not really a green lane at all; the Stormont Brake is "practically useless", and the Framework itself has no exit, other than through a highly complex legal process.' Had such a verdict been delivered in the forty-eight hours after the deal was signed, it might have had an impact. Published when a relieved Parliament seemed ready to embrace the Windsor Framework, it seemed like the bellow of a group of Lears raging at the dying of the light. A Sunak ally said, 'The fact that the ERG could find nothing positive to say about any of it did not help them.'

The star chamber took issue even with the name. 'Claims this amounts to a new framework or structure are not correct,' they wrote, asserting that it 'makes only limited legal changes' to the protocol. 'At most there has been "keyhole" surgery within the scope of these laws.' Keyhole surgery, of course, can be life-saving.

On the Stormont Brake, the complaint was that it covered 'a limited range' of EU laws relating to goods and not those on state aid, tax and customs. A 'good faith' threshold had to be cleared otherwise 'adjudicators could find against the UK and reapply the law'. Far from celebrating the end of the ratchet of EU law in the province, the ERG spied the potential for more alignment. 'In practice the Windsor deal will incentivise the UK and its future governments to copy future EU rules, and adjustments to existing rules, so as to avoid the imposition of new checks across the Irish Sea,' they concluded.

Finally, Northern Ireland continuing to receive 'different treatment under a treaty with a foreign power' meant they would not trade on the same terms as the rest of the UK. Pretty much every business group in the province had celebrated Northern Ireland's inclusion in both the UK and EU markets. 'The best of both worlds,' Sunak argued on a visit to Belfast. To the ERG this was a problem.

The anger of the ERG was sincerely held. But once again what was pure principle and consistent ideology was bad politics and it contributed to a sense that they had missed their moment. The growing view among MPs, voiced by one Brexiteer was this: 'No one cares what the ERG thinks any more.'

A leading figure on the Eurosceptic right, privy to ERG WhatsApp exchanges, said that, as the group shrank, it had been radicalised by researchers like Christopher Howarth. 'Whenever anything happened they'd say, "It's conspiracy, they're lying, they're cheating us, only the bill will do,"' the MP said. Howarth, the ERG man who had paid the key trip to Michael Spicer's deathbed in 2019,[7] was so attached to the view that the Paleosceptics, not Vote Leave, won the 2016 referendum, he even claimed Dominic Cummings was not in charge of the campaign. Now, he claimed that the Stormont Brake would 'never be used'.

Those involved in the talks with Brussels insisted the ERG had misunderstood the significance of the brake. 'It would be used nearly every week,' one official said. 'It's very hard to complain about the imposition of laws when you have the power to stop it, but you refused to exercise it.' Another negotiator said, 'There's no dynamic alignment. There's some sensible cooperation, but with sovereignty clauses', on 'table food stuffs' such as oranges, where the EU feared contaminated fruit entering their market. 'Otherwise, there were absolutely no obligations.'

The whips won over some Brexiteers by pointing out that the EU had conceded that membership of the single market did not require standardised rules. 'Suddenly, you have an actor in a single market who can operate to lighter, less stringent regulation,' a Downing Street source said. 'Imagine that happening twenty times a year for ten years.' Time would gradually cleave Northern Ireland away from the EU market.

The whips held their nerve ahead of the big vote, even when, the night before, word reached them of a drinks do being held by Liz Truss, a 'gathering of the clans' for the right. Johnson is said to have attended. One of those present called it an attempt to coordinate opposition. But a 'temperature check' by the whips found that even close allies of the two ex-prime ministers were planning to back Sunak.

Since the Stormont Brake required a statutory instrument to be passed, the government decided to confine the vote just to the brake, rather than the entire deal, and granted only a ninety-minute debate. This was cynical and ruthless, but there was little fuss from MPs. 'The whipping operation was much more about making sure that everyone understood it,' a Number 10 official said. 'Normally you want to squeeze people down and fuck them over.' For the hold-outs there were always 'a few well-placed slips' so people could be absent. Chris Heaton-Harris, who had the double distinction of being a former chief whip and a former ERG chairman, told his Brexiteer colleagues, 'If we'd been offered this three years ago, we would have bitten their arms off.'

The main drama on the day, Wednesday 22 March, was created by Downing Street's scheduling of the vote slap bang in the middle of Boris Johnson's marathon cross examination by the Privileges Committee on whether he had lied to the Commons about partygate. It effectively made the point that Sunak was fixing problems while the predecessor who had helped create them remained mired in controversy. The signature moment came when the hearing was suspended so Johnson could leave to vote against the Stormont Brake. His decision had little influence on others. Two aspects of the deal irked him: first, the fact that goods manufactured in Northern Ireland would still have to meet EU regulations; second, the small print of the deal which some saw as making it more difficult for the UK as a whole to diverge from EU rules. 'Windsor won't really fix the problems,' he said. 'It will still be hard to get stuff into Northern Ireland.' The bigger issue, he told allies, was that he was 'burned' by his experience of negotiating what he thought were fair and flexible deals in 2019 and 2020 – only to find that the EU took, what he considered, a too literal interpretation of their provisions. He told one confidant, 'The fatal mistake was leaving them with the power to decide how to operate that deal. The Windsor Framework looks better, but the problem is that authority is retained by the EU.'

Even close allies thought Johnson should not have let himself become isolated with the hardliners. 'He could have stayed out of it,' Eddie Lister said. 'The Windsor Framework – that was what we wanted. I remember having long conversations with the head of HMRC about having a red lane and a green lane. If we could have got that in 2019, it would've been so different. It was a hell of a breakthrough for Rishi to get it. My simple view was, on the one hand, you've got civil war in Ireland. On the other hand, you've got a trade war with Europe. Whatever you get in between those two things is good.'

While Sunak was exploiting the collective desire in Tory ranks to 'get Brexit done', the man who had made the phrase famous seemed to have forgotten its unifying power. When Johnson walked through the No lobby at 2.21 p.m., he found just 21 other Tory MPs and seven from the DUP.[8] The rebels included three former Tory leaders – Johnson, Truss and Iain Duncan Smith – but just 12 of the original 28 Spartans.

On the other side of the House, Sunak positioned himself at the entrance to the Yes lobby and shook the hand of all 515 MPs who voted for the deal. It was something he had done before on budget votes as chancellor to thank his Tory colleagues, but this time meant shaking the hands of opposition MPs too, including Keir Starmer. Those backing the brake included Labour, the Lib Dems, the SNP, Plaid Cymru, the Green Party, plus the SDLP and Alliance parties from Northern Ireland and nine independents. Among the 282 Tory hands he shook were eight of the Spartans: Steve Baker, John Baron, Suella Braverman, Marcus Fysh, Philip Hollobone, Ranil Jayawardena, Julia Lopez and Lee Rowley. 'That vote was a collector's item in all the Brexit votes,' an ally said. 'It was the first time there had been real cross-party support for anything. This is Rishi's party now.' It was all downhill from there.

When the result was in, Sunak returned to 10 Downing Street. Liam Booth-Smith was at his desk outside the prime minister's study when he got back. 'How many?' he asked.

'Twenty-two,' the chief of staff replied. Sunak just gave a nod. Then he gave Booth-Smith a hug.

While Johnson entered the second hour of his evidence session, Sunak went down to the Number 10 garden for an impromptu game of cricket. He was clean bowled by an eight-year-old from the Ace academy for aspiring black cricketers. Sunak later described it as one of the rare enjoyable moments of his premiership. He talked to the youngsters about his favourite players, who included Michael Atherton and Rahul Dravid, careful players who got their heads down, a sporting metaphor for the style of leadership which had secured the Windsor Framework. Watching from the sidelines was another cricket fan with a taste for dour players – Theresa May, whose hero was Geoffrey Boycott. She turned to Booth-Smith and said simply, 'Well done,' then carried on watching the game. 'She looked very happy,' a witness said.

Sunak's one unlikely cricketing hero was the maverick, flamboyant and priapic Shane Warne, a match-winning weapon who delighted the fans and drove his captains mad – the cricketing equivalent of Johnson. Some in the Tory Party hoped the two men could find a way of working together. Those around Sunak just wanted to ensure Johnson never returned as skipper. In Johnson's old paper, the *Daily Telegraph*, Camilla Tominey pronounced the last rites: 'The cults of Boris and Brexit are simultaneously imploding.' This was premature, of course, but it was a week for symbolism.

Perhaps the most poignant moment came on Friday 24th when Steve Baker began removing names from the ERG WhatsApp group, destroying the weapon he had wielded against successive prime ministers. Iain Duncan Smith called him irrational before he, too, was kicked out.[9]

The Windsor Agreement was not the end of Brexit but after seven years of turmoil, it was a rare example of successful political operations. The difficulty for Sunak was that many of the problems which had caused Brexit (including a cost of living crisis that made people feel left behind) and many of the problems caused *by* Brexit (economic sluggishness among them) were unresolved. The psychodrama which gripped the Conservative Party was not over and the man who made Brexit happen still had the ability to steal the limelight.

As he wrestled with these problems over the next year, Sunak's premiership spiralled into the same crisis of leadership which had derailed his three predecessors, until he reached a point where, eight years after the referendum, SW1 was obsessed again with David Cameron, Boris Johnson, uncontrolled immigration and yet another plot to oust a sitting prime minister. It left Sunak with nowhere to go but to present his credentials to a vengeful electorate, with consequences that were predictably catastrophic for him and his party.

'THE JUDDERING CLIMAX'

Boris, Rishi, Dom and the Pivot

November 2022 to November 2023

'Operation Juddering Climax is coming
to its final shuddering surge'

– Boris Johnson, May 2016

Afterwards, when Rishi Sunak's team wondered where his premiership went wrong, several of them pointed to the incident with the soup.

It was Saturday 3 December 2022, and he had been prime minister for less than six weeks. Sunak's close aides – Liam Booth-Smith, the chief of staff, and Dougie Smith, the veteran of the dark arts, among them – pushed for a proper sit-down with his team to work out a political strategy to win the next general election. Sunak's aides envisaged an intense weekend at Chequers with an overnight stay, with presentations on polling and messaging and a proper discussion with a whiteboard to map out their immediate priorities and long-term goals.

Sunak had no interest in such an exercise. He believed in governing quietly and competently, not in selling a vision of Ronald Reagan's 'shining city on a hill' to the electorate. Pressed, he told one minister, 'I can run a bloody government, right?' as if that was enough. 'Right' was a verbal tick of Sunak's, demanding affirmation for things he thought should be obvious to others, the word spoken with a rising inflection that was pure California. 'He was not keen,' one adviser said.

Even close cabinet allies were frustrated by his outlook. 'Rishi is a fundamentally very decent man, a very hard-working man, and somebody who, for good or ill, I thought had the capability to lead the country,' one said. 'But, on the flip side, he never really owned a vision for the country, or believed the vision thing was that important. He felt he could delegate that, but a leader has to own the vision. He always thought that was bullshit. He felt that meetings like that were a waste of his time.' After twelve years of turbulent Tory rule, Sunak, a keen cricketer, had come to the crease at the tail end of a limited overs game, many wickets down and many runs to chase. But he seemed determined to play like a test match batsman, content to occupy the crease, rather than focus on the target and chase it hard to win.

Eventually, Sunak agreed to invite some of his team to Chequers, but only for the day. When they arrived, armed police kept them waiting for half an hour in the walled gravel car park outside. 'He's not ready yet,' a protection squad officer said. This was particularly embarrassing for Oliver Dowden, whose Cabinet Office role meant he was chairman of the Chequers Trust, which ran the grace and favour property.

When they were finally admitted, there was 'no apology' from Sunak, who seemed in an 'off mood'. Upstairs in the dining room, the main event was a presentation by Isaac Levido, who Booth-Smith had been instrumental in re-hiring as the election campaign director. Polling data, showing the Tories on course for just 170 seats, was presented by Joe Slater of Stack Data Strategy, a firm spun out of Hanbury Strategy, run by Tory veterans Paul Stephenson and Ameet Gill, both of whom were also present. 'Basically, people were enraged and had really switched off us,' said another aide present.

Levido gave a PowerPoint presentation outlining the mood of voters: 'I quite like Rishi. He seems competent and the right man for the job right now – even if I don't like how he got it. And Keir Starmer is a bit bland – he wouldn't be terrible, but he doesn't fill me with confidence. But I'm sick of politics and arguments – I don't want to think about it right now. I just want to see progress on the issues that affect my life. And the next election is two years away, so I don't need to make a decision now.' This last bit was in red and underlined. 'So I'm going to wait and see if Rishi does a good job. And then I will decide who to vote for.' Levido urged Sunak to focus on delivery. In his mind, this was a combination of two things: a tried and tested technique and a new reality. The former was to echo the 'long-term economic plan' which David Cameron and George Osborne had peddled under Lynton Crosby's tutelage. Post-Covid, the public expected accountability – they wanted to look online and see whether the government was making progress towards its goals, just as they had with testing or the vaccine rollout. 'Come up with five or six priorities,' Levido said. He suggested targets on inflation, debt and growth, plus NHS waiting lists and immigration. He also proposed a sixth, 'education?', since it was one of Sunak's passions. 'Ultimately, this is a matter for you,' he told the PM. 'It's got to be true to you, and you've got to have confidence about the deliverability of most of them before you put your neck on the line.'

'Makes sense,' the prime minister said.

Levido gave a very clear warning about the mountain that lay ahead. In his 'key takeaways' he concluded, 'Economic management is all we have. Performance/delivery is the only thing that matters to voters. They are not going to engage, so we should not expect any significant recovery in headline vote next year.' The last bit was a message he repeated to cabinet and to Conservative MPs. To many of those present, this was common sense, but some found the presentation 'underwhelming' and 'low energy', a problem exacerbated by Sunak's impatience. Some (Dowden and Smith among them) thought this too convenient an argument for Levido to advance. 'Dougie thought we were being "managed" by consultants who wanted to be paid for twelve months without getting any results,' one witness said.

Things got worse when they broke for lunch. 'Okay, guys,' said Sunak, 'thanks for coming.' They were dismissed. An incredulous Smith, exhibiting signs of being 'hangry', complained, 'You're not going to give us any food?'

Sunak grumpily relented and, after an awkward wait, bowls of soup were eventually produced. Theresa May had attracted ridicule for serving her team with a bland concoction of chicken lasagne and boiled potatoes during a Chequers meeting ahead of the 2017 election, but this was another level of horror for a trencherman like Smith. 'I couldn't even tell what flavour it was,' another participant admitted. The real problem was that the meeting itself was thin gruel, politically, but the 'soupgate' summit became notorious.

'We needed a vision and a narrative for the public of where he wanted to take the country,' said one Tory strategist. Another veteran said, 'We needed to sit down for a couple of days with a white board and work out a strategy to get us to the election. He had no interest in it. He seemed irritated that people were trying to pin him down. He just thought if he governed competently the public would see him as a responsible guy they can trust.'

Levido flew home to Australia for Christmas. The first he knew of what Sunak had decided was the day before he told the country.

Colleagues said Dougie Smith was already irritated that he was not consulted by Sunak about the appointment of Amber de Botton, the ITV political producer who had masterminded the broadcaster's coverage of partygate, as director of communications. 'Dougie went nuts,' a witness recalled, since Smith did not regard her as a Conservative and wanted his old friend Robbie Gibb to return to the role he had held under Theresa May. Booth-Smith had pressed for de Botton's appointment, leaving Nissy Chesterfield to continue as press secretary. He also brought in Eleanor Shawcross, a veteran Tory adviser to George Osborne, as head of policy and persuaded Will Tanner, a veteran of Theresa May's Number 10, to return as his deputy. Booth-Smith knew the government's predicament demanded an extreme level of political creativity. He wasn't sure he could provide that and run Number 10. He persuaded Sunak to see Dominic Cummings. The Vote Leave man was toxic for Tory MPs. The meeting was off the books in Booth-Smith's flat in Pimlico, just the three of them. Most of Downing Street had no idea it had taken place for another year.

Sunak outlined his steady-as-she-goes approach to the economy. Cummings told him it would be 'a complete disaster'. He said, 'You just had Boris and Truss create this utter shitshow. You've got to have an emergency budget early in the new year, and you've got to say that Boris's tax rises in quarter three 2021 were wrong and should never have happened, that you disagree with them, and that we should never have broken a manifesto pledge.' Sunak was raking in income tax by freezing thresholds, but Cummings said, 'We should do the opposite. We should increase the 40 per cent income tax threshold to 100 grand and take millions of people out of the 40 per cent tax bracket.'

The government was in a pay dispute with the junior doctors and nurses. The junior doctors wanted a 35 per cent rise. Cummings told Sunak to settle the strikes 'immediately' and 'make rebuilding the NHS one of your core two or three priorities that everyone can see week in, week out, you're working on. Make a huge national effort in the spirit of the vaccine taskforce.'

He also told the prime minister to withdraw from the European Convention on Human Rights (ECHR) so he could tackle illegal migration. Cummings outlined his proposals in a short memo. 'This is Dom, so there was two-thirds of a page of things he would do and then five pages of things he wanted,' a source said. Cummings explained, 'I said I was only prepared to build a political machine to smash Labour and win the election if he would commit to Number 10 truly prioritising the most critical things, like the scandal of nuclear weapons infrastructure, natural and engineered pandemics, the scandal of MoD procurement, AI and other technological capabilities, and the broken core government institutions which we started fixing in 2020 but Boris abandoned.'

Sunak listened but afterwards he did not have the stomach for Cummings' proposals. 'The parliamentary party was in an absolutely horrific state,' an ally recalled. 'He thought it would drive a coach and horses through our attempt to try and bring everyone together.' Booth-Smith disagreed but accepted the decision. He, de Botton and Dougie Smith all believed Sunak needed to 'index for the voters, not the MPs' in drawing up his priorities, while Forsyth and Rupert Yorke, whose job it was to interact with MPs, understandably focused on the mood in the parliamentary party.

In common with Suella Braverman, the home secretary, Smith believed that to stop the boats and make the Rwanda policy work, Sunak had to be more radical in derogating from the ECHR in asylum cases. That meant passing legislation containing notwithstanding clauses like those used in the Northern Ireland Protocol Bill – but just as Sunak was trying to negotiate them out of existence with Brussels.

To those in the maximalist camp, Sunak's appointments of Victoria Prentis as his attorney general and Alex Chalk as justice secretary were emblematic of the PM's caution. As AG, Braverman's position on parliamentary sovereignty and its supremacy to international law made her and her successor, Michael Ellis, 'our flexible friends', one of the hardliners joked, ready to give 'legal top cover' to political decisions. Prentis, by contrast, was passionate about Britain's international legal obligations. 'I think he gave her the job as a human shield,' an ally of Braverman concluded later, 'to protect himself from having to make any difficult decisions.' Angry about the Prentis and de Botton appointments and Sunak's offhand approach at Chequers, Smith vowed to have it out with the PM, demanding a meeting where he could press his views one final time. Sunak received Smith, along with Dowden and Booth-Smith, in his study one evening. The chief of staff ordered pizza. 'Dougie just let rip,' a witness said: 'Do not rule out derogating or notwithstanding clauses ... You're not going to win unless you go in this direction ... Do not delude yourself that you're going to solve it any other way.' Sunak responded with a detailed legal analysis, quoting James Eadie, the Treasury solicitor. 'Enough!' Smith erupted. He had helped Sunak for years because he regarded him as good 'horse flesh', as he liked to describe political talent. But the racehorse no longer wanted a trainer. 'Dougie did his thing and told him what he thought,' a witness said. 'Rishi reacted very negatively to it, more negatively than I'd ever seen him react.' Another said, 'He totally lost his rag.'

The prime minister was enraged, out of his seat, up and at Smith, finger pointing, grievances once internalised, now flowing. 'You know what? You and Olive betrayed me!' Sunak shouted, referring to the leadership contest. 'You walked away from me. Once it became clear I wasn't going to win, you both went on holiday!' This was true in so far as it went, but both had cancelled family holidays to help out until there was no point working fourteen hours a day. The die was cast. Smith kept his Number 10 pass, but he was seldom seen in meetings with Sunak after that. The confrontation was a lesson for the prime minister's other aides in how little he relished robust challenge.

Having achieved little at Chequers, Booth-Smith called a meeting of senior staff in the Thatcher study, upstairs at Number 10, just before Christmas. Sixteen political aides attended, including Smith, de Botton and Shawcross. 'We need to step it up a gear,' he said. On a whiteboard they mapped out Labour's vulnerabilities, Sunak's opportunities and possible announcements for the government grid. 'This was the meeting we should have had at Chequers,' an adviser said.

The upshot of this activity was announced on 4 January 2023, also the day James Forsyth started in Number 10 as political secretary. Sunak gave a speech outlining five priorities for his government and vowed to deliver on each of them within a year. They could be summarised in just thirteen words: 'Halve inflation, grow the economy, reduce debt, cut waiting lists, stop the boats.' The sixth prospective pledge on education fell by the wayside.

The prime minister marked his one hundredth day in office on 2 February, a week after inviting his senior ministers to Chequers for their first political cabinet. 'In September. I was trying to get into my local cricket club,' he said. 'And now I'm here.' Over a chicken buffet lunch and dinner of duck, he attempted to instil some optimism. Levido gave a presentation showing 20 per cent of the electorate was undecided about how they would vote. Including those who might change their mind, 'a third of the electorate is soft', he explained. William Hague, Sunak's mentor from Richmond, compared the PM to John Major in 1990: 'We got a new leader who was more popular than the party and won in 1992', before adding, 'At my first party conference [in 1997] we were 40 points behind. I ended up losing by 9 points [in 2001], so if I can make up 31 points on Labour you can too.'

A week later, the PM played host to Volodymyr Zelensky, who addressed Parliament to press his demands for more help to fight the Russians. They breakfasted together in the Number 10 flat before Sunak had to leave for PMQs. Afterwards, Zelensky asked, 'How did it go?' The Ukrainian president's presence had led Keir Starmer to pull his punches. 'Sorry I can't come every week,' Zelensky joked.

Booth-Smith took Cummings' advice to heart and, in January 2023, began secret negotiations with Pat Cullen, the general secretary of the Royal College of Nursing. They met in the cafe at the John Lewis department store on Oxford Street. 'Liam put a lot of time and capital into it,' a Number 10 source said. 'Rishi was always more hawkish [in resisting pay demands]. He had a natural distrust that they would ever get it over the line.'

Efforts to talk to the British Medical Association (BMA), which was demanding a 35 per cent pay increase for junior doctors, got nowhere. 'They were so far off the reservation that you couldn't negotiate with them,' the source said.

However, the nurses were part of the separate 'Agenda for Change' pay scale. Their strike, encompassing one million NHS workers, was settled in May 2023 for a 5 per cent pay rise. Despite Cullen's recommendation that her union accept it, the RCN membership voted against, but the deal was carried. It was still a political win.

The following month, Sunak and Hunt launched the first ever NHS workforce plan, a long-term strategy to get the health service the staff it needed, which was welcomed by the royal colleges. But waiting lists were creeping up. 'I certainly felt towards the end that, with hindsight, we should have settled all the NHS disputes, but I was not an advocate at the time,' a senior cabinet minister said. 'It would have had a massive knock-on effect across the public sector, which would have hit both debt and inflation.' Explaining Sunak's view, a close aide said, 'He was prepared to do things politically, but he didn't like doing things politically which he thought were actively wrong for the country.'

At a Tory MPs' away day on 1 March, Levido talked MPs through the polling around the five priorities plan. He was staggered when several complained they could not be expected to remember all the pledges.[1]

Within hours, Sue Gray, the mandarin who wrote the partygate report, quit the civil service to join Labour as Keir Starmer's chief of staff. Johnson was 'absolutely furious' when he heard the news, telling his team, 'This whole thing absolutely stinks.' An ally said, 'It just proves everything Boris has been saying – that his removal was a stitch-up with the connivance of Labour.'

The Gray appointment was followed, two days later, on Friday 3 March, by the release of an interim report by the Privileges Committee, which was investigating whether Johnson lied to the Commons about the Downing Street parties during lockdown. It included new photographs of Johnson at several gatherings.

When the committee was tasked with the inquiry in April 2022, the chairman, Labour's Chris Bryant, recused himself on the ground that he had made several public statements denouncing Johnson. Yet Harman, who had said she thought he had 'misled' MPs and 'lied repeatedly', was appointed to replace him without resistance from Tory MPs.

The inquiry turned on the thorny issue of parliamentary lying, a charge that normally cannot even be levelled at a fellow MP. Commons convention was that ministers who misled the House should correct themselves at the despatch box. But in a world of high political controversy, where few facts were accepted by both sides, the committee had, effectively, to peer inside Johnson's head to divine whether he intended to mislead. 'Liar' had been the favourite charge of Johnson's critics for years. Rory Stewart, his former leadership rival, described Johnson as 'the most accomplished liar in public life – perhaps the best liar ever to serve as prime minister'. He wrote in the *Times Literary Supplement*, 'He has mastered the use of error, omission, exaggeration, diminution, equivocation and flat denial. He has perfected casuistry, circumlocution, false equivalence and false analogy. He is equally adept at the ironic jest, the fib and the grand lie; the weasel word and the half-truth; the hyperbolic lie, the obvious lie, and the bullshit lie – which may inadvertently be true.'[2] Even those who had broken with Johnson thought things more complicated than this. One estranged aide observed, 'His version of lying is really, really complicated, where he can just decide this is what he believes to be true at the time, and this is now the version of events, and therefore he's right.' Johnson was far from the only politician of whom this was true.

The interim report suggested Johnson must have misled MPs about whether the Downing Street parties broke the pandemic lockdown rules. The Committee would now have to decide whether this was 'inadvertent, reckless, or intentional'. Proving intention would be a difficult hurdle to clear, but Johnson loyalists saw the lesser charge of recklessness as rewriting of the rules to trip up their man. Nonetheless, Johnson and his team were quick to point out that there was no 'smoking gun' which proved an intent to mislead. In one exchange, Jack Doyle, his director of communications, discussed the birthday event for which Johnson was fined, saying, 'I'm struggling to come up with a way this was within the rules.' But that only showed that his aides expressed that view to each other, not to Johnson.

As the Privileges Committee inquiry unfolded like a slow-motion car crash, Johnson came to see both Gray and Harman as part of a Remainer conspiracy with 'some deep forces in the British political establishment' to undermine Brexit. He told friends it was a 'fatal mistake' to hand the initial inquiry to Gray. 'What you've got to understand is that the civil servants of this country are on a long-term mission to try to reverse Brexit,' he told one confidant. 'I really believe this. Even if they don't articulate this to themselves, that's what actually in secret they're all trying to do. They needed me out of the way as fast as possible.' A close friend of Johnson added, 'We are very, very clear-sighted that the endgame is to finish Boris as an electoral threat to Labour on Starmer's behalf in the near term. Harriet Harman is an openly biased judge. She made up her mind before this process even began. This is a political show trial with an outrageous level of bias that would make Stalin blush.'

Several ministers blamed Simon Case, the cabinet secretary, for pushing Gray into the arms of Labour by thwarting her ambitions to become a permanent secretary. 'The fact she's now working in the leader of the opposition's office is because Case blocked her for a perm sec role,' one said. 'She applied weeks before she went. Case made it pretty clear she would not even be shortlisted.'

Even before Johnson's imbroglio with the Privileges Committee, there was a reminder of how his personal circumstances contributed to the chaos of his premiership. On 21 January, the *Sunday Times* revealed that Sam Blyth, a Canadian multimillionaire and distant cousin of Johnson, had offered to guarantee an £800,000 loan to help bail him out of the cost of his divorce and Carrie's renovations to the Downing Street flat. Blyth had asked advice from a friend, Richard Sharp, who then discussed the matter with Case and introduced Case to Blyth. Sharp then became Johnson's choice as the next BBC chairman. In December 2020, the Cabinet Office propriety and ethics team told Johnson to stop seeking Sharp's advice about his personal finances. Sharp acknowledged connecting Blyth and Case but denied giving financial advice.[3]

After the story broke, word reached Case that Johnson was blaming him for the affair becoming public, a claim which infuriated the cabinet secretary, who felt he had been dragged against his will into the chaos of Johnson's finances. Told that Johnson was bad-mouthing him, Case put his head in his hands in front of one of Sunak's senior aides and said, 'Why does he have to be such a cunt?'

Johnson wasn't the only ethical nuisance for Sunak. On 29 January, he was in Richmond when he received a report, at 7 a.m., from his ethics adviser, Sir Laurie Magnus, detailing how Nadhim Zahawi, the Tory chairman, had paid a £4.7 million tax settlement, more than £1 million of which was a penalty. Zahawi had twice misled the propriety and ethics team – when he was appointed education secretary and chancellor – about being under investigation by HMRC. By 9 a.m., Sunak had sacked him, but the loss of another prominent minister, after Williamson's departure, was wounding.

On 21 April, Dominic Raab resigned as deputy prime minister after Adam Tolley KC found that Raab acted in an 'intimidating' and 'aggressive' way towards officials when he was Johnson's justice secretary and foreign secretary. Greg Hands became party chairman and Oliver Dowden was elevated to deputy prime minister.

Between these blows, on 4 February, Liz Truss surfaced with a four-thousand-word defence of her premiership which seemed both premature to voters and tin-eared to many MPs. There was a brief discussion in Number 10 about whether Sunak should use the occasion to distance himself more aggressively from the inheritance of both Johnson and Truss. When he took over aides, and some ministers, including Michael Gove, pressed Sunak to publicly denounce Truss, but it was not Sunak's style. 'Rishi's natural instinct was to try and unite the tribe,' a senior aide said.

However, some in Sunak's inner circle later concluded failing to create clear blue water with his predecessors was one of their biggest mistakes. 'He probably should have just done it and done it ruthlessly,' one adviser said. 'I think a show of strength at the beginning would have helped. The problem was that because we didn't do that from the off, it was very difficult to do that down the line.' The danger, as another put it, was that a course of action which 'would have been net positive in the country' could have left the party looking like 'rats in a sack' again.

But by 2024, three senior cabinet ministers believed he should have gone on the attack. 'The biggest mistake of all was right from the start,' one said. 'We, as Westminster insiders, knew there couldn't be anything more different from Liz Truss than Rishi. Therefore, we thought it was evident that it would be a massive change in the eyes of the country – and it wasn't.' A second said, 'He should have said to the parliamentary party, "I told you Liz Truss would be a disaster. You chose Truss. It was a disaster." The country would have thought: fair enough.' Like Theresa May in 2018 and 2019, Sunak put party unity ahead of good politics. The third cabinet minister said, 'When he came in, the party was fracturing. I was as guilty as anyone of going safety first. But I felt more and more as we went on that we should have been more willing to risk blowing up the party. If I was to have my time again, I would say, "Be comfortable if they boot you out after six months, more fool them."'

Johnson prepared diligently for his appearance before the Privileges Committee on 22 March, spending weeks absorbing the detail in a way he had never bothered to when first confronting partygate. In an ironic twist, his leading barrister was David Pannick, the peer who led the case against him in the Supreme Court over prorogation in 2019. In response to the interim report, Johnson's team submitted a written statement on the morning of 21 March, published later that day, turning his testimony into a two-day media circus. The document conceded that Johnson's statements to Parliament were misleading but argued that they were inadvertent. Pannick maintained that the charge of recklessness was open to abuse and would become a partisan battering ram, just as impeachment had become in the United States.

Johnson made his case that he was only attending the drinks dos to thank staff for their hard work or bid them goodbye. Allies even suggested he found it 'helpful for him because it has given him a chance to say what he wanted to say'. Some wished he had been clearer a year earlier, when his job depended on it. He had an uncomfortable time under cross-examination from Bernard Jenkin, one of the four Tory Brexiteers who formed the majority on the seven-member committee. Nonetheless, when Johnson finished giving evidence he told his team, 'I think we did a good job.' He put both thumbs up, a characteristic pose in better times. His team was confident that the evidence, showing multiple aides failing to advise him that the parties broke the rules, meant he could not be found to have deliberately misled the Commons. They were wrong.

From October 2022 to March 2023, Sunak stabilised the government, vowing to 'focus on the fundamentals and ignore the noise' of the day-to-day political drama. Post-Windsor, the polls began, gradually, to improve. Between 17 and 30 March, the Tories were at or above 30 per cent in seven of the sixteen national surveys.

On 15 March, Jeremy Hunt produced his first proper budget, announcing an extension of the energy support package for a further three months, at a cost of £3 billion, so household bills did not rise in April, just as the local election campaign started. He also announced £27 billion of tax cuts for business to encourage investment. The main retail offer was thirty hours of free childcare for parents in England with children over the age of nine months.

Nonetheless, there was irritation from the Tory right that both Sunak and Hunt still opposed cuts in personal taxation. MPs blamed the PM, seeing Hunt as a cipher for the 'First Lord of the Treasury'. One ally suggested he had gone from 'the most powerful chancellor in history' when drafted in by Truss to 'one of the least powerful' alongside Sunak. In fact, Hunt and Sunak agreed that they needed to control inflation – still over 10 per cent – before cutting personal taxes, but the childcare package was pushed by Hunt against Sunak's wishes. 'All the big signature pieces in every budget came from Jeremy,' a minister said. A senior

Sunak aide said, 'The big difference between them was that Jeremy always wanted to increase public spending, and Rishi was always incredibly hostile to doing that and wanted to use any money available to cut taxes. Rishi never wanted to do the childcare expansion. That was money that could have paid for an income tax cut.'

On 29 March, Sunak addressed the 1922 Committee of Tory back-benchers, warning that while they were 'making real progress', they 'shouldn't expect the voters to reward that hard work'. The PM warned them to prepare for a tough time in the local elections, where election experts Michael Thrasher and Colin Rallings were predicting the Conservatives would lose 1,000 council seats. Privately, CCHQ, now under the command of party chairman Greg Hands, expected losses of between 500 and 600 seats.

In the event, the local elections on 4 May were far worse than anyone had predicted. Labour won, with a national equivalent vote share of 36 per cent to the Tories on 29 per cent, within expectations for a mid-term government. However, a series of narrow defeats meant this translated to a disastrous loss of 1,063 seats and forty-eight councils.

Labour's headline figures – 22 councils and 537 councillors gained – masked some inconsistencies. The national swing to Labour was 4 per cent, but only half that in the North. But with King Charles's coronation on the Saturday, by dawn on Friday Morgan McSweeney, Starmer's chief strategist, decided they should make the case Starmer was on course to win the general election. A Labour official said, 'If people sitting in pubs saw one thing on the ticker tape, we wanted it to be "Starmer says Labour on course to win".'

At noon, the Labour leader arrived back at party headquarters and addressed a sea of exhausted yet jubilant workers. 'I know how long you've waited for nights like this,' he said. 'Doesn't it feel good to be back on the march? Doesn't it feel good to win?'

On the Tory side, defeat raised questions about CCHQ's expectation management and the match fitness of the Conservative machine, as well as concerns about the huge scale of anti-Tory tactical voting, aided in some areas by a 'progressive alliance' pact that saw opposition parties stand aside in some wards. In Bracknell Forest, the Tories got 46 per cent, more than double Labour or the Liberal Democrats, but won just ten seats to Labour's twenty-two and seven for the Lib Dems.

Supporters of Boris Johnson saw Sunak presiding over the collapse of his 2019 coalition. 'We are losing in council estates in Stoke; we are losing in places in Kent where they have three BMWs,' one said. 'We are getting smashed.' Peter Cruddas, who had recently founded a new grassroots group, the Conservative Democratic Organisation (CDO), widely seen as a 'bring back Boris' front (it denied this), directed the blame at MPs who ousted Johnson. 'These local election results and the dire polls leading into them are a reflection of the disunity in the Conservative Party caused by the 1922 committee and MPs removing two sitting prime ministers and installing a leader rejected by the members,' he wrote on Twitter. The psychodrama was back.

For two of Sunak's most senior advisers, it was the 2023 local elections that knocked his premiership off course. 'We were building momentum up until that point,' one said. 'Then we got the expectation management wrong.' The other said, 'That snapped our momentum and created a problem where MPs began to look at the result in their patch and worry.'

Relations with Johnson turned truly toxic two weeks later, when sixteen entries from Johnson's official diaries as prime minister were passed to Thames Valley Police and the Met. On 16 May, lawyers for the government legal service, who were helping Johnson to put together his statement for the upcoming Covid inquiry, came across entries which suggested there had been gatherings in Chequers and Number 10 which may have breached the Covid guidelines. They were shown to Alex Chisholm, the permanent secretary at the Cabinet Office, in his role as 'accounting officer', since the taxpayer was footing Johnson's legal bill. Cabinet Office officials say he was duty-bound to pass the material to the police, which he did on 18 May.

The following day, at around 3 p.m., Darren Tierney, the head of propriety and ethics in the Cabinet Office, called Johnson's office to inform him. When Johnson found out, he was in the United States, a visit that culminated in dinner with Donald Trump. He and his team called David Pannick to take over Johnson's evidence to the Covid inquiry as well as the Privileges Committee. 'Boris was completely flabbergasted, and he suspects foul play,' a close ally said. 'He has been spitting feathers.' By 9 p.m. Pannick's team had determined that every one of the gatherings in the diary entries was defensible.

There it might have remained, had the diary entries not then been passed to the Privileges Committee. Harman's committee wrote to Johnson's lawyers, claiming 'an assessment by the government legal department' had concluded they 'could reasonably be considered to constitute breaches of Covid regulations'. In fact, no assessment of the legal merits of the entries had been conducted at all, but this wording fuelled Johnson's paranoia. 'The only assessment we did was whether we should pass it to the police,' a senior Cabinet Office official said. 'It is a matter for the police to decide whether it constitutes grounds for an investigation. It would have been totally inappropriate to block it.'

Those closest to Johnson blamed Oliver Dowden and Jeremy Quin, the senior ministers in the Cabinet Office, for plotting the entire affair in a bid to end his political career. The Cabinet Office admitted that Quin, the paymaster general, had approved the decision to pass the material to the Privileges Committee. An ally of Johnson charged, 'This is a political stitch-up concocted in an attempt to smear Boris.' Dowden insisted he had no idea about the diaries before the police were called. Johnson, he said, wanted him to 'interfere with a police matter', which would have been 'completely inappropriate'. A minister said, 'Boris was seeing things which weren't there.'

This was all a nightmare for Sunak. 'The last thing we want is another load of headlines about Boris and parties,' a senior aide admitted. 'We want to move past all that.' Sadly for them, it then got worse.

On Friday 2 June Johnson and Sunak met in the prime minister's House of Commons office. If the purpose of the meeting was peace, its outcome was war. The two men met at 4.30 p.m., with James Forsyth, Sunak's political secretary, also present. They talked for forty-five minutes. The first twenty-five were cordial and productive as Sunak picked Johnson's brain about the best ways of taking the fight to Starmer and Labour. 'Boris made some bridge-building efforts,' an ally said. 'He wants to win the next election. He wants to beat Starmer. He basically offered to put the leadership question off the table.'

Then Johnson raised the issue of peerages, and the atmosphere chilled. Number 10 had made clear in advance that Sunak did not want to discuss honours. 'I don't want to talk about that,' the PM said.

'We must talk about it,' Johnson replied. He proceeded to press for assurances that MPs who had been submitted for peerages – Dorries, Alok Sharma and Nigel Adams – could wait and join the Lords later, noting how undesirable by-elections would be at that time. Sunak said it was 'their decision' whether to go or not. He would approve whatever list was put in front of him by officials. Sunak was explicit that he would not intervene. He told Johnson, 'I don't want you to leave this room thinking I have made you a promise, as that will be a problem in our relationship going forward.'

To Sunak, this meant he would leave the House of Lords Appointments Commission (HOLAC) to vet the list and then nod it through without intervention. Johnson took it to mean that Sunak would sign off on his original list. The prime minister was, they claim, 'Sphinx-like, not saying much, not giving much away.'

After the meeting, Johnson messaged Dorries to say, 'Just finished the meeting with Rishi. List being published imminently. You're on it.' When the list finally dropped on Friday, there was no mention of peerages for Dorries, Adams and Sharma, or gongs for Tory donors David Ross and Stuart Marks. Dorries, Sharma and Adams were removed by HOLAC since, under the rules, for them to remain on Johnson's list, they would have to resign as MPs within six months. None of them signalled to HOLAC they would do so.

This technical process appears to have been lost on Johnson and his nominees, who were under the mistaken belief that they could be automatically re-vetted every six months without needing to be renominated.

Dorries first got wind that there might be a problem at around 7 p.m. on Thursday when Steven Swinford of *The Times* contacted her having been tipped off that she was no longer on the list. In conversations with the chief whip, Simon Hart, on Friday morning, Dorries repeatedly stated that Johnson had been given personal assurances that she could be re-vetted and nominated at a later date. She was informed that Johnson was in no position to give her assurances, and that she would have needed to have either resigned already, or have notified HOLAC of her intention to do so. Dorries then asked whether it was possible for her to be put back on the list if she resigned that day, to which she was told no. She then asked whether Sunak would submit her name for a peerage at the next election in 2024. She was told the PM would not be making personal assurances to anyone, though Dorries claimed Hart hinted that she might be in luck if she kept her nose clean. 'It was the sheer audacity of the chief whip thinking … he could dangle some kind of stick and carrot: "Be a good girl and we'll make sure something's sorted for you in the future", which is basically what he was saying to me … That was what made me

... make my decision to resign.'[4] Hours later she said she was quitting.

'The key information was deliberately withheld,' Dorries told the author later. 'I think there was something devious and sinister about it. They wanted Boris and his allies out of Westminster.' She told TalkTV's Piers Morgan she was 'broken-hearted' and accused Sunak and Forsyth, 'two privileged posh boys', of 'duplicity and cruelty' in tricking a woman who grew up in working-class poverty out of a place in the Upper House.[5] Privately she called Sunak 'a dishonourable swindler'.

Sunak's team said it was Johnson who did not understand the rules, that it was, in effect, he who was responsible for Dorries' predicament. The government took the highly unusual step of declassifying the final list that had been approved by HOLAC. It showed that the commission had not approved peerages for Dorries, Adams or Sharma, meaning they were not submitted to the PM and were therefore not sent on by him to the King for approval. A senior Sunak aide said, 'If anyone is taken off the list by Downing Street, HOLAC has to declare that. They haven't. There was no intervention by the PM at all.'

At noon that Thursday, 8 June, Johnson was on a plane to Cairo, where he was due to give a speech, when he received an email from the Privileges Committee with a letter from Harriet Harman attached informing him that he had been found guilty of contempt of Parliament. Johnson erupted with rage as he and Ross Kempsell read the email with disbelief. A hard copy of the report was handed to Pannick, Johnson's lawyer, that afternoon. The committee found Johnson deliberately lied to MPs, not just that he had made recklessly inaccurate statements. The report concluded that in defending himself, Johnson had made further inaccurate claims under oath, which were also a contempt of Parliament.

Johnson, believing the report to be 'nakedly political and transparently biased', told Kempsell, 'This just confirms all of our worst suspicions. It's a total stitch up and they're not even bothering to hide it.' An incredulous ally said, 'They are effectively claiming to have gone back in time and put themselves inside his brain and claim with 100 per cent certainty that they know what he was thinking, when there was not one email or WhatsApp showing that he set out to lie.'

Johnson was particularly shocked because his team had, until two weeks earlier, been assured by Tory whips that MPs on the committee were leaning towards a suspension from Parliament of less than ten days

– the threshold needed to trigger a recall vote in an MP's seat, which, if lost, would force a by-election. That back channel went quiet around the time of the row about Johnson's diary entries. His team believed that when ministers agreed to send that material to the Privileges Committee, they gave tacit approval to move against him. 'Number 10 tipped the Tories on the committee the wink that they could throw the book at Boris,' an ally said. Johnson was warned his suspension from Parliament would 'significantly exceed' ten days. He personally sounded out senior ministers to ask whether the government could whip Tory MPs to vote against the sanction. He was informed that it would be a free vote. 'Well, I'm fucked in that case,' he concluded.

Furious at his treatment and about what had happened to Dorries, he resigned his seat, denying MPs the opportunity to kick him out. He privately raged at the prospect of dozens of Tory MPs voting against him: 'Don't these people realise they are only in Parliament because of me?' Johnson's one-thousand-word resignation letter was blistering, condemning the Privileges Committee and Sunak's drift away from what he regarded as proper Conservative policies. He claimed there was a 'witch-hunt under way, to take revenge for Brexit and ultimately to reverse the 2016 referendum result'. Dorries had quit a few hours earlier. A friend said, 'They've done a Thelma and Louise.'

While Johnson's decision was animated by fury, there was also an element of weariness. Visitors to Millbank Tower in the preceding weeks had found a man ground down by having to spend a large amount of his time with lawyers refighting old battles. A close ally said, 'When you feel like everyone is against you and you're facing a kangaroo court, that is going to get you down. He has felt a bit helpless. That's why he has thrown in the towel.'

Sunak was chairing a cabinet committee meeting on small boats when Johnson resigned. Aides did not interrupt proceedings but told him as he left the Cabinet Room. 'He was disappointed in a way but sanguine in another,' one source said Delphically. A senior government source added, 'There are three courts who decide the fate of a politician. There is the House, there is the Privileges Committee and there is the electorate – and Boris has decided that he doesn't want to face any of them.'

Johnson's rivals rejoiced. George Osborne tweeted, 'What a lovely evening.' David Cameron joked with friends, 'Who knew my recall law was so powerful; everyone called it feeble at the time.' Keir Starmer was at a dinner in Derby celebrating Margaret Beckett's forty years as an MP, when it was announced from the stage that Johnson had gone. 'There was a lot of cheering,' a source said. 'Keir just smiled.'

On 16 June, Johnson marked his fifty-ninth birthday quietly in Oxfordshire with family and friends. 'Ironically, he's the last person to convene a party,' a close friend said. 'He doesn't like parties.' When an ally told him he was getting old, Johnson shot back, 'Churchill did not become prime minister until he was sixty-five.'

The day before, the 108-page final report of the Privileges Committee was published, finding him guilty of 'repeated contempts of Parliament'. It identified five offences: deliberately misleading MPs when he said that no Covid rules were broken, deliberately misleading the committee when he reiterated the same argument; leaking the report in advance when he announced his resignation as an MP; 'Impugning' the committee by calling it a 'witch hunt' and a 'kangaroo court'; and complicity in a 'campaign of abuse and attempted intimidation of the committee' by his supporters. If Johnson had not already resigned, the committee said it would have recommended a 90-day suspension from the Commons. Instead, he would be denied a parliamentary pass, a traditional perk for ex-MPs.

'There is no precedent for a prime minister having been found to have deliberately misled the House,' the report read. 'He misled the House on an issue of the greatest importance ... and did so repeatedly.' Johnson's defence, the MPs concluded, was 'no more than an artifice' and defied the 'plain meaning' of his statements from the despatch box. The assurances he said he had received from officials that rules had not been broken 'were not accurately represented by him to the House'. The committee found Johnson 'closed his mind' to the facts and engaged in 'after-the-event rationalisations' in which he sought to 'rewrite the meaning of the rules and guidance to fit his own evidence'.

Before the leak, Johnson's suspension would have been twenty days, still enough to force a recall. Minutes of the committee's final meeting, on 13 June, showed that Labour's Yvonne Fovargue and Allan Dorans of the SNP wanted Johnson expelled completely from Parliament, a punishment last used in 1947. This was voted down. In order not to delay publication of the report, the MPs did not even consider the new evidence from Johnson's diaries.

When Johnson read the final report, he saw it as overkill. 'If the committee wanted to bury me, they have massively cocked that up,' he told an aide. 'It just proves our point.' Someone who spoke to him that week reported, 'He's been a lot more chipper than I expected. It has fuelled the martyrdom narrative. Instead of quietly euthanising him, the Privileges Committee and his opponents in the government have blown life into the next episode of the Boris Johnson box set.'

One close ally outlined circumstances in which he might stage a comeback: 'His strategy is: see what happens in the election. Let there be an interim leader of the opposition, and as soon as that guy or girl wobbles, that's when he will probably strike.' That pointed to a possible return in 2026. In the meantime, Johnson was able to 'put hay in the barn', earning £250,000 per speech and around £1.5 million for his memoirs. That weekend he began a *Daily Mail* column which paid 'north of £500,000, south of £1 million'.

At 9.26 p.m. the following Monday, 19 June, MPs voted by 354 votes to 7 to accept the report and bring down the curtain on Johnson's parliamentary career. Most Conservatives, on a one-line whip, stayed away, including Sunak. Only Bill Cash, Nick Fletcher, Adam Holloway, Karl McCartney, Joy Morrissey, Desmond Swayne and Heather Wheeler supported Johnson. Notable Conservatives who voted to condemn him included Theresa May, Penny Mordaunt, Steve Baker, Geoffrey Cox, Julian Smith, Tom Tugendhat and Graham Brady. 'For the last few weeks, we have been dominated by stuff that is very unhelpful,' a Sunak ally complained. 'Everything going back to Boris again.'

By the end of June, the local election setback, the Johnson circus, stubborn inflation (still 8.7 per cent in June) and Labour's continuing commanding position in the polls had sent Sunak into a deep funk. A senior adviser said, 'At that point, Rishi was punch drunk. He spent a lot of his time in a very bad place. He goes through long periods of just being really down because he can't understand why it's happening. He doesn't really get it.' To many longstanding friends and colleagues, Sunak's inability to move the dial with the public was the first major failure of his professional life. His incomprehension at his lack of success said a lot about his relative inexperience and naivety about politics. In one outburst he complained, 'Why do people not realise I'm right?'

On Wednesday 28 June, rising stars Claire Coutinho and Craig Williams hosted a summer gathering for Sunak loyalists and junior ministers in Mayfair. Sunak worked the room in a desultory fashion, thanking people for their support but appearing tired and irritable. 'He keeps saying how difficult everything is,' said a friend who was there. After Winchester, Oxford, Stanford and Goldman Sachs, another friend said, 'His whole life has been an equation – "the harder I work, the better I do" – and politics doesn't work like that.' A cabinet minister said, 'In his mind, the deal he struck with the universe is not working. He knows with cleverness comes responsibility to graft. But if you work hard and do the right thing, the universe will reward you and, in his mind, the universe is not keeping its side of the bargain. He's the kid who does all his homework and can't understand why he hasn't got an A. He couldn't understand how Boris could be prime minister when he didn't do his homework.'

One old friend concluded that Sunak's whirlwind political rise had upended his political creed: 'He has lost his political moorings. He used to be the most right-wing person I know. He wanted to cut tax to boost growth before Liz Truss did. He once thought the NHS should be privatised. But his public career has coincided with Covid and an economic crisis and the huge expansion of the state, and I think he's lost his understanding of who he is and what he thinks.'

Sunak's working methods, which cut out his ministers and made him seem distant and arrogant, also left him in lonely isolation when things went wrong. 'He never had Boris's animal instinct for politics,' a senior strategist said. 'He would never pick up the phone and just have a chat or text with one of the cabinet.' Michael Gove, Alister Jack and others encouraged Sunak to set up a kitchen cabinet to bounce ideas off. 'Rishi doesn't kibitz with other elected politicians,' a minister said. 'In politics, however super smart the adviser, it's not the same as having other politicians in the room. Rishi finds open criticism difficult, and he doesn't put himself in a position where that occurs.'

Fundamentally, Sunak did not think he had much to learn. 'He's an analyst,' a close ally explained. 'He goes off to do the work himself and then comes to a view.' It made him resistant to those who relied on political instinct alone. 'It's not that no one else's views are valid. The view could be valid if you've done the work. His perspective was, "I've just sat down for four hours and read everything, formed a view, and I know where all the pitfalls are. If you're just coming to me with an opinion and you haven't read anything, and I've got a bunch of reasons why what you're saying is bullshit, why are you here telling me I should do that?

You don't understand the facts." That's his logic.' In politics, as Gordon Brown and Theresa May discovered, diligence is not a substitute for good judgement and political skill. Levido told colleagues Sunak was a 'teacher-leader, not a preacher-leader', but the latter was increasingly what his party wanted.

Senior aides, including Booth-Smith and Chesterfield, tried to get Sunak to understand that he had to play the game, but he refused. 'He is just someone who has not accepted the terms of the game of politics,' one senior adviser said. 'He thinks it's bullshit. He has a very fundamental view that the focus should be: what is your record? What have you done? I said to him multiple times, starting with the non-dom stuff, "These are the rules of the game. You need to get on the pitch and play it." I have a huge amount of respect for him for saying, "I don't want to do it like that."' While his aides admired him, ministers despaired. They knew that refusing to play the game was a very simple way to lose it.

Booth-Smith felt the need for more 'political muscle'. Knowing Levido could work with Cummings, he persuaded the Vote Leave director to visit Sunak at his constituency home in Yorkshire in early July. The pair had dinner and spoke for two hours. No one else was present. Hardly anyone even knew about the meeting. It followed the same pattern as their November talk, Cummings pitching a strategy but also demanding Sunak's attention for what he saw as the rotten sink holes of the British state. 'My price for bailing the Tories out is that you put your authority in Number 10 behind actually solving these problems.'

Sunak still couldn't see Cummings back in government: 'It will be far too controversial. The MPs will go crazy. This has to be secret.'

'I understand your concerns,' Cummings replied, 'but I've got no fundamental interest in secretly helping the Conservatives win the election. The only point of it, from my point of view, is that we start tackling these problems, which is why I did Brexit in the first place, why I came in in 2019 and what I was trying to do in 2020.'

Cummings again pressed for Sunak to announce withdrawal from the European Convention on Human Rights – and not just so he could tackle the small boat crossings. 'There's lots of fundamental problems that we can't solve unless you sort out the ECHR,' he said. 'In 2020, I got all the government lawyers in, we red-teamed it with external experts and everyone was completely clear. It's impossible to stop this boats problem unless you're prepared to repeal the Human Rights Act and say that we're not going to be bound by Strasbourg court decisions on the subject. In terms of crime and antiterrorism, it imposes insane restrictions. We can't even keep convicted terrorists in Belmarsh under proper supervision. It's complete insanity.' He urged Sunak to declassify the details and explain fully to the public how the ECHR was binding the government's hands. 'It's good for the country to sort this out. And secondly, it will crack open the Labour Party and give them a massive strategic problem. It's the right thing to do and it's great politics.'

Sunak was cautious. 'The system will go crazy,' he said.

'Of course!' Cummings said. 'But look at the situation that you're in. Boris and Truss have driven the country into a massive crater and there is no calm, easy way out of it. If you just go along with the establishment view, tweak a few things here and there, then the country is going to keep on disintegrating and politically, you're going to disintegrate. If you listen to all the establishment characters who are saying, "Steady as she goes", a year from now, you'll be completely, utterly sunk.'

Once more, Cummings urged Sunak to settle the NHS strikes so he could get on top of waiting lists, but he found the prime minister 'more fatalistic' than he had been in November, 'more desperate' too though. 'Very interesting,' the prime minister said as they parted. 'If we're going to do a deal, we should sort it out next week.'

Cummings had a separate conversation with James Forsyth, who he found concerned about the growing insurrection among Tory MPs. 'That's really not the point,' Cummings told him. 'You need a completely different approach. If you get that right, you will go up in the polls and that will solve your problem with the MPs. But if you just tack around, you will never solve the strategic problem and you will end up completely broken.' Dougie Smith agreed, growling at one colleague, 'Desperate diseases require desperate remedies.'

Later, when Sunak had again rejected his advice, Cummings said, 'The post-2016 Tories are summed up by the fact that Sunak, like Johnson, would rather lose than take government seriously.' Asked after the general election whether Cummings should have been brought in, Booth-Smith told a friend, 'The MPs would have hated it, but would they have hated 150 seats more?'

*   *   *

Sunak had four set-piece opportunities to set a new narrative – the party conference, an autumn statement, a King's Speech and a budget the following spring. A crisis meeting to agree a new strategy was held over a dinner attended by a large group on Sunday 16 July at the Londoner Hotel. Levido and Brooks gave another polling presentation. Those present included the usual inner circle plus Will Tanner, party treasurer Stephen Massie and former Cameron strategist Ameet Gill. 'The group was far too large for the type of frank discussion we needed to have,' one said. Sunak was on edge, snapping at one of those present, 'Why are you even here?' One diner recalled, 'That was an appalling meeting.'

Dowden listened to the presentation and then laid into Levido, questioning why 'we're just going to keep going on inflation' when experts doubted the figure would have halved by January 2024, the target the PM had set. This had seriously rattled Sunak. 'He's a glass half empty guy,' an adviser said. 'It's always worst-case scenario with him.'

The following evening, Levido and Brooks went to Downing Street to thrash things out with Sunak, Booth-Smith and Forsyth. This was a franker conversation. The polling showed that voters wanted change. Both Levido and Booth-Smith believed they would have to offer change, in the form of forward-looking policies, at some point. 'The decision was made to do it in the autumn rather than at the start of 2024,' a source said. Levido thought it early but went along with it. An insider said, 'If the next election is Tories v Labour, we lose. If it's Conservatives v change, we lose. If it's change by Rishi Sunak v change by Keir Starmer, that's a contest where we have a chance.'

Part of the rationale for the pivot was to provide therapy for Sunak. 'He was very down,' a senior adviser said. 'A big part of Liam's job was finding ways of keeping the guy up, because the show had to be kept on the road. There was still a country to govern. Psychologically, giving him a new chapter of the project to focus on and have ownership of was important for keeping him positive and engaged.'

Following his meeting with Cummings, the PM had engaged in a process of self-analysis, working out what he had learned in his nine months in charge and asked himself what he wanted to achieve with what remained of his time at the top. His conclusion was: 'Short-term decision-making leads to long-term failure.' One of those present explained, 'He wants to do the things others have found too difficult and have left to fester.'

*　*　*

Nadine Dorries had announced she was standing down, but then did not, remaining as MP for Mid Bedfordshire to spite Sunak. She was quickly dubbed the 'mid beds blocker'. Boris Johnson's and Nigel Adams's resignations as MPs for Uxbridge and South Ruislip and Selby and Ainsty, plus that of David Warburton, the MP for Somerton and Frome, who had been photographed with what looked like cocaine, meant Sunak faced the prospect of a triple by-election defeat on 20 July. The 'tri-election' showdown was called 'B-Day' by sarcastic backbenchers who thought three losses would consign Tory general election hopes to the toilet and perhaps trigger a vote of no confidence against Sunak.

Focus groups conducted in the three seats by More in Common showed that Sunak, who had begun his premiership with personal approval ratings twenty points higher than his party, was now a drag on Tory fortunes. Asked what animal the PM reminded him of, Craig, thirty-nine, a software tester from Selby, said: 'A dodo.'

In Selby and Ainsty, Labour overturned a majority of more than 20,000, with the second biggest swing in by-election history from the Conservatives. Somerton and Frome fell to the Lib Dems on a 29 per cent swing. However, in Uxbridge, the Tories miraculously clung on by 495 votes because they managed to turn the by-election into a referendum on Labour mayor Sadiq Khan's extension of an Ultra Low Emission Zone (ULEZ), which hit drivers of older cars and vans with a £12.50 a day levy. Sunak arrived in Uxbridge the next morning beaming. That week inflation had also fallen to 7.9 per cent, the first stroke of luck the PM had had in several months.

When he departed for California on holiday the following week, he did so knowing that the course of his premiership was set. 'He was in a grey T-shirt and old jeans and trainers,' an aide recalled. 'It is the happiest I have ever seen him.' Before he left, Sunak told the 1922 Committee, 'In the coming months, I am going to set out more of what I would do if I had a full term.' He added, 'When we come back in September, we have a choice to make, all of us. Do we come together and throw everything at winning the next election or not? I've made my choice, I'm all-in.'

He would have to fight without his communications director. Amber de Botton left by mutual agreement. She had a family illness to attend to, but she was also frustrated that her view that Sunak should take more risks had not been embraced. 'For whatever reason, Amber and the PM didn't quite gel,' admitted one of de Botton's supporters in Number 10. Another special adviser said, 'The PM started turning on her in meetings, saying, "This isn't working."' Some said de Botton was too focused on broadcasters, rather than newspapers. There were also tensions in the communications team. Nissy Chesterfield, who understood Sunak better, was promoted to communications director.

The real culprit when it came to media mismanagement was the prime minister himself. Sunak had a reputation for sucking up to proprietors, bypassing their editors. They found him too transactional and frequently offhand when he didn't get the coverage he wanted. 'He's an investor,' a strategist explained. '"I invest here, where's my return?" But he's new to this. He doesn't understand that these relationships are an ongoing conversation.' It was another example of how Sunak's ignorance of, or impatience with, the rules of the game cost him.

After the July strategy meeting, Sunak commissioned a range of work streams on different problems he wanted to tackle. They were given codenames after trees. After the win in Uxbridge, Sunak's team thought there was political traction in challenging the stampede towards net zero. The first project to bear fruit was 'Cedar', a plan to delay some of the plans to achieve that target by 2050. Sunak was due to make an announcement on Friday 22 September that a boiler scrappage scheme was delayed and the move to ban the sale of new petrol and diesel cars would be delayed from 2030 to 2035, the deadline in the rest of Europe. However, the plan leaked, and the speech was brought forward two days amid a chorus of complaints from the green lobby. On the podium at Sunak's press conference was his new slogan: 'Long-term decisions for a brighter future.' It lacked the punch of 'Take back control' or 'Get Brexit done', but it was the first time the government had dominated the news bulletins by design for seven months. 'They made the weather in a way they had planned for the first time since Windsor,' a senior Tory said.

The same week, Keir Starmer said he planned to renegotiate a closer Brexit deal with the EU in 2025 and would not want to diverge from EU regulations. The Labour leader even hinted at, then retracted, the suggestion that he might do a migration returns deal with Brussels. The Tory attack machine, with Cameron aide Adam Atashzai now in harness, calculated that if the UK took migrants in the same ratios as EU member states, it would mean accepting an extra 130,000 people per year. As conference season arrived, there were signs of life for the Tories.

The Conservative conference in Manchester killed them. The 'let Sunak be Sunak' plan produced a bizarre smorgasbord of policies, which failed to hang together or support the headline 'change' message. James Nation and Eleanor Shawcross in the policy unit put out a call for ideas. 'Lots of people wrote up their pet projects,' a Number 10 adviser recalled. 'They put together this policy book. It was like an Argos catalogue of ideas and Rishi went through it and just randomly picked anything he liked the look of.'

First Sunak scrapped the northern leg of HS2 between Birmingham and Manchester. 'Rishi thought it was a total waste of money when he was chancellor and was always trying to get Boris to scrap it,' a source said. The prime minister who claimed education as his greatest passion then said he would abolish A-levels and replace them with an English baccalaureate to ensure all pupils studied maths and English until the age of eighteen. The new exam was to be called the 'Advanced British Standard', which sounded like a washing machine regulation. Finally, he announced plans to phase out smoking. 'It was so Rishi,' an adviser said. 'It's not just like he doesn't smoke. He hates smoking and thinks that anybody who smokes is basically morally degenerate. That's him at his most narrow, puritanical, Californian.' An aide countered, 'It polled remarkably well.'

However, Tory MPs looked with incredulity at a prime minister boasting about long-term decisions while scrapping the best-known infrastructure project in the country – in the city which was set to benefit from it. Sunak had been persuaded not to ditch HS2 before the local elections after an intervention by Andy Street, the mayor of the West Midlands. Now, an apoplectic Street got as far as telling the *Sunday Times* he would resign at the conference, before he was talked out of it.

Levido had helped save HS2 before the 2019 election, when Sunak and Cummings had both wanted to scrap it, since he believed that cut across Johnson's levelling up message. He now regarded Sunak's plan as 'dissonant' from his main message. But he didn't rock the boat. Levido knew there were two ways to do the job of campaign director. The first was to emulate his old boss, Lynton Crosby, who 'threatened to resign every day if he didn't get his way'. The other way was to accept that the decision maker was the one with his name on the ballot paper.

One of Sunak's closest aides admitted they 'indulged him' at conference. 'Everyone kept saying to him, "What do you want to do?" He said, "These are the things I think are important. I care about them, and I think the country will be better and healthier and stronger as a result."' For many, however, this was Sunak's best chance to get the public to look at him afresh – and he had blown it. 'That was the last straw,' a Number 10 veteran said. 'Different people got off the bus at different points, but that was quite a significant moment.'

The backlash led to forthright criticism of Sunak's team. 'These people love Rishi and think he is brilliant,' a cabinet minister complained. 'They think the public just needed to see more of him and they would fall in love too.' Insiders said Booth-Smith had a 'special dispensation' to challenge, but once Sunak had made his mind up, he had to withdraw or risk being frozen out. Fairly or not, the appointment of Forsyth, the prime minister's best friend, was seen as emblematic of Sunak's desire for cheerleaders not challengers. A senior Tory said, 'Since James arrived, Rishi always had someone to tell him "You're right" and encouraged the "Poor me, it's all so unfair" attitude, which has been fatal.' Chesterfield's office as director of comms was lined with family portraits – not of her family but of Sunak's. One visitor described it as 'a shrine'.

Pumping out a raft of new policies was not inherently misguided. It could have allowed Sunak to dictate the political weather that autumn. 'The way to make it work was to significantly increase the pace of politics and announce big things over and over again that tell a story,' a senior figure said. 'Labour wouldn't have known what to say until they did ten focus groups. But you have to keep going. He started, but then he stopped because it wasn't working.' They had also run out of policies. A senior aide admitted, 'We stripped the cupboard bare.'

When Sunak hosted the world's first summit on the opportunities and threats of artificial intelligence on 3 November at Bletchley Park, home of the wartime codebreakers, the public saw a prime minister more at home with the West Coast 'tech bros' than the red wall. Interviewing Elon Musk, the founder of Open AI who was in the process of transforming Twitter into X, Sunak behaved like an eager fan boy. 'I suppose it's a win,' a minister said. 'People seem to have noticed what we are doing on AI. At least we aren't talking about bloody Boris.'

The King's Speech on 9 November would have been a good moment to seize the news agenda again but it was a lacklustre collection of bills which had already been announced.

By then, Westminster was consumed again by the 'bloody Boris' era, as the Covid inquiry got going with a (literal) vengeance. Cummings and Lee Cain gave evidence on 1 November, Johnson on 6/7 December. The inquiry barrister, Hugo Keith KC, seemed more interested in the lurid WhatsApp messages which had been released than in a lessons-learned exercise. Cummings gave evidence about his description of MPs as 'useless fuckpigs'. It wasn't Sunak's government on trial, but a Tory peer observed, 'There isn't much differentiation in the public's mind on this stuff between Rishi and Boris. It's all pretty bad.'

To compound the psychodrama, the publication of Nadine Dorries' book *The Plot* advanced the theory that Sunak was the beneficiary of a conspiracy run by a cabal called The Movement, which included Cummings, Michael Gove and Dougie Smith – plus a man she named Dr No to circumvent the libel laws, whose bestiality extended to butchering a rabbit belonging to the brother of an ex-girlfriend when she dumped him, nailing the quartered corpse to a door.

In this morass of infighting, the autumn statement on 22 November, Sunak's last opportunity in 2023 to capture the public imagination, failed to move the dial. Hunt and Sunak decided to spend £20 billion on reducing business taxes and cutting 2p from National Insurance Contributions (NICs), rather than income tax, which most Tory MPs thought politically more potent. 'It was the best tax cut in terms of economic impact and growth,' a Downing Street source said. 'You can do National Insurance far quicker than income tax. It's also UK-wide, which income tax no longer is. And it's not inflationary.' Hunt told MPs the reduction would kick in from January, rather than the end of the tax year in April, fuelling speculation about a spring election. Still the polls didn't shift. 'All the other squeezes on people's income meant that people didn't feel it,' a Sunak aide said later. 'The great irony is if we'd sent everyone a cheque for the money, people would have felt different.'

By far the most significant development of November, however, was that in the nine days before the autumn statement, Sunak had sacked his home secretary and lost a Supreme Court case on the Rwanda policy. It capped a year of turmoil over the original Brexit issue, immigration, and brought the PM close to the brink of resignation.

DEJA BLUE II
Dave, Rwanda and the Grid of Shit
January 2023 to May 2024

'Plus ça change, plus c'est la même chose' (The more things change, the more they stay the same)

– Jean-Baptiste Alphonse Karr

Sunak fired Suella Braverman by phone at 8.30 a.m. on Monday 13 November after a week dominated by her claims that homeless people had made a 'lifestyle choice' to live in tents. Over the previous year she had seemed, to Number 10, to prioritise her role as a professional provocateur over that of running the Home Office. Cabinet ministers grew tired of being asked whether they agreed with her latest outburst whenever they did broadcast interviews. This was the 'final straw', but it was a convenient one for the prime minister, who had been thinking about firing Braverman for six months. 'She just didn't give a fuck or respect his leadership,' recalled a senior cabinet minister in whom Sunak confided. 'Rishi was always very worried that it could be the beginning of the end by getting rid of her. He was both emotionally highly desirous of doing it, but thought, "Are we just going to blow this whole bloody thing up?"'

From the beginning of his premiership, Sunak and Braverman had been locked in a stand-off about how to stop the boats. The home secretary believed a maximalist approach was necessary – withdrawing from the European Convention on Human Rights, or passing legislation ordering the courts to ignore the rulings of the European Court of Human Rights on asylum cases, so illegal arrivals could be sent to Rwanda. Sunak believed he could get planes in the air to Rwanda with less inflammatory action. The High Court had ruled in December 2022 that the plan to send asylum seekers there for processing was lawful. Senior aides were adamant Sunak was relaxed about ECHR withdrawal. 'He was intellectually very comfortable with it, but he thought the party would have torn itself to pieces.'

Braverman's team thought failure to go hard would prevent them getting flights off to Rwanda before the general election. 'Rishi and Liam [Booth-Smith] thought they could try their version first, see if that works. If it fails, they would come back with a stronger bill,' a Braverman ally said. 'We said, "You haven't got time to do that. The Court of Appeal could turn this over. You need to get rid of the problem."'

Sunak was also listening to Victoria Prentis, the attorney general, and James Eadie, the Treasury counsel, who warned that Braverman's 'full fat' proposals might breach international law. The home secretary sought outside counsel. 'We had legal opinion which said that we had a respectable argument for what we were proposing,' an aide said. The row reached an impasse. Sunak wanted his version of the bill passed but, constitutionally, it had to be introduced by the home secretary. Braverman flatly refused, playing chicken with Downing Street for three months. 'Number 10 were trying to force her to bring forward their bill,' a Home Office adviser said. Braverman's response, an aide recounted, was, 'Fire me and get somebody else to do it. If you don't do it right it will be my head on the chopping block, and you will fail the country.' She did not threaten to resign, but it was implicit in her actions. Little by little, the home secretary won concessions – some language on Clause 39, the disapplication of some elements of the Human Rights Act – but not what she regarded as enough.

When Sunak secured the Windsor Framework on 27 February, Braverman had little choice but to accept it. An ally recalled, 'We no longer had the ability to apply pressure because he could just say, "Fuck you. Everyone thinks I'm a genius." He was on the crest of a wave.' Dougie Smith brokered a compromise to allow the bill to proceed. On 3 March 2023 Sunak unveiled the new Illegal Migration Bill. Those coming to the UK through an unofficial route would be detained for up to twenty-eight days and then sent to their home country or Rwanda.

In the backlash, Gary Lineker, the football presenter, called a video of Braverman promoting the plan 'beyond awful' and compared the government to the Nazis. 'This is just an immeasurably cruel policy directed at the most vulnerable people in language that is not dissimilar to that used by Germany in the 30s,' Lineker tweeted. The outburst was perversely pleasing for Braverman's team, though, who thought the policy weak. 'Gary Lineker attacking us was the best thing that could have happened,' one said. 'It made us look so tough.'

The first half of the year was also filled with a running 'battle' over legal migration. Braverman's advisers found Sunak and Booth-Smith focused instead on illegals. 'Liam's argument was that the public do not give a fuck about legal migration, all they care about is the illegal stuff,' a source close to Braverman said. 'If you solve that, everything will fall into place.' Downing Street was also mindful that the OBR's growth figures were based on annual net migration of 250,000 and cutting it would narrow their room for manoeuvre economically. Braverman's team thought this complacent, along with the view in Number 10 that the Rwanda scheme would survive the courts. 'In their mind,' a Braverman ally said, 'we don't need this legal migration stuff. These guys are just clowns trying to force us into doing things that we don't want to do.'

New annual net migration figures were due at the end of May. Two weeks before that, on 15 May, Braverman addressed the first National Conservatism conference at the Emmanuel Centre in Westminster. 'We thought, "Fuck it, let's make something of it,"' an ally recalled. Jake Ryan, Braverman's spokesman, issued three paragraphs of quotes from her speech to the media the night before, showing them to Downing Street, where the comms team seemed not to register the impact they might have. They splashed five papers that Monday morning. In her speech, Braverman said, 'We need to get overall immigration numbers down' to the tens of thousands, before calling for British workers to be trained as 'HGV drivers, butchers or fruit pickers'. The speech was seen as a transparent leadership pitch. Just before the official figures were released, Number 10 'caved', agreeing to a crackdown on student numbers, banning most of them bringing family members to the UK. The new figures showed a huge surge in net migration from 504,000 in 2022 to 606,000, more than double the figure before Brexit. This could have been a moment for Sunak, as Braverman was doing privately, to blame Boris Johnson for opening the doors, but again he did not take it.

A dozen Tory MPs from red wall seats, including the party's deputy chairman, Lee Anderson, and the Stoke MP Jonathan Gullis, set up the

New Conservatives, a pressure group which developed the kind of nuisance value the ERG had previously enjoyed.

The other Brexit legacy issue which became a running sore was the Retained EU Law (REUL) Bill. The brainchild of Jacob Rees-Mogg, it was supposed to throw out as many as 5,000 Brussels-made laws in one fell swoop. But in early May, Kemi Badenoch, the business secretary who had taken over the bill, announced that only 800 laws would initially be scrapped. Rees-Mogg accused civil servants of deliberately dragging their feet. Badenoch's argument was that it was better to scrutinise everything more deliberately, since officials were erring on the side of retaining laws that could be scrapped. But one of the organisers of NatCon warned, 'We needed it to be impossible for Starmer to undo when he gets in. On the REUL bill, it will be a piece of piss for Starmer to unpick. Most of the EU acquis [the body of EU laws] will still be in place at the time of the next election.' However, Sunak and his senior aides invited in key players such as Bill Cash, listened to them and made several tweaks to the text of the bill. Not one Tory MP voted against the plans.

The Rwanda policy followed a similar path to Johnson's prorogation. After a four-day hearing in April, the Court of Appeal ruled two-to-one against the government on 29 June 2023, overturning the ruling of the High Court. On the upside, the lord chief justice ruled in their favour, and the court concluded that Rwanda itself was a safe destination – it was the risk of people being sent home from there, or to third countries, which caused concern.

Braverman argued that Sunak should 'pull the bill' and replace it with her version. The government vowed to appeal to the Supreme Court. 'They thought they would win in the Supreme Court,' a Home Office adviser said. 'But that didn't matter because if it was contentious in our courts Strasbourg would interfere anyway.'

Relations between Number 10 and Braverman turned truly toxic in August, when Downing Street put a 'small boats week' in the grid and sought to highlight the progress they had been making on illegal migration. Robert Jenrick, the immigration minister, had two significant announcements: increasing the civil penalties for working illegally and unveiling the first stage of a deal with Turkey, which Jenrick and Sunak hoped would pave the way for the Erdoğan government taking Turkish illegals back. A similar deal with Albania had already reduced arrivals by 90 per cent compared with the year before. Both were overshadowed by a briefing, blamed on Braverman's aides, that she was considering sending asylum seekers to Ascension Island, a remote Atlantic outpost. 'It's a completely mad policy and it isn't happening,' said one senior government source.

Downing Street had planned for Braverman to do a series of media appearances alongside Jenrick. 'She kept pulling out,' a source said. 'It was clearly a Home Office week, and the fact she didn't do anything went down very badly.' Her allies said she had warned that the entire idea was likely to blow up in their faces. 'Small boats week is a good example of what happens when the home secretary's views are ignored by Number 10,' an MP said. 'All it did was raise the salience of a difficult issue.' To cap it all, the *Bibby Stockholm*, a barge hired to accommodate some of the 50,000 asylum seekers living in hotels, was found that week to have traces of legionella bacteria in the showers. In Labour HQ there was hilarity. 'The only boat they were able to stop was their own barge,' Morgan McSweeney told his colleagues.

The tensions between Braverman and Jenrick were now nearly as bad as those between the home secretary and Number 10. Jenrick had visited Italy, Tunisia and Algeria to find ways of sharing intelligence and intercepting the criminal gangs 'upstream'. The home secretary thought this pointless. 'Suella thinks it's absolutely crackers to think we can arrest our way out of the problem in foreign jurisdictions,' an aide said. 'We need the deterrent of deporting people. Everything else is window dressing.'

Downing Street was, by now, tearing its hair out at the operational failures in the Home Office. 'The biggest challenge with Suella was that she saw every problem as a legal problem,' a senior Sunak adviser said. 'She was completely uninterested in actually running the Home Office. All she wanted to do was reach for all the legal levers rather than use the administrative ones. She was convinced we were going to fire her, so she became more and more rogue.'

Everything came to a head in the month after 7 October, when Hamas gunmen from Gaza entered Israel on a bestial orgy of slaughter, capturing grandparents and children, butchering and raping young women – prompting Israel to respond by invading Gaza. The prime minister demanded 'unequivocal' support for Israel and 'unequivocal condemnation' of Hamas. 'There can be no grey areas,' he told aides. Not everyone agreed. The BBC refused to call Hamas 'terrorists' and the brutality of Israel's response, in which thousands of children died, prompted protests from pro-Palestinian groups which went on for months.

In a meeting with Mark Rowley, the Met Commissioner, Braverman became 'deranged' by the marches, shouting and screaming at the police, 'What the hell are you doing? I've given you a chance, this is appalling, it's horrific.' Senior officers and Home Office officials watched incredulously as the home secretary became obsessed with protesters waving Palestinian flags. 'Flags! They're waving flags and nobody seems to stop them. The flags! I've seen it, it's terrible!'

Rowley calmly intervened and explained, 'Home Secretary, we can't do anything unless they are the flags of a terrorist organisation.' A witness said, 'It was bordering on mad. We couldn't believe it and you could see even her own officials were shocked. It was deranged in a way that was improper for a home secretary. She was totally unfit for the job.'

In a further sign of her skewed priorities, officials say Braverman spent 'whole afternoons' in October demanding and examining details of all the DEI – diversity, equity and inclusion – courses being run by the department. 'She wanted to scrap them,' one said. 'Officials had to spend hours and hours collating this stuff. She had lost all perspective.'

By November, with protests planned for Armistice Day, Braverman wrote an article for *The Times* accusing the Met of bias. 'Senior officers play favourites when it comes to protesters,' she wrote. 'Right-wing and nationalist protesters who engage in aggression are rightly met with a stern response, yet pro-Palestinian mobs displaying almost identical behaviour are largely ignored, even when clearly breaking the law.' Five days earlier she had claimed homeless encampments were 'occupied by people, many of them from abroad, living on the streets as a lifestyle choice'.

On the morning of *The Times*'s article, the Supreme Court announced that it was going to reveal its verdict on the Rwanda plan the following Wednesday. An aide warned Braverman she would be sacked: 'They'll come for you but not before the Supreme Court decision, because they'll want you to own whatever happens either way.' He was wrong.

The war in the Middle East, which was occupying a lot of Sunak's time, when he needed to focus on domestic issues, gave the prime minister an idea. In the week after the Hamas attack, he picked up the phone to

David Cameron and found his advice useful. 'Rishi was always keen on ancestor worship,' an aide said. The idea dawned that he would make a good foreign secretary.

When Sunak had scrapped part of HS2, a project Cameron had initiated, the former prime minister tweeted that it was 'the wrong' decision and bemoaned that a 'once-in-a-generation opportunity was lost'. Ten days after the party conference, Isaac Levido went to see Cameron, accompanied by Adam Atashzai, a former Cameron aide back in Number 10. 'He was pretty angry, and Isaac went to calm him down,' a source said. Oliver Dowden, another former Cameroon, also helped smooth relations. Sunak invited Cameron to his Downing Street flat on Tuesday 31 October to sound him out about a seat in the Lords and the cabinet. Cameron asked for time to consider. He had several further conversations with Dowden and consulted William Hague and former aides Liz Sugg, Gabby Bertin, Kate Fall and Andrew Feldman. Two days later, he accepted. After divesting himself of his business interests, the deal was done by Remembrance Sunday. Cameron nearly gave the game away. After the ceremony at the Cenotaph, he said to the PM, 'See you tomorrow.' He was overheard by a cabinet minister, but the secret was so outlandish it held.

The appointment was an exquisitely executed piece of political theatre. When Cameron's blacked-out people carrier pulled up in Downing Street the following day, there were gasps from the waiting journalists when the former prime minister got out and walked to the famous black door. Barely a dozen people knew what was planned.

Sunak's main motivation was administrative. He was approaching an election year, with wars in Ukraine and Gaza needing his attention, and China threatening Taiwan. 'I'm going to have much less time, and I want to make sure we don't drop the ball,' he said. Modern diplomacy was increasingly leader-to-leader, rather than foreign ministry to foreign ministry, particularly in the Middle East. 'Lots of Cameron's contacts were still there, and they were perfectly happy to deal with him in a way that they would not have been happy to deal with anyone who was not a former prime minister,' a senior Sunak aide said.

There was also a political win. Warned by his deputy chief of staff, Will Tanner, that Braverman might resign, Sunak finally decided to sack her. James Cleverly, the foreign secretary, was the obvious replacement. When he consulted Dowden about the Cameron plan, he correctly predicted, 'That would be the story, not the sacking of Suella.'

From Cameron's perspective the attractions were obvious. One confidant said, 'You do get to the stage where you're thinking, "Is that going to be it then for me for the rest of my life?" There has been a dawning realisation that it's not straightforward for ex-PMs to start a business, and David has always wanted to be in public service.' His new role elevated Andrew Mitchell to deputy foreign secretary. When he heard the news that his old boss was returning, Mitchell told colleagues, 'I nearly had an orgasm.' How nearly was not recorded.

Within twenty-four hours the new foreign secretary was conducting an all-staff meeting with stunned Foreign Office officials and diplomats around the world, winning over the sceptics with a self-deprecating talk in which he recounted how Barack Obama had once described them both as 'the best-looking horses in the glue factory'. Freed from the glue factory, Cameron joined a list of former prime ministers who became foreign secretary which included Alec Douglas-Home, Arthur Balfour, Lord John Russell and the Duke of Wellington.

Politics was so strange in the Brexit years that it is worth pausing to reflect on the sheer baroque absurdity of where it now stood. A prime minister who called a referendum to settle the European question that had dogged his party for decades and to stop his MPs 'banging on about Europe', had lost and was exiled, but now returned seven years later to a party more divided than ever. Immigration, the issue through which he had tried to reshape relations with the EU, had returned more pungent than ever. The furore had put air in the wings of Reform, the grandchild party of UKIP, which had menaced Cameron in 2014 and which Johnson and Cummings thought they had slain in 2019. Cameron had originally called the referendum, in part, because he feared being ousted as Tory leader. In the intervening years, Brexit and the divisions fuelled by it had cost his three successors their jobs. Now he returned at the behest of a fourth PM whose removal of Braverman was about to provoke one last leadership plot. *Plus ça change*, as they say.

Cameron quickly proved his worth as both 'prime minister for the world' and in cabinet, where he outshone his colleagues. Returning from his first meeting, he told his private office, 'No one says anything! What is the decision-making meeting in this government? Because it isn't cabinet, and I need to be in *that* meeting.' That soon changed. 'He definitely raised cabinet discussion,' a senior Sunak aide said. 'Not just by his contributions, but everyone felt they had to up their game.'

The appointment was, however, an acknowledgement that Sunak's 'change' strategy was dead, just six weeks after it was launched. Nor was Cameron's return clearly a vote winner. Many Lib Dem-facing Remain voters in the South had not forgiven him for calling the referendum.

The Tory right thought sacking Braverman would leave Nigel Farage rubbing his hands. In the first four polls after the reshuffle the Tories were on just 20 per cent, six points lower than the average of the eight polls the week before. The Brexit Party had risen from 7 per cent to 10 per cent in a week. A Braverman ally said, 'She's not got a broad appeal. People don't like her. But with that Reform vote, she was so popular that it became a real problem for Rishi.'

Despite being fired, Braverman issued a departure letter as if she had walked. She was canny enough to let the media frenzy over Cameron's appointment play out, waiting until the following day to publish her three-page Exocet to ensure maximum publicity. The centrepiece of the letter was her revelation that she had done a deal with Sunak the previous autumn – the first time that had been made public. She told the prime minister he had been 'rejected by a majority of party members' and had 'no personal mandate' but said she backed him 'because of the firm assurances you gave me'. She complained, 'You have manifestly and repeatedly failed to deliver on every single one of these key policies. Either your distinctive style of government means you are incapable of doing so. Or, as I must surely conclude now, you never had any intention of keeping your promises.' Her ideas were 'met with equivocation, disregard and a lack of interest', she complained.

Turning to asylum, Braverman accused Sunak of 'a betrayal' both of their agreement and 'your promise to the nation that you would do "whatever it takes" to stop the boats'. She said Sunak was guilty of 'magical thinking' over Rwanda, 'believing that you can will your way through this without upsetting polite opinion' rather than 'make hard choices'. She added, 'If we lose in the Supreme Court, an outcome that I have consistently argued we must be prepared for, you will have wasted a year and an act of Parliament, only to arrive back at square one.'

Braverman concluded with a blast of fury about the 'hate marches', where she said Sunak was 'uncertain, weak, and lacking in the qualities of leadership that this country needs', accusing the PM of 'occupying the office as an end in itself'. The only moment of self-reflection came when she conceded, 'I may not have always found the right words, but I have always striven to give voice to the quiet majority that supported us in 2019.' Even Braverman's special advisers, who were renowned for their studs-up approach, thought the letter 'monstrous' and 'pretty wild' and toned it down before publication. It was still the most outspoken missive of its kind ever written. 'That letter could have targeted Rishi on the policy of small boats and left out the personal animosity,' one noted.

In Number 10, they regarded the letter as 'faintly ridiculous' – further evidence of Braverman's presumption and destructiveness. A source said, 'It was absurd, but everyone indulged it. This was someone who continually did not hold the line, caused consistent parliamentary handling problems and had an operation that willingly just reaped chaos and madness, and was constantly stepping over the line of propriety.'

There was also frustration in Downing Street that Braverman refused to publicly make the argument that the government was driving down the numbers of asylum seekers crossing the Channel. At Prime Minister's Questions that Wednesday, Sunak did so himself: 'The number of illegal Albanian arrivals is down by 90 per cent. Some 20,000 people have been returned this year. The number of crossings is down by a third.' To Braverman's loyalists, this was proof that Sunak did not understand the politics of immigration. 'The public doesn't care about a 30 per cent cut in arrivals,' one said. 'They care that 30,000 people have come here this year on small boats. We wouldn't talk about the reduction because we knew the numbers were going to go back up.'

Looking back, Sunak's team saw Braverman's letter as trigger for 'a bloodletting' where critics like Danny Kruger and Miriam Cates, joint chairs of the New Conservatives, also let rip. 'All of them spent the best part of eight months going on telly and writing op-eds saying the Conservative Party has betrayed Britain,' said one loyalist. 'Then they all acted surprised when Reform did better than expected at the election. They were equal stakeholders in what was a corporate failure.'

At the time, however, Sunak's allies were dismissive of Braverman and her advisers, believing they could probably only muster twenty to thirty MPs in her support. 'She will now drop like a stone,' a cabinet minister predicted, 'leaving ripples in the pond which will fade away as the waters close over her head.' Asked about the threat, a Number 10 adviser said, 'Suella and whose army?' These jibes would have consequences.

*   *   *

On Wednesday morning, 15 November, Sunak got the news he had waited all year for, that inflation had fallen to 4.6 per cent, less than half the level it had been when the PM issued his five priorities in January. Any satisfaction was fleeting.

Within an hour, the Supreme Court delivered a crushing verdict declaring the Rwanda repatriation scheme unlawful, throwing the government's policy on illegal immigration into disarray. The ruling was far tougher than the Court of Appeal's and more problematic than government legal advisers had expected. Sunak called a press conference to announce that he would introduce emergency legislation to satisfy the court. As Braverman's team had predicted, having failed with Plan A, he needed a Plan B. But in classic Sunak fashion, it took him more than three weeks to act, at the end of which Robert Jenrick, the immigration minister, resigned calling it still inadequate.

The options became identified in the media by different grades of milk, 'from low fat to full fat'. The red-top low-fat version was to sign a new treaty with Rwanda, ensuring that those deported from Britain could not be sent elsewhere and for a Parliament vote to say Rwanda was a safe country. The green-top semi-skimmed option meant disapplying the Human Rights Act in the area of asylum claims, forcing a claimant to take their case to the European Court of Human Rights in Strasbourg, a process which would take time, a period in which its advocates hoped the policy could be shown to have worked. The full-fat bluetop option would also see the government remove the right of judicial review and include notwithstanding clauses, giving the government the ability to ignore the European Convention on Human Rights in the area of asylum without leaving the treaty.

Jenrick had been radicalised by his experiences and favoured the most robust option. He told friends, 'When we have very little time, there is no point having a fight to pass a bill which won't work. Politically, it would be much better to put forward a bill which will work, and if it is blocked by the House of Lords, the blame will rest with Labour and the Lib Dems.' That would have created a dividing line with Keir Starmer at the general election.

Sunak still feared going full Braverman would lead to a rebellion on the One Nation wing of the party and from his attorney general. The PM's tough rhetoric was also undermined by one of the first interviews James Cleverly gave as the new home secretary, in which he said the

Rwanda scheme was not the 'be all and end all' of plans to tackle illegal immigration. To make matters worse for the government, on 23 November the Office for National Statistics revised upwards the net migration figure for 2022 to 745,000, a staggering 139,000 higher than they had estimated in May.

By then Sunak was facing a plot to unseat him directed by Braverman's former special advisers, who were enraged at Downing Street briefing against them ('Suella and whose army?'), which they used as motivation in the way a football manager puts inspirational quotes on the dressing room walls. MPs from the National Conservatives began drumming up letters of no-confidence against the prime minister. This time fifty-three were needed to force a vote. Jake Ryan, the media spokesman, and Joel Winton, her political adviser, were identified by Number 10 as plotters, alongside Sam Armstrong, a political consultant. Theirs was partly a mission of revenge. 'It was made very clear to people in Number 10 that we wouldn't go quietly if they got rid of us,' one said. 'Suella had also made it known, "Come for me and I'll come for you." It was the law of the jungle.' They quickly won the backing of donors who wanted Sunak gone, who paid for an office in Soho. *The Times* later tracked them to Golden Cross House, a block of rented offices off Trafalgar Square, the entrance to which was next to a drag club called Halfway to Heaven.[1]

The advisers, who knew where most of the bodies were buried on the immigration issue, began releasing stories to the media designed to damage Sunak and expose how he had watered down Braverman's proposals. 'We just went for them,' a plotter said, 'it was indiscriminate – bang, bang, bang. We drew up a grid.' Armstrong christened their attack plan 'the grid of shit'. Ryan, who had been a reporter for the *Mail on Sunday* before his incendiary spell in the Home Office, briefed former journalistic colleagues in upmarket restaurants. Glen Owen, the political editor, dubbed the conspirators 'the pasta plotters' after a lunch at Giovanni's, an Italian in Covent Garden run by Sicilian aristocrat Count Pino Ragona, where the walls were covered with photos of celebrity patrons from Frank Sinatra to Liz Truss.[2]

When they began, the plotters lacked more than a hardcore of twenty MPs. The campaign was designed to convince others that Sunak was leading the party to electoral oblivion. 'Their whole plan was to drive the poll numbers down so Rishi was replaced,' a Number 10 adviser said. 'It didn't work, but it was detrimental quite significantly to everyone's re-election prospects.'

The conspirators had no idea how close their plan was to working.

On multiple occasions between September and December 2023, Rishi Sunak openly discussed with his closest confidants whether to resign as prime minister and let someone else lead the Conservatives into the general election. Sunak's personal confidence was shot by his failure to turn around his party's fortunes. 'He definitely, over the autumn period, gave consideration to whether he was the right person to lead it forward,' said one of those in whom he confided. 'He thought about that both before and after the party conference', peaking 'in the month before Christmas'. Aides say Sunak 'flagged it a couple of times in small groups' and spoke to both Oliver Dowden, his deputy, and Julian Smith, the former chief whip who had licence to drift in and out of Downing Street. 'He just posed the question,' one adviser said, '"Is it better that I go and leave it to someone else?" He wasn't trying to cling on. He was thinking, "What's the best thing for the party?" He understood that there were clear downsides to him.'

From each of these confidants, Sunak got the same message, summarised by one of them: 'The idea that we should have another prime minister is clearly mental. That would be terrible for the party. Another revolution at the top is just not going to help.' Sunak eventually agreed but kept asking the question. The PM was 'so loose' that he 'would drop his guard completely and just say what he was thinking in front of officials'. Political aides had to 'grab him' and warn 'You really can't say stuff like that' with civil servants present. Fortunately for Sunak, this agonising never leaked. If it had become public that he was tethered prey, it would have emboldened the plotters and convinced more MPs to turn on him.

The plotters were also unaware that if they had managed to drum up the letters to force a vote, Sunak would almost certainly have walked. A senior Downing Street figure said, 'He would have fought the confidence motion, won it, and probably then at that point said, "Thanks, but no thanks." I think he would have proved the point that he had won, but then said, "Anyone who's had a confidence motion in the last six years has basically been a dead man walking for months. I'm not going to hang around while you guys take pops at me."'

*   *   *

Robert Jenrick's resignation, on 6 December, was a mess of Sunak's creation. When Braverman was fired, Jenrick had asked Number 10 for 'a
proper job'. The assumption in Whitehall was that he expected to be home
secretary, but he actually wanted the Foreign Office. Booth-Smith recommended that he get a promotion. Given his hardening views on
immigration, there was a case for getting him out of the Home Office. But
'Rishi didn't want to do it', an aide said. Again, Sunak's technocratic tenden-
cies trumped shrewd politics. A senior figure said, 'Rishi's view was, "Rob's
done a very good job and we need good people because it's a really important brief." Which is like saying, "I'm actually paying you a compliment by
not promoting you." We should have promoted him and saved ourselves
the hassle because I don't believe that he really cares about the issue at all.'

Home Office officials said this was a misreading of Jenrick. 'Everyone
in Number 10 thought he was a client they could control,' said one. 'Rob
didn't agree at all times with Suella's language, but he thought her position was right – and that's where his constituents [in Newark] were. He
didn't want to take that bill through the House.'

Sunak held three lengthy meetings with Jenrick to try to persuade him
not to go. The first, on the evening of Wednesday 29 November in the
PM's Downing Street study, led to a decision the following Sunday and
an announcement on Monday 4 December to toughen the rules on legal
migration. Cleverly announced that the government would hike the
salary threshold for migrants, scrap the shortage occupation list and
place further limits on the number of family members who could be
brought in – measures calculated to reduce the numbers by 300,000 per
year. But Jenrick was amazed that Sunak had to be dragged kicking and
screaming to do anything. He said later, 'The prime minister was
completely disinterested in this issue ... He only discussed it with me
when I made clear that this was unsustainable, and I would have to leave
the government if we didn't resolve it. I was frankly outraged by the lack
of grip by some within the government on the sheer numbers of people
coming in both legally and illegally.'[3]

Sunak and Jenrick met again for an hour after cabinet on the Tuesday.
Both men left the meeting expecting Jenrick to resign, but they had
further conversations that day to try to improve the bill. In one exchange,
Sunak told Jenrick, 'You would be willing to stand at the despatch box
and say that sometimes vital national interests override contested notions
of international law. I'm not. That's a red line for me.' This account of

Sunak's views contradicted the one briefed by his aides. Jenrick saw a final version of the Safety of Rwanda (Asylum and Immigration) Bill on Tuesday evening and slept on it before deciding it would still not work. He concluded that Downing Street only wanted to get a few token flights to Rwanda in the air before the general election, rather than create a genuine deterrent to asylum seekers. They had another hour-long conversation in Sunak's study after Prime Minister's Questions on Wednesday, but Jenrick resigned around 5 p.m.

While the bill stated that Rwanda was a safe country and disapplied the use of the Human Rights Act in general, Jenrick was concerned it did not disapply it for individual cases. 'Everyone we attempt to remove to Rwanda will mount the argument that whilst Rwanda is generally safe, it is not safe for me,' a Home Office veteran said, 'because I'm a political dissident, I'm LGBT, I have mental health issues.'

Downing Street contested this, saying the loophole would only apply to known dissidents of the Rwandan regime. Sunak's aides were accused of 'cajoling' the Rwandans into publicly distancing themselves from the full-fat option. Shortly after details of the bill were published, Rwanda's minister of foreign affairs Vincent Biruta issued a statement saying it had to 'meet the highest standards of international law' and warning they might pull the plug on the deal. A Jenrick ally complained, 'At the eleventh hour, Rishi invented a further defence, which is that the government of Rwanda wouldn't support the strongest measures. No one said that until after Robert told Rishi he was going to resign.' Those who read 'absolutely stinging' diplomatic telegrams from Kigali say the Rwandans were genuinely stung by criticism in the Supreme Court ruling.

It was not just Jenrick who questioned the efficacy of the bill, however. James Eadie, the Treasury devil, warned that there was a 50 per cent chance that the European Court in Strasbourg would issue an interim injunction preventing flights to Rwanda from taking off. In this event, Sunak's team claimed he would use powers restated in the emergency legislation to allow ministers to ignore such Article 39 rulings. In a meeting with senior aides, the PM said, 'If we are being blocked by a foreign court, I will have no qualms in saying, "Parliament is sovereign."' This was to be his line until polling day in 2024.

Cabinet ministers thought Sunak's handling of Jenrick, once a close ally, inept. 'Rob was overlooked once too often,' a cabinet minister said. 'Rishi shouldn't have allowed that to happen.' Another said, 'When the arse-kisser is kicking you in the arse, you know you have a problem.'

Leadership contenders scented blood. Cabinet colleagues accused Kemi Badenoch, the trade secretary, of calling around to say, 'The ship is heading for the rocks. What are we going to do about the captain?'

Jenrick's departure also led to an audacious suggestion to Sunak's team by Alister Jack, the Scottish secretary. Having seen David Cameron ennobled, he told James Forsyth, 'You should offer Nigel Farage a peerage and make him immigration minister. If he does it, he's responsible, and if he says "No", then you've got him. We go public and we say he was offered the job and bottled it.' It was Sunak who bottled it.

However, Downing Street and the whips were now clever. Rather than ram through the emergency legislation before Christmas, as they had time to do, provoking a huge rebellion which might mortally wound the prime minister, they decided just to have a second reading of the bill. By convention, MPs vote at second reading on the principles of a new law, with a view to ironing out the details at committee and report stages. This put right-wingers, who approved of the idea of the bill but not its execution, in a difficult position. 'It was a clever move because everyone knew that if you voted against him, he'd be gone,' a plotter said, 'but to vote against the second reading is so improper.' At a huge meeting of right-wingers, many rebels concluded they would have to abstain.

In the second reading vote on 12 December, the government won by 313 votes to 269. Some 38 Tories, including Braverman and Jenrick, abstained. Sunak had finally won a battle. His aides mockingly briefed journalists that 'the grid of shit turned out to be just a shit grid'.

The day after Jenrick quit, the plotters gained a new recruit. David Frost wrote an article for the *Telegraph* on 7 December warning that the emergency bill 'won't do the job it's supposed to do'. Five days later, just after the second reading vote, a group of right-wingers met in the office of Iain Duncan Smith to decide what to do next. Will Dry, a young researcher who worked for Booth-Smith in Number 10 but who had grown disillusioned with Sunak, pushed the idea that they should get YouGov to produce a new MRP poll, their first since the 2019 election, to illustrate the dire straits the party was in and shock MPs out of their torpor. 'He was the driving force on the questions and getting YouGov on board,' a colleague said. A donor was found to pay the £100,000 cost of the poll. To disguise the source of the money, a front organisation was created called the Conservative Britain Alliance. Frost agreed to be the face of it.

After fieldwork over Christmas, the plotters gave the poll to the *Telegraph*, which splashed on 14 January with the news that the Tories were on course for a landslide defeat on the scale of Tony Blair's 1997 win, retaining just 169 seats, the greatest government collapse since 1906. YouGov calculated that Reform would not win any seats but would be a major factor in 96 Tory losses.

Dry was only in his mid-twenties, but he had already been on a roller-coaster political journey, from an enthusiastic member of the People's Vote campaign, via a spell as an adviser to Michael Gove, before he badgered Booth-Smith into giving him a job in the Treasury when Sunak was chancellor. After working on the leadership campaign, he went into Number 10 where his mentor was Dougie Smith. Dry was also close to Joel Winton. Friends say Dry went from a 'wishy-washy fan' of Sunak to 'total disillusionment' in a few months. When the poll dropped, Booth-Smith recalled the morning after Braverman was fired. In the 8 a.m. meeting Dry had looked 'like someone had nicked his lunch money', a colleague recalled. Before Christmas, he left Number 10.

Booth-Smith tried calling Dry, who rang back and confessed his role: 'I've been helping out with this poll.' They had a civil conversation, after which Dry called Jake Ryan and predicted, 'They're going to have my name out there within days.' Ryan thought this stupid, since it would highlight how Downing Street had harboured a double agent. But a little later he took a call from Steven Swinford of *The Times*, who had been tipped off about Dry. Later, Swinford told Ryan that he was thinking of not naming Dry, a young man at the start of his political career. But when Ryan informed Dry, he said, 'If they're going to come for me, I'm going to come for them. I'm sick of all the cloak and dagger stuff. Make sure my name goes in the paper.'

It was a curiosity of the grid of shit plot that some of its members remained friends with Tory advisers, even though they knew what was afoot. That evening Ryan was drinking with Harry Cole of the *Sun* and Alex Wild, the CCHQ director of communications. Cole was growing impatient for a statement from Dry. It was suggested Dougie Smith, who was helping to support Dry, had not yet approved it. Wild reported back to Number 10 that Smith was involved with the plotters. When Booth-Smith called Smith, Dark Arts Dougie told him, cryptically, 'I'm not actually doing anything, but I'm aware of things because people tell me things.'

'Why don't you tell us?' the chief of staff asked.
'I'm not at liberty to tell you things,' Smith said.

Nine days later, on 23 January, another bomb dropped on Downing Street. Simon Clarke, a key figure in the Truss government, called for Sunak to stand down. 'The unvarnished truth is that Rishi Sunak is leading the Conservatives into an election where we will be massacred,' he wrote in the *Telegraph*. Clarke said Sunak's 'uninspiring leadership is the main obstacle to our recovery' and predicted that if Nigel Farage returned to frontline politics the Tories would face 'extinction'. He concluded, 'I know many MPs are afraid another change of leader would look ridiculous. But what could be more ridiculous than meekly sleepwalking towards an avoidable annihilation.'

The intervention electrified the media, but it was one without momentum. The plotters tried to find others to break cover, but Clarke, who was in close touch with those drumming up letters, was a lone wolf. 'A couple indicated that they were going to go over the top', but they were deterred by the backlash. Sunak was fortunate that it was not in the interests of potential leadership candidates to strike before the election. Priti Patel, the former home secretary, made a conspicuous display of loyalty, accusing Clarke of 'engaging in facile and divisive self-indulgence'. Even Truss's spokesman distanced her from Clarke. The whips did not think the tally of letters was higher than the 'mid-twenties'.

In the midst of this chaos, Sunak had one of his final political successes, an update to the Windsor Agreement, which enabled the DUP to return to power sharing in Northern Ireland.

The work began, in secret, as soon as the Windsor deal was concluded. Believing Brussels could concede nothing further on the Stormont Brake that would satisfy the DUP, Sunak and his team changed their approach. 'Instead of trying to focus on the return of the institutions,' a senior adviser said, 'we focused instead on the problems that a lack of institutions had created.' Sunak told Chris Heaton-Harris, the Northern Ireland secretary, 'We've got a real-world problem to solve and then we've got a theoretical problem to solve. And the theoretical problem is getting [the DUP] back in. But the real-world thing is pressing – their budget deficit is growing, public services aren't being delivered.'

Heaton-Harris maintained a 'relentless optimism' that progress could be made. John Bew in Downing Street, and the civil servants Brendan Threlfall and Mark Davies helped with the detail. The key figure, however, was Julian Smith, the former chief whip, who was 'critical' to what came next. A senior figure said, 'He was of the prime minister, but not of the government', which meant he was 'trusted by everyone', including the DUP leader Jeffrey Donaldson. 'That meant he could pick up conversations, smooth things out or ginger them up in a way that didn't mean we were ever overcommitted or ever reneging. It was his work that created the space for it to happen.'

By May, Smith thought there was a chance of success. Unlike the Windsor deal, there was no crunch moment, just 'attritional' negotiating. It resulted in some changes to the checks on goods. Second, the government produced a command paper and a small piece of legislation which reasserted the importance of the Act of Union, symbolism vital to the Unionist community. 'That gave Jeffrey the space to go to his people and face them down.' By November, Sunak was talking to Donaldson directly. By mid-December there were regular meetings 'letting him know that if he jumped, we would jump'.

The EU was happy to see changes within the parameters of Windsor. 'The bigger thing with the EU was presentational, because the DUP were incentivised to make it sound as big as possible and the EU were incentivised to make it as small as possible,' a Downing Street adviser said. Sunak resisted DUP demands that the text describe Windsor as 'fundamentally changed'. There was no mention of a new 'framework' or an 'agreement'; it was just a tidying up exercise.

The price, as usual, was cold hard cash. Sunak began saying Belfast had to raise all the extra money it needed in tax, but ended up handing over £3 billion. The PM also had to face down ERG hardliners, including Christopher Howarth, David Frost and Boris Johnson, who tried to reopen the issue of regulatory divergence. The DUP wobbled, but when Donaldson decided to accept the deal, the ERG realised (to use a wildly inappropriate phrase) 'They could not be more Catholic than the Pope'. A senior source said, 'The real hero in the end was Jeffrey Donaldson, who had the political bravery to act.'

On 30 January, Donaldson announced that the DUP would re-enter power sharing. Eight weeks later, he was arrested on charges of historic sexual offences against two children. Political life comes at you fast.

* * *

From January 2024, Isaac Levido moved full-time to CCHQ and was in Number 10 two or three times a day. The main subject of discussion was when to call the election. Sunak had asked Booth-Smith to draw up a list of possible dates the previous October. The options he presented were: December, March, 2 May to coincide with the local elections, June/July or October/November. A senior source said, 'At the very start of the year the consensus amongst pretty much everyone was that we were going to go long, that things would hopefully improve.' By law, Sunak could call the vote as late as January 2025, but on 18 December he had stated publicly that the election would be in 2024.

In the first week of January the media spent three days in a row asking when the election date would be, a parlour game which risked swamping Downing Street's messaging – that voters faced a 'choice' between two visions for the economy and two leaders, Sunak and Starmer, whose personal ratings, while better than the PM's, were mediocre. Booth-Smith and Levido drew up a form of words: 'Our working assumption is the second half of the year', an attempt to hint at an autumn election while leaving the door open for the spring.

Sunak's team, meanwhile, finally found an effective way of selling him to the public, posting social media videos of Sunak marking progress on his five priorities using flip charts and graphs of falling inflation and reductions in the number of boats. These were not universally popular with MPs, who felt they were patronising and emphasised the geek in Sunak. But a Tory source said, 'Those things tested incredibly well.'

Whatever slender Tory hopes remained depended on the fact that 20 per cent of voters had yet to make up their minds who to vote for – double the usual number at this stage of the electoral cycle. 'Most of them say they will only decide when they have to,' a Tory aide said. Levido's figures showed that only 50 per cent of voters who had backed Boris Johnson in 2019 were still supporting Sunak's Conservatives. Those who had switched to Labour, around 15 per cent, were lost for good. The battle would be to win over some of those who were likely to sit on their hands and win back some who had switched to Reform.

The events of February made this more difficult.

At first it seemed like Labour were the ones struggling with a smaller party leeching votes from their political flank. The arena was the Leave-supporting town of Rochdale, where a by-election was caused by the death of former Labour minister Tony Lloyd. In Labour's candidate selection, Azhar Ali, who had stood twice in Pendle in 2015 and 2019, beat Paul Waugh, a lobby journalist, and Nazia Rehman, a Wigan councillor. Within a fortnight, the *Mail on Sunday* obtained a recording of a meeting in which Ali suggested that Israel had allowed Hamas' 7 October attack to go ahead, in order to 'green light' an invasion of Gaza. Ali was forced to apologise, but Starmer stood by him. However, no one at Labour HQ bothered to listen to the recording, which was emailed to them by the newspaper. When the *Daily Mail* published further comments on 12 February in which Ali attacked 'people in the media from certain Jewish quarters', Labour withdrew support from their candidate. Ali remained on the ballot paper, but the row opened the door to George Galloway, running under the banner of the Workers Party, to campaign on the issue of Palestinian rights. He swept to an easy win on 29 February, declaring, 'This is for Gaza.'

This was the backdrop when Lee Anderson, the former poster child for the red wall Tories, was accused of Islamophobia during a discussion on GB News. The MP for Ashfield took aim at Sadiq Khan, the Labour mayor of London. 'I don't actually believe that the Islamists have got control of our country,' he said, 'but what I do believe is they've got control of Khan and they've got control of London, and they've got control of Starmer as well.' Asked to apologise, he refused.

Sunak, desperate to show greater strength than Starmer, who had taken forty-eight hours to move against Ali, stripped Anderson of the whip on 24 February, defying the advice of both Levido and Booth-Smith, who feared a backlash from Reform-leaning voters.

To placate the right, and disgusted by Galloway's win, Sunak made a speech on the evening of Friday 1 March, denouncing extremism. It was so dark in Downing Street that hardly anyone noticed it was raining. Another episode with implications later.

Events then moved with dizzying speed. Anderson had previously claimed he was offered 'a lot of money' by 'a political party that begins with an R' to defect. Richard Tice, the leader of Reform, denied this but the day after his suspension, Anderson met Tice and on 11 March he joined Reform as their first MP. Farage's former pollster, Chris Bruni-Lowe, told him that if he returned to lead Reform they would overtake the Tories 'within forty-eight hours'. Farage, earning a good crust from

GB News and with the promise of lucrative media deals in the US if Donald Trump returned to the White House, was torn. He admitted UKIP's performance in 2015, when it secured 4 million votes and just one seat, 'haunts me'. He said, 'I don't need to do that again. But if I think we really can break through in a big way and totally realign the centre-right, that's the key factor. The historical odds say I'd be wasting my time, but somehow things just do feel a little bit different.'

Sunak's government now seemed paralysed and listless. The week Anderson defected, Number 10 spent several days failing to close down a story about the Conservative Party's biggest donor, Frank Hester, making racist remarks. The Yorkshire businessman told colleagues Labour's Diane Abbott made him 'want to hate all black women' and that she 'should be shot'. First Downing Street defended him, then refused to say the comments were racist.

Even loyal ministers were now in despair at how decisions 'disappear into the building', never to emerge from the 'black hole'. The usually mild-mannered Alex Chalk, the justice secretary, had a blazing row with Will Tanner, the deputy chief of staff, over prison capacity. For weeks the Ministry of Justice had been pressing to introduce legislation on sentencing to ease the pressure on prison places. It was politically unpalatable, but so was the alternative. 'Pass the bill or start releasing people early,' Chalk shouted. 'Those are your only choices. Would you please just pick one!' They didn't.

Watching this rolling barrage of disaster, the plotters remarked that Sunak was doing their work for them. The notorious media plan was re-branded again as 'The grid of *their* shit'.

They had just one play left, to find an alternative candidate who could step in if the local elections were a disaster for Sunak. Having concluded that Braverman would not command the necessary support, the plotters met in Henson's Bar and Social, an oak-panelled cocktail lounge with red velvet curtains in Soho. There they decided to explore whether a deal could be done with Penny Mordaunt, who was topping the ConservativeHome poll of grassroots supporters. Mordaunt would have to make the right moves on immigration if they were to avoid a protracted leadership battle. The story got legs when one of the plotters and several journalists shared a box, and a considerable volume of alcohol, at the Cheltenham Festival in mid-March.

In grave danger of losing her seat, Mordaunt had a bigger incentive to move against Sunak than the other frontrunner, Kemi Badenoch. Her outriders, including Nicola Richards, held arm's-length talks with the rebels, sounding each other out. A plotter said, 'Penny had two meetings in her parliamentary office with leading figures from the right.' One of these was Simon Clarke. 'She was asking for people's support but keeping it implicit. Her outriders had more detailed conversations about whether there could be a coronation and who she might need to give jobs to.' But senior MPs on the right, such as John Hayes, still opposed Mordaunt over her position on trans rights and made clear they would not back a coronation. Mordaunt dismissed claims she was plotting as 'nonsense'. David Davis, an ally, said, 'These stories have been put around by her enemies, not her friends.'

While Anderson's defection undermined the Tory effort to woo Reform, the OBR had thwarted Sunak and Hunt's hopes of offering sweeping tax cuts in the budget on 6 March. The chancellor was in his office in 11 Downing Street on the evening of Wednesday 28 February when the email arrived which helped make the case for an early general election. Entitled 'EFO' – Economic and Fiscal Outlook – the email contained what aides call 'the holy figure', the amount of 'headroom' in the government accounts which could go on tax cuts or extra public spending. At the start of that week, the chancellor thought he had around £15 billion to play with. The new email revealed that the number was down to £12.8 billion. 'Cumulatively, they knocked £2 billion off,' a Treasury source said.

Over the previous six weeks, the OBR had provided half a dozen updates and each left the government with less money. At the start of the process, it was £30 billion. That Friday, when the final figure was sent to the Treasury, it was down to £12.5 billion. Hunt scrapped a plan to abolish inheritance tax. Most of the changes were the result of an evolving macroeconomic picture. However, the £2 billion taken away that Wednesday was lost because the OBR ruled that a series of pro-growth reforms the Treasury had counted in the budget 'scorecard' would not raise as much money as Hunt hoped.

Ministers and Sunak's aides regarded this as a deliberate effort by the OBR to thwart pre-election tax cuts. 'They have deliberately screwed us,' a senior minister said. One of Sunak's closest aides agreed: 'The OBR kept taking away the headroom because they knew we were going to use it for tax cuts. They decided they didn't think that was responsible or good governance.'

By budget day, the following Wednesday, Hunt had found enough money to cut National Insurance by another 2p in the pound. But having received little political benefit from doing so before, MPs despaired. Sunak and Hunt agreed on the plan but some of their advisers and most of their MPs wanted an income tax cut, which would have helped pensioners, who did not pay National Insurance. In a bid to shoot Labour's fox, Hunt announced the phasing out of the non-dom tax regime. Rachel Reeves, the shadow chancellor, was relying on scrapping it to pay for several pledges. Hunt then signalled that he would like to scrap National Insurance altogether when it was affordable to do so, calling it a 'double tax on work'.

When they realised what he had said, Reeves and her shadow Treasury team immediately began crunching numbers. She said, 'We've got to grab this.' An aide recalled, 'We had a press release out that night saying this is going to cost £46 billion.' The Tories contested that saying it was an aspiration, not a costed policy, but Labour exploited a misunderstanding among some voters that NICs paid for the state pension and the NHS, to ask which of them would be cut to pay for the plan.

The immediate takeaway for Hunt, however, was that the OBR would make it impossible for him to cut taxes in an autumn statement, which had been seen as a vital curtain raiser to an autumn election.

In the first half of March, Sunak and his team had dinner in the Thatcher study in Number 10 and debated whether to cut and run and call the election for 2 May, the day of the local elections. While Simon Hart, the chief whip, was 'quite keen' so he did not have to deal with the parliamentary fallout of a heavy defeat, Andy Street, the mayor of the West Midlands, had very firmly asked for Sunak to avoid that date since he was up for re-election and did not want to be dragged down by the national campaign. 'The one firm decision coming out of that was that we're definitely not doing it on May 2nd,' an aide said.

However, word of the discussions spread and on Thursday 14th rumours swept Westminster that Sunak would go to the palace the following Monday. In Labour headquarters, Morgan McSweeney put his candidates on alert. Sunak's aides exchanged messages. There was 'total unanimity' he should publicly rule out a May election. One of them called the PM, who was campaigning in the West Country. He delivered the line in a local broadcast interview.

The truth, however, was that Sunak doubted the situation was sustainable for another six months. A senior cabinet minister added, 'With every passing month, the economy looks better, but with every passing month the Tory Party looks more ungovernable.' Conversations which were sporadic in January and February became more regular. Members of Sunak's inner circle were growing spooked by their 'lived experience' of government. 'Shit was going wrong,' a source said. 'There were concerns about more by-elections, concerns about the result of the locals and the fear that things would get worse.'

There were three or four major conversations in April. As deputy prime minister, Dowden saw it as his job to ask the question. He told friends he had no strong view, but others were clear he was keenest to move quickly. 'Olive was the firmest,' a colleague said, using Dowden's nickname. 'James [Forsyth] was more open-minded but responsive to the PM's mood', which was now leaning towards getting on with it. 'Liam had worries about holding the building together over what would have been a pretty dicey summer'. Another aide said, 'Rupert [Yorke] saw problems around every corner and just wanted everything to end. He and Nerissa [Chesterfield] were exhausted. They were worried Rishi would limp through the local elections and then face an assassination attempt by the MPs, which would leave him mortally wounded and limping on.'

The discussions increasingly focused on upcoming problems, of which overcrowding in prisons was a concern of Dowden's. The bigger problem was imminent public sector pay deals, where the unions could hold the government to ransom. Finally, there was illegal migration, with a new armada of small boats predicted and the issue of whether they would be able to get a repatriation flight to Rwanda in the air before polling day.

The pay deals were a particular concern for the prime minister. 'He is flinty about public money,' a close aide said. 'He knew that in those summer pay negotiations we would be in a very weak position. The unions had basically said, "If you don't want us to strike and destroy your election chances, we want inflation-busting pay rises all round." He really didn't like the idea of being forced into that.'

On Rwanda, whatever Braverman said, the team thought they had a workable solution which would put flights in the air eventually – and soon if they won the election. But with the chance to run out the clock before polling day, the courts might thwart them. 'We would have faced legal challenge on Rwanda,' a senior adviser said. 'If everyone knew that we had five years to make Rwanda work, some of the legal challenges would have become pointless. Given that we had six months to run, you are at high risk.' Sunak's team thought the British courts would find against them in order to delay a showdown with the European Court of Human Rights. 'If you are the judiciary, the last thing you wanted was a confrontation between us and Strasbourg before the election. They would have put themselves in between us and a showdown with Strasbourg. I think we would have really struggled to get the flights off.'

Rwanda was a symptom of a problem they all felt: the almost palpable erosion of power. 'Everyone knew we had to have an election, everyone could read the polls, and it was very difficult to get through what we wanted to get through. Rishi felt that renewed political authority to push things through both the civil service and the parliamentary party was necessary.'

The only problem with this growing consensus was that the man who had been hired to run the election disagreed. Isaac Levido, the campaign director, thought strategically that autumn would be the best time to maximise the Conservative vote, once optimism about the economy had begun to influence voting intention. There was the chance of an interest rate cut over the summer, which he saw as a more concrete symbol of revival than falling inflation. Levido was also struck that most of 'the good, hard-working MPs' wanted to go long. 'We'll be surprising and pissing them off,' he warned. This message was repeated by Craig Williams, Sunak's parliamentary private secretary: 'Your first rule of politics is don't surprise your colleagues.'

On 3 April, Levido and his sidekick Michael Brooks penned a memo for Sunak outlining the case to delay. 'It is strategically most beneficial to have an autumn election in October or November,' they explained. 'Choosing to go earlier in summer sacrifices strategic value in order to mitigate issues related to party management and governance.'

Levido said the Tory framing of the campaign, 'Stick with the plan vs back to square one', would not change. However, he warned that its 'potency' would be 'impacted by the timing of the election'. They would need to name the date 'in line with an inflection point which is emblematic of things improving'. He suggested this could be 'inflation reaching

2 per cent or interest rates being cut (ideally successively)' allowing them to argue 'we have steadied the ship and now we must look forwards'.

'Leveraging economic progress and future economic competency lends itself to a later election,' the memo argued. 'We need as much time as possible for economic metrics to improve and for voters to feel better off. An earlier election gives us less scope to communicate about economic progress, because voters are less likely to feel financially optimistic.' An early election would leave them 'fewer economic proof points' and 'less able to credibly assert the risks of Labour taking over the economy and how that would impact voters, because in the eyes of voters, there would be no "stronger economy" that Labour might jeopardise'. The paper also argued that moving before summer would remove the 'potential positive psychological effects of summer', including 'lower energy bills', 'holidays', 'better weather', the Euro 24 football tournament and the Olympics.

The memo acknowledged the concerns of Sunak's team, that a late election 'could leave us vulnerable to internal party division and other off-message distractions and policy challenges (e.g. strikes, increased Channel crossings)'. But going early meant the Tories would have to deploy more 'wedge' issue policies 'because we would have less ammunition to fight on the economy'. Levido warned, 'This approach comes with inherent risks of its own, such as dividing the party on contentious issues and then lacking coherence in its communication.'

The memo concluded, 'The election will be a fist fight, and we want to be able to throw punches with both fists – our "economy fist", and our "policy platform/reform fist" … In summer, our ability to fight on the economy will be weaker, meaning we will have to punch harder with our reform fist in order to hurt Labour and inject urgency into the campaign. Whereas in autumn, our ability to throw punches on the economy will be stronger, meaning we can hit Labour hard with both fists.'

Senior figures in CCHQ agreed and told Sunak, in writing, that they were not ready to fight an election. 'There was a paper trail from CCHQ, from the chairman and others,' a senior Tory said. More than 100 seats had no candidate and fundraising was in a parlous state, with donors reluctant to pay for Sunak to get a shellacking. 'Every month they write to the prime minister about election readiness. We did not have enough candidates and we did not have enough money.'

When all this was discussed, Levido realised his strategic rationale might have to defer to tactical issues. This he dealt with calmly. 'He was a sceptic not a screamer,' said a cabinet minister. 'Nobody was a screamer.' A senior aide agreed: 'It was finely balanced. No one was 100 per cent one way or the other. Everyone was 60–40 maximum level of confidence. There was not an easy answer anywhere.'

They all hoped for an interest rate cut, but the prospect 'kept receding' and the political benefit was less easy to calculate than in decades past. Booth-Smith, Forsyth and Dowden all warned that interest rate cuts no longer fed through immediately to mortgage rates with so many families on long-term fixed rates. In February a friend of Booth-Smith's in the City told him, 'Forget the polls, this is the key number – 100,000 people every single month are having to remortgage onto much higher rates from a fixed rate. In the time you've been in office, nearly two million people are physically paying the price of the mini-budget. No tax cut is going to make up for a five grand a year increase in your mortgage.'

In the end, they could all see that Sunak was at the end of his tether. 'Every day was grinding him down,' a minister said. 'He was dragging himself along for public service, for the sake of the party and the country, making himself do it. He was not enjoying office. In the end, his approach was, "Nothing else is working. Just bring it on."' A close aide agreed, 'I think, for him, it was a sense of taking initiative.' Like Corbyn before him in 2019, Sunak seemed to be choosing 'suicide by electorate'.

By the final week of April, the decision to go in July was made – they just needed to see the outcome of the local elections. Two days before that vote, knowing he was still opposed to the idea, Sunak called Levido back into his office after a meeting. He had found a glimmer of hope in the numbers. 'You never know, things might be a bit better than expected,' said Sunak. 'Maybe we will have some options.'

'Yes, maybe we will have some options, Prime Minister,' Levido replied.

It wasn't to be. Alex Wild and Nissy Chesterfield had successfully spun that the real test of Tory credibility was not council seats but whether they could hang on to both the mayoralties in the West Midlands and the Tees Valley. In the North-East, Ben Houchen was returned with a much reduced majority.

In Birmingham, Andy Street was fighting for his political life, running virtually as an independent with no Conservative branding on his literature, let alone mentions of Sunak. The decision to cancel HS2 had hurt a candidate who most neutrals felt had done a good job, but Labour-run Birmingham Council falling into bankruptcy had kept him competitive. Both Levido and Labour strategist Morgan McSweeney expected Street to cling on by the slenderest of margins, but McSweeney threw the kitchen sink at it, pulling all his ground staff out of the Tees Valley with more than a week to go and sending all available resources to Birmingham. After a full recount, Labour's Richard Parker won by just 1,508 votes, a margin of 0.3 per cent. Street had every reason to resent Sunak. 'Andy absolutely despises him,' a minister said. A former Number 10 aide explained, 'When Rishi was chancellor, Andy found him haughty, arrogant, patronising and dismissive.' Now, a drag-anchor too.

Labour gained nearly 200 council seats while the Tories lost more than 500 and fell behind the Liberal Democrats for the first time since 1996. Starmer spent the morning studying the swings and vote shares in key seats, a man more similar to Sunak than either of them cared to admit. 'You don't need to tell Keir to stay focused,' a Labour official said. 'He's like a football manager with five games to go in the title race, doing the quick fist pump to the crowd, then getting down the tunnel. No celebrating at this stage.'

The good news for Sunak was that he was safe from another parliamentary coup. The plotters had met three weeks earlier at an office in Soho and decided they would 'pull our punches' unless three trip wires were triggered on 2 May. Both Houchen and Street would have to lose and the Tories come in third behind Reform in the Blackpool South by-election, held the same day. In Blackpool, the Conservatives held on to second place by just 117 votes, but the rebels decided Sunak should 'own' the general election defeat to which they had all contributed.

Shortly afterwards Jake Ryan ran into Jamie Njoku-Goodwin from Downing Street in the gents at the Arts Club in Chelsea, a favoured haunt of the Westminster nocturnal set. Sunak had survived the onslaught, though the plotters had inflicted huge damage to the government's credibility on immigration and capped eight years of infighting with a leadership plot worthy of Gilbert and Sullivan. No one had won. They exchanged expressions of 'no hard feelings'. In that moment, the grid of shit was finally flushed down the pan. The damage done meant the Conservative Party was at risk of following it.

The local election campaign was not entirely wasted for the Tories.

Sunak used it to unveil new policies which Levido had warned in his memo would be needed if they went early. On 19 April, Sunak gave a speech on welfare, setting out plans to strip GPs of their power to sign people off work in an attempt to tackle the 'sick note culture' which had left 2.8 million people economically inactive due to sickness. On the evening of 22 April, the Rwanda bill finally completed its passage through Parliament. The following day, the prime minister announced a plan to increase defence spending to 2.5 per cent of GDP by 2030 at a cost of £75 billion. This would be paid for by axing 72,000 officials, returning the civil service to its pre-pandemic size – a move which meant Labour did not rush to support it.

In Labour headquarters in Southwark, McSweeney looked at the policy onslaught and concluded a general election was close. 'It's very unusual for a party of government to be spending £70 billion the week before local elections,' a source said. Nationwide, Labour made gains where they needed to win seats at the general election, such as Hartlepool and Redditch. McSweeney's favourite win was Rushmore, a seat which included Aldershot. 'Sunak tried pushing defence spending and security as an election issue and now he's lost the home of the British Army,' a Labour official crowed. Despite Houchen's win in the mayoral contest, the swing to Labour in the Tees Valley was big enough for Labour to reclaim every parliamentary seat in that red wall heartland.

Labour officials reflected on a visit to party HQ the week before by Nancy Pelosi, former speaker of the House of Representatives. In an address to staff, she commented on Starmer's winning mindset: 'He made a decision to win, and he's made every decision along the way in favour of winning. Sometimes, that changes things.' She added, 'This election is a heartbeat away. It's right around the corner, so thank heavens you're so ready and organised.'

In CCHQ, Levido and his team found crumbs of comfort that Labour's lead was lower when the public cast real votes. Labour won the national equivalent vote by 35 per cent to 26, a nine-point lead, when most polls had them 20 to 25 points ahead. In London, the Tory mayoral candidate Susan Hall lost to Sadiq Khan by 11 points, half the margin YouGov was predicting with two days to go. The Tories also clung to the hope that Reform's 17 per cent showing in the Blackpool by-election meant they were underperforming relative to UKIP in 2014 and 2015. It would prove to be a hope that killed.

Suella Braverman came out swinging, with another *Telegraph* piece blasting Sunak's 'managerialism'. The collector's item was the intro, in which she said it was too late to change leader. 'The hole to dig us out is the PM's, and it's time for him to start shovelling', a sentence which made no sense practically, gramatically or politically. 'It looked bitter and cheap when councillors were getting wiped out,' a plotter remarked. 'She had very little to say except "I told you so".'

The lack of a miracle revival meant Sunak was resolved to call the election for July. On Monday 13 May he made his last big pre-election speech, at the Policy Exchange think tank: 'The choice at the next election is: who do you trust to keep you safe?' It tied together economic safety with global security (branding Russia, China and Iran an 'axis of authoritarian states'), the challenges of illegal migration, violent protests and 'gender activists hijacking children's sex education'.

Three days later, Starmer unveiled a new Labour pledge card, the top item of which was 'economic security'. That Friday, Jeremy Hunt tried to frame the economic battle lines, revealing costings showing, he claimed, that Labour had a £38 billion 'black hole' in its spending plans which it would need to plug with tax rises. Labour was still campaigning on the claim that the Tory desire to abolish National Insurance had left a £46 billion gap. As Levido's memo explained, going early meant going harder, because Sunak had to raise the threat of Labour in voters' minds. Sunak had presented himself to the public as a technocrat who could deliver, but in his own terms he had failed. Of the five tests he had outlined in January 2023 only two or three – halving inflation, getting the economy growing and getting debt down after five years – could be said to have been met, and the latter relied on a projection. NHS waiting lists had been falling for six months but were still above the level he inherited. The boats had not been stopped. Just one migrant had been returned to Rwanda, three weeks earlier on a voluntary scheme, after the government handed him £3,000 to go.

Most of the cabinet had no idea what was coming and many of them thought Sunak's team was not ready. Penny Mordaunt went to see the prime minister on the third weekend in May. She had worked on George W. Bush's election in 2000. She gave the PM a list of Republican contacts in Washington who were willing to help the Tories. One call from Sunak and they would come. She told him he needed better support, 'especially on communications', and 'owed it to everyone to mount the best campaign he could'.[4] Mordaunt heard nothing more.

That Sunday, Sunak told the chief whip, Simon Hart, and his parliamentary aide Craig Williams that he was going to call a snap election, a conversation which would have disastrous consequences.

On Tuesday evening, 21 May, Sunak asked David Cameron to see him. The foreign secretary was due to travel to Albania the following day. In his study in Number 10, the PM told his predecessor he would have to return early the following afternoon for the election announcement. Cameron, surprised, said, 'It's the most difficult decision you have to take as prime minister. I totally respect you.' He told a colleague later, 'It was too late to say anything, other than to offer my support.'[5] Liam Booth-Smith called Jeremy Hunt to give him a heads-up too.

On the morning of Wednesday 22 May, official figures said inflation was down to 2.3 per cent, virtually back on target. Sunak gave the final 'go' order. Policies like his smoking ban would have to be abandoned in the 'wash-up' in Parliament. An aide said, 'He didn't want to cling on and be dragged out like Gordon Brown and John Major.'

At 3.30 p.m. Sunak called in eight senior ministers to tell them. Alongside Cameron, they included James Cleverly, Michael Gove, Grant Shapps, Kemi Badenoch, Simon Hart and Alister Jack. Some of those summoned, knowing that an election was on the cards, were delighted the PM had finally decided to consult his senior elected colleagues. Then Sunak opened his mouth and said, 'I have been to see the King. This is my decision. I'll explain it to you and then, when we go next door, I'll call on you to speak, and I want you to back me.' The ministers were not a kitchen cabinet, they were expected to rubber stamp a decision already made. Sunak explained that he wanted to 'turn the spotlight on Starmer' and that only by calling an election could the Tories force the public to listen to their arguments or face 'the choice' between two prime ministers.

Gove offered the motto of the SAS: 'Who dares wins!' Cameron mused that having been prime minister under the Fixed-term Parliaments Act, 'I never had to make this decision.' He called it 'tough' for Sunak and added, 'It either works for you or it doesn't. If you think Labour isn't ready, then you've got my full support.' Those watching thought this less than fulsome. The foreign secretary repeated his comments in the cabinet which followed at 5 p.m. but told a friend that week it was a 'bad idea'. The friend said, 'He doesn't think the country wants an election. No one in the cabinet supports this, apart from Dowden.'

Shapps was uncomfortable, telling Sunak in the pre-meeting that he would not have chosen that moment 'if it was my decision'. Others said Kemi Badenoch 'looked unhappy – a bit windy', though she did not vocalise any doubts. In the main cabinet meeting that followed, Shapps was not called on to speak. Esther McVey and Chris Heaton-Harris both made clear they did not agree with the decision either. 'Esther spoke out very strongly against it,' a colleague said. Everyone else muttered supportive bromides. They were then forced to wait so they could watch Sunak tell the nation.

The rain was already falling when Nissy Chesterfield went to talk to Sunak in his study. She had told the broadcasters to be ready in ten minutes. She remembered the extremism speech he had given in the rain a few weeks earlier. No one in the media had cared because it was dark. Now it was light. 'It's manageable,' she said. 'What do you think?'

They looked at weather apps, but they were already running late. 'What's the alternative?' Sunak asked. The team had set up the pillared state room upstairs as a possible launch venue. It would be chaotic, though. Civil service staff could not help with a political announcement. It would take half an hour to get the broadcasters into the building and set up. They would miss the top of the six o'clock news. Chesterfield envisaged newspaper reports criticising Sunak as too weedy to go out in the rain. The prime minister was adamant he wanted to do it: 'This is a big moment. It needs to be on the steps.'

They considered a coat or an umbrella but concluded that would invite a 'wally with the brolly' headline. Sunak was trying to spring a political surprise, but it was him who looked unprepared. As he stepped into the street, the persistent rain became a downpour of biblical proportions. Sunak's jacket first darkened in great gobs of black as if he had been hit by a sniper aiming waterbombs, then it saturated until it could absorb no more, the water gathering in iridescent pools which resembled the shiny cloth of an overused cheap suit – the multimillionaire in his bespoke two-piece trapped behind his lectern like a defendant in the dock dressed in a polyester blend from Man at C&A. Torrents of water ran down his face as Sunak, never smaller, peered grimly through the murk, chin raised in vain defiance as he gravely intoned, 'These uncertain times call for a clear plan.'

He didn't seem even to have a plan for the English weather.

Worse, those watching at home could hardly hear what he was saying. In front of the Downing Street gates, anti-Brexit campaigner Steve Bray had pointed two huge speakers up the street and was drowning out the prime minister's address to the nation with the New Labour theme tune, 'Things Can Only Get Better'. 'We spoke to the cops at the front gate three or four times,' a Number 10 aide complained. 'But they said, "We can't do anything," which is great.' The festival of democracy in all its horrific glory. Only when Bray's two enormous amplifiers were 'soaked and blown' did the music stop.

In the Cabinet Room, where a television had been set up, ministers stared open-mouthed. 'What is that?' asked an incredulous Esther McVey. 'What are we watching?' One minister who had been in on the decision shrank into his seat. 'Occasionally you have just very, very bad moments in politics,' he recalled. 'As the speech started and the rain poured, I just wanted the ground to swallow me up.'

Back inside, Sunak laughed and 'shook his arms', water spraying off him like a whippet who has made an impromptu diversion into a pond, the sodden cloth of his suit steaming in the warmth, a spent racehorse.

Westminster mocked. Levido and Brooks commissioned a focus group to see how bad it was. 'The voters didn't care,' a campaign official recalled. One poll found that just 30 per cent thought it damaging. When one veteran of SW1 told a campaign chief that Liz Sugg, Cameron's formidable head of operations, would never have let him walk into a downpour like that, the sanguine reply came: 'Mate, she'd have gone outside and looked at the rain and it would have stopped.' That Sunak had no one like that was part of the issue.

The bigger issue was that he had fired the starting gun on a general election for which his opponents were better prepared.

PART SEVEN

OVER AND OUT

THE 2024 GENERAL ELECTION

June to July 2024

'There are times, perhaps once every thirty years, when there is a sea-change in politics. It then does not matter what you say or what you do'

– James Callaghan, 1979

OUT OF THE WILDERNESS

How Keir Got Here

May 2021 to June 2024

Labour stole a six-hour head start on the Tories. The day before, Morgan McSweeney, the campaign director, had received a text message from a friend in the polling industry who kept an eye on the betting markets. There had been a surge of money for a July election. McSweeney had always suspected Sunak would go early and had only recently accepted that an autumn vote was on the cards, booking a family holiday for July. Now his antennae were twitching. 'I think they're going to do it,' he said. The next morning speculation was rife that the election could be called. At 10.24 a.m., another text, this time from a senior journalist: 'I'm getting silence from the usual election deniers. We have also booked a holiday. FFS.' In Parliament, Keir Starmer was preparing for Prime Minister's Questions. They talked. By the time PMQs began at noon, McSweeney was back at Labour head-quarters in Southwark, sure enough that he fired the starting gun on Labour's campaign.

The choreography had been planned for months, the launch grid writ-ten and rewritten, the vital first few hours meticulously planned. First impressions count. In quick succession, McSweeney and his fellow campaign chief, Pat McFadden, signed off a target seats list and took a final decision on the slogan: 'Change'. 'It is who we are, it is what we are offer-ing, but mostly it is what we are asking voters to do,' McSweeney said. 'It is an ask.' The design team descended: 'Do you want it lower case or upper case? Do you want a full stop?' Capitals, white letters on a red background, no full stop, an arrow-shaped flag in the corner. All printed and on a lectern ready for Starmer's launch speech, which had to fit into a fifteen-minute window between Sunak's and the top of the six o'clock news – impossible if they had waited.

In Labour's computer system already sat copies of the freepost leaflets, each of their candidates would send to Royal Mail for distribution to voters. 'All the photographs were done, the contact details, the endorsements, the scripts, everything was online,' a Labour official said, 'because we made every candidate do it. We got all of the YouTube videos ready for our candidates.'

Some things, involving large sums of money, had to wait until everything was confirmed. When Sunak emerged from the black door of Number 10 for his drenching, Tom Lillywhite, Labour's head of digital, turned to McSweeney and pointed out that it was still possible to purchase banner adverts for election week on a host of key websites, including YouTube and the home pages of the *Sun*, *Mail* and *Express* newspapers. 'They haven't bought them; shall we buy them?'

'Yes!' said McSweeney. He had money in the bank and had agreed protocols with the other key players on how decisions would be made; there did not need to be a meeting. 'We had a culture where we could sign things off quickly,' a party official said.

In Conservative campaign headquarters, McSweeney's opposite number Isaac Levido had lost the element of surprise in a campaign where he had warned that it was one of the few cards they held. Worse, he did not realise it. Worst, he would later discover it was down to betrayal in Conservative ranks. It was strange that the campaign springing the surprise had not bought the digital advertising already – it was a key trick Levido's digital team had pulled in 2019. What Labour did not know yet was that the Tories were very tight on cash.

Around 5.45 p.m. Starmer took to his own podium, inside, 'CHANGE' emblazoned in front of him and declared, 'A vote for Labour is a vote for stability, economic and political, a politics that treads more lightly on all our lives. A vote to stop the chaos.'

McSweeney and Levido were similar characters in many ways: watchful, intense, bearded, not shouters, people who commanded a room by a sort of inner force and presence rather than demonstrations of profane despotism. Neither was English. McSweeney grew up in Cork, in southwest Ireland, in a Fine Gael family. Only one could win. They both had known defeat and the sweet catharsis of triumph. They both retained a humble understanding of how fine a line there sometimes was between the two. The difference between them? Levido's party had lost the discipline and memory of how to win. McSweeney had, in Starmer, helped forge a leader with the will and belief to do so.

History shows that Labour won the 2024 general election. Every amateur historian knows that 'governments lose elections, oppositions don't win them'. But to take advantage of failing governments, oppositions must look like a credible alternative. The roots of Keir Starmer's victory lay as much in the events of the previous three years on Labour's side as it did the six weeks after McSweeney took that call about suspect betting patterns.

The events depicted in *No Way Out* showed Starmer understood how to use power to push Labour towards backing a referendum, an exercise he knew was necessary to secure the party leadership. After an initial period in 2020 and 2021 where he sought an accommodation with the left, Starmer and McSweeney put in place an uncompromising strategy, which they pursued with discipline and relentlessness. Theirs was an application of power in pursuit of a clear goal which matched in intensity that of Boris Johnson and Dominic Cummings in 2019 but far exceeded it in longevity.

It did not always look like that would be the case. On the eve of Labour's 2021 party conference, a member of Starmer's team told the columnist Dan Hodges that, during the leadership contest of 2020, Starmer had made a startling confession: 'You know, I don't get politics. I don't understand it. And I don't really like it.'[1] The conclusion of many by the autumn of 2021, with Boris Johnson riding high in the polls, was that Starmer had already blown it. In fact, that was the eve of his boldest action to put things back on track.

When he took over, just as the pandemic was beginning, Starmer had a three-stage plan: change the party; introduce himself to the electorate and prosecute the case against the government; then convince voters Labour was a government in waiting. He had been talent-spotted by McSweeney, who had run Liz Kendall's 2015 leadership bid, which garnered just 4.4 per cent of the vote in Jeremy Corbyn's landslide win. The Irishman was working for Labour Together when he decided Starmer was the most likely candidate to win a general election and vowed to make him so. That he was not a political obsessive helped. In Labour's endless internal tribal wars Starmer was a clean skin. 'That's one of his greatest strengths,' a frontbencher said. 'He's not part of a faction.

He's not associated with Brownites or Blairites. He just doesn't think in those terms. He doesn't have that baggage, so he can move faster because he's travelling light.' He was also more open to advice than most politicians in their late-fifties making a bid for the top job.

Initially, Starmer tried to unite the warring factions, issuing pledges during the leadership election to woo Corbyn supporters (all of which he later ditched). 'He thought if you ran the operation better, we could make it work,' a close aide said. 'He was struck by the utter incompetence of his predecessors, but I think he underestimated some of the malign activity that would happen.' An MP said, 'To start with he thought you could do business with the hard left, but when he realised that was impossible he knew he had to cut them off at the knees.'

In October 2020, he did so. Corbyn responded to a damning report by the Equalities and Human Rights Commission into antisemitism in the party by claiming the problem had been dramatically overstated for political reasons. Starmer stripped him of the whip. When the party's ruling National Executive Committee recommended it be restored, the leader refused. A senior member of the shadow cabinet said, 'That was the moment, for me, when I turned to colleagues and said, "This guy is the real deal."'

The first year was difficult, though. Covid meant Starmer struggled to differentiate himself from a government he had, in some regards, to support. Boris Johnson was an elusive target for a forensic lawyer who had never faced such bluster in court. The turning point was the Hartlepool by-election in May 2021, a seat once held by Peter Mandelson, where the Tories won with a 16 per cent swing. Starmer nearly resigned but was persuaded to stay and clear out his team.

In came Deborah Mattinson, Gordon Brown's former pollster, as director of strategy, and Matthew Doyle, a Blair era veteran, as director of communications. Jill Cuthbertson, an aide to both Brown and Ed Miliband, became gatekeeper to professionalise Starmer's office. McSweeney moved to take over planning for a general election at party headquarters, where his skillset was better suited. Mandelson said later, 'Keir's leadership has been a game of two halves. The first was Covid and clearing up after Corbyn. The second half has been post the calamity of the Hartlepool by-election.'

That autumn, with Labour seemingly as distant from power as ever, Starmer and McSweeney plotted their boldest move – changing party rules to reduce the power of members to elect the leader, the key move in preventing a resurgence of the hard left. McSweeney saw it as protecting 'the soul' of the party. 'Keir took power away from party members,' an aide said. 'No party has ever done that before.' The trap had to be sprung at the last moment, with the agenda for the key meeting kept blank to wrong-foot their opponents. The leadership of Unite, the party's biggest paymaster, was implacably opposed. A friend of Starmer's died the weekend before the party conference, a bereavement which was much on his mind as he made what allies thought his most important decision as leader. 'He knew it was very tight,' an aide said, 'but he knew it was vital.' On a Zoom call with McSweeney and his new chief of staff Sam White, he said, 'Let's go for it.'

The crunch came late at night when Paddy Lillis of Usdaw told Starmer he would support him. It was gone midnight when Gary Smith of the GMB, who had been stuck in a reception all evening, visited Starmer in his suite. 'If we're with you, what are the numbers?' Smith asked.

'50.3 per cent,' said McSweeney.

'Are you sure?' The margin was razor thin. There was no room for error. It was not worth Smith helping if they were going to lose anyway. The plan would have to be pulled or Starmer's authority would be shot. 'Yes,' McSweeney said. Smith wanted to speak to his lawyer.

McSweeney went with him. They also talked to Matt Pound, who had worked on Starmer's leadership election and was now head of political organising for the party. It was 2 a.m. when McSweeney returned to Starmer's suite and said, 'Gary is with us.' Starmer hugged him. 'Keir is not a hugger,' an aide observed.

Then Unison had a delegation meeting. Christina McAnea, the general secretary, decided she did not want to be left on the sidelines. McSweeney got a text message: 'We're not abstaining, we're backing you.' Starmer won with 53.67 per cent of the vote. McSweeney said to Starmer, 'We've got our party back.'

Now all they had to do was turn it into an election-winning machine. That same month, September 2021, Starmer was interviewed by Laura Kuenssberg. 'What is more important,' she asked, 'unity or winning?' One of those who joined after Hartlepool said, 'I think at one stage Keir would have said, "It's not a choice, you need to be united to win." But he immediately said, "Winning." At that point, I realised I had made the right choice.'

Those who didn't think Starmer was fanatical about winning had never seen him on a football field. 'He's a bloke in his sixties who still plays five-a-side,' one witness said. 'He's the captain, in the middle, doing all the shouting. And if he's not winning, he shouts a lot.' Alastair Campbell, Blair's spin doctor, called him 'a dirty footballer', intended as praise. Aides spoke with amused awe at a game Starmer made them play against the Scottish Labour Party. 'We were losing at half time and he said we were all fired if we didn't win,' one recalled. 'As soon as we took the lead, he said the game was over.'

The other big move, post-Hartlepool, was a ruthless reshuffle in May 2021. The most significant change was replacing his shadow chancellor, Anneliese Dodds, with Rachel Reeves. Dodds, academically clever but politically inexperienced, represented the woolly and earnest Starmer. The appointment of Reeves, a former Bank of England official, showed he meant business. Together Starmer and Reeves began instilling discipline in the shadow cabinet, refusing to support ad hoc spending commitments. A shadow cabinet colleague said, 'The appointment of Rachel was a real game changer.'

McSweeney decided that the way to beat the Tories was not to avoid their traditional strength – the economy – but to eliminate it as a strength. In early 2022, he gave a presentation to the shadow cabinet in which he displayed a picture of the Death Star from *Star Wars*, which gives the empire its strength but is then destroyed. 'The economy is the flaw in this massive weapon the Tories seem to have built,' he said. A Labour source explained, 'They had traditional Tory voters that wanted to focus on growth and smaller state and then a newer coalition that was more interested in better public services and levelling up. What they ended up with was George Osborne levels of public services and John McDonnell levels of taxation.'

Then, in September 2022, came Liz Truss's mini-budget, an event which presented a great political opportunity but which meant an incoming Labour government would have far less money to spend. Reeves was watching the Laura Kuenssberg show in her hotel room at Labour's conference in Liverpool. Starmer was on. Chancellor Kwasi Kwarteng said there was 'more to come' by way of tax cuts. 'The first thing Keir and Rachel both said when they saw each other was, "How are markets going to respond?"' a senior adviser recalled. The pound duly tanked and the duo realised their own economic plans would have to change. 'It showed why discipline really matters – in opposition but also in government,' the adviser said. 'That had a material effect on our ability to do what we want to do.'

In February 2023, Starmer tried to give shape to his election offer, responding to Sunak's five priorities with five missions for his premiership: to secure the highest sustained growth in the G7; to make Britain a 'clean energy superpower'; to build an NHS 'fit for the future'; to make Britain's streets safe; and to 'break down the barriers to opportunity at every stage'. These remained frustratingly vague even a year later, but they would provide the structure for the manifesto.

A core part of Starmer and McSweeney's success was that they learned from their setbacks. In July 2023 Labour narrowly lost the Uxbridge by-election after the Tories seized on Sadiq Khan's plans to extend the ULEZ clean air levy on motorists. This convinced Sunak he could win favour with his party by opposing green policies. It convinced McSweeney that Labour governments ought to listen to voters when they said they didn't like new taxes. 'They decided to focus on their party not on the voters,' a party official said. 'We did the opposite.'

At the party's National Policy Forum (NPF) in Nottingham two days later, where the leadership presented its plans for the next manifesto, Starmer pressed the unions to back tight fiscal rules and continuing with the two-child cap on child benefit payments, a policy loathed by his party but popular with the public. Ben Nunn, Reeves's spokesman, stuck a Post-it note above his desk to remind him of her top priority. It said simply 'trust'. Voters needed to look at Labour for the first time in two decades and trust them with their money. Everything else was secondary. At the shadow cabinet meeting beforehand, Starmer made clear this was not just for show. A frontbencher said, 'Keir was clear we could not go to the NPF saying, "Let's agree this language, but don't worry, when we're in power we'll do something softer." He said there couldn't be side deals, or nudges and winks. We have to be honest with ourselves and the country.' A party official added, 'We made sure that the whole weekend was focused on outcomes for voters.'

The loss in Uxbridge also prompted McSweeney to conduct a 'top to bottom' review of Labour's election machine to see how messaging and voter targeting could be improved. Reviewing the data he was pleased to find that Labour's 'vote efficiency' was now much better, picking up support in marginals, rather than stacking it up in safe seats. 'In 2019 if we had beaten the Tories by 12 per cent we would have got a majority of one, because of where our votes were,' an official explained. 'We thought we could change that with two types of voters: non-graduate voters in England and voters in Scotland. Because of voter efficiency the winning line is no longer a 12-point lead, it is much lower.' Around 5.3 per cent, according to one calculation.

In every area Labour was getting more professional. Hollie Ridley had conducted 'the biggest overhaul of field operations since the mid-nineties', a senior figure said, hauling a machine still using techniques pioneered by Bill Clinton's New Democrats into the twenty-first century. The attack unit under Paul Ovenden, advised by Damian McBride, the once notorious, still brilliant, spin doctor for Gordon Brown, was causing the Tories difficulties.

Another reason Labour was more match fit was their response to the Tories introducing laws to make it mandatory for voters to show photo ID at polling booths. This came into force for the local elections in May 2023. Most Labour activists thought it was an attempt at voter suppression. McSweeney was sick of his party behaving like 'victims' and 'a bunch of losers'. His order went out, 'I don't want people on Twitter talking about how the election is fixed with voter ID. Nearly every single voter has a necessary ID, and voters think it's a sensible idea. We might not like it. We are not going to get mad; we're going to get even.' Data showed that the single biggest thing you could do to increase the likelihood of a supporter voting was to get them to fill in a postal vote, and the best way of persuading them to do that was to just ask them. McSweeney ordered activists not to leave the doorstep until they had asked Labour voters to apply for a postal vote. Labour's postal votes rose by 20 per cent.

In September 2023, Starmer had the confidence to go after the government on immigration, traditionally a Tory strong suit, vowing to 'smash the gangs' trafficking migrants in small boats. The Tories regarded this as breathtakingly naive about how difficult it was to stop illegal migration, but it showed Starmer's willingness to park his tanks on their lawn. It was a theme he had been encouraged to tackle by Australia Labor strategists, who had been advising Labour after beating Isaac Levido in the previous Australian election.

Tackling immigration was also a way of trying to win back Labour's key audience – what strategist and pollster Deborah Mattinson identified as 'hero voters'. These were one-time Labour supporters who backed Brexit and then voted Tory in 2019.

September also brought a reshuffle billed as a return of the Blairites. But it was much more about putting in place people with experience who were ready to run a government. Witness the promotion of Pat McFadden, the return of Hilary Benn, the positioning of former Brown aide Jonathan Ashworth at the heart of preparations for government, the return of Liz Kendall, a former special adviser – most of all the hiring of Sue Gray, the veteran civil service fixer, as chief of staff.

Party conference that autumn was designed to answer the question, 'If not the Conservatives, why Labour?' To prevent complacency, MPs, unions and others hosting parties and fringe meetings were banned from introducing Starmer as 'the next prime minister'. Later that month, they won the Mid-Bedfordshire by-election, a 'proof point' that they were now competitive in rural areas.

In October, the Tories changed the law to increase the spending limit in general elections to £34 million. Instead of complaining, McSweeney said, 'They must have £34 million; we must raise £34 million too.' A party official said, 'It was one of the most successful fundraising drives in our history.' It turned out, the Tories had nothing like £34 million.

When 2024 began, the policy offerings were in place, with one exception. The Tories were making hay with Labour's pledge to commit £28 billion to hitting net zero targets, calling it a 'black hole'. If it was not dealt with, it would be the central plank of the Conservative election campaign. Despite a protracted rearguard action by Ed Miliband, the shadow minister responsible, Starmer, with Reeves's backing, announced in February that Labour would now only commit £8 billion to the goal, calling the pledge no longer affordable.

McSweeney was able to force the pace, since from the end of 2023 he had insisted that the party be ready for a general election on 2 May. When Jeremy Hunt used his autumn statement in November 2023 to cut National Insurance from January, rather than April as was usual, McSweeney told colleagues: 'They say autumn, but they act like it's May. That's a £2.5 billion tax cut. That's a lot of money to spend giving yourself options. It would be the most expensive bottle job in history.'

What mattered, though, was not what the campaign director thought but what he did. 'Morgan didn't just say, "We need to be ready for May,"' a colleague recalled. 'He told everyone, "The general election is going to be in May." He did presentations for the shadow cabinet with "Polling Day, May 2nd" on them, working backwards saying when the election would be called. Manifesto submissions had to be in by 8 February. He had no interest in a parlour game about when the election might be. Everyone was told they had to be ready. It was a bit like a religious cult. No one was allowed to talk that way.' McSweeney also ran a 'McCarthyite war on complacency'. A senior Labour source said, 'It's like *Minority Report*, where they try to prevent crimes in advance by knowing what you are thinking. Morgan ran around saying, "I heard you told your mum that you are feeling confident. Don't."' When anyone did question his decision to prepare for May, or sought to psychoanalyse Rishi Sunak, McSweeney snapped, 'It all just comes down to one thing: what's in the head of one man that none of us has ever really met. You've no qualifications; you never met the guy. So stop talking and just prepare.'

Preparing meant working out every possible date Sunak might fire the starting gun and constantly updating Labour's plan. 'What if he calls it on a Monday? What if he calls it on Tuesday? What if he calls it after a cabinet meeting? What if he calls it at noon just before PMQs? What if he calls it after PMQs? If he calls it at 5 p.m. is that still day one on the grid, or is it day zero?' And when Sunak did not opt for 2 May, preparing meant using the local elections to road test Starmer's messaging, as well as the ground campaign. 'We changed two regional directors in local elections,' a campaign source said.

All the leaflets which candidates had submitted for the general election were checked to ensure consistency in the messaging. One candidate had a draft rejected several times because it didn't contain a Union Jack. 'Fucking everything has to have a fucking flag on it,' said another candidate.[2]

McSweeney drew up a four-point plan for power. Jonathan Ashworth, the shadow Cabinet Office minister, relayed it to Labour aides before Christmas: 'The first point is that the country needs change. The second is that the Tories have already failed. The third is that Keir has changed the Labour Party. The final leg is to show that we have a plan for changing the country.'

Preparing meant getting staff who had never fought an election up to speed – and reminding those who had what was involved. Starmer gave several pep talks to rally the troops. There was more practical advice from the big names of triumphs past. Few who saw it quickly forgot

Alastair Campbell's thoughts on remaining hydrated: 'Yellow piss is losers' piss!'[3]

Preparing meant updating the battleground. Labour was hugely ambitious. Jeremy Corbyn had won 202 seats in 2019. By the time Parliament was dissolved, that had risen to 205. In June 2023, more than a year out, McSweeney drew up a list of targets which would take them to 400 seats. These were divided into seven different categories, one defensive and six attack:

0: Labour-held seats but where boundary changes made them more vulnerable, or which would have been lost in 2019 if the Brexit Party vote had collapsed
1: Tory or SNP-held seats which ought to fall easily
2: Seats needed to remove the Conservatives from government
3: Seats needed to make Labour the largest party
4: Seats needed to secure a Labour majority
5: Seats needed for a 'strong majority'
6: Those which would bring Labour to 400 seats, a majority of 150

'We kept monitoring and supporting activity in all of those seven types of seats,' a Labour official said. 'What we assumed is that we would shrink down in the election.' In the end, they didn't need to.

In February 2024, George Galloway's win in the Rochdale by-election created an eighth category of seat and a new unit in Labour HQ to handle them – those with a significant number of voters motivated by Labour's stance on the war in Gaza. After the 7 October attack, Starmer stated his support for Israel, a position abhorred by many MPs and activists, for whom Palestinian rights was a driving passion. He moved, crablike, towards backing a ceasefire, but not quickly enough for his critics.

There was an immediate impact on Labour support in their internal polling. 'From October last year, we had multiple problems,' a party official said. 'We lost some Muslim voters', but just as concerning were those who didn't vote. A list of twelve seats where this was an issue was drawn up, including three in Birmingham, two in Bradford and Blackburn, and two in Tower Hamlets. The list did not include Leicester South, where Jonathan Ashworth was MP. 'We had a unit focused on that. It was like a separate region focusing on those twelve seats, with their own plan and resources. We had to build a different coalition of voters to win.' Grimly, it also meant 'making sure the police are on top of any threats' to Labour's candidates, who were routinely being accused of complicity in genocide by Islamists. The complication was that almost none of the seats had ever been marginals, so there was a lack of campaigning infrastructure on the ground. At a shadow cabinet meeting after Rochdale, McSweeney said, 'We will have a Rochdale in the general election.'

Labour's final road test during the local election campaign came on 7 April when Labour put out an extremely aggressive attack ad against the prime minister. Tory voices were trying to link Labour to Asian grooming gangs in Rochdale. The digital team under Tom Lillywhite and Caitlin Roper produced a picture of a beaming PM with the words, 'Do you think adults convicted of sexually assaulting children should go to prison? RISHI SUNAK DOESN'T.' There was a factual basis for it. Some 4,000 were given community sentences or suspended sentences after child sex abuse cases.

Since the 2022 local elections McSweeney had instituted a 'Tinkerbell rule' to Labour campaigning: 'If you're on the Tory grid, a Labour councillor dies.' He wanted to see if he could take control of the news agenda. 'We knew it would create a row,' a source said. 'We wanted to see if we could grab hold of the microphone.'

McSweeney flew up to Scotland for Good Friday. When he got off the plane, his phone exploded with hundreds of messages. The reaction was highly negative. John McDonnell declared, 'We, the Labour Party, are better than this.' Some elements of the left called the advert racist. 'Staff were upset and worried,' a Labour official recalled. 'They didn't like being called racist on Twitter. A lot of people hated it.' It was now a test of nerve. The following morning, McSweeney chaired a meeting about a second advert, which said, 'Do you think an adult convicted of possessing a gun with intent to harm should go to prison? RISHI SUNAK DOESN'T.' An official said, 'Everyone was very nervous, but we decided to put it out. That was probably the most important decision of any campaign to do the second ad.' This was the Vote Leave manual: always double down.

The third ad turned the spotlight on Sunak's wife Akshata Murty's non-dom tax status: 'Do you think it's right to raise taxes for working people when your family benefited from a tax loophole? RISHI SUNAK

DOES.' Shadow ministers badmouthed the campaign and avoided broadcast interviews. Four out of ten did not tweet any of the adverts. But the Labour official said, 'When we did the third one it was clear we were not fucking about. We needed to tell the whole organisation that we were strong. People could see that they couldn't break us, and we would keep going.' They did a fourth one too and then stopped. The point was proved. They were blooded. They were finally ready.

While McSweeney prepared for the election, Sue Gray prepared for power, running transition talks between the party and the civil service. Inevitably there were briefings about a power struggle between the two, some denouncing 'the boys club' in the campaign, a monicker directed at McSweeney, Pat McFadden and Doyle, whom Gray was rumoured to be trying to freeze out, a campaign dubbed 'just stop Doyle'.[4] The tone of the briefings 'pissed off' Mattinson, Cuthbertson, Ridley, Marianna McFadden, and all the other senior women on the campaign. Starmer put a stop to it, making a speech on 17 April at HQ saying he would sack anyone, 'whoever they are', caught briefing against his team.[5]

Starmer and McSweeney were both mild-mannered men, but in each other they had found a kindred spirit who understood power like they did. A former cabinet minister said, 'What Keir has done is get us in a position where, when the apple fell from the tree, it did actually fall into our laps.' A leading broadcaster, who spoke regularly to Starmer, thought he knew why: 'He has become a ruthless bastard – and that's a good thing. He really, really wants to win.' When he was elected, people had thought Starmer might, at best, be another Neil Kinnock, there to prevent oblivion and begin the rebuild. But as Mandelson observed, 'It took Neil Kinnock and Tony Blair fourteen years to do what Keir has done in four years.' The game of politics might not have appealed to Starmer. In truth, it still didn't. 'Some people like the sport of politics,' a senior aide said. 'His conclusion, from the jobs he did before, was that politics was the best vehicle for change.' Unlike Sunak, Starmer realised that to achieve change you needed to play the game and play it to win.

When they saw the prime minister standing like a drowned rat outside Number 10, there was hilarity at Labour HQ. McSweeney joked with colleagues, 'I've been telling you for months that we have to be absolutely prepared and up to speed to take on the might of the Tory campaign machine. And then that happens.'

31

'APRÈS LE DELUGE'

The Campaign

22 May to 4 July 2024

'Whenever any form of Government becomes destructive ...
it is the right of the People to alter or to abolish it,
and to institute new Government'

– Thomas Jefferson, Declaration of Independence

The team gathered in Conservative campaign headquarters in Matthew Parker Street knew they had to come out fighting. Isaac Levido's plan was to grab the attention of the public early and hope to drive up the Tory poll numbers. So much depended on getting close enough to Labour that he could put the squeeze on voters who had defected to Reform and did not want Keir Starmer to be prime minister, but did not think the Conservatives had any chance of winning.

Sunak certainly grabbed public attention in the first two days of the campaign – for all the wrong reasons. The prime minister began with visits to England, Wales and Northern Ireland, each of them memorable for a gaffe. Two Conservative councillors were unmasked asking him questions on a visit to a warehouse in Derbyshire. In Barry, south Wales, Sunak asked whether everyone was looking forward to 'all the football'. Wales had not qualified for the Euros. Then, on a trip to the Harland & Wolff shipyard in Belfast, he spent time in the Titanic Quarter. 'Are you captaining a sinking ship going into this election?' was the first question. Sunak said, 'Our plan is working.' It wasn't.

Some of these were Sunak's fault, some were basic failures of operational planning, the kind of thing an experienced advance team would prevent. Ruth Davidson, the former Tory leader in Scotland, tweeted, 'Is there a double agent in CCHQ? ... Our candidates deserve better.' Levido's problem was that the campaign was short of both experienced operators and money. The Tories had raised more than Labour in 2023, but a party official admitted, 'That only made up for a barren 2022 when Boris and Liz were having all those problems.' As Sunak failed to make any impression, promised donations dried up.

The morning after the election was called, Liam Booth-Smith, the chief of staff, summoned special advisers for a 10 a.m. meeting in Downing Street. Many were still smarting that their summer plans had been disrupted and their ministerial bosses risked losing their seats. Those not in the key security departments would lose their jobs and were encouraged to join the campaign. They would work for free, living off their government pay-offs – but since Sunak had not been prime minister for two years these would be smaller than usual. If he had waited until at least 25 October this would not have been the case. Then Booth-Smith said any spads not taking part should come to see him. In his mind, he wanted to ensure their pay-offs were arranged quickly. What they heard was different. 'Liam basically said that if we weren't going to join the campaign we should come and explain why not,' one said. Around half of government special advisers never even collected their pass for CCHQ, still less helped out. While Levido had built up a twenty-strong digital team, senior Tories had expected CCHQ to hire the New Zealanders of Topham Guerin again. Bluntly, they couldn't afford to.

False rumours spread in the first week that veterans like Lynton Crosby and George Osborne would return to bolster the campaign. Crosby was in Australia and a friend of Osborne said this was not only untrue but impossible: 'George thinks Rishi is hopeless. He's always thought he doesn't have a big political brain and that Rishi has made two big calls in his career – backing Brexit and backing Boris – and that those are the two most catastrophic things to happen to this country in the last decade.' Johnson was another who was out of the country when Sunak called the election. Speaking trips and a family holiday would keep him out of the country for most of the campaign.

In the parliamentary party there was cold fury that the prime minister seemed prepared to sacrifice so many of his MPs and incredulity that the campaign opening was so shambolic. Many were furious that they had little time to prepare for the end of their careers.

Sunak tried to raise morale, visiting CCHQ on the first Saturday of the campaign to give a pep talk to the staff. The PM handed out a fluffy kangaroo and koala to the 'Tory of the day' and the 'Tory of the week', Levido's way to reward junior staff for their contributions and maintain morale. Then he said, 'Labour are sitting there thinking they can waltz into Downing Street without saying what they want to do with the great privilege and power of being in office. They think they can take the British people for granted and it's our job not to let that happen.'

While Labour wrote most of their manifesto in March, the Tory document was still a work in progress and key aides, such as Will Tanner, the deputy chief of staff, left to seek a safe seat. 'They were still recruiting people to work on the manifesto last week,' an insider said at the time. Tanner, who was selected as the candidate in Bury St Edmunds and Stowmarket, was one of several parachuted in to discover there was no such thing as a safe seat any more. His was one of one hundred rushed selections which caused bad blood with grassroots campaigners just as they were needed on the ground campaign. Other favoured sons – including special advisers Henry Newman and Declan Lyons and the journalist turned think tanker Seb Payne – narrowly missed out on selection having been put on shortlists of three drawn up by CCHQ. In Tunbridge Wells, James Forsyth insisted the broadcaster Iain Dale be put on the shortlist in his hometown. Three days later he had withdrawn after a podcast recording emerged in which Dale had said he 'never liked' the town and 'would happily live somewhere else'.[1] None was more controversial than the 'chicken run' of party chairman Richard Holden from the red wall to Basildon and Billericay, where there was no shortlist at all. Holden was simply imposed. Disgusted local activists went to campaign in other seats.

What Levido did have, in line with his April memo, were two major policy announcements to try to attract the attention and votes of Reform-leaning voters. 'The first rule of politics on any campaign is you've got to try and unite your base first and then you worry about swing voters,' a campaign official said. 'The two biggest groups were those who were defecting to "don't know", and those who were defecting to just Reform. We also had some problems with pensioners.'

Tory hopes that some of these votes could be clawed back intensified the day after the election was called when Nigel Farage announced that he would not be running for Parliament, saying it was 'not the right time' for him to return. He confirmed he wanted to be free to campaign for Donald Trump: 'Important though the general election is, the contest in the United States of America on 5 November has huge global significance.' Curiously, Farage also told his employer GB News that he had been planning to launch a campaign the following week to become an MP but pulled it because he did not have several months to do it properly. Sunak's team congratulated themselves on wrong-footing Reform. Farage's announcement overshadowed confirmation, the same day, that no flights to Rwanda would be leaving before the election.

On 26 May, the Tories announced a policy calling for compulsory national service for eighteen-year-olds. Sunak said it would create 'a shared sense of purpose among our young people and a renewed sense of pride in our country'. The reaction from young people, however, was more a shared sense of outrage. It was, as one Tory aide put it, David Cameron's 'National citizens' service on crack'.

The national service policy suffered from two problems. While the headline was eye-catching, the policy was more subtle. Only 30,000 teenagers who took part each year would be on a military placement, the rest would have been doing community service. This was missed by some voters. Second, there was confusion about how teenagers would be compelled to join the scheme. James Cleverly, the home secretary, had to be sent out to say that no one would go to jail, but military men pointed out that the last thing an overstretched army needed was to have to deal with thousands of untrained youths each year.

McSweeney leapt on the confusion, telling colleagues, 'They've exposed the throat. It looks chaotic. We can attack it from so many angles. We can mobilise the youth vote. We can get ex-military personnel to attack them for undermining the army.' On a video call with candidates, McSweeney said the opening salvos proved the Conservative manifesto would be 'an eighty-page panic attack'. When Jonathan Ashworth used the line on television, McSweeney was 'told off' for using mental health as an attack line.

However, as an attention-grabber the policy did its job effectively. 'Everyone was running around with their head on fire,' a Conservative campaign official said, 'but the goal was to dominate the agenda and it worked. We knew Labour would be saying nothing. We had to try to narrow the gap in the polls in the first week – then the media narrative around it would have been "game on".' Despite the criticisms, Tory candidates reported back that national service had 'huge cut through' on the doorstep. Jeremy Hunt, who was fighting to hold his Surrey seat, made the case that, despite being chancellor, he was a dedicated local MP. One voter expressed surprise: 'I didn't realise you were chancellor, but I did hear about national service.'

Two days later, on 28 May, Sunak unveiled what he called the 'triple lock plus'. In future, not only would the state pension rise by the highest of average earnings, inflation or 2.5 per cent, the income tax personal allowance for pensioners would also increase so it remained above the threshold at which people start paying income tax. When Labour refused to match this pledge, the Tories were able to claim that Starmer was planning a £275 million income tax raid on pensioners between 2027, when the state pension was expected to rise above the basic rate threshold, and 2030. Those of a cynical disposition noted that it was Sunak as chancellor who froze income tax thresholds in 2021, and Sunak as prime minister who kept them frozen, which created the problem in the first place – but this was an effective wedge issue.

Starmer, Reeves and McSweeney came to an agreement in October 2023, when Hunt was preparing his autumn statement, that they would 'support every tax cut' the Tories made 'for working people' while they were still in government. 'We wouldn't have followed them on inheritance tax, if they'd done that, but we did on National Insurance,' a source said. However, for the campaign the decision was made, 'We weren't going to match their manifesto.' These were forward-looking ideas from a Tory Party which was unlikely to be in government. 'We took a decision not to chase them on taxes during the campaign. We could have said we would put a billion in to move the threshold so that no pensioners would have to pay taxes. But our argument was, "The country can't afford these tax cuts." If we had tried to solve that problem in that way, we'd have created a bigger problem for ourselves.'

Labour's decision not to engage put them momentarily on the back foot. Reeves had ruled out increases in income tax and National Insurance but in the first week of the campaign had repeatedly ducked saying the same about VAT. On the evening of 29 May, Hunt went on the attack. In an article for the *Telegraph*, published at 10.30 p.m., he condemned Labour's 'higher taxes for millions of pensioners' and wheeled out the £38.5 billion 'black hole' identified in Labour's plans during the local elections. It would, he wrote, mean 'they would have to increase taxes on working families by £2,094 over the next Parliament'. He warned that plugging the gap would be the equivalent of putting VAT up from 15 per cent to 21p in the pound.

After crisis calls, Labour issued a late-night press release in which Reeves said it was 'absolute nonsense' she was secretly planning to hike VAT. 'Labour will not be increasing income tax, National Insurance or VAT,' she declared. In CCHQ they celebrated a win. The Tories got a small bump out of this double whammy of big news policies. But the undecided voters were not returning in sufficient numbers. 'One of the things I got wrong', a Sunak adviser said, 'was that I underestimated how many of the undecided voters had decided not to vote for us – they just hadn't decided who to vote for.'

Nonetheless, despite a sticky start, national service and the triple lock plus made the Tories feel like they were in the game, not least because Labour were having their worst moment of the campaign.

One of Starmer and McSweeney's big successes early in his leadership was expelling hard left Corbynites from the candidates list. When the election was called, they seized the opportunity to purge further ideological undesirables and parachute in key allies likely to be loyal, dubbed 'Starmtroopers'. Georgia Gould, the leader of Camden Council; former Starmer aide Chris Ward; Luke Akehurst, a veteran bête noire of the hard left; and Josh Simons, director of Labour Together, all landed safe seats. Paul Waugh was selected for Rochdale with the unenviable task of taking on George Galloway, and Heather Iqbal, an aide to Rachel Reeves, was given Dewsbury and Batley, another seat where passions were inflamed by the war in Gaza.

Faiza Shaheen, known as the 'Chingford Corbynista', was blocked from standing against Iain Duncan Smith, who she had come within a thousand votes of ousting in 2019, after an investigation of her social media posts. Lloyd Russell-Moyle, the MP for Brighton Kemptown since 2017, was suspended following a complaint about his behaviour dating back eight years, which prevented him standing. He blamed a 'vexatious and politically motivated' claim. Corbyn, meanwhile, launched his campaign to run as an independent in his Islington North seat.

All of that paled into nothing next to the Diane Abbott affair. The seventy-year-old MP for Hackney and Stoke Newington had been suspended by Labour in April 2023 after she said Jewish people were victims of prejudice not racism. In March, Starmer told Radio 2 the investigation was still ongoing, when it had concluded four months earlier. With the deadline for nominations approaching, a decision had to be made on whether to give Abbott back the whip.

Starmer's closest advisers say that while Abbott was a Corbynista, he had always viewed her differently to the other members of the hard left campaign group. She was Britain's first Black woman MP, party royalty, something akin to a national treasure. 'I know Keir was told she wanted to retire with dignity,' a senior adviser recalled. 'He always put her in a different category.' They decided to restore the whip in the expectation that she would then announce her retirement. 'I think he was given wrong information, and I think he was let down.'

Someone in Labour high command briefed *The Times* on the evening of Tuesday 28 May that Abbott would not be endorsed by Labour's ruling National Executive Committee and that she was therefore banned from standing as a Labour candidate. Someone close to Abbott confirmed to Politico overnight that she had offered to 'stand down with dignity' and was blindsided by the story. 'They couldn't even let her have her moment. It's unkind and unfair.'

If she had been planning to go quietly, Abbott now U-turned and vowed to stay – noisily. On Wednesday morning she said she was 'dismayed' to be barred and announced her intention to stand again. A day set aside in McSweeney's grid for attacking Tory failures in the NHS descended into chaos and backbiting.

Support was quick in coming. Sadiq Khan, the London mayor, said she should be 'given the respect she deserves'. Jess Phillips called the episode 'unedifying' and said Abbott should be able to stand. Starmer, lamely, said, 'No decision has been taken barring her,' but failed to clarify if she would be allowed to be a Labour candidate. The row led the BBC's *News at Ten* and was the splash in the *Guardian*, the *Telegraph* and the *i*, while the *Daily Mail* called it a 'crass error' to treat the first Black woman MP in such a 'brutal' way. That Thursday, Angela Rayner weighed in. 'I don't see any reason why Diane Abbott can't stand as a Labour MP going forward,' the deputy leader said, branding the briefings against her 'disgraceful'. Labour HQ would not say whether this was an authorised intervention, though one senior campaign official privately called it 'deeply unhelpful'. Starmer repeated his line that 'no decision has been taken to bar her' but seemed to soften his line, calling Abbott a 'trailblazer'.

It was not until the next day, Friday 31 May, that Starmer finally relented, saying Abbott was 'free to go forward as a Labour candidate', at least forty-eight hours after it would have been sensible to do so. She, like all the others, was rubber-stamped by the NEC the following Tuesday. 'It dragged on far too long,' a senior figure in the campaign admitted. It was by far Labour's worst unforced error of the campaign, noticed by two-thirds of voters, more than half of whom thought it reflected poorly on the campaign, according to a 'gaffe-o-meter' poll by More in Common at the end of the campaign. But the Tories had four gaffes more noticed and three more damaging. At CCHQ, the tracking poll showed that Starmer's personal favourability had taken a hit. On 29 May it was at +9. Three days later it had fallen eleven points to -2.

It made little difference to the overall picture, however. Ten days in, McSweeney committed to fighting all seven categories of target seats, approaching two hundred attack seats, to bring them up to around 400 MPs. That was spreading resources thin in a lot of marginal constituencies, but he was now confident that the national swing would take care of those in the lower categories, those necessary for a majority. He was ruthless with candidates in unwinnable seats, who begged for just one leaflet, arguing it would 'distract the Tories' into wasting resources. He told his team, 'My job is to say "No" out of love.' He regarded even experienced MPs as 'addicts' once they became candidates.

For Labour's campaign director, the most important phase of the campaign was the opening, where you tried to define the question every voter would be asking themselves as their pencil hovered over the ballot paper in the polling booth. He knew what Sunak and Levido would be asking voters: 'Is Labour ready for government?' He told colleagues, 'They want to make the whole thing a referendum on Labour.' Their job was to get voters to ask themselves a different question: 'Isn't it time for change after fourteen years?' The closing argument was simple: 'If you want change, you have to vote for change.'

On 27 May, Starmer gave a big speech on why voters could trust Labour, designed to answer the Tory polling booth question. There was also an event with Labour candidates from military backgrounds, where he dismissed Sunak's national service plan as a 'teenage *Dad's Army*'. On 3 June, he unveiled a 'triple lock' commitment to the Trident nuclear deterrent, calling it 'the foundation of any plan to keep Britain safe'. Wes Streeting said Labour would pay for '40,000 more appointments every week' in the NHS and clear the backlog of patients waiting more than eighteen weeks for treatment within five years.

The main arguments made, McSweeney and Pat McFadden, the campaign coordinator, saw their jobs after that as simply 'solving problems' both big and small. They sat on a hub in the centre of the Labour war room with Tom Lillywhite, the head of digital, their fastest hotline to the voters; Ellie Reeves, McFadden's deputy; Deborah Mattinson, the pollster and head of strategy; Jonathan Ashworth and Matt Pound, from the general secretary's office. But for several hours a day, the pair took themselves to a smaller room with plain walls, a whiteboard and a map, which came to feel like a cell. From 6 a.m. they solved problems. Marianna McFadden – deputy to McSweeney, wife to Pat, mind of an engineer – built meetings around them and forced decisions.

At first people brought them pizzas, like a couple of housebound pensioners, until McSweeney decided no one should wait on him hand and foot, and he might catch scurvy. He began going out for food.

The day began with a chat with Starmer, who was 'having a great time because he was out on the road meeting people', then a strategy meeting chaired by McFadden and a delivery meeting run by McSweeney. Others followed with the regional directors in England and the campaigns in Scotland and Wales, plus the digital team.

The Right Honourable Sir Edward Jonathan Davey, twenty-five years a Member of Parliament, candidate once more for Kingston and Surbiton, former cabinet minister, current Privy Counsellor, fellow of the Royal Society of Arts and leader of the Liberal Democrats, took up position on the paddle board. He was wearing a wetsuit, a red life vest and a slightly worried grin. He began in a kneeling position, wobbling awkwardly to his feet. Once upright, he caressed the water with the paddle, grinned for the cameras and offered a word to the waiting media. But as he did so, he leaned to his left as he was expecting the paddle to meet solid ground, rather than the turbid waters of Lake Windermere. First the arms went, then the legs, the lean became a plummet and the former minister of the crown launched himself backwards, the paddle board skidding forwards as, arms raised like the crucified Christ, he plunged, backside first, into the water. Anyone tempted to feel sorry for Davey need not have, since his plunge was all part of the plan. He 'fell' into the water four times to ensure that the cameramen and photographers got what they needed.

There was a serious point to it all, of course: to highlight the 27,000 tons of untreated sewage which had been pumped into the lake since 2020.

Further stunts followed, turning it from an oddity into a campaign theme as journalists and voters waited to see what he would do next. A waterslide, an obstacle course like something from *It's a Knockout*, cycling down a steep hill, wheelbarrow racing, aqua aerobics, swing dancing, playing 'We Will Rock You' with drumsticks on an exercise ball, performing CPR to the Bee Gees' 'Stayin' Alive', culminating in a bungee jump. These were often the brainchild of Rhiannon Leaman, described by one colleague as 'the strategic genius behind a lot of the air war stuff', and Olly Grender, the director of communications. 'Rhiannon worked intensively with Ed on how he wanted to come across as a person during the campaign, how that looked visually, how we got the message across.' The vibe was of centrist dad, game for anything, but the visual stunts were (usually) tied to a policy pledge, ensuring they got some airtime for their priorities. Davey said, 'We're making serious points, and the election is a serious matter. But I think you can do it in a slightly fun way.'[2] A Lib Dem staffer said, 'We ran out of space in the storage space under the bus because of all the random stuff like wheelbarrows in there.'

The Lib Dem campaign manager in 2024 was Dave McCobb, who had run the field operation in 2019. McCobb then had tried in vain to keep the party's target seats to a manageable size, rather than get carried away with visions of being competitive in 180. This time he was master of the Lib Dem battleground. McCobb began the long trek with two, slightly contradictory, thoughts in his head – avoid the mistakes of 2019; and an understanding that most campaigns failed because they overcompensated for the mistakes of the previous campaign. He put every seat in Britain in one of four tiers based on winnability, itself a combination of how close the Lib Dems had got last time, plus the strength of organisation on the ground, a significantly bigger factor for the Lib Dems than for the Tories or Labour.

There were two categories of target seats: those which were within reach even if the Tories closed the gap to Labour and were able to start to 'squeeze' Lib Dem voters – and those 'stretchier targets' which would be in play if the Conservatives did not begin to turn things around. A party official said, 'We wanted to make sure we had a really robust plan in place, both if that Tory vote recovered in the campaign, but also if it didn't.' At this point there were 35 seats on the target list.

Many were in commuter communities in Surrey and Oxfordshire, where long-term demographics were moving in the direction of the Lib Dems and away from the Conservatives. Target voters here they called 'the Surrey shufflers', Labour supporters who 'move out from London into the commuter belt and find themselves in a place where Labour can't win'. They were joined in suburban seats by 'Waitrose woman', who were once Conservative voters but socially liberal and environmentally conscious. They were turned off by partygate, general Tory incompetence and by the state of local health services.

A Lib Dem official said, 'We also noticed we were starting to get much bigger returns from campaign activity in the south-west.' Here the key voters were retired professionals who culturally would have been Conservative and wanted a common-sense approach on the economy. They didn't like what Johnson was about, but a lot of them held their noses in 2019 because there was a risk of Corbyn. Over the course of the Parliament, things like partygate and the successive scandals detached more of those voters from the Conservatives.'

By the halfway point in the Parliament, the old West Country vote began to recover. Since 2016, Brexit had driven a wedge between the Lib Dems and their former voters, many of whom backed the Leave campaign. 'A lot of people voted for Brexit because they were frustrated with the status quo and they thought that this was something they could do to try and change some of these things,' a party strategist said. 'And people were noticing that things were getting progressively worse, not better. It meant that dividing line on Brexit just wasn't there in the same way.' While the 2019 Tory coalition was disintegrating, McCobb was quietly reconstructing the Lib Dem voter base from their glory years between 1997 and 2010, when they held between 46 and 62 seats.

In each of the target seats the focus was on building up a more effective ground organisation and using systematic doorstep engagement to inform which issues to campaign on. This paid huge dividends in the Chesham and Amersham by-election, in June 2021, when the Lib Dems were quick to respond to widespread concerns about the state of the local environment. After Owen Paterson resigned from the Commons in December 2021, McCobb himself went to his North Shropshire seat to test the waters. He was immediately struck by the number of voters who had a family member, neighbour or a friend who had called an ambulance that did not turn up, or that took hours. He made ambulance services a focus of the campaign. They could tell things were going well when a local bus pulled up while Helen Morgan, the Lib Dem candidate, was campaigning in the high street. 'The bus driver got out just to shake Helen's hand. And rather than being annoyed that their bus had been delayed, all the passengers on the bus broke into applause.'

The most important meeting for the Liberal Democrat general election campaign took place almost exactly a year before polling day, two weeks into the Somerton and Frome by-election campaign. The Lib Dem campaign headquarters in Frome was based in a caricature of a Lib Dem safe space, a complex near the station where a vegan curry house sat cheek by jowl with an art gallery, a dance studio and a 'very, very nice bakery'. McCobb took his senior staff to a burrito bar and said, 'This is going so well, we need to have a plan for what happens if the general election goes like this. We need to take significantly more seriously the prospect that the Tory vote doesn't recover.' McCobb nearly doubled the number of target seats to 65. After the local elections in May 2024, three more seats which had shown they could build a good organisation and get good results were added to the list. By polling day there were 80 on McCobb's target whiteboard.

Every night during the campaign, McCobb left Lib Dem headquarters on Vincent Square and went for a walk with Grender, Leaman and Mike Dixon, the chief executive. They did two laps of the square, asking themselves what they could do better and when the squeeze from the Tories was going to bite? McCobb also had four regional directors reporting directly to him. Twice they all got together in person for a deep dive into every facet of the campaign. 'Ten days in, we couldn't see how we weren't already above 30 seats,' a senior official said. 'And twenty days in, we couldn't see how we weren't already above 50.'

The person who convinced them the squeeze would never come was the mother of one of the senior staff, who lived in the new constituency of Goole and Pocklington, to the west of Hull, where David Davis was the Conservative candidate. He had held the predecessor seats of Haltemprice and Howden, and Boothferry, since 1987, and boundary changes had removed the west Hull suburbs and made it theoretically safer for the Tories. But when she and her friends, all retired teachers, had lunch together, they realised two of them had been targeted by the same telephone pollster. 'They had been phoned by the Tories running their national voter modelling script, where they asked voters to rank their likelihood of voting for each party,' a campaign official said. One of the women said to the caller, 'The problem with this scale is that you're asking me to rank my likelihood to vote for the Conservative Party from one to ten. You haven't given me the option of zero. And the answer is zero.' The person making the call said, 'I'm really sorry. I don't like them either. I'm just paid to do this.'[3]

When McCobb heard about the poll, he told colleagues, 'If they're worried about seats like that, they're definitely worrying about being under 100 seats.'

Leaman and Grender persuaded Davey to be filmed talking about his disabled son John for the party election broadcast – a highly affecting short film which introduced a veteran politician but a new leader to a voting public who did not know him. He only agreed to do it after a 'long chat' with his wife, Emily. The film showed him cooking and hugging and playing games with the teenager to highlight the party's policy of giving more help to carers. 'It's not always been comfortable, talking about that, but it's a serious message,' he explained. 'It's just telling my story and hoping – because there are millions of people like me – that I can bring the caring issue out of the shadows.'[4] McCobb noticed a small uptick in the party's internal canvassing numbers after the film went out. It received universally positive notices.

On Monday 3 June, any progress the Tories were making was stopped dead. Nigel Farage announced he had changed his mind and was now going to stand for Parliament in the Essex seaside town of Clacton, the seat which Douglas Carswell had held for UKIP in the 2015 election and where Farage's old Brexit bad boy Arron Banks had conducted a poll a few months earlier to show that he could win. Farage announced at the same time that he would be taking over as leader of the party from Richard Tice. He had tried and failed seven times to become an MP, but the prospect of watching others succeed where he had previously failed was too much for Farage. If the Reform wave was going to slam into the Tory beach, he wanted his surfboard atop it.

In CCHQ, where the mood had been one of grim determination, campaign staff stared blankly at the television. 'It was funereal,' one said. In his press conference, Farage said he wanted to lead a 'political revolt – a turning of our backs on the political status quo. Nothing in this country works any more.' Predicting defeat and opposition for the Tories, he declared, 'They are split down the middle on policy, and frankly, right now they don't stand for a damn thing.' He then roamed the room riffing with journalists, glass of red wine in hand.

The following day, he turned up in Clacton telling his prospective constituents, and a travelling circus of journalists, delighted to have something interesting to cover, 'Send me to Parliament to be a bloody nuisance.' His main rival, Tory MP Giles Watling, who had appeared in the 1980s sitcom *Bread*, observed that Farage 'doesn't give two hoots' about Clacton. 'This is all about Nigel, as ever.' There were two immediate effects in the Tory Party. Some MPs began openly voicing the idea that Farage might be elected and then cross the floor to rejoin the Conservatives, a party he had left in 1992. For months there had been talk of a 'realignment of the right' or a 'reverse takeover' by the Faragistes. Jacob Rees-Mogg even predicted he might become leader: 'I'm a huge admirer of Nigel's, and I think he should hold high office within the Conservative Party.'

There was also soul searching about the decision to call a snap election. Privately, Tory chiefs pondered whether they would have been better to wait until the autumn, when it was possible Farage would have been based full-time in America. One friend had even suggested Farage would take a job working for Donald Trump if he became US president again after November's election.

'It is much, much, much, much less likely that Farage would have done this if the election had been in the autumn,' one senior Tory suggested. But even Levido knew there was no guarantee that Farage would have stayed stateside if they had waited until October or November. The consensus among Sunak's aides was that he would not have been able to resist temptation. 'I think the idea that Farage would not have run in the autumn is for the birds,' a senior adviser said. 'Some people talk as if we live in the era of the packet steamer. He would have loved nothing more than to open the Trump rally in Milwaukee, get on a plane and fly to Clacton. I think as soon as he began to get the sense that it was happening, he wasn't going to miss out on being the one who was there when it happened. I don't think Richard Tice getting elected and not him was on his wish list.'

In the end, it was irrelevant. Levido was fond of telling campaign colleagues, 'Focus on the things you can control.' Nigel Farage was never going to be one of those things. 'That guy's going to do what he's going to do,' he reasoned. He wasn't surprised when Farage stood down, and he wasn't surprised when he came bouncing back.

It was a 'big, big blow' though, one of three crushing setbacks for the Conservatives in a campaign which had to be perfect to get anywhere. There were two reasons it was damaging. The first was that Reform was proportionately leeching more votes from the Conservatives than the Brexit Party had done, which also stole a lot of votes from Labour in 2019. Second, Tory campaign squeeze messaging for the second half of the campaign required them to noticeably close the gap to Labour in the first two weeks. Their failure to do so, in turn, meant voters stopped taking their policy announcements seriously.

A close confidant of the prime minister said, 'The biggest challenge for the campaign was we needed the polls to tighten at the beginning. When they didn't, people's eyes glazed over at our positive offer. We were offering what I objectively think are a popular series of tax cuts. If we had been eight or nine points behind, maybe we could have got people to consider the tax cuts.' It was a vicious circle. 'The more people went Reform, the more other people went Reform, because of the further behind we fell. The pool of undecided voters, who we thought would come to us, were breaking to Reform.' A Conservative campaign source said. 'Rishi couldn't get his head around the idea that Boris was a great hero for these people when he was the one who massively increased immigration and he was the champion of net zero.'

Farage's entry into the race led to Reform closing to within two points of the Tories. Coincidentally, on the day Farage entered the fray, both YouGov and More in Common released their first MRP polls of the campaign, showing the Tories on course for a wipeout of historic proportions. YouGov's poll for Sky News gave Labour 422 seats, with the Tories down to just 140. More in Common had Labour on 382 seats, with the Tories on 180. The first 'crossover poll' which put Reform ahead came on 13 June, ten days after Farage returned.

Labour's data experts had calculated that if the Tories were able to squeeze the Reform vote, it might limit Starmer to around 375 seats, enough for a majority of 100. Farage's move meant there were legitimate hopes of a Blair-scale landslide. When Sunak became Tory leader, McSweeney's view was that he had a choice: either run a 'broad tent strategy' embracing Reform, or 'destroy them'. His conclusion was that

Sunak had done neither. 'They neither shot the fox or domesticated the fox, and now the fox has eaten them,' he told colleagues.

Farage's entry into the race also had knock-on effects on Labour's vote share, which declined by five or six points throughout the campaign. Some of this 'fragmentation' was people concluding that Reform had made it impossible for the Tories to win and reasoning that it was safe for them to vote for the Greens. It contributed to the lowest collective vote for the two main parties (57.4 per cent) for decades. The second leak came in seats where Labour was not the main challenger to the Conservatives. 'We lost a percentage or two immediately to people who were open to change and voted tactically for the Liberal Democrats,' a source said. 'That was the initial squeeze. We were completely unfazed by it, because it didn't have an impact in any seats that we were going for.' Corbyn's team had chased vote share rather than seats by enthusing left-wing voters in party strongholds. Labour in 2024 would do the opposite.

It became a talking point after the election that it was the worst Tory campaign in living memory. That was true of the outcome, but in the three days after Farage's entry, when the first leaders' debate dominated the campaign, Levido's team showed they could run a professional oper-ation, and there was a glimpse of the performer Sunak might have been if he had been willing to listen to advice earlier in his premiership.

Sunak spent the weekend before the showdown on ITV in a debate camp at a studio in Soho run by Brett O'Donnell, the American who prepared Johnson for his debates during the EU referendum campaign in 2016 and the 2019 leadership election and who helped Tom Tugendhat emerge victorious from the first leaders' debate in 2022. He was assisted by Adam Atashzai, a veteran of fifteen debates since 2010, with Oliver Dowden playing Starmer. 'Rishi was a bit unsure about Brett to begin with,' an aide said. 'They met over Zoom a few weeks earlier.' At that point O'Donnell had no idea there was going to be an election. 'Brett is very unassuming. He's got no ego about him, which is very disarming.' Like Boris Johnson before him, Sunak learned that this manner disguised his effectiveness.

Sunak's style at Prime Minister's Questions was to tell Starmer he was wrong and reel off a range of facts from the folder in front of him, an approach which sometimes made him seem cocksure and complacent about Britain's problems. Like his staff, the prime minister was frustrated that, after Truss in 2022, he was going to lose to a second opponent he thought wrong and who had escaped proper scrutiny by the media. Sunak's initial approach to the debate, an aide said, was this: 'I know all the details in answers to the question. You guys just need to write what you want me to say, and I'll go there and say it.' This was exactly what they were worried about. O'Donnell studied videos of Sunak and Starmer. Then he told the prime minister, 'You're not there to win the argument. I know you know all the stats, but when you're explaining and going through stats, you're on defence. You've got to get onto offence as soon as possible.' This, Sunak 'learned very well'. The chosen line of attack was to pin the idea of a £2,000 tax rise on Labour. 'All that matters is winning the top line of the debate,' O'Donnell counselled.

Not all Sunak's problems were so easily resolved, including the question of how much he distanced himself from Johnson and Truss. 'One of the things that Brett was always saying was, "You need to bookend this thing. You need to talk about *your* time in office." But arguably we hadn't done the work to be able to have that book-ending.' One senior aide, watching the prep session, told friends later that it was the most nervous he had been in the campaign, since Dowden was a highly effective Starmer. 'If Rish tried to say, "Here's some good news, things are getting better", Olive just said, "This just shows how complacent and out of touch you are. You want people to think everything's fine." Every time Rish came out with anything that was a new idea, he would come back, "You've had fourteen years and you're just proposing this. If this was such a good idea, why didn't you do it years ago?" That one-two punch was almost impossible to escape.' In the first debate, Dowden would prove to be a better Starmer than Starmer.

Sunak had two more, shorter, sessions in Manchester, where the debate was to take place, honing his attack. As he left for the studio, the prime minister said, 'Well at least Keir Starmer's got to answer questions now and it's not like PMQs.'

Starmer had his own debate camp in north London, where he was put through his paces by Matthew Doyle, his personal spinner Steph Driver, and Paul Ovenden, the party's head of attack, who wrote a lot of Starmer's best lines in PMQs. Sunak was played by Tom Webb, the director of policy, who did the same role in PMQ prep. On the Sunday, both McSweeney and Pat McFadden went to watch. 'Keir knew how he wanted to present himself to the country,' a senior Labour source said. 'He wanted to connect with people in the room. He didn't want to speak over Julie Etchingham. He knew Sunak would do that.' However, Starmer spent the afternoon of the debate alone in his hotel room, something he insisted on to prepare himself. It showed.

In the studio, Sunak seemed markedly the better prepared of the two as he sought to pin the £2,000 tax tag on Labour. He risked appearing aggressive, constantly interrupting Starmer and talking over Etchingham to land his attacks.

Starmer said Labour would not pay a 35 per cent rise but insisted he could 'resolve' the junior doctors' strike by just getting in a room with the unions. However, Starmer blushed as Sunak hit back: 'Just standing there saying "I'll resolve it" isn't an answer. That's not a plan.' Sunak used the same approach when Starmer vowed to axe the Rwanda scheme, repeatedly asking, 'What are you going to do? What are you going to do with illegal migrants?' Answer came there none. The Labour leader was visibly discombobulated – closing his eyes and tilting his head to the heavens. Etchingham had to intervene when it descended into a babble of cross talk. 'Please, gentlemen! We will lower our voices,' she interjected.

It was not all one-way traffic. Starmer had a good moment when he attacked on NHS waiting lists, leaving Sunak to explain that despite the total number of people waiting having increased since he took over, 'They are coming down from when they were higher.' There were groans from the audience.

However, it was the tax attack which was cutting through. Left-wing social media commentators went from attacking Sunak for bringing it up repeatedly to wondering why Starmer was not responding directly to it at all. In the Tory green room they could not believe their luck. 'What I found surprising was for someone whom it has literally been his job to argue and win a case, he was so flat-footed,' one said. 'Rishi smashed it.' At the half-time advert break, one person from each team was allowed to speak to their leader. In Labour HQ, McSweeney and McFadden were messaging the team in the green room, who relayed the message to Matthew Doyle in the studio that Starmer had to rebut the £2,000 claim. He went to speak to Starmer. Sunak's team decided to leave their man. 'We resolved we were only going to go out and talk to him if there was a problem,' one said. 'We just let him roll.'

When hostilities resumed, Starmer shoehorned a rebuttal of the £2,000 tax charge into his first answer, dismissing the figure as 'absolute garbage'. By then it was forty minutes into the debate. The damage was done. 'Obviously, he did push back, but it was not as quick as we wanted,' an aide admitted.

YouGov's snap poll of debate viewers gave the win to Sunak by 51 per cent to 49 per cent, which considering the Tories were trailing by 20 points in most polls suggested a clear win.

Neither leader thought they had done well. 'Keir was annoyed after the debate,' a Labour aide said. 'He felt he hadn't pushed back early enough, and he wanted to fix it. He is a very competitive guy and wants to win on everything.' Sunak was also 'quite pessimistic' about his performance, according to those waiting for him afterwards. 'He walked into the green room after the ITV debate and he thought it had gone badly,' one said. 'There were a few of us clapping and cheering and saying "Well done", and he didn't really believe us.' Then one of them showed him the WhatsApps they had been getting from Conservative MPs. There was even one from Wendy Morton, a usually hostile member of Team Truss, saying, 'Give Rishi a big hug from me, that was excellent.' Sunak called Levido and thanked him for bringing in O'Donnell. The campaign professionals had got their main argument into public minds. 'By the middle of the campaign we had got to where we wanted,' one said. 'We had what the party and the government had been struggling to get for a year – a very clear, simple message.'

In Labour HQ the next morning, with the papers running with the £2,000 tax claim, McSweeney recognised Labour had suffered 'a serious blow', though not one which seemed in danger of derailing the campaign. At the first moment when some voters would have been paying attention the Tories had won the day. To engage with the tax argument would elevate it further, just as the row over Vote Leave's claim that Brexit would lead to £350 million a week for the NHS put that issue at the top of the agenda. 'All that matters now is how we are going to fight this,' McSweeney told the other campaign chiefs.

Before the election, he had studied other winning campaigns, notably David Cameron's surprise win in 2015. He concluded that the Tories had actually made more mistakes than Labour on that occasion – Cameron triggering leadership speculation by saying he would only serve one more term, then forgetting which football team he supported. On polling day, the entire Tory data operation had failed – but on each occasion they had responded better. When he addressed the shadow cabinet at the start of the campaign, he said, 'We can't build a perfect campaign machine that will make no mistakes. What matters is what you do next. At some point in the campaign, you will fall down a hole. When you do, I will jump in there with you, and I will get you out. If you happen to see me and another shadow cab member in a hole, your job is not to kick dirt in the hole. Your job is to reach your hand in and pull us out. Mistakes will happen. What matters is how you respond to them, not whose fault they were.' Now it was Starmer in the hole and McSweeney jumped in.

Darren Jones, the shadow chief secretary, had written to James Bowler, the permanent secretary at the Treasury, on 24 May, to clarify how much of the £2,000 claim was the work of civil servants. When he first made the attack, Jeremy Hunt had said the numbers came 'from the Treasury and independent sources'. This subtlety had been lost in Sunak's debate attacks. Many of the calculations were official government figures, but some were not, and the overall number was the work of Tory political advisers. Bowler wrote that the calculation of a £38 billion black hole in Labour's plans 'includes costs beyond those provided by the civil service' and that the assessment 'should not be presented as having been produced by the civil service'. The campaign team knew nothing of the letter until the morning after the debate – otherwise they could have deployed it in the spin room after. Labour now issued the letter to the media and used it to argue that the Tory claims were unfair. Their plans were fully costed. These were the taxes they were raising; these were the areas which were protected.

Plan A lasted for an hour. At 10.30 a.m. Tom Lillywhite, the head of digital, turned to McSweeney and pointed to the coverage on the news channels, which was still dominated by the £2,000 claim. 'It's not work-ing,' Lillywhite said. 'All we're doing is amplifying their argument. All anyone's talking about is £2,000. You are on their grid. We have to get off their grid.' McSweeney was breaking his own Tinkerbell rule.

It called for a much more robust approach. The only problem was that the entire senior communications team were stuck on a train on the way back from the debate in Manchester. McSweeney and McFadden called in Damian McBride, Ovenden's deputy in the attack and rebuttal team, who had spent the campaign gathering damaging intelligence on rival candidates, everything from lewd behaviour to offensive Facebook posts, and pumping out stories for the media. He was to land more than 150 stories during the campaign.[5] 'Right, we're going to flip this,' McSweeney said. 'We're going to get into a fight with them and we're just going to call them liars. They lied that the number was from an independent and credible source. We're going to punch hard.' That day, Labour showed it could fight and win the day. That evening, the story was the claim the Tories had distorted the figures. When More in Common polled at the end of the week, the £2,000 claim remained slightly more salient with voters than the lying claim, but by 42 per cent to 29 per cent voters believed Labour, not the Tories.

The following day, 6 June, the eightieth anniversary of the D-Day landings in Normandy, brought the second great campaign calamity for the Tories. Sunak was in France for the commemorations. He spent the morning in several events with all the remaining British veterans. It was something he cared about. Both Sunak and his wife, Akshata, donated to veterans' charities. She had hosted a Number 10 reception for Chelsea Pensioners to mark Remembrance Day.

It was one of those days where the campaign grid was blocked out for this official government event. They had discussed Sunak's schedule in the three-day look-ahead meeting in CCHQ on Monday at which most of Sunak's key aides were present, including Levido, James Forsyth and Nissy Chesterfield. But the minute-by-minute level of detail you would have for a political event in a campaign was missing. 'We knew he was leaving early and missing stuff, but not really what it was,' one campaign official said.

The afternoon event was an international leaders' reception. The collective view was that Sunak did not need to be there. 'It was billed as a lunch, and we were told [Joe] Biden wouldn't be there either.' Sunak was due to see the US president, Volodymyr Zelensky, Emmanuel Macron and Olaf Scholz earlier in the day, and they were all expected at the G7 summit in Italy the following week. Those liaising with the private office in Downing Street said the official advice was that the leaders' event was 'optional', and it had been agreed weeks before that Sunak would not stay, returning home a little after the King. There was no question that Keir Starmer, who was also travelling to France, would attend the event.

The decision to stick to the plan was confirmed in a 6.30 a.m. daily campaign meeting on Thursday, D-Day itself. The official advice from the civil service was that the PM should stay at least as long as the King.

Only Lucy Noakes, the press secretary, seemed to smell danger. 'Are we sure about this?' she asked. 'Lucy flagged it,' a colleague confirmed. Knowing Sunak was coming back, Levido scheduled a meeting on the Conservative manifesto for 6 p.m. Nissy Chesterfield also found time for Sunak to do an interview with ITV's Paul Brand before that.

The idea, discussed in these meetings and peddled afterwards, that the civil service signed off on the decision to leave early was far from the full truth. Officials were adamant it was a 'political decision' to cut things short. There was a communication breakdown between the government and the campaign. Between the original decision to leave and 6 June, the international event had evolved into a major part of the day. 'The information that it was evolving into a memorial thing didn't make its way to the campaign proper,' a party official said. 'It was a communication breakdown between Number 10 and the campaign.'

Nonetheless, the changing plans of the French were sufficiently well-known for David Lammy, the shadow foreign secretary, to lobby the French government to allow both him and Starmer to attend. He became aware of diplomatic rumblings that the Élysée Palace was upset by Sunak's decision to avoid the French-led part of the commemoration. With help from Jill Cuthbertson and Sue Gray in Starmer's office and the British embassy in Paris, they accomplished their aim. There was no excuse for Sunak's aides to have been so blindsided.

The prime minister duly flew home and underwent a twenty-five-minute grilling from Brand, who asked him a series of questions about whether his wealth made him out of touch. Sunak said, 'I went without lots of things because my parents wanted to put everything into our education.' Asked what those things were, it became excruciating viewing as Sunak squirmed – a repeat of the horror in Theresa May's eyes when asked, in 2017, about the naughtiest thing she had ever done. Sunak might still have saved himself if he'd had the presence of mind to joke that he had been forced to grow up with no fields of wheat to run through, but instead he blurted, 'There are all sorts of things that I wanted as a kid that I couldn't have, famously Sky TV! That was something that we never had growing up.'

If the 'famously' was odd, Chesterfield immediately knew the rest of it would reinforce the widespread view that Sunak did not understand those less fortunate than himself. Worse, it would be hanging over them for days. The interview was not due to air until the following

Wednesday. 'That was what they were worried about,' said a political source. 'That he was beaten up over the money.' It was soon the least of their worries.

While Sunak was on his way home, Starmer had been hobnobbing with world leaders in front of the cameras. Macron greeted him like a lost brother. When Labour heard Zelensky was coming, Jill Cuthbertson, Starmer's gatekeeper, reached out to contacts she had made in Kyiv when they had visited the Ukrainian president, to discuss the possibility of a meeting. Zelensky was keen so they stayed in touch, exchanging messages and sharing their locations until they found each other in the crowd. The handshake and picture was a triumph for Starmer's team.

When the formal part of proceedings began, David Cameron stood in for Sunak, but oddly had no officials or political aides with him at all. He went to sit with Starmer. They were supposed to be joined by Grant Shapps, the defence secretary. But then they all watched as Shapps arrived and was given the full red carpet welcome. Greeted by Macron, he was ushered into the VVIP section with the foreign secretary still in the cheap seats. But Cameron did not become prime minister without fierce competitive instincts and a degree of low cunning. When the ceremonial element was over, the Labour delegation was held back by security to allow heads of state and prime ministers to go to the reception. On the other side of the crowd, they could see Biden, Macron and Scholz gathering for a team picture. The last they saw of Cameron was the back of his head as he worked his way effortlessly through the crowd and 'accidentally' found himself in the right place at the right time to join them. Reuters photographer Benoit Tessier clicked his shutter and Sunak immediately had a bigger problem.

When the first pictures of the foursome appeared on television, late in the day, a voice was heard in the CCHQ war room exclaiming, 'What the fuck is this?' It was the first they had known of the photocall.

One of Cameron's closest allies let it be known that they had advised Sunak to 'do' the full schedule. A Whitehall source said Cameron was 'apoplectic' about Sunak's decision but, when asked why he had not 'picked Sunak up by his lapels', he said, 'There is only so much I can do.' Another friend of Cameron contested this description: 'He was not apoplectic at all … he was fucking furious.' Those who knew him best, smiled and concluded that Cameron was probably not that upset to find himself once more in the heart of the action.

The affair got more difficult when lobby journalists worked out that Sunak had recorded the ITV interview – though they were mistaken in assuming that was why he had come home. It looked as though he had abandoned the veterans to attack Starmer on tax. It gave rise to headlines like 'he left them on the beaches' and 'infighting on the beaches'.

The broadcaster then put out pre-interview footage of Sunak apologising to Brand that the D-Day commemorations 'all just ran over', breaking a deal with Downing Street that they would not release footage of the interview until near broadcast time.

The next morning the full scale of the disaster was clearer, the *Mirror* splashing on 'PM DITCHES D-DAY', the broadcasters following in their slipstream. Levido and Forsyth were both in early at CCHQ. They agreed what needed to be done. At around 6 a.m. Levido said, 'Come on, let's call him.' They dialled Sunak. He sounded half-asleep but soon woke up as they explained what had been happening.

The prime minister was incredulous. 'What? We followed all the official advice?' There it was again, an echo of the non-dom story and the green card. He had done the right thing, followed all the rules. Process above political judgement.

'You're going to have to apologise,' Levido said. 'We'll do a tweet.' 'Absolutely,' he agreed, getting it. Sunak was 'crestfallen', thinking of all the people he had let down, 'despondent' when he thought about the veterans he had worked with. Those in Matthew Parker Street that day were 'mortified for him', each of them knowing that, in some small way, they had all 'failed him'. 'It really hurt our guy,' a senior figure said. 'It was really bad on the doorsteps.'

Liam Booth-Smith did not attend the campaign morning meetings. He had agreed with Levido that he wouldn't cut across him, just as Cummings had remained out of view in 2019. He woke on 7 June to around sixty messages on his phone, several saying Sunak was going to apologise. He called Levido: 'Are we sure apologising is the right move here?' Booth-Smith had not yet fully processed the public reaction. Levido was sure. Sunak and every other frontbencher would be dogged in every broadcast interview until the prime minister said sorry.

The chief of staff then called Number 10 to speak to Elizabeth Perelman, Sunak's principal private secretary, to find out what had happened. She was clear that the foreign affairs team in Downing Street had recommended that Sunak attend everything on D-Day. Officials had only admitted parts of it were voluntary because it was clear political aides wanted to get the PM home.

There was also no way Sunak's spinners could make the point to the media that Charles III had already gone home when the prime minister left, since that risked dragging the monarch into the row. Indeed, there was irritation at Buckingham Palace, where courtiers pointed out that the King, who was being treated for cancer, was advised not to travel but was determined to do so. 'He's been in pain, and they had to pump him full of drugs, but he's a trouper,' said a source close to the royal household.

A final footnote. As the row erupted, the French played a comedically cynical diplomatic game. One of Macron's aides contacted Labour to say Macron 'really liked' Starmer and was 'fascinated by men like him who can suddenly achieve stunning results'. Another called a member of Sunak's team to commiserate, telling them, 'This is all completely confected nonsense. How can we help?'

Afterwards, criticism focused on the comms team under Nissy Chesterfield and Eden Barnes, the head of operations, but in truth it was a collective failure. Ultimately it was Sunak's error to want to come home, a personal oddity that he didn't want to play at being prime minister a little longer for the cameras. If that reflected well on his seriousness and substance over surface image, it was also a signature Sunak moment, a man little given to the poetry of politics, happiest returning home to a manifesto meeting to ponder the prose of policy instead.

The context made it worse. Sunak had framed the election in a speech about security in April. His big line in the sand was defence spending of 2.5 per cent. His first announced policy of the campaign was compulsory national service. His biggest threat was from Reform, whose new leader had complained just three days earlier that widespread ignorance about D-Day was one of his motivations for returning to frontline politics. Cabinet ministers responded with impotent rage, criticising Sunak's appetite for the job. The prime minister, they said, had repeatedly complained privately that he had little interest in the ceremonial aspects of his job. A Tory who was no fan of either of them said, 'There is absolutely no way that if you presented this to Boris or indeed to Theresa, telling them it was a waste of time, that they would not have overruled that advice. This is the worst operation I have ever seen.'

Farage's entry into the race had been a crippling blow for the Tories, though not one they could control. The D-Day debacle was a disaster of their own making. It raised serious questions about the judgement of the prime minister and his aides. Both overshadowed an effective debate performance by Sunak. When Penny Mordaunt, a Royal Navy reservist fighting for her political life in Portsmouth North, was sent out to represent the government in a seven-way BBC debate that Friday evening, she had no choice but to denounce him. 'What happened was completely wrong, and the prime minister has rightly apologised.'

In the debate, Nigel Farage called Sunak's behaviour 'a disgrace'. He went further on Laura Kuenssberg's Sunday show, making an accusation which a lot of people saw as a racist 'dog whistle'. The Reform leader declared, 'It shows the man doesn't understand. He is not patriotic – he doesn't care about our history, our culture.'

That weekend, Sunak was in a black despair. According to one minister who saw him, he talked about stepping back from the campaign. 'Should I just leave it to others?' he asked. Aides said it was not a serious consideration. Nor was responding to Farage. When his team told him what had been said, the PM said, 'I'm not going anywhere near it. I know what he's doing. He just wants to be in the news.'

That didn't mean Sunak didn't feel the snide asides about his race. One close ally said, on his arrival in North Yorkshire he had faced racism, taking a year or more to win over the local community, before people approached him and shook his hand and said, 'I was wrong about you.' He felt it when people criticised his connection with California, saw it as 'an othering' of him. 'No one would bat an eyelid if George Osborne or David Cameron had a house in California,' another aide said. He felt it when Liz Truss's campaign called him 'slick' in 2022. Ostensibly directed at his flashy graphics on social media, his team heard more than that. '"Slick" is a racist trope,' one said. 'It's a reference to untrustworthy, rich, brown men who have cars with blacked-out windows and are doing dodgy things. They knew exactly what they were doing.'

Labour watched all this with detached bemusement, keen not to interrupt their enemy while he was making a major mistake. There were implications for them, however. 'I think D-Day hurt us, bizarrely,' a Labour official said. 'It started to get written up as if the election was over. It became harder to argue up the jeopardy of the election.' McSweeney worried it would drive turnout down, as well as more voters into the hands of the Lib Dems and the Greens.

* * *

The following week was manifesto week. The Lib Dems went on Monday 10 June, their location a funfair, their flagship policy still free personal care for the elderly. This time Ed Davey did an interview on a spinning teacup ride. The Tories had theirs a day later and Labour on the Thursday. The Conservatives unveiled their seventy-six-page document at Silverstone, home of Formula One. The dire straits they were in was highlighted by the absence of Penny Mordaunt, who had been given special dispensation to stay and fight for her seat.

The most interesting Conservative policy was the one they did not put in their manifesto. Prior to the campaign, Tory officials drew up a fifty-page policy paper which would have called time on British membership of the European Convention on Human Rights. The original plan was to drop it into the media the weekend before the Tory manifesto. Two days of the campaign media grid were set aside for it. Modelled on the 'Change or Go' document drawn up by Business for Britain before David Cameron's abortive renegotiation with the EU, it would have seen Sunak send an ultimatum to the court in Strasbourg detailing reforms the UK needed to see to end the meddling in asylum decisions. A senior Tory involved in the campaign said, 'We would have published this big document outlining the reforms. It was very well thought through, and it was written by lawyers. It was proper.'

Sunak's team felt they could use the plan as a wedge issue with Labour, but it was not clear it would work with Reform's support rising. A party official said, 'Farage made it too difficult, because we're never going to be able to have a position as hard as his. It would have split the party, and Labour would have been able to say, "Look at the Tories, fighting amongst themselves again." It was also very complicated, so we would have spent our entire time talking about it rather than talking about Labour and taxes.' Even devout Brexiteer Alex Wild, the director of comms for the party, while agreeing with the policy, argued against deploying the plan. Forsyth, another Brexiteer, and Levido were of the same mind. Forsyth thought leaving the ECHR may well be necessary, but it was not a simple exercise. He warned his colleagues, 'We will always be outbid on this stuff.' He also believed that a negotiation could bear fruit. In his analysis, Cameron's renegotiation had failed in 2016 because Britain's natural allies, the Poles and other Eastern Europeans, were fans of free movement and access to welfare, the very things he was trying to limit. But on the ECHR, all EU governments were struggling with the same problem of mass migration. Forsyth also thought that if they won the election, the court in Strasbourg would 'blink' rather than override a sovereign parliament.

From a comms point of view, Chesterfield argued that Sunak's position was basically the same as the new plan anyway. She said, 'Why complicate things?' Their campaign successes had been on tax, that was where they needed to focus their efforts.

The Tory campaign was now locked in a terrible stasis, but it did not descend into a death spiral – something ministers and advisers attributed to Levido. After a visit to CCHQ, Laura Trott, the chief secretary to the Treasury, said, 'Isaac kept the show on the road. In most other circumstances, with this position in the polls, it would have been a nest of vipers, and it wasn't like that at all.'

Levido was having to fight with a much-reduced team and dwindling resources. At one point he had to turn off digital advertising to save money. Donors were refusing to give while Sunak remained leader.

Levido could still see a gossamer thin path to a hung Parliament, but it meant winning back half of all voters who had defected to Reform and half those who had switched to the Lib Dems. He had one card left to play. On 10 June he penned a memo on 'Mid-Campaign Strategic Imperatives'. First, the good news. There wasn't much of it. Their policy offerings had 'significant cut through'. 68 per cent of voters had heard of national service and 46 per cent of triple lock plus. 'Voters, especially 2019 Conservatives, support these policies.' That had translated into a 6-point Tory rise on the economy and a 5-point bounce on pensions.

Then the bad news. The polls had got worse because 'voters have seen frequent polling and media commentary that Labour are expected to win, and win big'. Levido revealed, 'Our own polling shows that only 20 per cent of voters think that the Conservatives will win.' The consequence was that while liking Tory policies, 'voters do not believe they will ever be introduced'. It was impossible to force people into a 'binary choice between Labour and Conservative ... Our polling shows that 57 per cent of voters think that "Labour are going to win no matter how I vote", rising to 65 per cent among Conservative defectors.'

Finally, the plan. 'We must reframe the choice at this election to harness expectations that Labour will win to our advantage', warning voters Starmer would be 'unaccountable and free to do things that are unpopular with voters'. Levido spelled out the concerns voters had about a big Labour win:

1. Labour will do things they're not telling me if they win, especially increasing taxes
2. Labour will change election laws to favour them (votes at sixteen already announced, 'votes for migrants and prisoners coming next?'), meaning they'll be in power for a long time
3. Left-wing factions will take over Labour (because Starmer is weak), and Rayner could replace [him].

The memo said, 'The campaign must vocalise that Labour are on course to win a large majority, or "supermajority". That such a supermajority presents a grave and lasting risk to issues that voters care about. And that the Conservatives are the only party able to prevent that undesirable outcome.' Even as he sent the memo, Levido had authorised targeted digital advertising, since postal votes had started arriving in people's homes.

'This does not mean that the campaign, or the prime minister, should concede defeat,' Levido cautioned. 'It is a tactical communications device to force voters (particularly defectors to Reform, the Lib Dems and undecided) to consider the consequence of their vote.' If the plan helped make it a more competitive race, they could pivot to talking about policies again. If the polls did not tighten, 'the campaign may wish to switch to advocating for the Conservatives to be a strong opposition', though he made clear that would be a 'significant decision' for Sunak, not him.

On Wednesday 12 June, Grant Shapps, a former party chairman who had spoken to Levido, did a broadcast round. He warned it would be 'very bad news' if the polls were right and there was a Labour 'supermajority'. The defence secretary was not sent out expressly to use the term, but he was aware of the plan.

That week, Sunak snapped out of his despair. He began tying the supermajority concept together with the threat of tax rises by talking about stopping Starmer having a 'blank cheque'. One of those who was on his 2022 leadership team, said, 'He's like he was then. He was down for the first half of the campaign and then he decided he was just going to throw everything at it. His attitude is that he has to go out and swing for the fences.' Others felt liberated by the pivot. Levido told his team, 'People think a supermajority is bad. We need to make it terrifying. We now have a very simple message, and Labour has a complicated one.'

Sunak would need all this new determination. That Wednesday, ITV released the Paul Brand interview, and the PM faced another barrage of criticism for his comments about not having Sky TV growing up. That evening he went to Grimsby for a Sky News town hall-style debate. On the train up, Chesterfield put him through his paces ahead of a 'huddle' with lobby journalists. She warned him he would face questions about youthful privations. He said, 'Well, I used to wear second-hand clothes, but I don't want to get into every little bit of my childhood.' It was a much better answer, but he never used it, and Chesterfield knew there was only so far she could, or wanted to, push him.

After the Sky News event, Sunak flew to Italy for the G7 summit. Again, Chesterfield prepped him, this time for a huddle on the plane out. The hacks might ask whether he had apologised to the other leaders for leaving Omaha Beach early, she suggested. Sunak snapped, 'Well, I've had conversations with all of them, and all of them think it's completely ridiculous, and our UK media is a joke.'

'Maybe don't say that,' Chesterfield advised.

It was perhaps understandable he was under pressure again. In Grimsby he and Starmer were quizzed by Beth Rigby before facing questions from the audience. Rigby gave them both a hard time, skewering Sunak over his failure to deliver on his five priorities. When he explained that NHS strikes had hindered efforts to cut waiting lists, he was booed. He apologised twice for the D-Day debacle and looked flat and broken by the end of it. Starmer, far more energised than in the first debate, won the snap poll with 64 per cent of the vote.

What the audience did not know was that before he went on stage, Sunak was braced for the publication of a story in the *Guardian* by Pippa Crerar that Craig Williams had placed a £100 bet at 5–1 on a July election on 19 June, the day sources told the author he was informed about the prime minister's decision to call a snap election. Not only had the prime minister's parliamentary aide inadvertently helped give Labour a vital head start, he was now under investigation by the Gambling Commission. The bet had been flagged to them by bookmaker Ladbrokes because Williams was a 'politically exposed person'. The Cabinet Office had been informed five days earlier, since Williams was a minister there. CCHQ assumed it had been leaked by a civil servant. Sunak regarded it as a highly personal betrayal. 'He was crushed,' a close aide said. 'Craig was someone he trusted and was close to.' Sunak did not speak to Williams again.

Labour's manifesto, published that Thursday, was largely a non-event, the focus on public service reform rather than tax and spend, the usual bread and butter of a Labour manifesto. McSweeney's line with colleagues and commentators was, 'Labour used to make the argument that the pie ought to be more equitably distributed. But the Tories have eaten all of the pie and burned down the kitchen.' The campaign director had also lobbied for policies he thought politically damaging to be removed or watered down. He insisted it was written clearly that Labour did not back 'self-ID' on trans rights. He demanded that money to fill potholes be written in – a key retail policy. He told colleagues several 'zombies' remained which he had only 'half-killed'.

The manifesto ruled out rises to income tax, VAT and National Insurance. The next morning, the Tories put out a dossier detailing eighteen other taxes that Starmer had not ruled out. On Thursday night they sent out Penny Mordaunt into another seven-way debate to raise the spectre of capital gains tax rises, including the imposition of CGT on primary properties. Labour frontbenchers and officials put out a range of responses, alternately ruling it out and leaving the door open until Starmer quashed the idea the following day. After VAT, it was another tactical win for the Tory campaign machine.

Labour was surprised, however, that in focusing on the hidden agenda not listed in the manifesto, the Tory attack machine had not unpicked what was actually there.

'We were expecting at least for the Tories to challenge our spending assumptions,' said Darren Jones, the shadow chief secretary. 'I was expecting a wonky fight about forecasts.'[6]

The next week, the Tories continued to attack on tax and warn about a supermajority; Labour pumped out policies: 100,000 childcare places, 650,000 new jobs from £7.3 billion of green investment, planning reforms, improvements to the NHS dentistry and GP reforms.

Then, on 20 June, eight days after the Craig Williams scoop, it was revealed that one of Sunak's police protection officers had been arrested for placing a bet on the date of the election as well. He was one of those who had been told the election date a week in advance so they could plan security arrangements for the PM. Journalists became convinced a cabinet minister had placed a bet, until it turned out the protection officer had the same name as a senior minister. This time the BBC gave the scandal huge amounts of air time – inevitably dubbed 'gamblegate'.

In quick succession Tony Lee, the head of campaigning at CCHQ, and his wife Laura Saunders, the Tory candidate in Bristol North West, were revealed to have been caught in the dragnet. Lee was forced to take a leave of absence. Two weeks before polling day, the Conservatives had lost a key figure in their ground game. 'Colleagues were quick to confirm that Lee was one of those who were in the loop about the election date. 'He fucking knew,' one of them said.

Liam Booth-Smith, who a colleague described as being consumed by 'white-hot anger' at the betrayals, became the point man for the campaign with the Gambling Commission. He and others wanted to kick Saunders out of the party, but they were warned that they could not interfere with the investigation or even talk to their own staff about whether they had placed bets. Afterwards several thought they should have just ignored that. A colleague said, 'They just say, "We're looking into this person. As part of investigations, can you confirm whether or not this person is an employee or a candidate?" Then we just say "Yes" or "No". But you're not allowed to actually tell the person they're looking into them.' Investigators, with no understanding of politics, then came to Conservative HQ. 'They went through a very laborious process of asking every basic question you can possibly imagine and then wrote it up in front of you. By hand.' The process was paralysing at a key point in the campaign.

Tory officials found that once they confirmed names to the Commission, they leaked within a matter of hours. When potential criminal charges were in play, the names were also passed to Scotland Yard, where several police officers had now been arrested. Tory chiefs believed it was the Met leaking the names to provide a diversion from the potential corruption of their own officers. Suspicion focused on one senior figure at the Yard who had previously worked in Whitehall. 'It was definitely the Met,' a senior adviser said. 'They were up to their fucking necks in it.' Booth-Smith contacted Andrew Rhodes, the CEO of the Gambling Commission, urging him to tighten information security: 'It's getting out of control.'

Because of the leaks to the media, names were then put to Alex Wild in CCHQ by journalists before anyone there had heard about them from the Gambling Commission. One of those was Nick Mason, the chief data officer, who the *Sunday Times* revealed was under investigation on 23 June. He had placed around forty bets, each of them under £100, on the election date, though insiders said that while he might have worked things out, he was not in the circle of trust about the date in advance.

Tory poll numbers went backwards, and this time there seemed no way back. Sunak's approval rating fell from -22 to -41 over the next four days, the Conservative Party's to -47. It was more damaging than the D-Day debacle, which had cost Sunak 5 favourability points, but then rebounded. It was a reminder of the casual rule-breaking of partygate and the stench of sleaze which had brought down John Major's government. A senior cabinet minister said, 'Before the gambling stuff people would say, "We don't want Labour, we don't want to reward you, but we might vote for you." Then we slapped those people in the face with another fucking awful Tory thing. It was catastrophic because it suggested that Starmer was right that we were party before country, which is a travesty of the truth, but it resonated with voters.'

For Sunak it was the final brutal stake through the heart. A close confidant who discussed it with him said, 'He just felt like he could never catch a fucking break over anything. Every single thing would turn out on the shittier side. He would say, "What more can I do? Here's another shitty thing. Come on, chuck another fucking brick at me!"'

It was only on 25 June, thirteen days after the *Guardian* scoop, that the Tories officially withdrew support from Williams and Saunders.[7] The same day, Starmer made a point of immediately suspending Kevin Craig, Labour's candidate for Central Suffolk and North Ipswich, after he was informed that Craig had bet £8,000 on himself to lose the seat. Labour also returned £100,000 Craig had given to the party.

In the third and final head-to-head debate on the BBC, the following day, Starmer linked gamblegate to partygate and accused Sunak of inaction until he was 'bullied' into moving. Both leaders were at their best, but it was not enough for one questioner, who said, 'Are you two seriously the best we have got to be the next PM of our great country?'

Sunak was again well prepared and repeatedly urged voters not to 'surrender' to Labour. On immigration he quoted Roy Scheider's character from *Jaws*, 'If Labour win, the people smugglers are going to need a bigger boat. Don't surrender our borders to the Labour Party.' When the Labour leader suggested he would process migrants much quicker and do more returns deals with other countries, Sunak pointed out that that just meant allowing migrants to stay in the UK since most asylum seekers came from Iran, Syria and Afghanistan. 'Will you sit down with the Ayatollahs? Are you going to try to do a deal with the Taliban? It's completely nonsensical – you are taking people for fools,' he added. Sunak used his thirty-second closing statement to reiterate his controversial £2,000 tax claim, prompting Keir Starmer to shout, 'That is a lie.' His closing riff was to tell people that if they wanted change, 'you have to vote for it'. YouGov's snap poll scored it a dead heat.

The situation was getting bleaker, however. After D-Day did its damage, Levido changed his targets, burrowing deeper and deeper into the Tory heartlands, until some seats with huge majorities were also included. MPs who were toast were quietly asked if they would like to help a friend who was still savable. 'We pushed further and further down the list,' a source said. 'By the end there were not a huge number of seats' with large enough majorities to escape the list.

If Levido was uncomfortable with sending scarce resources to shore up seats with majorities over 20,000, McSweeney felt equally strange with a target seat list which included constituencies where Labour had literally never campaigned before and where they lacked any old canvass returns to fall back on. Labour's internal numbers fluctuated through the campaign but never fell below the 'high 300s' in terms of seats. Once the number got as high as 440, but it was usually in the 'low 400s'. By polling day, it was showing 'mid-420s'. Tony Blair had won 419 seats in 1997.

Things might have been worse for the Tories but for a couple of setbacks late in the campaign for Nigel Farage. On 21 June, in a *Newsnight* interview, Farage claimed the West 'provoked' Russia's invasion of Ukraine by expanding the EU and Nato eastwards. This gave Vladimir Putin a 'reason' to tell the Russian people 'they're coming for us again'. This was a mainstream view on the MAGA[8] right-wing of the Republican Party which backed Donald Trump's isolationism. But it was not calculated to appeal to Reform voters, and it immediately drew fire from Tory politicians, undermining the idea that Farage might work with them to realign the right. Boris Johnson dismissed Farage's argument as 'nauseating ahistorical drivel' and 'Kremlin propaganda'. A Conservative peer close to CCHQ said, 'I think it was a massive fuck-up. His so-called reverse takeover of the Tories is just not going to happen.'

The second problem was one Farage confronted in both UKIP and the Brexit Party. On 27 June, *Channel 4 News* ran an exposé of racism in Reform UK, including undercover footage of three activists in Clacton. One suggested using illegal migrants for 'target practice', called Islam a 'cult', suggested turning mosques into Wetherspoons pubs and described the prime minister as 'a fucking Paki'. Farage said he was 'dismayed' and that the three men would play no further role on the campaign.[9]

As July began, Theresa May was fighting hard. She had stood down from her Maidenhead seat, but an MRP poll had put the Lib Dems within a point of seizing it. She was one of several grandees invited to CCHQ to give a pep talk to staff. While she was there, she complained about the supermajority strategy, warning that it was hurting morale among canvassers. Levido explained his rationale. May never said a peep in public about her concerns. 'She's a class act,' a source said. On 1 July footage emerged of her ringing the video doorbell of a voter who was out as she pounded the streets. May introduced herself before informing the homeowner she was putting a leaflet through their door.

It is just possible that her example helped Boris Johnson decide that he ought to put his own shoulder to the wheel in the final week. At the start of the campaign, Johnson had concluded that any public appearance would, in his words, 'turn into a royal goat fuck'. Instead, he contributed videos and endorsements for two dozen MPs around the country.

Levido was in regular contact with Johnson and spoke three times a day to Ross Kempsell, Johnson's right-hand man. Both were keen that Johnson get involved. They concluded using him to deliver the final squeeze message to Reform voters was the best bang for their buck. Johnson was also growing 'existentially worried' about the prospect of a landslide for Starmer, the leader he had written off in 2021. 'He's been around long enough to be sceptical of the polls,' a friend said. 'But it dawned on him quite strongly in the past couple of weeks that this is actually happening.'

There was already a rally planned at the National Army Museum in London, where Sunak was due to speak. Johnson thought helping was the 'right thing to do', but he was also beginning to conclude that if he wanted ever to stage another comeback it would be sensible to look as if he had made more effort to help. This was a train of thought Levido sought to encourage. 'He fucking got rid of me,' Johnson complained in one conversation. 'Why should I be helping his re-election?'

'Don't worry about him, mate,' Levido said. 'This isn't about the election.' To Levido it very much was. 'This is about what it means for you inside the party going forward. Do it on that basis.'

However, for months, even when he and Sunak exchanged messages, the prime minister had never once asked Johnson to do so – an act of obeisance which Johnson wanted. 'There hadn't been what Boris considered a personal request,' a close ally said. 'He had this position all the way through, which was, "Sunak's got to ask me directly."'

A week before the end of the campaign, Sunak finally texted Johnson to say 'thanks very much' for his cheerleading *Daily Mail* columns. Sunak added, 'Boris, can you please do everything possible in the next week to help the campaign?'

Levido and Kempsell thrashed out the details. Johnson did not want to share a stage with the man he blamed for his fall. Levido arranged it so he could turn up, park, get into the venue, mic up and leave again without bumping into Sunak or Gove. But it was Johnson who said, 'I need to introduce Rishi.'

'I agree,' said Levido, grateful this had been volunteered.

The campaign director had two man-management issues. 'Sunak didn't actually know until the late afternoon of the day' that Johnson was doing the rally, a source said. In the car on the way there it was not clear Johnson would go through with it. He announced that he felt 'physically sick' that he was going to help Sunak. 'Why should I help this fucker? Why am I doing this? This guy's a fucking cunt.' Turning to Kempsell, he complained, 'You and Isaac stitched this up.' Gradually, the view that it was good news that the party needed him and sensible for him to help out reasserted itself.

Johnson's prepared remarks had been seen by Levido, whose big ask was that he do a riff on the supermajority theme and attack Farage – the only Tory who could call on similar loyalty from Leave voters. Pushing his luck a little, Levido sounded out Johnson about whether he would be content to shake Sunak's hand backstage and be pictured doing so. Johnson was 'not very keen'. Carrie, who accompanied him, was grateful that Levido did not push too hard.

Gove listed Tory achievements of the last fourteen years: a reformed welfare state, 'closing a huge school-attainment gap between rich and poor'. He urged activists to 'fight, fight, fight to the end', but some reflected that Gove himself had given up, deciding not to stand again in Surrey Heath, which duly fell to the Lib Dems later that week.

Johnson was due on stage at 9.30 p.m. His car pulled up at 9.25 p.m., and he walked with Carrie down a back corridor toward the stage. Levido suggested to Sunak that he leave the green room to say hello. 'Thank you for doing this,' Sunak said, hands firmly by his sides. 'It means a lot.'

Johnson replied, 'Happy to do it. It's the right thing to do for the campaign.' Watched by Levido, Kempsell, Carrie and Nissy Chesterfield, for 'three or four minutes' they discussed how best to attack Starmer. 'He's going to be a disaster,' Johnson said. It was the first time they had looked each other in the eye since the showdown in Millbank Tower. When things seemed to flag, Carrie kept them going, echoing her husband's criticisms of Starmer, but adding, 'We've all got to come together.' Those within earshot said it was 'cordial' but there was an atmosphere. 'The mutual antipathy rises off both of them,' one witness said. Johnson had still not forgiven Sunak for his role in his downfall. He did not confront this head on, but there was a reference: 'Obviously, I would have loved to keep going.'

Johnson arrived at the podium to chants of 'Boris! Boris! Boris!', before saying it was 'past Sir Keir Starmer's bedtime', a reference to the Labour leader saying he did not want to work past 6 p.m. on Fridays. Johnson's prepared remarks did not refer to the prime minister by name, but on stage he referred to Rishi. Addressing the crowd, he said, 'Is it not the height of insanity, if these polls are right, that we are about to give Labour a supermajority?' Reform UK voters, he warned, would end up with 'exactly the opposite of what they want', ushering 'in the most left-wing Labour government since the war'. He then rounded on Farage, branding him one of the 'Kremlin crawlers' and 'Putin's pet parrots' who 'make excuses for the invasion of Ukraine … Shame on them … Don't let the Putinistas deliver the Corbynistas.'

When Johnson left the stage, he passed very closely by Sunak in the narrow corridor, but they did not speak to each other. 'It was pretty icy,' another witness recalled. For Fraser Nelson, editor of Johnson's old magazine, the *Spectator*, the event was the coda to an entire era, Johnson and Gove's the 'best two speeches I heard from anyone in the campaign', the rally a 'requiem to what might have been'.

Before the requiem, there had to be a funeral. Senior Tories had now given up. Mel Stride, the work and pensions secretary, said, 'Tomorrow is likely to see the largest Labour landslide, the largest majority this country has ever seen.' Just as Suella Braverman had jumped the gun in 2022, announcing that she was running for leader before Johnson had even left, so this time she penned an article for the *Telegraph*, published on Tuesday evening, attacking her own government and praising Farage. 'It's over and we need to prepare for the reality and frustration of opposition,' she wrote.[10] A ministerial adviser who had previously sympathised with Braverman said, 'At that point Farage was trying to kill the party. MPs were still canvassing trying to save their seats.'

The only question left was how many of them would succeed.

32

IN

(and Out)

4 to 5 July 2024

'Gods watch from above and wonder what went wrong
The entropy of what once was strong
The survivors of man stay up late to pray
That the world will again be theirs one day ...'

– Abney Park, 'The End of Days'

At 4 p.m. on election day they called Rishi Sunak to read him the last rites. Isaac Levido, Liam Booth-Smith and James Forsyth had all planned to fly to Yorkshire to see the prime minister the night before to show him the internal numbers. Sunak was reluctant. He was with his family. 'I'll go to vote early and then I'm just going to switch my brain off,' he said.

'We can easily do this in the afternoon when we've got a bit more visibility from the ground,' Levido offered. Sunak sounded relieved. In any case, the numbers hadn't changed that much. There was no late surge from undecided voters breaking for the Tories.

At four, they dialled Sunak. Levido and his senior field staff were there, Oliver Dowden had dialled in as well. They walked through the possibilities. A lot of seats were very marginal, calling them was difficult, which gave a wide range of outcomes. 'At the low end you're looking at around 87 seats,' Levido revealed. Catastrophe. Some public MRPs had them in the fifties, behind the Lib Dems. 'Top end looks like 130,' he said. Disaster and a humiliation but not actually an extinction-level event. Sunak was matter-of-fact. The man holding the baby when the music stopped after eight years of political carnage.

It was a measure of the unity of Sunak's team that they nearly reached the end without falling apart and turning on each other. Nearly but not quite. On Thursday evening, Levido hosted a dinner at the St Ermin's Hotel in Westminster, a Tory polling day tradition. He went around the tables thanking each of those present. When he got to Booth-Smith, the chief of staff who Sunak had just handed a seat in the House of Lords, there was vocal dissent from other members of the inner circle. Rupert Yorke, the deputy chief of staff and Sunak's main point man with Tory MPs, was described as 'livid' at the way the announcement – which went public during the meal – had been handled. Multiple sources claimed he muttered uncomplimentary epithets about Booth-Smith.

Close aides had told Sunak not to include any political advisers in the dissolution honours – usually saved for a separate resignation honours list – and felt they had been 'lied to' about it. For a tight-knit team which, largely, did not leak or backbite, this was an astonishing breakdown at the final hurdle. Nissy Chesterfield was equally incensed. A former Downing Street source confirmed, 'Advice was given that no spads should be on the list for good reason. That was what was expected until suddenly it wasn't the case.' To a witness at the dinner though, 'Other people were pissed off they didn't get what they wanted when they thought they were going to get it. Alcohol doesn't mix well with frustration.' Yorke denied he had been drinking.

They returned to watch the exit poll, the campaign's appointment with fate. Levido thought they would get more than 100 seats, but he would not have been surprised if they were in single digits.

In Vincent Square, Dave McCobb of the Liberal Democrats went through in his head what he hoped for. The public MRPs had been all over the place, predicting everything between 30 and 72 seats, the number in the final YouGov model, the one which had proved most accurate in 2019. However, he was encouraged because, whatever base the Lib Dems had begun on with each pollster's model, each successive megapoll had shown them rising. So too did their own canvass returns.

For the last year he had had 65 seats on his target list; there were now 80. At the last election they had won 11, a number swelled to 15 in by-elections. Trying to keep everyone's feet on the ground, McCobb had spent the last week reminding his team, 'If we make twenty-six gains or more, that will be the best result ever in terms of seats gained for the party,' beating Paddy Ashdown in 1997. He spent the last ten days checking every single bit of data they had. Anything less than 35, the number of seats he had been targeting for most of the Parliament, would have been a disappointment. As the clock ticked down to 10 p.m. he reasoned that anything in the 50s or 60s would guarantee they had more seats than the SNP and would return to being the third party in Westminster.

Keir Starmer had borrowed a friend's house to watch the exit poll, gathered with his family and a dozen of his closest aides. At 9 p.m., McSweeney called him to say he expected to win somewhere around 422 seats, a majority of 194. He was planning to stay at party headquarters, for the 1 per cent chance that things had gone horribly wrong.

As 10 p.m. approached, the Labour leader was on a sofa with his wife Vic and their two teenage children. It was a poignant scene for others present, a man on the cusp of history with those dearest to him, tense as they approached the moment which would define the rest of their lives. Starmer's son consciously casual in the shirt of Arsenal, the team he and his father worshipped. His daughter the light relief. When Starmer's face appeared on screen, she let out a long 'Ewww' to laughter from the back of the room. With a minute to go, Starmer and his wife stretched an arm around each other's shoulders, reaching for the other's spare hand – two become one.[1]

Bong. Britain's most famous bell tolled for him. 'As Big Ben strikes ten, the exit poll is predicting a Labour landslide,' said the BBC's Clive Myrie. 'Keir Starmer will become prime minister with a majority of around 170 seats.'

Then: silence. Tom Baldwin, Starmer's biographer, who was there, thought it lasted two full minutes. 'Some sobbed as aching exhaustion mixed with relief and joy,' he wrote. Starmer 'wrapped both his arms around his wife to share an extravagant kiss'. Then he embraced his thirteen-year-old daughter, a hug that morphed into a protective embrace. Asked a week ago what he was frightened of as prime minister, Starmer had said that it would lead to intrusion into his children's lives. Baldwin 'looked away … The room suddenly felt hot … I knew this was intruding on something very personal.'[2]

The silence was broken by Matthew Doyle, the director of communications: 'Well, we won,' he said, deadpan, the ice broken. Starmer toured the room embracing his team, who finally had an appetite for the buffet.

Then the internet went down and with it the television. 'That's a bit frustrating,' said the prime minister elect. No drama Starmer.[3]

In Labour headquarters, the reaction was more raucous. McSweeney, the McFaddens, Lillywhite and the rest gathered by the bank of TV screens next to the press desk. They stood together, shoulder to shoulder, like a team of footballers in the centre circle anxiously watching a teammate trudge off alone to take a penalty in the shootout. Waiting for a number. Bong. Labour: 415 seats. 'Everyone just erupted.'

It went as he expected for Rishi Sunak. Bong. The exit poll predicted 131 seats for the Tories, at the top end of Levido's predictions. Sunak was 'very matter-of-fact', an ally said. 'He had internalised it all at four o'clock.'

In CCHQ, those who had known how bad things were allowed themselves a micro sigh of relief. Levido was straight into the small print of the poll. A large number of seats were too close to call. 'Cautiously optimistic' they might even be able to 'move up', win a few more, he stood on a desk and said, 'Obviously this is pointing towards a disappointing result. It's a projection, not a result, but this election is going to be a defining moment for our party and how we conduct ourselves over the next few hours will determine our future.' Then, a message for those who had walked into this on their first campaign. 'This is the hardest campaign you're ever going to work on. It will never be tougher than this.'

The thing Sunak did ask about was the exit poll's prediction that Reform would win thirteen seats – well above what anyone expected. 'Where is this Reform vote coming from?' Booth-Smith went to Chris Scott, the party's director of insights, who said, 'I cannot see from the numbers how that is possible.' By ten past ten they were calling Sunak again: 'We don't think the Reform number is accurate.'

In Vincent Square, the Lib Dem campaign team had moved their television to a better spot so the entire office could enjoy the show. Bong. Their number: 61. A gain of 46 seats, Paddy Ashdown's record smashed. 'Everyone just went mad, cheering, hugging,' a senior official said. 'Then they went back to work in a wonderfully Lib Dem way.'

McCobb, Dixon and Grender made a Zoom call to Ed Davey, who was at home. When the leader came online, all four of them just screamed at each other, a cathartic release. No words, just emotion.

There was another sweet moment for the Lib Dems. On ITV's panel, alongside George Osborne and Ed Balls, sat the SNP's Nicola Sturgeon. When the exit poll dropped, it predicted just 10 seats for the Nationalists, who had dominated politics north of the border for seventeen years. Sturgeon it was who had called the election a 'de facto referendum'. Five years earlier she had pumped her fists like a coked-up footballer when the Lib Dem leader Jo Swinson lost her seat to the SNP. As reality bit, Sturgeon became still, trying to control her emotions, lips pursed. Images of her constipated fury circulated on Lib Dem WhatsApp groups. A Swinson ally mocked up a 'how it started, how it's going' meme with the two pictures. Swinson approved.

For most of the night there was no 'Portillo moment', a shock defeat for a major player, just a series of skittles tumbling – Robert Buckland, Alex Chalk, Simon Clarke, Thérèse Coffey, David T. C. Davies, Michelle Donelan, Lucy Frazer, Damian Green, Greg Hands, Mark Harper (by 300 votes), Simon Hart, Gillian Keegan, Victoria Prentis, Jacob Rees-Mogg and Grant Shapps.

One of the biggest surprises was not a loss but a win. Clinging defiantly to the rocks in Godalming and Ash, as the tidal wave swept a generation of Conservatives away, was Jeremy Hunt. Levido always thought Hunt would win. There were many Conservatives in the old blue wall in the South who barely visited their seats, never went canvassing and when they tried to run a local campaign ('Forget about the government, vote for me because I'll fight for you'), they had no credibility. Not Hunt. It was his patch and he worked it hard. His final election message was to report to some constituents who had been without water that safe drinking water was back. 'It was the greatest closing message in history,' Levido told colleagues.

The other hero in CCHQ was Matt Vickers in Stockton West, the lone blue brick left in a reconstructed wall of solid red across the North-East. 'He's just a fucking good local campaigner,' a source said.

As Reform began to underperform the exit poll, which had given them 13 seats, Tory hopes rose. At 3.30 a.m., Sir John Curtice, who led the team behind the exit poll, revised their seat number up to 154. 'Everyone was quite excited then,' a campaign source said. But it was not to be. A series of narrow losses, mostly to the Lib Dems, meant they ended up with just 121 seats. They lost more than forty by margins of less than 2,000 votes.

Richard Holden, the party chairman, won by 20 votes, Greg Hands, his predecessor, lost by 147. 'If we'd had a bit of luck we might have got to 170 and then we'd have looked like geniuses,' a CCHQ official said. 'But we didn't have any luck in the campaign, so I shouldn't have expected any on election night.'

By 1 a.m. it was clear that it was over. Booth-Smith phoned his fellow chief of staff Sue Gray. 'It seems pretty clear the prime minister is going to have to give Sir Keir a call,' he said, keen to ensure they were ready. 'I'll get him to do it via switch,' he said.

At 3 a.m. Sunak made the call. After all the debates and attacks and the brutality of narrow differences, it was an 'incredibly courteous' conversation. Sunak congratulated his successor. 'It's a very difficult job, but massively rewarding.' He wished Starmer 'the best of luck with it' and added, something they both felt deeply, 'I hope your family will deal with it okay. It is a difficult transition.'

Starmer reflected that the campaign had been relatively clean. 'It's been incredibly tough, but thank you for the way we've been able to conduct this. It's been very hard, but it has not tipped over the edge.'

Sunak had a final thought and an offer, one he had taken up repeatedly. 'You're going to have your own ideas about pretty much everything you want to do. Good luck with it. But on anything to do with national security, I've made a point of talking to my predecessors, because they had a history and knowledge that I didn't have. If you ever wanted to discuss anything or just get my sense of what I've been told before on any national security matters, don't hesitate to pick up the phone. I'll always be there to help you.' It was the part of the job that surprised even those who had prepared for years. Sending men and women to fight and die for their country was the loneliest element of command. Only those who had experienced it could truly understand.

And thus was completed the moment when democracy asserts its superiority over other forms of government – the transfer of power. Its strength is not the voting or the counting of votes, but the accepting of them by the defeated, the willingness of a government of fourteen years to vacate the pitch when told to do so by the booing crowd in the stands. As Donald Trump had shown after the 2020 presidential election and his supporters had shown on 6 January 2021 when they stormed the US Capitol, there was nothing inevitable about this.

It was Sunak who first told the nation. Labour had not yet quite reached the 326 seats they needed for a simple majority when the prime minister took to the stage at his count in Richmond around 4.45 a.m. and declared, 'The Labour Party has won this general election, and I have called Sir Keir Starmer to congratulate him on his victory. Today, power will change hands in a peaceful and orderly manner, with good will on all sides. The British people have delivered a sobering verdict tonight,' he said. 'There is much to learn and reflect on – and I take responsibility for the loss.' To those who had lost their seats, he said, 'I am sorry ...'

Starmer headed from his count to Tate Britain for the victory party. At 3.30 a.m. he was met outside by McSweeney. They had won, in part, because they were both hyper-competitive. 'Where are the numbers going to finish up?' Starmer asked.

'They might be a little bit north of 410,' he replied. 'It might be a bit higher than the exit poll.' They walked and talked, into a lift, Vic Starmer with them. 'I'm not sure it's going to beat 1997,' McSweeney added.

It was a small sadness, but they both felt it. They were on course for 412 seats,[4] a gain of 211, one more than Stanley Baldwin in 1931, three fewer than the Liberal landslide of 1906. Yet Tony Blair, Starmer's benchmark, had won 419 seats in 1997. Their victory over the Tories was more emphatic, but McSweeney admitted, 'It irritates me a bit.' Starmer agreed. They both knew Mandelson and Campbell would have some fun with them, and it pissed them off.

'This is just a ridiculous kind of conversation to be having,' declared Vic Starmer, speaking for normal people.

The number might have been higher, but it was already evident there were problems. Starmer was worried about Jonathan Ashworth, who it was clear was going to lose his Leicester South seat thanks to the surge of votes for independents campaigning on Palestinian rights. Ashworth's had not even been one of the twelve seats monitored by the unit set up the previous year. McSweeney had warned colleagues that every campaign ends in some sort of failure. This was one problem he was not able to fix.

To those for whom Gaza was the greatest moral issue of the time, it seemed natural that it should be a driver of votes. To many others the sight of sectarian voting was a retrograde step which transported vicious passions into politics. Heather Iqbal, who had been subjected to vile abuse by fanatics who stood at polling stations yelling, 'You're not a Muslim if you vote Labour', lost by nearly 7,000 votes in Dewsbury and Batley. The same effect helped Jeremy Corbyn win again in Islington North. Independents also won Blackburn and Birmingham Perry Barr. The 'Chingford Corbynista' Faiza Shaheen got 12,445 votes, just 79 fewer than the Labour candidate in Chingford and Woodford Green, allowing Iain Duncan Smith to hold the seat by nearly 5,000 votes. Rushanara Ali, who was defending a majority of more than 37,000 in Bethnal Green and Stepney, would only cling on by 1,689 after a campaign in which she was given the kind of police protection usually reserved for a prime minister following a series of credible death threats. In Ilford North, Wes Streeting survived by just 528 votes.

Jess Phillips saw off a challenge from George Galloway's Workers Party in Birmingham Yardley by 693 votes and then denounced the behaviour of the baying mob at the count who disrupted her acceptance speech with pro-Palestinian chants. 'This election has been the worst election I have ever stood in,' she said. One of her young team, a 'brilliant community activist', was abused by her opponents. 'People filmed her on the streets and slashed her tyres.' The family of Jo Cox, murdered in 2016, had planned to join her at the count, but Phillips said, 'There was absolutely no way that I could have allowed them to see aggression and violence in our democracy.' For many, the sweetest win of the night was when Paul Waugh, once a jobbing hack, now the slayer of dragons, took Rochdale from Galloway.

The damage wrought by independents on the main parties was a score draw in the end. Reform UK won five seats, the same as the Gaza-focused independents. Lee Anderson held Ashfield and was joined by Richard Tice in Boston and Skegness, Rupert Lowe in Great Yarmouth and James McMurdock in South Basildon and East Thurrock. It was eighth time lucky for Nigel Farage, who won Clacton with a majority of 8,405. The BBC cut away from Corbyn's acceptance speech just before 4 a.m. to go to Farage – the anti-establishment baton passed. Farage pledged to 'put Clacton on the map' and declared, 'My plan is to build a mass national movement over the course of the next few years' and 'challenge properly at the general election in 2029'. He added, 'This is just the first step of something which is going to stun all of you.'

*   *   *

Starmer took to the stage at Tate Modern at 5 a.m. to a huge uproar of support. Now it was official, Labour had crossed the threshold of 326 seats. Starmer's grin was that of a man liberated by success, glowing as he spoke a little like a revivalist preacher about 'the sunlight of hope, pale at first but getting stronger through the day, shining once again'. In front of him, hundreds of delirious party activists, many of them too young to remember the last Labour election victory, still less the moment they last took power. He declared, 'You campaigned for it, you fought for it, voted for it and now it has arrived – change begins now. And it feels good, I have to be honest.' Their task, he said, 'is nothing less than renewing the ideas that hold this country together'. It would need 'hard work, determined work, patient work'.

Most Tory candidates were gracious towards Labour and showed humility about Tory failures. An emotional Jeremy Hunt, victorious as an MP, defeated as a cabinet minister, wished Starmer and Reeves well, calling them dedicated public servants. Suella Braverman was not even gracious in victory. It was 5.20 a.m. when she thanked the people of Farnham and Waterlooville for returning her to Parliament, before proving once more that it's not just what you say in politics that matters, but when you choose to say it. Wearing Thatcher blue and her hair expensively coiffured for the cameras, Braverman said, 'I want to briefly address the result in the rest of the country', before a melodramatic mea culpa: 'There is one thing I can say … Sorry … I'm sorry … I'm sorry that we didn't listen to you.' Each pause was delivered with the doe-eyed determination of a trainee method actor seeking to project sincerity. 'The Conservative Party has let you down. You, the great British people, voted for us over fourteen years and we did not keep our promises.' It was an inelegant 'I told you so', and most of her fellow Tories did not want to hear it. Three weeks later she was finished as a leadership candidate.

If there was a 'Portillo moment', it came at 7 a.m. when Liz Truss lost her South West Norfolk seat. Many MPs, seeing beloved colleagues swept away, found catharsis in the fact that one of those responsible paid her own high price. The crowd slow hand-clapped until she came to the stage for the returning officer to pronounce sentence. Truss lost to Labour's Terry Jermy by 630 votes and was only 1,200 ahead of the third-placed Reform UK candidate. An independent conservative, James Bagge, siphoned off more than 6,000 votes in a successful effort to force her out.

Her right-hand man, Jonathan Isaby, wept when the result was declared.

When Jermy had finished his victory speech, Truss gave one of her enigmatic smiles, half-pain, half-smirk. The other candidates and the returning officer looked her way. She had been the MP there for fourteen years, the prime minister of the country. They clearly expected her to speak, to offer something. She turned and walked from the stage.

Sunak flew down from his count and arrived at CCHQ as Truss was losing. He thanked staff for their hard work and apologised: 'I'm sorry I wasn't able to deliver the result that everyone deserved.' He looked tired, his voice hoarse. He praised the campaign for putting Labour on the spot over tax. 'The party must now move into opposition and the work the campaign has done will give us an effective platform to do that.'

At 9.25 a.m., Sunak addressed an all-staff meeting in the pillared state room in Number 10. 'The country voted for change, but that is a verdict on me and my party. It should not make you feel any less proud of what we've achieved together.' He thanked everyone, from the cafe, who kept him 'caffeinated', to the private office, who 'kept the whole show on the road, in spite of my handwriting'. Listing their achievements, he included 'returned the economy to stability', 'delivered the Windsor Framework' and 'completed 127 three-page briefs' – able to laugh at his demands for detail. Sunak had asked so many questions that the average length of a 'three-pager', someone calculated, was 'five to six pages'. When he left with Akshata, one present recalled, 'I think we were clapping for fifteen or twenty minutes because he wanted to stop and talk to everyone. Whatever his skills as a politician, he's a decent, genuine man.'

Two weeks later McSweeney, now permanently in a suit, sat in the wood-panelled surroundings of the Old War Office, the Raffles Hotel on Whitehall. Tea was still his drink of choice. Across the room, a member of Sunak's Downing Street team, in combats and a T-shirt, was drinking with a Tory MP who had just clung on. 'Seven years ago, I was working for an organisation which didn't have an office,' he reflected. Now his office was the most famous address in the country.

The Tories suffered their worst general election result in history, but it might have been worse. 'The Conservative Party still exists,' one campaign chief said. 'We are the official opposition and we're twice as big as the next best party. Given all the shit that has happened over the last four years, it could have been a hell of a lot worse.' In CCHQ, officials were only too happy to hand responsibility back to the MPs. 'They can deal with the consequences of their actions,' one said.

A Tory post-election analysis of what went wrong showed clearly that the roots of the disaster lay in events which pre-dated Sunak. Asked why they did not vote Conservative, 33 per cent said, 'They have not delivered enough in the last fourteen years', followed by 'it was time for a change', mentioned by 27 per cent.

'The chaos of leadership changes and division' motivated 21 per cent of non-Tory voters. Just 5 per cent, one in twenty, cited 'Sunak leaving D-Day' and 'they ran a bad election campaign', and 3 per cent mentioned the gambling scandal. Asked for their reasons for backing Labour, 53 per cent said for 'change/get rid of the Conservatives'. 'To stop the Conservatives' was also the number-one motivation for Lib Dem voters, cited by 27 per cent. Top of the list for Reform voters, with 46 per cent, was 'Conservatives/Labour/establishment have failed'.

Asked how he would apportion blame between Johnson, Truss and Sunak, one senior figure said, '50 per cent Truss, 25 per cent the other two.' Truss's culpability was reinforced by the voters in 2024 who had seen interest rates and mortgage rates soar after the mini-budget. 'Outright mortgage holders really punished us,' a Sunak adviser said. 'It's the same truth we learned on Black Wednesday – don't fuck with a man's castle.' A senior cabinet minister said, 'My experience in the election campaign of the reasons people weren't voting for us were: number one, "How can I endorse you guys after all the shit of the past five years?" Then it was, "The NHS is falling to pieces. It's like a war zone." Third was, "What the fuck are you doing about immigration?"'

While Johnson undoubtedly tarnished both his and the Tory brand, when viewed from Labour headquarters, it was removing him which put Starmer in front. A senior Labour official put it pithily, 'The biggest mistake the Tories made electorally was they panicked and got rid of Boris Johnson, who is a winner, and replaced him first with a lunatic [Liz Truss] and then with a loser [Sunak].'

Allied to this was a sentiment common on the doorstep with Leave voters that it was their responsibility, not the job of MPs, to send Johnson packing. 'You shouldn't underestimate the public's anger that the Tory Party had three prime ministers since the last election,' a senior Sunak aide said. 'There was a real feeling of "I voted for Boris, but it should have been up to me to decide whether to kick him out or not".'

All of this was a difficult 'inheritance' for Sunak. A senior cabinet minister said, 'Boris destroyed trust in the Conservatives and trust in competence. Liz finished off the job on competence and on the economy. Rishi was dealt a bad hand.' In the final week of the campaign, Sunak said the quiet bit out loud. 'There's no point sitting there going "I wish someone had given me four aces",' he told reporters on the Tory battle bus. 'You've got to play the cards you're dealt.'

Allies believed Sunak the right man at the wrong time. His incremental approach might have worked if he had had five years, but he was peculiarly unsuited to a two-year sprint to an election. Lacking political pizzazz he asked the electorate to judge him solely on delivery of their priorities, then failed to deliver.

Sunak did not see the danger of allowing the junior doctors' strike to derail his efforts to bring down waiting lists, an issue Dominic Cummings identified in November 2022 and again in July 2023. Flash forward to the election campaign, and polling by More in Common found that 'failing to reduce NHS waiting times' was the top grievance of voters – selected by 33 per cent, compared with 23 for failing to stop the boats. Luke Tryl said, 'In our focus groups everyone had a story about a relative who was on a waiting list. I can't forget the man who drove himself to hospital while having a heart attack. Dominic Cummings was right.'

Those on the right blamed Sunak for embracing the Rwanda plan and then not leaving the ECHR. 'If he'd done what we wanted I don't think he could have won the election,' a ministerial aide said. 'However, I think we would have been ten points closer, and I think the ten points is his fault. It was bad managerialism.'

A lot of heat was created debating whether Sunak was right to call the election early, rather than wait for the autumn. Levido never changed his mind that it would have been better to wait, but he didn't disagree violently with the verdict of one Sunak adviser, who concluded, 'I don't think you can believe that the timing would substantially have changed the result.' More intriguing was the suggestion of two senior figures that he called the election 'far too late'. 'Everyone's conventional wisdom says he went too early,' a senior figure said. 'We should have gone in May 2023.' Booth-Smith had raised the idea that January but not pushed it. No one at the time thought it credible.

Some viewed it as a terrible campaign, but if the campaign is what you plan and how you react, that was unfair. 'The three biggest events that hurt us were Farage coming back, D-Day and gambling,' a senior figure said. Of those, only D-Day was something those in charge could control. Levido's gameplan was effective in challenging Labour on tax, while the supermajority gambit contributed to the decline in Labour's poll numbers. The problem was that the gaffes were highly emblematic – D-Day of the sense that Sunak didn't 'get it', gambling a reminder of the wrongdoing of partygate. A senior minister concluded, 'If Farage hadn't stood and we hadn't had gambling, then we could easily have been in a position where we won more like 200 seats.'

Coulda, woulda, shoulda. You play by the rules of the game. The same went for Labour. Much commentary afterwards (not least from the Corbynites who got more votes) suggested Starmer's was a 'wide but shallow' landslide. Yet if anyone followed LBJ's instruction for politicians to learn to count, it was McSweeney. Winning 412 seats from 33.7 per cent of the vote was the most efficient winning performance in the history of British politics. Yes, the size of Starmer's majority was a function of the cleavage on the right between the Tories and Reform, just as Margaret Thatcher's two landslides in the 1980s followed the SDP split from Labour on the left. But that did not make her victories any less valid or politically far-reaching. The differential between vote share and seats revived talk about proportional representation being fairer. But if there was PR, Labour would have devised a different strategy to squeeze the Greens and target different voters.

The 2024 election did raise legitimate questions about the influence of public polls. The Tories won 23.7 per cent, exactly 10 points less than Labour, half the gap in most polls. 'If we'd ever had a poll that reflected the actual result, the squeeze message would have started to work,' a senior Sunak aide said. 'Our biggest problem with Reform voters was they did not think we could win.'

It was hard to avoid the conclusion, however, that the main reason for the Tory defeat was eight years of chaos which followed the EU referendum, the failure of Britain's leaders to resolve the differences which had caused Brexit or the new political pressures it unleashed. Ultimately it was a story of power failure.

Conclusion

POWER FAILURE

'Power doesn't always corrupt. Power can cleanse.
What I believe is always true about power is
that power always reveals'

– Robert Caro

Napoleon once said, 'What is history, but a fable agreed upon?' The Brexit referendum already feels like ancient history, but the world it created is the one we live in, and its effects will be living history for decades. The divisions it revealed and then created mean it is a fable that is very far from agreed upon.

The years between 2016 and 2024 were the most sustained period of domestic political drama in Britain since the Second World War and arguably far longer than that. It was an important, gripping, exciting, binary battle for power and the political soul of a nation refracted through the result of the referendum on 23 June 2016. It was also tedious, depressing, complicated and unedifying, a sapping banal, partisan process when politicians behaved like children.

The Roman Empire had six emperors in AD 238, there were four Popes in 1276, and before 2022 you had to go back to 1868 to find three prime ministers in a calendar year, or 1834 when there were four premiers, and the Duke of Wellington ruled for less than a month, to match the chaos of 2022. Yet in 2022 there was no shock election result as in 2017 and 2019, no seismic referendum as there was over Scotland in 2014 and Europe in 2016, no Covid pandemic as in 2020 and 2021. The parliamentary turmoil was nothing compared with 2018 and 2019 (for my money, the most dramatic year of the lot).

The turbulence engulfed every party. According to the Nuffield guide to the 2019 election, in 'the Brexit Parliament' between 2017 and 2019, there were 'eighty-nine changes of allegiance by MPs (involving some fifty-two different MPs), easily a post-war record. There were also record levels of ministerial resignations, more than any government for over a century, as well as Commons defeats for the government on an unprecedented scale'.[1] That is before the defenestration of Boris Johnson, where sixty-two frontbenchers resigned.

And yet it will be very possible, in years to come, to write a history of Brexit and the political tumult it unleashed which makes very little reference to the events in this book (and its three predecessors). Andrew Marr, in reviewing *All Out War*, remarked that 'I think we voted to leave because so many British people had been left behind economically and culturally for so long, and were furious about it; and because, from the 2008 financial crisis onwards, they had accumulated so much contempt for the political elites. In these circumstances any referendum narrows down to a single question: "Are you happy with the way things are?" The answer was "no".' I don't disagree. However, this was not a uniquely British situation. Countries around the world experienced the same economic pressures post-2008. 'Politics everywhere entered a period of upheaval,' a cabinet minister said. 'It led, in France, to the collapse of the Gaullists and the socialists and the rise of Macron; it led to the migration crisis, Trump in America; in the UK, Brexit was the manifestation of that and [Jeremy] Corbyn's victory as well. Every so often there are convulsions in politics, and it takes time for Parliament and the political system to adjust.'

Brexit was seen by critics as either a uniquely awful political mistake, or as a carbon copy of Trumpism. It was neither. While the broad trends can help explain the contemporary rise of Trump or Germany's Alternative für Deutschland, each had their own domestic characteristics. Brexit combined legitimate questions about the UK's compatibility with the goals of the European Union, and the internal dynamics of the Tory Party with the politics of austerity and immigration. Brexit was an expression of some of these forces, the result of others and in turn unleashed consequences of its own. It became a full spectrum political event where even things with no causal link to Brexit were experienced and understood by people on both sides in the context of Brexit.

Some of my writing during this period has been challenged for emphasising personal ambition and the political game as the driver of events. Where, wail some commentators (mostly far removed from the dirty business of news gathering), is the political analysis?

There is, of course, a fine tradition, pioneered by Lewis Namier's writings on the structure of politics at the accession of George III, which shows that faction, party, family and personal feuding is often as vital a catalyst for great political events as economics and social change. The better comparison is scholarship around the origins of the First World War. When I first became interested in the subject, in the 1980s, explanations of the war saw it as an inevitable consequence of impersonal forces like nationalism and imperialism. Most striking to this budding historian was the observation of A.J.P. Taylor that train timetables, which forced Russia to mobilise first, coupled with the great power alliance system created a man-made inevitability to the war. However, the two masterpieces of scholarship produced for its centenary in 2014 – Christopher Clark's *The Sleepwalkers* and *July Crisis* by T.G. Otte – emphasise the pivotal role played by individuals, their world views, their mistakes and their interactions.

It seems obvious to me that while Brexit was the product of broader trends, the specific path it took is impossible to understand without close study of the actions, views, ambitions and abilities of the key players. Within that, the battle for power, as much as the exercise of it, was what drove people, every bit as much as ideology. My argument is summed up by the aide to Liz Truss who remarked that 'politics is personality', and one of her cabinet ministers, who concluded, 'Leadership matters.'

Brexit was so disruptive and compelling that it disturbed the constitutional settlement which had largely kept the UK one of the least violent political spheres in the world since the seventeenth century.

'In as much as it works, the reason the government works, is because the executive derives its power from our legislature and our legislature derives its power from the people,' a Number 10 adviser under Theresa May observed. 'Throw the grenade of a direct democratic decision into that and the executive is no longer deriving power from its legislature.' To complicate matters, two thirds of the members of the legislature opposed the decision of the people. Consequently, arguments usually settled inside the legislature increasingly became a stand-off between the executive and the legislature, until eventually the courts intervened. It would take three further major national votes – the 2019 European elections and two general elections in 2017 and 2019 – to resolve the situation.

Our story encompasses multiple negotiations that exposed differing political traditions in Britain and the EU. 'For strong Brexiteers, the whole point of Brexit was a purity of a sovereign, autonomous democracy for the whole of the UK,' a Downing Street aide under May said. 'For the EU, it was the autonomy of its legal order and the integrity of the single market.' Eurosceptics, who had spent years complaining that the EU was a federalist political project, rather than an economic union, suddenly seemed to believe that Brussels would prioritise economics in the negotiations with the UK. Part of the problem was that at dawn on 24 June 2016, with the votes counted and a historic decision made, even Brexiteers disagreed on what Brexit was and what it meant.

When Theresa May pronounced that 'Brexit means Brexit' she was ridiculed, though the phrase has an enduring resonance precisely because people have been trying to define it ever since. May's words were no sort of answer (and indeed were intended to be ambiguous), but they were a very good question.

Brexit was an event and a process. The 2016 referendum result was a seismic *moment* but its meaning was defined by what followed – in the negotiations, Parliament and society – not by what preceded it in the campaign. At the time of writing, Brexit had been defined by Theresa May's inner cabinet in February 2018, again at Chequers in July 2018, then in the initial withdrawal agreement and political declaration in November 2018, a deal clarified by Jean-Claude Juncker and Donald Tusk in a letter to May in January 2019, further tweaked at Strasbourg in March 2019. A further expression was contemplated in the cross-party talks in April and May 2019. Boris Johnson then finalised a different withdrawal agreement in November 2019 and a trade deal, the Trade and Commerce Agreement (TCA), on Christmas Eve 2020. There then followed a series of grace periods to mitigate problems with the Northern Ireland Protocol in 2021 and 2022, before Rishi Sunak signed the Windsor Framework in February 2023. Even this was tweaked and updated in January 2024. Keir Starmer had been prime minister less than a week when he began the process of seeking renewed closeness with the EU. I have never forgotten the words of Alexandre Fasel, the Swiss ambassador in London, who told me when he arrived in 2017, 'Brexit will be a never-ending negotiation. We are negotiating with the EU every day.'

*　*　*

Brexit was a revealer. The referendum campaign did not create two tribes in British society, it was a barium meal on the body politic, lighting up latent divisions which were already there and then reinforcing them. What began as a debate between Eurosceptics and pro-Europeans quickly exposed differences between left and right on economics, between free traders and protectionists, libertarians and authoritarians, regulators and deregulators, optimists and defeatists.

Brexit was a political feeling and a tribal signifier. University-educated metropolitan elites and Home Counties professionals had looked down on working-class 'chavs' and blue collar workers for decades, but both sides probably felt they shared enough traditions: tolerance; a love of roast beef and fish and chips, *EastEnders* and *The X Factor*, queuing and complaining about the weather; and a discreet patriotism that was quietly proud of the armed forces and the Queen and noisily despairing of the England football team. But Brexit gave these divisions expression and a name and made it more respectable to put others in a box and ascribe them a label. Differences of class, race, education and origin all became refracted through the prism of Brexit. While this faded in the 2019–24 Parliament, it did not disappear. Claire Fox compared this to the way the choices people made in the great political battle of the 1980s lived permanently in the background of their lives. 'I don't think people will walk round, saying, "I'm a Leaver." It will be like the miners' strike … Were you a miner, were you a copper, were you a scab mattered, in those communities, for a long time.'[2]

Brexit as a cultural signifier became a significant factor for successive British prime ministers. The story of *No Way Out* is of Theresa May, a Remain voter, racing to establish her credentials with the Leavers in her party, then withdrawing from the hardline position she adopted in the autumn of 2016. She ended up trusted by neither wing of the party, both of which struggled to grasp what she really believed. Everyone knew what Liz Truss believed, but on Brexit, hers was the zeal of the convert – from energetic Remain campaigner to devout advocate of 'no-deal if necessary'. The most interesting conundrum was the way Boris Johnson and Rishi Sunak were perceived. Johnson was Mr Brexit, but also the most left-wing Tory leader on public spending since the days of Butskellism. It was his immigration reforms which opened the door to net migration approaching 750,000. Yet the Tory right regarded him as their figurehead and pined for his return once he had left. Sunak backed Brexit before

Johnson and was, by any conventional standards, hardline on immigration. Yet the Tory right saw him as a rich internationalist who was culturally from the Remain camp. That perception prevented him winning the leadership in 2022 and dogged his entire premiership.

Brexit was such a powerful idea that for years it drowned out other political issues, to the point that Brexit was then assumed to be responsible for everything good and bad in British politics.

Brexit was a radicaliser. Through the Brexit years, politicians adopted progressively extreme positions. In the autumn of 2016, a soft Brexit was membership of the single market and the customs union and a hard Brexit meant leaving both. By mid-2019, a hard Brexit meant no-deal and the alternative was a second referendum or revoking Brexit.

Another element of the radicalisation in Parliament was the 'boredom' of MPs and 'frustrated ego' from politicians 'who just felt that they should be part of it', another of May's aides said, pointing to the emergence of a phenomenon common in the US. 'A hung Parliament means every amendment has someone's name on it. You come up with a plan and once you've floated it you're then stuck with that plan.'

Part of this was the product of technology. People increasingly got their news from social media. Twitter, in particular, delivered pressure and abuse to force people to conform with a position – and to do so instantly. The advent of WhatsApp messaging, which allowed whole groups of people to communicate instantly made plotting and resistance easier. In her study of four US presidents, Doris Kearns Goodwin noted, 'When angry at a colleague, [Abraham] Lincoln would fling off what he called a "hot" letter, releasing all his pent wrath. He would then put the letter aside until he cooled down and could attend the matter with a clearer eye. When Lincoln's papers were opened at the turn of the twentieth century, historians discovered a raft of such letters, with Lincoln's notation underneath; "never sent and never signed".[3] In the Brexit years, people instantly tweeted their rage and often ill-informed and ill-formed views.

All of this meant that the art of compromise was lost. I began *No Way Out* with Bismarck's dictum that 'politics is the art of the possible' but too often campaigners on both sides sought what was politically impossible. Julian Smith put it best: 'It was frustrating that there wasn't huge sex appeal around compromise.'[4]

It depended on your political views as to whether you saw the ERG or the Bresistance as the more intransigent. In truth, they contributed to each other's refusal to budge. Gavin Barwell, May's chief of staff after the 2017 election, recalled, 'I can remember a meeting, once, with a group of Conservative MPs. There were some people who were from the ERG, or that wing of the party, and some people who were from the second referendum camp. It got quite heated. They were both, basically, having a go at me from completely different perspectives. I just, at some point, put my papers down and said, "Look, why don't we all just level with each other? Either we compromise or some of you are going to win and some of you are going to lose and possibly end up leaving the party." They both simultaneously said, "Yes, we're not going to compromise because we're going to win." That was the problem. It got into a winner-takes-it-all, and they both decided that risk was worth taking.'[5]

Oliver Letwin, a key figure in the Bresistance but also an ally of the May regime, noted, 'There is real merit in competitive democracy ... There's real merit in debate, in bringing out the arguments on either side and in letting people gradually understand the pros and cons ... But if that just turns into catcalling and a refusal to accept that the other side is motivated by anything other than low motives, the system will not work properly. It has to be a discussion between grown-ups who accept that people can honestly and rationally hold differing views.'[6] Too often in the Brexit years, it was not.

It is a truism that revolutions end up destroying the revolutionaries but it is still one of the most striking outcomes of Brexit that it nearly destroyed the Conservative Party, widely regarded as the most effective election-winning force in the Western world. Surveying the wreckage ahead of the 2024 general election, Andrew Neil, the leading political broadcaster of the period, said, 'The repeal of the Corn Laws [in the 1840s] destroyed that Conservative Party and a new one had to rise from the ashes. Brexit has destroyed the Conservative Party as we know it. It's divided it, it's exhausted it, it's made it almost childish as they changed leader after leader. The prime ministership became a game of Tory musical chairs.'[7]

The story of that game is the spine of this quartet and it tells us much about leadership; the pursuit, retention, use and loss of power. If there is one conclusion the Westminster class ought to take from nearly 2,700 pages of internecine warfare it is this: the craft of politics matters just as much as a commitment to public service or a particular political mission.

Being good at the 'political game' is not a sordid sideline for snake oil salesmen, it ought to be the basic requirement expected of all frontline politicians. That it is not explains a good deal of what you have read in these pages. Leaders need a view and from it a derived goal, plus an understanding of how to achieve what they want and an ability to take people – MPs and voters – with them to that destination. In most other walks of life, this would be the bare minimum expected of leaders.

The Brexit Britain ended up with was the result of a lot of people being very bad at politics and, just occasionally, very good.

The view that politics was a 'shitshow' in these years was all pervasive. Yet in their very different ways many of the key players displayed great ability: Theresa May in surviving (until her government had run out of people to alienate), Oliver Robbins in negotiating a deal which reconciled May's confused wishes with the parameters of EU tolerance; Michel Barnier in keeping his coalition of the twenty-seven countries together; Steve Baker and the ERG in plotting the downfall of that deal; Dominic Grieve and Oliver Letwin in dreaming up constitutional innovation that helped prevent no-deal; Boris Johnson in defying every prediction of his irrelevance before joining Leo Varadkar to grasp together history's passing vine; Dominic Cummings in authoring a political strategy that converted the Brexit he had won in 2016 into an election victory which delivered his goals in 2019.

Take also the case of Philip Hammond, whose reputation was as one of the most 'tin-eared' and inept political operators of the era. Yet there is a case that Hammond understood the exercise of real power better than most. Knowing his public persona would help him achieve little above the waterline, he focused on subterranean activities to move things in the direction he wanted. Hammond insisted on the Brexit transition phase before anyone else and co-opted David Davis as an ally to make it happen. He consciously made no-deal preparations difficult through most of 2018 by refusing to fund them; he joined the Bresistance full time in mid-2019, using his reading of Johnson's character to beef up the Benn Act and make a deal more likely. That will make him a villain to many but, having concluded that stopping no-deal was his most important legacy, he achieved that goal (and had the pragmatism to do a deal to secure a peerage as well).

The picture of how the Brexit prime ministers exercised power was, to be generous, mixed. As *All Out War* shows, David Cameron miscalculated in a way that would shape his life and his country to an extent that he deplored. Clear enough about his destination, a referendum win, the path he chose was distorted by his misunderstanding the views of the public and the target voters he would need – leading to fatal overconfidence about his ability to win them around.

As *Fall Out* and *No Way Out* demonstrated, Theresa May set out not knowing where she was going, took too long to decide on a viable destination and by the time she did, in the summer of 2018, she had successively alienated both wings of her party. Her secrecy meant she lacked the inclination to take people with her and when it became imperative to do so, she showed herself wholly inadequate for the task of public communication and persuasion.

In the negotiations, May played by rules made and refereed in Brussels, ignoring Brexiteer pleading that she turn over the table and fight. It is hard to escape the conclusion that she went too passively to her fate. Boris Johnson's first months in office went some way to confirming the view that playing hardball might have been worth a try – though his and David Frost's no-holds-barred approach also limited some of what Britain gained in 2020. Rishi Sunak's Windsor Framework showed that a more conciliatory approach could also bear fruit.

A Truss-era cabinet minister said, 'These prime ministers are significant figures for all time. With Theresa, it was what she didn't do which is so significant. She was an agent of history by dint of her failure.' May's semi-memoir was called *The Abuse of Power*. 'The real abuse of power was not delivering what she promised the British people she would,' the minister added. 'All the problems, all the instability stems from the sheer inadequacy of her personal leadership.'

This sequence of books is ostensibly about Brexit and the impact it had on British politics and British politicians, but at heart it is the story of Boris Johnson. 'The central figure is Boris, inescapably,' said Michael Gove. It is difficult to imagine Brexit happening without Gove or Dominic Cummings; it is impossible to do so without Boris.

Let us give him the name by which the public knew him. To do so is not to grant him the indulgence of familiarity, it is to acknowledge that he was a rarity, a public figure known by a single name and, in Johnson's case, as one of his biographers[8] has shown, 'Boris' was a character, a creation by Alexander Johnson to carry him away from the demons of his childhood. It is wrong to see the entire period of British politics as the plaything of Johnson's desire since childhood to be 'World King', but that is closer to the truth than simply saying he was flotsam on the grand waves of history. Brexit's shape was determined more by Johnson's trials and tribulations than the actions of anyone else.

In hundreds of interviews for these books I heard but one view of Theresa May from MPs, ministers, special advisers, civil servants and Eurocrats: that she was a decent person dedicated to public service who was, in essence, unknowable. Everyone had a different opinion about Boris – and they tended to veer to the extremities. His character was an infuriating combination of near-feral political genius and a level of self-indulgence and erratic governance which it is hard to fathom could share the same body with someone as attuned to the gut instincts of the British public. Johnson 'got' the voters better than any other politician of his generation and they returned the favour – both recognising their own base instincts in the other.

Johnson sought to emulate the erratic rise of his political spirit animal Winston Churchill. The comparisons are not as vulgar as Johnson's detractors charge. Churchill too was a One Nation Tory who became vociferously associated with divisive political concerns that were anathema to polite opinion (most notoriously, in his case, opposition to Indian self-government), an adroit writer and phrasemaker, changeable in his alliances, distrusted by the vast bulk of the Conservative Party, who saw in him a man driven only by his hopes for himself and for the country, rather than the party.

When Johnson's greatest tests arrived in 2019 and 2020, he did not ascend to the pantheon of Britain's great statesmen, as Churchill did in 1940. Yet there is an argument too that (what should properly be called) the Vote Leave government's handling of the Brexit crisis in the second half of 2019, reprehensible as it was to their opponents, was the one time politics was conducted on the Tory side with purpose, skill and élan in the period between the referendum and the 2024 general election.

The Johnson–Cummings strategy in 2019 was widely seen as an appalling subjugation of democracy, Parliament and the constitution itself – a view fuelled by the Supreme Court ruling and the idea that Johnson had lied to one of the most revered monarchs in British history. But, as Cummings argued, the Grieve–Letwin manoeuvres to seize the Commons timetable from the government relied on an activist speaker prepared to change established conventions. By contrast, Johnson's prorogation, while questionable, was seen as lawful by every government lawyer; it was the Supreme Court which made new law. It is also wrong to see Vote Leave's strategy as wholly cynical. Those who had won the referendum did feel responsible for delivering it and sincerely believed it was better if the result was honoured.

It is wrong to see Johnson as solely the puppet of Cummings. Their success also relied heavily on Johnson's personal abilities, one specific, one abstract. The first is that he had the charisma to woo Leo Varadkar, something which had been beyond May. 'He took really big risks,' Philip Rycroft observed. 'But he got a deal, and credit to him.'

Second, when it came to Brexit, Johnson's ability to speak out of both sides of his mouth enabled people to invest in the part of his claimed reality which best suited them, without him having to resolve the contradictions in his different public utterances. To his critics, Johnson was either ignorant or a liar when he adopted mutually incompatible positions. But all political deals in Northern Ireland are a fudge. Johnson not only recognised this, he embodied it. In this regard, he was perhaps the only politician who could have successfully navigated his way, Janus faced, through the minefield of Brexit in the second half of 2019.

The same duality allowed him to hold the traditional Tory heartlands in the 2019 election with a message of One Nation conservatism and fiscal responsibility (at least relative to Jeremy Corbyn) and, simultaneously, to make deep inroads into the red wall seats of the north.

Brexit gave him a theme in 'levelling up' but this was never translated into a concrete strategic goal, still less a tactical delivery plan. A Tory grandee once remarked that Johnson was a political cat, preening, independent and selfish but one with ninety-nine lives. He defied political gravity for so long, landing on his paws whatever the height of the skyscraper he had plunged from, that he believed he would always do so. This conditioned him to complacency during the various crises of his final nine months in Number 10.

By convincing himself he had a personal mandate from the electorate, he neglected the group who, in reality, were the only ones who could do him out of a job before 2024: Conservative MPs. The blame for all this was his own.

I've never forgotten Johnson's self-assessment in one of our conversations: 'I think what I'm good at is getting an awful lot of shit done very,

very fast – if I have the right team with me and everybody's going in the same direction and we're all having fun.' From the dawn of the pandemic, things were never fun again for Johnson and he found himself increasingly at odds with Cummings.

Johnson's one solace in this battle of the silverbacks was this, said sadly but proudly to one friend: 'People kept coming to me to make the decision. They didn't go to him.' Having baulked at the way Cummings tried to control him, Johnson vowed that no aide would ever threaten his supremacy again. This simply acted as a force multiplier, amplifying his defects across government, rather than neutralising them as a good political operation should. That he preferred the spurious control this chaos gave him to a tight ship which drove through his policy priorities is telling. The government was the man.

Was Johnson brought down by a 'plot'. In part. Cummings is very open that he led a systematic attempt to undermine him. 'I and others always knew he was not fit to be PM but in 2019 we thought trying to control him was the best of a bad job. In 2021 we decided to remove him and started a concerted effort to put him under constant pressure so he'd blow himself up. We were helped by officials in Number 10 and 70 Whitehall appalled by his behaviour. We were mainly helped by his combination of pathological lying and surrounding himself with courtier-fools.'[9] Dougie Smith shared this desire to see him gone, as did many of those around Rishi Sunak. One of Johnson's closest aides said, 'The fact that the prime minister of this country can be decided by a group of people, basically who are pissed off former employees, is quite a big deal in a democracy. And I think that that's really what happened.'

The 'plot' was not a coherent conspiracy and even if you accept its separate elements as the driving force of Johnson's downfall, his allies need to ask why people wanted him out. He ultimately resigned because his behaviour sabotaged the trust of his ministers and sixty-two of them quit, rendering him unable to form a viable government. They lost faith not because of what Cummings revealed but because of the way Johnson and his team responded to each successive crisis with a combination of sophistry, delay and U-turn. Eddie Lister, another loyal retainer, told one friend, 'The mistakes that matter are his mistakes.'

Even as his campaign against Johnson began, Cummings concluded it was still right to have helped him become PM. 'If the 2019 Parliament had staggered into 2020 without Brexit solved, imagine the scene. Brexit would have been postponed indefinitely. The handling of the Covid crisis would have been even more chaotic. Creating the Vaccine Taskforce would have been much harder if we'd still been in the EU ... Did we misjudge things? For sure. But we solved the constitutional crisis, ensured the biggest democratic vote in our history was respected, removed Corbyn, and began an important set of policy and structural changes.'[10]

Despite everything, 'Boris' was the most compelling political character of his era, Johnson the most consequential prime minister of it too. If regret in life is confined to the things you do not do, Johnson could rest easy. Theresa May was defined by the things she failed to do, Johnson by the things he did – both excellent and execrable.

What came next was also a function of Johnson and his government. It is not fair to blame him for all the problems that flowed from the 2019 deal. It was right, for the sake of stability and democracy, to grasp at any deal which was practically achievable, even if that meant revisiting aspects of it later. But in deciding to take a hard ball approach with Brussels in 2021 and 2022, rather than admit the compromises he had been forced to strike in 2019 and 2020, he put relations with the EU on a collision course that his successors would have to resolve. By July 2022, Johnson was 'done', Brexit still was not.

Liz Truss need not detain us long here. She had a very clear political goal, sustained by a coherent ideological world view. But Truss had no idea how to construct a tactical plan to get there – and was unable to build a team to do so, or even listen to those who had helped her win the premiership in the first place. Instead of mapping a path through the political undergrowth, she parachuted straight to her destination, only to find it heavily defended by the people she had spent months antagonising. In her own words, she hit the ground on day one (without a parachute).

Rishi Sunak's MO was to work hard, rule competently and seek marginal advantage where it could be achieved. In Brexit this was effective. The Windsor Framework was an intelligent and pragmatic solution to some of the worst legacy issues of Johnson's two deals. It did not go far enough for the Paleosceptic ultras but Sunak and his party managers effectively marginalised dissent (including that of Johnson and Truss) to pass the deal with the overwhelming support of the Commons. Seventeen months later, when he left government, it was still his signal achievement.

Sunak found that his approach was less suited to domestic political problems, where years of Tory chaos required a compelling story about how he might improve the lives of voters. 'He's so ignorant about politics that he doesn't know what he doesn't know,' a Number 10 veteran complained. In his final year, Sunak wrestled with further legacies of the Brexit process, notably soaring immigration, where his incremental approach neither solved the problem nor satisfied his party or the voting public – and where the lack of a driving political vision gave him no political cover from failures of delivery.

Between 1721 when Robert Walpole took over and Sunak's departure in 2024, Britain had fifty-seven prime ministers. The job is difficult – Anthony Seldon suggested it might even be 'impossible' – and only fifteen truly rose above its demands to stand out for their achievements or longevity: Walpole, the elder and younger Pitts, Lord Liverpool, Robert Peel, Palmerston, Gladstone, Disraeli, Salisbury, Asquith, Lloyd George, Churchill, Attlee, Thatcher and (arguably) Blair, who won three substantial election victories and made lasting changes to the UK's political economy. Some of these figures rode out crises, others came of age in moments of historical crescendo. The Brexit PMs do not make the grade.

David Cameron had the right temperament for the job and successfully negotiated his political times, winning two general elections and two referendums – until he didn't. His return as foreign secretary in 2023 gave hints that he remained a class above his peers. His is the division which includes Harold Wilson and nineteenth-century Tory the Earl of Derby, the winners of four and three general elections respectively, but whose policy achievements are harder to discern. Harold Macmillan won fewer elections but was even more emblematic of his times. Yet none of the others made a decision as personally calamitous as Cameron's to call the 2016 referendum. If he is admitted to this division, he must be considered at permanent threat of relegation.

Cameron should perhaps be bracketed with Lord North, Britain's sixth-longest serving premier but whose obituary was only going to have one opening: that he presided over the loss of America. That would place them with the group of leaders who were highly consequential but otherwise unsuccessful. Lord Gray, pilot of the 1832 Reform Act, Henry Campbell-Bannerman, in whose premiership the welfare state began, and Ted Heath, who took Britain into the EEC, did hugely consequential things but were otherwise not prime ministers of note.

It is in this basket that we must place Boris Johnson. His record on Brexit and Covid was a score draw and on the war in Ukraine he came closest to being the leader he wanted himself to be, but he had little understanding of how to govern when the barbarians were not at his gate and he allowed his government to sink into a political morass shaped by his personal foibles. Of the great rogues who have held the top job, he is far behind Palmerston, Disraeli or Lloyd George. The best we might say is that he was a photographic negative of Asquith. The great Liberal leader was a great domestic reformer who failed as a war leader; Johnson was a chaotically effective crisis manager who was unable to convert a huge majority into domestic reform – a man who seemed barely cognizant that to construct a wood you need to plant and nurture trees.

Theresa May bears comparison with Gordon Brown as someone who was an effective senior minister but who misjudged the leap between cabinet and the premiership, whose penchant for staring at trees precluded the ability to see the wood. Both, like the Duke of Wellington, were better at the job for which they were known before acceding to the premiership. To be fair to Brown, as chancellor at least, he was a titan and gifted at the art of politics, but he seemed to leave those skills at the door of Number 10 on the way in. What separates them is that, when he was really tested, Brown handled the 2008 crash with determination and vision, eclipsing Stanley Baldwin's response to the Great Depression, though he was a less enduring figure than the grey man of the 1930s.

May, however, is a division lower alongside Chamberlain and Callaghan, decent and sometimes canny operators whose premierships were dominated by a single great challenge (Hitler and industrial relations), which defeated them as Brexit defeated May. She was every bit the same victim of parliamentary arithmetic as Ramsay MacDonald and every bit the same captive of her party as John Major.

Liz Truss we must place in the lowest category, the Vauxhall Conference of prime ministers, alongside Anthony Eden, the worst premier of the twentieth century. Both were temperamentally unsuited to leadership and their personal instibility turned drama into crisis.

Rishi Sunak deserves credit for providing calm after the storm and his reworking of the Brexit deal showed what could be achieved by a diligent political leader who was across the detail. But his absence of politics rendered him a transitional figure who seemed out of touch with the feelings of the electorate, a twenty-first-century Alec Douglas-Home.

There was the makings of an exceptional prime minister in the raw materials of those who held the job – a combination of Cameron's temperament, Johnson's campaigning charisma and optimism, May's devotion to duty and public service, Sunak's diligence and hard work and Truss's clarity of goal, determination and sheer bloody-mindedness. Yet Brexit Britain needed someone clever enough to understand the complications of unweaving Britain's relationship with the EU, with a clear vision of the future relationship, a willingness to tell the truth to voters and MPs about the trade-offs, an ability to persuade them that theirs was the best solution and negotiate a deal. May failed in pretty well all these regards, Johnson and Sunak succeeded only fleetingly.

Collectively, their performance was an exercise in power failure.

In criticising those who held the highest position, it must be remembered that almost everyone miscalculated during the Brexit years. 'That period from 2016 was a massive political failure,' Julian Smith said. 'Everybody has to share some of the blame for that – all parties, all leaders.' One of Theresa May's Brexit advisers said, 'You will get people telling you that it was the political machine that failed or it was the official machine that failed but it was both of them.'

Throughout 2018 and 2019, the Bresistance held a majority in the House of Commons for a 'soft Brexit' but they never delivered it to the same voting lobby. Efforts in the spring of 2018 to coalesce around customs union membership came too early for the Labour front bench and the Remainers in ministerial ranks. By the time they arrived on the scene, in early 2019, the Bresistance had fractured into small groups who refused to support rival solutions they saw as second best. When Parliament voted twice on indicative options, each one was voted down. Bismarck would have been spinning in his grave.

The cabinet Rebel Alliance – Amber Rudd, David Gauke, Greg Clark and Philip Hammond – who might have provided a galvanising identity to the Bresistance were too late to the battlefield, only beginning to rebel in January and February 2019. Phillip Lee, an early Tory referendum backer, complained, 'This was all too little, too late.'

The cabinet Brexiteers were similarly negligent in seizing the initiative. Johnson and Davis, with the willing support of Philip Hammond, should probably have removed May immediately after the 2017 election, but Davis's personal loyalty to a prime minister who had salvaged his career, his distrust of Johnson and Johnson's misguided belief that May would still deliver the Brexit he wanted, meant she stumbled on. The Joint Report in December 2017, which created the Northern Ireland backstop, should have been a 'wake up and smell the coffee' moment, but Johnson, Michael Gove and Liam Fox all accepted the bromides offered by Number 10 that it was not a binding agreement and ducked the challenge. Davis, who probably understood better what it meant, still thought he could influence events from inside. The first Brexit secretary wrote a series of prescient letters to May throughout the first half of 2018, correctly predicting that her deal was doomed but did not act on them himself. He nearly resigned in June that year but only did so a month later, after Chequers, and even then did not bring down the prime minister. His successor, Dominic Raab, along with Esther McVey, quit over the withdrawal agreement in November 2018, but others like Fox, Penny Mordaunt, Chris Grayling and Andrea Leadsom all stayed. Another moment to change the course of events was lost.

Business leaders, represented by the CBI, thought Brexit an economic disaster for their members but were cowardly about saying so publicly. Caroline Flint, a rare Labour backer of May's deal, said 'I couldn't understand why industry seemed to just hide behind "say no to no-deal" and did not lobby MPs to back a deal.'

Did any group miscalculate to their own disadvantage more than the DUP? The Democratic Unionists got money and political influence from propping up the May government, but in their Brexit stance the DUP put an ideological belief about Northern Ireland being identical to Great Britain above the opportunities to be a member of both the EU and UK markets. It was well into 2019 before they realised their allies in the ERG put a hard Brexit before the integrity of the Union. The result was a customs border in the Irish Sea which took three years to mitigate.

What of those other two key players, the civil service and the European Union? Neither was blameless. From the beginning, senior officials failed to prepare properly for Brexit. After Covid, Mark Sedwill concluded, 'I think if there's one really big lesson, it's that we don't put enough effort, resourcing, and talent into contingency planning.'[11]

Oliver Robbins completed a technically accomplished negotiation to get the deal which May wanted, but he was sometimes too slow to tell May when she was barking up the wrong tree and failed to appreciate that his efforts would be in vain if they did not command majority support in the Conservative Party. In focusing on what was negotiable in Brussels, he too often ignored what was negotiable at home.

Ministers, not all of them Brexiteers, complained that the mandarins, particularly those in the Treasury, were institutionally opposed to Brexit. Steve Baker, when he was a Brexit minister, said, 'We've ended up with a governing class that likes being in the EU and trying to overturn the referendum result.' David Frost, interestingly, did not find the civil service so obstructive. He 'found very few cases' where officials let their personal views 'interfere in what they were doing day-to-day'. Their bias was 'to being nice to people' and a reluctance to be 'a bit firmer, just a bit more unambiguous, even though there is a price of upsetting the people we are talking to'.[12]

Jonathan Jones, the head of the government legal service for much of the period, said, 'I think the civil service has actually survived this remarkably well. We took everything that was thrown at us, and we did what the politicians asked, whatever our personal views ... Brexit was done, in the end, to the timetable, according to the wishes of the politicians. The big problem is, I'm afraid, on the political side, whether the politicians really did accept and understand what they were doing.'[13]

However, even some mandarins thought the civil service just as detached from reality. Philip Rycroft said, 'People did not understand the extent of disaffection with the political system, the sense of disenfranchisement ... It is quite extraordinary how little Whitehall understood about its own country. It took us by surprise because we did not spend time in town halls in Wakefield or Gateshead, to just get a better feel for where the population was at. We were detached. That, I think, is a failure of the civil service. It has become disassociated, if you like, from its own country.'[14]

The EU institutions were players in the game as well as the referee and while, tactically, they were brutally effective, strategically the EU was lacking. As Camilla Cavendish, Cameron's former head of policy, put it, 'No one who matters in the EU seems to have asked themselves why one of the largest members and biggest contributors is leaving. There has been no soul-searching of the kind that might have led to reform, or an attempt to meet Britain halfway.'[15] In making Brexit as unattractive as possible for other member states, they frequently overreached, boxing May into a corner unnecessarily, a position from which they repeatedly had to rescue her. The EU left it to Britain to define the future and offered few ideas about what a future partnership would look like. Stefaan De Rynck said it 'was just too toxic to have a rational discussion with the UK, on a strategic perspective, longer-term'. But had the EU taken a bigger-picture approach during Cameron's renegotiation, recognising that mass migration was making freedom of movement politically unpalatable for many, it might have enabled him to win the referendum.

The EU's strategic myopia was most questionable in the way Brussels weaponised the situation in Northern Ireland to extract concessions from the UK, demanding that the border issue be settled up front rather than as part of a trade deal, turning the Joint Report into a legally fossilised backstop which took more than five years, from December 2017 to February 2023, to make operable in practice. 'I do think the European Union has deliberately exploited the Northern Irish issue to try and keep us as near to being in the tent as it can,' Chris Grayling said. 'The only solution, really, is the alternative arrangements … In today's world, it is possible to manage the flow of goods with a combination of targeted enforcement and electronic systems.'[16] That, in the end, was what the Windsor deal created, with a real-time computer system proving threats to the single market were minimal. It was not beyond the wit of man to get there several years earlier.

Yet nothing is black and white. As *No Way Out* demonstrated, the member states were, in general, less helpful to Britain than the Commission, which was wrongly perceived to be the unbending guardian of EU orthodoxy. A lesson for Keir Starmer and his successors was that it was the Commission (which negotiates for a living) that was prepared to innovate to find a deal – once it found prime ministers who knew what they wanted. Barnier was consistent that there could be 'no cherry picking' over the single market. But in Martin Selmayr, during May's premiership, and Stéphanie Riso under Johnson and Sunak, the EU had two dealmakers who were prepared to go behind Barnier's back in the interests of pragmatism. Among the treasured possessions of Selmayr, one of the most deliciously arch political operators this author has ever met (think the sinuousness of Mandelson and the ruthlessness of Cummings), were letters of thanks from both Cameron and May.

'They know what we have done,' he said. 'We helped as much as possible without betraying our principles.'

Nothing was inevitable about what happened. But several counterfactual propositions have excited debate since 2016. Three stand out. Should Remainer MPs and Labour have backed Theresa May's deal? The bottom line is that May and Robbins produced a softer Brexit than Johnson and Frost. MPs who bemoan the harder version had numerous opportunities to accept her withdrawal agreement. A more dynamic Labour leader than Jeremy Corbyn would also have seen advantages in getting Brexit done and then turning his guns on the government on issues where Labour led in the polls. There were several opportunities to try this – at MV2 and MV3 and again after the cross-party talks in May 2019, when backbenchers could have presented the agreement thrashed out by the two sides (May's deal plus pledges on workers' rights) and tried to push it through. MPs could equally well have presented the same Labour-friendly version of the deal in the autumn before Johnson did his deal with Varadkar.

However, all of these opportunities required supporters of a second referendum to put aside that dream. Tom Baldwin of the People's Vote said, 'My job was not to try and find the least damaging form of Brexit. My job, very specifically, was to win the campaign for a People's Vote … My honest view is also that a soft Brexit of the sort proposed by Theresa May's deal, or by the Norway Group … was inherently unstable and possibly unsustainable … People just didn't want it. They either wanted proper Brexit or they wanted no Brexit.'[17] Justine Greening, who wanted a referendum, agreed: 'The polling showed that Theresa May's deal was less popular than the poll tax.'

What if there had been a second referendum? The People's Vote got close to achieving the numbers needed. Would a second referendum have solved the problems of the first? 'I will regret forever that we didn't prevail because a new referendum could – and I emphasise could – have been a healing, unifying thing for the country,' Baldwin argued. 'When we were thinking about how we would conduct a referendum campaign if we got it, it would have been building on the first referendum campaign and saying that, "Yes, we have heard that the country can't be the same again. Yes, we do have to tackle some of these issues which have left people frustrated and angry." Maybe that referendum campaign could have been a way for this country to move forward together.'[18] Dominic Grieve also concluded, 'I think a properly conducted remain campaign might have worked. I think we could have found the emotional arguments, but whether we could have found the leadership to do it I think is more questionable.'

This seems like the purest 'hopeium' to me and to most people I interviewed for this book. The reason people like David Gauke did not back a referendum was because they thought it would deepen Britain's divisions not ease them. Some Bresisters believed they would win because the evidence against Brexit was so overwhelming. This seems vanishingly unlikely. A combination of Johnson, Cummings and Farage, armed with the slogan 'tell them again', seems like a winning proposition. 'It wouldn't be about Brexit but about how much the public likes Parliament and MPs,' Cummings observed. 'They'd have been trounced.'[19]

Those who disagreed seemed blind to the wider issue of how a rerun would have been received by voters who backed Leave precisely because they thought the political class in Westminster out of touch with their concerns and needs. As Cummings put it, 'The great irony is that the people who were pushing hardest for the second referendum are the people who babble on most about Trump's "coup" and the anti-democratic nature of Trump.'[20] And what if Remain had won? Cummings' prediction of political violence doesn't seem unrealistic to me.

The most intriguing counterfactual, which really might have changed the course of Britain's political history, was what would have happened if a Brexiteer had become prime minister in 2016, rather than Theresa May. This was entirely possible. If Michael Gove had not knifed Boris Johnson, he would have made the run-off and would surely have beaten May with the membership.

Johnson had made Brexit happen; there was a logic to him being the one to deal with it. As a Brexiteer he would not have had to tack to the hard Brexit extremes as May did on taking office. He could have reached out to the 48 per cent. Johnson also had the political capital to make and sell compromises to Brexiteers in Parliament and Leave voters in the country. As David Davis, no fan, observed, 'A bit of Boris's genius is he saw that, as long as you could put a label on it saying "Brexit done", almost irrespective of the bends and twists and the plumbing, it's what people wanted.'[21] A senior civil servant also concluded, 'If you'd had a leading Brexiteer as prime minister after Cameron went, I think things would've been very different. They'd have been able to sell something.'

Johnson would also have been accompanied by Cummings, who would have insisted that the UK not trigger Article 50, putting Britain on the clock. In this he would have been strongly supported by Ivan Rogers, Britain's ambassador to the EU, who was drummed out by May's advisers for being too negative. From their very different perspectives they understood better than anyone I spoke to in 2016 and 2017 how Brexit would unfold. Without the traumas of 2016–19, the Vote Leavers would not have had to behave as they did in the second half of 2019.

(A footnote: Rogers' personality was a reverse Cleopatra's nose, a seemingly insignificant but decisive historical factor. Had she been less attractive, would Julius Caesar and Mark Antony have fought over her? Had Rogers been less obstreperous, might May and her team have listened more to his generally prescient advice?)

Even if such a compromise did not happen, and Johnson settled immediately on the form of Brexit he eventually championed, it is hard to avoid the conclusion that he would have arrived at a Canada Plus-style trade deal up to two years earlier, preventing the parliamentary agony which ensued. 'It would have been some version of Canada plus, in the end,' Gove concluded. 'We would have had a free trade agreement with nobs on.' Doing it quicker would also have reduced the lengthy process of entrenchment which made the situation so intractable.

Settling Northern Ireland would still have been very difficult, but as a Vote Leaver pointed out, 'Dom and Boris would not have allowed the sequencing which meant progress at the rate and on the terms that the EU dictated. I don't think that they would have allowed Northern Ireland to become elevated in the way that it was.'

We know enough of Johnson's leadership credentials to know it would have been messy, that he would have been exasperated by the details and got into fights with the Commission and his own backbenchers. The balance of forces in the Commons – with two out of three MPs declared Remainers – would still have been a giant hurdle. Another civil servant who worked on Brexit in Number 10 said, 'Had Boris come in and picked a Brexiteer cabinet, he could have probably smashed through a negotiation in a different way. But you still had a Remainer Parliament, and he'd have had to fight a parliamentary battle one way or another. It might have all blown up much sooner.'

In Brussels, a senior Council official said, 'Had there been a majority for a particular form of Brexit early on, then we would have had a credible negotiating partner. If we had, then we might have been able to close it earlier. But that is not a matter of Johnson versus May, that is a matter of whether it is a prime minister backed by a clear majority or not.'

The answer to this point is surely that Johnson would have had the credibility to call a general election in 2017 just like May did, but would have had the campaigning ability to win it much more clearly, arguing that he needed a majority to override the votes of Remainer MPs, just as he did in 2019. 'What you needed was somebody who moved fast in 2016, before everybody recovered from their shock and started deciding that they wanted to either have no-deal or stop the whole thing,' Nicky Morgan said. 'I think that if Michael and Boris had got their act together and not taken out and shot each other in 2016, we would have been in a lot better place.' Gove himself concluded it would have been better if he had bitten his tongue in 2016. 'I've asked myself this question a million times,' he said. 'There is no perfect answer. But I think, on balance, it would probably have been better for the country, for Brexit, and least important, me, if I just swallowed my doubts.'

None of which means Johnson would have enjoyed any more longevity than he did in Number 10. One aide said, 'I think we would have ended up where we are now. Boris would still have cut his own throat somehow, but we might have at least avoided a couple of years of total misery – and weirdly, we might have ended up with Theresa May.'

Had that happened, May's brand of deliberative diligence might have been better suited than Johnson to handling the pandemic (though it is difficult to see her driving the vaccine programme with anything like the same verve). Even leading Bresisters agree this scenario would have been preferable. Damian Green said, 'It was a terrible period. The sight of Parliament being completely paralysed month after month was quite frightening for those of us who believe in parliamentary democracy. The world and everyone [would have been] happier if Boris became prime minister in 2016, and had got Brexit done then so we didn't have those horrible few years. And then maybe when the pandemic came, and we wanted somebody who caught every detail then Theresa would be better. They were, in a sense, prime minister in the wrong order.'[22]

* * *

I have tried to make this quartet a study of the politics and people of Brexit, rather than a discussion of its merits and drawbacks. Calculating the costs and benefits of Brexit is always going to be a work in progress.

The vast majority of mainstream economists regarded Brexit as economically damaging. The Office of Budget Responsibility accepted models suggesting Brexit 'will reduce long-run productivity by 4 per cent relative to remaining in the EU'. British exports fell from 70,000 product types to 42,000, according to Aston Business School. Trade deals with Australia and New Zealand in no way plugged the gap, lifting GDP by 0.08 per cent and 0.03 per cent respectively.[23]

These statistics were challenged by Brexit-backing commentators, such as Derrick Berthelsen, who pointed out that the OBR based its figures on thirteen estimates from eleven independent providers, which ranged from a 0.6 per cent hit to GDP to a World Bank estimate of 10 per cent. A large part of the downside in these models was also not a direct consequence of the trade barriers erected by Brexit, but a calculation about reduced trade intensity hurting British productivity. Some also included assumptions about reduced immigration, at a time when net migration was actually rising.[24]

The point is not to arbitrate between these different claims but to highlight that even in the supposedly scientific assessment of what Brexit meant, people fell back into their old camps. Remainers wanted to blame Brexit for Britain's ills, to the point of minimising obvious difficulties which had lingered since the 2008 crisis or new problems caused by the pandemic (and the political response to Covid). Supporters of Brexit searched high and low for evidence that nothing was the fault of Brexit, or if it was, it was the result of not doing it properly.

The creation of the Covid vaccine programme in 2020 was the obvious case where the ability to do things differently at pace paid rich dividends. Johnson called this 'cut and dried' because Britain was outside the EU's vaccine procurement process. But all too often there was little evidence of Downing Street or Whitehall prioritising such gains.

Allied to this was the difficulty of measuring what Leave voters valued. How do you put a price on national sovereignty, the feeling of independence and the right to make Britain's own decisions – what Johnson once described to me as 'the idea of being free and different'?

In one area, foreign affairs, the ledger was more positive. Much was made of the hit to Britain's international reputation from Johnson's casual approach to international treaties. But Brexit gave a country which had always been proactive on the world stage a nimbleness it had lacked for a generation. John Bew, one of the quiet heroes of the period, used successive defence and security reviews to embed an approach that called for ad-hoc coalitions as events arose. Joining the Aukus defence pact with the US and Australia and signing up to the CPTPP Asia–Pacific trade bloc gave the UK more influence in the Far East. Britain worked with Canada on the issue of Hong Kong and the Baltic and Scandinavian countries to arm Volodymyr Zelensky's Ukrainian government. Johnson was clear, 'The Ukraine thing would never have happened, I promise you', if the UK had remained in the EU. 'Under our duty of sincere cooperation with the EU, we would've had to defer.' It was no coincidence that when Starmer took over in 2024 the first conversations with Brussels were about a defence and security deal to formalise Britain's pivotal status as a keystone of European defence.

Brexit neither solved Britain's problems as its supporters hoped, nor rendered it impossible to do so, as its critics maintained. The advent of the pandemic so soon afterwards reinforced the claims Cummings made about a rotten Whitehall system unfit for the modern world – though no-deal prep was some use in coping with lockdown. 'The whole fucking thing did fall apart like a deck of cards,' Cummings argued. 'These institutions … need to be ripped up and rebooted in all sorts of ways.'[25]

The passage of Brexit had not satisfied a large number of people who voted for it in the hope of being heard in Westminster. Those disillusioned by the failure of Parliament to deliver the referendum result in 2019 were, by 2024, disillusioned with a Conservative Party which had failed to deliver the benefits promised by Boris Johnson and had turned once more to Nigel Farage and Reform UK.

As I said at the end of *All Out War*, Brexit was a brutal process that churned up and spat out careers, broke friendships and strained people's sanity. The Cameroons, the Mayites, even the Vote Leavers became victims of the processes they set in train, the revolution consuming its architects and children, just as it had in France nearly two and a half centuries earlier. It is as well for George Osborne, Nick Timothy, Gavin Barwell and Dominic Cummings that we have moved on from the guillotine as a way of settling political argument.

It seemed at times like democracy could not cope with the passions unleashed. But Claire Fox, the Brexit Party MEP, saw it as 'a moment of great democratic flowering'. She said, 'It's completely politicised and transformed ordinary people's experience of politics … People felt free enough, treated as equals, and not looked down upon. I think to even taste that and savour it for some moments was, and has been, hugely historically important, and people won't forget it.'[26]

Brexit strained the British economy; it tested its democracy and its unwritten constitution, which came under assault from both Vote Leave and the Bresistance. But in the end the system coped. The political class delivered the wishes of the people. Failing leaders were evicted from power peacefully. The centre – perhaps deservingly battered, bruised and bedraggled – held. Just.

What will the future bring? The advantages of divergence are likely to become more apparent with changes in technology and the dawn of AI. The same tension will remain between market access to the EU and the level of regulatory alignment required to achieve it. The first time I talked to Ivan Rogers he predicted that Britain would initially have to go a long way out from the EU, to convince Brexiteers that the UK had truly left and to show the other member states that leaving was not worth their while – but that after a decade it would suit both sides to seek a closer relationship. Starmer's Labour, eight years into the process, began to explore that approach.

Making the best of leaving required a fundamental change in mindset. David Frost observed that EU membership meant 'We got used to having rules set by others … We had got used to not devising solutions for ourselves and not used to thinking hard about the world and what was in our interests.'[27] If Brexit had one true legacy, as the events of these books illustrate, it was that a country which had for years tended to blame Brussels for its own problems, now had the freedom to make its own mistakes. It was a freedom the British political class would exercise repeatedly.

The decision made in 2016 and enacted in 2019 and 2020 is now part of our national story, woven tight into the fabric of our political history. But it has ceased to be a discreet subject, it is now just integral to everything else in politics. There will be myriad futures that flow from the decisions made in these four books. There will be endless drafts of the Brexit story. I hope this one is seen as a fair basis on which to begin that discussion.

Over and out.

Tim Shipman, Umbria, August 2024

ILLUSTRATIONS

Election night (Andrew Parsons/Parsons Media)
Brexit night (Andrew Parsons/Number 10)
Johnson (X/@BorisJohnson)
Stéphanie Riso (Thierry Monasse/Getty Images)
David Frost and Oliver 'Sonic' Lewis (Thierry Monasse/Getty Images)
Cummings and Lee Cain (PA Images/Alamy Stock Photo)
Kwasi Kwarteng (PA Images/Alamy Stock Photo)
Liz Truss (WPA Pool/Pool/Getty Images)
Liz Truss leaves Downing Street (Uwe Deffner/Alamy Stock Photo)
Rishi Sunak and Ursula von der Leyen (The Canadian Press/Alamy
    Stock Photo)
Dougie Smith (Steve Back)
Liam Booth-Smith (Ben Cawthra/Shutterstock)
David Cameron joins Emmanuel Macron, Olaf Scholz and Joe Biden
    (Abaca Press/Alamy Stock Photo)
Sunak was better prepared (PA Images/Alamy Stock Photo)
Nigel Farage (BEN STANSALL/Getty Images)
Le Deluge (Imageplotter/Alamy Stock Photo)
Morgan McSweeney (ZUMA Press, Inc./Alamy Stock Photo)
Sue Gray (ZUMA Press, Inc./Alamy Stock Photo)
Brexit looming in the background (PA Images/Alamy Stock Photo)

NOTES

A full index of Brexit Witness Archive interviews, by UK in a Changing Europe, can be found online at: https://ukandeu.ac.uk/the-brexit-witness-archive/

Each transcript is available at: https://ukandeu.ac.uk/the-brexit-witness-archive/firstname-surname/

Chapter 1: 'By Any Means Necessary …'

1. Cummings gave evidence to the Commons Science and Technology Committee in March 2021. He wrote a blog about why he went into government in July 2021. He gave an interview to Suzanne Moore in May 2022 and another with Steve Hsu for the *Manifold* podcast in January 2023. The account here is supplemented by my own reporting. Despite their differences, Johnson has never disputed the broad details of the deal they did prior to entering Downing Street
2. Dominic Cummings: Vote Leave, Brexit, COVID, and No. 10 with Boris, interview with Steve Hsu, *Manifold* podcast, Ep. 28, 19 Jan 2023
3. Dominic Cummings, oral evidence to the Commons Science and Technology Committee, 17 Mar 2021
4. The 17,410,742 people who voted to leave the EU in 2016 was higher than the 17,378,581 people who voted to stay in the European Community in the 1975 referendum. However, the 52 per cent mark was exceeded by the 1975 Yes vote (67 per cent), the 68 per cent who voted against changing to the Alternative Vote (AV) electoral system in 2011 and the Conservative Party performance at the 1931 general election (55 per cent)
5. Dominic Cummings interview with Steve Hsu, *Manifold* podcast, Ep. 28, 19 Jan 2023
6. Dominic Cummings interview, Letters from Suzanne Substack, 29 May 2022
7. A few months later, Johnson said, 'I don't remember that', about one of his promises to Cummings. 'Should I get the email we agreed?' Cummings asked. Johnson smiled knowingly
8. Why I went to No10 in summer 2019, Dominic Cummings, Substack, 5 Jul 2021
9. Ibid.

10. Bower, Tom, *Boris Johnson: The Gambler*, WH Allen, 2020, p.392
11. Stephen Hammond interview with Matt Chorley, The Exit Interviews, Ep. 14, Times Radio, 4 Mar 2024
12. In 2023, Cummings published a 400-page 'timeline' of Bismarck's career, seeking to demonstrate how a skilled political operator shapes and responds to events. See #1 Bismarck: The ultimate practical education in the 'unrecognised simplicities' of high performance politics/government, Dominic Cummings, Substack, 14 Dec 2023
13. Dominic Cummings interview with Steve Hsu, *Manifold* podcast Ep. 28, 19 Jan 2023
14. Why I went to No10 in summer 2019, Dominic Cummings, Substack, 5 Jul 2021
15. Dominic Cummings interview with Steve Hsu, *Manifold* podcast, Ep. 28, 19 Jan 2023
16. See *No Way Out*, p.629
17. Mark Sedwill, 22 Jun 2021, Brexit Witness Archive, UKICE, p.17
18. No-deal looms as leak reveals Dominic Cummings considers EU negotiations a 'sham', *Daily Telegraph*, 2 Sep 2019
19. Revealed: Tory tycoon Christopher Moran's links to sex for sale in Chelsea Cloisters, *Sunday Times*, 25 Nov 2018
20. Trains and Buses was so named because several of its members had once been their party's transport lead. Anna Soubry of Change UK was also given to hastily switching to a discussion of failing railway services when a government whip approached. See *No Way Out*, p.330
21. Only a government of national unity can deliver us from no-deal, *Guardian*, 5 Aug 2019
22. Phillip Lee, 9 Apr 2021, Brexit Witness Archive, UKICE, p.20
23. Ibid.
24. See *No Way Out*, chapter 6
25. See ibid., chapter 1
26. Johnson, Boris, *Unleashed*, William Collins, 2024, p.37
27. Ibid., pp.37–8
28. Ibid., p.574

Chapter 2: Without Bounds

1. Hilary Benn, (undated), Brexit Witness Archive, UKICE, p.18
2. Oliver Letwin, 11 Dec 2020, Brexit Witness Archive, UKICE, p.23
3. Mark Sedwill, 22 Jun 2021, Brexit Witness Archive, UKICE, p.17
4. John Bercow, 21 Jul 2020, Brexit Witness Archive, UKICE, pp.28–9
5. Former Philip Hammond aide is FROGMARCHED out of Downing Street by police after being accused of LEAKING Brexit secrets by Boris Johnson's top adviser Dominic Cummings, *Daily Mail*, 30 Aug 2019
6. Seldon, Anthony and Newell, Raymond, *Johnson at 10*, Atlantic, 2023, p.269
7. Explosion of loathing at No10: Inside the incendiary row between ex-Chancellor Philip Hammond and table-thumping Boris Johnson that led to Tory defeat, *Daily Mail*, 4 Sep 2019
8. Phillip Lee, 9 Apr 2021, Brexit Witness Archive, UKICE, p.22
9. Oliver Letwin, 11 Dec 2020, Brexit Witness Archive, UKICE, p.23
10. Stephen Hammond interview with Matt Chorley, The Exit Interviews, Ep. 14, Times Radio, 4 Mar 2024
11. Bower, *Boris Johnson: The Gambler*, p.406
12. Dominic Cummings interview, Letters from Suzanne Substack, 29 May 2022
13. John Bercow, 21 Jul 20, Brexit Witness Archive, UKICE, pp.28–9
14. Dominic Cummings interview with Steve Hsu, *Manifold* podcast, Ep. 28, 19 Jan 2023
15. The author

Chapter 3: Outlaws

1. Scottish judges decide Boris Johnson misled the Queen, *Financial Times*, 11 Sep 2019
2. Lady Hale, *Spider Woman: A Life*, Bodley Head, 2021, p.236
3. Ibid., p.237
4. Ibid.
5. Ibid., p.238
6. Ibid., p.239
7. Ibid.
8. David Davis, 8 July 2021, Brexit Witness Archive, UKICE, p.38
9. Supreme Court ruling is the natural result of Boris Johnson's constitutional vandalism, *The Times*, 24 Sep 2019
10. Jonathan Jones, 6 May 2021, Brexit Witness Archive, UKICE, pp.19–20
11. John Bercow, 21 Jul 2020, Brexit Witness Archive, UKICE, p.28
12. 'Who runs this country?': Boris Johnson's allies blast 'constitutional coup' after judges rule PM broke the law by suspending Parliament and he's forced to fly back from New York TODAY to face a furious resumed Commons, *Daily Mail*, 24 Sep 2019
13. Boris hasn't given the Prince respect he deserves, *Mail on Sunday*, 11 Jun 2022
14. Up close and personal with Prince William: An intimate portrait of the future king, *Sunday Times Magazine*, 20 Mar 2021
15. Bercow, John, *Unspeakable: The Autobiography*, Weidenfeld & Nicolson, 2020, p.1
16. Oliver Letwin, 11 Dec 2020, Brexit Witness Archive, UKICE, pp.23–4

Chapter 4: Out of the Blue

1. Boris Johnson thinks he's in control, *The Atlantic*, 31 Oct 2019
2. Aiming to reach a deal with the European Union, letter from Julian Smith to Boris Johnson, 8 Sep 2019
3. The fevered weeks which sealed an 'impossible' deal: How Boris Johnson crafted his Brexit plan in face of EU hostility, *Daily Telegraph*, 19 Oct 2019
4. Ibid.
5. David Frost speech: The Northern Ireland Protocol: How we got here and what should happen now, Policy Exchange, 27 Apr 2022
6. John Bercow, 21 Jul 2020, Brexit Witness Archive, UKICE, p.27
7. No 10 probes Remain MPs' 'foreign collusion' amid plot to allow John Bercow to send 'surrender letter' to Brussels asking for a delay to Brexit, *Mail on Sunday*, 28 Sep 2019
8. Stefaan De Rynck, 1 & 15 Mar 2021, Brexit Witness Archive, UKICE, p.26
9. David Frost speech, The Northern Ireland Protocol, 27 Apr 2022
10. Sebastian Payne, *The Fall of Boris Johnson*, Macmillan, 2022, pp.194–5
11. Brexit is 'unsettling' the civil service, cabinet sec admits in leaked letter, Sky News website, 30 Sep 2019
12. Bower, *Boris Johnson: The Gambler*, p.415
13. Ibid.
14. Stefaan De Rynck, 1 & 15 Mar 2021, Brexit Witness Archive, UKICE, p.30
15. Johnson, *Unleashed*, pp.43–4
16. David Frost speech, The Northern Ireland Protocol, 27 Apr 2022
17. The fevered weeks which sealed an 'impossible' deal: How Boris Johnson crafted his Brexit plan in face of EU hostility, *Daily Telegraph*, 19 Oct 2019
18. David Frost speech, The Northern Ireland Protocol, 27 Apr 2022
19. A knife-edge day of fresh shirts, Shawshank Redemption jokes and tortuous talks that see-sawed between hope and despair – but did DUP leader Arlene Foster have the last laugh?, *Daily Mail*, 16 Oct 2019
20. Ibid.
21. David Frost speech, The Northern Ireland Protocol, 27 Apr 2022

Chapter 5: Extension Rebellion

1. See *All Out War*, chapter 9
2. Oliver Letwin, 11 Dec 2020, Brexit Witness Archive, UKICE, p.25
3. Ibid., pp.27–8
4. Gavin Barwell, 1 & 25 Sept 2020, Brexit Witness Archive, UKICE, p.48
5. The fevered weeks which sealed an 'impossible' deal: How Boris Johnson crafted his Brexit plan in face of EU hostility, *Daily Telegraph*, 19 Oct 2019
6. David Frost speech, The Northern Ireland Protocol, 27 Apr 2022
7. The 19 Labour rebels were: Kevin Barron, Sarah Champion, Rosie Cooper, Jon Cruddas, Gloria De Piero, Jim Fitzpatrick, Caroline Flint, Mike Hill, Dan Jarvis, Emma Lewell-Buck, John Mann, Grahame Morris, Lisa Nandy, Melanie Onn, Stephanie Peacock, Jo Platt, Ruth Smeeth, Laura Smith and Gareth Snell
8. Andrew Fisher, 15 Jun 2022, Brexit Witness Archive, UKICE, pp.32–3
9. Oliver Letwin, 11 Dec 2020, Brexit Witness Archive, UKICE, p.26

Chapter 6: Rudd, Sweat and Tears

1. Alastair Campbell, 5 Mar 2021, Brexit Witness Archive, UKICE, p.12
2. How People's Vote destroyed itself, *New Statesman*, 20 Nov 2019
3. How People's Vote collapsed after Roland Rudd's boardroom coup, *Guardian*, 20 Nov 2019
4. Tom Baldwin, 5 Jul 2021, Brexit Witness Archive, UKICE, p.25
5. Ibid., p.8
6. Ibid.
7. Ibid., p.9
8. Ibid., p.10
9. Ibid., p.17
10. Ibid., p.11
11. Ibid., p.14
12. Ibid., p.16
13. Ibid., p.13
14. Alastair Campbell, 5 Mar 2021, Brexit Witness Archive, UKICE, p.13
15. Phillip Lee, 9 Apr 2021, Brexit Witness Archive, UKICE, p.15
16. How People's Vote collapsed after Roland Rudd's boardroom coup, *Guardian*, 20 Nov 2019
17. Tom Baldwin, 5 Jul 2021, Brexit Witness Archive, UKICE, p.12
18. Alastair Campbell, 5 Mar 2021, Brexit Witness Archive, UKICE, p.24
19. Ibid., p.23
20. How People's Vote destroyed itself, *New Statesman*, 20 Nov 2019
21. Ibid.
22. Hilary Benn (undated), Brexit Witness Archive, UKICE, p.19
23. Phillip Lee, 9 Apr 2021, Brexit Witness Archive, UKICE, p.5
24. Philip Hammond, 13 & 20 Nov 2020, Brexit Witness Archive, UKICE, p.39
25. Tom Baldwin, 5 Jul 2021, Brexit Witness Archive, UKICE, p.23
26. Ibid., p.11
27. How People's Vote destroyed itself, *New Statesman*, 20 Nov 2019
28. Alastair Campbell, 5 Mar 2021, Brexit Witness Archive, UKICE, p.13
29. People's Vote officials say Stephen Dorrell sent the emails to Roland Rudd by mistake
30. People's Vote coup plotters, *Mail on Sunday*, 20 Oct 2019
31. How People's Vote destroyed itself, *New Statesman*, 20 Nov 2019
32. Alastair Campbell, 5 Mar 2021, Brexit Witness Archive, UKICE, p.24
33. How People's Vote destroyed itself, *New Statesman*, 20 Nov 2019
34. Tom Baldwin, 5 Jul 2021, Brexit Witness Archive, UKICE, p.26

Chapter 7: Going for Gold

1. MRP stands for 'multi-level regression and post-stratification'
2. Lib Dems' secret plan for general election victory is called 'Project 320', *Daily Mirror*, 1 Oct 2019
3. The limit was calculated on the basis of £30,000 per seat, or £18.9

million for parties standing in all 650 seats. Individual candidates could spend £8,700 plus 6p per registered elector.

4. Phillip Lee, 9 Apr 2021, Brexit Witness Archive, UKICE, p.23
5. Ibid., p.13
6. Richard Tice, 11 Sep 2020, Brexit Witness Archive, UKICE, p.16
7. Richard Corbett, Brexit Witness Archive, UKICE, pp.20–1
8. Will the Lib Dems seize their chance to replace the Tories?, *New Statesman*, 22 Feb 2024
9. Ibid.
10. Conservative Anthony Browne eventually won by fewer than 3,000 votes
11. Tom Baldwin, 5 Jul 2021, Brexit Witness Archive, UKICE, p.21
12. Phillip Lee, 9 Apr 2021, Brexit Witness Archive, UKICE, p.24
13. Ibid.

Chapter 8: Isaac not Ishmael

1. See *Fall Out*, chapter 26, for Theresa May's disastrous handling of the aftermath of the fire
2. Ford, Robert, Bale, Tim, Jennings, Will and Surridge, Paula, *The British General Election of 2019*, PalgraveMacmillan, 2021, p.19
3. See *Fall Out*, chapter 18
4. Election Considerations, Memo, Isaac Levido and Michael Brooks, to prime minister, cc Dominic Cummings, 24 Oct 2019
5. Levido document: Agenda – PM Campaign Meeting 03/11/19
6. Levido document: Draft PM visits grid 03/11/19
7. *The Inside Story of Election 19*, BBC Radio 4, 25 Feb 2020
8. General Election 2019 Campaign Strategy Update, Memo, Isaac Levido and Michael Brooks, to prime minister, cc Dominic Cummings, 9 Oct 2019
9. Ibid.

10. Levido deck: Political Cabinet Campaign Update, 5 Nov 2019
11. Dominic Cummings interview with Steve Hsu, *Manifold* podcast, Ep. 28, 19 Jan 2023
12. An intelligence report will say UK spy agencies found no evidence of Russian state interference in the outcome of the Brexit referendum, BuzzFeed News, 1 Nov 2019
13. Revealed: The extraordinary offer made by Tory fixers to 'bribe' Nigel Farage with a knighthood and peerages – and why it's sown the seeds of disaster for Rishi, *Mail on Sunday*, 27 Apr 2024
14. Richard Tice, 11 Sep 2020, Brexit Witness Archive, UKICE, pp.19–20
15. Ibid., p.17
16. Ibid., p.18
17. Ibid.
18. Ibid., p.20
19. Pogrund, Gabriel and Maguire, Patrick, *Left Out: The Inside Story of Labour Under Corbyn*, Bodley Head, 2020, pp.307–8

Chapter 9: 'Refighting the Last War …'

1. *The Inside Story of Election 19*, BBC Radio 4, 25 Feb 2020
2. See *Fall Out*, chapter 17
3. Pogrund and Maguire, *Left Out*, p.230
4. *Corbynism: The Post-Mortem*, Ep. 4: The 2019 General Election Defeat, 7 Feb 2020
5. Ibid.
6. The Tories think their election ground game is strong, but they are losing the air war, BuzzFeed News, 16 Nov 2019
7. Ibid.
8. Andrew Fisher, 15 Jun 2022, Brexit Witness Archive, UKICE, p.38
9. *Corbynism: The Post-Mortem*, Ep. 5: Life for Labour's Jewish MPs, 14 Feb 2020
10. Ibid., Ep. 9: The Red Wall Crumbles, 13 Mar 2020

11. Ibid., Ep. 4: The 2019 General Election Defeat, 7 Feb 2020
12. Pogrund and Maguire, *Left Out*, pp.300–1
13. Ibid., pp.301–2
14. *The Inside Story of Election 19*, BBC Radio 4, 25 Feb 2020
15. Andrew Fisher, 15 Jun 2022, Brexit Witness Archive, UKICE, p.39
16. Ibid., p.32
17. Ibid., p.37
18. Pogrund and Maguire, *Left Out*, p.230
19. Pogrund and Maguire, *Left Out*, p.312
20. Ibid., pp.305–6
21. *The Inside Story of Election 19*, BBC Radio 4, 25 Feb 2020
22. Pogrund and Maguire, *Left Out*, p.304
23. Ibid., p.319
24. Ibid., p.310
25. Ibid., p.319
26. Lib Dem leader Jo Swinson forced to deny shooting stones at squirrels after spoof story goes viral, *Independent*, 9 Nov 2019
27. Hilary Benn, Brexit Witness Archive, UKICE, p.25
28. *Corbynism: The Post-Mortem*, Ep. 9: The Red Wall Crumbles, 13 Mar 2020
29. Pogrund and Maguire, *Left Out*, pp.320–1
30. Ibid., p.323

Chapter 10: Wobbles
1. *The Inside Story of Election 19*, BBC Radio 4, 25 Feb 2020
2. Ibid.
3. *The Inside Story of Election 19*, BBC Radio 4, 25 Feb 2020
4. Pogrund and Maguire, *Left Out*, p.326
5. Ibid., p.327
6. *The Inside Story of Election 19*, BBC Radio 4, 25 Feb 2020
7. Ibid.
8. Dominic Cummings, Twitter, 18 Jun 2021
9. 'You are the 120th interview I've done, and I'm proud to be doing it', *Sunday Times*, 8 Dec 2019

10. Ford et al., *The British General Election of 2019*, pp.331–4
11. Corbyn could win without gaining a seat, *Daily Telegraph*, 10 Dec 2019
12. *The Inside Story of Election 19*, BBC Radio 4, 25 Feb 2020
13. Ibid.

Chapter 11: Wipeout
1. *The Inside Story of Election 19*, BBC Radio 4, 25 Feb 2020
2. James Schneider interview with James Butler, Novara Media, 31 Jan 2020
3. Ibid.
4. Listen to Boris Johnson's private victory speech to Conservative Party aides, BuzzFeed News, 13 Dec 2019
5. *Corbynism: The Post-Mortem*, Ep. 4: The 2019 General Election Defeat
6. Ford et al, *The British General Election of 2019*, p.473. For a full discussion of the impact of the Brexit Party see pp.468–74

Chapter 12: Falling Out
1. Richard Corbett, Brexit Witness Archive, UKICE, p.29
2. Dominic Cummings interview with Steve Hsu, *Manifold* podcast, Ep. 28, 19 Jan 2023
3. Dominic Cummings interview with Suzanne Moore, Letters from Suzanne Substack, 29 May 2022
4. Why I went to No10 in summer 2019, Dominic Cummings, Substack, 5 Jul 2021
5. It's not Princess Nut Nuts, it's Princess Nut Nut: Cummings allies' nasty nickname for Carrie Symonds 'has been used for MONTHS', *Mail on Sunday*, 15 Nov 2020
6. Dominic Cummings interview with Suzanne Moore, Letters from Suzanne Substack, 29 May 2022
7. The quote featured in a piece by Simon Walters in 2021 but the author has corroborated it with others. See Boris said 'being PM is too much hard work and like pulling a jumbo

jet down a runway every day' and he 'can't wait to have fun and make money', *Daily Mail*, 16 Jun 2021

8. Boris Johnson and the Lebedevs: How I exposed the prime minister's defining scandal, *Guardian*, 16 Jul 2022

9. Morning after: Boris Johnson recovers from Lebedev's exotic Italian party, *Guardian*, 26 Jul 2019

10. Boris Johnson and the Lebedevs: How I exposed the prime minister's defining scandal, *Guardian*, 16 Jul 2022

11. Boris Johnson's Russian crony Evgeny Lebedev got peerage after spies dropped warning, *Sunday Times*, 5 Mar 2022

12. Dominic Cummings interview with Suzanne Moore, Letters from Suzanne Substack, 29 May 2022

13. Boris Johnson evidence to the Liaison Committee, 6 July 2022, https://committees.parliament.uk/oralevidence/10543/pdf/

14. PM's father Stanley Johnson passed on Chinese message to minister, *Guardian*, 6 Feb 2020

15. https://www.instagram.com/p/CWbqKBHMMnl/?utm_medium=twitter

16. https://www.instagram.com/p/CclWuxHspcA/

17. https://www.instagram.com/p/Ce6w8tNsfXJ/

18. Quoted in: Stanley Johnson calls for Parliament ban on 'agreeable' Chinese ambassador to be lifted, *Independent*, 22 Jun 2022

19. https://www.instagram.com/stanleyjohnson/p/CvLMohNsZ3V/

20. https://www.instagram.com/stanleyjohnson/p/CwnNu83sM0F/

21. See *Fall Out*, pp.439, 458

22. Seldon and Newell, *Johnson at 10*, pp.279–80

23. Ibid., p.283

24. Ibid., p.284

Chapter 13: A Frosty Reception

1. Stefaan De Rynck, 1 & 15 Mar 2021, Brexit Witness Archive, UKICE, p.37

2. David Frost, 24 Jun 2021, Brexit Witness Archive, UKICE, pp.3–4

3. David Frost speech: The Northern Ireland Protocol, 27 Apr 2022

4. Stefaan De Rynck, 1 & 15 Mar 2021, Brexit Witness Archive, UKICE, p.32

5. Ibid., p.36

6. The EU ambassador eventually got full diplomatic status in May 2021

7. Stefaan De Rynck, 1 & 15 Mar 2021, Brexit Witness Archive, UKICE, p.38

8. David Frost, 24 Jun 2021, Brexit Witness Archive, UKICE, p.19

9. Inside story of how the Brexit deal was done, *The Times*, 24 Dec 2020

Chapter 14: Out of Breath

1. Dominic Cummings interview with Suzanne Moore, Letters from Suzanne Substack, 29 May 2022

2. Dominic Cummings, evidence to the Health and Social Care Committee and Science and Technology Committee, 26 May 2021

3. Ibid.

4. Dominic Cummings interview with Suzanne Moore, Letters from Suzanne Substack, 29 May 2022

5. Downing St dog to be reshuffled, *The Times*, 11 Mar 2020

6. Carrie Symonds, Twitter, 8.03 a.m., 11 Mar 2020

7. Dominic Cummings interview with Suzanne Moore, Letters from Suzanne Substack, 29 May 2022

8. Dominic Cummings, evidence to the Health and Social Care Committee and Science and Technology Committee, 26 May 2021

9. Dominic Cummings interview with Suzanne Moore, Letters from Suzanne Substack, 29 May 2022

10. Dominic Cummings, evidence to the Health and Social Care Committee and Science and Technology Committee, 26 May 2021
11. Ibid.
12. Dominic Cummings interview with Steve Hsu, *Manifold* podcast, Ep. 28, 19 Jan 2023
13. Ibid.
14. Ibid.
15. Dominic Cummings, evidence to the Health and Social Care Committee and Science and Technology Committee, 26 May 2021
16. Ibid.
17. Ibid.
18. Dominic Cummings interview with Steve Hsu, *Manifold* podcast, Ep. 28, 19 Jan 2023
19. Dominic Cummings, evidence to the Health and Social Care Committee and Science and Technology Committee, 26 May 2021
20. Covid Inquiry: WhatsApp, Dominic Cummings to Lee Cain, 19 Mar 2020, 15.36, 16.48, 16.48 and 17.59
21. Covid Inquiry: WhatsApp, Lee Cain to Dominic Cummings, 19 Mar 2020, 16.49
22. Mark Sedwill, 22 Jun 2021, Brexit Witness Archive, UKICE, p.21
23. At this point Covid-19 was thought to have originated at a 'wet market' in Wuhan where live animals were sold. Support later grew for the theory that the virus escaped from the Wuhan Institute of Virology, which studied coronaviruses
24. Covid Inquiry: WhatsApp, Dominic Cummings to Lee Cain, 3 Mar 2020, 12.06
25. Exclusive: How Boris Johnson's former aide had to 'nanny' him through lockdown, *Tatler*, 18 Nov 2022
26. *Dominic Cummings: The Interview*, BBC 2, 19 Jul 2021
27. Exclusive: How Boris Johnson's former aide had to 'nanny' him through lockdown, *Tatler*, 18 Nov 2022
28. Dominic Cummings interview with Steve Hsu, *Manifold* podcast, Ep. 28, 19 Jan 2023
29. Ibid.
30. Helen MacNamara, evidence to the Covid Inquiry
31. Mark Sedwill, 22 Jun 2021, Brexit Witness Archive, UKICE, p.21
32. 'No 10 was a plague pit': How Covid brought Westminster to its knees, *Guardian*, 12 Mar 2021
33. Boris Johnson, 'How Covid nearly killed me', *Daily Mail*, 27 September 2024
34. Dominic Cummings statement, Downing Street rose garden, 25 May 2020
35. Johnson, *Unleashed*, p.447
36. Doctors waiting at St Thomas' hospital for Boris Johnson to arrive only realised he wasn't coming when they saw him clapping the NHS on TV, reveals HARRY COLE, as he shares the dramatic inside story of the PM's coronavirus battle, *Mail on Sunday*, 11 Apr 2020
37. Guto Harri, *Unprecedented podcast*, Ep. 4: The Road to Peppa Pig
38. 'No 10 was a plague pit': How Covid brought Westminster to its knees, *Guardian*, 12 Mar 2021
39. Interview with David Wooding, Docs were ready for me to die, *Sun on Sunday*, 2 May 2020
40. Johnson, *Unleashed*, p.451
41. Exclusive: How Boris Johnson's former aide had to 'nanny' him through lockdown, *Tatler*, 18 Nov 2022
42. Tom Bower, *Boris Johnson: The Gambler*, p.484
43. Doctors waiting at St Thomas' hospital for Boris Johnson to arrive only realised he wasn't coming when they saw him clapping the NHS on TV, reveals HARRY COLE, as he shares the dramatic inside story of the PM's coronavirus battle, *Mail on Sunday*, 11 Apr 2020

44. Guto Harri, *Unprecedented podcast*, Ep. 4: The Road to Peppa Pig
45. Johnson, *Unleashed*, p.458
46. Guto Harri, *Unprecedented podcast*, Ep. 4: The Road to Peppa Pig
47. Exclusive: How Boris Johnson's former aide had to 'nanny' him through lockdown, *Tatler*, 18 Nov 2022
48. David Frost, Twitter, 3.42 p.m., 16 Apr 2020
49. Stefaan De Rynck, 1 & 15 Mar 2021, Brexit Witness Archive, UKICE, p.32
50. Guto Harri, *Unprecedented* podcast, Ep. 4: The Road to Peppa Pig
51. Hancock's 'Give me a break' bust-up with PM, *Mail on Sunday*, 10 May 2020
52. Dominic Cummings interview with Steve Hsu, *Manifold* podcast, Ep. 28, 19 Jan 2023
53. Docs were ready for me to die, *Sun on Sunday*, 2 May 2020
54. Seldon and Newell, *Johnson at 10*, p.299
55. Ibid., p.301
56. Ibid., p.299
57. Exclusive: How Boris Johnson's former aide had to 'nanny' him through lockdown, *Tatler*, 18 Nov 2022
58. Sue Gray Report, 22 May 2022, pp.16–17. https://assets.publishing. service.gov.uk/government/uploads/ system/uploads/attachment_data/ file/1078404/2022-05-25_FINAL_ FINDINGS_OF_SECOND_ PERMANENT_SECRETARY_INTO_ ALLEGED_GATHERINGS.pdf
59. Dominic Cummings, evidence to the Health and Social Care Committee and Science and Technology Committee, 26 May 2021
60. Exclusive: How Boris Johnson's former aide had to 'nanny' him through lockdown, *Tatler*, 18 Nov 2022
61. Dominic Cummings, Twitter, 12.53 p.m., 25 May 2022
62. Why I went to No10 in Summer 2019, Dominic Cummings, Substack, 5 Jul 2021
63. Exclusive: How Boris Johnson's former aide had to 'nanny' him through lockdown, *Tatler*, 18 Nov 2022
64. Civil servant branded a 'c***' by Dominic Cummings at Covid Inquiry, *Daily Mail*, 1 Nov 2023
65. Why I went to No10 in Summer 2019, Dominic Cummings, Substack, 5 Jul 2021
66. Putting PM out to stud, *The Times* Diary, 25 Aug 2020
67. Johnson has stuck his foot in Dominic Cummings's hornets' nest, *The Times*, 24 Apr 2021
68. Covid Inquiry, 30 Oct 2023, pp.97–8: https://covid19. public-inquiry.uk/wp-content/ uploads/2023/10/30203506/2023-10- 30-Module-2-Day-14-Transcript.pdf
69. Covid Inquiry, 30 Oct 2023. Extract of letter from Dominic Cummings to the Inquiry titled 'Evidence of Dominic Cummings', dated 11/11/2022, p.56
70. Covid Inquiry, 30 Oct 2023, pp.97–8: https://covid19. public-inquiry.uk/wp-content/ uploads/2023/10/30203506/2023-10- 30-Module-2-Day-14-Transcript.pdf
71. Boris: 'Let the bodies pile high in their thousands', *Daily Mail*, 25 Apr 2021
72. Ibid.
73. Dominic Cummings, evidence to the Health and Social Care Committee and Science and Technology Committee, 26 May 2021

Chapter 15: The Madman Strategy II

1. Inside story of how the Brexit deal was done, *The Times*, 24 Dec 2020
2. David Frost, 24 Jun 2021, Brexit Witness Archive, UKICE, p.2
3. Inside story of how the Brexit deal was done, *The Times*, 24 Dec 2020
4. David Davis, 8 Jul 2021, Brexit Witness Archive, UKICE, p.41

5. Stefaan De Rynck, 1 & 15 Mar 2021, Brexit Witness Archive, UKICE, p.34
6. Inside story of how the Brexit deal was done, *The Times*, 24 Dec 2020
7. David Frost speech: The Northern Ireland Protocol, 27 Apr 2022
8. David Frost, 24 Jun 2021, Brexit Witness Archive, UKICE, p.2
9. Jonathan Jones, 6 May 2021, Brexit Witness Archive, UKICE, p.23
10. UK plan to undermine withdrawal treaty puts Brexit talks at risk, *Financial Times*, 6 Sep 2020
11. Inside story of how the Brexit deal was done, *The Times*, 24 Dec 2020
12. Jonathan Jones, 6 May 2021, Brexit Witness Archive, UKICE, p.24
13. David Frost speech: The Northern Ireland Protocol, 27 Apr 2022
14. Stefaan De Rynck, 1 & 15 Mar 2021, Brexit Witness Archive, UKICE, p.38
15. Risk, aggression, Brexit and Article 16: Advice to Tory MPs: Triggering A16 would be another trolley disaster, Dominic Cummings, Substack, 12 Nov 2021
16. Inside story of how the Brexit deal was done, *The Times*, 24 Dec 2020
17. Barnier, *My Secret Brexit Diary*, Polity Press, 2021, p.370
18. Ibid., p.371
19. Ibid., p.374

Chapter 16: Cummings and Goings
1. Sky's Sophy Ridge: 'I survived Theresa May's death stare', *Sunday Times*, 10 Sep 2023
2. 'If leaks carry on, we'll start shooting people': The chilling warning sent to government special adviser NEIL TWEEDIE just before Boris Johnson's bruiser Lee Cain unjustly fired him – as he reveals how he was … whacked by the No.10 Mafiosi, *Daily Mail*, 14 Nov 2020
3. Why I went to No10 in Summer 2019, Dominic Cummings, Substack, 5 Jul 2021

4. Seldon and Newell, *Johnson at 10*, p.303
5. Why I went to No10 in Summer 2019, Dominic Cummings, Substack, 5 Jul 2021
6. Seldon and Newell, *Johnson at 10*, p.462
7. Ibid., p.463
8. Simon Case admits discussing work 'opportunities' for Carrie Johnson, *Guardian*, 23 Jun 2022
9. Partygate: Inside the storm, *Panorama*, BBC, 30 May 2022
10. Get out, Johnson told Dominic Cummings and Lee Cain, *The Times*, 14 Nov 2020
11. Dominic Cummings interview with Steve Hsu, *Manifold* podcast, Ep. 28, 19 Jan 2023
12. Exclusive: How Boris Johnson's former aide had to 'nanny' him through lockdown, *Tatler*, 18 Nov 2022

Chapter 17: The Nightmare Before Christmas
1. Barnier, *My Secret Brexit Diary*, pp.380–1
2. Ibid., p.384
3. Ibid., pp.385–6
4. Ibid., p.391
5. Inside story of how the Brexit deal was done, *The Times*, 24 Dec 2020
6. Risk, aggression, Brexit and Article 16: Advice to Tory MPs: Triggering A16 would be another trolley disaster, Dominic Cummings, Substack, 12 Nov 2021
7. Stefaan De Rynck, 1 & 15 Mar 2021, Brexit Witness Archive, UKICE, pp.36–7

Chapter 18: Fatal Distractions
1. Johnson has stuck his foot in Dominic Cummings's hornets' nest, *The Times*, 24 Apr 2021
2. Ibid.
3. Statement regarding No10 claims today, Dominic Cummings's Blog, 23 Apr 2021

4. Ibid.

5. The departing Downing St aide, Dilyn the dog … and a cocked leg that stunned a No10 gathering, *Daily Mail*, 19 Feb 2021

6. PM's secret fund for Carrie's No10 decor, *Daily Mail*, 2 Mar 2021

7. 'She's buying gold wallpaper. It's costing tens and tens of thousands … I can't afford it': Boris Johnson's despairing cry to Downing St aides about lavish new No 10 decor – as revealed in definitive account of THAT scandal, *Daily Mail*, 27 Apr 2021

8. Ibid.

9. PM fears Carrie's No10 decor may cost £200,000, *Daily Mail*, 5 Mar 2021

10. No10 decor scandal: Tory HQ 'cover-up' exposed, *Daily Mail*, 6 Mar 2021

11. Secrets of the money trail behind Carrie's No10 makeover, *Daily Mail*, 13 Mar 2021

12. No10 makeover scandal: New incendiary email revealed, *Daily Mail*, 21 Apr 2021

13. Electoral probe into No10 decor scandal, *Daily Mail*, 20 Mar 2021

14. Statement regarding No10 claims today, Dominic Cummings's Blog, 23 Apr 2021

15. My four year affair with Boris, *Sunday Mirror*, 28 Mar 2021

16. Tom Baldwin, *Keir Starmer: The Biography*, William Collins, 2024, pp.310–11

17. US kept Britain in dark over deal that led Taliban back to power, *Sunday Times*, 14 Aug 2022

18. Dominic Dyer, Twitter, 25 May 2022, 8.03 a.m.

19. Johnsonian French for 'get a grip' and 'give me a break'.

20. Johnson used this phrase, lifted from a Kipling poem, predicting doom when he messaged David Cameron to say he was backing the Leave campaign. See *All Out War*, p.177

21. Columnist Sarah Vine opens up about her divorce from Michael Gove, *Tatler*, 5 Jan 2022

22. SARAH VINE: The problem with the wife who's been with you for ever is that she knows you're not the Master of the Universe you purport to be, *Mail on Sunday*, 26 Jun 2021

23. Gimson, Andrew, *Boris Johnson: The Rise and Fall of a Trouble Maker at Number 10*, Simon & Schuster, 2022, p.233

24. Ibid., pp.369–71

25. Ibid., pp.367–8

26. https://www.gov.uk/government/ speeches/pm-speech-at-the-un-general-assembly-22-september-2021

27. Payne, Sebastian, *The Fall of Boris Johnson*, Macmillan, 2022, pp.2–3

28. Exclusive: Boris Johnson's callous jibe about married life with Carrie Symonds, *New European*, 17 Nov 2021

29. Payne, *The Fall of Boris Johnson*, p.16

30. No 10 'yes men' blamed for Johnson's troubles, *The Times*, 6 Nov 2021

31. Ibid.

Chapter 19: Frosty the No Man

1. David Frost speech, The Northern Ireland Protocol, 27 Apr 2022

2. Ibid.

3. Ibid.

4. EU in U-turn over move to control vaccine exports to Northern Ireland, *Guardian*, 29 Jan 2021

5. Johnson, *Unleashed*, p.537

6. David Frost speech, The Northern Ireland Protocol, 27 Apr 2022

7. Ibid.

8. Ibid.

9. Ibid.

10. David Frost, 24 Jun 2021, Brexit Witness Archive, UKICE, p.14

11. Ibid., p.13

12. Ibid., p.12

13. How Boris Johnson sold out Britain's farmers over dinner with the Australian PM, Politico, 1 Jun 2023

14. Michel Barnier: Why is the EU's former Brexit chief negotiator sounding like a Eurosceptic?, *Observer*, 26 Sep 2021
15. Barnier's Brexit lesson: 'Less bureaucracy, more democracy' needed in Brussels, Politico, 4 May 2021
16. Barnier, *My Secret Brexit Diary*, pp.115–16
17. Michel Barnier: Why is the EU's former Brexit chief negotiator sounding like a Eurosceptic?, *Observer*, 26 Sep 2021
18. https://ec.europa.eu/commission/presscorner/detail/en/ip_21_5215
19. https://www.gov.uk/government/news/lord-frost-statement-on-the-protocol-on-irelandnorthern-ireland-17-december-2021--2
20. David Frost speech, The Northern Ireland Protocol, 27 Apr 2022
21. The 185,000 refugees included 100,000 British Nationals Overseas threatened by draconian security laws in Hong Kong, 20,000 refugees from Syria, 13,000 from Afghanistan and around 50,000 fleeing the war in Ukraine
22. Guto Harri, *Unprecedented* podcast, Ep. 5: Boris's Big Fat Hairy Promise
23. The UK's new points-based immigration system, House of Commons Library, 27 Sep 2022
24. Prince Charles: Flying migrants to Rwanda is 'appalling', *The Times*, 10 Jun 2022
25. Guto Harri, *Unprecedented* podcast, Ep. 5: Boris's Big Fat Hairy Promise
26. Ibid.
27. Ibid.
28. David Frost speech, The Northern Ireland Protocol, 27 Apr 2022

Chapter 20: Partied Out

1. Seldon and Newell, *Johnson at 10*, p.541
2. No one was fined for participating in this event
3. Payne, *The Fall of Boris Johnson*, p.55
4. 'I'm with the gays': How new revelations of Carrie Johnson gathering on Boris's birthday may derail his premiership, *Daily Telegraph*, 29 May 2022
5. Guto Harri, *Unprecedented* podcast, Ep. 3: Clusterf**k
6. Payne, *The Fall of Boris Johnson*, p.68
7. Guto Harri, *Unprecedented* podcast, Ep. 1: An Orgy of Pain
8. Ibid., Ep. 2: Conflict, Chaos and Another C**t
9. Harry Yorke interview with Nadhim Zahawi, an edited version of which appeared in the *Sunday Times*, 19 May 2024
10. *Putin vs the West*, BBC, Episode 3: A Dangerous Path, 30 Jan 2023
11. Payne, *The Fall of Boris Johnson*, p.94
12. *Putin vs the West*, BBC, Episode 3: A Dangerous Path, 30 Jan 2023
13. Boris Johnson interview with CNN, 23 Nov 2022
14. Guto Harri, *Unprecedented* podcast, Ep. 2: Conflict, Chaos and Another C**t
15. Ibid.

Chapter 21: Out of Step

1. See *Fall Out*, chapter 18
2. Now Boris accuses Sunak of 'a failure of political judgment', *Mail on Sunday*, 8 Aug 2021
3. Payne, *The Fall of Boris Johnson*, p.94
4. Guto Harri, *Unprecedented* podcast, Ep. 5: Boris's Big Fat Hairy Promise
5. Rishi Sunak's Russian hypocrisy shows who he is really protecting, *Byline Times*, 25 Mar 2022
6. Johnson, *Unleashed*, p.704
7. Guto Harri, *Unprecedented* podcast, Ep. 3: Clusterf**k
8. Ibid.
9. On Friday 8 July 2022, Starmer and Rayner and all other attendees were cleared by Durham Constabulary who concluded that the gathering was reasonably necessary for work purposes

10. Guto Harri, *Unprecedented* podcast, Ep. 4: The Road to Peppa Pig
11. Ibid.
12. Ibid.

Chapter 22: Out of Excuses

1. Seldon and Newell, *Johnson at 10*, p.544
2. Payne, *The Fall of Boris Johnson*, p.133
3. Ibid., p.138
4. The Streisand effect refers to the way attempts to censor information only draw attention to it after the actress and singer attempted in 2003 to suppress publication of a photograph of her clifftop residence in Malibu
5. Seldon and Newell, *Johnson at 10*, p.548
6. Ibid.
7. Payne, *The Fall of Boris Johnson*, p.134
8. Conversation reconstructed from: Payne, *The Fall of Boris Johnson*, pp.142–3; and Seldon and Newell, *Johnson at 10*, p.546
9. Guto Harri, *Unprecedented* podcast, Ep. 4: The Road to Peppa Pig
10. Payne, *The Fall of Boris Johnson*, p.166
11. Simon McDonald: Why I had to call out Boris Johnson's untruths about Christopher Pincher, *Civil Service World*, 12 July 2022
12. Ibid.
13. Seldon and Newell, *Johnson at 10*, p.552
14. Johnson, *Unleashed*, p.705
15. Guto Harri, *Unprecedented* podcast, Ep. 1: An Orgy of Pain
16. Payne, *The Fall of Boris Johnson*, p.180
17. Ibid., p.183
18. Seldon and Newell, *Johnson at 10*, p.553
19. Harry Yorke interview with Nadhim Zahawi, an edited version of which appeared in the *Sunday Times*, 19 May 2024
20. Ibid.
21. Seldon and Newell, *Johnson at 10*, p.553
22. Author's research and Payne, *The Fall of Boris Johnson*, p.193
23. Harry Yorke interview with Nadhim Zahawi, an edited version of which appeared in the *Sunday Times*, 19 May 2024
24. Seldon and Newell, *Johnson at 10*, p.556
25. Ibid.
26. Payne, *The Fall of Boris Johnson*, p.205
27. Ibid., p.210
28. Seldon and Newell, *Johnson at 10*, p.557
29. Harry Yorke interview with Nadhim Zahawi, an edited version of which appeared in the *Sunday Times*, 19 May 2024
30. Ibid.
31. Greenhalgh, an ally of Johnson, later posted screenshots from the chat on Twitter, describing himself and Hughes as 'the counter herd'. See: Kemi Badenoch is accused of pressuring junior colleague into joining putsch against Boris Johnson just hours after she had resigned herself, *Daily Mail*, 26 Feb 2023
32. Author's research and Payne, *The Fall of Boris Johnson*, p.210
33. Seldon and Newell, *Johnson at 10*, p.561
34. Ibid., p.562
35. Johnson, *Unleashed*, p.705
36. Seldon and Newell, *Johnson at 10*, p.562
37. Harry Yorke interview with Nadhim Zahawi, an edited version of which appeared in the *Sunday Times*, 19 May 2024
38. Seldon and Newell, *Johnson at 10*, p.564
39. Guto Harri, *Unprecedented* podcast, Ep. 3: Clusterf**k
40. Johnson, *Unleashed*, p.466
41. Ibid., pp.705–6
42. Gimson, *Boris Johnson*, p.256
43. Ibid., p.249

44. Karl Marx on Palmerston, 1853. Quoted in Gimson, *Boris Johnson*, pp.397–9
45. Seldon and Newell, *Johnson at 10*, pp.1–3

Chapter 23: Knife Fight in a Phone Box

1. Truss, Liz, *Ten Years to Save the West*, Biteback, 2024, p.182
2. How to prepare a secret Tory leadership campaign, Politico *Westminster Insider* podcast, 10 May 2024
3. Cole, Harry and Heale, James, *Out of the Blue: The Inside Sory of the Unexpected Rise and Rapid Fall of Liz Truss*, HarperCollins, p.229
4. How to prepare a secret Tory leadership campaign, Politico *Westminster Insider* podcast, 10 May 2024
5. I'd love to be Chancellor … but I don't want success just because I've got a pair of boobs, *Daily Mail*, 29 Nov 2018
6. Truss, *Ten Years to Save the West*, pp.187–8
7. Cole and Heale, *Out of the Blue*, p.238
8. Payne, *The Fall of Boris Johnson*, p.235
9. How to prepare a secret Tory leadership campaign, Politico *Westminster Insider* podcast, 10 May 2024
10. Tom Tugendhat: Wounded in a 10hr firefight in Iraq, now he is set for a new battle, *Sunday Times*, 10 Jul 2022
11. Payne, *The Fall of Boris Johnson*, p.225
12. Cole and Heale, *Out of the Blue*, p.243
13. Ibid.
14. Ibid., p.246
15. Truss, *Ten Years to Save the West*, p.196
16. Ibid.
17. Cole and Heale, *Out of the Blue*, p.250
18. PM compares premiership to Typhoon flight, implies he'd like to send Rishi into orbit, Guido Fawkes, 18 Jul 2022

19. Cole and Heale, *Out of the Blue*, pp.251–2
20. Ibid., p.265
21. What is good in life, Theresa? All good things come to an end; and Boris too, *The Critic*, 20 Jul 2022
22. Truss, *Ten Years to Save the West*, p.199
23. When David Willetts contemplated switching from David Davis to David Cameron in 2005, Davis's campaign whip, the later disgraced Derek Conway, told the author, 'Willetts thinks he's switching, but I've got his wife and children locked in the cellar.'
24. Cole and Heale, *Out of the Blue*, pp.270–1
25. Ibid., p.3
26. Johnson, *Unleashed*, p.727
27. Truss, *Ten Years to Save the West*, p.2

Chapter 24: Going Big

1. 49 days of Liz Truss: The inside story, Politico *Westminster Insider* podcast, 17 May 2023
2. Cole and Heale, *Out of the Blue*, p.271
3. Truss, *Ten Years to Save the West*, p.200
4. Kremlin 'hacked Truss's mobile', *Mail on Sunday*, 29 Oct 2022
5. A proposal she rejected in an interview with the *Financial Times* on 6 Aug 2022
6. Ibid., pp.234–5
7. The inside story of Liz Truss's disastrous 44 days in office, *Financial Times*, 9 Dec 2022
8. Truss, *Ten Years to Save the West*, p.224
9. Truss, *Ten Years to Save the West*, p.246
10. Simon Clarke, How did it all go so wrong for Liz Truss?, *The Critic*, Dec/ Jan 2023
11. 49 days of Liz Truss: The inside story, Politico *Westminster Insider* podcast, 17 May 2023

12. Simon Clarke, How did it all go so wrong for Liz Truss?, *The Critic*, Dec/Jan 2023

13. 49 days of Liz Truss: The inside story, Politico *Westminster Insider* podcast, 17 May 2023

14. Truss, *Ten Years to Save the West*, p.250

15. Simon Clarke, How did it all go so wrong for Liz Truss?, *The Critic*, Dec/Jan 2023

16. How to prepare a secret Tory leadership campaign, Politico *Westminster Insider* podcast, 10 May 2024

17. Truss, *Ten Years to Save the West*, pp.210–12

18. Ibid., p.215

19. 'She's totally lost it': Inside story of the unravelling of Liz Truss's premiership, *Guardian*, 1 Sep 2023

20. Cole and Heale, *Out of the Blue*, p.276

21. Truss, *Ten Years to Save the West*, p.220

22. 49 days of Liz Truss: The inside story, Politico *Westminster Insider* podcast, 17 May 2023

23. The inside story of Liz Truss's disastrous 44 days in office, *Financial Times*, 9 Dec 2022

24. Cole and Heale, *Out of the Blue*, p.280

25. Truss, *Ten Years to Save the West*, p.5

26. Ibid., pp.5–6

27. Ibid., p.218

28. 49 days of Liz Truss: The inside story, Politico *Westminster Insider* podcast, 17 May 2023

29. The inside story of Liz Truss's disastrous 44 days in office, *Financial Times*, 9 Dec 2022

30. 49 days of Liz Truss: The inside story, Politico *Westminster Insider* podcast, 17 May 2023

31. Ibid.

32. Ibid.

33. Truss, *Ten Years to Save the West*, p.248

34. Truss, *Ten Years to Save the West*, p.251

35. Connoisseurs of irony also enjoyed the front-page advert for a souvenir pound coin collection commemorating the late Queen, the value of which were already in steep decline

36. 49 days of Liz Truss: The inside story, Politico *Westminster Insider* podcast, 17 May 2023

Chapter 25: Going Home

1. 49 days of Liz Truss: The inside story, Politico *Westminster Insider* podcast, 17 May 2023

2. Kwasi Kwarteng interview with TalkTV, 10 Nov 2022

3. Liz Truss exclusive: 'I assumed upon entering Downing Street my mandate would be respected. How wrong I was', *Sunday Telegraph*, 4 Feb 2023

4. Truss, *Ten Years to Save the West*, p.256

5. Ibid., p.259

6. 49 days of Liz Truss: The inside story, Politico *Westminster Insider* podcast, 17 May 2023

7. Truss, *Ten Years to Save the West*, p.237

8. Ibid., p.259

9. 'Sadistic' Gove told: Stop plots or let in Starmer, *Mail on Sunday*, 9 Oct 2022

10. Truss tells MPs: Unite or face disaster, *Sunday Telegraph*, 9 Oct 2022

11. What went wrong for Liz Truss?, Politico *Westminster Insider* podcast, Series 9 Episode 1

12. Cole and Heale, *Out of the Blue*, p.313

13. The inside story of Liz Truss's disastrous 44 days in office, *Financial Times*, 9 Dec 2022

14. Truss, *Ten Years to Save the West*, p.241

15. Ibid., pp.267–8

16. Kwasi Kwarteng interview with TalkTV, 16 Feb 2024

17. Truss, *Ten Years to Save the West*, p.270

18. Kwasi Kwarteng interview with TalkTV, 16 Feb 2024

19. Truss, *Ten Years to Save the West*, p.273
20. Ibid.
21. Ibid., p.280
22. Ibid., p.206
23. Ibid., p.274
24. 49 days of Liz Truss: The inside story, Politico *Westminster Insider* podcast, 17 May 2023
25. Conversation reconstructed from author's research: The inside story of Liz Truss's disastrous 44 days in office, *Financial Times*, 9 Dec 2022; Cole and Heale, *Out of the Blue*, p.299
26. Truss, *Ten Years to Save the West*, p.275
27. Kwasi Kwarteng interview with TalkTV, 16 Feb 2024
28. Liz Truss interview, *Sunday Morning with Trevor Phillips*, Sky News, 21 Apr 2024
29. Truss, *Ten Years to Save the West*, p.276
30. See chapter 14
31. Truss, *Ten Years to Save the West*, pp.238–9
32. Cole and Heale, *Out of the Blue*, p.307
33. Craig Whittaker interview with Matt Chorley, *The Exit Interviews*, Ep. 22, Times Radio, 6 May 2024
34. Ibid.
35. Ibid.
36. Ibid.
37. 49 days of Liz Truss: The inside story, Politico *Westminster Insider* podcast, 17 May 2023
38. Cole and Heale, *Out of the Blue*, p.309
39. Truss, *Ten Years to Save the West*, p.278
40. Ibid., p.279
41. Ibid., pp.209–10
42. Cole and Heale, *Out of the Blue*, p.310
43. Truss, *Ten Years to Save the West*, p.279
44. Cole and Heale, *Out of the Blue*, p.311
45. Peter Walker, Twitter
46. Simon Clarke, How did it all go so wrong for Liz Truss?, *The Critic*, Dec/Jan 2023

47. Cole and Heale, *Out of the Blue*, p.313
48. Ibid.
49. The inside story of Liz Truss's disastrous 44 days in office, *Financial Times*, 9 Dec 2022
50. Liz Truss exclusive: 'I assumed upon entering Downing Street my mandate would be respected. How wrong I was', *Sunday Telegraph*, 4 Feb 2023
51. Truss, *Ten Years to Save the West*, p.245
52. Simon Clarke, How did it all go so wrong for Liz Truss?, *The Critic*, Dec/Jan 2023
53. The inside story of Liz Truss's disastrous 44 days in office, *Financial Times*, 9 Dec 2022
54. 49 days of Liz Truss: The inside story, Politico *Westminster Insider* podcast, 17 May 2023
55. Ibid.
56. How to prepare a secret Tory leadership campaign, Politico *Westminster Insider* podcast, 10 May 2024

Chapter 26: Princes in the (Millbank) Tower

1. Kemi Badenoch backs Rishi Sunak as Tory Right splits its forces, *Sunday Telegraph*, 22 Oct 2022
2. Suella Braverman, Rishi Sunak is the only candidate that fits the bill for prime minister, *Daily Telegraph*, 23 Oct 2022
3. Ibid.
4. David Frost, Twitter, 12.03 p.m., 22 Oct 2022

Chapter 27: The Third Protocol

1. Inside the deal: How Boris Johnson's departure paved the way for a grand Brexit bargain, *Politico*, 28 Feb 2023
2. Ibid.
3. Revealed: Secret cross-party summit held to confront failings of Brexit, *Observer*, 11 Feb 2023

4. Has Rishi Sunak got a good Brexit deal? *Times* writers give their verdicts, *The Times*, 27 Feb 2023
5. BBC *Newsnight*, Twitter, 8.24 p.m., 27 Feb 2023
6. Sunak's deal will help, but it remains a bitter pill to swallow, *Daily Telegraph*, 28 Feb 2023
7. See *No Way Out*, pp.530–1
8. The 22 Tory MPs who made up the 2023 Spartans who voted against the Stormont Brake were: Adam Afriyie, Sir Jake Berry, Peter Bone, Andrew Bridgen, Sir Christopher Chope, Simon Clarke, Richard Drax, Sir James Duddridge, Sir Iain Duncan Smith, Mark Francois, Jonathan Gullis, Adam Holloway, Andrea Jenkyns, Boris Johnson, David Jones, Danny Kruger, Craig Mackinlay, Matthew Offord, Priti Patel, John Redwood, Jacob Rees-Mogg and Liz Truss
9. Harry Cole, Twitter, 1.28 p.m., 24 Mar 2023

Chapter 28: 'The Juddering Climax'
1. How Starmer slaughtered the Tories: Inside Labour's march to victory, UnHerd, 5 Jul 2024
2. Lord of Misrule, *Times Literary Supplement*, 6 Nov 2020
3. The BBC chairman, the prime minister and the £800,000 loan guarantee, *Sunday Times*, 21 Jan 2023
4. Nadine Dorries interview, Piers Morgan Uncensored, TalkTV, 12 Jun 2023
5. Nadine Dorries interview, Piers Morgan Uncensored, TalkTV, 12 Jun 2023

Chapter 29: Deja Blue II
1. The peer, the pollster and the rumblings of a plan to oust Rishi Sunak, *The Times*, 23 Feb 2024
2. The 'pasta plotters' cooking up scheme to oust Rishi Sunak revealed, *Mail on Sunday*, 9 Dec 2023

3. Sunak only went ahead with net migration measures after I threatened to quit, says Jenrick, *Daily Telegraph*, 28 Mar 2024
4. How the Tory election campaign melted down in 6 disastrous weeks, *Politico*, 5 Jul 2024
5. How the Tory election campaign melted down in 6 disastrous weeks, *Politico*, 5 Jul 2024

Chapter 30: Out of the Wilderness
1. The brutal truth is Labour leader Sir Keir Starmer is no good at politics and has already blown it, argues DAN HODGES, *Mail on Sunday*, 25 Sep 2021
2. How the Tory election campaign melted down in 6 disastrous weeks, *Politico*, 5 Jul 2024
3. Ibid.
4. West Wing Sue … and her battle with Keir's boys, *Mail on Sunday*, 31 Mar 2024
5. Keir Starmer vows to sack critics behind 'boys' club' briefings, *The Times*, 17 Apr 2024

Chapter 31: 'Après le Deluge
1. Conservative Tunbridge Wells hopeful Iain Dale said he 'never liked the place' and 'would happily live somewhere else', *Byline Times*, 29 May 2024
2. Liberal Democrats election broadcast shows Ed Davey with disabled son, *Guardian*, 5 Jun 2024
3. Davis ended up winning Goole and Pocklington with a majority of 3,572, on a swing of 18.8 per cent away from the Tories
4. Liberal Democrats election broadcast shows Ed Davey with disabled son, *Guardian*, 5 Jun 2024
5. How the Tory election campaign melted down in 6 disastrous weeks, *Politico*, 5 Jul 2024
6. Ibid.

7. Craig Williams finished third in his Montgomeryshire and Glyndwr seat behind both Labour and Reform UK. Laura Saunders was also third in Bristol North West
8. Make America Great Again
9. https://www.channel4.com/news/exclusive-undercover-inside-reforms-campaign-evidence-of-homophobia-and-canvassers-racism
10. The Tories are in no position to attack Farage, *Daily Telegraph*, 2 Jul 2024

Chapter 32: In
1. Stunned silence, hugs and a very big kiss: at home with the Starmers on election night, *Observer*, 7 Jul 2024
2. Ibid.
3. Ibid.
4. This number includes the Speaker, Lindsay Hoyle, who ran uncontested in Chorley

Conclusion
1. Ford et al., *The British General Election of 2019*
2. Claire Fox, 6 Nov 2020, Brexit Witness Archive, UKICE, p.30
3. Doris Kearns Goodwin, *Leadership: Lessons from the Presidents in Turbulent Times* (Penguin, 2019)
4. Julian Smith, 20 Jul 2020, Brexit Witness Archive, UKICE, p.9
5. Gavin Barwell, 1 & 25 September 2020, Brexit Witness Archive, UKICE, pp.44–5
6. Oliver Letwin, 11 Dec 2020, Brexit Witness Archive, UKICE, pp.31–2
7. *Spectator* podcast, 23 Jun 2024, https://www.youtube.com/watch?v=ewqMFSJnuUI
8. See Sonia Purnell's *Just Boris* (Aurum)

9. #3 The Startup Party: Reflections on the last 20 years, what could replace the Tories, and why, Dominic Cummings, Substack, 9 Jun 2023
10. Why I went to No10 in summer 2019, Dominic Cummings, Substack, 5 Jul 2021
11. Mark Sedwill, 22 Jun 2021, Brexit Witness Archive, UKICE, p.22
12. David Frost, 24 Jun 2021, Brexit Witness Archive, UKICE p.18
13. Jonathan Jones, 6 May 2021, Brexit Witness Archive, UKICE, p.25
14. Philip Rycroft, 26 Jun 2020, Brexit Witness Archive, UKICE, p.27
15. Theresa May's Brexit battle plan falls at the gates of Fort Macron, *Sunday Times*, 5 Aug 2018
16. Chris Grayling, 21 Oct 2020, Brexit Witness Archive, UKICE, p.25
17. Tom Baldwin, 5 Jul 2021, Brexit Witness Archive, UKICE, p.24
18. Ibid.
19. Dominic Cummings interview with Steve Hsu, *Manifold* podcast, Ep. 28, 19 Jan 2023
20. Ibid.
21. David Davis, 8 Jul 2021, Brexit Witness Archive, UKICE, p.15
22. Damian Green interview, GB News, 18 Jul 2022
23. Assembling a better British relationship with Europe, *Economist*, 5 Jan 2023
24. Why the OBR is wrong about Brexit, *The Critic*, 25 Mar 2024
25. Dominic Cummings interview with Suzanne Moore, Letters from Suzanne Substack, 29 May 2022
26. Claire Fox, 6 Nov 2020, Brexit Witness Archive, UKICE, pp.31–2
27. David Frost, 24 Jun 2021, Brexit Witness Archive, UKICE, pp.19–20